W9-CZF-704

THE EXPOSITOR'S
GREEK TESTAMENT

EDITED BY THE REV.
W ROBERTSON NICOLL, M.A., LL.D.
EDITOR OF "THE EXPOSITOR," "THE EXPOSITOR'S BIBLE," ETC.

VOLUME V

WM. B. EERDMANS PUBLISHING COMPANY
GRAND RAPIDS, MICHIGAN

PHOTOLITHOPRINTED BY GRAND RAPIDS BOOK MANUFACTURERS, INC.
GRAND RAPIDS, MICHIGAN, UNITED STATES OF AMERICA
1967

THE EXPOSITOR'S
GREEK TESTAMENT

I

THE FIRST EPISTLE GENERAL OF PETER

BY THE REV.

J. H. A HART, M.A.

II

THE SECOND EPISTLE GENERAL OF PETER

BY THE REV.

R. H. STRACHAN, M.A.

III

THE EPISTLES OF JOHN

BY THE REV.

DAVID SMITH, M.A., D.D.

IV

THE GENERAL EPISTLE OF JUDE

BY THE REV.

J. B. MAYOR, LITT.D.

V

THE REVELATION OF ST. JOHN THE DIVINE

BY THE REV.

JAMES MOFFATT, D.D.

THE FIRST EPISTLE GENERAL

OF

PETER

INTRODUCTION

In the case of this document a question preliminary to the ordinary heads of Introduction arises; the question of *the Unity of the Epistle.* For it contains *two* formal and solemn conclusions. The first[1] is "*That in all things God may be glorified through Jesus Christ to Whom belongs the glory and the victory to the ages of the ages. Amen;*" and the second,[2] "*Now the God of all grace, he who called you to his eternal glory in Christ, himself shall refit you after brief suffering, shall confirm you, shall strengthen you, shall establish you. His is the victory to the ages of the ages. Amen.*" The latter conclusion is followed by a postscript which ends with yet another formula of conclusion[3] "*Peace to you all who are in Christ*".

The address[4] at the head of the document stamps it as a circular letter or an encyclical epistle. The three conclusions divide it into three parts. Of these the last and shortest part may fairly be taken as a true postscript. The writer (we may suppose) takes the pen from the secretary, to whom he has been dictating, and appends a greeting in his own handwriting. St. Paul did the same thing in the Epistle to the Galatians.[5] In such a case the value of the postscript would be greater than in the case of a circular letter addressed to widely separated churches in different provinces or countries. The Galatian letter would naturally be preserved in the chest of the chief church of the province; and St. Paul's autograph would be prized as proof of the authenticity of the exemplar, copies of which were doubtless made and supplied as need and demand arose. But in this case also the autograph has a value of its own, inasmuch as it gives the credentials of the bearer, who presumably went from place to place and read it out to the assembled Christians, letting them see the postscript before he travelled on. So the third part of the letter may well be an integral portion of this encyclical.

But this postscript is preceded not by one conclusion but by two; and in this the document bears witness *against* its own unity. And

[1] iv. 11. [2] v. 10 f. [3] v. 14. [4] i. 1. [5] Gal. vi. 11-17.

further it is to be noted that the first conclusion is followed by a general form of address—"*Beloved*"—which has occurred at an earlier point.[1] In fact, apart from the formal superscription—X to Y greeting—the second part[2] of the Epistle is a complete epistle in itself. And it is natural enough that a circular letter, addressed to different communities, should contain alternative or additional letters, if the writer was aware that the conditions or circumstances were not identical in every case. The formal severance of the second part may, therefore, be taken as indicating that *all* the communities addressed were *not* necessarily in the condition, which that part implies.

1. *The Recipients.*—Eusebius of Cæsarea, whose Ecclesiastical History belongs to the beginning of the fourth century, is the earliest (extant) writer, who inquired systematically into the origins of the Christian literature. For him there is no question about the nationality of the first recipients of this document: they are *Hebrews* or Jewish Christians. He insists that the compact made between St. Peter and St. Paul at Jerusalem[3] was faithfully observed, as their respective writings and the evidence of St. Luke agree to testify: "That Paul, on the one hand, preached to those of Gentile origin and so laid the foundations of the churches from Jerusalem and round about as far as Illyricum is plain from his own statements and from the narratives, which Luke gives in the Acts. And, on the other hand, from the phrases of Peter it is clear in what provinces he for his part preached the Gospel of Christ to those of the Circumcision and delivered to them the message of the New Covenant—I mean, from his acknowledged epistle in which he writes *to those of Hebrew origin* in the dispersion of Pontus and Galatia, Cappadocia and Asia and Bithynia.[4]

Just before this[5] plain statement Eusebius quotes verbally from Origen's exegetical commentary upon Genesis: "Peter seems to have preached in Pontus and Galatia and Bithynia, in Cappadocia and Asia *to the Jews in dispersion*". Origen's assertion rests presumably on the authority of the address of our document, although the order of the provinces differs in respect of Bithynia from the generally accepted text. When Eusebius speaks for himself he restores the conventional order of the provinces and explicitly quotes the authority of "the acknowledged Epistle". It does not seem at all probable that either Eusebius or Origen had any other evidence for their belief than such as is preserved for modern investigation. Both knew of

[1] ii. 11. [2] iv. 12-v. 11. [3] Gal. ii. 7-9.
[4] Eus. *H. E.* iii. 4. [5] Eus. *H. E.* iii. 1.

the compact, in virtue of which Peter was to continue his work among the Jews: both construed the direction of the Epistle as proof that the writer had preached the Gospel to his readers: therefore in virtue of the compact his readers were *Jews*—Jews of the Dispersion, but still Jews.

The evidence upon which both Eusebius and Origen seem to rely is extant; the deduction drawn—characteristic as it is of patristic exegesis—is not necessarily valid, and it is not supported by any pretence of independent tradition.

The compact to which James and Cephas and John, on the one side, and Paul and Barnabas, on the other, were consenting parties, cannot be held to prove these Christians to be Jewish Christians—even if it could be made out that St. Peter "the Apostle of the Cir cumcision," who writes to them, converted them to Christianity.

The appellation *of the Dispersion* is on the face of it a weightier argument, because *Dispersion* is a technical term and comprises in itself all the Jews who lived outside Palestine. Whatever its *provenance*, the term is Jewish through and through, for it insists upon the First Cause of all such scattering and upon the central shrine from which the exiles are removed. The mere Greek spoke and thought of exiles as fugitives and had a collective term φυγή to correspond with the Jewish διασπορά. But the Jewish word recognises that those dispersed are placed here and there—as exiles, traders and what not?—by God. Jewish as it is, this appellation is capable of extension to the new Israel and does not necessarily imply that the persons addressed were born Jews. Ultimately and fundamentally it does not denote privilege like the term *Israel* but rather penalty—removal from the place which was traditionally associated with the visible presence of Jehovah. The writer may, perhaps, be taken to use it without a precise definition of a centre corresponding to the Holy Land of the Jew; but there is no valid ground for doubting that he could apply it to Gentiles, who were in the world and not of it by virtue of their faith in Christ. Situated as they were among unfriendly friends these *Gentile* churches are collectively the new Dispersion.

These *Gentile* Churches—for there is more than one passage in our document which seems to settle the point, apart from general probabilities to be derived from the traditions of St. Paul's missionary activity. In the first place, St. Peter[1] applies to his readers the words of Hosea[2]; ye who were once no People but now are God's People, who were not in a state of experiencing His mercy, but now have

[1] ii. 10.

[2] See Hosea ii. 23.

come under its influence." At a definite time God had shown mercy to these Christians, who before—according to the strict Jewish point of view—had been outside the pale of His mercy. And, if we may argue from silence as from the tenses employed, they were formerly *not a people at all*, to say nothing of their being no people of God. In fact they were just *tribes* and *Gentiles*—not a λαός but just ἔθνη. It is true that Hosea was speaking of the children of Israel, who had apostatized, and of the final restoration, when all the dispersed should be gathered together. It is true, again, that St. Paul[1] uses the prophecy conformably with the apparent intention of the prophet; but he cites it more fully than St. Peter in connexion with the calling of the Gentiles.[2] The Christian Church is God's, Israel the heir of His promises; and—who knows?—the writer may have added the title *of the Dispersion* partly because it is written in the book of Hosea,[3] "and I will sow her unto myself upon the earth, and I will love her who was not beloved, and I will say to Not-my-people, Thou art my people and he shall say, Thou art the Lord my God". It is a great prophecy and a Jewish Christian would be slow to forget its first intention. No line of argument can exclude the possibility that *some* of the Christians, to whom his letter is addressed, were born Jews. And if he thought less of them and most of the aliens, who, perhaps, outnumbered them, at anyrate his own mind was Jewish and he spoke to his Jewish self, before he wrote or dictated his letter. It must have been a strange experience for a Jew to preach a Messiah, whom his Nation had rejected, to a motley collection of Gentile believers and to use such prophecies as this.

But whatever emotions the words stirred up within his heart they remained there. The thought of his countrymen does not shake him visibly as it shook St. Paul;[4] and from this self-repression one might conclude that the Jewish element in these churches was insignificant, or that the decree which severed him and them from the unbelieving Jews was already made absolute.

The probable significance of this use of Hosea's phrase is supported by the words, "*For ye were once wanderers like sheep but now ye have returned to the shepherd and overseer of your souls*".[5] It is, of course, possible to exaggerate the force of ἐπεστράφητε, *ye have returned*, as if it implied a previous association with God. But the word means no more than obedience to the invitation *Repent*, which Christian missionaries addressed to all the world; in the Septuagint it is used of Jewish *apostasy* without implying previous

[1] Rom. xi. 28-32 [2] Rom. ix. 24-26. [3] Hosea ii. 23 (LXX).
[4] Rom. ix. 1 ff, [5] ii. 25.

apostasy, and here it is fitly applied to the adherence of Gentiles, who previously had no faith in God. In fact its proper force is represented by *turn* rather than *return*.

Another capital passage would seem to be sufficient in itself to show that the writer regarded the churches to whom he speaks, as composed of Gentile Christians : "*Sufficient is the time that is past for the accomplishment of the ideal of the Gentiles, when you walked in . . . unlawful idolatry*".[1] If they were Jews by birth, who are so reproached for their pre-Christian life, it is clear that they must have been renegades, who had forfeited their title to be reckoned as Jews. For so great an apostasy there is no evidence whatever. That individuals in the Dispersion did succumb to the attractions of the life outside the ghetto is probable enough. Philo, for example, warns his fellow countrymen against the seductions of pagan mysteries; and his own nephew gave up his faith in order to become a soldier of fortune. But the interpretation, which makes Jews of the readers, involves an impossible assumption of wholesale perversion. The persons in question are, surely, Gentiles; before their conversion they lived as their neighbours lived, and, after their conversion, they excited the surprise of their neighbours by their change of life.[2]

The internal evidence of the Epistle is borne out by what is known of the evangelisation of the provinces named. With the exception of Cilicia all Asia Minor is included and Asia Minor was the great field of the labours of St. Paul and his companions. There is nothing to suggest that St. Peter was addressing converts of his own as Origen and Eusebius[3] seem to assume.

The Author.—The beginning and the final conclusion of this document certify it to be the letter or epistle of *Peter the Apostle of Jesus Christ*, who speaks of Silvanus and Mark as his companions and writes from "Babylon". The certificate was accepted and remained unquestioned until quite modern times. Irenæus, whose connexion with Polycarp is certain, quotes the document as written by *the* Peter of the Church—Simon, son of John, to whom Jesus gave the name of *Cephas* or (in Greek) *Peter*. When F. C. Baur (for example) speaks of the "alleged apostolic authorship of writings which bear the marks of pseudonymity so plainly on their face,"[4] he illustrates the reaction which ran riot, when once the doctrine of the inspiration and authority of canonical books was called in question. The authorship of this document does not

[1] iv. 3. [2] iv. 4. [3] See above page 4.

[4] *Church History* (English translation: London, 1878), p. 131 (note) in reference to the Epistle of James and the First Epistle of Peter.

necessarily decide the question of its authority—all or none—as it did in the time of uncritical devotion to the letter of Scripture. But Baur's brave words do no more to solve the problem than the stolid reiteration of traditional dogmas. And it is to be remembered that Catholic traditions have often been rehabilitated by critical researches.

To the question, "Do you at this time of day venture to attribute this document to Simon Peter?" the answer is, "Why not?"

Such a conservative attitude excites the pity—if not the contempt—of the "advanced" critics. They find no difficulty in treating the Canonical Epistles as most men have treated the Epistles of Phalaris—ever since Bentley wrote his dissertation. Bentley said[1] out of Galen, "*That in the age of the* Ptolemies *the trade of coining false Authors was in greatest Practice and Perfection. . . . When the* Attali *and the* Ptolemies *were in Emulation about their Libraries, the knavery of forging Books and Titles began. For there were those that to enhance the price of their Books put the Names of great Authors before them, and so sold them to those Princes.*" But Bentley proceeded to demonstrate that the Epistles of Phalaris contained blunders incompatible with their authenticity; and—for all their exquisite reasons—the critics, who treat the First Epistle of Peter as falsely so-called, have not yet found their Bentley. Indeed, their reasons are chiefly interesting as symptoms of presuppositions inherited from past controversies. They reveal (for example) a tendency to resent the attribution of divine authority to the Apostles, and a tendency—which others share—to ignore the relatively mature theology to which, as a matter of fact, the first Christian missionaries were bred, before ever they became missionaries or Christians at all. For those who believe that the Church has been directed by the Holy Spirit it is not easy to suppose that others than James and Peter, Jude and John were as destitute as they were full of divine inspiration. And it is not difficult to acquiesce in the excommunication of Marcion and all others who regard Christianity as a new thing descended from heaven with no affinity to any earthly antecedents.

In a natural and simple phrase this document professes to be written by Peter. But Harnack[2] has put forward the hypothesis that the opening and closing sentences[3] are an interpolation by another hand and argues against the assumption that the whole is a forgery. "If," he says, "the hypothesis here brought forward should prove erroneous, I shouid more readily prevail upon myself to regard the improbable as possible and to claim the Epistle for Peter him-

[1] Wagner's edition (London, 1883), pp. 80, 81.

[2] *Chronologie*, p. 457 ff.

[3] i. 1, 2 and v. 12-14.

self than to suppose that a *Pseudo-Petrus* wrote our fragment as it now stands from the first verse to the last, soon after A.D. 90, or even from ten to thirty years earlier. Such an assumption is, in my opinion, weighed down by insuperable difficulties.[1]

So far as extant evidence goes Harnack's hypothesis of interpolation has nothing on which to rest. It remains to consider the chief objections which have been urged to prove that the traditional view is improbable. Peter cannot have written the Epistle (it is said) because (1) it is clearly indebted to Paulinism, (2) it contains no vivid reminiscences of the life and doctrine of Jesus, (3) it is written in better Greek than a Galilean peasant could compass, and (4) it reflects conditions which Peter did not live to see.

The first reason is regarded as decisive by Harnack:[2] "Were it not for the dependence [of 1 Peter] on the Pauline Epistles, I might perhaps allow myself to maintain its genuineness: that dependence however, is not accidental, but is of the essence of the Epistle". Dr. Chase has examined the affinities between 1 Peter and the Epistles of the N.T., and it is sufficient to state the results at which he arrives. "The coincidences with St. James can hardly be accounted for on the ground of personal intercourse between the two writers. . . . The coincidences with the Pauline Epistles other than Romans and Ephesians are not very close and are to be accounted for as the outcome of a common evolution of Christian phrases and conceptions rather than as instances of direct borrowing. . . . There is no doubt that the author of 1 Peter was acquainted with the Epistle to the Romans. Nor is this surprising if the writer is St. Peter. . . . The connexion of Ephesians with 1 Peter (here he adopts the words of Hort) is shown more by the identities of thought and similarity in the structure of the two Epistles as wholes than by identities of phrase. . . ." In his summing-up he says: "All that we learn of St. Peter from the New Testament gives us the picture of a man prompt and enthusiastic in action rather than fertile in ideas. His borrowing from St. James' Epistle shows that his mind was receptive and retentive of the thoughts of others. The Epistle undoubtedly owes much to St. Paul. But it is only when the Pauline element is isolated and exaggerated that it becomes a serious argument against the Petrine authorship of the Epistle."[3]

It is to be remembered, also, that St. Paul did not invent Paulinism and that St. Peter manifests (according to the narrative of

[1] *Die Chronologie*, 464 f. (quoted by Chase, Hastings' *Dictionary of the Bible*, vol. iii. p. 786 b).

[2] *Chron.* p. 364 (quoted by Chase).

[3] Hastings' *Dictionary of the Bible.* vol. iii. pp. 788 f.

Acts) a disinclination to associate with the Gentile which suggests that he also was a strict Pharisee. There can be no doubt that of the Apostles of Christianity, who are known to us, St. Paul's was the master-mind. And there can be no doubt that St. Paul brought to the service of the Church a body of doctrine which he had inherited from Gamaliel and the masters of Gamaliel. The common notion that Christianity was something absolutely new planted by St. Paul and watered—watered *down*—by St. Peter and finally by St. John is inconsistent with known facts and with general probability. It is, indeed, the vicious product of the artificial isolation of the New Testament literature from the literature and the life of Judaism.

Others than St. Paul modified their inherited theology in the light of their belief, that Jesus, having been raised from the dead, was the promised and anointed deliverer—the Messiah, who by revealing God's will more fully than the prophets or the scribes, but not independently of either, introduced to men more fully the Sovereignty of Heaven, under whose yoke he lived and died. Inevitably and insensibly the first Christian teachers learned from each other and profited by their own and each other's experience. But they all inherited and already possessed the presuppositions and categories of the Scribes, whose teaching their Master had endorsed and extended. Into this body of theology they fitted the new fact of a crucified Messiah—into the framework of Pharisaism—as Pharisees fitted all new facts which threw fresh light upon the will of God. If St. Paul was the first (as our fragmentary evidence suggests) to find a deep significance in it, it is not derogatory to St. Peter to suggest that he may have been indebted to St. Paul both here and elsewhere, and such indebtedness is not necessarily an argument against the authenticity of this Epistle of Peter.

The second objection is that our document contains no vivid reminiscences of the life and doctrine of Jesus such as we should expect from a personal disciple.

The alleged expectation is not altogether a reasonable one. If the document is, as an unbroken chain of tradition affirms, a pastoral letter addressed to Christian Churches already in being, there is no reason to expect reminiscences of the life and teaching of Jesus. The Church was built upon the belief that Jesus was raised from the dead and so declared to be the promised deliverer. His submission to death—and the death of the cross—was the crown and the summary of His life as it was the fulfilment of His teaching. So far as other facts and traditions were relatively necessary to the faith of the converts they were naturally communicated—formally or informally—by those who founded or confirmed the Churches. But in an epistle like this they would have been irrelevant and inconclusive. The occasion called for the emphatic isolation of the glorious resurrection, which followed the culmination of the sufferings of Jesus and in which His past miracles were swallowed up like stars in the sunshine. As for the teaching of Jesus our records are plainly incomplete, and, whether the Fourth Gospel be permitted to give evidence or not it is quite clear that the arguments used by Jesus and the topics He treated were determined for Him by the character of those to whom He addressed Himself. When the Christian missionaries addressed themselves to men of different nationalities, they could not presume in them knowledge of Jewish presuppositions and therefore, quite apart from its relative insignificance they postponed indefinitely much of the teaching of Jesus. For in any case this teaching was relatively insignificant in their view; the essence of their message was Jesus and the Resurrection. Particular incidents and particular sayings may have their value as links in the chain of proof that—witness here and witness there—Jesus was He of whom Moses and the Prophets had spoken. But such proof belongs properly to the controversy with the Jews and, in many cases, not to the original phase of it. Historical or biographical sermons upon which the Gospel according to St. Mark is by tradition asserted to be based, were a sequel to the summons, "Repent and believe". It may well be that St. Peter did so preach, and that he dwelt rather upon the record of Jesus' life in Galilee of the Gentiles, because his own audience had little in common with the Jews of Jerusalem; but his reminiscences of the ministry prior to the Passion were *not*, as has been said,[1] "the best, the most inspiring message that he could deliver at such a critical time". He himself had seen and heard these things; yet, when the crisis came, he himself denied and repudiated Jesus. The impressiveness of these things, which failed to convince an eye-witness, was not likely to be heightened, when he repeated them to strangers. And there can be little doubt that, if he had inserted a reference to the Transfiguration (for example), it would be said nowadays that this was the mark of a sedulous forger, anxious to keep up the part he was playing. In his intercourse with Jesus St. Peter had learned and unlearned here a little and there a little. But at the last his faith was not

[1] Von Soden, *Early Christian Literature* (English Translation), London, 1906, pp. 278 f.: "It is evident that St. Peter cannot have written this epistle. The oldest personal disciple of our Lord would never have omitted the slightest reference to that which must above all things have distinguished him in the eyes of his readers. And how, especially at such a critical time, could he have refrained from speaking of reminiscences which formed the best, the most inspiring, message that he could deliver?"

proof against the appearance of failure. When, therefore, he converted and began to establish his brethren, he imparted to them the convictions he had acquired, and did not parade the diverse and devious steps by which he had painfully reached that height.

A third objection is that the Greek of this Epistle is better than a Galilean peasant could compass and that a Palestinian Jew would not possess such a familiar knowledge of the Old Testament in Greek.

Such an objection seems to take no account at all of certain known facts and of general probability. Even a Galilean peasant, who stayed in his native place, needed and presumably acquired some knowledge of the Greek language in his intercourse with the non-Jewish inhabitants of the land, whom Josephus calls indifferently *Greeks* and *Syrians*. If he went up to Jerusalem for the feasts he there came into contact with Jews of the Dispersion, most of whom lived in the Greek-speaking world. The part played by these assemblies in cementing the solidarity of the whole nation is commonly overlooked; and therefore it is worth while to quote Philo's explicit statement on the subject.[1] "The Temple made with hands," he says, "is necessary for men in general. They must have a place where they can give thanks for benefits and pray for pardon when they sin. So there is the temple at Jerusalem and no other. They must rise up from the ends of the earth and resort thither, if they would offer sacrifice. They must leave their fatherland, their friends and their kinsfolk, and so prove the sincerity of their religion. And this they do. At every feast myriads from East and West, from North and South repair to the Temple to be free for a little space from the business and the confusion of their lives. They draw breath for a little while, as they have leisure for holiness and the honouring of God. *And so they make friends with strangers hitherto unknown to them; and over sacrifices and libations they form a community of interests which is the surest pledge of unanimity*." In the face of this, it seems impossible to accept the modern distinction between Alexandrian and Palestinian Judaism as corresponding to an absolute severance in life, language and religion in the first century of the present era. Apart from this normal intercourse of all classes of religiously minded Jews, those who aspired to direct their fellows as Sages or Scribes seem to have travelled in foreign countries as a part of their training. And further, it is known that the delivery of the Temple dues at Jerusalem was regarded as a pious duty which the foremost members of each

[1] *De specialibus legibus*, i. (*de templo*), §§ 67-70 (Cohn and Wendland, vol. v. pp. 17 f.; ii. p. 223, Mangey).

community were selected to perform. In these and other ways the Jews of Palestine became acquainted with the Greek language and, so far as they engaged in religious discussion with their visitors or hosts of the Dispersion, with the Old Testament in Greek also. The translation known as the Septuagint was still a triumphant achievement, through which the Jews of the Greek world were retained within the fold of Judaism and the Greeks outside were offered knowledge of the Law. And even when the Christian missionaries began to utilise in the interests of their own creed the laxities of the Septuagint, the non-Christian Jews produced the Greek versions of Aquila Symmachus and Theodotion. In fact, so far as and as long as any sect of Judaism engaged in missionary enterprise knowledge of the Greek language and the Greek Bible was indispensable to its agents.

It is therefore entirely in keeping with the tradition that this document is the Epistle General of St. Peter, the Apostle of the Circumcision, that it should be written in passable Greek and bear evident traces of familiarity with the Septuagint. In order to prove that Jesus was the deliverer for whom the prophets had looked, he was bound to appeal to the Scriptures, and to the Scriptures in that version which was established as the Bible of the Greek Dispersion.

If in spite of these and other considerations it is felt that the general style of the Epistle is too literary for one who had lived the life and done the work of St. Peter, there is still another line of defence for the traditional view. In other words, it is still possible to believe that the document as it stands gives a just and true account of its own origin. In the postscript[1] the author says, "*I write* (or *I have written*) *to you, briefly by means of Silvanus the faithful brother, as I reckon him*".

If the phrase *I write by means of Silvanus* may be taken to imply that Silvanus was not only the bearer of the Epistle but also the trusted secretary who wrote out in his own way St. Peter's message, then all the difficulties derived from the style of the document and its use of Pauline ideas vanish at once. And in any case this mention of Silvanus proves that St. Peter was closely associated with the sometime colleague of St. Paul, who had actually helped to preach the Gospel in Syria, Cilicia and Galatia.[2] For there seems to be no reason for questioning the identification of the Silas of the *Acts* with the Silvanus of the Pauline Epistles and this Epistle.

The interpretation of the phrase διὰ Σιλουανοῦ is still in dispute. Professor Zahn[3] maintains the view that "Silvanus' part in the

[1] v. 12. [2] See Acts xv. 23, 40 f.; xvi. 1-8.

[3] *Introduction to the New Testament* (English Translation, 1909), vol. ii. p. 150.

composition was so important and so large that its performance required a considerable degree of trustworthiness. . . . It purports to be a letter of Peter's; and such it is, except that Peter left its composition to Silvanus because he regarded him as better fitted than himself . . . to express in an intelligible and effective manner the thoughts and feelings which Peter entertained toward the Gentile Christians of Asia Minor".

Dr. Chase[1] quotes Professor Zahn as arguing that Silvanus "must have been *either* a messenger who conveyed the letter *or* a friend who put St. Peter's thoughts into the form of a letter". Against this interpretation, he says, four "considerations seem together decisive"; and he concludes that Silvanus carried the Epistle and did *not* write it. It is of course possible that the phrase may bear this meaning, but the other is not to be excluded. The parallels quoted are, with two exceptions, ambiguous, and of the exceptions each supports one of the rival views. In Acts xv. 22, for example, it is said that the Apostles chose Judas and Silas and *wrote by their hand*.[2] Clearly they were the bearers of the letter, as it is said that they delivered it at Antioch;[3] and "being prophets they exhorted and confirmed the brethren".[4] But it is certainly possible if not definitely probable that they actually wrote each a copy of the letter for himself at the dictation of St. James. The case on which Dr. Chase chiefly relies is the postscript of Ignatius' letter to the Romans: "I write these things to you by the worthy Ephesians: Crocus whom I love is by my side with many others".[5] But even here the other interpretation is not impossible. They certainly were the bearers, but for safety's sake each may have written his own copy of the letter. The journey from Smyrna to Rome was long and dangerous, and apart from considerations of safe delivery each of them may well have desired to have his own copy. And there is one clear case in which this ambiguity disappears: Dionysius, Bishop of Corinth, writes to Soter, Bishop of Rome, in acknowledgment of a letter received from the Roman Church, which (he says) "we shall always have to read for our admonition like the former

[1] Hastings' *Dictionary of the Bible* (1900), vol. iii. p. 790.

[2] γράψαντες διὰ χειρὸς αὐτῶν.

[3] Acts xv. 30, οἱ μὲν οὖν ἀπολυθέντες κατῆλθον εἰς Ἀντιόχειαν καὶ συναγαγόντες τὸ πλῆθος ἐπέδωκαν τὴν ἐπιστολήν.

[4] Acts xv. 32.

[5] *Ad Romanos*, xiv. 1, γράφω δὲ ὑμῖν ταῦτα ἀπὸ Cμύρνης δι' Ἐφεσιων τῶν ἀξιομακαρίστων. ἔστιν δὲ καὶ ἅμα ἐμοὶ σὺν ἄλλοις πολλοῖς καὶ Κρόκος τὸ ποθητόν μοι ὄνομα.

Epistle written to us *through* Clement".[1] Here the preposition clearly denotes the interpreter who writes in the name of the Church and cannot cover the messenger also, because the bearers of the Epistle—Claudius Ephebus, Valerius Bito, and Fortunatus—are named at the end.[2]

Since, therefore, διά can in such contexts designate the *writer* as well as the *bearer* of an Epistle, it is hardly safe to say that Silvanus cannot have been *both* in this case. If St. Peter had not so far profited by his general experience and in particular by his association with Silvanus and other missionaries as to write moderately good Greek and to employ "Pauline" ideas, then we may suppose that he permitted Silvanus to write the Epistle for him. He was none the less the real author if he employed a letter-writer whose position and experience enabled him to supplement the author's alleged deficiencies in respect of the language and modes of thought familiar to the persons addressed. The postscript indicates St. Peter's approval of the draft thus made and submitted to him. The tone of authority which is used in the addresses to separate classes is naturally reproduced by the secretary from his recollection of what St. Peter had said. The secretary's intervention affects only the manner of the Epistle at most. If Silvanus had really contributed to the matter he would have been joined with St. Peter in the salutation. On the other hand, there is every reason to suppose that Silvanus was also St. Peter's messenger plenipotentiary and would, as when he was sent by the Apostles of Jerusalem, "proclaim the same things by word of mouth".[3]

The fourth objection to the traditional view is that the Epistle reflects conditions which were definitely later than the date of St. Peter's death. No other book of the New Testament offers any plain information about St. Peter at any time after the hypocrisy he practised at Antioch.[4] But Christian tradition connects him not only with Antioch[5] and Asia Minor[6]—statements which are probably simple inferences from the statements of St. Paul's Epistle to the

[1] Τὴν σήμερον οὖν κυριακὴν ἅγιαν ἡμέραν διηγάγομεν ἐν ᾗ ἀνέγνωμεν ὑμῶν τὶν ἐπιστολήν· ἣν ἕξομεν ἀεί ποτε ἀναγινώσκοντες νουθετεῖσθαι ὡς καὶ τὴν προτέραν ἡμεῖν διὰ Κλήμεντος γραφεῖσαν (Eusebius, *Historiae Ecclesiae*, iv. 23. 8).

[2] Clement, *ad Corinthios*, lxv. [3] Acts xv. 27. [4] Gal. ii.

[5] So Origen (*in Lucam Homilia*, vi.): "Eleganter in cuiusdam martyris epistola scriptum repperi, Ignatium dico, *episcopum Antiochiae post Petrum secundum*, qui in persecutione Romae pugnavit ad bestias, 'principem saeculi huius latuit virginitas Mariae'."

[6] So Origen (fragment in Eusebius, *Historiae Ecclesiae*, iii. 1): Πέτρος δὲ ἐν Πόντῳ καὶ Γαλατίᾳ καὶ Βιθυνίᾳ Καππαδοκίᾳ τε καὶ Ἀσίᾳ κεκηρυχέναι τοῖς ἐκ διασπορᾶς Ἰουδαίοις ἔοικεν.

Galatians and the First Epistle of St. Peter respectively—but also with Rome. For this part of the tradition there is no obvious hint in the New Testament which can be used to explain away its origin, unless it be supposed that the bare mention of Babylon in the First Epistle of St. Peter is sufficient of itself to have given birth to so complete a legend. It is not surprising that Babylon should have been interpreted as meaning Rome from the first; but the tradition, that St. Peter died at Rome under Nero, has nothing on which to rest in the Epistles or elsewhere.

Tertullian is the first to state this tradition explicitly. We read, in the *Lives of the Cæsars*, "Nero first laid bloody hands upon the rising faith at Rome. Then was Peter girded by another when he was bound to the cross."[1] But apart from the definite date, the tradition is as old as Clement of Rome, who cites St. Peter and St. Paul as "noble examples of our own generation" in his Epistle to the Corinthians: "By reason of envy and jealousy the great and righteous Pillars were persecuted and struggled on till they died. Let us put before our eyes the good Apostles—Peter, who by reason of unrighteous envy endured not one or two but many labours and so became a martyr and departed to the place of glory which was his due".[2] A brief account of St. Paul's sufferings, based largely on New Testament evidence, follows; and the conclusion that St. Peter suffered before St. Paul and both at Rome is commonly drawn. After this Clement goes on to say: "To these men of holy life was gathered a great multitude of elect persons who by reason of envy suffered many outrages and torments and so became a noble example among us".[3] This further illustration of the terrible effects of envy and jealousy—the theme to which all these references are incidental—is most naturally interpreted as describing the victims of the Neronian persecution of A.D. 64, of whom Tacitus[4] speaks as "a huge multitude". If, then, Clement has put his illustrations in

[1] *Vitas Caesarum legimus: Orientem fidem Romae primus Nero cruentavit. Nunc Petrus ab altero cingitur, cum cruci adstringitur* (*Scorpiace*, 15). The fact is so stated as to indicate the fulfilment of the word of Jesus reported in John xxi. 18:

[2] διὰ ζῆλον καὶ φθόνον οἱ μέγιστοι καὶ δικαιότατοι στύλοι (cf. Gal. ii. 9) ἐδιώχθησαν καὶ ἕως θανάτου ἤθλησαν. λάβωμεν πρὸ ὀφθαλμῶν ἡμῶν τοὺς ἀγαθοὺς ἀποστόλους Πέτρον ὃς διὰ ζῆλον ἄδικον οὐχ ἕνα οὐδὲ δύο ἀλλὰ πλείονας ὑπήνεγκεν πόνους καὶ οὕτω μαρτυρήσας ἐπορεύθη εἰς τὸν ὀφειλόμενον τόπον τῆς δόξης (1 *Clementis ad Corinthios*, v. 2-4).

[3] τούτοις τοῖς ἀνδράσιν ὁσίως πολιτευσαμένοις συνηθροίσθη πολὺ πλῆθος ἐκλεκτῶν οἵτινες πολλὰς αἰκίας καὶ βασάνους διὰ ζῆλος παθόντες ὑπόδειγμα κάλλιστον ἐγένοντο ἐν ἡμῖν (1 *Clementis ad Corinthios*, vi. 1).

[4] *Annals*, xv. 44.

chronological order, he agrees with Tertullian in asserting that St. Peter died as a martyr under Nero and, being a conspicuous pillar of the Church, before the mass of the Christians. To this assertion Origen, quoted by Eusebius,[1] adds the statement that "at the end Peter being at Rome was crucified head-downwards having himself requested that he might so suffer".

Eusebius in his account of the Neronian persecution endorses this tradition of St. Peter's martyrdom and cites evidence to prove its truth: "So then at this time this man who was proclaimed one of the foremost fighters against God was led on to slaughter the Apostles. It is related that Paul was beheaded in Rome itself and that Peter was likewise crucified in his reign. And the history is confirmed by the inscription upon the tombs there which is still in existence. It is also confirmed by an ecclesiastic named Gaius, who lived at the time when Zephyrinus was Bishop of Rome, who writing to Proclus, the leader of the Phrygian heresy, says these very words about the places where the sacred tabernacles of the aforesaid Apostles are deposited, 'But I can shew the trophies of the Apostles. For if you will go to the Vatican or to the Ostian Way you will find the trophies of those who founded this Church. And that they both became martyrs at the same time Dionysius, Bishop of Corinth, writing to the Romans proves in this way. You also by such admonition have compounded the plant of Romans and Corinthians which came from Peter and Paul. For they both of them came to our Corinth and planted us, teaching like doctrine, and in like manner they taught together in Italy and became martyrs at the same time."[2]

All the other extant evidence[3] agrees with this, and we may fairly conclude that from the end of the first century it has been the unchallenged belief of the Christian Church that St. Peter was put to death at Rome in A.D. 64. The question therefore arises, Is this tradition compatible with the traditional ascription of this document to St. Peter?

DATE, CIRCUMSTANCES, AND PURPOSE.

If St. Peter was the author of this document and if St. Peter perished in the persecution under Nero, it follows that the document

[1] *Historiae Ecclesiasticae*, iii. 1: **ὃς καὶ ἐπὶ τέλει ἐν Ῥώμῃ γενόμενος ἀνεσκολοπίσθη κατὰ κεφαλῆς οὕτως αὐτὸς ἀξιώσας παθεῖν.**

[2] *Historiae Ecclesiasticae*, ii. 25.

[3] See Dr. Chase's article on Peter (Simon) in Hastings' *Dictionary of the Bible* vol. iii.

must have been written before A.D. 64. The conclusion is challenged on the ground of the circumstances implied by the document and consequently one or other of the premises is invalidated. The circumstances implied and indicated are suppposed to belong to a date definitely later than the time of Nero; and from this supposition it follows *either* that St. Peter did not write the Epistle *or* that he did not perish under Nero. In either case the Epistle is now commonly assigned to the reign either of Domitian (A.D. 81-96) or of Trajan (A.D. 98-117). Professor Gunkel (for example) in a popular commentary recently published[1] ends his introduction with the words: "The more precise dating of the Epistle must be determined in accordance with the persecutions above mentioned, with which, it must be confessed, we are not perfectly acquainted. Now the Neronian persecution affected only Rome and not the provinces. On the other hand more general persecutions seem to have taken place under Domitian. The time of Trajan, under whom a persecution (A.D. 112) to which the letters of Pliny to the emperor testify, certainly took place in Asia Minor, is open to the objection that then the Christians were compelled to offer sacrifice—to which the Epistle has no reference. Our Epistle is therefore best assigned to the early period of Domitian's reign. A still later dating (*sc.* than the reign of Trajan ?) is excluded by the lack of references to *Gnosis* and the Episcopate."

Professor Ramsay similarly suggests, on the basis of the contents of the Epistle: "The First Epistle of Peter then must have been written soon after Vespasian's resumption of the Neronian policy in a more precise and definite form. It implies relations between Church and State which are later than the Neronian period, but which have only just begun."[2]

Professor Cone[3] urges that the conditions implied by the Epistle fit the time of Trajan, and argues, as against Professor Ramsay, that "since they also fit the later date, they furnish no ground for excluding it in favour of the earlier". His conclusion is: "The data supplied in the Epistle and in known and precisely determinable historical circumstances do not warrant us in placing its composition more definitely than in the last quarter of the first, or the first quarter of the second, century". For this he relies partly on Professor Ramsay's opinion that "the history of the spread of Chris-

[1] *Die Schriften des Neuen Testaments neu übersetzt und für die Gegenwart erklärt* . . . Gottingen, 1908.

[2] *The Church in the Roman Empire* (sixth edition: London, 1893), p. 282. He assigns it, therefore, to *c.* A.D. 80 at the end of Vespasian's reign.

[3] *Encyclopedia Biblica III.*, "Peter, the Epistles of".

tianity imperatively demands for 1 Peter a later date than A.D. 64"; and from it he deduces the corollary: "The later date renders it very probable that Babylon is employed figuratively for Rome, according to Rev. xiv. 8, xvi. 19, xvii. 5, xviii. 2, 10, 21".

Professor Cone's corollary deserves attention. He seems to assume that the Christians started afresh—*de novo* or *ex nihilo*—to evolve modes and idioms of thought for themselves. Such an assumption is demonstrably untenable. In the particular case of such cipher-language as this, it is certain that the Christians appropriated the inventions of the Jews, who in their own oppressions and their own persecutions had learned to veil their hopes from all but the initiated. Babylon was the great and typical oppressor, and her successors in the part naturally received her proper name. Rome was not the declared and inflexible enemy of the Jewish nation as a whole before the time of Caligula; but Rome stood behind Herod the Great, and Pompey had desecrated the Temple at Jerusalem. Philo might forgive and forget the outrages which Pompey and Herod had perpetrated in order to heighten the enormity of Caligula's offences, but the Psalms of Solomon and the evidence of Josephus suffice to prove that for some Rome was already the enemy in the last century B.C. Formal proof that the Jews actually spoke of Rome by the name of Babylon before the destruction of Jerusalem in A.D. 70 is, indeed, wanting. But the identification of Rome with Babylon and the consequent transference of the paraphernalia of Babylon to Rome is part and parcel of the apocalyptic vocabulary and passed over into the language of the Rabbis. The author of the Epistle had no more need to explain his use of Babylon than had the Jewish poet who wrote in the name of the Sibyl and said in reference to Nero:—

"Poets shall mourn for thee, thrice-hapless Greece,
What time the mighty king of mighty Rome,
Coming from Italy, shall pierce thine Isthmus—
A God-like mortal, born (they say) of Zeus
By lady Hera, who with dulcet songs
Shall slay his hapless mother and many more.
A shameless prince and terrible! He shall fly
From *Babylon* . . ."[1]

And again he prophesied that after a time and times and half a time[2]

[1] Oracula, *Sibyllina*, v. 137-143 (Geffcken: Leipzig, 1902).
[2] *Ibid.* 154: "ἐκ τετράτου ἔτεος"; compare Daniel vii. 25.

"From heav'n into the sea a star shall fall
That shall consume with fire the ocean wide,
And *Babylon* herself, and Italy . . ."[1]

Nero's achievements added matricide to the specification of Antichrist; but the book of Daniel and other apocalypses, which were directly or indirectly inspired by the experience of the Jews under Antiochus Epiphanes, had long ago established the code of language by which each particular persecutor was identified with the vanished type. In the time of Antiochus such disguise was a necessary pre caution; and it was so again in the time of Nero or Vespasian, of Domitian or Trajan. In fact, Professor Cone's corollary has nothing to do with his conclusion. Whenever any Christian community became exposed for whatever reason to attack by any representative of the State, the State became for them the enemy, and therefore Babylon.

For Trajan's attitude towards the Christians of Bithynia we have ample testimony—thanks to the lack of independence displayed by his legate, the younger Pliny. In A.D. 112 Bithynia was in a bad state. There were many abuses which called for remedies, and the province was distracted by factions.[2] The law which forbade the formation of clubs or associations for different purposes had fallen into abeyance, and Pliny began by re-enacting it in accordance with Trajan's mandate.[3] On this policy Trajan insisted so strongly that he refused to authorise a fire brigade in Nicomedia, in spite of Pliny's protestations that only 150 men would be enrolled, only carpenters, and for the sole purpose of dealing with such a conflagration as had recently devastated the city.[4] From experience he held that all corporations, whatever name they bore, quickly became political associations.[5] This rigid interpretation of the law made the ordinary meetings of the Christians at once illegal; and there were so many Christians in Bithynia that the temples were almost deserted and the customary sacrifices were omitted. When the edict was

[1] Or. *Sib.* v. 158-160.

[2] Trajan to Pliny, xxxii. (xli.): "Meminerimus idcirco te in istam provinciam missum, quoniam multa in ea emendanda apparuerint; xxxiv. (xliii.) meminerimus provinciam istam . . . factionibus esse vexatam".

[3] Pliny to Trajan, xcvi. (xcvii.): "Edictum meum quo secundum mandata tua hetaerias esse vetueram".

[4] Pliny to Trajan, xxxiii. (xlii.): "Tu, domine, dispice an instituendum putes Collegium fabrorum dumtaxat hominum Cl. Ego attendam ne quis nisi faber recipiatur neve iure concesso in aliud utatur; necerit difficile custodire tam paucos".

[5] Trajan to Pliny, xxxiv. (xliii.): "Quodcumque nomen ex quacumque causa dederimus eis qui in idem contracti fuerit. . . . hetaeriae que brevi fient".

published, some Christians — apparently renegades, who abjured Christianity when challenged by Pliny—asserted that either they or the Christians generally gave up either the practice of meeting for a common meal or their religious meetings also. It is improbable that those who persisted in their wicked and immoderate superstition should have abandoned their weekly assemblies at which they recited a hymn to Christ as God, but it is unnatural to distinguish between these assemblies and the subsequent meetings for the common meal, and the statement of the renegades may reasonably be confined to their own obedience to the edict.

Professor Ramsay, however, infers from Pliny's language that the statement refers to the Christians as a whole: "They had, indeed, been in the habit of holding social meetings, and feasting in common; but this illegal practice they had abandoned as soon as the governor had issued an edict in accordance with the Emperor's instructions, forbidding the formation or existence of *sodalitates*".[1] And he asserts that Pliny's language implies a distinction between the illegal meetings of the evening and the legal meetings of the morning: "The regular morning meetings which Pliny speaks about and which, as we know, must have been weekly meetings, were not abandoned, and Pliny obviously accepts them as strictly legal. Amid the strict regulations about societies the Roman government expressly allowed to all people the right of meeting for purely religious purposes. The morning meeting of the Christians was religious; but the evening meeting was social, including a common meal, and therefore constituted the Christian community a *sodalitas*. The Christians abandoned the illegal meeting, but continued the legal one. This fact is one of the utmost consequence. It shows that the Christian communities were quite alive to the necessity of acting according to the law, and of using the forms of the law to screen themselves as far as was consistent with their principles."[2]

Against this view it must be urged, in the first place, that the common meal of the Christian community had a definitely religious character and could not be abandoned without a breach of their principles; and, in the second place, that Pliny's language is by no means so explicit and clear as is suggested. The authors of the statement are a large number of persons accused of Christianity, either by an anonymous letter or by an informer: all of them convinced Pliny that they had never been Christians, or had ceased to be Christians, by offering sacrifice to idols and blas-

[1] *The Church in the Roman Empire*, p. 206.
[2] *Ibid.* pp. 219 f.

pheming Christ.[1] As regards their past Christianity—if ever they had practised Christianity—they affirmed that this was the sum and substance of their crime, that they had been accustomed to assemble on a fixed day before sunrise and to repeat alternately a hymn to Christ as God, and to bind themselves by an oath—not to commit any crime, but—to abstain from theft, brigandage, adultery, breach of faith, and refusal of any deposit; which done they usually departed and assembled again to take food, which food was taken by all together, and involved no crime. And even this, they said, they had ceased to do after the edict.[2]

Here, surely, Pliny is concerned only with renegades who proved to him that the Christian faith which they had abandoned had led them into no crimes of which he must take cognisance. Their oath was not proof of conspiracy and their meal was not a cannibal feast. To satisfy himself that their denial of the charges brought against them was well founded, Pliny examined two slaves, who were called deaconesses, under torture. Finding nothing in them but a foul immoderate superstition, he submitted the case to the Emperor.[3]

The fact is that the large number of persons involved and the doubt whether those who had repented of their Christianity had thereby deserved free pardon, gave Pliny food for reflexion. Christianity had been rampant in his province, but his experience of these apostates gave him good hope that it might be checked. Apostates would naturally be more zealous heathens, and therefore good

[1] Pliny to Trajan, xcvi. (xcvii.): "Propositus est libellus sine auctore multorum nomina continens. Qui negabant esse se Christianos aut fuisse cum praeeunte me deos appellarent et imagini tuae, quam propter hoc iusseram cum simulacris nominum adferri, ture ac vino supplicarent, praeterea male dicerent Christo, quorum nihil posse cogi dicuntur qui sunt se vera Christiani, dimittendos esse putavi. Alii ab indice nominati esse se Christianos dixerunt et mox negaverunt; fuisse quidem, sed desisse, quidam ante plures annos non nemo etiam ante viginti quoque. Omnes et imaginem tuam deorumque simulacra venerati sunt et Christo maledixerunt."

[2] Pliny to Trajan, xcvi. (xcvii.): "Adfirmabant autem hanc fuisse summam vel culpae suae vel erroris quod essent soliti stato die ante lucem convenire carmenque Christo quasi deo dicere secum invicem, seque sacramento non in scelus aliquod obstringere, sed ne furta, ne latrocinia ne adulteria committerent, ne fidem fallerent, ne depositum appellati abnegarent; quibus peractis morem sibi discedendi fuisse, rursusque ad capiendum cibum, promiscuum tamen et innoxium; quod ipsum facere desisse post edictum meum, quo secundum mandata tua hetaerias esse vetueram".

[3] Pliny, *ibid.*: "Quo magis necessarium credidi ex duabus ancillis quae ministrae dicebantur, quid esset veri et per tormenta quaerere. Nihil aliud inveni quam superstitionem pravam immodicam. Ideo dilata cognitione ad consulendum te decucurri".

citizens, in future. To execute them all would have been to diminish seriously the population of his province.[1] As a conscientious governor, he was anxious to bring this section of his subjects to their senses, and he believed that the extension of clemency to those who repented of their Christianity would be the means most likely to secure that end.[2] If room for repentance was given, all the Christians might be induced to recant. He does not contemplate a policy of religious toleration at all. Though there might be no crimes inherent in the profession of Christianity, Christians were still guilty of *sacrilegium* when they refused to worship the gods of the Empire, even if they satisfied Pliny that their meetings were purely religious in character and, therefore, did not constitute them a *sodalitas* within the meaning of the law. Obstinate Christians had three opportunities of recantation: if they did not take advantage of their opportunities, they were executed summarily—or, if they were Roman citizens, they were transported to Rome. It was an accepted and a familiar fact that a Christian was, as such, a criminal[3]—so familiar, indeed, that Pliny leaves their crime of sacrilege to be inferred from the sacrifice required of those who would prove their apostasy. He confesses that he never occupied such an official position as to be called on to decide or advise in the case of Christians, and was therefore ignorant of the precise nature of the proceedings.[4] But he did not hesitate to condemn the obdurate,[5] although he might doubt whether the name itself, if it involved no crime, or the crimes attaching to the name were thereby punished.[6]

[1] *Ibid.*: "Visa est enim mihi res digna consultatione maxime propter periclitantium munerum. Multi enim omnis aetatis, omnis ordinis utriusque sexus etiam, vocantur in periculum et vocabuntur. Neque civitates tantum sed vicos etiam atque agros superstitionis istius contagio pervagata est; *quae videtur sisti et corrigi posse.* Certe satis constat prope iam desolata templa coepisse celebrari et sacra sollemnia diuintermissa repeti pastumque venire victinarum cuius adhuc rarissimus emptor."

[2] *Ibid.*: "Ex quo facile est opinari quae turba hominum emendari possit si sit paenitentiae locus".

[3] *Ibid.*: "Interrogari ipsos an essent Christiani. Confitentes iterum ac tertio interrogari, supplicium miratus: perseverantes duci iussi. *Neque enim dubitatum, qualecumque esset quod faterentur, pertinaciam certe et inflexibilem obstinationem debere puniri.* Fuerunt alii similis amentiae quos, quia cives Romani erant, adnotari in urbem remittendos."

[4] Professor Ramsay's paraphrase of Pliny's words (*ibid.*): "Cognitionibus de Christianis interfui numquam; ideo nescio quid et quatenus aut puniri soleat aut quaeri".

[5] See note (1) *supra*.

[6] *Ibid.*: "Nec mediocriter haesitavi sitne aliquod discrimen aetatum an quamlibet teneri nihil a robustioribus differant, detur paenitentiae venia an eï qui omnino Christianus fuit desisse non prosit. nomen ipsum, si flagitiis careat, an flagitia cohaerentia nomini puniantur".

Such doubts as this arose from his examination of the renegades and the slaves who were called deaconesses, in which he learned that there were no crimes other than *sacrilegium* involved in the name, and, therefore, was emboldened to suggest that renegades should be pardoned.

Trajan's answer authorises the policy suggested: "Any one who denies that he is a Christian and gives plain proof of his truthfulness, that is, by worshipping our gods, though his past may not be above suspicion, shall obtain pardon by his repentance".[1] No anonymous accusations are to be entertained,[2] and Christians are not to be sought out. If they are brought before the governor and convicted of being Christians they must, of course, be punished. Pliny did well to investigate the cases of the so-called Christians, who had been brought before him.[3] No general policy can be laid down. Trajan is content to endorse the existing practice of punishing obdurate Christians as Christians, and to sanction the pardon of such Christians as were prepared to renounce their Christianity and to ratify their renunciation by performance of heathen rites.

Trajan's endorsement of the action which Pliny took without hesitation against the Christians *as such*, proves that "persecution for the name" was already an established and familiar part of Roman policy. If Pliny had been present at trials of Christians before becoming governor of Bithynia, he might have learned that the vulgar were wrong in ascribing foul crimes to the Christians, as such. But there is no question that Christians, as such, were liable to capital punishment. In the first instance, when he had only to do with those Christians who refused to apostatize, Pliny condemned them to death almost instinctively as a matter of routine and immemorial tradition.

Under Domitian (according to Dio Cassius) Flavius Clemens was put to death on the charge of atheism, and many others who embraced the customs of the Jews were condemned to death or

[1] Trajan to Pliny, xcvii. (xcviii.). . . . puniendi sunt ita tamen ut qui negaverit se Christianum esse idque re ipsa manifestum fecerit, id est supplicando dis nostris, quamvis suspectus in praeteritum, veniam ex paenitentia impetret".

[2] *Ibid.*: "Sine auctore vero propositi libelli in nullo crimine locum habere debent. Nam et pessimi exempli nec nostri saeculi est."

[3] *Ibid.*: "Actum quem debuisti, mi Secunde, in excutiendis causis eorum qui Christiani ad te delati fuerunt secutus es. Neque enim in universum aliquid quod quasi certam forman habeat constitui potest. Conquirendi non sunt: si deferantur et arguantur, puniendi sunt". . . .

deprived of their goods. His wife Domitilla, a relative of the Emperor, was merely banished to Pandateria.[1]

Suetonius[2] describes Flavius Clemens as a man of contemptible inactivity—a conventional description of Christians[3]—and says that he was put to death on the barest suspicion. Eusebius[4] asserts explicitly that Domitilla was banished with many others, because she bore witness to Christ. Probably the Christians were regarded as a Jewish sect who could not claim the privileges of Jews proper. Evidently the sect was proscribed. A Christian as such was liable to death, banishment, or confiscation of his goods. Domitian (as Eusebius[5] says) was the second persecutor of the Christian Church and made himself the heir of Nero's battle with God. But according to Hegesippus,[6] as reported by Eusebius,[7] Domitian stopped the persecution after examining the grandsons of Judas, the brother of Jesus.[8]

[1] lxvii. 14 (epitome of Xiphilinus): Κἀν τῷ αὐτῷ ἔτει (A.D. 95) ἄλλους τε πολλοὺς καὶ τὸν Φλάβιον Κλήμεντα ὑπατεύοντα, καίπερ ἀνεψιὸν ὄντα, καὶ γυναῖκα καὶ αὐτὴν συγγενῆ ἑαυτοῦ Φλαουίαν Δομιτίλλαν ἔχοντα, κατέσφαξεν ὁ Δομετιανός· ἐπηνέχθη δὲ ἀμφοῖν ἔγκλημα ἀθεότητος, ὑφ' ἧς καὶ ἄλλοι εἰς τὰ τῶν Ἰουδαίων ἔθη ἐξοκέλλοντες πολλοὶ κατεδικάσθησαν, καὶ οἱ μὲν ἀπέθανον, οἱ δὲ τῶν γοῦν οὐσιῶν ἐστερήθησαν· ἡ δὲ Δομιτίλλα ὑπερωρίσθη μόνον εἰς Πανδατερίαν.

[2] *Domitian* xv. Denique Flavium Clementem patruelum suum contemptissimae inertiae . . . repente ex tenuissima suspicione tantum non ipso eius consulatu interemit: quo maxime facto maturavit sibi exilium.

[3] Compare Tertullian's *Apology*, xlii.: "Sed alio quoque iniuriarum titulo postulamur et infructuosi in negotiis dicimur. . . . Quomodo infructuosi videmur negotiis vestris, cum quibus et de quibus vivimus, non scio. Sed si carimonias tuas non frequento, attamen et illa die homo sum."

[4] *Historiae ecclesiasticae*, iii. 18: "εἰς τοσοῦτον δὲ ἄρα . . . ἡ τῆς ἡμετέρας πίστεως διέλαμπε διδασκαλία, ὡς καὶ τοὺς ἄποθεν τοῦ καθ' ἡμᾶς λόγου συγγραφεῖς μὴ ἀποκνῆσαι ταῖς αὐτῶν Ἱστορίαις τόν τε διωγμὸν καὶ τὰ ἐν αὐτῷ μαρτύρια παραδοῦναι. οἵγε καὶ τὸν καιρὸν ἐπ' ἀκριβὲς ἐπεσημήναντο, ἐν ἔτει πεντεκαιδεκάτῳ Δομετιανοῦ μετὰ πλείστων ἑτέρων καὶ Φλαυίαν Δομετίλλαν ἱστορήσαντες, ἐξ ἀδελφῆς γεγονυῖαν Φλαυίου Κλήμεντος, ἑνὸς τῶν τηνικάδε ἐπὶ Ῥώμης ὑπάτων, τῆς εἰς Χριστὸν μαρτυρίας ἕνεκεν, εἰς νῆσον Ποντίαν κατὰ τιμωρίαν δεδόσθαι."

[5] *Historiae ecclesiasticae*, iii. 17: "Τῆς Νέρωνος θεοεχθρίας τε καὶ θεομαχίας διάδοχον ἑαυτὸν κατεστήσατο. δεύτερος δῆτα τὸν καθ' ἡμῶν ἀνεκίνει διωγμόν, καίπερ τοῦ πατρὸς αὐτοῦ Οὐεσπασιανοῦ μηδὲν καθ' ἡμῶν ἄτοπον ἐπινοήσαντος."

Hegesippus was an Eastern—probably a native of Palestine. He visited Rome in the episcopate of Anicetus (? A.D. 155-156) and published his five books of *Memoranda* or *Memoirs* (ὑπομνήματα) in A.D. 180. See Bardenhewer, *Geschichte der altkirchlichen Literatur*, i. pp. 483-490.

Historiae ecclesiasticae, iii. 20: "ἐφ' οἷς μηδὲν αὐτῶν κατεγνωκότα τὸν Δομετιανόν, ἀλλὰ καὶ ὡς εὐτελῶν καταφρονήσαντα, ἐλευθέρους μὲν αὐτοὺς ἀνεῖναι, καταπαῦσαι δὲ διὰ προστάγματος τὸν κατὰ τῆς ἐκκλησίας διωγμόν

Eusebius[1] quotes Tertullian[2] to the same general effect: "Domitian, a semi-Nero in cruelty, attempted to condemn the Christians; but, being also a man, he readily stopped the course of action he had begun, and even recalled those whom he had banished".

But Nero was the first to persecute the Christians[3] and something is known of his procedure from Tacitus,[4] who represents his persecution as a final effort to divert from himself the suspicion of having given orders for the fire of Rome. Human assistance, public largesses, services of expiation, all failed to banish the calumny. So to put an end to the rumour, Nero made the Christians, as they were commonly called by the vulgar who hated them for their crimes, scape-goats in his place and visited them with the most elaborate penalties. Christ from whom their name was derived was executed by the procurator Pontius Pilate in the reign of Tiberius. For a time this fatal superstition was suppressed, but it broke out afterwards not only in Judaea, the birthplace of the mischief, but also in Rome . . . Accordingly, in the first instance those who confessed were arrested; and afterwards on their information a huge multitude were sent to join them not so much on the charge of arson as on that of hatred of the human race.

Tacitus emphasises the fact that the Christians were guilty and deserved to suffer the last penalty of the law.[5] Public feeling condemned them as enemies of civilised society; but the outrageous mockery with which Nero had them executed, and the common suspicion that the alleged arson was a mere pretence produced a revul-

[1] *Historiae ecclesiasticae*, iii. 20.

[2] *Apology* v.: "Temptaverat et Domitianus, portio Neronis de crudelitate; sed qua et homo (ἀλλ' οἶμαι ἅτε ἔχων τι συνέσεως, Eusebius) facile coeptum repressit, restitutis etiam quos relegaverat.

[3] Tertullian, *Apology*, v.: "Consulite commentarios vestros; illic reperietis primum Neronem in hanc sectam cum maxime Romae orientem Caesariano gladio ferocisse. Sed tali dedicatore damnationis nostrae etiam gloriamur. Qui enim scit illum, intelligere potest non nisi grande aliquod bonum a Nerone damnatum."

[4] *Annals*, xv. 44: "Sed non ope humana, non largitionibus principis aut deum placamentis decedebat infamia, quin iussum incendium crederetur. Ergo abolendo rumori Nero subdidit reos, et quaesitissimis poenis affecit, quos per flagitia invisos vulgus Chrestianos (*sic*) appellabat. Auctor nominis eius Christus, Tiberio imperitante, per procuratorem Pontium Pilatum supplicio affectus erat. Repressaque in praesens exitiabilis superstitio rursus erumpebat, non modo per Judaeam originem eius mali sed per urbem etiam. . . . Igitur primo correpti qui fatebantur, deinde indicio eorum multitudo ingens, haud perinde in crimine incendii quam odio humani generis coniuncti sunt."

[5] *Ibid.*: "sontes et novissima exempla meritos".

sion in their favour.[1] The bare punishments—crucifixion, burning at the stake, and death by wild beasts—were right and proper. But the people to whom Nero threw open his gardens, in order that they might witness such sights, found Nero himself among them dressed in the garb of a charioteer[2]—the ancient equivalent of a jockey. If the Christians were really magicians, as their punishments implied,[3] and their stories of healings may have suggested, the situation was too serious for such buffoonery. Nero's conduct was enough to discredit his plea of reasons of state.

It is clear, then, that Christians, who confessed their Christianity or were denounced as Christians by such confessors, were put to death by Nero after the great fire of Rome in A.D. 64. It was alleged that they were incendiaries or magicians, but these allegations were not proven. The reference to the execution of the founder of the sect suggests that they were, in accordance with that precedent, liable to capital punishment in Rome or in the provinces.

Suetonius records that under Nero many practices were severely punished and prohibited and many others set up. No food was henceforth to be sold in the cook shops (for example) except vegetables; and punishments were inflicted upon the Christians—a kind of men who embraced a new and maleficent superstition.[4]

The natural inference that Nero's action in the matter of the Christians formed a precedent which was followed generally and in the provinces unless further regulations were introduced by himself or his successors, is probable in the nature of the case, and it is expressly asserted by Sulpicius Severus, who follows Tacitus, and may have known parts of his *Annals* which are no longer extant. This, he says, was the beginning of the savage treatment of the Christians.

[1] *Annals*: "pereuntibus addita ludibria, ut ferarum tergis contecti, laniatu canum interirent, aut crucibus affixi, aut flammandi, atque ubi defecisset dies in usum nocturni luminis urerentur . . . Unde . . . miseratio oriebatur, tamquam non utilitate publica sed in saevitiam unius absumerentur."

[2] *Ibid.*: "Hortos suos ei spectaculo Nero obtulerat et Circense ludicrum edebat, habitu aurigae permixtus plebi vel circulo insistens".

[3] So Ramsay, *Church in the Roman Empire*, p. 236: "*Odium humani generis* was, as Arnold aptly points out, the crime of poisoners and magicians. . . . The punishments inflicted on the Christians under Nero are those ordered for magicians. Paulls, Sentent. v. 23 M.: "Magicae artis conscios summo supplicio affici placuit, id est, bestiis obici aut cruci suffigi. Ipsi autem magi vivi exuruntur."

[4] *Vita Neronis*, xvi.: "Multa sub eo et animadversa severe et coercita nec minus instituta . . . interdictum, ne quid in popinis cocti praeter legumina aut holera veniret cum antea nullum non obsonii genus proponeretur; adflicti suppliciis Christiani, genus hominum superstitionis novae ac maleficae."

Afterwards also laws were laid down by which the religion was proscribed and edicts were issued by which it was publicly declared illegal to be a Christian. Then Paul and Peter were condemned to death.[1]

To the three first persecutors of the Church—Nero, Domitian, and Trajan—Sulpicius Severus suggests that Titus should be added. If he is following good authority—say, Tacitus, here as elsewhere—Titus held a council to decide the fate of the Temple, when Jerusalem was taken in A.D. 70. Of his councillors some urged that a consecrated house famous beyond all mortal things ought not to be destroyed. Its preservation would bear witness to Roman moderation; its ruin would be an eternal mark of their cruelty. Others, and among them Titus himself, held the Temple should be destroyed at once, in order that the religion of the Jews and Christians might be more completely undone; inasmuch as these religions, though opposed to one another, nevertheless came from the same parent stock. The Christians sprang from the Jews. If the root were taken away the branch would naturally perish.[2]

From this survey of the evidence it appears that the non-Christian authorities bear out the assertion of Tertullian that from the year 64 A.D. Christianity was distinguished from Judaism and, therefore, proscribed. It had lost the protection of the ancient and famous lawful religion, which sheltered it at the first.[3] Nero set the law in motion against it for his own purposes and attempted to justify his action to the people. But such action once taken, persecution of the Church was part of the law of the Empire, as Suetonius, Sulpicius Severus, and Tertullian aver.[4] There is nothing in the evidence to

[1] *Chronicon*, ii. 29: "Hoc initio in Christianos saeviri coeptum. Post etiam datis legibus religio vetebatur, palamque edictis propositis Christianum esse non licebat. Tum Paulus et Petrus capitis damnati."

[2] *Chronicorum*, ii. 30: "Fertur Titus adhibito consilio prius deliberasse an templum tanti operis everteret. Etenim nonnullis videbatur aedem sacratam ultra omnia mortalia illustrem non oportere deleri, quae servata modestiae Romanae testimonium, diruta perennem crudelitatis notam praeberet. At contra alii et Titus ipse evertendum imprimis templum censebant, quo plenius Judaeorum et Christianorum religio tolleretur: quippe has religiones, licet contrarias sibi, isdem tamen ab auctoribus profectas: Christianos ex Judaeis extitisse: radice sublata stirpem facile perituram."

[3] Tertullian, *Apology*, xxi.: "Antiquissimis Judaecorum instrumentis sectam . . . suffultam . . . sub umbraculo insignissimae religionis certe licitae".

[4] In addition to passages quoted above, see Tertullian, *ad Nationes*, i. 7: "Principe Augusto nomen hoc ortum est: Tiberio disciplina eius inluxit: sub Nerone damnatio invaluit ut iam hinc de persona persecutoris ponderetis, si pius ille princeps, impii Christiani . . . si non hostis publicus, nos publici hostes: quales simus damnator ipse demonstravit, utique aemula sibi puniens: et tamen permansit erasis

suggest that the Neronian persecution slackened, because the citizens of Rome saw through the pretexts of arson and witchcraft. On the contrary the evidence suggests that the name was condemned by Nero.

It was still possible for Titus and for Dio Cassius to recall the fact that Christianity was a sect—a schismatic sect of Judaism. Perhaps the condemnation of the sect carried with it a partial proscription and prohibition of its name. But there is no trace of any real change of attitude between the policy, on which Nero embarked in sudden desperation, and the action taken by Pliny, when he began to put the affairs of Bithynia in order. Pliny assumed that the name of Christian was proof of guilt and only inquired why, when he found himself dealing with special and extenuating circumstances. Nero in special circumstances had sought to save himself from popular suspicion by making the name of Christian proof, first of special and then of general guilt.

It remains to examine the relations of the Christian Church and the Roman State, as they are reflected in the First Epistle of St. Peter, and to inquire which of the first three persecutions known to us they best fit.

In the first part of the Epistle, which ends at iv. 11, the writer speaks generally of manifold temptations.[1] "He exhorteth them—to quote the summary of the revisers of 1611—from the breach of charity . . . he beseecheth them also to abstain from fleshly lusts, to be obedient to magistrates, and teacheth servants how to obey their masters, patiently suffering for well-doing after the example of Christ. He teacheth the duty of wives and husbands to each other, exhorting all men to unity and love, and to suffer persecution. . . . He exhorteth them to cease from sin by the example of Christ, and the consideration of the general end that now approacheth. . . .

In the second part of the Epistle the writer "comforteth them against persecution. He exhorteth the elders to feed their flocks, the younger to obey, and all to be sober, watchful, and constant in the faith : to resist the cruel adversary the devil." Here only it is suggested that Christians may be put to death for the Name. For certain churches, to whom the bearer would read this part of the letter and whose special circumstances the writer had in mind, a trial[2] was imminent : their adversary the devil was walking about, as a roaring lion,

omnibus hoc solum institutum Neronianum: iustum denique, ut dissimile sui auctoris".

[1] i. 6. [2] iv. 12.

seeking whom he might devour.[1] In the earlier and general part the references to persecution and persecutors are vaguer, and stress is laid upon the railing or reviling[2] to which the Christians are exposed, but must not retaliate in kind. In both parts the example of Christ is put before them as their model—He suffered and they must suffer *as* He suffered—but only in the second part is it added that they must commit the keeping of their souls to God, as He did.[3] The first part, in fact, does not seem to contemplate state-persecution so much as the discredit and discomfort inevitably incurred by those who dissent from an established religion.

But such a distinction between the two parts of the Epistle, even if it be accepted as valid, does not relegate the second part to a later period. In some of the Churches of Asia Minor, at any rate—and there is no evidence to show which—the conditions described in the second part existed already. And so the evidence of the Epistle as a whole must be taken.

The faith of the Christians addressed is undergoing a trial : for a season (if need be) they are in heaviness through manifold temptations.[4] In different ways their faith is being tested. The tests—whatever they are—cause a temporary grief in the midst of their permanent joy, but will only refine their faith and purge it of dross. Half-hearted Christians will fall away. They have already purified their souls by obedience to the truth revealed to them,[5] and must lay aside all malice and all guile and hypocrisies and envies and all evil speakings.[6] They must abstain from fleshly lusts which war against the soul, and, by their good conduct, refute the common rumour which speaks of them as evildoers.[7] Pending the visitation of God, they are exhorted to be obedient to the Emperor and his officers, and as loyal citizens stop the mouths of ignorant fools.[8] There is no room, here, for the later test of their loyalty : the writer could not exhort them to offer sacrifice to Cæsar. No one can really harm them, if they obey these commands ; but they may have to suffer for righteousness' sake.[9] They must not be afraid. They must be ready to defend themselves and to reply to every one who inquires about their hope. Good behaviour and gentle answers may put their calumniators to shame ; in any case it is essential.[10]

In certain places Christians are already sharing in the sufferings of Christ, and therefore must rejoice therein. Their suffering may be misrepresented as the just punishment of murderers, thieves,

[1] v. 8. [2] iii. 9 with ii. 21-23. [3] iv. 19 with ii. 23. [4] i. 6 f.
[5] i. 22. [6] ii. 1. [7] ii. 11 f.. [8] ii. 13. [9] iii. 13 f. [10] iii. 15 f.

criminals or busybodies: they must correct by word or deed all such misrepresentations and make it clear that they are reproached—or what not?—simply because they are Christians.[1] Their adversary the devil—in the persons of all his agents—goes about seeking whose faith he may destroy; they must resist him and survive the ordeal.[2] Throughout the world the Christian brotherhood is exposed to the same temptations and varied persecutions.

From this evidence Professor Ramsay[3] concludes that the Epistle belongs to the time when Vespasian revived the policy of Nero. "The Christian communities of Asia Minor north of the Taurus are regarded as exposed to persecution (i. 6), not merely in the form of dislike and malevolence on the part of neighbours, . . . but persecution to the death (iv. 15, 16), after trial and question (iii. 15). The persecution is general, and extends over the whole Church (v. 9). The Christians are not merely tried when a private accuser comes forward against them, but are sought out for trial by the Roman officials (v. 8, iii. 15). They suffer for the Name (iv. 14-16) pure and simple; the trial takes the form of inquiry into their religion, giving them the opportunity of 'glorifying God in this name'."

Of this persecution by Vespasian there is no evidence except an inference from the statement of Sulpicius Severus, that Titus his son and successor wished to exterminate both Judaism and Christianity, and the general deduction from the letter of Pliny, that persecution for the Name was an established practice. Apart from this objection, it may fairly he said that even the rigorous interpretation which Professor Ramsay puts upon different passages is not necessarily inconsistent with the conditions of the reign of Nero when persecution of the Church did, as a fact, begin. If the vague terms, in which the various sufferings of Christians are described, are to be pressed and limited to mean State persecution and persecution to the death, there still remain indubitable references to unofficial persecution which did not go to such lengths. The author, as Professor Ramsay himself says, looks *forward* to a period of persecution as the condition in which Christians have to live. Further he exhorts Christians to be loyal subjects and therein proves that the obvious test of loyalty had not yet been applied to them. And he definitely excludes the narrow interpretation of the roaring lion, when he urges the Christians to resist it.

For these and other reasons, Professor Ramsay's theory is re-

[1] iv 13-16. [2] v. 8 f.:
[3] *The Church in the Roman Empire*, pp. 279 ff.

jected by Dr. Chase on the one hand and Professor Schmiedel[1] on the other. But many of his arguments hold good against the date under Trajan, to which Professor Schmiedel adheres. Pliny's correspondence with Trajan, however, is not easily made to fit the state of things reflected in the First Epistle of St. Peter. For one thing, in Pliny's time Bithynia was so far infected by real or nominal Christianity that the temples were deserted. The unlawful superstition was so far predominant that many of its adherents conformed without any conviction. Pliny's anticipation that clemency shown to such penitents would result in the annihilation of Christianity suggests an altogether different state of things.

On the whole—whether St. Peter perished under Nero or, as Professor Ramsay urges, at a later date—the Epistle may not unreasonably be referred to the time when Nero inaugurated the attack upon the provincial Roman Christians and gave the cue to all provincial governors who wished to earn his favour by endorsing the rightfulness of his action under whatever pretext. Already they were distinguished from the Jews, and, therefore, stood under the ban of the law as an unlicensed corporation. They were magicians who prophesied the destruction of the world, and the fire of Rome was proof of their power. They might plead innocence of crimes associated with the name by vulgar suspicion; but even when they cleared their name it was in itself sufficient to condemn them. That is the pagan view. The Christian view is that Christ suffered and they must follow in His steps. No colour must be given to the misrepresentations of their enemies. They must take every opportunity of removing them. This done, though death be their penalty, they will die to the glory of God, resisting the slanderer and remaining firm in their faith.

Canonicity.

There are two different ways of treating the fact that any given book of the New Testament Canon is first quoted as authoritative Scripture and as the work of its commonly reputed author by a later writer of known date and recognised authority. You may say that the said book is thereby recognised as canonical and as authentic either *not before* or *as early as* such and such a date. In the former case the endorsement of tradition is regarded as an innovation, in the latter as an explicit regularisation of previous, but inarticulate, practice.

[1] *Encyclopædia Biblica*, vol. i.: "Christian, name of".

The former interpretation of such facts has the advantage of appearing to appeal to what is apparent and to nothing else. But it involves axioms which require to be proved. We must suppose that the Canon was definitely fixed by authority and was not a thing of gradual growth. And, if we are to argue from the silence of ecclesiastical writers, we must ignore the fact that many of them are no longer extant and postulate for them an interest in such matters as canonicity equal to our own. In fact it seems more reasonable to allow ourselves the exercise of a sober imagination in dealing with the evidence. In the case of 1 Peter at all events there is no sign of any attempt to force a new forgery upon the acceptance of the Church. It contains no innovation of doctrine such as might need the support of Apostolic authority.

The Epistle, then (we may say), is used by Irenæus *as early as* the third quarter of the second century. Behind Irenæus in all probability there lies a period, in which the idea of the New Testament Canon grew up and in which its contents were gradually reduced for reasons which appeared to those in authority to be adequate. Of that period we certainly do not know everything. All the Gnostics whom Irenæus has pilloried are represented only by fragments and summaries of their doctrines contemptuously preserved by their opponents at a later time. But, even so, it appears that the Gnostics in their efforts to elucidate the philosophy of the Christian religion and to advance to something higher than the somewhat pedestrian and commonplace theology of the ordinary ecclesiastic laid stress upon Scripture. And in so far as they tended to relegate the Old Testament to a definitely inferior place in the development of true religion they necessarily devoted themselves to the writings of the Apostles—the Scriptures of the New Testament. Inevitably the Gospels, which contained the sayings of Jesus, and the works of St. Paul occupied the first place in their estimation. The Lord and *the* Apostle exercised an authority to which the Church must bow. So the Gnostics applied themselves to New Testament exegesis—not always for the purposes of theological controversy. The controversies, which ensued upon the deductions they drew from such exegesis, led to the delimitation of the Canon and there is a strong presumption in favour of the traditional view of the books which survived the ordeal. 1 Peter is not a book which was likely to be much to the mind of daring thinkers who could discriminate between the different degrees of inspiration latent in different sayings of the Lord and who were determined to be done with Judaism. The Gnostics professed to be wiser than the Apostles—Irenæus their posthumous conqueror asserts. 1 Peter is a book more congenial to such a man as Polycarp, who was more fitted to be a simple recipient of the general tradition. And it is to be remembered that Polycarp takes us back to a time when the idea of a Canon of New Testament Scripture was in its infancy.

Our document is first quoted with the formula *Peter* or *Peter in his Epistle says* in the latter part of the second century.

Irenæus, the disciple of Polycarp, whose book *Against Heresies* was written while Eleutherus was Bishop of Rome (A.D. 175-189),[1] is the earliest witness to its reception as such. He appealed to it (for example) along with Paul and Isaiah: "et Petrus ait in epistula:[2] *Quem non videntes diligitis*, inquit, *in quem nunc non videntes credidistis, gaudebitis gaudio inenarrabili*".[3] In another place it is quoted after Moses and the Lord: "et propter hoc Petrus, ait, *non velamentum malitiae habere nos libertatem*[4] sed ad probationem et manifestationem fidei".

Tertullian, a little later, puts Peter on a level with Paul in respect of his inspiration, and explains their agreement as due to the fact that they were inspired by the same spirit: "de modestia quidem cultus et ornatus aperba praescriptio est etiam Petri cohibentis eodem ore quia eodem et spiritu quo Paulus, et vestium gloriam et auri superbiam et crinium lenoniam operositatem".[5] In his *Antidote* to the poison of the Gnostics, which may perhaps be dated A.D. 213, he cites 1 Peter as addressed to the natives of Pontus: "Petrus quidem ad Ponticos, *Quanta enim*, inquit, *gloria si non ut delinquentes puniamini, sustinetis. Haec enim gratia est, in hoc et vocati estis, quoniam et Christus passus est pro nobis, relinquens vobis exemplum semetipsum, uti adsequamini vestigia ipsius.* Et rursus *Dilecti ne expavescatis ultionem quae agitur in vobis in temptationem, quasi novum accidat vobis; etenim secundum quod communicatis passionibus Christi, gaudete, uti et in revelatione gloriae eius gaudeatis exultantes: si dedecoramini nomine Christi, beati estis, quoniam gloria et dei spiritus requiescat in vobis, dum ne quis vestrum patiatur, ut homicida aut fur aut maleficus aut alieni speculator. Si autem ut Christianus, ne erubescat, glorificet autem dominum in nomine isto.*[6]

[1] "νῦν δωδεκάτῳ τόπω τὸν τῆς ἐπισκοπῆς ἀπὸ τῶν Ἀποστόλων κατέχει κλῆρον Ἐλεύθερος." Irenæus, *Adv. Haer.*, iii. 3. 3 (Harvey's edition).

[2] *Adv. Haer.* iv. 19, 2 = 1 Peter i. 8. [3] *Adv. Haer.* iv. 28. [4] 1 Peter ii. 16.

[5] *De Oratione*, xv. referring to 1 Peter iii. 3 and Tim. ii. 9; compare Clement of Alexandria, *Paedagogus*, III., xi. 66, quoted above.

[6] Scorpiace xii. = 1 Peter ii. 20, 21 and iv. 12-15.

Clement of Alexandria (A.D. 150-(?) 210) commented on 1 Peter in his Hypotyposes, but the commentary is only preserved in a Latin abridgment.[1] In his extant works he quotes freely from the Epistle and uses it as if it were familiar to his readers. In the *Paedagogus*[2] (for example), which is addressed to catechumens, he says: ἐγνωκότες οὖν τὸ ἑκάστου ἔργον, ἐν φόβῳ τὸν τῆς παροικίας ὑμῶν χρόνον ἀναστράφητε, εἰδότες ὅτι οὐ φθαρτοῖς, ἀργυρίῳ ἢ χρυσίῳ, ἐλυτρώθημεν ἐκ τῆς ματαίας ἡμῶν ἀναστροφῆς πατριπαραδότου, ἀλλὰ τιμίῳ αἵματι ὡς ἀμνοῦ ἀμώμου καὶ ἀσπίλου Χριστοῦ. ἀρκετὸς οὖν ὁ παρεληλυθὼς χρόνος—ὁ Πέτρος φησί—τὸ βούλημα τῶν ἐθνῶν κατειργάσθαι, πεπορευμένους ἐν ἀσελγείαις, ἐπιθυμίαις, οἰνοφλυγίαις, κώμοις, πότοις. καὶ ἀθεμίτοις εἰδωλολατρείαις.[3] And in the *Stromateis*,[4] which were intended for more advanced Christians, he has, after quotations from the Second Epistle to the Corinthians: διὸ καὶ ὁ θαυμάσιος Πέτρος φησίν· ἀγαπητοί, παρακαλῶ ὡς παροίκους καὶ παρεπιδήμους ἀπέχεσθαι τῶν σαρκικῶν ἐπιθυμιῶν, αἵτινες στρατεύονται κατὰ τῆς ψυχῆς, τὴν ἀναστροφὴν ὑμῶν καλὴν ἔχοντες ἐν τοῖς ἔθνεσιν. ὅτι οὕτως ἐστὶ τὸ θέλημα τοῦ θεοῦ, ἀγαθοποιοῦντας φιμοῦν τὴν τῶν ἀφρόνων ἀνθρώπων ἐργασίαν, ὡς ἐλεύθεροι καὶ μὴ ὡς ἐπικάλυμμα ἔχοντες τῆς κακίας τὴν ἐλευθερίαν, ἀλλ' ὡς δοῦλοι θεοῦ. On one occasion[5] he fuses together the sumptuary laws for women laid down by St. Paul and St. Peter: προσιέναι δὲ αὐτὰς ὁ παιδάγωγος κελεύει. ἐν καταστολῇ κοσμίῳ, μετὰ αἰδοῦς καὶ σωφροσύνης κοσμεῖν ἑαυτάς,[6] ὑποτασσομένας τοῖς ἰδίοις ἀνδράσιν, ὡς καὶ εἴ τινες ἀπειθοῖεν τῷ λόγῳ, διὰ τῆς τῶν γυναικῶν ἀναστροφῆς ἄνευ λόγου κερδηθήσονται, ἐποπτεύσαντες, φησί, τὴν ἐν λόγῳ ἁγνὴν ἀναστροφήν ὑμῶν· ὧν ἔστω οὐχ ὁ ἔξωθεν ἐμπλοκῆς καὶ περιθέσεως χρυσίων ἢ ἐνδύσεως ἱματίων κόσμος, ἀλλ' ὁ κρυπτὸς τῆς καρδίας ἄνθρωπος ἐν τῷ ἀφθάρτῳ τοῦ πραέος καὶ ἡσυχίου πνεύματος, ὅ ἐστιν ἐνώπιον τοῦ θεοῦ πολυτελές.[7] This fusion is characteristic: both St. Paul and St. Peter wrote Scripture, and Clement follows popular usage, which never has insisted upon a nice discrimination between the authors of "texts". Indeed in another place[8] he refers part of the first Epistle to Timothy[9] to St. Peter:

[1] Potter's edition, pp. 1006 f. [2] III., xii. 85. [3] 1 Peter i. 17-19, iv. 3.
[4] III., xi. 75. [5] *Paedagogus*, III., xi. 66. [6] 1 Tim. ii. 9.
[7] 1 Peter iii. 1-4. [8] *Paedagogus*, II., xii. 127. [9] Tim. ii. 9 f.

πάνυ γοῦν θαυμασίως ὁ Πέτρος ὁ μακάριος γυναῖκας, φησίν, ὡσαύτως μὴ ἐν πλέγμασιν ἢ χρυσῷ ἢ μαργαρίταις ἢ ἱματισμῷ πολυτελεῖ, ἀλλ' ὃ πρέπει γυναιξὶν ἐπαγγελλομέναις θεοσέβειαν, δι' ἔργων ἀγαθῶν σφᾶς αὐτὰς κοσμούσων.

The fact of the matter is that even Clement used, at any rate in his *Paedagogus*, manuals of extracts from Scripture classified according to their subjects. His *Paedagogus* or instructor is the distinguished successor of a line of humbler books of the same kind. The Christian catechist had his armoury of appropriate texts just as the missionary to the Jews had his. The extracts were arranged under headings: sayings of Moses, the Prophet, the Psalmist, the Sage, the Lord and the Apostle followed each other in various orders and with different degrees of precision in attribution. The inevitable results were that the extracts were affected by their new neighbours in respect of their text, and that their proper ascription was lost sight of. As the learning and the security of the Church increased, these results were corrected. Complete Bibles in the Church chests superseded the manuals, and Origen (for example) laboured to restore the purity of the text. The new state of things is reflected in the *Stromateis* of Clement: there Jesus Son of Sirach receives credit for his wisdom, which in the *Paedagogus* is ascribed to wisdom, the Paedagogue, or Solomon; and the text of the extracts conforms to the standard of the uncial manuscripts. But the literature which preceded Clement was popular rather than scholarly, and the phenomena presented by his use of Scripture in the *Paedagogus* contribute to confirm the conclusion that the argument based upon the silence of his predecessors is fallacious, and that their silence can fairly be construed as a denial of the Petrine origin or authorship of 1 Peter.

These examples of the use of 1 Peter made by Irenæus, Tertullian, and Clement of Alexandria have been given in full to show what the raw material of the evidence really is. Samples only as they are, they suffice to show that 1 Peter was recognised as St. Peter's Epistle about A.D. 200 in Gaul, Africa, and Alexandria. By a stretch of the imagination it might be supposed that Tertullian was dependent upon Clement for this knowledge; but Irenæus and Clement represent a tradition which they inherited independently from a distant past. Now Clement was the earliest Christian *scholar*, whose works have come down to us, and Irenæus is linked to the apostolic age by his connexion with Polycarp.

In his Epistle to the Philippians, Polycarp, Bishop of Smyrna, who died a martyr on 23rd February, A.D. 155 at the age of 86 years,[1] has left, as Eusebius noted, a valuable witness to the earlier history of the New Testament Canon.

So far as the Canonicity of 1 Peter is concerned the evidence of the Epistle is overwhelming. It is true that Polycarp does not give the name of the authority, which he uses so often. It would be unreasonable to expect that he should. "Paul" and "the Lord" are the only authors named. The words of the Lord have naturally a higher authority than those of His Apostles—at any rate at this stage in the development of the Canon. And St. Paul as the founder of the Church at Philippi had a special claim upon their obedience: "Neither I (Polycarp says) nor anyone like me can attain to the wisdom of the blessed and glorious Paul, who, when he came among you, before the face of the men of that time taught accurately and surely the word of truth, who also when he was absent wrote letters to you into which if you look you will be able to be built up in the faith given unto you."[2] Other Scriptures, even the first Epistle of St. John, Polycarp's teacher, are used just as 1 Peter is used—anonymously and not always with a clear formula to stamp the quotations as quotations.

The following passages contain clear cases of Polycarp's use of 1 Peter:—

(I. 1-3) συνεχάρην . . . ὅτι ἡ βεβαία τῆς πίστεως ὑμῶν ῥίζα . . . μεχρὶ νῦν διαμένει καὶ καρποφορεῖ εἰς τὸν κύριον ἡμῶν Ἰησοῦν Χριστὸν . . . εἰς ὃν οὐκ ἰδόντες πιστεύετε χαρᾷ ἀνεκλαλήτῳ καὶ δεδοξασμένῃ[3] εἰς ἣν πολλοὶ ἐπιθυμοῦσιν εἰσελθεῖν.[4]

II. διὸ ἀναζωσάμενοι τὰς ὀσφύας ὑμῶν[5] δουλεύσατε τῷ θεῷ . . . πιστεύσαντες εἰς τὸν ἐγείραντα τὸν κύριον ἡμῶν Ἰησοῦν Χριστὸν ἐκ νεκρῶν καὶ δόντα αὐτῷ δόξαν[6] καὶ θρόνον ἐκ δεξιῶν αὐτοῦ . . . μὴ ἀποδιδόντες κακὸν ἀντ κακοῦ ἢ λοιδορίαν ἀντὶ λοιδορίας[7] ἢ γρόνθον ἀντὶ γρόνθου ἢ κατάραν ἀντὶ κατάρας.[8]

V. καλὸν γὰρ τὸ ἀνακόπτεσθαι ἀπὸ τῶν ἐπιθυμιῶν τῶν ἐν τῷ κόσμῳ, ὅτι πᾶσα ἐπιθυμία κατὰ τοῦ πνεύματος στρατεύεται.[9]

VII. ἐπὶ τὸν ἐξ ἀρχῆς ἡμῖν παραδοθέντα λόγον ἐπιστρέψωμεν νήφοντες πρὸς τὰς εὐχὰς[10] καὶ προσκαρτεροῦντες νηστείαις.

[1] So Bardenhewer, *Geschichte der Altkirchlichen Litteratur*, i. p. 149.
[2] iii. 2. [3] 1 Peter i. 8. [4] Compare 1 Peter i. 12. [5] 1 Peter i. 3.
[6] 1 Peter i. 21. [7] 1 Peter iii. 9. [8] Compare 1 Peter iii. 9.
[9] 1 Peter ii. 11 conflated with Galatians v. 17. [10] Peter iv. 7.

VIII. προσκαρτερῶμεν τῇ ἐλπίδι ἡμῶν καὶ τῷ ἀρραβῶνι τῆς δικαιοσύνης ἡμῶν, ὅς ἐστιν Χριστὸς Ἰησοῦς, ὃς ἀνήνεγκεν ἡμῶν τὰς ἁμαρτίας τῷ ἰδίῳ σώματι ἐπὶ τὸ ξύλον,[1] ὃς ἁμαρτίαν οὐκ ἐποίησεν, οὐδὲ εὑρέθη δόλος ἐν τῷ στόματι αὐτοῦ.[2] ἀλλὰ δι' ἡμᾶς, ἵνα ζήσωμεν ἐν αὐτῷ, πάντα ὑπέμεινεν. μιμηταὶ οὖν γενώμεθα τῆς ὑπομονῆς αὐτοῦ καὶ ἐὰν πάσχωμεν διὰ τὸ ὄνομα αὐτοῦ, δοξάζωμεν αὐτόν.[3] τοῦτον γὰρ ἡμῖν τὸν ὑπογραμμὸν ἔθηκε δι' ἑαυτοῦ, καὶ ἡμεῖς τοῦτο ἐπιστεύσαμεν.[4]

X. In his ergo state et domini exemplar sequimini *firmi in fide et inmutabiles, fraternitatis amatores diligentes invicem. . . .*[5] *Omnes vobis invicem subiecti estote,*[6] *conversationem vestram inreprehensibilem habentes in gentibus, ut ex bonis operibus vestris* et vos laudem accipiatis *et dominus in vobis non blasphemetur.*[7]

[1] I Peter ii. 24.
[2] I Peter ii. 22.
[3] I Peter iv. 16.
[4] I Peter ii. 21.
[5] Compare I Peter iii. 8 (ii. 17).
[6] Compare I Peter v. 5.
[7] I Peter ii. 12: the paraphrase of the latter part of the verse (**ἐποπτεύοντες δοξάσωσι τὸν θεόν**) is due to the next quotation (Isaiah lii. 5), vae autem, per quem nomen domini blasphematur.

NOTE.

This edition is based on a course of lectures delivered, in the first instance, to a class of honours men who were expected to use the late Professor Bigg's commentary as a text-book. The lectures were, therefore, made independently of that commentary and with a view to the exhibition of new material and processes rather than results. In particular, an attempt was made to illustrate the reference of the Septuagint and Jewish literature generally to the exegesis of the New Testament. In the reduction of these notes to their present form the commentaries of Alford, Bigg, Hort, Kühl-Meyer, and Von Soden were consulted.

The text is taken from the facsimile of the great Vatican Codex (B), the lines of which are indicated by spaces.

The editor gratefully acknowledges the kindness of the Rev. George Milligan D.D., and the Rev. R. St. John Parry, B.D., who read the commentary in proof.

⁻πέτρου Ā.

ΠΕΤΡΟΣ ἀπόστολος ιῦ χῦ[1] ἐκλεκτοῖς παρε πιδήμοις δια- I. 1
σπορᾶς Πόντου Γαλατίας Καπ παδοκίας Ἀσίας κατὰ 2

[1] ιῦ χῦ is the normal contraction of Ἰησοῦ Χριστοῦ: so κῦ = κυρίου, Θῦ = Θεοῦ. After Ἀσίας all other manuscripts and all the versions add καὶ βιθυνίας: the original scribe of Codex Vaticanus (B*) stands alone in the omission.

Chapter I.—Vv. 1, 2. Peter the High Commissioner of Jesus, who is Messiah of Greeks as of Jews, sends greeting after the Christian fashion, in which the Greek and Jewish formulæ have been combined and transformed, to the Churches of Northern Asia Minor. They are the dispersion of the New Israel, chosen out of the whole world in accordance with God's foreknowledge of their fitness, to undergo the hallowing of His Spirit, and with a view to their reception into His Church. For the result, and therefore the purpose, of their election is that they may profess obedience and receive the outward sign of sprinkling, being baptised into the death of Jesus Christ. For them may grace (and not mere greeting) and peace (God's peace not man's) be multiplied! For discussion of writer and readers see Introduction.

Ver. 1. **ἐκλεκτοῖς παρεπιδήμοις διασπορᾶς,** *elect sojourners of dispersion*, a combination of titles of Israel appropriated to Christians in accordance with the universal principle of the early Church. (i.) The Jews were the *chosen race* (ii. 9 from Isa. xliii. 20) as Moses said, *Because He loved thy fathers therefore He chose their seed after them* (Deut. iv. 37; *cf.* Rom. xi. 28). So Jesus said to His disciples, *I have chosen you* (John xv. 16, 19, etc.), and refers to them in the eschatological discourse as *the elect* (Mark xiii. 20). (ii.) Being *chosen out of the world—in the world*, indeed, *but not of it*, John xv. 16 ff.—Christians are *alien sojourners* during their life on earth. Their fatherland is *the city that hath foundations* (i. 7, ii. 11; Heb. xiii. 14; Phil. iii. 20). In Heb. xi. 9-13 the Patriarchs are credited with the same idea and Philo says that the sages of Moses' school are all introduced as *sojourners* (p. 416 M). So Abraham said to the Sons of Heth, "I am a stranger and sojourner (πάροικος καὶ παρεπίδημος = גר ותושב) with you" (Gen. xxiii. 4); Jacob speaks of *the days of the years of my pilgrimage* (מגורי ἃς παροικῶ); and the Psalmist anticipates Peter and Heb. in the generalisation *I am a stranger and sojourner* (πάροικος καὶ παρεπίδημος) *in the earth as all my fathers were* (Ps. xxxix. 13). Deissmann (*Bible Studies*, p. 149) quotes two examples of παρεπίδημος from wills of the third century B.C., one of a Jew resident in the Fayyüm (Ἀπολλώνιον [παρεπ]ίδημον ὃς καὶ συριστὶ Ἰωνάθας). In P. Tor. 8 (B.C. 118) παρεπιδημοῦντες and κατοικοῦντες are contrasted. (iii.) Moses said to Israel *thou shalt be scattered among the kingdoms of the earth* (Deut. xxviii. 25); and the rendering of the LXX διασπορά is probably the earliest example of the technical designation (*cf.* John vii. 35) of the Jews, who—for whatever reason—lived outside the Holy Land. The collective term (Rabbinic גולה) implies the real unity of these scattered communities, whose scattering is no longer regarded as God's punishment for sin. It thus serves well the purpose of one, who, like St. Paul, insists on the unity of the whole brotherhood of Christians (*e.g.*, v. 9); but this application of the principle that the Church is the Israel of God is subordinate to others which imply that there is

προγνωσιν ΘΥ[1] πατρος εν αγιασμω πνευμα τος εις υπακοην
και ραντισμον αιματος ΙΥ ΧΥ· χαρις υμιν και ειρηνη

[1] ΘΥ is the normal contraction of Θεοῦ.

no earthly correlative to it. When St. James addresses *the twelve tribes which are in Dispersion*, he may on the other hand be contrasting the saints of Jerusalem with those abroad (as St. Paul did in the matter of the Collection) if indeed he is not speaking simply to his fellow-countrymen as a Jew to Jews. But St. Peter writes from "Babylon" and the capital of Christendom is no longer Jerusalem. The collocation of **παρεπιδήμοις** and **διασπορᾶς** implies that this scattering, which in the case of the type was God's punishment for sin, will not be permanent for the antitype. For the Christian Church the Jewish hope of the ingathering will be fulfilled, as is indicated by the emphatic **ἐκλεκτοῖς**—for Jesus said, "*The Son of Man . . . shall gather together his elect . . . from the uttermost part of the earth to the uttermost part of heaven*" (Mark xiii. 26, 27; *cf.* Deut. xxx. 4). Compare Didache ix. 4, "For as this was broken [bread] scattered over the hills and being gathered together became one, so may thy Church be gathered together from the ends of the earth *into thy kingdom*," and Justin Martyr, *Dial.* 113, "As Moses . . . so also Jesus the Christ (corresponding to J., the Son of Nun) shall turn again the Dispersion of the People . . . shall give us the possession eternally".

Πόντου . . . Ἀσίας. The order indicates the route of the messenger, who landed presumably at Sinope or Amastris and, if the omission of **καὶ Βιθυνίας** be accepted, left the country at Ephesus or Smyrna. The (Armenian) Acta of Phocas (Martyr of Sinope under Trajan) are addressed to the brethren dwelling in Pontus and Bithynia in Paphlagonia and in Mysia in Galatia and in Cappadocia and in Armenia (Conybeare, *Monuments of Early Christianity*, p. 103). See Introduction.

Ver. 2. The three clauses **κατὰ . . .**, **ἐν . . .**, and **εἰς . . .** qualify **ἐκλεκτοῖς** and perhaps also **ἀπόστολος** (as Oecumenius) Peter himself is *elect* and shares their privileges but had no need to magnify his office, as had St. Paul. Yet see Acts xv. 7 ff.

κατὰ πρόγνωσιν. . . . The noun occurs only in Acts ii. 23 (speech of St. Peter) in reference to the slaying of Christ **τῇ ὡρισμένῃ βουλῇ καὶ προγνώσει τοῦ θεοῦ**, *cf.* i. 20. The use of nouns instead of verbs is characteristic of this Epistle. The same idea is expressed more elaborately by St. Paul in Rom. viii. 29 (*q.v.*). *Cf.* Origen, *Philocalia*, xxv. Oecumenius infers that the Apostle is thus the equal of the prophets, especially Jeremiah (*v.* Jer. i. 5).—**ἐν ἁγιασμῷ πνεύματος,** subjective genitive like **θεοῦ**, being elect they are within the sphere of the proper work of the Holy Spirit. The context excludes the rendering *hallowing of the* (*human*) *spirit*. Peter uses the stereotyped phrase; *cf.* 2 Thess. ii. 13 (which corresponds exactly to the whole context) **εἵλατο ὑμᾶς ὁ θεὸς ἀπ' ἀρχῆς (κατὰ πρ. θ. π.) . . . ἐν ἁγιασμῷ πνεύματος καὶ πίστει ἀληθείας (εἰς ὑπ.).—εἰς ὑπακοὴν . . . Ι. Χριστοῦ,** the goal or purpose of their election. *Obedience* is a technical term: sc. *to* God; *cf.* i. 14, where it is contrasted with the ignorant disobedience of their past lives (i. 22). As Christians, they obeyed God and not men (Acts iv. 19, v. 29); God gives His Holy Spirit to them that obey Him (Acts v. 32). Compare the Pauline *obedience of faith*. This obedience implies a change of mind in Jew and in Gentile, which is effected by the *sprinkling of blood of Jesus Christ*. They are now cleansed from sin, which is disobedience in Jew or Gentile. Jesus Christ, the mediator of the new covenant, sprinkles those whom God selected with His own blood, as Moses sprinkled the children of Israel who had promised obedience with the blood of oxen (Exod. xxiv. 7 f.; *cf.* Heb. ix. 19). But references to other sprinklings of the O.T., unconnected with obedience, must not be excluded. The word **ῥαντισμός** is appropriated, for example, to the water in which the ashes of the heifer were dissolved (Num. xix.); and a less obvious explanation is supported by Barnabas, "that by the remission of sins we might be purified, that is in the sprinkling of His blood for it stands written . . . *by His bruise we were healed* (Isa. liii. 5)". Indeed the best commentary is supplied by the Epistle to the Hebrews in which evidence of the O.T. is reviewed and the conclusion drawn that according to the

πληθυνθείη. εὐλογητὸς ὁ Θς̄[1] καὶ πα τὴρ τοῦ Κῡ ἡμῶν Ιῡ 3
Χῡ ὁ κατὰ τὸ πολὺ αὐτοῦ ἔλεος ἀναγεννήσας ἡμᾶς[2] εἰς

[1] Θς̄ is the normal contraction of Θεός: so Χς̄ = Χριστός, κς̄ = κύριος, Ις̄ = Ἰησοῦς.

[2] For ἡμᾶς a few cursives read ὑμᾶς: the words are practically interchangeable in manuscripts.

law everything is cleansed by blood. All the types were summed up in the fulfilment (see especially Heb. ix.) whether they related to the Covenant or to the Worship. So in Heb. xii. 24 the blood of Abel the first martyr is drawn into the composite picture of typical blood sheddings. It would be possible to take ὑπακοήν with Ιησοῦ Χριστοῦ, and to render either that ye might obey Jesus Christ (*cf.* i. 22; 2 Cor. x. 5) being sprinkled with His blood or that ye might obey as He obeyed even unto death (*cf.* Heb. v. 8; Phil. ii. 8). **χάρις . . . πληθυνθείη.** This full formula is found also in 2 Peter and Jude. For precedent see Dan. iii. 31. Its use here is not merely a convention peculiar to the Petrine school; grace and peace are multiplied to match the growth of hostility with which the Christians addressed are confronted, lest the word of Jesus be fulfilled διὰ τὸ πληθυνθῆναι τὴν ἀνομίαν ψυγήσεται ἡ ἀγάπη τῶν πολλῶν (Matt. xxiv. 12); *cf.* Rom. v. 20 f. In the Pastoral Epistles ἔλεος (*cf.* ver. 3) is inserted between χ. and εἰρ., so 2 John 3. From Gal. vi. 16 it appears that ἔλεος stood originally in the place which χάρις usurped (as distinctively Christian and reminiscent of the familar χαίρειν); so that the source will be Num. vi. 24-26. κύριος . . . ἐλεήσαι σε . . . καὶ δῴη σοι εἰρήνην.

Vv. 3-12. *Benediction of the Name.* The mention of God is followed by the Benediction of the Name as Jewish piety prescribed; the formula *the Holy One, blessed be He*, being amplified by the Christian appreciation of their fuller knowledge. The Apostle surpasses the fervour of the Psalmist, Blessed be the Lord God of Israel inasmuch as the last mighty work surpasses all previous deliverances. It falls naturally into three divisions. Vv. 3-5 have as their central figure the Father, vv. 6-9 the Son, and vv. 10-12 the Spirit who is at last given, who inspired the prophets of old and now inspires the Christian missionaries. From the past which preceded their acceptance of God's choice of them and its outward sign St. Peter turns to consider their present condition and to illuminate it with the light of the future glory.

Vv. 3-5. Blessed be God whom we have come to know as the God and Father of our Lord Jesus Christ! For He has granted to us the crowning manifestation of His great mercy. He has raised Jesus Christ from the dead and us thereby to newness of life. So you may hope for and in part enjoy the inheritance which was prefigured by the Promised Land. This heavenly treasure God has kept for those whom He guards with His power. So your faith respond, He is guarding you for the salvation which will be revealed at the last.

Ver. 3. **εὐλογητός.** The verbal adjective is recognised, perhaps coined by the LXX as proper to the Benediction of the Name. This usage is reflected in N.T., Rom. i. 25, ix. 5; 2 Cor. i. 3, xi. 31; Eph. i. 3; note Mark xiv. 61. **ὁ θεὸς . . . ἡμῶν,** part of the formula (*cf.* 2 Cor. i. 3; Eph. i. 3)—based on the saying "I ascend to your father and my father, unto your God and my God" (John xx. 17). **κατὰ τὸ πολὺ ἔλεος,** the more elaborate κατὰ τὸ πλοῦτος τῆς χάριτος αὐτοῦ of Eph. i. 7 (*cf.* ii. 4). **ἀναγεννήσας** (*cf.* i. 23). Else the verb only occurs in N.T. as variant to γεννηθῇ ἄνωθεν in Old Latin (and Irenæus) text of John iii. 5, which prompted St. Peter's Christian use of the word, see especially i. 23. Later it is used to describe the outward sign of baptism (*e.g.*, Justin Apol. i. 51) for the benefit of pagans as to the limitation of worshippers of Isis (Apuleius, *Met.* xi. 26, ut renatus quodammodo staatim sacrorum obsequio desponderetur). And of Mithras (in aeternum renati). Here the regeneration of the Christian corresponds to the resurrection of Christ (Chrysostom on John) and implies a previous mystical or figurative death to sin—see ii. 24; iii. 17 f.; iv. 1—which is repeated in the practice of their unnatural virtue (iv. 1-4). The simple idea of regeneration underlies St. Paul's elaborations of the doctrine of the καινὴ κτίσις. Hort refers to Philo, *de incorruptibilitate mundi* (ii. 489 M.) where ἀναγέννησις is used for the more usual παλιγγενεσία—rebirth of the world—of the Stoics. **ἐλπίδα ζῶσαν.** The omission of the definite article is characteristic of St Peter. The *Hope*

4 ἐλπίδα ζῶσα⁻[1] δι' ἀναστάσεως Ιῦ Χῦ ἐκ νεκρῶν εἰς κληρο
νομίαν ἄφθαρτον ꝁ[2] ἀμίαντον καὶ ἀμάρα⁻ τον τετηρημένην ε⁻
5 οὐρανοῖς εἰς ὑμᾶς τοὺς ἐν δυνάμει Θῦ φρου ρουμένους διὰ

[1] **ζωσα⁻** = **ζῶσαν**: the sign ⁻ for ν is apt to be absorbed in the preceding line and so disregarded: it is used at the end of the line or *sichu*, whether or not the word in which it occurs has come to its end.

[2] **ꝁ** is the common abbreviation for **καί**: it is probably derived from cursive writing in which letters were joined together and so varied in shape according to their companions.

is a recognised technical term (Acts xxiii. 6, etc.) of the Pharisees, corresponding to בטחון. **ζῶσαν** stamps the Christian hope as Divine since life is God's prerogative (*cf.* i. 23 and the *living* bread, water of John) and effective (*cf.* the corresponding use of dead faith, Jas. ii. 17, 26). *Cf.* Sap. iii. 4, **ἡ δὲ ἐλπὶς αὐτῶν ἀθανασίας πλήρης. δι' ἀ.** with **ἀναγεννήσας** rather than **ζῶσαν**: three prepositional clauses are thus attached to **ἀ.** as to **ἐκλεκτοῖς** (and **ἀπόστολος**) in ver. 2. The resurrection of Jesus is the means and guarantee of the spiritual resurrection of the Christian (1 Cor. xv. 14, 17) from the death of the sinful and fleshly life.

Ver. 4. **εἰς κληρ. . . . ἀμάραντον,** as God's sons in virtue of their regeneration they are God's heirs (Gal. iv. 7) and have an heavenly inheritance. The accumulated adjectives recall various images employed to describe it—and emphasise the fact that it is eternal (Heb. ix. 15) and spiritual. It is **ἄφθαρτον,** *incorruptible* (*cf.* i. 23, iii. 4) because it belongs to the future life which the risen dead (1 Cor. xv. 52) share with God Himself (Rom. i. 23; 1 Tim. i. 17). It is set where "moth doth not corrupt (**διαφθείρει**, Luke xii. 33: Matt. vi. 19 ff. has **ἀφανίζει**)," apart from this corruptible world (*cf.* Isa. xxiv. 3). It is the incorruptible crown (1 Cor. ix. 25). The second epithet **ἀμίαντον** is applied to the great High Priest, Heb. vii. 26 (*cf.* Heb. xiii. 4; Jas. i. 27) and implies again separation from this sinful world of which it is written **ἐμιάνατε τὴν γῆν μου καὶ τὴν κληρονομίαν μου ἔθεσθε εἰς βδέλυγμα** (Jer. ii. 7). Compare the description of virtue in Sap. iv. 2, **στεφανηφοροῦσα πομπεύει τὸν τῶν ἀμιάντων ἄθλων ἀγῶνα νικήσασα. ἀμάραντον** is peculiar to 1 Peter in N.T., *cf.* **ἀμαράντινον** (v. 4): it is perhaps derived from Sap. vi. 12, **ἀμάραντός ἐστιν ἡ σοφία,** and thus presupposes the identification of eternal life with knowledge of God (John xvii. 3). Compare the application of Isa. xl. 6 f. (cited *infra* 24) in Jas. i. 11. All three suit or are associated with the wreath presented to the victor in the games—a metaphor which the Lord Himself used according to the Apocalypse (ii. 10, *cf.* 1 Peter v. 4; Jas. i. 12). Origen (?) in Cramer's *Catena* notes that the words contradict Chiliasm. **τετηρημένην εἰς ὑμᾶς,** *reserved* (1) *with a view to you*, *cf.* John xii. 7, **ἵνα εἰς τὴν ἡμέραν . . . τηρήσῃ,** 2 Peter ii. 4, **εἰς κρίσιν τηρουμένους**; for same use of **εἰς** in similar context see Rom. viii. 18. (2) . . . *until you came*—a sense which would suit the other examples of **τηρεῖν εἰς.** (3) . . . *for you*, **εἰς** = ל = dative (so Syriac), the writer or translator being influenced by **εἰς** above and below. The inheritance is still, as it has always been, kept back, but the Christians are sure to succeed to it. So Enoch refers to the secrets of the righteous which shall be revealed (xxxviii. 3); the lot of the righteous which the Son of Man preserves (xlviii. 7); and says Blessed are ye ye righteous and elect for glorious will be your lot . . . it will be said to the holy that they should seek in heaven the secrets of righteousness the heritage of faith (lviii. 5).

Ver. 5. The Christians addressed are—to complete the metaphor from other passages in the Epistle—a spiritual house (ii. v.), which is besieged by the devil (v. 8) but guarded and garrisoned by God's Power. So long as they have faith (v. 9) they are safe: "our faith lays hold upon this power and this power strengthens faith and so we are preserved" (Leighton). Without responsive faith God's power is powerless to heal or to guard (*cf.* Mark vi. 5 f. and accounts of Jesus' miracles generally, Jas. i. 6 f.). The language seems to echo Rom. i. 16, **δύναμις θεοῦ εἰς σωτηρίαν παντὶ τῷ πιστεύοντι,** combined with Gal. iii. 23 (*cf.* Phil. iv. 7) where also the distinctive **φρουρεῖν** occurs in similar context. The ***Power***

πίστε ως εἰς σωτηρίαν ἑτοί μην ἀποκαλυφθῆναι ἐν καιρῷ
ἐσχάτω· ἐν ῷ ἀγαλλιᾶσθε ὀλίγον ἄρ τι εἰ δέον[1] λυπηθέντες[2] 6

[1] Codex Alexandrinus with others adds **ἐστι** after **δέον.**

[2] **λυπηθέντες** is probably right, **εἰ δέον** being parenthetical: the variants **λυπηθέντας** (first hand of Codex Sinaiticus and many cursives) and **λυπηθῆναι** (one cursive and the Vulgate) are due to the connexion of **δέον** with its context, the parenthetical character of the phrase being disregarded.

(גבורתא) *of God* is put for *Jehovah* in the Targum of Isa. xxxiii. 21; and the corresponding use of **ἡ δύναμις** is found in Mark xiv. 62 (see Dalman, 200 f.; and add **ἡ μεγαλωσύνη**, a more exact rendering, of Heb. i. 3, viii. 1). In Philo God's powers are personified self-manifestations. **εἰς σωτηρίαν, κ.τ.λ.,** is probably the third clause qualification of **φρουρ.** (*cf.* 2, 3). Below, the salvation of souls is described as the goal of faith (9) in a passage where the **ἑτοίμην, κ.τ.λ.,** qualify **σωτηρίαν** rather than **κληρονομίαν** which is explained by **σωτ. . . . ἐσχάτῳ.** Salvation is to St. Peter that salvation which is to be revealed in the future (*cf.* i. 9, ii. 2; so Rom. xiii. 11, **νῦν ἐγγύτερον . . . ἡ σωτηρία**). Partial anticipations he neglects; for them as for Christ the glory follows the present suffering. The idea of the revelation of salvation comes from Ps. xcviii. 2 (*cf.* Isa. lvi. 1) which has influenced St. Paul also (Rom. i. 16 f.). **ἑτοίμην** seems to be simply the equivalent of עתיד *prepared*, which St. Paul renders with more attention to current usage than etymology by **μέλλουσαν** (Rom. viii. 18; Gal. iii. 23; so 1 Peter v. 1). This weaker sense begins with Deut. xxxii. 35 (LXX, **πάρεστιν ἕτοιμα.** as Peter here) and prevails in new Hebrew (Tarphon said . . . the recompense of the reward of the righteous is for *the time to come.* העתיד לבא, Aboth, ii. 19). But the proper significance of the word is recognised and utilised in the Parables of Jesus, Matt. xxiv. 4, 8.

καιρῷ ἐσχάτῳ, still anarthrous as being technical term—indefinite as the time is unknown as well as in accordance with authors' custom (*cf.* **δύναμις, πιστέως, σωτηριαν** above); *cf.* John ii. 18.

Vv. 6-9. Exult then. These various temptations to which you are exposed cause present grief. But they are part of God's plan for you. Even material perishable gold is tried in the fire. So is your faith tested that it may be purged of its dross and the good metal be discovered when Jesus Christ is revealed. You love Him whom you never saw; though you see Him not you believe on Him. Exult then with joy that anticipates your future glory. You are winning the prize of your faith, the ultimate salvation of souls. St. Peter returns to the present and regards it from the point of view of those whom God is guarding—but only to advance again to the glorious future (7 fin, 9) when Jesus Christ the present object of their love and faith shall be revealed. He is the central figure of this section which is based upon two of His sayings which are appropriate to the circumstances of these His persecuted followers (so iv. 13) *v.* Matt. v. 12 = Apoc. xix. 7 from Ps. xxi. 1, cxviii. 24. Compare Jas. i. 2-4 and John cited below.

Ver. 6. **ἐν ᾧ.** There are four possible antecedents. (1) **καιρῷ,** (2) Jesus Christ, (3) God, (4) the state of things described in 3-5. (1) would imply that they must live in the future and is least probably right. (2) is supported by 8 but is unlikely at this point. The choice lies between (3), God being hitherto the dominating figure; and (4): *cf.* Luke i. 47 = 1 Sam. ii. 1 **α—ἀ.** with **ἐν** in LXX as well as **ἐπί. ἀγαλλιᾶσθε.** Indicative (with or without quasi future meaning) rather than Imperative. Bye form of **ἀγάλλομαι** (Homer downwards) first found in LXX especially as assonant rendering of גיל: used later in bad sense (**λοιδορεῖται,** Hesych): here borrowed from Matt. v. 11 f. **χαίρετε καὶ ἀγαλλιᾶσθε. ὀλίγον,** (1) *for a little time,* or (2) *to a small extent* (contrast John xvi. 6, **ἡ λύπη πεπλήρωκεν ὑμῶν τὴν καρδίαν**). **εἰ δέον,** they cannot but feel grief at their trials (John xvi. 20, **ὑμεῖς λυπηθήσεσθε ἡ δὲ λύπη ὑμῶν εἰς χαρὰν γενήσεται**), but they must not indulge their natural weakness. To take the "necessity" as referring to their trials (for not all the Saints are oppressed, Oec.) limits **λυπ.** to the external sense of vexation without reference to the feelings of the grieved corresponding to the feelings implied in **ἀγ.** The contrast is thus destroyed, but this sense *harass* would suit the other military metaphor, **τοὺς φρουρουμένους.—ἐν ποικίλοις πειρασμοῖς,** the adjective rules out the

7 ἐν ποικίλοις πειρασμοῖς ἵνα τὸ δοκίμιον[1] ὑμῶ̄ τῆς πίστεως
πολυτει[2] μότερον χρυσοῦ τοῦ ἀπολλυμένου διὰ πυ ρὸς δὲ

[1] For **δοκίμιον** three cursives read **δόκιμον**, a more familiar form of the adjective.

[2] The **ει** in **πολυτειμότερον** is used in place of the conventional **ι** to show that the syllable is long: so **τειμήν**, etc. The secondary uncials have **πολὺ τιμίωτερον.**

limitation of **π.** to external trials which St. James who has the entire phrase seems to put upon it.

Ver. 7. **τὸ δοκίμιον.** The evidence of the papyri (Deissmann, *Bible Studies*, pp. 259 ff.) shows that **δοκίμιος** is a bye form of the adjective **δόκιμος** *approved*; so Ps. xii. 7, **ἀργύριον πεπυρωμένον· δοκίμιον** (*cf.* 1 Chron. xxxix. 4; Zech. xi. 3, where it occurs as *v.l.* for **δόκιμον**). Hence the phrase (here and in Jas. i. 3?) corresponds exactly to St. Paul's **τὸ τῆς ὑμετέρας ἀγάπης γνήσιον**—"the genuineness of your faith or "the approvedness"). So Arethas on Apoc. ix. 4, **οἱ δὲ τὸ δοκίμιον ἑαυτῶν διὰ πυρὸς παρεχόμενοι.** The substantive **δ.** = "means of trial, testing" which does not suit this context, or a specimen of metal to be tested.—**πολυτιμότερον,** to justify the common rendering (A.V., R.V.) according to which **π. κ.τ.λ.** are taken as in apposition to **τὸ δοκ., ὄν** must be supplied as if omitted by haplography after **πολ.** But there is no need for emendation, if **πολ.** be taken as predicate thrown forward for the sake of emphasis.—**χρυσοῦ κ.τ.λ.** St. Peter adapts the familiar comparison of man's suffering to the fining-pot of precious metal, insisting on the superiority of the spiritual to the material gold. The stress lies on **διὰ πυρός.** True faith is tested by trials, just as gold is proved by fire. It is more valuable than gold which is perishable. If men test gold thus, much more will God test faith which outlives the present age, *cf.* Hebrew ix. 23. *Cf.* use of **πύρωσις,** iv. 12. For the image, Zech. xiii. 9, **δοκιμῶ αὐτοὺς ὡς δοκιμάζεται τὸ χρυσίον**; Ps. lxvi. 10; Prov. xvii. 3; Sir. ii. 5, etc.—**Τοῦ ἀπολλυμένου,** *cf.* John vi. 27, **τὴν βρῶσιν τὴν ἀπ.** (contrasted with imperishable food; here gold generally is contrasted with faith) and **φθαρτοῖς ἀργυρίῳ καὶ χρυσίῳ** below.—**εὑρεθῇ,** *cf.* 2 Peter iii. 14, **σπουδάσατε ἄσπιλοι καὶ ἀμώμητοι αὐτῷ εὑρεθῆναι ἐν εἰρήνῃ**; Ps. xvii. 3, **ἐδοκίμασας τὴν καρδίαν μου . . . καὶ οὐχ εὑρέθη ἐν ἐμοὶ ἀδικία.**—**εἰς ἔπαινον . . .** must be taken with the whole sentence, unless **ὄν** be supplied. So **εἰς** might introduce the predicate (better ∵ stronger) of **εὑρ.**, *cf.* Rom. vii. 10. **εἰς** taken as = לְ expressing transition into a new state or condition (as Rom. vii. 10).—**ἔπαινον** is the verdict. "Well done good and faithful servant; enter thou into the joy of thy Lord." The Christian is the true Jew and receives at last the *praise* which the name Judah signifies. In Rom. ii. 29, **ὁ ἐν τῷ κρυπτῷ Ἰουδαῖος . . . οὗ ὁ ἔπαινος οὐκ ἐξ ἀνθρωπων ἀλλ' ἐκ τοῦ θεοῦ,** Paul follows the alteration of the original **ἐξομολόγησις** (Gen. xxix. 35, LXX, and Philo) consequent upon the transference of the praise (תודה) from God to men (*cf.* Gen. xlix. 8, **Ἰούδα σε αἰνέσαισαν οἱ ἀδελφοί σου**). The old Israel set their hope on praise from the congregation (Sir. xxxix. 10) or glory from men, John v. 44; xii. 42 f. The new Israel looked for praise from God to balance the dispraise of men (Matt. v. 11 f.); so St. Peter adds **ἐπ.** to the usual formula **δόξαν καὶ τιμήν**, Rom. ii. 7, 10 (Ps. viii. 6) **δόξῃ καὶ τιμῇ ἐστεφάνωσας ἄνθρωπον,** *cf.* **σκεῦος εἰς τιμήν**, Rom. ix. 21, for the less obvious word. Hort compares Marcus Aurelius xii. 11, **μὴ ποιεῖν ἄλλο ἢ ὅπερ μέλλει ὁ θεὸς ἐπαινεῖν.**—**ἐν ἀποκαλύψει Ἰυ. Χυ.,** *when Jesus Christ is revealed.* The expression is derived from the saying **κατὰ τὰ αὐτὰ ἔσται ᾗ ἡμέρᾳ ὁ υἱὸς τοῦ ἀνθρώπου ἀποκαλύπτεται** (Luke xvii. 30). As Judge He will pronounce the verdict of approval and bestow glory and honour. The reference to present *glorified joy* in the midst of trial suggests that the writer has advanced beyond the simple belief in a final theophany and contemplates a spiritual revelation of Jesus Christ as each Christian (*cf.* Gal. i. 16) realises the meaning of His Resurrection; but *cf.* **μὴ ὁρῶντες** below.

Ver. 7. The Christians addressed were not personal disciples of Jesus but converts of the Apostles (12). As such they could claim Beatitude **μακάριοι οἱ μὴ ἰδόντες καὶ πιστεύσαντες** (John xx. 29). Their love began and continues without sight of Him; even now when they expect His coming they must still believe without seeing Him and exult. The Latin version of Augustine, gives

δοκιμαζομένου εὑρεθῇ εἰς ἔπαινον ϗ δόξαν καὶ τειμὴν ἐν
ἀποκαλύψει Ιῦ Χῦ ὃν οὐχ[1] ἰδόντες[2] ἀγαπᾶτε εἰς ὃν ἄρτι μὴ 8
ὁρῶντες πιστεύοντες δὲ ἀγαλ λιᾶτε χαρᾷ ἀνεκλαλή τῳ καὶ
δεδοξασμένῃ κομιζόμενοι τὸ τέλος τῆς πίστεως σωτηρί αν 9
ψυχῶν. περὶ ἧς σω τηρίας ἐξεζήτησαν ϗ ἐξηραύνησαν προ- 10
φῆ ται οἱ περὶ τῆς εἰς ὑμᾶς χάριτος προφητεύσᾱ τες

[1] The first hand of Codex Vaticanus is alone in reading **οὐχ**, which could only be justified if followed by an aspirate.

[2] For **ἰδόντες** many manuscripts, headed by Codex Alexandrinus, read **εἰδότες**: this confusion between **ἰδεῖν** and **εἰδέναι** is common.

three distinct clauses referring to the past, the present and the future climax *whom you knew not; in whom now—not seeing ye believe; whom when you see you will exult*. But for lack of support it must be set aside in favour of the Greek text (which regards present as leading up to future culmination without a break) as being a redaction of the passage for separate use. **εἰς ὅν**, with **πιστεύοντες, μὴ ὁρῶντες** being parenthesis added to explain force of **πιστ.** (Heb. xi. 1; Rom. viii. 24).—**χαρᾷ ἀνεκλαλήτῳ καὶ δεδοξασμένῃ.** Their faith enables them to pass beyond their present sufferings to the joy which belongs to the subsequent glories. Thus their joy being heavenly is *unspeakable* and *glorified*. Language cannot express the communion with God which the Christian like St. Paul may enjoy (2 Cor. xii. 3 f.); compare Rom. viii. 26, **αὐτὸ τὸ πνεῦμα ὑπερεντυγχάνει στεναγμοῖς ἀλαλήτοις.** And this joy is *glorified* because it is an earnest of the glory which shall be revealed; *cf.* iv. 14.

Ver. 9. The connexion with mention of persecution suggests that the writer is here thinking of the saying, *in your patience ye shall win your souls* and perhaps also of the contrast between the persecutor who has only power over the body. Whatever happen to the body the conclusion — the consummation of their faith—is assured them.—**κομιζόμενοι** implies that already they are receiving what is due to them (*cf.* v. 4) and therefore they rejoice with Hannah in God the Saviour. In the Attic Orators who use a refined form of colloquial Greek the verb is common in the sense of *recovering* debts, as in Matt. xxv. 27, **ἐκομισάμην ἂν τὸ ἐμόν.** St. Paul applies it to future recompense (2 Cor. v. 10, **ἵνα κομίσηται ἕκαστος τὰ διὰ τοῦ σώματος**; Eph. vi. 8; Col. iii. 25; *cf.* 2 Macc. viii. 33, **τὸν ἄξιον τῆς δυσσεβείας ἐκομίσατο μισθόν**); in Heb. iii. 4, it is used of receiving promises.—**τὸ τέλος.** The common meaning *fulfilment* or *consummation* gives a fair sense but the connection with **κομιζόμενοι** is thus somewhat strange. The parallel of v. 4, taken with Pindar, Ol. x(xi.) 81, **Δόρυκλος δ' ἔφερε πυγμᾶς τέλος,** suggests as a possible rendering *because ye receive the reward*. The Septuagint, again (Num. xxxi. 28, etc.), uses **τ.** to translate מכס = *proportion to be paid, tax*. And this use is well established in Greek literature for **τὰ τέλη,** *cf.* **λυσιτελεῖν,** etc. Accordingly Suidas defines **τέλος** as **τὸ διδόμενον τοῖς βασιλεῦσι.** The particular connotations can hardly be pressed here but these uses give some colour of support to the Syriac rendering *recompense* and the *mercedem* of Augustine; *cf.* Rom. vi. 22.—**σωτηρίαν ψυχῶν** = **σωτηρίαν** above. **ψυχῶν** is added to console the readers for their sufferings in accordance with Mark viii. 35, **ὃς δ' ἂν ἀπολέσει τὴν ψυχὴν αὐτοῦ ἕνεκεν τοῦ εὐαγγελίου σώσει αὐτήν** = John xii. 25; *cf.* Luke xxi. 19; Jas. i. 21. The soul for St. Peter is the self or personality as for Jesus Himself.

Vv. 10-12.—The ancient prophets prophesied concerning the grace which was destined for you and enquired diligently about this salvation. They were the unconscious instruments of the revelation of God and their first duty done continued to pore over the inspired descriptions of the sufferings and subsequent glories of the Messiah. They asked themselves to whom does this refer and when shall these things be. And to them the revelation was made that they were only the administrators of an estate which others —you in fact should enjoy. The subjects of their prophecies have now been proclaimed to you by your Christian teachers who, like the prophets, were inspired by

11 ἐραυνῶντες εἰς τίνα ἢ ποῖον καιρὸν ἐδήλου τὸ ἐν αὐτοῖς πνεῦμα [1] προμαρτυρό μενον [2] τὰ εἰς Χρειστὸ παθήματα καὶ τὰς

[1] Codex Vaticanus is alone in omitting Χριστοῦ after πνεῦμα.
[2] Codex Alexandrinus with others has προμαρτυρουμενον.

the Holy Spirit—with this difference that now the Spirit has been sent from heaven whereas of old He dwelt only in minds of a few. And these are the mysteries into which angels long to peep.

St. Peter has utilised a saying of Jesus to explain the great problem of unfulfilled prophecy and expounded it. Among the prophets he includes the so-called apocalyptic writers like Daniel and his successors. Gradually the coming of the Messiah and the dawn of the new age had been pushed further and further back until the inspired prophets realised that —as the Christians held—the Messiah would only come just before the end of all. The Messiah was not Hezekiah despite the Rabbis, nor yet the best of the Hasmonean house as Enoch hoped. ἀπεκαλύφθη. Such was the revelation or Apocalypse from which the latest of the prophets derive their common name; and St. Peter credits all the line with the curiosity which characterised the last of them and his own contemporaries; *cf.* Acts ii. and Heb. xi. 13 ff. The saying in question on which St. Peter builds is reported differently: According to Matt. xiii. 17, Jesus said, πολλοὶ προφῆται καὶ δίκαιοι ἐπεθύμησαν . . . according to Luke x. 24, προφῆται καὶ βασιλεῖς ἠθέλησαν . . . according to St. Peter προφῆται (10) καὶ ἄγγελοι. The mention of the *righteous* derives support from Heb. xi. 13-16, and John viii. 56, and an original ישרים "the righteous" would easily be altered in the course of transmission into שרים = *princes* earthly or heavenly (*cf.* Dan. x. 21; LXX, Μιχαὴλ ὁ ἄγγελος). The motive which prompted the interpretation ἄγγελοι is due to the influence of the Book of Enoch (see note below) which explains the writer's conception of the prophets.

Ver. 10. The prophets were concerned with the Messianic salvation and searched their own writings and those of their predecessors for definite information about it. They are honoured by the Christians who realise that as a matter of fact they prophesied concerning the grace which was destined for the Christian Church.—τῆς εἰς ὑμᾶς χάριτος, *the grace which belongs to you*, *cf.* τὰ εἰς χριστὸν παθ. (11).

Ver. 11. The construction of εἰς τ.κ.π. καιρόν and of προμαρτ. is doubtful. ἐραυνῶντες takes up ἐξεζήτησαν κ.τ.λ. (10); the run of the sentence seems to naturally connect τὰ . . . δόξας with προμαρτ. and εἰς . . . καιρόν with ἐδήλου. So Vulgate *in quod vel quale tempus significaret . . . spiritus . . . praenuntians . . . passiones.* But if εἰς . . . καιρὸν be unfit to be a direct object and προμαρτ., perhaps, to have one of this kind, τὰ . . . δόξας must be governed by ἐδήλου. It is possible also to dissociate τίνα from καιρὸν and to render *in reference to whom and what time the Spirit signified . . .*; *cf.* Eph. v. 22, ἐγὼ δὲ λέγω εἰς Χριστόν, Acts ii. 25. If τίνα be taken with καιρόν, the two words correspond to the two questions of the disciples, *When? . . .* and *what shall be the sign?* (Mark xiii. 4). Failing to discover *at what time*, the prophets asked *at what kind of time*; their answer received a certain endorsement in the eschatological discourse of Jesus (Mark xiii. 5 ff. and parallels).—ἐδήλου, *cf.* Heb. ix. 8, τοῦτο δηλοῦντος τοῦ Πνεύματος. The word implies discernment on the part of the student (Heb. xii. 27, τὸ δὲ ἔτι ἅπαξ δηλοῖ . . .). *What time . . . did point unto* of R.V. is unjustifiable; a simple accusative is required, *i.e.*, either (i.) ποῖον κ. or (ii.) τίνα ἢ π. κ. (εἰς being deleted as dittography of -ες) or (iii.) τὰ . . . δόξας.—τὸ πνεῦμα [Χριστοῦ], the full phrase is a natural one for a Christian to employ—Christ being here the proper name = Jesus Christ and not the title. κύριος in the O.T. was commonly interpreted as referring to Our Lord; and ΧC. is a frequent *v.l.* for ΚC. Hence Barnabas (*v.q.*), οἱ προφῆται ἀπ' αὐτοῦ ἔχον τὴν χάριν εἰς αὐτὸν ἐπροφήτευσαν.—προμαρτυρόμενον only occurs here. If μαρτύρομαι (the proper sense) determine the meaning of the compound render "*protesting* (*calling God to witness*) *beforehand*". If usage justify confusion with μαρτυρεῖν, *be witness* [*of*] render *testifying beforehand* or (*publicly*.)—τὰ εἰς Χν παθήματα, the doctrine that the Messiah must suffer and so enter into His glory was stated by the prophets (*e.g.* Isa. iii.) but neglected by the Jews of the first century (John xii. 34). Believers were reminded of it by the risen Lord Himself (Luke xxiv. 26, 46) and put it in the forefront of their *demonstratio*

με τὰ ταῦτα δόξας οἷς ἀ πεκαλύφθη ὅτι οὐχ ἑ αυτοῖς 12
ὑμῖν δὲ διηκό νουν[1] αὐτὰ ἃ νῦν ἀνηγ γέλη ὑμῖν διὰ τῶν εὐ

[1] For **διηκόνουν** Dr. Rendel Harris (*Side-Lights on New Testament Research*, p. 207) conjectures that **διενοοῦντο** should be read in accordance with the statement of the Book of Enoch, "I contemplated them (the things heard in the vision) not for the present generation but for one that was far distant". See Henoch, i. 2, **καὶ οὐκ ἐς τοῦ νῦν γενεὰν διενοούμην ἀλλὰ ἐπὶ πόρρω ἤνσαν ἐγὼ λαλῶ. διανοίας** of verse 13 is cited in confirmation of the conjecture.

evangelica (Acts iii. 18, xvii. 3, xxvi. 23). The phrase corresponds exactly to the original "חבלי שלי": **εἰς** standing for the ל (periphrasis for construct. state).—**τὰς μετὰ ταῦτα δόξας,** the plural *glories* implies some comprehension of the later doctrine, *e.g.*, John, which recognised that the glory of Jesus was partially manifested during His earthly life; although the definition *subsequent* reflects the primitive simplicity and if it be pressed the glories must be explained as referring to the resurrection ascension triumph over angels as well as the glorious session (viii. 21 f.).—**οἷς ἀπεκαλύφθη,** so St. Peter argues that Joel prophesied the last things (*cf.* Sir. xlviii. 24) and that David foresaw and spoke concerning the resurrection (Acts ii. 17, 31, *cf.* iii. 24). Compare Dan. ix. 2, xii. 4, etc., for examples of partial revelations of this kind proper to apocalyptic writers. Heb. l.c. *supr.* credits the Patriarchs with the same insight.—**οὐχ ἑαυτοῖς ὑμῖν δέ,** negative and positive presentation of the past for emphasis is common in this Epistle.—**διηκόνουν αὐτά,** "they were supplying, conveying the revelations granted to them—primary the prophecy and the revealed solution of it alike," *cf.* iv. 10, **εἰς ἑαυτοὺς αὐτὸ διακονοῦντες.** The context shows, if the word **διακονεῖν** does not itself connote **it,** that herein they were stewards of God's manifold grace—channels of communication. For Acc. with **διακον.** *cf*, 2 Cor. iii. 3, **ἐπιστολὴ Χριστοῦ διακονηθεῖσα ὑφ' ἡμῶν,** viii. 19, **τῇ χάριτι ταύτῃ τῇ διακονουμένῃ ὑφ' ἡμῶν,** from which it may be inferred that **δ.** connotes what the context here suggests, *cf.* **ἃ νῦν ἀνηγγέλη,** *have been at the present dispensation declared*; **ἀ.** is taken from the great proof text relating to the calling of the Gentiles, **οἷς οὐκ ἀνηγγέλη ἀκούουσιν,** Isa. lii. 15 cited Rom. xv. 21. "But St. Peter probably meant more by the word . . . the phrase includes not only the announcement of the historical facts of the Gospel, but, yet more, their implicit teachings as to the counsels of God and the hopes revealed for men" (Hort).—**διὰ τῶν εὐαγγ. ὑμας,** God spake *through* the evangelists (*cf.* Isa. lxi. 1, apud Rom. x. 15) as *through* the prophets, Matt. i. 22, ii. 15, etc. Both are simply God's messengers. For accusative after **εὐαγγ.** *cf.* use of בשר = *gladden with good tidings* (Isa. lxi. 1). So **πτωχοὶ εὐαγγελίζονται** (Matt. xi. 5; Luke vii. 22) is substituted for the original **πτωχοῖς εὐαγγελίζεσθαι** (Luke iv. 18 = Isa. lxi. 1) if the prophecy which Jesus appropriated and which forms the basis of the Christian use of the word.—**πνεύματι κ.τ.λ.** The evangelists preached *by the Spirit*, as Stephen spoke (Acts vi. 10), **τῷ πνεῦματι ᾧ ἐλάλει.** In Sir. xlviii. 24, if the Greek and Hebrew texts are trustworthy, **πνεύματι** the simple Dative (**πνεύματι μεγάλῳ εἶδεν τὰ ἔσχατα** *i.e.* Isaiah) corresponds to ברוח : *cf.* insertion of **ἐν** here in *v.l.* The visible descent of the Holy Spirit is contrasted with the indwelling Spirit which inspired the prophets. The Holy Spirit was given, when Jesus was glorified, as never before, **οὐκ ἐκ μέτρου** (John iii. 34). Vulgate renders by ablative absolute.—**εἰς ἃ . . . παρακύψαι,** after expanding the first part of Jesus' saying (and its context *ye see*) St. Peter at last reaches the second in its secondary form. He combines with it as its proper Scripture, the prophecy of Enoch (ix. 1) **καὶ ἀκούσαντες οἱ τέσσαρες μεγάλοι ἀρχάγγελοι . . . παρέκυψαν ἐπὶ τὴν γῆν ἐκ τῶν ἁγίων τοῦ οὐρανοῦ.** St. Paul spiritualises the idea "to me . . . this grace was given to preach to the Gentiles . . . in order that now might be made known to the principalities and the authorities in heavenly places by means of the Church the very-varied wisdom of God" (Eph. iii. 8 ff.). St. Peter reproduces faithfully the simplicity of the original and represents this longing as still unsatisfied since the Church is not yet perfect or complete. It thus becomes part of the sympathetic groaning and travailing of the whole creation (Rom. viii. 22 f.). In iii. 21 St. Peter states on the same authority that

αγγελισαμένων ὑμᾶς πνεύματι [1] ἁγίω ἀπο σταλέντι ἀπ' οὐρανοῦ
13 εἰς ἃ ἐπιθυμοῦσιν ἄγ γελοι παρακύψαι. διὸ ἀναζωσάμενοι
τὰς ὀσφύας τῆς διανοίας ὑμῶν νέφοντες [2] τε λείως ἐλπίσατε
14 ἐπὶ τὴ̄ φερομένην ὑμῖν χάρι̅ ἐν ἀποκαλύψει Ιῦ Χῦ. ὡς

[1] To πνεύματι Codex Sinaiticus, with other manuscripts of less weight, prefixes ἐν.

[2] νέφοντες for νήφοντες.

Christ preached to the spirits in prison; adding that when he ascended all angels were subjected to Him. The apparent contradiction is due to the discrepancy between the ideal and its gradual realisation and not to an imperfect coordination of these conceptions of the universal sovereignty of God. See 1 Cor. xv. 25 f., Heb. ii. 7 f., *not yet do we see . . .*—**παρακύψαι** has lost its suggestion of peeping through its use in the LXX for שקף *look forth* though it is not employed by them in the places where God is said to *look down from* heaven (Ps. xiv. 2, etc.). The patristic commentators seem to hold by the Evangelist rather than the Apostle in respect to the saying, as they refer exclusively for illustration to the O.T. figures, Moses (Heb xi. 26), Isaiah (John xii. 41). Oecumenius notes that Daniel is called by the angel *a man of longings* (Dan. ix. 25). That the angels of Peter are due to Enoch and secondary seems to be borne out by the Targum of Eccles. i. 8, "In all the words that are prepared (about) to come to pass in the world the ancient prophets wearied themselves and could not find their ends".

Vv. 13-21. *Practical admonitions.* In this section St. Peter is engrossed with the conception of the Church as the new Israel which has been delivered from idolatry—the spiritual Egypt—by a *far more excellent sacrifice.* Jesus Himself endorsed such adaptation of the directions given for the typical deliverance (Luke xii. 35) and the principle that the worshippers of Jehovah must be like Him (John iv. 23 f.; Matt. v. 48, etc.).

Ver. 13. **διό** introduces the practical inference. —**ἀναζωσάμενοι, κ.τ.λ.**, the reference to the directions for celebration of the Passover (Exod. xii. 11, **οὕτως δὲ φάγεσθε αὐτό· αἱ ὀσφύες ὑμῶν περιεζωσμέναι . . . μετὰ σπουδῆς**) is unmistakable. The actual deliverance of the Christians is still in the future; they must be always ready against the coming of the Lord. Oec. refers to Job xxxviii, 3. The particular compound occurs only twice in LXX—once in this phrase of the manly woman in Prov. xxxi. 17, **ἀναζωσαμένη ἰσχυρῶς τὴν ὀσφὺν αὐτῆς**, where it implies preparation for serious work. In 2 Kings iv. 29 ff. (Elisha's mission of Gehazi which is in some ways a type fulfilled by Jesus' mission of the Seventy, *cf.* Luke x. 4), **ζῶσαι τὴν ὀσφύν σου** is the preparation for an urgent errand. The addition of **τῆς διανοίας** implies that the readiness required is spiritual. St. Paul uses **καρδία** in the same way (Eph. i. 18, **πεφωτισμένους τοὺς ὀφθαλμοὺς τῆς καρδίας ὑμῶν**) and from Mark xii. 30 = Deut. vi. 4 f. it appears that **διάνοια** is a recognised equivalent of לבב *heart.* —**νήφοντες τελείως.** In cases like this it is natural to take the adverb with the preceding verb. **τελείως** (only here in N.T.) has much the same force as **τῆς διανοίας**; so the adjective is applied to the antitype as contrasted with the type in Heb. ix. 11, **τῆς . . . τελειοτέρας σκηνῆς** and Jas. i. 25, **νόμον τέλειον τὸν τῆς ἐλευθερίας.** For **νήφοντες** *cf.* iv. 7 and v. 8, **νήψατε γρηγορήσατε**, 1 Thess. v. 8, **γρηγορῶμεν καὶ νήφωμεν.** Sobriety is necessary to watchfulness. The origin of this use of the word (not in the LXX) is to be found in the parable of Luke xii. 45 f.; it has special point in view of the **κώμοις** and **πότοις**, in which they were prone to indulge.—**τὴν φερομένην ὑμῖν χάριν** is an adaption of the common Greek idiom (Homer downwards) **φέρειν χ.**, *to confer a favour* (*cf.* Sir. viii. 19, **μὴ ἀναφερέτω σοι χάριν**) and is thus analogous to St. Paul's use of **χαρίζεσθαι** (see Rom. viii. 32). The present participle has its natural force. Peter does not distinguish between the present and the climax; already the new age which is the last has begun. The **χάρις** is the final deliverance and its use here is another link with the type: **ἔδωκεν ὁ Κύριος τὴν χάριν τῷ λαῷ αὐτοῦ** (Exod. xii. 36).—**ἐν ἀποκαλύψει Ἰησοῦ Χριστοῦ**, Jesus Christ is being revealed *or* is revealing the salvation. The revelation began with the resurrection *cf.* **φανερωθέντος** and continues to the culmination (7).

Ver. 14. **ὡς**, *inasmuch as you are*, *cf.*

τέκνα ὑπακοῆς· μὴ συσχηματιζόμε ναι [1] ταῖς πρότερον ἐν
τῇ ἀγνοίᾳ ὑμῶν ἐπι θυμίαις· ἀλλὰ κατὰ τὸ̄ καλέσαντα ὑμᾶς 15
ἅγιο̄ καὶ αὐτοὶ ἅγιοι ἐν πά σῃ ἀναστροφῇ γενή θητε·
διότι γέγραπται ὅτι ἅγιοι ἔσεσθε ὅτι ἐ γὼ ἅγιος· καὶ εἰ 16, 17
πατέρα ἐπικαλεῖσθε τὸν ἀπρο σωπολήμπτως κρί νοντα κατὰ
τὸ ἑκάστου ἔργον ἐν φόβῳ τὸν τῆς παροικίας ὑμῶν χρόνον

[1] The termination **συσχηματιζόμεναι** is probably due to the following **ταῖς**.

ii. 2, 5, iii. 7, etc.—**τέκνα ὑπακοῆς**, *obedient* corresponds to St. Paul's **υἱοὶ τῆς ἀπειθείας** (Col. iii. 6; Eph. ii. 2, v. 6). Both phrases reflect the Hebrew use of בֵּן, "followed by word of quality characteristic, etc." (B.D.B., *s.v.*, 8). For **τέκνα** in place of usual **υἱοί** in this idiom, *cf.* Hos. 9, **τέκνα ἀδικίας** and Eph. ii. 3, **τέκνα ὀργῆς**. Here it suits better with **βρέφη** (ii. 1).—**συσχηματιζόμεναι**, from Rom. xii. 2, **μὴ συσχηματίζεσθε τῷ αἰῶνι τούτῳ**. The feminine is peculiar to B whose scribe was perhaps influenced by the Alexandrian identification of woman with the flesh (John i. 13) or regarded such conformity as womanish. The participle has the force of an imperative. The Christians needed to be warned against conformity to the manners and morals of their countrymen, which were incompatible with their new faith (see v. 2-4). The use of **σχῆμα** in Isa. iii. 17, perhaps assists the use of **συσχ.** in connection with lusts.—**ἐν τῇ ἀγνοίᾳ ὑμῶν**. It was a Jewish axiom that the Gentiles were *ignorant* (Acts xvii. 30; Eph. iv. 17 f.). Christian teachers demonstrated the equal ignorance of the Jews (Peter, Acts iii. 17; Paul, in Rom.). So Jesus had pronounced even the teachers of Israel to be blind and promised them knowledge of the truth (John viii. 32 ff., *cf.* interview with Nicodemus); whereas speaking to the Samaritan woman He adopted the Jewish standpoint (John iv. 22)—*cf.* 2 Kings xvii. 29-41 with Isa. ii. 3; Baruch. iv. 4, **μακάριοί ἐσμεν Ἰσραὴλ ὅτι τὰ ἀρεστὰ τοῦ θεοῦ ἡμῖν γνωστά ἐστιν.**

Vv. 15 f. The command *Ye shall be holy for I am holy* is connected originally with the deliverance from Egypt and the distinction between clean and unclean, which lays down the principle of separation involved in the Exodus (Lev. xi. 44-46, etc.; *cf.* Isa. lii. 11). St. Peter combines the Scripture with the Word of Jesus for **κατὰ τὸν . . .** corresponds to **ὡς** of Matt. v. 48. Gentiles needed God's summons before they could regard Him as their heavenly Father; hence *Him that called you.* Compare Deut. xviii. 13 (whence **τέλειος** of Matt. *l.c.*) where also contrast with abominations of the the heathen.—**ἅγιον** is better taken as predicate than as substantive, since **ὁ καλέσας** (**καλῶν**) is well-established as a title of God in His relation to Gentile Christians (*cf.* ii. 9, etc.).—**ἐν πάσῃ ἀναστροφῇ**, *cf.* i. 18, ii. 12, iii. 1, 2, 16; Tobit iv. 19, **ἴσθι πεπαιδευμένος ἐν πάσῃ ἀ. σου.** The corresponding verb, **ἀναστρέφεσθαι** is found as rendering of הלך in the same sense (Prov. xx. 7, **ἀναστρέφεται ἄμωμος**); both verb and noun are so used in late Greek authors (especially Epictetus).—**γενήθητε** *become as you were not* OR *show yourselves as you are*; the latter sense suits **ἀ.** which is distinctively outward behaviour.

Ver. 17, *cf.* Rom. ii. 10 f., **εἰ πατέρα ἐπικαλεῖσθε**, *if ye invoke as Father*:—reminiscence of Jer. iii. 19, **εἰ πατέρα ἐπικαλεῖσθέ με** (so Q. perhaps after 1 Peter, for **εἶπα πατέρα καλέσετέ με**) *cf.* Ps. lxxxix. 27, **αὐτὸς ἐπικαλέσεταί με Πατήρ μου εἶ σύ.** There may be a reference to the use of the Lord's Prayer (*surname the Judge Father*); but the context of Jer. *l.c.* corresponds closely to the thought here: "All the nations shall be gathered . . . to Jerusalem, neither shall they walk any more after the stubbornness of their evil heart. In those days . . . Judah and Israel shall come together out of the land of captivity . . . and I said 'My father ye shall call me'."—**ἀπροσωπολήμπτως** summarises St. Peter's inference from experience at Caesarea (Acts x. 34) **καταλαμβάνομαι ὅτι οὐκ ἔστιν προσωπολήμπτης ὁ θεός.** Adjective and adverb are formed from **λαμβάνειν πρόσωπον** of LXX = נשא פני *receive* (*lift up*) *the face of*, *i.e.*, *be favourable* and later *partial*, *to.* The degeneration of the phrase was due to the natural contrast

18 ἀναστράφη τε· εἰδότες ὅτι οὐ φθαρ τοῖς ἀργυρίῳ ἢ χρυσίῳ
ἐλυτρώθητε ἐκ τῆς ματαίας ὑμῶν ἀναστρο φῆς πατροπαρα-
19 δότου· ἀλλὰ τιμίῳ αἵματι ὡς ἀμνοῦ ἀμώμου καὶ ἀ σπίλου

between the face and the heart of a man, which was stamped on the Greek equivalent by the use of **πρόσωπον** for *mask* of the actor or *hypocrite*.—**κρίνοντα.** If the tense be pressed, compare the saying of Jesus recorded in John xii. 31, **νῦν κρίσις ἐστιν τοῦ κόσμου τούτου.** Rom. ii. 16 is referred to the last Judgment by **διὰ Χριστοῦ Ἰησοῦ.** But the present participle may be timeless as in **ὁ καλῶν, ὁ βαπτίζων,** etc.—**κατὰ τὸ ἑκάστου ἔργον**, a commonplace Jewish and Christian, *cf.* Ps. xii. 12 (cited Rom. ii. 6), **σὺ ἀποδώσεις ἑκάστῳ κατὰ τὰ ἔργα αὐτοῦ** (Hebrew has *the work*). R. Aqiba used to say . . . The world is judged by grace and everything is according to the work (*Pirqe Aboth.*, iii. 24). For collective singular *lifework*, *cf.* also 1 Cor. iii. 13-15, etc.—**ἐν φόβῳ,** *Fear* is not entirely a technical term in N.T. Christians needed the warning to fear God (so Luke xii. 5; 2 Cor. v. 10), although love might be proper to the perfect—Gnostic or Pharisee—1 John iv. 18. The natural and acquired senses exist side by side, as appears in the use of **ἄφοβος.** Compare **ἄφοβος οὐ δύναται δικαιωθῆναι** (Sir. i. (22 with **ἐν τούτῳ ἄφοβός εἰμι** (Ps. xxvii. 2, Symmachus) = *in Him I am confident*.—**τὸν τῆς παροικίας χρόνον**, *during your earthly pilgrimage*, which corresponds to the sojourn of Israel in Egypt (Acts xiii. 17). If God is their Father, heaven must be their home (i. 4); their life on earth is therefore a sojourn (see on i. 1). St. Paul has his own use of the metaphor (Eph. ii. 19). Gentile Christians are no longer strangers and sojourners, but fellow-citizens of the saints.

Ver. 18. Amplification of Isa. lii. 3 f., **Δωρεὰν ἐπράθητε καὶ οὐ μετὰ ἀργυρίου λυτρωθήσεσθε** (*cf.* xlv. 13) . . . **εἰς Αἴγυπτον κατέβη ὁ λαός μου τὸ πρότερον παροικῆσαι ἐκεῖ.** The deliverance from Babylon corresponds to the deliverance from Egypt. To these the Christians added a third and appropriated to it the descriptions of its predecessors.—**οὐ φθαρτοῖς, κ. τ. λ.** The preceding negative relief to positive statement is characteristic of St. Peter, who here found it in his original (Isa. *l.c.*). **φθαρτοῖς** echoes **ἀπολλυμένου** and is probably an allusion to the Golden Calf of which it was said *These be thy gods O Israel, which brought thee up out of the land of Egypt* (Exod. xxxii. 14). According to Sap. xiv. 8, it is the proper name for an idol: **τὸ δὲ φθαρτὸν θεὸς ὠνομάσθη.** So the dative represents the agent and not only the instrument of the deliverance.—**ματαίας** supports the view taken of **φθ.,** for *the gods of the nations are vanity*, **μάταια** הבל (Jer. x. 3, etc.).—**πατροπαραδότου**, *ancestral*, *hereditary*. The adjective indicates the source of the influence, which their old way of life—*patrius mos, patrii ritus*—still exercised over them. The ancient religion had a strength—not merely *vis inertiae*—which often baffled both Jewish and Christian missionaries: "to subvert a custom delivered to us from ancestors the heathen say is not reasonable" (Clem. *Ac. Protr.* x.). This power of the dead hand is exemplified in the pains taken by the Stoics and New Pythagoreans to conserve the popular religion and its myths by allegorical interpretation. Among the Jews this natural conservatism was highly developed; St. Paul was a *zealot for the ancestral laws*. But the combination of patriarch and tradition does not prove that the persons addressed were Jewish Christians. The law, according to which the Jews regulated their life, was Divine, its mediator Moses; and there is a note of depreciation in the words *not that it is derived from Moses only from the Fathers* (John vii. 22). **πατρο** is contrasted with **πατέρα (17) as παραδότου** with the direct calling.

Ver. 19. The blood of Christ, the true paschal lamb, was the (means or) agent of your redemption. The type contemplated is composite; the *lamb* is the *yearling sheep* (שה **πρόβατον**, but Targum-Onkelos has אמר *lamb* and שה is rendered **ἀμνός** in Lev. xii. 8; Num. xv. 11; Deut. xiv. 4) prescribed for the Passover (Exod. xii. 5). But the description *perfect* (**τέλειον** תמים) is glossed by **ἀμώμου** (*cf.* Heb. xii. 14), which is the common translation of תמים in this connection, and **ἀσπίλου** which summarises the description of sacrificial victims generally (*v.* Lev. xxii. 22, etc.). **ἄμωμος** would be unintelligible to the Gentile, because it has acquired a peculiar meaning from the

Χῦ προεγνωσ μένου μὲν πρὸ κατα βολῆς κόσμου φανε 20, 21
ρωθέντος δὲ ἐπ' ἐσχά του τῶν χρόνων δι' ὑμᾶς τοὺς δι' αὐτοῦ

Hebrew מוּם *blemish.* **ἄσπιλος** is used by Symmachus in Job xv. 15, for זַךְ· Hesychius treats **ἄσπιλος. ἄμωμος** and **καθαρός** as synonyms.—**τιμίῳ** is set over against **φθαρτοῖς** as **πολυτιμ.** against **ἀπολλυμένου**; *cf.* Ps. cxvi. 15, **τίμιος ἐναντίον Κυρίου ὁ θάνατος τῶν ὁσίων** and **λίθον . . . ἔντιμον** (ii. 4).

Ver. 20. As the paschal lamb was taken on the tenth day of the month (Exod. xiii. 3) so Christ was foreknown before the creation and existed before His manifestation. The preexistence of Moses is stated in similar terms in *Assumption of Moses*, i. 12-14, "God created the world on behalf of His people. But He was not pleased to manifest this purpose of creation from the foundation of the world in order that the Gentiles might thereby be convicted. . . . Accordingly He designed and devised me and He prepared me before the foundation of the world that I should be the mediator of His Covenant." So of the Messiah, Enoch (xlviii. 3, 6) says: "His name was called before the Lord of spirits before the sun and the signs of the zodiac were created. . . . He was chosen and hidden with God before the world was created. At the end of time God will reveal him to the world." Alexandrian Judaism took over from Greek philosophy (Pythagoras, Plato, Aristotle) the doctrine of the preexistence of all souls. So in the *Secrets of Enoch* (xxiii. 5) it is said "Every soul was created eternally before the foundation of the world". The author of Wisdom *was a goodly child and obtained a good soul or rather being good came into a body undefiled* (Sap. viii. 19 f.); and Philo found Scriptural warrant in the first of the two accounts of Creation (Gen. i. 26 f.). Outside Alexandria, apart from the Essenes (Joseph, B. J., ii. 154-157) the general doctrine does not appear to have been accepted. But the belief in the preexistence of the Name of the Messiah if not the Messiah Himself was not unknown in Palestine and was latent in many of the current ideals. The doctrine of Trypho was probably part of the general reaction from the position reached by the Jewish thinkers (A.D.) and appropriated by the Christians. There are many hints in the O.T. which Christians exploited without violence and the development of angelology offered great assistance. Current conceptions of Angels and Wisdom as well as of the Messiah all led up to this belief. Apart from the express declarations of Jesus recorded by St. John, it is clear that St. Peter held to the real and not merely ideal pre-existence of Christ, not deriving it from St. Paul or St. John and Heb. It is no mere corollary of God's omniscience that the spirit of Christ was in the prophets.—**προεγνωσμένου**, *cf.* **κατὰ πρόγνωσιν**, ver. 2; only here of Messiah, perhaps as a greater Jeremiah (*cf.* Jer. i. 5)—but see the description of Moses cited above.—**πρὸ καταβολῆς κόσμου.** The phrase does not occur in LXX but Matt. xiii. 35 = Ps. lxxviii. 2 renders מִנִּי קֶדֶם by **ἀπὸ καταβολῆς** (LXX **ἀπ' ἀρχῆς**) Philo has **καταβολὴ γενέσεως** and **αἱ καταβολαὶ σπερμάτων** and uses **ἐκ κ.** = afresh. In 2 Macc. ii. 29, **καταβολή** is used of the foundation of a house; *cf.* **κατασκευάζειν** in Heb.—**φανερωθέντος**, of the past manifestation of Christ. In v. 1 of the future implies previous hidden existence, *cf.* 1 Tim. iii. 16 (quotation of current quasi-creed) **ἐφανερώθη ἐν τῷ κόσμῳ.** The manifestation consists in the resurrection and glorification evidenced by descent of spirit (21): *cf.* Peter's sermon in Acts ii., *risen, exalted, Jesus has sent the spirit: therefore let all the house of Israel know surely that God hath made Him both Lord and Christ.* St. Paul speaks in the same way of the *revelation of the secret, which is Christ in you*; see especially Col. i. 25-27. Compare John i. 14.—**ἐπ' ἐσχάτου τῶν χρόνων**, *at the end of the times*, *cf.* **ἐπ' ἐσχάτου τῶν ἡμερῶν** (Heb. i. 1 and LXX). The deliverance effected *certo tempore* by Christ's blood is eternally efficacious, *cf.* **αἰώνιον λύτρωσιν εὑράμενος** Heb., ix. 12 and the more popular statement of the same idea in Apoc. xiii. 8, the lamb slain from the *foundation of the world.*

Ver. 21. **δι' ὑμᾶς**, *for the sake of you Gentiles*, *i.e.*, **ἵνα ὑμᾶς προσαγάγῃ τῷ θεῷ**, iii. 18. The resurrection of Jesus and His glorification are the basis of their faith in God and inspire not merely faith but hope.—**δι' αὐτοῦ.** Compare for form Acts iii. 16, **ἡ πίστις ἡ δι' αὐτοῦ** and for thought Rom. v. 2; Eph. ii. 18—**πιστοὺς εἰς θεόν.** This construction occurs not infrequently in the Bezan text and is simply equivalent to **π.** with

πιστοὺς[1] εἰς Θν̄ τὸν ἐ γείραντα αὐτὸν ἐκ νε κρῶν καὶ δόξαν
αὐτῷ δόντα· ὥστε τὴν πί στιν ὑμῶν καὶ ἐλπίδα εἶναι εἰς
22 Θν̄· τὰς ψυχὰς ὑμῶν ἡγνικότες ἐν τῇ ὑπακοῇ τῆς ἀληθεί
ας[2] εἰς φιλαδελφίαν ἀνυπόκριτον· ἐκ καρ δίας ἀλλήλους

[1] For **πιστοὺς** Codex Sinaiticus and others substitute the participle **πιστεύοντας** in order to avoid the unfamiliar construction with the adjective.

[2] Manuscripts of secondary importance add **διὰ πνεύματος** after **τῆς ἀληθείας** and (with the original hand of Codex Sinaiticus) **καθαρᾶς** before **καρδίας**. The latter addition might be regarded as a mistaken emendation of an accidental repetition of **καρδίας**; but in the course of transmission such safeguards are commonly added to Scriptural texts. The third hand of Codex Sinaiticus substitutes **ἀληθινῆς** after **καρδίας**.

the Dative (Acts xvi. 15) corresponding to נאמן ל'. But **π.** keeping construction has changed its meaning. Already it is semi-technical = *believing*, *sc.* in Jesus and here **πίστιν . . . εἰς θεόν** follows immediately. So the verb **πιστεύοντας** is a true gloss; the addition of **εἰς θεόν** corrects the common conception of faith, which ultimately gave rise to a distinction between belief in Christ and belief in God.—**δόξαν αὐτῷ δόντα**, so *e.g.*, the prophecy (Isa. lii. 13) **ὁ παῖς μου . . . δοξασθήσεται σφόδρα** was fulfilled when the lame man was healed by St. Peter and St. John; **ὁ θεὸς Ἀβραὰμ . . . ἐδόξασεν τὸν παῖδα αὐτοῦ Ἰησοῦν** (Acts iii. 13). But the glory is primarily and generally the glorious resurrection and ascension, in which state Jesus sent the Holy Spirit (**ἦν τὸ πνεῦμα ὅτι οὔπω ἐδοξάσθη**, John). —**ὥστε . . . θεόν. καὶ ἐλπίδα** may be part of the subject of **εἶναι εἰς θεόν**, *so that your faith and hope are in God*, *or* predicate *so that your faith is also hope in God*. In either case **ἐλπίς** is rather *confidence* than *hope*, in accordance with LXX usage (= בטחה), and supplies an adequate climax—patient faith leads up to the appropriation of the Hope of Israel.

Vv. 22-25. The combination of purification of souls with love of the brotherhood suggests that the temptations to relapses were due to former intimacies and relationships which were not overcome by the spiritual brotherhood which they entered. Different grades of society were doubtless represented in all Christian churches and those who were marked out for leaders by their wealth and position were naturally slow to love the slaves and outcasts. As at Corinth old intimacies and congenial society led the better classes (iv. 3 f.) to fall back on the clubs to which they had belonged and in the company of their equals to sneer at their new brothers—"the brethren" (ii. 1). St. Peter reminds them that they must purify their souls from the taint—with a side-glance perhaps at the rites proper to the associations in question. They must love the brotherhood and its members as such. Earthly relationships are done away by their regeneration; they have exchanged the flesh for the spirit. The section is full of echoes; compare **ἡγνικότες** with **ἅγιοι** (15), **ἐν ἁγιασμῷ** (2), **τῇ ὑπακοῇ** with **τέκνα ὑ.** (14), **ἀναγεγεννημένοι** with **ἀναγεννήσας** (3), **φθαρτῆς** with **φθαρτοῖς** (18), **εὐαγγελισθέν** with **τῶν εὐαγγελισαμένων** (12). It should be compared throughout with Eph. iv. 18-24.—**τὰς . . . ἡγνικότες** from Jer. vi. 16, "*see what is the good way and walk in it and you shall find purification* (**ἁγνισμόν** LXX) *to your souls.* **ἁ.** usually of ceremonial purification in LXX. Compare Jas. iv. 8, **ἁγνίσατε καρδίας δίψυχοι** (*cf.* **ἀνυπόκριτον**). The perfect participle is used as indicating the ground of the admonition, so **ἀναγεγεννημένοι** (23). Pagan rites professed to purify the worshipper but cannot affect the soul, the self or the heart any more than the Jewish ceremonies can (Heb. ix. 9 f.). Scripture declares **ὁ φόβος Κυρίου ἁγνός** (Ps. xix. 10). They must realise that they have cleansed themselves ideally at baptism, *cf.* 1 John iii. 3 and 15 f. above with context.—**ἐν τῇ ὑπακοῇ τῆς ἀληθείας**, in your obedience to the truth, *cf.* Jer. *l.c.* above. They are no longer ignorant (14) but have learned the truth (*cf.* John xvii. 17-19, and **γνώσεσθε τὴν ἁ.**, John viii. 32) from the missionaries. They must persist in the obedience to it which they then professed, in contrast with those who *are disobedient to the truth* (Rom. ii. 8; *cf.* 2 Thess. ii. 12). Hort says: "St. Peter rather means the dependence of Christian obedience on the possession

ἀγαπή σατε ἐκτενῶς ἀναγε γεννημένοι οὐκ ἐκ σπορᾶς[1] 23
φθαρτῆς ἀλλὰ ἀφθάρτου διὰ λόγου ζῶντος Θῦ καὶ μένο-
τος.[2] διότι πᾶσα σὰρξ ὡς χόρτος καὶ πᾶσα δόξα αὐτῆς ὡς 24
ἄνθος χόρτου ἐξηράνθη ὁ χόρτος καὶ τὸ ἄνθος ἐξέπεσεν
τὸ δὲ ῥῆμα Κῦ μένει εἰς τὸν αἰῶ να· τοῦτο δέ ἐστιν τὸ 25

[1] The three great uncials (Sinaiticus, Alexandrinus and Ephraemi Rescriptus) put **φθορᾶς** for **σπορᾶς** keeping **φθαρτῆς**: the variant was probably a paraphrase of the whole phrase and possibly implied the identification of **ἀφθάρτου** with **ζῶντος Θεοῦ καὶ μένοντος.**

[2] The addition of **εἰς τὸν αἰῶνα** to **μένοντος** is due to verse 25.

of the truth," relying on Eph. iv. 24, and the probability that "St. Peter would have distinctly used some such language as **ἐν τῷ ὑπακούειν τῇ ἀληθείᾳ**". In regard to the latter point it should be observed that St. Peter is curiously fond of using nouns instead of verbs (*e.g.*, 2).—**εἰς φιλαδελφίαν**, *love of the brethren*, Vulgate, *in fraternitalis amore*, mutual love which exists between brothers. It is the primary Christian duty, Matt. xxiii. 8, the first fruits of their profession of which St. Paul has no need to remind the Thessalonians, 1 Thess. iv. 9.—**ἀνυπόκριτον**, *unfeigned*, contrasted with the love which they professed towards their fellow Christians (*cf.* ii. 1) which was neither hearty nor eager. There was pretence among them whether due to imperfect sympathy of Jew for Gentile or of wealthy and honourable Gentiles for those who were neither the one nor the other. For a vivid illustration of this feigning see Jas. ii. 15 f. and ii. 1-5, etc., for the friction between rich and poor.—**ἀλλήλους ἀγαπήσατε.** St. John's summary of the teaching of Jesus (John xiii. 34 f., xv. 12, 17) which he repeated in extreme old age at Ephesus, till the disciples were weary of it: "Magister quare semper hoc loqueris". His answer was worthy of him: "Quia praeceptum Domini est et si solum fiat sufficit (Hieron. in Gal. vi. 10).—**ἐκτενῶς**, *intentius* (Vulg.), in LXX of "*strong* crying to God" (Jonah iii. 8 = בחזקה *violently*, *cf.* Jud. iv. 12; Joel i. 14; 3 Macc. v. 9: in Polybius of a warm commendation (xxxi. 22, 12) a warm and friendly welcome (viii. 21, 1), a warm and magnificent reception (xxxiii. 16 4).

Ver. 23. **ἀναγεγεννημένοι.** So St. John **ἀγαπῶμεν ἀλλήλους ὅτι . . . πᾶς ὁ ἀγαπῶν ἐκ τοῦ θεοῦ γεγέννηται**; *cf.* Eph. iv. 17, v. 2.—**ἐκ σπορᾶς ἀφθάρτου**, *i.e.*, of God regarded as Father and perhaps also as Sower (*cf.* ver. 24); the two conceptions are combined in 1 John iii. 9, **πᾶς ὁ γεγεννημένος ἐκ τοῦ θεοῦ ἁμαρτίαν οὐ ποιεῖ ὅτι σπέρμα αὐτοῦ μένει.** Compare Philo, *Leg. All.*, p. 123 M. **Λείαν . . . ἐξ οὐδενὸς γεννητοῦ λαμβάνουσαν τὴν σπορὰν . . . ἀλλ' ὑπ' αὐτοῦ τοῦ θεοῦ.**—**διὰ λόγου . . . μένοντος**, the connection of **ζῶντος κ. μέν.** is doubtful; the following quotation might justify *the abiding word* and Heb. iv. 22, the living *word* in accordance with Deut. xxxii. 47—*cf.* 3, **ἐλπίδα ζῶσαν.** On the other hand the rendering of the Vulgate, *per verbum dei vivi et permanentis*, is supported by Dan. vi. 26 (**αὐτὸς γάρ ἐστιν θεὸς μένων καὶ ζῶν**) and supports St. Peter's argument: earthly relationships must perish with all flesh and its glory; spiritual kinship abides, because it is based on the relation of the kinsfolk to *God living and abiding*. For *the word of God* as the means of regeneration, *cf.* Jas. i. 18, **βουληθεὶς ἀπεκύησεν ἡμᾶς λόγῳ ἀληθείας.** For its identification with **ῥῆμα** of the quotation, *cf.* Acts x. 36 f.

Ver. 24 f. = Isa. xl. 6-8, adduced as endorsement of the comparison instituted between natural generation and divine regeneration, with gloss explaining the saying of Jehovah (*cf.* Heb. i. 1 f.). The only divergences from the LXX (which omits—as Jerome notes, perhaps through homœdeuton—quia spiritus dei flavit in eo: vere foenum est populus; asuit foenum cecidit flos) are that **ὡς** is inserted before **χ.** (so Targum), and that **αὐτῆς** is put for **ἀνθρώπου** (so Heb., etc.) and **Κυρίου** for **τοῦ θεοῦ ἡμῶν** (in accordance with the proper reading of *Jehovah* in the omitted verse).

Ver. 25. **τὸ εὐαγγελισθὲν** comes from **ὁ εὐαγγελιζόμενος Σειὼν** of Isa. xl 9 which the Targum explains as referring to the prophets.

II. 1 ῥῆμα τὸ εὐαγγελισθὲ̄ εἰς ὑμᾶς. ἀποθέμενοι οὖν πᾶσαν
κακίαν καὶ πάντα δόλον καὶ ὑπό κρισιν καὶ φόνους[1] ꝁ πάσας
2 καταλαλιὰς ὡς ἀρτιγέννητα βρέφη τὸ λογικὸν ἄδολον

[1] **φόνους** is an error (peculiar to Codex Vaticanus) for **φθόνους**.

Chapter II.—Vv. 1-10. Continuation of practical admonition with appeal to additional ground-principles illustrating the thesis of i. 10.

Ver. 1. *Put away then all malice—all guile and hypocrisy and envy—all backbiting.* **οὖν** resumes **διό** (i. 13). The faults to be put away fall into three groups, divided by the prefix *all*, and correspond to the virtues of i. 22 (**ὑπόκρισιν ἀνυπόκριτον**). The special connection of the command with the preceding Scripture would require the expression of the latent idea, that such faults as these are inspired by the prejudices of the natural man and belong to *the fashion of the world*, which *is passing away* (i. John ii. 17).—**ἀποθέμενοι**, *putting off*. Again participle with imperative force. St. Peter regards the metaphor of removal as based on the idea of washing off filth, *cf.* **σαρκὸς ἀπόθεσις ῥύπου** (iii. 21). St. James (i. 21, **διὸ ἀποθέμενοι πᾶσαν ῥυπαρίαν καὶ περισσείαν κακίας**) which seems to combine these two phrases and to deduce the familiarity of the spiritual sense of *filth* (*cf.* Apoc. xxii. 11, **ῥυπαρὸς κἄγιος**). St. Paul has the same word but associates it with the putting off of clothing (Col. iii. 5 ff.; Eph. iv. 22; Rom. xiii. 12—all followed by **ἐνδύσασθαι**).—**κακίαν**, probably *malice* rather than *wickedness*. Peter is occupied with their mutual relations and considering what hinders brotherly love, not their vices, if any, as vice is commonly reckoned. So James associates the removal of **κακία** with *courtesy*; and St. Paul says *let all bitterness and anger and wrath and shouting and ill-speaking be removed from you with all malice* (Eph. iv. 31; *cf.* Col. iii. 8). **κ.** is generally eagerness to hurt one's neighbour (Suidas)—the feeling which prompts *backbitings* and may be subdivided into *guile, hypocrisy, and envy*.—**δόλον**, *Guile* was characteristic of Jacob, the eponymous hero of the Jews, but not part of the true Israelite (**ἴδε ἀληθῶς Ἰσραηλίτης ἐν ᾧ δόλος οὐκ ἔστιν** John i. 47). It was also rife among the Greeks (**μεστοὺς . . . δόλου**, Rom. i. 29) as the Western world has judged from experience (Greek and grec = cardsharper; compare characters of Odysseus and Hermes). **δ.** is here contrasted with *obedience to the truth* (i. 22), vii. 22, iii. 10.—**ὑπόκρισιν** is best explained by the saying *Isaiah prophesied about you hypocrites. . . . This people honours me with their lips but their heart is far away from me* (Mark vii. 6 f. = Isa. xxix. 13). It stands for חנף *profane, impure* in Symmachus' version of Ps. xxxv. 16; so **ὑποκριτὴς** in LXX of Job (xxxiv. 30, xxxvi. 13), and Aquila (Prov. xi. 9), etc. In 2 Macc. vi. 25, **ὑ** is used of (unreal ?—not secret) *apostasy* perhaps in accordance with the earlier sense of ח', which only in post-Biblical Hebrew and Aramaic = *hypocrisy*. In His repeated denunciations of the hypocrites Jesus repeated the Pharisees description of the Sadducees *that live in hypocrisy with the saints* (Ps. Sol. iv. 7). Polybius has **ὑ.** in the classical sense of oratorical delivery, and once contrasted with the purpose of speakers (xxxv. 2, 13).—**καταλαλιάς**, *detractiones* (Vulgate), of external slanders in ii. 12, iii. 11. For internal calumnies, *cf.* Jas. iv. 11; 2 Cor. xii. 20 illustrates one special case, for **φυσιώσεις καταλαλιαὶ** correspond to **εἷς ὑπὲρ τοῦ ἑνὸς φυσιοῦσθε κατὰ τοῦ ἑτέρου** of 1 Cor. iv. 6 (*cf.* i. 12).

Ver. 2. **ὡς**, *inasmuch as you are newborn babes*; *cf.* **ἀναγεγεννημένοι** (i. 23). The development of the metaphor rests upon the saying, *unless ye be turned and become as the children* (**ὡς τὰ παιδία**) *ye shall not enter into the kingdom of heaven* (Matt. xviii. 3).—**βρέφη** (only here in metaphorical sense) is substituted for **παιδία** (preserved by St. Paul in 1 Cor. xiv. 20) as = *babes at the breast*. A **παιδίον** might have lost its traditional innocence but not a **βρέφος** (= either *child unborn* as Luke i. 41, or *suckling* in classical Greek). For the origin of the metaphor, which appears also in the saying of R. Jose, "the proselyte is a child just born," compare Isa. xxviii. 9, *Whom will he teach knowledge? . . . Them that are weaned from the milk and drawn from the breasts*, which the Targum renders, *To whom was the law given? . . . Was it not to the house of Israel which is beloved beyond all peoples?*—**τὸ . . . γάλα.** The quotation of ver. 3 suggests that the *milk* is Christ;

γά λα ἐπιποθήσατε ἵνα ἐν αὐτῷ αὐξηθῆτε[1] εἰς σωτηρίαν 3, 4
εἰ ἐγεύσα σθε ὅτι χρηστὸς ὁ Κς̄ πρὸς ὃν προσερχόμε νοι
λίθον ζῶντα ὑπ' ἀ̄ θρώπων μὲν ἀποδε δοκιμασμένον παρὰ δὲ
Θῶ ἐκλεκτὸν ἔντει μον· καὶ αὐτοὶ ὡς λίθοι ζῶντες οἰκοδο- 5
μεῖσθε οἶκος πνευματικὸς εἰς ἱεράτευμα ἅγιον ἀνενέγκαι

[1] The variant ἀξιωθῆτε for αὐξηθῆτε illustrates the possibilities of variation and consequently of emendation: at the same time it directs attention to the omnipotence of God and the relative impotence of man.

compare St. Paul's explanation of the tradition of the Rock which followed the Israelites in the desert (1 Cor. x. 4) and the *living water* of John iv. 14. Milk is the proper food for babes; compare Isa. lv. 1, *buy . . . milk* (LXX, στέαρ) *without money* (*cf.* i. 18). This milk is *guileless* (*cf.* δόλον of ver. 1) *pure* or *unadulterated* (*cf.* μηδὲ δολοῦντες τὸν λόγον τοῦ θεοῦ, 2 Cor. iv. 2). The interpretation of λογικόν (pertaining to λόγος) is doubtful. But the use of λόγος just above (i. 23) probably indicates the sense which St. Peter put upon the adjective he borrowed (?) from Rom. xii. 1, τὴν λογικὴν λατρείαν. There and elsewhere λ. = *rationabilis*, *spiritual*; here belonging to contained in the Word of God, delivered by prophet or by evangelist. St. Paul in his use of λ. and of the metaphor of *milk* (solid food, 1 Cor. iii. 1 ff.) follows Philo and the Stoics.—**ἵνα . . . σωτηρίαν**, *that fed thereon ye may grow up* (*cf.* Eph. iv. 14 f.) *unto salvation*; *cf.* Jas. i. 21, "receive the ingrafted word which is able to save your souls".

Ver. 3. St. Peter adopts the language of Ps. xxxiv. 9, omitting καὶ ἴδετε as inappropriate to γάλα. χρηστός (identical in sound with χριστός) = *dulcis* (Vulg.) or *kind* (*cf.* χρηστότης θεοῦ, Rom. ii. 4, xi. 22). Compare Heb. vi. 4 f. γευσαμένους τῆς δωρεᾶς τῆς ἐπουρανίου . . . καὶ καλὸν γευσαμένους θεοῦ ῥῆμα.

Vv. 4-10. Passages of scripture proving that Christ is called stone are first utilised, then quoted, and finally expounded. The transition from *milk* to the *stone* may be explained by the prophecy *the hills shall flow with milk* (Joel iii. 18), as the stone becomes a mountain according to Dan. iii. 21 f.; or by the legend to which St. Paul refers (1 Cor. x. 4); compare also ποτίσαι of Isa. xliii. 20, which is used in ver. 9. This collection of texts can be traced back through Rom. ix. 32 f. to its origin in the saying of Mark xii. 10 f.; Cyprian (Test. ii. 16 f.) gives a still richer form.

Ver. 4. **πρὸς ὃν προσερχ.** from Ps. xxxiv. 6, προσελθόντες πρὸς αὐτὸν (Heb. and Targum, *they looked unto Him*; Syriac, *look ye . . .*). Cyprian uses Isa. ii. 2 f.; Ps. xxiii. 3 f. to prove that the stone becomes a mountain to which the Gentiles *come* and the just ascend. —**λίθον ζῶντα**, a paradox which has no obvious precedent in O.T. Gen. xlix. 24 speaks of the Shepherd the stone of Israel, but Onkelos and LXX substitute אביך *thy father* for אבן *stone*. The Targum of Isa. viii. 14, however, has אבן מחי *a striking stone*, for אנגף which might be taken as meaning *reviving* or *living stone*, if connected with the foregoing instead of the following words. The LXX supports this connection and secures a *good* sense by inserting a negative; the Targum gives a *bad* sense throughout. **ὑπ' . . . ἔντιμον**, *though by men rejected, yet in God's sight elect precious*. ἀποδεδοκ. comes from Ps. cxviii. 22 (see ver. 7); ἐκλ. ἐντ. from Isa. xxviii. 6 (see ver. 6). ἀνθρώπων is probably due to Rabbinic exegesis "read not בונים *builders* but בני אדם *sons of men*". St. Peter insists upon the contrast between God's judgment and man's in the sermon of Acts ii.

Ver. 5. Fulfilment of the saying, Destroy this temple and in three days I will raise it (John ii. 19). Christians live to God through Jesus Christ (Rom. vi. 11). For this development of the figure of building, *cf.* especially Eph. ii. 20 ff.—**οἰκοδομεῖσθε**, indicative rather than imperative. "It is remarkable that St. Peter habitually uses the aorist for his imperatives, even when we might expect the present; the only exceptions (two or three) are preceded by words removing all ambiguity, ii. 11, 17, iv. 12 f." (Hort).—**οἶκος . . . ἅγιον**, *a spiritual house for an holy priesthood*. The connection with *priesthood* (Heb. x. 21) and the offering of sacrifices points to the special sense of the House of God, *i.e.*,

6 πνευματι κὰς θυσίας εὐπροσδέ κτους Θῶ διὰ Ιῦ Χῦ δι ὅτι
περιέχει ἐν γραφῇ ἰδοὺ τίθημι ἐν Σειὼν λίθον ἐκλεκτὸν
ἀκρο γωνιαῖον ἔντειμον καὶ ὁ πιστεύων ἐπ' αὐ τῷ οὐ μὴ
7 καταισχυν θῇ· ὑμῖν οὖν ἡ τειμὴ τοῖς πιστεύουσιν· ἀπι
στοῦσιν[1] δὲ λίθος ὃν ἀ πεδοκίμασαν οἱ οἰκο δομοῦντες οὗτος
ἐ γενήθη εἰς κεφαλὴν γωνίας καὶ λίθος προσ κόμματος καὶ

[1] For **ἀπιστοῦσιν** Codex Alexandrinus, with others, reads **ἀπειθοῦσιν.**

the Temple; (*cf.* (iv. 17; 1 Tim. iii. 5) **ναὸς ὅς ἐστε ὑμεῖς**, 1 Cor. iii. 16; Eph. ii. 21. So Heb. iii. 5 f., **οὗ (Χριστοῦ) οἶκός ἐσμεν ἡμεῖς . . .**—**Ἱεράτευμα**, *body of priests*, in Exod. xix. 6 (Heb. *priests*) xxiii. 22; 2 Macc. ii. 17; *cf.* 9 *infra.* Here Hort prefers the equally legitimate sense, *act of priesthood.* Usage supports the first and only possible etymology the second. The ideal of a national priesthood is realised, Isa. lxi. 6.—**ἀνενέγκαι . . . Χριστοῦ.** *to offer up spiritual sacrifices acceptable to God through Jesus Christ.*—**διὰ Ἰησοῦ Χ.** is better taken with **ἀν.** than **εὐπροσδ.**; *cf.* Heb. xiii. 15, **δι' αὐτοῦ**, where the thankoffering is singled out as the fit type of the Christian sacrifice. Spiritual sacrifices are in their nature acceptable to God (John iv. 23) and Christians are enabled to offer them through Jesus Christ. **ἀναφέρειν** in this sense is peculiar to LXX, Jas. and Heb.

Ver. 6. **περιέχει ἐν γραφῇ**, *it is contained in Scripture.* The formula occurs in Josephus (Ant. xi. 7, **βούλομαι γενέσθαι πάντα καθὼς ἐν [τῇ ἐπιστολῇ] περιέχει**) and is chosen for its comprehensiveness.—**περιέχει** is intransitive as the simple verb and other compounds often are; *cf.* **περιοχή**, *contents*, Acts viii. 32.—**γραφῇ**, being a technical term, has no article.—**ἰδοὺ . . . καταισχυνθῇ**, formal quotation of Isa. xxviii. 16, preceding quotation from Psalms, as prophets always precede the writings. The LXX has **ἰδοὺ ἐμβάλλω ἐγὼ εἰς τὰ θεμέλια** (unique expansion of normal **θεμελιῶ** = יסד of Heb., *cf.* **εἰς τὰ θ.** below; Targum, ממני *I will appoint*) **Σειὼν λίθον πολυτελῆ** (**π.** duplicate of **ἔντιμον**; Heb., *a stone a stone;* Targum, *a king a king;* pointing to Jewish Messianic interpretation) **ἐκλεκτὸν ἀκρ. ἔντ. εἰς τὰ θεμέλια αὐτῆς** (*a foundation a foundation*, Heb.) **καὶ ὁ πιστεύων** (+ **ἐπ' αὐτῷ** ℵAQ) **οὐ μὴ καταισχυνθῇ** (= יבוש for יחיש of Heb. = *shall not make haste*; Targum, *when tribulation come shall not be moved*). The chief difference is that St. Peter omits all reference to the *foundation*, and substitutes **τίθημι**; LXX is conflate, **ἐμβάλλω εἰς** being the original reading and **τὰ θεμ.** added by some purist to preserve the meaning of the Hebrew root. This omission may be due to the fact that Christians emphasised the idea that the stone was a corner stone binding the two wings of the Church together (Eph. ii. 20) and regarded this as inconsistent with **εἰς κεφ.**

Ver. 7 f. The second quotation is connected with the first by means of the parenthetic interpretation: *The "precious"-ness of the stone is for you who believe but for the unbelievers it is . . . "a stone of stumbling".* It is a stereotyped conflation of Ps. cxviii. 22 and Isa. viii. 14, which are so firmly cemented together that the whole is cited here where only the latter part is in point. The same idea of the two-fold aspect of Christ occurs in St. Paul more than once; *e.g.*, *Christ crucified to Jews a stumbling-block . . . but to you who believe . . .* 1 Cor. i. 23. The problem involved is discussed by Origen who adduces the different effects of the sun's light.—**ἡ τιμή**, the **τιμή** involved in the use of the adjective **ἔντιμον.**, or rather Heb. יקרה underlying it. The play on the peculiar sense thus required does not exclude the ordinary meaning *honour* (for which *cf.* i. 7; Rom. ii. 10).—**λίθος ὃν . . . γωνίας** = Ps. *l.c.* (LXX)—the prophetic statement in scriptural phrase of the fact of their unbelief. The idea may be that the raising of the stone to be head of the corner makes it a stumbling-block but in any case **λίθος . . . σκανδάλου** is needed to explain this.—**λίθος προσκόμματος κ. π. σκ.** from Isa. viii. 14; LXX paraphrases the original, which St. Peter's manual preserves, reading **καὶ οὐχ ὡς λίθῳ προσκόμματι συναντήσεσθε οὐδὲ ὡς πετρας πτώματι** (common confusion of construct. with Gen.).—**οἱ . . . ἀπειθοῦντες**, des-

πέτρα σκανδάλου οἱ προσκό πτουσιν τῷ λόγῳ ἀπι στοῦντες 8
εἰς ὃ καὶ ἐτέ θησαν· [1] ὑμεῖς δὲ γένος ἐκλεκτὸν βασίλειον 9
ἱεράτευμα ἔθνος ἅγιο͞ λαὸς εἰς περιποίησιν· ὅπως τὰς ἀρετὰς
ἐξαγ γείλητε τοῦ ἐκ σκότους ὑμᾶς καλέσαντος εἰς τὸ

[1] In view of "the argument which is intended to carry one back to the opening of the prophetic passage," Dr. Rendel Harris (*Side-Lights on New Testament Research*, pp. 209 f.) proposes to substitute **ἐτέθη** for **ἐτέθησαν**.

cription of the unbelieving in terms of the last quotation, *who stumble at the word being disobedient.* **τῷ λόγῳ** is probably to be taken with **πρ.** or both **πρ.** and **ἀ.** in spite of the stone being identified with the Lord. Stumbling at the word is an expression used by Jesus (Mark iv. 17, **διὰ τὸν λόγον σκανδαλίζονται**; Matt. xv. 12, **ἀκούσαντες τὸν λόγον ἐσκανδαλίσθησαν**; John vi. 60, **τοῦτο—ὁ λόγος οὗτος—ὑμᾶς σκανδαλίζει**). For **ἀ.** *cf.* iv. 17, **τῶν ἀπειθούντων τῷ τοῦ θεοῦ εὐαγγελίῳ.—εἰς ὃ καὶ ἐτέθησαν**, *whereunto also* (*actually*) *they were appointed.* **ἐτέθησαν** comes from **τίθημι** (6); stone and stumbler alike were appointed by God to fulfil their functions in His Purpose. For the sake of the unlearned he only implies and does not assert in so many words that God appointed them to stumble and disobey; but his view is that of St. Paul (see Rom. ix., xi., especially ix. 17, 22); *cf.* Luke ii. 34. Didymus distinguishes between their voluntary unbelief and their appointed fall. If any are tempted to adopt such ingenious evasions of the plain sense it is well to recall the words of Origen: "If in the reading of scripture you stumble at what is really a noble thought, *the stone of stumbling and rock of offence*, blame yourself. You must not despair of this stone . . . containing hidden thoughts so that the saying may come to pass, *And the believer shall not be shamed.* Believe first of all and you will find beneath this reputed stumbling-block much holy profit (in Jer. xliv. (li.) 22, Hom. xxxix. = Philocalia x.).

Vv. 9 f. The Church, God's new people, has all the privileges which belonged to the Jews. In enumerating them he draws upon a current conflation of Isa. xliii. 20 f., **ποτίσαι τὸ γένος μου το ἐκλεκτὸν** (1) **λαόν μου ὃν περιεποιησάμην** (4) **τὰς ἀρετάς μου διηγεῖσθαι** with Exod. xix. 65, **ὑμεῖς δὲ ἔσεσθέ μοι βασίλειον ἱεράτευμα** (2) **καὶ ἔθνος ἅγιον** (3) **ἔσεσθέ μοι λαὸς περιούσιος** (4) **ἀπὸ πάντων τῶν ἐθνῶν** (1); and Ps. cvii. 14, **καὶ ἐξήγαγεν αὐτοὺς καὶ ἐκ σκιᾶς θανάτου . . . ἐξομολογησάσθων τῷ κυρίῳ τὰ ἐλέη αὐτοῦ καὶ τὰ θαυμάσια αὐτοῦ τοῖς υἱοῖς τῶν ἀνθρώπων**—to which is appended Hos. i. 6, 8.—**γένος ἐκλεκτόν**, Isa. *l.c.* LXX (Heb., *my people my chosen*); **γένος**, *race* implies that all the individual members of it have a common Father (God) and are therefore brethren (*cf.* **υἱοὶ γένους Ἀβραάμ**, Acts xiii. 26); *cf.* i. 1, 6.—**βασίλειον ἱεράτευμα**, *a royal priesthood*, from Exod. *l.c.* LXX (Heb., *a kingdom of priests* = Apoc. i. 6, **βασιλείαν ἱερεῖς**). Christians share Christ's prerogatives. The *priesthood* is the chief point (see ii. 5) it is *royal*. Clement of Alexandria says: "Since we have been summoned to the kingdom and are anointed (*sc.* as Kings)". The comparison of Melchizedek with Christ perhaps underlies the appropriation of the title.—**ἔθνος ἅγιον**, to the Jew familiar, with the use of **ἔθνη** for Gentiles, as much a paradox as *Christ crucified.* But **λαός**, the common rendering of עם in this connexion is wanted below, and St. Peter is content to follow his authority.—**λαὸς εἰς περιποίησιν**, *a people for possession* = עם סגלה. The source of the Greek phrase is Mal. iii. 17, but the Hebrew title variously rendered occurs in the two great passages drawn upon. Deut. (vii. 6, etc.) has **λαὸς περιούσιος** which is adopted by St. Paul (Tit. ii. 14); but the phrase **εἰς π.** is well established in the Christian vocabulary, Heb. x. 39; 1 Thess. v. 9; 2 Thess. ii. 14, and the whole title is apparently abbreviated to **περιποίησις** in Eph. i. 14.—**ὅπως . . . ἐξαγγείλητε**, from Isa. *l.c.* + Ps. *l.c.*, the latter containing the matter of the following designation of God. In Isa. **τὰς ἀρετάς μου** stands for תהלתי *my praise;* and this sense reappears in Esther xiv. 10. **ἀνοῖξαι στόμα ἐθνῶν εἰς ἀρετὰς ματαίων**, *the praises of idols.* Elsewhere it stands for הוד, *glory* (Hab. iii. 3; Zach. vi. 13). In the books of Maccabees (especially the fourth) it has its ordinary sense of *virtue*, which cannot

10 θαυμαστὸν αὐτοῦ φῶς· οἵ ποτε οὐ λαὸς νῦν δὲ λαὸς Θῦ οἱ
11 οὐκ ἠ λεημένοι νῦν δὲ ἐλε ηθέντες. ἀγαπητοὶ παρακαλῶ
ὡς παροίκους καὶ παρεπιδήμους ἀπέ χεσθαι[1] τῶν σαρκικῶ̄
12 ἐπιθυμιῶν αἵτινες στρατεύονται κατὰ τῆς ψυχῆς τὴν ἀνα
στροφὴν[2] ὑμῶν ἐν τοῖς ἔθνεσιν καλὴν ἵνα ἐν ῷ καταλαλοῦσιν

[1] For ἀπέχεσθαι Codex Alexandrinus and others read ἀπέχεσθε: ε and αι are interchangeable in the manuscripts.

[2] Codex Vaticanus omits ἔχοντες, which is formally required to govern ἀναστροφὴν. If ἀπέχεσθαι represents the infinitive, ἔχοντας would be more grammatical.

be excluded altogether here. The whole clause is in fact the pivot on which the Epistle turns. Hitherto Peter has addressed himself to the Christians and their mutual relations, now he turns to consider their relations to the outside world (i. 11 f.). In 2 Peter i. 3, ἀ. corresponds to θεία δύναμις, a sense which might be supported by Ps. *l.c.* (for discussion of other — very uncertain — evidence see Deissmann, *Bible Studies*, pp. 95 ff., 362) and the events of Pentecost (see especially Acts ii. 11).—τοῦ . . . φῶς is derived from Ps. *l.c.*; the natural antithesis *light* is readily supplied (*cf.* Eph. v. 8, 14); *darkness* = heathenism in *cf.* 10.

Ver. 10, from Hosea i. 6, ii. 1(3); *cf.* Rom. ix. 25 (has καλέσω κάλεσον of Hos.); the terms are so familiar that μου is omitted by Peter as unnecessary (*cf.* γένος ἐκ. for τὸ γ. μου ἐ.).

Vv. 11 f. indicate generally the subject to be discussed. Beloved I exhort you to abstain from the lusts of the flesh, because they wage war against the soul. Slanders and even torments can only affect the body. But the lusts natural or acquired which you have renounced may hinder your salvation, as they have already impeded your mutual love. For the sake of your old friends and kinsfolk refuse to yield to their solicitations. If rebuffed they resort to persecution of whatever kind, remember that it is only a passing episode of your brief exile. Let your conduct give them no excuse for reproach; so may they recognise God's power manifest not on your lips but in your lives.—ἀγαπητοί, not an empty formulæ but explanation of the writer's motive. He set before them the great commandment and now adds to it as Jesus did, Love one another as I have loved you, John xiii. 34.—ὡς π. καὶ παρεπιδήμους with ἀπεχ. (motive for abstinence in emphatic position) rather than παρακαλῶ (as νουθετεῖτε ὡς ἀδελφόν, 2 Thess. iii. 15—the motive of exhortation is here expressed by ἀγ.) echoes παρεπιδήμοις of i. 1 and παροικίας of i. 17. The combination (= גר ותושב) occurs twice in LXX (Gen. xxxiii. 4; Ps. xxxix. 13). Christians are in the world, not of the world.—ἀπέχεσθαι, *cf.* Plato, *Phaedo*, 82 C, true philosophers, ἀπέχονται τῶν κατὰ τὸ σῶμα ἐπιθυμιῶν ἁπάσων—not for fear of poverty, like the vulgar, nor for fear of disgrace, like the ambitious, but because only so can he, departing in perfect purity, come to the company of the gods".—τῶν σαρκικῶν ἐπιθυμιῶν, *the lusts of the flesh.* St. Peter borrows St. Paul's phrase, ἡμεῖς πάντες ἀνεστράφημέν ποτε ἐν ταῖς ἐπιθυμίαις τῆς σαρκὸς ἡμῶν ποιοῦντες τὰ θελήματα τῆς σαρκὸς καὶ τῶν διανοιῶν (Eph. ii. 3), but uses it in his own way in a sense as wide as τὰς κοσμικὰς ἐ. (Tit. ii. 12). For the flesh is the earthly life (*cf.* Col. iii. 5) the transitory mode of existence of the soul which is by such abstinence to be preserved (i. 9).—αἵτινες . . . ψυχῆς, *because they are campaigning against the soul.*—στρατεύονται (*cf.* iv. 1 f., for military metaphor) perhaps derived from Rom. vii. 23, "I perceive a different law in my members warring against (ἀντιστρατευόμενον) the law of my mind;" *cf.* Jas. iv. 1, the pleasures which war in your members, and 4 Macc. ix. 23, ἱερὰν καὶ εὐγενῆ στρατείαν στρατεύσασθε περὶ τῆς εὐσεβείας.—κατὰ τῆς ψυχῆς. The lusts of this earthly life are the real enemy for they affect the soul. Compare Matt. x. 28, which may refer to the Devil and not to God, and the Pauline parallel, ἡ σὰρξ ἐπιθυμεῖ κατὰ τοῦ πνεύματος . . . ταῦτα γὰρ ἀλλήλοις ἀντικεῖται (Gal. v. 17).

Ver. 12. Adaptation of the saying, ὅπως ἴδωσιν ὑμῶν τὰ καλὰ ἔργα καὶ δοξάσωσιν τὸν πατέρα ὑμῶν τὸν ἐν τοῖς οὐρανοῖς (Matt. v. 16). The good behaviour on which the resolved ἀναστρέφεσθαι permits stress to be laid is the

ὑ μῶν ὡς κακοποιῶν ἐκ τῶν καλῶν ἔργων ἐποπτεύοντες
δοξά σωσι τὸν Θν̅ ἐν ἡμέρα ἐπισκοπῆς. ὑποτά γητε 13
πάσῃ ἀνθρωπί νῃ κτίσει διὰ τὸν Κν̅ εἴτε βασιλεῖ ὡς
ὑπε ρέχοντι εἴτε ἡγεμό σιν ὡς δι᾽ αὐτοῦ πεμ πομένοις εἰς 14
ἐκδίκη σιν κακοποιῶν ἔπαι νον δὲ ἀγαθοποιῶν· ὅτι οὕτως 15
ἐστὶν τὸ θέλημα τοῦ Θῦ ἀγαθο ποιοῦντας φειμοῦ τὴν

fruit of the abstinence of ver. 11; *cf.* Heb. xiii. 8; Jas. iii. 13. This second admonition is disjointed formally—against formal grammar—from the first; *cf.* Eph. iv. 1 f., **παρακαλῶ . . . ὑμᾶς . . . ἀνεχόμενοι.**—**ἐν τοῖς ἔθνεσιν**, *the people of God* (ii. 9) is a correlative term and implies the existence of *the nations*, who are ignorant and disobedient. The situation of the Churches addressed justifies the use of Dispersion in i. 1. But the point of the words here is this: you—the new Israel must succeed where the old failed, as it is written my name is blasphemed **ἐν τοῖς ἔθνεσιν** on your account (Isa. lii. 5; LXX, cited Rom. ii. 24).—**ἵνα . . . ἐπισκοπῆς**, *in order that as a result of your good works they may be initiated into your secrets and come to glorify God in respect to your conduct when He at last visits the world, though now they calumniate you as evildoers in this matter.*—**ἐν ᾧ** in the case of the thing in which, *i.e.*, your behaviour generally; *cf.* iii. 16, iv. 4, and for **δοξ. τὸν θεὸν ἐν**, iv. 11, 16. —**καταλαλοῦσιν ὡς κ.** Particular accusations are given in iv. 15. This popular estimate of Christians is reflected in Suetonius' statement: Adflicti suppliciis Christiani, genus hominium superstitionis novae et *maleficae* (Ner. 16).—**ἐποπτεύοντες** takes Acc. in iii. 2 (*overlook, behold*, as in Symmachus' version of Ps. x. 14, xxxiii. 13); but here the available objects are either appropriated (**θεόν** with **δοξ.**) or far off (**ἀναστροφήν**). It will therefore have its ordinary sense of *become* **ἐπόπτης**, *be initiated.* The Christians were from the point of view of their former friends members of a secret association, initiates of a new mystery, the secrecy of which gave rise to slanders such as later Christians brought against the older mysteries and the Jews. St. Peter hopes that, if the behaviour of Christians corresponds to their profession, their neighbours will become initiated into their open secrets (for as St. Paul insists this hidden mystery has now been revealed and published).—**δοξάσωσιν τὸν θεόν**, *come to glorify God*—like the centurion, who said of the crucified Jesus, *Truly this was the Son of God* (Mark xv. 39)—*i.e.*, recognise the finger of God either in the behaviour of the Christians or in the whole economy (see Rom. xi.).—**ἐν ἡμέρᾳ ἐπισκοπῆς**, from Isa. x. 3, *What will ye do*—ye the oppressors of the poor of my people—*in day of visitation* (יום פקדה) *i.e.* (Targum), *when your sins are visited upon you.* But St. Peter looks for the repentance of the heathen at the last visitation (*cf.* iv. 6), though the prophet found no escape for his own contemporaries. Compare Luke xix. 44.

Vv. 13-17. The duty of the Christian towards the State; compare Rom. xiii. 1-7.—**πάσῃ ἀνθρωπίνῃ κτίσει**, *every human institution*, including rulers (14), masters (18), and husbands (iii. 1). **κτίζειν** is used ordinarily in many senses, *e.g.*, of peopling a country, of founding a city, of setting up games, feasts, altar, etc. In Biblical Greek and its descendants it is appropriated to *creation.* Here **κτίσις** is apparently selected as the most comprehensive word available; and the acquired connotation—creation by God—is ruled out by the adjective **ἀνθρωπίνῃ.** It thus refers to all human institutions which man set up with the object of maintaining the world which God created. —**διὰ τὸν κύριον**, *for the sake of the Lord.* **διά** may be (1) retrospective—*i.e.*, because Jesus said, Render what is Cæsar's to Cæsar *or*, generally, because God is the source of all duly-constituted authority; *or* (ii.) prospective *for the sake of Jesus* (*Jehovah*); your loyalty redounding to the credit of your Master in heaven.—**βασιλεῖ**, the Roman Emperor, as in Apoc. xvii. 9, etc.; Josephus B.J., v. 136, *v. infra.*—**ὑπερέχοντι**, *pre-eminent*, *supreme*, *absolute*, as in Sap. vi. 5, where **τοῖς ὑπερέχουσιν** corresponds to *those who are underlings of His Sovereignty* (4), to whom *power was given from the Lord* (3); *cf.* **δι᾽ αὐτοῦ** below.—**ἡγεμόσιν**, properly *Governors of provinces*, but Plutarch uses the singular = *Imperator.* Peter rather follows the conventional rendering of the saying of Jesus, **ἐπὶ ἡγεμόνων καὶ βασιλέων σταθήσεσθε,** interpreted in the light of popular usage

16 τῶν ἀφρόνων ἀνθρώπων ἀγνωσίαˉ· ὡς ἐλεύθεροι καὶ μὴ
ὡς ἐπικάλυμμα ἔχοˉ τες τῆς κακίας τὴν ἐλευθερίαν ἀλλ' ὡς
17 Θῦ δοῦλοι πάντας τιμή σατε· τὴν ἀδελφότη τα ἀγαπᾶτε
18 τὸν Θν̄ φο βεῖσθε, τὸν βασιλέα τει μᾶτε. οἱ οἰκέται ὑπο
τασσόμενοι ἐν παντὶ φόβῳ τοῖς δεσπόταις, οὐ μόνον τοῖς
19 ἀγαθοῖς καὶ ἐπιεικέσι ἀλλὰ καὶ τοῖς σκολιοῖς. τοῦτο

(*cf.* Luke xxi. 12) or of Jer. xxxix. 3, **ἡγεμόνες βασιλέως Βαβυλῶνος.** Contrast vague general term, **ἐξουσίαις ὑπερεχ· ὡς . . .** which St. Paul employed before his visit to Rome.—**πεμπ.**, *as being sent through the Emperor.* **διά** implies that the governors are sent by God acting through the Emperor; so Rom. xiii. 1-7 (*cf.* Sap. vi. 3) and John xix. 11, **εἰ μὴ ἦν δεδομένον σοι ἄνωθεν.**—**εἰς ἐκδίκησιν, κ.τ.λ.** The ruler executes God's vengeance (Rom. xii. 19) and voices God's approval (Ps. xxii. 25, **παρὰ σοῦ ὁ ἔπαινός μου**). The former function of governors has naturally become prominent, the latter is exemplified in the crowns, decrees and panegyrics with which the Greek and Jewish States rewarded their benefactors if not mere well-doers.—**οὕτως . . .** *since this is so* (referring to 13 f.) *God's will is that . . .* (*cf.* Matt. xviii. 14, **οὕτως οὐκ ἔστιν θέλημα** where **οὕτως** refers to the preceding parable) rather than *God's will is thus namely that . . .* or . . . *well-doing thus.* Since God has set up governors who express His approval of well-doers, you as well-doers will receive official praise and thus be enabled to silence the slanderers. St. Peter is thinking of the verdict pronounced in the case of St. Paul and of Jesus himself.—**φιμοῦν**, (1) *muzzle* (1 Cor. ix. 9), (2) *silence* as Jesus did (Matt. xxii. 34, **ἐφίμωσεν τοὺς Σαδδουκαίους**).—**τὴν ἀγνωσίαν**, a rare word—perhaps borrowed from Job xxxv. 16, **ἐν ἀγνωσίᾳ ῥήματα βαρύνει**, *He multiplieth words without knowledge.* In 1 Cor. xv. 34, **ἀγνωσίαν γαρ θεοῦ τινες ἔχουσιν**, it is derived from Sap. xiii. 1, **οἷς παρῆν θεοῦ ἀγνωσία.** It is the opposite of **γνῶσις** (**ἀγνωσίας τε καὶ γνώσεως**, Plato, Soph., 267 B) *cf.* **ἄγνοια**, of Jews who crucified Jesus, Acts iii. 17.—**τῶν ἀφρόνων** = the foolish men who calumniate you (12). **ἀ.** is very common in the Wisdom literature (especially Proverbs); as used by Our Lord (Luke xi. 40) and St. Paul (2 Cor. xi.); it implies lack of insight, a point of view determined by external appearances.

Ver. 16. **ὡς ἐλεύθεροι**, the contrast with **τῆς κακίας** supports the connection of **ἐ.** in thought with **ἀγαθοποιοῦντας**, which explains the nature of the self-subjection required. Christians are *free* (Matt. xvii. 26 f. *q.v.*; John viii. 36; Gal. ii. 4) and therefore must submit to authority. Peter generalises summarily St. Paul's argument in Gal. v. 13, which refers to *internal* relations.—**καὶ μὴ . . . ἐλευθερίαν**, *and not having your freedom as a cloak of your malice.* For **ἐπ.** *cf.* Menander (apud Stobaeum Florileg.) **πλοῦτος δὲ πολλῶν ἐπικάλυμμ' ἐστιν κακῶν.** The verb is used in Ps. cited Rom. iv. 7 = כפר; and this sense may perhaps be contemplated here; early Christians regarded their freedom as constituting a propitiation for future as for past sins.

Ver. 17. Sweeping clause based partly on Rom. xiii. 7 f. (*cf.* Matt. xxii. 21), partly on Prov. xxiv. 21, **φοβοῦ τὸν θεὸν υἱὲ καὶ βασιλέα καὶ μηθετέρῳ αὐτῶν ἀπειθήσῃς.**—**πάντας τιμήσατε.** The aorist imperative is used because the present would be ambiguous; *cf.* **ἀπόδοτε**, Rom. *l.c.*, and for matter, Rom. xii. 10, **τῇ τιμῇ ἀλλήλους προηγούμενοι**, since **πάντας** covers both *the brotherhood* and *the emperor.*—**οἱ οἰκέται**, vocative; the word is chosen as being milder than **δοῦλος** and also as suggesting the parallel between slaves and Christians who are God's household (ii. 5).—**ὑποτασσόμενοι** has force of imperative resuming **ὑποτάγητε** or goes with **τιμήσατε** (17) as being a particular application of that general principle.—**τοῖς δεσπόταις**, *to your masters*, not excluding God, the Master of all, as is indicated by the insertion of *in all fear* (*cf.* 17, etc.) and **τοῖς ἀγαθοῖς καὶ ἐπιεικέσιν** (*cf.* Ps. lxxxvi. 4, **σὺ κύριος χρηστὸς καὶ ἐπιεικής**).—**τοῖς σκολιοῖς**, *the perverse*, *cf.* Phil. ii. 15, **ἵνα γένησθε . . . τέκνα θεοῦ ἄμωμα μέσον γενεᾶς σκολιᾶς καὶ διεστραμμένης**, where the full phrase is cited from Deut. xxxii. 5 (**σκ.** = עקש). The Vulgate has *dyscolis* = **δυσκόλοις**; Hesychius, **σκολιός· ἄδικος**; Prov. xxviii. 18, **ὁ σκολιαῖς ὁδοῖς πορευόμενος χ. ὁ πορευόμενος δικαίως.**

Vv. 19 f. Summary application of the teaching of Jesus recorded in Luke vi. 27-

γὰρ χάρις εἰ διὰ συνίδη σιν Θ̅ῦ ὑποφέρει τις λύπας πάσχων
ἀδίκως. ποῖον γὰρ κλέος εἰ ἁ μαρτάνοντες καὶ κο λαφιζό- 20
μενοι[1] ὑπομε νεῖτε; ἀλλ' εἰ ἀγαθοποι οῦντες καὶ πάσχον τες
ὑπομενεῖτε, τοῦ το χάρις παρὰ Θ̅ῷ. εἰς τοῦτο γὰρ ἐκλήθητε 21
ὅτι καὶ Χ̅ς̅ ἔπαθεν ὑ πὲρ ὑμῶν ὑμῖν ὑπο λιμπάνων ὑπογραμ
μὸν ἵνα ἐπακολουθή σηται τοῖς ἴχνεσιν αὐτοῦ· ὃς 22
ἁμαρτίαν οὐκ ἐποίησεν οὐδὲ εὑρέθη δόλος ἐν τῷ στόματι
αὐτοῦ ὃς λοι δορούμενος οὐκ ἀν τελοιδόρει πάσχων οὐκ 23

[1] The third corrector of Codex Sinaiticus puts **κολαζόμενοι** for **κολαφιζόμενοι** with the assent of some cursives. Such variations may be due to careless copying or they may result from erroneous expansion and interpretation of abbreviations.

36 = Matt. v. 39-48.—**χάρις** seems to be an abbreviation of the O.T. idiom *to find favour* (חן) *with God*—*cf.* **χάρις παρὰ θεῷ** (20)—taken from St. Luke's version of the saying, **εἰ ἀγαπᾶτε τοὺς ἀγαπῶντας ὑμᾶς, ποία ὑμῖν χάρις ἔστιν** (vi. 32).—Compare **χάριτας** = רצון *that which is acceptable* in Prov. x. 32.—**διὰ συνείδησιν θεοῦ**, (i.) *because God is conscious of your condition* (**θεοῦ** subjective genitive), a reproduction of *thy Father which seeth that which is hidden* . . . (Matt. vi. 4, etc.); so **συνείδ.** in definite philosophical sense of *conscience* is usually followed by possessive genitive OR (ii.) *because you are conscious of God* (**θ.** objective genitive), *cf.* **σ. ἁμαρτίας**, Heb. x. 2. The latter construction is preferable: the phrase interprets **διὰ τὸν κύριον** with the help of the Pauline expression **διὰ τὴν σ.** (Rom. xiii. 5; 1 Cor. x. 25) employed in the same context.—**πάσχων ἀδίκως**, emphatic. Peter has to take account of the possibility which Jesus ignored, that Christians might deserve persecution; *cf.* 20, 25.—**ποῖον κλέος**, *what praise* rather than *what kind of reputation* (**κλ.** neutral as in Thuc. ii. 45) *cf.* **ποία χάρις τίνα μισθόν**, Matt. **κλ.** (only twice in Job in LXX) corresponds to **ἔπαινος** above: **χάρις παρὰ θεῷ** shows that the praise of the Master who reads the heart is intended.—**κολαφιζόμενοι**, from description of the Passion, Mark xiv. 65, **ἤρξαντό τινες . . . κολαφίζειν αὐτόν**: *cf.* Matt. v. 39, **ὅστις σε ῥαπίζει**. So also St. Paul recalls the parallel between Christ's and the Christians' sufferings (1 Cor. iv. 11) **κολαφιζόμεθα**.—**ἀγαθοποιοῦντες**, opposed to **ἁμαρτάνοντες**, explains **ἀδίκως** (19).—**χάρις**, see on **χ.** ver. 19.

Ver. 21. **εἰς τοῦτο**, *sc.* to do well and to suffer, if need be, without flinching, as Christ did.—**ἐκλήθητε**, *sc.* by God; *cf.* **διὰ τὴν συνείδησιν θεοῦ**.—**ἔπαθεν ὑπὲρ ἡμῶν**, ver. 22 supplies the essential point, which would be readily supplied, but Christ's suffering was undeserved (**δίκαιος ὑπὲρ ἀδίκων**, iii. 18).—**καί** *also* with reference to the similar experience of Christians; so Phil. ii. 5, **τοῦτο φρονεῖτε ἐν ὑμῖν ὃ καὶ ἐν Χριστῷ**.—**ὑπογραμμόν** (1) *outline*, 2 Macc. ii. 28, *to enlarge upon the outlines of our abridgment*; (2) *copy-head, pattern*, to be traced over by writing-pupils (Plato, *Protag.*, 227 D; Clement of Alexandria, *Strom.*, v. 8, 49, gives three examples of which **βεδιζαμψχθωπληκτρον σφιγξ** is one).—**ἐπακολουθήσητε**, reminiscence of Jesus' word to Peter, **ἀκολουθήσεις ὕστερον**, John xiii. 36.

Ver. 22 = Isa. liii. 9, **ἁμ.** being put for **ἀνομίαν** (חמס) and **εὑρ. δόλος** (so $\aleph^{ca}$ AQ, etc.) for **δόλον** (= Heb.) of LXX. The latter variation is due to conjunction of Zeph. iii. 13, **οὐ μὴ εὑρεθῇ ἐν τῷ στόματι αὐτῶν γλῶσσα δολία**: Christ being identified with the Remnant. The former appears in the Targum: "that they might not remain who work sin and might not speak guile with their mouth".

Ver. 23. Combination of the Scripture **οὐκ ἀνοίγει τὸ στόμα** (Isa. liii. 7) with the saying **ὅταν ὀνειδίσωσιν και διώξωσιν** (Matt. v. 11). For **λοιδ.** *cf.* 1 Cor. iv. 12. **λοιδορούμενοι εὐλογοῦμεν** (**εἴπωσιν πᾶν πονηρόν** of Matt. *l.c.*), John ix. 28, the Jews **ἐλοιδόρησαν** the once blind man as Jesus' disciple and, for O.T. type Deut. xxxiii. 8, **ἐλοιδόρησαν αὐτὸν ἐπὶ ὕδατος ἀντιλογίας** (Levi = Christ the Priest, *cf.* **ἀντιλογία**, Heb. xii. 3).—**οὐκ ἠπείλει**, the prophecy **ἀπειλήσει τοῖς ἀπειθοῦσιν** (Isa. lxvi. 14) is yet to be fulfilled (Luke xiii. 27). Oec. notes that He threatened Judas, seeking to deter him and reviled the Pharisees, but not in re-

24 ἠπείλει παρεδί δου δὲ τῷ κρείνοντι δικαίως · ὃς τὰς ἁμαρτίας
ὑμῶν αὐτὸς ἀνή νεγκεν ἐν τῷ σώμα τι αὐτοῦ ἐπὶ τὸ ξύλο̅
ἵνα ταῖς ἁμαρτίαις ἀ πογενόμενοι τῇ δικοσύνῃ ζήσωμεν · οὗ
25 τῷ μώλωπι [1] ἰάθηται. ὡς πρόβατα πλανώμε νοι ἀλλὰ ἐπε-
στράφη τε νῦν ἐπὶ τὸν ποιμέ να καὶ ἐπίσκοπον τῶ ψυχῶν
III. 1 ὑμῶν. ὁμοί ως γυναῖκες ὑποτασ σόμεναι τοῖς ἰδίοις

[1] The superfluous **αὐτοῦ** after **οὗ τῷ μώλωπι** is omitted by Codex Vaticanus and other authorities. It would be repugnant to the ear of a Greek, but is not therefore to be regarded as necessarily absent from the original.

tort.—**παρεδίδου.** It is doubtful what object, if any, is to be supplied. The narrative of the Passion suggests two renderings: (i.) *He delivered Himself* (**ἑαυτὸν** omitted as in Plato, *Phaedrus*, 250 E). *Cf.* Luke xxiii. 46 (Ps. xxxi. 5), **παρατίθεμαι τὸ πνεῦμά μου** and Isa. liii. 6; **κύριος παρέδωκεν αὐτόν**, *ib.* 12 **παρεδόθη.** (ii.) *He delivered the persecutors* (latent in passive participles **λοιδ.** and **πάσχων**), when He said *Father forgive them.* In ordinary Greek **παραδίδωμι** without object = *permit*; but this hardly justifies the rendering *He gave way to* (*cf.* **δότε τόπον τῇ ὀργῇ**, Rom. xii. 19), *i.e.*, permitted God to fulfil His will. But most probably **παρ. τῷ . . .** represents the Hebrew ellipse, גל אל י״ *commit to Jehovah* (Ps. xxii. 9) for the normal *commit, way, works, cause*; LXX (Syriac) has **ἤλπισεν** = Matt. xxvii. 43. Compare Joseph. Ant. vii. 9, 2, David **περὶ πάντων ἐπιτρέψας κριτῇ τῷ θεῷ.—τῷ κρίνοντι δικαίως**, *cf.* i. 17; the award was the glory.

Ver. 24. Christ was not only *well-doer* but *benefactor.*—**τὰς ἁμ. . . . ἀνήνεγκεν** comes from Isa. liii. 12, LXX, **καὶ αὐτὸς ἁμαρτίας πολλῶν ἀνήνεγκεν** (נשׂא usually translated **λαμβάνειν**), used also Heb. ix. 28. Christ is the perfect sin-offering: "Himself the victim and Himself the priest. The form of expression *offered up* our sins is due to the double use of חטאה for sin and sin-offering.—**ἐν τῷ σώματι αὐτοῦ**, a Pauline phrase derived from the saying, *This is my body which is for you* (1 Cor. xi. 24), explaining **αὐτός** of Isa. *l.c.*—**ἐπὶ τὸ ξύλον**, replaces the normal complement of **ἀναφέρειν**, **ἐπὶ τὸ θυσιαστήριον**, in view of the moral which is to be drawn from the sacrificial language adopted. So Jas. ii. 21, **ἐπὶ τὸ θυσιαστήριον** is substituted for **ἐπάνω τῶν ξύλων** of the original description of the offering of Isaac, Gen. xxii. 9. Christ died because He took our sins upon Himself (*cf.* Num. iv. 33, **οἱ υἱοὶ ὑμῶν . . . ἀνοίσουσιν τὴν πορνείαν ὑμῶν**). Therefore our sins perished and we have died to them, Col. ii. 14.—**ἵνα . . . ζήσωμεν.** Compare Targum of Isa. liii. 10, "and from before Jehovah it was the will to refine and purify the remnant of His people that He might cleanse from sins their souls: they shall see the kingdom of His Christ and . . . prolong their days".—**ἀπογενόμενοι** = (i.) *die* (Herodotus, Thucydides) as opposite of **γενόμενοι**, *come into being* OR (ii.) *be free from*, as in Thuc. i. 39, **τῶν ἁμαρτημάτων ἀπογενόμενοι.** The Dative requires (i.), *cf.* Rom. vi. 2, **οἵτινες ἀπεθάνομεν τῇ ἁμαρτίᾳ.** The idea is naturally deduced from Isa. liii., Christ bore our sins and delivered His soul to death, therefore He shall see His seed living because sinless.—**οὗ . . . ἰάθητε** from Isa. liii. 5; **μώλωπι**, properly the *weal* or *scar* produced by scourgeing (Sir. xxviii. 17, **πληγὴ μάστιγος ποιεῖ μώλωπας**) thus the prophecy was fulfilled according to Matt. xxvii. 26, **φραγελλώσας.** The original has **ἰάθημεν.** The paradox is especially pointed in an address to slaves who were frequently scourged.

Ver. 25 = Isa. liii. 6, **πάντες ὡς πρόβατα ἐπλανήθημεν** combined with Ez. xxxiv. 6, where this conception of the people and their teachers (*the shepherds of Israel*) is elaborated and the latter denounced because **τὸ πλανώμενον οὐκ ἐπεστρέψατε.** Further the use of this metaphor in the context presupposes the saying *I am the good shepherd. . . . I lay down my life for the sheep* (John xii. 15).—**ἐπίσκοπον**, *cf.* Ez. xxxiv. 11, **ἰδοὺ ἐγὼ ἐκζητήσω τὰ πρόβατά μου καὶ ἐπισκέψομαι αὐτά.** It is to be noted that the command which Jesus laid on Peter, *feeding sheep*, comes from Ez. *l.c.*

CHAPTER III.—Vv. 1-6. Duty of wives (Eph. v. 21-24; Col. iii. 18; Tit. ii. 4)—Submissiveness and true adorn-

ἀνδράσιν· ἵνα εἴ τινες[1] ἀπειθοῦσιν τῶ λόγω διὰ τῆς τῶν γυναικῶ̄
ἀναστροφῆς ἄνευ λό γου κερδηθήσονται ἐποπτεύσαντες 2
τὴ̄ ἐν φόβω ἁγνὴν ἀνα στροφὴν ὑμῶν. ὧν ἔστω οὐχ ὁ 3
ἔξωθεν ἐμπλοκῆς τριχῶν κ̔ περιθέσεως χρυσίω̄ ἢ ἐνδύσεως
ἱματίω̄ κόσμος· ἀλλ' ὁ κρυπτὸς τῆς καρδίας ἄνθρωπος 4

[1] The variant **οἵτινες** for **εἴ τινες** serves as a reminder that in uncial manuscripts **Є** is apt to be confused with **O** and that words were not written separately from one another.

ment.—**τοῖς ἰδίοις ἀνδράσιν,** *your own husbands*, the motive for submissiveness, Eph. v. 22; Tit. ii. 4. St. Peter assumes knowledge of the reason alleged by St. Paul (Eph. *l.c.*; 1 Cor. xi. 3) after Gen. iii. 16, **αὐτός σου κυριεύσει.—καὶ εἰ . . . λόγῳ,** *even if in some cases your husbands are disobedient to the word* (ii. 8), *i.e.*, remain heathens in spite of the preaching of the Gospel. St. Paul found it necessary to impress upon the Corinthian Church that this incompatibility of religion did not justify dissolution of marriage (1 Cor. xii. 10 ff.).—**ἄνευ λόγου,** *without word from their wives.* Peter deliberately introduces **λ.** in its ordinary sense immediately after the technical **τῷ λ.**—an example of what the grammarians call antanaclasis and men a pun. In his provision for the present and future welfare of the heathen husbands whose wives come under his jurisdiction he echoes the natural aspiration of Jews and Greeks; so Ben Sira said, *a silent woman is a gift of the Lord . . . a loud crying woman and a scold shall be sought out to drive away enemies* (Sir. xxvi. 14, 27) and Sophocles, *Silence is the proper ornament* (**κόσμος**) *for women* (Ajax 293). St. Paul forbids women to preach or even ask questions at church meeting (1 Cor. xiv. 34: at Corinth they had been used to prophesy and pray).—**ἵνα . . . κερδηθήσονται,** *be won, cf.* **ἵνα κερδήσω** in 1 Cor. ix. 20 ff. = **ἵνα . . . σώσω,** *ib.* 22, (*cf.* vii. 16.).

Ver. 2. **ἐποπτεύσαντες,** *having contemplated*; see on ii. 12. **τὴν . . . ὑμῶν. ἐν φόβῳ,** *cf.* i. 17 and Eph. v. 21. **ὑποτασσόμενοι ἀλλήλοις ἐν φόβῳ Χριστοῦ· αἱ γυναῖκες**: as no object is expressed, **τοῦ θεοῦ** must be supplied.—**ἁγνήν,** not merely *chaste* but *pure, cf.* i. 22 and iii. 4.

Ver. 3. The description of the external ornaments proper to heathen society seems to be based on Isa. iii. 17-23, where the destruction of the hair, jewels and raiment of the daughters of Zion is foretold.—**ἐμπλοκῆς τριχῶν,** *braiding of hair.* 1 Tim. ii. 19, **πλέγμασιν καὶ χρυσίῳ** refers to the golden combs and nets used for the purpose; *cf.* **ἐμπλόκια,** Isa. iii. 18, for שְׁבִיסִים. Juvenal describes the elaborate coiffures which Roman fashion prescribed for the Park and attendance at the Mysteries of Adonis: tot premit ordinibus tot adhuc compagibus altum aedificat caput (Sat. vi. 492-504). Clement of Alexandria quotes 1 Peter iii. 1-4, in his discussion of the whole subject (*Paed.*, III. xi.); and in regard to this particular point says **ἀπόχρη μαλάσσειν τὰς τρίχας καὶ ἀναδεῖσθαι τὴν κόμην ἐντελῶς περόνῃ τινι λιτῇ παρὰ τὸν αὐχένα . . . καὶ γὰρ αἱ περιπλοκαὶ τῶν τριχῶν αἱ ἑταιρικαὶ καὶ αἱ τῶν σειρῶν ἀναδέσεις . . . κόπτουσι τὰς τρίχας ἀποτίλλουσαι ταῖς πανούργοις ἐμπλοκαῖς,** because of which they do not even touch their own head for fear of disturbing their hair—nay more sleep comes to them with terror lest they should unawares spoil **τὸ σχῆμα τῆς ἐμπλοκῆς** (p. 290 P).—**περιθέσεως χρυσίων,** *i.e.*, rings bracelets, etc., enumerated in Isa. *l.c.*—**ἐνδύσεως ἱματίων.** Stress might be laid on **κόσμος,** or the crowning prohibition regarded as an exaggeration intended to counteract an ingrained bias. In either case the expression points to a remarkable precedent for this teaching in Plato's *Republic* IV., iii. ff. "Plato's assignment of common duties and common training to the two sexes is part of a well-reasoned and deliberate attempt by the Socratic school to improve the position of women in Greece. . . . Socrates' teaching inaugurated an era of protest against the old Hellenic view of things. . . . In later times the Stoics constituted themselves champions of similar views" (Adam, *ad loc.*). Accordingly gymnastics must be practised by women as by men: **ἀποδυτέον δὴ ταῖς τῶν φυλάκων γυναιξὶν ἐπείπερ ἀρετὴν ἀντὶ ἱματίων ἀμφιέσονται.**

Ver. 4. *Yours be the secret man of the heart not the outward ornament.* A better antithesis and a pretty paradox would be

ἐν τῶ ἀφθάρτῶ τοῦ ἡσυχίου καὶ πραέως πνεύματος ὅ ἐστιν
5 ἐνώπιον τοῦ Θῦ πολυ τελές. οὕτως γάρ πο τε καὶ αἱ ἅγιαι
γυναῖκες αἱ ἐλπίζουσαι εἰς Θν̀ ἐκόσμουν ἑαυτὰς ὑ ποτασ-
6 σόμεναι τοῖς ἰδίοις ἀνδράσιν· ὡς Σάρρα ὑπήκουεν τῶ
ʽΑβραὰμ κύριον αὐτὸν καλοῦσα. ἧς ἐγενήθη τε τέκνα, ἀγα-
7 θοποιοῦ σαι, καὶ μὴ φοβούμε ναι μηδεμίαν πτόησι̅.[1] ἄνδρες

[1] **πτῶσιν** for **πτόησιν** illustrates the danger of cursive writing, in which the ligature of two letters is apt to alter the normal shape of one or both.

secured by supplying **ἄνθρωπος** with **ὁ ἔξωθεν** and taking **κ.** as predicate: your ornament be *cf.* **οὕτως ἐκόσμουν ἑαυτάς** (ver. 5). But the order in ver. 3 is against this and a Greek reader would naturally think of the other sense of **κ.** = world universe and remember that man is a microcosm and "the universe the greatest and most perfect *man*" (Philo, p. 471 M.).—**ὁ κρυπτὸς τῆς καρδίας ἄνθρωπος**, *the hidden man that is the heart* (or *which belongs to the heart*) is the equivalent of the Pauline *inner man* (Rom. vii. 22), *i.e.*, Mind as contrasted with *the outward man*, *i.e.*, flesh (Rom. *l.c.*, *cf.* 2 Cor. iv. 16). St. Peter employs the terms used in the Sermon on the Mount; *cf.* St. Paul's **ὁ ἐν τῷ κρυπτῷ Ἰουδαῖος** and **περιτομὴ καρδίας**, Rom. ii. 29.—**ἐν τῷ ἀφθάρτῳ**, *clothed in the incorruptible thing* (or *ornament*, sc. **κόσμῳ**) contrasted with corruptible *goldens*; *cf.* Jas. ii. 2, **ἀνὴρ . . . ἐν ἐσθῆτι λαμπρᾷ.**—**τοῦ . . . πνεύματος**, *namely*, *the meek and quiet spirit*. The adjectives are perhaps derived from the version of Isa. lxvi. 2, known to Clement of Rome (Ep. i. xiii. 4), **ἐπὶ τίνα ἐπιβλέψω ἀλλ' ἢ ἐπὶ τὸν πρᾳὺν καὶ ἡσύχιον καὶ τρέμοντά μου τὰ λόγια.** Jesus professed Himself, **πρᾳὺς καὶ ταπεινὸς τῇ καρδίᾳ.** For **πνεύματος** compare **πνεῦμα ἁγιωσύνης**, Rom. i. 4. In Rom. ii. 29, **πν.** is coupled with *heart* as contrasted with *flesh* and outwardness. **ὅ** *which spirit* or *the posssesion of which* reference.—**πολυτελές** suggests use of conception of Wisdom which is *precious* above rubies (Prov. iii. 15, etc.); *cf.* Jas. i. 21, iii. 13, **ἐν πρᾳύτητι σοφίας** and description of *the wisdom from above*, *ib.* 17.

Ver. 5. **ποτε** refers vaguely to O.T. history as part of **αἱ . . . θεόν.** References to the holy women of the O.T. are rare in N.T. and this appeal to their example illustrates the affinity of Peter to Heb. (xi. 11, 35). Hannah is the obviously appropriate type (*cf.* Luke i. with 2 Sam. 1 f.); but Peter is thinking of the traditional idealisation of Sarah.

Ver. 6. **ὡς . . . καλοῦσα.** The only evidence that can be adduced from the O.T. narrative is *Sarah laughed within herself and said . . . "but my lord is old"* (Gen. xviii. 12). The phrase, if pressed, implies a nominal subjection as of a slave to her lord, but the context at any rate excludes *any hope in God*. Philo, who starts with the assumption that Sarah is Virtue, evades the difficulty; her laughter was the expression of her joy, she denied it for fear of usurping God's prerogative of laughter (*de Abr.*, ii. p. 30 M). The Rabbinic commentaries dwell upon the title accorded to Abraham and draw the same inference as Peter; but there are also traces of a tendency to exalt Sarah "the princess" as superior to her husband in the gift of prophecy, which St. Peter may wish to correct (as St. James corrects the exaggerated respect paid to Elijah, Jas. v. 17).—**ἧς . . . τέκνα.** Christian women became children of Sarah who is Virtue or Wisdom (Philo) just as men became children of Abraham. But the fact that they were Christians is still in the background; the essential point is that they must do the works traditionally ascribed to Sarah (*cf.* Rom. iv.; John viii.) and so justify their technical parentage, whether natural or acquired. Oec. compares Isa. li. 2, *Sarah your mother*.—**ἀγαθοποιοῦσαι**, the present participle emphasises the need for continuance of the behaviour appropriate to children of Sarah.—**μὴ . . . πτόησιν**, from Prov. iii. 25, LXX. Peter regards Sarah's falsehood (Gen. *l.c.*) as the yielding to a sudden terror for which she was rebuked by God. Fearlessness then is part of the character which is set before them for imitation and it is the result of obedience to the voice of Wisdom. Rabbinic exegesis associates the ideas of *ornament* with the promised child and that of peace between husband and wife with the whole incident.

Ver. 7. *Duty of husbands to their wives*. Application of principle **πάντας τιμήσατε.**—**κατὰ γνῶσιν**, for the

ὁμοίως συνοι κοῦντες κατὰ γνῶσι ὡς ἀσθενεστέρω σκεύ ει
τῶ γυναικείω ἀπο νέμοντες τειμὴν ὡς καὶ συγκληρονόμοις
χάριτος ζωῆς εἰς τὸ μὴ ἐγκόπτεσθαι ταῖς προσευχαῖς ὑμῶν.
τὸ δὲ τέλος, πάντες ὁ μόφρονες συμπαθεῖς φιλάδελφοι 8
εὔσπλαγ χνοι ταπεινόφρονες· μὴ ἀποδιδόντες κακὸ ἀντὶ κακοῦ 9
ἢ λοιδορί αν ἀντὶ λοιδορίας· τοὐ ναντίον δὲ εὐλογοῦ τες,
ὅτι εἰς τοῦτο ἐ κλήθητε, ἵνα εὐλογία κληρονομήσητε. ὁ 10

woman is the weaker vessel—the pot—which the stronger—the cauldron—may easily smash (Sir. xiii. 2). **ὡς, κ.τ.λ.** point with comma after **γνῶσιν** and **τιμήν.** **σκεύει.** The comparison of Creator and creature to potter and clay is found first in Isa. xxix. 16, but is latent in the description of the creation (יצר) of Adam from the dust of the earth (Gen. ii. 7 f.). In the prophets it is developed and applied variously (Isa. xlv. 9 f., lxiv. 8; Jer. xviii. 6). In Sap. xv. 7, there is an elaborate description of the maker of clay images, in which **σκεῦος** replaces **πλάσμα** and *vessels which serve clean uses* are distinguished from *the contrary sort.* Thence St. Paul adopts the figure and employs it to illustrate the absolute sovereignty of the Creator, as Isaiah had done (see Rom. ix. 21), distinguishing *vessels intended for honour* from those *intended for dishonour.* Lastly 2 Tim. ii. 20 exemplifies the particular application of the figure, on which Peter's use of **σκεῦος** rests—**ἐν μεγάλῃ δὲ οἰκίᾳ** (1 Peter ii. 5, iv. 17) . . . **κ.τ.λ.** The comparative **ἀσθενεστέρῳ** proves that both husband and wife are *vessels* and assists to exclude the notion that St. Paul could mean to call a wife the vessel of her husband in 1 Thess. iv. 4.—**ὡς . . . ζωῆς,** *inasmuch as they are also heirs with you of the grace* (i. 10, 13) *of life* (ii. 24): the heavenly inheritance is not distributed according to earthly custom, which gave the wife no rights of her own.—**εἰς . . . ὑμῶν.** If the prayers are those of all (ver. 8) compare 1 Cor. vii. (**τὴν ὀφειλὴν ἀποδιδότω . . . ἵνα σχολάσητε τῇ προσευχῇ**). Peter teaches that married life need not—if the wife be properly honoured—hinder religious duties, as St. Paul feared (*ib.* 32 ff.). If **ὑμῶν** = *you husbands* (as *v.l.* **συγκληρονόμοι** requires) *cf.* Jas. v. 4.

Vv. 8 f. Sweeping clause addressed to all, inculcating detailed **φιλαδελφία** after Rom. xii. 10, 15-17.

Ver. 8. **τὸ . . . τέλος,** *finally.* Oecumenius brings out the possible connotations of the word *goal* and also the law for all love since love is the end of the law.—**ὁμόφρονες,** *of one mind, united,* an Epic word. St. Paul's **τὸ αὐτὸ φρονεῖν** but here wider than parallel expressing Rom. xii. 16, **τὸ αὐτὸ εἰς ἀλλήλους φρονοῦντες.**—**συμπαθεῖς** summarises **χαίρειν μετὰ χαιρόντων κλαίειν μετὰ κλαιόντων** of Rom. xii. 15; *cf.* Heb. iv. 15 (of Christ), x. 34 (particular example of sympathy with "the prisoners").—**φιλάδελφοι,** *cf.* i. 22; Rom. xii. 10, **τῇ φιλαδελφίᾳ εἰς ἀλλήλους φιλόστοργοι.**—**εὔσπλαγχνοι,** *kind-hearted,* in Eph. iv. 32 (only here in N.T.) coupled with *kind . . . forgiving one another;* epithet of Jehovah in Prayer of Manasses, ver. 7 = *compassionate,* in accordance with metaphorical use of **σπλάγχνα κ.τ.λ.** derived from different senses of רחם. Here = **ἐνδύσασθε . . . τὰ σπλάγχνα τῆς χρηστότητος,** Col.—**ταπεινόφρονες = τοῖς ταπεινοῖς συναπαγόμενοι,** Rom. xii. 16, *cf.* Prov. xxix. 23, LXX, *insolence humbleth a man but the humble* (**ταπεινόφρονας**) *Jehovah stayeth with glory* (**κ. ὕβρις**).

Ver. 9. **μὴ . . . κακοῦ,** from Rom. xii. 17; *cf.* 1 Thess. v. 15; Prov. xx. 22, *Say not I will recompense evil* (LXX **τίσομαι τὸν ἐχθρόν**): an approximation to Christ's repeal of the *lex talionis* (Matt. v. 38 ff.) which Plato first opposed among the Greeks (see *Crito.*, p. 49, with Adam's note).—**λοιδορίαν ἀντὶ λοιδορίας** refers to pattern left by Christ (ii. 23).—**τοὐναντίον,** *contrariwise.*—**εὐλογοῦντες** with **λοιδ.,** 1 Cor. iv. 21; *cf.* Rom. xii. 14, **εὐλογεῖτε τοὺς διώκοντας** = Luke vi. 28.—**ὅτι . . . κληρονομήσητε,** Christians must do as they hope to be done by. They are the new Israel called to inherit blessing in place of the Jews, who are reprobate like Esau; *cf.* Heb. xii. 17, **ἴστε γὰρ ὅτι καὶ μετέπειτα θέλων κληρονομῆσαι τὴν εὐλογίαν ἀπεδοκιμάσθη.** So St. Paul reverses the current view which identified the Jews with Isaac and the Gentiles with Ishmael (Gal. iv. 22 ff.).

Vv. 10-12 = Ps. xxxiv. 12-17*a*. intro-

γὰρ θέλων ζωὴν ἀγαπᾶ̄, καὶ ἰδεῖν ἡμέρας ἀγα θάς,
παυσάτω τὴν γλῶσ σαν ἀπὸ κακοῦ, καὶ χεί λη τοῦ μὴ λαλῆσαι
11 δό λον. ἐκκλεινάτω δὲ ἀπὸ κακοῦ καὶ ποιη σάτω ἀγαθόν·
12 ζητη σάτω εἰρήνην, καὶ δι ωξάτω αὐτήν, ὅτι ὀ φθαλμοὶ Κῡ
ἐπὶ δικαί ους, καὶ ὦτα αὐτοῦ εἰς δέησιν αὐτῶν· πρόσωπον
13 δὲ Κῡ ἐπὶ ποιοῦντας κακά. καὶ τίς ὁ κακώσων ὑμᾶς,
14 εἰ τοῦ ἀγαθοῦ ζη λωταὶ[1] γένοισθε[2] ἀλ λ' εἰ καὶ πάσχοιτε δι ὰ
δικαιοσύνην, μακά ριοι. τὸν δὲ φόβον αὐ τῶν μὴ φοβηθῆτε

[1] For **ζηλωταὶ** three secondary uncials substitute **μιμηται**.

[2] Codex Vaticanus is alone in reading **γένοισθε** for **γενησθε** (the first hand of Codex Sinaiticus has **γενεσθαι**).

duced by mere **γάρ** as familiar. The lips of Christians who wish to love life must be free from cursing and from guile as were Christ's (*cf.* Isa. *apud* ii. 23). If Jehovah is to hear their petition as He heard Christ's they also must turn from evil and do good (*cf.* **ἀγαθοποιεῖν** above) seeking peace within and without the Church.

Ver. 10. Peter omits the rhetorical question **τίς ἐστιν ἄνθρωπος**, which introduces **ὁ θέλων** in the original (LXX = Hebrew) but is influenced by it in the substitution of the third for the second person throughout. The change of **ἀγαπῶν** (= Hebrew) to **ἀγαπᾶν καὶ** removes the barbarisms **θέλων ζωήν** and **ἀγαπῶν ἰδεῖν** (= Hebrew) and secures the balance between the clauses disturbed by the omission of the opening words.—**ἰδεῖν ἡμ. ἀγαθάς** is the natural sequel of the alteration of the original (*days to see good*), which is already found in the LXX (**ἡμ. ἰ. ἀγαθάς**).—**ζωήν** = *earthly life* in the original corresponding to *days*. The text adopted by Peter makes it mean *eternal life*, parallel *good days*. Only with this interpretation is the quotation pertinent to his exhortation : *cf. that ye might inherit blessing* (9) with *fellow-inheritors of the grace of life* (7).—**παυσάτω, κ.τ.λ.**, parallel **μὴ . . . λοιδορίαν** (9); *cf.* ii. 22 f.

Ver. 12. **πρόσωπον Κυρίου**, *Jehovah's face, i.e., wrath* (Targum, *the face of Jehovah was angry*) as the following clause, *to cut off the remembrance of them* . . . shows; *cf.* Lam. iv. 16; Ps. xxi. 9. But Peter stops short and leaves room for repentance.

Ver. 13. **κακώσων** echoes **ποιοῦντας κακά** (as **ζηλ. τοῦ ἀγ.** echoes **ποιησάτω ἀγαθόν**); but the phrase comes also from O.T.: Isa. l. 9, **Κύριος βοηθήσει μοι· τίς κακώσει με;**—**τοῦ ἀγαθοῦ ζηλωταί.** The phrase sums up ver. 11. All that was good in Judaism, however it may have been perverted, finds its fulfilment in the new Israel (Rom. x. 2). *Some* Jews were zealots, boasting their zeal for the Lord or His Law, like Phinehas and the Hasmonaeans (1 Macc. ii. *passim*): *all* Christians should be *zealots for that which is good.* So Paul says of himself as Pharisee that he was *a zealot for his ancestral traditions* (Gal. i. 14). For him as for the colleague of Simon the Zealot the word retained a flavour of its technical sense; *cf.* Tit. ii. 14, *that He might cleanse for Himself a peculiar people, zealot of good* (**καλῶν**) *works*; *cf.* similar use of **ἀφωρισμένος** = Pharisee (Rom. i. 1). **τοῦ ἀγ.** in emphatic position.

Ver. 14. **ἀλλ' . . . μακάριοι.** *Nay if ye should actually suffer*—if some one, despite the prophet (13), should harm you—*for the sake of righteousness, blessed are ye.* Peter appeals to the saying, **μακάριοι οἱ δεδιωγμένοι ἕνεκεν δικαιοσύνης** (Matt. v. 10).—**πάσχοιτε, εἰ** with optative (*cf.* 17, **εἰ θέλοι**) is used to represent anything as generally possible without regard to the general or actual situation at the moment (Blass, *Grammar*, p. 213). The addition of **καί** implies that the contingency is unlikely to occur and is best represented by an emphasis on *should*. The meaning of the verb is determined by **κακώσων** above, *if ye should be harmed, i.e.*, by persons unspecified (**αὐτῶν**).—**δικαιοσύνην** perhaps suggested **ζηλωταί**, *cf.* 1 Macc. ii. 27-29, **πᾶς ὁ ζηλῶν τῷ νόμῳ . . . ἐξελθέτω . . . τότε κατέβησαν πολλοὶ ζητοῦντες δικ. καὶ κρίμα.**—**τὸν δὲ φόβον . . . ὑμῶν.** An adaptation of Isa. viii. 12 f. LXX, **τὸν δὲ φόβον αὐτοῦ μὴ φοβηθῆτε οὐδὲ μὴ ταραχθῆτε· κύριον αὐτὸν ἁγιάσατε καὶ αὐτὸς ἔσται σου φόβος.** The scripture

Κ͞ν δὲ τὸν Χ͞ν[1] ἁγιάσατε ἐν ταῖς καρδίαις ὑμῶν ἕτοιμοι ἀεὶ 15
πρὸς ἀπολογίαν παντὶ τῷ αἰτοῦντι ὑμᾶς λογο̄ περὶ τῆς
ἐν ὑμῖν ἐλπίδος· ἀλλὰ μετὰ πραΰτητος καὶ φόβου
συνείδησιν ἔχοντες ἀγαθήν· ἵνα ἐν ᾧ καταλαλεῖσθε[2] κατ- 16
αισχῡθῶσιν οἱ ἐπηρεάζοντες ὑμῶν τὴν ἀγαθὴ̄ ἐν Χ͞ω
ἀναστροφήν· κρεῖττον γὰρ ἀγαθοποιοῦντας εἰ θέλοι 17

[1] Three secondary uncials read **θεόν** (Θ͞Ν) for **Χριστόν** (Χ͞ν).

[2] For **ἐν ᾧ καταλαλεῖσθε** Codex Sinaiticus with other authorities reads **ἐν ᾧ καταλαλῶσιν ὑμῶν ὡς κακοποιῶν**—an assimilation of the text to ii. 12.

corresponding to the saying, *Fear not them that kill the body; but fear rather him that can destroy both soul and body* (Matt. x. 28 parallels Luke xii. 4 f. where the description of God is modified). The sense of the original, *fear not what they (the people) fear; Jehovah of Hosts Him shall ye count holy and let Him be the object of your fear*, has been in part abandoned. For it is simpler to take *the fear* as referring to the evil with which their enemies try to terrify them, than to supply the idea that their enemies employ the means by which they themselves would be intimidated. Compare iii. 6.—**τὸν χριστόν**, gloss on **κύριον** = Jehovah; *cf.* ii. 3.—**ἐν ταῖς καρδίαις** *sc.* mere profession. Peter is probably thinking of the prescribed prayer, *Hallowed be thy name*, elsewhere in N.T. it belongs to God to sanctify Christ and men.—**ἕτοιμοι ἀεὶ πρὸς ἀπολογίαν**, *ready for reply*. The contrast between the inward hope (parallels sanctification of Christ in the heart) and the spoken defence of it is not insisted upon; the second **δέ** is not to be accepted. The use of the noun in place of verb is characteristic of St. Peter. The play upon **ἀπολογίαν** *back-word* and **λόγον** cannot be reproduced. Properly *speech in defence*, **ἀ.** is used metaphorically (NB **παντί**) here as by St. Paul in 1 Cor. ix. 3, **ἡ ἐμὴ ἀπολογία τοῖς ἐμὲ ἀνακρίνουσιν**; where also, though another technical word is introduced, no reference is intended to formal proceedings in a court of law. St. Peter is thinking of the promise which he himself once forfeited for unworthy fear, *I will give you mouth and wisdom* (Luke xxi. 14 f., xii. 11, uses **ἀπολογεῖσθαι**; Matt. x. 19, **λαλεῖν**).—**παντὶ . . . λόγον**, *to every one* (for dative *cf.* 1 Cor. ix. 3) *that asketh of you an account*. The phrase (compare *Demosthenes Against Onetor*, p. 868, **ἐνεκάλουν καὶ λόγον ἀπῄτουν**) recalls the Parable of the Steward of Unrighteousness, of whom his lord demanded an account (Luke xvi. 1 ff.), as also the metaphor of iv. 10, **ὡς καλοὶ οἰκονόμοι**.—**μετὰ πραΰτητος καὶ φόβου**, *with meekness* (*cf.* ver. 4) *and fear of God* (Isa. *l.c.* has the same play on the senses of *fear*).—**συνείδησιν ἔχοντες ἀγαθήν**, intermediate step between **διὰ σ. θεοῦ** and the quasi-personification of **σ. ἀ.** in ver. 21; so St. Paul says **οὐδὲν γὰρ ἐμαυτῷ σύνοιδα** (1 Cor. iv. 4) but goes on beyond the contrast between self-judgment and that of other men to God's judgment. Ver. 17 supplies the explanation here.—**ἵνα . . . ἀναστροφήν**, generalisation of Peter's personal experience at Pentecost, when the Jews first scoffed and then were pierced to the heart (Acts ii. 13, 37). Misrepresentation is apparently the extent of their present suffering (17) and this they are encouraged to hope may be stopped. The heathen will somehow be put to shame even if they are not converted (ii. 12).—**ἐν ᾧ**, *in the matter in respect of which*; see ii. 12.—**ἐπηρεάζοντες**, occurs in Luke vi. 28, **προσεύχεσθε περὶ τῶν ἐπηρεαζόντων ὑμᾶς**, and therefore constitutes another hint of contact between St. Luke and Peter (*cf.* **χάρις**, ii. 19). Aristotle defines **ἐπηρεασμός** as "hindrance to the wishes of another not for the sake of gaining anything oneself but in order to baulk the other"—the spirit of the dog in the manger. Ordinarily the verb means *to libel*, *cf.* **λαλῆσαι δόλον** (10).—**ὑμῶν . . . ἀναστροφήν**, *your* (possessive genitive precedes noun in Hellenistic Greek) *good-in-Christ behaviour*: **ἐν Χριστῷ** (iv. 14, 16) is practically equivalent to *Christian*, *cf. if any is in Christ a new creature*.

Ver. 17. **κρεῖττον**, *cf.* ii. 19 f., where **χάρις κλέος** correspond to **μισθὸν περισσόν** of the sources.—**εἰ θέλοι τὸ θέλημα θεοῦ.** Again optative implies that it is a purely hypothetical case (*cf.* ver. 14). For the semi-personification

18 τὸ θέλημα τοῦ Θῦ πά σχειν ἢ κακοποιοῦν τας· ὅτι καὶ Χς
ἅπαξ πε ρὶ ἁμαρτιῶν ἔπαθεν δίκαιος ὑπὲρ ἀδίκω ἵνα
ἡμᾶς προσαγάγῃ θανατωθεὶς μὲν σαρ κὶ ζωοποιηθεὶς δὲ

of *the will of God* compare Eph. i. 11, where the **θέλημα** has a **βουλή**; so Paul is Apostle *through the will of God* (1 Cor. i. 1; 2 Cor. i. 1). For the pleonastic expression *cf.* the verbal parallel **ἐάν τις θέλῃ τὸ θέλημα αὐτοῦ ποιεῖν**, John vii. 17. So *God's patience was waiting* (ver. 20).

Ver. 18. The advantage of suffering for well-doing is exemplified in the experience of Christ, who gained thereby quickening (ver. 21) and glory (ver. 22). How far the pattern applies to the Christian is not clear. Christ suffered *once for all* according to Heb. ix. 24-28; the Christian suffers *for a little* (v. 10). But does the Christian suffer also *for sins?* St. Paul and Ignatius speak of themselves as **περίψημα περικαθάρματα**; compare the value of righteous men for Sodom. But even if Peter contemplated this parallel it is quite subordinate to the main idea, *in which* (*spirit*) *even to the spirits in prison he went and preached them that disobeyed once upon a time when the patience of God was waiting in the days of Noah while the ark was being fitted out. . . .* The spirits who disobeyed in the days of Noah are the sons of God described in Gen. vi. 1-4. But there as in the case of Sarah St. Peter depends on the current tradition in which the original myth has been modified and amplified. This dependence supplies an adequate explanation of the difficulties which have been found here and in ver. 21, provided that the plain statement of the preaching in Hades is not prejudged to be impossible. The important points in the tradition as given in the Book of Enoch (vi.-xvi. *cf.* Jubilees v.) are as follows: the angels who lusted after the daughters of men descended in the days of Jared as his name (Descent) shows. The children of this unlawful union were the Nephilim and the Eliud. They also taught men all evil arts so that they perished appealing to God for justice. At last Enoch was sent to pronounce the sentence of condemnation upon these watchers, who in terror besought him to present a petition to God on their behalf. God refused to grant them peace. They were spirits eternal and immortal who transgressed the line of demarcation between men and angels and disobeyed the law that spiritual beings do not marry and beget children like men. Accordingly they are bound and their children slay one another leaving their disembodied spirits to propagate sin in the world even after it has been purged by the Flood. But Christians believed that Christ came to seek and to save the lost and the captives; all things are to be subjected to Him. So Peter supplements the tradition which he accepts. For him it was not merely important as connected with the only existing type of the Last Judgment or an alternative explanation of the origin and continuance of sin but also as the greatest proof of the complete victory of Christ over the most obstinate and worst of sinners.—**ἐν ᾧ** *sc.* **πνεύματι**: as a bodiless spirit in the period between the Passion (18) and the Resurrection-Ascension (22).—**καί**, *even* to the typical rebels who had sinned past forgiveness according to pre-Christian notions.—**τοῖς ἐν φυλακῇ πνεύμασιν**, *the spirits in prison*, *i.e.*, the angels of Gen. *l.c.* who were identified with *my spirit* of Gen. vi. 3, and therefore described as having been sent to the earth by God in one form of the legend (Jubilees, *l.c.*). The name contains also the point of their offending (Enoch summarised above); *cf.* 2 Peter ii. 4; Jude 6; and the prophecy of Isa. lxi. 1 (which Jesus claimed, Luke iv. 8 f.), **κηρῦξαι αἰχμαλώτοις ἄφεσιν.** These spirits were *in ward* when Christ preached to them in accordance with God's sentence, *bind them in the depths of the earth* (Jub. v. 6).—**ἐκήρυξεν = εὐηγγελίσατο**, *cf.* Luke iv. 8. Before Christ came, they had not heard the Gospel of God's Reign. Enoch's mediation failed. But at Christ's preaching they repented like the men of Nineveh; for it is said that *angels subjected themselves to Him* (22. *cf.* **ὑποτάσσεσθαι**, throughout the Epistle.—**ἀπειθήσασίν ποτε**, their historic disobedience or rebellion is latent in the narrative of Gen. vi. and expounded by Enoch; *cf.* ii. 7 f., iii. 1, iv. 17. In LXX **ἀπ.** commonly = rebel (מרה).—**ἀπεξεδέχετο . . . μακροθυμία**, *God's long-suffering was waiting.* The reading **ἅπαξ ἐξεδέχετο** is attractive, as supplying a reference to the present period of waiting which precedes the second and final Judgment (Rom. ii. 4, ix. 22). The tradition lengthens the period of **πάρεσις** (Rom. iii. 25); but

πνεύματι · ἐν ᾧ καὶ[1] τοῖς ἐν φυλακῇ πνεύμα σιν πορευθεὶς 19
ἐκήρυ ξεν ἀπειθήσασίν πο ε ὅτε ἀπεξεδέχετο[2] ἡ τοῦ Θῦ 20
μακροθυμία ἐν ἡμέραις Νῶε κατα σκευαζομένης κειβώ
του εἰς ἣν ὀλίγοι του τέστι ὀκτὼ ψυχαὶ διεσώθησαν δι' ὕδατος · ὃ καὶ ὑμᾶς ἀντίτυπο νῦν σώζει βάπτισμα οὐ σαρ- 21
κὸς ἀπόθεσις ῥύ που ἀλλὰ συνειδήσε ως ἀγαθῆς ἐπερώτη

[1] Dr. Rendel Harris would restore Ἑνὼχ after ἐν ᾧ καὶ (ϗ), supposing that a scribe has blundered "in dropping some repeated letters" (a case of *haplography*). See *Side-Lights on New Testament Research*, p. 208.

[2] Erasmus supposing an haplography read ἅπαξ ἐξεδέχετο for ἀπεξεδέχετο.

St. Peter limits it by adding *while the Ark was being fitted out* in accordance with Gen. If Adam's transgression be taken as the origin of sin the long-suffering is still greater. The idea seems to be due to ἐνεθυμήθην, *I reflected*, of the LXX, which stands for the unworthy anthropomorphism of the Hebrew *I repented* in Gen. vi. 6. Compare for language Jas. v. 7; Matt. xxiv. 37 f.; Luke xvii. 26 f.—εἰς ἥν, *sc. entered and.*—ὀλίγοι, κ.τ.λ. St. Peter hints that here in the typical narrative is the basis of the disciple's question, εἰ ὀλίγοι οἱ σωζόμενοι (Luke xiii. 23).—ὀκτὼ ψυχαί, so Gen. vii. 7; ψ. = *persons* (of both sexes), *cf.* Acts ii. 41, etc. The usage occurs in Greek of all periods; so נפש in Hebrew and *soul* in English.—διεσώθησαν δι' ὕδατος, *were brought safe through water.* Both local and instrumental meanings of δί are contemplated. The former is an obvious summary of the whole narrative; *cf.* also διὰ τὸ ὕδωρ (Gen. vii. 7). The latter is implied in the statement that the water *increased and lifted up the ark* (*ib.* 17 f.); though it fits better the antitype. So Josephus (Ant. I., iii. 2) says that "the ark was strong so that from no side was it worsted by the violence of the water and Noah with his household διασώζεται". Peter lays stress on the water (rather than the ark as *e.g.*, Heb. xi.) for the sake of the parallel with Baptism (Rom. vi. 3; *cf.* St. Paul's application of the Passage of the Red Sea, 1 Cor. x. 1 f.).

Ver. 21. Baptism is generally the antitype of the deliverance of Noah. Christians pass *through water* (in both senses) to salvation; in each microcosm are the sins which must be washed away and the remnant which is to be saved. Therefore the antitypical water saves us (ὃ = τὸ ὕδωρ > δι' ὕδατος) being οὐ σαρκός, κ.τ.λ.; *cf.* Tit. iii. 5.—βάπτισμα, if not an interpolation explains ὁ ἀντ. *which corresponding to the* (pre-existent) *type* (*cf.* Heb. ix. 24 the earthly temple is ἀντίτυπα τῶν ἀληθινῶν). The following definition by exclusion contrasts Christian baptism with Jewish and pagan lustrations and also with the Deluge which was a removal of sin-fouled flesh from the sinners of old (iv. 6); the former affected the flesh and not the conscience (Heb. ix. 13 f.), the latter removed the flesh but not the spiritual defilement proceeding from past sin. σαρκός and συνειδήσεως stand before their belongings for emphasis and not merely in accordance with prevalent custom. For ἀπόθεσις ῥύπου compare Isa. iv. 4 (sequel of the description of the daughters of Zion which is used above iii. 3), *Jehovah shall wash away their filth* (τὸν ῥύπον: LXX chivalrously prefixes *of the sons and*). ἐπερώτημα is explained by Oecumenius as meaning *earnest*, *pledge* as in Byzantine Greek law. Its use for the questions put to the candidate in the baptismal service (dost thou renounce . ..?) is probably due to St. Peter here. In ordinary Greek (Herodotus and Thucydides) it = *question* (ἐπ. having no force, as if implying a second additional question arising out of the first). Here the noun corresponds to the verb as used in Isa. lxv. 1, quoted by St. Paul in Rom. x. 20, ἐμφανὴς ἐγενόμην τοῖς ἐμὲ μὴ ἐπερωτῶσι = (1) a seeking, quest after God or (2) *request addressed to God* (supported by εἰς; *cf.* the formula ἔντευξις εἰς τὸ βασίλεως ὄνομα, a petition addressed to the king's majesty). In the latter case Peter will still be thinking as above and below of the disobedient spirits who presented a petition (ἐρώτησις) to God inspired by an evil conscience (see Enoch summarised above). At any rate συνειδ. is probably subjective or possessive rather than objective genitive. The believer who comes to baptism has believed in Christ and repented of his past sins, renounces them and the

22 μα εἰς Θν̄ δί ἀναστάσε ως Ιῦ Χῦ ὅς ἐστιν ἐν δε ξιᾷ Θῦ[1] πορευθεὶς εἰς οὐρανὸν ὑποταγέν των αὐτῷ ἀγγέλων ϗ ἐξου-
IV. 1 σιῶν καὶ δυνάμε ων Χῦ οὖν παθόντος[2] σαρκὶ[3] καὶ ὑμεῖς τὴν
αὐ τὴν ἔννοιαν ὁπλίσα σθε· ὅτι ὁ παθὼν σαρκὶ πέπαυται
2 ἁμαρτίαις[4] εἰς τὸ μηκέτι ἀνθρώ πων ἐπιθυμίαις ἀλλὰ
θελήματι Θῦ τὸν ἐπί λοιπον ἐν σαρκὶ βιῶ σαι χρόνον·
3 ἀρκετὸς γὰρ[5] ὁ παρεληλυθὼς χρόνος[6] τὸ βούλημα τῶ̄

[1] After **θεοῦ** the Vulgate adds *degluttiens mortem ut vitae aeternae heredes efficiamur.*

[2] The variant **αποθανόντος** for **παθόντος** is a simple case of erroneous transcription which does not affect the sense. Codex Alexandrinus adds the Christian gloss **ὑπὲρ ἡμῶν.**

[3] To **σαρκὶ** two secondary uncials prefix the preposition **ἐν.**

[4] For **ἁμαρτίαις** most manuscripts have **ἁμαρτίας.**

[5] After **γὰρ** the secondary uncials supply **ἡμῖν,** and the first hand of Codex Sinaiticus with many cursives **ὑμῖν.**

[6] The secondary uncials add **τοῦ βίου** to **χρόνος** and substitute **θέλημα** for **βούλημα.**

spirits which prompted them and appeals to God for strength to carry out this renunciation in his daily life.—**δι᾽ ἀναστ.** with **σώζει**; compare 1 Cor. xv. 13-17.

Ver. 22. Christ went into Heaven—and now is on God's right hand (Ps. cx. 1)—when angels and authorities and powers had subjected themselves to Him in accordance with prophecy (Ps. viii. 7; *cf.* Heb. ii. 8; 1 Cor. xv. 24 ff.). For the orders of angels see also Rom. viii. 38; Eph. i. 21. Clearly they include the rebels of ver. 19 f. whom Jubilees calls *the angels of the Lord* (Jub. iv. 15) and Onkelos *the sons of the mighty* and their children (?) *the giants.*

Chapter IV.—Ver. 1. *Christ having died to flesh, arm yourselves with the same thought that* (or *because*) *he that died hath ceased to sins.*—**παθόντος σαρκί.** Peter goes back to the starting point of iii. 18 in order to emphasise the import of the first step taken by Christ and His followers, apart now from the consequences. The new life implies death to the old.—**τὴν αὐτὴν ἔννοιαν.** **ἐ.** only occurs once elsewhere in N.T., Heb. iv. 12, **τῶν ἐνθυμήσεων καὶ ἐννοιῶν καρδίας**, but is common in LXX of Proverbs; compare (*e.g.*) Prov. ii. 11, **ἔννοια ὁσία** (תבונה, *discernment*) *shall keep thee.* Here it is the noun-equivalent of **φρονεῖτε ὃ καὶ ἐν Χριστῷ** (Phil. ii. 1). Christ's *thought* (*or purpose*) which He had in dying is shared by the Christian: and it is defined by **ὅτι, κ.τ.λ.**—**ὁπλίσασθε**, *sc.* for the fight with sin and sinners whom you have deserted.—**ὅτι . . . ἁμαρτίαις.** This axiom is better taken as explaining *the same thought* than as motive for **ὁπλ.** St. Paul states it in other words, **ὁ γὰρ ἀποθανὼν δεδικαίωται ἀπὸ τῆς ἁμαρτίας**; compare the death-bed confession of the Jew, "O may my death be an atonement for all the sins . . . of which I have been guilty against thee". One dead—literally or spiritually—hath rest in respect of sins assumed or committed; so Heb. ix. 28 insists that after His death Christ is **χωρὶς ἁμαρτίας.** **πέπαυται** echoes **παυσάτω** of iii. 10. In the Greek Bible the perfect passive occurs only once (Exod. ix. 34) outside Isa. i.-xxxix., where it is used three times to render שבת (*cf.* **σαββατισμός**, Heb. iv. 9). The dative **ἁμ.** is analogous to that following **ζῆν ἀποθανεῖν** (**παθεῖν**); the *v.l.* **ἁμαρτίας** is due to the common construction of **παυ.**

Ver. 2. Christians who were baptised into Christ's death and resurrection (Rom. vi. 2-11) are not taken *out of the world* at once (John xvii. 15); they have to live in the flesh but not to the flesh, because *they have been born not of the will of the flesh nor of man but of God* (John i. 13). Their duty is to their new Father.—**εἰς τό . . .** gives the result of **ὅτι κ.τ.λ.** which must be achieved by, and is therefore also the object of, the required ornament.

Ver. 3. The use of the rare **ἀρκετός** indicates the saying which St. Peter here

ἐθνῶν κατειργάσθαι · πεπορευμένους ἐν ἀσελγείαις ἐπίθυμι
αις οἰνοφλυγίαις κώ μοις πότοις καὶ ἀθε μίτοις εἰδωλολατρεί
αις ἐν ᾧ ξενίζονται μὴ συντρεχόντων ὑμῶν εἰς τὴν αὐτὴν 4
τῆς ἀσωτίας ἀνάχυσι̅ βλασφημοῦνταις οἳ ἀποδώσουσι λόγον 5

applies, *sufficient unto the day* [that is past] *its evil*. Compare Ezek. xliv. 6, **ἱκανούσθω ὑμῖν ἀπὸ πασῶν τῶν ἀνομιῶν ὑμῶν.** The detailed description of *the evil* follows the traditional redaction of the simple picture of absorption in the ordinary concerns of life which Jesus is content to repeat (Matt. xxiv. 37, etc.). Eating, drinking, marrying were interpreted in the worst sense to account for the visitation and become gluttony, drunkenness and all conceivable perversions of marriage; see Sap. xiv. 21-27, followed by Rom. i. 29, etc.—**τὸ . . . πεπορευμένους**, from 2 Kings xvii. 8, **ἐπορεύθησαν τοῖς δικαιώμασιν τῶν ἐθνῶν.** The construction is broken (for the will . . . *to have been accomplished . . . for you walking*) unless **κατ.** be taken as if middle to **πεπορ.** as subject.—**ἀσελγείαις**, *acts of licentiousness* (as in Polybius); so Sap. xiv. 26. Earlier of wanton violence arising out of drunkenness (Demosthenes).—**οἰνοφλυγίαις**, *wine-bibbings*, Deut. xxi. 20, **οἰνοφλυγεῖ** = סבא. Noun occurs in Philo coupled with **ἀπλήρωτοι ἐπίθυμίαι.**—**κώμοις**, *revellings* associated with *alien rites*, Sap. xiv. 26. For **πότοις** *cf.* **ποτήριον δαιμόνων**, 1 Cor. x. 14 ff.—**ἀθεμίτοις εἰδωλολατρίαις**, a Jew's description of current Pagan cults, which were often *illicit* according to Roman law. For **ἀ.** *cf.* Acts x. 28, *it is unlawful for a Jew to associate with a foreigner*, and 2 Macc. vi. 5, vii. 1 (of swine flesh).

Ver. 4. **ἐν ᾧ**, *whereat, i.e.* (i.) at your change of life (2 f.) explained below by **μὴ συντρεχ.** . . . or (ii.) *on which ground*, because you lived as they did.—**ξενίζονται**, *are surprised*, as in ver. 12, where this use of **ξ.** (elsewhere in N.T. *entertain*, except Acts xvii. 20, **ξενίζοντα**) is explained by **ὡς ξένου . .. συμβαίνοντος.** Polybius has it in the same sense followed by dative, acc., **διά** with acc. and **ἐπί** with dative. So in Josephus Adam was *surprised* (**ξενιζόμενον**) that the animals had mates and he none, Ant., i. 1, 2) and the making of garments *surprised* God (*ib.* 4).—**συντρεχόντων**, from Ps. l. 18, LXX, *if thou sawest a thief*, **συνέτρεχες αὐτῷ**, *and with adulterers thou didst set thy portion*; where תרץ *consent* has been rendered as if from רוץ *run*. It thus corresponds to St. Paul's **συνευδοκεῖν** (Rom. i. 32).—**ἀσωτίας**, *profligacy*. According to Aristotle **ἀ.** is the excess of liberality, but is applied in complex sense to **τοὺς ἀκρατεῖς καὶ εἰς ἀκολασίαν δαπανηρούς.** Prodigality is in fact a destruction of oneself as well as one's property (*Eth. Nic.*, iv. 13).—**ἀσελγείαις . . . πότοις.** Violence and lust are classed with drunkenness, which breeds and fosters them. **ἀ.** is wanton violence as well as licentiousness. So the classic Christian example of the word is exactly justified; see Luke xv. 13, the Prodigal Son *squandered his substance, living* **ἀσώτως.**—**ἀνάχυσιν**, *excess, overflow*, properly of water (Philo ii. 508 f., description of evolution of air from fire, water from air, land from water). In Strabo (iii. 1, 4, etc.) = estuary. St. Peter is still thinking of the narrative of the Deluge, which was the fit punishment of an inundation of prodigality.—**βλασφημοῦντες**, put last for emphasis and to pave the way for ver. 5 in accordance with the saying, *for every idle word* (*cf.* Rom. iii. 8). The *abuse* is directed against the apostate heathens and implies blasphemy in its technical sense as opposed to the *giving glory to God* (ii. 12).

Ver. 5. **ἀποδώσουσιν λόγον**, *will render account* — if of their blasphemy, *cf.* Matt. xii. 36, if of their **ἀσωτία** (see note) *cf.* the steward of Luke xvi. 2.—**τῷ ἑτοίμως κρίνοντι**, *i.e.*, to Christ rather than to God (as i. 17). The Christians took over the Jewish doctrine that every man must give an account of his life (Rom. xiv. 10). As already Enoch (lxix. 27 = John v. 22, 27) taught that this judgment was delegated to Messiah. So St. Peter said at Caesarea *this is he that hath been appointed by God judge of living and dead* (Acts x. 43). Compare Matt. xxv. 31 ff. for a more primitive and pictorial statement. The use of **ἑτοίμως** probably represents עתיד (see i. 5) *i.e.*, *the future judge*; Greek readers would understand *the imminent judge* (*cf.* use of **ἑτοίμως** = *ready, sure to come*, Homer, *Il.*, xviii. 96, etc.). The *v.l.*

6 τῷ ἑτοίμως κρείνοντι[1] ζῶντας καὶ νεκροὺς εἰς τοῦτο γὰρ
καὶ νε κροῖς εὐηγγελίσθη ἵ να κριθῶσι μὲν κατὰ ἀνθρώ-
7 πους σαρκὶ ζῶ σι δὲ κατὰ Θ͞ν πνεύματι. πάντων δὲ τὸ τέλος
ἤγγικεν· σωφρονήσα τε οὖν καὶ νήψατε εἰς προσευχάς·
8 πρὸ πάντω͞ τὴν εἰς ἑαυτοὺς ἀγάπη͞ ἐκτενῆ ἔχοντες ὅτι
9 ἀγάπη καλύπτει πλῆ θος ἁμαρτιῶν· φιλόξε νοι εἰς ἀλλή-

[1] Codex Sinaiticus with the bulk of the manuscripts has **ἔχοντι κρῖναι** for **κρίνοντι.**

ἑ. ἔχοντι κρῖναι softens the rugged original.

Ver. 6. The judgment is imminent because all necessary preliminaries have been accomplished. There is no ground for the objection "perhaps the culprits have not heard the Gospel". As regards the living, there is a brotherhood in the world witnessing for Christ in their lives and the missionaries have done their part. As regards the dead Christ descended into Hades to preach there and so was followed by His Apostles. And the object of this was that though the dead have been judged as all men are in respect of the flesh they might yet live as God lives in respect of the spirit.—**εἰς τοῦτο**, with a view to the final judgment or = **ἵνα, κ.τ.λ.**.—**νεκροῖς**, *to dead men* generally, but probably as distinct from the rebel spirits who were presumably immortal and could only be imprisoned. Oecumenius rightly condemns the view, which adds *in trespasses and sins* or takes *dead* in a figurative sense, despite the authority of *e.g.*, Augustine (*Ep.*, 164, §§ 1-18).—**εὐηγγελίσθη**, the Gospel was preached, the impersonal passive leaves the way open for the development of this belief according to which not Christ only but also the Apostles preached to the dead. Hermas, *Sim.*, ix. 165-167; *Cl. Al. Strom.*, vi. 645 f. So was provision made for those who died between the descent of Christ and the evangelisation of their own countries.—**ἵνα, κ. τ. λ.**, *that though they had been judged in respect of flesh as men are judged they might live in respect of spirit as God lives.* The parallel between the dead and Christ is exact (see iii. 20). Death is the judgment or sentence passed on all men (Ecclus. xiv. 17 = Gen. ii. 17, iii. 19). Even Christians, who have died spiritually and ethically (Rom. viii. 10), can only hope wistfully to escape it (2 Cor. v. 2 ff.). But it is preliminary to the Last Judgment (Heb. ix. 27), at which believers, who are quickened spiritually, cannot be condemned to the second death (Apoc. xx. 6).

Ver. 7. But the end of all things and men has drawn nigh; Christians also must be ready, *watch and pray*, as Jesus taught in the parable of Mark xiii. 34-37 (*cf.* xiv. 38).—**σωφρονήσατε** parallels **ἀσελγ. ἐπιθυμίαις** (ver. 3) *cf.* 4 Macc. i. 31, *temperance is restraint of lust.* In Rom. xii. 3 St. Paul plays on the meaning of the component parts of **σω-φρονεῖν**, *cf.* **εἰς σωτηρίαν ψυχῶν** above.—**νήψατε**, corresponds to **οἰνοφλυγίαις κώμοις πότοις** (ver. 3); *cf.* i. 13, v. 8. St. Paul also depends on parable of Luke xii. 42-46 in 1 Thess. v. 6 ff.—**εἰς προσευχάς**, the paramount duty of Christians is prayer especially for the coming of the Lord (Apoc. xxii. 20; Luke xi. 2; *cf.* iii. 7).

Ver. 8. **πρὸ πάντων**, St. Peter emphasises the pre-eminent importance of love of man as much as St. John; *cf.* i. 22.—**ἑαυτούς** put for **ἀλλήλους** in accordance with the saying *thou shalt love thy neighbour as thyself* as much as with the contemporary practice.—**ὅτι . . . ἁμαρτιῶν**, quotation of Prov. x. 12, *love hides all transgressions* which was adduced by Jesus (Luke vii. 47). The plain sense of the aphorism has been evaded by the LXX (**πάντας τοὺς μὴ φιλονεικοῦντας καλύπτει φιλία**) and Syriac translators substitutes *shame* for *love.* The currency of the true version is attested by Jas. v. 20, he that converted a sinner . . . **καλύψει πλῆθος ἁμαρτιῶν.**

Ver. 9. Hospitality is the practical proof of this *love*; its practice was necessary to the cohesion of the scattered brotherhood as to the welfare of those whose duties called them to travel. The inns were little better than brothels and Christians were commonly poor. Chrysostom cites the examples of Abraham and Lot (*cf.* Heb. xiii. 2). The united advocacy of this virtue was successful—so much so that the Didache has to provide against abuses such as Lucian depicts in the biography of Peregrinus "a Christian traveller shall not remain more than two or three days . . . if he wishes to settle . . . is unskilled and

λους ἄνευ γογγυσμοῦ· ἕκαστος καθὼς ἔλαβεν χάρισμα 10
εἰς ἑαυτοὺς αὐτὸ δια κονοῦντες ὡς καλοὶ οἰκονόμοι ποικίλης
χάριτος Θῦ· εἴ τις λαλεῖ ὡς λόγια Θῦ· εἴ τις διακο 11
νεῖ ὡς ἐξ ἴσχυος ἧς χο ρηγεῖ ὁ Θς̅· ἵνα ἐν πᾶσιν δοξάζηται
ὁ Θς̅ διὰ Ιῦ Χῦ ᾧ ἐστιν ἡ δόξα καὶ τὸ κράτος εἰς τοὺς αἰ
ῶνας τῶν αἰώνων ἀμήν. ἀγαπητοί, μὴ ξενίζεσθε τῇ ἐν 12
ὑμῖ̄ πυρώσει πρὸς πειρα σμὸν ὑμῖν τεινομέ νῃ ὡς ξενοῦ

will not work he is a **Χριστέμπορος**, makes his Christian profession his merchandise."—**ἀλλήλους**, used despite **ἑαυτούς** above and below, perhaps because the recipients of hospitality belong necessarily to other Churches.—**ἄνευ γογγυσμοῦ**, St. Peter guards against the imperfection of even Christian human nature. Ecclus. xxix. 25-28 describes how a stranger who outstays his welcome is first set to menial tasks and then driven out.

Vv. 10 f. supplement the foregoing directions for the inner life of the Church and rest partly on Rom. xii. 6 (with simpler classification of *gifts*), partly on the conception of disciples as *stewards* (Luke xii. 42) serving out rations in God's house.—**διακονοῦντες**, in the widest sense (as **διακονία** in Acts vi. 1, 4; 1 Cor. xii. 5) in accordance with the saying, *the Son of Man came . . . to minister* (Mark x. 45), which is interpreted here, as part of the pattern, by the addition of an object (only here and i. 12); *cf.* 2 Cor. viii. 19, **τῇ χάριτι . . . τῇ διακονουμένῃ ὑφ' ἡμῶν**.—**οἰκονόμοι**. The title is applied to all and not only to the governors as by St. Paul (1 Cor. iv. 1; Tit. i. 7); compare the question of St. Peter which precedes the source (Luke xii. 41 f.).

Ver. 11 follows the primitive division of ministry into that of the word and that of tables (Acts vi. 2-4); compare *prophecy* and ministry (in narrower sense like **διακονεῖ** here) of Rom. xii. 6.—**λαλεῖ** covers all the speaking described in 1 Cor. xii. 8, 10, *to one by means of the spirit hath been given a word of wisdom*, etc. . . . xiv. 6, 26.—**ὡς λόγια θεοῦ** (perhaps echoes **κατὰ τὴν ἀναλογίαν** of Rom. xii. 6) *as being God's oracles* or *as speaking God's oracles*. The Seer is the model for the Christian preacher: Num. xxiv. 4, **φησὶν ἀκούων λόγια θεοῦ**. His message is the particular grace of God which he has to administer like the prophets and evangelists, i. 10-12.—**διακονεῖ** includes all forms of the ministration of God's gifts other than those of speech—primarily almsgiving, hospitality and the like.—**ἵνα, κ. τ. λ.** A liturgical formula such as this is necessarily capable of many special meanings.—**ἐν πᾶσιν** may refer particularly to the gifts or their possessors—hardly to the Gentiles as Oec. suggests (Matt. v. 16)—but so to limit it would be a gratuitous injustice to the author. The saying **ἐν τούτῳ ἐδοξάσθη ὁ πατήρ μου ἵνα καρπὸν πολὺν φέρητε καὶ γενήσεσθε ἐμοὶ μαθηταί** is sufficient to justify this appendix to the exhortation *love one another in deed*—**διὰ Ἰησοῦ Χριστοῦ**, *through Jesus Christ* through whom the spirit descended on each of you, Acts ii. 33, through whom you offer a sacrifice of praise (Heb. xiii. 15); *cf.* **δοξαζέτω τὸν θεὸν ἐν ὀνόματι τούτῳ**.—**ᾧ . . .** The insertion of **ἐστιν** changes the doxology to a statement of fact and thus supports the interpretation of **ᾧ** as referring of the immediate antecedent *Jesus Christ*. Already He possesses the glory and the victory; realising this His followers endure joyfully their present suffering and defeat.

Ver. 12. **ἀγαπητοί** marks the beginning of the third division of the Epistle in which Peter having cleared the ground faces at last the pressing problem.—**ξενίζεσθε**, *be surprised*, as in ver. 4.—**τῇ ἐν ὑμῖν πυρώσει**, *the ordeal which is in your midst* or rather *in your hearts*.—**ἐν ὑμῖν**, *cf.* **τὸ ἐν ὑμῖν ποίμνιον** (v. 1) but the test is internal—in what frame of mind will they meet it? Will they regard it as a strange thing or as a share in Christ's sufferings, part of the pattern?—**πυρώσει**. This conception of suffering as a trial not vindictive is stated in Jud. viii. 25, 27, **ἐκείνους ἐπύρωσεν εἰς ἐτασμὸν καρδίας αὐτῶν**; compare Zach. xiii. 19, **πυρώσω αὐτοὺς ὡς πυροῦται ἀργύριον**, Prov. xxvii. 21, **χρυσῷ πύρωσις** parallels *but a man is tried* . . . **π.** also occurs in the sense of *blasting*, Amos iv. 9; Apoc. xviii. 9, 18.

13 ὑμῖν συμβαίνοντος· ἀλλὰ καθὸ κοινωνεῖτε τοῖς τοῦ Χῦ
παθήμασιν χαίρετε ἵνα καὶ ἐν τῇ ἀποκαλύψει τῆς δόξης
14 αὐτοῦ χαρῆτε ἀγαλλιώμενοι· εἰ ὀνειδίζεσθε ἐν ὀνόματι
Χῦ μακάριοι ὅτι τὸ τῆς δόξης[1] καὶ τὸ τοῦ Θῦ πνεῦμα ἐφ᾽ ὑμᾶς
15 ἀναπαύεται·[2] μὴ γάρ τις ὑμῶν πασχέτω ὡς φονεὺς ἢ κλέπτης

[1] After **δόξης** the first hand of Codex Sinaiticus with the consent of many manuscripts adds **καὶ τῆς δυνάμεως αὐτοῦ.**

[2] At the end of the verse the secondary uncials add **κατὰ μὲν αὐτοὺς βλασφημεῖται κατὰ δὲ ὑμᾶς δοξάζεται.**

Ver. 13. **καθό**, *so far as, i.e.*, so far as your suffering is undeserved and for Christ's name.—**κοινωνεῖτε . . . παθήμασιν**, *ye share the sufferings of the Messiah.* The dative after **κ.** usually denotes the partner; here the thing shared as in Rom. xv. 27; 1 Tim. v. 22; 2 John 11; and in LXX; Sap. vi. 23; 3 Macc. iv. 11. This idea is expressed even more strongly by St. Paul **ἀνταναπληρῶ τὰ ὑστερήματα τῶν θλίψεων τοῦ Χριστοῦ** (Col. i. 24). It is derived from such sayings as *the disciple is as his Master* (Matt. x. 24 f.)—*the sons of Zebedee must drink his cup, be baptised with his baptism* (Mark x. 38 f.). To suffer in Christ's name is to suffer as representing Christ and so to share His sufferings.—**ἵνα κ. τ. λ.,** from Matt. v. 12, **χαίρετε καὶ ἀγαλλιᾶσθε.** But St. Peter postpones the exultation. St. James (v. 10) follows Jesus in appealing to the pattern of the prophets. **ἀποκαλύψει**, the final *revelation* represents an original wordplay גלה on the quoted **ἀγαλλιώμενοι** = גיל.

Ver. 14. The Beautitude, **μακάριοι . . . ὅταν ὀνειδίσωσιν ὑμᾶς ἕνεκεν ἐμοῦ** is supported by prophecy which referred originally to the root of Jesse. Both are partially paraphrased for sake of clearness. For **ἐν ὀνόματι**; *cf.* Mark ix. 41, **ἐν ὀνόματι ὅτι Χριστοῦ ἐστε.** For the reproach *cf.* Heb. xiii. 13, *let us come out to him bearing His reproach*, with Ps. lxxxix., *so remember Lord the reproaches* (**ὀνειδισμῶν** LXX) *of thy servants.*—**ὅτι . . . ἀναπαύεται**, quoted from a current Targum of Isa. xi. 1 f., *a branch* (נצר: LXX, **ἄνθος**: Targ. *Messiah*) *from his roots shall grow and there shall rest upon him the spirit of Jehovah.* An elaborate description of this *spirit* follows, which Peter summarises by **τὸ τῆς δόξης.** The Glory is a name of God in the Targums (so John xii. 41 = Isa. vi. 5; Onkelos has יקרא די׳ for י׳) and its use here is probably due to the juxtaposition of Isa. xi. 10, *his rest shall be glorious.* It is not impossible that **καὶ τοῦ θεοῦ** is an insertion by first or later scribes for the benefit of Greek readers.

Ver. 15. **γάρ.** I assume that you suffer in Christ's name as representing Him and bearing only the reproach which attaches to it *per se.* The crimes of which slanderers had accused Christians are given in the order of probability and are selected as belonging to the pattern. Christ Himself was implicitly accused thereof by His persecutors and acquitted of each by independent witnesses, as the Gospels are at pains to show. He suffered the fate from which the *murderer* was preserved (Acts iii. 14) by the petition of the Jews; shared it with *thieves* or brigands, being delivered up to the secular arm as a *malefactor* (John xviii. 30). Such slanders the Christian must rebut for the credit of his Lord; that he must not be guilty of such crimes goes without saying.—**ἀλλοτριεπίσκοπος** is distinguished from the preceding accusations by the insertion of **ὡς**; it is also an addition to the *pattern* of Christ, unless stress be laid on the sneer, *He saved others.* The word was apparently coined to express the idea of the itinerant philosopher of whatever sect current among the unphilosophical. Epictetus defends the true Cynic against this very calumny; he is a messenger sent from Zeus to men to show them concerning good and evil (Arrian, iii. 22, 23) . . . a spy of what is helpful and harmful to men . . . he approaches all men, cares for all (*ib.* 81) . . . neither meddler—**περίεργος**—nor busybody is such an one; for he is not busy about alien things—**τὰ ἀλλότρια πολυπραγμονεῖ**—when he inspects the actions and relations of mankind—**ὅταν τὰ ἀνθρώπινα ἐπισκοπῇ** (*ib.* 97). This zeal for the welfare of others was certainly the most obvious charge to bring against Christians, who indeed were not always content to

ἢ κακοποιὸς ἢ ὡς ἀλ λοτριεπίσκοπος· εἰ δὲ ὡς Χρειστιανὸς 16
μὴ αἰσχυνέσθω δοξαζέ τω δὲ τὸν Θν̅ ἐν τῷ ὀνό ματι[1] τούτῳ
ὅτι ὁ και ρὸς τοῦ ἄρξασθαι τὸ κρίμα ἀπὸ τοῦ οἴκου τοῦ 17
Θυ̅ εἰ δὲ πρῶτον ἀ πὸ ἡμῶν τί τὸ τέλος τῶν ἀπειθούντων
τῷ τοῦ Θυ̅ εὐαγγελίῳ· καὶ εἰ ὁ δίκαιος μόλις σώζεται ὁ δὲ 18
ἀσεβὴς καὶ ἁμαρτωλὸς ποῦ φανεῖται· ὥστε καὶ οἱ πάσ- 19
χοντες κατὰ τὸ θέλημα τοῦ Θυ̅ πιστῷ κτιστῇ παρατιθέσθω
σαν τὰς ψυχὰς ἐν ἀ γαθοποιΐᾳ. πρεσβυ τέρους οὖν ἐν ὑμῖν V. 1

[1] The secondary uncials have **μέρει** for **ὀνόματι.**

testify *by good behaviour without word.* St. Paul heard of some at Thessalonica, **μηδὲν ἐργαζομένους ἀλλὰ περιεργαζομένους** (2 Thess. iii. 11). Women generally if unattached were prone to be not merely idle but *meddlers speaking what they should not* (1 Tim. v. 13). So St. Peter (*cf.* 1 Cor. x. 27) has emphasised the duty of all Christians—even of the wives of heathen husbands—to preach Christianity only by example and now deprecates their acquiescence in what some might reckon a title of honour. The fate of Socrates is the classical example of the suffering of such; and later one philosopher was scourged and another beheaded for denunciation of the alliance of Titus with Berenice (*Dio Cassius*, lxvi. 15). Punishment of this offence would depend on the power of the other man concerned who, if not in authority, would naturally utilise mob-law like Demetrius (Acts xix.).

Ver. 16. **εἰ δὲ ὡς χριστιανός,** *if one suffers as a follower of Christ, in the name of Christ* (14). See on Acts ix. 26 and Introduction.—**μὴ αἰσχυνέσθω** echoes the saying, *Whosoever shall be ashamed of me and my words of him also the Son of Man shall be ashamed when He cometh in the glory;* so St. Paul says *I suffer thus but am not ashamed* (2 Tim. i. 12; *cf.* 8).—**δοξαζέτω τὸν θεόν,** by martyrdom if necessary, for this sense the phrase has acquired already in John xxi. 19.—**ἐν τῷ ὀνόματι τούτῳ** = Mark ix. 41.

Ver. 17. That Judgment begins at the House of God is a deduction from the vision of Ezek. ix. (*cf.* vii. 4, *the* **καιρός** *has come*); the slaughter of Israelites who are not marked with Tau, is ordained by the Glory of the God of Israel; the Lord said, **ἀπὸ τῶν ἁγίων μου ἄρξασθε** and the men began at (**ἀπό**) the elders who were within in the house. The new Israel has precedence like the old even in condemnation; *cf.* Rom. ii. 8 f., **τοῖς . . . ἀπειθοῦσι τῇ ἀληθείᾳ . . . ὀργὴ ἐπὶ . . . ψυχὴν . . . Ἰουδαίου τε πρῶτον.—τῷ . . . εὐαγγελίῳ**, *cf.* Mark i. 14. The Gospel or Word, which God *spake in a Son,* succeeds to the law as the expression of the will against which all but the remnant (Ez. *l.c.*) rebel.

Ver. 18. To the summary excerpt from Ezekiel Peter appends the Septuagint version of Prov. xi. 31, which is followed by the Syriac and partially by the Targum: The original—according to the Masoretic text—is *Behold* or *if the righteous will be punished on the earth: how much more the wicked and the sinner.* The Greek, which probably represents a different Hebrew text, is more apt to his purpose and to the teaching of Jesus, which provoked the question, *Who then can be saved* (Mark x. 24-26).

Ver. 19. *So let even those who suffer in accordance with the will of God with a faithful Creator deposit their souls in well-doing.* The Christian must still follow the pattern. It is God's will that he share Christ's sufferings in whatever degree; let him in this also copy Christ, who said, *Father into thy hands I commit my spirit* (Luke xxiii. 46 = Ps. xxxi. 6) and bade His disciples lose their souls that they might find them unto life eternal. With this teaching Peter combines that of the Psalmist which is assumed by Jesus (Matt. vi. 25 ff.), *Jehovah knows His creature.* He the God of faithfulness (אל אמת, Ps. *l.c.*) is the faithful Creator to whom the soul He gave and redeemed (Ps. *l.c.*) may confidently return.

Chapter V.—Ver. 1. **οὖν**, *therefore*—since your suffering is according to God's will and calls only for the normal self-devotion, which Christ required of His disciples—go on with the duties of the station of life in which you are called.—**πρεσβυτέρους**, not merely *older men* as contrasted with *younger* (ver. 5),

παρακαλῶ ὁ συμπρε σβύτερος καὶ μάρτυς τῶν τοῦ Χ͞υ
παθημά των ὁ καὶ τῆς μελλού σης ἀποκαλύπτεσθαι
2 δόξης κοινωνὸς ποι μάνατε τὸ ἐν ὑμῖν ποίμνιον τοῦ Θ͞υ μὴ
ἀναγκαστῶς ἀλλὰ ἑ κουσίως μὴ δὲ αἰσχρο κερδῶς ἀλλὰ

but *elders*, such as had been appointed by Paul and Barnabas in the Churches of Southern Asia (Acts xiv. 23). The collective **τῶν κλήρων** (ver. 3) and the exhortation, *shepherd the flock* (ver. 2) prove that they are the official heads of the communities addressed. Similarly St. Paul bade *the elders of the Church* (Acts xx. 17) at Ephesus *take heed to themselves and to all the flock in which the Holy Spirit appointed you overseers.* The use of the term in direct address here carries with it a suggestion of the natural meaning of the word and perhaps also of the early technical sense, one of the first generation of Christians Both Jews and Gentiles were familiar with the title which was naturally conferred upon those who were qualified in point of years; the youthful Timothy was a marked exception to the general rule (1 Tim. iv. 12).—**ἐν ὑμῖν.** Peter does not address them as mere officials, *your elders*, but prefers a vaguer form of expression, *elders who are among you; cf.* **τὸ ἐν ὑμῖν ποίμνιον**, which also evades any impairing of the principle, *ye are Christ's.*—**ὁ συμπρεσβύτερος . . . κοινωνός.** This self-designation justifies Peter's right to exhort them. He is *elder* like them, in all senses of the word. If their sufferings occupy their mind, he was witness of the sufferings of Christ; of his own, if any, he does not speak. He has invited them to dwell rather on the thought of the future glory and this he is confident of sharing.—**μάρτυς . . . παθημάτων.** Such experience was the essential qualification of an Apostle in the strict sense; only those who were companions *of the Twelve in all the time from John's baptism to the Assumption* or at least *witnesses of the Resurrection* (Acts i. 22) were eligible; as Jesus said, the Paraclete shall testify and do you testify because ye are with Me from the beginning (John xv. 27). That he speaks of the sufferings and not of the resurrection which made the sufferer Messiah, is due partly to the circumstances of his readers, partly to his own experience. For him these sufferings had once overshadowed the glory; he could sympathise with those oppressed by persecution and reproach, who understood now, as little as he then, that it was all part of the sufferings of the Messiah. He had witnessed but at the last test refused to share them.—**ὁ . . . κοινωνός.** Peter will share the future glory which Christ already enjoys for it was said to him, *Thou shalt follow afterward* (John xiii. 36). St. Paul has the same idea in a gnomic form, **εἴπερ συνπάσχομεν ἵνα καὶ συνδοξασθῶμεν** (Rom. viii. 17; *cf.* 2 Cor. iv. 10) which presupposes familiarity with the teaching of the risen Jesus *that the Christ must suffer and so enter into His glory*, Luke xxiv. 46; *cf.* i. 5, 13, iv. 13.

Ver. 2. The command laid upon St. Peter, *shepherd my sheep* (John xxi. 19) became the charge delivered to succeeding elders (*v.* Acts xx. 28) and a familiar description of the Christian pastor (*e.g.*, 1 Cor. ix. 7) who must copy the good Shepherd who obeyed where His predecessors fell short (Ez. xxxiv.).—**τὸ ἐν ὑμῖν ποίμνιον τοῦ θεοῦ.** Christendom is God's flock among you—not yours but God's.—**ἀναγκαστῶς.** *As a matter of constraint* contrasted with **ἑκουσίως**, *willingly*—not as pressed men but as volunteers. In times of persecution lukewarm elders might well regret their prominence; hence the need for the aphorism *if any aspire to oversight he desireth a noble work* (1 Tim. iii. 1). So of gifts of money St. Paul requires that they be **μὴ ἐξ ἀνάγκης** (2 Cor. ix. 7). It is possible that St. Paul's words, **ἀνάγκη μοι ἐπικεῖται** (1 Cor. ix. 16) had been wrested.—**αἰσχροκερδῶς.** If the work be voluntarily undertaken, the worker has a reward according to St. Paul (1 Cor. ix. 16 f.). Base gainers are those who wish to make gain whence they ought not (Aristotle, *Nic. Eth.*, v. 1, 43).—**προθύμως.** The adverb occurs in 2 Chron. xxix. 34, LXX, where the Levites eagerly purified themselves; Heb. the Levites upright of heart to . . . The verb **προθυμεῖν** is used in Chron. to render נדב *offer freewill offerings.*

Ver 3. Application of the saying, *the reputed rulers of the nations lord it* (**κατακυριεύουσιν**) *over them . . . not so among you; but whosoever would be great among you he shall be your servant . . . for the Son of Man came . . . to serve* (Mark x. 42 f.).—**τῶν κλήρων**, the lots, *i.e.*, the portions of the new Israel who fall to

προθύ μως[1] καὶ φανερωθέν τος τοῦ ἀρχιποίμενος κομιεῖσθε 4
τὸν ἀμαρᾱ τινον τῆς δόξης στέ φανον· ὁμοίως νεώ τεροι 5
ὑποτάγητε πρε σβυτέροις· πάντες δὲ ἀλλήλοις τὴν τάπει
νοφροσύνην ἐγκομ βώσασθε[2] ὅτι Θς̄ ὑπε ρηφάνοις ἀντι-
τάσ σεται ταπεινοῖς δὲ δίδωσιν χάριν· ταπει νώθητε 6

[1] Codex Vaticanus is alone in omitting verse 3, **μηδ' ὡς κατακυριεύοντες τῶν κλήρων ἀλλὰ τύποι γινόμενοι τοῦ ποιμνίου.**

[2] For the unfamiliar **ἐγκομβώσασθε** two cursives read **ἐγκολπίσασθε,** whence *insinuate* of the Vulgate.

your care as Israel fell to that of Jehovah (Deut. ix. 29, **οὗτοι λαός σου καὶ κλῆρός σου**). The meaning is determined by the corresponding **τοῦ ποιμνίου** and supported by the use of **προσεκληρώθησαν** *were made an additional portion* in Acts xvii. 4. So it is said of God's servant that He **κληρονομήσει πολλούς** (Isa. liii. 12). The Vulgate has *dominantes in cleris*, and Oecumenius following the usage of his time explains the phrase likewise as equivalent to **τὸ ἱερὸν σύστημα**, *i.e.*, the inferior clergy.—**τύποι γεινόμενοι**, *i.e.*, as servants according to Mark *l.c.*; *cf.* 1 Thess. i. 7; 1 Tim. iv. 12.

Ver. 4. **φανερωθέντος τοῦ ἀρχιποίμενος**, *at the manifestation of the chief Shepherd*, *i.e.*, Christ. **ἀρχιποίμην** is the equivalent of **ὁ ποίμην ὁ μέγας** of Heb. xiii. 20, being formed on the analogy of **ἀρχιερεύς** = כהן הגדל; else it occurs only as Symmachus' rendering of נקד (LXX, **νωκηδ**) in 2 Kings iii. 4 and in a papyrus. *Cf.* appeal to Jehovah, **ὁ ποιμαίνων τὸν Ἰσραὴλ . . . ἐμφάνηθι** of Ps. lxxx. 1.—**τὸν . . . στέφανον** = the *crown of life which He promised* (Jas. i. 12). The metaphor is probably derived from the wreath of fading flowers presented to the victor in the games (*cf.* **ἀμαράντινον**); but it may also be due to the conception of the future age as a banquet, at which the guests were crowned with garlands (Sap. ii. 8, **στεψώμεθα ῥόδων κάλυξιν πρὶν ἢ μαρανθῆναι**). See on i. 4.

Ver. 5. **νεώτεροι,** the younger members of each Church were perhaps more or less formally banded together on the model of the **σύνοδοι τῶν νέων**, which are mentioned in inscriptions as existing distinct from the Ephebi in Greek cities, especially in Asia Minor (Ziebarth Die Griechische Vereine, 111-115). Compare the modern Guilds and Associations of Young Men. In 1 Tim. iv. 1, these natural divisions of *elders* and *youngers* are also recognised.—**πάντες δὲ . . .** Elders must serve; youngers submit. May all be lowly-minded towards one another—there is no need to add detailed commands. —**ἐγκομβώσασθε** is explained by Oecumenius as **ἐνειλήσασθε περιβάλεσθε** (wrap yourselves in, put round you), so the command corresponds to **ἐνδύσασθε . . . ταπεινοφροσύνην** of Col. iii. 12. But the choice of this unique word must have some justification in associations which can only be reconstructed by conjecture. The lexicographers (Hesychius, Sindas, etc.) give **κόμβος κόσυμβος** and **ἐγκόμβωμα** as synonyms. Pollux explains **ἐγκομβ.** as the apron worn by slaves to protect their tunic; so Longus, *Pastoralia*, ii. 35 f., in "casting his *apron*, naked he started to run like a fawn". Photius (Epistle 156) takes George Metropolitan of Nicomedia to task for his suggestion that it was a barbarous word: "You ought to have remembered Epicharmus and Apollodorus . . . the former uses it frequently and the latter in the 'Runaway' (a comedy) says **τὴν ἐπωμίαν πτύξασα διπλῆν ἄνωθεν ἀνεκομβωσάμην.**" But the LXX of Isa. iii. 18 has **τοὺς κοσύμβους** = *front-bands* and Symmachus **τὰ ἐγκομβώματα** in ver. 20 for *bands* or *sashes*. Peter is therefore probably indebted again to this passage and says *gird* yourselves with the humility which is the proper ornament of women. If the word be taken in this sense a reference to John xiii. 4 ff., *Taking a napkin He girded Himself*, may be reasonably assumed —**θεὸς . . . χάριν** = Prov. iii. 34, LXX (**θεός** being put for **κύριος,** which to a Christian reader meant Christ); the Hebrew text gives *scoffers he scoffs at but to the humble he shows favour.* The same quotation is employed in similar context by St. James (iv. 6); the devil (see below) is the typical *scoffer.*

Ver. 6. **ταπεινώθητε οὖν** echoes the exhortation and its accompanied

οὖν ὑπὸ τὴ̄ κραταιὰν χεῖρα τοῦ Θῦ ἵνα ὑμᾶς ὑψώσῃ ἐν
7 καιρῷ· πᾶσαν τὴν μέ ριμναν ὑμῶν ἐπιρεί ψαντες ἐπ' αὐτὸν
8 ὅτι αὐτῷ μέλει περὶ ὑμῶ̄ νήψατε γρηγορήσα τε ὁ ἀντίδικος ὑμῶ̄ διάβολος ὡς λέων ὠ ρυόμενος περιπατεῖ
9 ζητῶν καταπιεῖν ᾧ ἀντιστῆτε στερεοὶ τῇ πίστει εἰδότες τὰ
αὐτὰ τῶν παθηματω̄ τῇ ἐν τῷ κόσμῳ ὑμῶ̄ ἀδελφότητι
10 ἐπιτε λεῖσθε· ὁ δὲ Θς̄ πάσης χάριτος ὁ καλέσας ὑ μᾶς

scripture in ver. 5—obey in order that the promise (Luke xiv. 11) may be fulfilled for you, *he that humbleth himself shall be exalted* (*sc.* by God). So too St. James, *subject yourselves therefore to God* (iv. 7).—**τὴν κραταιὰν χεῖρα.** God's *mighty hand* is a common O.T. expression; see Exod. iii. 19, etc. for connexion with deliverance and especially Ez. xx. 33 f., **ἐν χειρὶ κραταιᾷ καὶ . . . ἐν θυμῷ κεχυμένῳ βασιλεύσω ἐφ' ὑμᾶς.**

Ver. 7. **τὴν μέριμναν . . . αὐτόν** comes from Ps. lv. 12, **ἐπίριψον ἐπὶ Κύριον τὴν μέριμνάν σου,** which is the source of part of the Sermon on the Mount (Matt. vi. 25 ff.).—**ὅτι . . . ὑμῶν** substituted for **καὶ αὐτός σε διαθρέψει** of Ps. *l.c.* in accordance with Jesus' amplification and application of the metaphor. God cares for His flock as the hireling shepherd does not (**οὐ μέλει αὐτῷ περὶ τῶν προβάτων,** John x. 13).

Ver. 8. **νήψατε γρηγορήσατε,** *cf.* i. 13, iv. 7. So St. Paul, **γρηγορῶμεν καὶ νήφωμεν . . . ἡμέρας ὄντες νήφωμεν** (1 Thess. v. 6, 8) drawing upon the common source in the Parables of the Householder and Burglar, etc. (Matt. xxiv. 42 ff.) which set forth the sudden coming of the Kingdom.—**ὁ ἀντίδικος ὑμῶν διάβολος,** *your adversary, Satan*—**ἀ.** (properly *adversary in law suit*) is used in the general sense of enemy in LXX. Of the description of Satan, *as a roaring lion* comes from Ps. xxii. 14, **ὡς λέων ὁ ἁρπάζων καὶ ὠρυόμενος**; *walketh* from Job i. 7, where Satan (**ὁ διάβολος** LXX, **Σατάν,** Aq.) **περιελθὼν τὴν γῆν καὶ ἐμπεριπατήσας τὴν ὑπ' οὐρανὸν πάρειμι**; *seeking to devour* identifies him with Hades the lord of death; *cf.* Prov. i. 12, where the wicked say of the righteous man, **καταπίωμεν αὐτὸν ὥσπερ ᾅδης ζῶντα.** The present sufferings of the Christians are his handiwork as much as the sufferings of Jesus (1 Cor. ii. 6, 8) and of Job.

Ver. 9. **ᾧ ἀντίστητε.** St. James adds the same exhortation to his quotation of Prov. The connexion is not obvious but is perhaps due to the traditional exposition of לֵץ = **ὑπερηφάνοις** as referring to the Devil and his children. As God ranges Himself against scoffers, so must Christians resist the Devil who is working with their slanderous tempers. Oecumenius and Cramer's *Catena* both appeal to an extract from Justin's book against Marcion (?) which is preserved in Irenæus and quoted by Eusebius. The main point of the passage is that before Christ came the devil did not dare to blaspheme against God, for the prophecies of his punishment were enigmatic; but Christ proclaimed it plainly and so he lost all hope and goes about eager to drag down all to his own destruction.—**στερεοὶ τῇ πίστει,** *rock like in your faith,* abbreviation of **ἐπιμένετε τῇ πίστει τεθεμελιωμένοι καὶ ἑδραῖοι,** Col. i. 23; *cf.* **τὸ στερέωμα τῆς εἰς Χριστὸν πίστεως,** Col. ii. 5 and Acts xvi. 5, **αἱ . . . ἐκκλησίαι ἐστερεοῦντο τῇ πίστει.** The metaphorical use of **στ.** in a good sense is not common. Peter perhaps thinks of the **στερεὰ πέτρα** (צוּר) of Isa. li. 1 and warns them against his own failing.—**εἰδότες . . . ἐπιτελεῖσθαι.** The rendering (first suggested by Hoffmann) *knowing how to pay* (that you are paying) *the same tax of sufferings as the brotherhood in the world is paying* seems preferable to the common *knowing that the same kinds of sufferings are being accomplished for* (*by*) . . . it assumes the proper idiomatic force of **ἐπιτελεῖσθαι** and accounts for **τὰ αὐτά** (*sc.* **τέλη**) followed by the genitive. Xenophon who is a good authority for Common Greek uses **ἐ.** thus twice:—Mem. iv. 8. 8, "but if I shall live longer perhaps it will be necessary to pay the penalties of old age (**τὰ τοῦ γήρως ἐπιτελεῖσθαι**) and to see and hear worse . . ." *Apol,* 33 nor did he turn effeminate at death but cheerfully welcomed it and paid the penalty (**ἐπετελέσατο**). For the dative with **τὰ αὐτά** *same as, cf.* 1 Cor. xi. 5, **ἓν καὶ τὸ αὐτὸ τῇ ἐξυρημένῃ.**

Ver. 10. Your adversary assails you,

εἰς τὴν αἰώνιον αὐτοῦ δόξαν ἐν τῷ Χῶ ὀλίγον παθόντας αὐ
τὸς καταρτίσει στηρί ξει σθενώσει· αὐτῷ τὸ κράτος εἰς 11
τοὺς αἰ ῶνας ἀμήν. διὰ Ϲιλ βανοῦ ὑμῖν τοῦ πιστοῦ 12
ἀδελφοῦ ὡς λογίζο μαι δι᾽ ὀλίγων ἔγραψα παρακαλῶν καὶ
ἐπι μαρτυρῶν ταύτην εἶναι ἀληθῆ χάριν τοῦ Θῦ εἰς ἣν

but God has called you to His eternal glory; first for a little you must suffer, His grace will supply all your needs. Ver. 9 is practically a parenthesis; **ὁ θεός** stands over against **ὁ ἀντίδικος** (ver. 8) as **δέ** shows.—**ὁ καλέσας**, for the promise of sustenance implied in the calling; *cf.* 1 Thess. v. 23 f.; 1 Cor. i. 8 f.—**ἐν Χριστῷ** goes with **ὁ . . . δόξαν**; God called them in Christ and only as they are in Christ can they enter the glory; *cf.* 2 Cor. v. 17-19, **εἴ τις ἐν Χριστῷ καινὴ κτίσις . . . θεὸς ἦν ἐν Χριστῷ κόσμον καταλλάσσων ἑαυτῷ.**—**ὀλίγον παθόντας**, *after you have suffered for a little while.* The same contrast between temporary affliction and the eternal glory is drawn by St. Paul in 2 Cor. iv. 17, **τὸ παραυτίκα ἐλαφρὸν τῆς θλίψεως . . . αἰώνιον βάρος δόξης κατεργάζεται**, where in addition to the antithesis between eternal glory and temporary suffering the *weight* of glory (play on meanings of root יקר) is opposed to *the lightness* of tribulation.—**αὐτός** has the force of **πιστὸς ὁ καλῶν** (1 Thess. v. 24).—**καταρτίσει**, *shall perfect.* When Simon and Andrew were called to leave their fishing and become fishers of men James and John were themselves also in a boat mending—**καταρτίζοντας**—their nets (Mark i. 16-19). The process was equally necessary in their new fishing and the word was naturally applied to the mending of the Churches or individual Christians who by their good behaviour must catch men (see *e.g.*, 1 Cor. i. 10). Only God can fully achieve this mending of all shortcomings; *cf.* Heb. xiii. 21.—**στηρίξει**, *shall confirm; cf.* 2 Thess. ii. 17, etc.; when the Kingdom of Heaven was stormed the stormers needed confirmation (Acts xviii. 23). This was the peculiar work assigned to St. Peter—*thou having converted confirm*—**στήρισον**—*the brethren* (Luke xxii. 32).—**σθενώσει** is only apparently unique, being equivalent to **ἐνισχύσει** or **δυναμώσει** (Hesychius) *cf.* Col. i. 11, **ἐν πάσῃ δυνάμει δυναμώμενοι κατὰ τὸ κράτος τῆς δόξης αὐτοῦ** and Heb. xi. 34, **ἐδυναμώθησαν ἀπὸ ἀσθενείας** (parallel to **ὀλίγον παθ.** above).

Ver. 11. Liturgical formula, adapted in iv. 11 (**ἐστιν**), which occurs in 1 Tim. vi. 16; John 25; Apoc. i. 6; v. 13.

Vv. 12-14. Postscript in St. Peter's own handwriting, like Gal. vi. 11-18 (**ἴδετε πηλίκοις ὑμῖν γράμμασιν ἔγραψα τῇ ἐμῇ χειρί**); 2 Thess. iii. 17 f. (**ὁ ἀσπασμὸς τῇ ἐμῇ χειρὶ Παύλου**).—**διὰ Σιλουανοῦ**, *by the hand of my scribe S.;* so Ignatius writes **διὰ Βύρρου** to the Philadelphians (xi. 2) and the Smyrnaeans (xii. 1), but wishes to keep him with himself (Eph. ii. 1). That S. was also the bearer of the Epistle is indicated by the recommendation which follows. There does not seem to be any good reason for refusing to identify this S. with the companion of St. Paul and Timothy who wrote with them to the Church of Thessalonica and preached with them at Corinth (2 Cor. i. 19).—**τοῦ πιστοῦ ἀδελφοῦ ὡς λογίζομαι.** One main object of the postscript is to supply S. with a brief commendation. He is presumably the appointed messenger who will supplement the letter with detailed application of its general teaching and information about the affairs of the writer. So St. Paul's Encyclical ends with *that ye may know my circumstances how I fare Tychicus the beloved brother and faithful minister in the Lord shall make known all things to you* (Eph. vi. 21 f.). S. was known probably to some of the Churches as St. Paul's companion: in case he was unknown to any, St. Peter adds his own certificate. For this use of **λογίζομαι** compare 1 Cor. iv. 1, **οὕτως ἡμᾶς λογιζέσθω ἄνθρωπος**; 2 Cor. xi. 5, **λογίζομαι γὰρ μηδὲν ὑστερηκέναι τῶν ὑπερλίαν ἀποστόλων.**—**παρακαλῶν . . . θεοῦ**, motive and subject of the Epistle. St. Peter wrote *exhorting* as he said *I exhort you* (ii. 11, v. 1) and the general content of his exhortation may be given by the subordinate clause which follows: "That you stand in the grace, which I bear witness is truly God's grace". The acquired sense of the verb *comfort* (LXX for נחם) is not directly contemplated. The Epistle is a **λόγος παρακλήσεως** in the sense of **ὁ παρακαλῶν ἐν τῇ παρακλήσει**, Rom. xii. 8.—**ἐπιμαρτυρῶν**, *testifying to . . .* not *. . . in addition.* The verb does not

13 στῆτε· ἀσπάζεται ὑμᾶς ἡ ἐ͞ Βαβυλῶνι συνεκλε κτὴ καὶ
14 Μᾶρκος ὁ υἱός μου· ἀσπάσασθε ἀλλή λους ἐν φιλήματι ἀ
γάπης· εἰρήνη ὑμῖν πᾶσι τοῖς ἐν Χῷ.

occur elsewhere in O.T. (LXX has ἐπιμαρτύρομαι) or N.T.; but Heb. ii. 4 has the compound συνεπιμαρτυροῦντος τοῦ θεοῦ.—**ταύτην . . . θεοῦ**, *that this is true grace of God*, *i.e.*, the grace—in the widest sense of the word which is theirs (i. 10) which God gives to the humble (v. 5). St. Peter was witness of the sufferings of Christ which they now share; he witnesses from his experience that the grace which they possess is truly God's grace, though sufferings are a passing incident of their sojourn nere.—**εἰς ἣν στῆτε**, paraenetic summary of τὴν προσαγωγὴν ἐσχήκαμεν εἰς τὴν χάριν ταύτην ἐν ᾗ ἑστήκαμεν (Rom. v. 2), from which the easier reading ἑστήκατε is derived.—**ἡ . . . συνεκλεκτή**. As *the co-elder* exhorts *the elders* so *the co-elect* (woman) greets the *elect sojourners* (i. 1). The early addition of *Church* represents the natural interpretation of the word, which indeed expresses the latent significance of ἐκ-κλησία, *the called out*, compare St. Paul's use of ἡ ἐκλογή in Rom. xi. 7. In v. 1 ff. Peter addresses bodies rather than individuals and in v. 9 he uses a collective term embracing the whole of Christendom. Accordingly the woman in question is naturally taken to mean the Church—and not any individual (see on Μᾶρκος). Compare the woman of Apoc. xii. 1 f. who is Israel—a fragment which presupposes the mystical interpretation of Canticles (see Cant. vi. 10) and generally the conception of Israel as the bride of Jehovah, which St. Paul appropriated, as complement of the Parables of the Marriage Feast, etc., and applied to the Church in Corinth (2 Cor. xi. 2). So in Hermas' *Visions* the Church appears as a woman. **ἐν Βαβυλῶνι**, *in Rome*, according to the Apocalyptic Code, the use of which was not merely a safeguard but also a password. Compare Apoc. xvii. 5, *on the forehead of the woman was written a mystery*, "*Babylon the great*," xiv. 8, xvi. 19, xviii. 2; Apoc. Baruch, xi. 1. So Papias reports a tradition ("they say") that Peter composed his first Epistle in Rome itself and signifies this by calling the city allegorically Babylon. The point of the allegory is that Rome was becoming the oppressor of the new (and old) Israel, not that it was the centre of the world (Oec.). Literal interpretations (i.) Babylon, (ii.) Babylon in Egypt are modern.—**Μᾶρκος ὁ υἱός μου**. Oecumenius interprets *son* of spiritual relationship and adds noting that some have dared to say that M. was the fleshly son of St. Peter on the strength of the narrative of Acts xii. where P. is represented as rushing to the house of the mother of John M. as if he were returning to his own house and lawful spouse. So Bengel, "Cöelecta sic coniugem suam appellare videtur; *cf.* iii. 7, Erat enim *soror*; 1 Cor. ix. 5, Et congruit mentio *filii* Marci". But granting that Petronilla (?) was missionary and martyr and that Peter may well have had a son—though Christian tradition is silent with regard to him—what have they to do sending greetings to the Churches of Asia Minor in this Encyclical?

Ver. 14. **φιλήματι ἀγάπης**. So St. Paul concludes 1 Thess. with greet all the brethren with an holy kiss (v. 26; *cf.* 1 Cor. xvi. 20; 2 Cor. xiii. 12; Rom. xvi. 16). "Hence," says Origen, "the custom was handed down to the Churches that after prayers (so Justin Apol., i. 65) the brethren should welcome one another with a kiss." Chrysostom (on Rom. *l.c.*) calls it "the peace by which the Apostle expels all disturbing thought and beginning of smallmindedness . . . this kiss softens and levels". But the practice was obviously liable to abuse as Clement of Alexandria shows, "love is judged not in a kiss but in good will. Some do nothing but fill the the Churches with noise of kissing. . . . There is another—an impure—kiss full of venom pretending to holiness" (Paed., iii. 301 P.). Therefore it was regulated (Apost. Const., ii. 57, 12, men kiss men only) and gradually dwindled.—**εἰρήνη**. The simple Hebrew salutation is proper to Peter's autograph postscript and links it with the beginning.—**τοῖς ἐν Χριστῷ**, *cf.* iii. 16, v. 10, and the saying, *Thus have I spoken to you that in me ye might have peace: in the world ye have tribulation but be of good cheer I have conquered the world* (John xvi. 33).

THE SECOND EPISTLE GENERAL

OF

PETER

INTRODUCTION.

CHAPTER I.

AUTHENTICITY AND DATE.

External Evidence.

Fourth Century.—In considering the external evidence for the authenticity of 2 Peter, it will be found most convenient to proceed from the earliest date when its place was fixed in the Canon of the New Testament. This date must be found in the fourth century A.D. Even then, the Epistle was rejected by the Syrian Church, where it was not accepted till early in the sixth century, and only by the Monophysites. The view of the Church of Rome is represented chiefly by JEROME, whose influence was paramount in the formation of the Vulgate Canon. He mentions the doubts raised by the differences in style and character between 1 and 2 Peter (*Quæst. ad Hedib.* Migne, *Pal. Lat.*, xxii. 1002). Jerome, however, is clearly expressing only the objections of scholars. He says: "Scripsit duas epistulas, quae Catholicae nominantur; quarum secunda a plerisque eius esse negatur, propter stili cum priore dissonantiam," where "a plerisque," and the nature of the difficulty expressed, both point to the opinion of the learned class, which he does not himself share. The Epistle is quoted in the last quarter of the fourth century by "AMBROSIASTER"[1] and by AMBROSE OF MILAN (*de Fide*, iii. 12). In an African list, CANON MOMMSENIANUS, belonging to the middle of the fourth century, 2 Peter is found inserted, but with a protest, which indicates rejection in the mind of the scribe. DIDYMUS, who wrote a commentary on 2 Peter, towards the end of the fourth century, uses the following words, which are a fragment come down to us in a Latin translation, "non igitur ignorandum *praesentem epistolam esse falsatam*, quae licet publicetur, non tamen in canone est". How are we to explain the words in italics, in view of the fact that in the *De Trinitate*, a later treatise, Didymus quotes repeatedly from 2 Peter? Chase suggests that the phrase represents the Greek words ὡς νοθεύεται αὕτη ἡ ἐπιστολή, which would

[1] *Cf.* Souter, *Study of Ambrosiaster*, p. 196 f., *Pseudo-Augustine Quaestiones*, etc. (Vindob. 1908), p. 499.

mean that the writer was only stating the opinion of others, more or less contemporary. Zahn (*Gesch. Kan.*, I. i. p. 312) urges that Didymus is here recording a judgment of the second or third century, but there appears to be no conclusive reason to doubt that he is recording a contemporary opinion. EUSEBIUS (*H. E.*, iii. 3) discusses the canonicity of 2 Peter, and makes the following important statement: τὴν δὲ φερομένην αὐτοῦ δευτέραν οὐκ ἐνδιάθηκον μὲν εἶναι παρειλήφαμεν, ὅμως δὲ πολλοῖς χρήσιμος φανεῖσα μετὰ τῶν ἄλλων ἐσπουδάσθη γραφῶν. "The opinion has been handed down to us that the so-called Second Epistle (of Peter) is not canonical, but it has been studied along with the other Scriptures, as it appears profitable to many". In the *H. E.*, iii. 25, 2 Peter is placed among the ἀντιλεγόμενα, although "accepted by the majority" (γνωρίμων δ' οὖν ὅμως τοῖς πολλοῖς). Eusebius had a second class of ἀντιλεγόμενα which he regarded also as spurious (νόθα), and 2 Peter is classed with James, Jude, 2 and 3 John as disputed books which were also γνώριμα. The evidence of Eusebius is specially valuable (1) because he records the opinion that in his day 2 Peter was regarded as uncanonical; (2) because he records a judgment of the past against it; (3) he failed to find any recognition of the book as Petrine in the earlier literature known to him, and his knowledge was wide. There can be little doubt that Eusebius himself rejected the idea of Petrine authorship, but he was also one of those to whom it was a "profitable" book. Constantine entrusted Eusebius with the preparation, for use in the new Capital, of fifty copies of the Scriptures, which contained 2 Peter. This quasi-official standard practically did away with the distinction between 'acknowledged' and 'disputed' books (Chase, *H. D. B.*, iii. 806 a).

Another indication of fourth century opinion is the inclusion of 2 Peter in the catalogues of GREGORY NAZIANZEN (d. 391), CYRIL OF JERUSALEM (d. 386), and ATHANASIUS (d. 373). One catalogue which is contained in the CODEX CLAROMONTANUS (sixth century), and regarded by Tischendorf and Westcott as earlier than the fourth century, recognises seven Catholic Epistles, together with the Shepherd of Hermas, Acts of Paul, and Apocalypse of Peter. On the other hand, in the list of AMPHILOCHIUS, Bishop of Iconium (c. 380), only one Epistle of Peter is recognised. We have already seen that the Syriac-speaking churches unanimously rejected 2 Peter, and considerable importance is to be attached to the fact that CHRYSOSTOM acknowledges only the Catholic Epistles, and that THEODORE OF MOPSUESTIA describes five Epistles, among which is 2 Peter, as "mediae auctoritatis". "Since Chrysostom's expositions, at any rate, were addressed to popular audiences, the rejection of the Epistle by the great teachers in question must have reflected the usage of the Antiochene Church in general." (Chase, *op. cit.*, iii. 805.)

If we pass in review the evidence afforded by the usage of the fourth century in regard to this Epistle, we find that there was a considerable prevailing feeling of doubt as to the Petrine authorship, along with instances of definite rejection. It is, however, specially significant, in view of the modern tendency to depreciate the Epistle, that it seems to have gained a place in the Canon by virtue of its contents and its useful opposition to the doctrines of false teachers.

Third Century.—Methodius, a bishop of Lycia at the end of the third century, who suffered in the Diocletian persecution, explicitly quotes 2 Peter iii. 8 in the fragment *De Resurrectione.* Zahn (*Gesch. Kan.*, I. i. p. 313) has collected some passages in the same treatise which seem to echo 2 Peter iii. 10-13, and while in these the thought, rather than the language, recalls 2 Peter, there seems no reason to doubt the reference. Methodius regards the Apocalypse of Peter also as inspired (Comm.; Virg., ii. *b*). A further presumption in favour of the use by Methodius of 2 Peter is found in the Dialogue of Adamantius, written probably in the later years of Constantine, which makes large use of the works of Methodius. In this work 2 Peter is quoted. Firmilian, bishop of Cæsarea in Cappadocia, evidently refers to 2 Peter in a letter to Cyprian (No. 75). His words are: "Stephanus adhuc etiam infamans Petrum et Paulum beatos apostolos . . . qui in epistolis suis haereticos exsecrati sunt, et ut eos evitemus monuerunt". The allusion to heretics applies only to 2 Peter.

We come now to the evidence of Origen. In his extant Greek works there is a reference to 2 Peter of a somewhat ambiguous kind. "Peter left one recognised Epistle, and perhaps a second; for it is disputed" (Πέτρος δέ . . . μίαν ἐπιστολὴν ὁμολογουμένην καταλέλοιπεν· ἔστω δὲ καὶ δευτέραν· ἀμφιβάλλεται γάρ); (quoted Eusebius, *H. E.*, VI. xxv. 8). In the Latin translation of his works by Rufinus there are some passages expressly quoting 2 Peter, *e.g.*, 2 Peter, i. 4, "ad participationem capiendam divinae naturae sicut Petrus Apostolus edocuit" (*Ep. ad Rom.* iv. 9. Ed. Lomm., vi. 302). 2 Peter, i. 2, "Petrus in epistola sua dicit. Gratia uobis et pax multiplicatur in recognitione Dei" (*ib.*, viii. 6. Ed. Lomm., vii. 234). 2 Peter, ii. 19, "Scio enim scriptum esse, quia unusquisque a quo vincitur huic et servus addicitur" (*in Exod.* xii. 4. Ed. Lomm., ix. p. 149). Also in a passage which contains an allegorical use of the trumpet blasts before Jericho, it is written, "Petrus etiam duabus epistolarum suarum personat tubis" (*Hom. in Jos.*, xii. 1. Ed. Lomm., xi. 62). These passages have had grave doubt cast on their genuineness by Dr. Chase (*op. cit.*, p. 803*b*). There can, at least, be no doubt, judging from the one undisputed reference, that Origen reflects a serious division of opinion in his time, and that his own opinion tends towards rejection (ἔστω δὲ καὶ δευτέραν) of the Petrine authorship.

As regards CLEMENT OF ALEXANDRIA, the main question to be settled is whether in the *Hypotyposeis* he comments on 2 Peter. If we are to take the statements of Eusebius (*H. E.*, VI. xiv. 1) and Photius (*Bibliothec*, 109), he commented "on all the Catholic Epistles". On the other hand, Cassiodorus, who wrote some 300 years afterwards, gives most conflicting evidence. At one time he says that Clement expounded the Scriptures of the Old and New Testaments "from beginning to end," and in another passage, where he is giving a list of the canonical Epistles expounded by Clement, he omits 2 Peter. Moreover, in Cassiodorus' translation of Clement's Expositions, none are given of 2 Peter. The difficulty may be solved by supposing that in Clement's work, 2 Peter had a place beside the Apocalypse of Peter, which was included in the *Hypotyposeis*. (So Chase, *op. cit.*, 802 *a*, and Zahn. *Forsch.* iii. p. 154.) Clement distinctly quotes the Apocalypse of Peter as the work of Peter, and as Scripture (*Eclogæ ex Script. Proph.*, xli., xlviii., xlix). Accepting the statements of Eusebius and Photius quoted above, and supposing that for purposes of exposition 2 Peter was merged in the Apocalypse of Peter, we may find confirmation of the first statement of Cassiodorus in certain passages of Clement's writing which have been collected by Mayor (*The Epistle of St. Jude and the Second Epistle of St. Peter*, *Introd.*, cxix.) and Bigg (*Commentary on First and Second Peter*, p. 202). In these the word-parallels are striking, but they would not necessarily constitute valid evidence in themselves.

In the writings of CYPRIAN we find no trace of 2 Peter, but it must not be forgotten that Firmilian's letter to him, quoted above, contains a clear allusion. In HIPPOLYTUS there are found passages that point to acquaintance with 2 Peter (Chase, 804 *b*, Bigg, p. 203). A portion of evidence that must not be omitted here is afforded by the division of sections in CODEX B. In this manuscript there are two divisions of sections, and one is older than the other. The double division is preserved in all the Catholic Epistles except 2 Peter, where the older division is wanting. The conclusion is inevitable that in the older form of Codex B, 2 Peter was wanting.

To sum up the evidence of the third century, we find that 2 Peter was in use so far as to influence the thought of Hippolytus in Rome, to be commented on by Clement of Alexandria, and to be expressly quoted by Firmilian and Methodius in Asia Minor. Although no reference is found in the writings of Cyprian of Carthage, yet Firmilian's letter with the quotation is addressed to him. This is scarcely evidence, but it certainly implies Cyprian's knowledge of the Epistle, and also that he would concur in its use as a source of quotation. Again, the two great Egyptian versions of this century, the SAHIDIC and BOHAIRIC, both contain 2 Peter. If we accept a conjectural emendation of Zahn's in the language of the MURATORIAN CANON, there is contained in it a reference to the division of opinion in the Church with regard to this Epistle (*Gesch. Kan.* i., p. 110 n.).[1] Origen's statement that "it is disputed," represents a widespread doubt as to its genuineness. This attitude, combined with a general willingness to respect its contents, must be regarded as the mind of the church about 2 Peter in the third century.

Second Century.—In a document which is preserved in a seventh century MS. entitled ACTUS PETRI CUM SIMONE (xx., ed. Lips., p. 67) there occurs a passage which contains several striking parallels with 2 Peter. The following phrases may be noted (1) "majestatem suam videre in monte sancto," (2) "vocem eius audivi talem qualem referre non possum". In (2) there is a parallel to the rather remarkable phrase, φωνῆς τοιᾶσδε, of 2 Peter i. 17. It is true that the extant MS. only represents a Latin translation of the original Greek, and that editors and translators *may* interpolate. At the same time, it is difficult not to regard Chase as over-sceptical in seeking to discredit the parallel by regarding the whole passage as an interpolation (*op. cit.*, 802 *b*). There seems no reason why we should not accept the passage as an important second century attestation of 2 Peter, and as an indication that the Epistle had already some position in the Church. Turning next to the CLEMENTINE LITERATURE, we have in the *Recognitions* (v. 12) what appears to be a reference to 2 Peter ii. 19: "Unusquisquis illius fit servus cui se ipse subjecerit". Rufinus

[1] The passage in question reads, as amended by Zahn, "Apocalypses etiam Johannis et Petri (unam) tantum recipimus (epistulam; fertur etiam altera), quam quidam ex nostris legi in ecclesia nolunt". The emendations are apt, but is it possible, if we have regard to the loose grammatical construction everywhere in the document, that no change is needed? The Apocalypse of Peter may be referred to as the document "quam quidam, etc.," and we have seen reason to believe (*e.g.*, in case of Clement of Alexandria), that 2 Peter and the Apoc. Petri were sometimes regarded as one whole.

is again the translator of the *Recognitions,* and we are reminded of his translation of Origen (*In Exod. Hom.*, 12), "Unusquisque a quo vincitur huic et servus addicitur". The translations are both of the same passage in 2 Peter, and the variety in the language, so far from countenancing a theory of interpolation on the part of Rufinus may well indicate that he is translating at different times separate references to the same passage. In the *Homilies* (xvi. 20) there occurs a reference, pointed out by Salmon (*Introduction*, p. 488 n.) to 2 Peter iii. 9, τοὐναντίον μακροθυμεῖ, εἰς μετάνοιαν καλεῖ. The context also is confirmatory. Peter is speaking of the blasphemies of Simon Magus, which appear to have been similar in character to the false teaching that is denounced in 2 Peter. All things have been as they were from the foundation of the world. The earth has not opened; fire has not come down from heaven; rain is not poured out; beasts are not sent forth from the thicket to avenge their spiritual adultery. Then come the words quoted, "But, on the contrary, he is long-suffering, and calls to repentance". Yet Chase says, "It is difficult to see what there is in the context which specially recalls 2 Peter." The coincidences mentioned by Salmon (*op. cit.*, p. 488) in the writing of THEOPHILUS OF ANTIOCH are inconclusive, although the words in ii. 9, οἱ δὲ τοῦ θεοῦ ἄνθρωποι πνευματόφοροι πνεύματος ἁγίου καὶ προφῆται γενόμενοι recall 2 Peter i. 21. In ii. 13, ὁ λόγος αὐτοῦ, φαίνων ὥσπερ λύχνος ἐν οἰκήματι συνεχομένῳ, may be compared with 2 Peter i. 19. Similarly, in TATIAN, *Or. ad Graecos*, 15 (Otto vi., p. 70), σκήνωμα (= body) is reminiscent of its similar use in 2 Peter i. 13. To found an argument, however, for the use of 2 Peter by these writers on such single words and expressions is precarious. They might well be part of the current vocabulary. In the *Apology* of ARISTIDES (129-130) a passage occurs that naturally suggests 2 Peter i. 11 and ii. 2. ἡ ὁδὸς τῆς ἀληθείας ἥτις τοὺς ὁδεύοντας αὐτὴν εἰς τὴν αἰώνιον χειραγωγεῖ βασιλείαν (*Apolog.*, xvi). IRENÆUS introduces a quotation from 1 Peter with the words, "Petrus ait in epistola sua" (iv. 9, 2), but this does not necessarily imply that he knew only one Petrine letter. He knew 2 John, and yet quotes 1 John in the same phrase. The phrase in 2 Peter iii. 8 occurs in Irenæus v. 23, 2, "Dies Domini sicut mille anni," and in v. 28, 3, ἡ γὰρ ἡμέρα κυρίου ὡς χίλια ἔτη. In both passages, however, the words are connected with Chiliasm, which is absent from the thought of 2 Peter. In THE EPISTLE OF THE CHURCHES OF LYONS AND VIENNE, with which Irenæus was closely connected (date 177-179) we find the words ὁ δὲ διὰ μέσου καιρὸς οὐκ ἀργὸς αὐτοῖς οὐδὲ ἄκαρπος ἐγίνετο (*cf.* 2 Peter i. 8).

The most important question in the external evidence of the second century arises in connexion with the Apocalypse of Peter, to which Harnack assigns the date 110-160, or probably 120-140. The work is used by the Viennese Church, and therefore the earlier date is more likely. Only a fragment of the Apocalypse is preserved to us, in which there are some striking coincidences with 2 Peter (*cf.* M. R. James, *A Lecture on the Revelation of Peter*). Some of these may be quoted here: (1) πολλοὶ ἐξ αὐτῶν ἔσονται ψευδοπροφῆται, καὶ ὅδους καὶ δόγματα ποικίλα τῆς ἀπωλείας διδάξουσιν· ἐκεῖνοι δὲ υἱοὶ τῆς ἀπωλείας γενήσονται. καὶ τότε ἐλεύσεται ὁ θεός . . . καὶ κρινεῖ τοὺς υἱοὺς τῆς ἀνομίας (Apoc. § 1; *cf.* 2 Peter ii. 1, iii. 7, 12.) (2) ὁ Κύριος ἔφη, Ἄγωμεν εἰς τὸ ὄρος . . . ἀπερχόμενοι δὲ μετ' αὐτοῦ ἡμεῖς οἱ δώδεκα μαθηταί (Apoc. § 2; *cf.* 2 Peter i. 18). The passage goes on to say that the Apostles desired "that He would show them one of our righteous brethren who have departed," ἵνα ἴδωμεν ποταποί (2 Peter iii. 11) εἰσι τὴν μορφήν, καὶ θαρσήσαντες παραθαρσύνωμεν καὶ τοὺς ἀκούοντας ἡμῶν ἀνθρώπους (*cf.* ἐγνωρίσαμεν ὑμῖν, 2 Peter i. 16); ἔχομεν βεβαιότερον (i. 19). (3) τόπον . . . αὐχμηρὸν πάνυ; . . . σκοτεινὸν εἶχον αὐτῶν τὸ ἔνδυμα κατὰ τὸν ἀέρα τοῦ τόπου (§ 6; *cf.* i. 19). (4) A frequent use of κολάζειν, or the noun (*cf.* §§ 6, 7, 10, 11, 2 Peter ii. 9). (5) οἱ βλασφημοῦντες τὴν ὁδὸν τῆς δικαιοσύνης (§ 6; *cf.* § 13 and 2 Peter ii. 2, 21). (6) (*a*) λίμνη τις . . . πεπληρωμένη βορβόρου (§ 8. βόρβορος occurs in § 9 twice, and in § 16); (*b*) ἐκυλίοντο (§ 15; *cf.* ii. 22). (7) ἀμελήσαντες τῆς ἐντολῆς τοῦ θεοῦ (§ 15; *cf.* ii. 21, iii. 2). (8) (*a*) ἡ γῆ παραστήσει πάντας τῷ θεῷ ἐν ἡμέρᾳ κρίσεως καὶ αὐτὴ μέλλουσα κρίνεσθαι σὺν καὶ τῷ περιέχοντι οὐρανῷ (quoted by Macarius Magnes, *Apocritica* iv. 6). (*b*) τακήσεται πᾶσα δύναμις οὐρανοῦ, καὶ ἑλιχθήσεται ὁ οὐρανὸς ὡς βιβλίον, καὶ πάντα τὰ ἄστρα πεσεῖται Mac. Magn. *op. cit.* iv. 7; *cf.* 2 Peter iii. 10-13; see Mayor, ed. pp. cxxx. ff.).

All scholars are agreed that these and other coincidences are more than accidental (*cf.* Salmon, *op. cit.*, p. 591). Various hypotheses to account for them are suggested.

(1) Did 2 Peter borrow from the Apocalypse? (Harnack, *Chronologie*, p. 471). A comparison, however, of the language of the two documents suggests that 2 Peter is simpler and shorter in the expression of the same ideas; and in some cases, ideas and phrases, separated in 2 Peter, are gathered together in one passage in the Apocalypse (*cf.* (1), (2), (8) above). Bigg (*op. cit.*, p. 207) also contends against this hypothesis on the ground that the description of hell is suggested by Plato, Aristophanes, Homer, and especially Virgil, and points to a later date than the Epistle. The rare word ταρταρώσας is indeed used by 2 Peter of the punishment of the wicked after death, and the conception is undoubtedly derived from heathen

mythology. The word, however, is found in Jewish writings, which 2 Peter may have read (see note on ii. 4).

(2) Are 2 Peter and the Apocalypse by the same author? (Sanday, *Inspiration*, p. 347). This view is opposed by Chase (*op. cit.*, 815) on the ground of the difference in style. "The Apocalypse," he says, "is simple and natural in its style. There is nothing remarkable in its vocabulary." The argument would seem to be conclusive, as the style of 2 Peter is unmistakable, and would be easily recognised. At the same time, the undoubted similarity between the two writings "not only in words or indefinitely marked ideas, but also in general conceptions—*e.g.*, in both there is the picture drawn of Christ on the mountain with His Apostles, the latter being admitted to a secret revelation which they should afterwards use for the confirmation of their disciples—seems to be an argument of some strength in favour of the view that the two documents are the product of the same school" (Chase).

(3) Does the Apocalypse borrow from 2 Peter? Some of the arguments already adduced against the contrary hypothesis (i.) are really in favour of this supposition. The "naturalness of the words and phrases as they stand in their several contexts in the Apocalypse," which is brought forward by Chase as an argument against this third hypothesis (*op. cit.*, p. 815 *b*) is really only a compliment to the style of the writing, and an indication that the writer has no intention of slavishly imitating 2 Peter, or of forming a kind of mosaic of his own and another's diction. As regards the absence in the Apocalypse of the strange and remarkable phrases of 2 Peter that they were strange and remarkable might be precisely the reason why they were avoided or modified. ἐβασάνιζεν in 2 Peter ii. 8 is rendered by δοκιμάζω in Apocalypse, § 1; the reference to the Transfiguration in the Apocalypse is fuller than in 2 Peter, and would seem to indicate reflection on the Petrine narrative (*e.g.*, *cf.* addition of οἱ δώδεκα μαθηταί to simple ἡμεῖς in 2 Peter i. 18; and expression τὸ ὄρος for τῷ ἁγίῳ ὄρει). Such a phrase as ἐν τόπῳ σκοτεινῷ, might well be a paraphrase of ἐν αὐχμηρῷ τόπῳ, a much rarer word, and it is extremely unlikely that αὐχμ. would be substituted for σκοτεινός. It is therefore most probable that the Apocalypse is indebted to 2 Peter, which would suggest a date for the Epistle earlier than 120-140 (*cf.* p. 181).

In the so-called SECOND EPISTLE OF CLEMENT (130-170) there is a passage deserving of notice. γινώσκετε δὲ ὅτι ἔρχεται ἤδη ἡ ἡμέρα τῆς κρίσεως ὡς κλίβανος καιόμενος καὶ τακήσονται αἱ δυνάμεις τῶν οὐρανῶν καὶ πᾶσα ἡ γῆ ὡς μόλυβδος ἐπὶ πυρὶ τηκόμενος καὶ τότε φανήσεται τὰ κρύφια καὶ φανερὰ ἔργα τῶν ἀνθρώπων (xvi. 3). One or two interesting points are raised by this passage.

(1) Where does the writer derive the conception of the day of judgment as meaning the destruction of the universe by fire? He clearly quotes Mal. iv. 1, Isa. xxxiv. 4, but these passages are not sufficient to suggest the idea unless to one already familiar with the doctrine. Bigg (*Comm.* pp. 214-15) argues at some length that this doctrine is ultimately to be traced to 2 Peter. Justin (*Apol.*, i. 20) traces the belief in the world-fire to the Sybil (Book iv.) and Hystaspes. Bigg holds that both these belong to the same family as the pseudo-Petrine literature. The destruction of the world by fire was not an article of faith among the Jews, and Philo argues strongly against it (*On the Incorruptibility of the World*). The office of fire in the O.T. is to purify, and not to destroy (Isa. xxxiv. 4, li. 6, lxvi. 15, 16, 22; Mal. iv. 1). In the N.T. (*e.g.*, Heb. xii. 26-29; 1 Cor. iii. 13; 2 Thess. i. 8; Apoc. xxi. 1) the conception of fire is distinctly that of a purifying agency. It is to be noted, however, against Bigg's view, that the conception of 2 Peter is not altogether at variance with the doctrine of the N.T. about the office of fire. The destruction of the present universe is vividly described in Chapter III., but the writer evidently has the idea of purification in his mind, and not of annihilation. "Nevertheless we, according to His promise, look for new heavens and a new earth wherein dwelleth righteousness" (iii. 13). Accordingly, if the passage quoted from 2 Clement is to be taken in the sense of annihilation by fire, it cannot be regarded as founded exclusively on 2 Peter.

(2) Is there anything in the language to connect the two? ἡμέρα κρίσεως is found in N.T. only in St. Matthew's Gospel (x. 15, xi. 22, 24), in 1 John (iv. 17), and in 2 Peter (ii. 9, iii. 7). In 2 Peter iii. 10, however, the expression is ἡμέρα κυρίου. τήκομαι is also a word common to 2 Peter (iii. 12) and the passage in 2 Clem. An important coincidence is φανήσεται . . . ἔργα, which may be an attempt to make sense of the very doubtful reading in 2 Peter iii. 10 (ἔργα εὑρεθήσεται). On the whole, the similarity of language and the affinity of thought in the two passages must be regarded as establishing a connexion. (For other coincidences, see Spitta, *Der zweite Brief des Petrus und der Brief des Judas*, p. 534 n.)

In the Epistle of Barnabas (130-31, Harnack), in a Chiliastic passage, the words occur, ἡ γὰρ ἡμέρα παρ' αὐτῷ χίλια ἔτη. αὐτὸς δέ μοι μαρτυρεῖ λέγων, ἰδοὺ ἡμέρα Κυρίου ἔσται ὡς χίλια ἔτη (xv. 4). It has been pointed out that παρ' αὐτῷ is very close to 2 Peter's παρὰ κυρίῳ and the repetition of the words points to the quotation of some recognised utterance of Scripture. Barnabas, also, is in the habit of using λέγει to introduce his quotations from Scripture. The question is whether he is quoting 2 Peter iii. 8 or some other source. The context in Barnabas is different from that in 2 Peter. He is dealing with the mystical interpretation of the passage Gen. ii. 16. Also, in 2 Peter no Chiliastic meaning is attached, as in Barnabas. In all probability, 2 Peter iii. 8 is regarded by Barnabas as an authority for Chiliasm, along with Rev. xx. 4 ff., which he quotes. In The Shepherd of Hermas (110-140, Harnack) there are certain words and phrases that are found only in 2 Peter, μιασμός (Sim. v. 1, 2); βλέμμα (in different sense = *appearance;* Sim. vi. 2, 5); δυσνόητος (Sim. ix. 14, 4); αὐθάδεις, applied to false teachers (Sim. ix. 22, 1.)[1] In Clement of Rome (93-95, Harnack) we find several phrases which, in N.T., are peculiar to 2 Peter: τοὺς δὲ ἑτεροκλινεῖς ὑπάρχοντας εἰς κόλασιν καὶ αἰκισμὸν τίθησιν (xi. 1); ἐπόπτης (used, however, of God) (lix. 3); αὐθάδη (i. 1); μῶμος (lxiii. 1); μεγαλοπρεπεῖ δόξῃ αὐτοῦ (ix. 2), but μεγαλοπρεπεῖ βουλήσει occurs previously in same paragraph; Νῶε ἐκήρυξεν μετάνοιαν (vii. 6). The passage in Clem. xxxiv. may also be noted: εἰς τὸ μετόχους ἡμᾶς γενέσθαι τῶν μεγάλων κ. ἐνδόξων ἐπαγγελιῶν αὐτοῦ (*cf.* 2 Peter i. 4).[2] These coincidences in Barnabas, in Clement, and in the Didache are scarcely conclusive as quotations, but they suggest a *milieu* of thought corresponding to 2 Peter.

To what conclusion does the evidence of the second century lead? Chase says, "If we put aside the passage from the Clementine Recognitions and that from the Acts of Peter, as open to the suspicion of not accurately representing the original texts, there does not remain, it is believed, a single passage in which the coincidence with 2 Peter can, with anything approaching confidence, be said to imply literary obligation to that Epistle" (*cf.* Bacon, *Introd.*, 173). It ought, however, to be noted that the passage in the Clementine Recognitions can only be set aside on the ground that Rufinus can fairly be accused of interpolation; and the evident coincidences in the *Actus Petri cum Simone* can be dismissed only on account of distrust of the Latin translator of the work. We have also the evidence of

[1] Of the passages collected by Zahn (*der Hirt der Hermas*, p. 431) as having affinity with 2 Peter, the most striking is Sim. vi. 4, 4: τῆς τρυφῆς καὶ ἀπάτης ὁ χρόνος ὥρα ἐστὶ μία. τῆς δὲ βασάνου ἡ ὥρα τριάκοντα ἡμέρων δύναμιν ἔχει. ἐαν οὖν μίαν ἡμέραν τρυφήσῃ τις καὶ ἀπατηθῇ κ.τ.λ. (*cf.* 2 Peter ii. 13).

[2] Spitta, p. 534 n., points out a passage in the Didache (iii. 6-8) having a remarkable affinity with Jude and 2 Peter. γόγγυσος, a rare word (Jude 16) is used. βλασφημία, αὐθάδης and τρέμων are twice repeated (*cf.* 2 Peter ii. 10).

dependence in the Apocalypse of Peter. It is doubtful whether any of the Apostolic Fathers make use of the Epistle, but the coincidences in word and thought in 2 Clement, Barnabas, Hermas, Didache, and Clement of Rome cannot be ignored. They at least suggest a possible atmosphere of thought for 2 Peter. On the whole, the evidence of the second century would suggest a date for the Epistle not much later than the first decade. There is an entire absence of evidence tor the Petrine authorship.

CHAPTER II.

INTERNAL EVIDENCE OF AUTHENTICITY.

1. The obvious first step to be taken is to examine the *References to the Gospel History* in the Epistle, and to consider what light they may throw on the authorship of the Epistle.

(1) Chap. i. 3. **τοῦ καλέσαντος ἡμᾶς.** The reference of the participle is to Ἰησοῦ τοῦ κυρίου ἡμῶν (*cf.* note). Does ἡμᾶς refer to the Apostles, and in particular to the call of St. Peter? This interpretation involves that ἡμῖν in i. 1 likewise refers to the Apostles. Other indications, however, in the Epistle point to a group of scattered Christian communities in Asia Minor as the recipients of the letter, and the sense in i. 1 seems to be that the readers of the letter, who are isolated and harassed by false teachers, are set on equal terms with "us," who occupy a less difficult position, and enjoy greater outward privileges. Again, in i. 4 the best attested reading is ἡμῖν (not ὑμῖν), and clearly there the reference is to the writer and readers together. So ἡμῶν ought to be taken in i. 2. ἡμᾶς must therefore consistently be referred to the body of readers with whom 2 Peter identifies himself in thought, as united in their common faith, and not to the Apostles alone. Spitta (*op. cit.*, pp. 37 ff.), arguing for the reference to the Gospel History, takes ἡμᾶς as referring to the calling of the immediate Apostles, in contrast to those who believed in response to their preaching. Such a sense would by no means suit ἡμῖν in i. 4. Also, in i. 10 κλῆσιν clearly refers to writer and readers taken together. Moreover, καλεῖν in N.T. is by no means confined to the call of the first disciples (*cf.* Matt. ix. 13). In Rom. ix. 24 the thought is almost exactly parallel to this passage, "even us, whom he hath called, not of the Jews only, but also of the Gentiles".

(2) Chap. i. 16 ff.—*The Transfiguration.*—If we compare the reference here with the Synoptic accounts, there emerge some interesting points of difference. All three Synoptics speak as though the glory had its source from within. Such can only be the significance of μετεμορφώθη (Matt. and Mark): and the ἐγένετο . . . ἕτερον of

Luke is an indication that he interpreted the phenomenon as an inward change. He also tells us that it was ἐν τῷ προσεύχεσθαι, "as he was praying," that the change took place (Luke ix. 29). 2 Peter, on the other hand, seems to think of the glory as having an outward source, like what happened in the case of Moses (Exod. xxxiv. 29 ff.; 2 Cor. iii. 7 ff.), as a *reflexion* of the glory of God, an outward attestation in addition to the voice (λαβὼν γὰρ παρὰ θεοῦ πατρὸς τιμὴν καὶ δόξαν, i. 17). Spitta argues that this is a more natural and primitive account, and therefore independent of the account in the Synoptics, which shows traces of later thought playing upon the incident. There can be no doubt that the conception of the glory as *external* is found in 2 Peter, but it is not regarded as an attestation previous to the voice, as in the Synoptics. On the contrary, the two aorist participles imply coincident action, the first really taking the place of a finite verb (*cf.* the common phrase, ἀποκριθεὶς εἶπεν). "He received honour and glory when there came to Him," etc. Moreover, τιμή can only refer to the attestation of the voice (see note on passage). To this extent 2 Peter differs from the Synoptic gospels. Are we then justified in regarding the disparity as a mark of the eye-witness? There are, however, other characteristics of the passage in 2 Peter which rather point to *literary* dependence on the Synoptic account. (*a*) The reading of ℵACKL, adopted in the text, is οὗτος ἔστιν ὁ υἱός μου ὁ ἀγαπητός, εἰς ὃν ἐγὼ εὐδόκησα, which differs from Matt. xvii. 5 only in respect that (α) εἰς ὃν is substituted for ἐν ᾧ (see note on passage), (β) ἐγώ is inserted, and (γ) ἀκούετε αὐτοῦ is omitted. Again, σκηνώματι (ii. 12) σκηνώματος (ii. 14) and ἔξοδον (v. 15) occurring together, seem to indicate that the vocabulary of the Synoptic account was lingering in the mind of the writer. σκήνωμα, a rare and unusual word in this sense, is used characteristically in the sense of the ordinary σκῆνος, and may have been suggested by the σκήνη of the Gospel narrative. ἔξοδος belongs to Luke's own vocabulary in reporting the conversation of the three men, and its employment indicates acquaintance with his Gospel. "Omission of details of the history (*e.g.*, the presence of Moses and Elias) in an allusion contained in a letter cannot reasonably be taken to show that a writer is giving an account independent of, or more primitive than, that of the Synoptists" (Chase, *op. cit.* iii. 809 *b*, but *cf.* Zahn, *Introd.* II., pp. 217 f.). Moreover, ἐν τῷ ἁγίῳ ὄρει indicates a later stage of thought than the simple εἰς ὄρος ὑψηλὸν (Mark, ix. 2; Matt. i. 7), or εἰς τὸ ὄρος (Luke ix. 26). It implies not only the assignment of a definite locality, but also the ascription of a "sacred" site, "a known mountain which had now become consecrated as the scene of the vision" (Mayor, *op. cit.*, cxliv.). It is, of course, also possible to take ἐν τῷ ἁγίῳ ὄρει in sense of Isa. xi. 9, lxii. 25 where it is used of the Messiah's kingdom. "Perhaps 2 Peter means that in the Transfiguration the three Apostles were admitted to behold the glories of that kingdom, without alluding to any particular Jewish mountain" (Mayor, iv., note 1). The passage betrays reflexion on the original incident, and is written from the standpoint of one who is concerned chiefly to interpret the "glory" of Jesus on the Mount of Transfiguration as prophetic of His δύναμιν καὶ παρουσίαν, which is the theme of the Epistle (ἐπόπται γενηθέντες τῆς ἐκείνου μεγαλειότητος), and as establishing the truthfulness of the Apostles who preached the παρουσία.

(3) Chap. i. 14: *Prophecy of the death of St. Peter.*—ταχινή ἐστιν ἡ ἀπόθεσις . . . καθὼς καὶ ὁ κύριος ἡμῶν Ι. Χ. ἐδήλωσεν μοι. Clearly there is here a reference to the incident in John xxi. 18. In the notes, ταχινή is taken to mean "imminent" and not in the sense of sudden death Spitta, amongst others, has argued strongly (pp. 88 f., 491 f.) that there is here no reference to the Gospel history, and is supported by Mayor. It is contended that the words ὅταν γηράσῃς, in John xxi. 15, imply that death was not imminent, and that in old age a man does not require a prophecy to tell him that death is near. Moreover, in the Johannine passage, the emphasis is not on the time but on the *manner* of St. Peter's death. It is further suggested that some special revelation by Jesus to St. Peter of the near approach of death, not recorded in Scripture, must be meant, and that a reference may be intended to the story contained in the legend, "Domine quo vadis?" found in the Clementine Homilies, and in the Apocalypse of Peter. The foregoing argument is founded on the supposition that καθὼς necessarily refers to the whole preceding clause, ὅτι . . . μου. It need not be so. The writer speaks as an old man, and the reference would then be to the prophesied death in old age. The objection that old age in itself is a warning of approaching death seems trivial. That fact would not prevent the mention of a prophecy regarding it. Again, it is not necessary to suppose that 2 Peter actually has the passage John xxi. 18 in his mind. He may be referring independently to the incident. It is suggestive to compare the use of καθὼς καὶ here with iii. 15. There the καθὼς καὶ is added as a kind of afterthought, and is not really dependent on the principal verb ἡγεῖσθε. It has really the significance of another principal clause. The syntax would seem to be similar in i. 14. The matter of knowledge (εἰδὼς) is that death is near at hand, however that knowledge is suggested to him, and the clause καθὼς καὶ is added by way of further illustration. It is unreasonable to demand that the thought in 2 Peter

must be an exact replica of the passage in John, if the reference is to be the same.

(4) Chap. ii. 20 (γέγονεν αὐτοῖς τὰ ἔσχατα χείρονα τῶν πρώτων) is clearly a reminiscence of the words of Jesus recorded in Matt. xii. 45, Luke xi. 29.

These four references to the Gospel history have now been examined. The first may be set aside, and the other three may be regarded as indicating no more than a knowledge of the Gospels, and especially of two incidents in the life of St. Peter. They do not nearly amount to evidence that the writer is the Apostle himself.

The paucity of references to the Gospel history, in an Epistle purporting to be written by the Apostle Peter, is remarkable. It contains only one reference to the actual words of Jesus (ii. 20), but indirectly these may be referred to in ii. 1 = Matt. x. 33; i. 8 = Luke xiii. 7-8; iii. 4 = Matt. xxiv. 37-42. We would expect that the mind of an intimate disciple would have been saturated with reminiscences of our Lord's teaching, and would have dwelt easily on the great events of His Life. In this respect we may compare 2 Peter most unfavourably with the genuine first Epistle. In the former there is no mention of the Passion or Resurrection, and there is a strange absence of that vivid sense of the Risen Lord as living and reigning in grace, which is so characteristic of the writings of the Apostles, who "had been begotten again unto a living hope". It is also a matter for serious consideration as against the genuineness of the Epistle, that the references to the Gospel history are introduced apparently to support the character of one writing as St. Peter, and to distinguish his statements from σεσοφισμένοι μῦθοι (i. 16). (But *cf.* Bigg. p. 231.)

2 *The Personality of St. Peter in the Epistle.*—(1) Chap. i. 1: Συμεὼν Πέτρος δοῦλος καὶ ἀπόστολος Ἰησοῦ Χριστοῦ. The significance of the form Συμεὼν is very obscure. The point to be emphasised at present is that St. Peter is here represented as the writer of the Epistle. If, however, the Petrine authorship is untenable, how is the expression to be justified? In this connexion, one or two questions call for consideration.

(*a*) Does the form of the words afford any indication that the name of St. Peter is being used by a later writer? His own description of himself in 1 Peter i. 1 is Πέτρος ἀπόστολος Ἰησοῦ Χριστοῦ. The form Συμεὼν is used only in one other passage, *viz.*, Acts xv. 14, in the address of St. James at the Council of Jerusalem. δοῦλος is found in Jude 1, and in view of the evident dependence of 2 Peter on Jude, this fact may be regarded as significant. Again, if Spitta is right in supposing that by the use of the pre-Christian name, Συμεὼν, the writer puts himself on a level with those whom he addresses, and prepares the way for the epithet ἰσότιμον ("equally privileged," as between Jew and Gentile), it is evident that the whole title given to St. Peter is carefully chosen by a process of reflection. There is, therefore, a presumption that another mind is at work here, which has also borrowed largely from Jude in chap. ii.

(*b*) If the name of St. Peter has been thus used, the Epistle is pseudonymous. What is the distinction between pseudonymity in early Christian writings and forgery? Does pseudonymity imply ethical fault, and does it affect the authority of a writing? A most uncompromising position in this regard is characteristic of the older criticism. Westcott (*Canon*, pp. 352 f.) in speaking of the disputed books of the Canon, says: "The Second Epistle of St. Peter is either an authentic work of the Apostle, or a forgery; for in this case there can be no mean. . . . It involves a manifest confusion of ideas to compensate for a deficiency of historical proof by a lower standard of canonicity. The extent of the Divine authority of a book cannot be made to vary with the completeness of the proof of its genuineness. The genuineness must be admitted before the authority can have any positive value, which from its nature cannot admit of degrees; and till the genuineness be established, the authority remains in abeyance." In a note, Westcott adds, "These books (2 Peter, James, Jude, Hebrews) have received the recognition of the Church in such a manner that, if genuine, they must be canonical".

The use of the term "forgery" in such a connexion ought to be avoided.[1] In the first place, the expression is an entire misunderstanding of the origin of much of the pseudepigraphic literature of the time, and on other grounds the term is equally objectionable. It is, in effect, an attempt to browbeat the judgment into the acceptance of such books as genuine, on account of the difficulty of believing that the Church could accept into the Canon what is supposed to be the product of fraud and deceit. The question of pseudonymity cannot be settled "by a profession of moral indignation". The idea that literary property is guarded by ethical considerations is essentially modern. "Believers frequently borrowed from the books of other believers or of unbelievers, without mentioning any source, and without considering themselves in any way as thieves." "With the best intentions and with the clearest consciences they put such words into the mouth of a revered Apostle as they wished to hear enunciated with Apostolic authority to their contemporaries, while yet they did not regard themselves in the smallest degree as liars and

[1] Zahn, who himself upholds the Petrine authorship, says "The mere occurrence of Peter's name in an ancient writing is no proof of authorship" (*Introd.*, ii., p. 270).

deceivers" (Jülicher, *Introd.*, E. Tr., p. 52). The standard of genuineness applied to the early Christian writings, and especially in the formation of the Canon, was their conformity to the teaching of the Church. Were they orthodox or heretical? A case in point is the story related by TERTULLIAN (*De Baptismo*, xvii.) of the writer of the Acts of Paul and Thecla, who was compelled to give up his office "on the ground that he imputed to Paul an invention of his own" (quasi titulo Pauli de suo cumulans). He defended himself by saying that he wrote out of regard for Paul, and that therefore he had not an evil conscience. The plea was evidently accepted, and he was convicted, not of literary fraud as such, but because he dared to advocate the heretical view that women had a right to preach and to baptise. We must also take into account in our estimate of pseudepigraphy what Jülicher calls "the boundless credulity of ecclesiastical circles to which so many of the N.T. Apocrypha have owed their lasting influence". Eusebius (*H. E.*, i. 13) quotes as genuine an Epistle purporting to be written by Christ to Agbarus. "It is evident," says Mayor (p. xxv., note 1), "that there were among the early Christians good and pious men who had no scruple about impersonating not saints alone, but the Lord of saints Himself. We should gather the same from the readiness with which the orthodox worked up and expurgated the religious romances by which the heretics sought to popularise their doctrines."

The practice of pseudepigraphical writing is exemplified in the O.T. in Ecclesiastes, and in the apocryphal books of Wisdom, Esdras, Baruch, Enoch, and the Sibylline Oracles. The second century produced many pseudonymous books, such as the Gospel of Peter, which, after being read in the churches of Cilicia for some time, was at length forbidden by Serapion, bishop of Antioch, about the end of the century, on account of its docetic teaching. The unknown writer of 2 Peter made use of the name of St. Peter, both in order to mark his views as important, and because he believed them to be in accordance with what would have been St. Peter's teaching under similar circumstances.

(*c*) The foregoing may enable us to rid our minds of prejudice when we come to consider the question as to whether any genuine teaching of St. Peter is contained in this Epistle. Are there contained in the Epistle any actual reminiscences of St. Peter's teaching, and is the work written by a disciple of St. Peter?[1] No attempt, of course, can be made to disentangle from the rest of the writing

[1] *Cf.* Ramsay, *Church in Roman Empire*, pp. 492-3; Moffatt, *Historical New Testament*, p. 598.

what might be regarded as the utterances of the Apostle, but a presumption in favour of the hypothesis of actual reminiscence may be obtained from a comparison of 1 and 2 Peter (see chap. iv.). Weiss has said that "no document in the N.T. is so like 2 Peter as 1 Peter". Moreover, there is probably a reference in the second Epistle itself (i. 15), which is corroborated by tradition, to the fact that St. Peter's teaching was subsequently embodied in the Gospel of St. Mark (so Jülicher, *Introd.*, E. Tr., p. 240). Mayor (p. cxliii. ff.) also favours this view, and successfully defends it against the objections of Zahn (*Introd.*, ii., pp. 200-9).[1] Bigg considers that the statement in i. 15 gave rise to the whole body of pseudo-Petrine literature (*op. cit.* p. 265). It is to be noted also that in two passages in the Epistle the pseudonymous writer betrays the consciousness that he is faithfully and honestly setting forth nothing inconsistent with the teaching of the Apostle. In iii. 1 he is not afraid to set the contents of his Epistle alongside those of 1 Peter without fear of contradiction,[2] and again in iii. 15, his concern is evidently to show that there is no inconsistency between the Petrine and the Pauline teaching. These, and the other considerations adduced above ought to be a guarantee at least of the good faith of the writer of this Epistle.

(2) Another instance where the personality of St. Peter is allowed to obtrude itself is found in i. 16, in the use of the word ἐπόπται. The word means eye-witness, with perhaps an added sense, derived from Gnostic sources, of spiritual vision. In the Apocalypse of Peter, there is an account of the Transfiguration which contains the words ἡμεῖς οἱ δώδεκα μαθηταὶ ἐδεήθημεν ὅπως δείξῃ ἡμῖν ἕνα τῶν ἀδελφῶν . . . τῶν ἐξελθόντων ἀπὸ τοῦ κόσμου, ἵνα ἴδωμεν ποταποί εἰσι τὴν μορφήν (*cf.* Mayor, cxxv. note). Similarly in i. 18, of the Voice at the Transfiguration, 2 Peter has ἡμεῖς ἠκούσαμεν. Jülicher, in commenting on the pseudepigraphic character of 2 Peter, says that "the author never loses consciousness of the part he is playing," and "constructs his fiction methodically". Among other instances, he cites this passage describing the Transfiguration. He sees in the structure of the Epistle only "an artificial production of learned ingenuity" (*Introd.*, E. Tr., pp. 240, 241). It may be granted that the choice

[1] If the words μετὰ τὴν ἐμὴν ἔξοδον are taken as implying that the Apostle was not yet dead, we are immediately involved in all the insuperable difficulties connected with a date for the Epistle earlier than A.D. 64, the traditional date of Peter's martyrdom. On the other hand, it is easy to see how this expression might be put into the mouth of Peter by a later disciple, who well knew his mind and the preparations he had made for preserving his teaching after his death.

[2] For consideration of the question whether the reference here is really to 1 Peter, see p. 113.

of the Transfiguration as the only incident in the Synoptic account of St. Peter's life, to which reference is made, is an indication that the writer has made choice of this incident as suitable to his theme. At the same time, if it was legitimate for him to write under the honoured name at all, he could hardly have done so more naturally than he does in i. 16-18, especially as it is extremely probable that here he is making use of an actual reminiscence of the teaching of St. Peter himself (*cf.* notes on the passage).

(3) Chap. iii. 15.—ὁ ἀγαπητὸς ἡμῶν ἀδελφὸς Παῦλος. The examination of the whole passage in the Commentary leads to the conclusion that the Epistles of St. Paul are regarded as in the same rank with the O.T. Scriptures. The date thus implied makes it impossible that the actual writer is St. Peter. Why, then, the conjunction of the two names? There can be little doubt that 2 Peter wishes to impress upon his readers the consistency of the teaching of St. Peter and St. Paul against the Antinomian interpretation of the Christian faith. The affectionate terms in which St. Paul is spoken of are exactly those that might have been used by St. Peter himself of his fellow-apostle, and if St. Peter were known to be already dead, how could there be any sane intention to deceive the readers? The phrase ὁ ἀγαπητὸς ἡμῶν ἀδελφὸς is used by St. Paul of Tychicus (Eph. vi. 21; Col. iv. 7) and of Onesimus (Col. iv. 9; Philem. v. 16). No doubt the readers of this Epistle were acquainted with the disagreement between the two Apostles described in Galatians ii. 11-14. 2 Peter only reiterates the fact that there was never any fundamental opposition between their teaching. St. Peter's full sympathy with the Pauline teaching is evident in the First Epistle, and this passage may easily be true to his mind. It is indeed significant that the attitude taken up towards the Pauline teaching is not without reserve (iii. 16, ἐν αἷς ἐστὶν δυσνόητά τινα), but the warm-hearted reference may be a real reminiscence.

CHAPTER III.

INTERNAL EVIDENCE AS TO DATE.

We have next to examine any hints that may be given in the Epistle itself as to the Date of its composition.

(1) Chap. i. 15.—Here reference is made to the death of St. Peter as imminent. Other considerations render it impossible to hold that this Epistle was published during the lifetime of the Apostle who died *c.* 64 A.D. (see pp. 97 f.). The context shows that if the words μετὰ τὴν ἐμὴν ἔξοδον are put into the mouth of St. Peter by a later writer, the period of writing must have been some time after his decease. ἑκάστοτε (as occasion arises) in v. 15 implies that occasion has arisen more than once to refer to the posthumous teaching. ἔχειν ὑμᾶς, κ.τ.λ., implies a document or documents already in the possession of the Church. Again, if we are to see in this verse a reference to the tradition connecting St. Peter with the Gospel of Mark, we know that this tradition is at least much earlier than the time of Papias (140-160), who is quoted by Eusebius (*H. E.*, iii. 39) as saying, καὶ τοῦτο ὁ πρεσβύτερος ἔλεγε, Μᾶρκος μὲν ἑρμηνευτὴς Πέτρου γενόμενος ὅσα ἐμνημόνευσεν ἀκριβῶς ἔγραψεν, οὐ μέντοι τάξει, τὰ ὑπὸ τοῦ Χριστοῦ ἢ λεχθέντα ἢ πραχθέντα. Papias himself is reporting the testimony which he had received orally from the Presbyter. From the perfectly natural way in which the reference is introduced, we would conclude that 2 Peter has not in view a tradition which he found in such a writer as Papias, but betrays either a personal knowledge of the intentions of St. Peter himself, or an acquaintance with those who did know his mind. Hence a date not very much later than the end of the first century is probable.

(2) In chap. iii. 4 the words occur, ἀφ' ἧς γὰρ οἱ πατέρες ἐκοιμήθησαν, πάντα οὕτως διαμένει ἀπ' ἀρχῆς κτίσεως. Here οἱ πατέρες refers to the immediately preceding generation of Christians. The whole sentence reflects the disappointment and disillusionment experienced by those who saw men and women believing in the coming of the Lord in their life-time, and dying without having realised their expectation, and who felt that all signs of an immediate coming in their

own day were absent. Such an atmosphere of thought would be most intense in the second generation of Christians, and much of the Epistle is meant for the encouragement of those who still expected the delayed Parousia of the Lord, and whose minds were likely to feel the element of truth in the words of the false teachers. ἀφ' ἧς need not denote a long interval of time (*cf.* Luke vii. 45). It may therefore be possible that the Epistle is addressed to the second generation of Christians. Moreover, chap. i. 16-18 is most naturally regarded as addressed to those "who have not seen, and yet have believed," and the superior position of the eye-witnesses therein implied is an idea that would be most prominent in sub-Apostolic times.

(3) Chap. iii. 8.—As an indication of an early date for the Epistle, the absence of any millennial significance in this passage has been adduced (Bigg, pp. 214, 295). Against this, Mayor (*op. cit.* cxxvi. has pointed out that we learn from Justin Martyr (*Dial.*, chap. 80) that there were also many orthodox believers in his time who refused to accept the millenial teaching. It may, however, be noted that the passage in Justin hardly negatives Dr. Bigg's conclusion. There it is said that "many think otherwise," *i.e.*, in opposition to a millenial doctrine. In 2 Peter, the context in which the words are used is entirely apart from any millenarian notion at all. The significant thing is that 2 Peter, unlike all subsequent writers does not employ Psalm xc. 4. in connection with the idea. He is dealing with the very verse out of which Chiliasm arose, and he could hardly have so completely ignored the opinion unless he had been writing at a date previous at least to its later widespread acceptance in the Church.

At what time the view became common in the Early Church is uncertain. In Barnabas xv. 5 we meet with the conception, but there is no trace of the doctrine in either 1 Clem., Ignatius, Polycarp, the Epistle to Diognetus, or the Didache. Hermas is not uninfluenced by the idea. In none of the apologists, except Justin, is there any trace of Chiliasm. 2 Peter iii. 8, therefore, with its peculiar use of Psalm xc. 4 would indicate a date certainly much earlier than Justin Martyr (140-161), who refers to the belief as a tenet of the orthodox faith, and probably earlier than Barnabas. If the absence of reference to millenial doctrine in 1 Clem., Ignatius, and the Didache means the same as in 2 Peter, a date at the very end of the first century and the very beginning of the second is probable for our Epistle.

(4) Chap. iii. 2.—τῶν ἀποστόλων ὑμῶν. The writer must be regarded as including himself among the Apostles (*cf.* i. 1), and not as

making any distinction between himself and them. The phrase need not necessarily mean "the Twelve," but rather missionaries from whom the knowledge of the Gospel was first received.[1] Of these the writer is one (i. 16). ἀπόστολος is so used Phil. ii. 25, 2 Cor. viii. 23 (*cf.* discussion of term in Harnack, *Expansion of Christianity*, Bk. iii. ch. i.). The passage, therefore, does not exclude a date later than the Apostolic Age.

(5) Chap. iii. 16.—Two considerations are suggested by this reference to St. Paul that have a bearing on the date of the Epistle. (*a*) Paul's Epistles are included in a body of writings called γραφαί, and we have reason to suppose that τὰς λοιπὰς γραφάς probably refers to the O.T. Scriptures. (*b*) The "unlearned and unstable" distort these Epistles of Paul to their own destruction. Both these statements require that the date of the Epistle be postponed so as to leave room for them. (*a*) renders it quite impossible to fix a date in the life-time of Peter. The statement implies not necessarily a collection of Pauline letters such as we have in the Canon of the N.T., but the epithet γραφή would be applied if certain letters of Paul were accustomed to be read in the churches. That interpretation would not require a date later than the end of the first century. At the same time (*b*) demands that time must be allowed to enable the Pauline Epistles to gain such a position of recognised authority in the Church as Scripture that they can be misinterpreted by "unlearned and unstable souls". All these circumstances would be met by a date quite early in the second century.

(6) Chap. ii.—The resemblances in this chapter to the Epistle of Jude are undoubted. There are parallels in thought and language also in Jude 1, 2=2 Peter i. 1, 2; Jude 3, 2=Peter i. 12; Jude 17-19 =2 Peter iii. 1-3; Jude 20-25=2 Peter iii. 14-18. Spitta, Zahn, and Bigg are among the foremost defenders of the view that 2 Peter is prior to Jude. Irresistible arguments, however, may be adduced for the opinion that the relationship is the other way. For the discussion of the question the reader may be referred to the Introduction to Jude. At the moment we are concerned with the question only in so far as it has a bearing on the date of 2 Peter. A date not later than A.D. 90 is assigned to Jude by Chase, Mayor, Salmon, Plummer, Spitta. The limits 100-180 are accepted by

[1] Two conceptions of the term "apostle" are found in the early church, a wider, based on the Jewish official use of the term, and a narrower, confined to the "Twelve". The two conceptions existed side by side, and "the narrower was successful in making headway against its rival" (Harnack, *Expansion of Christianity*, i. p. 408). If the wider use is found here, it would amount to an argument for an early date to the epistle.

Jülicher and Harnack. The arguments for the second century date are examined by Chase (*op. cit.*, pp. 803 f.), and found insufficient.[1]

If the date in the last decade of the first century be accepted for Jude, 2 Peter must be later; but there is not that evidence of advance in the Gnostic views opposed in 2 Peter upon those in Jude to warrant our assigning to 2 Peter a date much later than Jude.

To sum up the *internal* evidence for the date of 2 Peter, the considerations adduced in (3) would fix the *terminus ad quem* at least previous to 140-160, the probable date of Justin, in whose day Chiliasm was an orthodox belief. On the other hand, (1), (2), (5) would render it possible to regard the Epistle as the product of a time not very much later than the apostolic, and perhaps (4) may also be regarded as confirmatory in this connexion. The relationship to Jude would suggest a date not earlier than A.D. 100. The *external evidence,* as we have seen, would render possible a date not later han the first decade of the second century. Perhaps A.D. 100-115, may be tentatively suggested as the extreme limits.

[1] A summary of the evidence may here be given :—

1. πίστις, spoken of in Jude 3-20, as a formulated deposit, is used in practically the same way in Gal. i. 23, iii. 23, vi. 10, etc.

2. In ver. 17 the language need not imply that the apostolic period is long past. The mention of oral instruction (ἔλεγον) would quite suit a date in early sub-apostolic times, when some of the Apostles were dead and some scattered.

3. The argument from the use of apocryphal books is invalid. Of the two quoted by Jude, Enoch is assigned by most scholars to a date B.C., and the Assumption of Moses was probably written within the first thirty years A.D.

4. The Gnostic views attacked in the Epistle are not necessarily of late date.

CHAPTER IV.

RELATION TO 1 PETER.

It is a very generally accepted result of criticism that the two Epistles of Peter are not by the same hand. Jerome (*Script. Eccles.*, 1), in connexion with 2 Peter, remarked on the "stili cum priore dissonantiam" (see p. 175). So marked are these differences between the two Epistles, that even Spitta and Zahn, who defend the authenticity of 2 Peter, are therefore obliged to give up the real Petrine authorship of 1 Peter. They admit that 2 Peter is a letter from the Apostle's own hand, and attribute the First Epistle to Silvanus, under the direction of the Apostle, in accordance with their interpretation of 1 Peter v. 12 (Spitta, *op. cit.*, pp. 530 ff.; Zahn *Introd.* II., pp. 149 ff.).

Space does not permit of a full discussion of this question, and the reader is referred to the minute and elaborate treatment of the subject in Mayor's edition (pp. lxviii. ff.). Reference may be made briefly to the following points:—

1. *Resemblances in Vocabulary and Style.*—(1) *Vocabulary*— (*a*) χάρις ὑμῖν καὶ εἰρήνη πληθυνθείη, 2 Peter i. 2, 1 Peter i. 2; use of καλεῖν, 2 Peter i. 3 and 1 Peter i. 15, ii. 9, 21, iii. 9, v. 10; with κλῆσιν καὶ ἐκλογὴν, 2 Peter i. 10, may be compared the foregoing references to use of καλεῖν in 1 Peter, and the use of ἐκλεκτός, 1 Peter i. 1, ii. 4, 9; θέλημα 2 Peter i. 21, and 1 Peter ii. 15, iii. 17, iv. 2, 19; with ἐν ἐπιθυμίαις σαρκὸς ἀσελγείαις *cf.* πεπορευμένους ἐν ἀσελγείαις, ἐπιθυμίαις 1 Peter iv. 3; ἐπόπται, 2 Peter i. 16, and ἐποπτεύοντες, 1 Peter ii. 12, iii. 2; ἄσπιλοι καὶ ἀμώμητοι, 2 Peter iii. 14, and ἄμωμος καὶ ἄσπιλος, 1 Peter i. 19; ἀκαταπαύστους ἁμαρτίας, 2 Peter ii. 14, and πέπαυται ἁμαρτίας, 1 Peter iv. 1.

The foregoing resemblances are remarkable as extending to the uses of the same words or ideas in similar connexions. The following single words may be noted as being largely confined, in their use in the N.T. to 1 and 2 Peter:—

	2 Peter.	1 Peter.	Rest of N.T.
ἀναστροφή . .	2	5	5
ἀπόθεσις . .	1	1	0
ἀρετή . . .	3	1 (pl.)	1
ἀσεβής . . .	1	1	6 (3 in Jude.)
ἀσέλγεια . .	3	1	6 (1 in Jude.)
ἄσπιλος . . .	1	1	2
προγινώσκω .	1	1	3

(*b*) Including these already mentioned, Mayor, *op. cit.*, pp. lxix., lxx. gives a list of 100 words common to both Epistles. He also gives a list of 369 words occurring in 1 Peter and not in 2 Peter, 230 words occurring in 2 Peter and not in 1 Peter.

(*c*) One remarkable difference is in the word used for the Second Advent. In 2 Peter παρουσία (i. 16, iii. 4, 12), in 1 Peter ἀποκάλυψις (i. 7, 13, iv. 13) is used.

The facts contained in (*a*) are sufficient at least to suggest literary dependence between the two Epistles, but (*b*) and (*c*) entirely negative the possibility that they are by the same hand.

(2) *Style.* "The style of 1 Peter is simple and natural, without a trace of self-conscious effort. The style of 2 Peter is rhetorical and laboured, marked by a love for striking and startling expressions" (Chase, *D. B.*, iii. 812 *a*). As against this estimate, it may be questioned whether the two Epistles are so far apart in style as it is usual to say they are. Mayor says, "There can be no doubt that the style of 1 Peter is, on the whole, clearer and simpler than that of 2 Peter, but there is not that chasm between them which some would try to make out" (p. civ.). As regards *grammatical similarity*, he sums up the results of a most learned discussion (chap. iv.) as follows: "As to the use of the article, they resemble one another more than they resemble any other book of the N.T. Both use the genitive absolute correctly. There is no great difference in their use of the cases or of the verbs, except that 1 Peter freely employs the articular infinitive, which is not found in 2 Peter. The accusative with the infinitive is found in both. The accumulation of prepositions is also common to both. The optative is more freely used in 1 Peter than in 2 Peter. In final clauses 2 Peter conforms to classical usage in attaching the subjunctive to ἵνα, while 1 Peter, in one place, has the future indicative. 2 Peter is also more idiomatic in the use of such elliptical forms as ἕως οὗ, ἐφ᾽ ὅσον, ἀφ᾽ ἧς. On the other hand, 1 Peter shows special elegance in his use of ὡς in comparisons, and emphasises the contrast between the aorist and the present imperative by coupling τιμήσατε with τιμᾶτε in ii. 7" (pp. civ., cv.). It is

incumbent on scholars to give every weight to these utterances, especially in view of such extreme criticism of the style of 2 Peter as that of Dr. E. A. Abbott (*Exp.*, ii., vol. iii.; *From Letter to Spirit*, §§ 1123-1129).

2. *Attitude to the Old Testament.*—It has been reckoned by Hort (Appendix, *Notes on* 1 *Peter*, p. 179) that there are thirty-one quotations from the O.T. in 1 Peter as against five in 2 Peter. Also, an examination of the quotations in 2 Peter (ii. 2, 22, iii. 8, 12, 13), and of the references to O.T. history (Noah, ii. 5; Lot, ii. 6-9; Balaam, ii. 15-16) show that they are not only much fewer in number, but that 2 Peter never formally quotes the O.T., and that the actual allusions are of a much less intimate and spiritual character than in 1 Peter. Incidentally it may be pointed out (*cf.* Chase, *op. cit.*, p. 813 *a*) that this is the opposite of what we would expect if St. Peter wrote the Epistle to Jewish Christians (so Spitta and Zahn).

3. *Relation to the Pauline Epistles.*—1 Peter displays a close connexion of thought with Romans and Ephesians in particular. "The connexion though very close, does not lie on the surface. It is shown more by identities of thought and similarity in the structure of the two Epistles as wholes than by identities of phrase" (Hort, *1 Peter*, p. 5). 2 Peter, on the other hand, is extremely non-Pauline in thought. The idea of the μακροθυμία of God in chap. iii. might easily be the common property of the Christian consciousness. Even granting that there were special circumstances in the origin of 1 Peter, that would largely account for the presence of Pauline thought in the mind of St. Peter as he wrote (*cf.* Chase, *D. B.*, 788, 789), it cannot be regarded as possible that the difference in the circumstances both of writer and readers which we find in 2 Peter would lead to such a complete freedom from Pauline influence.

4. *Devotional Expression.*—There is a great contrast in devotional thought and feeling between the two Epistles. It has already been noted (pp. 186-9) that the references to the great events in the life of Christ are strangely few. The only allusion to His sufferings and death is contained in τὸν ἀγοράσαντα αὐτοὺς δεσπότην (ii. 1). The only crisis in His life that is mentioned is the Transfiguration. No mention is made of the Holy Spirit except as the source of inspiration of the ancient prophets (i. 21). Prayer is not alluded to. The Apostles were essentially witnesses to the Resurrection, but on the Resurrection 2 Peter is silent. Instead, the writer guarantees the truth of the Apostolic teaching by an appeal to the Transfiguration (*cf.* 1 Peter i. 2, 3, 11, 19-21, ii. 24, iii. 18, 21, 22).

There is also a striking difference between the two writers in their personal attitude and relationship towards Jesus Christ. A warmth and intensity of feeling is apparent all through 1 Peter, which displays a much more vivid and tender sense of the reality of the grace and presence of the Risen Christ in the individual heart (*cf.* i. 8, 18, ii. 9, 21, iv. 12 f., v. 16) than the second epistle. "The flame of love," so bright in the first epistle, burns but dimly in the second. 2 Peter contains what Mayor calls "reverential periphrases," such as θεία φύσις, θεία δύναμις, μεγαλειότης, μεγαλοπρεπὴς δόξα, κυριότης. ἐπίγνωσις, ἐπιγινώσκω are the only words that are used of the deepest and most intimate religious experience, communion of heart with the Living Christ. It is true that the thoughts of God's long-suffering (iii. 9-15) and His care of the righteous (ii. 9) are full of tender meaning, but we do not find in 2 Peter that sense of personal relationship to Christ, founded on memories of past, and an actual sense of present discipleship, which transfuses the thought of the first epistle, and we miss the penitential sense of cleansing through the death of Christ so prominent in 1 Peter (*cf.* 1 Peter i. 18-19, ii. 21-23). The references to the Risen Lord in 2 Peter are few, and are pervaded chiefly by a sense of His majesty (*cf.* i. 16, ii. 1, 3, 12, 17, 20, 21, iii. 7, 10, 12). Even where the language is purely hortatory, as in 2 Peter, chap. i., the difference of tone and manner compared with 1 Peter is quite clearly marked. Thus the religious and devotional atmospheres in the two Epistles are far apart. Allowance must no doubt be made for the varying circumstances under which they were written. The one is written to a scattered body of Christians who are suffering persecution, and are in special need of spiritual comfort and stimulus; the other is directed against the immoral influences of false teaching. At the same time external circumstances are quite insufficient to account for these fundamental differences in the religious attitude of the two writings. Such a change could not take place in the history of a single personality, unless through some crisis completely revolutionising thought and feeling.

CHAPTER V.

VOCABULARY AND STYLE OF 2 PETER.

THE extreme limit of depreciatory criticism of the style of 2 Peter is reached in the epithet applied by Dr. E. A. Abbott, (*Expositor* ii., vol. iii.; *From Letter to Spirit* 1121-1135), who describes it as "Baboo Greek". The most moderate treatment of the subject is found in the article, so often referred to, by Dr. Chase. We may briefly summarise the chief points of criticism.

*1. *The large number of words found in 2 Peter, and nowhere else in the N.T.* The full list may be given: ἄθεσμος,[1] ἀκατάπαυστος, ἅλωσις,[1,2] ἀμαθής,[2] ἀμώμητος,[2,3] ἀποφεύγειν,[1,2] ἀργεῖν,[1,2,3] ἀστήρικτος,[2] αὐχμηρός,[2] βλέμμα,[2] βόρβορος,[1,2,3] βραδύτης,[2] διαυγάζειν, δυσνόητος, ἐγκατοικεῖν,[2] ἑκάστοτε,[2,3] ἔκπαλαι,[3] ἔλεγξις,[1] ἐμπαιγμονή, ἐντρυφᾶν,[1] ἐξακολουθεῖν,[1,3] ἐξέραμα, ἐπάγγελμα,[2] ἐπόπτης,[1,2,3] ἰσότιμος, κατακλύζειν,[1,3] καυσοῦσθαι, κύλισμα, λήθη,[1] μεγαλοπρεπής,[1,3] μέγιστος,[1,3] μίασμα,[1,2] μιασμός,[1] μνήμη,[1,3] μυωπάζειν, μῶμος,[1] ὀλίγως, ὁμίχλη,[1,2] παραφρονία, παρεισάγειν, παρεισφέρειν,[2,3] πλαστός,[2] ῥοιζηδόν, σειρός, στηριγμός,[2,3] στοιχεῖον[1] (in sense of physical elements), στρεβλοῦν,[1,2] ταρταροῦν, ταχινός,[3] τεφροῦν, τήκεσθαι, τοιόσδε, τολμητής, ὗς,[1,3] φωσφόρος,[3] ψευδοδιδάσκαλος.

One or two remarks on the list may be offered.

(1) Largely on the ground of the use by 2 Peter of such a remarkably long list of ἅπαξ λεγόμενα the vocabulary of 2 Peter has been characterised as an "ambitious" one (Chase). It has also been described as "bookish," ** with a strong inclination for striking and poetical words.

It is undoubtedly true that many of the words marked [2] are found only in the Greek dramatists or historians, but it is rash to conclude that at the time 2 Peter was written all of them were still poetical words. Moreover, the use of poetical language is not incompatible with the prophetic tone in 2 Peter. The words marked [3] are found in various Papyri, representing the vernacular of daily life, in which much of the N.T. was written. It will be noted that

* Words marked [1] are found in LXX, [2] in classical writers, [3] in Papyri (for reff. see *Comm.*).

** *E.g.* Moulton, *Proleg.*, pp. 97-8. But *cf.* note on II. 5 in *Comm.*

in four cases the so-called ἅπαξ λεγόμενα of 2 Peter are found both in the classics and in the vernacular. This suggests that most ordinary of all occurrences in the history of words, the passing of a word from the language of literature into the language of common speech. Again, the case of words such as ἀμώμητος, ἀργεῖν, etc., taken along with the fact that the study of colloquial Greek is in its infancy, suggests that caution is required in peremptorily condemning the use of certain words in 2 Peter as barbarisms. No less than sixteen words in the above list are found in Papyri.

(2) At the same time it is undoubtedly true that the style of 2 Peter is often rhetorical, and contains some most successful attempts after sonorous effect, (*e.g.*, note the rhythm of ii. 4-9, and *cf.* the remarks of Mayor, p. lviii. and Bigg, pp. 227 ff.). The writer is himself impressed with the majesty of his theme, and it is of great interest to note that in some cases he may probably be making use of the liturgical language of his day. An inscription has been discovered in Stratonicea in Caria, dating from the early imperial period, containing a decree of the inhabitants in honour of Zeus Panhemerios and of Hekate. Deissmann (*Bible Studies*, E. Tr., pp. 360 ff.) has pointed out one or two most suggestive parallels in the inscription with 2 Peter i. 3 ff. The phrases τῆς θείας δυνάμεως ἀρετάς, τῶν κυρίων Ῥωμαίων αἰωνίου ἀρχῆς, πᾶσαν σπουδὴν εἰσφέρεσθαι, and the superlative μεγίστων (θεῶν) occur. In the case of θεία δύναμις, where 2 Peter was usually supposed to be employing philosophical language, he appears really to be quoting a current religious term, well known perhaps to the very readers of his Epistle. With the phrase θείας κοινωνοὶ φύσεως (i. 4) may be compared φύσεως κοινωνοῦντες ἀνθρω[πί]νης from a religious inscription of Antiochus I. of Kommagene (middle of first century B.C.). It is probable, also, that the use of words like μεγαλοπρεπής, ταρταροῦν and εὐσέβεια (which also occurs in the Carian inscription, and is a common N.T. word); δωρέομαι, ἀρέτη (i. 3), ἐπιχορηγεῖν, and phrases like διεγείρειν ἐν ὑπομνήσει may be traced to the same liturgical source.

2. *Solecisms.*—Chase gives a list of certain expressions in the Epistle "which, *so far as our knowledge of the language goes*, appear to be contrary to usage." These are βλέμμα (ii. 8), καυσοῦσθαι (iii. 10-12), μελλήσω (i. 12), μνήμην ποιεῖσθαι (i. 15), μυωπάζεν (i. 9), παρεισφέρειν (i. 5), σειρός (ii. 4). For discussion as to the meaning of these see the *Commentary in loc.* That something may be said for their use is proved by the remarks of Mayor (pp. lx. ff.).

3. *Reiteration of Words.*—There is a well-marked reiteration of words in the vocabulary of 2 Peter, *e.g.*, ἐπιχορηγεῖν (i. 5, 11); βέβαιος

(i. 10, 19); ὑπομιμνήσκειν, ἐν ὑπομνήσει, μνήμην ποιεῖσθαι (i. 12, 13, 15; iii. 1); ἐνεχθείσης, ἐνεχθεῖσαν (i. 17, 18); ἀπώλεια (ii. 13, iii. 7-16); ἐφείσατο (ii. 4, 5); τηρεῖν (ii. 4, 9, 17; iii. 7); στοιχεῖα καυσούμενα (iii. 10, 12).

Chase asserts that "the extraordinary list of repetitions" stamps the vocabulary as "poor and inadequate" (*op. cit.*, 808). In reply, it may be urged, (1) This sweeping condemnation is scarcely consistent with the occasional use of very rare words on the part of the writer. (2) Reiteration may arise from other causes than a limited vocabulary. It may arise "either from a liking for resonant sounds, or from a desire to give emphasis by the use of line upon line, or from both" (Mayor, p. lvii. f.). (3) A similar habit of repeating words is found in 1 Peter (*cf.* Bigg, pp. 226 f.).

The foregoing remarks on the vocabulary and style of 2 Peter are necessary and timely, in view of the current tendency to depreciate these. Many of the phrases in 2 Peter have found a permanent place in the religious language of the Christian Church. It would be rash to acquit the writer entirely of all faults of style that have been attributed to him, but his ordinary intelligence must at least be vindicated. Chap. iii., "On the Style of 2 Peter," of Mayor's edition is worthy of close study, as tending to restore the style of 2 Peter to that respect which enabled it to be studied in the time of Aurelius, though not regarded as canonical, along with other Scriptures, "as it appears profitable to many".

CHAPTER VI.

CIRCUMSTANCES OF WRITING.

1. *Readers.*—To whom was the Epistle written? The crucial passage in this connexion is iii. 1, where the Epistle referred to is most naturally understood to be 1 Peter. The objection is urged by Spitta, Zahn, and more recently by Mayor, that the description of the contents in iii. 1, 2 is inapplicable to 1 Peter. Yet in 1 Peter i. 10-12 we have almost an exact parallel to τῶν προειρημένων ῥημάτων ὑπὸ τῶν ἁγίων προφητῶν, and 1 Peter is full of reminiscences of the teaching and example of Jesus (τῆς . . . ἐντολῆς τοῦ κυρίου καὶ σωτῆρος) (*cf.* 1 Peter i. 15, 16, ii. 13-17, 23, etc.; *cf.* also ii. 1, τοῦτο δέ ἐστιν τὸ ῥῆμα τὸ εὐαγγελισθὲν εἰς ὑμᾶς). The ethical difficulty caused by this interpretation of the reference, if the two Epistles are not by the same author, is no greater than that aroused by the use of the apostolic name in i. 1 (see *Introd.*, pp. 97-99). Moreover, we have no reason to expect anything but a statement in iii. 1 of what the two Epistles have in common. The words do not exclude the supposition that their contents differ in many respects. The readers, then, are, in general, those mentioned in 1 Peter i. 1, *viz.*, Christian communities of Asia Minor.

Mayor (*op. cit.*, pp. cxxxvii. ff.) has again defended the view that 2 Peter is written to the Roman Church.[1] He founds his argument on 2 Peter iii. 15, καθὼς καὶ ὁ ἀγαπητὸς ἡμῶν Παῦλος ἔγραψεν ὑμῖν, holding that καθώς must be explained by the immediately preceding admonition, τοῦ κυρίου ἡμῶν μακροθυμίαν σωτηρίαν ἡγεῖσθε, which is more distinctly stated in Romans ii. 4, iii. 25, 26, ix. 22, than elsewhere. Various objections may be urged against this view. (1) It is extremely doubtful whether the reference καθώς can be thus narrowed, so as to include only ver. 14. The introduction of the comparison with Paul seems to arise from a desire to show that in general there is no discrepancy between the Petrine and the Pauline teaching. (2) Even although the Epistle to the Romans is meant, it would be no proof that 2 Peter was written to the Roman Church, as it is evident from

[1] So Grotius, Dietlein.

ἐν πάσαις ἐπιστολαῖς, and τὰς λοιπὰς γραφὰς (ver. 16), that the Epistles of Paul had reached the rank of γραφαί, and were known to the Church at large. (3) Even if the narrower reference of καθὼς is adopted, the idea of μακροθυμία is echoed also in 1 Corinthians and Thessalonians (1 Cor. xv. 2; 2 Thess. ii. 16). If the wider reference is taken, almost any of the Pauline Epistles may be meant, as the doctrine of God's free grace is reflected in many of them. It is also, of course, quite possible that the reference may be to a lost Epistle.[1]

That practically the same class of readers as in 1 Peter is meant, is confirmed by τοῖς ἰσότιμον ἡμῖν λαχοῦσιν πίστιν (i. 1).[2] The phrase may be regarded as referring in general to the isolated position of the readers, who are made to feel, as in 1 Peter i. 1, 2, that they too are recipients of the grace of God and objects of His special choice. The words in 2 Peter may well be a succinct expression of the idea in the opening verses of the First Epistle. In the one case the readers are suffering persecution; in the other, they are being led astray and harassed by false teaching. In both cases the words carry a message of comfort.

The question may be raised whether i. 16, ἐγνωρίσαμεν ὑμῖν τὴν τοῦ κυρίου . . . δύναμιν καὶ παρουσίαν, implies that the Apostle himself had preached to these readers, and whether this is compatible with an Asiatic community as recipients of the letter. In 1 Peter the Apostle does not appear to have been personally acquainted with his readers or to have himself laboured among them, and there is no trace in the career of St. Peter of an Asiatic ministry. The words, however, do not necessarily imply that Peter had himself preached the Gospel to those who are addressed. The plural may be used of a single person (*cf.* Moulton, *Proleg.*, p. 86). The mask would seem to be thrown off for the moment, and the actual personality of the unknown writer to obtrude itself in this pseudonymous Epistle. That he should have taken no special pains to prevent this, is itself an indication of good faith on the writer's part, and of his lack of any intention to deceive. He himself is the preacher.

The general character of the address in 2 Peter is undoubted. The Epistle is written to a wide class of Christians readers

[1] Hofmann (vii. 2, 113 ff.) argues that the reference is to Ephesians. An important discussion of whole question is found in Spitta (pp. 286-88).

[2] In connexion with these words, it has been argued whether they indicate Jewish or Gentile Christians. The presumption is in favour of the latter (see *Commentary in loc.*). The use of a word like ταρταρώσας (ii. 4) indicates a Hellenic atmosphere of thought, and the phrase in ii. 20, ἀποφυγόντες τὰ μιάσματα τοῦ κόσμου seems most applicable to Gentiles.

who are not recent converts (i. 12), "ein für weite Kreise der Kirche bestimmtes pastorales Rundschau" (Spitta, *op. cit.*, p. 483). 1 Peter also is general in its destination. 2 Peter may well be addressed to the same localities as 1 Peter, although to a later generation of Christians, under different circumstances. This would also supply a motive for the use of the Apostle's name.

2. *False Teachers.*—The description of the false teachers given in chap. ii. is taken in the main from the Epistle of Jude. It ought to be noted, however, that the object in view in the two Epistles is somewhat different. Jude is, above all, a polemic against the false teaching. 2 Peter is written with a view to confirming the faith of the Christian communities in the face of the delayed Parousia. The false teachers in 2 Peter "have brought a new idea into the field. . . . They cast doubt on the Christian eschatological expectation . . . appealing in support of their view to a deeper knowledge of Christ (i. 2, 3, iii. 18, *cf.* i. 16-18), a particular conception of the O.T. (i. 20, iii. 16), and certain Pauline positions (iii. 15 f., *cf.* ii. 19)" (Von Soden, *op. cit.*, p. 194). They are "mockers" (ἐμπαῖκται) who say, ποῦ ἐστὶν ἡ ἐπαγγελία τῆς παρουσίας αὐτοῦ; (iii. 4). In this fact, we may find a partial explanation of the use made by 2 Peter of Jude. He makes use of an authoritative description of their real character, making certain changes dictated by his own views as to the use of apocryphal books (*e.g.*, omission of story of Michael), and by the special circumstances of those he addresses.

A remarkable circumstance in the language employed is that the writer speaks at one time of the false teachers as about to come (ii. 1 f., iii. 3), at another as though they were already active (ii. 11, 12, 17 f., 20, iii. 5, iii. 16). All such explanations as that the writer projects himself into the future, and from that point of view vividly regards future events as actually happening; or that he is at one time thinking of communities where the ψευδοδιδάσκαλοι are actually at work, and at another of communities where their influence has not yet penetrated, may be set aside. The simplest explanation seems to be that again the writer, when he speaks of them in the present tense, throws off the prophetic mask, and depicts what he knew was actually happening.[1]

Do the characteristics mentioned in this Epistle point to a Gnostic sect? It has been pointed out that there is one important difference between the libertines of Jude's Epistle and those of

[1] Henkel suggests that the False Teachers, who are active in other communities, are regarded as presenting only an imminent possible danger to the readers of 2 Peter (*Der Zw. B. des Apostelfürsten Petrus*, p. 37 ff.).

2 Peter (*cf.* Chase, *op. cit.*, iii. 811). In the former, not so much teaching as practice, was in question, while, in 2 Peter, they are called ψευδοδιδάσκαλοι, and seem to have been engaged in the active propagation of false doctrine. The use of γνῶσις in i. 5 f. can scarcely be without reference to that intellectualism, with its hidden wisdom, and exclusive mysteries, so characteristic of Gnosticism (*cf.* Lightfoot, *Colossians*, pp. 73-113). The word ἐπόπτης (i. 16) is a Gnostic term meaning one who has been initiated into the mystery. Jude, on the other hand, seems to feel that the movement he combats is also doctrinal in its import; for he urges his readers "to contend for the faith once delivered to the saints" (ver. 3), and the heresy he opposes must have had a certain materialistic basis (κυριότητα δὲ ἀθετοῦσιν, δόξας δὲ βλασφημοῦσιν, ver. 8). There is also implied a certain doctrinal process in the words, χάριτα μετατιθέντες εἰς ἀσέλγειαν καὶ τὸν μόνον δεσπότην καὶ κύριον ἡμῶν Ἰησοῦν Χριστὸν ἀρνούμενοι (ver. 4). Thus, in both cases, the readers are warned against what was really a matter both of life and of doctrine, and the situation in 2 Peter need not necessarily imply a stage at least much later in the development of the false teaching. In these Epistles it can scarcely be doubted that we are in the presence of an incipient Gnosticism, and the two directions in which the Gnostic tendency led, *viz.*, Intellectualism and Antinomianism, are clearly marked. On this latter aspect, the emphasis is laid, not only in the Epistles, but in the N.T. generally. The new movement caused great anxiety to the leaders of the Church, owing chiefly to its immoral tendency. For long the heretics were in communion with the Christian Church, and it was not until the second century that the cleavage widened out to its true limits (*cf.* E. F. Scott, *Apologetic of the N.T.*, pp. 146 ff.). These false teachers in Jude and 2 Peter were partakers in the rites of the Christian Church (Jude 12; 2 Peter ii. 13). Incidentally, it may be mentioned that their description in 2 Peter does not in itself warrant a date for its composition in the second century, and certainly not a date so much later than Jude, as is usually supposed.

2 Peter, then, gives us in general a picture of the prevalence of Antinomian heresy, which has as its results the corruption of morals, and a certain materialistic tendency which led to disbelief in the Person of Christ (ii. 1), and a denial of the ethical nature of God (iii. 8, 9; *cf.* also Philipp. iii. 18 f). 2 Peter is throughout eminently ethical in its tone. Religion and life are inseparably connected, ὡς πάντα ἡμῖν τῆς θείας δυνάμεως αὐτοῦ τὰ πρὸς ζωὴν καὶ εὐσέβειαν δεδωρημένης διὰ τῆς ἐπιγνώσεως τοῦ καλέσαντος ἡμᾶς (i. 3). The true γνῶσις must contain ethical qualities (i. 6). The Christian must take pains "to

make his calling and election sure" by godliness of life (i. 10). We are not, however, left without traces of the doctrinal position of these false teachers. The Gnostic position which demanded γνῶσις, or a hidden wisdom which leads to perfection, is tacitly opposed in the use of the word ἐπίγνωσις, which is used by St. Paul to denote "complete knowledge" or "saving knowledge" (*cf.* 1 Cor. xiii. 12; Philem. 6). Mayor suggests (*op. cit.*, p. 171) that ἐπίγνωσις came into use to distinguish the "living knowledge of the true believer from the spurious γνῶσις which had then begun to ravage the Church". The true ἐπίγνωσις carries with it "all that is needed for life and godliness" (i. 3). These Gnostics evidently held that Revelation in itself was incomplete. Those, however, who possess ἐπίγνωσις are made θείας κοινωνοὶ φύσεως, a phrase which originates in a philosophic atmosphere, and no doubt reflects a sense of opposition to the pure intellectualism of these false teachers, who would claim to be κοινωνοὶ θείας φύσεως by means of wisdom or γνῶσις alone. τυφλός ἐστιν μυωπάζων (i. 9) is a reference to the darkness which was mistaken for light, because the γνῶσις that accompanied it was so unethical (*cf.* the whole passage, i. 5-9). σεσοφισμένοις μύθοις (i. 16) refers to those fictions connected with the emanation of æons, so characteristic of the Gnostic system (*cf.* 1 Tim. i. 4, iv. 7; 2 Tim. iv. 4; Tit. i. 14), by virtue of which the Person of Christ was regarded as the emanation of an æon, in union with a human body. In contrast to this idea, the writer claims that the Apostles were ἐπόπται . . . τῆς ἐκείνου μεγαλειότητος. The Voice proclaims Him to be actually ὁ υἱός μου ὁ ἀγαπητός μου (i. 17). What seems to be a denial of the Person and Work of Christ is referred to in i. 1 τὸν ἀγοράσαντα αὐτοὺς δεσπότην ἀρνούμενοι. πλαστοῖς λόγοις (fictitious words) of i. 3 may be compared with σεσοφισμένοις μύθοις of i. 16. κυριότητος καταφρονοῦντας (ii. 10), δόξας οὐ τρέμουσιν (ii. 11) evidently cannot refer to any denial of human authority, but rather to sceptical views regarding the influence of spiritual powers, good or evil, upon the life of the individual. Such a belief was part of the orthodox Jewish thought of the time (see *Commentary in loc.*). ἐλευθερίαν . . . ἐπαγγελλόμενοι (ii. 19) may be set alongside the passage dealing with the misuse and misinterpretation of the Pauline doctrine of free grace (iii. 16), which provided the theoretic basis for Antinomianism. These false teachers questioned the truth of the Parousia expectation (iii. 4) on the ground (1) *of the uniformity of nature* (πάντα οὕτως διαμένει ἀπ' ἀρχῆς κτίσεως) which is met by the argument that the heavens and the earth were created by the word of God, and that the earth has already been flooded by the same divine agency (iii. 5-7). (2) *The indestructibility of matter*, against which it is asserted that in the day of the Lord οἱ οὐρανοὶ ῥοιζηδὸν παρελεύσονται, στοιχεῖα δὲ καυσούμενα λυθήσεται (iii. 10). Finally, we are told that the false teachers use the Scriptures of the O.T. as a basis for their heretical teaching (iii. 16).

It is thus apparent that in 2 Peter, far more than in Jude, the doctrine as well as the life of the false teachers is in question. Their ethical character is described in words largely borrowed from Jude, and in no measured terms. They speak evil of the way of truth (ii. 2); make merchandise of their followers (ii. 3); are fleshly and lustful (ii. 10-12); practise a vulgar hedonism (ii. 13); defile the love-feasts by their presence (13); deceive the hopes of their followers, like waterless fountains (16). They are Christians in name, steal into the Church without disclosing their impious views (ii. 1, 20, 21), and are boastful and irreverent (ii. 10, 18).

The question arises whether these false teachers can be identified with any known heretical sect. Some critics have sought to distinguish between the libertines of chap. ii. and the mockers of chap. iii., but there is really no difficulty in identifying the two.[1] The denial of the Parousia by the mockers is really the outcome of a materialistic philosophy, and the denial of a future judgment would have the tendency to emancipate from all moral restraint. "There may have been shades of difference between them; some, perhaps, had a philosophy, and some had not; but in the eyes of a Christian Preacher, judging the party as a whole by its practical results, they would all seem to wear the same livery" (Bigg, *op. cit.*, p. 239, *cf.* Henkel, *op. cit.*, p. 37).

Harnack, who holds that Jude was written 100-130, suggests that the attack in that Epistle is aimed at some of the older forms of Gnosticism, among which he mentions the Nicolaitans. This sect is known to have had considerable influence in Asia Minor, and is mentioned by name in Rev. ii. 6, 15, in the Epistles to Ephesus and to Pergamum. In the case of the latter Church they are represented as existing side by side, and probably as identical with a sect of "Balaamites" (ii. 14). No doubt the same sect is accused of immorality in the Epistle of Thyatira (ii. 20). In 2 Peter ii. 15, 16 the example of Balaam is adduced as a parallel to the conduct of the false teachers, and it would appear that the name of Balaamites was given as a nickname to the Nicolaitans. Irenæus (iii., c. 1) tells us that the Nicolaitans held the doctrine of two Gods—the God who created the world, and the Father of Jesus; that an æon descended upon Jesus, and again returned into the Pleroma before the Cruci-

[1] *Cf.* Henkel, *op. cit.*, pp. 21 ff., where the question is fully discussed.

fixion. The language of 2 Peter iii. 5-9, relative to the creation and the present government of the world, through the long-suffering of the Creator, might well have in view some such doctrine as this. The accusation, also, of distorting the Scriptures of the O.T. (iii. 16) would also be explained, as also the statement in Jude 4 and 2 Peter ii. 1 about the heretics' denial of Christ. It is probable that these views were common to the Nicolaitans along with other early Gnostic sects, such as the followers of Simon Magus (*cf.* Mayor, *op. cit.*, pp. clxxviii. ff.).

On the intellectual side, Gnosticism originated in a compromise with Greek thought, and an attempt to adapt the Christian teaching to the current philosophy. It is probable that, on the side of conduct, the immoralities that are so vividly denounced in Jude and 2 Peter were due to a similar compromise with the customs and ideas of the Græco-Roman society of the day. The Nicolaitan teaching, as described in Rev. ii., was "evidently an attempt to effect a reasonable compromise with the established usages of Græco-Roman society, and to retain as many as possible of those usages in the Christian system of life. It affected most of all the educated and cultured classes in the Church, those who had most temptation to retain as much as possible of the established social ideas and customs of the Græco-Roman world, and who by their more elaborate education had been most fitted to take a somewhat artificial view of life, and to reconcile contradictory principles in practical conduct through subtle philosophical reasoning" (Ramsay, *The Letters to the Seven Churches*, pp. 337 ff.).

It had evidently become the custom in the Early Church to use the most unsparing language in denouncing these Gnostic errors. Both in Revelation and in Jude, the language is violent, and 2 Peter deals with the false teachers in the same temper. This may render it difficult, at the present day, to understand the exact theoretic position of a sect like the Nicolaitans, and it is a well-known fact that certain philosophic positions in religion, adopted and advocated by men who are themselves of blameless life, may really lead in the case of weaker followers to great moral laxity. If we consider the picture of Græco-Roman society drawn by St Paul in Romans i., it is not to be wondered at that these heresies, which led to such moral compromises, should be vigorously denounced by the Christian teacher. Nothing else "could have saved the infant Church from melting away into one of those vague and ineffective schools of philosophic ethics. . . . An easy-going Christianity could never have survived; it could not have conquered and trained the world; only the most convinced, resolute, almost bigoted adherence to the most uncompromising interpretations of its own principles could have gained the Christians the courage and self-reliance that were needed" (Ramsay, *op. cit.*, *ibid.*).

3. *Place of Writing.*—On this topic, there is very little ground for judgment beyond vague conjecture. Chase favours the view that 2 Peter is of Egyptian origin. He founds his opinion (1) on the supposition that the Apocalypse of Peter and 2 Peter belong to the same school, (2) that Clement of Alexandria appears to have placed the two documents side by side, and commented on them together in his Hypotyposeis, (3) certain resemblances in thought and word with Philo and Clement of Alexandria (*op. cit.*, p. 816 f.). Jülicher (*Introd.*, E. Tr., p. 239) suggests that the Epistle originated either in Egypt or in Palestine. Palestine is selected on the ground that the Epistle is directed against one of the earlier and less known Gnostic sects which flourished in that country or in Syria. Deissmann, on the basis of the Stratonicean inscription already quoted (*op. cit.*, pp. 367 f.) inclines to the view that the local colouring of the Epistle belongs to Asia Minor. He awaits the result of further inquiry "how far its peculiar vocabulary has points of contact with that of literary sources (of the imperial period) from Egypt, or Asia Minor, including those of the papyri and the inscriptions". There can be little doubt that the readers are in Asia Minor, but does not the form of address, τοῖς ἰσότιμον ἡμῖν λαχοῦσιν πίστιν, point to a writer at some distance from his readers, though well acquainted with their circumstances? (*cf.* p. 114).

LITERATURE.

Friederich Spitta. *Der zweite Brief des Petrus und der Brief des Judas.* 1885.

H. v. Soden. *Hand-Commentar Zum N.T.*, vol. iii., 1892.

F. H. Chase. Art. 2 Peter in Hastings' *Dictionary of the Bible.*, vol. iii., 1900.

Charles Bigg. "A Critical and Exegetical Commentary on the Epistles of St. Peter and St. Jude (*International Critical Commentary*). 1901.

J. B. Mayor. *The Epistle of St. Jude and the Second Epistle of St. Peter.* 1907.

Amongst older commentaries of the present century referred to are those of Alford (ed. 1898), Hofmann (1875), Huther (in Meyer, 1852. E. Tr., 1881), A. Wiesinger (in Olshausen, *Bibelwerk*, 1862), Dietlein (1851).

The general question of authenticity is discussed in the following:—

Salmon's *Introduction*, pp. 481, ff. 1894.

Jülicher's *Introduction*, E. Tr., 1904, pp. 232 ff.

Zahn's *Introduction*, E. Tr., 1909, vol. ii., pp. 134 ff.

B. Weiss. *Studien und Kritiken*, 1866, pp. 256 ff.

Grosch. *Die Echtheit des zweiten Briefes Petri*, 1889.

McGiffert. *History of Christianity in the Apostolic Age*, 1897, pp. 600 ff.

Sanday. *Inspiration*, 1893, pp. 346 ff., 382 ff.

E. A. Abbott. *Expositor*, Jan.-March, 1882. "From Letter to Spirit," §§ 1121-1135.

Karl Henkel. *Der zweite Brief des Apostelfürsten Petrus, geprüft auf seine Echtheit.* (From R. C. Standpoint), 1904.

ABBREVIATIONS OF REFERENCES TO PAPYRI AND INSCRIPTIONS.

P. Amh. *The Amherst Papyri*, edd. B. P. Grenfell and A. S. Hunt. (London, 1900-01.)

P. Fay. *Fayûm Towns and their Papyri*, edd. B. P. Grenfell, A. S. Hunt and D. G. Hogarth (Egyptian Exploration Fund. London, 1900.)

P. Fior. *Papiri Fiorentini*, ed. G. Vitelli. (Milan, 1905-06.)

P. Gen. *Les Papyrus de Genève*, 1. *Papyrus Grecs*, ed. J. Nicole. (Genève, 1896-1900.)

P. Grenf. I. *An Alexandrian Erotic Fragment and other Greek Papyri, chiefly Ptolemaic*; ed. B. P. Grenfell. (Oxford, 1896.) II. *New Classical Fragments and other Greek and Latin Papyri*, edd. B. P. Grenfell and A. S. Hunt. (Oxford, 1897.)

P. Hib. *The Hibeh Papyri* I., edd. Grenfell and Hunt. (Egyptian Exploration Fund. London, 1906.)

P. Lond. *Greek Papyri in British Museum*, 3 vols. (London, 1893, 1898, 1907.)

P. Oxy. *The Oxyrhynchus Papyri*, edd. Grenfell and Hunt. (Egyptian Exploration Fund. London, 1898, 1899, 1903, 1904.)

P. Par. Paris Papyri in *Notices et Extraits*, xviii., ii., ed. Brunet de Presle. (Paris, 1865.)

P. Petr. *Flinders Petrie Papyri* in Proceedings of the Royal Irish Academy, "Cunningham Memoirs" (Nos. viii., ix., xi.), 3 vols. (Dublin, 1891-1893.)

P. Tebt. *The Tebtunis Papyri*, 2 vols. (University of California Publications. London, 1902, 1907.)

B.G.U. *Griechische Urkunden*, from the Berlin Museum.

C.I.A. *Corpus Inscriptionum Atticarum.* Berlin, 1873- .

O.G.I.S. *Orientis Graeci Inscriptiones Selectae*, ed. W. Dittenberger, 2 vols. (Leipzig, 1903-05.)

For the references to Papyri I am indebted to the "Lexical Notes from the Papyri," appearing in *Expositor*, 1908-9, by Rev. Professor J. H. Moulton, D.D., D.Lit., and the Rev. George Milligan, D.D., and to private communications from these scholars.

OTHER ABBREVIATIONS.

ZNTW. Zeitschrift für die neutestamentliche Wissenschaft, herausgegeben von Erwin Preuschen.

MME. Notes from the Papyri in *Expositor*, 1908, by Professor Moulton and Dr. Milligan.

Moulton Proleg. Grammar of New Testament Greek, vol. i. Prolegomena by Professor J. H. Moulton.

Abbott, J. G. Johannine Grammar by Edwin A. Abbott.

WM. Winer's Grammar of N.T. Greek, 3rd edition, by W. F. Moulton.

H.D.B. Hastings' Dictionary of the Bible (5 vols.).

ΠΕΤΡΟΥ ΕΠΙΣΤΟΛΗ Β̄.

I. 1. **ΣΥΜΕΩΝ**[1] Πέτρος δοῦλος καὶ ἀπόστολος Ἰησοῦ Χριστοῦ τοῖς
ἰσότιμον ἡμῖν λαχοῦσιν πίστιν ἐν δικαιοσύνῃ τοῦ Θεοῦ ἡμῶν καὶ
σωτῆρος Ἰησοῦ Χριστοῦ· 2. χάρις ὑμῖν καὶ εἰρήνη πληθυνθείη ἐν

[1] Συμεων ℵAKLP syrr., Treg., Ti., WH^m; Σιμων B, vulg., sah., boh., WH.

Chapter I. Vv. 1-2. *The Greeting.* "Simeon Peter, slave and apostle of Jesus Christ, to those who have obtained a faith of equal honour with our own, through the justice of our God and Saviour Jesus Christ. Grace and peace be multiplied unto you in the saving knowledge of our Lord."

Ver. 1. The form **Συμέων** is only once used elsewhere of Peter in Acts xv. 14. **τοῖς κ.τ.λ.** The question as to who are the actual recipients of the letter, is matter for discussion in the Introduction (chap. vi. 1). The presumption is in favour of a body of non-Jewish Christians. **ἡμῖν.** probably means, in accordance with its use elsewhere in the chapter, the whole Christian community to which the writer belongs (see Introd. p. 49). **ἰσότιμον.** It is doubtful whether **ἰσοτ.** means "like in honour" or "like in value". Both meanings are found (*cf.* Mayor, p. 80). We may compare the sense of **τιμή** in v. 17 (see note), where the sense is clearly of an honour conferred (*cf.* 1 Peter i. 7), which would suggest the same meaning here. **ἐν δικαιοσύνῃ . . . Χριστοῦ.** **ἐν** is instrumental,. **δικ.** has the sense of "justice" or "impartiality," and is opposed to **προσωποληµψία.** God is no respecter of persons. There is no distinction in His sight between the faith of an eye-witness, and the faith of those "who have not seen". With this non-theological sense of **δικ.** *cf.* **ἄδικος** in Hebrew vi. 10; also 1 John i. 9. **Θεοῦ** refers to Christ, *cf.* John xx. 28. **σωτῆρος,** a title used by the Emperor. "Familiarity with the everlasting apotheosis that flaunts itself in the papyri and inscriptions of Ptolemaic and Imperial times, lends strong support to Wendland's contention (ZNTW, pp. 335 ff.) that Christians from the latter part of i. A.D. onward, deliberately assumed for their Divine Master the phraseology that was impiously arrogated to themselves by some of the worst of men" (*i.e.,* the Emperors). Moulton, *Proleg.* p. 84 (*cf.* Spitta, p. 523; Chase, *D. B.* iii. 796). **πίστιν ἐν δικ.** can hardly be taken together (*cf.* Eph. i. 15, 1 Tim. iii. 13), as the relation of the believer to Christ in this epistle is rather that of **γνῶσις** or **ἐπίγνωσις** (*cf.* v. 2). (*Cf.* Zahn. *Introd.* ii. pp. 218-9).

Ver. 2. **χάρις . . . πληθυνθείη.**: the same form of salutation as in 1 Pet. i. 2. **ἐν ἐπιγνώσει τοῦ Κυρίου ἡμῶν.** (For history of **ἐπίγνωσις** see Mayor's note, pp. 171 ff.; Robinson's *Excursus* in *Ephesians.*) **ἐπίγνωσις** in this epistle corresponds to **πίστις** in the Pauline sense (Spitta, p. 522). In Rom. i. 21 **γνόντες** is used of the imperfect knowledge of God possessed by the heathen world, and in v. 28 he contrasts it with the Christian or perfect knowledge of God. (**καθὼς οὐκ ἐδοκίμασαν τὸν Θεὸν ἔχειν ἐν ἐπιγνώσει.**) *Cf.* 1 Cor. xiii. 12, Col. i. 9. "**ἐπίγνωσις,** involving the complete appropriation of all truth and the unreserved acquiescence in God's will, is the goal and crown of the believer's course" (Lightfoot, note on Col. i. 9). *Cf.* Introd. p. 117; note v. 8; Paget, *Spirit of Discipline,* pp. 112 ff. **ἐπίγνωσις** implies a more intimate and personal relationship than **γνῶσις.** It would be a useful word, seeing that **γνῶσις** had become associated with Gnosticism, then incipient in the Church. Mayor quotes Clem. Alex. *Strom.* i. p. 372, and *Str.,* vi., p. 759, where **κατ' ἐπίγνωσιν** is twice opposed to **κατὰ περίφασιν** (= on a broad general view, *cf.* Mayor's note, p. 213). Grace and peace are multiplied in and through this more

a 1 Cor. iv. 18, Xen. Cyr. 3, 3, 4. Mem. 1, 6, 5.

ἐπιγνώσει τοῦ κυρίου ἡμῶν,[1] 3. ᵃὡς πάντα ἡμῖν τῆς θείας δυνάμεως αὐτοῦ τὰ πρὸς ζωὴν καὶ εὐσέβειαν δεδωρημένης διὰ τῆς ἐπι-

[1] του θεου και Ιησου του κυριου ημων MSS. generally, Ti., Treg., WH; om. του θεου καὶ Ιησου P, vulg., Minusc., 69, 137, 163, Spitta, Zahn., Nestle. A strong argument in favour of omission is the fact that consistently throughout the epistle Jesus alone appears as the object of επιγνωσις or γνωσις. Additional confirmation is the use of αυτου (sing.) in v. 3.

intimate heart knowledge of Jesus Christ, in contrast to a mere barren γνῶσις.

Vv. 3, 4. *The Promises and their Source.* "Inasmuch as His Divine Power has granted us all things that are needed for life and piety, by means of the personal knowledge of One who called us by the impression of his own glory and excellency; and through this glory and excellency have been granted promises that are precious to us and glorious, in order that, by means of these, ye might be partakers of the Divine Nature, escaping the corruption that is in the world owing to lust."

Throughout this passage, the contrast between ἡμῖν, ἡμᾶς, and 2 p. plur. in γένησθε (ver. 4) must be preserved. ἡμῖν implies the apostolic circle, who, by virtue of their own experience of the δόξα and ἀρετή of Christ, are able to transmit to these readers certain promises "precious to us, and glorious." (So Spitta, Van Soden).

Ver. 3. τῆς θείας δυνάμεως is originally a philosophic term (Plato, *Ion.* 534 C., Arist. *Pol.* vii. 4) *cf.* τὸ θεῖον as used by St. Paul in speaking to philosophers at Athens (Acts xvii. 29). The subject is Christ (*cf.* δύναμις κυρίου, Luke x. 17; 1 Cor. v. 4; 2 Cor. xii. 9; and v. 16, of this chapter). The phrase θεία δύναμις is contained in an inscription of Stratonicea in Caria in honour of Zeus Panhemerios and Hekate, belonging to the early Imperial period. 2 Peter would thus be availing himself of one of "the familiar forms and formulæ of religious emotion" (Deissmann, *Bible Studies*, p. 367). αὐτοῦ is taken as referring to Κυρίου in ver. 2, which would confirm the reading adopted. πάντα . . . τὰ πρὸς ζωὴν καὶ εὐσέβειαν. ζωή is the new life that belongs to believers in Christ. εὐσέβεια is also found in the inscription quoted above. This word and its cognates are found in N.T. only in Acts, this Epistle, and in the Pastoral Epistles. They are also common in inscriptions of Asia Minor, and were apparently familiar terms in the religious language of the Imperial period. In εὐσέβεια, the emphasis of meaning lies towards "godliness" in its practical, rather than its devotional aspect, *i.e.*, what God requires of man "pious conduct". In 1 Tim. iii. 16 Christ is spoken of as "the secret of piety" (τὸ τῆς εὐσεβείας μυστήριον). The conjunction of the two ideas ζωή and εὐσέβεια is significant. Religion does not narrow, but expand the province of life. The life in Christ is not "a little province of peculiar emotion . . . . If we fear that it may lose itself in the vast and often lawless universe of life beneath, the danger is to be averted not by wilfully contracting it within a narrower field, but by seeking greater intensity of life in deeper and more submissive communion with the Head Himself in the heavens" (Hort, *The Way, the Truth, and the Life*, p. 147). δεδωρημένης (="gifted" or "granted"). This word and its cognates always carry a certain regal sense describing an act of large-handed generosity. *Cf.* Mark xv. 45 of the giving by Pilate of the body of Jesus to Joseph; John iv. 10; James i. 17. The same sense is found in Gen. xxx. 20, Prov. iv. 2, Isa. lxii. 3; and O.G.I.S. 517[7] (iii. A.D.) with reference to the gift by Marcus Aurelius of a new law-court, ὁπότε ἐδω[ρ]ήσατο τῆι πατρίδι ἡμῶν [τ]ὴν ἀγορὰν τῶν δικῶν. τοῦ καλέσαντος ἡμᾶς. Judging from usage elsewhere in N.T., the reference would here be to God, who is always the Caller. 2 Peter, however, shows great independence of thought in other directions, and it is more likely that the reference is to Christ, especially as ἐπίγνωσις is used consistently in relation to Christ (i. 8, ii. 20). (So Spitta, Von Soden, Mayor). "Cognitionem dei praesupponit haec epistula, ver. 3. Cognitionem autem Domini nostri, nempe Jesu Christi urget proprie" (Bengel). *Cf.* 2. Clem. ix. 5. χριστὸς . . . ἐγένετο σὰρξ καὶ οὕτως ἡμᾶς ἐκάλεσεν. ἰδίᾳ δόξῃ καὶ ἀρετῇ. Has ἰδίᾳ an intensive force here, or has it an exhausted sense

γνώσεως τοῦ καλέσαντος ἡμᾶς ἰδίᾳ δόξῃ καὶ ἀρετῇ,[1] 4. δι' ὧν τὰ τίμια ἡμῖν καὶ μέγιστα[2] ἐπαγγέλματα δεδώρηται, ἵνα διὰ τούτων γένησθε θείας κοινωνοὶ φύσεως, ἀποφυγόντες τῆς ἐν τῷ κόσμῳ ἐν

[1] **δια δοξης και αρετης** BKL, 31, WH. Recurrence of **δια** in vv. 3, 4 would lead to dittography, and correction to genitive easily follows. The versions are unanimous in favour of the reading adopted.

[2] **τιμια και μεγιστα ημιν** B, syrp, spec., WH, Mayor; **μεγιστα και τιμια ημιν** ACP, syrp (A, syrp **υμιν**), 13, 31 + Treg.

merely equivalent to a personal pronoun? The emphasis conveyed in the former interpretation would better carry on the sense of **πάντα. δόξα** is used in sense of John i. 14. **ἀρετή** is an interesting word. There is considerable evidence to prove that it is not used here in the ordinary Greek philosophical sense of "virtue," although the combination of **δόξα** and **ἀρετή** is not infrequently found in philosophical writings (*cf.* Plat. *Symp.* 208 D. Plut. *Mor.* 535). Deissmann, following the Stratonicean inscription already mentioned, renders "manifestation of power," *i.e.*, in miracle (*op. cit.* pp. 95-97). In 1 Pet. ii. 9 it is used in plural, in LXX sense = "praises" (תְּהִלָּה). (*Cf.* Thuc. i. 33.) In P. Hib. xv. 8 3 ff. (iii. B.C.) the younger men are exhorted to employ their bodies **εὐκαίρως τὴν ἀπόδειξιν ποιησαμένους τῆς αὐτῶν ἀρετῆς,** "in a timely display of their prowess" (G. and H.). In later papyri **ἀρετή** is used as title of courtesy, *e.g.*, P. Oxy. 71, ii. 18 (iv. A.D.). **εἴ σου δόξειεν τῇ ἀρετῇ** = "if it please your Excellency". Foucart defines **ἀρετή** as "vim divinam quae mirabilem in modum hominibus laborantibus salutem afferret" (*cf.* Hort's note, 1 Peter, p. 129 and MME, Sept. 1908).

The phrase **τοῦ καλέσαντος . . . ἀρετῃ** contains one of the finest ideas in the N.T. What could be a more effective answer to the intellectualism of the Gnostic teachers or its modern equivalent, than the impression produced on the lives of men, and especially the early disciples, by the Personality of Jesus? They beheld His glory in the evidences of miraculous knowledge and power which Jesus showed at the time of their call (John i. 42, 47-51; Luke v. 4). Their sense of His moral greatness overcame all resistance on their part (Luke v. 8; John i. 49). If 2 Pet. is lacking in devotional expression, his apologetic for the person of Christ is cast on most effective lines. Reason can only compass the facts of Revelation, in terms of antinomies, and it is vain to meet inadequate theories of the person of Christ by dogmatic subtlety. The Life and Death of our Lord, if its significance is to be fully understood, must be looked upon largely as an acted parable, and Christian experience—the *impression* of **δόξα καὶ ἀρετή**—is an indispensable constituent of dogmatic *expression.*

Ver. 4. **δι' ὧν.** Reference is to **δόξῃ καὶ ἀρετῇ** (so Kühl, Dietlein, Wiesinger, Brückner, Mayor) **ἐπαγγέλματα** = "promised blessings". No doubt what 2 Peter has chiefly in view is the particular comprehensive **ἐπάγγελμα** of His Second Coming (*cf.* iii. 4, **ἐπαγγελία** and iii. 13). The Parousia will be the vindication of all moral and spiritual effort. Christ promised forgiveness to the sinful, rest to the weary, comfort to the sad, hope to the dying and life to the dead. If the reference adopted above of **δι' ὧν** is correct, the sense would be that in the character and deeds of the Incarnate One, we have a revelation that is itself a promise. The **ἐπαγγέλματα** are given, not only in word but also in deed. The very life of Christ among men, with its **δόξα** and **ἀρετή** is itself the Promise of Life, and the Parousia expectation is also a faith that He lives and reigns in grace, having "received gifts for men". **δεδώρηται.** Passive, see note on ver. 3. **ἵνα διὰ τούτων . . . φύσεως. τούτων** refers to **ἐπαγγέλματα.** The hope and faith kindled in us by the promises are a source of moral power. "The history of the material progress of the race is the history of the growing power of man, arising from the gradual extension of his alliances with the forces which surround him. . . . He arms himself with the strength of the winds and the tides. He liberates the latent energy which has been condensed and treasured up in coal, transforms it into heat, generates steam, and sweeps across a continent without weariness, and with the swiftness of a bird. . . . Moving freely among the stupendous energies by which he is encompassed, he is strong in their strength, and they give to his volitions—powerless apart from them—a large and effective expression. The his-

ἐπιθυμίᾳ [b] φθορᾶς. 5. καὶ αὐτὸ [c] τοῦτο δὲ σπουδὴν πᾶσαν παρεισενέγκαντες ἐπιχορηγήσατε ἐν τῇ πίστει ὑμῶν τὴν ἀρετήν, ἐν δὲ τῇ
ἀρετῇ τὴν γνῶσιν, 6. ἐν δὲ τῇ γνώσει τὴν ἐγκράτειαν, ἐν δὲ τῇ

b Gen. after ἀποφυγ. found here only.
c Xen. *Anab.* i, 9, 21, Plat· *Protag.* 310e.

tory of man's triumphs in the province of his higher and spiritual life is also the history of the gradual extension of his alliance with a Force which is not his own. . . . In Christ we are 'made partakers of the divine nature'" (Dale, *Atonement*, pp. 416, 417). **θεία φύσις** is originally a philosophic term, *cf.* Plat. *Symp.* ii. 6, Philo (ed. Mangey), ii. pp. 51, 647; ii. 22, 143, 329, 343. **θεῖος** is found in a papyrus of 232 A.D. = "imperial" (Deissmann, *op. cit.* p. 218, note 2). Probably 2 Peter is here again making use of a current religious expression (*cf.* note on **θεία δύναμις**, ver. 3). **ἀποφυγόντας . . . φθορᾶς.** The aorist participle is used of coincident action. Moral emancipation is part of the **κοινωνία θείας φύσεως.** The idea of participation in the Divine Nature is set between the two pictures, one of hope, **τὰ τίμια ἡμῖν καὶ μέγιστα ἐπαγγέλματα,** the other of despair, **τῆς ἐν τῷ κόσμῳ ἐν ἐπιθυμίᾳ φθορᾶς.** The way to God is through the Redemption of Christ. The approach to God is an "escape," and not an act of intellectual effort. **φθορά** in philosophic writers is the counterpart of **γένεσις,** *cf.* Plat. *Rep.* 546A, *Phaed.* 95E. Aristot. *Phys.* 5, 5, 6. It expresses not sudden but gradual dissolution and destruction. The scriptural meaning alternates between destruction in the moral, and in the physical sense. In the N.T. the significance is physical, in 1 Cor. xv. 42, 50, Col. ii. 22, Gal. vi. 8, ii. Pet. ii. 12; moral here, as in 2 Pet. ii. 19, Rom. viii. 21. Man becomes either regenerate or degenerate. Either his spiritual and moral powers are subject to slow decay and death, the wages of sin (**ἐν ἐπιθυμίᾳ**), or he rises to full participation in the Divine. **ἐν ἐπιθυμίᾳ,** a compact phrase. The corruption consists in **ἐπιθυμία,** which may be interpreted in the widest sense of inordinate affection for earthly things. **ἐν τῷ κόσμῳ**; *cf.* Rom. viii. 21. **φθορά** becomes personified as a world-wide power to which all creation including man is subject. In Mayor's edition there is a valuable study of **φθορά** and cognates (pp. 175 ff.). The idea contained in **φθορά,** moral decay, is illustrated in Tennyson's "Palace of Art," and "Vision of Sin"; also in Byron, *e.g.*, "Stanzas for Music".

Vv. 5-7. *Faith is not only illumination but character.* "Nor is this all. On your part bring the utmost earnestness to bear, and in your faith supply moral energy, and in your moral energy understanding, and in your understanding self-control, and in your self-control patient endurance, and in patient endurance piety, and in piety brotherly love, and in brotherly love love."

Ver. 5. **καὶ αὐτὸ τοῦτο δὲ,** a phrase that emphasises the fact of the **δώρημα** as having its logical outcome in character. "The soul of religion is the practick part" (Bunyan). On the other hand, 2 Peter here teaches that so-called practical Christianity without the spiritual motive is incomplete and unintelligent. **σπουδὴν πᾶσαν παρεισενέγκαντες,** an impressive phrase. *Cf.* similar ideas in Rom. xii. 11, Heb. vi. 11. It is a warning against sluggishness and self-indulgence in the spiritual life. **ἐπιχορηγήσατε.** The A.V. trans., "add to," is insufficient. **χορηγός** in Attic drama is one who defrays the cost of the chorus, at the bidding of the State, as an act of citizenship (Dem. 496, 26). It was a duty that prompted to lavishness in execution. Hence **χορηγέω** came to mean "supplying costs for any purpose," a public duty or **λειτουργία,** with a tendency, as here, towards the meaning, "providing more than is barely demanded". In P. Oxy. 282[6] ff. (30-35 A.D.), a man complains that his wife had deserted him, although **ἐπεχορήγησα αὐτῇ τὰ ἑξῆς καὶ ὑπὲρ δύναμιν** ("I provided for her suitably and beyond my resources"). **ἐπι-** denotes a particular application of **χορηγέω** (*cf.* Moulton, *Proleg.* p. 113). **ἐν** "is used each time of that which is supposed to be theirs" (Alford). **ἀρετή**: "strenuus animae tonus ac vigor" (Bengel) — a manifestation of moral power. **γνῶσιν,** understanding, implying insight, circumspection, discretion, discernment (*cf.* 1 Cor. xvi. 18). *Cf.* Didache, ix. 3 (in Eucharistic prayer), xi. 2, where **γν.** is conjoined with **δικαιοσύνη.**

Ver. 6. **ἐγκράτειαν**: "self-control": accompanied by, and arising from, knowledge, and not a mere product of fear or submission to authority. **ὑπομονήν**: "steadfastness"—not turned aside from the faith by trial and suffering (*cf.* Luke viii. 15, Rom. v. 3 ff.). The desponding

ἐγκρατείᾳ τὴν ὑπομονήν, ἐν δὲ τῇ ὑπομονῇ τὴν εὐσέβειαν, 7. ἐν δὲ
τῇ εὐσεβείᾳ τὴν φιλαδελφίαν, ἐν δὲ τῇ φιλαδελφίᾳ τὴν ἀγάπην. 8.
ταῦτα γὰρ ὑμῖν ὑπάρχοντα καὶ πλεονάζοντα οὐκ ἀργοὺς οὐδὲ ἀκάρπους καθίστησιν εἰς τὴν τοῦ κυρίου ἡμῶν Ἰησοῦ Χριστοῦ ἐπίγνωσιν.
9. ᾧ γὰρ [d] μὴ πάρεστιν ταῦτα, τυφλός ἐστιν μυωπάζων, λήθην λαβὼν

[d] Acts xv. 29 (D), 1 John iv. 3, Tit. i. 11.

doctrine of the false teachers would itself call for **ὑπομονή** in the readers. Mayor compares the Aristotelian **καρτερία** (*cf.* Heb. xi. 27). **εὐσέβειαν.** In the Epistle the false teachers are **ἀσεβεῖς** (*cf.* note on v. 3).

Ver. 7. **φιλαδελφίαν**: "affection towards the brethren," *i.e.*, of the same Christian community. **ἀγάπην**: probably love towards all, even enemies; not directed by sense and emotion, but by deliberate choice (*cf.* Matt. v. 44). Mayor interprets: "Love to God manifesting itself in love to man and to the whole creation, animate and inanimate".

Vv. 8-11. *Further emphasis on the connexion between faith and morality, and its reward.* "If you have these virtues, and are not sparing in your use of them, you will not be ineffective and unfruitful in the direction of deepening your Christian experience. Where these virtues are not present a man is blind, near-sighted as it were, and entirely forgetful of the great fact that he is purified from the sins of the past. With this danger in view, your earnest purpose ought to be to make sure your calling and election. Steadily practise these virtues and you will not stumble; for thus there will be ministered unto you an abundant entrance into the eternal kingdom."

Ver. 8. **πλεονάζοντα**: "abound". In classical use = "exaggerate". The word here again emphasises the display of a regal, uncalculating and unwearied spirit in the practice of the Christian graces. **ἀργοὺς.** Perhaps "ineffective" or "ineffectual," a meaning which is further emphasised in **ἀκάρπους.** In The Didache, 12, are given directions for discriminating genuine from false among the itinerant teachers. "If he wishes to settle with you and is a tradesman, let him work and let him eat. If he has no trade, according to your wisdom provide how he shall live as a Christian among you, but not in idleness (**μὴ ἀργός**). If he will not do this, he is making merchandise of Christ. Beware of such men." Here is illustrated the passage from the ordinary sense of **ἀργός,** which really signifies "idle" for want of occupation, and not by choice, to the ethical significance. *Cf.* James ii. 20, "Faith without works is **ἀργή**". Matt. xx. 6, "Why stand ye here all the day, **ἀργοί**?" and the reply. *Cf.* also use of **ἀργεῖ** in ii. 3. In P. Par. II. 4(9)[4] (iii. B.C.), certain quarrymen complain that they "are idle (**ἀργοῦμεν**) for want of slaves to clear away the sand". *Cf.* P. Par. II. 20. **ὅπως . . μὴ ἀργῆι τὰ πλοῖα.** P. Lond. 208[10] (ii. A.D.). **λόγος ἐργατῶν ἀργησάντων.** In P. Lond. III. p. 27 (a census-return of 160 or 161 A.D.) a certain Apollonius is described as belonging to "the leisured class of Memphis". (**τῶν ἀπὸ Μέμφεως ἀργῶν**). P. Fior. I. P. Amh, 97? (both ii. A.D.) **ἐλαιουργίου ἀργοῦ** = "an oil-press which is out of working order" **εἰς τὴν . . . ἐπίγνωσιν.** Here the writer returns to the idea, introduced by **ἀποφυγόντες . . . φθορᾶς** in v. 4, that morality and religion are intimately connected. Some have sought to interpret the words as meaning "with reference to the knowledge of our Lord Jesus Christ," on the ground that **ἐπίγνωσις** has already been postulated as the source of "all things needed for life and godliness," and cannot now be regarded as an end to be attained. Yet **ἐπίγνωσις** may be regarded as both the beginning and the end of morality (*cf.* iii. 18, Col. i. 6 ff. Phil. i. 9). The translation of A.V. is correct (**εἰς** = in, expressive of result). **ἐπίγν.** contrasted with **γνῶσις** marks "a higher degree of intensity, an energy of deeper penetration. It is not a quiescent state, the resting in an acquirement, but the advance of one to whom easy attainment is but the impulse of fresh effort; one who is not content to know, but ever, in Hosea's words (vi. 3), follows on to know" (Paget, *Spirit of Discipline*, p. 112). Each advance in the Christian life deepens and widens our spiritual understanding. "Die **ἐπίγν.** ist ihrer Natur nach etwas, was wächst" (Von Soden).

Ver. 9. **μυωπάζων**: "short-sighted". Only once elsewhere in Greek literature in Ps. Dionys. *Eccl. Hier.* ii. 3. This is one of the words to which exception has been taken in 2 Peter. It is both rare, and it seems to contradict **τυφλός.** Spitta and Von S. translate "wilfully blind". Mayor (p. lxi.) (fo lowing Beza

e Heb. i. 3. τοῦ καθαρισμοῦ τῶν πάλαι αὐτοῦ ᵉἁμαρτιῶν. 10. διὸ μᾶλλον,
ἀδελφοί, σπουδάσατε βεβαίαν ὑμῶν τὴν κλῆσιν καὶ ἐκλογὴν
f Moulton, *Proleg.* ποιεῖσθαι· ταῦτα γὰρ ποιοῦντες οὐ ᶠμὴ πταίσητέ ποτε· 11. οὕτως
pp. 188 ff. γὰρ πλουσίως ἐπιχορηγηθήσεται ὑμῖν ἡ εἴσοδος εἰς τὴν αἰώνιον
g Matt. xxiv. 6 βασιλείαν τοῦ κυρίου ἡμῶν καὶ σωτῆρος Ἰησοῦ Χριστοῦ.
only. 12. Διὸ ᵍμελλήσω[1] ἀεὶ ὑμᾶς ὑπομιμνήσκειν περὶ τούτων,

[1] **μελλησω** ℵABCP, vg., Ti., Treg., WH; **ουκ αμελησω** KL, syrr. The analogy of **σπουδασω** in ver. 15 favours reading adopted. Yet, in MSS., there is frequent confusion between **μελλω** and **μελω**, *e.g.*, John xii. 6, 1 Peter v. 7, Matt. xxii. 16, where **μελλω** is incorrect. Field (*Notes on Trans. of N.T.* p. 240) suggests that true reading here is **μελησω** (*cf.* on **σπουδαζω** ver. 15).

Grotius, Huther, etc.) interprets the word as limiting **τυφλός**. "He who is without the virtues mentioned in i. 5-7 is blind, or to put it more exactly is short-sighted; he cannot see the things of heaven, though he may be quick enough in regard to worldly matters." **λήθην λαβών**. A periphrastic form. *Cf.* Jos. *Ant.* ii. 6, 9; also 2 Tim. i. 5, Heb. xi. 29. **τοῦ καθαρισμοῦ τῶν πάλαι αὐτοῦ ἁμαρτιῶν.** Is the reference to baptism? This view is rendered very probable by the use of **πάλαι**. For the idea of cleansing from pre-baptismal sin, *cf.* Barnabas, xi. 11, Hermas, *Mand.* iv, 3. *Vis.* ii. 1. Spitta adheres to the general interpretation of **καθ.** as the work of Christ on the moral life. *Cf.* ii. 20-22, 1 Jn. iii. 3. While **καθαρισμός** is used of the ceremonial washings of the Jews, John iii. 25, it is also used of the work of Christ in Heb. i. 3 (*cf.* Zahn. *Introd.* ii. 232).

Ver. 10. **σπουδάσατε**. An Imperative. "A sharp and urgent form" (Moulton, *Proleg.* i. 173). **βεβαίαν**. *Cf.* Deissmann, *B. S.* pp. 105 ff. The word has a legal sense. **βεβαίωσις** is the legal guarantee, obtained by a buyer from a seller, to be gone back upon should any third party claim the thing. Here the readers are exhorted to produce a guarantee of their calling and election. This may be done by the cultivation of the Christian graces, *Cf.* Eph. iv. 1. "To walk worthily of the calling wherewith ye are called." **κλῆσιν καὶ ἐκλογὴν**. What is the difference between these two? **καλέω** used in Gospels = "bid to a feast". **κλητοί** would, therefore, imply those bidden; **ἐκλεκτοί** = those who have become true partakers of God's salvation. *Cf.* Matt. xxii. 14. Not all who hear the Divine Voice (**κλῆσιν**) progress in Christian conduct, which is the token of **ἐκλογήν**. **οὐ μὴ πταίσητε**, as a blind or short-sighted person might do.

Ver. 11. Note the accumulation in this verse of words suggesting splendour and fulness. **ἐπιχορηγηθήσεται.** *Cf.* note on v. 5. Mayor says that here the word "suggests the ordering of a triumphal procession," and compares Plut. Vit. 994, **ὁ δῆμος ἐθεᾶτο τὰς θέας ἀφειδῶς πάνυ χορηγουμένας. εἴσοδος.** *Cf.* Heb. x. 19. In a theatre, **εἰσ.** is the place of entrance for the chorus (Ar. *Nub.* 326; *Av.* 296), and in P. Par. ii. 41, we find **εἴσοδος κοινή** = of the door of a house. The great description of the entrance of the pilgrims into the celestial city in Bunyan's *Pilgrim's Progress*, Pt. i., may be quoted in illustration. **αἰώνιον βασιλείαν.** does not occur elsewhere in N.T. or Apostolic Fathers (*cf.* Aristotle's *Apol.* xvi., and Clem. *Hom.* x. 25), but **αἰωνίου ἀρχῆς** occurs in the Stratonicean inscriptions already quoted (Deissmann, *op. cit.* p. 361).

Vv. 12-15. *The aim of the writer, and the urgency of his message.* "You are already acquainted with and established in the truth, so far as revealed to you, but, in view of the great issues, I shall always be prepared to awaken you to a sense of these things. In my lifetime I feel bound to do so, especially as I know that death is imminent, as Jesus declared to me. I shall also do my best to enable you to refer to these things as opportunity occurs, even after my decease."

Ver. 12. **μελλήσω.** What is the exact significance of the future? It can hardly be simply a periphrastic future. "The idea is rather that the writer will be prepared in the future, as well as in the past and in the present to remind them of the truths they know, whenever the necessity arises" (Zahn. *Introd.*, ii., p. 211; quoted with approval by Nestle. *Text. Criticism of N.T.* pp. 333-34). **ἐστηριγμένους.** This word is used by Jesus in the warning given of Peter's fall, and its spiritual result. **καὶ σύ ποτε ἐπιστρέψας στήρισον τοὺς ἀδελφούς σου** (Lk. xxii. 32). *Cf.* 1 Pet. v. 10, 2 Pet. iii. 17, where **στηριγμός** = "stead-

ʰ καίπερ εἰδότας καὶ ἐστηριγμένους ἐν τῇ παρούσῃ ἀληθείᾳ. 13.
δίκαιον δὲ ἡγοῦμαι, ἐφ᾽ ὅσον εἰμὶ ἐν τούτῳ τῷ σκηνώματι, διεγείρειν ὑμᾶς ἐν ὑπομνήσει, 14. εἰδὼς ὅτι ταχινή ἐστιν ἡ ἀπόθεσις
τοῦ σκηνώματός μου, καθὼς καὶ ὁ κύριος ἡμῶν Ἰησοῦς Χριστὸς
ἐδήλωσέν μοι. 15. σπουδάσω[1] δὲ καὶ ἑκάστοτε ⁱ ἔχειν ὑμᾶς μετὰ

h Phil. iii. 4, Heb. v. 8, vii. 5, xii. 17.
i For construction of ἔχειν with infin. see Matt. xviii. 25, Eph. iv. 28

[1] σπουδαζω ℵ 31, arm., syrp, "an intentional alteration . . . copyists and translators could not bring themselves to read here again a promise of Peter's, which he seemed not to have fulfilled" (Zahn, Introd. ii. p. 212). These remarks apply also to variants for μελλησω (ver. 12) (*ibid. cf.* Nestle, *Textual Criticism of N.T.* p. 324).

fastness of mind". **ἐν τῇ παρούσῃ ἀληθείᾳ.**—"in the present truth," *i.e.* in so far as you yet have experience of it. *Cf.* note on v. 8.

Ver. 13. **δίκαιον δὲ ἡγοῦμαι.** "I consider it a duty." The language in vv. 13, 14, is studiously solemn and impressive. **σκηνώματι**, used in literal sense of "tent" in Deut. xxxiii. 18. In Acts vii. 46, it is used of the Tabernacle of God. Elsewhere in N.T. **σκῆνος** is used in the metaphorical sense of human existence. *Cf.* 2 Cor. v. 4. A similar use of **σκήνωμα** is found in *Ep. ad Diogn.* 6. **ἀθάνατος ἡ ψυχὴ ἐν θνητῷ σκηνώματι κατοικεῖ.** **σκηνή** is the word used by Peter in the transfiguration story (Matt. xvii. 4; Mark ix. 5; Luke ix. 33). **διεγείρειν ὑμᾶς ἐν ὑπομνήσει· διεγ.** is always used in N.T. = "awaken" or "rouse from sleep" (except in Jn. vi. 18 of the sea); significant in view of the reference to the Transfiguration in vv. 16 ff. *Cf.* **διαγρηγορήσαντες** ("fully awake") in St. Luke's account; *Introd.* p. 95.

Ver. 14. **ταχινή** "imminent," *cf.* ii. 1. A poetical word peculiar to 2 Peter in N.T. The *process* described by **ἀπόθεσις** can hardly be "sudden," Plat. *Rep.* 553D, but there is always an impression of suddenness to the onlooker, who lifts up his eyes some morning, and finds the tent or the encampment gone where he had seen it yesterday. An inscription in C.I.A. III. 1344^{3}, reads **ζωῆς καὶ καμάτου τέρμα δραμὼν ταχινόν**, where sense can only be "brief" (but see discussion in Zahn. *Introd.*, ii., pp. 212 f.). **ἀπόθεσιν τοῦ σκην.** **ἀποτίθεμαι** is used of "putting off a garment" (Acts vii. 58); and might here be connected with the idea of taking off a tent-cover (So Spitta). Probably "removal" is the proper translation. In B.G.U. 606^{5} (iv. A.D.) **[πρὸς ἀ]πόθεσιν ἀχύρου** (for removal of a chaff-heap) is found. *Cf.* 1 Pet. iii. 21, **οὐ σαρκὸς ἀπόθεσις ῥύπου.** **καθὼς καὶ . . . ἐδήλωσέν μοι.** There seems no reason to doubt the reference here to John xxi. 18, 19, as Spitta and others have done (see Introduction, pp. 96 f.).

Ver. 15. **σπουδάσω.** The form is used by Polybius and later writers for the classical **σπουδάσομαι.** **ἑκάστοτε** goes with **ἔχειν** = "on each occasion when you have need". The word is found apparently in the same sense in P. Gen. 31^{3f}. (ii. A.D.), **ἑκάστοτέ σοι κατ᾽ ἐπιδημίαν παρενοχλῶν** ("causing you annoyance on each occasion when you are at home"). **τὴν τούτων μνήμην ποιεῖσθαι.** What is the reference in **τούτων**? It must have the same reference as in verse 12, *viz.* to the practice of the Christian graces, and the larger reference must be to some systematic body of instruction. This might easily take the form of reminiscences of the example of Jesus Himself, and the allusion may be to the Petrine reminiscences contained in the Gospel of St. Mark (*cf.* **μετὰ δὲ τὴν τούτων** (Peter and Paul) **ἔξοδον Μᾶρκος τὰ ὑπὸ Πέτρου κηρυσσόμενα ἐγγράφως ἡμῖν παραδέδωκεν** Iren. iii. 1. 1.). "He has already referred to Christ (v. 3), as having called them **ἰδίᾳ δόξῃ καὶ ἀρετῇ**"; surely nothing could be more appropriate, more helpful to a godly life, than that Peter should leave behind the picture of this **δόξα καὶ ἀρετή** drawn from his own recollection. And the following words, **οὐ γὰρ σεσοφισμένος κ.τ.λ.** (v. 16) seem to imply a statement of facts" (Mayor, cxliii., where see whole discussion against Zahn. *Introd.* II. pp. 199 ff.). **ἔξοδον.** The same word is used in Luke ix. 31 of the death of Christ. It seems to include the thought of subsequent glory (*cf. Expositor*, vi. ii. pp. 73 f. Smith, *Days of His Flesh*, pp. 274 f.) The meaning "death" is found in B.G.U. 168^{14f}. (ii.-iii. A.D.). **ἐπιγνοῦσα τὴν (το)ῦ Εὐδαίμονος ἔξοδον.**

τὴν τούτων μνήμην ποιεῖσθαι: "refer

τὴν ἐμὴν ἔξοδον τὴν τούτων μνήμην ποιεῖσθαι. 16. οὐ γὰρ
σεσοφισμένοις μύθοις [k] ἐξακολουθήσαντες ἐγνωρίσαμεν ὑμῖν τὴν τοῦ
κυρίου ἡμῶν Ἰησοῦ Χριστοῦ δύναμιν καὶ παρουσίαν, ἀλλʼ ἐπόπται
γενηθέντες τῆς ἐκείνου μεγαλειότητος. 17. λαβὼν γὰρ παρὰ
Θεοῦ πατρὸς τιμὴν καὶ δόξαν, φωνῆς ἐνεχθείσης αὐτῷ τοιᾶσδε

k Amos ii. 4, Isa. lvi. 11, *cf.* 2 Peter ii. 2, 15.

to"; always in Greek writers, from Herodotus down = "mentionem facere, "make mention of" (*cf.* Grimm-Thayer under **μνήμη**). The sense here seems much the same. The document "referred to" would be an authentic source of information. *Cf.* P. Fay, 19^{10} (ii. A.D.) **[ἀκριβ]εστάτην μνήμην ποιούμενος.**

Vv. 16-18. *The fact of the Transfiguration a guarantee of the writer's truthfulness.* "For we are not without facts to rest upon. Our preaching of the power and coming of Jesus Christ was not based on sophistical myths. We were eye-witnesses of His Majesty. For He received from God the Father honour and glory, a voice coming to Him through the splendour of the glory, 'This is my beloved Son in whom I am well pleased'. This voice we heard, as it was borne from heaven, when we were with Him in the Holy Mount." (For a comparison of this passage, with the Synoptic account, see Introduction, pp. 94 ff.).

Ver. 16. **σεσοφισμ. μύθ.** *Cf.* **σεσοφισμένη μήτηρ**.. "suppositious mother". Greg. Nyss. i. 171 D. This is evidently the character attributed to the facts of the Christian Gospel by the False Teachers. They specially sought to discredit the outlook for the Second Advent. **μῦθοι** is often used in the Pastoral Epistles of the fanciful Gnostic genealogies (1 Tim. i. 4, iv. 7; Tit. i. 14). **ἐγνωρίσαμεν.** Used in N.T. of preaching the Gospel (*e.g.* 1 Cor. xv. 1). **δύναμιν καὶ παρουσίαν.** For collocation of words, *cf.* Matt. xxiv. 30, Mark ix. 1. For **δύναμις**, see note on verse 3. **παρουσίαν.** Chase (*op. cit.* 797*a*) regards the word here as denoting the first coming of Christ, because (1) the context speaks of history and not of prophecy; (2) the word itself naturally bears this meaning. He admits, however, that elsewhere in the N.T and in this Epistle it is used of the Second Coming (*cf.* Ignat. *Philad.* 9). Justin (*Dialogue* 32) distinguishes "two advents,—one in which He was pierced by you; a second, when you shall know Him, Whom you have pierced". There is, however, no real difficulty here in taking **παρ.** in the usual sense, which, indeed, is more in harmony with the context. The Transfiguration itself, as used by this writer, is regarded as a basis for belief in the Second Advent, against the False Teachers.

Dr. Milligan, in his recent edition of Thessalonians, gives a valuable note on **παρουσία** (p. 145). He mentions that it occurs frequently in the Papyri as a kind of *terminus technicus* with reference to the visit of the king, or some other official. (P. Petr. ii. 39 (*e*), 18 (iii. B.C.). P. Tebt. 48, 13 f. (ii. B.C.), 116 (ii. B.C.). P. Gren., ii. 14 (*b*), 2 (iii. B.C.)). Dittenberger, *Sylloge*, 226, 84 ff. (iii. BC.). **τῶν δὲ ἀρχόντων συναγαγόντων ἐκλησίαν καὶ τήντε παρουσίαν ἐμφανισάντωντοῦ βασιλέως.** "We fall back upon" these examples of the word "the more gladly because for this particular sense of the word the Jewish sacred writings give us little help" (*ibid.*). The word must, therefore, have come into use, in this application to the Second Advent, in apostolic times, as faithfully representing the meaning of Jesus Himself (*cf.* Matt. xxiv. 3, 27, 37, 39). The usual classical sense of the word as "presence" must not be disregarded. Taken together with the other meaning illustrated by the **Κοινή**, **παρουσία** would thus seem to combine in itself the meaning of "actual presence," and a near "coming". This combination of meaning in the consciousness of the early Church, with its perplexity as to the interpretation of our Lord's promise, would seem to be reflected in John xvi. 16-18. **ἐπόπται**: used of those who had attained the highest degree of initiation into the Eleusinian mysteries. Judging from the use of **ἐποπτεύω** in 1 Peter, the word may have passed into ordinary speech, but no doubt is used here to enhance the splendour of the vision, and the honour done the disciples, at the Transfiguration—"admitted to the spectacle of His grandeur' (Moffat, *H. N. T.* p. 600). **ἐπόπτης** is applied to God in Esth. v. 1, 2 Macc. vii. 35, *cf.* O.G.I.S., 666^{25} **τὸν Ἥλιον Ἄφμαχιν ἐπόπτην καὶ σωτῆρα** (reference to an Egyptian Sun-god). Hofmann holds that the reference is rather to the Resurrection and Ascension. **μεγαλειότητος.** *Cf.* Luke ix. 43, Acts xix. 27.

ὑπὸ τῆς μεγαλοπρεποῦς[1] δόξης Ὁ υἱός μου ὁ ἀγαπητός μου οὗτός ˡ
ἐστιν, εἰς ὃν ἐγὼ ˡεὐδόκησα,—18. καὶ ταύτην τὴν φωνὴν ἡμεῖς
ἠκούσαμεν ἐξ οὐρανοῦ ᵐἐνεχθεῖσαν σὺν αὐτῷ ὄντες ἐν τῷ ἁγίῳ
ὄρει· 19. καὶ ἔχομεν βεβαιότερον τὸν προφητικὸν λόγον, ᾧ καλῶς
ποιεῖτε ⁿπροσέχοντες ὡς λύχνῳ φαίνοντι ἐν αὐχμηρῷ τόπῳ, ᵒἕως οὗ
ἡμέρα διαυγάσῃ καὶ φωσφόρος ἀνατείλῃ ἐν ταῖς καρδίαις ὑμῶν·

l Matt. iii. 17, xvii. 5, Mark i. 11, Luke iii. 22.
m Acts ix. 12, x. 3, xi. 3, xxvi. 13, Luke x. 18.
n 3 John vi., Acts x. 35, Phil. iv. 14.
o Mark xiv. 32 Luke xiii. 8.

[1] απο της μεγαλοπ. syrr.

Ver. 17. **λαβὼν.** It is well-nigh impossible to say what is the case agreement of the participle here. It is at least certain that the subject is Jesus. Dietlein, Schott, Ewald, and Mayor agree that the writer intended to go on, **ἐβεβαίωσεν τὸν προφητικὸν λόγον,** for which he substitutes **καὶ ἔχομεν βεβαιότερον,** after the parenthetic 18th verse. **παρὰ Θεοῦ πατρός.** See Hort's note, 1 Pet. i. 2. The usage (without the article) indicates the growth of a special Christian terminology. The two words are treated as one proper name. **τιμὴν καὶ δόξαν.** A frequent combination, *cf.* Ps. viii. 6, Job. xl. 10, 1 Peter i. 7, Rom. ii. 7, 10, 1 Tim. i. 17, Heb. ii. 7, 9. **τιμή** is the personal honour and esteem in which Jesus is held by the Father, *cf.* Hort's note on 1 Pet. i. 7. "Honour in the voice which spoke to Him; glory in the light which shone from Him" (Alford). **φωνῆς . . . τοιᾶσδε.** This is the only instance of **τοιόσδε** in N.T. = "to the following effect". **ὑπὸ τῆς μεγαλοπρεποῦς δόξης.** Retaining reading **ὑπὸ,** we may regard **μεγ. δόξα** as a vehicle of expression. The voice expresses its significance. It is not a mere accompanying phenomenon of the voice. *Cf.* the instrumental dative in i. 21 after **ἠνέχθη.** **μεγ. δόξης** corresponds to "the bright cloud" (**νεφέλη φωτεινή**) of the Synoptics. **οὐρανός** is used in verse 18 to describe the source from which the voice came; "the sky," *cf.* iii. 12, 13. **εἰς ὃν ἐγὼ εὐδόκησα.** Moulton (*Proleg.* p. 63) points out that tendency in N.T. is for **εἰς** to encroach on the domain of **ἐν.** *Cf.* John i. 18, **ὁ ὢν εἰς τὸν κόλπον** (*ib.* p. 235).

Ver. 18. **ἐν τῷ ὄρει τῷ ἁγίῳ.** The phrase indicates a view of the place and incident which has been taken up into and sanctified in the religious consciousness of the Church. *The Gnostic Acts of Peter* use the phrase "in monte sacro". **ἅγιος** signifies a place where Jehovah manifested Himself, *cf.* Exod. iii. 5, Isa. lii. 1.

Vv. 19-21. *The Transfiguration confirms Prophecy.* "Thus we have still further confirmation of the words of the prophets, a fact to which you would do well to give heed, as to a lamp shining in a murky place, meant to serve until the Day break and the Day-Star arise in your hearts. Recognise, above all, this truth, that no prophecy is restricted to the particular interpretation of one generation. No prophecy was ever borne through the instrumentality of man's will, but men spoke, direct from God, impelled by the Holy Spirit."

Ver. 19. **βεβαιότερον.** Originally a legal term. See note v. 10; *cf.* Phil. i. 7, 2 Cor. i. 21. **τὸν προφητικὸν λόγον,** *i.e.* all in the O.T. scriptures that points to the Coming of the Messiah. The prophecy is now supported by its partial fulfilment in the Transfiguration. **ᾧ καλῶς ποιεῖτε προσέχοντες.** "to which ye do well to take heed". "**καλ. ποιήσεις** c. aor. part. is the normal way of saying 'please' in the papyri, and is classical" (Moulton *Proleg.* p. 228). **ὡς λύχνῳ . . . καρδ. ὑμῶν.** Spitta would eliminate the words **ἕως οὗ . . . ἀνατείλῃ** as a gloss founded on Ps. cxix. 105 and 4 Esdras xii. 42. **αὐχμηρῷ τόπῳ,** properly = "dry" or "parched": then "squalid" or "rough". Here it means "murky". In Aristot. *de Color.* 3 **τὸ αὐχμηρόν** is opposed to **τὸ λαμπρόν.** **φωσφόρος.** "Morning-star." Not found elsewhere in Biblical Greek. The LXX word is **ἑωσφόρος.** In the poets, the word is always applied to Venus (Cicero, *Nat. Deorum*, 2, 20).

This verse has been much discussed. It may be well to mention three grammatical points that emerge. (1) The reference of **ᾧ.** It is simplest to understand it as referring to *the content of the preceding clause*, and not to **τὸν προφ. λόγον** alone, *viz.* the fact that the **προφ. λογ.** is now **βεβ.** on account of the Transfiguration. (2) **ἕως οὗ κ.τ.λ.** is to be taken with **φαίνοντι,** not with **προσέχοντες.** (3) **ἐν τ. κ. ὑμῶν** is connected

20. τοῦτο [p] πρῶτον γινώσκοντες ὅτι πᾶσα προφητεία γραφῆς ἰδίας
[q] ἐπιλύσεως οὐ γίνεται· 21. οὐ γὰρ θελήματι ἀνθρώπου ἠνέχθη
προφητεία ποτέ, ἀλλὰ ὑπὸ πνεύματος ἁγίου φερόμενοι ἐλάλησαν
ἀπὸ Θεοῦ [1] ἄνθρωποι.

p Peter iii. 3, 1 Tim. ii. 1. q Heb. xii. 11, x. 39. Art. absent owing to growth of a special Christian terminology. *Cf.* Jude 8, 2 Peter ii. 10, ii. 18, i. 20. (Mayor, *Ed.* xxvii. ff.).

[1] απο Θεου BP, syr[h], boh., WH, Ti.; αγιοι Θεου ℵKL, syr[p] + Treg.; αγιοι sah.; αγιοι του Θ. A; αγιοι απο θ. C.

with ἀνατείλῃ alone, and not with διαυγάσῃ. With these presuppositions we may briefly consider the two leading interpretations.

1. Mayor may be taken as representative of the view that the verse is wholly an exhortation to "search the Scriptures". There are three stages: the prophetic lamp (τὸν προφ. . . . τόπῳ); the Gospel dawn (ἡμέρα διαυγ.); the inner light of the spirit (φωσφόρος . . . ὑμῶν.). "The lower degree of faith in the written word will be followed by divine insight". He compares Euth. Zig. ὁ προφητικὸς λόγος τοὺς ἐν ἀγνοίᾳ φωταγωγεῖ ἕως καθαρὸν ὑμῖν τὸ φῶς τοῦ εὐαγγελίου διαφανῇ καὶ ὁ νοητὸς ἑωσφόρος, τουτέστι Χριστός, ἐν ταῖς καρδίαις ὑμῶν ἀνατείλῃ. (*cf.* Huther, Alford). The objection to this view is that it seems to ignore the place given to the Transfiguration as a religious fact for writer and readers alike (ἔχομεν).

2. Another and more probable view naturally takes ἕως οὗ . . . ὑμῶν as referring to the Second Advent. This preserves the usual meaning of ἡμέρα in the Epistle, and it also gives point to the striking sequence of metaphors. The λύχνῳ φαίνοντι is the confirmation of the prophetic word by the Transfiguration which the writer has given them (*cf.* v. 16); and this is made all the more probable if we take the reference suggested for φ in (1) above. The αὐχμ. τόπῳ would be the world in which they live (*cf.* Ps. cxix. 105). This lamp is meant to serve until the glorious appearing. One objection to the eschatological interpretation of ἕως οὗ κ.τ.λ. is the phrase ἐν ταῖς καρδίαις ὑμῶν which implies an inward Coming. This is largely repelled if we accept its grammatical connection with ἀνατείλῃ alone ((3) above). "The Morning-Star arises in their hearts, when the σημεῖα of the approaching Day are manifest to Christians. The fulfilment of their hope is at the door: the Lord is at hand" (von Soden). See note on ver. 9.

Ver. 20. τοῦτο πρῶτον γινώσκοντες. "Recognising this truth above all else" (in your reading of Scripture). The False Teachers appealed to the O.T. scriptures in support of their doctrine. ὅτι πᾶσα . . . οὐ γίνεται. πᾶσα . . . οὐ need not be regarded as a Hebraism. It is as normal as in 1 Jn. ii. 21, Jn. iii. 16. ἰδίας ἐπιλύσεως. This passage is a noted crux. (1) Hardt, followed by Lange, Spitta and others interpret ἐπιλυσ. = *dissolutio*. "No prophecy of S. is of such a kind that it can be annulled". But no satisfactory instance of ἐπιλυσ. in this sense can be adduced. (2) Accepting the sense of ἰδ. ἐπιλ. = "private," or "human interpretation," Von Soden sees a reference to the methods of the false teachers in their attitude to Scripture (*cf.* v. 16, ii. 1). ἰδίας "is opposed to the φωνὴ ἐνεχθεῖσα of i. 17". (3) It seems most satisfactory to understand ἰδ. ἐπιλ. as the meaning of the prophet himself, or what was in the prophet's mind when he wrote; the fulfilment in any particular generation or epoch. "The special work of the prophet is to interpret the working of God to his own generation. But in doing this, he is laying down the principles of God's action generally. Hence there may be many fulfilments of one prophecy, or to speak more exactly, many historical illustrations of some one principle of Providential Government" (Mayor, p. 196). The genitive ἐπιλύσεως is gen. of definition and not of origin. "No prophecy is of such a nature as to be capable of a particular interpretation."

Ver. 21. οὐ γὰρ θελήματι ἀνθρώπου ἠνέχθη προφητεία ποτέ. With ἠνέχθη *cf.* vv. 17, 18. ἀλλὰ ὑπὸ πνεύμ. . . . φερόμενοι, *cf.* Acts ii. 2. ὥσπερ φερομένης πνοῆς βιαίας. Here we have the only reference to the Holy Spirit in the Epistle, and only in this connexion, *viz.* as the source of prophetic inspiration. The spirit is an agency rather than an agent. The men speak. The spirit impels. It is of much signific-

II. 1. Ἐγένοντο δὲ καὶ ψευδοπροφῆται ἐν τῷ λαῷ, ὡς καὶ ἐν a Vv. 4, 10,
ὑμῖν ἔσονται ψευδοδιδάσκαλοι, οἵτινες παρεισάξουσιν αἱρέσεις ᵃ ἀπω- Jas. i. 25. See
λείας, καὶ τὸν ἀγοράσαντα αὐτοὺς δεσπότην ἀρνούμενοι, ἐπάγοντες Moulton, *Proleg.* 74.

ance for the interpretation of the whole passage that **ἄνθρωποι** occupies a position of emphasis at the end of the sentence, thus bringing into prominence the human agent. The prophets were not ignorant of the meaning of their prophecies, but they saw clearly only the contemporary political or moral situation, and the principles involved and illustrated therein.

CHAPTER II.—Vv. 1-3. *The False Teachers and their Judgment.* "Yet there were also false prophets in the ancient community, just as among you there will be false teachers. They will not hesitate to introduce alongside the truth corrupting heresies, even denying their Redeemer, and bringing on themselves swift destruction. Many will imitate their vicious example, and thereby the way of truth will be discredited. Nay, further, actuated by covetousness, they will make merchandise of you by lying words. Yet you must not think that the judgment passed on all such long ago is inactive. Their destruction is awaiting them."

Ver. 1. **ψευδοπροφῆται ἐν τῷ λαῷ. ἐν τῷ λαῷ** is used for the chosen people in LXX. **ψευδοπροφῆται.** A class of False Prophets is frequently mentioned in the O.T. In the earlier ages it is not suggested that there was conscious deceit on the part of the prophet. His prophecy is false, if it is proved so by the event (Jer. xxviii. 9). "When a prophet lies, without being inspired by a false or impotent god, it is because God in His anger against Israel's sin means to destroy him, and therefore put into the prophets 'a lying spirit'". (Schulz. *O.T. Th.* i. 257). *Cf.* 1 Kings xxii. 5 ff. These are the prophets who cry "peace, peace," when God is really going to bring judgment. In the later period superstitious acts and pagan practices, such as spiritualism, ventriloquism, professional soothsaying, became common (*e.g.* Jer. xxvii. 9; Isa. viii. 19). The cardinal distinction between the true and the false prophet lay in the moral character of their teaching (Jer. xxiii. 21, 22). **ψευδοδιδάσκαλοι.** The characteristics of their teaching are well-marked in this Epistle. See Introduction, pp. 115 ff. Compare Phil. iii. 18 f., "enemies of the Cross," who brought tears of shame to the eyes of the Apostle; the abuses of the Lord's Supper in 1 Cor. xi.; also Galat. ii. 4, 2 Cor. xi. 13.

παρεισάξουσιν. What is the force of **παρα-**? The idea of "stealth" or "secrecy"—"stealthily to introduce"—is hardly in accord with their character described elsewhere as **τολμηταὶ αὐθάδεις, δόξας οὐ τρέμουσιν βλασφημοῦντες** (ii. 10). Rather the idea seems to be of the introduction of false teaching alongside the true, whereby the **ὁδὸς ἀληθείας** is brought into disrepute. *Cf.* **παρεισενέγκαντες,** i. 5. The idea of stealth is present in **παρεισάκτους** (Gal. ii. 5). **αἱρέσεις.** Clearly **αἵρεσις** here is used in original sense of "tenet" ("animus," "sententia") (So Spitta, von Soden, Weiss; but *cf.* Zahn., *op. cit.* ii. 233). In Galat. v. 20, 1 Cor. xi. 19, the sense is "dissensions," arising from such diversity of opinion. It is used in the sense of "sect" in Acts v. 17, xv. 5, xxiv. 5. The **ψευδοδιδάσκαλοι** were within the Church. Even the "Alogi," who disputed the fourth Gospel in second century, were not excommunicated. They were, as Epiphanius says, "one of ourselves". *Cf.* MME., *Expos.* Feb. 1908. **αἱρέσεις ἀπωλείας.** The Genitive contains the qualifying idea—"corrupting tenets". Our identification with a great cause may be maintained, as in the case of the false teachers, but personal motives may sadly deteriorate, and the influence of the life may breed corruption. *Cf.* Ignat. *Trall.* vi. 1; *Eph.* vi. 2. **καὶ τὸν ἀγορ. . . . ἀρνούμενοι. καὶ** = "even". *Cf.* Mark i. 27. If the ordinary use of **δεσπότης** in early Christian writers is followed here, *viz.*, as referring to God, **ἀγοράζω** would also be used of God, who redeemed Israel out of Egypt (2 Sam. vii. 23). The reference here, however, is to Christ (*cf.* Mayor, p. xvii.). The N.T. use of **ἀγορ.** is illustrated in 1 Cor. vi. 20, where reference might be to God; but in *ib.* vii. 23 reference is clearly to Christ. So in Rev. v. 9. *Cf.* our Lord's words in Mark x. 45, about "giving his life a ransom" and Jude v. 4. The "denial" seems to have consisted in an inadequate view of the Person and Work of Christ, and their relation to the problem of human sin. *Cf. Epp. of Peter*, J. H. Jowett, pp. 230 ff. **ταχινήν.** See note on i. 14. **ἐπάγοντες.** The

b 1 Tim. ii. 1, 2 Cor. ii. 1, viii. 2, Luke i. 44.
c Ezek. xxvii. 21.
d Acts iii. 13, 1 Cor. viii. 6.

ἑαυτοῖς ταχινὴν ἀπώλειαν· 2. καὶ πολλοὶ ἐξακολουθήσουσιν αὐτῶν
ταῖς ἀσελγείαις, δι' οὓς ἡ ὁδὸς τῆς ἀληθείας βλασφημηθήσεται· 3.
καὶ [b] ἐν πλεονεξίᾳ πλαστοῖς λόγοις ὑμᾶς [c] ἐμπορεύσονται· οἷς τὸ
κρίμα ἔκπαλαι οὐκ ἀργεῖ, καὶ ἡ ἀπώλεια αὐτῶν οὐ [d] νυστάζει. 4.
εἰ γὰρ ὁ Θεὸς ἀγγέλων ἁμαρτησάντων οὐκ ἐφείσατο, ἀλλὰ σειραῖς [1]

[1] **σειραις** KLP, vulg., syrr., boh. +; **σειροις** ABC, WH, Treg.; **σιροις** ℵ, Ti. The two last are mere variations in spelling: the last gives a different word which seems less applicable to **ζοφου**. The difficulty is, however, partially explained by regarding **σειραις** as suggested by **δεσμοις** of Jude 6. **σειρος** or **σιρος** is a pit for the storage of grain, and so far as known, the word "does not seem to suggest anything awful or terrible" (Mayor). The presumption, considering dependence of whole chapter on ideas of Jude, is in favour of **σειραις**.

middle might have been expected. *Cf.* v. 5, where the active is suitably used.

Ver. 2. **ἀσελγείαις.** are "acts of lasciviousness". **ὁδὸς τῆς ἀληθείας.** **ἀληθεία** contains the root-idea of "genuineness". It combines the ideas of the knowledge of God and His purposes in Christ; and of the human obligation to right living that springs from it. "He that doeth truth cometh to the light." The writer of 2 Peter is, as always, concerned to oppose a merely intellectual Gnosticism, which has its ultimate fruit in immorality. *Cf.* Ps. cxix. 29, 30. **βλασφημηθήσεται.** The whole Church suffered in reputation because of these men. *Cf.* Rom. ii. 24, 1 Tim. vi. 1.

Ver. 3. **ἐν** is causal. **πλεονεξίᾳ** = "covetousness". *Cf.* Luke xii. 15. **πλαστοῖς**: here only in N.T., "manufactured," "feigned," "artificial". **ἐμπορεύσονται** Originally used in intrans. sense = "go a-trading". *Cf.* Jas. iv. 13. Then = "import," in trans. sense. Here = "make gain of," "exploit". *Cf.* 2 Cor. ii. 17, 1 Tim. vi. 5.

οἷς τὸ κρίμα ἔκπαλαι οὐκ ἀργεῖ: 'whose judgment has for long not been nactive," although there is an appearance of delay. This delay is the argument used by the false teachers. **ἔκπαλαι** occurs in O.G.I.S., 584[5] (ii. A.D.), **δι' ὧν ἔκπαλαι αὐτὴν** (sc. **τὴν πατρίδα**) **εὐεργέτ[ησεν]**. (*Cf.* iii. 4 and ii. 1, **ἐπάγοντες ἑαυτοῖς ταχινὴν ἀπώλειαν.**) For **ἀργεῖ** see note on i. 8. The judgment has long been gathering, and is impending. **νυστάζει.** The word used of the slumbering virgins in Matt. xxv. 5. In Isa. v. 27 it is used of the instruments of God's anger employed against those guilty of social abuses.

Vv. 4-10*a*. *A historical illustration of the Divine judgment on the wicked, and care of the righteous.*

"God spared not angels who sinned, but having cast them into Tartarus, gave them over to chains of darkness, reserving them for judgment. He spared not the ancient world, but guarded Noah, with seven others, while the impious world was overwhelmed by a flood. So Divine judgment was extended to the cities of Sodom and Gomorrah, which were overwhelmed by ashes, and overthrown by earthquake, as an example of what is in store for impious persons, while righteous Lot was delivered, grieved and wearied as he was by the profligate life of the lawless. For day after day this man with his righteous instincts, in his life among them, was vexed with the sight and sound of their lawless deeds. In all this we have a proof that the Lord knows how to deliver the godly out of trial, and to keep the ungodly under discipline until the day of judgment, especially those who follow the polluting lusts of the flesh and despise authority."

Ver. 4. **εἰ γὰρ ὁ θεός . . .** introducing a series of conditional sentences. The apodosis is found in **οἶδεν κύριος** . . . of v. 9. **σειραῖς**. No doubt a rendering of **δεσμοῖς** in Jude 6, agreeably to the practice of this writer, who is somewhat fond of using rarer words, instead of the more commonplace. **σειρά** usually means a "cord" or "rope" (Homer, *Il.* xxiii., 115, *Od.* xxii., 175). It would seem to mean "a golden chain" in *Il.* viii., 19, 25, *cf.* Plato. *Theatetus*, i. 53 C The meaning "fetters" is peculiar to 2 Peter (for *var. lect.* **σειροῖς**, see textual note). **ταρταρώσας** = "cast into Tartarus". The verb is a **ἅπαξ λεγ.** **τάρταρος** occurs in three passages of LXX. (Job xl. 15 (20), xli. 22 (23), Prov. xxiv. 51 (xxx. 16): but in none of these is there any corresponding idea in the Hebrew. The word also occurs in Enoch xx. 2, where Gehenna is the place of

ζόφου [1] ταρταρώσας παρέδωκεν εἰς κρίσιν τηρουμένους,[2] 5. καὶ ἀρχα- [e]
ίου κόσμου οὐκ ἐφείσατο, ἀλλὰ [e]ὄγδοον [f]Νῶε δικαιοσύνης κήρυκα
ἐφύλαξεν, κατακλυσμὸν κόσμῳ ἀσεβῶν [g]ἐπάξας· 6. καὶ πόλεις
Σοδόμων καὶ Γομόρρας τεφρώσας [h]καταστροφῇ κατέκρινεν, ὑπόδειγμα
μελλόντων ἀσεβέσιν [3] τεθεικώς, 7. καὶ δίκαιον Λὼτ καταπονούμενον ὑπὸ τῆς τῶν ἀθέσμων [i]ἐν ἀσελγείᾳ ἀναστροφῆς ἐρύσατο,—

e Plato, *Legg.* 3, 695c, Plut. *Pelop.* c. 13, Dem. i. 812, 3 Macc. v. 27.

f Art. absent ii. 7, *cf.* Abbott, J. G. pp. 57 f.

g Luke xiii. 34, Acts xiv. 27.

h Matt. xx. 18.

i 1 Pet. iii. 2.

[1] ζοφου ℵBCKLP, Ti., Treg., WH; ζοφοις ℵA. "The latter reading may have arisen from a marginal -οις intended to connect σειραις, but wrongly applied to ζοφου" (Māyor, *Ed.* p. cxciv.).

[2] τηρουμενους BCKLP, syr[h] + Ti., Treg., WH; κολαζομενους τηρειν ℵA, latt., Syr[p], boh., sah.

[3] ασεβεσιν BP, syr[h], syr[p], WH; τοις ασεβεσιν sah., boh.; ασεβειν ℵACKL, vulg., Treg., Ti.

punishment for apostate Jews, and Tartarus for the fallen angels. In Homer (*e.g. Il.* viii. 13) Hades is the place of confinement for dead men, and Tartarus is the name given to a murky abyss beneath Hades in which the sins of fallen Immortals (Kronos, Japetos, and the Titans) are punished (*cf.* Salmond, *H.B.D.* ii. 344 *a*). Hence 2 Peter uses this word in agreement with the Book of Enoch and Greek mythology, because he is speaking of fallen angels and not of men. As regards the cosmology that is here implied, it has been suggested that the earth is not regarded as flat, but the universe is conceived as two concentric spheres, the outer heaven, the inner the earth. The nether half of heaven is Tartarus, and the nether half of the earth is Hades (St. Clair, *Expositor*, July, 1902). The use of the word by 2 Peter is remarkable as implying an atmosphere of Greek thought in the circle in which he moved, and for which he wrote. **ζόφος** in Homer is used of the gloom of the nether world, *Od.* xx. 356, *cf.* Heb. xii., 18. Also v. 17 and Jude 6, 13. It is implied that fallen angels and unrighteous men alike undergo temporary punishment until the day of their final doom, *cf.* ver. 9. Enoch x. 4, 12, lxxxviii. 2.

Ver. 5. **ἀρχαίου κόσμου.** The article is omitted, which is not a mark of illiteracy. This chapter is prophetic in form, and the omission of the article is characteristic of that style. *Cf.* Job. iii. 10, Judges v. 5. (See Mayor, *Ed.* xxxiv. xxxv.). **δικαιοσύνης κήρυκα. κηρ.** in this sense is used in N.T. only here, and in 1 Tim. ii. 7, 2 Tim. i. 11. 2 Peter again borrows from Jewish tradition as to the preaching of Noah. *Cf.* Jos. *Antiq.* i. 3, 1, Clem. Rom. i. 7. **κατακλυσμόν**, *cf.* Matt. xxiv. 38, 39, Luke vii. 27, Gen. vi. 17. **ἐπάξας.** Aorist participle implies co-incident action. "He saved N. . . . while he sent, etc." **ἐπάγω** is used of "setting-on," "letting loose," *e.g.* "dogs". *Odyssey*, xix. 445, Xen. *Cyr.* x. 19. **ὄγδοον.** "with seven others". Classical Greek usage is to add **αὐτόν.** There is much difficulty as to the significance of the numeral. The reference is no doubt to the number of Noah's family. The numeral is placed in a prominent place in the sentence to lay stress on the small number saved out of the inhabited world, as a striking example of mercy in the midst of judgment, *cf.* 1 Pet. iii. 20. *Cf.* P. Petr. iii. 28. **ὅτι ἐδραγματοκλέπτει τρίτος ὤν** (*bis*), *cf.* Abbott, J. G. § 562

Ver. 6. **πόλεις Σοδ. καὶ Γομορρ.** Not genitive of apposition, but cities of the district, where Sodom and Gomorrah were situated. *Cf.* Jude 7. **Σ. καὶ Γ. καὶ αἱ περὶ αὐτὰς πόλεις καταστροφῇ κατέκριεν. καταστροφῇ** is dative of instrument, "condemned them by overthrow". Gen. xix. 24, 25 seems to imply some further destruction after the fire. Perhaps an earthquake is meant, a common accompanying phenomenon of volcanic disturbance. **ὑπόδειγμα . . . τεθεικώς**, "constituting them an example to ungodly persons of things in store for them." With **μελλ.** *cf.* Heb. xi. 20, Col. ii. 17. **τεφρώσας** = "cover up with ashes" (not "reduce to ashes") —found in a description of the eruption of Vesuvius. (Dio. Cass. lxvi. p. 1094).

Ver. 7. **καταπονούμενον**, the word applied to the condition of the slave whom Moses delivered, Acts vii. 24. It implies outward discomfort. **ἀθέσμων.** *Cf.* iii. 17,

8. βλέμματι γὰρ καὶ ἀκοῇ δίκαιος[1] ἐνκατοικῶν ἐν αὐτοῖς ἡμέραν ἐξ
ἡμέρας ψυχὴν δικαίαν ἀνόμοις ἔργοις ἐβασάνιζεν,—9. οἶδεν Κύριος
εὐσεβεῖς ἐκ πειρασμοῦ [k]ῥύεσθαι, ἀδίκους δὲ εἰς ἡμέραν κρίσεως
κολαζομένους τηρεῖν, 10. μάλιστα δὲ τοὺς ὀπίσω σαρκὸς ἐν ἐπιθυμίᾳ
[l]μιασμοῦ πορευομένους καὶ κυριότητος καταφρονοῦντας. τολμηταὶ

k Infinit. with οἶδα 1 Tim. iii. 5, Jas. iv. 17, Matt. vii. 11, Phil. iv. 12, 1 Thess. iv. 4, classical.

l Luke iv. 22, Col. i. 13, Rom. i. 26.

[1] **ο δικαιος** ℵACKLP, syrr., Treg., Ti.; om. **ο** B, vulg., WH.

"a stronger word than **ἄνομος,** because **θεσμός** is used especially of a divine ordinance, a fundamental law" (Mayor).

Ver. 8. **βλέμματι γὰρ καὶ ἀκοῇ.** Two interpretations are possible (1) Instrumental dative after **ἐβασάνιζεν.** "He vexed his righteous soul by what he saw and heard." The objections are (*a*) the long interval that separates **βλ. κ.τ.λ.** from **ἐβασάνιζεν,** (*b*) that **βλέμμα** is never elsewhere used of the thing seen, but is used of sight from the subjective, emotional, and volitional point of view. Hence (2), reading **δίκαιος** without the article, and taking **βλ. κ.τ.λ.** with that word, we may translate with the Vulgate "aspectu et auditu justus". His instincts of eye and ear were nobler than those of the society around him. **ἡμέραν ἐξ ἡμέρας.** "Day in, day out." *Cf.* **ἡμέρα καθ ἡμέραν** in Ps. lxviii. 19. **ἐβασάνιζεν.** It is somewhat peculiar that the active should be used. "He vexed, distressed his righteous soul." May it not be that in the use of the active a certain sense of personal culpability is implied? Lot was conscious that the situation was ultimately due to his own selfish choice (*cf.* von Soden).

Ver. 9. **οἶδεν Κύριος, κ.τ.λ.** Apodosis to protasis begun in ver. 4. **πειρασμοῦ.** See Mayor's note on Jas. i. 2. The idea here is primarily of those surroundings that try a man's fidelity and integrity, and not of the inward inducement to sin, arising from the desires. Both Noah and Lot were in the midst of mockers and unbelievers. This **πειρασμός** is the atmosphere in which faith is brought to full development. It was a condition even of the life of Jesus. **ὑμεῖς δὲ ἐστε οἱ διαμεμενηκότες μετ' ἐμοῦ ἐν τοῖς πειρασμοῖς μου** (Luke xxii. 28). It is the word used by St. Luke of the Temptation (Luke iv. 13). On the one hand, **πειρασμός** is not to be lightly sought (Luke xi. 4), or entered into carelessly (Mark xiv. 38); the situation of **πειρασμός** may itself be the result of sin (1 Tim. vi. 9). On the other hand, it is a joyous opportunity for the development of spiritual and moral strength (Jas, i. 2, 12). **πειρασμός** becomes sin only when it ceases to be in opposition to the will. The word is peculiar to the N.T. **ἀδίκους δὲ εἰς ἡμέραν κρίσεως κολαζομένους τηρεῖν**: "to keep the unrighteous under punishment until the day of judgment". The reference may be the same as in 1 Pet. iii. 19, **τοῖς ἐν φυλακῇ πνεύμασιν,** if we interpret "spirits in prison" as meaning those who had disobeyed the preaching of Noah, and to whom Christ preached. *Cf.* Book of Enoch, x. 4 f. **ἡμέραν κρίσεως.** This day is also the day of Parousia. The same expression is used in iii. 7. It is called **ἡμέρα κυρίου** (iii. 10); **ἡ τοῦ θεοῦ ἡμέρα** (iii. 12). Three great results are brought about on that day. (1) The ungodly will suffer **ἀπώλεια** (iii. 7; *cf.* ii. 1, iii. 16). It is noteworthy that the ultimate fate of the fallen angels is not described except as **κρίσις** (ii. 4). (2) Dissolution of the material universe by fire (iii. 11, iii. 7, iii. 12, iii. 10). (3) The righteous are promised "new heavens and a new earth". In this new universe, or environment, righteousness has its home (iii. 13). The difficult passage (i. 19), about the day-star, has reference to this **ἡμέρα κυρίου,** when the great Day shall dawn, and the sign of it shall cheer the hearts of the faithful, and the lamp of prophecy will be no longer needed.

Ver. 10*a*. **μάλιστα δὲ τοὺς ὀπίσω σαρκὸς . . . πορευομένους,** "especially those who follow the flesh as their leader". *Cf.* Matt. iv. 19, 1 Tim. v. 15. In Isa. lxv. 2 we have **πορευομένοις . . . ὀπίσω τῶν ἁμαρτιῶν αὐτῶν.** The writer now passes from the sin of Sodom to the sin of the Libertines. **ἐπιθυμίᾳ μιασμοῦ. ἐπιθυμίᾳ** is used of strong desire generally; "lust" in its older meaning. *E.g.* Luke xxii. 15. **μιασμοῦ** is a qualitative genitive, as in ii. 1. **αἱρέσεις ἀπωλείας**: "a polluting desire". **κυριότητος καταφρονοῦντας. κυρ.** cannot be taken in a purely abstract sense, "despising authority". **κυριότης**

αὐθάδεις, δόξας οὐ τρέμουσιν βλασφημοῦντες. 11. **ὅπου ἄγγελοι ἰσχύϊ καὶ δυνάμει μείζονες ὄντες οὐ φέρουσιν κατ' αὐτῶν παρὰ**

is used in the abstract sense of the Lordship of Christ in Didache iv. 1. Honour him who speaks the word of God, **ὡς κύριον, ὅθεν γὰρ ἡ κυριότης λαλεῖται, ἐκεῖ κύριός ἐστιν.**

As is suggested by this passage in the Didache, we may conclude that by **κυριότητος καταφρονοῦντας** is meant a despising of the Lordship of Christ, which was the central theme of the apostolic teaching and preaching. The writer in ver. 10*b*, goes on to speak of their attitude towards **δόξας**, or "angelic beings". *Cf.* Jude 8, **κυριότητα δὲ ἀθετοῦσιν, δόξας δὲ βλασφημοῦσιν.** It is true that in Col. i. 16, **κυριότητες** form one of the ranks of angels in the false Gnostic teaching, but there is no indication that the Libertines here spoken of taught any elaborate angelology. On the contrary, they spoke lightly of the Unseen Powers generally. Their teaching seems to have been materialistic in tone. They were **ὡς ἄλογα ζῷα γεγεννημένα φυσικὰ** (ver. 12)—creatures of natural instinct, not employing the higher powers of reason (**ἄλογα**).

Vv. 10*b*-14 *Further description of the False Teachers.* "Presumptuous and arrogant, they do not shrink from irreverent speech about the unseen powers, while even angels, who are far superior to these false teachers in greatness and might, do not dare to bring against these powers an irreverent accusation. Their irreverence is therefore of an ignorant type, as of unreasoning animals, who are born creatures of instinct, and are fitted only for capture and destruction. Their destruction will be in keeping, and they will be defrauded of what is really the wages of fraud. Their notion of pleasure is to spend the day in delicate living. They are spots and blemishes, luxuriating in their pleasures, while they feast with you. Their eyes are full of adultery, and they are insatiable in sin, alluring unstable souls. With hearts experienced in covetousness, they are children of the curse."

Ver. 10*b*. **τολμηταὶ αὐθάδεις. αὐθ.** is to be taken as an epithet of **τολμηταί.** The idea in **τολμ.** is of shameless and irreverent darlng. **αὐθάδεις** (**αὐτὸς** and **ἥδομαι**) = "self-willed," "arrogant". In 1 Tim. i. 7, the **ἐπίσκοπος** must not be **αὐθάδης,** where the thought seems to be of irresponsibility in regard to the community. *Cf.* Didache iii. 6, **μὴ γίνου γόγγυσος· ἐπειδὴ ὁδηγεῖ εἰς τὴν βλασφημίαν· μηδὲ αὐθάδης μηδὲ πονηρόφρων. ἐκ γὰρ τούτων ἁπάντων βλασφημίαι γεννῶνται.** The false teachers push forward their views, regardless of consequences. *Cf.* P. Amh. 78, 13 f. (ii. A.D.), **μ[ου] πλεονεκτῖ ἄνθρωπος ἁ(υ)θάδης.** "An audacious man is taking advantage of me." **δόξας οὐ τρέμουσιν βλασφημοῦντες. δόξας** is used of Unseen Powers whether good or evil. How can **βλασφημ.** be used of evil powers? It is obvious that we must find some sense for **βλασφημεῖν** here; and also in Jude 8, that will be applicable to **δόξας,** apart altogether from their moral character. In Plato, *Rep.* 381 E, there occurs a passage dealing with the popular conception of the gods, which holds that they may sometimes change their form, and "in the likeness of wandering strangers, bodied in manifold forms, go roaming from city to city" (*cf.* Homer, *Od.* xvii. 485). By such notions, as taught for example by mothers to their children, men may be said, "**εἰς θεοὺς βλασφημεῖν**". Not only are these a misrepresentation of the Divine, but their tendency is to make light of it, belittle it, detract from its dignity. Some such sense of **βλ.** seems to be required here. The false teachers may have scoffed at the idea both of angelic help, and of diabolic temptation. Their tendency seems to have been to make light of the Unseen, to foster a sense of the unreality both of sin and of goodness, and to reduce the motives of conduct to a vulgar hedonism (*cf.* Mayor's note, p. 74).

Ver. 11. **ὅπου** = "whereas". The interpretation of this verse turns on the meaning of **κατ' αὐτῶν.** Does it refer to the false teachers, or to a distinction between two sets of angels, which finds an illustration in the contest between Michael and Satan for the body of Moses? (Jude, 9). In the latter case **κατ' αὐτῶν** would refer to the fallen angels. Another possible interpretation is that **ἄγγελοι ἰσχύϊ καὶ δυνάμει μείζονες ὄντες** are a superior class of archangels (Spitta), and **κατ' αὐτῶν** would refer to the **δόξαι** in general. Chase suggests that the reference is to the false teachers, and angels are represented as bringing before the Lord tidings as to the conduct of created beings, whether angels or men (*op. cit.* 797 *b*).

m Κυρίῳ βλάσφημον κρίσιν. 12. οὗτοι δέ, ὡς ἄλογα ζῷα γεγεννημένα φυσικὰ εἰς ἅλωσιν καὶ φθοράν, ἐν n οἷς ἀγνοοῦσιν βλασφημοῦντες, ἐν τῇ φθορᾷ αὐτῶν καὶ φθαρήσονται, 13. ἀδικούμενοι[1] μισθὸν ἀδικίας· ἡδονὴν ἡγούμενοι τὴν ἐν ἡμέρᾳ τρυφήν, σπίλοι καὶ μῶμοι

m Use of dat. instead of accus. indicates progress towards extinction of prepp. with three cases (Moulton, *Proleg.* 106). Luke v. 25. n Rom. x. 14, vi. 21, xiv. 21, John xix. 37,

[1] αδικουμενοι ℵ BP, syr^h + WH; κομιουμενοι ACKLℵ^c, boh., spec., syr^h + Ti., Treg.

We may note the tendency in 2 Peter exemplified here to put in general terms what Jude states in the particular, in the story of Michael and Satan. The particulars of Jude are omitted (as also the name Enoch afterwards) in order to avoid direct reference to apocryphal writings. Accordingly the sentence, οὐ φέρουσιν κατ' αὐτῶν βλάσφημον κρίσιν, is only intelligible by reference to Jude 9, where Michael does not himself condemn Satan, but says ἐπιτιμήσαι σοι κύριος. *Cf.* note on βλασφημοῦντες, v. 10.

Ver. 12. γεγεννημένα φυσικὰ—"born creatures of instinct". Instinct is here distinguished from the rational centres of thought and judgment. They are ἄλογα ζῷα. Their chief characteristic is that they are "alive," and have no sense of the moral issues of life. Like animals, they exist εἰς ἅλωσιν καὶ φθοράν. ἐν οἷς ἀγνοοῦσιν βλασφημοῦντες = ἐν τούτοις ἃ . . . "Speaking lightly of things they are ignorant of". Spiritually they are incapable. They know not what they do, in thus clouding moral issues. ἐν τῇ φθορᾷ αὐτῶν καὶ φθαρήσονται. Here is a subtle example of the dependence of this epistle upon Jude. In Jude 10, we have ἐν τούτοις φθείρονται, referring to ὅσα δὲ φυσικῶς . . . ἐπίστανται. The sense in 2 Peter is confused, and there is no distinction between the two kinds of knowledge, although the intended meaning in both passages is the same. *Cf.* Rom. viii. 5, 6.

Ver. 13. ἀδικούμενοι μισθὸν ἀδικίας (*cf.* v. 12). This playing upon words is characteristic of 2 Peter, ἀδικεῖν has usually the sense of "doing harm to" (*cf.* Acts xxxv. 10; Galat. iv. 12). Here it would seem to mean "being defrauded of the wages of fraud," or "being done out of the wages of wrong-doing". It has been customary to see in this phrase an illustration of the irresponsible use of words in 2 Peter. "Another example of the author's love of far-fetched and artificial expressions" (Mayor). In P. Eleph., however $27a^{24}f$ (iii. B.C.), the writers ask for a receipt with reference to a certain business transaction. τούτου δὲ γενομένου ἐσόμεθα οὐκ ἠδικημένοι "this having been arranged, we shall not be defrauded". To this may be added Mayor's citation of Plut. Cato Mi. 17 (p. 766) εὑρὼν χρέα παλαιὰ τῷ δημοσίῳ πολλοὺς ὀφείλοντας καὶ πολλοῖς τὸ δημόσιον, ἅμα τὴν πόλιν ἔπαυσεν ἀδικουμένην καὶ ἀδικοῦσαν. The accusative *rei* after ἀδικ. is very unusual. In classical writers it is found only with ἀδίκημα. μισθὸν ἀδικίας suggests the experience of Balaam, of whom the same expression is used in ver. 15, who never received his promised hire from Balak (Num. xxiv. 11). Death deprives the false teachers of all their reward. For significance of the name "Balaam," in connexion with the false teachers, see Introduction, p. 118. ἡδονὴν in N.T. only in a bad sense, *cf.* Luke viii. 14, Tit. iii. 3, Jas. iv. 1-3. τρυφή only in N.T. in Luke vii. 25 where it is used of "delicate living," a luxurious life, but with no special blame attached. The word is also used of gifts of wisdom in Prov. iv. 9, *cf.* Ps. xxxvi. 8, "the river of thy pleasures". Eden is called παράδεισος τῆς τρυφῆς, Gen. ii. 15, iii. 13, 24. ἐν ἡμέρᾳ "in the day-time,", 'in broad day-light". σπίλοι καὶ μῶμοι, *cf.* Ephes. v. 27, 2 Pet. iii. 14, 1 Pet. i. 19, Jude 12. μῶμος "reproach," "disgrace". *Cf.* Hort. on 1 Pet. i. 19, where he traces the way in which μῶμος and ἄμωμος, came to be used with superficial meaning of "blemish," *cf.* Ephes. i. 4, v. 27, Heb. ix. 14. ἐντρυφῶντες: "to be luxurious," *cf.* Xen. *Hell.* iv. 1, 30. ἐν ταῖς ἀπάταις αὐτῶν: to be taken with ἐντρυφ. ἀπάτη is a favourite word of Hermas (*Mand.* viii. 5) and is frequently joined by him with τρυφή (*Mand.* xi. 12 and throughout *Parable* 6). According to Deissmann, ἀπάτη in popular Hellenistic has the meaning "pleasure". *Cf.* Matt. xiii. 22 = Mark iv. 19 (Luke viii. 14), (see his *Hellenisierung des semitischen Monotheis-*

ἐντρυφῶντες ἐν ταῖς ἀπάταις [1] αὐτῶν συνευωχούμενοι ὑμῖν, 14. ᵒ
ὀφθαλμοὺς ἔχοντες μεστοὺς ᵒ μοιχαλίδος καὶ ἀκαταπαύστους [2]
ᵖ ἁμαρτίας, δελεάζοντες ψυχὰς ἀστηρίκτους, καρδίαν γεγυμνασμένην
ᵖ πλεονεξίας ἔχοντες, κατάρας τέκνα· 15. καταλείποντες εὐθεῖαν
ὁδὸν ἐπλανήθησαν, ἐξακολουθήσαντες τῇ ὁδῷ τοῦ Βαλαὰμ τοῦ Βόσορ [3]

o Matt. x. 10, Heb. iii. 1, Eph. ii. 12.
p 1 Peter iv. 1, Jas. i. 13.
q Heb. iii. 12.

[1] **απαταις** ℵACKLP, syr^h (mg. **αγαπαις**), WH, Ti.; **αγαπαις** A²B, sah., syr^p + Treg., WHm. At first sight it would seem probable that 2 Peter has misread **ἀγαπαις** in Jude 12. Confusion is common in MSS. of O.T. between **ἀγαπαω** and **ἀπαταω, ἀγαπη** and **ἀπατη** (*e.g.*, Ps. lxxviii. 36). Yet **ἀπατη, ἀπαταω** has been proved to be the correct reading in many cases. **αὐτων** here is an argument in its favour. Nestle (*op. cit.* pp. 324 ff.) and Zahn (*op. cit.* ii. p. 235 f.) argue strongly for **αγαπαις** and omission of **υμιν** (**συνευωχουμενοι** = "feasting with one another") (Mayor, *Ed.* cxcvii).

[2] **ακαταπαυστους** ℵCKLP, 13, 31, Ti., Treg.; **ακαταπαστους** AB, WH. The latter reading "may have originated in a faulty pronunciation on the part of the reader, or the **υ** may have been accidentally omitted at the end of the line, as in **B**, where one line ends with **πα-** and the next begins with **-στους**" (Mayor, *Ed.* cxcvii. *cf.* Moulton, *Proleg.* p. 47).

[3] **Βοσορ** ℵ^cACKLP, boh., syr^h, Ti., Treg.; **Βεωρ** B, syr^p, sah., WH, Weiss; **Βεωρσορ** ℵ. There can be little doubt that **Βοσορ** is the correct reading. The reading of ℵ is manifestly due to a combination of **Βοσορ** and a marginal correction **-εωρ**. Zahn. (*op. cit.* ii. p. 292) says that everywhere in LXX, Josephus, Philo, only the forms **Βεορ** or **Βαιορ** occur, and that **Βοσορ** is inexplicable except as a mistake on the part of 2 Peter due to "imperfect pronunciation or defective hearing". Nestle, however (*op. cit.* p. 244), after Holmes-Parsons, cites **υιον του Βοσορ** in the Georgian version of Jos. xiii. 22. **Βοσορ** also occurs as name of a place in Deut. iv. 43, 1 Sam. xxx. 9, 1 Macc. v. 26. "The support of the ordinary name by **B** against the other MSS. may be compared with its support of **Σιμων** against **Συμεων** in i. 1" (Mayor, *Ed.* cxcviii.).

mus, (*Neue Jahrb. f. d. Klass. Altertum*, 1903), p. 165, n. 5).

Ver. 14. **ἀκαταπαύστους ἁμαρτίας.** For use of genitive with this verb, *cf.* 1 Pet. iv. 1. See Grammatical Note. **δελεάζοντες.** *Cf.* v. 18 and Mayor's note on Jas. i. 14, "entice or catch by a bait". **κατάρας τέκνα.** *Cf.* **τέκνα ὑπακοῆς**, 1 Pet. i. 14.

Vv. 15, 16. *Example of Balaam.* "They have left the straight way and wandered from it, having followed the way of Balaam, who loved the ways of wickedness, and was rebuked for his transgression, when a dumb ass spoke with a man's voice, and forbade the infatuation of the prophet."

Ver. 15. **τῇ ὁδῷ τοῦ Βαλαάμ.** The comparison of the conduct of the False Teachers to that of Balaam is significant as determining their character and motive (see Introduction, pp. 115 ff.). The writer of 2 Peter takes the miraculous narrative in Numbers xxii. 21-35 literally. It is no disparagement of the value of the illustration that we, in our day, can no longer do so. Balaam had the gift of real spiritual vision. He is described in Numbers xxiv. 36 as one "whose eye was closed," *i.e.* to outer things, and also as one "which seeth the vision of the Almighty, falling down and having his eyes open," *i.e.* to spiritual vision. Balaam was one who allowed the greed of gain to become stronger than the prophetic impulse. He is conscious that he is tempting God, and an evil conscience makes him irritable. He fears lest God may yet interfere to rob him of his reward. When the ass starts aside he beats it, but ultimately his passion is subdued by the momentary triumph of his higher spiritual instincts, when he begins to suspect that in the stubbornness of the animal there is really the power of God exercised to hinder him in his course. The angel with the drawn sword is often the form that men's religion takes who are disobeying the voice of conscience. "There is a strange depth of meaning in the appealing eye of an ill-treated animal. It is an appeal, in the first place, to whatever remnant of pity and generosity may still survive in the heart of the man who ill-treats it, but it is an appeal, in the second place, to the

ὃς μισθὸν ἀδικίας ἠγάπησεν, 16. ἔλεγξιν δὲ ἔσχεν ἰδίας παρα-
νομίας· ὑποζύγιον ἄφωνον ἐν ἀνθρώπου φωνῇ φθεγξάμενον ἐκώλυσεν
τὴν τοῦ προφήτου παραφρονίαν. 17. οὗτοί εἰσιν πηγαὶ ἄνυδροι
καὶ ὁμίχλαι ὑπὸ λαίλαπος ἐλαυνόμεναι, οἷς ὁ ζόφος τοῦ σκότους
τετήρηται. 18. ὑπέρογκα γὰρ ματαιότητος φθεγγόμενοι δελεάζουσιν ἐν ἐπιθυμίαις σαρκὸς ἀσελγείαις τοὺς ὀλίγως [1] ἀποφεύγοντας τοὺς
ἐν πλάνῃ ἀναστρεφομένους, 19. ἐλευθερίαν αὐτοῖς ἐπαγγελλόμενοι,

[1] **ολιγως** ABℵ^c, vg., syrr., sah., boh., Treg., Ti., WH; **οντως** ℵCKLP; **οντως** would require aor.; **αποφυγοντας** ("clean escaped" A.V.), read by KLP. In the MSS. **οντως** is hardly distinguishable from **ολιγως** (Mayor, *Ed.* cxcviii.).

justice of the God who made them both, a cry of which we may be sure it has entered into the ears of the Lord of Sabaoth. When animals are put to unnecessary suffering, either in the shambles or as beasts of burden, or in the interests of science or sport, or for any other reason, cases are sure to arise in which we may justly apply the words of our Epistle, and say of such poor tortured creatures that with their dying gaze, no less clearly than if they had spoken with man's voice, they forbade the madness of their torturers" (Mayor, p. 203). *Cf.* F. W. Robertson, *Sermons*, *Ser.* iv. pp. 40 f.

Ver. 16. **ἔλεγξιν δὲ ἔσχεν**, a periphrasis for the passive of **ἐλέγχω**, = "was rebuked". **ἰδίας παρανομίας**, emphatic, "his own transgression". Two interpretations of **ἰδίας** are possible. (1) The **παρανομ.** is a characteristic trait in Balaam (Keil. Weiss). (2) As prophet, Belaam was expected to do and teach God's law. He whose duty it is to rebuke others is himself rebuked for his own transgression" (Hundhausen, Wiesinger). **παρανομία** = "a particular transgression" as distinct from **ἀνομία** = "disobedience in general". **παραφρονίαν**, "infatuation". Balaam is proceeding against what he knows to be the Divine will.

Vv. 17-19. *The Libertines are themselves slaves.* "They are like waterless wells, and mists that the wind disperses. For them is reserved the fate of gloomy darkness. They utter ponderous nothings, and allure through their lusts those who were just escaping from the temptations of heathen life. Promising freedom to others, they are themselves slaves of corruption. Every one is a slave to that which has mastered him."

Ver. 17. **πηγαὶ . . . ἐλαυνόμεναι.** It is interesting to compare the expressions in 2 Peter here with Jude 12. It would appear as though he had felt that **νεφέλαι ἄνυδροι** was a contradiction in terms, and instead he substituted **πηγαί**. **λαίλαπος** is a strong expression = "gale," a "storm of wind". *Cf.* Mk. iv. 37, Lk. viii. 23. **οἷς ὁ ζόφος . . . τετήρηται** is somewhat out of place here, and is used appropriately of meteors in Jude 13.

Ver. 18. **ὑπέρογκα.** *Cf.* Jude 16. No doubt the reference is to the use of Gnostic terms. **ματαιότης**, used specially of moral insincerity. *Cf.* **ματαίας ἀναστροφῆς**, "heartless conduct," 1 P. i. 18. There is no corresponding reality behind their words. **σαρκὸς**, to be taken with **ἀσελγείαις**, which is in apposition to **ἐπιθυμίαις**. **τοὺς ὀλίγως ἀποφεύγοντας**: "those who are just escaping"; who have been impressed with Christian truth, and have had strength to separate themselves from their old surroundings and customs; but are led to return through the compromises suggested by the false teachers. The phenomenon is not uncommon in all missionary work, of men who have escaped from "Gentile vices, but are not yet established in Christian virtues" (Bigg). **τοὺς ἐν πλάνῃ ἀναστρεφομένους** = governed by **ἀποφεύγοντας**: "(escaping from) those who live in error"; *i.e.* from their old heathen companionships. "There is great passion in the words. Grandiose sophistry is the hook, filthy lust is the bait, with which these men catch those whom the Lord had delivered, or was delivering" (Bigg).

Ver. 19. **ἐλευθερίαν.** Doubtless that Antinomianism is indicated to which the doctrine of Grace has ever been open. *Cf.* Galat. v. 13. It arises from the ever-recurring confusion of liberty and license. The training of conscience is contemporaneous with the growth of Christian character. The Pauline teaching, which abrogated external legality, was open to

αὐτοὶ δοῦλοι ὑπάρχοντες τῆς φθορᾶς· ᾧ γάρ τις ἥττηται, τούτῳ
δεδούλωται. 20. εἰ γὰρ ἀποφυγόντες τὰ μιάσματα τοῦ κόσμου ἐν
ἐπιγνώσει τοῦ κυρίου καὶ σωτῆρος Ἰησοῦ Χριστοῦ, τούτοις ʳ δὲ πάλιν
ἐμπλακέντες ἡττῶνται, γέγονεν αὐτοῖς τὰ ἔσχατα χείρονα τῶν
πρώτων. 21. κρεῖττον γὰρ ˢ ἦν αὐτοῖς ᵗ μὴ ἐπεγνωκέναι τὴν ὁδὸν
τῆς δικαιοσύνης ἢ ἐπιγνοῦσιν ὑποστρέψαι ἐκ τῆς παραδοθείσης
αὐτοῖς ἁγίας ἐντολῆς· 22. συμβέβηκεν αὐτοῖς τὸ τῆς ἀληθοῦς

r Acts xi. 17 (Rec.). s Rom. ix. 3, 2 Cor. xii. 11, Matt. xxv. 27, xxvi. 9, 24, Arist. *Nub.* 1215, Xen. *Anab.* 7, 7. 40. t Luke xvii. 1 (*om.* (?) τουξ).

abuse, and might easily be dangerous to recent converts from heathenism. **φθορᾶς.** See Mayor's note, ed. p. 175. **φθορά** is that gradual decay of spiritual and moral sense that follows on wilful self-indulgence. **ᾧ γάρ . . . διδούλωται.** *Cf.* Rom. vi. 16, viii. 21, John viii. 34.

Vv. 20-23. *The consequences of falling away.* "The case of their victims is a serious one. They have escaped from the pollutions of the world through the knowledge of Jesus Christ, and are once more entangled and worsted by these. Their last state becomes worse than the first. It were better for them not to have known the way of righteousness, than in spite of such knowledge, to depart from the holy commandment committed to them. They illustrate the truth of the proverb: 'the dog that turned back to his own vomit, and the sow that went to bathe to wallowing in the mud'."

Ver. 20. Here, again, **γὰρ** loosely introduces the subject of the victims allured by the false teachers away from their former faith. **τὰ μιάσματα τοῦ κόσμου.** (Lev. vii. 8, Jer. xxxix. 34), occurs only here in N.T. In LXX the word seems to have a technical religious sense, the profanation of flesh by ordinary use which is set apart for sacrifice. This sense lingers here. The body is sacred to God, and to give licentious rein to the passions is **μίασμα.** *Cf.* **μιασμός**, v. 10, and **μιαίνω**, Jude 8. **τοῦ κόσμου** is the world in the sense of the heathen society and its practises. **ἐπιγνώσει.** See note on i. 2. **τούτοις** is governed by **ἐμπλακέντες** = "entangled by these". *Cf.* 2 Tim. ii. 4, **γέγονεν αὐτοῖς, κ.τ.λ.** *Cf.* Matt. xii. 45, Luke xi. 26, and Heb. vi. 4-8, x. 26.

Ver. 21. **ὁδὸν τῆς δικαιοσύνης.** Also called "the way of truth," ii. 2, "the straight way," ii. 15. **ἐντολῆς.** Elsewhere in N.T. the singular is used to mean a particular precept. *Cf.* Rom. vii. 12, 1 Tim. vi. 14. It is characteristic of this writer to emphasise the aspect of Christianity, not only as faith, but as the moral law **ἁγίας ἐντολῆς.** *Cf.* i. 5. **ἐν τῇ πίστει ὑμῶν τὴν ἀρετήν.** A strong ethical note pervades the teaching of 2 Peter.

Ver. 22. **τὸ τῆς ἀληθοῦς παροιμίας**: "the content of the true proverb" has been "verified," or "realised" in their case. The first proverb is found in Prov. xxvi. 11. The second is apparently not derived from a Hebrew source. Both are quoted familiarly in an abbreviated form (*cf.* WM. p. 443). The interpretation of the second is an exegetical crux. Bigg takes **λουσαμένη** = "having bathed itself in mud". The sense is, "not that the creature has washed itself clean in water (so apparently the R.V.), still less that it has been washed clean (as A.V.), and then returns to the mud; but that having once bathed in filth it never ceases to delight in it". This, however, is to force the meaning of **λουσαμένη,** which is consistently used of washing with water. Again, the *point* of the proverb is to illustrate **τὰ ἔσχατα χείρονα τῶν πρώτων.** The dupes of the false teachers were cleansed and returned to pollution.

The question is important whether **λουσαμένη** is Middle or Passive? Dr. Rendel Harris (*Story of Ahikar*, p. lxvii.) may have discovered the original proverb in the following, appearing in some texts of Aḥikar. "My son, thou hast behaved like the swine which *went to the bath* with people of quality, and when he came out, saw a stinking drain, and went and rolled himself in it". If this be the source of the **παροιμία, λ.** is Middle (Moulton, *Proleg.* pp. 238-39).

A friend of my own, with a knowledge of animals, tells me that the pig is often washed in certain forms of dishealth, to open the pores of the skin. The animal, being unprotected by hair, finds the sun's heat disagreeable, and wallows again in the mud for coolness. The dried mud protects the skin from the rays. **βόρβορος** found only here and in

[u] παροιμίας, Κύων ἐπιστρέψας ἐπὶ τὸ ἴδιον ἐξέραμα, καί Ὗς [v] λουσαμένη εἰς κυλισμὸν βορβόρου.

III. 1. Ταύτην ἤδη, ἀγαπητοί, δευτέραν ὑμῖν γράφω ἐπιστολήν,
ἐν αἷς διεγείρω ὑμῶν ἐν ὑπομνήσει τὴν εἰλικρινῆ διάνοιαν, 2.
[a] μνησθῆναι τῶν προειρημένων ῥημάτων ὑπὸ τῶν ἁγίων προφητῶν
καὶ τῆς τῶν ἀποστόλων ὑμῶν ἐντολῆς τοῦ κυρίου καὶ σωτῆρος, 3.
τοῦτο πρῶτον [b] γινώσκοντες ὅτι ἐλεύσονται ἐπ᾽ ἐσχάτων τῶν ἡμερῶ-
ἐν ἐμπαιγμονῇ ἐμπαῖκται κατὰ τὰς ἰδίας ἐπιθυμίας αὐτῶν πορευόν

u Luke xx. 25, Jas. iv. 1 Cor. vii. 33.
v Mid.? Matt. xxvii. 5.
a For this use of so-called epexegetical infinitive see Moulton, *Proleg.* pp. 203-204.
b Col. iii. 16, 2 Cor. vii. 5, ix. 10, Phil. i. 29.

Jer. xxxviii. 6. *Cf.* Acta Thomae, 53. **εἶδον βόρβορον . . . καὶ ψυχὰς ἐκεῖ κυλιομένας.** In the *Legends of Pelagia*, which, though late, are written in good vernacular Greek, both noun and corresponding verb are found. **ἐλθοῦσα περιστερὰ μελάνη καὶ βεβορβορωμένη περιεπέτατό μοι, καὶ τὴν δυσωδίαν τοῦ βορβόρου αὐτῆς οὐκ ἠδυνάμην φέρειν.** (*Die Pelag. Legend.*, ed. Usener, p. 21). Bishop Wordsworth suggested that the double proverb is an inexact quotation of two iambic lines—

εἰς ἴδιον ἐξέραμ᾽ ἐπιστρέψας κύων
λελουμένη θ᾽ ὗς εἰς κύλισμα βορβόρου.

If he is right, 2 Pet. cannot be charged with the use of the two rare words, **βορβόρου** and **ἐξέραμα.** Bigg suggests (ed., p. 228) that the Proverbs of Solomon had been unified by some Jewish paraphrast, and this one of the pig added to the canonical collection.

CHAPTER III.—Vv. 1-4. *Prophets and apostles have warned us that delay will lead to denial of the Second Advent.*

"I am now writing my second letter to you. In both I seek to rouse you to honest reflection on the words formerly spoken by the holy prophets, and on the commandment of our Lord delivered by your missionaries. Especially realise the truth of their warning, that there will come in the last days scoffers, with scoffing questions, walking after their own lusts, and saying, 'Where is the promise of His appearing? For,' say they, 'from the time the fathers fell asleep, everything remains as it has been from the beginning of creation'."

Ver. 1. For **ἤδη** with numeral, *cf.* John xxi. 14. **δευτέραν ἐπιστολήν.** Does this refer to 1 Peter? See Introduction, p. 113. **ἐν αἷς**: "in both of which," *constructio ad sensum.* **διεγείρω . . . ὑπομνήσει**: *cf.* i. 13. **εἰλικρινῆ**: *cf.* 1 Cor. v. 8, 2 Cor. i. 12, ii. 17, Phil. i. 10. **εἰλικρινῆ διάνοιαν** is a technical philosophic term used by Plato. *Phaed.* 66 A = "pure reason," such as the geometer employs. In *Phaed.* 81 C, **εἰλικρινὴς ψυχή** is opposed to **ψ. μεμιασμένη καὶ ἀκάθαρτος.** 2 Peter here cannot be acquitted of a confusion in the use of philosophic terms, probably picked up loosely in conversation. At the same time, **διάνοια** is also used in the philosophic sense of **ψυχή** in Gen. xvii. 17, Deut. vi. 5, Num. xv. 39; also in N.T. Coloss. i. 21, 1 Pet. i. 13. **εἰλικρινής** is of doubtful etymology, and signifies ethical purity, a mind uncontaminated and unwarped by sensual passion. The opposite state is described in Plato, *Phaed.* 81, "She thinks nothing true, but what is bodily, and can be touched and seen, and eaten and drunk, and used for men's lusts".

Ver. 2. Borrowed from Jude 17. **μνησθῆναι**: epexegetical infinitive. See grammatical note. **καὶ τῆς τῶν ἀποστόλων, κ.τ.λ.** Double possessive genitive "of the Lord's command delivered by your apostles". Chase (*op. cit.* p. 811 *a*) suggests that **διά** should be inserted after **τῆς,** and compares the title of the Didache, **διδαχὴ κυρίου διὰ τῶν δώδεκα ἀποστόλων τοῖς ἔθνεσιν. ἐντολή** = teaching of our Lord on the fulfilment of the moral law, *cf.* ii. 21, John xii. 50. **ἀποστόλων**: Are the Twelve meant? *cf.* Introd. pp. 103-4. Probably **ἀπ.** signifies just those from whom they received the first knowledge of the gospel, accredited missionaries of the Church. The word is used of Epaphroditus, Phil. ii. 25, and of other than apostles, 2 Cor. viii. 23.

Ver. 3. **τοῦτο πρῶτον γινώσκοντες.** Accusative is required, but all MSS. have nominative, *cf.* Jude 18. **ἐπ᾽ ἐσχάτων τῶν ἡμερῶν.** Mockers are one of the signs of the approach of the end, *cf.* 1 John ii. 18. **ἐν ἐμπαιγμονῇ ἐμπαῖκται**:

μενοι, 4. καὶ λέγοντες Ποῦ ἐστὶν ἡ ἐπαγγελία τῆς παρουσίας [c]αὐτοῦ;
ἀφ' ἧς γὰρ οἱ πατέρες ἐκοιμήθησαν, πάντα οὕτως [d]διαμένει ἀπ'
ἀρχῆς κτίσεως. 5. λανθάνει γὰρ αὐτοὺς τοῦτο θέλοντας ὅτι οὐρανοὶ
ἦσαν ἔκπαλαι καὶ γῆ ἐξ ὕδατος καὶ δι' ὕδατος συνεστῶσα τῷ τοῦ
Θεοῦ [e]λόγῳ· 6. δι' ὧν ὁ τότε κόσμος ὕδατι κατακλυσθεὶς ἀπώλετο·

c 1 John ii. 12 2 John 6.
d John xv. 27, viii. 58, 1 John iii. 8, Jer. i. 5, Ps. lxxxix. 2.
e Rom. iii. 24, Eph. ii. 8.

ἐμπαίκτης is an unclassical form, *cf.* Mark xv. 20. This verse is not part of the prophetic or apostolic message of ver. 2, but a particular caution of the writer, based on Jude.

Ver. 4. **ποῦ ἐστὶν, κ.τ.λ.** The coming of our Lord in the near future was evidently an integral part of the apostolic teaching, *cf.* i. 16. "There is no sure evidence that Jesus sought to undermine the assumption of His followers, that the final glory would be manifested in their day; and even this we may fairly qualify with the remembrance that a main motive of the principal eschatological discourse, reported by the Synoptists, is to warn the disciples against premature expectations" (J.H. Muirhead, *Eschatology of Jesus*. pp. 126, 127). **τῆς παρουσίας**: See note on i. 16. **ἀφ' ἧς γὰρ, κ.τ.λ.** "The fathers," must mean those of the preceding generation, in whose life-time the **παρουσία** was expected. **οὕτως**=*in statu quo*. **ἀπ' ἀρχῆς κτίσεως**, *i.e.*, "contrary to all previous human experience". The Teaching of our Lord Himself in one aspect would imply that the actual **παρουσία,** would be attended with no outward previous disturbance of life to act as a warning. Men would be engaged in their ordinary occupations and pleasures (Matt. xxiv. 36-42). The development and ripening of the moral and spiritual issues of men's lives are often not outwardly apparent (*cf.* Paget's "*Studies in the Christian Character*,"—"*The Hidden Issues*," pp. 89 ff).

Vv. 5-7. *The first part of the argument against the scoffers.* "It is not true that the course of the world is unchanging. They have wilfully forgotten that the heavens existed originally, and the earth was formed out of water, and by means of water, by the Word of God. By this very water and Word the world, as it then was, was overwhelmed and perished. The present heavens and earth, by the same Word, are treasured up for fire, being reserved for the day when impious men shall meet their doom and destruction."

Ver. 5. **λανθάνει γὰρ αὐτοὺς τοῦτο.** "This escapes their notice." **τοῦτο** is nominative. **θέλοντας**: "wilfully" "of their own purpose". **ἔκπαλαι** (*cf.* note, ii. 3): "originally," *i.e.* before the creation of the world. The Rabbinical school of Shammai held that Gen. i. 1, **ἐν ἀρχῇ ἐποίησεν ὁ θεὸς τὸν οὐρανὸν καὶ τὴν γῆν** meant that the heaven was in existence before the six days' work, *i.e.* **ἔκπαλαι.** Perhaps this notion is present here. **ἐξ ὕδατος καὶ δι' ὕδατος.** Two kinds of water are meant. The first may refer to the primeval watery chaos—"the face of the waters" (Gen. i. 2). The second is perhaps connected with the formation of the dry land by "the gathering together of the waters into one place" (Gen. i. 9). But the meaning is obscure (*cf.* Mayor, ed. lxxxiii.; Chase, *op. cit.* 797). **συνεστῶσα**="was formed". *Cf.* Philo, i. p. 330. **ἐκ γῆς καὶ ὕδατος καὶ ἀέρος καὶ πυρὸς συνέστη ὅδε ὁ κόσμος.**

The above interpretation is in substantial agreement with Alford's, who distinguishes "the waters above the firmament," and "the fountains of the great deep". The Hebrew had no notion of evaporation. The rivers run into the sea, and the water returns subterraneously to their sources again (Eccles. i. 7).

Ver. 6. **δι' ὧν.** Mayor and Schmeidel, against the evidence of nearly all manuscripts, read **δι' ὅν.**. This is rendered unnecessary (1) if the above rendering of **ἐξ ὕδατος κ.τ.λ.** is taken, and the plural **δι' ὧν** refers to the two waters. **δι' ὅν** would refer to **λόγῳ** alone, or (2) if **δι' ὧν** refers to **ὑδάτων** and **λόγῳ** taken together, which would in some ways suit the sense of the whole passage better. The false teachers had ignored the agency of the Divine word. **κατακλυσθείς**; **ἅπ. λεγ.** in N.T.; found several times in P.Tebt. *e.g.* 54^{17}*ff* (B.C. 86) **[ὥστε] . . . συμβεβηκότων κατακλυσθῆναι.** "So that in consequence of what happened, it was flooded"; 56^{5}*f* (late ii. B.C.) **γείν[ωσ]κε δὲ περὶ τοῦ κατακεκλῦσθαι τὸ πεδίον** "but know about our plain having been inundated".

7. οἱ δὲ νῦν οὐρανοὶ καὶ ἡ γῆ τῷ αὐτῷ[1] λόγῳ τεθησαυρισμένοι εἰσὶν
πυρὶ τηρούμενοι εἰς ἡμέραν κρίσεως καὶ ἀπωλείας τῶν ἀσεβῶν
ἀνθρώπων. 8. Ἓν δὲ τοῦτο μὴ λανθανέτω ὑμᾶς, ἀγαπητοί, ὅτι μία
ἡμέρα παρὰ Κυρίῳ ὡς χίλια ἔτη καὶ χίλια ἔτη ὡς ἡμέρα μία. 9.
οὐ βραδύνει Κύριος τῆς ἐπαγγελίας, ὥς τινες βραδύτητα ἡγοῦνται,
f WM. iii. § xix. 2 (b). ἀλλὰ μακροθυμεῖ εἰς ὑμᾶς, μὴ βουλόμενός τινας ἀπολέσθαι ἀλλὰ
πάντας εἰς μετάνοιαν χωρῆσαι. 10. Ἥξει δὲ [f] ἡμέρα Κυρίου ὡς

[1] τῳ αυτῳ ABP, vulg., sah., boh., WH, Ti.; τῳ αυτου ℵCKL, syrr., Treg.

Ver. 7. **πυρὶ τηρούμενοι.** According to the Jewish conception of the rainbow promise, water would not again be the destructive agency. The heaven and the earth are reserved for destruction by fire. **τεθησαυρισμένοι**: "set apart for". The writer means that both the rainbow promise and the delay are not to be regarded as implying that there will be no more great cosmical changes.

The idea of the association of a great cosmical change with the coming of Christ is an interesting one. It involves the question of our environment when the natural is exchanged for the spiritual body. This writer evidently expects not complete annihilation of the present environment, but a "new heaven and a new earth, wherein dwelleth righteousness" (v. 13). St. Paul speaks of "the deliverance of the creation itself from the bondage of corruption into the glory of the liberty of the children of God". "We are not informed as to the nature of our future environment, yet it must be such as to satisfy all the longings, and give scope for all the activities of a perfected humanity" (Mayor, ed. p. 207. See also his most interesting and suggestive note: "*Answer to the objection that no change is possible in the material universe*"; and with whole passage, vv. 5-7, *cf.* Ruskin, *Sesame and Lilies*, p. 24.)

Vv. 8-10. *A further argument to explain the apparent delay.* "One thing beloved, you must not forget. The sense of the duration of time in the Divine Mind is not the same as in the human. One day is the same to God as a thousand years, and a thousand years as one day. God must not be judged as slack by human standards, in the fulfilment of His promise. He is better than the promise. He is long-suffering to usward, not willing that some should perish, but that all should come to repentance. We know not when His long-suffering will be exhausted. The day of the Lord will come as a thief. Then the heavens will pass away with hurtling noise, and the elements being burned, shall pass away, and the earth and the works of men contained in it, will be made manifest."

Ver. 8. **μία ἡμέρα, κ.τ.λ.** *Cf.* Ps. xl. 4. The literal application of this statement to the story of creation, employed by patristic writers, in which one day is interpreted as 1000 years, and therefore the creation in six days really means 6000 years, is of course absurd. On the other hand, it can scarcely be said that the writer of 2 Peter has attained to the conception that the category of time does not exist for the Divine Mind. Rather the meaning is that infinite compassion overrides in the Divine Mind all finite reckoning. *Cf.* Barnabas, 15, Justin, *Dialogue*, 81.

Ver. 9. **οὐ βραδύνει . . . ἡγοῦνται.** The idea that is combated is that God has made a promise and has not kept it, He is, however, better than His promise. The additional element of His **μακροθυμία** is brought into play. God is greater than men's conception of Him, especially if theirs is a mechanical view of the universe.—**ὥς τινες βραδύτητα ἡγοῦνται.** As nowhere else in the Epistle, here the writer of 2 Peter enables us to view the summit of the Christian Faith, and to rise to a magnificent conception of God. **μὴ βουλόμενός, κ.τ.λ.** Delay does not spring from an unwillingness or impotence to perform. His will is not even that "some" should perish, though that is regarded by the writer as inevitable. Are we to see here opposition in the writer's mind to the purely logical interpretation of the Pauline teaching on Predestination? Some will perish, but it is not His Will. His Will is that all should come to repentance. The goodness of God should lead to repentance.

Ver. 10. **ἡμέρα Κυρίου.** No distinction is made between the Day of the Lord, and the Coming of Christ. This is remarkable, as excluding any idea of mil-

κλέπτης, ἐν ᾗ οἱ οὐρανοὶ ῥοιζηδὸν [g] παρελεύσονται, στοιχεῖα δὲ
καυσούμενα λυθήσεται, καὶ γῆ καὶ τὰ ἐν αὐτῇ ἔργα εὑρεθήσεται.[1]
11. Τούτων οὖν πάντων λυομένων ποταποὺς δεῖ ὑπάρχειν ὑμᾶς

g John xix. 31, Rev. xxi. 12, 1 Tim. v. 25, Luke xxiv. 11, Xen. *Anab.* 1, 7, 17.

[1] **ευρεθησεται** ℵBKP, syr[p]; **ουχ ευρεθησεται** sah.; **κατακαησεται** AL, syr[h], Ti.; **καυθησεται** vel.; **κατακαυθησονται** al.; **αφανισθησονται** C; om. **και γη . . . ευρεθησεται** vulg.; om. **ευρεθησεται** spec. Both Nestle and Mayor agree in suggesting the passive of a compound of **ρεω** (**καταρυησεται** or **διαρρυησεται**. I am indebted to Professor J. H. Moulton for the information that the late Henry Bradshaw, of Cambridge, suggested the reading **εργα αργα ευρεθησεται.** As against this, and in favour of the text as it stands, we have 2 Clem. xvi. 3, which seems to be a paraphrase of this passage. **καὶ πᾶσα ἡ γῆ ὡς μόλυβδος ἐπὶ πυρὶ τηκόμενος, καὶ τότε φανήσεται τὰ κρύφια καὶ φανερὰ ἔργα τῶν ἀνθρώπων.**

lenarian teaching, which speedily made its appearance in the Early Church. **ὡς κλέπτης**, *cf.* 1 Thess. v. 2, Matt. xxiv. 43, Luke xii. 39, Apoc. iii. 3, xvi. 15. That day will surprise those who are clinging to the idea that no change is possible. **ῥοιζηδὸν**, onomatopoetic, expressing the sound produced by rapid motion through the air, *e.g.*, flight of a bird, or an arrow. It is also used of the sound of a shepherd's pipe. No doubt the sound of a fierce flame is meant. "It is used of thunder in Luc. *Jup. Trag.* 1; of the music of the spheres in Iamblich, *Vit. Pyth.* c. 15; Oecumenius says the word is especially used of the noise caused by a devouring flame" (Mayor, *ed.* p. 157). **στοιχεῖα**. Spitta interprets **στ.** as being the spirits that preside over the various parts of nature. But the situation of **στ.** between **γῆ** and **οὐρανοὶ** makes it practically certain that the heavenly bodies are meant. The universe consists of **οὐρανοί, στοιχεῖα** and **γῆ**. **οὐρανοὶ** is the vault of heaven, "the skies". **στ.** would therefore mean sun, moon and stars. *Cf.* Justin. *Apol.* ii. 5, *Trypho.* 23. *Cf.* Isa. xxxiv. 4, Joel ii. 30, 31, Matt. xxiv. 29, Apoc. vi. 12-14 in illustration of the Jewish belief that the stars will share in the final destruction of the Last Day. **καυσούμενα.** A medical term, used of the heat of fever (**καῦσος**). This is the only known use of the word applied to inanimate objects. Whether the writer of 2 Peter has here indulged a fondness for unusual words, or whether **καυσόομαι** was ever used in other than a medical sense in the **Κοινὴ**, it is impossible as yet to say. In any case it denotes a violent consuming heat. **εὑρεθήσεται**. The only alternative reading that is worthy of notice in connexion with this difficult passage is **κατακαήσεται,** but one would expect a word expressing dissolution, like **παρελεύσονται,** or **λυθήσεται.** **εὑρεθήσεται** is found in an absolute sense in Clement, *Cor.* ix. 3 (of Enoch) **οὐχ εὑρέθη αὐτοῦ θάνατος,** "his death was not brought to light". In 2 Clem. xvi. (see textual note) **φανήσεται** is the paraphrase of **εὑρεθήσεται** (*cf.* Introd. pp. 90 f.).

Vv. 11-16. *The ethical value of the Parousia expectation.* "Seeing then that all these things are to be dissolved, how great an effect it ought to exercise on our whole moral and religious life, as we look forward to and hasten the coming of the day of God. The skies shall be set on fire and dissolved, and the elements shall melt with fiercest heat, but we look for new skies and a new earth according to His promise, in which righteousness shall find a home. Wherefore, beloved, with such expectations, endeavour to be found in peace, spotless and blameless. Do not reckon the long-suffering of our Lord as an opportunity for licence, but as a means of salvation, as our beloved brother Paul wrote you in the wisdom granted to him. He indeed spoke in all his letters of these things, in which there are some things hard to be understood, which ignorant and unstable persons wrest, as they do the other Scriptures, to their own destruction."

Ver. 11. **λυομένων.** Present used for a future. Mayor translates "are in process of dissolution," as though the principle of **φθορά** were already at work; but this is a conception foreign to the mind of the writer, who uses it only in a moral significance. Nature is "reserved" (**θησαυρίζεσθαι**) for destruction. Dissolution is the goal in sight. **ποταπούς.** "What sort of men." A later form of **ποδαπός.** **ὑπάρχειν** implies not merely existence, but existential character. **ἀναστροφαῖς καὶ εὐσεβείαις.** The use

ἐν ἁγίαις ἀναστροφαῖς καὶ εὐσεβείαις, 12. προσδοκῶντας καὶ
σπεύδοντας τὴν παρουσίαν τῆς τοῦ Θεοῦ ἡμέρας, δι' ἣν οὐρανοὶ
πυρούμενοι λυθήσονται καὶ στοιχεῖα καυσούμενα τήκεται. 13.
καινοὺς δὲ οὐρανοὺς καὶ γῆν καινὴν κατὰ τὸ ἐπάγγελμα αὐτοῦ
προσδοκῶμεν, ἐν οἷς δικαιοσύνη κατοικεῖ. 14. Διό, ἀγαπητοί,
h 2 Cor. xii. 20. ταῦτα προσδοκῶντες σπουδάσατε ἄσπιλοι καὶ ἀμώμητοι [h] αὐτῷ
εὑρεθῆναι ἐν εἰρήνῃ, 15. καὶ τὴν τοῦ κυρίου ἡμῶν μακροθυμίαν
σωτηρίαν ἡγεῖσθε, καθὼς καὶ ὁ ἀγαπητὸς ἡμῶν ἀδελφὸς Παῦλος
κατὰ τὴν δοθεῖσαν αὐτῷ σοφίαν ἔγραψεν ὑμῖν, 16. ὡς καὶ ἐν πάσαις[1]

[1] **πασαις ταις** ℵKLP, Ti.; om. **ταις** ABC, Treg., WH, Weiss.

of the plural in cases of abstract nouns is peculiar to the writer and to 1 Peter. He emphasises once more the close connexion between morality and religion.

Ver. 12. **σπεύδοντας.** Either (1) "earnestly desiring," *cf.* Isa. xvi. 5, **σπεύδων δικαιοσύνην**, or (2) preferably, "hastening the coming". "The Church may be said to bring the day nearer when it prays, 'Thy kingdom come'" (Bigg). The writer is here referring to the Jewish idea that the sins of men prevented Messiah from appearing. "Si Judaei poenitentiam facerent una die, statim veniret Messias, filius David."

The words are capable of a still more spiritual meaning, which, however, is rather beyond the consciousness of this writer. The kingdom of God is "within" us, and Christians may be said to hasten this coming by holiness of life. Christian conduct is itself both a rebuke to vice and a realisation of the presence of Christ in the hearts of His disciples.

τήκεται. Again present for future. The phrases in this verse are repeated from ver. 10 in order to introduce the more impressively the idea in ver. 13.

Ver. 13. **καινοὺς δὲ οὐρανοὺς . . . προσδοκῶμεν.** *Cf.* Isa. lxv. 17. **ἔσται γὰρ ὁ οὐρανὸς καινὸς καὶ ἡ γῆ καινή.** Enoch xci. 16. See note on ver. 7. **οὐρανός** might appropriately be translated "sky". **ἐν οἷς δικαιοσύνη κατοικεῖ**; "wherein righteousness dwells," or "has its home". In the word there is both the sense of permanence and of persuasive influence. Both in the hearts of men, and the new environment, there will be nothing that militates against righteousness. The Parousia is both judgment on the wicked and triumph for the kingdom. *Cf.* v. 7.

Ver. 14. **ἄσπιλοι καὶ ἀμώμητοι αὐτῷ. αὐτῷ** is dative = "in relation to Him," or "in His sight". *Cf.* Rom. vii. 10. **εὑρέθη μοι ἡ ἐντολὴ ἡ εἰς ζωὴν αὕτη εἰς θάνατον**; Ephes. i. 4, **εἶναι ἀμώμους κατενώπιον αὐτοῦ.** For **ἄσπιλοι καὶ ἀμώμητοι**, *cf.* note on v. 13. **ἀμώμητος** occurs in *Epistle of Aristeas* (ed. Wendland), with reference to sacrificial victims. **ἐν εἰρήνῃ.** Peace and righteousness are one. *Cf.* Ps. lxxxv. 10. The "well-doers" will be able to meet the Parousia with calm expectation.

Ver. 15. **καὶ τὴν τοῦ κυρίου . . . ἡγεῖσθε.** *Cf.* v. 9. The Divine long-suffering is capable of interpretation as "slackness," or as opportunity for license instead of as **σωτηρίαν**, an opportunity for repentance. **καθὼς καὶ ὁ ἀγαπητὸς . . . ἔγραψεν ὑμῖν.** The interpretation here largely depends on (1) whether the reference of **καθὼς** is confined to the idea in the first clause of the verse, or (2) is to be extended to include **ἄσπιλοι καὶ ἀμώμητοι . . . εἰρήνῃ** in ver. 14, or (3) is still further extended to include the whole treatment of moral disorder arising from delayed Parousia. In the case of (1) Romans would be the most appropriate among the known canonical epistles. In that epistle the idea of God's long-suffering is most prominent (*cf.* ii. 4, iii. 25, 26, ix. 22, 23, xi. 22, 23). (2) Almost any of St. Paul's epistles might be meant. (3) If the question of moral disorder arising from difficulties about the **παρουσία** is placed in the foreground, "none of the existing Pauline Epistles can be in question except 1 Corinthians (in this Church there were very similar extravagances, and the Resurrection was by some denied) and Thessalonians" (Bigg). A decision on this point involves the discussion on the destination of the epistle, for which see Introduction, pp. 205 f. (*cf.* Zahn., *Introd.* ii., pp. 211-2). **ὁ ἀγαπητὸς . . . Παῦλος** need not imply that Paul was alive. **κατὰ τὴν δοθεῖσαν αὐτῷ σοφίαν.** *Cf.* 1 Cor. iii. 10, Gal. ii. 9, 1 Cor. iii. 66, Col. i. 28.

Ver. 16. **ὡς καὶ ἐν πάσαις ταῖς**

ταῖς ἐπιστολαῖς λαλῶν ἐν αὐταῖς περὶ τούτων, ἐν αἷς ἐστιν δυσνόητά
τινα, ἃ οἱ ἀμαθεῖς καὶ ἀστήρικτοι στρεβλοῦσιν ὡς καὶ τὰς λοιπὰς
γραφὰς πρὸς τὴν ἰδίαν [1] αὐτῶν ἀπώλειαν. i Acts ii. 8, Tit. i. 12.

17. Ὑμεῖς οὖν, ἀγαπητοί, προγινώσκοντες φυλάσσεσθε ἵνα μὴ τῇ

ἐπιστολαῖς. This statement implies neither the inclusion of all the epistles that have come down to us, nor the formation of a canon. It is much more natural to take it as referring to a collection of letters made not long after Paul's death, and read in the churches. The term **ὁ ἀγαπητὸς ἡμῶν ἀδελφὸς** in ver. 15 would seem to refer to one whose memory is still quite fresh in the hearts of the readers. **λαλῶν ἐν αὐταῖς περὶ τούτων**: "where he touches on these subjects" (Mayor). **περὶ τούτων** indicates a widening of the reference to include Paul's treatment of the whole question of the Second Coming. The mention of Paul's name here implies a desire on the part of the writer to show that on this point the Pauline and Petrine teaching are at one. The false teachers founded their Antinomian doctrine on Paul's teaching about the Grace of God. **ἐν αἷς, κ.τ.λ.** This clearly involves that a collection of letters is meant. **δυσνόητά τινα.** "What are the **δυσνόητά** referred to? "Probably St. Paul's doctrine of God's free grace (Rom. iii. 5-8), with his apparent disparagement of the law in Rom. iii. 20-28, iv. 15, v. 20, vi. 4, vii. 4-11; his teaching with regard to the **πνευματικοί**, 1 Cor. i. 15; with regard to the strong, whom he seems to justify in their neglect of the rule made at the Apostolic Council, as to **εἰδωλόθυτα** (Acts xv. 29; Rom. 14; 1 Cor. viii., x. 25); as regards the Resurrection in baptism (Rom. vi. 3-11; Col. iii. 1; 1 Cor. xv. 12); perhaps as regards predestination (Rom. ix. 11-21), and the Parousia (2 Th. ii.)" (Mayor). **οἱ ἀμαθεῖς καὶ ἀστήρικτοι.** **ἀμαθής** is not used elsewhere in the N.T. It signifies not so much "unlearned" as "uneducated"; a mind untrained and undisciplined in habits of thought, lacking in the moral qualities of a balanced judgment. **ἀστήρικτοι** refers more to conduct, those whose habits are not fully trained and established. The reference of **ἀμ. καὶ ἀστηρ.** is of course not to the Libertines, but to a class among the readers. In ver. 17 **στηριγμός** is used of the readers, in distinction to the False Teachers, who are called **ἀθέσμων.** **στρεβλοῦσιν**: of persons, "to torture," of things, "to wrest" or "twist".

ὡς καὶ τὰς λοιπὰς γραφάς. (1) There has been much discussion among commentators as to the meaning of **γραφάς.** Spitta takes **γραφάς** in sense of "writings," and concludes that these were by companions of the Apostle Paul; but this is a very unusual sense of **γραφή** unless the name of an author is given. Mayor and others interpret as the O.T. Scriptures; while some who are prepared to assign a late date in the second century to the epistle, think that both Old and New Testament Scriptures are meant. On every ground the hypothesis of **γραφάς** = O.T. Scriptures is to be preferred. (2) The difficulty in connexion with the meaning of **γραφάς** is largely occasioned by the phrase **τὰς λοιπὰς γρ.** Does this mean that the Epistles of St. Paul are regarded as Scripture? Attempts have been made (*e.g.*, by Dr. Bigg) to cite classical and other parallels that would justify the sense for **τὰς λοιπὰς**, "the Scriptures as well". In these, certain idiomatic uses of **ἄλλος** and other words are referred to, but no real parallel to this sense of **λοιπός** can be found, and the connexion implied in **λοιπός** is closer than **ἄλλος.** The result of the whole discussion is practically to compel us to take **τὰς λοιπὰς γραφάς** in the obvious sense "the rest of the Scriptures," and we cannot escape the conclusion that the Epistles of Paul are classed with these. The intention of the author of 2 Peter seems to be to regard the Pauline Epistles, or those of them that he knew, as **γραφαί,** because they were read in the churches along with the lessons from the O.T.

Vv. 17, 18. *Final exhortation.* "Having then, brethren, been forewarned, be on your guard lest you fall from your own foundation, carried away by the error of lawless men. Grow in the grace and knowledge of Our Lord and Saviour Jesus Christ. To Him be glory both now and in the day of eternity."

Ver. 17. This verse gathers up various thoughts that appear elsewhere in the epistle. **Προγινώσκοντες** repeats **τοῦτο πρῶτον γινώσκοντες** of i. 20, iii. 1; **ἀθέσμων** occurs ii. 7; **πλάνη** ii. 18. **συναπαχθέντες** (*cf.* Galat. ii. 13), "carried away". **ἀθέσμων,** see note ii. 7.

k Gal. ii. 13. **τῶν ἀθέσμων πλάνῃ [k] συναπαχθέντες ἐκπέσητε τοῦ ἰδίου στηριγμοῦ,**
18. **αὐξάνετε δὲ ἐν χάριτι καὶ γνώσει τοῦ κυρίου ἡμῶν καὶ σωτῆρος**
Ἰησοῦ Χριστοῦ. αὐτῷ ἡ δόξα καὶ νῦν καὶ εἰς ἡμέραν αἰῶνος.

στηριγμοῦ, "steadfastness"; perhaps "foundation" is better, although in this sense we would expect **στήριγμα.** There is, however, a tendency in N.T. to confuse words in **-μα -μος.** *Cf.* **κύλισμα** (2 Pet. ii. 22). **ἁρπαγμός** (Phil. ii. 6). The foundation is the **χάρις** and **γνῶσις** of v. 18. **ἰδίου** is in emphatic contrast to the untrustworthy basis of the Libertine teaching.

Ver. 18. **ἐν χάριτι καὶ γνώσει τοῦ Κυρίου, κ.τ.λ.** The genitive is to be taken with both words. **γνῶσις** here means "spiritual instruction," a knowledge that has its source in Christ Himself, as distinct from **ἐπίγνωσις**, which is personal communion with Christ (see note i. 5). **γνῶσις** is the privilege of the "friend" of Christ. *Cf.* John vii. 17, xv. 15. **αὐτῷ.** Note that the doxology is addressed to Christ, and, therefore, **κυρίου ἡμῶν.** also refers to Him. **εἰς ἡμέραν αἰῶνος**: "in the day of eternity". The meanings of **εἰς** and **ἐν** in later Greek are somewhat interchangeable (*cf.* Moulton, *Proleg.* 234 f.). **ἡμ. αἰῶνος** is a very rare phrase not found elsewhere in N.T. It is found in Sir. xviii. 10, where the phrase is **ἐν ἡμέρᾳ αἰῶνος.** The more usual expression is **εἰς τοὺς αἰῶνας τῶν αἰώνων.** "**εἰς τοὺς αἰῶνας** becomes so immediately the ruling phrase that this Petrine doxology cannot have been written after liturgical expressions had become in any degree stereotyped" (Bigg).

THE EPISTLES

OF

ST. JOHN

INTRODUCTION.

The First Epistle.

The first Epistle differs from all the other N.T. Epistles save the Epistle to the Hebrews in this, that it is anonymous. The author, however, claims to have been an eye-witness of the Word of Life (i. 1-3) and speaks throughout in a tone of apostolic authority, and there is abundance of primitive and credible testimony that he was St. John, "the disciple whom Jesus loved," and the last survivor of the Apostle-company.

1. *The MSS. Titles.*—AB Ἰωάνου (-άννου) α: ℵ Ἰωάννου ἐπιστολὴ α: L ἐπιστολὴ καθολικὴ τοῦ ἁγίου ἀποστόλου Ἰωάννου: P Ἰωάννου τοῦ εὐαγγελιστοῦ καὶ ἀποσ(τόλου ἐπιστολὴ) α. Two later MSS. have interesting titles—13 ἐπιστολὴ α Ἰωάννου· εὐαγγελικὴ θεολογία περὶ χῡ: f βροντῆς υἱὸς Ἰωάννης τάδε χριστιανοῖσιν.[1]

2. *Patristic Evidence.*—Polycarp. *ad Philipp.* viii.: πᾶς γὰρ ὃς ἂν μὴ ὁμολογῇ Ἰησοῦν Χριστὸν ἐν σαρκὶ ἐληλυθέναι, ἀντίχριστός ἐστιν—a manifest echo of 1 John iv. 2, 3. This proves the early date of our Epistle and the esteem in which it was held, and if it does not attest the Johannine authorship, it at least suggests it. Polycarp had known several of the Apostles and of those who had seen the Lord; he had been a disciple of St. John and had been ordained by him bishop of Smyrna; and he was the leading ecclesiastic in the whole of Asia. *Cf.* Jer. *Script. Eccles.*; Iren. III. iii. 4.

Eusebius (*H. E.* iii. 39) says that Papias, whom Irenæus had called "a hearer of John and a comrade of Polycarp, an ancient man

[1] St. Augustine's discourses on the First Epistle are entitled "Ten Treatises on the Epistle of John to the Parthians (*In Epistolam Joannis ad Parthos Tractatus Decem*)," and he elsewhere quotes from the Epistle under this strange title (*Quæst. Ev.* ii. 39). Probably the Epistle was entitled in some MS. Ἰωάννου τοῦ παρθένου, as the Apocalypse is entitled in 30 αποκαλυψ. του αγιου ενδοξοτατου αποστολου και ευαγγελιστου παρθενου ηγαπημενου επιστηθιου ιωαννου θεολογου, and ΤΟΥ-ΠΑΡΘΕΝΟΥ was mistaken for ΠΡΟΣΠΑΡΘΟΥΣ. The Latin frag. of Clem. Alex.'s exposition of the Second Epistle begins: "Secunda Joannis epistola quæ ad virgines scripta," where "Joannis ad virgines" probably represents Ἰωάννου τοῦ παρθένου.

('Ιωάννου μὲν ἀκουστὴς Πολυκάρπου δὲ ἑταῖρος γεγονώς, ἀρχαῖος ἀνήρ)," "used testimonies from the first (former) epistle of John (κέχρηται δ' ὁ αὐτὸς μαρτυρίαις ἀπὸ τῆς 'Ιωάννου προτέρας ἐπιστολῆς)". προτέρας is merely a grammatical inaccuracy, as conversely πρῶτος for πρότερος in Matt. xxi. 36; Acts i. 1; 1 Cor. xiv. 30; Heb. x. 9; Rev. xxi. 1. *Cf.* Eus. *H. E.* iii. 24; ἡ προτέρα τῶν ἐπιστολῶν . . . αἱ λοιπαὶ δύο.

Irenæus, a disciple of Polycarp[1] and bishop of Lyons, quotes 1 John ii. 18, 19, 21, 22, iv. 1, 3, v. 1, and says expressly that he is quoting from the Epistle of St. John.[2]

The Muratorian Canon (about A.D. 170) includes our epistle and ascribes it to St. John: "Quid ergo mirum si Johannes tam constanter singula etiam in epistulis suis proferat, dicens in semetipso: *Quæ vidimus oculis nostris, et auribus audivimus, et manus nortræ palpaverunt, hæc scripsimus?*" *Cf.* 1 John i. 1.[3]

These testimonies are primitive, and there is no need to adduce in addition the later and abundant testimonies of Clement of Alexandria, Tertullian, Origen, Jerome, Augustine, Athanasius.

With no less unanimity and emphasis does ancient tradition ascribe the Fourth Gospel to St. John, and it hardly admits of reasonable doubt that the Gospel and the Epistle are from the one pen. They agree in style, language, and thought. They have the same Hebraistic style, abounding in parallelism (*e.g. cf.* 1 John ii. 10, 11 with John iii. 18, 20, 21) and parataxis (the co-ordinating καί is the favourite conjunction). Their style is identical, and it is unique in the N.T. They have, moreover, common phrases and expressions *Cf.* Ep. i. 1, 2 with Gosp. i. 1, 2, 4, 14; Ep. i. 4 with Gosp. xv. 11, xvi. 24; Ep. ii. 1 with Gosp. xiv. 16, 26, xv. 26, xvi. 7; Ep. ii. 8 with Gosp. xiii. 34, xv. 10, 12; Ep. ii. 11 with Gosp. xii. 35; Ep. iii. 8, 15 with Gosp. viii. 44; Ep. iii. 11, 16 with Gosp. xv. 12, 13; Ep. iii. 12 with Gosp. vii. 7; Ep. iii. 13 with Gosp. xv. 18, 19; Ep. iii. 14 with Gosp. v. 24; Ep. iv. 6 with Gosp. viii. 47; Ep. iv. 12 with Gosp. i. 14; Ep. iv. 14 with Gosp. iii. 17; Ep. v. 3 with Gosp. xiv. 15, 21; Ep. v. 6-8 with Gosp. xix. 34, 35; Ep. v. 9 with Gosp. v. 32, 34, 36, viii. 17, 18; Ep. v. 10 with Gosp. iii. 33; Ep. v. 12 with Gosp. iii. 15, 36; Ep. v. 13 with Gosp. xx. 31; Ep. v. 14 with Gosp. xiv. 13, 14, xvi. 23; Ep. v. 20 with Gosp. xvii. 3. Then they have in common certain fundamental conceptions which are thus defined and enumerated by Dr. H. J. Holtzmann: "the Son of God in the Flesh, the Life, which has its source in Him and is identical with Him, the Being in Him, the Abiding in God, the Love of God actualised in the Sending of

[1] Jer. *Script. Eccles.* [2] Iren. III. xviii. 5, 8.

[3] The Mur. Can. is given in Routh's *Reliq. Sacr.*, i. pp. 394 seq.

the Son, the resultant Commandment of Brotherly Love, the Walking in the Light, the Begetting of God, the Overcoming of the World, etc.; the antitheses of Life and Death, Light and Darkness, Love and Hate, Truth and Lying, Father and World, God and Devil, Children of God and Children of the Devil." Thus inextricably are the two works intertwined. "Our Epistle," says Rothe, "has throughout as its presupposition the peculiar conception of the person and history of the Redeemer, in general the peculiar conception of Christianity, which prevails in the Gospel. Consequently, if the Fourth Gospel is a work of the Apostle John, our Epistle also belongs as indubitably to him; as in the contrary case our Epistle could be no composition of the Apostle John."

The common authorship has nevertheless been called in question on the ground of certain alleged divergences which, says Schmiedel, "are explained much more easily on the assumption that the two writings come from different writers though belonging to one and the same school of thought." The divergences are (1) linguistic, and (2) doctrinal.[1]

(1) The words ἀγγελία, ἐπαγγελία, διάνοια, παρουσία, ἐλπίς, ἀνομία and others occur in the Epistle and not in the Gospel. But what then? A writer need not exhaust his entire vocabulary in a single writing: that would argue extreme barrenness of mind. Does it follow that the Third Gospel and the Book of Acts are by different authors because ἐλπίς never occurs in the former and eight times in the latter, or that the Epistle to the Romans is not St. Paul's because ἱλαστήριον occurs in it and in no other of his Epistles? The only reasonable inference from the occurrence of words in the Epistle which are absent from the Gospel is that the former is not an imitation of the latter.

(2) The following instances of doctrinal divergence are adduced: (*a*) ἱλασμός in Ep. ii. 2, iv. 10 and nowhere else in the N.T.; whereas, says Martineau, "the gospel knows nothing of an atoning or propitiatory efficacy in the blood of Christ". It is true that the word is not found in the Gospel, but the idea is. *Cf.* i. 29, x. 11, 15, xi. 49, 52. (*b*) χρῖσμα (Ep. ii. 20, 27) is another ἅπαξ λεγόμενον. The very idea, however, is found in the Gospel (xiv. 26, xvi. 13). (*c*) The Gospel is more spiritual in its eschatology, representing the Judgment not as future but as present (iii. 18) and the Coming of Christ as happening in the experience of each believer (xiv. 3); whereas the

[1] See Holtzmann's *Einl. in das N.T.*, and his elaborate discussion: *Das Probl. des erst. johann. Br. in sein. Verhält. zum Ev.* in *Jahrb. f. prot. Theol.* (1881-82); Martineau's *Seat of Auth.*, p. 509; Schmiedel in *Encycl. Bibl.*, vol. ii., cols. 2556-7.

Epistle represents the παρουσία (ii. 28) as "a visible individual occurrence" on a particular day (iv. 17). This is simply erroneous. The Gospel also speaks of a final and universal Judgment (v. 29), "the last day" (vi. 39, 40, 44, 54; xi. 24), and a personal Coming of Christ (xxi. 22, 23).[1] (*d*) The Παράκλητος is the Holy Spirit in the Gospel, Jesus in the Epistle. Here, however, there is no divergence. The doctrine of the Epistle explains the Gospel's ἄλλον Παράκλητον (xiv. 16). See commentary on ii. 1.

It is beyond reasonable doubt that the Epistle and the Gospel are from the same pen. "The identity of authorship in the two books," says Lightfoot,[2] "though not undisputed, is accepted with such a degree of unanimity that it may be placed in the category of acknowledged facts." And they have a very intimate connection. This is abundantly apparent from internal evidence. The Epistle opens with a reference to the Gospel-narrative, and there is an unmistakable relation between 1 John v. 13 and John xx. 31 (see commentary). Indeed the Epistle throughout has the Gospel as its background and is hardly intelligible without it. It is, in the language of Lightfoot,[3] "a devotional and moral application of the main ideas which are evolved historically in the sayings and doings of Christ recorded in the Gospel". And it is significant that the Muratorian Canon mentions the First Epistle in connection with the Gospel, and the Second and Third Epistles after an interval in their natural place among the other Epistles of the N.T.

The precise connection between them is nowhere indicated, but it appears from a consideration of the historical situation. The fall of Jerusalem in A.D. 70 dispersed the Church, and a colony of disciples found a home in Asia Minor. It was a considerable and increasingly influential community, including, in the phrase of Polycrates of Ephesus, "great luminaries (μεγάλα στοιχεῖα)"—not only the Apostles Philip[4] and Andrew[5] but, according to abundant and trustworthy tradition, St. John.[6] The latter fixed his residence at Ephesus, where there was a church founded by St. Paul.[7] It was the proudest boast of Ephesus that she was "the Temple-sweeper (νεωκόρος) of Artemis" (Acts xix. 35), and the Temple which she had reared for her goddess was one of the Seven Wonders of the ancient

[1] John xxi. is an addition to the Gospel. but it is by the same hand, "a postscript from the same pen as the rest" (Renan).

[2] *Ess. on Sup. Rel.*, pp. 186 f.

[3] *Ibid.*, p. 188.

[4] Eus. *H. E.* iii. 31, v. 24.

[5] *Mur. Can.*

[6] On the credibility of this tradition see Drummond, *The Char. and Auth. of the Fourth Gospel*, pp. 814 ff.

[7] Iren. III. iii. 4.

world; and in that historic and brilliant city St. John exercised his ministry to the end of his long life, which lasted until the reign of Trajan (A.D. 98-117).[1]

It was an active and gracious ministry. It had Ephesus for its headquarters, but it comprehended a wide area. St. John took oversight of all the Christian communities in the surrounding country—such as the churches of Smyrna, Pergamum, Thyatira, Sardis, Philadelphia, Laodicea (*cf.* Rev. ii.-iii.), counselling and strengthening them by letters and visitations. "He would go away when invited," says Clement of Alexandria,[2] "to the neighbouring districts of the Gentiles, here to appoint bishops, there to form new churches, and there to put into the office of the ministry some one of those that were indicated by the Spirit." And Clement proceeds to relate an interesting story, μῦθον οὐ μῦθον. The Apostle once visited a neighbouring city—Smyrna, according to the Alexandrian Chronicle—and saw there a lad of stalwart form, charming face, and ardent spirit. "I deposit this lad in thy keeping," he said to the bishop, "with all earnestness, taking the Church and Christ to witness." The bishop accepted the trust and, when St. John returned to Ephesus, took the lad home, nurtured him, and finally baptised him. Then, thinking he had done enough, he let him alone, and the lad fell into evil company, committed a crime, and, fleeing to the mountains, became the captain of a band of brigands. By and by St. John revisited that city, and after settling the business which had brought him, he said: "Now then, bishop, restore us the deposit which the Saviour and I entrusted to thee". The bishop was thunderstruck, supposing that he was being accused of some pecuniary intromission. "It is the lad that I am requiring," explained St. John, "and the soul of the brother." The bishop groaned and wept: "He is dead!" "How? When? And what death?" "He is dead to God," said the bishop, and told the story. The Apostle rent his robe and with a loud cry smote his head. "A fine guardian of the brother's soul did I leave in thee! Let me have a horse forthwith and some one to show me the way." And he rode off and found the lost youth, and by tender entreaties won him to penitence and brought him back to the Church.

Such was the ministry of St. John at Ephesus, and it was far on in the course of it that he wrote his Gospel, "having employed all the time an unwritten message".[3] He wrote it, says the Muratorian Canon, "at the exhortation of his fellow-disciples and bishops," *i.e.*, his own congregation at Ephesus and his colleagues in the neigh-

[1] Iren. III. iii. 4. [2] *De Div. Serv.* 42. [3] Eus. *H. E.* iii. 24.

bouring churches within the circuit of his supervision. It was intended for the instruction and edification of the Christians all over that extensive area. And the Epistle is, in the phrase of Lightfoot, a "commendatory postscript" to the Gospel. This explains the circumstance of its having neither address nor signature. It was not sent to a particular community, and since it was an appendix to the Gospel, it had no need to be inscribed with the author's name.

The aim of the Epistle is twofold—polemical and religious. Irenæus says[1] that "John the disciple of the Lord desired by the declaration of his Gospel to remove the error which had been sown among men by Cerinthus and, much earlier, by those who are called Nicolaitans". And this is borne out by the companion Epistle. It is against these two heresies that the polemic of the latter is directed.

1. It is said that the Nicolaitans were the followers of Nicolas, one of the seven deacons (Acts vi. 5),[2] and this strange story is told of him by Clement of Alexandria[3]: "He had, they say, a beautiful wife, and after the Ascension of the Saviour, being taunted by the Apostles with jealousy, he brought the woman forward and gave who would permission to marry her. This, they say, is in accordance with that expression of his: 'We must abuse the flesh'. And indeed the adherents of his sect follow up the incident and the saying absolutely and unquestioningly and commit fornication without restraint". Clement proceeds to attest the moral purity of Nicolas and explain his action as an inculcation of ascetic self-restraint, but certainly the sect which bore his name was given over to licentiousness. Clement says elsewhere[4] that they were "dissolute as he-goats," and others bear like testimony.[5] They were Antinomians, disowning moral obligation, *nullam differentiam esse docentes in mœchando et idolothyton edere*;[6] herein being forerunners of the Gnostics and justifying Tertullian's classification of them with the Cainites.[7] This heresy was rampant among the churches of Asia Minor in St. John's day (*cf.* Rev. ii. 6, 14, 15), and he deals with it in our Epistle. See i. 5-ii. 6, 15-17, iii. 3-10.

2. Cerinthus also was an Antinomian,[8] but his distinctive heresy was a theory of the Person of Christ. He taught in Asia, but he had been trained in Egypt,[9] and the foundation of his system, as of

[1] III. xi. 7. [2] Iren. I. xxiii.

[3] *Strom.* iii. 4; *cf.* Eus. *H. E.* iii. 29. [4] *Strom.* ii. 20.

[5] *Cf.* Tert. *Adv. Marc.* i. 29; Hippol. *Phil.* vii. 36.

[6] Iren., *l.c.* [7] *De Præscript. Hær.* 33.

[8] Dionysius of Alexandria in Eus. *H. E.* iii. 28.

[9] Theodoret. *H. E.* ii. 3.

Marcion's, was that postulate of Greek philosophy—the inherent and necessary evil of matter. "He said that the world had not been made by the First God, but by a power which is separate from the Authority which is over the Universe and ignorant of the God who is over all. And he supposed that Jesus had not been begotten of a virgin, but had been born of Joseph and Mary as a son in like manner to all the rest of men, and became more righteous and prudent and wise. And after the Baptism the Christ descended into him from the Sovereignty which is over the Universe, in the form of a dove; and then He proclaimed the unknown Father and accomplished mighty works, but at the end the Christ withdrew from the Jesus, and the Jesus had suffered and been raised, but the Christ had continued throughout impassible, being spiritual."[1] The essence of this is the dissolution (λύσις) of the Person of our Lord, the distinction between the human Jesus and the divine Christ. St. John encountered Cerinthus at Ephesus, and strenuously controverted his error. Irenæus and Eusebius quote a story of Polycarp's that the Apostle once visited the public baths, and, seeing Cerinthus within, sprang out of the building. "Let us flee," he cried, "lest the building fall, since Cerinthus, the foe of the Truth, is within it!"[2] And all through our Epistle he has the heresy in view. See ii. 18-23, iv. 1-6, 13-15, v. 1-12.

The Epistle has also a religious purpose. Its key-note is Love. "Locutus est multa," says St. Augustine, "et prope omnia de caritate." Its doctrine of love is distinctive and profound. The love which it inculcates is love for God and love for the brotherhood of believers—love for God manifesting itself in love for the brotherhood, and love for the brotherhood inspired by the love wherewith the Father has loved all His children. Special emphasis is laid on the latter. It is the whole of religion, it is all that God requires (*cf.* ii. 8-11, iii. 10-18, iv. 7-v. 2); for it implies love for God, and love for God implies a right attitude of heart and mind toward Him. This is the dominant doctrine of the Epistle, and it was the constant message of the Apostle's later ministry, so much so that, it is said, his people grew weary of its incessant reiteration. See St. Jerome's story quoted in commentary on iv. 7.

This had not always been his manner. He had not always been the Apostle of Love. He had once been the precise opposite—self-seeking (*cf.* Mark x. 35-45 = Matt. xx. 20-28), fiery, passionate, and vindictive (*cf.* Luke ix. 51-56), meriting the title which Jesus gave him "the Son of Thunder" (Mark iii. 17). His doctrine of

[1] Iren. I. xxi. [2] Iren. III. iii. 4; Eus. *H. E.* iv. 14.

the Supremacy of Love was a late discovery, and he proclaims it as such (see commentary on ii. 7-11). It was not merely an article of his polemic, a protest against the loveless intellectualism wherewith St. Ignatius charges the heretical teachers (τοὺς ἑτεροδοξοῦντας), who had "no concern for love, none for the widow, none for the orphan, none for the distressed, none for the bondman, none for the hungry or the thirsty."[1] It was a personal confession. That was an aspect of the Gospel which St. John had himself too long failed to perceive; and it may be that it had been revealed to him by two life-transforming experiences. (1) His Exile in Patmos (Rev. i. 9).[2] During that season of retirement he could look back over his interrupted ministry and review his methods. Incidents like his encounter with Cerinthus would recur to him, and would appear to his chastened spirit ill accordant with "the meekness and sweet reasonableness of Christ" (2 Cor. x. 1). It was right that he should contend for the Truth, but had not his intemperate zeal too often caused needless offence and defeated its own end by hardening the hearts of his opponents? He would discover the truth of St. Paul's precept that "the Lord's servant must not strive, but be gentle towards all" (2 Tim. ii. 24). (2) The writing of his Gospel. As he lived over again those three years of blessed fellowship and told "what he had heard and seen concerning the Word of Life," he would realise the pity and patience of the gentle Jesus, and feel as though he had never until that hour understood the Gospel-story. And he would address himself to what remained of his ministry in a new spirit. "Little children, love one another." "Master, why do you always say this?" "Because it is the Lord's commandment, and if only it be done, it is enough."

The Second and Third Epistles.

There is no doubt that the Second and Third Epistles are from the same hand. *Cf.* 2 John 1 with 3 John 1; 2 John 4 with 3 John 3, 4; 2 John 10 with 3 John 8; 2 John 12 with 3 John 13, 14. Are they also the work of St. John?

This was a disputed question in the early Church. Eusebius in his chapter "On the Acknowledged Divine Scriptures and those that

[1] *Ad Smyrn.* vi. *Cf.* Barn. *Ep.* xx. 2: οὐκ ἐλεῶντες πτωχόν, οὐ πονοῦντες ἐπὶ καταπονουμένῳ . . . ἀποστρεφόμενοι τὸν ἐνδεόμενον καὶ καταπονοῦντες τὸν θλιβόμενον.

[2] Put by Eus. *H. E.* iii. 23 in the reign of Domitian (A.D. 81-96), by Epiphan. *Haer.* li. 33 in that of Claudius (A.D. 41-54).

are not such (περὶ τῶν ὁμολογουμένων θείων γραφῶν καὶ τῶν μὴ τοιούτων)"[1] includes the Second and Third Epistles of John (ἡ ὀνομαζομένη δευτέρα καὶ τρίτη Ἰωάννου) among "those that are controverted yet recognised by most (τῶν ἀντιλεγομένων, γνωρίμων δ' οὖν ὅμως τοῖς πολλοῖς)". So Origen:[2] "He (John) has left an epistle of a very few lines; also, let it be granted, a second and a third, since not all allow that these are genuine. However, there are not a hundred lines in them both." And in the fourth century an opinion was put forward, which still finds favour, that their author was indeed John, only not John the Apostle but another John denominated "the Presbyter".[3]

There is, however, very strong evidence, both internal and external, on the other side. They exhibit coincidences of thought and language which link them with the First Epistle. *Cf.* 1 John ii. 7 with 2 John 5; 1 John ii. 18, iv. 1-3 with 2 John 7; 1 John ii. 23 with 2 John 9; 1 John iii. 6, 9 with 3 John 11. And the external testimony, though scanty, is weighty. The Muratorian Canon, despite the corruption of the passage, plainly attests the two epistles as works of the Apostle John and as accepted in the Catholic Church (*superscripti Johannis duas in catholica habentur*). Irenæus[4] quotes 2 John 11 with the preface Ἰωάννης δὲ ὁ τοῦ Κυρίου μαθητὴς ἐπέτεινε τὴν καταδίκην αὐτῶν μηδὲ χαίρειν αὐτοῖς ὑφ' ὑμῶν λέγεσθαι βουληθείς. And again, after a reference to the First Epistle, he quotes 2 John 7, 8 as a saying of the Lord's disciple John "in the aforesaid epistle".[5] This slip of memory only makes the attestation more effective. Irenæus knew that it was a saying of St. John that he was quoting: the Second Epistle no less than the First was the Apostle's. Clement of Alexandria too recognised more than one Epistle of St. John, for in one place he quotes 1 John v. 16 as occurring "in his larger Epistle (ἐν τῇ μείζονι ἐπιστολῇ),"[6] and elsewhere he speaks of "the Second Epistle of John".[7]

The ground for the ascription of the two smaller epistles to John the Presbyter is the fact that their author styles himself ὁ πρεσβύτερος. But it can hardly be maintained in view of his self-revelation in the Third Epistle. He appears there as exercising authoritative supervision over a wide circle of churches, writing to them, visiting them, interfering in their dissensions and settling these by his personal and solitary arbitrament, sending deputies and receiving their

[1] *H. E.* iii. 25.
[2] *Comm. in Ev. Joan.* v. 3 (ed. Lommatzsch, vol. i., p. 165).
[3] Eus. *H. E.* iii. 39; *cf.* Jer. *Script. Eccles.* under *Joannes Apostolus; Papias.*
[4] I. ix. 3. [5] III. xvii. 8. [6] *Strom.* ii. 15.
[7] *Adumbrat. in Ep. Joan.* ii.

reports. This is precisely the sort of ministry which, as we have seen,[1] St. John exercised in Asia Minor, and it would have been impossible for any lesser personage than an Apostle.[2] It may, moreover, be questioned whether such slight compositions as these two little letters would have won recognition had they not been recommended by the name of the Apostle John. And it was natural that the latter should style himself ὁ πρεσβύτερος. The term was not only an official designation (*cf.* 1 Tim. v. 1, 17, 19). The second generation of Christians used it of their predecessors, "the men of early days," *Männer der Vorzeit*, who had witnessed the great beginnings. Thus, Papias uses it of the Apostles,[3] and Irenæus in turn uses it of Papias and his contemporaries.[4] It was therefore natural that St. John, the last of the Apostles, the sole survivor of "the elder men," should be known among the churches of Asia as ὁ πρεσβύτερος.

And indeed it is very questionable whether this John the Presbyter ever existed. He was discovered by Eusebius in the preface to Papias' work *Expositions of Dominical Oracles*, but "it is well," remarks Barth, "to distinguish between what Papias really says and what Eusebius has made of his words". Here are the words of Papias: "I shall not hesitate to incorporate for you with my interpretations as many things as I once learned well from the elders (τῶν πρεσβυτέρων) and remembered well, guaranteeing their truth. For I did not, like so many, take pleasure in those that have so much to say but in those that teach the truth, nor in those that remember alien commandments but in those that remember the commandments that have been given by the Lord to the Faith and come from the Truth itself. Now if anywhere one came in my way who had been a follower of the elders (τοῖς πρεσβυτέροις), I would search[5] the words of the elders—what Andrew or Peter had said (εἶπεν), or what Thomas or James, or what John or Matthew, or any other of the Lord's disciples; and (I would search) the things which Aristion and the elder John (ὁ πρεσβύτερος Ἰωάννης), the Lord's disciples, say (λέγουσιν)".[6]

[1] See p. 155.

[2] *Cf.* Barth, *Die Hauptprobl.*, S. 26: "In der That nun ist diese 'patriarchalisch-monarchische' Autorität unerklärlich bei einem einfachen Presbyter einer Localgemeinde; sie erklärt sich aber vollkommen, wenn der πρεσβύτερος wie Paulus ein Apostel gewesen ist."

[3] Eus. *H. E.* iii. 39.

[4] V. xxxvi. *et passim*. Similarly in Heb. xi. 2.

[5] ἀνέκρινον, not "enquire about". Jerome (*Script. Eccles.* under *Papias*) rightly renders *considerabam*.

[6] Eus. *H. E.* iii. 39.

And this is what Eusebius makes of the passage: "Here it is worthy of observation how he twice enumerates the name of John. The former of these he reckons along with Peter and James and Matthew and the rest of the Apostles, plainly indicating the Evangelist; and the other John after an interval he ranks with others outside the number of the Apostles, having put Aristion before him, and he plainly names him 'an elder (πρεσβύτερον)'; so that the truth of their story is hereby demonstrated who have said that two persons in Asia have had the same name, and there are two tombs in Ephesus and each is called John's to this day."[1] Eusebius had a theological interest in putting this construction on the passage. He disliked the Chiliasm of the Apocalypse, and he was glad to find a second John to whom he could ascribe its authorship. And he has certainly perverted the passage. Papias is here defining the plan of his work. His method was (1) to quote a *logion* of Jesus, (2) to interpret it, and (3) to illustrate it by any story which he had gleaned from oral tradition. Such stories he derived from two sources. One was their followers' reports of what they had heard from the lips of "the elders," *i.e.*, as Papias used the term, the Apostles. These reports he "searched" for suitable illustrations. But he was not wholly dependent on hearsay. Two of the men who had been with Jesus were still alive in the earlier years of Papias—Aristion, not an Elder or Apostle but a disciple of the Lord, and the Elder John; and he enjoyed the advantage of hearing their living voices, and he "would search" their discourses for the material he required. The transition from "had said (εἶπεν)" to "say (λέγουσιν)," though ignored by Eusebius, is significant and explains the double mention of St. John. Papias had derived his knowledge of St. John's teaching from two sources: (1) from the reports of men who had companied with him and the other Apostles while they still tarried at Jerusalem, and (2) from his own lips after his settlement at Ephesus, where, Irenæus says,[2] Papias had been one of his "hearers". ὁ πρεσβύτερος Ἰωάννης must mean "the Apostle John," since the Apostles have just been called "the Elders" (τοῖς πρεσβυτέροις), and it is impossible that the term should bear different meanings within the compass of a single sentence. In his phrase "from the Truth itself (ἀπ' αὐτῆς τῆς ἀληθείας)" Papias echoes 3 John 12, and this renders it more than likely that he called St. John ὁ

[1] Eusebius probably had this story from Dionysius of Alexandria (*cf. H.E.* vii. 25). It means simply that in the fourth century there were two rival sites for St. John's burial-place.

[2] See p. 151.

πρεσβύτερος because the latter had so styled himself in each of the Epistles.[1]

The Second Epistle is addressed ἐκλεκτῇ κυρίᾳ καὶ τοῖς τέκνοις αὐτῆς, and the meaning of the address is a disputed question.[2] It was supposed by St. Jerome,[3] and the idea is approved by many moderns, that "the elect lady"[4] is a figurative appellation, signifying either the whole Church (Hilgenfeld, Mangold) or a particular community (Hofmann, Ewald, Huther, Wieseler). The main arguments are that the universal affection spoken of in verse 1 could hardly have been felt for an individual, and that it is "not improbable" that this is the Epistle referred to in 3 John 9.[5] The metaphor is indeed paralleled by Eph. v. 22-33 and Rev. xxi. 9; but it is the Church which is thus designated, not a particular community, and, on the ecclesiastical interpretation, it is a particular community that is here addressed, since St. John sends greetings to the "elect lady" from "the children of her elect sister" (verse 13), *i.e.*, presumably, his own congregation. And, moreover, the simplicity of the little letter precludes the possibility of so elaborate an allegory, while the tenderness of its tone stamps it as a personal communication.

It is therefore not a church but a lady that is addressed, and there are authority and reason for regarding Κυρία as her name.[6] The name was common in those days, and it occurs, *e.g.*, in the Oxyrhynchus Papyri, 498: Ἀντωνίᾳ Ἀσκληπιάδι τῇ καὶ Κυρίᾳ. 914: Αὐρήλιος Ἀπφοῦτος υἱὸς Ἁρεοῦτος μητρὸς Κυρίας. It is the Greek form of Martha, which means "mistress (*domina*)". The objection has been urged that, if it be a proper name, St. John must have written not ἐκλεκτῇ Κυρίᾳ but Κυρίᾳ τῇ ἐκλεκτῇ on the analogy of Γαΐῳ τῷ ἀγαπητῷ in 3 John 1; but either construction is permissible. The former is paralleled by 1 Peter i. 1: ἐκλεκτοῖς παρεπιδήμοις, and if

[1] On the identity of John the Presbyter and John the Apostle see Barth, *Hauptprobl.*, S. 26-29; Farrar, *Early Days*, Exc. xiv.

[2] *Cf.* scholium quoted by Euth. Zig.: ἢ πρὸς ἐκκλησίαν γράφει ἢ πρός τινα γυναῖκα διὰ τῶν εὐαγγελικῶν ἐντολῶν τὴν ἑαυτῆς οἰκίαν οἰκονομοῦσαν πνευματικῶς.

[3] *Ep. ad Ageruchiam.*

[4] The words, however, can hardly mean more than "*an* elect lady".

[5] Schmiedel in *Encycl. Bibl.*, vol. ii., col. 2560. *Cf.* B. Weiss, *Einleit.*

[6] Others take Ἐκλεκτῇ as the name ("the lady Electa"). Clem. Alex.: "ad quandam Babyloniam (probably a confused reference, for which the translator is responsible, to 1 Peter v. 13) *Electam* nomine". Clement apparently took Electa as the Church personified, for he proceeds: "significat electionem ecclesiæ sanctæ". But then Ἐκλεκτῆς in verse 13 must also be a proper name, and two sisters can hardly have borne the same name.

there be any irregularity, it is in the latter, where τῷ ἀγαπητῷ is a defining after-thought (*cf.* 1 John i. 2: τὴν ζωὴν τὴν αἰώνιον, "the life, the eternal life"). Carpzov would identify Kyria (Martha) with the sister of Lazarus and Mary. The family of Bethany disappear from the Gospel-story after the feast in Levi's house at the beginning of the Passion-week. They probably fled to escape the fury of the rulers, and it is just possible that they had found a home in Asia Minor like so many other refugees from Palestine.[1] And now Martha is living in one of the cities of St. John's diocese, a widow with a grown-up family; and it is natural that she should be dear to the Apostle and honoured by the whole Church. This is a pleasant fancy, but it is nothing more.

The facts are sufficiently interesting. The epistle is addressed to a devout lady named Kyria, who resided in one of the cities near Ephesus with a grown-up family. It is remarkable how large a part was played by women in the life of the primitive Church, especially in Asia Minor,[2] and Kyria was an honourable and influential personage not only in her own community but all over that wide area (verse 1). It is probable that, like that of Nympha at Colossæ,[3] her house was the meeting-place of the Church, according to the custom of those days when there were no ecclesiastical edifices; and it appears from verse 10 that she afforded hospitality to the itinerant evangelists of whom the Third Epistle speaks. A sister of Kyria, presumably deceased, had a family resident at Ephesus and connected with St. John's congregation; and several of Kyria's sons had visited their cousins. The Apostle had met with them and found them earnest Christians, and in the gladness of his heart he wrote to their mother, testifying his gratification, giving some kindly counsel very needful in those days of intellectual unrest, and expressing the hope that he might ere long visit her.

The Third Epistle is addressed to "Gaius the beloved". Gaius (never Caius) was one of the commonest of names, and there are three who bear it in the N.T. (1) Gaius of Macedonia (Acts xix. 29), (2) Gaius of Derbe (Acts xx. 4), and (3) Gaius of Corinth (Rom. xvi. 23; 2 Cor. i. 14). The name being so common, our Gaius may very well have been different from all these, but it is affirmed in the interesting *Synopsis Sacræ Scripturæ* ascribed to St. Athanasius that St. John composed his Gospel during his exile in Patmos and that Gaius of Corinth acted as his amanuensis and

[1] See p. 154. [2] *Cf.* Ramsay, *The Church in the Rom. Emp.*, p. 67.
[3] Col. iv. 15: Νύμφαν καὶ τὴν κατ' αὐτῆς ἐκκλησίαν (WH Nest).

published it at Ephesus.[1] And it appears from the "Apostolic Constitutions" (vii. 46) that one Gaius was ordained by St. John first "bishop" of Pergamum.

Whatever be the value of these traditions, it is evident that Gaius was a prominent personage, probably bishop or presbyter, in one of the churches of Asia Minor, and St. Paul's description of Gaius of Corinth, "the host of me and of the whole Church," might have been written of him. Trouble had arisen in his congregation, the ringleader being Diotrephes, probably a wealthy layman. The primitive Church was rent by factions, each swearing by one or other of the great teachers (*cf.* 1 Cor. i. 10-17), and it may be that Diotrephes belonged to the Pauline faction and abjured St. John and disowned his authority.[2] The actual truth, however, is that he was an opinionative and domineering man who insisted on having his own way in everything. The occasion of the trouble was a visit which had been paid to the Church of Gaius by a company of itinerant evangelists (*wandernde Glaubensboten*). This order of "prophets" was a recognised institution. Their office was to travel about preaching to the Gentiles and seeking to win them to the Faith. There were sometimes unworthy men among them who traded on the Gospel and merited the stinging epithet of "Christ-traffickers (χριστέμποροι)," and very stringent regulations are laid down regarding them in the *Didache*;[3] but their ministry was a needful and heroic one. They abandoned everything for Christ's sake and, to obviate misrepresentation, took nothing from the Gentiles—no food, no lodging. Thus they were dependent on the good offices of the believers wherever they went, and it was a debt of honour to see that they suffered no lack. Gaius had given a hospitable welcome to that company of "prophets"; but Diotrephes, disowning the Apostle's authority, opposed the reception of his emissaries and would have denied them entertainment. On their return to Ephesus they reported the incident at a meeting of the Church; and St. John wrote this letter and sent it by Demetrius, commending the action of Gaius and intimating his intention of

[1] τὸ δὲ κατὰ Ἰωάννην εὐαγγέλιον ὑπηγορεύθη τε ὑπ' αὐτοῦ τοῦ ἁγίου Ἰωάννου τοῦ ἀποστόλου καὶ ἠγαπημένου, ὄντος ἐξορίστου ἐν Πάτμῳ τῇ νήσῳ, καὶ ὑπὸ τοῦ αὐτοῦ ἐξεδόθη ἐν Ἐφέσῳ διὰ Γαΐου τοῦ ἀγαπητοῦ καὶ ξενοδόχου τῶν ἀποστόλων, περὶ οὗ καὶ Παῦλος Ῥωμαίοις γράφων φησί· ἀσπάζεται ὑμᾶς Γάϊος ὁ ξένος μου καὶ ὅλης τῆς ἐκκλησίας.

[2] It has been thought incredible that the great Apostle should have been so cavalierly treated (*cf.* verses 9, 10), but great men are usually less honoured by their contemporaries than by after generations.

[3] xi.-xiii. *Cf.* 2 John 10, 11.

visiting his Church at an early date and reducing the recalcitrant Diotrephes to order.

The Text of the Epistles.

The accompanying Greek text is the *regia editio* (1560) of Robert Stephanus (Etienne), commonly known in England as the *Textus Receptus*.[1] Constructed from a few late and inferior MSS. when the science of Textual Criticism was yet unborn, it is far from satisfactory; and the principal variants are presented in the critical notes, The long and patient labours of Mill, Bentley, Griesbach, Lachmann. Tregelles, Tischendorf, and Westcott and Hort have cleared away the rubbish of corruption and reduced uncertainty to a minimum; and Dr. Eberhard Nestle's text (British and Foreign Bible Society) is probably a very close approximation to the sacred autographs. It is "the resultant of a collation" of the monumental recensions of Tischendorf (8th edition, 1869-72), Westcott and Hort (1881), and Bernhard Weiss (2nd edition, 1905). "The readings adopted in the text are those in which at least two of these editions agree."

The *materia critica* is copious and excellent. 1. Greek MSS.:—

ℵ Codex Sinaiticus, 4th c. Discovered by Tischendorf in 1844 and 1859 in the monastery of St. Catherine at the foot of Mount Sinai. Now at St. Petersburg.

A Codex Alexandrinus, 5th c. Brought from Alexandria to Constantinople by Cyril Lucar, Patriarch of Constantinople (d. 1638), and sent by him to King Charles I. in 1628 by the hand of Thomas Roe on the return of the latter from a Turkish embassy. Now in the British Museum.

B Codex Vaticanus, 4th c. In the Vatican Library at Rome.

C Codex Ephraemi, 5th c. A rescript or palimpsest, written over in 12th c. with a Greek version of thirty-eight treatises of Ephraemus Syrus. In the National Library at Paris. In 1834-35 the librarian Carl Hase had the original writing revived by a chemical process, the applica- of Giobertine tincture. The codex was written, probably in Egypt, in 5th c.; corrected first, probably in Palestine, in 6th c. (C^2), then, probably at Constantinople, in 9th c. (C^3).

K Codex Mosquensis, 9th c. Brought to Moscow from the monastery of St. Dionysius at Mount Athos.

[1] See C. R. Gregory's *Prolegomena* to Tischendorf's *Nov. Test. Gr.*, pp. 212 *sqq*.

L Codex Angelicus Romanus, 9th c. In the Angelic Library of the Augustinian monks at Rome.

P Codex Porfirianus, 9th c. A palimpsest found by Tischendorf in 1862 among the books of Bishop Porfirius Chiovensis.

D Codex Bezæ, 5th or 6th c. In the Library of the University of Cambridge, to which it was presented by Theodore Beza in 1581. The Greek text with a slavish Latin translation. Much mutilated, our Epistles being represented only by the Latin version of 3 John 11-15.[1]

These manuscripts are uncials,[2] and there are besides upwards of two hundred minuscules or cursives, ranging in date from 9th c. to 16th c.[3]

2. Ancient Versions:[4]—

Syriac—

(1) **Syr^{vg}** Peshitto or Vulgate, 3rd (?) c. Contains the First Epistle.

(2) **Syr^{ph}** Philoxenian or Heraclean Version, 6th c. The three Epistles.

(3) **Syr^{bo}** Pococke's edition (1630) of 2 Pet. and 2 and 3 John from codex in Bodleian Library, Oxford.

Vg Latin Vulgate, St. Jerome's revision (A.D. 382-84). The three Epistles.

Egyptian—

(1) **Cop** Memphitic Version, 3rd (?) c. The three Epistles.

(2) **Sah** Thebaic Version, 3rd (?) c. The three Epistles.

Aeth Ethiopic Version, from 4th to 6th c. The three Epistles.

Arm Armenian Version, 5th c. The three Epistles.

These versions have no small value for the determination of the original text. It is usually plain which of several disputed readings the translator had before him, and whether his MS. contained a word or passage of doubtful authenticity.

Literature.

Clem. Alex. *Adumbrationes in Epp. Joan.* i., ii. (a rude Latin translation); Didymus, the blind teacher of St. Jerome in the Catechetical School of Alexandria (A.D. 308-95), commentary on the

[1] Gregory, pp. 345 *seq.*

[2] The signs $^{*\ 2\ 3\ a\ b\ c}$ affixed to uncials denote corrections by later hands.

[3] Gregory, pp. 616 *seq.* [4] *Ibid.*, pp. 803 *seq.*

Cath. Epp., translated into Latin by Epiphanius Scholasticus; Aug., *In Epistolam Joannis Tractatus Decem* (1st Ep., stopping abruptly at v. 3); Bede, *Expos.;* Euthymius Zigabenus (12th c.).

Erasmus, *In N. T. Annotat.;* Luther; Calvin (1st Ep.); Beza; Carpzov, *Commentatio in Ep.* 2 *Joan.; in Joan. Ep.* 3 *Brevis Enarratio;* Wetstein; Bengel; Lücke; Olshausen; Neander (1st Ep.); Düsterdieck; Huther in Meyer (translated by T. & T. Clark); Braune in Lange; Alford; Haupt (1st Ep., translated by T. & T. Clark); Rothe, *Der erste Brief Johannis practisch erklärt* (a beautiful work); Alexander in *Speaker's Commentary;* Plummer in *Cambridge Bible;* Westcott, *The Epistles of St. John;* H. J. Holtzmann in *Hand-commentar zum Neuen Testament;* Bernhard Weiss, *Die drei Briefe des Ap. Joh.;* Farrar, *Early Days of Christianity,* chaps. xxxi-vii.; Cox, *Private Letters of St. Paul and St. John;* Maurice, *Epistles of St. John;* Findlay, *Fellowship in the Life Eternal;* Law, *Tests of Life* (Lectures on 1st Ep.).[1]

[1] The two last appeared after this commentary was written.

ΙΩΑΝΝΟΥ ΤΟΥ ΑΠΟΣΤΟΛΟΥ

ΕΠΙΣΤΟΛΗ ΚΑΘΟΛΙΚΗ ΠΡΩΤΗ[1].

I. 1. Ὃ [a] ἮΝ [b] ἀπ' ἀρχῆς, ὃ ἀκηκόαμεν, ὃ [c] ἑωράκαμεν τοῖς ὀφθαλμοῖς ἡμῶν, ὃ [d] ἐθεασάμεθα, καὶ [2] αἱ χεῖρες ἡμῶν [e] ἐψηλάφησαν περὶ

a Rev. i. 4. 8.
b John i. 1.
c 2 Peter i. 16.
d John i. 14.
e Luke xxiv. 39; John xx. 27.

[1] See Introd., p. 151.

[2] Tert. (*de Anim.* 17; *adv. Prax.* 15) quotes thus: *quod vidimus, quod audivimus, oculis nostris vidimus et manus nostræ contrectaverunt de sermone vitæ*, as though reading ὃ ἐθεασάμεθα, ὃ ἀκηκόαμεν, ἑωράκαμεν τοῖς ὀφθαλμοῖς ἡμῶν, κ.τ.λ.

The First Epistle.

Chapter I.—Vv. 1-4. The Preface. "That which was from the beginning, which we have heard, which we have seen with our eyes, which we beheld and our hands felt, concerning the Word of Life—and the Life was manifested, and we have seen and testify and announce to you the Life, the Eternal Life, which was with the Father and was manifested to us—that which we have seen and heard, we announce to you also, that ye also may have fellowship with us. Yea, and our fellowship is with the Father and with His Son Jesus Christ. And these things we are writing that our joy may be fulfilled."

The Apostle here characterises and commends his Gospel (*cf.* Introd. p. 154). 1. *Its theme*—the earthly life of Jesus. No mere biography, since Jesus was not one of the children of men but the Eternal Son of God, the Word made flesh. (*a*) An ineffable wonder but no dream, an indubitable reality. His readers might doubt it, since they belonged to a later generation and had never seen Jesus; but St. John had seen Him, and he assures them, with elaborate iteration, that it is no dream: "These eyes beheld Him, these hands felt Him". "Because," says Calvin, "the greatness of the thing demanded that its truth should be certain and proved, he insists much at this point". (*b*) His narrative was necessarily incomplete, since the infinite revelation was larger than his perception or understanding of it. "He would give only a little drop from the sea, not the sea itself" (Rothe). A complete biography of Jesus is impossible, since the days of His flesh are only a segment of His life, a moment of His eternal years. 2. *His purpose in writing it:* (*a*) that his readers might share his heavenly fellowship; (*b*) that his joy might be fulfilled.

Ver. 1. ὃ, *i.e.* the Logos and the Eternal Life which He manifested. *Cf.* v. 4: πᾶν τὸ γεγεννημένον with note. ἦν, "verbum æternitatis significativum non habentis initium" (Clem. Alex.). It "was" ere it "was manifested". ἀπ' ἀρχῆς, בְּרֵאשִׁית (Gen. i. 1). The Logos already was when time began. "The design of the Apostle is to remove the idea of novelty which could lessen the dignity of the Gospel" (Calvin). *Cf.* Athan., *Synops. Script. Sacr.:* θεολογῶν δὲ ἐξηγεῖται μὴ νεώτερον εἶναι τὸ καθ' ἡμᾶς μυστήριον ἀλλὰ καὶ ἐξ ἀρχῆς μὲν ἀεὶ τυγχάνειν αὐτὸ νῦν δὲ πεφανερῶσθαι ἐν τῷ Κυρίῳ. ἀκηκόαμεν, "we have heard"; either the editorial "we" (*cf.* Rom. i. 5; Col. iv. 3); or, with Lightfoot, St. John and the elders of Ephesus who had certified the authorship and authenticity of the Gospel (xxi. 24); or "I and the rest of the Apostles"—not hearsay but the testimony of eye-witnesses. ἐθεασάμεθα, "we beheld"—a spectacle which broke on our astonished vision. This seems to be the force of the transition from perfect to aorist, though it may be simply an instance of the decay of the distinction between perfect and aorist

[f] τοῦ λόγου τῆς ζωῆς· 2. καὶ ἡ ζωὴ ἐφανερώθη, καὶ ἑωράκαμεν,
καὶ [g] μαρτυροῦμεν, καὶ ἀπαγγέλλομεν ὑμῖν τὴν ζωὴν τὴν αἰώνιον,
[h] ἥτις ἦν [1] πρὸς τὸν πατέρα, καὶ ἐφανερώθη ἡμῖν· 3. ὃ ἑωράκαμεν καὶ
ἀκηκόαμεν, ἀπαγγέλλομεν ὑμῖν,[1] ἵνα καὶ ὑμεῖς [k] κοινωνίαν ἔχητε
μεθ' ἡμῶν· καὶ [l] ἡ κοινωνία δὲ ἡ ἡμετέρα μετὰ τοῦ πατρὸς καὶ μετὰ
τοῦ υἱοῦ αὐτοῦ Ἰησοῦ Χριστοῦ· 4. καὶ ταῦτα [m] γράφομεν ὑμῖν, ἵνα

f John i. 1, 4. g John i. 7, xxi. 24; Acts i. 8, ii. 32. h Heb. viii. 6; Mark iv. 20; Phil. iv. 3. i John i. 1, 2. k Acts ii. 42. l ii. 24; John xvii. 21; 2 Cor. xiii. 13. m ii. 12, 13.

[1] και υμιν ℵABCP, Syr[vg], Sah., Aeth., Arm., edd.

(see Moulton's *Gram. of N.T. Gk.*, i. pp. 142 f.). **ἐψηλάφησαν**: the word is used of the fumbling of a blind man in Gen. xxvii. 12 LXX **μή ποτε ψηλαφήσῃ με ὁ πατήρ**. **περὶ**, *in Betreff des Wortes des Lebens* (Holtzmann); *i.e.* "We did not grasp all the wonder but only its skirts". "*Vom Worte des Lebens* will er verkündigen, denn *ihn selbst* verkündigen zu können, dazu fühlte er sich nicht in Stande" (Rothe). **τοῦ Λόγου τῆς ζωῆς**, "the Word who gives life," "des Wortes, ohne welches es kein Leben gibt" (Holtzmann). Calvin: "Genitivus loco epitheti pro Vivifico". Rothe's "das Wort vom Leben (the word concerning life)" is Pauline (*cf.* Phil. ii. 16) but not Johannine.

Ver. 2. A parenthesis reiterating the assurance of the reality of the manifestation. The Apostle heaps assurance upon assurance with elaborate emphasis, and the cumbrousness of his language should not be removed by devices of construction or punctuation, making ver. 1 a complete sentence: (1) "That which was from the beginning (is) that which we have heard, etc."; (2) "That which was from the beginning, which we have seen . . . beheld, our hands also handled". *Cf.* Tert. in crit. n. **μαρτυροῦμεν**, according to the Lord's parting charge (*cf.* John xv. 27; Luke xxiv. 48; Acts i. 8). **ἡ μαρτυρία Ἰησοῦ Χριστοῦ** (Rev. i. 2, 9, xix. 10) was the apostolic **ἀπαγγελία**. **ἀπαγγέλλομεν, κ. τ. λ.**: "Whence we gather that Christ cannot be preached to us without the Heavenly Kingdom being opened to us, so that, being wakened from death, we may live the life of God" (Calvin). Observe the note of wonder in the Apostle's language. Speech fails him. He labours for expression, adding definition to definition.

Ver. 3. **ὃ ἑωρ. καὶ ἀκ.**, not merely a resumption but a reiteration of the protasis. **καὶ ὑμεῖς**, "ye also" who have not seen Jesus. **κοινωνίαν**, not merely knowledge through hearsay of what the Apostles had known as eye-witnesses, but personal and direct communion with the living Lord. This St. John proceeds to make plain. The phrase **καὶ . . . δὲ**, *et . . . vero, atque etiam*, introduces an important addition or explanation (*cf.* John vi. 51, viii. 16, 17, xv. 27; Acts xxii. 29; Heb. ix. 21; 2 Peter i. 5). "Christ walks no longer in the flesh among us, but He appears still continually to the world of men and reveals Himself to those who love Him. Through faith a real personal contact with the Christ now glorified in the Spirit is possible" (Rothe). There is a gracious constraint on all who know this blessed fellowship to bring others into it. *Cf.* 1 Cor. ix. 16. Bunyan, preface to *The Jerusalem-Sinner Saved*: "I have been vile myself, but have obtained mercy, and I would have my companions in sin partake of mercy too, and therefore I have writ this little book".

Ver. 4. **ἡμεῖς**, clearly the editorial plural. The reading **ὑμῶν** seems at the first glance more attractive than **ἡμῶν** as evincing a generous solicitude on the part of the Apostle for the highest good of his readers, *viz.*, the fulfilment of their joy. Rothe: "Wer es weis, dass das uranfängliche Leben erschienen ist und er mit demselben und dadurch mit dem Vater Gemeinschaft haben kann, dessen Herz muss hoch schlagen". In truth, however, **ἡμῶν** evinces a still more generous solicitude—the very spirit of Jesus. As He could not be happy in Heaven without us, so the Apostle's joy was incomplete unless his readers shared it. *Cf.* Samuel Rutherford:—

"Oh! if one soul from Anwoth
Meet me at God's right hand,
My heaven will be two heavens
In Immanuel's land."

Vv. 5-10. The Message of the Incarnation and the Duty which it brings. "And this is the message which we have heard from Him and are announcing to you, that God is light, and darkness—in Him there is none. If we say

[n] ἡ χαρὰ ἡμῶν [1] ᾖ πεπληρωμένη. 5. Καὶ αὕτη ἐστὶν [2] ἡ [o] ἐπαγγελία [3]
ἣν ἀκηκόαμεν ἀπ' αὐτοῦ, καὶ [p] ἀναγγέλλομεν ὑμῖν, ὅτι ὁ Θεὸς φῶς
ἐστι, καὶ [q] σκοτία ἐν αὐτῷ οὐκ ἔστιν οὐδεμία. 6. [r] ἐὰν εἴπωμεν ὅτι
κοινωνίαν ἔχομεν μετ' αὐτοῦ, καὶ ἐν τῷ σκότει περιπατῶμεν, ψευδόμεθα, καὶ οὐ ποιοῦμεν τὴν ἀλήθειαν· 7. [s] ἐὰν δὲ ἐν τῷ φωτὶ
περιπατῶμεν, ὡς αὐτός ἐστιν ἐν τῷ φωτί, κοινωνίαν ἔχομεν μετ'
ἀλλήλων, καὶ [t] τὸ αἷμα Ἰησοῦ Χριστοῦ [4] τοῦ υἱοῦ αὐτοῦ καθαρίζει [5]

n John iii. 29, xv. 11, xvi. 24, xvii. 13; 2 John 12. With ἡμῶν cf. 3 John, 4.
o iii. 11.
p Matt. xxviii. 11; John iv. 25, xvi. 12, 14, 15; 1 Peter i. 12.
q John i. 4, 5, 8, 9, viii. 12, ix. 5; James i. 17.
r ii. 4, John iii. 19-21; John, viii. 12, xii. 35, 36.
s Exod. x. 22, 23.
t Heb. ix. 13, 14.

[1] υμων ACKP, Syrph., Vg., Cop., Aeth., Arm., Aug.; ημων ℵBL, many minusc., Syrvg, Sah., edd.

[2] εστιν αυτη ℵBCKLP, edd.

[3] αγγελια ℵcABKL, Syrvg., Vg. (*annuntiatio*), Aeth., Arm., Aug. (*annuntiatio*), edd.

[4] Ιησου Χριστου AKL, Syrph, Vg., Cop., Tert. (*de Pudic.* 19), Aug.; om. Χριστου ℵBCP, Syrvg, Sah., Arm., edd.

[5] καθαρισει or καθαριει some lesser authorities, Cop., Sah., Aug. (*purgabit*).

that we have fellowship with Him and be walking in the darkness, we lie and are not doing the Truth; but if we be walking in the light, as He is in the light, we have fellowship with one another, and the blood of Jesus His Son cleanseth us from every sin. If we say that we have not sin, we are deceiving ourselves and the Truth is not in us. If we confess our sins, faithful is He and righteous to forgive us the sins and cleanse us from every unrighteousness. If we say that we have not sinned, we are making Him a liar and His Word is not in us."

Ver. 5. **ἀγγελία** in N.T. only here and iii. 11. **ἐπαγγελία** could only mean "promise" (*cf.* ii. 25). **ἀπαγγέλλειν** and **ἀναγγέλλειν** both mean "announce," the former with reference to the source of the message (**ἀκηκόαμεν ἀπ' αὐτοῦ**) and the latter to its destination. "*Quod Filius annunciavit, renunciat apostolus*" (Haupt). **οὐκ ἔστιν οὐδεμία**: the double negative makes a stronger negative (*cf.* Luke xxiii. 53). The manifestation of God in Christ was to those who beheld it a splendid glory, the breaking of a great light into the darkness of a sinful and sorrowful world. *Cf.* Matt. iv. 14-16. Light means warmth, health, sight, in a word "life" (*cf.* ver. 2).

Light is given that we may "walk in it" and enjoy its blessings. It is thus that the Gospel attains its end and fulfils its purpose in us. The Apostle now proceeds to warn his readers against two heresies which ignored this condition of heavenly fellowship.

Vv. 6, 7. The heresy of Antinomianism, represented by the Nicolaitans (*cf.* Introd. p. 156). **ἐὰν εἴπωμεν**, a gentle and charitable hypothesis. He does not charge his readers with actually holding this pernicious doctrine, and he includes himself ("we," not "ye"). **περιπατεῖν**, Heb. הָלַךְ, of the whole course of life. The Greek phrase is **ἀναστρέφεσθαι** (*conversari*). God is light and sin darkness, *peccata tenebræ sunt* (Aug.), and it is impossible to be living in sin or compromising with it and at the same time be enjoying fellowship with God. **ψευδόμεθα**: we may believe the lie, being self-deceived (ver. 8); for disobedience to the Truth blinds us to it. Knowledge comes by doing (*cf.* John vii. 17). **τὴν ἀλήθειαν,** see note on ver. 8. "Walking in the light" has two blessed results: (1) "fellowship with one another," which may mean either *fellowship with God—He with us and we with Him* (Aug., Calv.), or *communion of saints—our fellow-believers with us and we with them.* In fact the one idea implies the other. They are inseparable. Communion with our brethren is the consequence and evidence of communion with God. *Cf.* iv. 20. (2) "Cleansing in the blood of Jesus." **τὸ αἷμα Ἰησοῦ,** God's Infinite Sacrifice for the sin of the world—a N.T. phrase of peculiar poignancy and fragrance. *Cf.* Ignat. *ad Rom.* vii.: **τὸ αἷμα αὐτοῦ, ὅ ἐστιν ἀγάπη ἄφθαρτος.** When we walk in the light, that demonstration of the length to which God has gone in sacrifice for our sakes, is ever before us, and the amazing spectacle subdues our hearts, takes possession of them, and drives out every evil affection. *Cf.* Catherine of Siena: "The blood and tears of the Divine Son are able

ἡμᾶς ἀπὸ πάσης ἁμαρτίας. 8. Ἐὰν εἴπωμεν ὅτι [u] ἁμαρτίαν οὐκ
ἔχομεν, ἑαυτοὺς [v] πλανῶμεν, καὶ [w] ἡ ἀλήθεια οὐκ ἔστιν ἐν ἡμῖν. 9.
[x] ἐὰν ὁμολογῶμεν τὰς ἁμαρτίας ἡμῶν, πιστός ἐστι καὶ δίκαιος, ἵνα
ἀφῇ ἡμῖν τὰς ἁμαρτίας, καὶ καθαρίσῃ ἡμᾶς ἀπὸ πάσης ἀδικίας.
10. ἐὰν εἴπωμεν ὅτι οὐχ ἡμαρτήκαμεν, [z] ψεύστην ποιοῦμεν αὐτόν,
καὶ [a] ὁ λόγος αὐτοῦ οὐκ ἔστιν ἐν ἡμῖν.
II. 1. [a] Τεκνία μου, ταῦτα γράφω ὑμῖν, ἵνα μὴ ἁμάρτητε· καὶ

u John ix. 41, xv. 22, 24, xix. 11.
v ii. 26, iii. 7, iv. 6; Rev. ii. 20, xii. 9; Matt. xxii. 29, xxiv. 4, 5, 11, 24.
w ii. 4.
x Ps. xxxii. 5; Prov. xxviii. 13.
(T.R., WH). *Cf.* comm.
y Rom. iii. 26.
z Rom. iii. 4.
a i. 8, ii. 4; John v. 38, viii. 37.
a Gal. iv. 19

to cleanse us from head to foot". **πάσης ἁμαρτίας,** "every sin,' *i.e.* every outbreak of the sinful principle; not "all sin" (**πάσης τῆς ἁμαρτίας**). *Cf.* Rom. iii. 19: **πᾶν στόμα . . . πᾶς ὁ κόσμος.**

Vv. 8-10. The heresy of Perfectionism. Some might not say, with the Antinomians, that they were absolved from the obligation of the moral law, but they maintained that they were done with sin, had no more sinful propensities, committed no more sinful acts. In opposition hereto the Apostle asserts two facts: (1) *Inherent corruption.* Distinguish **ἁμαρτίαν ἔχειν** ("to have sin") and **ἁμαρτάνειν** ("to sin"), corresponding to the sinful principle and its manifestation in specific acts. Our natures are poisoned, the taint is in our blood. Grace is the medicine, but recovery is a protracted process. It is begun the moment we submit ourselves to Christ, but all our lives we continue under treatment. **πλανῶμεν,** "lead astray" (*cf.* Matt. xviii. 12). **ἡ ἀλήθεια,** in Johannine phraseology not simply "der Wahrheitssinn, die Wahrhaftigkeit der Selbstprüfung und der Selbsterkenntniss" (Rothe), but the revelation of "the True God" (ver. 20; John xvii. 3), which came "through Jesus Christ" (John i. 17), Himself "the Truth" (John xiv. 6). Nearly equivalent to **ὁ λόγος** (ver. 10). The Truth is a splendid ideal, never realised here, else it would cease to be an ideal; always as we pursue it displaying a fuller glory, And thus the nearer we approach it the further off it seems; when we walk in the light we see faults which were hidden in the darkness. Self-abasement is a characteristic of the saints. When Juan de Avila (A.D. 1500-69) was dying the rector of his college approached him and said: "What joy it must be to you to think of meeting the Saviour!" "Ah!" said the saint, "rather do I tremble at the thought of my sins." (2) *The frequent falls of the believer.* We all "have sinned (**ἡμαρτήκαμεν**)," *i.e.*, committed acts of sin (**ἁμαρτίας**) manifesting the strength and activity of the sinful principle (**ἡ ἁμαρτία**) in our souls. This, however, is no reason for despair. There is a remedy—forgiveness and cleansing in the blood of Jesus; and there is a way of obtaining it—confession. **πιστός,** *i.e.*, to His promise (*cf.* Heb. x. 23). **δίκαιος**: He would be unrighteous if He broke His promise ratified by the blood of Jesus. Peace is not got by denying our sinfulness and our sins, but by frankly confessing them and availing ourselves, continually and repeatedly, of the gracious remedy. "Woe to that soul which presumes to think that he can approach God in any other way than as a sinner asking mercy. Know yourself to be wicked, and God will wrap you up warm in the mantle of His goodness" (Juan de Avila). "Remission of sins cannot be sundered from penitence, nor can the peace of God belong to consciences where the fear of God does not reign" (Calv.).

Perfectionism has two causes: (1) *The stifling of conscience*: "we make Him a liar, *i.e.*, turn a deaf ear to His inward testimony, His voice in our souls. (2) *Ignorance of His Word*: it "is not in us". Such a delusion were impossible if we steeped our minds in the Scriptures. Consider the lapses of the saints, *e.g.*, David, Peter.

CHAPTER II.—Vv. 1, 2. The Remedy for the Sins of Believers. 'My little children, these things I am writing to you in order that ye may not sin. And if any one sin an Advocate have we with the Father—Jesus Christ, a righteous One. And He is Himself the propitiation for our sins, and not for ours only but also for the whole world."

Ver. 1. Observe the sudden change in the Apostle's manner. His heart is very tender toward his people, and he adopts an affectionate and personal tone: (1) He passes from the formal "we" to "I". (2, He styles them **τεκνία μου,** *filioli mei*, *meine Kindlein*—his favourite appellation (*cf.* ii. 12, 28; iii. 7, 18; iv. 4; v. 21). Not only was it very suitable

ἐάν τις ἁμάρτῃ, [b] παράκλητον ἔχομεν [c] πρὸς τὸν πατέρα, Ἰησοῦν
Χριστὸν [d] δίκαιον· 2. καὶ αὐτὸς [e] ἱλασμός ἐστι [f] περὶ τῶν ἁμαρτιῶν

b *Cf.* comm. c i. 2.
d Matt. xxvii. 19; Luke xxiii. 47; Acts vii. 52, xxii. 14; 1 Peter iii. 18.
e In N.T. only here and iv. 10, ἱλαστήριον Rom. iii. 25; Heb. ix. 5; ἱλάσκεσθαι Luke xviii. 13; Heb. ii. 17.
f Rom. viii. 3.

on the lips of the aged teacher, but it was a phrase of Jesus (*cf.* John xiii. 33). St. John had caught the phrase and its spirit. He remembered how the Master had dealt with His disciples, and he would deal with his people after the same fashion and be to them what Jesus had been to himself—as gentle and patient.

He assumes this tone because he is about to address a warning to them, and he would fain take the sting out of it and disarm opposition. He foresees the possibility of a two-fold perversion of his teaching: (1) "If we can never in this life be done with sin, why strive after holiness? It is useless; sin is an abiding necessity". (2) "If escape be so easy, why dread falling into sin? We may sin with light hearts, since we have the blood of Jesus to cleanse us." "No," he answers, "I am not writing these things to you either to discourage you in the pursuit of holiness or to embolden you in sinning, but, on the contrary, in order that (ἵνα) ye may not sin." *Cf.* Aug.: "Lest perchance he should seem to have given impunity to sins, and men should now say to themselves, 'Let us sin, let us do securely what we will, Christ cleanses us; He is faithful and righteous, He cleanses us from all iniquity,' he takes from thee evil security and implants useful fear. It is an evil wish of thine to be secure; be anxious. For He is faithful and righteous to forgive us our sins, if thou art always displeasing to thyself and being changed until thou be perfected." As a physician might say to his patient: "Your trouble is obstinate; the poison is in your blood, and it will take a long time to eradicate it. But I do not tell you this to discourage you or make you careless; no, on the contrary, to make you watchful and diligent in the use of the remedy"; so the Apostle says: "My little children, these things I am writing to you in order that ye may not sin".

If, however, we fall into sin, let us not lose heart, for **Παράκλητον ἔχομεν πρὸς τὸν Πατέρα. παράκλητος,** "one called to your side," so, in a forensic sense, "one who undertakes and champions your cause," "an advocate". Vulg., *Advocatus;* Luth., *Fürsprecher bei dem Vater.* Here of the ascended Jesus; in John xiv. 16, 26, xv. 26, xvi. 7, of the Holy Spirit, where Vulg. simply transliterates *Paracletus*, and both our versions give "Comforter," Luth., *Tröster*—an impossible rendering, since the word is not act. but pass. Render "Advocate" in every case. *Cf.* saying of R. Li'ezer ben Jacob: "He who does one commandment has gotten him one advocate (פרקליט, **παράκλητος**), and he who has committed one transgression has gotten him one accuser (קטיגור, **κατήγορος**). Repentance and good works are as a shield in the face of punishment." In the days of His flesh Jesus was God's Advocate with men. He told the Eleven in the Upper Room that, though He was going away, God would not be left without an Advocate on the earth to plead His cause and win men to faith (John xvi. 16, 17). The Holy Spirit has come in the room of Jesus, and still from age to age performs the office of God's Advocate with men. Nor has the advocacy of Jesus ceased. He is our Advocate in Heaven, pleading our cause with God. The history of redemption is thus a progressive economy of grace: (1) the O.T. dispensation, when God was conceived as remote in high Heaven; (2) that of the Incarnation, when He revealed Himself as a Father and, by the advocacy of His Eternal Son, made His appeal to the children of men; (3) that of the Holy Spirit, under which we live in the enjoyment of a double advocacy—our Glorified Redeemer's, who "maketh intercession for us" (Rom. viii. 34) in the Court of Heaven (*cf.* Christina Rossetti's *Verses*, p. 41: "Day and night the Accuser"), and the Holy Spirit's down here, wooing us to faith by His gracious importunities. **δίκαιον,** Rothe: "Only the righteous One, the guiltless, the One that is separate from sin, can be the Advocate with God for sinners, in general the Mediator of salvation, and make His friendship for us prevalent with God, because only such a one has access to God and fellowship with God (Heb. vii. 26; 1 Peter iii. 18; John xvi. 8, 10)". "What better advocate could we have for us, than He that is appointed to be our judge?" (Jer. Taylor, *The Great Exemplar*, I. i. 3).

Ver. 2. Our Advocate does not plead that we are innocent or adduce extenuating circumstances. He acknowledges our guilt and presents His vicarious

ἡμῶν· οὐ περὶ τῶν ἡμετέρων δὲ μόνον, ἀλλὰ καὶ περὶ ὅλου [g] τοῦ
κόσμου. 3. Καὶ [h] ἐν τούτῳ γινώσκομεν ὅτι ἐγνώκαμεν αὐτόν, ἐὰν
[i] τὰς ἐντολὰς αὐτοῦ τηρῶμεν. 4. ὁ λέγων,[1] "Ἔγνωκα αὐτόν," καὶ
τὰς ἐντολὰς αὐτοῦ μὴ τηρῶν, ψεύστης ἐστί, καὶ [k] ἐν τούτῳ ἡ ἀλήθεια
οὐκ ἔστιν· 5. ὃς δ' ἂν [l] τηρῇ αὐτοῦ τὸν λόγον, ἀληθῶς ἐν τούτῳ ἡ

g John i. 29, iii. 16. h John xiii. 35. i John xiv. 15, 21, xv. 10; Rev. xii. 17, xiv. 12; Matt. xxviii. 20; 1 Cor. vii. 19. k i. 6, 8. l John viii. 51, 52, 55, xiv. 23, xv. 20, xvii. 6; Rev. iii. 8.

[1] λεγων οτι ℵAB, edd.

work as the ground of our acquittal. He stands in the Court of Heaven **ἀρνίον ὡς ἐσφαγμένον** (Rev. v. 6) and the marks of His sore Passion are a mute but eloquent appeal: "I suffered all this for sinners, and shall it go for naught?" **περὶ ὅλου τοῦ κόσμου**, *pro totius mundi* (Vulgate), "for *the sins* of the whole world". This is grammatically possible (*cf.* Matt. v. 20), but it misses the point. There are *sins*, special and occasional, in the believer; there is *sin* in the world; it is sinful through and through. The Apostle means "for our sins and that mass of sin, the world". *Cf.* Rothe: "Die 'Welt' ist ihrem Begriff zufolge überhaupt sündig, ein Sündenmasse, und hat nicht blos einzelne Sünden an sich". The remedy is commensurate with the malady. Bengel: "Quam late patet peccatum, tam late *propitiatio*".

Observe how the Apostle classes himself with his readers: "*we* have," "*our* sins"—a rebuke of priestcraft. *Cf.* Aug.: "But some one will say: 'Do not holy men pray for us? Do not bishops and prelates pray for the people?' Nay, attend to the Scriptures, and see that even the prelates commend themselves to the people. For the Apostle says to the common folk 'withal praying for us'. The Apostle prays for the folk, the folk for the Apostle. We pray for you, brethren; but pray ye also for us. Let all the members pray for one another, let the Head intercede for all."

Vv. 3-6. The Proof of our Interest in Christ's Propitiation and Advocacy. "And herein we get to know that we know Him—if we observe His commandments. He that saith 'I know Him,' and observeth not His commandments, is a liar, and in this man the Truth is not; but whosoever observeth His Word, truly in this man the love of God hath been carried to its end. Herein we get to know that we are in Him; he that saith he abideth in Him is bound, even as the Lord (**ἐκεῖνος**) walked, himself also so to walk." The Apostle foresees a question which may be raised: "How can I be assured that Christ is all this to *me*—*my* Propitiation, *my* Advocate? And how can I be assured that I have an abiding interest in Him?" He answers: (1) We attain to personal and conscious acquaintance with Christ by observance of His commandments (3-5*a*); (2) we attain to assurance of abiding union with Him by "walking even as He walked" (5*b*, 6).

Ver. 3. The principle is that it is not enough to understand the theory; we must put it into practice. *E.g.*, what makes an artist? Not merely learning the rules of perspective and mixture of colours, but actually putting one's hand to brush and canvas. First attempts may be unsuccessful, but skill comes by patient practice. *Cf.* Rembrandt's advice to his pupil Hoogstraten: "Try to put well in practice what you already know; and in doing so you will, in good time, discover the hidden things which you inquire about'. To know about Christ, to understand the doctrine of His person and work is mere theory; we get to know Him and to know that we know Him by practice of His precepts. **γινώσκω** (*cognosco*) is to **οἶδα** (*scio*) as **γίνομαι** (*fio*) to **εἰμί** (*sum*). **ἐγνώκαμεν**, *cognovimus*, "we have got to know," *i.e.* "we know". **τηρεῖν**, "keep a watchful eye upon". *Cf.* Matt. xxvii. 36: **καὶ καθήμενοι ἐτήρουν αὐτὸν ἐκεῖ.**

Ver. 4. **μὴ τηρῶν**, in classical Greek a gentle hypothesis, merely suggesting a possible case; but in later Greek **μή** is the regular negative with participles. It was an actual error, else the Apostle would hardly have spoken so emphatically about it. **ψεύστης**, see note on **i.** 6. **ἀλήθεια**, see note on i. 8.

Ver. 5. **ἡ ἀγάπη τοῦ Θεοῦ**, "the love of God," is ambiguous like אַהֲבַת יְהוָֹה, *amor Dei*, *l' amore di Dio*, *l'amour de Dieu*, *die Liebe Gottes*. It might be objective genitive, "love for God," "die Liebe zu Gott" (Rothe). But the believer's love for God is never perfected in this life. The genitive is subjective (*cf.* iv. 9), *amor Dei erga hominem*, *per Christum nobis reconciliatus* (Bengel),

[m] **ἀγάπη τοῦ Θεοῦ τετελείωται.** ἐν τούτῳ γινώσκομεν ὅτι ἐν αὐτῷ
[n] **ἐσμεν.**[1] 6. ὁ λέγων [o] ἐν αὐτῷ μένειν, [p] **ὀφείλει, καθὼς** [q] **ἐκεῖνος περιε-**
πάτησε, καὶ αὐτὸς οὕτω [2] [r] **περιπατεῖν.** 7. **ἀδελφοί,**[3] **οὐκ** ἐντολὴν
[s] **καινὴν** γράφω ὑμῖν, **ἀλλ'** ἐντολὴν **παλαιάν,** [t] **ἣν εἴχετε ἀπ' ἀρχῆς·**
ἡ ἐντολὴ ἡ **παλαιά** ἐστιν ὁ **λόγος** ὃν ἠκούσατε **ἀπ' ἀρχῆς.**[4] 8.
πάλιν ἐντολὴν καινὴν γράφω ὑμῖν, ὅ ἐστιν **ἀληθὲς** ἐν αὐτῷ **καὶ** ἐν

m iv. 12, 17, 18; Luke xiii. 32, John iv. 34, v. 36, xvii. 4, 23 Heb. ii. 10, x. 1, 14, xi. 40
n 2 Cor. v. 17.
o John xv. 4-7.
p iii. 16, iv. 11; 3 John 8; John xiii. 14; Matt. xxiii. 16, 18; Luke xvii. 10; Rom. xv. 1 Heb. v. 12.
q *Cf.* comm.
r Eph. v. 2; Col. ii. 6.
s Matt. xiii. 52, xxvi. 28, 29, xxvii. 60 Mark i. 27.
t John xiii. 34, xv. 12; Mark xii. 29-31.

[1] Punct. **ἐσμεν ·** WH, Nest.

[2] **και αυτος ουτως** ℵCKP, Syr^{ph}, Cop., Arm., Tisch., Nest.; om. **ουτως** AB, Vg. Sah., Aeth., Aug., WH.

[3] **αγαπητοι** ℵABCP, Syr$^{vg\ ph}$, Vg., Cop., Sah., Arm., Aug., edd.

[4] **απ αρχης** om. ℵABCP, many minusc., Syr$^{vg\ ph}$, Vg., Cop., Sah., Aeth., Arm. Aug., edd.

and the idea is that the redeeming love of God has attained its end in the man who observes His Word. *Cf.* Isa. liii. 11. St. Augustine understands "the love of God" as His love for sinners, a forgiving love like that of Jesus when He prayed on the Cross "Father, forgive them". "What is the perfection of love? It is both to love one's enemies and to love them in order that they may be brethren." By cultivating a love like this we get to know that we know Him. **ἐν τούτῳ** (*b*) points forward to **ὁ λέγων, κ.τ.λ.**, introducing a second assurance. It is not enough to know Him; we must be sure of continuing in fellowship with Him, of "abiding in Him" to the end. This assurance comes by "walking even as He walked"; *i.e.* the conformation of our lives to His is an evidence of our abiding interest in Him, our vital union with Him. We get like Him by imitating Him, and our likeness to Him is an irrefragable evidence to ourselves and the the world that we are His, as a son's likeness to his father proves their relationship. **ὀφείλει,** "is bound," "ist schuldig" (Rothe), of *moral obligation.* The claim (**λέγων**) must be honourably attested. **αὐτὸς** in this section refers grammatically to Jesus Christ vv. 1, 2). The change of pronoun (**ἐκεῖνος**) does not imply a change of person, since here as in iii. 3, 5, 7, 16, iv. 17, **ἐκεῖνος** is not a mere pronoun. It is used like *ille*, and signifies "that great One," "the Master". *Cf.* 2 Tim. ii. 12, 13. **περιπατεῖν,** see note on i. 6. Aug.: "Perhaps He admonishes us to walk in the sea. Far from it! He admonishes us to walk in the way of righteousness."

Vv. 7-11. A New Meaning in an Old Commandment. "Beloved, it is no new commandment that I am writing to you, but an old commandment which ye had from the beginning. The old commandment is the word which ye heard. Again, it is a new commandment that I am writing to you—a thing which is true in Him and in you, because the darkness is passing away and the light, the true light, is already shining. He that saith he is in the light and hateth his brother is in the darkness even until now. He that loveth his brother abideth in the light, and there is no stumbling-block in his way; but he that hateth his brother is in the darkness, and walketh in the darkness, and knoweth not where he is going, because the darkness hath blinded his eyes."

St. John has lately discovered the supremacy of Love in the Christian revelation (see Introd. pp. 157 f.). His imperfect realisation of this has been the defect of his teaching hitherto, and he would now repair it: "It is not a new commandment that I am writing to you; it is part of the Gospel which I have been preaching to you all along. But I have never adequately understood it, and therefore it is new to your ears as it is to my heart."

Ver. 7. **ἀγαπητοί,** St. John's favourite style (*cf.* iii. 2, 21, iv. 1, 7, 11). About to enjoin love, he begins by loving. **καινός,** "novel," "new *in kind*" (*novus*) as distinguished from **νέος,** "new *in time*" (*recens*). **ἀπ' ἀρχῆς,** here not as in i. 1, but "from the beginning of your Christian life". **ἡ ἐντολὴ ἡ παλαιά,** *cf.* i. 2: **τὴν ζωὴν τὴν αἰώνιον.**

Ver. 8. **πάλιν,** "again," *i.e.* in another sense, from another point of view, not in itself but in our recognition of it, "it is a new commandment". **ὅ ἐστιν ἀληθές,** in apposition to **ἐντολήν**—"a thing which is true," *viz.*, the paramount

ὑμῖν · ὅτι [u] ἡ σκοτία [v] παράγεται, καὶ [w] τὸ φῶς τὸ ἀληθινὸν ἤδη [x] φαίνει.
9. [y] ὁ λέγων ἐν τῷ φωτὶ εἶναι, καὶ τὸν ἀδελφὸν αὐτοῦ μισῶν, ἐν τῇ
σκοτίᾳ ἐστὶν ἕως ἄρτι. 10. [z] ὁ ἀγαπῶν τὸν ἀδελφὸν αὐτοῦ, ἐν τῷ φωτὶ
μένει, καὶ [a] σκάνδαλον ἐν αὐτῷ οὐκ ἔστιν.[1] 11. ὁ δὲ μισῶν τὸν
ἀδελφὸν αὐτοῦ, [b] ἐν τῇ σκοτίᾳ ἐστί, καὶ ἐν τῇ σκοτίᾳ περιπατεῖ, καὶ
οὐκ οἶδε [c] ποῦ ὑπάγει, ὅτι ἡ σκοτία ἐτύφλωσε τοὺς ὀφθαλμοὺς αὐτοῦ.

u i. 5-7. v Ver. 17; 1 Cor. vii. 31. w John i. 9. x John i. 5, v. 35; Rev. i. 16, viii. 12, xviii. 23, xxi. 23. y iv. 20. z i. 5-7; Ps. xxxvi. 9. a Johann. only here and Rev. ii. 14; σκανδαλίζειν John vi. 61, xvi. 1. b John iii. 8, viii. 14, xii. 35, xiii. 36, xiv. 5, xvi. 5. c John xi. 9, 10, xiv. 35, 36; Is. vi. 10 (John xii. 40).

[1] **εν αυτω ουκ εστιν** BKLP, WH, Nest.; **ουκ εστιν εν αυτω** ℵAC, Tisch., WH (marg).

necessity of Love. This truth, though unperceived, is contained in the revelation of Jesus Christ (**ἐν αὐτῷ**) and proved in the experience of believers (**ἐν ὑμῖν**). It is a fact that hatred of one's brother clouds the soul and shuts out the light. "I know this," says the Apostle, "because the darkness is passing away and the light, the true light, is already shining," *i.e.* my eyes are getting accustomed to the light of the Gospel-revelation, and I have seen this truth which at first was hidden from me. Adjectives in **-ινός** denote the material of which the thing is made; and **ἀληθινός** is used of the real as opposed either to the type (*cf.* John vi. 32, xv. 1; Heb. viii. 2, ix. 24) or to the counterfeit (*cf. Symb. Nic.*: **Θεὸν ἀληθινὸν ἐκ Θεοῦ ἀληθινοῦ** "very God of very God," *i.e.* the real God as opposed to false gods, idols, which were "things of naught"). The opposite of **τὸ φῶς τὸ ἀληθινόν** is, on the one hand, the dim light of the Jewish Law (the type) and, on the other, the false light of human speculation (the counterfeit).

Ver. 9. He says and perhaps thinks he is in the light, but he has never seen the light; it has never shone on him. **ἀδελφόν**, on the lips of Jesus a fellow-man (*cf.* Matt. v. 45; Luke xv. 30, 32), in the apostolic writings a fellow-Christian (*cf.* v. 1-2, 16)—one of the apostolic narrowings of the Lord's teaching. *Cf.* "neighbour"—with the Rabbis, a fellow-Jew; with Jesus, a fellow-man (*cf.* Luke x. 25-37). There is no contradiction between this passage and Luke xiv. 26. The best commentary on the latter is John xii. 25.

Ver. 10. **ἐν τῷ φωτὶ μένει**: he does not merely catch glimpses of the light but "abideth in it," being of one mind with God, the common Father, who "is light" (i. 5). **σκάνδαλον οὐκ ἔστιν ἐν αὐτῷ**, "there is no occasion of stumbling, nothing to trip him up and make him fall, in his case"—an echo of John xi. 9, 10. Another interpretation, less agreeable to the context but more consonant with the common use of **σκάνδαλον** (*cf.* Matt. xiii. 41, xviii. 7; Rom. xiv. 13), is: Because he is winsome and gracious, there is in him no stumbling-block to others, nothing to deter them from accepting the Gospel. The love of the primitive Christians impressed the heathen. *Cf.* Tert. *Apol.* 39: "Vide, inquiunt, ut invicem se diligant: ipsi enim invicem oderunt; et ut pro alterutro mori sint parati: ipsi enim ad occidendum alterutrum paratiores erunt". *Ep. ad Diogn.* 1: **καὶ τίνα φιλοστοργίαν ἔχουσι πρὸς ἀλλήλους.** This spirit disappeared, and in view of the bitter controversies of the 4th century the Pagan historian Ammianus avowed that "the enmity of the Christians toward each other surpassed the fury of savage beasts against man". Another interpretation takes **αὐτῷ** as neuter: "There is no occasion of stumbling in it," *i.e.*, in the light. *Cf.* John xi. 9.

Ver. 11. St. John recognises no neutral attitude between "love" and "hatred". Love is active benevolence, and less than this is hatred, just as indifference to the Gospel-call amounts to rejection of it (*cf.* Matt. xxii. 5-7). Observe the climax: "in the darkness is, and in the darkness walketh, and knoweth not where he is going". **ἐτύφλωσεν**, aor. of the *indefinite past*, where we would use the perf. (*cf.* Moulton, *Gram. of N. T. Gk.*, i. pp. 135 ff.). The penalty of living in the darkness is not merely that one does not see, but that one goes blind. The neglected faculty is atrophied. *Cf.* the mole, the *crustacea* in the subterranean lakes of the Mammoth Caves of Kentucky.

Observe how St. John emphasises and elaborates the old-new commandment "Love thy brother," reiterating it, putting it negatively and positively.

Vv. 12-17. The Appeal of Experience. "I am writing to you, little children, because your sins have been forgiven you for His name's sake; I am writing to you, fathers, because ye have got to know Him that it is from the beginning

12. γράφω ὑμῖν, τεκνία, ὅτι ἀφέωνται ὑμῖν αἱ ἁμαρτίαι [d] διὰ τὸ
ὄνομα αὐτοῦ. 13. Γράφω ὑμῖν, πατέρες, ὅτι ἐγνώκατε τὸν [e] ἀπ᾽
ἀρχῆς. γράφω ὑμῖν, [f] νεανίσκοι, ὅτι [g] νενικήκατε [h] τὸν [1] πονηρόν.
γράφω [2] ὑμῖν, [1] παιδία, ὅτι ἐγνώκατε τὸν πατέρα. 14. [i] Ἔγραψα ὑμῖν,
πατέρες, ὅτι ἐγνώκατε τὸν [3] ἀπ᾽ ἀρχῆς. [i] Ἔγραψα ὑμῖν, νεανίσκοι, ὅτι
[k] ἰσχυροί ἐστε, καὶ [l] ὁ λόγος τοῦ Θεοῦ ἐν ὑμῖν μένει, καὶ νενικήκατε τὸν

d Matt. x 22, xxiv. 9; John xv. 21 Rev. ii. 3. e i. 1. f Matt. xix. 20, 22 Acts, ii. 17. g John xvi. 33; Rom. xii. 21. h iii. 12, v. 18, 19; John xvii. 15; Matt. v. 37, vi. 13, xiii. 19, 38. i Ver. 18, iii. 17 (v.l.). k Eph. vi. 10. l i. 10 reff.

[1] το ℵ.

[2] γραφω K, Vg., Aug.; εγραψα ℵABCLP, Syr^vg ph, Cop., Sah., Aeth., Arm., edd.

[3] το B.

I am writing to you, young men, because ye have conquered the Evil One. I wrote to you, little ones, because ye have got to know the Father; I wrote to you, fathers, because ye have got to know Him that is from the beginning; I wrote to you, young men, because ye are strong, and the Word of God abideth in you, and ye have conquered the Evil One. Love not the world, nor the things that are in the world. If any one loveth the world, the love of the Father is not in him; because everything that is in the world—the lust of the flesh, and the lust of the eyes, and the braggart boast of life—is not of the Father but is of the world. And the world is passing away and the lust of it, but he that doeth the will of God abideth for ever."

The Apostle has been setting forth searching truths and is about to make an exacting claim; and here he pauses and with much tenderness reassures his readers: "I am not addressing you as unbelievers or casting doubt upon the sincerity of your faith. On the contrary, it is because I am assured thereof that I am writing this letter to you and wrote the Gospel which accompanies it".

Ver. 12. **τεκνία,** all the Apostle's readers, his customary appellation (see n. on ii. 1). **ἀφέωνται**, perf., the Doric form of **ἀφεῖνται**. **τὸ ὄνομα αὐτοῦ,** the character, mind, purpose of God revealed in Christ. "The name of God" is "whatsoever there is whereby he makes himself known" (*Westm. Larg. Catech.*).

Ver. 13. He now subdivides **τεκνία** into **πατέρες**, *i.e.*, mature believers with a long and ever-deepening (**ἐγνώκατε**) experience behind them, and **νεανίσκοι,** who, though **ἡ ἐπιθυμία τῆς σαρκός** is strong within them, have conquered the Evil One by the aids of grace—an evidence of the reality of their interest in Christ. **ἀπ' ἀρχῆς**, as in i. 1. The ancient interpreters took **τεκνία, πατέρες, νεανίσκοι** as a threefold classification, according to age (Aug., Athan.) or according to Christian experience, **κατὰ τὸν ἔσω ἄνθρωπον** (Euth. Zig.); but the order would then be either **τεκνία, νεανίσκοι, πατέρες** or **πατέρες, νεανίσκοι, τεκνία.** According to the variant **γράφω ὑμῖν, παιδία, τεκνία** is a general appellation subdivided into **πατέρες, νεανίσκοι, παιδία.** Ver. 14 should begin with **ἔγραψα ὑμῖν, παιδία.** The aor. **ἔγραψα** is most simply and reasonably explained as a reference to the Apostle's Gospel (see Introd. p. 154). Having assured them of his present conviction of the sincerity of their faith, he now goes on to assure them that he had entertained a like opinion when he wrote the Gospel for their instruction. His tone is much like that of 2 Pet. i. 12. Other explanations: (1) The reference is to a former epistle (*cf.* 3 John 9)—a gratuitous and unnecessary hypothesis. (2) The Apostle resumes after a pause whether in composition or in thought, and reiterates what he "has written". (3) An emphatic form of expression, like "we decree and have decreed". (4) Calvin, reading **γράφω ὑμῖν, παιδία,** regards **πατέρες . . . πονηρόν** as an interpolation. This is to cut the knot instead of untying it. **παιδία**, a general appellation for all the Apostle's readers, practically identical with **τεκνία.** Strictly **τεκνία** carries the idea of relationship by *birth-regeneration; cf.* Aug.: "*Quia remittuntur vobis peccata per nomen ejus,* et regeneramini in novam vitam, ideo filii". **παιδία**, on the other hand, are merely "children," *pueri* (Aug.), *infantes* (Vulg.), and the distinction is **ὅτι ἐγνώκατε τὸν Πατέρα.** All men are children of God, believers are children who "have got to know the Father'

Ver. 14. The Apostle gives the same reason as before for writing to the fathers, as though there could be none

πονηρόν. 15. μὴ ἀγαπᾶτε τὸν κόσμον, μηδὲ τὰ ἐν τῷ κόσμῳ· [m] ἐάν
τις ἀγαπᾷ τὸν κόσμον, οὐκ ἔστιν ἡ ἀγάπη τοῦ πατρὸς [1] ἐν αὐτῷ·
16. ὅτι πᾶν τὸ ἐν τῷ κόσμῳ, [n] ἡ ἐπιθυμία τῆς σαρκός, καὶ ἡ ἐπιθυμία
τῶν ὀφθαλμῶν, καὶ ἡ [o] ἀλαζονεία [2] τοῦ [p] βίου, οὐκ ἔστιν ἐκ τοῦ πατρός,
ἀλλ᾽ [3] [q] ἐκ τοῦ κόσμου ἐστί. 17. καὶ ὁ κόσμος [r] παράγεται, καὶ ἡ
ἐπιθυμία αὐτοῦ· ὁ δὲ [s] ποιῶν τὸ θέλημα τοῦ Θεοῦ, μένει εἰς τὸν αἰῶνα.

m James iv. 4. n Rom. xiii. 14; Gal. v. 16. 24; Eph. ii. 3; 1 Peter ii. 11; 2 Peter ii. 10, 18; 2 Peter ii. 14; Mark iv. 19. o James iv. 16; Rom. i. 30; 2 Tim. iii. 2 (ἀλαζών). p Luke viii. 14; 2 Tim. ii. 4 q iv. 5; John viii. 23, xv. 19. r Ver. 8 reff. s John iv. 34; Matt. vii. 21, xxiv. 39; 1 Peter iv. 2.

[1] **του πατρος** ℵBKLP, Syr vg ph, Vg., Cop., Sah., Arm., Aug., edd.; **του θεου** AC, several minusc., Aeth.; **του θεου και πατρος**, several minusc.

[2] **αλαζονεια** B³K; **αλαζονια** ℵAB*LP, edd. [3] **αλλ** ℵAKL; **αλλα** BC, edd.

greater. He gives the same reason also for writing to the young men, but he amplifies it: they have the strength of youth, but it is disciplined by the in-dwelling Word, and therefore they have conquered.

Ver. 15. He is dealing with believers who have a large experience of the grace of Christ, and on this fact he proceeds to base an appeal, a call to further advancement and higher attainment: "Love not the world". Yet God "loved the world" (John iii. 16). Observe that the Apostle does not say that the world is evil. It is God's world, and "God saw every thing that He had made, and, behold, it was very good" (Gen. i. 31). His meaning is: "The things in the world are transient. Do not set your affection on them, else you will sustain a bitter disappointment. The world is a good and beautiful gift of God, to be used with joy and gratitude; but it is not the supreme end, it is not the home of our souls". "Let the Spirit of God be in thee," says St. Augustine, "that thou mayest see that all these things are good; but woe to thee if thou love created things and forsake the Creator! . . . If a bridegroom made a ring for his bride and, when she got it, she were fonder of the ring than of the bridegroom who made the ring for her, would not an adulterous spirit be detected in the very gift of the bridegroom, however she might love what the bridegroom gave? . . . God gave thee all those things: love Him who made them. There is more which He would fain give thee, to wit, Himself who made these things". Again: "There are two loves—of the world and of God. If the love of the world inhabit, there is no way for the love of God to enter. Let the love of the world retire and that of God inhabit, let the better get room. . . . Shut out the evil love of the world, that thou mayest be filled by the love of God. Thou art a vessel, but thou art still full; pour out what thou hast, that thou mayest get what thou hast not". **ἡ ἀγάπη τοῦ Πατρός**, like **ἡ ἀγάπη τοῦ Θεοῦ** (ver. 5), either (1) "love for the Father," in antithesis to **ἀγαπᾷ τὸν κόσμον**, or (2) "the love which the Father feels for us". In fact the one implies the other. The sense of the Father's love for us awakens in us an answering love for Him. *Cf.* iv. 19.

Ver. 16. **ἡ ἐπιθυμία τῆς σαρκός**, not object. gen. (Aug.: "desiderium earum rerum quæ pertinent ad carnem, sicut cibus et concubitus, et cætera hujusmodi,") but subject.: "the lust which the flesh feels, which resides in the flesh". *Cf.* **ἡ ἐπιθυμία τῶν ὀφθαλμῶν. ἀλαζονία**, vain pretension, claiming what one really has not. *Def. Plat.*: **ἕξις προσποιητικὴ ἀγαθοῦ ἢ ἀγαθῶν τῶν μὴ ὑπαρχόντων.** Suid.: **ἀλαζόνας τοὺς ψεύστας ἐκάλουν, ἐπεὶ λέγειν ἐπαγγέλλονται περὶ ὧν μὴ ἴσασιν.** Theophr. *Char.* vi.: **προσδοκία τις ἀγαθῶν οὐκ ὄντων. ζωή**, the vital principle (*vita qua vivimus*), **βίος**, the outward life (*vita quam vivimus*) or livelihood (*victus*). There is here a summary of all possible sins, exemplified in the temptations of Eve (Gen. iii. 1-6) and our Lord (Matt. iv. 1-11). *Cf.* Aug.; Lightfoot, *Hor. Heb.*, on Matt. iv. 1. (1) "The lust of the flesh": *cf.* "The tree was good for food"; "Command that these stones become loaves". (2) "The lust of the eyes": *cf.* "It was a delight to the eyes"; "Cast thyself down"—a spectacular display. (3) "The braggart boast of life": *cf.* "The tree was to be desired to make one wise": "All the kingdoms of the world and the glory of them".

Ver. 17. An explanation, especially of **ἡ ἀλαζονία τοῦ βίου.** To set one's affection on the things in the world is "braggart boasting"; for they are not ours, they are transient. *Cf.* Mohammed: "What have I to do with the

18. [t] Παιδία, [u] ἐσχάτη [v] ὥρα ἐστί· καὶ καθὼς [w] ἠκούσατε ὅτι [1] ὁ [2] [x] ἀντίχριστος [y] ἔρχεται, καὶ νῦν ἀντίχριστοι πολλοὶ γεγόνασιν· [z] ὅθεν

t Ver. 13 reff. u John vi. 39, 40, 44, 54, xi. 24; Acts ii. 17; 1 Cor. xv. 52; 2 Tim. iii. 1; James v. 1; 1 Peter i. 5; 2 Peter iii. 3. v John v. 28. w Matt. xxiv. 5, 24. x Ver. 22, iv. 3; 3 John 7. y John iv. 25. z Acts xxvi. 19; Heb. ii. 17, iii. 1, vii. 25, ix. 18.

[1] **οτι** ℵBCKP, Syr[vg ph], Vg., Cop., Aug., edd.; om. AL, several minusc.

[2] **ο** ℵ[c]AKL; om. ℵ*BC, Arm., edd.

comforts of this life? The world and I—what connection is there between us? Verily the world is no otherwise than as a tree unto me: when the traveller hath rested under its shade, he passeth on." Aug. on iv. 4: "Mundus iste omnibus fidelibus quærentibus, patriam sic est, quomodo fuit eremus populo Israel". **αὐτοῦ**, subjective genitive like **σαρκός** and **ὀφθαλμῶν**. **τὸ θέλημα τοῦ Θεοῦ**, alone permanent amid the flux of transitory things. *Cf.* Aug.: "Rerum temporalium fluvius trahit: sed tanquam circa fluvium arbor nata est Dominus noster Jesus Christus. Assumpsit carnem, mortuus est, resurrexit, ascendit in cœlum. Voluit se quodammodo circa fluvium temporalium plantare. Raperis in praeceps? tene lignum. Volvit te amor mundi? tene Christum."

Vv. 18-29. A Warning against Heretical Teaching. "Little ones, it is the last hour; and, as ye heard that Antichrist is coming, even now have many antichrists arisen; whence we recognise that it is the last hour. From our company they went out, but they were not of our company; for, if they had been of our company, they would have abode in our fellowship; but the purpose of it was that it may be manifested that they all are not of our company. And *ye* have a chrism from the Holy One, and ye all know. I did not write to you because ye did not know the Truth, but because ye know it and because every lie is not of the Truth. Who is the liar but he that denieth that Jesus is the Christ? This is the Antichrist—he that denieth the Father and the Son. Every one that denieth the Son neither hath he the Father; he that confesseth the Son hath the Father also. As for you, that which ye heard from the beginning, let it abide in you. If that abide in you which ye heard from the beginning, ye also in the Son and in the Father will abide. And this is the promise which He Himself promised us—the Life, the Eternal Life. These things I wrote to you regarding them that would lead you astray. And as for you, the chrism which ye received from Him abideth in you, and ye have no need that any one should teach you; but, as His chrism is teaching you regarding all things, and is true and is not a lie, and even as it taught you, abide in Him. And now, little children, abide in Him, that, if He be manifested, we may have boldness and not be shamed away from Him at His advent. If ye know that He is righteous, recognise that every one also that doeth righteousness hath been begotten of Him."

A heresy had arisen in the bosom of the Church (see Introd. pp. 156 f.). It was a fatal heresy, a denial of the possibility of the Incarnation, and therefore of the relation of fatherhood and sonship between God and man. St. John's emphatic condemnation of it was justified, but his apprehension was groundless. He shared the prevailing expectation of the imminence of the Second Advent (*cf.* 1 Cor. x. 11, xv. 51; Phil. iv. 5; 1 Thess. iv. 15 *sqq.*; Heb. x. 25; James v. 8; 1 Peter iv. 7; Rev. i. 1, 3, iii. 11, xxii. 7, 10, 12, 20), and saw in the heresy an evidence that the end was at hand. It was rather an evidence that the Gospel was winning its way. The era of simple and unquestioning faith in the apostolic testimony was past, and men were beginning to enquire and reason. A heresy has the same use in theology as a mistaken hypothesis in science: it provokes thought and leads to a deeper understanding. What seemed to the Apostle the pangs of dissolution were in reality "growing pains".

Ver. 18. Aug.: "Pueros alloquitur, ut festinent crescere, quia novissima hora est. . . . Proficite, currite, crescite, novissima hora est". Ver. 28 puts it beyond doubt that **ἐσχάτη ὥρα** means "the end of the world," and rules out various attempts which have been made to give it another reference and absolve the Apostle from the current misconception: (1) Aug. says vaguely: "the last hour is of long duration, yet it is the last" (*novissima hora diuturna est; tamen novissima est*). And Calv.: "Nothing any longer remains but that Christ should appear for the redemption of the world. . . . He calls that 'the last time' in which all things are being so completed that nothing is left except the last revelation of Christ". (2) Lightfoot, *Hor. Heb.*, on

γινώσκομεν ὅτι ἐσχάτη ὥρα ἐστίν. 19. [a] Ἐξ ἡμῶν ἐξῆλθον,[1] ἀλλ'
οὐκ ἦσαν [b] ἐξ ἡμῶν· εἰ γὰρ ἦσαν ἐξ ἡμῶν,[2] μεμενήκεισαν ἂν [c] μεθ' ἡμῶν·
ἀλλ' [d] ἵνα [e] φανερωθῶσιν ὅτι οὐκ εἰσὶ πάντες ἐξ ἡμῶν. 20. Καὶ ὑμεῖς
[f] χρίσμα [3] ἔχετε ἀπὸ [g] τοῦ ἁγίου, καὶ [h] οἴδατε πάντα.[4] 21. οὐκ ἔγραψα

a Acts xv. 24, xx. 30. b John iii. 1. c Matt. i. 23, xxvi. 29, 38, 58, 69; Acts i. 26. d 1 Cor. xi. 19. e John iii. 21; 2 Cor. iii. 3. f Ver. 27. g *Cf.* Comm. h 1 Cor. ii. 15.

[1] **εξηλθον** ℵKLP; **εξηλθαν** ABC, edd.

[2] **ησαν εξ ημων** ℵAKLP, Tisch.; **εξ ημων ησαν** BC, WH, Nest.

[3] **χρίσμα** WH; **χρῖσμα** Tisch., Nest.; *cf. v.* 27.

[4] **παντα** ACKL, Syr[vg] (understanding **πάντα ἄνθρωπον**) [ph], Vg., Cop., Aeth., Arm.; **παντες** ℵBP, Sah., edd.

John xxi. 22, compares אַחֲרִית הַיָּמִים *i.e.*, "the last times of the Jewish city, nation, and dispensation," and remarks: "Gens ista vergit jam quam proxime in ruinam, cum enatus jam sit ultimus et summus apex infidelitatis, apostasiæ et nequitiæ". (3) Beng. with unwonted ineptitude: The advanced age of St. John and his contemporaries in contrast to his "little children". "*Ultima*, non respectu omnium mundi temporum: sed in antitheto *puerulorum* ad *patres*, et ad *juvenes*". (4) Westcott: "a last hour," *i.e.*, "a period of critical change". This is possible but improbable. The omission of the def. art. in the pred. is regular. **Ἀντίχριστος** (anarthrous) is a proper name. Nowhere in N.T. but in the Johannine Epp. It may mean (1), on the analogy of **ἀντιφιλόσοφος, ἀντικάτων, ἀντικείμενος, ἀντίθεσις**, "adversary of Christ," *Widerchrist* (Luth.); *cf.* Orig. *C. Cels.* vi. 45: **τὸν τούτῳ κατὰ διάμετρον ἐναντίον,** Tert. *De Praescript. Hær.*: "antichristi, Christi rebelles," Aug.: "Latine Antichristus contrarius est Christo"; (2), on the analogy of **ἀντιβασιλεύς, ἀνθύπατος** (*proconsul*), "antipope," a "rival of Christ," usurping His name, a **ψευδόχριστος** (*cf.* Matt. xxiv. 24 = Mark xiii. 22); *cf.* Aristoph. *Eq.* 1038 *sq.*: **ἐγὼ γὰρ ἀντὶ τοῦ λέοντός εἰμί σοι. / καὶ πῶς μ' ἐλελήθης Ἀντιλέων γεγενημένος;** St. John seems to combine both ideas. The heresy arose in the bosom of the Church and claimed to be an enlightened Christianity; yet, while calling themselves Christians, Cerinthus and his followers were adversaries of Christ. Wetst.: "Qui se pro Christo gerit, ideoque ei contrarius est". **ἀντίχριστοι πολλοί,** the exponents and representatives of the antichristian movement were a numerous party. **γεγόνασιν,** "have arisen," in contrast to the true Christ who "was in the beginning". *Cf.* the contrast between the Word and the Baptist in John i. 1, 6.

Ver. 19. *Cf.* Aug.: "Sic sunt in corpore Christi quomodo humores mali. Quando evomuntur, tunc relevatur corpus: sic et mali quando exeunt, tunc Ecclesia relevatur. Et dicit quando eos evomit atque projicit corpus: Ex me exierunt umores isti, sed non erant ex me. Quid est, non erant ex me? Non de carne mea præcisi sunt, sed pectus mihi premebant cum inessent". **ἵνα,** sc. **ἐξῆλθαν** or **γέγονε τοῦτο**—a frequent Johannine ellipse: *cf.* John i. 8, ix. 3, xiii. 18, xv. 25.

Ver. 20. An expression of confidence in his readers: they will not be led astray; they have received "a chrism," the enlightening grace of the Holy Spirit, "which He poured forth upon us richly through Jesus Christ our Saviour" (Tit. iii. 6). Baptism was called **χρῖσμα** in later days (Greg. Naz. *Orat.* xl. 4) because of the rite of baptismal anointing (*cf.* Tert. *De Bapt.* 7: "Exinde egressi de lavacro perungimur benedicta unctione de pristina disciplina, qua ungi oleo de cornu in sacerdotium solebant"; Aug.: "Unctio spiritalis ipse Spiritus sanctus est, cujus sacramentum est in unctione visibili"); but there is no reference here to this rite, which was of a later date and was derived from our passage. **χρῖσμα** is suggested by **ἀντίχριστοι.** "They are **ἀντίχριστοι,** you are **χριστοί.**" *Cf.* Ps. cv. (civ. LXX) 15: **μὴ ἅψησθε τῶν χριστῶν μου. τοῦ Ἁγίου,** not the Holy Spirit. St. John has **τὸ Πνεῦμα** in Epp. and Rev., but never **τὸ Πνεῦμα τὸ Ἅγιον.** Either (1) Christ (*cf.* Rev. iii. 7) or (2) God the Father (*cf.* Acts x. 38; Heb. i. 9). The latter is preferable. The Spirit **παρὰ τοῦ Πατρὸς ἐκπορεύεται** (John xv. 26)—from (**ἀπό**) the Father through (**διά**) Christ (*cf.* Tit. iii. 6).

Ver. 21. **ἔγραψα,** "I wrote," may refer to the Gospel, which is an exposition of the Incarnation, **ἡ τοῦ Σωτῆρος ἡμῶν Ἰησοῦ Χριστοῦ ἔνσαρκος οἰκονομία** (*cf.* note on ver. 14); but more probably "aor. referring to the moment just past" (Jebb on Soph. *O.T.* 337). The aor. is appro-

ὑμῖν, [i] ὅτι οὐκ οἴδατε τὴν ἀλήθειαν, ἀλλ' ὅτι οἴδατε αὐτήν, καὶ ὅτι
πᾶν ψεῦδος [k] ἐκ τῆς ἀληθείας οὐκ ἔστι.[1] 22. Τίς ἐστιν ὁ [l] ψεύστης,
εἰ μὴ ὁ ἀρνούμενος ὅτι Ἰησοῦς [m] οὐκ ἔστιν ὁ Χριστός; οὗτός ἐστιν ὁ
ἀντίχριστος, ὁ ἀρνούμενος τὸν πατέρα καὶ τὸν υἱόν. 23. [n] πᾶς ὁ
ἀρνούμενος τὸν υἱόν, οὐδὲ τὸν πατέρα ἔχει.[2] 24. Ὑμεῖς οὖν[3] ὃ
ἠκούσατε [o] ἀπ' ἀρχῆς, ἐν ὑμῖν μενέτω. ἐὰν ἐν ὑμῖν μείνῃ ὃ ἀπ'
ἀρχῆς ἠκούσατε, [p] καὶ ὑμεῖς ἐν τῷ υἱῷ καὶ ἐν τῷ πατρὶ μενεῖτε.
25. καὶ αὕτη ἐστὶν [q] ἡ ἐπαγγελία, ἣν αὐτὸς ἐπηγγείλατο ἡμῖν, τὴν
ζωὴν τὴν αἰώνιον. 26. ταῦτα ἔγραψα ὑμῖν περὶ τῶν πλανώντων
ὑμᾶς. 27. Καὶ ὑμεῖς τὸ χρίσμα[4] ὃ ἐλάβετε ἀπ' αὐτοῦ, ἐν μῖν
μένει,[5] καὶ οὐ [s] χρείαν ἔχετε ἵνα τις διδάσκῃ ὑμᾶς· ἀλλ' ὡς [t] τὸ[6] αὐτὸ[7]
χρίσμα[8] διδάσκει ὑμᾶς περὶ πάντων, καὶ ἀληθές ἐστι, καὶ οὐκ ἔστι

i 2 Peter 12.
k Ver. 16.
l ii. 4.
m Luke xx. 27; Gal. v. 7.
n iv. 15; John v. 23, xv. 23.
o Ver. 7.
p John xv. 7, 23.
q Luke xxiv. 49; Acts i. 4; 1 Tim. iv. 8; 2 Tim. i. 1; Heb. iv. 1.
r i. 8 reff.
s Heb. v. 12.
t John xiv. 26; xvi. 13; Gal. i. 12; Heb. viii. 11 (Jer. xxxi. 34)

[1] **εστιν** edd.

[2] Add **ὁ ὁμολογῶν τὸν υἱὸν καὶ τὸν πατέρα ἔχει** ℵABCP, many minusc., Syrvg ph. Vg., Cop., Sah., Aeth., Arm., Aug., edd.

[3] **ουν** om. ℵABCP, Syrph, Vg., Arm., edd.

[4] **χαρισμα** B.

[5] **μενει εν υμιν** ℵABCP, Vg., Cop., Sah., Aeth., Arm., edd.

[6] **αλλ ως το** ℵACKLP, Vg., Sah., edd.; **αλλα το** B, Aeth.

[7] **αυτο** AKL, Cop.; **αυτου** ℵBCP, Syrvg ph, Vg., Sah., Aeth., Arm., Aug., edd.

[8] **πνευμα** ℵ*, Cop., Aeth.

priate. No sooner has he spoken of the antichrists than he hastens to reiterate his assurance of confidence in his readers. **τὴν ἀλήθειαν**, see note on i. 8. **ἐκ**, of parentage (*cf.* iii. 8-10). His readers had only to be reminded of their experience (**οἴδατε**), and it would keep them from being led astray. An experience is an anchor to the soul in time of storm. "Tell me," said the dying Cromwell to a minister, "is it possible to fall from grace?" "No, it is not possible." "Then I am safe, for I know that I was once in grace" (Morley's *Oliver Cromwell*, V. x.).

Ver. 22. **ψεύστης**, *cf.* n. on i. 6. The Cerinthian distinction between Jesus and the Christ was a denial of the possibility of the Incarnation, *i.e.*, of the filial relation of man to God. **οὐκ** in dependent clause after **ἀρνεῖσθαι** is a common Gk. idiom, not unknown in English; *cf.* Shakespeare, *Comedy of Errors*, IV. ii. 7: "He denied you had in him no right".

Ver. 23. Since the Father is manifested and interpreted in the Son. *Cf.* John i. 18, xiv. 9.

Ver. 24. **ἀπ' ἀρχῆς**, as in ver. 7. The significant iteration of **μένειν** is lost in A.V. ("abide . . . remain . . . continue"). **ἐν τῷ Υἱῷ καὶ ἐν τῷ Πατρί**: observe the order. The Son is the manifestation of the Father; through Him we reach the Unseen Father (*cf.* John xiv. 9).

Ver. 25. **ἐπαγγελία**, *repromissio*, "promise"; only here in the Johannine writings (see note on i. 5). **αὐτός**, *i.e.*, the Father. God is the Promiser, and His promises are made in Christ (*cf.* 2 Cor. i. 20).

Ver. 26. **ἔγραψα**, see note on ver. 21. **τῶν πλανώντων**, the heretical teachers. Pres. partic., "are leading astray" but unsuccessfully.

Ver. 27. The ground of the Apostle's confidence in his readers. They need not be taught but only reminded. **ἀλλ' ὡς, κ.τ.λ.**, a single sentence with one apodosis. Vulg. makes it a double sentence with two apodoses: "as His chrism is teaching you regarding all things, it is indeed true and is not a lie; and even as it taught you, abide in Him". Reading **ἀλλά**, translate: "ye have no need that any one should teach you, but His chrism is teaching you . . . a lie; and even as, etc." **διδάσκει**, of the continued teaching by the grace of the Spirit; **ἐδίδαξεν**, of the illumination at the hour of conversion. **μένετε**, plainly imperat. in next ver., can hardly be indicat. here ("ye are abiding"). The reading **μενεῖτε** ("ye shall abide") would express the Apostle's confidence in the steadfastness of his

ψεῦδος · καὶ καθὼς ἐδίδαξεν ὑμᾶς, μενεῖτε [1] ἐν αὐτῷ. 28. [u] Καὶ νῦν,
τεκνία, μένετε ἐν αὐτῷ · ἵνα ὅταν [2] [v] φανερωθῇ, ἔχωμεν [3] [w] παρρησίαν,
καὶ μὴ [x] αἰσχυνθῶμεν ἀπ' αὐτοῦ, ἐν τῇ [y] παρουσίᾳ αὐτοῦ. 29. [z] ἐὰν
εἰδῆτε ὅτι δίκαιός ἐστι, [a] γινώσκετε ὅτι [4] πᾶς ὁ ποιῶν τὴν δικαιοσύνην,
ἐξ αὐτοῦ γεγέννηται.

III. 1. [a] Ἴδετε ποταπὴν ἀγάπην δέδωκεν [5] ἡμῖν ὁ πατήρ, ἵνα
τέκνα Θεοῦ [b] κληθῶμεν [6] · διὰ τοῦτο ὁ κόσμος οὐ γινώσκει ἡμᾶς, ὅτι

u John xvii. 5.
v i. 2; John i. 31, xxi. 1, 14; Col. iii. 4; 1 Peter v. 4.
w iii. 21, iv. 17, v. 14; Eph. iii. 12; Heb. iv. 16, x. 19.
x Mark viii. 38; Rev. iii. 18.
y Matt. xxiv. 3, 27, 39; 1 Cor xv. 23; 1 Thess. ii. 19; iii. 13.
z Phil. ii. 1.
a John xv. 18.
a Matt. viii. 27; Mark xiii. 1; Luke i. 29, vii. 39; 2 Peter iii. 11.
b Matt. v. 9, xxiii. 7, 8, 9, xxvii. 8; Luke i. 32, 35; John i. 43.

[1] **μενειτε** KL; **μενετε** ℵABCP, many minusc., Syrvg ph, Vg., Cop., Sah., Aeth., Arm., Aug., edd.

[2] **οταν** KL, Syrvg ph, Vg., Aug.; **εαν** ℵABCP, Cop., Sah., Arm., edd.

[3] **εχωμεν** ℵ*KL; **σχωμεν** ℵcBCP, edd.

[4] **οτι** BKL, Syrph, Cop., Aeth., Arm., Aug., WH; **οτι και** ℵACP, Syrvg, Vg. Sah., Tisch., Nest.

[5] **δεδωκεν** ℵABCKP, edd.; **εδωκεν** AL.

[6] **κληθωμεν και εσμεν** ℵABCP, Syrvg, Vg. (*et simus*), Cop., Sah., Aeth., Arm., edd.

readers, like "England expects every man to do his duty". *Cf.* Matt. v. 48: **ἔσεσθε οὖν ὑμεῖς τέλειοι. ἐν αὐτῷ**, *in eo* (Vulg), "in Him," *i.e.*, in Christ and therefore in God (*cf.* ver. 24). According to Aug., "in it," *i.e.*, the chrism, *unctio* (*permanete in ipsa*).

Ver. 28. **καὶ νῦν**, continuing and reinforcing the exhortation. **ἐὰν φανερωθῇ**: the uncertainty is not in the manifestation but in the time of it, and this is the reason for steadfast abiding in Him. *Cf.* unwritten saying of Jesus: **ἐφ' οἷς γὰρ ἂν εὕρω ὑμᾶς, φησὶν, ἐπὶ τούτοις καὶ κρινῶ. σχῶμεν**, aor. marking the suddenness of the crisis. **παρρησία**, properly "freedom of speech" (*cf.* Mark viii. 2; John vii. 13, xvi. 29, xviii. 20; Acts ii. 29, iv. 29, 31, xxviii. 31); then "confidence," "boldness," especially before God (*cf.* Heb. iv. 16; 1 John iii. 21, iv. 17, v. 14), the attitude of children to their father in contrast with that of slaves to their master (*cf.* Sen. *Ep.* xlvii.: "Infelicibus servis movere labra ne in hoc quidem ut loquantur licet. Virga murmur omne compescitur: . . . nocte tota jejuni mutique perstant"). **καὶ μὴ αἰσχυνθῶμεν**, in contrast to **σχῶμεν παρρησίαν. παρουσία**, frequent in N.T. but only here in the Johannine writings. Not simply "presence" but "arrival," "advent" (*adventus*); *cf.* Luke xiii. 1: **παρῆσαν**, Matt. xi. 50, John xi. 28.

Ver. 29. In view of the preceding verse **δίκαιος** must refer to Christ (*cf.* ii. 1), and it is equally certain that **ἐξ αὐτοῦ** refers to the Father, since "begotten of Christ" (*cf.* Tennyson s "our fair father Christ") is not a Scriptural idea. The abrupt transition evinces St. John's sense of the oneness of the Father and the Son (*cf.* ver. 24; John x. 30). **γινώσκετε**, *scitote* (Vulg.), rather *cognoscite* (Calv.), "get to know," "recognise" (see note on ver. 3); perceive the blessed inference, appropriate your birthright. It enfeebles the sentence to take the verb as indicat.

Chapter III. Vv. 1-3. Our Present Dignity and Our Future Destiny. "See what unearthly love the Father hath given us, in order that we may be styled 'children of God'; and so we are. It is for this reason that the world doth not recognise us, because it did not recognise Him. Beloved, now are we children of God, and it was not yet manifested what we shall be. We know that, if it be manifested, we shall be like Him, because we shall see Him even as He is. And every one that hath this hope resting on Him purifieth himself even as the Lord is pure."

Ver. 1. St. John has been speaking of the salvation which Jesus has brought—His Propitiation and Advocacy, and he sees and would have his readers see in it an amazing expression of the love of God. *Cf.* John iii. 16. **ποταπός (ποδαπός)**, properly *cujas*, "of what country," though approximating in late Greek to **ποῖος**, *qualis*, "of what sort" (*cf.* Moulton, *Gram. of N.T. Gk.*, i. p. 95), retains something of its proper and original signification. The love of God in Christ is foreign to this world: "from what far realm? what unearthly love?" *Cf.* Matt. viii. 27: "What unearthly personage?" 2 Peter iii. 11: "How other-worldly". **ἵνα, κ.τ.λ.**, the purpose of this amazing

οὐκ ἔγνω αὐτόν. 2. ἀγαπητοί, νῦν [d] τέκνα Θεοῦ ἐσμεν, καὶ οὔπω [c] ἐφανερώθη τί ἐσόμεθα· οἴδαμεν δὲ [1] ὅτι [e] ἐὰν φανερωθῇ, ὅμοιοι αὐτῷ
ἐσόμεθα, ὅτι ὀψόμεθα αὐτὸν καθώς ἐστι. 3. Καὶ πᾶς ὁ ἔχων τὴν
ἐλπίδα ταύτην [f] ἐπ᾽ αὐτῷ, [g] ἁγνίζει ἑαυτόν, καθὼς ἐκεῖνος [h] ἁγνός ἐστι.

c John i. 26, xvi. 3, xvii. 25. d Rom. viii. 16, 17. e Col. iii. 4; 2 Cor. iii. 18; Phil. iii. 21; Exod. xxxiv. 29. f 1 Tim. iv. 10; Acts xxiv. 15; Col. iv. 27; Ps. lxxviii. 7, cxlvi. 5. g John xi. 55; Acts xxi. 24; James iv. 8; 1 Peter i. 22. h 2 Cor. xi. 2; 1 Tim. v. 22.

[1] δε om. ℵABCP, Syrph, Vg., Sah., Arm., edd.

gift; a wise, holy love, concerned for our highest good; not simply that we may be saved from suffering and loss but "in order that we may be styled 'children of God'". And we have not only the name but the character: "so we are". Vulg. and Aug. give *simus*, as though reading ὦμεν for ἐσμὲν: "that we should be styled and be". *Cf.* Aug.: "Nam qui vocantur et non sunt, quid illis prodest nomen ubi res non est? Quam multi vocantur medici, qui curare non norunt? quam multi vocantur vigiles, qui tota nocte dormiunt?" **διὰ τοῦτο**, not anticipative, of **ὅτι**, but retrospective: "for this reason," *viz.*, because we are children of God. **ὅτι** explains the inference: "(and no wonder) because it did not recognise Him," *i.e.* the Father as revealed in His Son (*cf.* note on ii. 29). We must accept what our high dignity as children of God involves in a world alienated from God. On **ὁ κόσμος** see note on ii. 15. *Cf.* Aug.: "Jam cum auditis mundum in mala significatione, non intelligatis nisi dilectores mundi. . . . Ambulabat et ipse Dominus Jesus Christus, in carne erat Deus, latebat in infirmitate. Et unde non est cognitus? Quia omnia peccata arguebat in hominibus. Illi amando delectationes peccatorum non agnoscebant Deum: amando quod febris suadebat, injuriam medico faciebant."

Ver. 2. Having spoken of our present dignity, the Apostle goes on to speak of our future destiny. The Incarnation manifested our standing as children of God, but "it was not yet manifested what we shall be". The aorist **ἐφανερώθη** (*cf.* **ἔγνω** in previous verse) refers to the historic manifestation in Jesus Christ. The N.T. says nothing definite about the nature of our future glory. With our present faculties we cannot conceive it. It must be experienced to be understood. Jesus simply assures us of the felicity of the Father's House, and bids us take His word for it (*cf.* John xiv. 2). **ἐὰν φανερωθῇ**, "if (*cf.* note on ii. 28) it may be manifested," taking up **οὔπω ἐφανερώθη**. This obvious connection is decisive against the rendering "if He shall be manifested" (*cf.* ii. 28; Col. iii. 4). **ὅτι, κ.τ.λ.**: What we shall be was not manifested, but this we know that we shall be like Him. And how do we know it? From His promise that "we shall see Him even as He is" (*cf.* John xvii. 24). The argument is two-fold: (1) Vision of God implies likeness to Him in character and affection (*cf.* Matt. v. 8); (2) the vision of God transfigures (*cf.* 2 Cor. iii. 18), even in this life.

"Ah! the Master is so fair,
  His smile so sweet to banished men,
That they who meet it unaware
  Can never rest on earth again."

And how will it be when we "see Him face to face" (1 Cor. xiii. 12)? St. Augustine expresses much of the Apostle's thought in a beautiful sentence: "Tota vita Christiani boni sanctum desiderium est".

Ver. 3. The duty which our destiny imposes. **ἐπ᾽ αὐτῷ**, "resting on Him," *i.e.*, on God as Father. *Cf.* Luke v. 5: **ἐπὶ τῷ ῥήματί σου**, "relying on Thy word". **ἐκεῖνος**, Christ; see note on ii. 6. **ἁγνός** also proves that the reference is to Christ. As distinguished from **ἅγιος**, which implies absolute and essential purity, it denotes purity maintained with effort and fearfulness amid defilements and allurements, especially carnal. *Cf.* Plat. *Def.*: **ἁγνεία εὐλάβεια τῶν πρὸς τοὺς θεοὺς ἁμαρτημάτων· τῆς θεοῦ τιμῆς κατὰ φύσιν θεραπεία.** Suid.: **ἐπίτασις σωφροσύνης.** God is called **ἅγιος** but never **ἁγνός**. Christ is **ἁγνός** because of His human experience. The duty of every one in view of his appearing before God, his presentation to the King, is **ἁγνίζειν ἑαυτόν**, like the worshippers before the Feast (John xi. 55), like the people before the Lord's manifestation at Sinai (Exod. xix. 10-11, LXX). It is his own work, not God's, or rather it is his and God's. *Cf.* Phil. ii. 12-13. Aug.: "Videte quemadmodum non abstulit liberum arbitrium, ut diceret, *castificat semetipsum*. Quis nos castificat nisi Deus? Sed Deus te nolentem non castificat. Ergo quod adjungis voluntatem tuam Deo, castificas teipsum."

4. Πᾶς ὁ ποιῶν τὴν ἁμαρτίαν, καὶ [i] τὴν ἀνομίαν ποιεῖ· καὶ ἡ ἁμαρτία
ἐστὶν [k] ἡ ἀνομία. 5. καὶ οἴδατε ὅτι ἐκεῖνος [l] ἐφανερώθη, ἵνα τὰς
ἁμαρτίας ἡμῶν [1] [m] ἄρῃ· καὶ ἁμαρτία ἐν αὐτῷ οὐκ ἔστι. 6. πᾶς
ὁ [n] ἐν αὐτῷ μένων, [o] οὐχ ἁμαρτάνει· πᾶς ὁ ἁμαρτάνων, οὐχ ἑώρακεν
αὐτόν, οὐδὲ ἔγνωκεν αὐτόν. 7. Τεκνία,[2] μηδεὶς πλανάτω [p] ὑμᾶς·

i Matt. vii. 23, xiii. 41; Heb. x. 17 (Jer. xxxi. 34). k John i. 4; 1 Cor. xv. 56. l ii. 28 reff. m John i. 29; Col. ii. 14. n ii. 6 ref. o Rom. vi. 14. p i. 8 reff.

[1] **αμαρτιας ημων** ℵCKL, Syr[vg], Vg., Sah.; om. **ημων** ABP, Syr[ph], Cop., Aeth., Arm., Tert. (*de Pudic.* 19), Aug., edd.

[2] **τεκνια** ℵBKL, edd.; **παιδια** ACP, WH (marg.).

Vv. 4-12. The Obligation of our Dignity as Children of God. "Every one that doeth sin doeth also lawlessness; and sin is lawlessness. And ye know that He was manifested that He might take away the sins; and sin in Him there is not. Every one that abideth in Him doth not keep sinning; every one that keepeth sinning hath not seen Him nor got to know Him. Little children, let no one lead you astray: he that doeth righteousness is righteous, even as He is righteous; he that doeth sin is of the Devil, because from the beginning the Devil keepeth sinning. To this end was the Son of God manifested, that He might undo the works of the Devil. Every one that hath been begotten of God doeth not sin, because His seed in him abideth; and he cannot keep sinning, because of God he hath been begotten. Herein are manifest the children of God and the children of the Devil: every one that doeth not righteousness is not of God, and he that loveth not his brother. Because this is the message which ye heard from the beginning, that we love one another. Not as Cain was of the Evil One and slew his brother. And wherefore did he slay him? Because his works were evil, but his brother's righteous."

Vv. 4-8. The Incompatibility of Sonship with Continuance in Sin.

Ver. 4. **ὁ ποι. τὴν ἁμ.**, the converse of **ὁ ποι. τὴν δικ.** (ii. 29). **νόμος,** the revelation of God's will, the Father's requirement of His children, an expression of the true law of their nature. **ἡ ἁμ. ἐστ. ἡ ἀν.**: the article in both subject and predicate make "sin" and "lawlessness" convertible and co-extensive terms.

Ver. 5. The purpose of the Incarnation was to "take away the sins"—atone for the sins of the past and prevent sins in the future. **αἴρειν**, properly "lift up and carry away" (*cf.* Mark vi. 29; John ii. 16), but the idea of expiation is involved since it is "the Lamb of God" that "taketh away the sins". **ἐκεῖνος,** see note on ii. 6. **ἁμαρτία,** "sin," *i.e.* the sinful principle; see note on i. 8.

Ver. 6. This seems a stark contradiction of i. 8-ii. 2. (1) St. Augustine first limits the statement: "In quantum in ipso manet, in tantum non peccat," and then narrows the idea of "sin" by defining it as "not loving one's brother" (vers. 10). (2) St. Bernard (*De Nat. et Dign. Am. Div.* vi.) compares Rom. vii. 17, 20: "secundum hoc quod natus est ex Deo, id est secundum interioris hominis rationem, in tantum non peccat, in quantum peccatum quod corpus mortis foris operatur, odit potius quam approbat, semine spiritualis nativitatis quo ex Deo natus est eum interius conservante". (3) Romanists limit "sin" to "mortal sin". (4) Many commentators say that St. John is thinking only of the ideal. All these simply explain away the emphatic declaration. There is really no contradiction, and the Apostle's meaning appears when account is taken of the terms he employs with accurate precision. In the earlier passage he says that there is indwelling sin in the believer. The sinful principle (**ἁμαρτία**) remains, and it manifests its presence by lapses from holiness—occasional sins, definite, isolated acts of sin. This is the force of the aorists, **ἁμάρτητε, ἁμάρτῃ** in ii. 1. Here he uses the present **ἁμαρτάνειν** (varied by **ποιεῖν τὴν ἁμαρτίαν**) with the implication of *continuance in sin.* The distinction between present and aorist is well exemplified by Matt. vi. 11: **δὸς σήμερον** as contrasted with Luke xi. 3: **δίδου τὸ καθ' ἡμέραν**, and Matt. xiv. 22: **ἐμβῆναι . . . καὶ προάγειν.** The distinction was obvious to St. John's Greek readers, and they would feel no difficulty when he said, on the one hand: **ἐάν τις ἁμάρτῃ, Παράκλητον ἔχομεν**, and, on the other: **πᾶς ὁ ἁμαρτάνων οὐχ ἑώρακεν αὐτόν.** The believer may fall into sin but he will not walk in it. "Hath not seen Him," because he is "in the darkness" (*cf.* i. 5-7).

Ver. 7. An affectionate warning against Nicolaitan Antinomianism (*cf.* note on i. 6-7). The Apostle cuts away vain pretences by a sharp principle: a

ὁ [q] ποιῶν τὴν δικαιοσύνην, δίκαιός ἐστι, καθὼς ἐκεῖνος [r] δίκαιός
ἐστιν. 8. ὁ ποιῶν τὴν ἁμαρτίαν, [s] ἐκ τοῦ διαβόλου ἐστίν· ὅτι
[t] ἀπ' ἀρχῆς ὁ διάβολος ἁμαρτάνει. εἰς τοῦτο [u] ἐφανερώθη ὁ υἱὸς
τοῦ Θεοῦ, ἵνα [v] λύσῃ [w] τὰ ἔργα τοῦ διαβόλου. 9. πᾶς ὁ γεγεννημένος [x] ἐκ τοῦ Θεοῦ, ἁμαρτίαν οὐ ποιεῖ, ὅτι σπέρμα αὐτοῦ ἐν αὐτῷ
μένει· καὶ οὐ δύναται ἁμαρτάνειν, ὅτι ἐκ τοῦ Θεοῦ γεγέννηται.
10. ἐν τούτῳ [y] φανερά ἐστι τὰ τέκνα τοῦ Θεοῦ καὶ τὰ τέκνα τοῦ
διαβόλου. Πᾶς ὁ μὴ [z] ποιῶν δικαιοσύνην, οὐκ ἔστιν ἐκ τοῦ Θεοῦ,
καὶ ὁ μὴ ἀγαπῶν τὸν ἀδελφὸν αὐτοῦ. 11. ὅτι αὕτη ἐστὶν ἡ [a] ἀγγελία
ἣν [b] ἠκούσατε ἀπ' ἀρχῆς, ἵνα ἀγαπῶμεν ἀλλήλους· 12. οὐ καθὼς
[c] Κάϊν ἐκ [d] τοῦ πονηροῦ ἦν, καὶ [e] ἔσφαξε τὸν ἀδελφὸν αὐτοῦ· καὶ χάριν
τίνος ἔσφαξεν αὐτόν; ὅτι τὰ ἔργα αὐτοῦ πονηρὰ ἦν, τὰ δὲ τοῦ

q ii. 29, ver. 10.
r ii. 1 reff.
s iv. 7.
t John viii. 44.
u ii. 28 reff.
v *Cf.* comm.
w Matt. xi. 2; John vii. 7, ix. 3, 4, x. 37; Rom. xiii. 12; Gal. v. 19.
x iv. 7, v. 18.
y 1 Cor. iii. 13. xi. 19; Gal. v. 19.
z Ver. 7.
a i. 5.
b ii. 7; John xiii. 34, xv. 12.
c Gen. iv. 8.
d ii. 13 reff.
e Rev. v. 6, 9, 12, xiii. 3, 8, xviii. 24.

righteous character expresses itself in righteous conduct. Christ (**ἐκεῖνος**) is the type. He was "the Son of God," and if we are "children of God," we must be like Him.

Ver. 8. **ὁ ποι. τὴν ἁμ.**, an emphatic and interpretative variation of **ὁ ἁμαρτάνων**—"he that makes sin his business or practice". **ἐκ** of parentage (*cf.* vers. 9); "hoc est, ex patre diabolo" (Clem. Alex.). **ἀπ' ἀρχ.**, a vague phrase. In i. 1 "ere time began"; in ii. 7, iii. 11, "from the beginning of your Christian life". Here "from the beginning of his diabolic career"; "a quo peccare cœpit incontrovertibiliter in peccando perseverans" (Clem. Alex.). **λύσῃ**, "loose," metaphorically of "loosening a bond," "relaxing an obligation" (Matt. v. 19; John v. 18), "pulling to pieces" (John ii. 19).

Ver. 9. The Reason of the Impossibility of a Child of God continuing in Sin. The germ of the divine life has been implanted in our souls, and it grows—a gradual process and subject to occasional retardations, yet sure, attaining at length to full fruition. The believer's lapses into sin are like the mischances of the weather which hinder the seed's growth. The growth of a living seed may be checked temporarily; if there be no growth, there is no life. This is the distinction between **ἐάν τις ἁμάρτῃ** and **ὁ ἁμαρτάνων**. Alexander in Speaker's Comm. understands: "His seed," *i.e.*, whosoever is born of God (*cf.* Isa. liii. 10, lxvi. 22), "abideth in Him," *i.e.*, in God. This is Pauline but not Johannine. "He cannot keep sinning," as the seed cannot cease growing.

Vv. 10-12. The Evidence of Divine Sonship, *viz.*, Human Brotherhood.

Ver. 10. The Apostle reiterates the "old commandment" (ii. 7-11) as not only the paramount duty of believers but the evidence of their divine sonship. He has said that the evidence lies in "doing righteousness," and now he defines **ποιεῖν δικαιοσύνην** as **ἀγαπᾶν τὸν ἀδελφὸν αὐτοῦ.** See note on ii. 9. The "righteousness" of the Pharisees consisted in ritual observance, that of Jesus in love. **δίκαιος** had the meaning "kind," "sweetly reasonable". See Hatch, *Ess. in Bib. Gk.*, p. 50 ff. On Matt. i. 19 St. Chrysostom remarks: **δίκαιον ἐνταῦθα τὸν ἐνάρετον ἐν ἅπασι λέγει. ἔστι μὲν γὰρ δικαιοσύνη καὶ τὸ μὴ πλεονεκτεῖν· ἔστι δὲ καὶ ἡ καθόλου ἀρετή. . . . δίκαιος οὖν ὢν, τούτεστι χρηστὸς καὶ ἐπιεικής.**

Ver. 11. **ἵνα** ecbatic, expressing not the aim but simply the substance of the message. *Cf.* John xvii. 3. See Moulton's *Gram. of N.T. Gk.*, p. 206; Moulton's *Winer*, p. 425.

Ver. 12. **οὐ καθὼς, κ.τ.λ.**, a loose, almost ungrammatical expression, analogous to John vi. 58. Were there no **οὐ**, ver. 11 might be regarded as a parenthesis: "he that loveth not his brother, even as Cain was, etc.". The phrase is elliptical: "We must not hate our brethren, even as Cain was, etc.". **τοῦ πον.**, see note on ii. 18. **ἔσφαξεν**, a strong word, "slaughtered," "butchered," properly by cutting the throat (*jugulare*), like an ox in the shambles.

Vv. 13-24. The Secret of Assurance. "Wonder not, brethren, if the world hateth you. *We* know that we have migrated out of the domain of death into the domain of life, because we love the brethren. He that loveth not abideth in the domain of death. Everyone that

ἀδελφοῦ αὐτοῦ δίκαια. 13. μὴ [1] θαυμάζετε, ἀδελφοί μου,[2] εἰ [f] μισεῖ
ὑμᾶς ὁ κόσμος. 14. Ἡμεῖς οἴδαμεν ὅτι [g] μεταβεβήκαμεν ἐκ τοῦ
[h] θανάτου εἰς τὴν ζωήν, [i] ὅτι ἀγαπῶμεν τοὺς ἀδελφούς· ὁ μὴ ἀγαπῶν
τὸν ἀδελφόν,[3] μένει ἐν τῷ θανάτῳ. 15. πᾶς ὁ μισῶν τὸν ἀδελφὸν αὐτοῦ,[4] [k] ἀνθρωποκτόνος ἐστί· καὶ οἴδατε ὅτι πᾶς ἀνθρωποκτόνος
οὐκ ἔχει ζωὴν αἰώνιον ἐν αὐτῷ [5] μένουσαν. 16. Ἐν τούτῳ ἐγνώκαμεν τὴν ἀγάπην,[6] ὅτι [l] ἐκεῖνος ὑπὲρ ἡμῶν [m] τὴν ψυχὴν αὐτοῦ ἔθηκε·
καὶ ἡμεῖς [n] ὀφείλομεν ὑπὲρ τῶν ἀδελφῶν τὰς ψυχὰς τιθέναι.[7] 17.
ὃς δ' ἂν ἔχῃ τὸν [o] βίον τοῦ κόσμου, καὶ [p] θεωρῇ τὸν ἀδελφὸν αὐτοῦ

f John xv. 18, 19; Matt. v. 11.
g John v. 24.
h Matt. iv. 16.
i iv. 19.
k Only here and John viii. 44 in N.T.
l ii. 6.
m John x. 11, 15, 17, 18, xiii. 37, 38, xv. 13.
n ii. 6 reff.
o Mark xii. 44; Luke viii. 43; xv. 12, 30.
p John xvii. 24, xx. 6, 12, 14; Matt. xxvii. 55, xxviii. 1; Mark v. 15, 38; Luke x. 18.

[1] **μη** ABCKL, Syr[ph], Vg., Cop., Sah., Aug., WH, Nest.; **και μη** אC*P, Syr[vg], Aeth., Arm., Tisch.

[2] **μου** om. אABCP, Vg., Arm., Aug., edd.

[3] **τον αδελφον** om. אAB, Vg., Arm., Aug., edd.

[4] **εαυτου** B. [5] **εαυτω** אACLP, Tisch., WH (marg.); **αυτω** BK, WH, Nest.

[6] **την αγαπην του θεου** one minusc., Vg. [7] **θειναι** אABCP, edd.

hateth his brother is a murderer, and ye know that every murderer hath not life eternal abiding in him. Herein have we got to know love, because He laid down His life for us; and we are bound to lay down our lives for the brethren. But whosoever hath the world's goods, and beholdeth his brother in need, and locketh up his compassion from him, how doth the love of God abide in him? Little children, let us not love with word nor with the tongue, but in deed and truth. Herein shall we get to know that we are of the Truth, and in His presence shall assure our heart, whereinsoever our heart may condemn us, because greater is God than our heart, and He readeth everything. Beloved, if the heart condemn not, we have boldness toward God, and whatever we ask we receive from Him, because we observe His commandments and do the things that are pleasing in His sight. And this is His commandment, that we believe the name of His Son Jesus Christ and love one another, even as He gave a commandment to us. And he that observeth His commandments in Him abideth and He in him; and herein we get to know that He abideth in us—from the Spirit which He gave us."

Ver. 13. It is natural that the world (see notes on ii. 15, iii. 1) should hate those whose lives contradict its maxims and condemn its practices. St. John frequently addresses his readers as **τεκνία** and **ἀγαπητοί**, here only as **ἀδελφοί**. The term suits the context, where he enforces love of the brethren. It is no wonder if the world hate us, and its judgment is not decisive. Nevertheless our business is not to be hated by the world, but to commend Jesus to it and win it. We must not impute to the world's hostility to goodness the consequences of our own unamiability or tactlessness. "It is not martyrdom to pay bills that one has run into one's self" (Geo. Eliot).

Ver. 14. **ἡμεῖς** emphatic: "Whatever the world may say, *we* know". The test is not its hatred but our love. **μεταβεβήκαμεν**, "have migrated". The word is used of transition from one place to another (John vii. 3, xiii. 1), of passing from one form of government to another (Plat. *Rep.* 550 D), of the transmigration of souls (Luc. *Gall.* 4).

Ver. 15. An echo of the teaching of Jesus. See Matt. v. 21-22 and *cf.* Smith, *The Days of His Flesh*, pp. 96-98.

Ver. 16. **τὴν ἀγάπην**, "the thing called 'love'". The love of God in Christ Jesus our Lord is the perfect type. Till the world saw that, it never knew what love is. **ἐκεῖνος**, Christ; see note on ii. 6. **ἡμεῖς** emphatic, "we on our part". **ὀφείλομεν**, see note on ii. 6.

Ver. 17. Love must be practical. It is easy to "lay down one's life": martyrdom is heroic and exhilarating; the difficulty lies in doing the little things, facing day by day the petty sacrifices and self-denials which no one notices and no one applauds. **τὸν βίον τοῦ κόσμου**, "the livelihood of the world"; see note on ii. 16. **θεωρῇ**, *of a moving spectacle; cf.* Matt. xxvii. 55. **κλείσῃ**, *schliesst;* the metaphor is locking the chamber of the heart instead of flinging

[q]χρείαν ἔχοντα, καὶ [r]κλείσῃ τὰ [s]σπλάγχνα αὐτοῦ ἀπ' αὐτοῦ, [t]πῶς ἡ
ἀγάπη τοῦ Θεοῦ μένει ἐν αὐτῷ; 18. τεκνία μου,[1] μὴ ἀγαπῶμεν
[u]λόγῳ μηδὲ[2] γλώσσῃ, ἀλλ' ἔργῳ[3] καὶ ἀληθείᾳ. 19. Καὶ[4] ἐν
τούτῳ γινώσκομεν[5] ὅτι ἐκ τῆς ἀληθείας ἐσμέν, καὶ ἔμπροσθεν αὐτοῦ
πείσομεν τὰς καρδίας[6] ἡμῶν· 20. ὅτι[7] [v]ἐὰν καταγινώσκῃ ἡμῶν ἡ
καρδία, ὅτι[8] μείζων ἐστὶν ὁ Θεὸς[9] τῆς καρδίας ἡμῶν, καὶ γινώσκει

q Mark ii. 25; Eph. iv. 28.
r Matt. xxiii. 14, xxv. 10; Luke iv. 25; John xx. 19, 26.
s Luke i. 78; 2 Cor. vi. 12; Phil. i. 8, ii. 1.
t iv. 20; James ii. 15, 16.
u James i. 22, 23, 25.
v Mark vi. 23 (ὅ, τι ἐάν).

[1] μου om. ℵABCP, Syrph, Arm., Aug., edd.

[2] μηδε τη ABCKL, edd. [3] εν εργω ℵABCLP, Arm., edd.

[4] και ℵCKLP, Syrvg, Sah., Aeth., Arm., Tisch.; om. AB, Syrph, Vg., Cop., Aug., WH, Nest.

[5] γνωσομεθα ℵABCP, Cop., Sah., Arm., edd.

[6] τας καρδιας ℵA²CKLP, Syrph, Vg., Cop., Arm., Tisch.; την καρδιαν A*B, Syrvg, Sah., Aeth., Aug., WH, Nest.

[7] Punct. ημων ο τι.

[8] οτι om. A, several minusc., Vg., Cop., Sah., Aeth., Arm., Aug. [9] κυριος C.

it wide open and lavishing its treasures. **σπλάγχνα**, רַחֲמִים, *viscera*, "the inward parts," viewed by the ancients as the seat of the affections. *Cf.* Col. iii. 12: **σπλάγχνα οἰκτιρμοῦ**. **ἡ ἀγ. τ. Θ.**, "love for God" (objective genitive), inspired by and answering to the love which God feels (subjective genitive). *Cf.* note on ii. 5.

Ver. 18. Observe the transition from instrumental dative to preposition **ἐν**: "not with word and the tongue but in the midst of deed and truth"—not in empty air but amid tangible realities. *Cf.* Bunyan, *Good News*: "Practical love is best. Many love Christ with nothing but the lick of the tongue." Sheridan, *Sch. for Scand.* v. i.: "He appears to have as much speculative benevolence as any private gentleman in the kingdom, though he is seldom so sensual as to indulge himself in the exercise of it".

Vv. 19-20. A *crux interpretum*. Read **τὴν καρδίαν ἡμῶν ὅ, τι ἐάν** (*i.e.* **ἄν**), and take the subsequent **ὅτι** as "because". The foregoing exhortation may have awakened a misgiving in our minds: "Am I loving as I ought?" Our failures in duty and service rise up before us, and "our heart condemns us". So the Apostle furnishes a grand reassurance: "Herein shall we get to know that we are of the Truth, and in His presence shall assure our heart, whereinsoever our heart may condemn us, because, etc.". The reassurance is two-fold: (1) The worst that is in us is known to God (*cf.* Aug.: *Cor tuum abscondis ab homine; a Deo absconde si potes*), and still He cares for us and desires us. Our discovery has been an open secret to Him all along. (2) He "readeth everything"—sees the deepest things, and these are the real things. This is the true test of a man: Is the deepest that is in him the best? Is he better than he seems? His failures lie on the surface: is there a desire for goodness deep down in his soul? Is he glad to escape from superficial judgments and be judged by God who "readeth everything," who sees "with larger other eyes than ours, to make allowance for us all"? *Cf.* F. W. Robertson, *Lett.* lvi.: "I remember an anecdote of Thomas Scott having said to his curate, who was rather agitated on having to preach before him, 'Well, sir, why should you be afraid before me, when you are not afraid before God?' But how very easy it was to answer! He had only to say, God is not jealous, nor envious, nor censorious; besides, God can make allowances". So Browning:—

"Thoughts hardly to be packed
Into a narrow act,
Fancies that broke through language and
escaped;
All I could never be,
All, men ignored in me,
This, I was worth to God, whose wheel
the pitcher shaped."

ἔμπροσθεν αὐτοῦ, and what matter how we appear **ἔμπροσθεν τῶν ἀνθρώπων** (Matt. vi. 1.)? **πείσομεν**, "persuade," *i.e.* pacify, win the confidence, soothe the alarm, of our heart. *Cf.* Matt. xxviii. 14. Otherwise: "we shall persuade our heart . . . that greater is God". But

πάντα. 21. ἀγαπητοί, ἐὰν ἡ καρδία ἡμῶν[1] μὴ καταγινώσκῃ
ἡμῶν,[2] [w] παρρησίαν ἔχομεν πρὸς τὸν Θεόν, 22. καὶ [x] ὃ ἐὰν αἰτῶμεν,
λαμβάνομεν παρ'[3] αὐτοῦ, ὅτι τὰς ἐντολὰς αὐτοῦ τηροῦμεν, καὶ [y] τὰ
ἀρεστὰ [z] ἐνώπιον αὐτοῦ ποιοῦμεν. 23. καὶ αὕτη ἐστὶν ἡ ἐντολὴ
αὐτοῦ, ἵνα πιστεύσωμεν[4] τῷ ὀνόματι τοῦ υἱοῦ αὐτοῦ Ἰησοῦ Χριστοῦ,
καὶ ἀγαπῶμεν ἀλλήλους, [a] καθὼς ἔδωκεν ἐντολὴν ἡμῖν. 24. καὶ ὁ
τηρῶν τὰς ἐντολὰς αὐτοῦ, ἐν αὐτῷ μένει, καὶ αὐτὸς ἐν αὐτῷ. καὶ ἐν
τούτῳ γινώσκομεν ὅτι μένει ἐν ἡμῖν, [b] ἐκ τοῦ Πνεύματος οὗ ἡμῖν
ἔδωκεν.

IV. 1. Ἀγαπητοί, μὴ παντὶ πνεύματι πιστεύετε, ἀλλὰ [a] δοκιμάζετε

w ii. 28 reff. x John xiv. 13, 14, xv. 7, 16, xvi. 23. y John viii. 29. z Luke xii. 6, xv. 10, 18, xvi. 15; John xx. 30; Rom. iii. 20. a John vi. 29, xv. 17. b iv. 13; Rom. viii. 9. a Rom. ii. 18; 1 Cor. iii. 13, xi. 28; Gal. vi. 4; 1 Thess. v. 21.

[1] **ημων** ℵCKL, Syr$^{vg\ ph}$, Vg., Cop., Sah., Aeth., Arm., Tisch.; om. AB, several minusc., Aug., WH, Nest.

[2] **ημων** ℵAKL, Syr$^{vg\ ph}$, Vg., Cop., Sah., Aeth., Arm., Tisch.; om. BC, one minusc., WH, Nest.

[3] **απ** ℵABC, edd.

[4] **πιστευσωμεν** BKL, WH, Nest.; **πιστευωμεν** ℵAC, Tisch., WH (marg.).

how can love for the brethren yield this inference? **γινώσκει πάντα,** "readeth every secret". *Cf.* John ii. 25. A quite different and less satisfying sense is got by punctuating **τὴν καρδίαν ἡμῶν. ὅτι ἐάν, κ.τ.λ.** The second **ὅτι** is then a difficulty and has been dealt with in three ways: (1) It has been ignored as redundant: "For if our heart condemn us, God is greater, etc." (A.V. fortified by the omission of the participle in some inferior MSS.). (2) An ellipse has been assumed —either of the substantive verb: "because if our heart condemns us, (it is) because God, etc." (Alford), or of **δῆλον** (Field, who compares 1 Tim. vi. 7): "it is plain that God, etc.". (3) **ὅτι** has been conjecturally emended into **ἔτι** (Steph., Bez.): "still greater is God, etc.".

Vv. 21-22. **παρρησίαν,** see note on ii. 28. **ὃ ἐὰν αἰτῶμεν λαμβάνομεν,** though not always in the form we expect or desire; the answer may be different from but it is always better than our prayer. St. Augustine draws a distinction between the hearing of prayer "ad salutem" and "ad voluntatem," comparing the experience of St. Paul (2 Cor. xii. 7-9): "Rogasti, clamasti, ter clamasti: ipsum semel quod clamasti audivi, non averti aures meas a te; novi quid faciam; tu vis auferri medicamentum quo ureris; ego novi infirmitatem qua gravaris. Ergo iste ad salutem exauditus est, ad voluntatem non est exauditus. . . . Tu morbum confitearis, ille medicamentum adhibeat." *Cf.* Juan de Avila: "Go to prayer rather to hearken than to speak. Bend humbly and lovingly before God, expecting." **τηροῦμεν,** see note on ii. 3.

Ver. 23. *Cf.* our Lord's summary of the commandments in Matt. xxii. 34-40 = Mark xii. 28-31, and observe the apostolic narrowing of **τὸν πλησίον σου** (*cf.* Luke x. 29-37) to **ἀλλήλους,** *i.e.* **τοὺς ἀδελφούς** (see note on ii. 9). **τῷ ὀνόματι,** see note on ii. 12.

Ver. 24. **τὰς ἐντ. αὐτ.,** "the commandments of God," resuming ver. 22. *Cf.* iv. 15. **ἐκ,** the assurance is begotten of the Spirit; see note on ii. 21. **οὗ** for **ὅ**, by attraction to the case of the antecedent (*cf.* Luke ii. 20; Rev. xviii. 6). **ἔδωκεν,** "gave," *i.e.*, when first we believed. For the thought *cf.* 2 Cor. i. 21, 22; Eph. i. 13, 14; also Rom. viii. 15, 16.

Chapter IV.—Vv. 1-6. The Spirit of Truth and the Spirit of Error. "Beloved, believe not every spirit, but prove the spirits, whether they are from God; because many false prophets have gone forth into the world. Herein ye get to know the Spirit of God: every spirit which confesseth Jesus as Christ come in flesh, is from God: and every spirit which confesseth not Jesus, is not from God. And this is the spirit of the Antichrist, whereof ye heard that it is coming, and now it is in the world already. *Ye* are from God, little children, and have conquered them, because greater is He that is in you than he that is in the world. *They* are from the world; therefore from the world they talk, and the world hearkeneth to them. *We* are from

**τὰ πνεύματα, εἰ [b] ἐκ τοῦ Θεοῦ ἐστιν· ὅτι πολλοὶ [c] ψευδοπροφῆται
[d] ἐξεληλύθασιν εἰς τὸν κόσμον. 2. ἐν τούτῳ γινώσκετε [1] τὸ Πνεῦμα
τοῦ Θεοῦ· πᾶν πνεῦμα ὃ [e] ὁμολογεῖ Ἰησοῦν Χριστὸν ἐν σαρκὶ ἐληλυθότα,[2] ἐκ τοῦ Θεοῦ ἐστι. 3. καὶ πᾶν πνεῦμα ὃ μὴ ὁμολογεῖ [3] τὸν
Ἰησοῦν Χριστὸν [4] ἐν σαρκὶ ἐληλυθότα,[5] ἐκ τοῦ Θεοῦ οὐκ ἔστι· καὶ
τοῦτό ἐστι τὸ τοῦ ἀντιχρίστου, ὃ ἀκηκόατε ὅτι [f] ἔρχεται, καὶ νῦν ἐν**

b Ver. 2-6. *Cf.* comm.
c Matt. vii. 15, xxiv. 11, 24; Luke vi. 26; Acts xiii. 6.
d ii. 19; 3 John 7; John xiii. 3, xvi. 27, 28, 30, xvii. 8; 1 Cor. xiv. 36.
e John ix. 22; 2 John 7.
f ii. 18 reff.

[1] **γινωσκετε** ℵcABCL, Syrph, Cop., Sah., Aeth., edd.; **γινωσκεται** K, Syrvg, Vg., Aug.—an itacism.

[2] **εληλυθοτα** ℵACKL, edd.; **εληλυθεναι** B, Vg., WH (marg.).

[3] **μη ομολογει** all Gk. MSS. and all versions except Vg.; **λυει** Socr. *H. E.* vii. 32 (of Nestorius): **αὐτίκα γοῦν ἠγνόησεν ὅτι ἐν τῇ καθολικῇ Ἰωάννου ἐγέγραπτο ἐν τοῖς παλαιοῖς ἀντιγράφοις ὅτι πᾶν πνεῦμα ὃ λύει τὸν Ἰησοῦν ἀπὸ τοῦ θεοῦ οὐκ ἔστι. ταύτην γὰρ τὴν διάνοιαν ἐκ τῶν παλαιῶν ἀντιγράφων περιεῖλον οἱ χωρίζειν ἀπὸ τοῦ τῆς οἰκονομίας ἀνθρώπου βουλόμενοι τὴν θεότητα· διὸ καὶ οἱ παλαιοὶ ἑρμηνεῖς αὐτὸ τοῦτο ἐπεσημήναντο, ὥς τινες εἶεν ῥᾳδιουργήσαντες τὴν ἐπιστολήν, λύειν ἀπὸ τοῦ θεοῦ τὸν ἄνθρωπον θέλοντες.** Iren. III. xvii. 8: *et omnis spiritus qui solvit Iesum, non est ex Deo.* Orig. *in Matth. Comm. Ser.* 65 (Lomm. iv. p. 360). Vg.: *omnis spiritus qui solvit Iesum.* Aug.: *omnis spiritus qui solvit Christum* (after quoting *omnis spiritus qui non confitetur Jesus Christum in carne venisse*).

[4] **Χριστον** om. AB, Syrvg ph, Vg., Cop., Aeth., Arm., Iren., Orig., Socr., edd.; **κυριον** ℵ.

[5] **ἐν σαρκι εληλυθοτα** om. AB, Vg., Cop., Sah., Aeth., edd.

God; he that is getting to know God hearkeneth to us; one who is not from God, hearkeneth not to us. From this we get to know the Spirit of Truth and the spirit of error."

1. The Apostle has just said that the Spirit begets in us the assurance that God abideth in us. And this suggests a warning. The Cerinthian heresy also had much to say about "the spirit". It boasted a larger spirituality. Starting with the philosophical postulate of an irreconcilable antagonism between matter and spirit, it denied the possibility of the Incarnation and drew a distinction between Jesus and the Christ (see Introd., p. 157). Its spirit was not "the Spirit of Truth" but "a spirit of error," and thus the necessity arises of "proving the spirits". **δοκιμάζειν**, of "proving" or "testing" a coin (**νόμισμα**). If it stood the test, it was **δόκιμον** (*cf.* 2 Cor. x. 18); if it was found counterfeit (**κίβδηλον**), it was **ἀδόκιμον** (*cf.* 1 Cor. ix. 27; 2 Cor. xiii. 5-7). *Cf.* Jer. vi. 30 LXX: **ἀργύριον ἀποδεδοκιμασμένον . . . ὅτι ἀπεδοκίμασεν αὐτοὺς Κύριος. ἐκ**, here of *commission*, not *parentage*; "from God," as His messengers. *Cf.* John i. 24; xviii. 3; Soph., *O.C.*, 735-737: **ἀπεστάλην . . . οὐκ ἐξ ἑνὸς στείλαντος. πολλοί**: Cerinthus had a large following. **ἐξεληλ. εἰς τ. κόσμ.**, a monstrous reversal of John xvii. 18. They went forth from the Church into the world not to win but to deceive it.

2. The Test of the Spirits. **γινώσκετε**, as in ii. 29, may be either indicat. ("ye recognise") or, like **πιστεύετε, δοκιμάζετε**, imperat. ("recognise"). The former seems preferable. **ὁμολογεῖ Ἰησοῦν Χριστὸν ἐν σαρκὶ ἐληλυθότα**, "confesseth Jesus as Christ come in flesh," an accurate definition of the doctrine which the Cerinthian heresy denied. The argument is destroyed by the false variant **ἐληλυθέναι**, "confesseth that Jesus Christ hath come," *confitetur Jesum Christum in carne venisse* (Vulg.)

Ver. 3. The Test negatively expressed. Omit **Χριστὸν ἐν σαρκὶ ἐληλυθότα. τὸν Ἰησοῦν**, "the aforementioned Jesus," "Jesus as thus described". **μή** makes the statement hypothetical: "every spirit, if such there be, which doth not confess". The variant **λύει τὸν Ἰησοῦν**, *solvit Jesum* (Vulg., Aug.), "dissolveth" or "severeth Jesus," *i.e.*, separates the divinity and the humanity, aptly defines the Cerinthian heresy. It was much appealed to in later days against Nestorius. The ecclesiastical historian Socrates (see crit. note) says it was the primitive reading, and was altered by "those who wished to separate the deity from the man of the Incarnation". St. Augustine, defining heresy as schism due to lack of brotherly love, comments: "Ille venit

τῷ κόσμῳ ἐστὶν ἤδη. 4. Ὑμεῖς ἐκ τοῦ Θεοῦ ἐστε, τεκνία, καὶ
[g] νενικήκατε αὐτούς·[1] ὅτι μείζων ἐστὶν ὁ ἐν ὑμῖν ἢ [h] ὁ ἐν τῷ κόσμῳ.
5. Αὐτοὶ [i] ἐκ τοῦ κόσμου εἰσί· διὰ τοῦτο [k] ἐκ τοῦ κόσμου λαλοῦσι, καὶ
ὁ κόσμος αὐτῶν ἀκούει. 6. ἡμεῖς ἐκ τοῦ Θεοῦ ἐσμεν· ὁ γινώσκων
τὸν Θεόν, ἀκούει ἡμῶν· [l] ὃς οὐκ ἔστιν ἐκ τοῦ Θεοῦ, οὐκ ἀκούει ἡμῶν.
Ἐκ τούτου γινώσκομεν τὸ πνεῦμα τῆς ἀληθείας καὶ τὸ πνεῦμα τῆς
[m] πλάνης. 7. Ἀγαπητοί, [n] ἀγαπῶμεν ἀλλήλους· ὅτι ἡ ἀγάπη ἐκ τοῦ
Θεοῦ ἐστι, καὶ πᾶς ὁ ἀγαπῶν, [o] ἐκ τοῦ Θεοῦ γεγέννηται, καὶ γινώσκει

g John xvi. 33. h John xiv. 30. i ii. 16 reff. k John iii. 31, viii. 44. l John viii. 43, 47. m i. 8 reff; Matt. xxvii. 64; Eph. iv. 14; James v. 20. n ii. 7, iii. 11. o ii. 29, iii. 9.

[1] **αυτους** Aug. *eum.*, *i.e.*, *Antichristum.*

colligere, tu venis solvere. Distringere vis membra Christi. Quomodo non negas Christum in carne venisse, qui disrumpis Ecclesiam Dei, quam ille congregavit?" On the Antichrist see note on ii. 18. **ὃ ἀκηκόατε ὅτι ἔρχεται,** "which ye have heard that it is coming"—the regular Greek idiom. *Cf.* Luke iv. 34: **οἶδά σε τίς εἶ.**

Ver. 4. **ὑμεῖς** emphatic (*cf.* ii. 20, 27, iii. 14), as contrasted with the deluded world. The faithful are God's delegates (**ἐκ**), bearing their Master's commission and continuing His warfare (John xx. 21), and they have shared His victory (**νενικήκατε**). **αὐτοὺς**, *i.e.*, the false prophets (ver. 1). *Eum* (Vulg.); "Quem nisi Antichristum?" (Aug.). **ὁ ἐν ὑμῖν,** *i.e.*, God (*cf.* iii. 24); **ὁ ἐν τῷ κόσμῳ,** *i.e.*, **ὁ ἄρχων τοῦ κόσμου τούτου** (John xii. 31, xiv. 30).

Ver. 5. **αὐτοὶ** (as opposed to **ὑμεῖς**) **ἐκ τοῦ κόσμου εἰσίν,** as its delegates, messengers, representatives, and as such **ἐκ τοῦ κόσμου λαλοῦσιν. λαλεῖν,** not "speak" (**λέγειν**), but "talk," with a suggestion of prating (*cf.* John iv. 42). **ἀκούειν** takes accus. of the thing heard, genit. of the person from whom it is heard. *Cf.* Luke v. 1; Acts i. 4 (where both are combined). The world listens to those who speak its own language.

Ver. 6. Conversely, those who are getting to know God, understand the language of His messengers and listen to it. **ἐκ τούτου,** *i.e*, from their hearkening or not hearkening. Men's attitude to the message of the Incarnate Saviour ranks them on this side or on that—on God's side or the world's. Of course St. John does not ignore St. Paul's **ἀληθεύοντες ἐν ἀγάπῃ** (Eph. iv. 15). The message may be the truth and be rejected, not because of the hearers' worldliness, but because it is wrongly delivered—not graciously and winsomely. *Cf.* Rowland Hill's anecdote of the preaching barber who had made a wig for one of his hearers—badly made and nearly double the usual price. When anything particularly profitable escaped the lips of the preacher, the hearer would observe to himself: "Excellent! This should touch my heart; but oh, the wig!" **τῆς ἀληθείας,** see note on i. 8. **τὸ πν. τῆς πλάνης,** "the spirit that leadeth astray".

Vv. 7-21. The Blessedness of Love. "Beloved, let us love one another, because love is of God, and every one that loveth of God hath been begotten and is getting to know God. He that loveth not did not get to know God, because God is love. Herein was manifested the love of God in us, because His Son, His only-begotten, hath God commissioned into the world, that we may get life through Him. Herein is the love, not that *we* have loved God, but that *He* loved us and commissioned His Son as a propitiation for our sins.

"Beloved, if it was thus that God loved us, we also are bound to love one another. God—no one hath ever yet beheld Him: if we love one another, God abideth in us and His love is perfected in us. Herein we get to know that we abide in Him and He in us, because of His Spirit He hath given us. And we have beheld and testify that the Father hath commissioned the Son as Saviour of the world. Whosoever confesseth that Jesus is the Son of God, God in him abideth and he in God. And we have got to know and have believed the love which God hath in us.

"God is love, and he that abideth in love in God abideth, and God in him abideth. Herein hath love been perfected with us—so that we may have boldness in the Day of Judgment—because, even as He is, we also are in this world. Fear there is not in love, but the perfect love casteth out fear, because fear hath punishment; and he that feareth hath not been perfected in love. *We* love because *He* first loved *us*. If one say,

τὸν Θεόν· 8. ὁ μὴ ἀγαπῶν, [p] οὐκ ἔγνω τὸν Θεόν· ὅτι [q] ὁ Θεὸς ἀγάπη p ii. 3, 4,
ἐστίν. 9. Ἐν τούτῳ ἐφανερώθη ἡ ἀγάπη τοῦ Θεοῦ ἐν ἡμῖν, ὅτι τὸν iii. 23. q iv. 16.
υἱὸν αὐτοῦ τὸν [r] μονογενῆ [s] ἀπέσταλκεν ὁ Θεὸς εἰς τὸν κόσμον, ἵνα r John i. 14, 18, iii. 16,
ζήσωμεν δι' αὐτοῦ. 10. ἐν τούτῳ ἐστὶν ἡ ἀγάπη, [t] οὐχ ὅτι ἡμεῖς 18. s Matt. x.
ἠγαπήσαμεν[1] τὸν Θεόν, ἀλλ' ὅτι αὐτὸς ἠγάπησεν ἡμᾶς, καὶ ἀπέσ- 40; John iii. 17, xx.
τειλε τὸν υἱὸν αὐτοῦ [v] ἱλασμὸν περὶ τῶν ἁμαρτιῶν ἡμῶν. 11. ἀγαπη- 21. t John iii.
τοί, εἰ [w] οὕτως ὁ Θεὸς ἠγάπησεν ἡμᾶς, [x] καὶ ἡμεῖς [y] ὀφείλομεν ἀλλήλους 16. u Ver. 19. v ii. 2 reff.

w John iii. 16. x Rom. xiii. 8; Matt. xviii. 33; Rom. xv. 7; Eph. iv. 32; Col. iii. 13. y ii. 6 reff.

[1] ηγαπησαμεν ℵcKL, Tisch., WH (marg.)—an assimilation to the other aors.; ηγαπηκαμεν B, WH, Nest.

'I love God,' and hate his brother, he is a liar. For he that loveth not his brother whom he hath seen, God whom he hath not seen, he cannot love. And this commandment have we from Him, that he that loveth God love also his brother."

Ver. 7. St. John reiterates the "old commandment" (ii. 7-11). It is so all-important that he cares not though his readers be tired of hearing it. *Cf.* the anecdote which St. Jerome relates on Gal. vi. 10: "Beatus Joannes Evangelista cum Ephesi moraretur usque ad ultimam senectutem, et vix inter discipulorum manus ad Ecclesiam deferretur, nec posset in plura vocem verba contexere, nihil aliud per singulas solebat proferre collectas nisi hoc: Filioli, diligite alterutrum. Tandem discipuli et fratres qui aderant, tædio affecti quod eadem semper audirent, dixerunt: Magister, quare semper hoc loqueris? Qui respondit dignam Joanne sententiam: Quia præceptum Domini est, et si solum fiat, sufficit." Love is the divine nature, and those who love have been made partakers of the divine nature (2 Peter i. 4); and by the practice of love they "get to know God" more and more.

Ver. 8. Conversely, a stranger to love is a stranger to God. **οὐκ ἔγνω** "did not get to know," *i.e.*, at the initial crisis of conversion. On **μὴ** see note on ii. 4.

Ver. 9. The Incarnation is a manifestation of the love of God because it is a manifestation of the divine nature, and the divine nature is love. **ἐν ἡμῖν**, "in our souls"—an inward experience. *Cf.* Gal. i. 16: **ἀποκαλύψαι τὸν υἱὸν αὐτοῦ ἐν ἐμοί**. **μονογενῆ**, *cf.* Luke vii. 12, viii. 42, ix. 38. St. John applies the term exclusively to Jesus. It carries the idea of preciousness; *cf.* LXX Pss. xxii. 20, xxxv. 17, where יְחִידָתִי, "my dear life," is rendered **τὴν μονογενῆ μου**. **ἀπέσταλκεν**, "hath sent as an **ἀπόστολος**" (*cf.* Heb. iii. 1). An apostle is not simply *nuntius*, but *nuntius vices mittentis gerens*. *Cf. Bab. Ber.* 34, 2: "Apostolus cujusvis est sicut ipse a quo deputatur". The perf. is used here because the influence of the Incarnation is permanent. **ζήσωμεν**, ingressive or inceptive aor. *Cf.* Luke xv. 24, 32; Rev. xx. 4, 5. **ἵνα ζήσωμεν** reconciles **ἐφανερώθη ἡ ἀγάπη** with **ἡ ζωὴ ἐφανερώθη** (i. 2). The Incarnation manifested the love of God, and the love was manifested that we might get life. Eternal Life is not future but present: we get it here and now. *Cf.* John xvii. 3. Amiel: "The eternal life is not the future life; it is life in harmony with the true order of things—life in God".

Ver. 10. The love which proves us children of God is not native to our hearts. It is inspired by the amazing love of God manifested in the Incarnation—the infinite Sacrifice of His Son's life and death. Aug.: "Non illum dileximus prius: nam ad hoc nos dilexit, ut diligamus eum." **ἀπέστειλεν**: the aor. is used here because the Incarnation is regarded as a distinct event, a historic landmark.

Having inculcated love, the Apostle indicates two incentives thereto: (1) God's love for us imposes on us a moral obligation to love one another (11-16a); (2) If we have love in our hearts, fear is cast out (16b-18).

Ver. 11. Here, as in John iii. 16, **οὕτως** may denote either the extent or the manner of God's love—"to such an extent," going such a length (*cf.* Rom. viii. 32); "in such a manner," righteously, not by a facile amnesty but by a propitiation. **ὀφείλομεν**: see note on ii. 6. *Noblesse oblige.* If we are God's children, we must have our Father's spirit. *Cf.* Matt. v. 44-48. Thus we requite His love. Aug.: "*Petre*, inquit, *amas me?* Et ille dixit: *Amo. Pasce oves meas*" (John xxi. 15-17).

ἀγαπᾶν. 12. Θεὸν οὐδεὶς πώποτε τεθέαται· ἐὰν ἀγαπῶμεν ἀλλήλους, [a] ὁ Θεὸς ἐν ἡμῖν μένει, καὶ ἡ ἀγάπη αὐτοῦ [b] τετελειωμένη ἐστὶν
ἐν ἡμῖν.[1] 13. ἐν τούτῳ γινώσκομεν ὅτι ἐν αὐτῷ μένομεν, καὶ αὐτὸς
ἐν ἡμῖν, ὅτι [c] ἐκ τοῦ Πνεύματος αὐτοῦ δέδωκεν ἡμῖν.
14. Καὶ ἡμεῖς [d] τεθεάμεθα, καὶ [e] μαρτυροῦμεν ὅτι ὁ πατὴρ ἀπέσ-
ταλκε τὸν υἱὸν [f] σωτῆρα τοῦ κόσμου. 15. [g] ὃς ἂν ὁμολογήσῃ ὅτι
Ἰησοῦς ἐστιν ὁ υἱὸς τοῦ Θεοῦ, ὁ Θεὸς ἐν αὐτῷ μένει, καὶ αὐτὸς ἐν τῷ
Θεῷ. 16. Καὶ ἡμεῖς [h] ἐγνώκαμεν καὶ πεπιστεύκαμεν τὴν ἀγάπην ἣν
ἔχει ὁ Θεὸς [i] ἐν ἡμῖν. ὁ Θεὸς ἀγάπη ἐστί, καὶ ὁ μένων ἐν τῇ ἀγάπῃ,
[k] ἐν τῷ Θεῷ μένει, καὶ ὁ Θεὸς ἐν αὐτῷ.[2]
17. Ἐν τούτῳ [b] τετελείωται ἡ ἀγάπη μεθ' ἡμῶν, ἵνα [l] παρρησίαν
ἔχωμεν [m] ἐν τῇ ἡμέρᾳ τῆς κρίσεως, ὅτι [n] καθὼς ἐκεῖνός ἐστι, καὶ ἡμεῖς
ἐσμεν ἐν τῷ κόσμῳ τούτῳ. 18. φόβος οὐκ ἔστιν ἐν τῇ ἀγάπῃ, ἀλλ'
ἡ τελεία ἀγάπη [o] ἔξω βάλλει τὸν [p] φόβον, ὅτι ὁ φόβος [q] κόλασιν [r] ἔχει·
ὁ δὲ φοβούμενος οὐ [b] τετελείωται ἐν τῇ ἀγάπῃ. 19. [s] ἡμεῖς ἀγαπῶ-

z i. 1 ref.; John i. 18.
a Ver. 16, iii. 24.
b ii. 5 reff.
c iii. 24 reff.
d i. 1 ref.
e i. 2 reff.
f John iii. 17, iv. 42.
g Matt. xvi. 16, 17.
h John vi. 69.
i Ver. 9.
k Ver. 12.
l ii. 28 reff.
m Matt. x. 15, xi. 22, 24, xii. 36; 2 Peter ii. 9, iii. 7.
n John xx. 21.
o Matt. v. 13, xiii. 48; Luke xiv. 35.
p Rom. viii. 15; Heb. ii. 15.
q Matt. xxv. 46.
r James i. 4.
s Ver. 10.

[1] εν ημιν εστιν ℵB, edd.

[2] εν αυτω μενει ℵBKL, Syrph, Cop., Sah., Arm., Aug., Tisch., WH (brack.), Nest.

Ver. 12. "God—no one hath ever yet beheld Him". By and by "we shall see Him even as He is" (iii. 2), but even now, if we love, we are no strangers to Him: He abides and works in us. **τετελειωμένη**, "carried to its end"; see note on ii. 5.

Ver. 13. *Cf.* iii. 24. The argument is that God would not have granted us this priceless gift if he were not in intimate relation with us and had not a steadfast purpose of grace toward us.

Ver. 14. The apostolic testimony (*cf.* i. 1-3). **ἡμεῖς**, either the editorial "we" or "I and the rest of the Apostles who were eye-witnesses". **ἀπέσταλκεν**, see note on ver. 9.

Ver. 15. **ὁμολογήσῃ**, aor. of a definite confession born of persuasion. Such a conviction implies fellowship with God.

Ver. 16. **ἡμεῖς**, here "you and I," we believers. Observe the three stages: (1) "get to know" (**γινώσκειν**), (2) "believe" (**πιστεύειν**), (3) "confess" (**ὁμολογεῖν**). **ἐν ἡμῖν**, see note on ver. 9.

Another incentive to love: it casts out fear. **τῇ ἀγάπῃ**, "the love just mentioned". *Cf.* **τὸν φόβον, ὁ φόβος** (ver. 18).

Ver. 17. **τετελείωται**, *cf.* ver. 12. **μεθ' ἡμῶν**: love is a heavenly visitant sojourning with us and claiming observance. Love has been "carried to its end" when we are like Jesus, His visible representatives. **ὅτι** resumes **ἐν τούτῳ**, **ἵνα . . . κρίσεως** being parenthetical: "herein . . . because" (iii. 16, iv. 9, 10). **παρρησίαν**, see note on ii. 28. **ἐκεῖνος**, see note on ii. 6. **ἐστιν**, "is," not **ἦν**, "was". Jesus is in the world unseen, and our office is to make Him visible. We are to Him what He was to the Father in the days of His flesh—"Dei inaspecti aspectabilis imago".

Ver. 18. Bern.: "Amor reverentiam nescit". **φόβος**, the opposite of **παρρησία**. **κόλασιν ἔχει**, "implies punishment," the portion of slaves. The portion of slaves is punishment (**κόλασις**) and their spirit fear; the portion of sons is chastisement (**παιδεία**) and their spirit boldness (**παρρησία**). *Cf.* Heb. xii. 7, Clem. Alex.: "Perfectio fidelis hominis caritas est". Aug.: "Major charitas, minor timor; minor charitas, major timor". Bengel has here one of his untranslatable comments: "Varius hominum status: sine timore et amore; cum timore sine amore; cum timore et amore; sine timore cum amore".

Ver. 19. **ἀγαπῶμεν** has no accus. The thought is that the amazing love of God in Christ is the inspiration of all the love that stirs in our hearts. It awakens within us an answering love—a grateful love for Him manifesting itself in love for our brethren (*cf.* ver. 11). The insertion of **αὐτόν** is a clumsy and unnecessary gloss. Neither should **οὖν** be inserted and **ἀγαπῶμεν** taken as hortat. subjunctive. Vulg.: "Nos ergo diligamus Deum, quoniam Deus prior dilexit nos".

μεν αὐτόν,[1] ὅτι αὐτὸς[2] πρῶτος ἠγάπησεν ἡμᾶς. 20. [t]Ἐάν τις εἴπῃ,
"Ὅτι ἀγαπῶ τὸν Θεόν," καὶ τὸν ἀδελφὸν αὐτοῦ μισῇ, [u]ψεύστης
ἐστίν· ὁ γὰρ μὴ ἀγαπῶν τὸν ἀδελφὸν αὐτοῦ ὃν ἑώρακε, τὸν Θεὸν [v]ὃν
οὐχ ἑώρακε, πῶς δύναται ἀγαπᾶν;[3] 21. καὶ [w]ταύτην τὴν ἐντολὴν
ἔχομεν ἀπ' αὐτοῦ,[4] ἵνα ὁ ἀγαπῶν τὸν Θεόν, ἀγαπᾷ καὶ τὸν ἀδελφὸν
αὐτοῦ.

V. 1. Πᾶς ὁ πιστεύων ὅτι [a]Ἰησοῦς ἐστιν ὁ Χριστός, [b]ἐκ τοῦ Θεοῦ
γεγέννηται· καὶ [c]πᾶς ὁ ἀγαπῶν τὸν γεννήσαντα ἀγαπᾷ καὶ[5] τὸν
γεγεννημένον[6] ἐξ αὐτοῦ. 2. [d]ἐν τούτῳ γινώσκομεν ὅτι ἀγαπῶμεν τὰ
τέκνα τοῦ Θεοῦ, ὅταν τὸν Θεὸν ἀγαπῶμεν, καὶ τὰς ἐντολὰς αὐτοῦ
τηρῶμεν.[7] 3. [e]αὕτη γάρ ἐστιν ἡ ἀγάπη τοῦ Θεοῦ, ἵνα τὰς ἐντολὰς

t ii. 9, iii. 17 reff.
u i. 6 reff.
v Ver. 12 reff.
w ii. 7 reff.
a iv. 15 ref
b iii. 9 reff.
c 1 Peter i. 22, 23.
d 1 Cor. xiii. 4, 5.
e John xiv. 15, 23, 24.

[1] **αυτον** om. AB, Aeth., Aug., edd.; **τον θεον** ℵ, Syr[vg ph], Vg., Cop., Arm.

[2] **αυτος** ℵBKL, Syr[vg ph], Cop., Sah., Aeth., Arm., Aug., edd.; **ο θεος** A, Vg.

[3] **ου δυναται αγαπαν** ℵB, Syr[ph], Sah., edd.

[4] **απο του θεου** A, Vg.

[5] **αγαπα και** ℵAKLP, Syr[vg ph], Vg., Aeth., Arm., Tisch.; om. **και** B, Sah., Aug., WH, Nest.

[6] **το γεγεννημενον** ℵ.

[7] **τηρωμεν** ℵKLP—an assimilation to **τηρωμεν** in *v.* 3; **ποιωμεν** B, Syr[vg ph], Vg. Cop., Sah., Aeth., Arm., Aug., edd.

Ver. 20. Lest the vagueness of the objectless **ἀγαπῶμεν** encourage false security, St. John reiterates the old test: Love for the invisible Father is manifested in love for the brother by our side, the image of the Father. *Cf.* Whittier:—

"Not thine the bigot's partial plea,
  Nor thine the zealot's ban;
Thou well canst spare a love of thee
  Which ends in hate of man".

ψεύστης, see note on i. 6.

Ver. 21. The Old Commandment. *Cf.* ii. 7-11.

Chapter V.—Vv. 1-5. What makes the Commandments of God easy. "Every one that hath faith that Jesus is the Christ hath been begotten of God; and every one that loveth Him that begat loveth him that hath been begotten of Him. Herein we get to know that we love the children of God, whenever we love God, and do His commandments. For this is the love of God, that we should observe His commandments; and His commandments are not heavy, because everything that hath been begotten of God conquereth the world. And this is the conquest that conquered the world—our faith. Who is he that conquereth the world but he that hath faith that Jesus is the Son of God?"

Vv. 1-2. A reiteration of the doctrine that love for God = love for the brethren. Where either is, the other is also. Love for God is the inner principle, love for the brethren its outward manifestation. The argument is "an irregular Sorites" (Plummer):—

Every one that hath faith in the
  Incarnation is a child of God;
Every child of God loves the Father;
∴ every one that hath faith in the
  Incarnation loves God.
Every one that hath faith in the
  Incarnation loves God;
Every one that loves God loves the
  children of God;
∴ every one that hath faith in the
  Incarnation loves the children
  of God.

These are the two commandments of God, the fundamental and all-embracing Christian duties—*love God* and *love the brotherhood*. And faith in the Incarnation (**ὅτι Ἰησοῦς ἐστιν ὁ Χριστός**) is an inspiration for both.

πιστεύων corresponds to **πίστις** (ver. 4). The lack of a similar correspondence in English is felt here as in many other passages (*e.g.*, Matt. viii. 10, 13; ix. 28, 29). Latin is similarly defective: "omnis qui *credit*," "*fides* nostra".

Ver. 3. **ἡ ἀγ. τ. Θεοῦ**, here objective genitive; contrast ii. 5. **ἵνα** ecbatic (see

f Matt. xi. 28-30. g i. 1; John iii. 6. h Ver. i. ref. i John xvi. 33. k Ver. 1 ref. l Heb. ix. 11, 12. m John xix. 34.

αὐτοῦ τηρῶμεν· καὶ [f] αἱ ἐντολαὶ αὐτοῦ βαρεῖαι οὐκ εἰσίν. 4. ὅτι [1]
[g] πᾶν τὸ [h] γεγεννημένον ἐκ τοῦ Θεοῦ, νικᾷ τὸν κόσμον· καὶ αὕτη ἐστὶν
[i] ἡ νίκη ἡ νικήσασα τὸν κόσμον, ἡ πίστις ἡμῶν.[2] 5. τίς ἐστιν [3] ὁ
νικῶν τὸν κόσμον, εἰ μὴ ὁ πιστεύων ὅτι [k] Ἰησοῦς ἐστιν ὁ υἱὸς [4] τοῦ
Θεοῦ;
6. Οὗτός ἐστιν ὁ ἐλθὼν [l] δι᾽ [m] ὕδατος καὶ αἵματος,[5] Ἰησοῦς ὁ [6]

[1] Punct. εισιν, οτι edd. [2] ημων ℵABKP, Vg., edd.; υμων L, Aeth.

[3] τις εστιν AL, Vg., Sah., Tisch., Nest.; τις εστι δε B, WH (δε brack.); Syr[vg] *quis enim*, Aeth. *et quis*.

[4] ο χριστος ο υιος two minusc., Arm.

[5] και αιματος BKL, Syr[vg], Vg., Tert. (*de Bapt.*, 16: *venerat enim per aquam et sanguinem, sicut Ioannes scripsit*), edd.; add. και πνευματος ℵAP, many minusc., Syr[ph], Cop., Sah.

[6] ο om. ℵABL, Arm., edd.

Moulton's *Gram. of N. T. Gk.*, i. pp. 206-9), where the classical idiom would require τὸ ἡμᾶς τηρεῖν. *Cf.* John xvii. 3; Luke i. 43. τὰς ἐντ., the two commandments—"love God" and "love one another" (*cf.* iii. 23, where see note; iv. 21). καὶ αἱ ἐντ., κ.τ.λ.: *cf.* Herm. *Past. M.* xii. 4, § 4: οἱ δὲ ἐπὶ τοῖς χείλεσιν ἔχοντες τὸν κύριον, τὴν δὲ καρδίαν αὐτῶν πεπωρωμένην, καὶ μακρὰν ὄντες ἀπὸ τοῦ κυρίου, ἐκείνοις αἱ ἐντολαὶ αὗται σκληραί εἰσι καὶ δύσβατοι. Aug. *In Joan. Ev. Tract.* xlviii. 1: "Nostis enim qui amat non laborat. Omnis enim labor non amantibus gravis est."

Ver. 4. The reason why "His commandments are not heavy". Punctuate οὐκ εἰσίν, ὅτι πᾶν, κ.τ.λ. The neut. (πᾶν τὸ γεγ.) expresses the universality of the principle, "drückt die unbedingte Allgemeinheit noch stärker aus als 'Jeder, der aus Gott geboren ist'" (Rothe). *Cf.* John iii. 6. τὸν κόσμον, the sum of all the forces antagonistic to the spiritual life. "Our faith" conquers the world by clinging to the eternal realities. "Every common day, he who would be a live child of the living has to fight the God-denying look of things, to believe that, in spite of their look, they are God's, and God is in them, and working his saving will in them" (Geo. MacDonald, *Castle Warlock*, xli.). St. John says first "is conquering" (νικᾷ) because the fight is in progress, then "that conquered" (ἡ νικήσασα) because the triumph is assured.

Ver. 5. St. John says: "Everything that hath been begotten of God conquereth the world". But he has already said: "Every one that hath faith that Jesus is the Christ hath been begotten of God" (ver. 1). So now he asks: "Who is he that conquereth the world but he that hath faith that Jesus is the Son of God?" ("Son of God" being synonymous with "Christ," *i.e.*, "Messiah". *Cf.* John xi. 27, xx. 31). His doctrine therefore is that faith in the Incarnation, believing apprehension of the wonder and glory of it, makes easy the commandments of God, *i.e.*, love to God and love to one another. The remembrance and contemplation of that amazing manifestation drive out the affection of the world and inflame the heart with heavenly love. "What else can the consideration of a compassion so great and undeserved, of a love so free and in such wise proved, of a condescension so unexpected, of a gentleness so unconquerable, of a sweetness so amazing—what, I say, can the diligent consideration of these things do but deliver utterly from every evil passion the soul of him that considers them and hale it unto them in sorrow, exceedingly affect it, and make it despise in comparison with them whatsoever can be desired only in their despite?" (Bern. *De Dilig. Deo*). "There is no book so efficacious towards the instructing of a man in all all virtue and in abhorrence of all sin as the Passion of the Son of God" (Juan de Avila). "Fix your eyes on your Crucified Lord, and everything will seem easy to you" (Santa Teresa).

Vv. 6-8. The Threefold Testimony to the Incarnation. "This is He that came through water and blood, Jesus Christ; not in the water only, but in the water and in the blood. And it is the Spirit that testifieth, because the Spirit is the Truth. Because three are they that

Χριστός· οὐκ [n] ἐν τῷ ὕδατι μόνον, ἀλλ᾽ ἐν τῷ ὕδατι καὶ [1] τῷ αἵματι· n iii. 18. o Phil. ii.
καὶ τὸ πνεῦμά ἐστι [o] τὸ μαρτυροῦν ὅτι τὸ πνεῦμά ἐστιν [p] ἡ [q] ἀλήθεια. 13. p iii. 4 reff.
7. ὅτι τρεῖς [2] εἰσιν οἱ μαρτυροῦντες ἐν τῷ οὐρανῷ, ὁ Πατήρ, ὁ Λόγος, q i. 6 reff.
καὶ τὸ Ἅγιον Πνεῦμα· καὶ οὗτοι οἱ τρεῖς ἕν εἰσι.
8. καὶ τρεῖς
εἰσιν οἱ μαρτυροῦντες ἐν τῇ γῇ,[3] τὸ πνεῦμα, καὶ τὸ ὕδωρ, καὶ τὸ

[1] και εν ABLP, edd. [2] οι τρεις ℵ.

[3] εν τω ουρανω . . . εν τη γη a Latin interpolation, certainly spurious. (1) Found in no Gk. MS. except two late minuscules—162 (Vatican), 15th c., the Lat. Vg. Version with a Gk. text adapted thereto; 34 (Trin. Coll., Dublin), 16th c. (2) Quoted by none of the Gk. Fathers. Had they known it, they would have employed it in the Trinitarian controversies (Sabellian and Arian). (3) Found in none of the early versions—in Vg. but not as it left the hands of St. Jerome. (4) Quoted by no Latin writer until Priscillian (close of 4th c.). *Apparet igitur . . . verba quae de tribus testibus caelestibus dici solent nullam prorsus fidem, auctoritatem nullam habere, nec a gravi libidinis aut imprudentiae crimine liberari posse eos qui etiamnum, falsa quippe pietate ducti, libris sacris obtrudi patiuntur. . . . Error vero longe est gravissimus, si qui, quod de sancta trinitate ecclesia Christi praecepit, a verbis illis Johanni obtrusis vel maxime pendere opinati sunt* (Tisch.).

testify—the Spirit and the water and the blood, and the three are for the one end."

St. John has said that faith in the Incarnation makes the commandments easy, and now the question arises: How can we be assured that the Incarnation is a fact? He adduces a threefold attestation: the Spirit, the water and the blood. His meaning is clear when it is understood that he has the Cerinthian heresy (see Introd. pp. 156 f.) in view and states his doctrine in opposition to it. Cerinthus distinguished between Jesus and the Christ. The divine Christ descended upon the human Jesus at the Baptism, *i.e.*, He "came through water," and left him at the Crucifixion, *i.e.*, He did not "come through blood". Thus redemption was excluded; all that was needed was spiritual illumination. In opposition to this St. John declares that the Eternal God was incarnate in Jesus and was manifested in the entire course of His human life, not only at His Baptism, which was His consecration to His ministry of redemption, but at His Death, which was the consummation of His infinite Sacrifice: "through water and blood, not in the water only but in the water and in the blood".

Ver. 6. **οὗτος**, *i.e.*, this Jesus who is the Son of God, the Messiah whom the prophets foretold and who "came" in the fulness of the time. **ὁ ἐλθών**, not **ὁ ἐρχόμενος**. His Advent no longer an unfulfilled hope but an historic event. **διά**, of the *pathway* or *vehicle* of His Advent. **Ἰησοῦς Χριστός**, "Jesus Christ," one person in opposition to the Cerinthian "dissolution" (**λύσις**) of Jesus and Christ (see note on iv. 3). **ἐν**: He not only "came through" but continued "in the water and in the blood," *i.e.*, His ministry comprehended both the Baptism of the Spirit and the Sacrifice for sin. Perhaps, however, the prepositions are interchangeable; *cf.* 2 Cor. vi. 4-8; Heb. ix. 12, 25. **ἡ ἀλήθ.**: Jesus called Himself "the Truth" (John xiv. 6), and the Spirit came in His room, His *alter ego* (vv. 16-18).

Vv. 7-8. The Water (the Lord's consecrated Life) and the Blood (His sacrificial Death) are testimonies to the Incarnation, but they are insufficient. A third testimony, that of the Spirit, is needed to reveal their significance to us and bring it home to our hearts. Without His enlightenment the wonder and glory of that amazing manifestation will be hidden from us. It will be as unintelligible to us as "mathematics to a Scythian boor, and music to a camel". **τρεῖς οἱ μαρτυροῦντες**, masculine though **Πνεῦμα, ὕδωρ,** and **αἷμα** are all neuter, because agreeing **κατὰ σύνεσιν** with **τὸ Πνεῦμα**—a testimony, the more striking because involuntary, to the personality of the Spirit. **εἰς τὸ ἕν**, "for the one end," *i.e.* to bring us to faith in the Incarnation (**ὅτι Ἰησοῦς ἐστιν ὁ Υἱὸς τοῦ θεοῦ**). This was the end for which St. John wrote his Gospel (John xx. 31). There is no reference in the Water and the Blood either to the effusion of blood and water from the Lord's pierced side (John xix. 34) or to the two Sacraments.

r John xi. 52, xvii. 23.
s John v. 31-37, viii. 18.
t John v. 26; Heb. viii. 16, x. 16 (Jer. xxxi. 33).
u i. 10.
v i. 2; John v. 26.
w John iii. 36; 1 Cor. iii. 21-23.

αἷμα· καὶ οἱ τρεῖς [r] εἰς τὸ ἕν εἰσιν. 9. Εἰ τὴν μαρτυρίαν τῶν
ἀνθρώπων λαμβάνομεν, ἡ μαρτυρία τοῦ Θεοῦ μείζων ἐστίν· ὅτι αὕτη
ἐστὶν [s] ἡ μαρτυρία τοῦ Θεοῦ, ἣν[1] μεμαρτύρηκε περὶ τοῦ υἱοῦ αὐτοῦ.
10. ὁ πιστεύων εἰς τὸν υἱὸν τοῦ Θεοῦ, ἔχει τὴν μαρτυρίαν [t] ἐν ἑαυτῷ·[2]
ὁ μὴ πιστεύων τῷ Θεῷ,[3] [u] ψεύστην πεποίηκεν αὐτόν, ὅτι οὐ πεπίσ-
τευκεν εἰς τὴν μαρτυρίαν, ἣν μεμαρτύρηκεν ὁ Θεὸς περὶ τοῦ υἱοῦ
αὐτοῦ. 11. Καὶ αὕτη ἐστὶν ἡ μαρτυρία ὅτι ζωὴν αἰώνιον ἔδωκεν
ἡμῖν ὁ Θεός· καὶ [v] αὕτη ἡ ζωὴ ἐν τῷ υἱῷ αὐτοῦ ἐστιν. 12. [w] ὁ ἔχων
τὸν υἱόν, ἔχει τὴν ζωήν· ὁ μὴ ἔχων τὸν υἱὸν τοῦ Θεοῦ, τὴν ζωὴν οὐκ
ἔχει.

[1] **ην** KLP; **οτι** אAB, Vg. (*testimonium Dei, quod majus est, quoniam testificatus est*), Cop., Sah., Arm., edd. Punct. **ο τι**.

[2] **εαυτω** א; **αυτω** ABKLP; **αὐτῷ** Tisch., WH (marg.), Nest.; **αὑτῷ** WH.

[3] **τω θεω** אBKLP, Syr[vg], Cop., edd.; **τω υιω** A, Syr[ph], Vg.

Vv. 9-12. Our attitude to the Threefold Testimony. "If we receive the testimony of men, the testimony of God is greater, because this is the testimony of God—what He hath testified concerning His Son. He that believeth in the Son of God hath the testimony in himself. He that believeth not God hath made Him a liar, because he hath not believed in the testimony which God hath testified concerning His Son. And this is the testimony, that God gave us life eternal; and this life is in His Son. He that hath the Son hath the life; he that hath not the Son of God the life hath not."

Ver. 9. According to the Jewish law threefold testimony was valid (Deut. xix. 15; *cf.* Matt. xviii. 16; John viii. 17-18). Read (as in iii. 20) **ὅ, τι μεμαρτύρηκεν**, "what He hath testified concerning His Son," *i.e.* the testimony of His miracles and especially His Resurrection (Rom. i. 4). The variant **ἣν** is a marginal gloss indicating the relative (**ὅ, τι**), not the conjunction (**ὅτι**). The latter is incapable of satisfactory explanation. The alternatives are: (1) "Because the testimony of God is this—the fact that He hath testified," which is meaningless and involves an abrupt variation in the use of **ὅτι**. (2) "Because this is the testimony of God, because, I say, He hath testified," which is intolerable. The Apostle appeals here to his readers to be as reasonable with God as with their fellow men. *Cf.* Pascal: "Would the heir to an estate on finding the title-deeds say, 'Perhaps they are false'? and would he neglect to examine them?"

Ver. 10. A subtle and profound analysis of the exercise of soul which issues in assured faith. Three stages: (1) "Believe God" (**πιστεύειν τῷ Θεῷ**, *credere Deo*), accept His testimony concerning His Son, *i.e.*, not simply His testimony at the Baptism (Matt. iii. 17) but the historic manifestation of God in Christ, the Incarnation. God speaks not by words but by acts, and to set aside His supreme act, and all the forces which it has set in operation is to "make Him a liar" by treating His historic testimony as unworthy of credit. (2) "Believe in the Son of God" (**πιστεύειν εἰς τὸν Υἱὸν τοῦ Θεοῦ**, *credere in Filium Dei*), make the believing self-surrender which is the reasonable and inevitable consequence of contemplating the Incarnation and recognising the wonder of it. (3) The Inward Testimony (**τὴν μαρτυρίαν ἐν αὑτῷ**, *testimonium in seipso*). "Fecisti nos ad te, et inquietum est cor nostrum donec requiescat in te" (Aug.). The love of Jesus satisfies the deepest need of our nature. When He is welcomed, the soul rises up and greets Him as "all its salvation and all its desire," and the testimony is no longer external in history but an inward experience (*cf.* note on iv. 9: **ἐν ἡμῖν**), and therefore indubitable. These three stages are, according to the metaphor of Rev. iii. 20, (1) hearing the Saviour's voice, (2) opening the door, (3) communion.

Ver. 11. The Testimony of the Incarnation. *Cf.* i. 2. **ἔδωκεν**, "gave," aorist referring to a definite historic act, the Incarnation.

Ver. 12. **μή** with the participle does not necessarily make the case hypothetical (*cf.* note on ii. 4). St. John would have

13. Ταῦτα ἔγραψα ὑμῖν τοῖς πιστεύουσιν εἰς τὸ ὄνομα τοῦ υἱοῦ
τοῦ Θεοῦ,[1] ἵνα εἰδῆτε ὅτι ζωὴν ἔχετε αἰώνιον, καὶ ἵνα πιστεύητε[2]
εἰς τὸ [x] ὄνομα [y] τοῦ υἱοῦ τοῦ Θεοῦ. 14. Καὶ αὕτη ἐστὶν ἡ [z] παρρησία
ἣν ἔχομεν πρὸς αὐτόν, ὅτι [a] ἐάν τι αἰτώμεθα κατὰ [b] τὸ θέλημα αὐτοῦ,
ἀκούει ἡμῶν· 15. καὶ [c] ἐὰν οἴδαμεν ὅτι ἀκούει ἡμῶν, ὃ ἂν[3] αἰτώμεθα, οἴδαμεν ὅτι ἔχομεν τὰ [d] αἰτήματα ἃ ᾐτήκαμεν παρ᾽[4] αὐτοῦ.
16. Ἐάν τις ἴδῃ τὸν ἀδελφὸν αὐτοῦ [e] ἁμαρτάνοντα ἁμαρτίαν μὴ πρὸς

x ii. 12 reff., iii. 23.
y John xx. 31.
z ii. 28 reff.
a iii. 21 John xiv. 13, xvi. 23.
b Matt. vi. 10; Luke xxii. 42.
c *Cf.* 1 Thess. iii. 8 (ἐὰν στήκετε).
d Luke xxiii. 24; Phil. iv. 6.
e ii. 25; Mark iv. 41; John vii. 24; 1 Tim. i. 18; 2 Tim. iv. 7; Col. ii. 19; 1 Peter iii. 14.

[1] **τοις πιστευουσιν εις το ονομα του υιου του θεου** KLP; om. ℵAB, Syr$^{vg\ ph}$, Vg., Cop., Sah., Aeth., Arm., edd.

[2] **και ινα πιστευητε** KLP; **τοις πιστευουσιν** ℵ*B, Syr$^{vg\ ph}$, edd.; **οι πιστευοντες** ℵ^{c}A.

[3] **εαν** ℵLP, edd. [4] **παρ** AKLP; **απ** ℵB, edd.

only too many actual instances before him in those days of doctrinal unsettlement.

Vv. 13-21. The Epistle is finished, and the Apostle now speaks his closing words. "These things I wrote to you that ye may know that ye have eternal life, even to you that believe in the name of the Son of God. And this is the boldness which we have toward Him, that if we request anything according to His will, He hearkeneth to us. And if we know that He hearkeneth to us whatever we request, we know that we have the requests which we have made from Him. If any one see his brother sinning a sin not unto death, he shall make request, and he will give to him life, even to them that are sinning not unto death. There *is a* sin unto death; not concerning that do I say that he should ask. Every sort of unrighteousness is sin, and there is a sin not unto death. We know that every one that hath been begotten of God doth not keep sinning, but the Begotten of God observeth him, and the Evil One doth not lay hold on him. We know that we are of God, and the whole world lieth in the Evil One. And we know that the Son of God hath come, and hath given us understanding that we may get to know the True One; and we are in the True One, in His Son Jesus Christ. This is the True God and Life Eternal. Little children, guard yourselves from the idols."

Ver. 13. The purpose for which St. John wrote his Gospel was that we might believe in the Incarnation, and so have Eternal Life (xx. 31); the purpose of the Epistle is not merely that we may have Eternal Life by believing but that we may *know that we have it*. The Gospel exhibits the Son of God, the Epistle commends Him. It is a supplement to the Gospel, a personal application and appeal. **ἔγραψα**, "I wrote," looking back on the accomplished task. **εἰδῆτε**, "know," not **γινώσκητε**, "get to know". Full and present assurance.

Ver. 14. **παρρησία**, see note on ii. 28. As distinguished from **αἰτεῖν** the middle **αἰτεῖσθαι** is to pray *earnestly* as with a personal interest (see Mayor's note on James iv. 3). The distinction does not appear here, since **αἰτεῖν αἰτήματα** (cognate accusitive) is a colourless periphrasis for **αἰτεῖσθαι**. A large assurance: our prayers always heard, never unanswered. Observe two limitations: (1) **κατὰ τὸ θέλημα αὐτοῦ**, which does not mean that we should first ascertain His will and then pray, but that we should pray with the proviso, express or implicit, "If it be Thy will". Matt. xxvi. 39 is the model prayer. (2) The promise is not "He granteth it" but "He hearkeneth to us". He answers in His own way.

Ver. 15. An amplification of the second limitation. "We have our requests" not always as we pray but as we would pray were we wiser. God gives not what we ask but what we really need. *Cf.* Shak., *Ant. and Cleop.* I. ii.:—

> "We, ignorant of ourselves,
> Beg often our own harms, which the wise powers
> Deny us for our good; so find we profit,
> By losing of our prayers".

Prayer is not dictation to God but **ἀνάβασις νοῦ πρὸς Θεὸν καὶ αἴτησις τῶν προσηκόντων παρὰ Θεοῦ** (Joan. Damasc. *De. Fid. Orthod.*, iii. 24). Clem. Alex.: "Non absolute dixit quod petierimus sed quod oportet petere".

Ver. 16. After the grand assurance

f Matt. xiii. 31-32; Heb. vi. 4-6. g iii. 4. h iii. 9. i John xvii. 15. k ii. 13 reff.

θάνατον, αἰτήσει, καὶ δώσει αὐτῷ ζωήν, τοῖς ἁμαρτάνουσι μὴ πρὸς θάνατον. ἔστιν [f] ἁμαρτία πρὸς θάνατον· οὐ περὶ ἐκείνης λέγω ἵνα ἐρωτήσῃ· 17. [g] πᾶσα ἀδικία ἁμαρτία ἐστί· καὶ ἔστιν ἁμαρτία οὐ πρὸς θάνατον. 18. Οἴδαμεν ὅτι [h] πᾶς ὁ γεγεννημένος ἐκ τοῦ Θεοῦ, οὐχ ἁμαρτάνει· ἀλλ' ὁ γεννηθεὶς ἐκ τοῦ Θεοῦ, [i] τηρεῖ ἑαυτόν,[1] καὶ [k] ὁ

[1] αυτον A*B, Vg. (*generatio Dei conservat eum*), edd.

that prayer is always heard, never unanswered, the Apostle specifies one kind of prayer, *viz.*, Intercession, in the particular case of a "brother," *i.e.* a fellow-believer, who has sinned. Prayer will avail for his restoration, with one reservation—that his sin be "not unto death". The reference is to those who had been led astray by the heresy, moral and intellectual, which had invaded the churches of Asia Minor (see Introd. pp. 156 f.) They had closed their ears to the voice of Conscience and their eyes to the light of the Truth, and they were exposed to the operation of that law of Degeneration which obtains in the physical, moral, intellectual, and spiritual domains. *E.g.*, a bodily faculty, if neglected, atrophies (*cf.* note on ii. 11). So in the moral domain disregard of truth destroys veracity. Acts make habits, habits character. So also in the intellectual domain. *Cf.* Darwin to Sir J. D. Hooker, June 17, 1868: "I am glad you were at the *Messiah*, it is the one thing that I should like to hear again, but I daresay I should find my soul too dried up to appreciate it as in old days; and then I should feel very flat, for it is a horrid bore to feel as I constantly do, that I am a withered leaf for every subject except Science". And so in the spiritual domain. There are two ways of killing the soul: (1) The benumbing and hardening practice of disregarding spiritual appeals and stifling spiritual impulses. *Cf. Reliq. Baxter*, I. i. 29: "Bridgnorth had made me resolve that I would never go among a People that had been hardened in unprofitableness under an awakening Ministry; but either to such as had never had any convincing Preacher, or to such as had profited by him". (2) A decisive apostasy, a deliberate rejection. This was the case of those heretics. They had abjured Christ and followed Antichrist. This is what Jesus calls **ἡ τοῦ Πνεύματος βλασφημία** (Matt. xii. 31-32 = Mark iii. 28-30). It inflicts a mortal wound on the man's spiritual nature. He can never be forgiven because he can never repent. He is "in the grip of an eternal sin (**ἔνοχος αἰωνίου ἁμαρτήματος**)". *Cf.* Heb. vi. 4-6. This is "sin unto death". Observe how tenderly St. John speaks: There is a fearful possibility of a man putting himself beyond the hope of restoration; but we can never tell when he has crossed the boundary. If we were sure that it was a case of "sin unto death," then we should forbear praying; but, since we can never be sure, we should always keep on praying. So long as a man is capable of repentance, he has not sinned unto death. "Quamdiu enim veniæ relinquitur locus, mors prorsus imperium nondum occupat" (Calv.). **δώσει**, either (1) "he (the intercessor) will give to him (the brother)," **τοῖς ἁμαρτ.** being in apposition to **αὐτῷ**, "to him, *i.e.* to them that, etc."; or (2) "He (God) will give to him (the intercessor) life for them that, etc." The former avoids an abrupt change of subject, and the attribution to the intercessor of what God does through him is paralleled by James v. 20.

Ver. 17. A gentle warning. "Principiis obsta." Also a reassurance. "You have sinned, but not necessarily 'unto death'."

Vv. 18-20. The Certainties of Christian Faith. St. John has been speaking of a dark mystery, and now he turns from it: "Do not brood over it. Think rather of the splendid certainties and rejoice in them."

Ver. 18. Our Security through the Guardianship of Christ. **οὐχ ἁμαρτάνει**, see note on iii. 6. The child of God may fall into sin, but he does not continue in it; he is not under its dominion. Why? Because, though he has a malignant foe, he has also a vigilant Guardian. **ὁ γεννηθεὶς ἐκ τοῦ Θεοῦ**, *i.e.*, Christ. *Cf. Symb. Nic.*: **Κύριον Ἰησοῦν Χριστὸν, τὸν Υἱὸν τοῦ Θεοῦ, γεννηθέντα ἐκ τοῦ Πατρὸς.** As distinguished from **γεγεννημένος** the aor. **γεννήθεις** refers to the "Eternal Generation". The rendering "he that is begotten of God (the regenerate man) keepeth himself (**ἑαυτὸν**), *qui genitus est ex Deo, servat seipsum* (Calv.), is doubly objectionable: (1) It

πονηρὸς οὐχ [l] ἅπτεται αὐτοῦ. 19. οἴδαμεν ὅτι [m] ἐκ τοῦ Θεοῦ ἐσμεν,
καὶ ὁ κόσμος ὅλος [n] ἐν [k] τῷ πονηρῷ κεῖται. 20. οἴδαμεν δὲ ὅτι ὁ υἱὸς
τοῦ Θεοῦ [o] ἥκει, καὶ δέδωκεν ἡμῖν διάνοιαν ἵνα [p] γινώσκωμεν [1] τὸν
[q] ἀληθινόν· καί ἐσμεν ἐν τῷ [q] ἀληθινῷ, ἐν τῷ υἱῷ αὐτοῦ Ἰησοῦ
Χριστῷ· οὗτός ἐστιν ὁ [q] ἀληθινὸς Θεός, καὶ [r] ἡ [2] ζωὴ αἰώνιος. 21.
Τεκνία, [s] φυλάξατε ἑαυτοὺς [3] ἀπὸ τῶν [t] εἰδώλων. ἀμήν.[4]

l Luke vii. 14, 39; John xx. 17. m iii. 8. n Luke ii. 12, 16. o John viii. 42. p (-ομεν) 1 Cor. iv. 6; Gal. iv. 17.

q ii. 8. r i. 2. s Luke xii. 15; John xii. 25, xvii. 12; 2 Thess. iii. 3; 1 Tim. vi. 20; 2 Tim. i. 12, 14. t 1 Cor. x. 14; Eph. v. 5.

[1] γινωσκομεν ℵAB*LP, edd.—an itacism.

[2] η om. ℵAB, edd. [3] εαυτους ℵcAKP; εαυτα ℵ*BL, edd.

[4] αμην KLP, Vg.; om. ℵAB, Syrvg ph, Cop., Sah., Aeth., Arm., edd. A common ecclesiastical addition.

ignores the distinction between perf. and aor.; (2) there is no comfort in the thought that we are in our own keeping; our security is not our grip on Christ but His grip on us. Calvin feels this: "Quod Dei proprium est, ad nos transfert. Nam si quisque nostrum salutis suæ sit custos, miserum erit præsidium". Vulg. has *generatio Dei*, perhaps representing a variant **ἡ γέννησις τοῦ Θεοῦ. τηρεῖ**, see note on ii. 3. **ἅπτεται,** stronger than "toucheth," rather "graspeth," "layeth hold of". A reference to Ps. cv. (LXX civ.). 15: **μὴ ἅψησθε τῶν χριστῶν μου,** *Nolite tangere christos meos* (Vulg.).

Ver. 19. Our Security in God's Embrace. **ὁ κόσμος**: "Non creatura sed seculares nomines et secundum concupiscentias viventes" (Clem. Alex.). See note on ii. 15. **τῷ πονηρῷ**, masc. as in prev. vers. **κεῖται,** in antithesis to **οὐχ ἅπτεται.** On the child of God the Evil One does not so much as lay his hand, the world lies in his arms. On the other hand, the child of God lies in God's arms. *Cf.* Deut. xxxiii. 27. Penn, *Fruits of Solitude:* "If our Hairs fall not to the Ground, less do we or our Substance without God's Providence. Nor can we fall below the arms of God, how low soever it be we fall."

Ver. 20. The Assurance and Guarantee of it all—the fact of the Incarnation (**ὅτι ὁ Υἱὸς τοῦ Θεοῦ ἥκει**), an overwhelming demonstration of God's interest in us and His concern for our highest good. Not simply a historic fact but an abiding operation—not "came (**ἦλθε**)," but "hath come and hath given us". Our faith is not a matter of intellectual theory but of personal and growing acquaintance with God through the enlightenment of Christ's Spirit. **τὸν ἀληθινόν**, "the real" as opposed to the false God of the heretics. See note on ii. 8. **ἐν τῷ ἀληθινῷ**, as the world is **ἐν τῷ πονηρῷ.**

Ver. 21. *Filioli, custodite vos a simulacris* (Vulg.). The exhortation arises naturally. "This"—this God revealed and made near and sure in Christ—"is the True God and Life Eternal. Cleave to Him, and do not take to do with false Gods: guard yourselves from the idols." St. John is thinking, not of the heathen worship of Ephesus—Artemis and her Temple, but of the heretical substitutes for the Christian conception of God. **τεκνία** gives a tone of tenderness to the exhortation. **φυλάσσειν** is used of "guarding" a flock (Luke ii. 8), a deposit or trust (1 Tim. vi. 20; 2 Tim. i. 12, 14), a prisoner (Acts xii. 4). **φυλάσσειν,** "watch *from within*"; **τηρεῖν** (see note on ii. 3), "watch *from without*". Thus, when a city is besieged, the garrison **φυλάσσουσι,** the besiegers **τηροῦσιν.** The heart is a citadel, and it must be guarded against insidious assailants from without. Not **φυλάσσετε**, "be on your guard," but **φυλάξατε,** aor. marking a crisis. The Cerinthian heresy was a desperate assault demanding a decisive repulse.

ΙΩΑΝΝΟΥ ΤΟΥ ΑΠΟΣΤΟΛΟΥ.

ΕΠΙΣΤΟΛΗ ΚΑΘΟΛΙΚΗ ΔΕΥΤΕΡΑ.[1]

a 3 John i; 1 Tim. v. 1, 17, 19; Heb. xi. 2; 1 Peter v. 1.
b John xvii. 17, 19.
c 1 John ii. 4, 14, 24, 27, iii. 9.
d 1 John iv. 17.
e 1 Tim. i. 2; 2 Tim. i. 2.

1. [a] Ὁ ΠΡΕΣΒΥΤΕΡΟΣ ἐκλεκτῇ κυρίᾳ[2] καὶ τοῖς τέκνοις αὐτῆς, οὓς
ἐγὼ ἀγαπῶ [b] ἐν ἀληθείᾳ, καὶ οὐκ ἐγὼ μόνος, ἀλλὰ καὶ πάντες οἱ
ἐγνωκότες [b] τὴν ἀλήθειαν, 2. διὰ [b] τὴν ἀλήθειαν τὴν [c] μένουσαν[3] ἐν ἡμῖν,
καὶ [d] μεθ' ἡμῶν ἔσται εἰς τὸν αἰῶνα· 3. ἔσται[4] μεθ' ἡμῶν[5] [e] χάρις,

[1] ιωαννου β ℵ; ιωανου β B; επιστολη ιωαννου β P, 96; ιωαννου καθολικη δευτερα 99; ιωαννου επιστολη καθολικη β K, 101, 106; του αγιου αποστολου ιωαννου του θεολογου επιστολη δευτερα L; του αυτου αγιου ιωαννου του θεολογου επιστολη δευτερα 95; επιστολη δευτερα ιωαννου του επι στηθους 4.

[2] τη εκλεκτη κυρια 73; εκλεκτη τη κυρια 31; εκλεκτη τη και κυρια Aeth.; Κυρίᾳ Syr[vg ph], Tisch.; Ἐκλέκτῃ Κυρίᾳ WH (marg.).

[3] μενουσαν ℵBKLP, Vg., edd.; ενοικουσαν A.

[4] εσται δε 15, 36, Euth. Zig.

[5] ημων ℵBLP, Syr[bo], Sah., Aeth., edd.; υμων K, Vg. (*sit vobiscum gratia*), Cop., Syr[ph].

The Second Epistle.

Vv. 1-3. The Address. "The Elder to elect Kyria and her children, whom I love in Truth, and not I alone but also all that have got to know the Truth, because of the Truth that abideth in us; and with us it shall be for ever. Yea, there shall be with us grace, mercy, peace from God the Father and from Jesus Christ the Son of the Father in Truth and love."

Ver. 1. **ὁ πρεσβύτερος,** see Introd. pp. 159 ff. **ἐκλεκτῇ Κυρίᾳ,** see Introd. pp. 162 f. **οὓς,** *constructio* **κατὰ σύνεσιν,** because **τὰ τέκνα** were or included sons, not "weil an Gemeindeglieder gedacht ist" (Holtzmann). **ἐγώ**: according to the Greek idiom, when a man speaks of himself in the third person, he passes immediately to the first. *Cf.* Plat. *Euthyphr.* 5 A: **οὐδέ τῳ ἂν διαφέροι Εὐθύφρων τῶν πολλῶν ἀνθρώπων, εἰ μὴ τὰ τοιαῦτα πάντα ἀκριβῶς εἰδείην.** Soph. *Aj.*, 864-65. The construction is found in loose English; *cf.* Thackeray, *Barry Lyndon*, chap. xviii.: "I was a man who never deserved that so much prosperity should fall to my share". **ἐν ἀληθείᾳ** (see note on 1 John i. 8) defines the Elder's love for Kyria as fellowship in Christian knowledge and faith, in view perhaps of heathen accusations of licentiousness. His affection for her and her family was not merely personal; it was inspired by her devotion to the common cause and was shared by all the Christians in his extensive **διοίκησις.** *Cf.* 2 Cor. viii. 18: **οὗ ὁ ἔπαινος ἐν τῷ εὐαγγελίῳ διὰ πασῶν τῶν ἐκκλησιῶν. τὴν ἀλήθειαν,** "the Truth just mentioned".

Ver. 2. **μένουσαν ἐν ἡμῖν,** not merely apprehended by the intellect but welcomed by the heart. **μεθ' ἡμῶν,** *nobiscum*, *bei uns*, as our guest and companion.

Ver. 3. **ἔσται μεθ' ἡμῶν,** not a wish (1 Peter i. 2; 2 Peter i. 2) but a confident assurance. **χάρις,** the well-spring in the heart of God; **ἔλεος,** its outpourings; **εἰρήνη,** its blessed effect. They are evangelical blessings: (1) not merely "from God" but "from God the Father and from Jesus Christ the Son of the Father" who has interpreted Him and brought Him near, made Him accessible; (2) not merely "in Truth," enlightening the intellect, but "in love," engaging the heart.

ʼλεος, εἰρήνη παρὰ Θεοῦ πατρός, καὶ παρὰ Κυρίου[1] Ἰησοῦ Χριστοῦ
τοῦ υἱοῦ τοῦ πατρός, ἐν ἀληθείᾳ καὶ ἀγάπῃ.
4. [f] Ἐχάρην λίαν ὅτι εὕρηκα ἐκ τῶν τέκνων σου [g] περιπατοῦντας ἐν
ἀληθείᾳ, καθὼς ἐντολὴν ἐλάβομεν[2] παρὰ τοῦ πατρός. 5. καὶ νῦν
ἐρωτῶ σε, κυρία,[3] [h] οὐχ ὡς ἐντολὴν γράφω[4] σοι καινήν,[5] ἀλλὰ ἣν
εἴχομεν[6] ἀπ' ἀρχῆς, ἵνα ἀγαπῶμεν ἀλλήλους. 6. καὶ [i] αὕτη ἐστὶν
ἡ ἀγάπη, ἵνα [g] περιπατῶμεν κατὰ τὰς ἐντολὰς αὐτοῦ. [k] αὕτη ἐστὶν ἡ

f Matt. ii. 10; Mark xiv. 11; Luke xxiii. 8; John xx. 20.
g 1 John i. 6, 7, ii. 6, 11.
h 1 John ii. 7, iii. 11, 23.
i 1 John v 3 reff.
k 1 John iii. 23.

[1] **κυριου** ℵKLP, Syrph, Cop., Arm.; om. AB, several minusc., Syrbo, Vg. (*a Christo Jesu*), Aeth., edd.
[2] **ελαβον** ℵ. [3] **Κυρια** Tisch.
[4] **γραφω** several minusc., Aeth., Arm.; **γραφων** ℵABKLP, Vg., edd.
[5] **γραφων σοι καινην** BKLP, WH, Nest.; **καινην γραφων σοι** ℵA, Tisch.
[6] **ειχομεν** BKLP; **ειχαμεν** ℵA, edd.

Observe the high tribute which the Elder pays to Kyria: (1) He testifies to the esteem in which she is held; (2) he recognises her as a fellow-worker as though she were a fellow-apostle—the three-fold "us," not "you"; (3) he is about to speak of the danger from heretical teaching, but he has no fear of her being led astray: "You and I are secure from the deceiver. The Truth abideth in us; with us it shall be for ever; yea, there shall be with us grace, mercy, peace."

Ver. - The Occasion of the Epistle. "I was exceedingly glad because I have found some of thy children walking in Truth, even as we received commandment from the Father."

ἐχάρην, of a glad surprise (*cf.* Mark xiv. 11). He had been too often disappointed in lads like these (see Introd., p. 155). They had profited by the nurture of their godly home, the best equipment for the battle of life. "No man should ever leave money to his children. It is a curse to them. What we should do for our children, if we would do them the best service we can, is to give them the best training we can procure for them, and then turn them loose in the world without a sixpence to fend for themselves" (Cecil John Rhodes). **εὕρηκα,** "I have found". He sits down at once and writes to Kyria. How glad she would be that her lads, far away in the great city were true to their early faith! **ἐκ τῶν τέκνων,** "some of thy children" (a tenderer word than "sons," **υἱῶν**), "members of thy family," not implying that others had done ill; the lads who had come to Ephesus. **περιπατοῦντας, κ.τ.λ.,** *ambulantes in veritate, die in der Wahrheit wandeln,* "ordering their lives according to the precepts of the Gospel". See note on 1 John i. 6.

Vv. 5-6. The Comprehensive Commandment. "And now I ask thee, Kyria, not as writing a new commandment to thee but the one which we had from the beginning, that we love one another. And this is love—that we walk according to His commandments; this is the commandment, even as ye heard from the beginning—that we should walk in love,"

These counsels are just a summary of the doctrines expounded at large in the first Epistle. There is here a sort of reasoning in a circle: The commandment is Love; Love is walking according to His commandments; His commandments are summed up in one—Love.

Ver. 5. **ἀπ' ἀρχῆς,** "from the beginning of our Christian life". See note on 1 John ii. 7.

Ver. 6. **ἡ ἀγάπη,** "the love just referred to". **περιπ. κατὰ τὰς ἐντ. αὐτ.,** regulating our lives by their requirements; **περιπ. ἐν ἀληθείᾳ** (ver. 4), keeping within the limits of the Christian revelation and not straying beyond them —not **προάγοντες** (ver. 9). **αὐτῇ,** *i.e.,* "love," not "the commandment" (Vulg.: *Hoc est mandatum, ut . . . in eo ambuletis*). **περιπατεῖν ἐν ἀγάπῃ** is synonymous with **περιπατεῖν ἐν ἀληθείᾳ,** since Love is Truth in practice. *Cf.* the story of R. Hillel: A mocking Gentile promised to become a proselyte if he would teach him the whole Law while he stood on one foot—a gibe at the multitudinous precepts, reckoned at 613. "What is hateful to thyself," said the Rabbi, "do not to thy neighbour. This is the whole Law; the rest is commentary." ***Yalk. Chad.***, lix. 2; "qui justum cibat **frusto,**

ἐντολή,[1] καθὼς ἠκούσατε ἀπ' ἀρχῆς, ἵνα ἐν αὐτῇ περιπατῆτε· 7.
ὅτι πολλοὶ [l] πλάνοι [m] εἰσῆλθον [2] εἰς τὸν κόσμον, οἱ μὴ [n] ὁμολογοῦντες
Ἰησοῦν Χριστὸν ἐρχόμενον ἐν σαρκί· οὗτός ἐστιν ὁ [l] πλάνος καὶ ὁ
[o] ἀντίχριστος. 8. [p] βλέπετε ἑαυτούς, ἵνα μὴ ἀπολέσωμεν ἃ εἰργασά-
μεθα, ἀλλὰ [q] μισθὸν πλήρη ἀπολάβωμεν.[3] 9. πᾶς ὁ [r] παραβαίνων,[4]
καὶ μὴ [s] μένων ἐν τῇ διδαχῇ τοῦ Χριστοῦ, Θεὸν οὐκ ἔχει· ὁ μένων
ἐν τῇ διδαχῇ τοῦ Χριστοῦ,[5] οὗτος καὶ [t] τὸν πατέρα καὶ τὸν υἱὸν ἔχει.

l 1 John i. 8. m 1 John iv. 1 reff. n 1 John iv. 2. o 1 John ii. 18 reff. p Mark xiii. 9. q Matt. x. 41, 42, xx. 8; James v. 4. r Matt. ii. 9, xiv. 22; Mark x. 32; 1 Tim. v. 24 (προάγων). s 1 Tim. ii. 15; 2 Tim. iii. 14. t 1 John ii. 22, 23.

[1] **εστιν η εντολη** ℵLP; **η εντολη εστιν** ℵBK, edd.

[2] **εισηλθον** KLP; **εξηλθον** ℵAB, Syrbo, Vg., Sah., Arm., Iren. (III. xvii. 8), edd. (**-αν** A, Tisch., WH).

[3] **απολεσωμεν απολαβωμεν** KLP; **απολεσητε απολαβητε** ℵ* (**απολησθε**) AB, Syrvg ph, Vg., Cop., Sah., Aeth., Arm., Iren., edd.; **ειργασαμεθα** BKLP, Syrph (marg.), Sah.; **ηργ-**B*, WH, Nest.; **ειργασασθε** ℵA, Syrbo ph, Vg., Cop., Aeth., Arm., Iren., Tisch.

[4] **παραβαινων** KLP, Syrbo ph, Vg. (*qui recedit*), Cop., Arm.; **προαγων** ℵAB, Sah., Aeth., edd.

[5] **του χριστου** KLP, Cop., Aeth.; om. ℵAB, Syrph, Vg., Sah., Arm., edd.

perinde est acsi totum Pentateuchum servasset".

Vv. 7-8. A Warning against Heretical Teaching. "Because many deceivers went forth into the world—even they that confess not Jesus as Christ coming in flesh. This is the deceiver and the Antichrist. Look to yourselves, that ye may not lose what we wrought, but receive a full wage."

Ver. 7. **ὅτι** explaining **ἐρωτῶ σε**: "I ask you to obey the old commandment because seducers are at work". **ἐξῆλθον εἰς τὸν κόσμον,** see note on 1 John iv. 1. **οἱ μὴ ὁμολογοῦντες,** a definite and well-known sect. See note on 1 John ii. 4. **ἐληλυθότα** (1 John iv. 2) of the Advent, **ἐρχόμενον** of the continous manifestation of the incarnate Christ. *Cf.* John i. 14, where **σὰρξ ἐγένετο** corresponds to **ἐληλυθότα** and **ἐσκήνωσεν ἐν ἡμῖν** to **ἐρχόμενον**.

Ver. 8. **μισθόν**, *cf.* Matt. xx. 8; James v. 4. St. John here addresses not only Kyria but her family and "the Church in her house". He views them as his fellow-labourers in the Lord's vineyard: "We have worked together (**ἠργασάμεθα**): see that you do not forfeit the reward of your labour. Get a full wage. Be not like workmen who toward the close of the day fall off, doing their work badly or losing time, and get less than a full day's pay." **ἀπολέσητε . . . ἠργασάμεθα . . . ἀπολάβητε**: "We have been fellow-workers thus far, and I mean to be faithful to the last; see that you also be so". Their danger lay in taking up with false teaching and losing the comfort of the Gospel in its simplicity and fulness.

Ver. 9. Progress in Theological Thought. "Every one that 'progresseth' and abideth not in the teaching of the Christ hath not God; he that abideth in the teaching—this man hath both the Father and the Son."

ὁ προάγων: the Cerinthians (see Introd. pp. 156 f.) boasted of their enlightenment. They were "progressives," "advanced thinkers". **τῇ διδαχῇ τοῦ Χριστοῦ,** the teaching which recognises Jesus as the Christ (see note on 1 John iv. 1-2), *i.e.* the Messiah, the Saviour. **Θεὸν οὐκ ἔχει,** *i.e.* according to His true nature as the Father manifested in the Son (**καὶ τὸν Πατέρα καὶ τὸν Υἱόν**). It is necessary not merely to believe in God but to believe in Him "through Christ" (1 Peter i. 21).

St. John does not here condemn theological progress, which is a necessity of living and growing faith. A doctrine is a statement of Christian experience, and since there is always more in Christ than we have ever experienced, our doctrines can never be adequate or final. Theology is to God's revelation in Grace as Science is to His revelation in Nature; and just as Science is always discovering more of the wonders of the First Creation, so Theology is always entering more deeply into the glory of the New Creation and appropriating more of the treasures which are hidden in Christ. Even the inspired Apostles did not comprehend all His fulness. Each saw only so much as was revealed to him, and declared only so

10. [u]εἴ τις ἔρχεται πρὸς ὑμᾶς, καὶ ταύτην τὴν διδαχὴν οὐ φέρει,
μὴ λαμβάνετε αὐτὸν εἰς οἰκίαν, καὶ χαίρειν αὐτῷ μὴ λέγετε· 11. ὁ
γὰρ λέγων [1] αὐτῷ χαίρειν, [v] κοινωνεῖ [w] τοῖς ἔργοις αὐτοῦ τοῖς πονηροῖς.

u 2 Thess. iii. 6. v 1 John i. 3, 6, 7; 1 Tim. v. 22. w 1 John iii. 12.

[1] ο γαρ λεγων KLP, Iren. (I. ix. 3); ο λεγων γαρ ℵAB, edd.

much as he saw. Each approached the infinite wonder along the lines of his temperament and experience. St. John saw in it a revelation of Eternal Life; St. Paul the Reconciliation of sinners to God, the satisfaction of humanity's long desire and the completion of its long discipline under the Law; the author of the Epistle to the Hebrews the rending of the Veil and the opening of free Access to God. St. John does not condemn theological progress; he defines its limits: "abide in the teaching of the Christ". (1) We must never break with the past; the new truth is always an outgrowth of the old. A theology which is simply old is dead; a theology which is simply new is false (*cf.* Matt. xiii. 52). (2) We must maintain "the teaching of the Christ". Jesus is the Saviour, and no interpretation of Christianity is true which eliminates Redemption or obscures the glory of the Cross.

Vv. 10-11. Treatment of Heretical Teachers. "If any one cometh unto you and bringeth not this teaching, receive him not into your house, and bid him not farewell. For he that biddeth him farewell hath fellowship with his works, his evil works."

Ver. 10. **φέρει**, not "endureth" (*cf.* Rom. ix. 22; Heb. xii. 20), but "bringeth" as a precious boon (*cf.* Rev. xxi. 24, 26). **εἰς οἰκίαν** (*cf.* Mark ii. 1; iii. 19), *zu Hause; cf.* "to church," "to town," "to market," "to bed". See Moulton's *Winer*, pp. 148 ff. **χαῖρε**, like *ave*, *salve*, was used of both the salutation at meeting and the farewell at parting. The former is its prevailing use in N.T., but here, as in 2 Cor. xiii. 11, the latter. "Zum Abschied, wenn der Abgewiesene weiter ziehen muss" (Holtzmann).

Ver. 11. **κοινωνεῖ**, *cf.* 1 John i. 3. An unholy **κοινωνία**. **τοῖς ἔργ. αὐτ. τοῖς πον.**, *cf.* 1 John i. 2: **τὴν ζωὴν τὴν αἰώνιον.** The adjective is an emphatic afterthought.

This counsel recalls the story of St. John's behaviour to Cerinthus (see Introd. p. 157), and it was cited by Irenæus (I. ix. 3) as inculcating intolerance of heretics. If so, it is certainly an unChristian counsel, contrary to the spirit and teaching of our Lord (*cf.* Mark ix. 38-39; Luke ix. 51-56; Matt. xiii. 28-29). Heretics are our fellow-creatures; Jesus died for them also, and our office is to win them. If we close our doors and our hearts against them, we lose our opportunity of winning them and harden them in their opposition. There are two thoughts which may well teach us forbearance and humility: (1) The patience of the Lord. A Jewish fable tells how Abraham thrust an aged wayfarer from his tent because he asked no blessing on his food and avowed himself a fire-worshipper. And the Lord said: "I have suffered him these hundred years, although he dishonoured Me; and couldst not thou endure him for one night?" (2) The mystery of the things of God and the blindness of our intellects. "Illi," says St. Augustine (*Contra Epistolam Manichæi*, 2), "in vos sæviant, qui nesciunt cum quo labore verum inveniatur, et quam difficile caveantur errores". This counsel of the Apostle must be read in the light of local circumstances. There was need of caution and discrimination in receiving the itinerant "apostles and prophets" who went from church to church, lest they should prove "false apostles" (**ψευδαπόστολοι**) and "false prophets" (**ψευδοπροφῆται**). See *Didache*, xi.-xii., where the test is given: **οὐ πᾶς ὁ λαλῶν ἐν πνεύματι προφήτης ἐστίν, ἀλλ' ἐὰν ἔχῃ τοὺς τρόπους Κυρίου.** It is not until the second century that there is any appearance of buildings set apart for worship. The primitive **ἐκκλησίαι** met in private houses (*cf.* Rom. xvi. 5; 1 Cor. xvi. 19; Col. iv. 15; Philem. 2); and when St. John warns Kyria against "receiving into her house" a heretical teacher, it is not showing him hospitality that he forbids, but affording him an opportunity to unsettle the faith of the brethren. She must neither let him pervert "the church in her house" nor send him on his way to a neighbouring church with the recommendation of her confidence and goodwill. This is expressed, though somewhat vaguely, by Clem. Alex.: "Hoc in hujusmodi non est inhumanum, sed nec conquirere vel condisputare cum talibus admonet qui non valent intelligibiliter divina tractare, ne per eos traducantur a doctrina veri-

x 3 John 14.
y 1 John i. 4 reff.
z Ver. 1.

12. Πολλὰ ἔχων ὑμῖν γράφειν, οὐκ ἠβουλήθην[1] διὰ χάρτου καὶ
μέλανος· ἀλλὰ ἐλπίζω ἐλθεῖν[2] πρὸς ὑμᾶς, καὶ [x]στόμα πρὸς στόμα
λαλῆσαι, ἵνα ἡ χαρὰ ἡμῶν[3] ᾖ [y]πεπληρωμένη.[4] 13. ἀσπάζεταί σε
τὰ τέκνα τῆς ἀδελφῆς σου τῆς [z]ἐκλεκτῆς. ἀμήν.[5]

1 εβουληθην ℵABKLP, edd. 2 γενεσθαι ℵAB, Syrph, Vg., edd.

3 ημων ℵKLP, Tisch., WH (marg.), Nest.; υμων AB, Vg., WH.

4 η πεπληρωμενη AKLP; πεπληρωμενη η ℵB, edd.

5 αμην om. ℵABP, Vg., Cop., Sah., Aeth., Arm., edd.

tatis, verisimilibus inducti rationibus. Arbitror autem, quia et orare cum talibus non oportet, quoniam in oratione quæ fit in domo, postquam ab orando surgitur, salutatio gaudii est et pacis indicium."

Vv. 12-13. The Conclusion. "Though I have many things to write to you, I would not by paper and ink; but I hope to get to you, and talk face to face, that our joy may be fulfilled. The children of thine elect sister salute thee."

Ver. 12. Explanation of the brevity of the letter. **ὑμῖν**, *i.e.*, Kyria, her children, and the church in her house. **γράφειν** connected **ἀπὸ κοινοῦ** with **ἔχων** and **ἐβουλήθην**. **χάρτης**, a sheet of papyrus, like those exhumed at Oxyrhynchus (see Deissmann, *New Light on the New Test.*, pp. 12 ff.), the common material for letter-writing. **μέλαν**, *atramentum;* in N. T. only here, 3 John 13, 2 Cor. iii. 3. **γενέσθαι πρὸς ὑμᾶς** (*cf.* John x. 35; Acts x. 13; 1 Cor. ii. 3, xvi. 10): he was planning a visitation (see Introd. p. 155). **στόμα πρὸς στόμα**, "mouth answering mouth"; *cf.* LXX. Num. xii. 8; Jer. xxxii. (xxxix.), 4.

Why would he not write all that was in his mind? It was a deliberate decision ere he took pen in hand: this is the force of **οὐκ ἐβουλήθην**. His heart was full, and writing was a poor medium of communication (Beng.: "Ipsa scribendi opera non juvat semper cor affectu sacro plenum"); he was an old man, and writing was fatiguing to him (Plummer). The reason is deeper. The "many things" which he had in his mind, were hard things like his warning against intercourse with heretics, and he would not write them at a distance but would wait till he was on the spot and had personal knowledge. It is easy to lay down general principles, but their application to particular cases is a delicate task, demanding knowledge, sympathy, charity. (1) The sight of people's faces appeals to one's heart and softens one's speech. (2) When one meets with people and talks with them, one's judgment of them and their opinions is often modified. Writing from Ephesus, St. John might have condemned a teacher in a neighbouring town whose teaching he knew only by report; but perhaps, if he met the man and heard what he had to say, he might discover that there was nothing amiss, at all events nothing which called for excommunication. Dr. Dale of Birmingham was at first inclined to look with disfavour on Mr. Moody. He went to hear him, and his opinion was altered. He regarded him ever after with profound respect, and considered that he had a right to preach the Gospel, "because he could never speak of a lost soul without tears in his eyes". St. John shrank from hasty condemnation that there might be no after-regret—**ἵνα ἡ χαρὰ ἡμῶν πεπληρωμένη ᾖ**.

Ver. 13. See Introd. pp. 162 f.

ΙΩΑΝΝΟΥ ΤΟΥ ΑΠΟΣΤΟΛΟΥ.

ΕΠΙΣΤΟΛΗ ΚΑΘΟΛΙΚΗ ΤΡΙΤΗ.[1]

1. [a] Ὁ ΠΡΕΣΒΥΤΕΡΟΣ Γαΐῳ τῷ ἀγαπητῷ, ὃν ἐγὼ ἀγαπῶ [b] ἐν ἀληθείᾳ. a 2 John 1 reff.
2. Ἀγαπητέ, περὶ πάντων εὔχομαί σε [c] εὐοδοῦσθαι καὶ ὑγιαίνειν, b 2 John 1 ref.
καθὼς [c] εὐοδοῦταί σου ἡ ψυχή. 3. [d] ἐχάρην γὰρ [2] λίαν, ἐρχομένων c 1 Cor. xvi. 2.
ἀδελφῶν καὶ μαρτυρούντων σου τῇ ἀληθείᾳ, καθὼς σὺ [e] ἐν ἀληθείᾳ d 2 John 4.
περιπατεῖς. 4. [f] μειζοτέραν τούτων οὐκ ἔχω χαράν,[3] ἵνα ἀκούω τὰ e 2 John 4. f 1 John i. 4.

[1] ιωαννου γ̅ ℵ; ιωανου γ̅ B; ιωαννου επιστολη γ̅ C, many minusc.; ιωαννου επιστολη καθολικη γ̅ 101, 106; επιστολη τριτη του αγιου αποστολου ιωαννου L; του αυτου αγιου ιωαννου του θεολογου επιστολη τριτη 95; επιστολη του αγιου αποστολου και ηγαπημενου προς γαΐον ιωαννου 4.

[2] γαρ ABCKLP, Syr bo ph, Cop., WH, Nest.; om. ℵ, Vg., Sah., Aeth., Arm., Tisch.

[3] χαραν ℵACKLP, Tisch., WH (marg.), Nest.; χαριν B, Vg., Cop., WH.

THE THIRD EPISTLE.

Vv. 1-4. Address and Commendation. "The Elder to Gaius the beloved, whom I love in Truth. Beloved, in all respects I pray that thou mayest prosper and be in health, even as thy soul prospereth. For I was exceedingly glad when brethren would come and testify to thy Truth, even as thou walkest in Truth. A greater gladness than this I have not—that I should hear of my children walking in the Truth."

Ver. 1. **ὁ πρεσβύτερος**, see Introd. pp. 159 ff. **ἐγώ**, see note on 2 John i. **ἐν ἀληθείᾳ**, see note on 2 John i.

Ver. 2. *Cf.* Law, *Ser. Call*, chap. vii.: "Flavia would be a miracle of piety, if she was but half as careful of her soul as she is of her body. The rising of a pimple on her face, the sting of a gnat, will make her keep her room for two or three days, and she thinks they are very rash people that do not take care of things in time." Penn, *Fruits of Solitude:* "He is curious to wash, dress and perfume his Body, but careless of his Soul. The one shall have many Hours, the other not so many Minutes." **περὶ πάντων,** *de omnibus*, with **εὐοδοῦσθαι καὶ ὑγιαίνειν**, not *præ omnibus*, "above all things". The latter use is epic (*e.g.*, Hom. *Il.* i. 287: **περὶ πάντων ἔμμεναι ἄλλων**), and prosperity and health were not the *summa bona* in the Apostle's estimation. **εὐοδοῦσθαι**, "prosper" in worldly matters. Trouble tests character. "A good knight is best known in battle, and a Christian in the time of trouble and adversity"; and Gaius had stood the test. The hostility of Diotrephes, probably a well-to-do member of the Church, had lessened his maintenance (**εὐοδοῦσθαι**) and affected his health (**ὑγιαίνειν**), yet St. John has only admiration for the spirit he has manifested and commendation for the part he has played.

Ver. 3. **ἐχάρην**, see note on 2 John 4. **ἐρχομένων**, repeatedly, not on one particular occasion (**ἐλθόντων**). The itinerant brethren (*die reisenden Brüder*) were always at work, going out from Ephesus on their missions and returning with their reports. *Cf. vv.* 5-6. See Introd. p. 155.

Ver. 4. *Cf.* Senec. *Ep.* xxxiv.: "Si agricolam arbor ad fructum perducta delectat, si pastor ex fœtu gregis sui capit voluptatem, si alumnum suum nemo aliter intuetur quam adulescentiam illius

[g] ἐμὰ τέκνα ἐν[1] ἀληθείᾳ περιπατοῦντα. 5. Ἀγαπητέ, πιστὸν ποιεῖς
ὃ ἐὰν [h] ἐργάσῃ[2] εἰς τοὺς ἀδελφοὺς καὶ εἰς τοὺς[3] [i] ξένους, 6. οἳ ἐμαρ-
τύρησάν σου τῇ ἀγάπῃ [k] ἐνώπιον ἐκκλησίας· οὓς [l] καλῶς ποιήσεις
[m] προπέμψας [n] ἀξίως τοῦ Θεοῦ. 7. ὑπὲρ γὰρ [o] τοῦ ὀνόματος ἐξῆλθον[4]

g 1 Tim. i. 2; 1 Cor. iv. 15; Philem. 10; Gal. iv. 19. h Matt. xxvi. 10. i Heb. xiii. 1. k 1 John iii. 22 reff. l 2 Peter i. 19. m Acts xv. 3, xx. 38, xxi. 5; Rom. xv. 24; 1 Cor. xvi. 6, 11; 2 Cor. i. 16. n 1 Thess. ii. 12; Col. i. 10. o Acts v. 40, 41; 1 Peter iv. 14, 16.

[1] **εν** ℵC²KLP; **εν τη** ABC*, edd.

[2] **εργαση** ℵBCKLP, edd.; **εργαζη** A, Vg. (*quidquid operaris*).

[3] **εις τους** KLP; **τουτο** ℵABC, Vg., Syr$^{\text{bo ph}}$, Vg., Cop., Sah., Aeth., Arm., edd.

[4] **εξηλθαν** ℵB, edd.

suam judicet: quid evenire credis his qui ingenia educaverunt, et quæ tenera formaverunt adulta subito vident?" *Ev. sec. Heb.* (quoted by Jerome on Eph. v. 4): "Et numquam, inquit (Dominus), læti sitis nisi cum fratrem vestrum videritis in caritate". **μειζοτέραν**, a double compar.; *cf.* **ἐλαχιστοτέρῳ** (Eph. iii. 8); our "lesser"; Germ. *mehrere.* **τούτων**: this use of the plur. (**ταῦτα**) rather than the sing. (**τοῦτο**) is common. See Moulton's *Winer*, p. 201. **ἵνα**, epexegetic of **τούτων**. *Cf.* Luke i. 43 and see note on 1 John iii. 11. **τέκνα** implies that Gaius was a convert of St. John. *Cf.* marg. note.

Vv. 5-8. The Duty of Entertaining Itinerant Preachers. "Beloved, it is a work of faith that thou art doing in thy treatment of the brethren, strangers withal. They testified to thy love before the Church; and thou wilt do well in speeding them on their way worthily of God. For it was for the sake of the Name that they went forth, taking nothing from the Gentiles. We therefore are bound to undertake for such, that we may prove fellow-workers with the Truth."

A company of *reisende Brüder* had returned to Ephesus, and in reporting of their mission at a meeting of the Church had made special mention of the hospitality of Gaius. The Apostle commends him and bids him continue his good offices.

Ver. 5. The adjective **πιστός** is either act., "believing" (*cf.* John xx. 27), or passive, "worthy to be believed," "trustworthy" (*cf.* 2 Tim. ii. 2). It is passive here, and it is well explained by Œcumenius as equivalent to **ἄξιον πιστοῦ ἀνδρός.** The peculiarity is that, by a sort of hypallage, the adjective is transferred from the subjective to the objective. Transitive: "Thou makest whatever thou workest on the brethren a believing act, a work of faith". It was not mere hospitality but a religious service. Westcott's rendering: "thou makest sure whatsoever thou doest" gives **πιστόν** an unexampled and indeed impossible meaning. **ποιεῖς**, aor. of habitual and constant hospitality; **ἐργάσῃ**, aor. of each particular act. **καὶ τοῦτο**, "and that to"; more commonly **καὶ ταῦτα** (*cf.* Heb. xi. 12).

Ver. 6. On the anarthrous **ἐκκλησίας,** see note on 2 John 10. **καλῶς ποιήσεις** has the sense of "please" in the Oxyrhynchus Papyri; *e.g.*, 300, 3-6: **ἔπεμψά σοι διὰ τοῦ καμηλείτου Ταυρείνου τὸ πανάριον, περὶ οὗ καλῶς ποιήσεις ἀντιφωνήσασά μοι ὅτι ἐκομίσου,** "I sent you the bread-basket by the cameleer Taurinus; please let me have word again that you got it". **προπέμψας**: when a Rabbi visited a town, it was customary on his departure to escort him on his way (Lightfoot, *Hor. Heb.*, on Matt. v. 41). The gracious usage was observed in the primitive Church, and it appears to have included the furnishing of provision for the journey (*cf.* Tit. iii 13). *Cf.* Hom. *Od.* xv., 74: **χρὴ ξεῖνον παρεόντα φιλεῖν, ἐθέλοντα δὲ πέμπειν,** "welcome the coming, speed the parting guest". **ἀξίως τοῦ Θεοῦ,** "in a manner worthy of God," *i.e.* (1) "Since they are God's representatives (John xiii. 20), *weil ihr Evangelistenwerk Gottes Werk ist* (Holtzm.), treat them as you would treat God"; (2) "Since you are God's representatives, treat them as God would treat them".

Ver. 7. **τοῦ Ὀνόματος,** sc. of Jesus (*cf.* Acts v. 40, 41). There is perhaps a reference to this verse in Ignat. *ad Eph.* vii. 1: **εἰώθασι γάρ τινες δόλῳ πονηρῷ τὸ ὄνομα περιφέρειν, ἄλλα τινὰ πράσσοντες ἀνάξια Θεοῦ.** *Cf.* iii. 1: **δέδεμαι ἐν τῷ ὀνόματι. ἐξῆλθαν,** sc. from Ephesus, the seat of the Apostle and therefore the headquarters of the Church in Asia Minor. *Cf.* Introd. p. 155. **μηδέν,** see note on 1 John ii. 4. Winer (Moulton's Winer, p. 463, note 1) draws a distinction, perhaps too fine, between **λαμβάνειν παρά τινος** and **λαμβάνειν ἀπό τινος.**

μηδὲν λαμβάνοντες [q] ἀπὸ τῶν ἐθνῶν.[1] 8. ἡμεῖς οὖν [r] ὀφείλομεν ἀπο-
λαμβάνειν[2] τοὺς τοιούτους, ἵνα [s] συνεργοὶ [t] γινώμεθα τῇ ἀληθείᾳ. 9.
Ἔγραψα[3] τῇ ἐκκλησίᾳ· ἀλλ' ὁ [u] φιλοπρωτεύων αὐτῶν Διοτρεφὴς οὐκ
ἐπιδέχεται ἡμᾶς. 10. διὰ τοῦτο, ἐὰν ἔλθω, [v] ὑπομνήσω αὐτοῦ τὰ
ἔργα ἃ ποιεῖ, λόγοις πονηροῖς [w] φλυαρῶν ἡμᾶς· καὶ μὴ ἀρκούμενος
ἐπὶ τούτοις, οὔτε αὐτὸς ἐπιδέχεται τοὺς ἀδελφούς, καὶ τοὺς βουλο-
μένους [x] κωλύει, καὶ ἐκ τῆς ἐκκλησίας [y] ἐκβάλλει. 11. Ἀγαπητέ, [z] μὴ

p Acts xx. 35; 1 Cor. ix. 12-15. q 1 John v. 15. r 1 John ii. 6 reff. s Rom. xvi. 3, 9, 21; 1 Cor. iii. 9; 2 Cor. viii. 23. t Matt. v. 45.

u *Cf.* Matt. xx. 27. v John xiv. 26; 2 Tim. ii. 14; Tit. iii. 1. w 1 Tim. v. 13. x Mark ix. 38, 39. y John ix. 34. z Rom. xii. 9; Ps. xxxvii. 27.

[1] **εθνων** KLP; **εθνικων** ℵABC, edd.

[2] **απολαμβανειν** KLP; **υπολαμβανειν** ℵABC*, edd.

[3] **εγραψα**: add **τι** ℵABC, Cop., Sah., Arm., edd.

The former would have been used here had the Gentiles "*proferred* an acknowledgment; the latter implies *exaction*. The missionaries might have accepted maintenance (Matt. x. 10), but like St. Paul they waived their right, "that they might cause no hindrance to the Gospel of Christ" (1 Cor. ix.).

Ver. 8. **ἡμεῖς**, emphatic in contrast to the Gentiles. **ὀφείλομεν**, of moral obligation. See note on 1 John ii. 6. **ὑπολαμβάνειν**, *suscipere*, "receive hospitably" (*cf.* **ὑποδέχεσθαι**), "take under one's protection". Observe the *Wortspiel*—**λαμβάνοντες, ὑπολαμβάνειν. συνεργοὶ τῇ ἀληθείᾳ**: a division of labour. If we cannot preach the Gospel ourselves, we may help others to do it. William Carey, comparing his missionary enterprise to the exploration of a mine, said: "I will go down if you will hold the ropes".

Vv. 9-10. Churlishness of Diotrephes. "I wrote something to the Church, but Diotrephes, who loveth pre-eminence over them, doth not receive us. Therefore, if I come, I shall call to remembrance his works which he doeth, prating about us with evil words; and, not content therewith, neither doth he himself receive the brethren and them that would he preventeth and casteth out of the Church."

"Der Zweck des 3. Briefes liegt in der Empfehlung der Gastfreundschaft gegen wandernde Glaubensboten" (Holtzm.).

Ver. 9. **ἔγραψά τι**, a brief letter of commendation, **συστατικὴ ἐπιστολή** (2 Cor. iii. 1), introducing and authorising a company of itinerant brethren, probably those referred to in *v.* 5. **φιλοπρωτεύειν**, "love to be first, to be chief' (**ἅπαξ λεγόμενον**). The noun is **φιλοπρωτεία** and the adj. **φιλόπρωτος** (Polyb., Plut). **προάγειν** (2 John 9) and **φιλοπρωτεύειν** denote two tempers which disturbed the Christian life of Asia Minor—intellectual arrogance and personal aggrandisement. **αὐτῶν** refers **κατὰ σύνεσιν** to **ἐκκλησίᾳ**. **οὐκ ἐπιδέχεται ἡμᾶς**, "doth not receive me in the person of my delegates" (*cf.* Matt. x. 40), *i.e.*, "disowneth my authority".

Ver. 10. **ἐὰν ἔλθω**: the aged Apostle with his failing strength can only "hope" (*cf.* ver. 14) to undertake the journey. **ὑπομνήσω αὐτοῦ τὰ ἔργα**, not "remind him of his works" (contrast the "work" of Gaius in ver. 5), but "bring his works to remembrance," by reciting them at a meeting of the Church. St. John does not threaten excommunication or any sort of discipline, but simply that he will state the facts and let them speak for themselves. A terrible reckoning, like that of the Day of Judgment (*cf.* Rev. xx. 12)—to hear a recital of all one's passionate speeches and inconsiderate actions. Contrast St. Paul's threats (1 Cor. iv. 21; 2 Cor. x. 11, xiii. 1-3). St. John deserved to be called "the Apostle of Love". **φλυαρεῖν** (*nugari*, *verschwatsen*), of foolish chattering. Suid.: **φλύαρος· φλήναφος καὶ λῆρος καὶ μάταιος λόγος.** The chatter of Diotrephes was not only foolish but malevolent (**λόγοις πονηροῖς**). **μὴ ἀρκ.**, see note on 1 John ii. 4. **οὔτε . . . καί**, *cf.* John iv. 11. **κωλύει, ἐκβάλλει**, pres. implying not that he actually did it but that he tried to do it. **ἐκβάλλει**, here not of literal ejection (*cf.* John ii. 15 = Matt. xxi. 12 = Mark xi. 15) but of excommunication from the fellowship of the congregation.

Vv. 11, 12. Testimony to Demetrius. "Beloved, do not imitate what is bad but what is good. He that doeth what is good is of God; he that doeth what is bad hath not seen God. To Demetrius testimony hath been borne by all and by the Truth itself; yea, and we testify, and thou knowest that our testimony is true."

[a] μιμοῦ τὸ κακόν, ἀλλὰ τὸ ἀγαθόν. ὁ ἀγαθοποιῶν, ἐκ τοῦ Θεοῦ ἐστιν·
[b] ὁ δὲ[1] κακοποιῶν, οὐχ ἑώρακε τὸν Θεόν. 12. Δημητρίῳ [c] μεμαρτύρηται ὑπὸ πάντων, καὶ ὑπ᾽ αὐτῆς τῆς ἀληθείας· [d] καὶ ἡμεῖς δὲ
μαρτυροῦμεν, καὶ οἴδατε[2] ὅτι ἡ μαρτυρία ἡμῶν ἀληθής ἐστι.
13. Πολλὰ εἶχον γράφειν,[3] ἀλλ᾽ οὐ θέλω διὰ μέλανος καὶ καλάμου
σοι γράψαι·[4] 14. ἐλπίζω δὲ εὐθέως ἰδεῖν σε,[5] καὶ [e] στόμα πρὸς στόμα
λαλήσομεν. 15. [f] Εἰρήνη σοι. ἀσπάζονταί σε οἱ [g] φίλοι. ἀσπάζου
τοὺς [g] φίλους [h] κατ᾽ ὄνομα.

a Heb. xiii. 7.
b 1 John iii. 6.
c Heb. xi. 2, 4, 5, 39.
d John xix. 35, xxi. 24.
e 2 John 12.
f Matt. x. 13; Luke xxiv. 36; John xx. 19, 21, 36; 1 Peter v. 14.
g John xi. 11; Acts xxvii. 3.
h John x. 3.

[1] **ο δε** L, Cop., Aeth., Arm.; **ο** ℵABCKP, Syr^ph, Vg., Sah., edd.
[2] **οιδατε** KLP, Syr^bo ph, Aeth.; **οιδας** ℵABC, Vg., Cop., Sah., Arm.
[3] **γραφειν** KLP; **γραψαι σοι** ℵABC, edd.
[4] **γραψαι** KLP; **γραφειν** ℵABC, edd.
[5] **ιδειν σε** ℵKLP; **σε ιδειν** ABC, edd.

Ver. 11. A warning against evil example. The pres. participles **ἀγαθοποιῶν, κακοποιῶν** denote *continuance in and practice of* good or bad. See note on 1 John iii. 6. **ἐκ τοῦ Θεοῦ**, "a child of God" (*cf.* 1 John iii. 10). Observe the gentleness of the Apostle: the natural antithesis of **ἐκ τοῦ Θεοῦ** would be **ἐκ τοῦ διαβόλου** (1 John iii. 8), but he says **οὐχ ἑώρακεν τὸν Θεόν.**

Ver. 12. Application of the warning against evil example: Do not imitate Diotrephes, but imitate Demetrius. Demetrius was probably the bearer (*Ueberbringer*) of the epistle. There is no reason for identifying him with Demetrius the silversmith of Ephesus (Acts xix. 24). B. Weiss (*Einleit.*), supporting the ecclesiastical interpretation of 2 John (see Introd. p. 162) and finding a reference to it in 3 John 9, regards Demetrius as the recipient (*Empfänger*) of the former—a member of the Church and a striking contrast to his fellow-member Diotrephes. But evidently he was a stranger to Gaius and needed introduction and commendation. St. John gives him a threefold testimony: (1) that of the whole community at Ephesus (**ὑπὸ πάντων**); (2) that of "the Truth" (see note on 1 John i. 8): he fulfilled the requirements of the Gospel and exemplified its saving power; (3) that of the Apostle and his colleagues at Ephesus (**ἡμεῖς**): he has long been honoured by his community as an embodiment of the Truth (**μεμαρτύρηται**), and the Apostle testifies this when he is going among strangers ignorant of his past (**μαρτυροῦμεν**). **καὶ . . . δὲ**, see note on 1 John i. 3. **οἶδας ὅτι, κ.τ.λ.**: because St. John knew him so well. Demetrius belonged to the Church of Ephesus and was probably a convert of the Apostle.

Vv. 13-15. The Conclusion. "I had many things to write to thee, but I am not minded to be writing to thee by pen and ink. However, I hope presently to see thee, and we shall talk face to face. Peace to thee! The friends salute thee. Salute the friends by name."

Cf. 2 John, 12-13. The similarity of the conclusions suggests that the two epistles were written at the same time. The Apostle meditated a visitational circuit (see Introd. p. 155) in the course of which he would see both Kyria and Gaius.

Ver. 13. **γράψαι**, aor. of the complete composition in the Apostle's mind; **γράφειν**, pres. of the process of putting it on paper. **κάλαμος** (in full **κάλαμος γραφεύς**), a reed-pen, as distinguished from **γραφεῖον**, a sharp-pointed *stilus* for writing on waxed tablets. Plutarch (*Dem.*, 29, 3) says that Demosthenes, when meditating and writing, was accustomed to bite his **κάλαμος.**

Ver. 15. **εἰρήνη σοι**, *pax tibi*, the Jewish greeting, שָׁלוֹם לָךְ (Jud. vi. 23, xix. 20), **οἱ φίλοι**, those at Ephesus; **τοὺς φίλους**, those with Gaius. St. John knew all "by name," and would have named them had space permitted. He had the true shepherd's heart (*cf.* John x. 3, the only other place where **κατ᾽ ὄνομα** occurs in N.T.). Ignat., *ad Smyrn.*, xiii. 2: **ἀσπάζομαι Ἄλκην, τὸ ποθητόν μοι ὄνομα, καὶ Δάφνον, τὸν ἀσύγκριτον καὶ εὔτεκνον, καὶ πάντας κατ᾽ ὄνομα.**

THE GENERAL EPISTLE

OF

JUDE.

INTRODUCTION.

CHAPTER I.

Relation of the Second Epistle of Peter to the Epistle of Jude.[1]

THE general resemblance between the two Epistles will be apparent from the marginal references to my text. I propose here to compare them throughout, stating the reasons which have led me to believe that the epistle of Jude was known to the author of 2 Peter, not *vice versa.*[2]

To begin with, both style themselves servants of Jesus Christ and address themselves to those who in some way belong to God and to Jesus Christ, desiring that peace might be multiplied upon them. We notice here certain differences occasioned by the difference of the writers. J. marks his identity by naming his brother James; P. claims apostleship. J. adds the prayer for mercy and and love to that for peace; P. who is about to speak more fully of love immediately, omits it here, and changes ἔλεος into the wider χάρις. J. defines his readers as "the called who have been beloved by God the Father and kept safe in Jesus Christ"; P. defers the notion of "calling" to the third and tenth verses, and dwells here on God's free gift of faith (τοῖς λαχοῦσιν πίστιν) as characteristic of his readers. He adds two remarkable phrases (1) that, through the justice of our God and of our Saviour Jesus Christ, this faith is (2) equally privileged with that of the writer (whether we are to regard him as representing the Apostles, or the Jews, as seems to me more probable), and he emphasises this equality of Jew and Gentile by the unique use of his own double name, the Hebrew "Symeon" added to the Greek "Peter," suggesting that his sympathies embrace both. We may compare with this the friendly reference to St. Paul in iii. 15, and the association of Silvanus with the writer in 1 Peter.

[1] For the justification of the readings and interpretations adopted in the following chapters, see critical and explanatory notes.

[2] In what follows P. stands for 2 Peter, J. for Jude.

After this greeting J. turns at once to the immediate occasion for his letter. He had been preparing, he says, to write on the subject which is of highest interest to all Christians, *viz.*, salvation,[1] when news reached him of a new danger threatening the Church, against which he felt bound to warn his readers. It seems hardly possible to suppose that this note of alarm could have come to him through P., who writes in a much more leisurely way, not feeling it necessary at once to plunge into controversy and supply his readers with weapons for the defence of the faith. In fact the latter begins with the very subject which J. had felt himself obliged to omit, or at least to postpone to the end of his Epistle (ver. 20), *viz.* the doctrine of salvation. Thus we seem to lose sight of J. until the beginning of the second chapter of P., but we shall see that in the intervening passage of P. there is frequent recurrence to thoughts which are found in the former epistle.

After speaking generally of the blessings in store for man through the goodness of God, P. goes on (i. 5) to speak of the corresponding duty on man's part. We are to use every effort to build up the Christian life in its seven-fold completeness on the rock of faith. Towards the end of J. we find words which may very possibly have suggested to P. this idea of the seven ascending tiers rising on the foundation of faith and culminating in love (J. ver. 20), **ἐποικοδομοῦντες ἑαυτοὺς τῇ ἁγιωτάτῃ ὑμῶν πίστει . . . ἑαυτοὺς ἐν ἀγάπῃ Θεοῦ τηρήσατε.** The phrase **σπουδὴν πᾶσαν** of P. i. 5 occurs also in J. ver. 3. The mention of **εὐσέβεια** in P. i. 3, 6, 7 may be due to the prevalence of **ἀσέβεια** so often deplored by J. The verses which follow (i. 8-11) dwell on the importance of the cultivation of these virtues or graces. "Their continued growth will tend to make us not unfruitful (*cf.* J. ver. 12) in regard to that knowledge of God, out of which they grow. Their absence causes blindness, or at least limits us to narrow earthly views, and makes us forgetful of the baptismal cleansing from the sins of our old life. Remember that it is not enough simply to have been baptised. We have to make sure the calling and election of which baptism was the seal. If you are diligent in doing this, you will never stumble, but will have a glorious entry into the eternal kingdom of our Lord and Saviour Jesus Christ." Here too we find connecting links with the later verses of J. "Eternal life" is the goal in J. ver. 21, "the eternal kingdom," in P. i. 11. The **οὐ μὴ πταίσητε** and the **πλουσίως ἐπιχορηγηθήσεται** of P. remind us of J.'s summing up in ver. 24, "God our Saviour is able to *keep us without*

[1] The word **κοινήν** here may have suggested to P. his phrase **ἰσότιμον πίστιν.**

stumbling and to set us *before His glory* without blemish *in exceeding joy*".

P. continues (i. 12-15), "I know that you are established in this truth, but it will be always my care to remind you of it, as I am indeed bound to do, whilst I continue in this earthly habitation. Even after I leave it, as our Lord Jesus Christ has warned me that I must soon do, I hope to bequeath to you a legacy which will enable you to make mention of these things after my departure." We have here an echo of J. ver. 5, "I desire to put you in remembrance, though ye know all things," *i.e.*, as it is explained afterwards, though you are familiar with the examples of judgment contained in the O.T., including the punishment of the angels who sinned. P. addressing Gentiles, who could hardly be expected to be familiar with a narrative resting mainly on Jewish tradition, gives the phrase a more fitting application in reference to the general moral and religious teaching which precedes.

The connexion between the two Epistles is most conspicuous in the second chapter of P. In both, this section begins with a short Introduction (J. ver. 4, P. ii. 1-3), describing in general terms the innovators against whom the readers are warned. They steal into the Church, they deny the only Master (δεσπότην), their lives are impure, the verdict of heaven has long been pronounced against them. To this P. prefixes a clause to connect the new subject with that of the preceding chapter. The gift of prophecy was liable to misuse under the old dispensation (of which he presently quotes Balaam as an example, *cf.* P. ii. 15, 16, and J. ver. 11). Corresponding to this in the new dispensation will be the abuse of teaching (*cf.* James iii. 1-12); and these false teachers will introduce destructive heresies and bring on themselves swift destruction. [The word ἀπώλεια does not occur in J., but in the next verse he says that the Lord τοὺς μὴ πιστεύσαντας ἀπώλεσεν.] P. adds the Pauline epithet ἀγοράσαντα before δεσπότην. He foretells that many will follow the loose living of these teachers and that thus the way of truth (Ps. cxix. 30) will be evil spoken of (Isa. lii. 5). He speaks of their covetousness (*cf.* J. ver. 11 on Balaam) and of their glozing words. While J. denounces οἱ πάλαι προγεγραμμένοι εἰς τοῦτο τὸ κρίμα (where the reference in τοῦτο is obscure), P. has the fine phrase οἷς τὸ κρίμα οὐκ ἀργεῖ καὶ ἡ ἀπώλεια αὐτῶν οὐ νυστάζει. On the other hand we lose J.'s τὴν τοῦ Θεοῦ χάριτα μετατιθέντες εἰς ἀσέλγειαν, for which perhaps ἐλευθερίαν αὐτοῖς ἐπαγγελλόμενοι, αὐτοὶ δοῦλοι ὑπάρχοντες τῆς φθορᾶς (P. ii. 19) was intended as an equivalent, *cf.* Gal. v. 13, ἐπ' ἐλευθερίᾳ ἐκλήθητε· μόνον μὴ τὴν ἐλευθερίαν εἰς ἀφορμὴν τῇ σαρκί.

Then follow (J. vv. 5-7) three examples of judgment taken from the O.T.: Israel in the Wilderness, the offending angels, the sin of Sodom, which are repeated in P. ii. 4-9, except that the Deluge takes the place of the punishment of Israel. Why was this change made? Probably because the destruction of the world by water and the destruction of Sodom by fire were recognised types of Divine vengeance (Lk. xvii. 26-29), and also because P. is about to speak of the Deluge below (iii. 5-7) to show that there is nothing incredible in the destruction of the existing universe by fire. Moreover he had already referred to the case of Israel (ἐν τῷ λαῷ) in comparing the false prophets of the O.T. with the false teachers of the N.T. Perhaps, too, he wished to keep the chronological order in his three examples. It has been suggested in the note on τὸ δεύτερον that, in speaking of the destruction of Israel after their falling back into unbelief, J. may have had in his mind the question of the forgiveness of post-baptismal sin. There is perhaps a similar reference in P. i. 9, λήθην λαβὼν τοῦ καθαρισμοῦ τῶν πάλαι αὐτοῦ ἁμαρτιῶν as well as in P. ii. 20. With regard to P.'s triplet, it is to be noticed that it is given in a far more animated form than that of J., being used as a protasis to an apodosis applying the same principles to the persons addressed, εἰ γὰρ ὁ Θεὸς οὐκ ἐφείσατο κ.τ.λ. Of the angels P. says merely that they sinned, J. dwells on their pristine dignity, and follows the book of Enoch in making their sin to consist partly in the fall from their high estate, and partly in their going after σαρκὸς ἑτέρας, as the men of Sodom did afterwards τὸν ὅμοιον τρόπον τούτοις, J. ver. 7. If P. had J. before him, these omissions are natural; if J. wrote after P., he would scarcely have gone out of his way to insert particulars so derogatory to the angelic nature. As to their punishment, they are reserved, in both epistles, for judgment under darkness in chains.

It is interesting to compare what is said in the two Epistles about the two missionaries of the antediluvian world. In J. ver. 14 Enoch, the seventh from Adam, appears simply as the denouncer of vengeance to come: in P. Noah is a preacher of righteousness and he is the eighth saved. In my edition of 2 Peter I have suggested that the writer may have intended a mystical opposition between the two numbers; and, I think, this is confirmed by the way in which the number 8 is introduced in 1 P. iii. 20 (κιβωτοῦ) εἰς ἣν ὀλίγοι, τοῦτ' ἔστιν ὀκτὼ ψυχαί, διεσώθησαν δι' ὕδατος. The ark is here regarded as a symbol of the Church. What was the writer's motive in adding that it contained only a few, and further that these few, on being reckoned up, were found to amount to 8? Must he not have intended to signify that, while the visible Church consisted of a mere "remnant," a "little flock," yet these few represented all who share the Resurrection of Christ, "the general assembly and church of the first-born," which would be continually recruited not only from the living, but also from the dead by the ever-present, ever-active Spirit of Christ (1 P. iii. 19)? In the account of Sodom P. (ii. 6) differs from J. in laying stress on Lot's protest against surrounding wickedness, and on the mercy shown towards him, just as he had done before in regard to Noah (hereby illustrating the duty of the faithful under the present stress); and the moral he draws from the two stories is that "God knows how to deliver the godly from trial, as well as to keep the wicked under chastisement for the day of judgment". P. alone gives details as to the destruction of Sodom (τεφρώσας καταστροφῇ κατέκρινεν), while J. speaks of its present state as a warning to future ages. As regards this warning P.'s ὑπόδειγμα μελλόντων ἀσεβέσιν is better expressed than J.'s rather confused πρόκειται δεῖγμα πυρὸς αἰωνίου δίκην ὑπέχουσαι. In ver. 8 J. turns to the libertines and declares that they are guilty of like sins with these sinners of the old world: they defile the flesh, make light of authority and rail at "glories" (as the men of Sodom did towards the angels), and this they do because they are still buried in a carnal sleep (*cf.* Eph. v. 14). These men (ver. 10, οὗτοι δέ) rail at things beyond their ken, while they surrender themselves like brute beasts to the guidance of their appetites, and thus bring about their own destruction.[1] P. (ii. 10) combines part of J.'s description of the men of Sodom, who went ὀπίσω σαρκὸς ἑτέρας (for which he substitutes ὀπίσω σαρκὸς ἐν ἐπιθυμίᾳ μιασμοῦ πορευομένους) with J.'s condemnation of the libertines as despising authority,[2] and predicates both characteristics of the wicked, whom God keeps under chastisement for the day of judgment. Then turning to the libertines he exclaims against them as "headstrong and shameless (τολμηταί, *cf.* ἐτόλμησεν, J. ver. 9) men that shrink not from railing at glories" (ii. 10). In ii. 12 he goes on, as J. does in ver. 10, with a οὗτοι δέ, "these are like brute beasts". Apparently he wants to bring out more fully the force of J.'s ὅσα φυσικῶς ἐπίστανται, ἐν τούτοις φθείρονται by the periphrasis γεγεννημένα φυσικὰ εἰς ἅλωσιν καὶ φθοράν and ἐν τῇ φθορᾷ αὐτῶν φθαρήσονται. That is, while J. simply states that the libertines are destroyed through

[1] For the connexion between the darkened heart which refuses to know God, and the indulgence in the vilest lusts, see Rom. i. 21-28.

[2] It will be noticed that, while J. couples κυριότητα and δόξας as belonging to the same category, P. only names the abstract word κυριότητα here, and introduces δόξας later on as a concrete example.

their indulgence in their animal instincts, P. draws out the comparison to the brute beasts, "which are born mere creatures of instinct, with a view to capture and slaughter," and then adds that the libertines will share their fate, since they mock at that higher world which is beyond their ken. Here there can be no doubt that P.'s language is far more obscure than that of J. Even J. is not quite clear. The true antithesis would have been "they rail at what transcends the senses, they admire what appeals to the senses and appetites" (and yet these are the causes of their ruin). Is it possible that P., writing with an imperfect recollection of J., understood ἐν τούτοις φθείρονται to mean "perish among them," *i.e.*, among the brutes?

We have now to consider the very curious verse interposed between J. vv. 8 and 10, P. ii. 10 and 12. In J. it runs: "Michael, the archangel, when he was disputing with the devil about the body of Moses, did not venture to bring a judgment of railing, but said, 'the Lord rebuke thee'": in P. "whereas angels, though greater in power and might, do not venture to bring against them a railing judgment before the Lord". The former is a little difficult, but with the help of the *Assumptio Mosis* we can understand that, if the chief of the archangels abstained from using any contemptuous expression against Satan, and contented himself with making his appeal to God, much more should frail and sinful mortals abstain from slighting language about the powers of the invisible world. What, however, is to be made of P? Standing by itself, it is merely a riddle, for which the answer is to be found in J. That is to say, P. wrote with J.'s sentence in his mind, but for some reason or other chose to eliminate the points essential for its intelligibility. What was his reason? The same, I think, which led him to omit the details as to the fall of the angels, which are mainly derived from the Book of Enoch, in ii. 4, and the reference to the preaching of Enoch below. He objects, that is, to make use of these apocryphal writings, and generalises the story by dropping the proper names and by twice changing a singular into a plural (ἄγγελοι, αὐτῶν). So, too, a vague παρὰ Κυρίῳ takes the place of ἐπιτιμήσαι σοι Κύριος, and the vagueness is increased by the use of the indeterminate αὐτῶν and by the omission of the object of the comparative μείζονες. In fact the sentence is meaningless except to one who was already acquainted with its parallel in J., though it may perhaps be true, as Dr. Bigg suggests, that P. felt himself justified in his generalisation by the remembrance of an obscure passage in the Book of Enoch.

I go on to J. ver. 11, "Woe to them, for they have followed in the steps of Cain, and been carried away in the error of Balaam for gain, and lost themselves in the rebellion of Korah. These are sunken rocks in your love-feasts, where they join your feast without any feeling of religious reverence, caring only for their own enjoyment. They are clouds without water, scudding before the wind; trees without fruit in the fruit-bearing season, twice dead, torn up by the roots; raging waves foaming out their own shame; wandering stars for which the blackness of darkness is reserved for ever." This passage corresponds to P. ii. 13-17, but, in the latter, the order is considerably altered and there are various additions and omissions. Balaam (who is also prominent in the Apocalypse ii. 14) is the only one of the old hæresiarchs referred to, but his story is given at more length in ii. 15 16: "They (the libertines) have wandered from the straight path, following the path of Balaam, who loved the wages of unrighteousness and was convicted of his error by the dumb ass, which spoke with human voice and stayed the prophet's madness". Here P. clenches the comparison made before (ii. 1) between the false prophet of the O.T. and the false teacher of the N.T., and brings out again the motive of covetousness (see above ii. 3 and ii. 15). Has he any special reason for introducing the story of the ass rebuking the prophet? We may compare other passages in which God is represented as choosing the foolish things of this world to confound the wise (1 Cor. i. 27, Ps. viii. 2), or in which men are called upon to learn a lesson from animals, as Isa. i. 3, Jer. viii. 7, Prov. vi. 6, Job xii. 7. Possibly P. may be thinking of the scorn entertained for simple believers by those who called themselves Gnostics (see below ii. 18).

J. ver. 12 appears with some remarkable alterations in P. ii. 13, σπίλοι καὶ μῶμοι ἐντρυφῶντες ἐν ταῖς ἀπάταις αὐτῶν συνευωχούμενοι ὑμῖν. Here σπίλοι and ἀπάταις are substituted for σπιλάδες and ἀγάπαις in J. Some editors read ἀγάπαις with B, but the addition of αὐτῶν suits much better with ἀπάταις. J. speaks of ἀγάπαις ὑμῶν. It was natural of course that the wolves should seek to find their way into the sheep-folds; but can we suppose that the faithful would enter the love feasts of the libertines? Moreover the change of an original ἀγάπαις to ἀπάταις by a copyist is hardly conceivable, while the reverse change to suit J. is most natural. But how are we to account for the disappearance of the important—we might almost call it the indispensable word—ἀγάπη? In my edition of 2 P., p. cxcv., I have suggested that ἀγάπην was the original reading, instead of ἡδονήν, in the earlier part of this verse (ἡδονὴν ἡγούμενοι τὴν ἐν ἡμέρᾳ τρυφήν); where my explanatory note shows how hard it is to make a satisfactory distinction between ἡδονήν and τρυφήν. On the other hand ἀγάπην gives exactly the sense required "thinking that revelling in the daytime makes an ἀγάπη," as may be seen from the quotations from Clement given in the passage referred to (*cf.* too Rom. xiii. 13). I account for ἡδονήν by supposing that it was a marginal gloss on τρυφήν. The word ἀπάτη is often joined with τρυφή, as shown in the explanatory note, and it is wanted here to explain how the libertines managed to gain admission to the love-feasts of the Church. We have next to ask why σπιλάδες should have been changed to σπίλοι. The former word is a daring metaphor even among the metaphors which accompany it in J., but quite out of place here, and P. substitutes for it the similar sounding σπίλος found in Eph. v. 27, of which the derivatives ἄσπιλος and σπιλόω occur elsewhere in P. and J. Are we to suppose that P. intentionally replaced J.'s words by others of similar sound, in order not to startle people who were already familiar with them? or was it the unconscious action of the mind, calling up similar sounds, as in rhyming or alliteration? The latter seems to me the more probable explanation.

P. returns to J.'s metaphors in ii. 17, where he splits up νεφέλαι ἄνυδροι ὑπὸ ἀνέμων παραφερόμεναι into two, πηγαὶ ἄνυδροι and ὁμίχλαι ὑπὸ λαίλαπος ἐλαυνόμεναι, perhaps because he regarded J.'s expression as superfluous, and also because he thus provides distinct pictures of present disappointment (the well) and future uncertainty (the cloud). He omits the fruitless trees, the stormy waves and wandering stars as unsuited to his purpose, but inappropriately appends to his last metaphor, the clause in which J. describes the doom of the wandering stars, οἷς ὁ ζόφος τοῦ σκότους τετήρηται. Of course the gender shows that P. intends this clause to apply to the persons whom he has just figuratively described, as it is indeed applied by J. himself in ver. 6, but it loses the aptness which it has in J. ver. 13, and thus supplies another convincing proof of the priority of J. How could the latter have had the patience to gather the scattered fragments out of P. in order to form the splendid cluster of figures in vv. 12, 13? We have still to consider the insertion in P. (ii. 13), ἀδικούμενοι μισθὸν ἀδικίας, which commences the loose series of participles ending in ii. 15. If the participle is omitted, this phrase recalls J. ver. 11, τῇ πλάνῃ τοῦ Βαλαὰμ μισθοῦ ἐξεχύθησαν, and is repeated again in ii. 15; but ἀδικούμενοι is difficult. Apparently P. intends his paradoxical phrase to correspond to J.'s οὐαί: the libertines are miserable, because they are, as they think, "robbed of (or 'robbed as') the reward of their iniquity". The following participles gave a striking and powerful description of the evil influence which these men exercise over unstable souls, ὀφθαλμοὺς ἔχοντες μεστοὺς μοιχαλίδος καὶ ἀκαταπαύστους ἁμαρτίας, δελεάζοντες ψυχὰς ἀστηρίκτους (*cf.* γεγεννημένα εἰς ἅλωσιν, ii. 12), καρδίαν γεγυμνασμένην πλεονεξίας ἔχοντες, κατάρας τέκνα. Perhaps P. may intend this partly to take the place of J.'s fine figure κύματα ἄγρια θαλάσσης ἐπαφρίζοντα τὰς ἑαυτῶν αἰσχύνας.

In vv. 14, 15 J. gives the prophecy of Enoch, the seventh from Adam, which simply announces the future judgment on impious deeds and words. To this P. makes no direct reference, but, as I have before suggested, it may have been one reason for speaking of Noah as the eighth. In ver. 16 (perhaps taken from the *Assumption of Moses*) J. goes on to describe the libertines as "murmuring and discontented, walking after their own lusts, whose mouth λαλεῖ ὑπέρογκα, and who flatter others for the sake of advantage". To the same effect P. (ii. 18) speaks of them as uttering ὑπέρογκα ματαιότητος, by which they seduce through the lusts of the flesh those who were just escaping from heathen error. In ii. 19-22 P. is mostly independent of J., but I have already noticed that ἐλευθερίαν ἐπαγγελλόμενοι may be an echo of J. ver. 4, χάριτα μετατιθέντες εἰς ἀσέλγειαν. He continues, εἰ γὰρ ἀποφυγόντες τὰ μιάσματα τοῦ κόσμου ἐν ἐπιγνώσει τοῦ κυρίου καὶ σωτῆρος Ἰησοῦ Χριστοῦ, words which recall what he had said in i. 4, ἀποφυγόντες τῆς ἐν τῷ κόσμῳ ἐν ἐπιθυμίᾳ φθορᾶς, . . . διὰ τῆς ἐπιγνώσεως . . . τοῦ Θεοῦ καὶ Ἰησοῦ τοῦ κυρίου ἡμῶν, and goes on to give an impressive warning against the dangers of backsliding, in which he borrows from J. ver. 3, ὑποστρέψαι ἐκ τῆς παραδοθείσης αὐτοῖς ἁγίας ἐντολῆς, concluding with the proverb of the dog and the sow returning to their foulness after being cleansed from it.

In the third chapter of P. we go back again to J. The readers are addressed as ἀγαπητοί in P. iii. 1 as in J. ver. 17. In both, they are bidden to remember the words of the Apostles, warning them against mockers who should come in the last days, walking after their own lusts. To this P. adds (iii. 1, 2) "This is the second letter I am writing to you, and in both I stir up your sincere mind by calling on you to remember the command of the Lord and Saviour spoken by your Apostles". Since in i. 16, he had used the phrase ἐγνωρίσαμεν ὑμῖν τὴν τοῦ κυρίου ἡμῶν παρουσίαν, it would seem that P. must himself be included among "your Apostles". He further bids them "remember the words which were spoken before by the holy prophets," recurring in this to what he had said in i. 19. What are we to understand by the allusion to a previous letter? Our first thought is naturally of 1 P. But is there anything in it which would answer to the description here given? Many have denied this, because they thought that the contents of the prophecy, as given in J. ver. 18, were included in P.'s reference to an earlier Epistle. J. there says, ὅτι ἔλεγον ὑμῖν Ἐπ' ἐσχάτου χρόνου ἔσονται ἐμπαῖκται κ.τ.λ., that is, he asserts that the words quoted by him were words which were often in the mouth of the Apostles. On the other hand P. makes a clear separation between iii. 2 and iii. 3 by inserting the phrase τοῦτο πρῶτον γινώσκοντες, which he had previously used in i. 20, not to introduce a particular prophecy, but to lay down how prophecy was to be understood. The reference to a former letter is therefore restricted by P. to iii. 2, bidding the readers pay heed to the words of the prophets and the apostles. If we turn now to 1 P. i. 10-12, περὶ ἧς σωτηρίας ἐξεζήτησαν . . . προφῆται οἱ περὶ τῆς εἰς ὑμᾶς χάριτος προφητεύσαντες . . . οἷς ἀπεκαλύφθη ὅτι οὐχ ἑαυτοῖς, ὑμῖν δὲ διηκόνουν αὐτά, ἃ νῦν ἀνηγγέλη ὑμῖν διὰ τῶν εὐαγγελισαμένων ὑμᾶς πνεύματι ἁγίῳ (*cf.* 1 P. i. 16), we shall find an exact correspondence to what is stated here. The words τῶν προειρημένων ῥημάτων (J. ver. 17, P. iii. 2) remind us of J. ver. 4, οἱ πάλαι προγεγραμμένοι εἰς τοῦτο τὸ κρίμα (though no doubt the immediate reference there is to the prophecy of Enoch) and of P. ii. 3, οἷς τὸ κρίμα ἔκπαλαι οὐκ ἀργεῖ. In citing the prophecy, P. adds the emphatic ἐν ἐμπαιγμονῇ, which may be compared with ἐν τῇ φθορᾷ αὐτῶν καὶ φθαρήσονται of ii. 12, and with the reiterated ἀσεβεῖς of J. ver. 15 and κατὰ τὰς ἐπιθυμίας πορευόμενοι of J. vv. 16 and 18.

In iii. 4, P., omitting J.'s somewhat obscure ver. 19, οὗτοί εἰσιν οἱ ἀποδιορίζοντες, ψυχικοί, πνεῦμα μὴ ἔχοντες, goes on to specify in what the mockery of the ἐμπαῖκται consisted. They said that the promise of the coming of Christ (to which P. had borne witness in i. 16) remained unfulfilled, and that the world was not liable to the catastrophic changes predicted as accompaniments of the final judgment. There is a little awkwardness in P.'s wording, ἀπ' ἀρχῆς κτίσεως following ἀφ' ἧς ἐκοιμήθησαν, but it is a very natural blending of two objections. I cannot think that if J. had known this verse, which gives so much point to the preceding prophecy, he would have refrained from inserting it. P. gives a double answer in iii. 5-10: (*a*) as the world was created out of water by the word of God, so, owing to[1] the same word, it was destroyed through water, and will be destroyed again by fire on the day of judgment (*cf.* Jude vv. 6, 7, P. ii. 3, 4, 9); (*b*) God is not limited to days and years. If He waits, it is from His long-suffering patience, because He desires that all should repent and be saved. We may compare this with P.'s use of the O.T. types of judgment to point out proofs of mercy in the case of Noah and Lot (ii. 5, 7), in contrast with the severer tone of J. vv. 5-7. In iii. 10

[1] Reading δι' ὅν, for which see my edition of 2 P.

P. bids his readers make a practical use of the knowledge that the Lord is about to come unexpectedly. "Do not be blind to the symptoms of the breaking up of the frame of nature (perhaps a reference to volcanic eruptions and earthquakes). Make ready for the coming of the day of God by the practice of holiness and piety. Look forward to the fulfilment of the promise of the reign of righteousness in a new earth and heaven."

At this point J. and P. again come together in J. ver. 20 and P. iii. 14, both commencing a new section with ἀγαπητοί. J.'s exhortation to his readers "to build themselves up on their most holy faith and keep themselves in love" has been already used by P., as we have seen, in i. 5-7. His reference to the Spirit's help in prayer may be compared with P. i. 20 on the inspiration of the prophets. His phrase in ver. 21, προσδεχόμενοι τὸ ἔλεος τοῦ κυρίου ἡμῶν Ἰησοῦ Χριστοῦ εἰς ζωὴν αἰώνιον is taken up in the προσδοκῶντας of P. iii. 12 and προσδοκῶμεν of iii. 13, and again in iii. 14, while the goal εἰς ζωὴν αἰώνιον may be compared wlth εἰς τὴν αἰώνιον βασιλείαν in P. i. 11. P. inserts ἄσπιλοι καὶ ἀμώμητοι (*cf.* 1 P. i. 19) from J.'s ἀμώμους in ver. 24, and in contrast to his own σπίλοι καὶ μῶμοι in ii. 13, and to J.'s ἐσπιλωμένον in ver. 23. ἐν εἰρήνῃ looks back to J. ver. 2 and P. i. 2. While in vv. 22, 23 we have J.'s stern rule for the treatment of backsliders, P. gives utterance again (iii. 15) to the more hopeful view of iii. 9, and claims for it the inspired support of Paul. "Yet Paul's letters, wise and good as they are, offer some difficulties, which have been misunderstood and perverted, like the rest of the Bible,[1] by the unlearned and unstable to their own destruction." The word σωτηρία in iii. 15 reminds us that J. had originally intended to write περὶ τῆς κοινῆς σωτηρίας (ver. 3) and that his purpose is apparently carried out to a certain extent in these last verses from 20 onwards. In ver. 24 J. begins an Ascription partly borrowed from St. Paul, addressed "to Him who is able to *keep His people* free from *stumbling* (*cf.* P. i. 10) and present them before His glory in exceeding joy" (*cf.* P. i. 11). P. bids his readers, "knowing these things beforehand (see above i. 12, iii. 2) to be on their guard, that they may not be led away by the *error* (J. ver. 11, P. ii. 18) of the wicked (P. ii. 7, *cf.* J. ver. 23, ἐλεᾶτε ἐν φόβῳ), and so fall from their own steadfastness" (*cf.* P. i. 12, ii. 14, iii. 16). J.'s ἐν ἀγαλλιάσει soars higher than the lesson which P. here inculcates: it may be compared, as we have seen, with the πλουσίως ἐπιχορηγηθήσεται of i. 11. P. continues his exhortation in iii. 18, αὐξάνετε ἐν χάριτι καὶ γνώσει, for which

[1] For the justification of this rendering see explanatory notes in my edition of 2 P.

we may compare χάρις πληθυνθείη in i. 2 and ταῦτα πλεονάζοντα in i. 8, also J. ver. 4. The Ascription in P. is much simpler than that in J., being addressed to our Saviour Jesus Christ, while J.'s is addressed μόνῳ Θεῷ σωτῆρι ἡμῶν διὰ Ἰησοῦ Χριστοῦ τοῦ κυρίου ἡμῶν. P. has δόξα only, while J. has the full liturgical form, δόξα, μεγαλωσύνη, κράτος, καὶ ἐξουσία. P. has καὶ νῦν καὶ εἰς ἡμέραν αἰῶνος, while J. has πρὸ παντὸς τοῦ αἰῶνος καὶ νῦν καὶ εἰς πάντας τοὺς αἰῶνας, concluding with ἀμήν, which is omitted in P. by W.H. after Cod. B. *Cf.* A. J. Wilson, *J. of Theol. Stud.* vol. viii. 75 on Emphasis in N.T.

To sum up: What do we find to be the main points in which the two Epistles agree, what the points in which they differ? Both agree in making faith, which is itself the gift of God (P. i. 1, λαχοῦσιν πίστιν), the foundation of the Christian life (J. vv. 3, 20, P. i. 1, 5): both agree that its commencement lies in the divine call (J. ver. 1, P. i. 3, 10). The call was sealed in baptism for the forgiveness of sin (J. ver. 5 in connexion with 1 Cor. x. 1, 2, P. i. 9), but we have to make our calling sure through good works (P. i. 10), to build ourselves up on the foundation of the faith (J. ver. 20, P. i. 5-7), to keep ourselves in the love of God by praying with the help of the Holy Spirit (J. ver. 20), looking for the mercy of our Lord Jesus Christ (which shall be fully revealed) in the life eternal (J. ver. 21). God our Saviour is able to keep us without stumbling and to present us before His glory unblemished in joy (J. vv. 24, 25). P. does not expressly mention prayer, and he lays more stress on personal effort than J. in the words "give diligence that ye may be found in peace, without spot and blameless in His sight" iii. 14, "beware lest ye fall from your steadfastness, grow in grace" iii. 17, 18. So in i. 5-8 he bids his readers add all diligence to supply "in your faith energy, in your energy knowledge," etc., and goes on in ver. 10 to say "if ye do these things, ye shall never stumble: for thus shall be richly supplied to you the entrance into the eternal kingdom". At the same time he ascribes to the divine power "all that pertains to life and godliness, through the knowledge of Him who called us by the manifestation of His own goodness". That manifestation has been to us the guarantee of most blessed promises, through which we are enabled to become partakers of the divine nature (P. i. 3, 4).

The broad distinction between the two Epistles may be said to be that, while J. is throughout occupied with the denunciation of evil-doers, except in vv. 1-3 and 20-25, P.'s denunciations are mainly confined to a portion of chapter ii., and that the latter dwells more upon the mercy of God as shown even in his punishments.

The conclusion I have drawn from the above comparison of the two Epistles as to the priority of J., is confirmed by the general opinion of modern critics, as by Neander, Credner, Ewald, Hilgenfeld, Holtzmann, Harnack, Bernhard Weiss, Abbott, Farrar, Salmon, above all by Dr. Chase in his excellent article on the "Second Epistle of St. Peter" in Hastings' *D. of B.* It is true some of the best authorities speak very doubtfully both of this priority and of the authenticity of 2 P. Thus Döllinger, who, in his *First Age of the Church*, had maintained the priority of 2 P., wrote to Dr. Plummer in the year 1879 that he could no longer hold this opinion (Plummer's *St. James* and *St. Jude* 1891, p. 400). See also Plummer's *St. Jude*, p. 268: "While admitting that the case is by no means proved, we may be content to retain the priority, as well as the authenticity of 2 Peter, as at least the best working hypothesis". And Hort is quoted by Dr. Sanday (*Inspiration*, p. 347) as saying that "If he were asked he should say that the balance of argument was against the epistle; and the moment he had done so he should begin to think that he might be wrong". On the other hand three of the most recent critics, Spitta in his Commentary on the two Epistles, 1885, Dr. Bigg in his *International Critical Commentary*, ed. 2, 1902, and the veteran Zahn in his *Einleitung in das N.T.*, ed. 3, 1906, have no hesitation in maintaining the priority and authenticity of 2 P. I proceed to consider the arguments which have been adduced by them or by others in favour of that view.[1]

(1) Assuming the genuineness of the two Epistles, it is easier, in a case of evident borrowing, to suppose that the borrower should be the comparatively obscure Jude, rather than Peter, the foremost of the Apostles.

(2) Jude seems to acknowledge his obligations to Peter in ver. 4 οἱ πάλαι προγεγραμμένοι εἰς τοῦτο τὸ κρίμα . . . τὸν μόνον δεσπότην ἀρνούμενοι and in vv. 17, 18 μνήσθητε τῶν ῥημάτων τῶν προειρημένων ὑπὸ τῶν ἀποστόλων τοῦ κυρίου ἡμῶν Ἰησοῦ Χριστοῦ, ὅτι ἔλεγον ὑμῖν Ἐπ᾽ ἐσχάτου χρόνου ἔσονται ἐμπαῖκται κατὰ τὰς ἑαυτῶν ἐπιθυμίας πορευόμενοι, the former verse being regarded as an allusion to P.'s ii. 3 ἐν ὑμῖν ἔσονται ψευδοδιδάσκαλοι . . . τὸν ἀγοράσαντα αὐτοὺς δεσπότην ἀρνούμενοι . . . οἷς τὸ κρίμα ἔκπαλαι οὐκ ἀργεῖ, the latter to P. iii. 2, 3 μνησθῆναι τῶν προειρημένων ῥημάτων ὑπὸ τῶν ἁγίων προφητῶν καὶ τῆς τῶν ἀποστόλων ὑμῶν ἐντολῆς τοῦ κυρίου καὶ σωτῆρος, τοῦτο πρῶτον γινώσκοντες ὅτι ἐλεύσονται ἐπ᾽ ἐσχάτων τῶν ἡμερῶν ἐν ἐμπαιγμονῇ ἐμπαῖκται κατὰ τὰς ἰδίας ἐπιθυμίας αὐτῶν πορευόμενοι.

[1] I agree with Dr. Bigg that it is superfluous to consider theories which suppose 2 P. to be made up of two independent epistles. Its unity, as shown in the earlier part of this chapter, forces itself on the mind of any careful reader.

(3) The priority of P. is confirmed by the prevailing use of the future tense in regard to the innovators, whereas J. uses the past or the present; *cf.* P. ii. 1 ἔσονται, παρεισάξουσιν, ii. 2 ἐξακολουθήσουσιν, βλασφημηθήσεται, ii. 3 ἐμπορεύσονται, with J. ver. 4 παρεισεδύησαν, ver. 8 μαίνουσιν, ver. 10 βλασφημοῦσιν and the aorists in ver. 11.

Dealing with these objections in order, we may concede that, if both Epistles are genuine, we should rather have expected the borrowing to be on the side of the more obscure. Yet the probability is not one that can be pressed. Milton and Handel borrowed from men much inferior to themselves; Isaiah borrows from Micah, and 1 P. from James. If on the other hand we find reason to believe that 2 P. was not written by the Apostle, the objection only amounts to this, that, though St. Peter himself had borrowed from James in 1 P., an admirer of St. Peter could not have borrowed from Jude in 2 P. With regard to obj. (2), I have pointed out in my note that the word πάλαι in J. ver. 4 cannot refer to P., but must be understood of the prophecy of Enoch, quoted in J. ver. 15, in which the word ἀσεβεῖς (which sums up the judgment in ver. 4), occurs no less than four times (if we include the cognate verb and abstract noun). I have also pointed out that J. in ver. 17 refers not to any one writer, but to the oral teaching of the Apostles, and that P. in iii. 2 does not profess to utter any new prophecy, but simply adds to what Jude had said, that the teaching of the Apostles rested upon the authority of Christ, and that it was in agreement with the teaching of the prophets. As regards obj. (3), the difference of tense, P. is not consistent in his use of the future. We have the pres. in ii. 10 τρέμουσιν, ii. 17 εἰσίν, ii. 18 δελεάζουσιν, iii. 5 λανθάνει, from which we should conclude that the innovators had already begun their work, if not among those to whom he writes, yet among other churches, to which J. may have addressed himself. If the former Epistle is a product of the second century, the writer may have used the future tense to give it verisimilitude, while falling at times into the present from inadvertence.

(4) Spitta asks why, if P. is borrowing from J., he makes no reference to him, as he does to Paul? It might be enough to ask in reply, "Why, if J. borrows from P., does he make no definite acknowledgment of the fact"? But we have a parallel case, though no doubt on a smaller scale, in the unacknowledged borrowings from the Epistle of James in 1 Peter, on which see the Introduction to my edition of James, pp. xcviii to cii. The reason however for the mention of Paul in 2 P. is quite distinct from the acknowledgment of a debt. The libertines claimed his authority in behalf of their own views (*cf.* J. ver. 4), and it was necessary for P. to protest against this.

It would be endless to go into a minute examination of the parallel passages which have been cited to prove the priority of P. I have said all that I think need be said about them in the earlier part of this chapter and in the explanatory notes of my edition of 2 P. The impression which they leave on my mind is that in J. we have the first thought, in P. the second thought; that we can generally see a reason why P. should have altered J., but very rarely a reason why what we read in P. should have been altered to what we find in J. P. is more reflective, J. more spontaneous.

CHAPTER II.

The Epistle of Jude, Author, Style, Authenticity, Circumstances of Writing.—The name Judas (Ἰούδας) was naturally in very common use among the Jews at the time of the Christian era. It was dear to them as having been borne not only by the Eponymos of their tribe, but also by their great champion Judas the Maccabee. Two among the Twelve bore this name, Judas Iscariot, and the Judas not Iscariot (Jn. xiv. 22), who is also called Judas son of James (ὁ Ἰακώβου, Lk. vi. 16, Acts i. 13) and Thaddaeus (Mt. ix. 3, Mk. iii. 18, where some MSS. add Λεββαῖος). Besides these we meet with a Judas among the Brethren of the Lord (Mt. xiii. 55, Mk. vi. 3), Judas of Galilee (Acts v. 37), Judas surnamed Barsabbas (Acts xv. 22), Judas of Damascus (Acts ix. 11). It is therefore not surprising that the writer should have added a note of identification, δοῦλος Ἰησοῦ Χριστοῦ, ἀδελφὸς δὲ Ἰακώβου. The most famous James in the middle of the first century was the head of the Church at Jerusalem and brother of the Lord, who also begins his epistle by styling himself simply δοῦλος (Θεοῦ καὶ Κυρίου) Ἰησοῦ Χριστοῦ. Hence it seems probable that the addition was made, not merely for the purpose of identification, but, like the addition of ἀπόστολος δέ in Tit. i. 1, as giving a reason why his words should be received with respect, since he was brother of James and therefore one of the Brethren of the Lord. In my Introduction to the Epistle of St. James (pp. i-xlvii), I have endeavoured to show that the Brethren of the Lord were sons of Joseph and Mary, that they did not join the Church till after the Crucifixion, and that none of them was included among the Twelve.[1]

Other facts which we learn from the N.T. are (1) that Jude was probably either the youngest or the youngest but one of the Brethren of the Lord, as he is mentioned last among them in Mt. xiii. 55 οἱ ἀδελφοὶ αὐτοῦ Ἰάκωβος καὶ Ἰωσῆς καὶ Σίμων καὶ Ἰούδας, and last but one in Mk. vi. 3 ἀδελφὸς δὲ Ἰακώβου καὶ Ἰωσῆ καὶ Ἰούδα καὶ Σίμωνος; (2) that the Brethren of the Lord (of course exclusive of James, who

[1] See ver. 17, where the writer appears to distinguish between the Apostles and himself.

remained stationary at Jerusalem) were engaged in missionary journeys like St. Paul (1 Cor. ix. 5), but that they differed from him in the fact that they were married and were accompanied by their wives, and also, as we may suppose from Gal. ii. 9, Mt. x. 23, that their ministrations were mainly directed to the Jews. In my edition of James (p. cxv) I have argued that his Epistle was addressed to Jews of the eastern Diaspora and it seems not improbable that Jude, writing many years after his brother's death, may have wished to supply his place by addressing to the same circle of readers the warnings which he felt bound to utter under the perilous circumstances of the new age. His cousin Symeon, the son of his uncle Clopas, had succeeded to the bishopric of Jerusalem (Eus., *H.E.*, iii., 22, iv., 22, quoted in my edition of James pp. viii foll.), and is said to have been crucified A.D. 107 at the age of 120[1] (*cf.* Hegesippus *ap.* Euseb., *H.E.*, iii., 32, **ἀπὸ τούτων τῶν αἱρετικῶν κατηγοροῦσι τινὲς Συμεῶνος . . . ὡς ὄντος ἀπὸ Δαβὶδ καὶ Χριστιανοῦ. καὶ οὕτως μαρτυρεῖ ἐτῶν ὢν ἑκατὸν εἴκοσιν ἐπὶ Τραϊανοῦ Καίσαρος καὶ ὑπατικοῦ Ἀττικοῦ**).

Eusebius (*H.E.*, iii., 19) quotes again from Hegesippus an interesting story of the grandsons of Judas, "who were seized and carried to Rome by order of Domitian, whose fears had been excited by the report he heard of them as descendants of David, and akin to the Messiah. When they were brought before him, he quickly ascertained that they were poor men, and that the kingdom they looked forward to was not of this world, and accordingly dismissed them as men of no importance, and ceased from his persecution of the Church. When they returned home, they received special honours, as having witnessed to the truth, and also as being kinsmen of the Lord. They lived till the time of Trajan."

In my Introduction to St. James I have pointed out that his Epistle bears marked traces of some characteristics which are found in the Lord Himself. I propose to call attention here to some resemblances and differences between the Epistles of the two brothers.

A. (1) Among the former we may note the tone of undoubting and unquestioned authority which pervades the two Epistles, combined with the personal humility of the writers. They do not arrogate to themselves that relationship which constituted the ground of the reverence with which they were regarded by their fellow-believers. They are simply servants of Jesus Christ, the Lord of Glory, to whose coming, as the righteous Judge, they look forward, whose power still manifests itself in works of mercy (James i. 1, ii. 1, v. 8, 9, 14); of Jesus Christ, who keeps His people safe to the end, through whom

[1] More probably under 95.

they hope for eternal life, to deny whom is the climax of impiety, in whom the Father is glorified for ever (Jude vv. 1, 4, 21, 25). They are sharers of a common salvation (Jude ver. 3), they need forgiveness of sin like other men (James iii. 2).

(2) Mental characteristics as exhibited in the two Epistles.

In my edition of James (p. ccxxix.) I have summed up the more general qualities of his style in the words "energy, vivacity, and as conducive to both, vividness of representation, meaning by the last that dislike of mere abstractions, that delight in throwing everything into picturesque and dramatic forms, which is so marked a feature in our Epistle". To a certain extent this is true also of Jude, as shown in his imaginative power and his frequent use of figurative speech. *Cf.* Jude ver. 8, where the innovators are spoken of as dreamers polluting the flesh; ver. 12, where they are compared (1) to sunken rocks on which those who meet them at the love-feasts run aground and perish, (2) to waterless clouds driven by the wind, (3) to trees which have to be rooted up, because they bear no fruit in the fruit-bearing season, (4) to wild waves foaming out their own shame on the shore, (5) to falling stars which are extinguished in everlasting gloom. In ver. 20 the faithful are bidden to build themselves up on their most holy faith; in ver. 23, to save sinners, snatching them from the fire; to hate the garment spotted by the flesh. In regard to St. James I further illustrated the quality of vividness by "the frequent reference to examples such as Abraham, Rahab, Job, Elijah". In the same way St. Jude gives animation to his warnings by reference to the Israelites who perished in the wilderness for their unbelief after being saved from Egypt; to the fallen angels who are reserved for the judgment in everlasting chains; to Sodom and the neighbouring cities, which sinned in the same way as the angels, and now suffer the penalty of eternal fire (vv. 5-7). Reverence for the powers of the unseen world is commended by the pattern of the archangel Michael, who, even in his dispute with the devil for the body of Moses, refused to bring a railing accusation, but committed the case to God (vv. 8, 9). Cain and Balaam and Korah are cited as the predecessors of the present disturbers of the Church (ver. 11). Enoch the seventh from Adam has left us his warning against such men (vv. 14, 15). "You have yourselves heard the same warning from the Apostles" (ver. 17).

(3) For moral strictness and stern severity in rebuking sin, the whole of this short Epistle may be compared with such passages as James ii. 19, iii. 15, iv. 1-v. 6. For noble and weighty expression we may compare vv. 20, 21, ὑμεῖς δέ, ἀγαπητοί, ἐποικοδομοῦντες ἑαυτοὺς τῇ

ἁγιωτάτῃ ὑμῶν πίστει, ἐν πνεύματι ἁγίῳ προσευχόμενοι, ἑαυτοὺς ἐν ἀγάπῃ Θεοῦ τηρήσατε, προσδεχόμενοι τὸ ἔλεος τοῦ κυρίου ἡμῶν Ἰησοῦ Χριστοῦ εἰς ζωὴν αἰώνιον and the final doxology, with the passages which I have selected from St. James in p. ccxxviii. The appealing ἀγαπητοί, which is thrice found in St. James, is also thrice repeated in Jude. The warning against Respect of Persons is found in James ii. 1-9 and in Jude ver. 16: that against a murmuring discontented spirit in James i. 13, iv. 1, v. 9, in Jude vv. 15, 16; that against the misuse of the tongue in James iii. 1-10, in Jude ver. 16: the charge to labour for the salvation of others in James v. 19, 20, in Jude vv. 22, 23.

For special details of the style of St. Jude see my larger edition, pp. xxvi-lxvi: one point which may be noticed here is his fondness for triplets. Thus in ver. 2 we find ἔλεος[1] καὶ εἰρήνη[2] καὶ ἀγάπη[3] πληθυνθείη. In ver. 4 "the men who were designed for this judgment" are described as ἀσεβεῖς[1], τὴν τοῦ Θεοῦ χάριτα μετατιθέντες[2] εἰς ἀσέλγειαν, τὸν μόνον δεσπότην ἀρνούμενοι[3]. In vv. 3-7 three examples of punishment are adduced, Israel in the wilderness, the angels who sinned, the overthrow of Sodom. In ver. 8 the libertines, σάρκα μὲν μιαίνουσιν, κυριότητα δὲ ἀθετοῦσιν, δόξας δὲ βλασφημοῦσιν. [In vv. 9, 10 we have two couplets οὐκ ἐτόλμησεν—ἀλλὰ εἶπεν: ὅσα μὲν οὐκ οἴδασιν—βλασφημοῦσιν, ὅσα δὲ—φθείρονται.] In ver. 11 we return to the triplet, Cain, Balaam, Korah. [In vv. 12, 13 we have a quintet of metaphors, hidden rocks, rainless clouds, dead trees, turbid waves, falling stars. In ver. 15 again two couplets ποιῆσαι κρίσιν—ἐλέγξαι, περὶ πάντων ὧν ἠσέβησαν—ὧν ἐλάλησαν.] In ver. 16 we return to the triplet πορευόμενοι—λαλοῦντες (disguised in the form καὶ τὸ στόμα λαλεῖ ὑπέρογκα)—θαυμάζοντες. So in ver. 17, the word—the Apostles—the Lord. Ver. 18 does not admit of subdivision. Ver. 19 has the triplet ἀποδιορίζοντες, ψυχικοί, πνεῦμα μὴ ἔχοντες. Vv. 20 and 21 have a double triplet, ἐποικοδομοῦντες—προσευχόμενοι—προσδεχόμενοι and πνεῦμα ἅγιον—Θεός—Ἰησοῦς Χριστός. Ver. 22 has the marked triplet οὓς μὲν—οὓς δὲ—οὓς δέ. Ver. 24 has a couplet, φυλάξαι—στῆσαι. Ver. 25 has a quartet δόξα, μεγαλωσύνη, κράτος, ἐξουσία, followed by the triplet πρὸ παντὸς τοῦ αἰῶνος, καὶ νῦν, καὶ εἰς πάντας τοὺς αἰῶνας, thus closing with a septet. Compare the stress laid on the fact that Enoch was *seventh* from Adam, ver. 14.

There are some traces of the triplet in St. James, as in i. 14, ἕκαστος πειράζεται ὑπὸ τῆς ἰδίας ἐπιθυμίας—εἶτα ἡ ἐπιθυμία τίκτει ἁμαρτίαν, ἡ δὲ ἁμαρτία ἀποκύει θάνατον, ver. 19 ἔστω δὲ πᾶς ἄνθρωπος ταχὺς εἰς τὸ ἀκοῦσαι, βραδὺς εἰς τὸ λαλῆσαι, βραδὺς εἰς ὀργήν, ii. 23 ἐπίστευσεν Ἀβραὰμ τῷ Θεῷ, καὶ ἐλογίσθη αὐτῷ εἰς δικαιοσύνην, καὶ φίλος Θεοῦ ἐκλήθη, iii. 6, ἡ γλῶσσ ἡ σπιλοῦσα, καὶ φλογίζουσα—καὶ φλογιζομένη, iv. 8, ἐγγίσατε τῷ Θεῷ—καθαρίσατε χεῖρας—ἁγνίσατε καρδίας, so iv. 9, v. 17, 18. Perhaps we may find a septet in the beautiful description of heavenly wisdom (iii. 17) πρῶτον μὲν ἁγνή, ἔπειτα εἰρηνική, ἐπιεικής, εὐπειθής, μεστὴ ἐλέους καὶ καρπῶν ἀγαθῶν, ἀδιάκριτος, ἀνυπόκριτος. But the distinctive mark of St. James's style is "paronomasia" passing at times into such a climax as we find in i. 14, 15 quoted above and in i. 3, 4, τὸ δοκίμιον ὑμῶν τῆς πίστεως κατεργάζεται ὑπομονήν, ἡ δὲ ὑπομονὴ ἔργον τέλειον ἐχέτω, ἵνα ἦτε τέλειοι. See pp. ccxxii f. of my edition.

Another characteristic which may be noted is the love of forcible antithesis as in J. ver. 10, ὅσα μὲν οὐκ οἴδασιν βλασφημοῦσιν, ὅσα δὲ φυσικῶς ὡς τὰ ἄλογα ζῷα ἐπίστανται, ἐν τούτοις φθείρονται. As regards vocabulary, the most striking resemblance is the occurrence of ψυχικός as opposed to πνευματικός, of which the earliest biblical example is in James iii. 15, but this had been adopted by Paul (1 Cor. ii. 10 foll.) before it was made use of by Jude.

B. (1) The differences between the two Epistles are hardly less marked: Jude evidently belongs to a much later period of Christian development. James, as I have endeavoured to show in the Introduction to his Epistle, wrote about the year 45 A.D. before any of the other canonical books was in existence, and his theological position is that of the early Church described in the opening chapters of the Acts. Jude is familiar with the writings of St. Paul. He is familiar with the terms σωτήρ and σωτηρία (vv. 3 and 25): in vv. 20, 21 he brings together the three Persons of the Trinity; he addresses those to whom he writes in Pauline language as κλητοί (ver. 1) and ἅγιοι (ver. 3), and uses forms of ascription and doxology closely resembling those which occur in St. Peter and St. Paul. Their "most holy faith" is a "tradition once delivered to the saints" (vv. 4, 20): they are bidden to "remember the words of the Apostles, how they told them that in the last time there should come scoffers" (vv. 17, 18). The error which he combats appears to be a misgrowth of St. Paul's teaching in regard to a salvation of free grace, "not of works, lest any man should boast" (ver. 4). Many of the features which he distinguishes are such as we find delineated in St. Paul's farewell to the Ephesian Church, and in some of his Epistles, especially those to Titus and Timothy.

(2) Another difference might seem to be Jude's repeated references to Pseudepigrapha such as the book of Enoch and the Assumption of Moses (on which see the next chapter) and his readiness to give credence to fanciful legends such as the fall of the Watchers, and the contention for the body of Moses. Credulity of this kind seems to

be far apart from the strong practical sense of James. Yet there are signs that the latter was not unacquainted with rabbinical traditions. Spitta even goes so far as to trace most of his teaching to pre-Christian sources. I have argued against this view in ch. vii. 2 of my Introduction to his Epistle; but my notes on i. 8 (δίψυχος) and iv. 8, 9 ἁγνίσατε καρδίας, δίψυχοι· ταλαιπωρήσατε, suggest a connexion with an apocryphal writing quoted in Clem. Rom. i. 23 ἡ γραφὴ αὕτη, ὅπου λέγει Ταλαίπωροί εἰσιν οἱ δίψυχοι[1] and identified by Lightfoot and Spitta with *Eldad and Modad* (on which see Herm., *Vis.*, ii., 3), by Hilgenfeld with the *Assumption of Moses.* The phrase in iv. 14, ἀτμὶς γάρ ἐστε πρὸς ὀλίγον φαινομένη, has been traced by some to another apocryphal quotation found in Clem. i. 17 ἐγὼ δέ εἰμι ἀτμὶς ἀπὸ κύθρας, which Hilgenfeld also supposes to be taken from the *Assumption of Moses.* The phrase κόσμος ἀδικίας in James iii. 6 is found in Enoch xlviii. 7. The *Testaments of the Patriarchs*, which also contain quotations from Enoch (such as *Sim.* 5 ἑώρακα ἐν χαρακτῆρι γραφῆς Ἐνώχ, *Levi* 10 βίβλος Ἐνὼχ τοῦ δικαίου, *ib.* 14, ἔγνων ἀπὸ γραφῆς Ἐνὼχ ὅτι ἐπὶ τέλει ἀσεβήσετε, *ib.* 16, *Juda* 18, *Benj.* 9, *Zab.* 3, *Nepht.* 4. ἐν γραφῇ ἁγίᾳ Ἐνὼχ ὅτι . . . ποιήσετε κατὰ πᾶσαν ἀνομίαν Σοδόμων), furnish several parallels quoted in my note on James iv. 7 ἀντίστητε τῷ διαβόλῳ καὶ φεύξεται ἀφ' ὑμῶν. The words which immediately precede (ἐγγίσατε τῷ Θεῷ καὶ ἐγγίσει ὑμῖν) are not unlike another quotation which occurs in Herm. *Vis.* ii. 3, ἐγγὺς Θεὸς τοῖς ἐπιστρεφομένοις, ὡς γέγραπται ἐν τῷ Ἐλδὰτ καὶ Μωδὰτ τοῖς προφητεύσασιν ἐν τῇ ἐρήμῳ τῷ λαῷ. James has also been credited with a knowledge of the Sibylline writings on the ground of the phrase ἰοῦ θανατηφόρου which occurs in iii. 8 and also in Sib. *Prooem.* 71.

εἰσὶ θεοὶ μερόπων δηλήτορες[2] <οὗτοι> ἀβούλων,
τῶν δὴ κὰκ στόματος χεῖται θανατηφόρος ἰός.

But if there is borrowing, it is just as likely to be on the other side. The strange expression τροχὸς γενέσεως in iii. 6 is regarded as Orphic by some, but it seems to have been used by the Orphic writers in a different sense, *viz.* that of the endless changes of metempsychosis.

(3) Another difference which strikes one on reading the two epistles is that while the former is full of instruction for the present time, the bulk of the latter is made up of denunciations, which have very much lost their force. To a modern reader it is curious rather

[1] The quotation, as given more fully in Clem. Rom. ii. 11, contains the somewhat rare word ἀκαταστασία, which is also used by James iii. 16.

[2] MS. δολοητορες. Geffcken reads δόλῳ ἡγητῆρες.

than edifying, with the exception of the beginning and end (vv. 1, 2 and 20-25). This is no doubt to be explained by what is stated of the purport of the letter in ver. 3. It was called out by a sudden emergency, to guard against an immediate pressing danger, and was substituted for a treatise περὶ τῆς κοινῆς σωτηρίας which Jude had hoped to send (ver. 3), and which would probably have been more in the tone and spirit of vv. 20 f.

The Epistle of Jude was recognised as canonical in the Third Council of Carthage, A.D. 397 (Westcott on the Canon, p. 566), with which agree Jerome (Westcott, p. 580) and Augustine (*De Doctr. Christiana*, ii. 12). Jerome, however (*De vir. ill.* iv.), mentions that, owing to the use made of the apocryphal Enoch, the epistle of Jude *a plerisque reicitur*. So Eusebius *H.E.* ii. 23, "Not many old writers have mentioned the Epistle of James, nor yet the Epistle of Jude, which is also one of the seven so-called Catholic Epistles, though we know that these have been publicly used with the rest in most churches." *Ib.* iii. 25, "Among the controverted books, which are nevertheless well known and recognised by most, we class the Epistle circulated under the name of James and that of Jude." Cyril of Jerusalem (d. 386 A.D.) acknowledged both Jude and 2 P. In Asia Minor both Jude and 2 P. were recognised as canonical by Gregory Naz. (d. *c.* 391). In Alexandria Didymus (d. 394) wrote comments on the Catholic Epistles, especially defending Jude from the attacks made upon him as having made use of apocryphal books. Athanasius (d. 373) in his list of the books of the N.T. "agrees exactly with our own Canon" (Westcott, p. 520). Origen (*In Matt.* x. 17) says of Jude ἔγραψεν ἐπιστολήν, ὀλιγόστιχον μέν, πεπληρωμένην δὲ τῶν τῆς οὐρανίου χάριτος ἐρρωμένων λόγων. In the same treatise (xvii. 30) he quotes Jude 6, adding words which signify that it was not universally received, εἰ δὲ καὶ τὴν Ἰούδα πρόσοιτό τις ἐπιστολήν. Clement of Alexandria commented on Jude in his *Hypotyposes* (Eus. *H.E.* vi. 14)—the comment is still extant in the Latin translation—and quotes him by name (*Paed.* iii. 44, 45) with commendation, διδασκαλικώτατα ἐκτίθεται τὰς εἰκόνας τῶν κρινομένων. He quotes him again *Strom.* iii. 11, and, without naming him, in *Strom.* vi. 65. Tertullian (*De Cult. Fem.* 3) says "Enoch apud Judam apostolum testimonium possidet". It appears in the Muratorian Canon (*c.* 170 A.D.), "Epistola sane Judae et superscripti Johannis duae in catholicis habentur". Theophilus of Antioch (*ad Autol.* ii. 15) seems to allude to Jude 13 in the words quoted in my note on that verse. Athenagoras (*c.* 180) speaks (§ 24, p. 130 Otto) of the fallen angels in a manner which suggests acquaintance with

Jude ver. 6, ἀγγέλους τοὺς μὴ τηρήσαντας τὴν ἑαυτῶν ἀρχήν. (Of the angels some) ἔμειναν ἐφ' οἷς αὐτοὺς ἐποίησεν καὶ διέταξεν ὁ Θεός, οἱ δὲ ἐνύβρισαν καὶ τῇ τῆς οὐσίας ὑποστάσει καὶ τῇ ἀρχῇ, and he adds that he asserts this on the authority of the prophets, which may perhaps refer both to Enoch and Jude. The form of salutation in Jude 2 ἔλεος καὶ εἰρήνη καὶ ἀγάπη πληθυνθείη is found in *Mart. Polyc. Inscr.* and Polyc. *ad Phil.* The earliest reference however to Jude is probably to be found in 2 Pet., which, as we have seen in the preceding Chapter I., is largely copied from him. There appears also to be an allusion to it in *Didache* ii. 7, οὐ μισήσεις πάντα ἄνθρωπον, ἀλλὰ οὓς μὲν ἐλέγξεις, περὶ δὲ ὧν προσεύξῃ, οὓς δὲ ἀγαπήσεις, *cf.* Jude 22. Jude's epistle was included in the Old Latin Version, but not in the Peshitto.

The most important passage in Jude bearing upon the circumstances of its composition is ver. 17, where the readers are bidden to call to mind the words formerly spoken to them by the Apostles of our Lord Jesus Christ (which would fit in with the suggestion that it was addressed to the Syrian churches) ὅτι ἔλεγον ὑμῖν Ἐπ' ἐσχάτου χρόνου ἔσονται ἐμπαῖκται, the latter words showing that these communications of the Apostles had now ceased, either by their death or by their removal from Jerusalem. Jude recognises that "the last time," of which they had preached, had now arrived. The long retrospect which these words imply agrees with the far-away note of ver. 3, παρακαλῶν ἐπαγωνίζεσθαι τῇ ἅπαξ παραδοθείσῃ τοῖς ἁγίοις πίστει, as contrasted with such passages as Luke iv. 21 σήμερον πεπλήρωται ἡ γραφή αὕτη, though we must not forget that the idea of a Christian tradition is familiar to St. Paul, and that there are other examples in the N.T. of the objective use of πίστις.

It has been argued that this epistle must have been written before 70, or it would have contained some reference to the destruction of Jerusalem among the other notable judgments of God. We may grant that this is what we should have expected, if the letter were written shortly afterwards, though even then it is a possible view that a patriotic Jew might shrink from any further allusion to so terrible a subject, beyond the reference to the destruction in the wilderness (ver. 5); but this difficulty is lessened if we suppose the date of the Epistle to be nearer 80 than 70.

CHAPTER III.

Use of Apocryphal Books by Jude.—Clement of Alexandria in his *Adumbrationes* (Dind. vol. iii. p. 483), after quoting Jude 9, "Quando Michael archangelus cum diabolo disputans altercabatur de corpore Moysis," remarks "hic confirmat *Assumptionem Moysis*," *i.e.*, here the writer corroborates the *Assumption of Moses*; and again, in commenting on ver. 14, "Prophetavit autem de his septimus ab Adam Enoch," he adds "His verbis prophetam (*al.* prophetiam) comprobat".

The Hebrew original of the book of Enoch[1] is now lost. It was translated into Greek, of which only a few fragments remain, and this was again translated into Ethiopic, probably about 600 A.D. A copy of the last was found in Abyssinia in 1773 by Bruce, the famous traveller, and an English version was published by Abp. Laurence in 1821, followed by the Ethiopic text in 1838. The composite nature of the book is generally recognised. The latest editor, R. H. Charles, who is my authority for what follows, divides it into five sections and recognises many interpolations in these. He considers that the larger portion of the book was written not later than 160 B.C., and that no part is more recent than the Christian era. It exercised an important influence on Jewish and Christian literature during the centuries which followed being used by the author of the *Assumption of Moses* (written about the Christian era), also by the writers of the *Book of Jubilees*, the *Apocalypse of Baruch*, the *Fourth Book of Ezra*, and the *Testaments of the Twelve Patriarchs*. Mr. Charles traces its influence in the N.T. not merely in the epistles of St. Jude and the two epistles of St. Peter, but above all, in the Apocalypse; also in the Acts, and the epistle to the Hebrews, in some of the epistles of St. Paul, and in the Gospels. It is quoted three times (twice as Scripture) in the *Epistle of Barnabas*, is referred to, though not named, in Justin and Athenagoras, is cited by Irenæus, iv. 16. 2: "Enoch . . . cum esset homo, legatione ad angelos fungebatur et translatus est et conservatur usque nunc testis judicii Dei, quoniam angeli

[1] On which see Schürer, *Hist. of Jewish People*, vol. iii. pp. 54-73.

quidem deciderunt in terram in judicium" (En. xiv. 7). Tertullian quotes it as Scripture, calling Enoch the oldest of the prophets (*Idol.* xv., *Apol.* xxii.). He allows that its canonicity was denied by some, "quia nec in armarium Judaicum admittitur," and also because it was thought that, if it were a genuine writing of Enoch, it must have perished in the Deluge. He considers, however, that it should be received, because of its witness to Christ, and because it has the testimony of the Apostle Jude. It is twice quoted in Clement's *Ecl. Proph.* (Dind. iii. pp. 456, 474) as well as in *Strom.* iii. 9. Origen speaks doubtfully of the authority of Enoch: *cf. C. Celsum,* v. 54, ἐν ταῖς ἐκκλησίαις οὐ πάνυ φέρεται ὡς θεῖα τὰ ἐπιγεγραμμένα τοῦ Ἐνὼχ βιβλία, and *In Johannem,* vi. 25, ὡς ἐν τῷ Ἐνὼχ γέγραπται, εἴ τῳ φίλον παραδέχεσθαι ὡς ἅγιον τὸ βιβλίον, also *In Num. Hom.* xxviii. 2, *De Princ.* i. 3. 3. Hilary (*Comm. in Psalm.* cxxxii. 3) writes: "Fertur id, de quo etiam nescio cuius liber extat, quod angeli concupiscentes filias hominum, cum de caelo descenderent, in montem Hermon convenerant". Jerome says that the doubts entertained as to the epistle of St. Jude arose from his quoting an apocryphal book as an authority (*De Vir. Ill.* iv), "quia de libro Enoch, qui apocryphus est, in ea assumit testimonia, a plerisque reicitur". *Cf.* also *Comm. in Ps.* cxxxii. 3 and *Comm. in Titum,* i. 12. Augustine (*Civ. Dei,* xv 23. 4) and Chrysostom (*Hom. in Gen.* vi. 1) speak of the story of the angels and the daughters of men as a baseless fable. Still more severe is the condemnation passed on the book of Enoch with other apocryphal writings in *Const. Apost.* vi. 16. 2, as φθοροποιὰ καὶ τῆς ἀληθείας ἐχθρά.

Mr. Charles has also edited the *Assumption of Moses* (1897), which he regards as a composite work made up of two distinct books, the *Testament* and the *Assumption* of Moses.[1] "The former was written in Hebrew between 7 and 29 A.D., and possibly also the latter. A Greek version of the entire work appeared in the first century A.D. Of this only a few fragments have been preserved. The Greek version was translated into Latin not later than the fifth century" (pp. xiii., xiv.). "The book preserved in the incomplete Latin version, first published by Ceriani in 1861, is in reality a Testament and not an Assumption." "The editing of the two books in one was probably done in the first century, as St. Jude draws upon both in his epistle" (pp. xlvii and l.). Thus Jude ver. 9[2] is derived from the

Cf. Schürer, pp. 73-83.

[2] See note on this, and add to the illustrative passages there quoted a scholium printed for the first time in James' *Test. of Abraham*, p. 18: ὁ διάβολος ἀντεῖχεν θέλων ἀπατῆσαι, λέγων ὅτι Ἐμόν ἐστιν τὸ σῶμα, ὡς τῆς ὕλης δεσπόζων· καὶ ἤκουσεν τὸ Ἐπιτιμήσαι σοι Κύριος, τούτεστιν ὁ Κύριος ὁ πάντων τῶν πνευμάτων

Assumption, Jude 16 from the *Testament* (p. lxii.). On the latter Charles compares οὗτοί εἰσι γογγυσταί, μεμψίμοιροι, καὶ τὸ στόμα αὐτῶν λαλεῖ ὑπέρογκα, θαυμάζοντες πρόσωπα ὠφελίας χάριν with *Ass. M.* vii. 7, *quaerulosi*, vii. 9, et manus eorum et mentes *immunda tractantes et os eorum loquetur ingentia*, v. 5, *erunt illis temporibus mirantes personas . . . et accipientes munera* (MS. acceptiones munerum). He identifies the ἐμπαῖκται of Jude 18 with the *homines pestilentiosi* of *Ass. M.* vii. 3, and calls attention to the frequent recurrence of the word ασεβεῖς in the former (vv. 4, 15, 18) and *impii* in the latter: see vi. 1, facient facientes impietatem, vii. 3, pestilentiosi et impii, *ib.* 7, ix. 3, xi. 17.

Again there appears to be a reminiscence of the *Testaments of the Patriarchs*,[1] where the sin of the Watchers is connected with that of Sodom: cf. *Test. Nepht.* 3, ἥλιος καὶ σελήνη καὶ ἀστέρες οὐκ ἀλλοιοῦσι τὴν τάξιν αὐτῶν . . . ἔθνη πλανηθέντα καὶ ἀφέντα κύριον ἠλλοίωσαν τάξιν αὐτῶν . . . ἐξακολουθήσαντες πνεύμασι πλάνης. Ὑμεῖς μὴ οὕτως . . . ἵνα μὴ γένησθε ὡς Σόδομα, ἥτις ἐνήλλαξεν τάξιν φύσεως αὐτῆς. Ὁμοίως καὶ Ἐγρήγορες ἐνήλλαξαν τάξιν φύσεως αὐτῶν, οὓς κατηράσατο Κύριος ἐπὶ τοῦ κατακλυσμοῦ, *Test. Aser* 7, μὴ γίνεσθε ὡς Σόδομα ἥτις ἠγνόησε τοὺς ἀγγέλους κυρίου καὶ ἀπώλετο ἕως αἰῶνος. There seems to be more than a casual coincidence between these passages and Jude 6, 7 and 13, ἀγγέλους τοὺς μὴ τηρήσαντας τὴν ἑαυτῶν ἀρχὴν . . . ὡς Σόδομα . . . τὸν ὅμοιον τρόπον ἐκπορνεύσασαι καὶ ἀπελθοῦσαι ὀπίσω σαρκὸς ἑτέρας πρόκεινται δεῖγμα πυρὸς αἰωνίου . . . ἀστέρες πλανῆται.

We have seen how this use of apocryphal books was viewed by the early Christian writers. They were at first disposed to think that a book stamped with the approval of St. Jude must be itself inspired. Later on, the feeling changed: the authority of St. Jude was no longer sufficient to save the apocryphal writing: on the contrary the prejudice against the Apocrypha and its "blasphemous fables" (Chrys. *Hom.* 22 *in Gen.*) led many to doubt the authority of St. Jude: see above quotation from Jerome, who argues that the approval of the Apostle need not be supposed to extend to the whole of the book of Enoch, but only to the verses quoted by him. So Augustine (*Civ. Dei*, xv. 23, 4): "Scripsisse quidem nonnulla divina Enoch illum septimum ab

δεσπόζων· ἄλλοι δέ, ὅτι βουλόμενος ὁ Θεὸς δεῖξαι ὅτι μετὰ τὴν ἔνθενδε ἀπαλλαγήν, ταῖς ἡμετέραις ψυχαῖς ἀνθιστάμενοι <ἦσαν> δαίμονες πορευομέναις τὴν ἐπὶ τὰ ἄνω πορείαν, τοῦτο οὖν συνεχώρησεν ὁρᾶσθαι ἐπὶ τῆς Μωσέως ταφῆς· ἐβλασφήμει γὰρ καὶ ὁ διάβολος κατὰ Μωσέως, φονέα τοῦτον καλῶν διὰ τὸ πατάξαι τὸν Αἰγύπτιον· ὁ Μιχαὴλ ὁ ἀρχάγγελος, μὴ ἐνεγκὼν τὴν αὐτοῦ βλασφημίαν, εἴρηκεν αὐτῷ ὅτι Ἐπιτιμήσαι σοι Κύριος ὁ Θεός, διάβολε. ἔλεγε δὲ καὶ τοῦτο, ὅτι ἐψεύσατο ὁ Θεὸς εἰσαγαγὼν τὸν Μωσῆν ἔνθα ὤμοσεν αὐτὸν μὴ εἰσελθεῖν.

[1] An edition has lately been brought out by Charles.

Adam negare non possumus, cum hoc in epistola canonica Judas apostolus dicat" (although the book as a whole has been justly excluded from the Canon).

Some modern writers have endeavoured to avoid the necessity of allowing that an apocryphal writing is quoted as authoritative in the Bible, by the supposition that the words quoted may have come down by tradition and have been made use of by the inspired writer, independently of the book from which he is supposed to quote, or that they were uttered by immediate inspiration without any human assistance, or again, that the book of Enoch may be subsequent to that of Jude, and have borrowed from it. But the careful investigation of many scholars, as summed up by Charles, can leave little doubt in any candid mind as to the proximate dates, both of Enoch and of the Assumption. St. Jude does not put forward his account of the burial of Moses or the preaching of Enoch, as though it were something unheard of before. As regards the libertines described in the latter book, he uses the phrase προγεγραμμένοι, implying that he refers to a written prophecy. None of the early Fathers find a difficulty in supposing him to refer to a book which was not included in the Canon. Jews of that time were accustomed to accept rabbinical explanations or additions to Scripture as having authority. Thus St. Paul accepts the story of the Rock which followed the Israelites in their wanderings (1 Cor. x. 4), gives the names of the magicians who withstood Moses before Pharaoh (2 Tim. iii. 8), recognises the instrumentality of angels in the giving of the Law (Gal. iii. 19, *cf.* Heb. ii. 2, Acts vii. 53). So, too, Stephen speaks of Moses as learned in all the wisdom of the Egyptians (Acts vii. 2); the author of the epistle to the Hebrews (xi. 37) alludes to the tradition as to the death of Isaiah (see Charles' *Ascension of Isaiah*, pp. xlv. foll.), and James (v. 17) limits the drought predicted by Elijah to 3½ years.

CHAPTER IV.

The Story of the Fallen Angels.—St. Jude (vv. 5-8) introduces as examples of the divine wrath against those who had sinned after receiving favours from God (1) the Israelites who perished in the wilderness for unbelief after they had been saved from Egypt; (2) the angels who abandoned their original office and habitation, being led away by fleshy lusts, and are now kept in chains under darkness till the day of judgment; (3) the people of Sodom, who inhabited a land like the garden of the Lord (Gen. xiii. 10), who were rescued from Chedorlaomer by Abraham (Gen. xiv. 16, 17), and yet sinned after the fashion of the angels, and are now a warning to all, suffering the punishment of eternal fire. A similar account is given in 2 Pet. ii.4-9 where it is said (1) that God spared not the angels who sinned, but hurled them into Tartarus, to be detained there in chains (or pits) of darkness until the final judgment; (2) that He brought a flood on the world of the ungodly, while he spared Noah; (3) that He destroyed Sodom and Gomorrah, while he delivered righteous Lot; in all three cases punishing impurity and rebellion.

As is shown in the explanatory notes, this account of the Fall of the Angels is taken directly from the book of Enoch, which is itself an expansion from Jewish and Gentile sources of the strange narrative contained in Gen. vi. 1-4: "It came to pass, when men began to multiply on the face of the ground and daughters were born unto them, that the sons of God saw the daughters of men that they were fair; and they took them wives of all that they chose. . . . The Nephilim were in the earth in those days, and also after that, when the sons of God came in to the daughters of men, and they bare children unto them: the same were the mighty men which were of old, the men of renown" (R.V.). ἐγένετο ἡνίκα ἤρξαντο οἱ ἄνθρωποι πολλοὶ γίνεσθαι ἐπὶ τῆς γῆς καὶ θυγατέρες ἐγεννήθησαν αὐτοῖς, ἰδόντες δὲ οἱ ἄγγελοι τοῦ Θεοῦ τὰς θυγατέρας τῶν ἀνθρώπων ὅτι καλαὶ εἰσὶν ἔλαβον ἑαυτοῖς γυναῖκας ἀπὸ πασῶν ὧν ἐξελέξαντο . . . οἱ δὲ γίγαντες ἦσαν ἐπὶ τῆς γῆς ἐν ταῖς ἡμέραις ἐκείναις, καὶ μετ' ἐκεῖνο, ὡς ἂν εἰσεπορεύοντο οἱ υἱοὶ τοῦ Θεοῦ πρὸς τὰς θυγατέρας τῶν ἀνθρώπων καὶ ἐγέννωσαν ἑαυτοῖς, ἐκεῖνοι ἦσαν οἱ γίγαντες οἱ ἀπ' αἰῶνος, οἱ ἄνθρωποι οἱ ὀνομαστοί (LXX). That the version ἄγγελοι gives the true force of the original is evident from the other passages in which the phrase "sons of God" occurs, Job i. 6, ii. 1, xxxviii. 7, Dan. iii. 25, 28, Ps. xxix. 1, lxxxix. 6. It has been suggested that the phrase μετ' ἐκεῖνο may be a marginal note having reference to Num. xiii. 33, where the Nephilim are mentioned as a gigantic race, "in whose eyes the spies were as grasshoppers," inhabiting a part of Canaan at the time of the Exodus. The translation γίγαντες implies not only superhuman size, but also superhuman insolence and impiety. According to Greek mythology they were children of Heaven and Earth, who rose up in insurrection against the Gods and were hurled down to Tartarus or buried beneath the mountains. This resemblance is noted by Josephus in the passage quoted below.

It is evident that the passage in Gen. vi. is a fragment unconnected either with what precedes or follows. Driver says of it: "We must see in it an ancient Hebrew legend . . . the intention of which was to account for the origin of a supposed race of prehistoric giants, of whom no doubt (for they were 'men of name') Hebrew folk-lore told much more than the compiler of Genesis has deemed worthy of preservation". Ryle (*Early Narratives of Genesis*, pp. 91-95) speaks of it as "an extract from a very early legend which gives an alternative explanation of the Fall, in which woman is again tempted by one of higher race".

The story was variously commented on by later Jewish writers, most of whom supposed that the Nephilim were the offspring of the intercourse between the angels and the daughters of men, and that they were destroyed in the Flood.

The Fall of the Angels is largely treated of in the collection of treatises which goes under the name of the Book of Enoch. The earliest portion of the book is considered by the latest editor, Mr. R. H. Charles, to have been written in the first quarter of the second century B.C. Two hundred of the angels, or watchers, Ἐγρήγοροι as they are called in the Greek versions of Dan. iv. 13 by Aquila and Symmachus, conspired together under the leadership of Semjaza (elsewhere called Azazel, as in Enoch, chapters viii. and ix.) and descended on Mount Hermon in the days of Jared, father of Enoch (vi.). There they took to themselves human wives whom they instructed in magic and various arts, and begot giants, who afterwards begot the Nephilim: *cf.* viii., οἱ δὲ γίγαντες ἐτέκνωσαν Ναφηλείμ . . . μετὰ δὲ ταῦτα ἤρξαντο οἱ γίγαντες κατεσθίειν τὰς σάρκας τὰς ἀνθρώπων (like Polyphemus). Complaint having been made of the sin and misery thus introduced into the world, Raphael is sent down from heaven to bind Azazel hand and foot and shut him up in darkness till the judgment day, when he will be cast into eternal fire. Gabriel is at the same time sent to slay the giants (x. 9): the watchers will be bound under the hills for seventy generations, and then be confined for ever in the abyss of fire: the spirits of the slain giants become demons. In chap. xix., however, the demons are represented as existing before the fall of the watchers.

The prevailing demonology of the Book of Enoch is thus summed up by Dr. Charles (*Enoch*, p. 52). The angelic watchers who fell from lusting after the daughters of men have been imprisoned in darkness from the time of their fall. The demons are the spirits which proceeded from the souls of the giants who were their offspring. They work moral ruin on earth without hindrance till the final judgment. Satan is the ruler of a counter kingdom of evil. He led astray the angels and made them his subjects. He also tempted Eve. The Satans can still appear in heaven (as in Job). They tempt to evil, they accuse the fallen, they punish the condemned. In portions however of the Book of Enoch there is no mention of a Satan or Satans, but the angels are led astray by their own chief Azazel, or as he is sometimes called Semjaza (*En.* ix., x., xiii., liv.). Of the *Secrets of Enoch*, which is supposed to date from about the Christian era, Dr. Charles says:[1] "It is hard to get a consistent view of the demonology of the book; it seems to be as follows: Satan, one of the archangels, seduced the watchers of the fifth heaven into revolt in order to establish a counter kingdom to God. Therefore Satan or the Satans were cast down from heaven and given the air for their habitation. Some however of the Satans or Watchers went down to earth and married the daughters of men." Compare xviii. 3, "These are the Grigori, who with their prince Satanail rejected the holy Lord, and in consequence of these things they are kept in great darkness".

In chap. liv. there appears to be an attempt to connect the two different stories of the Fall: the guilt of the Watchers is said to have consisted in their becoming subject to Satan, who was either identified with the Serpent, as in Apoc. xii. 9, καὶ ἐβλήθη ὁ δράκων ὁ μέγας, ὁ ὄφις ὁ ἀρχαῖος, ὁ καλούμενος Διάβολος καὶ ὁ Σατανᾶς, ὁ πλανῶν τὴν οἰκουμένην ὅλην—ἐβλήθη εἰς τὴν γῆν, καὶ οἱ ἄγγελοι αὐτοῦ μετ᾽ αὐτοῦ ἐβλήθησαν; or else was supposed to have made use of the Serpent as his instrument, as in the *Assumption of Moses* quoted by Orig. *De Princip.* iii. 2. 1 (Lomm. vol. xxi. p. 303): "In Genesi serpens Evam seduxisse describitur, de quo in *Asc. Mosis* (cujus libelli meminit apostolus Judas) Michael Archangelus cum diabolo disputans de cor-

[1] See his note on pp. 36, 37.

pore Mosis ait a diabolo inspiratum serpentem causam exstitisse praevaricationis Adae et Evae ".[1]

The history of the gradual development of the belief in regard to Satan, as exhibited in the Bible, will be found in any of the Dictionaries of the Bible. Beside the attempt to harmonise the two Fall-stories by making Satan the cause of both, an attempt was made to arrive at the same result by ascribing to Satan or the Serpent the same motive which led to the fall of the angels. In Wisdom ii. 24 we read "By the envy of the devil death entered into the world". This envy is explained in rabbinical writings sometimes as occasioned by the dignity of Adam and his lordship over the creation, but more frequently by Satan's desire for Eve:[2] *cf.* 4 Macc. xviii. 8, οὐδὲ ἐλυμήνατό μου τὰ ἁγνὰ τῆς παρθενίας λυμεὼν ἀπάτης ὄφις. Sometimes again his fall is ascribed to the less ignoble motive of pride, as in the pseudepigraphic Life of Adam: "When God created Adam, He called upon the angels to adore him as His image. . . . Satan however refused, and on being threatened with the wrath of God said that he would exalt his throne above the stars of heaven" (Isa. xiv. 13). In other writings (*Life of Adam*, *Secrets of Enoch*) Satan refuses to worship God Himself, "entertaining the impossible idea that he should make his throne higher than the clouds over the earth, and should be equal in rank to [God's] power".[3]

There can be little doubt that the story of the punishment of the angels took its colouring from two passages of Isaiah, the fine imaginative description of the mighty king of Babylon, under the figure of the morning star, entering the realm of Hades (ch. xiv.) and what appears to be an account of the punishment of guardian angels for their neglect of the nations committed to their charge (ch. xxiv. 21 f.), "It shall come to pass in that day, that the Lord shall punish the host of the high ones on high, and the kings of the earth upon the earth. And they shall be gathered together as prisoners are gathered in the pit, and shall be shut up in the prison and after many days shall they be visited."

St. Jude's allusion to this story is merely parenthetical, to illustrate the law of judgment. He appears not to recognise any con-

[1] Cf. Tennant, *The Fall and Original Sin*, pp. 245, 246.

[2] See Tennant, pp. 152 foll.; Thackeray, *St. Paul and Jewish Thought*, pp. 50 foll.; Edersheim, *Life and Times of Jesus*, i. p. 165, ii. 753 foll. In the latter passage the rabbis are quoted to the effect that the angels generally were opposed to the creation of man, and that the demons were the offspring of Eve and male spirits, and Adam and female spirits, especially Lilith.

[3] See Tennant, pp. 199, 201, 206.

nection between the Fallen Angels and Satan. The former are suffering imprisonment in darkness till the final judgment: the latter was apparently able to confront the archangel on equal terms, when contending for the body of Moses. So the continued activity and even the authority of Satan and his angels in this world are asserted both in the O.T., as in Job i. 6 and Zech. iii. 1, 2, and in the N.T. as in James iv. 7, 1 P. v. 8, Eph. 6, 11, 12 (we have to stand against the wiles of the devil, . . . our warfare is not against flesh and blood, but) πρὸς τὰς ἀρχάς, πρὸς τὰς ἐξουσίας, πρὸς τοὺς κοσμοκράτορας τοῦ σκότους τοῦ αἰῶνος τούτου, πρὸς τὰ πνευματικὰ τῆς πονηρίας ἐν τοῖς ἐπουρανίοις, see Lightfoot on Col. ii. 15. In 2 Cor. iv. 4 Satan is spoken of as the god, in John xii. 31 and xvi. 11 as the prince of this world. He is the tempter and accuser of the brethren, and did not shrink even from assailing the Son of God Himself (Mt. iv. 3).

The above account of the Fall of the Angels was that usually accepted, with slight variations, both among Jews and Christians till towards the close of the fourth century A.D.

Julius Africanus is said to be the only one of the ante-Nicene Fathers who enunciated the view which afterwards prevailed, *viz.*, that "the sons of God were the descendants of Seth, and the daughters of men descendants of Cain".[1] See the quotation in Routh, *Rel. Sacr.* ii. p. 241, where he also gives the alternative explanation εἰ δὲ ἐπ' ἀγγέλων νοοῖτο τοῦτο, τοὺς περὶ μαγείας καὶ γοητείας . . . ἐσχολακότας συνιέντι χρὴ τῶν μετεώρων ταῖς γυναιξὶ τὴν γνῶσιν δεδωκέναι. Eusebius (*Pr. Ev.* v. 4, 11, 12) still keeps to the old view and compares the narrative of Gen. 6 to the stories of the Titans and Giants of Greek mythology. So Lactantius, *Div. Inst.* ii. 14: "Deus ne fraudibus suis diabolus, cui ab initio terrae dederat potestatem, vel corrumperet vel disperderet homines, quod in exordio rerum fecerat, misit angelos ad tutelam cultumque generis humani . . . Itaque illos cum hominibus commorantes dominator ille terrae fallacissimus consuetudine ipsa paullatim ad vitia pellexit et mulierum congressibus inquinavit . . . sic eos diabolus ex angelis Dei suos fecit satellites," etc. So Sulpicius Severus (*Chron.* i. 2): "Angeli quibus caelum sedes erat, speciosarum forma virginum capti . . . naturae suae originisque degeneres . . . matrimoniis se mortalibus miscuerunt." Julian, like Celsus, used this belief as a ground for attacking Christianity. Cyril of Alexandria, in his reply (ix. p. 296) repudiates the belief as altogether unworthy, and injurious to morality, since men plead the angels' sin as excuse for their own, and adopts the interpretation of "sons of God" previously

[1] It is also found in the apocryphal *Conflict of Adam and Eve* of uncertain date, on which see the art. "Adam, Books of," in the *D. of Christ. Biog.* i. 36 foll.

given by Africanus. Chrysostom deals at length with the subject in his 22nd homily on Genesis. He calls the old interpretation blasphemous, and holds that it is precluded by the words of Christ, that "in the resurrection men shall be like angels, neither marrying nor given in marriage". Augustine (*Civ. Dei*, xv. 23) thinks it cannot be denied "Silvanos et Faunos, quos vulgo incubos vocant . . . mulierum appetisse ac peregisse concubitum. . . . Dei tamen angelos sanctos nullo modo sic labi potuisse crediderim, nec de his dixisse Apostolum Petrum . . . sed potius de illis qui primum apostatantes a Deo cum diabolo principe suo ceciderunt," unless we are rather to understand this of the children of Seth. A little later Philastrius (*Haer.* 107) goes so far as to condemn the old opinion as a heresy.

The sympathies of Christians in the present day must assuredly be with those who endeavoured to eliminate from the Scriptures all that might seem to be dishonouring to God and injurious to men. But the methods employed with this view were often such as we could not now accept. For instance, the allegorical method borrowed from the Stoics by Philo, and adopted from him by many of the Fathers, is too subjective and arbitrary to be of any value in getting rid of moral difficulties. We have replaced this now by the historical method, first enunciated by our Lord, when he contrasted the spirit of the Gospel with that of the old Dispensation.[1] There is a continuous growth in the ideal of conduct as set before us in the Bible. Much that was commanded or permitted in the days of Abraham or Moses or David is forbidden to those who have received the fuller light of Christianity. So, what it was found possible for men to believe about God Himself and about the holy angels, is impossible for us now. The words put into the mouth of God in Gen. iii. 22, and in xi. 6, 7, we feel to be inconsistent with any true idea of the power and wisdom and love of God, and only suitable to a very low state of human development. So also for the story of the fall of the angels. But is it a satisfactory explanation of the latter to suppose that "sons of Seth" are meant by "sons of God"? Ryle (*Early Narratives of Genesis*, 91-95) points out that "there is nothing in the context to suggest this, no sign that the Sethites were distinguished for piety: they are not even exempted from the charge of general wickedness which brought on the Flood". Equally untenable is the Jewish explanation that "sons of God" are the nobles. I think no one who has studied with any care the recent investigations as to the origin of the book of Genesis, of which Driver's *Book of Genesis* may be taken as a specimen, can doubt that it contains much which is unhistoric, though full of moral and spiritual

[1] *Cf.* Matt. v. 21-48, xix. 8; Luke ix. 54-56.

teaching. The pre-Abrahamic narrative shows many resemblances to the Babylonian records, but in general the motive has been changed and purified.[1] Thus Driver says (p. lxiii.): "It is impossible, if we compare the early narratives of Genesis with the Babylonian narratives, from which in some cases they seem plainly to have been ultimately derived . . . not to perceive the controlling operation of the Spirit of God, which has taught these Hebrew writers . . . to take the primitive traditions of the human race, to purify them from their grossness and their polytheism, and to make them at once the foundation and the explanation of the long history that is to follow." Of the particular passage in question, however, Driver says (p. 83): "As a rule, the Hebrew narrators stripped off the mythological colouring of the piece of folklore which they record; but in the present instance it is still discernible".[2]

[1] Tennant, 20, 21, 41.

[2] For further information on this subject see Suicer's *Thesaurus* under **ἄγγελος**, and **'Εγρήγορος**, Hasting's *D. of B.* under "Angel," "Demon," "Fall," "Flood"; *Encycl. of B. Lit.* under "Angel," "Demon," "Deluge," "Nephilim," "Satan"; Maitland's *Eruvin* (Essays iv.-vi.), where the literal interpretation is defended; Hagenbach, *Hist. Doctr.* § 52 and § 132.

CHAPTER V.

Notes on the Text of the Epistle of Jude.—The Epistle of Jude is contained in the uncials ℵABCKLP. It is omitted in the Peshitto, but included in the later Syriac versions,[1] the Philoxenian and Harkleian, here distinguished as *syr^p^* and *syr^h^*. In citing the Egyptian versions I have used the notation *Boh.*, now commonly employed, instead of the less distinctive *Copt.*, employed by Tischendorf. The only other point which it may be well to mention is that, as in the Epistle of James, the symbol + is appended in the Critical Notes to signify that the reading in question is found in other authorities besides those previously mentioned. In discussing the readings I start with that of WH.

If we may judge from the number of "primitive errors" suspected by WH in the short Epistle of Jude, it would seem that the text is in a less satisfactory condition than that of any other portion of the New Testament. There are no less than four such errors in these twenty-five verses, the same number as are found in the eight chapters of the two Petrine Epistles, and in the forty-four chapters of the first two Gospels. I notice below some passages where the text presents special difficulties.

Ver. 5. ὑπομνῆσαι δὲ ὑμᾶς βούλομαι, εἰδότας ἅπαξ πάντα, ὅτι Κύριος λαὸν ἐκ γῆς Αἰγύπτου σώσας τὸ δεύτερον τοὺς μὴ πιστεύσαντας ἀπώλεσεν. I quote Tregelles' notes with additions from Tischendorf in round brackets, only changing the notation of the Egyptian and Syriac versions to prevent confusion, and correcting the citations in accordance with more recent collations.

εἰδότας *add.* "ὑμᾶς ℵKL. 31 syrr., *om.* ABC² 13 Vulg. Boh. Sah. Arm.," and so Tisch.

In point of fact however B reads εἰδότας ὑμᾶς, as any one may convince himself by looking at Cozza-Luzi's photographic reproduction. Also Dr. Gwynn reports that *h* and all the MSS. of *p* give the same reading, though he adds that the pleonastic idiom of the Syriac would lead the translators to supply the pronoun even if wanting in the Greek. The preponderance of authority is therefore

[1] See Dr. Gwynn's *Later Syriac Versions*, published in 1909.

in favour of this latter reading. The repeated ὑμᾶς emphasises the contrast between the readers ("to remind you, *you* who know it already") and the libertines previously spoken of. The repetition here may be compared with the repeated ὑμῖν of v. 3.

ἅπαξ *ante* πάντα ABCL. 13. 31. Vulg. *Ante* ὅτι K. *Ante* λαὸν . (Syrr.) Arm. *Ante* ἐκ γῆς Αἰγ. Clem. 280 (and 997) Did. Cassiod. ὅτι κύριος σώσας τὸν λαὸν ἐκ γῆς Αἰγ. ἅπαξ Sah., ὅτι ἅπαξ κύριος σώσας λαὸν αὐτοῦ Boh. *Om.* ἅπαξ Lucif. 28. [ἅπαξ is so placed in Syrr. as to be connected with σώσας "when he had once saved them," G.]

παντα ABCℵ 13 Vulg. Syr[h]. Boh. Arm. Aeth. Lucif. [In the *App.* to WH (*Sel. Readings*, p. 106) it is suggested that this may be a primitive error for πάντας (*cf.* 1 John ii. 20) found in Syr [1]], τοῦτο 31 KL. Sah.

ὅτι] *add.* ὁ C.[2] KL. 31. Arm. Clem. 280. *Om.* ABℵ 13.

κύριος] ℵCKL. Syr[h]. Θεὸς C.[2] Tol. Syr[p] Arm. Clem. Lucif. Ἰησοῦς AB 13 Vulg. Boh. Sah. Aeth. [In *App.* to WH. (*Sel. Readings*, p. 106) it is suggested that there may have been some primitive error, "apparently ΟΤΙΚ͞Ϲ (ὅτι Κύριος), and ΟΤΙΙ͞Ϲ (ὅτι' Ιησους) for ΟΤΙΟ (ὅτι ὁ)".]

γῆς] *om.* Syr[p].

It appears to me that the true reading of the passage is ὑπομνῆσαι δὲ ὑμᾶς βούλομαι, εἰδότας ὑμᾶς πάντα, ὅτι Κύριος ἅπαξ λαὸν ἐκ γῆς Αἰγύπτου σώσας τὸ δεύτερον [τοὺς] μὴ πιστεύσαντας ἀπώλεσεν. I see no difficulty in πάντα, which gives a reason for the use of the word ὑπομνῆσαι, "I need only *remind you*, because *you* already *know all* that I have to say". It was easy for the second ὑμᾶς to be omitted as unnecessary, and then the word ἅπαξ might be inserted in its place partly for rhythmical reasons; but it is really unmeaning after εἰδότας: the knowledge of the incidents, which are related in this and the following verses, is not a knowledge for good and all, such as the faith spoken of in ver. 3. On the other hand, ἅπαξ is very appropriate if taken with λαὸν σώσας (a people was saved out of Egypt once for all), and it prepares the way for τὸ δεύτερον. For the reading πάντας I see no reason. Can it be assumed that *all* who are addressed should be familiar with the legends contained in the Book of Enoch and the Assumption of Moses, to which allusion is made in what follows? It is surely much more to the point for the writer to say, as he does again below (ver. 17), that he is only repeating what is *generally* known, though it need not be known to every individual. As to Hort's suggestion on the word κύριος, that the original was ὅτι ὁ (λαὸν σώσας), I think the fact of the variants is better explained by Spitta, who considers that the abbreviations Ι͞Ϲ, Κ͞Ϲ, Θ͞Ϲ might easily be confused, if the first letter was faintly written, and that

[1] "This is an error: the two best MSS. of *p* represent πάντα." G.

the mention of τὸν μόνον δεσπότην καὶ Κύριον Ἰ. Χ. in the preceding verse would naturally lead a later copyist to prefer ΙΣ, a supposition which is confirmed by Cramer's *Catena*, p. 158, εἴρηται γὰρ πρὸ τούτων περὶ αὐτοῦ, ὡς εἴη ἀληθινὸς θεὸς οὗτος ὁ μόνος δεσπότης ὁ κύριος Ἰ. Χ., ὁ ἀναγαγὼν τὸν λαὸν ἐξ Αἰγύπτου διὰ Μωσέως. Spitta himself however holds that ΘΣ is the true reading, as it agrees with the corresponding passage in 2 Peter ii. 4, ὁ Θεὸς ἀγγέλων ἁμαρτησάντων οὐκ ἐφείσατο, and with Clement's paraphrase (*Adumbr*. Dind. iii. p. 482): "Quoniam Dominus Deus semel populum de terra Aegypti liberans deinceps eos qui non crediderunt perdidit". There is no instance in the New Testament of the personal name "Jesus" being used of the pre-existent Messiah, though the official name "Christ" is found in 1 Cor. x. 4, 9, in reference to the wandering in the wilderness. But in the second and later centuries this distinction was less carefully observed. Thus Justin M. (*Dial.* 120), speaking of the prophecy in Genesis xlix. 10, says that it does not refer to Judah, but to Jesus, τὸν καὶ τοὺς πατέρας ὑμῶν ἐξ Αἰγύπτου ἐξαγαγόντα, and this use of the name was confirmed by the idea that the son of Nun was a personification of Christ (see Justin, *Dial.* 75; Clem. Al. 183; Didymus, *De Trin.* 1. 19, Ἰούδας καθολικῶς γράφει, ἅπαξ γὰρ κύριος Ἰησοῦς λαὸν ἐξ Αἰγύπτου σώσας κ.τ.λ.; Jerome, *C. Jov.* 1. 12; Lact. *Inst.* 4. 17, "Christi figuram gerebat ille Jesus, qui cum primum Auses vocaretur, Moyses futura praesentiens jussit eum Jesum vocari"). In the explanatory note I have stated my reasons for considering that the article before μή did not belong to the original text.

Ver. 12. οὗτοί εἰσιν [οἱ] ἐν ταῖς ἀγάπαις ὑμῶν σπιλάδες συνευωχούμενοι ἀφόβως ἑαυτοὺς ποιμαίνοντες. The article here is omitted by ℵK and many inferior MSS. with vg. (but not syrr. or sah. or boh.), and some of the patristic quotations. I agree with Dr. Chase in thinking that it is out of place here, as in ver. 5 above. There is not only the difficulty of construction (οἱ . . . σπιλάδες), but the very bold assumption that the signification of σπιλάδες will be at once apparent. If we omit the article, ἀφόβως should be attached to συνευωχ. as by Ti. In syrr. it is joined with ποιμαίνοντες.

Ver. 19. οὗτοί εἰσιν οἱ ἀποδιορίζοντες, ψυχικοὶ πνεῦμα μὴ ἔχοντες.

ἀποδιορίζοντες *add.* ἑαυτούς C vulg. syrr. *Om.* ℵABKL 13, etc.

Schott, B. Weiss, and Huther-Kühl suppose the words ψυχικοὶ πνεῦμα μὴ ἔχοντες to be spoken by, or at least to express the feeling of οἱ ἀποδιορίζοντες: "welche Unterscheidungen machen, *sc.* zwischen Psychikern und Pneumatikern, wobei dann der Verfasser diese Unterscheidungen in seiner drastischen Weise sofort zu ihren Ungunsten umkehrt". This explanation seems to me to give a better sense than the gloss approved by Spitta, οἱ τὰ σχίσματα ποιοῦντες; for one cause of the danger which threatens the Church is that the innovators do not separate themselves openly, but steal in unobserved (παρεισεδύησαν, ver. 4), and take part in the love-feasts of the faithful, in which they are like sunken rocks (ver. 12); and, secondly, it is by no means certain that the word ἀποδιορίζω could bear this sense. ἀφορίζω is used in Luke vi. 22 of excommunication by superior authority, which of course would not be applicable here. On the other hand, it seems impossible to get the former sense out of the Greek as it stands. Even if we allowed the possibility of such a harsh construction as to put ψυχικοί in inverted commas, as the utterance of the innovators (and should we not then have expected the contrast ψυχικοί, πνευματικοί?), still we cannot use the same word over again to express Jude's "drastic" retort. This difficulty would be removed if we supposed the loss of a line to the following effect after ἀποδιορίζοντες:—

ψυχικοὺς ὑμᾶς (or τοὺς πιστοὺς) λέγοντες, ὄντες αὐτοὶ
ψυχικοὶ πνεῦμα μὴ ἔχοντες.

The opposition of ψυχικοί to πνευματικοί is familiar in the writings of Tertullian after he became a Montanist. The Church is carnal, the sect spiritual. So the Valentinians distinguished their own adherents as *pneumatici* from the *psychici* who composed the Church. These were also technical terms with the Naassenes and Heracleon (see my notes on James iii. 15), and were probably borrowed by the early heretics from St. Paul, who uses them to distinguish the natural from the heavenly body (1 Cor. xv. 44), and also to express the presence or absence of spiritual insight (1 Cor. ii. 14 f.) ψυχικὸς ἄνθρωπος οὐ δέχεται τὰ τοῦ πνεύματος τοῦ Θεοῦ, μωρία γὰρ αὐτῷ ἐστιν . . . ὁ δὲ πνευματικὸς ἀνακρίνει πάντα. The innovators against whom St. Jude writes seem to have been professed followers of St. Paul (like the Marcionites afterwards), abusing the doctrine of Free Grace which they had learnt from him (ver. 4 τὴν τοῦ Θεοῦ χάριτα μετατιθέντες εἰς ἀσέλγειαν), professing a knowledge of the βάθη τοῦ Θεοῦ (1 Cor. ii. 10), though it was really a knowledge only of τὰ βάθεα τοῦ Σατανᾶ (Apoc. ii. 24), and claiming to be the true δυνατοί and πνευματικοί, as denying dead works and setting the spirit above the letter. This explains the subsequent misrepresentation of St. Paul as a heresiarch in the Pseudo-Clementine writings.

Vv. 22, 23. (Text of Tischendorf and Tregelles) καὶ οὓς μὲν ἐλέγχετε διακρινομένους, οὓς δὲ σώζετε ἐκ πυρὸς ἁρπάζοντες, οὓς δὲ ἐλεᾶτε ἐν φόβῳ, μισοῦντες καὶ τὸν ἀπὸ τῆς σαρκὸς ἐσπιλωμένον χιτῶνα. (Text of WH. and

B. Weiss) καὶ οὓς μὲν ἐλεᾶτε διακρινομένους σώζετε ἐκ πυρὸς ἁρπάζοντες, οὓς δὲ ἐλεᾶτε ἐν φόβῳ μισοῦντες καὶ τὸν ἀπὸ τῆς σαρκὸς ἐσπιλωμένον χιτῶνα. In *App.* to WH. it is added, "Some primitive error probable: perhaps the first ἐλεᾶτε an interpolation" (*Sel. Readings*, p. 107).

22 ἐλέγχετε AC 13. Vulg. Boh. Arm. Aeth. (Eph. Theophyl. Oec. *Comm.* Cassiod.). ἐλεᾶτε ℵBC² Syrh. ἐλεεῖτε KLP (Theophyl. Oec. *txt.*), ἐκ πυρὸς ἁρπάζετε (hic) Syrp. Clem. 773.

διακρινομένους ABCℵ. 13. Vulg. Syrr. Boh. Arm. Clem. 773, διακρινόμενοι KLP +.

23. οὓς δὲ (1st) ℵACKLP 13 Vulg. Syrh. Boh. Arm. *Om.* B., δὲ Syrp. Clem

σώζετε ℵABC 13 Vulg. Boh. Arm. Aeth., ἐν φόβῳ σώζετε KLP +, ἐλεεῖτε Clem. 773 (quoted below), ἐλεᾶτε ἐν φόβῳ Syrp. ἐκ πυρὸς ℵABCKLP 13 Arm., ἐκ τοῦ π. Boh. *Om.* σώζετε ἐκ πυρὸς ἁρπάζοντες Syrp.

ἁρπάζοντες οὓς δὲ ἐλεᾶτε ἐν φόβῳ ABℵ 13. Vulg., Arm., *om.* ἁρπάζοντες Boh., ἁρπάζοντες ἐν φόβῳ C. Syrh, ἁρπάζοντες KLP +.

Tischendorf makes the matter clearer by giving the consecutive text of versions and quotations as follows: Vulg. *Et hos quidem arguite judicatos, illos vero salvate de igne rapientes, aliis autem miseremini in timore.* Are. *Et quosdam corripite super peccatis eorum, et quorundam miseremini cum fuerint victi, et quosdam salvate ex igne et liberate eos.* Arp. *Et signate quosdam cum dubitaverint orbos* (?) *et salvate quosdam territione, abripite eos ex igne.* Aeth. *quoniam est quem redarguent per verbum quod dictum est* (Aethp.p. *propter peccatum eorum*), *et est qui et servabitur ex igne et rapient eum, et est qui servabitur timore et poenitentia.* Arm. *Et quosdam damnantes sitis reprehensione, et quosdam salvate rapiendo ex igne, et quorundam miseremini timore judicando* (? *indicando*). Cassiodor. 142 *Ita ut quosdam dijudicatos arguant, quosdam de adustione aeterni ignis eripiant, nonnullis misereantur errantibus et conscientias maculatas emundent, sic tamen ut peccata eorum digna execratione refugiant.* Mr. Horner states that vv. 22, 23 are omitted in Sah. He translates Boh. as follows: καὶ οὓς μὲν ἐλέγχετε διακρινομένους, οὓς δὲ σώζετε ἐκ τοῦ πυρός (*al. om.* τοῦ), οὓς δὲ ἐλεᾶτε (*al.* φέρετε) ἐν φόβῳ. Commentaries of Theophylact and Oecumenius, κἀκείνους δέ, εἰ μὲν ἀποδιΐστανται ὑμῶν—τοῦτο γὰρ σημαίνει τὸ διακρίνεσθαι—ἐλέγχετε, τουτέστι φανεροῦτε τοῖς πᾶσι τὴν ἀσέβειαν αὐτῶν· εἴτε δὲ πρὸς ἴασιν ἀφορῶσι, μὴ ἀπωθεῖσθε, ἀλλὰ τῷ τῆς ἀγάπης ὑμῶν ἐλέῳ προσλαμβάνεσθε, σώζοντες ἐκ τοῦ ἠπειλημένου αὐτοῖς πυρός· προσλαμβάνεσθε δὲ μετὰ τοῦ ἐλεεῖν αὐτοὺς καὶ μετὰ φόβου.

In all these it will be observed that three classes are distinguished as in the text of Tregelles and Tischendorf, and in A, οὓς μὲν ἐλέγχετε διακρινομένους, οὓς δὲ σώζετε ἐκ πυρὸς ἁρπάζοντες, οὓς δὲ ἐλεᾶτε ἐν φόβῳ, and ℵ, οὓς μὲν ἐλεᾶτε διακρινομένους, οὓς δὲ σώζετε ἐκ πυρὸς ἁρπάζοντες, οὓς δὲ ἐλεᾶτε ἐν φόβῳ. We should draw the same conclusion from the seeming quotation in *Can. Apost.* vi. 4 (οὐ μισήσεις πάντα ἄνθρωπον, ἀλλὰ) οὓς μὲν ἐλέγξεις, οὓς δὲ ἐλεήσεις, περὶ ὧν δὲ προσεύξῃ (οὓς δὲ ἀγαπήσεις ὑπὲρ τὴν ψυχήν σου), which occurs also, with the omission of the cause οὓς δὲ ἐλεήσεις in the Didaché ii. 7.

Two classes only are distinguished in the following: Syr^{p}. *Et quosdam de illis quidem ex igne rapite; cum autem resipuerint, miseremini super eis in timore*, representing καὶ οὓς μὲν ἐκ πυρὸς ἁρπάζετε, διακρινομένους δὲ ἐλεᾶτε ἐν φόβῳ. Syr^{h}. *et hos quidem miseremini resipiscentes, hos autem servate de igne rapientes in timore*, representing καὶ οὓς μὲν ἐλεᾶτε διακρινομένους, οὓς δὲ σώζετε ἐκ πυρὸς ἁρπάζοντες ἐν φόβῳ. Clem. (*Adumbr.*) *quosdam autem salvate de igne rapientes, quibusdam vero miseremini in timore*,[1] representing οὓς δὲ σώζετε ἐκ πυρὸς ἁρπάζοντες, οὓς δὲ ἐλεᾶτε ἐν φόβῳ. Clem. *Strom.* vi. 773, καὶ οὓς μὲν ἐκ πυρὸς ἁρπάζετε, διακρινομένους δὲ ἐλεεῖτε, implying that he was acquainted with two different recensions. With these we may compare the texts of B, followed by WH. and B. Weiss, καὶ οὓς μὲν ἐλεᾶτε διακρινομένους σώζετε ἐκ πυρὸς ἁρπάζοντες, οὓς δὲ ἐλεᾶτε ἐν φόβῳ, of C, καὶ οὓς μὲν ἐλέγχετε διακρινομένους, οὓς δὲ σώζετε ἐκ πυρὸς ἁρπάζοντες ἐν φόβῳ, and of KLP, καὶ οὓς μὲν ἐλεεῖτε διακρινόμενοι, οὓς δὲ ἐν φόβῳ σώζετε ἐκ πυρὸς ἁρπάζοντες.

St. Jude's predilection for triplets, as in vv. 2, 4, 8, in the examples of judgment in vv. 5-7, and of sin in v. 11, is *prima facie* favourable to the triple division in this passage. Supposing we take A and א to represent the original, consisting of three members, *a b c*, we find B complete in *a* and *c*, but confused as to *b*. As it stands, it gives an impossible reading; since it requires οὓς μέν to be taken as the relative, introducing the subordinate verb ἐλεᾶτε, depending on the principal verb σώζετε; while οὓς δέ, on the other hand, must be taken as demonstrative. WH suggest that ἐλεᾶτε has crept in from below. Omitting this, we get the sense, "Some who doubt save, snatching them from fire; others compassionate in fear". It seems an easier explanation to suppose that ἐλεᾶτε was written in error for ἐλέγχετε and οὓς omitted in error after διακρινομένους. The latter phenomenon is exemplified in the readings of Syr^{p}. and Clem. *Str.* 773. The texts of C and KLP are complete in *a* and *b*, but insert a phrase from *c* in *b*. The most natural explanation here seems to be that the duplication of ἐλεᾶτε in *a* and *c* (as in א) caused the omission of

[1] The paraphrase continues, *id est ut eos qui in ignem cadunt doceatis ut semet ipsos liberent.* (It would seem that this clause has got misplaced and should be inserted after *rapientes.*) *Odientes, inquit, eam, quae carnalis est, maculatam tunicam; animae videlicet tunica macula* (read *maculata*) *est, spiritus concupiscentiis pollutus carnalibus.*

the second ἐλεᾶτε, and therefore of the second οὓς δέ. The reading διακρινόμενοι in KLP was a natural assimilation to the following nominative ἁρπάζοντες, and seemed, to those were not aware of the difference in the meaning of the active and middle of διακρίνω, to supply a very appropriate thought, viz., that discrimination must be used; treatment should differ in different cases.

The real difficulty however of the triple division is to arrive at a clear demarcation between the classes alluded to. "The triple division," says Hort (*App.* p. 107), "gives no satisfactory sense"; and it certainly has been very diversely interpreted, some holding with Kühl that the first case is the worst and the last the most hopeful: "Die dritte Klasse . . . durch helfendes Erbarmen wieder hergestellt werden können, mit denen es also nicht so schlimm steht, wie mit denen, welchen gegenüber nur ἐλέγχειν zu üben ist, aber auch nicht so schlimm, wie mit denen, die nur durch rasche, zugreifende That zu retten sind"; while the majority take Reiche's view of a climax: "a dubitantibus minusque depravatis . . . ad insanabiles, quibus opem ferre pro tempore ab ipsorum contumacia prohibemur". My own view is that Jude does not here touch on the case of the heretical leaders, of whom he has spoken with such severity before. In their present mood they are not subjects of ἔλεος, any more than the Pharisees condemned by our Lord, as long as they persisted in their hostility to the truth. The admonition here given by St. Jude seems to be the same as that contained in the final verses of the Epistle written by his brother long before: ἐάν τις ἐν ὑμῖν πλανηθῇ ἀπὸ τῆς ἀληθείας καὶ ἐπιστρέψῃ τις αὐτόν, γινώσκετε ὅτι ὁ ἐπιστρέψας ἁμαρτωλὸν ἐκ πλάνης ὁδοῦ αὐτοῦ σώσει ψυχὴν ἐκ θανάτου. The first class with which the believers are called upon to deal is that of doubters, διακρινόμενοι, men still halting between two opinions (*cf.* James i. 6), or perhaps we should understand it of disputers, as in Jude 9. These they are to reprove and convince (*cf.* John xvi. 8, 9, ἐλέγξει περὶ ἁμαρτίας ὅτι οὐ πιστεύουσιν εἰς ἐμέ). Then follow two classes undistinguished by any special characteristic, whose condition we can only conjecture from the course of action to be pursued respecting them. The second class is evidently in more imminent danger than the one we have already considered, since they are to be saved by immediate energetic action, snatching them from the fire; the third seems to be beyond human help, since the duty of the believers is limited to trembling compassion, expressing itself no doubt in prayer, but apparently shrinking from personal communication with the terrible infection of evil. We may compare with this St. Paul's judgment as to the case of incest in the Church of Corinth (1 Cor. v. 5), and the story told about Cerinthus and St. John.

ΙΟΥΔΑ ΕΠΙΣΤΟΛΗ.

1. **ἸΟΥΔΑΣ Ἰησοῦ Χριστοῦ δοῦλος, ἀδελφὸς δὲ Ἰακώβου, τοῖς**[1] **ἐν**

[1] **τοις θεῳ . . . και εν Ιησου** conj. H (*Sel. Read.* p. 106).

Vv. 1, 2.—*Salutation.* Jude a servant of Jesus Christ and brother of James, to those who have received the divine calling, beloved of the Father, kept safe in Jesus Christ. May mercy, peace and love be richly poured out upon you!

1. **Ἰησοῦ Χριστοῦ δοῦλος.** The same phrase is used by St. James in the Inscription to his epistle, also by St. Paul in Rom. and Phil. In 1 Pet. the phrase used is **ἀπόστολος Ἰ. Χ.**, in 2 Pet. **δοῦλος καὶ ἀπόστολος.** It is, I think, a mistake to translate **δοῦλος** by the word "slave," the modern connotation of which is so different from that of the Greek word (*cf.* 2 Cor. iv. 5). There is no opposition between **δουλεία** and **ἐλευθερία** in the Christian's willing service. It only becomes a **δουλεία** in the opposed sense, when he ceases to love what is commanded and feels it as an external yoke.

ἀδελφὸς δὲ Ἰακώβου. *Cf.* Tit. i. 1, **δοῦλος Θεοῦ, ἀπόστολος δὲ Ἰ. Χ.** See Introduction on the Author.

τοῖς ἐν Θεῷ πατρὶ ἠγαπημένοις καὶ Ἰησοῦ Χριστῷ τετηρημένοις κλητοῖς. On the readings see Introduction on the text. The easier reading of some MSS., **ἡγιασμένοις** for **ἠγαπημένοις,** is probably derived from 1 Cor. i. 2, **ἡγιασμένοις ἐν Χ. Ἰ.** There is no precise parallel either for **ἐν Θεῷ ἠγ.** or for **Χριστῷ τετ.** The preposition **ἐν** is constantly used to express the relation in which believers stand to Christ: they are incorporated in Him as the branches in the vine, as the living stones in the spiritual temple, as the members in the body of which He is the head. So here, "beloved as members of Christ, reflecting back his glorious image" would be a natural und easy conception. Lightfoot, commenting on Col. iii. 12, **ἐκλεκτοὶ τοῦ Θεοῦ, ἅγιοι καὶ ἠγαπημένοι,** says that in the N.T. the last word "seems to be used always of the objects of God's love," but it is difficult to see the propriety of the phrase, 'Brethren beloved by God in God". **Ἠγαπημένοι** is used of the objects of *man's* love in Clem. *Hom.* ix. 5, **τῶν αὐτοῖς ἠγαπημένων τοὺς τάφους ναοῖς τιμῶσιν,** and the cognate **ἀγαπητοί** is constantly used in the same sense (as below ver. 3), as well as in the sense of "beloved of God". If, therefore, we are to retain the reading, I am disposed to interpret it as equivalent to **ἀδελφοί,** "beloved by us in the Father," *i.e.*, "beloved with **φιλαδελφία** as children of God," but I think that Hort is right in considering that **ἐν** has shifted its place in the text. See his *Select Readings*, p. 106, where it is suggested that **ἐν** should be omitted before **Θεῷ** and inserted before **Ἰησοῦ**, giving the sense "to those who have been beloved by the Father, and who have been kept safe in Jesus from the temptations to which others have succumbed," **ἠγαπημένοις** being followed by a dative of the agent, as in Nehem. xiii. 26, **ἀγαπώμενος τῷ Θεῷ ἦν.**

κλητοῖς is here the substantive of which **ἠγαπημένοις** and **τετηρημένοις** are predicated. We find the same use in Apoc. xvii. 14 (**νικήσουσιν**) **οἱ μετ' αὐτοῦ κλητοὶ κ. ἐκλεκτοὶ κ. πιστοί,** in St. Paul's epistles, as in Rom. i. 6, **ἐν οἷς ἐστε καὶ ὑμεῖς, κλητοὶ Ἰησοῦ Χριστοῦ,** 1 Cor. i. 24, **κηρύσσομεν Χριστὸν ἐσταυρωμένον, Ἰουδαίοις μὲν σκάνδαλον . . . αὐτοῖς δὲ τοῖς κλητοῖς Χριστὸν Θεοῦ δύναμιν.** We have many examples of the Divine calling in the Gospels, as in the case of the Apostles (Matt. iv. 21, Mark i. 20) and in the parables of the Great Supper and the Labourers in the Vineyard. This idea of calling or election is derived from the O.T. See Hort's n. on 1 Pet. i. 1 **Ἰησοῦ Χριστοῦ ἐκλεκτοῖς**: "Two great forms of election are spoken of in the O.T., the choosing of Israel, and the choosing of single

Θεῷ πατρὶ ἠγαπημένοις[1] καὶ Ἰησοῦ Χριστῷ τετηρημένοις κλητοῖς.
2. ἔλεος ὑμῖν καὶ εἰρήνη καὶ ἀγάπη πληθυνθείη.
3. Ἀγαπητοί, πᾶσαν σπουδὴν ποιούμενος γράφειν ὑμῖν περὶ τῆς

[1] ηγαπημενοις AB א; ηγιασμενοις KLP.

Israelites, or bodies of Israelites, to perform certain functions for Israel. . . . The calling and the choosing imply each other, the calling being the outward expression of the antecedent choosing, the act by which it begins to take effect. Both words emphatically mark the present state of the persons addressed as being due to the free agency of God. . . . In Deuteronomy (iv. 37) the choosing, by God is ascribed to His own love of Israel: the ground of it lay in Himself, not in Israel. . . . As is the election of the ruler or priest within Israel for the sake of Israel, such is the election of Israel for the sake of the whole human race. Such also, still more clearly and emphatically, is the election of the new Israel." For a similar use of the word "call" in Isaiah, *cf.* ch. xlviii. 12, xliii. 1, 7. The chief distinction between the the "calling" of the old and of the new dispensation is that the former is rather expressive of dignity ("called by the name of God"), the latter of invitation; but the former appears also in the N.T. in such phrases as James ii. 7, **τὸ καλὸν ὄνομα τὸ ἐπικληθὲν ἐφ' ὑμᾶς**, and 1 Pet. ii. 9, **ὑμεῖς δὲ γένος ἐκλεκτόν, βασίλειον ἱεράτευμα . . . λαὸς εἰς περιποίησιν.** The reason for St. Jude's here characterising the called as beloved and kept, is because he has in his mind others who had been called, but had gone astray and incurred the wrath of God.

Ver. 2. For the Salutation see my note on **χαίρειν**, James i. 1, and Hort's excellent note on 1 Pet. i. 2, **χάρις . . . πληθυνθείη.** We find **ἔλεος** and **εἰρήνη** joined in Gal. vi. 16, and with the addition of **χάρις** in 1 Tim. i. 2, 2 Tim. i. 2, 2 John 3. The mercy of God is the ground of peace, which is perfected in the feeling of God's love towards them. The verb **πληθυνθείη** occurs in the Salutation both of 1 Peter and 2 Peter and in Dan. vi. 25 (in the letter of Darius), **εἰρήνη ὑμῖν πληθυνθείη**, *cf.* 1 Thess. iii. 12, **ὑμᾶς δὲ ὁ κύριος πλεονάσαι καὶ περισσεύσαι τῇ ἀγάπῃ εἰς ἀλλήλους. Ἀγάπη** (=the love of God) occurs also in the final salutation of 2 Cor. **ἡ χάρις τ. κυρίου Ἰησοῦ καὶ ἡ ἀγάπη τοῦ Θεοῦ,** and in Eph. **εἰρήνη τοῖς ἀδελφοῖς καὶ ἀγάπη μετὰ πίστεως ἀπὸ Θεοῦ πατρὸς καὶ Κυρίου Ἰ. Χ.** *Cf.* 1 John iii. 1, **ἴδετε ποταπὴν ἀγάπην δέδωκεν ἡμῖν ὁ πατὴρ ἵνα τέκνα Θεοῦ κληθῶμεν,** where Westcott's n. is "The Divine love is infused into them, so that it is their own, and becomes in them the source of a divine life (Rom. xiii. 10). In virtue of this gift they are inspired with a love which is like the love of God, and by this they truly claim the title of children of God as partakers in His nature, 1 John iv. 7, 19." The same salutation is used in the letter of the Smyrnaeans (*c.* 156 A.D.) giving an account of the martyrdom of Polycarp, **ἔλεος καὶ εἰρήνη καὶ ἀγάπη Θεοῦ πατρὸς καὶ Κυρίου ἡμῶν Ἰ. Χ. πληθυνθείη.** The thought of **ἔλεος** and **ἀγάπη** recurs again in ver. 21.

Vv. 3, 4.—*Reasons for Writing.* He had been intending to write to them on that which is the common interest of all Christians, salvation through Christ, but was compelled to abandon his intention by news which had reached him of a special danger * threatening the Gospel once for all delivered to the Church. His duty now was to stir up the faithful to defend their faith against insidious assaults, long ago foretold in ancient prophecy, of impious men who should change the doctrine of God's free grace into an excuse for licentiousness, and deny the only Master and our Lord Jesus Christ.

Ver. 3. **ἀγαπητοί** occurs in vv. 17 and 20, also in 2 Pet. iii. 1, 8, 14, 17, 1 Pet. ii. 11, iv. 12 and James. It is common in the Epistles of John and of Paul, sometimes with **μου** attached, as in 1 Cor. x. 14, Phil. ii. 12, and is often joined to **ἀδελφοί**, especially in James. The **ἀγάπη** of ver. 2 leads on to the **ἀγαπητοί** here. They are themselves **ἀγαπητοί** because the love of God is shed abroad in their hearts.

πᾶσαν σπουδὴν ποιούμενος. For **πᾶσαν**, see my n. on James i. 2, and *cf.* 2 Pet. i. 5, **σπουδὴν πᾶσαν παρεισενέγκαντες**, i. 15, **σπουδάσω ἔχειν ὑμᾶς μνήμην ποιεῖσθαι,** also Isocr. *Orat.* v. p. 91 *b*, **πᾶσαν τὴν σπουδὴν περὶ τούτου**

* For this see the Introduction on Early Heresies.

κοινῆς ἡμῶν[1] σωτηρίας ἀνάγκην ἔσχον γράψαι[2] ὑμῖν παρακαλῶν ἐπαγωνίζεσθαι τῇ ἅπαξ παραδοθείσῃ τοῖς ἁγίοις πίστει.

[1] κοινης ημων] κ. υμων boh.; om. ημων KLP + ; σωτηριας] add. και ζωης ℵ.
[2] γραψαι] γραφειν ℵ.

ποιεῖσθαι, Plato, *Euthyd.* 304 *e*, περὶ οὐδενὸς ἀξίων ἀναξίαν σπουδὴν ποιοῦνται. Jude was busy on another subject, when he received the news of a fresh danger to the Church, which he felt it his duty to meet at once. Whether he lived to carry out his earlier design, and whether it was of the nature of a treatise or of an epistle, we know not. It is noteworthy that there is a similar allusion in 2 Peter iii. 1 to an earlier letter now lost. Compare Barn. iv. 9, πολλὰ δὲ θέλων γράφειν . . . γράφειν ἐσπούδασα.

κοινῆς σωτηρίας. *Cf.* Tit. i. 4, κατὰ κοινὴν πίστιν, Ign. *Eph.* i., ὑπὲρ τοῦ κοινοῦ ὀνόματος καὶ ἐλπίδος with Lightfoot's n., Jos. *Ant.* 10. 1. 3 (Hezekiah besought Isaiah to offer sacrifice) ὑπὲρ τῆς κοινῆς σωτηρίας. Bede explains as follows: "omnium electorum communis est salus, fides, et dilectio Christi". Jude puts on one side the address he was preparing on the main principles of Christianity (probably we may take vv. 20 and 21 as a sample of what this would have been) and turns to the special evil which was then threatening the Church.

ἀνάγκην ἔσχον γράψαι. *Cf.* Luke xiv. 18, ἔχω ἀνάγκην ἰδεῖν αὐτόν, Heb. vii. 27, *al.*, also Plut. *Cato Mi.* 24, ἀνάγκην ἔσχεν ἐκβαλεῖν ἀσχημονοῦσαν τὴν γυναῖκα. There is a similar combination of γράφειν and γράψαι in 3 John 13. The aor. γράψαι, contrasted with the preceding pres. γράφειν, implies that the new epistle had to be written at once and could not be prepared for at leisure, like the one he had previously contemplated. It was no welcome task: "necessity was laid upon him".

ἐπαγωνίζεσθαι τῇ ἅπαξ παραδοθείσῃ τοῖς ἁγίοις πίστει. "To contend *for* the faith," almost equivalent to the ἀγώνισαι περὶ τῆς ἀληθείας in Sir. iv. 28, see 1 Tim. vi. 12, ἀγωνίζου τὸν καλὸν ἀγῶνα τῆς πίστεως, and εἰς ὃ κοπιῶ ἀγωνιζόμενος, Col. i. 29. We may compare ἐπαμύνειν, ἐπαναπαύειν νόμῳ, Rom. ii. 17 and Clem. *Strom.* iii., p. 553, ἐπαγωνιζόμενος τῇ ἀθέῳ δόξῃ. It is possible (as is shown by the following examples) for spiritual blessings, once given, to be lost, unless we use every effort to maintain them. The redemption from Egypt was a fact, as baptism into the name of Christ is a fact, but, unless it is borne in mind and acted upon, the fact loses its efficacy.

τῇ ἅπαξ παραδοθείσῃ τοῖς ἁγίοις πίστει. The word πίστις here is not used in its primary sense of a subjective feeling of trust or belief, but in the secondary sense of the thing believed, the Truth or the Gospel, as in ver. 20 below, Gal. i. 23, ὁ διώκων ἡμᾶς ποτε νῦν εὐαγγελίζεται τὴν πίστιν ἥν ποτε ἐπόρθει, also Gal. iii. 23, Phil. i. 27, συναθλοῦντες τῇ πίστει τοῦ εὐαγγελίου, where see Lightfoot, Acts vi. 7. In the same way ἐλπίς is used in a concrete sense for the object or ground of hope (as in Col. i. 5, τὴν ἐλπίδα τὴν ἀποκειμένην ὑμῖν, 1 Tim. i 1, Ἰησοῦ Χριστοῦ τῆς ἐλπίδος ἡμῶν, Tit. ii. 13, προσδεχόμενοι τὴν μακαρίαν ἐλπίδα), and φόβος for the object of fear, Rom. xiii. 3, 1 Pet. iii. 14.

ἅπαξ. Used here in its classical sense "once for all," as below ver. 5, and in Heb. vi. 4, τοὺς ἅπαξ φωτισθέντας, *ib.* ix. 26, 27, x. 2, 1 Pet. iii. 18. This excludes the novelties of the Libertines, *cf.* Gal. i. 9. The later sense "on one occasion" is found in 2 Cor. xi. 25, ἅπαξ ἐλιθάσθην, 1 Thess. ii. 18, καὶ ἅπαξ καὶ δὶς ἠθελήσαμεν ἐλθεῖν.

παραδοθείσῃ. *Cf.* Philo M. i. 387, πιστεύει τοῖς ἅπαξ παραδοθεῖσι. The Christian tradition is constantly referred to by the Fathers, as by Clem. Al. *Str.* vii. where we read of ἡ ἀληθὴς παράδοσις (p. 845), ἡ ἐκκλησιαστικὴ π. (p. 890), ἡ θεία π. (p. 896), ἡ πάντων τῶν ἀποστόλων π. (p. 900), αἱ τοῦ Χριστοῦ π. (p. 901), and even in the N.T. as in 1 Cor. xi. 2, κάθως παρέδωκα ὑμῖν τὰς παραδόσεις κατέχετε, 2 Thess. ii. 15, 1 Tim. vi. 20, τὴν παραθήκην φύλαξον. For an account of the gradual formation of the Creed, see A. E. Burn's *Introduction to the Creeds*, ch. ii., 1899, and compare the comment in my larger edition, p. 61 f.

τοῖς ἁγίοις. Used generally of Christians who were consecrated and called to be holy, as in 1 Cor. i. 2, Phil. i. 1, where see Lightfoot. The word contains an appeal to the brethren to stand fast against the teaching and practice of the Libertines.

4. παρεισεδύησαν[1] γάρ τινες ἄνθρωποι, οἱ πάλαι προγεγραμμένοι εἰς τοῦτο τὸ κρίμα, ἀσεβεῖς, τὴν τοῦ Θεοῦ ἡμῶν χάριτα μετατιθέν-

[1] παρεισεδυησαν B, WH; παρεισεδυσαν ℵACKLP + Ti., Treg.

Ver. 4. *Nature of the Threatened Danger.* It is stealthy; it is serious enough to have been predicted long ago; its characteristic is impiety, showing itself in the antinomian misuse of the Gospel of God's free grace, and in the denial of God and Christ.

Ver. 4. **παρεισεδύησαν γάρ τινες ἄνθρωποι.** For this form which is found in B and adopted by WH, Veitch cites **διεκδυῆναι** in Hippocr. i. 601, and compares **ἐφύην, ἐρρύην.** The aor. is here used with the perfect force, as in ver. 11 **ἐπορεύθησαν**, etc. *cf.* Blass, *Gr.* p. 199, my edition of St. James, p. ccii., and Dr. Weymouth there cited. The verb occurs in Demades 178, **ἄδικος παρεισδύνων λόγος εἰς τὰς τῶν δικαστῶν γνώμας οὐκ ἐᾷ συνορᾶν τὴν ἀλήθειαν**, Clem. Al. p. 659, **ὅπως εἰς τὴν τῶν αἰνιγμάτων ἔννοιαν ἡ ζήτησις παρεισδύουσα ἐπὶ τὴν εὕρεσιν τῆς ἀληθείας ἀναδράμῃ**, D. Laert. ii. 142, **λαθραίως παρεισδὺς εἰς τὴν πατρίδα**, Plut. *M.* p. 216 B, **τὰ ἀρχαῖα νόμιμα ἐκλυόμενα ἑώρα, ἄλλα δὲ παρεισδυόμενα μοχθηρά**, other examples in Wetst. The noun **παρείσδυσις** occurs in Barn. ii. 10, iv. 9, **ἀντιστῶμεν ἵνα μὴ σχῇ παρείσδυσιν ὁ μέλας**, Clem. Al. p. 189, **ἀκροσφαλὴς ἡ τοῦ οἴνου παρείσδυσις.** Similar compounds are **παρεισφέρω** in 2 Pet. i. 5, **παρεισάγω** in 2 Pet. ii. 1, **παρείσακτος** in Gal. ii. 4, **διὰ τοὺς παρεισάκτους ψευδαδέλφους οἵτινες παρεισῆλθον κατασκοπῆσαι τὴν ἐλευθερίαν ὑμῶν**, Rom. v. 20, 2 Macc. viii. 1 **παρεισπορευόμενοι λεληθότως εἰς τὰς κώμας**, so **παρεισέρπω, παρεισπέμπω, παρεισπίπτω.** The earliest prophecy of such seducers comes from the lips of Jesus Himself, Matt. vii. 15, **προσέχετε ἀπὸ τῶν ψευδοπροφητῶν, οἵτινες ἔρχονται πρὸς ὑμᾶς ἐν ἐνδύμασι προβάτων, ἔσωθεν δέ εἰσι λύκοι ἅρπαγες**, *cf.* Acts xx. 29, 30, and Introduction on the Early Heresies in the larger edition.

οἱ πάλαι προγεγραμμένοι εἰς τοῦτο τὸ κρίμα. "Designated of old for this judgment." *Cf.* 2 Pet. ii. 3, **οἷς τὸ κρίμα ἔκπαλαι οὐκ ἀργεῖ.** The word **πάλαι** precludes the supposition that the second epistle of Peter can be referred to.* The allusion is to the book of Enoch quoted in vv. 14, 15. In ver. 18 below the same warning is said to have been given by the Apostles. The phrase **οἱ προγ.** is in apposition to **τινες ἄνθρωποι**, *cf.* Gal. i. 7 with Lightfoot's n., Luke xviii. 9, **εἶπεν δὲ πρός τινας τοὺς πεποιθότας ἐφ' ἑαυτοῖς.** For **προγ.**, *cf.* Rom. xv. 4, **ὅσα γὰρ προεγράφη εἰς τὴν ἡμετέραν διδασκαλίαν ἐγράφη.** The word is intended to show that they are already doomed to punishment as enemies of God. As such they are to be shunned by the faithful, but not to be feared, because, dangerous as they may seem, they cannot alter the Divine purpose. Dr. Chase compares Hort's interesting note on 1 Peter ii. 8, **εἰς ὃ καὶ ἐτέθησαν.** By "this" Spitta understands "that judgment which I am now about to declare," *i.e.*, the condemnation contained in the word **ἀσεβεῖς** used by some ancient writer. Zahn however remarks that **οὗτος** usually refers to what precedes, and he would take **τοῦτο** here (with Hofmann) as referring to **παρεισεδύησαν.** Better than this logical reference to some preceding or succeeding word is, I think, Bengel's explanation "the now impending judgment," *Apostolo iam quasi cernente pœnam.*

ἀσεβεῖς. This word may be almost said to give the keynote to the Epistle (*cf.* vv. 15, 18) as it does to the Book of Enoch.

τὴν τοῦ Θεοῦ ἡμῶν χάριτα μετατιθέντες εἰς ἀσέλγειαν. With this we may compare 1 Peter ii. 16, **μὴ ὡς ἐπικάλυμμα ἔχοντες τῆς κακίας τὴν ἐλευθερίαν**, 2 Peter ii. 19, **ἐλευθερίαν ἐπαγγελλόμενοι**, iii. 16, **δυσνόητά τινα, ἃ οἱ ἀμαθεῖς στρεβλοῦσιν πρὸς τὴν ἰδίαν αὐτῶν ἀπώλειαν**, Rom. iii. 1, 2, 5-8 (If man is justified by free grace and not by works, then works are unnecessary), *ib.* vi. 1, 15, viii. 21, 1 Cor. vi. 12, x. 23 f., John viii. 32-36, Gal. v. 13, **ὑμεῖς ἐπ' ἐλευθερίᾳ ἐκλήθητε· μόνον μὴ τὴν**

* Zahn, it is true, following Schott and others, argues in favour of this reference, holding that **πάλαι** may be equivalent to "lately"; and the word is of course very elastic in meaning; but unless the contrast makes it clear that the reference is to a recent past, I think we are bound to assign to the word its usual force, especially here, where it stands first, giving the tone as it were to what follows, and is further confirmed and explained by **ἕβδομος ἀπὸ 'Αδάμ** in ver. 14.

τες εἰς ἀσέλγειαν καὶ τὸν μόνον δεσπότην[1] καὶ κύριον ἡμῶν Ἰησοῦν

[1] δεσποτην] add. θεον KLP, syrr. +.

ἐλευθερίαν εἰς ἀφορμὴν τῇ σαρκί. For μετατιθέντες see Gal. i. 6, for ἀσέλγειαν 2 Peter ii. 2, πολλοὶ ἐξακολουθήσουσιν αὐτῶν ταῖς ἀσελγείαις, *ib.* ii. 7, 18, 1 Peter iv. 3, and Lightfoot on Gal. v. 19, "A man may be ἀκάθαρτος and hide his sin: he does not become ἀσελγής until he shocks public decency. In classical Greek the word ἀσέλγεια generally signifies insolence or violence towards another. . . . In the later language the prominent idea is sensuality . . . *cf.* Polyb. xxxvii. 2, πολλή δέ τις ἀσέλγεια καὶ περὶ τὰς σωματικὰς ἐπιθυμίας αὐτῷ συνεξηκολούθει. Thus it has much the same range of meaning as ὕβρις". On the meaning of χάρις see Robinson, *Ephes.* p. 221 f. The form χάριν is used elsewhere in the N.T., except in Acts xxiv. 27.

τὸν μόνον δεσπότην καὶ κύριον ἡμῶν Ἰησοῦν Χριστὸν ἀρνούμενοι. So 2 Peter ii. 1, τὸν ἀγοράσαντα αὐτοὺς δεσπότην ἀρνούμενοι. On the denial of God and Christ see 1 John ii. 22, οὗτός ἐστιν ὁ ἀντίχριστος, ὁ ἀρνούμενος τὸν πατέρα καὶ τὸν υἱόν, Tit. i. 16, Θεὸν ὁμολογοῦσιν εἰδέναι, τοῖς δὲ ἔργοις ἀρνοῦνται βδελυκτοὶ ὄντες καὶ ἀπειθεῖς καὶ πρὸς πᾶν ἔργον ἀγαθὸν ἀδόκιμοι, Matt. x. 33, ὅστις ἂν ἀρνήσηταί με ἔμπροσθεν τῶν ἀνθρώπων, ἀρνήσομαι κἀγὼ αὐτὸν ἔμπροσθεν τοῦ πατρός μου, *ib.* xxvi. 70 (Peter's denial). Such denial is one of the sins noticed in the book of Enoch, xxxviii. 2: "When the Righteous One shall appear . . . where will be the dwelling of the sinners and where the resting-place of those who have denied the Lord of Spirits?" *Ib.* xli. 2, xlv. 2, xlvi. 7, xlviii. 10: "They will fall and not rise again . . . for they have denied the Lord of Spirits and His Anointed".

Two questions have been raised as to the meaning of the text, (1) is τ. μόνον δεσπότην to be understood of the Son, (2) what is the force of ἀρνεῖσθαι? The objection to understanding δεσπότης of our Lord is that in every other passage in the N.T., where δεσπότης occurs, except in 2 Peter ii. 1 (on which see n.), it is spoken of God the Father; that, this being the case, it is difficult to understand how Christ can be called τὸν μόνον δεσπότην. It seems to me a forced explanation to say that the phrase μόνος δεσπότης has reference only to other earthly masters. No Jew could use it in this connexion without thinking of the one Master in heaven. Again μόνος is elsewhere used of the Father only, as in John v. 44, τὴν δόξαν τὴν παρὰ τοῦ μόνου Θεοῦ οὐ ζητεῖτε, xvii. 3, ἵνα γινώσκωσίν σε τὸν μόνον ἀληθινὸν Θεον Rom. xvi. 27, μόνῳ σόφῳ Θεῷ διὰ Ἰησοῦ Χριστοῦ, 1 Tim. i. 17, τῷ βασιλεῖ τῶν αἰώνων . . . μόνῳ Θεῷ τιμὴ κ. δόξα, *ib.* vi. 15, 16, ὁ μακάριος κ. μόνος δυνάστης ὁ μόνος ἔχων ἀθανασίαν, and by Jude himself, below 25, μόνῳ Θεῷ σωτῆρι ἡμῶν διὰ Ἰ. Χ., τοῦ κυρίου ἡμῶν, δόξα. Wetst. quotes several passages in which Josephus speaks of God as ὁ μόνος δεσπότης. On the other hand, the phrase, so taken, seems to contradict the general rule that, where two nouns, denoting attributes, are joined by καί, if the article is prefixed to the first noun only, the second noun will then be an attribute of the same subject. In the present case, however, the second noun (κύριον) belongs to the class of words which may stand without the article, see Winer, pp. 147-163. A similar doubtful case is found in Tit. ii. 13, προσδεχόμενοι τὴν μακαρίαν ἐλπίδα καὶ ἐπιφάνειαν τῆς δόξης τοῦ μεγάλου Θεοῦ καὶ σωτῆρος ἡμῶν Χ. Ἰ. ὃς ἔδωκεν ἑαυτὸν ὑπὲρ ἡμῶν ἵνα λυτρώσηται ἡμᾶς, where also I should take τοῦ μεγάλου Θεοῦ to refer to the Father. Other examples of the same kind are Eph. v. 5, οὐκ ἔχει κληρονομίαν ἐν τῇ βασιλείᾳ τοῦ Χριστοῦ καὶ Θεοῦ (where Alf. notes "We cannot safely say here that the same Person is intended by Χ. κ. Θεοῦ merely on account of the omission of the art.; for (1) any introduction of such a prediction regarding Christ would here be manifestly out of place, (2) Θεός is so frequently anarthrous that it is not safe to ground any such inference on its use here)," 2 Thess. i. 12, ὅπως ἐνδοξασθῇ τὸ ὄνομα τοῦ κυρίου ἡμῶν Ἰησοῦ ἐν ὑμῖν καὶ ὑμεῖς ἐν αὐτῷ κατὰ τὴν χάριν τοῦ Θεοῦ ὑμῶν καὶ κυρίου Ἰησοῦ Χριστοῦ; 1 Tim. v. 21 (*cf.* 2 Tim. iv. 1), διαμαρτύρομαι ἐνώπιον τοῦ Θεοῦ καὶ Χριστοῦ Ἰησοῦ καὶ τῶν ἐκλεκτῶν ἀγγέλων, which Chrysostom explains μάρτυρα καλῶ τὸν Θεὸν καὶ τὸν υἱὸν αὐτοῦ; 2 Peter i. 1, ἐν δικαιοσύνῃ τοῦ Θεοῦ ἡμῶν καὶ σωτῆρος Ἰησοῦ Χριστοῦ, where see my n. The denial of the only Master and our Lord Jesus Christ may be implicit, shown by their conduct, though not asserted in

Χριστὸν ἀρνούμενοι. 5. Ὑπομνῆσαι δὲ ὑμᾶς βούλομαι, εἰδότας
πάντα,[1] ὅτι [2] Κύριος [3] ἅπαξ λαὸν [4] ἐκ γῆς Αἰγύπτου σώσας τὸ δεύτε-

υμας παντα ℵKL 31 syrr. Clem. Theoph. Oecon. + ; **υμας απαξ παντα** B ;. **απαξ παντα** AC² 13 vulg. + Ti. Treg. WH ; **απαξ παντας** H. (*Sel. Read.* p. 106)

οτι ℵAB syrh ; add. **ὁ** C²KL syrp.

[3] **κυριος** ℵCKL syrh ; **Ιησους** AB + ; **θεος** C² syrp, Clem.

[4] **απαξ λαον** ℵ, 68, tol., syrr., boh. (**οτι απαξ Ιησ. λαον**) sah. arm. Did. Cassiod. **λαον απαξ** Clem. ; **λαον** ABCL, Ti., Treg., WH.

word, as in Tit. i. 16 ; but it is more naturally taken as explicit, as in 1 John ii. 22, where Westcott notes that a common gnostic theory was that "'the Aeon Christ' descended upon the man Jesus at His baptism and left Him before His passion. Those who held such a doctrine denied . . . the union of the divine and human in one Person . . . and this denial involves the loss of the Father, not only because the ideas of sonship and fatherhood are correlative, but because . . . it is only in the Son that we have the [full] revelation of God as Father." The phrase **τὸν μόνον δεσπότην** might also refer to the heresy attributed to Cerinthus by Hippolytus (*Haer.* vii. 33, x. 21) **οὐχ ὑπὸ τοῦ πρώτου θεοῦ τὸν κόσμον γεγονέναι ἠθέλησεν ἀλλ' ὑπὸ δυνάμεώς τινος ἀγγελικῆς,** and Irenæus *Haer.* i. 26. See Introduction on Early Heresies in the large edition.

Vv. 5-13. *Illustrations of Sin and Judgment Derived from History and from Nature.* The judgment impending over these men is borne witness to by well-known facts of the past, and may be illustrated from the phenomena of nature. God showed His mercy in delivering the Israelites from Egypt, but that was no guarantee against their destruction in the wilderness when they again sinned by unbelief. The angels were blessed beyond all other creatures, but when they proved unfaithful to their trust they were imprisoned in darkness, awaiting there the judgment of the great day. The men of Sodom (lived in a land of great fertility, they had received some knowledge of God through the presence and teaching of Lot, they had been lately rescued from captivity by Abraham, yet they) followed the sinful example of the angels, and their land is still a prey to the fire, bearing witness to the eternal punishment of sin. In spite of these warnings the heretics, who are now finding their way into the Church, persist in their wild hallucinations, giving themselves up to the lusts of the flesh, despising authority, and railing at angelic dignities. They might have been taught better by the example of the archangel Michael, of whom we are told that, when disputing with the devil about the body of Moses, he uttered no word of railing, but made his appeal to God. These men however rail at that which is beyond their knowledge, while they surrender themselves like brute beasts to the guidance of their appetites, and thus bring about their own destruction, following in the wake of impious Cain, of covetous Balaam, and rebellious Korah. When they take part in your love-feasts they cause the shipwreck of the weak by their wantonness and irreverence. In greatness of profession and smallness of performance they resemble clouds driven by the wind which give no rain ; or trees in autumn on which one looks in vain for fruit, and which are only useful for fuel. By their confident speaking and brazen assurance they seem to carry all before them ; yet like the waves bursting on the shore, the deposit they leave is only their own shame. Or we might compare them to meteors which shine for a moment and are then extinguished for ever.

Ver. 5. **ὑπομνῆσαι δὲ ὑμᾶς βούλομαι, εἰδότας ὑμᾶς πάντα.*** *Cf.* 2 Pet. i. 12, **διὸ μελλήσω ὑμᾶς ἀεὶ ὑπομιμνήσκειν καίπερ εἰδότας,** *ib.* i. 13, **διεγείρειν ὑμᾶς ἐν ὑπομνήσει,** *ib.* iii. 1, **διεγείρω ὑμῶν ἐν ὑπομνήσει τὴν εἰλικρινῆ διάνοιαν,** Rom. xv. 14, **πέπεισμαι δὲ ὅτι καὶ αὐτοὶ μεστοί ἐστε ἀγαθωσύνης, πεπληρωμένοι πάσης τῆς γνώσεως . . . τολμηροτέρως δὲ ἔγραψα ὑμῖν|ἀπὸ μέρους ὡς ἐπαναμιμνήσκων ὑμᾶς.** The word **εἰδότας** justifies **ὑπομνῆσαι**: they only need to be reminded of truths already known, so that it is unnecessary to write at length. The repeated **ὑμᾶς** contrasts the readers with the libertines of the former verse. The words in themselves might be taken ironically of persons professing (like the Corinthians) to "know all things," but

*** On the readings see Introduction.**

ρον [τοὺς] μὴ πιστεύσαντας ἀπώλεσεν, 6. ἀγγέλους τε τοὺς μὴ τηρήσαντας τὴν ἑαυτῶν ἀρχὴν ἀλλὰ ἀπολιπόντας τὸ ἴδιον οἰκητή-

the broad distinction maintained throughout the epistle between **ὑμεῖς** and **οὗτοι** (the Libertines) forbids such an interpretation. If we read **ἅπαξ πάντα** with some MSS., it suggests something of anxiety and upbraiding, which may be compared with the tone of St. Paul in writing to the Galatians. See, however, the following note for the position of **ἅπαξ**. Instead of **πάντα** some MSS. have **τοῦτο**. The former finds some support in Enoch i. 2, "I heard everything from the angels," xxv. 2, "I should like to know about everything," *Secrets of En.* xl. 1, 2, "I know all things from the lips of the Lord . . . I know all things and have written all things in the books," lxi. 2 (quoted by Chase in *Dict. of the Bible*). It should probably be understood of all that follows, including the historical allusions, implying that those addressed were familiar not only with the O.T. but with rabbinical traditions: so Estius "omnia de quibus volo vos commonere". Bede's note is "omnia videlicet arcana fidei scientes et non opus habentes recentia quasi sanctiora a novis audire magistris". In what follows he takes **ἅπαξ** with **σώσας**, "ita clamantes ad se de afflictione Aegyptia primo salvavit humiles, ut secundo murmurantes contra se in eremo prosterneret superbos. . . . Meminerimus illum sic per aquas baptismi salvare credentes, ut etiam post baptismum humilem in nobis requirat vitam."

ὅτι Κύριος, ἅπαξ λαὸν ἐκ γῆς Αἰγύπτου σώσας, τὸ δεύτερον [τοὺς] μὴ πιστεύσαντας ἀπώλεσεν.] For text, see Introduction on Readings. Clement in his *Adumbrationes* gives the paraphrase "Quoniam Dominus Deus semel populum de terra Aegypti liberans deinceps eos qui non crediderunt perdidit".

τὸ δεύτερον has given rise to much discussion. According to the reading I have adopted, it contrasts the preceding *saving* with the following *destruction*. The deliverance from Egypt was the creation of a people once for all, but yet it was followed by the destruction of the unbelieving portion of the people, *i.e.* by all but Caleb and Joshua (Num. xiv. 27, 37). So in 1 Cor. x. we have the privileges of Israel allowed, and yet all was in vain because of their unbelief. There seems less force in the connection of **ἅπαξ** with **εἰδότας**: **ἤδη** would have been more suitable. For the opposition to **τὸ δεύτερον**, *cf.* Heb. ix. 28, **ὁ Χριστὸς ἅπαξ προσενεχθεὶς εἰς τὸ πολλῶν ἀνενεγκεῖν ἁμαρτίας ἐκ δευτέρου χωρὶς ἁμαρτίας ὀφθήσεται,** Theoph. *Autol.* ii. 26, **ἵνα τὸ μὲν ἅπαξ ᾖ πεπληρωμένον ὅτε ἐτέθη, τὸ δὲ δεύτερον μέλλῃ πληροῦσθαι μετὰ τὴν . . . κρίσιν,** Liban. *ap.* Wetst. **ἐμοὶ δὲ ἅπαξ ἀρκεῖ γέλωτα ὀφλεῖν, δεύτερον δὲ οὐκέτι.**

I am inclined to think that the article before **μή** is an intrusion, as it seems to be before **ἐν** in ver. 12. Omitting it, we can take **δεύτερον** with **μὴ πιστεύσαντας**, getting the sense: "In the 1st case of unbelief (in Egypt) * salvation followed; in the 2nd (in the wilderness) destruction," lit. "when they, a second time failed to believe, He destroyed them". If this was the original reading, it is easy to understand the insertion of **τούς** as facilitating the plural construction after **λαόν**. We may compare the solemn utterance in Heb. x. 26, **ἑκουσίως ἁμαρτανόντων ἡμῶν μετὰ τὸ λαβεῖν τὴν ἐπίγνωσιν τῆς ἀληθείας οὐκ ἔτι περὶ ἁμαρτιῶν ἀπολείπεται θυσία,** and the belief, apparently based upon it, in the early Church as to sin after baptism.

Ver. 6. **ἀγγέλους τε τοὺς μὴ τηρήσαντας τὴν ἑαυτῶν ἀρχὴν . . . εἰς κρίσιν . . . τετήρηκεν.**] *Cf.* Clem. Al. *Adumbr.* "Angelos qui non servaverunt proprium principatum, scilicet quem acceperunt secundum profectum." This of course supplies an even more striking instance of the possibility of falling away from grace, *cf.* Bede, "Qui angelis peccantibus non pepercit, nec hominibus parcet superbientibus, sed et hos quoque cum suum principatum non servaverint, quo per gratiam adoptionis filii Dei effecti sunt, sed reliquerint suum domicilium, id est, Ecclesiae unitatem . . . damnabit". On the Fall of the Angels see Introduction and the parallel passages in 2 Pet. ii. 4, and in Enoch, chapters 6-10.

ἀρχήν.] Used of office and dignity, as in Gen. xl. 21 of the chief butler: here perhaps of the office of Watcher, though Spitta takes it more generally of the sovereignty belonging to their abode in heaven = **τὸν ἄνω κλῆρον** in Clem. Al. 650 P. The term **ἀρχή** is used of the evil angels themselves in Eph. vi. 12. *Cf.* Enoch xii. 4, of the Watchers (angels)

* *Cf.* Exod. ii. 14, iv. 1, v. 21, vi. 9, xiv. 11, 12.

ριον εἰς κρίσιν μεγάλης ἡμέρας δεσμοῖς ἀϊδίοις ὑπὸ ζόφον[1] τετήρηκεν· 7. ὡς Σόδομα καὶ Γόμορρα καὶ αἱ περὶ αὐτὰς πόλεις, τὸν ὅμοιον τρόπον τούτοις[2] ἐκπορνεύσασαι καὶ ἀπελθοῦσαι ὀπίσω

[1] ζοφον] add. αγιων αγγελων speculum, Luc., *cf.* H. (*S. R.* p. 106); αγριων αγγ. Clem. p. 280; add. "in Tartaro constrictos" Orig.

[2] τροπον τουτοις ℵABC; τουτοις τροπον KL.

who have *abandoned the high heaven and the holy eternal place* and defiled themselves with women, *ib.* xv. 3. Philo says of the fallen angels (M. i. p. 268), καλὸν μὴ λιποτακτῆσαι μὲν τῆς τοῦ Θεοῦ τάξεως, ἐν ᾗ τοὺς τεταγμένους πάντας ἀριστεύειν ἀνάγκη, αὐτομολῆσαι δὲ πρὸς τὴν ἄνανδρον ἡδονήν. So Just. M. *Apol.* ii. 5, οἱ δ᾽ ἄγγελοι παραβάντες τήνδε τὴν τάξιν γυναικῶν μίξεσιν ἡττήθησαν with Otto's n.

ἀπολιπόντας τὸ ἴδιον οἰκητήριον. *Cf.* 2 Cor. v. 2, τὸ οἰκ. τὸ ἐξ οὐρανοῦ, and the quotation from Enoch in the last n. [For οἰκητήριον, *cf.* Enoch xv. 7 (the message of Enoch to the Watchers) "the spiritual have their dwelling in heaven" . . . ἡ κατοίκησις αὐτῶν ἔσται ἐπὶ τῆς γῆς. Chase.]

εἰς κρίσιν μεγάλης ἡμέρας δεσμοῖς ἀϊδίοις ὑπὸ ζόφον τετήρηκεν. *Cf.* 2 Pet. ii. 4 σειροῖς ζόφου ταρταρώσας, *ib.* ii. 9, ἀδίκους εἰς ἡμέραν κρίσεως κολαζομένους τηρεῖν, *ib.* iii. 7, τηρούμενοι εἰς ἡμέραν κρίσεως . . . τῶν ἀσεβῶν ἀνθρώπων, Joel ii. 31, ὁ ἥλιος μεταστραφήσεται εἰς σκότος . . . πρὶν ἐλθεῖν τὴν ἡμέραν Κυρίου τὴν μεγάλην καὶ ἐπιφανῆ, Apoc. vi. 17, ἦλθεν ἡ ἡμέρα ἡ μεγάλη τῆς ὀργῆς αὐτοῦ, *ib.* xvi. 14, συναγαγεῖν αὐτοὺς εἰς τὸν πόλεμον τῆς μεγάλης ἡμέρας τοῦ Θεοῦ τοῦ παντοκράτορος. Enoch x. 5, ἐπικάλυψον αὐτῷ (Azazel) σκότος, καὶ οἰκησάτω ἐκεῖ εἰς τὸν αἰῶνα, x. 12, δῆσον αὐτοὺς . . . μέχρι ἡμέρας κρίσεως αὐτῶν, *ib.* xxii. 11 (Gr. in Charles' *App.* C) μέχρι τῆς μεγάλης ἡμέρας τῆς κρίσεως, *ib.* liv. 6, note on xlv. 1. So ἡμέρα τοῦ κυρίου 1 Cor. i. 8, 2 Pet. iii. 10 *al.*, ἐκείνη ἡ ἡμέρα 2 Th. i. 10. On δεσμοῖς see En. liv. 3-5, "I saw how they made iron chains of immeasurable weight, and I asked for whom they were prepared, and he said unto me 'These are prepared far the hosts of Azazel'." *Cf.* δέσμιοι σκότους (Wisd. xvii. 2) of the plague of darkness.

ἀϊδίοις. The chains are called "everlasting," but they are only used for a temporary purpose, to keep them for the final judgment. It seems to be here synonymous with αἰώνιος in ver. 7. So too in the only other passages in which it occurs in the Bible, Wisdom vii. 26, ἀπαύγασμά ἐστι φωτὸς ἀϊδίου, and Rom. i. 20, ἡ ἀΐδιος αὐτοῦ δύναμις καὶ θειότης.

Ver. 7. ὡς Σόδομα καὶ Γόμορρα καὶ αἱ περὶ αὐτὰς πόλεις. The 3rd example of Divine judgment differs from the two others, as it tells only of the punishment, not of the fall from grace. Hence the difference of connexion ἀγγέλους τε. . . . ὡς Σόδομα. *Cf.* 2 Pet. ii. 6, πόλεις Σοδόμων καὶ Γομόρρας καταστροφῇ κατέκρινεν. The destruction was not limited to these two cities, but extended to all the neighbouring country (Gen. xix. 25, called Πεντάπολις in Wisd. x. 6), including the towns of Admah and Zeboim (Deut. xxix. 23, Hos. xi. 8). Zoar was spared at the request of Lot.

τὸν ὅμοιον τρόπον τούτοις ἐκπορνεύσασαι. For the adverbial acc., *cf.* Matt. xxiii. 37, ὃν τρόπον ἐπισυνάγει ὄρνις τὰ νοσσία, 2 Macc. xv. 39, ὃν τρόπον οἶνος . . . ἀποτελεῖ, οὕτω καὶ, Luc. *Catapl.* 6 τεθνᾶσι τὸν ὅμοιον τρόπον. "Like them," *i.e.* the fallen angels. The two judgments are similarly joined in *Test. Nepht.* 3, μὴ γένησθε ὡς Σόδομα, ἥτις ἐνήλλαξε τάξιν φύσεως αὐτῆς. Ὁμοίως δὲ καὶ οἱ Ἐγρήγορες ἐνήλλαξαν τάξιν φύσεως αὐτῶν, οὓς κατηράσατο Κύριος. Others understand τούτοις of the libertines who are subsequently referred to as οὗτοι (vv. 8, 10, 12, 16, 19); but the beginning of ver. 8 (μέντοι καὶ οὗτοι) seems to distinguish between them and the preceding. The verb ἐκπ. occurs in Gen. xxxviii. 24 of Tamar, Exod. xxxiv. 15, 16, (μή ποτε) ἐκπορνεύσωσιν ὀπίσω τῶν θεῶν αὐτῶν, Lev. xvii. 7, Hos. iv. 12, Ezek. xvi. 26, 28, 33.

ἀπελθοῦσαι ὀπίσω σαρκὸς ἑτέρας. In the case of the angels the forbidden flesh (lit. "other than that appointed by God") refers to the intercourse with women; in the case of Sodom to the departure from the natural use (Rom. i. 27), what Philo calls ἀνόμους καὶ ἐκθέσμους μίξεις (*de Gig.* M i. p. 267), *cf.* Exod. xxx. 9, οὐκ ἀνοίσεις θυμίαμα ἕτερον. For the post-classical phrase *cf.* 2 Pet. ii. 10, τοὺς ὀπίσω σαρκὸς ἐν ἐπιθυμίᾳ μιασμοῦ πορευομένους, Deut. iv. 3, ἐπορεύθη ὀπίσω Βεελφεγώρ, Jer. ii. 2, 3.

σαρκὸς ἑτέρας, πρόκεινται δεῖγμα πυρὸς αἰωνίου δίκην ὑπέχουσαι.
8. Ὁμοίως μέντοι καὶ οὗτοι ἐνυπνιαζόμενοι σάρκα μὲν μιαίνουσιν,

πρόκεινται δεῖγμα πυρὸς αἰωνίου δίκην ὑπέχουσαι. *Cf.* Enoch lxvii. 12, "this judgment wherewith the angels are judged is a testimony for the kings and the mighty," 2 Pet. ii. 6, **ὑπόδειγμα μελλόντων ἀσεβέσιν τεθεικώς,** 1 Cor. x. 6, 11 **τύποι ἐγένοντο,** Heb. iv. 11 **ἵνα μὴ ἐν τῷ αὐτῷ τις ὑποδείγματι πέσῃ τῆς ἀπειθείας.** The present aspect of the Lacus Asphaltites was a conspicuous image of the lake of fire and brimstone prepared for Satan and his followers, Apoc. xix. 20, xx. 10, xxi. 8. It is questioned whether **πυρός** is governed by **δεῖγμα** or **δίκην.** If by **δίκην,** then the burning of Sodom is itself spoken of as still going on (eternal), and this is in accordance with Jewish belief as recorded in Wisd. x. 7 (**πῦρ Πενταπόλεως**) **ἧς ἔτι μαρτύριον τῆς πονηρίας καπνιζομένη καθέστηκε χέρσος,** Philo (*De Abr.* M. ii. xxi.), **μέχρι νῦν καίεται. τὸ γὰρ κεραύνιον πῦρ ἥκιστα σβεννύμενον ἢ νέμεται ἢ ἐντύφεται. πίστις δὲ σαφεστάτη τὰ δρώμενα, τοῦ γὰρ συμβεβηκότος πάθους σημεῖόν ἐστιν ὅ τε ἀναδιδόμενος ἀεὶ καπνὸς καὶ ὃ μεταλλεύουσι θεῖον,** *ib. V. Moys.* M. ii. p. 143. Some disallow this sense of **αἰώνιος** and think that it can only be used of hell-fire, as in 4 Macc. xii. 12 (the words of the martyr contrasting the fires of present torture with the eternal flames awaiting the persecutor), **ταμιεύεταί σε ἡ θεία δίκη πυκνοτέρῳ καὶ αἰωνίῳ πυρί, καὶ βάσανοι εἰς ὅλον τὸν αἰῶνα οὐκ ἀνήσουσί σε.** For an examination of the word see Jukes, *Restitution of all Things*, p. 67 n. and *cf.* Jer. xxiii. 39, 40, Ezek. xvi. 53, 55 (on the restoration of Sodom); xlvii. 1-12 (a prophecy of the removal of the curse of the Dead Sea and its borders), Enoch. x. 5 and 12, where the **εἰς αἰῶνα** of the former verse is equivalent to seventy generations in the latter, also ver. 10 where **ζωὴ αἰώνιος** is reckoned at 500 years. As the meaning of **δεῖγμα** is made clear by the following participial clause, it seems unnecessary to take it with **πυρός** in the sense of "an example or type of eternal fire," which would escape the difficulty connected with **αἰωνίου,** but leaves **δίκην ὑπέχουσαι** (for which *cf.* Xen. *Mem.* ii. 1, 8, 2, Macc. iv. 48) a somewhat otiose appendage. In the book of Enoch (lxvii. 4 foll.) the angels who sinned are said to be imprisoned in a burning valley (Hinnom, ch. 27) in which there was a great swelling of waters, accompanied by a smell of sulphur; and "that valley of the angels burned continually under the earth". Charles notes on this that "the Gehenna valley here includes the adjacent country down to the Dead Sea. A subterranean fire was believed to exist under the Gehenna valley."

Ver. 8. **ὁμοίως μέντοι καὶ οὗτοι.** Notwithstanding these warnings the libertines go on in similar courses.

ἐνυπνιαζόμενοι σάρκα μιαίνουσιν Compare Acts ii. 17 (a quotation from Joel ii. 28), **οἱ πρεσβύτεροι ὑμῶν ἐνυπνίοις ἐνυπνιασθήσονται,** of those that see visions: and so Spitta (holding that Jude copied from 2 Peter), would render it here, prefixing the article to make it correspond with the **ψευδοπροφῆται** and **ψευδοδιδάσκαλοι** of 2 Peter ii. 1. Those who take the opposite view (*viz.* that 2 Peter was copied from Jude) will see nothing to justify the article. The word is used by Isa. lvi. 10 in connexion with the words **οὐκ ἔγνωσαν, οὐκ εἰδότες** (see ver. 10 below), **ἐνυπνιαζόμενοι κοίτην φιλοῦντες νυστάξαι,** which Delitsch explains "instead of watching and praying to see divine revelations for the benefit of the people, they are lovers of ease talkers in their sleep.

Bengel explains "Hominum mere naturalium indoles graphice admodum descripta est. Somnians multa videre, audire, etc. sibi videtur." And so Chase "they live in an unreal world of their own inflated imaginations," comparing the conjectural reading of Col. ii. 18, **ἀέρα κενεμβατεύων.** This accords with ver. 10: in their delusion and their blindness they take the real for the unreal, and the unreal for the real. The verb is used both in the active and middle by Aristotle, *Somn.* i. 1, **πότερον συμβαίνει ἀεὶ τοῖς καθεύδουσιν ἐνυπνιάζειν, ἀλλ οὐ μνημονεύουσιν;** *Probl.* 30, 14, 2, **οἱ ἐν τῷ καθεύδειν ἐνυπνιαζόμενοι ἱσταμένης τῆς διανοίας, καὶ καθ᾽ ὅσον ἠρεμεῖ, ὀνειρώττουσιν,** *cf.* Artem. *Oneir*, i. 1. Some interpret of polluting dreams (*cf.* Lev. 15); but the word **ἐνυπνιαζόμενοι** is evidently intended to have a larger scope, covering not merely **μιαίνουσιν** but **ἀθετοῦσιν** and **βλασφημοῦσιν.** We must also interpret **μιαίνω** here by the **ἀσέλγειαν** of ver. 4, the **ἐκπορνεύσασαι** and **σαρκὸς ἑτέρας** of ver. 7. This wide sense appears in Tit. i. 15, **τοῖς**

κυριότητα[1] δὲ ἀθετοῦσιν, δόξας δὲ βλασφημοῦσιν. 9. Ὁ δὲ

[1] κυριοτητα]—τητας ℵ Orig.

μεμιασμένοις οὐδὲν καθαρόν, ἀλλὰ μεμίανται αὐτῶν καὶ ὁ νοῦς καὶ ἡ συνείδησις.

κυριότητα δὲ ἀθετοῦσιν, δόξας δὲ βλασφημοῦσιν. On first reading one is inclined to take the words **κυριότης** and **δόξαι** simply as abstractions. The result of indulgence in degrading lusts is the loss of reverence, the inability to recognise true greatness and due degrees of honour. This would agree with the description of the libertines as sharing in the **ἀντιλογία** of Korah, as **κύματα ἄγρια θαλάσσης**, as **γογγυσταί** uttering hard speeches against God. When we examine however the use of the word **κυριότης** and the patristic comments, and when we consider the reference to the archangel's behaviour towards Satan, and the further explanation in ver. 10, where the **σάρκα** of ver. 8 is represented by **ὅσα φυσικῶς ἐπίστανται,** and the phrase **κυριότητα ἀθετοῦσιν, δόξας δὲ βλασφημοῦσιν** by **ὅσα οὐκ οἴδασιν βλασφημοῦσιν,** we seem to require a more pointed and definite meaning, not simply "majesty," but "the divine majesty," not simply "dignities," but "the angelic orders". *Cf.* 2 Pet. ii. 10, Eph. i. 21 (having raised him from the dead and set him on his right hand) **ὑπεράνω πάσης ἀρχῆς καὶ ἐξουσίας καὶ δυνάμεως καὶ κυριότητος,** Col. i. 16, **ἐν αὐτῷ ἐκτίσθη τὰ πάντα ἐν τοῖς οὐρανοῖς καὶ ἐπὶ τῆς γῆς, τὰ ὁρατὰ καὶ τὰ ἀόρατα, εἴτε θρόνοι εἴτε κυριότητες εἴτε ἀρχαὶ εἴτε ἐξουσίαι,** where Lightfoot considers that the words are intended to be taken in their widest sense, including bad and good angels, as well as earthly dignities. In our text, however, it would seem that the word should be understood as expressing the attribute of the true **κύριος,** *cf. Didache*, iv. 1 (honour him who speaks the word of God), **ὡς κύριον, ὅθεν γὰρ ἡ κυριότης λαλεῖται, ἐκεῖ κύριός ἐστιν,** Herm. *Sim*, v. 6, 1, **εἰς δοῦλου τρόπον οὐ κεῖται ὁ υἱὸς τοῦ Θεοῦ, ἀλλ' εἰς ἐξουσίαν μεγάλην κεῖται καὶ κυριότητα.** The verb **ἀθετέω** has God or Christ for its object in Luke x. 16, John xii. 48, 1 Thess. iv. 8, etc. We have then to consider how it can be said that the libertines (**οὗτοι**) "despise authority" in like manner to the above-mentioned offenders. For the former we may refer to ver. 4, **τὸν κύριον ἡμῶν ἀρνούμενοι,** for the latter to the contempt shown by the Israelites towards the commandments of God. So the desertion of their appointed station and abode by the angels showed their disregard for the divine ordinance, and the behaviour of the men of Sodom combined with the vilest lusts an impious irreverence towards God's representatives, the angels (Gen. xix. 5). *Cf.* Joseph. *Ant.* i. 11. 2, **εἰς ἀνθρώπους ἦσαν ὑβρισταὶ καὶ πρὸς τὸ θεῖον ἀσεβεῖς,** and *Test. Aser.* 7, where the sin of Sodom is expressly stated to have been their behaviour towards the angels, **μὴ γίνεσθε ὡς Σόδομα ἥτις ἠγνόησε τοὺς ἀγγέλους Κυρίου καὶ ἀπώλετο ἕως αἰῶνος.**

δόξας δὲ βλασφημοῦσιν. *Cf.* 2 Pet. ii. 10, **τολμηταὶ αὐθάδεις δόξας οὐ τρέμουσιν βλασφημοῦντες.** The only other passage in the N.T. in which the plural occurs is 1 Peter i. 11, where the sense is different. Dr. Bigg compares Exod. xv. 11, **τίς ὅμοιός σοι ἐν θεοῖς, Κύριε; τίς ὁμοιός σοι; δεδοξασμένος ἐν ἁγίοις, θαυμαστὸς ἐν δόξαις.** Clement's interpretation of this and the preceding clause is as follows: (*Adumbr.* 1008) "dominationem spernunt, hoc est solum dominum qui vere dominus noster est, Jesus Christus . . . majestatem blasphemant, hoc est angelos". The word **δόξα** in the singular is used for the Shekinah, see my note on James ii. 1. This suggests that Clement may be right in supposing the plural to be used for the angels, who are, as it were, separate rays of that glory. Compare Philo's use of the name **λόγοι** for the angels as contrasted with the divine **Λόγος.** In Philo, *Monarch.* ii. p. 18 the divine **δόξα,** is said to consist of the host of angels, **δόξαν δὲ σὴν εἶναι νομίζω τάς σε δορυφορούσας δυνάμεις.** See *Test. Jud.* 25, **Κύριος εὐλόγησε τὸν Λευί, ὁ ἄγγελος τοῦ προσώπου ἐμέ, αἱ δυνάμεις τῆς δοξης τὸν Συμεών,** also Luke ix. 26, where it is said that "the Son of Man will come in His own glory and in the glory of the Father and of the holy angels".* Ewald, *Hist. Isr.* tr. vol. viii. p. 142, explains **ἡ κυριότης** of the true Deity, whom they practically deny

* There is much said of the glory of the angels in *Asc. Isaiae*, pp. 47, 49 f. ed. Charles.

Μιχαὴλ ὁ ἀρχάγγελος, ὅτε[1] τῷ διαβόλῳ διακρινόμενος διελέγετο περὶ τοῦ Μωυσέως σώματος, οὐκ ἐτόλμησεν κρίσιν ἐπενεγκεῖν βλασ-

[1] **ο δε Μιχαηλ . . . οτε** ACKL, ℵ; **οτε Μιχ. . . . τοτε** B.

by their dual God; **αἱ δόξαι** as the angels, whom they blaspheme by supposing that they had created the world in opposition to the will of the true God, whereas Michael himself submitted everything to Him. This last clause would then be an appendage to the preceding, with special reference to the case of the Sodomites (*cf.* John xiii. 20). There may also be some allusion to the teaching or practice of the libertines. If we compare the mysterious reference in 1 Cor. xi. 10, **διὰ τοῦτο ὀφείλει ἡ γυνὴ ἐξουσίαν ἔχειν ἐπὶ τῆς κεφαλῆς διὰ τοὺς ἀγγέλους**, which is explained by Tertullian (*De Virg. Vel.* 7) as spoken of the fallen angels mentioned by Jude, "propter angelos, scilicet quos legimus a Deo et caelo excidisse ob concupiscentiam feminarum," we might suppose the **βλασφημία**, of which the libertines were guilty, to consist in a denial or non-recognition of the presence of good angels in their worship, or of the possibility of their own becoming **κοινωνοὶ δαιμονίων**; or they may have scoffed at the warnings against the assaults of the devil, or even at the very idea of "spiritual wickedness in high places". So understood, it prepares us for the strange story of the next verse.

Ver. 9. **ὁ δὲ Μιχαὴλ ὁ ἀρχάγγελος.** The term **ἀρχ.** occurs in the N.T. only here and in 1 Thess. iv. 16. The names of seven archangels are given in Enoch. The story here narrated is taken from the apocryphal *Assumptio Mosis*, as we learn from Clem. *Adumbr. in Ep. Judae*, and Orig. *De Princ.* iii. 2, 1. Didymus (*In Epist. Judae Enarratio*) says that some doubted the canonicity of the Epistle because of this quotation from an apocryphal book. In Cramer's *Catena* on this passage (p. 163) we read **τελευτήσαντος ἐν τῷ ὄρει Μωυσέως, ὁ Μιχαὴλ ἀποστέλλεται μεταθήσων τὸ σῶμα, εἶτα τοῦ διαβόλου κατὰ τοῦ Μωυσέως βλασφημοῦντος καὶ φονέα ἀναγορεύοντος διὰ τὸ πατάξαι τὸν Αἰγύπτιον, οὐκ ἐνεγκὼν τὴν κατ' αὐτοῦ βλασφημίαν ὁ ἄγγελος, Ἐπιτιμήσαι σοι ὁ Θεός, πρὸς τὸν διάβολον ἔφη.** Charles in his edition of the *Assumption* thus summarises the fragments dealing with the funeral of Moses: (1) Michael is commissioned to bury Moses, (2) Satan opposes his burial on two grounds: (*a*) he claims to be the lord of matter (hence the body should be handed over to him). To this claim Michael rejoins, "The Lord rebuke thee, for it was God's spirit which created the world and all mankind". (*b*) He brings the charge of murder against Moses (the answer to this is wanting). The story is based upon Deut. xxxiv. 6 (R.V.), "he buried him (*mg.* he was buried) in the valley . . . but no man knoweth of his sepulchre unto this day". Compare the vain search for Elijah (2 Kings ii. 16, 17). Further details in Josephus (*Ant.* iv. 8, 48), **νέφους αἰφνίδιον ὑπὲρ αὐτοῦ στάντος ἀφανίζεται κατά τινος φάραγγος. γέγραφε δὲ αὐτὸν ἐν ταῖς ἱεραῖς βίβλοις τεθνεῶτα, δείσας μὴ δι' ὑπερβολὴν τῆς περὶ αὐτὸν ἀρετῆς πρὸς τὸ θεῖον αὐτὸν ἀναχωρῆσαι τολμήσωσιν εἰπεῖν**, Philo i. p. 165, and Clem. Al. (*Str.* vi. § 132, p. 807) where it is said that Caleb and Joshua witnessed the assumption of Moses to heaven, while his body was buried in the clefts of the mountain. See comment in the larger edition, pp. 74-76.

διακρινόμενος. Here used in the sense of "disputing," as in Jer. xv. 10, **ἄνδρα διακρινόμενον πάσῃ τῇ γῇ**, Joel iii. 2, Acts xi. 2. See my note on James i. 6 and below ver. 22.

διελέγετο. *Cf.* Mark ix. 34, **πρὸς ἀλλήλους διελέχθησαν, τίς μείζων.**

οὐκ ἐτόλμησεν κρίσιν ἐπενεγκεῖν βλασφημίας. I take **βλασφημίας** to be *gen. qualitatis*, expressed by the adjective **βλάσφημον** in 2 Peter: see below on ver. 18, James i. 25, **ἀκροατὴς ἐπιλησμονῆς**, ii. 4 **κριταὶ διαλογισμῶν πονηρῶν**, iii. 6, **ὁ κόσμος τῆς ἀδικίας**, also 2 Peter ii. 1, **αἱρέσεις ἀπωλείας**, ii. 10, **ἐπιθυμίᾳ μιασμοῦ.** For **ἐπενεγκεῖν** see Plat. *Legg.* ix. 856 **προδόσεως αἰτίαν ἐπιφέρων**, *ib.* 943, **τιμωρίαν ἐπιφ.** The word occurs elsewhere in N.T. only in Rom. iii. 5. Field (*On Translation of N.T.* p. 244) compares Acts xxv. 18 **οἱ κατήγοροι οὐδεμίαν αἰτίαν ἔφερον ὧν ἐγὼ ὑπενόουν**, Diod. xvi. 29, **δίκην ἐπήνεγκαν κατὰ τῶν Σπαρτιατῶν**, *ib.* xx. 10, **κρίσεις ἀδίκους ἐπιφέροντες**, xx. 62, **φοβηθεὶς τὰς ἐπιφερομένας κρίσεις**, tom. x. p. 171 ed. Bip. **ἐπήνεγκαν κρίσιν περὶ ὕβρεως**, and

φημίας, ἀλλὰ εἶπεν Ἐπιτιμήσαι σοι Κύριος.[1] 10. Οὗτοι δὲ ὅσα μὲν οὐκ οἴδασιν βλασφημοῦσιν, ὅσα δὲ φυσικῶς ὡς τὰ ἄλογα ζῷα ἐπίστανται, ἐν τούτοις φθείρονται. 11. οὐαὶ αὐτοῖς, ὅτι τῇ ὁδῷ

[1] κυριος] ὁ θεος ℵ.

translates "durst not bring against him an accusation of blasphemy"; but surely that is just what he does in appealing to God. Besides such a statement would be altogether beside the point. The verse is introduced to show the guilt attached to speaking evil of dignities, *i.e.* of angels. If Michael abstained from speaking evil even of a fallen angel, this is appropriate; not so, if he simply abstained from charging the devil with speaking evil of Moses.

κρίσις, like **κρίνω**, has the two meanings of judgment and of accusation, *cf.* Lycurg. 31 where **οἱ συκοφαντοῦντες** are distinguished from **τῶν δικαίως τὰς κρίσεις ἐνισταμένων**.

ἐπιτιμήσαι σοι Κύριος. These words occur in the vision of Zechariah (iii. 1-10) where the angel of the Lord replies to the charges of Satan against the high priest Joshua with the words **ἐπιτιμήσαι Κύριος ἐν σοί, διάβολε, καὶ ἐπιτιμήσαι Κύριος ἐν σοί, ὁ ἐκλεξάμενος τὴν Ἱερουσαλήμ**. They were no doubt inserted as appropriate by the author of the *Ass. Mos.* in his account of the controversy at the grave of Moses. We may compare Matt. xvii. 18, **ἐπετίμησεν αὐτῷ ὁ Ἰησοῦς**.

Ver. 10. **οὗτοι δὲ ὅσα μὲν οὐκ οἴδασιν βλασφημοῦσιν**. The libertines do the contrary of what we are told of the respect shown by the angel even towards Satan: they speak evil of that spiritual world, those spiritual beings, of which they know nothing, *cf.* 2 Peter ii. 12. The common verb **βλασφ.** shows that the **δόξαι** of ver. 8 are identical with **ὅσα οὐκ οἴδασιν** here. For the blindness of the carnal mind to all higher wisdom *cf.* 1 Cor. ii. 7-16, a passage linked with our epistle by the distinction between the **ψυχικοί** and **πνευματικοί** and by the words **λαλοῦμεν Θεοῦ σοφίαν, ἣν οὐδεὶς τῶν ἀρχόντων τοῦ αἰῶνος τούτου ἔγνωκεν· εἰ γὰρ ἔγνωσαν οὐκ ἂν τὸν κύριον τῆς δόξης ἐσταύρωσαν**. See too John viii. 19, 1 Tim. vi. 4, **τετύφωται μηδὲν ἐπιστάμενος**. For the form **οἴδασιν** see my ed. of St. James, p. clxxxiii.

ὅσα δὲ φυσικῶς ὡς τὰ ἄλογα ζῷα ἐπίστανται. This stands for **σάρκα** in ver. 8 and is explained by **ἀσέλγειαν** in ver. 4, **ἐκπορνεύσασαι** in ver. 7, **μιαίνουσιν** in ver. 8, **κατὰ τὰς ἐπιθυμίας αὐτῶν πορευόμενοι** in ver. 16.

φυσικῶς, "by instinct," so Dion. L. x. 137, **φυσικῶς καὶ χωρὶς λόγου.** Alford cites Xen. *Cyrop.* ii. 3, 9, **μάχην ὁρῶ πάντας ἀνθρώπους φύσει ἐπισταμένους, ὥσπερ γε καὶ τἄλλα ζῷα ἐπίσταταί τινα μάχην ἕκαστα οὐδὲ παρ' ἑνὸς ἄλλου μαθόντα ἢ παρὰ τῆς φύσεως.**

ἐν τούτοις φθείρονται. The natural antithesis here would have been "these things they admire and delight in". For this Jude substitutes by a stern irony "these things are their ruin". *Cf.* Phil. iii. 19, where speaking of the enemies of the Cross the apostle says: **ὧν τὸ τέλος ἀπώλεια, ὧν ὁ θεὸς ἡ κοιλία, καὶ ἡ δόξα ἐν τῇ αἰσχύνῃ αὐτῶν**, Eph. iv. 22, **ἀποθέσθαι . . . τὸν παλαιὸν ἄνθρωπον τὸν φθειρόμενον κατὰ τὰς ἐπιθυμίας.**

Ver. 11. **οὐαὶ αὐτοῖς, ὅτι τῇ ὁδῷ τοῦ Καὶν ἐπορεύθησαν**. For the use of the aorist see note on ver. 4, **παρεισεδύησαν**: for the phrase *cf.* Blass, *Gr.* p. 119, and 2 Peter ii. 15, **ἐξακολουθήσαντες τῇ ὁδῷ τοῦ Βαλαάμ.** The phrase **οὐαί**, so common in Enoch, especially in cc. 94 to 100, and in the Gospels and Apocalypse, occurs in the epistles only here and in 1 Cor. ix. 16. The woe is grounded on the fate which awaits those who walk in the steps of Cain, Balaam and Korah. In 2 Peter Balaam is the only one referred to of the three leaders of wickedness here named by Jude. Cain, with Philo, is the type of selfishness (M. 1 p. 206), **πᾶς φίλαυτος ἐπίκλησιν Καὶν εὕρηκεν** (quoted by Schneckenb. p. 221); he is named as a type of jealous hate in 1 John iii. 11, 12, **ἵνα ἀγαπῶμεν ἀλλήλους. οὐ καθὼς Καὶν ἐκ τοῦ πονηροῦ ἦν καὶ ἔσφαξεν τὸν ἀδελφὸν αὐτοῦ· καὶ χάριν τίνος ἔσφαξεν αὐτόν; ὅτι τὰ ἔργα αὐτοῦ πονηρὰ ἦν, τὰ δὲ τοῦ ἀδελφοῦ αὐτοῦ δίκαια,** of unbelief in Heb. xi. 4, **πίστει πλείονα θυσίαν Ἄβελ παρὰ Καὶν προσήνεγκεν τῷ Θεῷ,** *cf* Philo, *De Agric.* 1 M. 300 f., and Targ. Jer. on Gen. iv. 7, cited by Schneckenburger, in which Cain is represented as saying "non est judicium, nec judex, nec est aliud saeculum, nec dabitur merces bona justis; nec ultio sumetur de improbis," etc. There seems no reason why we should not regard Cain here as symbolising the absence both of faith

τοῦ Καὶν ἐπορεύθησαν, καὶ τῇ πλάνῃ τοῦ Βαλαὰμ μισθοῦ ἐξεχύθησαν,

and of love, *cf.* 1 John iii. 23. Euthym. Zig. gives an allegorical explanation, **καὶ αὐτοὶ ἀδελφοκτόνοι εἰσί, δι' ὧν διδάσκουσι τὰς τῶν ἀπατωμένων ψυχὰς ἀποκτείνοντες.** Cain and Korah are said to have been objects of special reverence with a section of the Ophite heresy, which appears to have been a development of the Nicolaitans (Epiphan. *Pan.* i. 3, 37, 1, **οἱ Ὀφῖται τὰς προφάσεις εἰλήφασιν ἀπὸ τῆς Νικολάου καὶ Γνωστικῶν καὶ τῶν πρὸ τούτων αἱρέσεων**). They held that the Creator was evil, that the serpent represented the divine Wisdom, that Cain and his successors were champions of right (Epiphan. *ib.* 38, 1, **οἱ Καιανοί φασι τὸν Καὶν ἐκ τῆς ἰσχυροτέρας Δυνάμεως ὑπάρχειν καὶ τῆς ἄνωθεν αὐθεντίας**, and boast themselves to be of kin to Cain, **καὶ τῶν Σοδομιτῶν καὶ Ἠσαῦ καὶ Κορέ**, see too Iren. i. 51, Clem. *Str.* vii. § 108.)

τῇ πλάνῃ τοῦ Βαλαὰμ μισθοῦ ἐξεχύθησαν. Every word in this clause is open to question. The passive of **ἐκχέω**, to "pour out," is used to express either the onward sweeping movement of a great crowd, or the surrender to an overpowering motive on the part of an individual = *effusi sunt*,* as in Sir. xxxvii. 29, **μὴ ἐκχυθῇς ἐπ' ἐδεσμάτων**, *Test. Reub.* 1, **πορνείᾳ ἐν ᾗ ἐξεχύθην**, Clem. Al. *Str.* ii. p. 491, **εἰς ἡδονήν, τράγων δικήν, ἐκχυθέντες καθηδυπαθοῦσιν**, Plut. *V. Ant.* 21, **εἰς τὸν ἡδυπαθῆ καὶ ἀκόλαστον βίον ἐκκεχυμένος.** Such an interpretation seems not quite consistent with **μισθοῦ**, which implies cool self-interest. That covetousness, **αἰσχροκέρδεια**, was a common motive with false teachers is often implied or asserted by St. Paul and St. Peter in the passages quoted below: and this, we know, was the case with Balaam; but would it be correct to say either of him or of his followers, here condemned by St. Jude, that they ran greedily into (or "in") error for reward? Perhaps we should understand it rather of a headstrong will breaking down all obstacles, refusing to listen to reason or expostulation, as Balaam holds to his purpose in spite of the divine opposition manifested in such diverse ways. Then comes the difficulty, how are we to understand the dative **πλάνῃ**, and what is the reference in the word? Should we take **πλάνῃ** as equivalent to **εἰς πλάνην** (Winer, p. 268)? This is the interpretation given by Lucifer p. 219, "vae illis quoniam in seductionem B. mercede effusi sunt," but it is a rare use of the dative, and it seems more natural to explain **πλάνῃ** by the preceding **ὁδῷ** (dative of the means or manner), which is used in the same collocation in 2 Peter ii. 15. What then are we to understand by "they were hurried along on the line of Balaam's error"? What was his error? From Num. xxii., xxv. 1-3, and xxxi. 16, Neh. xiii. 2, **Μωαβῖται ἐμισθώσαντο ἐπ' αὐτὸν τὸν Βαλαὰμ καταράσασθαι**, Jos. *Ant.* iv. 6, 6, we learn that B. was induced by Balak's bribe to act against his own convictions and eventually to tempt Israel to fornication. This then is the error or seduction by which he leads them astray.† In rabbinical literature Balaam is a sort of type of false teachers (Pirke Aboth, v. 29, with Taylor's n.). Some suppose the name Nicolaitan (Apoc. ii. 6) to be formed from the Greek equivalent to Balaam = "corrupter of the people"; see however the passages quoted from Clem. Al. in the Introduction on Early Heresies. In Apoc. ii. 14 we read of some in Pergamum that held the teaching of Balaam, **ὃς ἐδίδασκεν τῷ Βαλὰκ βαλεῖν σκάνδαλον ἐνώπιον τῶν υἱῶν Ἰσραήλ, φαγεῖν εἰδωλόθυτα καὶ πορνεῦσαι.** There is no hint to suggest that the innovators, of whom Jude speaks, favoured idolatry, but they may have prided themselves on their enlightenment in disregarding the rule of the Apostolic Council as to the use of meats offered to idols (*cf.* 1 Cor. 8), and perhaps in burning incense in honour of the Emperor, see Ramsay, *Expositor* for 1904, p. 409, and July, pp. 43-60. On the other hand, Jude continually charges them with moral laxity, and we may suppose that this was combined with claims to prophetic power, and with the covetousness which is often ascribed to the false teachers of the early Church, as in 1 Thess. ii. 3 f., where

* I do not think the marginal reading in the R.V., "cast themselves away," is tenable.

† Zahn understands **πλάνη** in an active, not a passive sense, as the ruling principle of the **πλάνος** Balaam, not as the error into which others fell through his seductions. I do not think Jude discriminated between these meanings: **πλάνη** covers both.

καὶ τῇ ἀντιλογίᾳ τοῦ Κορὲ ἀπώλοντο. 12. οὗτοί εἰσιν[1] [οἱ]

[1] ουτοι εισιν] add. (ex. v. 16) γογγυσται—πορευομενοι ℵ C[2].

Paul asserts of his own ministry that it was οὐκ ἐκ πλάνης οὐδὲ ἐξ ἀκαθαρσίας οὐδὲ ἐν δόλῳ . . . οὔτε γὰρ ἐν λόγῳ κολακείας ἐγενήθημεν, οὔτε ἐν προφάσει πλεονεξίας, οὔτε ζητοῦντες ἐξ ἀνθρώπων δόξαν, 1 Tim. iii. 8, 9, διακόνους μὴ διλόγους, μὴ οἴνῳ πολλῷ προσέχοντας, μὴ αἰσχροκερδεῖς, ἔχοντας τὸ μυστήριον τῆς πίστεως ἐν καθαρᾷ συνειδήσει, Tit. i. 7, 11 διδάσκοντες ἃ μὴ δεῖ κέρδους χάριν, 1 Peter v. 2. For the gen. μισθοῦ *cf.* Winer, p. 258, Plat. *Rep.* ix. 575 B, μισθοῦ ἐπικουροῦσιν, 1 Cor. vii. 23, τιμῆς ἠγοράσθητε.

On the whole I understand the passage thus: Balaam went wrong because he allowed himself to hanker after gain and so lost his communion with God. He not only went wrong himself, but he abused his great influence and his reputation as a prophet, to lead astray the Israelites by drawing them away from the holy worship of Jehovah to the impure worship of Baal Peor. So these false teachers use their prophetical gifts for purposes of self-aggrandisement, and endeavour to make their services attractive by excluding from religion all that is strenuous and difficult, and opening the door to every kind of indulgence. See the notes and comments on the parallel passages of 2 Peter in my edition of that Epistle.

τῇ ἀντιλογίᾳ τοῦ Κορὲ ἀπώλοντο. For Korah's sin see Num. xvi. 1 f. and compare, for the same rebellious spirit in the Christian Church, 3 John, 9, 10 (of Diotrephes), Tit. i. 10, 11, εἰσὶ πολλοὶ ἀνυπότακτοι . . . οὓς δεῖ ἐπιστομίζειν, *ib.* i. 16; *ib.* iii. 10, 11, 1 Tim. i. 20 (among those who have made shipwreck of the faith mention is made of Hymenaeus and Alexander) οὓς παρέδωκα τῷ Σατανᾷ ἵνα παιδευθῶσιν μὴ βλασφημεῖν, *ib.* vi. 3-6, 2 Tim. ii. 16-18, ὁ λόγος αὐτῶν ὡς γάγγραινα νομὴν ἕξει, ὧν ἐστιν Ὑμέναιος καὶ Φίλητος, οἵτινες περὶ τὴν ἀλήθειαν ἠστόχησαν, *ib.* ii. 25, iv. 14, where the opposition of Alexander the coppersmith is noted; but especially iii. 1-9, which presents a close parallel to our passage, referring to a similar resistance to Moses in the case of the apocryphal Jannes and Jambres. For ἀντιλογία see Heb. xii. 3, ἀναλογίσασθε τὸν τοιαύτην ὑπομεμενηκότα ὑπὸ τῶν ἁμαρτωλῶν εἰς ἑαυτὸν ἀντιλογίαν. It is used as a translation of Meribah in Num. xx. 13 *al.* and (in relation to Korah) in *Protev. Jac.* 9, μνήσθητι ὅσα ἐποίησεν ὁ Θεὸς τοῖς Δαθάν, Κωρέ, καὶ Ἀβειράμ, πῶς ἐδιχάσθη ἡ γῆ καὶ κατέπιεν αὐτοὺς διὰ τὴν ἀντιλογίαν αὐτῶν.

Rampf draws attention to the climax contained in these examples. The sin of Cain is marked by the words ἐπορεύθησαν ὁδῷ, that of Balaam the gentile prophet by ἐξεχύθησαν πλάνῃ, that of the Levite Korah by ἀπώλοντο ἀντιλογίᾳ.

Ver. 12. **οὗτοί εἰσιν [οἱ] ἐν ταῖς ἀγάπαις ὑμῶν σπιλάδες συνευωχούμενοι.** Dr. Chase quotes Zech. i. 10 f., Apoc. vii. 14, Enoch xlvi. 3, *Secrets of Enoch*, vii. 3 xviii. 3, xix. 3, etc., for the phrase οὗτοί εἰσιν, adding that it was probably adopted by St. Jude from apocalyptic writings, for which he clearly had a special liking. On the early history of the Agape, see my Appendix C to Clem. Al. *Strom.* vii. The parallel passage in 2 Peter (on which see n.) has two remarkable divergencies from the text here, reading ἀπάταις for ἀγάπαις and σπῖλοι for σπιλάδες. There has been much discussion as to the meaning of the latter word. It is agreed that it is generally used of a rock in or by the sea, and many of the lexicographers understand it of a hidden rock, ὕφαλος πέτρα, see Thomas Mag., σπιλάς, Ἀττικῶς· ὕφαλος πέτρα, Ἕλληνες, Etymol. M., σπιλάδες . . . αἱ ὑπὸ θάλασσαν κεκρυμμέναι πέτραι, ὅθεν καὶ ὕφαλος ἄνθρωπος λέγεται ὁ κεκρυμμένος καὶ πανοῦργος, *ib.* κατασπιλάζοντες, κατακρύπτοντες, ἀπὸ μεταφορᾶς τῶν ὑφάλων πετρῶν, αἵτινες ὑπὸ ὕδατος καλυπτόμεναι τοῖς ἀπρούπτως προσπελάζουσι κίνδυνον ἐπιφέρουσι (both cited by Wetst.). The same explanation is given by the scholiast on Hom. *Od.* v. 401-405, καὶ δὴ δοῦπον ἄκουσε ποτὶ σπιλάδεσσι θαλάσσης . . . ἀλλ' ἀκταὶ προβλῆτες ἔσαν σπιλάδες τε πάγοι τε. See Plut. *Mor.* 101 B, εὐδία σπιλάδος, which Wytt. translates "tranquillitas maris caecam rupem tegentis," *ib.* 476 A, Oecumenius on this passage, αἱ σπιλάδες τοῖς πλέουσιν ὀλέθριοι, ἀπροσδοκήτως ἐπιγενόμεναι (? -νοις), and ἐξαίφνης, ὥσπερ σπιλάδες, ἐπάγοντες αὐτοῖς τὸν ὄλεθρον τῶν ψυχῶν. Wetst. also quotes Heliod. v. 31, θαλάσσῃ προσείκασας ἂν τοὺς ἄνδρας αἰφνιδίῳ σπιλάδι κατασεισθέντας. The compound κατασπιλάζω joined with the parallel case

ἐν ταῖς[1] ἀγάπαις[2] ὑμῶν[3] σπιλάδες, συνευωχούμενοι ἀφόβως,[4]

[1] **οι εν ταις**] om. **οι** ℵ K vulg. Luc. Theophl. Oecon. +, Chase.

[2] **αγαπαις** ℵ BKL syrr. sah. boh. + ; **απαταις** AC.

[3] **υμων**] **αυτων** A vulg. syrp +.

[4] **συνευωχουμενοι, αφοβως** syrr., Treg., WH; **συνευωχ. αφοβως**, Ti.

of **ὕφαλος** justifies, I think, this sense of **σπιλάς**, which is rejected by most of the later commentators.* *Cf.* also the use of **ναυαγέω** in 1 Tim. i. 19. *Scopulus* is used in a similar metaphoric sense, see Cic. *in Pis.* 41 where Piso and Gabinius are called "geminae voragines scopulique reipublicae". Others take **σπιλάδες** in the very rare sense of "spots," or "stains," like **σπίλοι** in 2 Peter. The only example of this sense seems to be in Orph. *Lith.* 614, but Hesych. gives the interpretation **σπιλάς, μεμιασμένοι.** I agree with Bp. Wordsworth and Dr. Chase in thinking that the metaphor of the sunken rocks is more in harmony with the context.

How are we to account for the gender in **οἱ . . . σπιλάδες συνευωχούμενοι**? Are we to suppose the gender of **σπιλάς** was changed or forgotten in late Greek (*cf.* Winer, pp. 25, 38, 73, 76)? If so, the forgetfulness seems to have been confined to this author. Or is this a *constructio ad sensum*, the feminine being changed to masculine because it is metaphorically used of men (Winer, pp. 171, 648, 660, 672), *cf.* Apoc. xi. 4, **οὗτοί εἰσιν αἱ δύο λυχνίαι αἱ ἐνώπιον τοῦ κυρίου ἑστῶτες** and B's reading **παραφερόμενοι** below? Or may we take **σπιλάδες** as expressing a complementary notion in apposition to **συνευωχούμενοι**? The last seems the best explanation though I cannot recall any exact parallel. An easier remedy would be to omit the article (with K and many versions), as suggested by Dr. Chase in Hastings' *Dictionary of the Bible*, ii. p. 799*b*, translating: "these are sunken rocks in your love-feasts while they feast with you".

συνευωχούμενοι. Is used in the parallel passage of 2 Peter with a dat. as in Luc. *Philops* 4, Jos. *Ant.* iv. 8, 7.

ἀφόβως ἑαυτοὺς ποιμαίνοντες. If we take **σπιλάδες** as complementary to **συνευωχούμενοι**, it is better to take **ἀφόβως** with **ποιμ.**: if we omit the article and take **σπιλάδες** to be the predicate, **συνευωχούμενοι** will be an epexegetic participle, which will require strengthening by **ἀφόβως.** Generally **ἀφ.** is used in a good sense, but we find it used, as here, of the want of a right fear in Prov. xix. 23, **φόβος Κυρίου εἰς ζωὴν ἀνδρί, ὁ δὲ ἄφοβος κ.τ.λ.**, *ib.* xv. 16, **κρεῖσσον μικρὰ μερὶς μετὰ φόβου Κυρίου ἢ θησαυροὶ μεγάλοι μετὰ ἀφοβίας,** Sir. v. 5, **περὶ ἐξιλασμοῦ μὴ ἄφοβος γίνου, προσθεῖναι ἁμαρτίαν ἐφ' ἁμαρτίαις.** The phrase **ἑαυτοὺς ποιμ.** recalls Ezek. xxxiv. 8, **ἐβόσκησαν οἱ ποιμένες ἑαυτούς, τὰ δὲ πρόβατά μου οὐκ ἐβόσκησαν,** but there does not seem to be any reference to spiritual pastors in Jude; and **ποιμαίνω** has probably here the sense "to fatten, indulge," as in Prov. xxviii. 7, **ὃς δὲ ποιμαίνει ἀσωτίαν, ἀτιμάζει πατέρα,** *ib.* xxix. 3, **ὃς δὲ ποιμαίνει πόρνας, ἀπολεῖ πλοῦτον,** Plut. *Mor.* 792 B, **Ἄτταλον ὑπ' ἀργίας μακρᾶς ἐκλυθέντα κομιδῇ Φιλοποίμην ἐποίμαινεν ἀτεχνῶς πιαινόμενον.** We may compare 1 Cor. xi. 27 f., James v. 5, 1 Tim. v. 6.

νεφέλαι ἄνυδροι ὑπὸ ἀνέμων παραφερόμεναι. The character of the innovators is illustrated by figures drawn from the four elements, air, earth, sea, heaven (**αἰθήρ**). Spitta points out the resemblance to a passage in Enoch (chapters ii.-v.), which follows immediately on the words quoted below, vv. 14, 15. The regular order of nature is there contrasted with the disorder and lawlessness of sinners. "I observed everything that took place in the heaven, how the luminaries . . . do not deviate from their orbits, how they all

* Dr. Bigg denies this meaning on the strength mainly of two quotations, Hom. *Od.* iii. 298, **ἀτὰρ νῆάς γε ποτὶ σπιλάδεσσιν ἔαξαν κύματα,** where, he says, the **σπιλάδες** are identical with **λισσὴ αἰπειά τε εἰς ἅλα πέτρη** of 293; and Anthol. xi. 390, **φασὶ δὲ καὶ νήεσσιν ἁλιπλανέεσσι χερείους τὰς ὑφάλους πέτρας τῶν φανερῶν σπιλάδων.** In both of these I think the word refers to the breakers at the bottom of the cliffs: in the latter it is said that hidden rocks are more dangerous than visible reefs. Compare Diod. iii. 43, **ὄρος δὲ ταύτῃ παράκειται κατὰ μὲν τὴν κορυφὴν πέτρας ἀποτομάδας ἔχον καὶ τοῖς ὕψεσι καταπληκτικάς, ὑπὸ δὲ τὰς ῥίζας σπιλάδας ὀξείας καὶ πυκνὰς ἐνθαλάττους.**

ἑαυτοὺς ποιμαίνοντες, νεφέλαι ἄνυδροι ὑπὸ ἀνέμων παραφερόμεναι,[1]

[1] παραφερομενοι B.

rise and set in order, each in its season, and transgress not against their appointed order. . . . I observed and saw how in winter all the trees seem as though they were withered and shed all their leaves. . . . And again I observed the days of summer . . . how the trees cover themselves with green leaves and bear fruit. . . . And behold how the seas and the rivers accomplish their task. But as for you, ye have not continued steadfast; and the law of the Lord ye have not fulfilled . . . and have slanderously spoken proud and hard words (below ver. 15, περὶ πάντων τῶν σκληρῶν ὧν ἐλάλησαν κατ' αὐτοῦ) with your impure mouths against his greatness." For the metaphor *cf.* Eph. iv. 14. In the parallel passage of 2 Peter the first figure is broken into two, πηγαὶ ἄνυδροι, ὁμίχλαι ὑπὸ λαίλαπος ἐλαυνόμεναι. Perhaps the writer may have thought that there was an undue multiplication of causes; if the clouds were waterless, it was needless to add that they were driven past by the wind. We find the same comparison in Prov. xxv. 14: "As clouds and wind without rain, so is he that boasteth himself of his gifts falsely". [The LXX is less like our text, suggesting that Jude was acquainted with the original Hebrew. C.] For the use of ὑπό with ἀνέμων see my note on James iii. 4.

δένδρα φθινοπωρινὰ ἄκαρπα. φθινοπωρινός is an adjective derived from τὸ φθινόπωρον, which is itself, I think, best explained as a compound of φθίνουσα ὀπώρα (*cf.* φθίνοντος μηνός), meaning the concluding portion of the ὀπώρα. This latter word is, according to Curtius, compounded of ὀπ-, connected with ὀπίσω, ὄπισθεν, and ὥρα = "the later prime". We find ὥρα used by itself both for the spring with its flowers and, more rarely, for the summer with its fruits, as in Thuc. ii. 52, ὥρα ἔτους. Perhaps from this double use of the word may have come the ambiguity in the application of ὀπώρα, of which Ideler says that "it originally indicated, not a season separate from and following after the summer, but the hottest part of the summer itself, so that Sirius, whose heliacal rising took place (in the age of Homer) about the middle of July, is described as ἀστὴρ ὀπωρινός *Il.* v. 5). In early times it would seem that the Greeks, like the Germans (Tac. *Germ.* 26), recognised only three seasons—winter, spring, summer, and that the last was indifferently named θέρος or ὀπώρα: compare Arist. *Aves* 709, πρῶτα μὲν ὥρας φαίνομεν ἡμεῖς ἦρος, χειμῶνος, ὀπώρας, with Aesch. *Prom.* 453, ἦν δ' οὐδὲν αὐτοῖς οὔτε χείματος τέκμαρ οὔτ' ἀνθεμώδους ἦρος οὔτε καρπίμου θέρους βέβαιον. But though ὀπώρα was thus used strictly for the dog-days, when the fruit ripened, it was also vaguely used for the unnamed period which ensued up to the commencement of winter. Thus Hesiod (*Op.* 674) μηδὲ μένειν οἶνόν τε νέον καὶ ὀπωρινὸν ὄμβρον καὶ χειμῶν' ἐπιόντα: and ὀπώρα appears as a definite season by the side of the others in a line of Euripides, qnoted by Plutarch (*Mor.* 1028 F), from which it appears that he assigned four months each to summer and winter, and two to spring and ὀπώρα:—

φίλης τ' ὀπώρας διπτύχους ἦρος τ' ἴσους

(where the epithet φίλης deserves notice). It is said that the author of the treatise *De Diaeta* (c. 420 B.C.), which goes under the name of Hippocrates, was the first to introduce a definite term (φθινόπωρον or μετόπωρον) for the new season, the word ὀπώρα being reserved for the late summer, according to the definition of Eustath. on *Il.* v. 5, ὀπώρα ὥρα μεταξὺ κειμένη θέρους καὶ τοῦ μετ' αὐτὴν μετοπώρου. And so we find it used by Aristotle (*Meteor.* ii. 5), αἱ χάλαζαι γίνονται ἔαρος μὲν καὶ μετοπώρου μάλιστα, εἶτα καὶ τῆς ὀπώρας, χειμῶνος δὲ ὀλιγάκις, and by Theophrastus (περὶ Σημείων, 44), ἐὰν τὸ ἔαρ καὶ τὸ θέρος ψυχρὰ γίνηται, ἡ ὀπώρα γίνεται καὶ τὸ μετόπωρον πνιγηρόν.

There is a good deal of inconsistency about the exact limits of the seasons, as is natural enough when we remember that they were first distinguished for purposes of agriculture and navigation, as we see in Hesiod's *Works and Days.* Each season brings its own proper work, and the farmer or merchant is reminded of the return of the season by various signs, the rising and setting of stars, especially of the Pleiades and Arcturus, the sun's passage through the signs of

**δένδρα φθινοπωρινὰ ἄκαρπα δὶς ἀποθανόντα ἐκριζωθέντα, 13. κύμ-
ατα ἄγρια θαλάσσης ἐπαφρίζοντα τὰς ἑαυτῶν αἰσχύνας, ἀστέρες**

the zodiac, the reappearance of the birds, etc. A more strictly accurate division was made by the astronomers, who distinguished between the various kinds of rising and setting of the stars, and divided the year into four equal parts by the solstices and equinoxes. In the year 46 B.C. Julius Caesar introduced his revised calendar, which assigned definite dates to the different seasons. Thus spring begins *a.d. vii. id. Feb.* (Feb. 7), summer *a.d. vii. id. Mai.* (May 9), autumn *a.d. iii. id. Sext.* (Aug. 11), winter *a.d. iv. id. Nov.* (Nov. 10).

To turn now to the commentators, I may take Trench as representing their view in his *Authorised Version*, p. 186, ed. 2, where he says, "The **φθινόπωρον** is the late autumn . . . which succeeds the **ὀπώρα** (or the autumn contemplated as the time of the ripened fruits of the earth) and which has its name **παρὰ τὸ φθίνεσθαι τὴν ὀπώραν,** from the waning away of the autumn and the autumn fruits. . . . The deceivers of whom St. Jude speaks are likened to trees as they show in late autumn, when foliage and fruit alike are gone."

I have stated above what I hold to be the origin of the word **φθινόπωρον.** Trench's explanation is ambiguous and unsuited to the facts of the case, as will be seen from the criticisms in Lightfoot's *Fresh Revision*, p. 135: "In the phrase 'autumn-trees without fruit' there appears to be a reference to the parable of the fig-tree. . . . At all events the mention of the season when fruit might be expected is significant." He adds in a note, "Strange to say, the earliest versions all rendered **φθινοπωρινά** correctly.* Tyndale's instinct led him to give what I cannot but think the right turn to the expression, 'Trees with out frute at gadringe (gathering) time,' *i.e.* at the season when fruit was looked for. I cannot agree with Archbishop Trench, who maintains that 'Tyndale was feeling after, though he has not grasped, the right translation,' and himself explains **φθινοπωρινὰ ἄκαρπα** as 'mutually completing one another, *without leaves, without fruit*'. Tyndale was followed by Coverdale and the Great Bible. Similarly Wycliffe has 'hervest trees without fruyt,' and the Rheims version 'trees of autumne unfruiteful'. The earliest offender is the Geneva Testament, which gives 'corrupt trees and without frute'. . . . The Bishops' Bible strangely combines both renderings, 'trees withered (**φθίνειν**) at fruite gathering (**ὀπώρα**) and without fruite,' which is explained in the margin, 'Trees withered in autumne when the fruite harvest is, and so the Greke woord importeth'."

The correctness of the interpretation, given by Lightfoot alone among modern commentators, is confirmed by a consideration of the context. The writer has just been comparing the innovators, who have crept into other Churches, to waterless clouds driven past by the wind. Just as these disappoint the hope of the husbandman, so do fruitless trees in the proper season of fruit. If **φθινοπωρινά** were equivalent to **χειμερινά,** denoting the season when the trees are necessarily bare both of leaves and fruit, how could a tree be blamed for being **ἄκαρπον**? It is because it might have been, and ought to have been a fruit-bearing tree, that it is rooted up.

δὶς ἀποθανόντα ἐκριζωθεντα. Schneckenburger explains, "He who is not born again is dead in his sins (Col. ii. 13), he who has apostatised is twice dead," *cf.* Apoc. xxi. 8, Heb. vi. 4-8, 2 Peter ii. 20-22. So the trees may be called doubly dead, when they are not only sapless, but are torn up by the root, which would have caused the death even of a living tree.

Ver. 13. **κύματα ἄγρια θαλάσσης ἐπαφρίζοντα τὰς ἑαυτῶν αἰσχύνας.** *Cf.* Cic. *Ad Herenn.* iv. 55, *spumans ex ore scelus.* The two former illustrations, the reefs and the clouds, refer to the specious professions of the libertines and the mischief they caused; the third, the dead trees, brings out also their own miserable condition; the fourth and fifth give a very fine description of their lawlessness and shamelessness, and their eventual fate. The phrase **ἄγρια κύματα** is found in Wisdom xiv. 1. The rare word **ἐπαφρίζω** is used of the sea in Moschus v. 5. It refers to the seaweed and other refuse borne on the crest of the waves and thrown up on the beach, to which are

* This agreement is probably owing to their dependence on the Vulgate "*arbores auctumnales infructuosae*".

πλανῆται[1] οἷς ὁ ζόφος τοῦ σκότους εἰς αἰῶνα τετήρηται. 14.
Ἐπροφήτευσεν[2] δὲ καὶ τούτοις ἕβδομος ἀπὸ Ἀδὰμ Ἐνὼχ λέγων

[1] πλανητες οις ζοφος σκοτους B.
[2] επροφητευσεν B^1; επροεφ. B^3; προεπροφ. ℵ; προεφ. ACKL al.

compared the overflowings of ungodliness (Ps. xvii. 4), the **ῥυπαρία καὶ περισσεία κακίας** condemned by James i. 21, where see my note. The libertines foam out their own shames by their swelling words (ver. 16), while they turn the grace of God into a cloak for their licentiousness (ver. 4). We may compare Phil. iii. 19, **ἡ δόξα ἐν τῇ αἰσχύνῃ αὐτῶν.**

ἀστέρες πλανῆται. This is borrowed from Enoch (chapters xliii., xliv.) where it is said that some of the stars become lightnings and cannot part with their new form, *ib.* 80, "In the days of the sinners, many chiefs of the stars will err, and will alter their orbits and tasks, *ib.* 86, where the fall of the angels is described as the falling of stars, *ib.* 88, "he seized the first star which had fallen from heaven and bound it in an abyss; now that abyss was narrow and deep and horrible and dark . . . and they took all the great stars and bound them hand and foot, and laid them in an abyss," *ib.* xc. 24, "and judgment was held first upon the stars, and they were judged and found guilty and were cast into an abyss of fire"; also xviii. 14 f.

It would seem from these passages, which Jude certainly had before him, that **πλανῆται** cannot here have its usual application, the propriety of which was repudiated by all the ancient astronomers from Plato downwards. *Cf.* Cic. *N. D.* ii. 51, "maxime sunt admirabiles motus earum quinque stellarum quae falso vocantur errantes. Nihil enim errat quod in omni aeternitate conservat motus constantes et ratos," with the passages quoted in my notes on that book.

Some commentators take it as applying to comets; perhaps the quotations from Enoch 44 and 80 fit better with shooting-stars, **ἀστέρες διάττοντες** (Arist. *Meteor.* i. 4, 7) which seem to rush from their sphere into darkness; compare Hermes Trismegistus *ap.* Stob. *Ecl.* i. 478, **κάτωθεν τῆς σελήνης εἰσὶν ἕτεροι ἀστέρες φθαρτοὶ ἀργοὶ . . . οὓς καὶ ἡμεῖς ὁρῶμεν διαλυομένους, τὴν φύσιν ὁμοίαν ἔχοντες τοῖς ἀχρήστοις τῶν ἐπὶ γῆς ζῴων, ἐπὶ ἕτερον δὲ οὐδὲν γίγνεται ἢ ἵνα μόνον φθαρῇ.** For the close relationship supposed by the Jews to exist between the stars and the angels, see my note on James i. 17, **φώτων.** In this passage, however, the subject of the comparison is men, who profess to give light and guidance, as the pole-star does to mariners (**ὡς φωστῆρες ἐν κόσμῳ**, Phil. ii. 15), but who are only blind leaders of the blind, centres and propagators of **πλάνη** (ver. 11), destined to be swallowed up in everlasting darkness. *Cf.* Apoc. vi. 13, viii. 10, 12, ix. 1, xii. 4.

οἷς ὁ ζόφος τοῦ σκότους εἰς αἰῶνα τετήρηται. See the parallel in 2 Pet. ii. 17, and above ver. 6.

Vv. 14-16.—*The Prophecy of Enoch.* The ancient prophecy, to which reference has been already made, was intended for these men as well as for the prophet's own contemporaries, where he says "The Lord appeared, encompassed by myriads of his holy ones, to execute justice upon all and to convict all the ungodly concerning all their ungodly works, and concerning all the hard things spoken against Him by ungodly sinners". (Like them) these men are murmurers, complaining of their lot, slaves to their own carnal lusts, while they utter presumptuous words against God, and seek to ingratiate themselves with men for the sake of gain.

Ver. 14. **ἐπροφήτευσεν δὲ καὶ τούτοις ἕβδομος ἀπὸ Ἀδὰμ Ἐνώχ.** "It was for these also (as well as for his own contemporaries) that the prophecy of Enoch was intended, far as he is removed from our time, being actually the sixth (by Hebrew calculation, seventh) descendant from Adam." For Enoch compare the allusions in Sir. xliv. 16, xlix. 14, Heb. xi. 5, Charles, *Introduction to Book of Enoch.* The prophecy is contained in En. i. 9 (Greek in Charles, *App. C.* p. 327), **ὅτι ἔρχεται σὺν τοῖς** (? **ταῖς**) **μυριάσιν αὐτοῦ καὶ τοῖς ἁγίοις αὐτοῦ ποιῆσαι κρίσιν κατα πάντων, καὶ ἀπολέσει τοὺς ἀσεβεῖς καὶ ἐλέγξει πᾶσαν σάρκα περὶ πάντων** <**τῶν**> **ἔργων αὐτῶν ὧν ἠσέβησαν κατ' αὐτοῦ ἁμαρτωλοὶ ἀσεβεῖς.** The phrase **ἕβδομος ἀπὸ Ἀδάμ** is also found in En. lx. 8, "My grandfather was taken up, the seventh from Adam," *ib.* xciii. 3, "And Enoch began to recount from the books and spake: I was born the seventh in the

Ἰδοὺ ἦλθεν Κύριος ἐν ἁγίαις μυριάσιν[1] αὐτοῦ, 15. ποιῆσαι κρίσιν
κατὰ πάντων καὶ ἐλέγξαι πάντας τοὺς ἀσεβεῖς[2] περὶ πάντων τῶν
ἔργων ἀσεβείας αὐτῶν[3] ὧν ἠσέβησαν καὶ περὶ πάντων τῶν σκληρῶν[4]
ὧν ἐλάλησαν κατ' αὐτοῦ ἁμαρτωλοὶ ἀσεβεῖς. 16. Οὗτοί εἰσιν

[1] αγιαις μυριασιν] μυριασιν αγιων αγγελων ℵ syrp. sah. arm. +.

[2] παντας τους ασεβεις] add. αυτων KL, Ti. (*incuria?*); πασαν ψυχην ℵ, syrp, sah.

[3] ασεβειας αυτων] om. ℵ sah. + ; [ασεβειας] αυτων Treg.

[4] σκληρων] add. λογων ℵC, Ti.

first week, while judgment and righteousness still tarried; and after me there will arise in the second week great wickedness," where Charles refers to *Jubilees*, 7. The genealogical order, as given in Gen. v. 4-20, is (1) Adam, (2) Seth, (3) Enos, (4) Cainan, (5) Mahalaleel, (6) Jared, (7) Enoch. It is probably the sacredness of the number 7 which led the Jewish writers to lay stress upon it in Enoch's case.

ἰδοὺ ἦλθεν Κύριος ἐν ἁγίαις μυριάσιν αὐτοῦ. Charles' translation from the Aethiopic is "And lo! He comes with ten thousands of his holy ones to execute judgment upon them, and He will destroy the ungodly and will convict all flesh of all that the sinners and ungodly have wrought and ungodly committed against Him". For μυριάσιν ἀγγέλων *cf.* Heb. xii. 22, Ps. lxviii. 17, Deut. xxxiii. 2. For the use of ἐν denoting accompanying circumstances see Blass, *Gr. N. T.* tr. p. 118, and Luke xiv. 31, εἰ δυνατός ἐστιν ἐν δέκα χιλιάσιν ἀπαντῆσαι τῷ μετὰ εἴκοσι χιλιάδων ἐρχομένῳ ἐπ' αὐτόν. The aorist here is the preterite of prophetic vision, as when Micaiah says, "I saw all Israel scattered," *cf.* Apoc. x. 7, xiv. 8.

Ver. 15. **ποιῆσαι κρίσιν κατὰ πάντων.** Follows exactly the Greek translation of Enoch given above, *cf.* Ael. *V. H.* ii. 6, Κρίτων ἔπειθεν αὐτὸν ἀποδρᾶναι καὶ τὴν κατ' αὐτοῦ κρίσιν διαφθεῖραι. On the distinction between the active ποιεῖν κρίσιν "to execute judgment" (as in John v. 27) and the periphrastic middle = κρίνειν (as in Isocr. 48 D) see my notes on αἰτεῖν and αἰτεῖσθαι, ἴδε and ἰδού (James iv. 3, *ib.* iii. 3).

ἐλέγξαι πάντας τοὺς ἀσεβεῖς περὶ πάντων τῶν ἔργων ἀσεβείας αὐτῶν ὧν ἠσέβησαν. Shortened from the Greek Enoch quoted above.

ἀσεβεῖς. *Cf.* vv. 4, 18. The word thrice repeated in this verse runs through the epistle as a sort of refrain.

περὶ πάντων τῶν σκληρῶν ὧν ἐλάλησαν. This is taken from Enoch xxvii. 2. Charles, p. 366 (To Gehenna shall come), πάντες οἵτινες ἐροῦσιν τῷ στόματι αὐτῶν κατὰ Κυρίου φωνὴν ἀπρεπῆ καὶ περὶ τῆς δόξης αὐτοῦ σκληρὰ λαλήσουσιν, *cf. ib.* v. 4, "The law of the Lord ye have not fulfilled, but . . . have slanderously spoken proud and hard words with your impure mouths against His greatness," *ib.* ci. 3, *al.*, Gen. xlii. 7, ἐλάλησεν αὐτοῖς σκληρά, 1 Kings xii. 13, ἀπεκρίθη πρὸς τὸν λαὸν σκληρά, Mal. iii. 13-15.

Ver. 16. **οὗτοί εἰσιν γογγυσταί, μεμψίμοιροι.** Charles thinks that we have here another case of borrowing from the *Assumption of Moses*, see his Introd. on Apocryphal Quotations. The word γογγυστής is used in the LXX, Exod xvi. 8, Num. xi. 1, 14-27, 29. The verb γογγύζω is found in John vii. 32 of the whispering of the multitude in favour of Jesus, but is generally used of smouldering discontent which people are afraid to speak out, as in 1 Cor. x. 10, of the murmurings of the Israelites in the wilderness; Matt. xx. 11 (where see Wetst.) of the grumbling of the labourers who saw others receiving a day's pay for an hour's labour; John vi. 41-43 of the Jews who took offence at the preaching of the Bread of Life. It is found in Epict. and M. Aur. but not in classical authors. γογγυσμός is used in 1 Peter iv. 9. See further in Phrynichus, p. 358 Lob. For the word μεμψίμοιρος see Lucian, *Cynic.* 17, ὑμεῖς δὲ διὰ τὴν εὐδαιμονίαν οὐδενὶ τῶν γιγνομένων ἀρέσκεσθε, καὶ παντὶ μέμφεσθε, καὶ τὰ μὲν παρόντα φέρειν οὐκ ἐθέλετε, τῶν δὲ ἀπόντων ἐφίεσθε, χειμῶνος μὲν θέρος εὐχόμενοι, θέρους δὲ χειμῶνα . . . καθάπερ οἱ νοσοῦντες, δυσάρεστοι καὶ μεμψίμοιροι ὄντες, and Theophr. *Char.* 17. It is used of the murmuring of the Israelites by Philo, *Vit. Mos.* i. 109 M. See other examples in Wetst. The same spirit is condemned in James i. 13.

γογγυσταί, μεμψίμοιροι, κατὰ τὰς ἐπιθυμίας αὐτῶν πορευόμενοι,
καὶ τὸ στόμα αὐτῶν λαλεῖ ὑπέρογκα, θαυμάζοντες πρόσωπα ὠφελίας
χάριν.
17. Ὑμεῖς δέ, ἀγαπητοί, μνήσθητε τῶν ῥημάτων τῶν προειρημένων ὑπὸ τῶν ἀποστόλων τοῦ κυρίου ἡμῶν Ἰησοῦ Χριστοῦ· 18. ὅτι

κατὰ τὰς ἐπιθυμίας αὐτῶν πορευόμενοι. *Cf.* 2 Pet. iii. 3 and ii. 10, below ver. 18, and see my notes on James iv. 1, 2. Plumptre notes "The temper of self-indulgence recognising not God's will, but man's desires, as the law of action, is precisely that which issues in weariness and despair . . *cf.* Eccles. ii. 1-20".

τὸ στόμα αὐτῶν λαλεῖ ὑπέρογκα. See Enoch v. 4, quoted on ver. 15, also Enoch ci. 3, "ye have spoken insolent words against His righteousness," Ps. xii. 4, Ps. lxxiii. 8, Dan. vii. 8, **στόμα λαλοῦν μεγάλα** and ver. 20 of the little horn; compare above vv. 4, 8, 11, and James iii. 5 foll. In classical writers **ὑπέρογκα** is generally used of great or even excessive size, in later writers it is also used of "big" words, arrogant speech and demeanour, see Alford's note on 2 Pet. ii. 18 and Plut. *Mor.* 1119 B (Socrates), **τὴν ἐμβροντησίαν ἐκ τοῦ βίου καὶ τὸν τῦφον ἐξήλαυνε καὶ τὰς ἐπαχθεῖς καὶ ὑπερόγκους κατοιήσεις καὶ μεγαλαυχίας**, *ib.* 7 A, where **ἡ θεατρικὴ καὶ παρατράγῳδος λέξις** is styled **ὑπέρογκος** in contrast with **ἰσχνὴ λέξις**, Plut. *Vitae* 505 B, **τοῦ βασιλέως τὸ φρόνημα τραγικὸν καὶ ὑπέρογκον ἐν ταῖς μεγάλαις εὐτυχίαις ἐγεγόνει.** It is found in 2 Peter ii. 18 and in Dan. xi. 36, **ὁ βασιλεὺς ὑψωθήσεται καὶ μεγαλυνθήσεται ἐπὶ πάντα θεόν, καὶ λαλήσει ὑπέρογκα.**

θαυμάζοντες πρόσωπα ὠφελίας χάριν The phrase occurs with the same force in Lev. xix. 15, **οὐ μὴ θαυμάσῃς πρόσωπον**, Job xiii. 10, see my note on James ii. 1, **μὴ ἐν προσωποληψίαις ἔχετε τὴν πίστιν τοῦ κυρίου ἡμῶν Ἰ. Χ.**, and *cf.* 1 Tim. iii. 8, quoted above on ver. 11. As the fear of God drives out the fear of man, so defiance of God tends to put man in His place, as the chief source of good or evil to his fellows. For the anacoluthon (**τὸ στόμα αὐτῶν λαλεῖ —θαυμάζοντες**) compare Col. ii. 2, **ἵνα παρακληθῶσιν αἱ καρδίαι ὑμῶν συμβιβασθέντες ἐν εἰρήνῃ**, where a similar periphrasis (**αἱ καρδίαι ὑμῶν = ὑμεῖς**) is followed by a *constructio ad sensum*, also Winer, p. 716. Perhaps the intrusion of the finite clause into a participial series may be accounted for by a reminiscence of Ps. xvii. 10, **τὸ στόμα αὐτῶν ἐλάλησεν ὑπερηφανίαν**, or Ps. cxliv. 8, 11, where a similar phrase occurs.

Vv. 17-19.—*The Faithful are bidden to call to mind the warnings of the Apostles.* The Apostles warned you repeatedly that in the last time there would arise mockers led away by their own carnal lusts. It is these that are now breaking up the unity of the Church by their invidious distinctions, men of unsanctified minds, who have not the Spirit of God. See Introduction on the Early Heresies in the larger edition.

Ver. 17. **ὑμεῖς δὲ, ἀγαπητοί, μνήσθητε τῶν ῥημάτων τῶν προειρημένων ὑπὸ τῶν ἀποστόλων.** The writer turns again, as in ver. 20 below, to the faithful members of the Church (ver. 3) and reminds them, not now of primeval prophecy, but of warning words uttered by the Apostles. Some have taken this as a quotation by Jude from 2 Peter iii. 3, where the quotation is given more fully. But, there also, the words are referred back to a prior authority, "holy prophets" and "your Apostles". The words **ὅτι ἔλεγον ὑμῖν**, which follow, imply that the warning was spoken, not written, and that it was often repeated.

Ver. 18. **ἐπ' ἐσχάτου χρόνου ἔσονται ἐμπαῖκται.** The parallel in 2 Peter iii. 3 is **ἐλεύσονται ἐπ' ἐσχάτων τῶν ἡμερῶν ἐν ἐμπαιγμονῇ ἐμπαῖκται**, where see note on the use of the article with **ἔσχατος**, *etc.* For **ἐπί**, *cf.* Arist. *Pol.* iv. 3, **ἐπὶ τῶν ἀρχαίων χρόνων.**

The prophecy of this mocking, as a mark of the future trials of the Church, has not come down to us. An example of it in the very beginning of the Church is given in Acts ii. 13, **ἕτεροι χλευάζοντες ἔλεγον ὅτι γλεύκους μεμεστωμένοι εἰσί.** In the O.T. we have such examples as 2 Chron. xxxvi. 16 (the summing up of the attitude of the Jews towards the prophets) **ἦσαν μυκτηρίζοντες τοὺς ἀγγέλους αὐτοῦ καὶ ἐξουθενοῦντες τοὺς λόγους αὐτοῦ καὶ ἐμπαίζοντες ἐν τοῖς προφήταις αὐτοῦ**, Jer. xx. 8, **ἐγενήθη λόγος Κυρίου εἰς ὀνειδισμὸν ἐμοὶ καὶ εἰς χλευασμὸν πᾶσαν ἡμέραν.** *Cf.* also the mockery at the crucifixion, and the declaration in Matt. x. 25 f., **εἰ τὸν οἰκοδεσπότην Βεεζέβοὺλ ἐπεκάλεσαν, πόσῳ μᾶλλον κ.τ.λ.** In 2

ἔλεγον ὑμῖν Ἐπ' ἐσχάτου[1] χρόνου[2] ἔσονται[3] ἐμπαῖκται κατὰ τὰς ἑαυτῶν ἐπιθυμίας πορευόμενοι τῶν ἀσεβειῶν.[4] 19. Οὗτοί εἰσιν οἱ ἀποδιορίζοντες,[5] ψυχικοί, πνεῦμα μὴ ἔχοντες.

[1] επ' εσχατου ℵB; οτι επ' εσχ. AC; [οτι] επ' εσχ. Treg.; ὅτι εν εσχατῳ KL P vulg. sah.

[2] χρονου BC; του χρονου ℵA; χρονῳ KL; τῳ χρονῳ P sah.; των χρονων boh. al.

[3] εσονται ℵBCKLP; ελευσονται ℵ[2]AC[2], sah. boh.

[4] των ασεβειων] οπισω ασεβειων syr[h]; οπισω ασεβειας syr[p].

[5] αποδιοριζοντες] add. εαυτους C vulg.

Peter the purport of this mockery is explained to be the unfulfilled promise of the Parusia. Here we must gather its meaning from the account already given of the libertines. If they turned the grace of God into licentiousness, they would naturally mock at the narrowness and want of enlightenment of those who took a strict and literal view of the divine commandments: if they made light of authority and treated spiritual things with irreverence, if they foamed out their own shame and uttered proud and impious words, if they denied God and Christ, they would naturally laugh at the idea of a judgment to come. On the form ἐμπαίκτης and its cognates, see note on 2 Peter.

τῶν ἀσεβειῶν. I am rather disposed to take τῶν ἀσεβειῶν here as a subjective genitive, "lusts belonging to, or arising from their impieties," *cf.* Rom. i. 28, καθὼς οὐκ ἐδοκίμασαν τὸν Θεὸν ἔχειν ἐν ἐπιγνώσει, παρέδωκεν αὐτοὺς ὁ Θεὸς εἰς ἀδόκιμον νοῦν. The position of the genitive is peculiar, and probably intended to give additional stress. We may compare it with James ii. 1, μὴ ἐν προσωπολημψίαις ἔχετε τὴν πίστιν τοῦ κυρίου ἡμῶν Ἰησοῦ Χριστοῦ, τῆς δόξης, where some connect τῆς δόξης with κυρίου in a qualitative sense.

Ver. 19. **οὗτοί εἰσιν οἱ ἀποδιορίζοντες.** "These are they that make invidious distinctions." See Introduction on the Text. The rare word ἀποδιορίζοντες is used of logical distinctions in Aristotle, *Pol.* iv. 43, ὥσπερ οὖν εἰ ζῴου προῃρούμεθα λαβεῖν εἴδη, πρῶτον ἂν ἀποδιωρίζομεν ὅπερ ἀναγκαῖον πᾶν ἔχειν ζῷον ("as, if we wished to make a classification of animals, we should have begun by setting aside that which all animals have in common") and, I believe, in every other passage in which it is known to occur: see Maximus Confessor, ii. p. 103 D, τὸ μὲν φυσικὸν ὥρισεν ἐπ' αὐτοῦ, τὸ δὲ γνωμικὸν ἀποδιώρισε, translated "naturali in eo (Christo) constituta voluntate, arbitrariam dispunxit," *ib.* p. 131 C, ὡς ὁ λόγος ἦν αὐτοῦ, μόνον τὸ ἐμπαθές, ἀλλ' οὐ τὸ φυσικὸν ἀποδιορίσασθαι θέλημα, "quod dixerat hoc solum spectare ut libidinosam, non ut naturalem voluntatem a Salvatore eliminaret," Severus *de Clyst.* xxxii., xxv., ὅταν ταῦτα τὰ συμπτώματα ὄψῃ παρόντα, ἀποδιόριζε τὴν ὀργανικὴν νόσον ἐκ τῆς ὁμοιομεροῦς. The simple διορίζω is found in Lev. xx. 24, διώρισα ὑμᾶς ἀπὸ τῶν ἐθνῶν "I separated you from the nations," Job xxxv. 11; so ἀφορίζω Matt. xxv. 32, ἀφορίζει τὰ πρόβατα ἀπὸ τῶν ἐρίφων, Acts xix. 9 (Paul left the synagogue) καὶ ἀφώρισεν τοὺς μαθητάς, 2 Cor. vi. 17, ἐξέλθατε ἐκ μέσου αὐτῶν καὶ ἀφορίσθητε, Luke vi. 22 (of excommunication) ὅταν ἀφορίσωσιν ὑμᾶς, Gal. ii. 12 (of Peter's withdrawal from the Gentiles) ὑπέστελλεν καὶ ἀφώριζεν ἑαυτόν.

ψυχικοί. Used of worldly wisdom in James iii. 15, where see note, distinguished from πνευματικός in 1 Cor. ii. 13-15, xv. 44, *cf.* the teaching of the Naassenes (*ap.* Hippol. p. 164) εἰς τὸν οἶκον θεοῦ οὐκ εἰσελεύσεται ἀκάθαρτος οὐδείς, οὐ ψυχικός, οὐ σαρκικός, ἀλλὰ τηρεῖται πνευματικοῖς.

πνεῦμα μὴ ἔχοντες. The subjective negative may be explained as describing a class (such as have not) rather than as stating a fact in regard to particular persons; but the use of μή is much more widely extended in late than in classical Greek, *cf.* such phrases as ἐπεὶ μή, ὅτι μή. It is simplest to understand πνεῦμα here of the Holy Spirit, *cf.* Rom. viii. 9, ὑμεῖς οὐκ ἐστὲ ἐν σαρκὶ ἀλλ' ἐν πνεύματι, εἴπερ πνεῦμα Θεοῦ οἰκεῖ ἐν ὑμῖν, 1 Cor. ii. 13, vii. 40, 1 John iii. 24, iv. 13, and the contrast in ver. 20, ἐν πνεύματι ἁγίῳ προσευχόμενοι. Others, *e.g.* Plumptre, prefer the explanation that "the false teachers were so absorbed in their lower sensuous nature that they no longer possessed, in any real sense of the word,

20. Ὑμεῖς δέ, ἀγαπητοί, ἐποικοδομοῦντες ἑαυτοὺς τῇ ἁγιωτάτῃ ὑμῶν πίστει, ἐν πνεύματι ἁγίῳ προσευχόμενοι,
21. ἑαυτοὺς ἐν ἀγάπῃ Θεοῦ τηρήσατε[1] προσδεχόμενοι τὸ ἔλεος τοῦ κυρίου ἡμῶν

[1] τηρησατε] τηρησωμεν BC.

that element in man's compound being, which is itself spiritual, and capable therefore of communion with the Divine Spirit".

Vv. 20-23. *The Final Charge to the Faithful.*—Use all diligence to escape this danger. Make the most of the privileges vouchsafed to you. Build yourselves up on the foundation of your most holy faith by prayer in the Spirit. Do not rest satisfied with the belief that God loves you, but keep yourselves in His love, waiting for the mercy of our Lord Jesus Christ which leads us to eternal life. And do your best to help those who are in danger of falling away by pointing out their errors and giving the reasons of your own belief; and by snatching from the fire of temptation those who are in imminent jeopardy. Even where there is most to fear, let your compassion and your prayers go forth toward the sinner, while you shrink from the pollution of his sin.

Ver. 20. **ὑμεῖς δὲ, ἀγαπητοί.** Contrasted with the libertines, as in ver. 17.

ἐποικοδομοῦντες ἑαυτοὺς τῇ ἁγιωτάτῃ ὑμῶν πίστει. For the spiritual temple, *cf.* 1 Pet. ii. 3-5; Col. i. 23; Eph. ii. 20-22, **ἐποικοδομηθέντες ἐπὶ τῷ θεμελίῳ τῶν ἀποστόλων καὶ προφητῶν, ὄντος ἀκρογωνιαίου αὐτοῦ Χριστοῦ Ἰησοῦ κ.τ.λ.**, 1 Cor. iii. 9-17, a passage which the writer may have had in his mind here and in ver. 23. Dr. Bigg compares Polyc. *Phil.* iii. "If ye study the epistles of the blessed apostle Paul, **δυνηθήσεσθε οἰκοδομεῖσθαι εἰς τὴν δοθεῖσαν ὑμῖν πίστιν.** Add Clem. *Strom.* v. p. 644, **ἡ κοινὴ πίστις καθάπερ θεμέλιον ὑπόκειται.** Usually Christ is spoken as the foundation or corner-stone of the Church, and we should probably assign an objective sense to **τῇ πίστει** here, as in ver. 3 above (**ἐπαγωνίζεσθαι τῇ πίστει**). Otherwise it might be explained of that faculty by which we are brought into relation with the spiritual realities (Heb. xi. 1, **πίστις ἐλπιζομένων ὑπόστασις, πραγμάτων ἔλεγχος οὐ βλεπομένων**), that which is the introduction to all the other Christian graces, see note on 2 Pet. i. 5, and which leads to eternal life (1 Pet. i. 5, and 9, **κομιζόμενοι τὸ τέλος τῆς πίστεως ὑμῶν, σωτηρίαν ψυχῶν**). The faith is here called "most holy," because it comes to us from God, and reveals God to us, and because it is by its means that man is made righteous, and enabled to overcome the world (1 John v. 4, 5). *Cf.* 1 Pet. v. 9, **ᾧ ἀντίστητε στερεοὶ τῇ πίστει.**

ἐν πνεύματι ἁγίῳ προσευχόμενοι. These words, contrasted with **πνεῦμα μὴ ἔχοντες** in ver. 19, show how they are to build themselves up upon their faith. I understand them as equivalent to James v. 16, **δέησις δικαίου ἐνεργουμένη,** where see note. Compare also Eph. vi. 18, **διὰ πάσης προσευχῆς προσευχόμενοι ἐν παντὶ καιρῷ ἐν πνεύματι,** Rom. viii. 26, 27.

Ver. 21. **ἑαυτοὺς ἐν ἀγάπῃ Θεοῦ τηρήσατε.** In ver. 1 the passive is used: those who are addressed are described as kept and beloved (*cf.* ver. 24, **τῷ δυναμένῳ φυλάξαι**): here the active is used and emphasised by the unusual order of words; each is to keep himself in the love of God, *cf.* James, i. 27, **ἄσπιλον ἑαυτὸν τηρεῖν,** Phil. ii. 12, **τὴν ἑαυτῶν σωτηρίαν κατεργάζεσθαι· Θεὸς γάρ ἐστιν ὁ ἐνεργῶν ἐν ὑμῖν.** Again in ver. 2 the writer invokes the divine love and mercy on those to whom he writes: here they are bidden to take steps to secure these. Compare Rom. v. 5, **ἡ ἀγάπη τοῦ Θεοῦ ἐκκέχυται ἐν ταῖς καρδίαις ἡμῶν διὰ πνεύματος ἁγίου τοῦ δοθέντος ἡμῖν,** *ib.* viii. 39, **πέπεισμαι ὅτι οὔτε θάνατος οὔτε ζωὴ . . . οὔτε τις κτίσις ἑτέρα δυνήσεται ἡμᾶς χωρίσαι ἀπὸ τῆς ἀγάπης τοῦ Θεοῦ,** John xv. 9, **καθὼς ἠγάπησέν με ὁ πατὴρ κἀγὼ ὑμᾶς ἠγάπησα, μείνατε ἐν τῇ ἀγάπῃ τῇ ἐμῇ. ἐὰν τὰς ἐντολάς μου τηρήσητε, μενεῖτε ἐν τῇ ἀγάπῃ μου.** The aor. imper. is expressive of urgency, see note on **ἡγήσασθε,** in James i. 2.

προσδεχόμενοι τὸ ἔλεος. *Cf.* Tit. ii. 13, **προσδεχόμενοι τὴν μακαρίαν ἐλπίδα καὶ ἐπιφάνειαν τῆς δόξης τοῦ μεγάλου Θεοῦ καὶ σωτῆρος ἡμῶν Ἰ. Χ.**, and 2 Pet. iii. 12, 13, 14. The same word is used of the Jews who were looking for the promised Messiah at the time of His first coming, Mark xv. 43, Luke ii. 25, 38.

εἰς ζωὴν αἰώνιον. Some connect this closely with the imperative **τηρήσατε,** but it seems to me to follow more natu-

Ἰησοῦ Χριστοῦ εἰς ζωὴν αἰώνιον. 22. Καὶ οὓς μὲν ἐλέγχετε[1]
διακρινομένους,[2] 23. οὓς δὲ[3] σώζετε[4] ἐκ πυρὸς ἁρπάζοντες, οὓς δὲ

[1] ελεγχετε AC vulg. boh. arm. + ; ελεατε ℵBC²; ελεειτε KLP +.

[2] διακρινομενους ℵABC; διακρινομενοι KLP.

[3] ους δε (1) ℵACKLP; om. B.

[4] σωζετε ℵABC; εν φοβῳ σωζετε KLP.

rally on the nearer phrase, πρ. τὸ ἔλεος: *cf.* 1 Pet. i. 37, εὐλογητὸς ὁ Θεὸς . . . ὁ κατὰ τὸ πολὺ αὐτοῦ ἔλεος ἀναγεννήσας ἡμᾶς εἰς κληρονομίαν ἄφθαρτον . . . τετηρημένην ἐν οὐρανοῖς εἰς ὑμᾶς τοὺς . . . φρουρουμένους . . . εἰς σωτηρίαν ἑτοίμην ἀποκαλυφθῆναι ἐν καιρῷ ἐσχάτῳ.

Ver. 22. **οὓς μὲν ἐλέγχετε διακρινομένους.** On the reading see the Introduction. For the form ὃς μέν instead of ὁ μέν, *cf.* Matt. xiii. 8, xxii. 5, Luke xxiii. 33, Acts xxvii. 44, Rom. xiv. 5, 1 Cor. vii. 7, xi. 21, 2 Cor. ii. 16, 2 Tim. ii. 20, not used in Heb., 1 and 2 Pet., James or John. The doubled ὃς δέ is found in Matt. xxi. 35, ὃν μὲν ἔδειραν, ὃν δὲ ἀπέκτειναν, ὃν δὲ ἐλιθοβόλησαν, *ib.* xxv. 15, ᾧ μὲν ἔδωκεν πέντε τάλαντα, ᾧ δὲ δύο, ᾧ δὲ ἕν. The use is condemned as a solecism by Thomas Magister and by Lucian, *Soloec.* 1, but is common in late Greek from the time of Aristotle, *cf.* Sturz. *Dial. Maced.* pp. 105 f. On the word ἐλέγχω (here wrongly translated "strafen," in the sense of excommunication, by Rampf), see *Const. Apost.* vii. 5, 3, ἐλεγμῷ ἐλέγξεις τὸν ἀδελφόν σου, and Hare's excellent note L in his *Mission of the Comforter*, where he argues that the conviction wrought by the Spirit is a conviction unto salvation, rather than unto condemnation; and quotes Luecke as saying that "ἐλέγχειν always implies the refutation, the overcoming of an error, a wrong, by the truth and right. When this is brought before our conscience through the ἔλεγχος, there arises a feeling of sin, which is always painful: thus every ἔλεγχος is a chastening, a punishment." Compare Grote's life-like account of the Socratic Elenchus in his *Hist. of Greece*.

This verse seems to be referred to in *Can. Apost.* vi. 4, οὐ μισήσεις πάντα ἄνθρωπον, ἀλλ' οὓς μὲν ἐλέγξεις, οὓς δὲ ἐλεήσεις, περὶ ὧν δὲ προσεύξῃ, οὓς δὲ ἀγαπήσεις ὑπὲρ τὴν ψυχήν σου, which is also found in the Didache ii. 7, with the omission of οὓς δὲ ἐλεήσεις. *Cf.* John xvi. 8, ἐκεῖνος ἐλέγξει τὸν κόσμον περὶ ἁμαρτίας καὶ περὶ δικαιοσύνης καὶ περὶ κρίσεως, 1 Cor. xiv. 24, ἐλέγχεται ὑπὸ πάντων (the effect of the prophets' teaching on an unbeliever), Tit. i. 13, ἔλεγχε αὐτοὺς ἀποτόμως ἵνα ὑγιαίνωσιν ἐν τῇ πίστει, *ib.* i. 9, τοὺς ἀντιλέγοντας ἐλέγχειν, 2 Tim. iv. 2 (the charge to Timothy) ἔλεγξον, παρακάλεσον ἐν πάσῃ μακροθυμίᾳ, Apoc. iii. 19, ὅσους ἐὰν φιλῶ ἐλέγχω καὶ παιδεύω, Eph. v. 13, τὰ δὲ πάντα ἐλεγχόμενα ὑπὸ τοῦ φωτὸς φανεροῦται. There is a tone of greater severity in the ποιῆσαι κρίσιν καὶ ἐλέγξαι of the 15th verse, but even there we need not suppose that the preacher is hopeless of good being effected. The point is of importance in deciding the mutual relations of the three cases here considered.

διακρινομένους. We should have expected a nominative here to correspond with ἁρπάζοντες and μισοῦντες in the following clauses, and so the *text. rec.* has διακρινόμενοι, wrongly translated in A.V., as if it were the active διακρίνοντες, "making a difference". This gives such a good sense that some commentators (*e.g.* Stier) have been willing to condone the bad Greek. It would have been better to alter the reading at once. Keeping the reading of the best MSS. we may either take the accusative as complementary to ἐλέγχετε (as we find in Plato, *Theaet.* 171 D, ἐμὲ ἐλέγξας ληροῦντα, Xen. *Mem.* 1, 7, 2, ἐλεγχθήσεται γελοῖος ὤν, Jelf, § 681), or simply as descriptive of the condition of the persons referred to. There is also a question as to the meaning we should assign to διακρ. Is it to be understood in the same sense as in James i. 6, ii. 4? In that case we might translate "convict them of their want of faith," taking the participle as complementary to the verb; or "reprove them because of their doubts". It seems more probable, however, that the meaning here is "convince them when they dispute with you," which we may compare with 1 Pet. iii. 15, ἕτοιμοι ἀεὶ πρὸς ἀπολογίαν παντὶ τῷ αἰτοῦντι ὑμᾶς λόγον . . . ἀλλὰ μετὰ πραΰτητος καὶ φόβου (*cf.* ἐν φόβῳ below). So taken, this first clause would refer to intellectual difficulties to be met by quiet reasoning; the force of διακρινόμενος being the same as that in ver. 9, τῷ διαβόλῳ διακρ., and in Socr. *E.H.* v. 5, ὁ λαὸς εἶχεν ὁμόνοιαν καὶ οὐκέτι πρὸς ἀλλήλους διεκρίνοντο.

Ver. 23. **σώζετε.** Here again a word

ἐλεᾶτε ἐν φόβῳ,[1] μισοῦντες καὶ τὸν ἀπὸ τῆς σαρκὸς ἐσπιλωμένον χιτῶνα.

24. Τῷ δὲ δυναμένῳ φυλάξαι ὑμᾶς[2] ἀπταίστους[3] καὶ στῆσαι

[1] ους δε (2) ελεατε εν φοβῳ ℵAB; om. KLP; εν φοβῳ C.
[2] υμας ℵBCL vulg. syrr. boh.; ημας A; αυτους KP.
[3] απταιστους] add. και ασπιλους C.

which is strictly applicable to God is transferred to him whom God uses as His instrument, *cf.* 1 Pet. iv. 11 and notes on τηρήσατε, ἐλέγχετε above, especially James v. 20, ὁ ἐπιστρέψας ἁμαρτωλὸν ἐκ πλάνης ὁδοῦ αὐτοῦ σώσει ψυχὴν ἐκ θανάτου.

ἐκ πυρὸς ἁρπάζοντες. The expression is borrowed from Amos iv. 11, κατέστρεψα ὑμᾶς καθὼς κατέστρεψεν ὁ Θεὸς Σόδομα καὶ Γόμορρα, καὶ ἐγένεσθε ὡς δαλὸς ἐξεσπασμένος ἐκ πυρός, καὶ οὐδ᾽ ὡς ἐπεστρέψατε πρός με, λέγει Κύριος, and Zech. iii. 3, οὐκ ἰδοὺ οὗτος δαλὸς ἐξεσπασμένος ἐκ πυρός; Both passages have further connexions with our epistle, the former from the reference to Sodom (see above ver. 7), the latter as following immediately on the words, ἐπιτιμήσαι σοι Κύριος quoted in ver. 9, and preceding a reference to filthy garments (see note below). In it the High Priest Joshua is a representative of Israel, saved like a brand from the captivity, which was the punishment of national sin. The image of fire is naturally suggested by the allusion to the punishment of Sodom in the passage of Amos, and of Korah (see above ver. 7) described in Num. xvi. 35, Ps. cvi. 18, ἐξεκαύθη πῦρ ἐν τῇ συναγωγῇ αὐτῶν καὶ φλὸξ κατέφλεξεν ἁμαρτωλούς. The writer may also have had in mind St. Paul's description of the building erected on the One Foundation (see above ver. 20), which, he says, will be tried by fire, 1 Cor. iii. 13-15, ἑκάστου τὸ ἔργον, ὁποῖόν ἐστιν, τὸ πῦρ αὐτὸ δοκιμάσει . . . εἴ τινος τὸ ἔργον κατακαήσεται, ζημιωθήσεται, αὐτὸς δὲ σωθήσεται, οὕτως δὲ ὡς διὰ πυρός. Such an one may be spoken of as "a brand snatched from the fire," not however as here, saved from the fire of temptation, but as saved through the agency of God's purgatorial fire, whether in this or in a future life.

ἐλεᾶτε ἐν φόβῳ. The faithful are urged to show all possible tenderness for the fallen, but at the same time to have a fear lest they themselves or others whom they influence should be led to think too lightly of the sin whose ravages they are endeavouring to repair. *Cf.* 2 Cor. vii. 1, καθαρίσωμεν ἑαυτοὺς ἀπὸ παντὸς μολυσμοῦ σαρκὸς καὶ πνεύματος ἐπιτελοῦντες ἁγιωσύνην ἐν φόβῳ Θεοῦ, Phil. ii. 12, 1 Pet. i. 17, iii. 15. For the confusion of the contracted verbs in -έω and -άω in late Greek see Jannaris, § 850. § 854 f., Winer p. 104. The best MSS. read ἐλεᾷ in Prov. xxi. 26, and ἐλεῶντος Rom. ix. 16, but ἐλεεῖ in Rom. ix. 18.

μισοῦντες καὶ τὸν ἀπὸ τῆς σαρκὸς ἐσπιλωμένον χιτῶνα. While it is the duty of the Christian to pity and pray for the sinner, he must view with loathing all that bears traces of the sin. The form of expression seems borrowed from such passages as Isa. xxx. 22, Lev. xv. 17, perhaps too from Zech. iii. 4, Ἰησοῦς ἦν ἐνδεδυμένος ἱμάτια ῥυπαρά. *Cf.* Apoc. iii. 4, οὐκ ἐμόλυναν τὰ ἱμάτια αὐτῶν, and *Apocal. Pauli* quoted by Spitta, ὁ χιτών μου οὐκ ἐρυπώθη. The derivatives of σπίλος are peculiar to late Greek: the only other examples of σπιλόω in Biblical Greek are James iii. 6, ἡ γλῶσσα . . . ἡ σπιλοῦσα ὅλον τὸ σῶμα and Wisd. xv. 4, εἶδος σπιλωθὲν χρώμασι διηλλαγμένοις. Compare for the treatment of the erring 2 Tim. ii. 25, 26, ἐν πραΰτητι παιδεύοντα τοὺς ἀντιδιατιθεμένους, μήποτε δῴη αὐτοῖς ὁ Θεὸς μετάνοιαν εἰς ἐπίγνωσιν ἀληθείας, καὶ ἀνανήψωσιν ἐκ τῆς τοῦ διαβόλου παγίδος.

Vv. 24, 25. *Final Benediction and Ascription.* I have bidden you to keep yourselves in the love of God; I have warned you against all impiety and impurity. But do not think that you can attain to the one, or guard yourselves from the other, in your own strength. You must receive power from above; and that it may be so, I offer up my prayer to Him, who alone is able to keep you from stumbling, and to present you before the throne of His glory, pure and spotless in exceeding joy. To Him, the only God and Saviour, belong glory, greatness, might, and authority throughout all ages.

Ver. 24. **τῷ δὲ δυναμένῳ φυλάξαι ὑμᾶς ἀπταίστους.** Apparently a reminis-

κατενώπιον τῆς δόξης αὐτοῦ ἀμώμους[1] ἐν ἀγαλλιάσει, 25. μόνῳ[2]

[1] αμωμους] αμεμπτους A. [2] μονῳ] add. σοφῳ KLP +.

cence * of Rom. xvi. 25 f., τῷ δὲ δυναμένῳ ὑμᾶς στηρίξαι . . . μόνῳ σοφῷ Θεῷ διὰ Ἰησοῦ Χριστοῦ, ᾧ ἡ δόξα εἰς τοὺς αἰῶνας τῶν αἰώνων. Similarly the noble doxology in Eph. iii. 20, commences τῷ δὲ δυναμένῳ. The reading ὑμᾶς is confirmed by the evidence of ℵ and B, which was unknown to Alford when he endeavoured to defend the reading αὐτούς, found in KP and some inferior MSS.

ἄπταιστος. Occurs in 3 Macc. vi. 39, μεγαλοδόξως ἐπιφάνας τὸ ἔλεος αὐτοῦ ὁ τῶν ὅλων δυνάστης ἀπταίστους αὐτοὺς ἐρρύσατο: used here only in the N.T. The verb πταίω has the same figurative sense in James ii. 10, iii. 2, εἴ τις ἐν λόγῳ οὐ πταίει, οὗτος τέλειος ἀνήρ, 2 Pet. i. 10, ταῦτα ποιοῦντες οὐ μὴ πταίσητέ ποτε.

στῆσαι κατενώπιον τῆς δόξης αὐτοῦ ἀμώμους ἐν ἀγαλλιάσει. *Cf.* Matt. xxv. 31-33, ὅταν δὲ ἔλθῃ ὁ υἱὸς τοῦ ἀνθρώπου ἐν τῇ δόξῃ αὐτοῦ . . . στήσει τὰ μὲν πρόβατα ἐκ δεξιῶν αὐτοῦ, Acts vi. 6, οὓς ἔστησαν ἐνώπιον τῶν ἀποστόλων, Col. i. 22, παραστῆσαι ὑμᾶς ἁγίους καὶ ἀμώμους καὶ ἀνεγκλήτους κατενώπιον αὐτοῦ (which Lightfoot refers to present approbation rather than to the future judgment of God, comparing Rom. xiv. 22, 1 Cor. i. 29, 2 Cor. ii. 17, iv. 2, vii. 12, xii. 19). In the present passage the addition of the words τῆς δόξης shows that the final judgment, the goal of φυλάξαι, is spoken of. Hort, in his interesting note on 1 Pet. i. 19, τιμίῳ αἵματι ὡς ἀμνοῦ ἀμώμου καὶ ἀσπίλου Χριστοῦ, traces the way in which the words μῶμος "blame," and ἄμωμος "blameless," come to be used (in "the Apocrypha, the N.T., and other books which presuppose the LXX") in the entirely unclassical sense of "blemish" and "unblemished" *cf.* Eph. i. 4, v. 27, Heb. ix. 14. In 2 Pet. iii. 14, ἀμώμητος seems to be used in the same sense. The word κατενώπιον is apparently confined to the Bible, where it occurs in Josh. i. 5, xxi. 42, Lev. iv. 17, Eph. i. 4, ἀμώμητος κατενώπιον αὐτοῦ ἐν ἀγάπῃ. κατένωπα is found in Hom. *Il.* xv. 320. For ἀγαλλίασις see Hort's note on 1 Pet. i. 6, ἐν ᾧ ἀγαλλιᾶσθε, "in whom ye exult". The verb with its cognate substantives "is unknown except in the LXX and the N.T. and the literature derived from them, and in the N.T. it is confined to books much influenced by O.T. diction (Matt., Luke, Acts, 1 Pet., Jude, John, including Apoc.), being absent from the more Greek writers, St. Paul, and (except in quot.) Heb. . . . It apparently denotes a proud exulting joy, being probably connected closely with ἀγάλλομαι, properly 'to be proud of,' but often combined with ἥδομαι and such words."

Ver. 25. μόνῳ Θεῷ σωτῆρι ἡμῶν. See above on ver. 4, τὸν μόνον δεσπότην. God is called σωτήρ in Isa. xlv 15, σὺ γὰρ εἶ Θεὸς . . . ὁ Θεὸς τοῦ Ἰσραὴλ σωτήρ, *ib.* ver. 21, Sir. li. 1, αἰνέσω σε Θεὸν τὸν σωτῆρά μου, Philo, *Confus. Ling.* § 20, i. p. 418 *fin.*, τίς δ' οὐκ ἂν . . . πρὸς τὸν μόνον σωτῆρα Θεὸν ἐκβοήσῃ (? -σαι); *cf.* Luke i. 47, ἠγαλλίασεν τὸ πνεῦμά μου ἐπὶ τῷ Θεῷ τῷ σωτῆρί μου, elsewhere in N.T. only in Tit. i. 3, ii. 10, iii. 4, ὅτε ἡ χρηστότης . . . ἐπεφάνη τοῦ σωτῆρος ἡμῶν Θεοῦ . . . κατὰ τὸ αὐτοῦ ἔλεος ἔσωσεν ἡμᾶς διὰ . . . πνεύματος ἁγίου οὗ ἐξέχεεν ἐφ' ἡμᾶς πλουσίως διὰ Ἰ. Χ. τοῦ σωτῆρος ἡμῶν, 1 Tim. i. 1, Παῦλος ἀπόστολος Ἰ. Χ. κατ' ἐπιταγὴν Θεοῦ σωτῆρος ἡμῶν καὶ Χ. Ἰ. *ib.* ii. 3, iv. 10. The later writers of the N.T. seem to have felt it needful to insist upon the unity of God, and the saving will of the Father, in opposition to antinomian attacks on the Law.

διὰ Ἰησοῦ Χριστοῦ. It seems best to take διά with δόξα and the following words. The glory of God is manifested through the Word, *cf.* 1 Pet. iv. 11, ἵνα ἐν πᾶσιν δοξάζηται ὁ Θεὸς διὰ Ἰ. Χ. ᾧ ἐστιν ἡ δόξα καὶ τὸ κράτος εἰς τοὺς αἰῶνας.

δόξα. The verb is often omitted in these ascriptions, *cf.* 2 Pet. αὐτῷ ἡ δόξα, Rom. xi. 36, xvi. 27, Gal. i. 5, Luke ii. 16, δόξα ἐν ὑψίστοις Θεῷ. In 1 Peter iv. 11 it is inserted, ᾧ ἐστιν ἡ δόξα καὶ τὸ κράτος, and, as we find no case in which ἔστω is inserted, and the indicative is more subject to ellipse than the imperative, it might seem that we should supply "is" here; but the R. V. gives "be," and there are similar phrases expressive of a wish or prayer, as the very common χάρις ὑμῖν καὶ εἰρήνη ἀπὸ Θεοῦ πατρός, where we must supply ἔστω or γένοιτο.

* For the position and genuineness of this doxology see the Introduction and notes in Sanday and Headlam's commentary, and the dissertations by Lightfoot and Hort in the former's *Biblical Essays*, pp. 287-374.

Θεῷ σωτῆρι ἡμῶν διὰ[1] Ἰησοῦ Χριστοῦ τοῦ κυρίου ἡμῶν δόξα μεγαλωσύνη κράτος καὶ ἐξουσία πρὸ παντὸς τοῦ αἰῶνος καὶ νῦν καὶ εἰς πάντας[2] τοὺς αἰῶνας· ἀμήν.

[1] δια Ι. Χ. του κυριου ημων] om. ΚΡ. [2] εις παντας] εις ℵ.

De Wette maintained that the following words **πρὸ παντὸς τοῦ αἰῶνος,** referring to already existing fact, were incompatible with a prayer; but it is sufficient that the prayer has regard mainly to the present and future; the past only comes in to give it a fuller, more joyful tone, reminding us of the eternity of God, as in the psalmist's words, "I said it is my own infirmity, but I will remember the years of the right hand of the Most High," and the close of our own doxology "as it was in the beginning, is now, and ever shall be". I do not see, however, that we need exclude either interpretation. The writer may exult in that which he believes to be already fact in the eternal world, and yet pray for its more perfect realisation in time, as in the Lord's Prayer, γενηθήτω τὸ θέλημά σου ὡς ἐν οὐρανῷ καὶ ἐπὶ γῆς. The omission of the verb allows of either or both views in varying proportion. **δόξα** by itself is the commonest of all ascriptions. It is joined with **τιμή** in 1 Tim. i. 17 and elsewhere, as here with **μεγαλωσύνη.** It is joined with **κράτος** in 1 Pet. iv. 11, v. 11, Apoc. i. 6. Fuller ascriptions are found in Apoc. iv. 11, ἄξιος εἶ, ὁ κύριος . . . λαβεῖν τὴν δόξαν καὶ τὴν τιμὴν καὶ τὴν δύναμιν, v. 13, τῷ καθημένῳ ἐπὶ τῷ θρόνῳ . . . ἡ εὐλογία καὶ ἡ τιμὴ καὶ ἡ δόξα καὶ τὸ κράτος εἰς τοὺς αἰῶνας τῶν αἰώνων, vii. 12, ἡ εὐλογία καὶ ἡ δόξα καὶ ἡ σοφία καὶ ἡ εὐχαριστία καὶ ἡ τιμὴ καὶ ἡ δύναμις καὶ ἡ ἰσχὺς τῷ Θεῷ ἡμῶν. Just before (ver. 10) we have the remarkable ascription ἡ σωτηρία τῷ Θεῷ ἡμῶν. Compare with this the ascription of David (1 Chron. xxix. 11), σοὶ Κύριε ἡ μεγαλωσύνη καὶ ἡ δύναμις καὶ τὸ καύχημα καὶ ἡ νίκη καὶ ἡ ἰσχύς, ὅτι σὺ παντων τῶν ἐν οὐρανῷ καὶ ἐπὶ γῆς δεσπόζεις. For a similar expression in regard to the future blessedness of man, see Rom. ii. 10, δόξα δὲ καὶ τιμὴ καὶ εἰρήνη παντὶ τῷ ἐργαζομένῳ τὸ ἀγαθόν.* An unusual form of ascription occurs in Clem. Rom. 59. 2, ἡ χάρις τοῦ κυρίου ἡμῶν Ἰησοῦ Χριστοῦ μεθ' ὑμῶν καὶ μετὰ πάντων πανταχῇ τῶν κεκλημένων ὑπό τοῦ Θεοῦ καὶ δι' αὐτοῦ· δι' οὗ αὐτῷ δόξα, τιμή, κράτος καὶ μεγαλωσύνη, θρόνος αἰώνιος ἀπὸ τῶν αἰώνων εἰς τοὺς αἰῶνας τῶν αἰώνων.

μεγαλωσύνη. Only found elsewhere in N.T. in Heb. i. 3, ἐκάθισεν ἐν δεξιᾷ τῆς μεγαλωσύνης ἐν ὑψηλοῖς, repeated in viii. 1. Dr. Chase notes that it occurs in Enoch v. 4, κατελαλήσατε μεγάλους καὶ σκληροὺς λόγους ἐν στόματι ἀκαθαρσίας ὑμῶν κατὰ τῆς μεγαλοσύνης αὐτοῦ, xii. 3, τῷ κυρίῳ τῆς μεγαλοσύνης, xiv. 16 (a house excelling) ἐν δόξῃ καὶ ἐν τιμῇ καὶ ἐν μεγαλοσύνῃ. It is coupled with **δόξα,** of which it may be regarded as an extension, in the doxology used by Clem. Rom. 20, 61. I am not aware of any other example of **ἐξουσία** in a doxology: compare, however, Matt. xxviii. 18, ἐδόθη μοι πᾶσα ἐξουσία ἐν οὐρανῷ καὶ ἐπὶ γῆς.

πρὸ παντὸς τοῦ αἰῶνος. *Cf.* 1 Cor. ii. 7 (τὴν σοφίαν) ἣν προώρισεν ὁ Θεὸς πρὸ τῶν αἰώνων εἰς δόξαν ἡμῶν, Prov. viii. 23, πρὸ τοῦ αἰῶνος ἐθεμελίωσέ με (*i.e.* σοφίαν), ἐν ἀρχῇ πρὸ τοῦ τὴν γῆν ποιῆσαι. An equivalent expression is **πρὸ καταβολῆς κόσμου** found in John xvii. 24, ἠγάπησάς με π. κ. κ. also Eph. i. 4, ἐξελέξατο ἡμᾶς ἐν αὐτῷ π. κ. κ. and 1 Pet. i. 20 (Χριστοῦ) προεγνωσμένου μὲν π. κ.κ., φανερωθέντος δὲ ἐπ' ἐσχάτου τῶν χρόνων. St. Jude speaks of one past age and of several ages to come. On the other hand St. Paul speaks of many ages in the past (1 Cor. ii. 7), and St. John of only one age in the future.

εἰς πάντας τοὺς αἰῶνας. This precise phrase is unique in the Bible, but **εἰς τοὺς αἰῶνας** is common enough, as in Luke i. 33, Rom. i. 25, v. 5, xi. 36, xvi. 27, 2 Cor. xi. 31, etc., so in LXX, Dan. ii. 4, 44, vi. 6, 26. The stronger phrase **εἰς τοὺς αἰῶνας τῶν αἰώνων** occurs in Gal. i. 5, Phil. iv. 20, 1 Tim. i. 17, 2 Tim. iv. 18, Heb. xiii. 21, 1 Pet. iv. 11, v. 11, Apoc. i. 6, etc. John uses only **εἰς τὸν αἰῶνα** apparently with the same meaning. Other variations are found in Eph. iii. 21, αὐτῷ ἡ δόξα ἐν τῇ ἐκκλησίᾳ καὶ ἐν Χ. Ἰ. εἰς πάσας τὰς γενεὰς τοῦ αἰῶνος τῶν αἰώνων, 2 Pet. iii. 18, αὐτῷ ἡ δόξα καὶ νῦν καὶ εἰς ἡμέραν αἰῶνος.

* For a full account of the early doxologies, see Chase on the Lord's Prayer (*Texts and Studies*, i. 3, p. 68 foll.). He states that the common doxology at the end of the Lord's Prayer (σοῦ ἐστιν ἡ βασιλεία καὶ ἡ δύναμις καὶ ἡ δόξα εἰς τοὺς αἰῶνας "appears to be a conflation of two distinct forms," and "was added to the Prayer in the 'Syrian' text of St. Matthew's Gospel".

THE REVELATION
OF
ST. JOHN THE DIVINE.

James Moffatt, D.D.

Longsuffering toward us here is the Most High:
    He hath shown us that which is to be,
    And hath not hidden from us what befalleth at the end.
For the youth of the world is over.
    Long since hath the strength of creation failed,
    And the advent of the times is at hand.
The pitcher is nigh to the cistern,
    The ship to the haven,
The caravan to the city,
    And life to its consummation.

—*The Syriac Apocalypse of Baruch* (lxxxv. 8, 10), A.D. 70-100.

INTRODUCTION.

§ 1. *The Text.*—The exceptionally corrupt state of the Textus Receptus in the Apocalypse is due to the fact that for this book Erasmus (to whose text it goes back) had access to only a single cursive[1] (numbered 1) of the twelfth or thirteenth century. Even that was inferior and incomplete. The MSS. which have become available since his day are neither ample nor faultless. Throughout the five uncials (two of which, *i.e.*, C and P, are defective palimpsests), over 1600 variants have been counted—excluding merely orthographical differences—in the 400 verses of the book; this proportion is considerably higher than in the Catholic epistles, for example, where 432 verses only yield about 1100 variants. The earliest uncial goes back to the fourth century (א); A and C, the most weighty, to the fifth; Q[2] to the eighth; and P to the ninth. Of these, אAQ are complete, while the Apocalypse in Q is bound up with the writings of Basil the Great and Gregory of Nyssa—"one of many instances in which the Apocalypse was bound up with ordinary theological treatises instead of with the other N.T. writings" (Gregory i. 121). C lacks i. 1, iii. 19-v. 14, vii. 14-17, viii. 5-ix. 16, x. 10-xi. 3, xiv. 13-xviii. 2, xix. 5-end. P is defective in xvi. 12-xvii. 1, xix. 21-xx. 9, xxii. 6-end.

אAC reflect a fairly uniform text, which seems to have been influenced by an older uncorrected text allied to that underlying the vulgate. Hence, as א in the Apocalypse, owing to its eccentric element, is not of exceptional value by itself (though supported by the cursives 95 and 36), AC vg. form an important group of witnesses, to which the minuscule 95 (like 68 and 38) and Syr. seem allied. The relation of P and Q is less obvious. Their differences (they agree

[1] Relatively high among the secondary documents, but woefully inferior to the uncials. On the performance of Erasmus, see Delitzsch's *Handschrifte Funde*, i. (1861), pp. 17 f., with A. Bludau's essay on the Erasmus editions of the N.T. in Bardenhewer's *Biblische Studien*, vii. 5.

[2] To avoid confusion with the B of Codex Vaticanus, it is better to cite this codex Vaticanus as Q (so, after Tregelles, Weiss, Haussleiter, Bousset, Swete) than as B (Tisch.) or B[2] (WH, Simcox).

only in about fifty cases against ℵAC) point either to two recensions of some older original (Bousset) or to a text based again upon some older revised text (Weiss). Q approximates rather to the cursives in text. But its archetype usually tallies with ℵAC, and is allied somehow to the text behind the so-called "Coptic"[1] version (*cf.* Goussen's "Theolog. Studia, fasciculus I.": *Apoc. S. Johannis apostoli versio sahidica*, 1895, pp. iv.-vii.), like a small group of cursives (Bousset's Q rel.). In no one MS. or group of MSS. is a neutral or fairly accurate text preserved. This is mainly due to the interval which elapsed before the Apocalypse became generally canonical, particularly in the East; its text was less carefully guarded during this period than any other portion of the N.T., and even by the time that the ℵAC text (or texts) came into being, the book had not secured its canonisation throughout the Eastern churches. In addition to this, the grammatical irregularities and anomalies[2] which studded its pages tempted many a scribe to correct and to conform the text. Systematic emendation of this kind must have begun very early (Weiss, pp. 144 f.).

This paucity and conflict of uncial evidence lends additional weight to the versions and patristic citations, especially as they reflect a text or texts which cannot be taken to be identical with, and yet must be older than, those underlying the MSS. Often, indeed, the versions themselves reproduce some of the most patent errors in the MSS., while the patristic texts are sometimes too

[1] In the textual notes = Sah. (*i.e.*, Sahidic): a further fragment is edited by J. Clédat in *Revue de l'Orient Chrétien* (1899), pp. 263-279. Gregory (pp. 546-547) throws both this and the later Bohairic or Memphitic version (= me.) back into the second century, but this is probably too early a date. All the extant fragments of the former are printed in Delaporte's *Fragments Sahidiques du N.T.* (Paris, 1906). For the latter, *cf.* Leipoldt in *Church Quart. Rev.*, 1906, pp. 292 f.

[2] These are not invariably Hebraisms, as Viteau and the older grammarians argue, but it is almost uncritical at the opposite extreme to rule out Hebraisms entirely. The Apocalypse is so saturated with the original text and the Greek version of the O.T., that there is more likelihood here than elsewhere in the N.T. of a grammatical solecism being due, directly or indirectly, to the influence of Semitic idiom. Even though a parallel instance can be adduced in some cases from the papyri or the κοινή elsewhere (*cf.* Helbing, p. iv.), this merely suggests a possible origin for the phrase in question. Besides, the Apocalypse is a piece of literary art. Where its eccentricities are not due to ignorance of Greek or to reminiscences of Hebrew idiom, they are deliberate violations of grammar and syntax in the interests of rhetoric or faith. That Greek was spoken in these Asiatic townships, although native dialects lingered in the country, is shown by L. Mitteis in his *Reichsrecht und Volksrecht in den östlichen Provinzen d. röm. Kaiserreiches* (1891), pp. 23 f.

insecure to admit of reliable inferences being drawn from their contents (*cf.* Bebb in *Studia Biblica*, ii. 195-240). Yet, even with these drawbacks, one need not despair of utilising either. Thus the Latin versions[1] and patristic citations—which are of special moment, since the Apocalypse was never absent from the Latin N.T., and since the fourth century version did not affect it seriously—reveal a fairly distinctive Greek text behind the type of African text preserved by Cyprian (third century, citations in his *Testimonia*), Primasius, the sixth century African commentator, and the fragmentary Fleury palimpsest (sixth or seventh century).[2] Critical opinion is still unsettled upon the precise connexion of this text with the uncials, or even with the citations of Latin fathers like Tertullian, Jerome and Augustine, to say nothing of Ticonius, Beatus (eighth century), Haymo (ninth century) and Cassiodorus (sixth century). Thus it is quite uncertain whether the idiosyncrasies of Tertullian's quotations reflect a private recension (so Haussleiter) or some ecclesiastical version, if they are not made directly from the Greek (*cf.* Nestle's *Einführung*, 94, 227 f., E. Tr. 119-20). Nevertheless, it is in this direction that the most promising outlook of textual criticism upon the Apocalypse lies. It has unique aid in the Latin versions. The greater respect shown by the ecclesiastical West to the Apocalypse must have conspired upon the whole to give its text a better chance of preservation than in the East. Certainly, the fragments of the so-called African text carry us back to a Greek text of the Apocalypse which was current in the middle of the third century, prior to the origin of any extant uncial, while the evidence of Dr. Gwynn's Syriac text comes only second in importance. The Greek citations of Clem. Alex. and Origen also echo a text which hardly corresponds to that of any of the uncials; but, where the latter writer agrees with ℵ, some early Alexandrian text may probably be discerned, which might be termed Western. His citations have also affinities with the text of S (*cf.* Gwynn, pp. lv. f.). As for the more important of the cursives, so far as they have been collated (*cf.* Gregory, i. 316-326, Scrivener's *Introd.*, 1894, i. 321-326), they seem mainly to corroborate other lines

[1] Dr. Armitage Robinson (*Cambridge Texts and Studies*, i. 2, pp. 73, 97 f.), followed by Dr. Salmon (*Introd. to N.T.*, pp. 567 f.), even argues from the Ep. Lugd., (Eus., *H. E.*, v. 1) that the Gallican churches must have had a Latin version of the N.T. (including the Apocalypse) by the middle of the second century, akin to the African old Latin.

[2] *Cf.* Gregory, 609, and Mr. E. S. Buchanan's collation in *Journ. Theol. Studies* viii., pp. 96 f.

of evidence. In the dearth of better witnesses, their place is occasionally more serious than some editors would allow; but no attempt at grouping them can be pronounced successful (about sixty contain the commentary of Andreas), and it is merely in the wake of earlier and heavier authorities that most of the minuscules can, as a rule, be employed with any safety.

In the main, however, there is a fair consensus of editors (*cf.* W.H ., ii., 260 f.) for the bulk of the text as printed in the following pages. Exigencies of space have obliged the present editor to omit nearly all the textual material which he had amassed, and the only variants noted, as a rule, are those of direct significance for the expositor. Once or twice a variant has some intrinsic interest of a special kind, or the reading has had to be justified, but the textual notes do not profess to provide anything like a complete textual conspectus. Thus there is no discussion upon the gloss of S on ἀνὰ in iv. 8, upon the curious Syriac rendering of viii. 13 (as if μεσ. = μέσος οὐρὰ αἷμα), or upon the interpolation at xi. 1. All that one has been able to do is to furnish the reader with as accurate a text as possible for that elucidation of the religious ideas of the book which it is the primary object of the Expositor's Greek Testament to facilitate.

Special Abbreviations (*cf.* others in vol. ii. 754-756, iii. 33-36, 413).

And. = comm.[1] of Andreas, bishop of Caesarea in Cappadocia (fifth or sixth century), author of first Greek edit. (ἑρμηνεία εἰς τὴν Ἀποκάλυψιν). *Cf.* von Soden's *die Schriften des N.T.*, i. 1, 472-475, 702 f., and Delitzsch's *Hands. Funde*, ii. (1862), pp. 29 f.

Areth. = comm. of Arethas, his successor (in 10th cent. ?), allied to Q (Delitzsch) as And. to A upon the whole.

Arm. = Armenian version. *Cf.* Conybeare's *Armenian Version of Rev.* (London, 1907), from codex 4 (12th cent.).

Bs. = Bousset's "Textkritische Studien zum N.T." (*Texte u. Untersuchungen*, xi. 4, 1-44), 1894.

edd. = consensus or large majority of editors: so min. (minuscules) MSS. (manuscripts), and vss. (versions).

[1] Extant in these forms: And^a = codex August., 12th cent. (14th, Gregory), And^c = codex Coisl. (10th cent.), And^{bav} = codex Bavaricus (16th cent.), And^{pal} = codex Palatinus (15th cent.). The newly discovered commentary of Oecumenius (6th cent., *cf.* Diekamp in *Sitzungsberichte der königl. preuss. Akad.*, 1907, 1046 f.), as yet unedited, may take the primacy from Andreas.

gig. = codex gigas Holmiensis (13th cent.), witness either to old Latin text or to "late European" type (Hort).

Pr. = Primasius, ed. Haussleiter in Zahn's *Forschungen zur Gesch. des NTlichen Kanons*, iv., pp. 1-224 (1891), a very important study. *Cf.* the same critic's essay on Vict., Tic., and Jerome in *Zeits. für Kirchl. Wiss. u. Leben* (1886), 237-257.

S. = Syriac Philoxenian recension (6th cent.), ed. Gwynn (1897); reflects a Greek text, which is mixed, but is in the main (lxi. f.) allied to the normal uncial text, and is especially close to C and Origen (lv. f.). *Cf.* Gregory, ii. 507, 509.

Spec. = pseudo-August. *Speculum* (8th or 9th cent.).

Syr. = Harkleian recension (represented by about eight considerable MSS.): posterior and inferior to S.

Tic. = "comm. in Apoc. homiliis octodecim comprehensus" of Tyconius the Donatist (end of 4th cent.).

vg. = vulgate (Jerome's version, 4th cent.), best preserved in codices Am. (= Amiatinus, 8th cent.), and Fuld. (= Fuldensis, 6th cent.), Harl. (= Harleianus, 9th cent.), and Tol. (= Toletanus, 8th cent.).

Vict. = comm. of Victorinus, bishop of Pettau in Pannonia (end of 3rd cent.).

Ws. = B. Weiss: "die Joh. Apk., textkritische Unters. u. Textherstellung" (*Texte u Unters.* vii. 1), 1891.

§ 2. *Analysis.*—The Apocalypse of John, which is thrown into epistolary form, is a slender book with a large design, After the title (i. 1-3) and prologue (i. 4-8) in which the prophet puts himself into relation with seven churches of Western Asia Minor, he proceeds to describe the vision of Jesus Christ (i. 9 f.) which furnished him with his commission to write.[1] The immediate outcome of the vision is a series of charges addressed to these churches (ii.-iii.).[2] Like the

[1] The phrase ἐν κυριακῇ (=imperial, *cf.* Deissmann's *Licht vom Osten*, 258 f.) ἡμέρᾳ (i. 10) denotes the Christian Sunday, not the day of judgment to which he was transported (so Wetstein, Weyland, Selwyn, Hort, Russell's *Parousia*, 371, 372, and Deissmann in *E. Bi.*, 2815). *The day of the Lord* is only twice used in the Apoc. (vi. 14, xvi. 14), and there in a special eschatological connexion and in its normal grammatical form. In the Apocalypse it means the day of judgment, whereas in i. 10 the words imply revelation, and the Apocalypse is not a mere revelation of the judgment-day. Besides, ἐν πν. must go here with ἐγεν. as in iv. 2, otherwise it would have a verb of transport (so xvii. 3, xxi. 10).

[2] These are addressed to tiny communities in the cities, not to the churches as being in any sense the cities. The character and history of the Christian community are by no means to be identified with those of the city; we have no reason to assume that the local Christians, who were ardently awaiting a citizenship from heaven,

author of the 50th Psalm, he tries to rouse God's people to the seriousness of their own position, before he enters into any predictions regarding the course of the outside world. The scene then changes to the celestial court (iv.-v.), where God appears enthroned in his presence-chamber over the universe, with Jesus installed as the divine revealer of providence in the immediate future. The description of the heavenly *penetralia* forms a series of weird Oriental arabesques, but the nucleus is drawn from the tradition of the later post-exilic prophets (especially Ezekiel). According to one phase of this tradition, the climax of things was to be heralded by physical and political disturbances; a regular crescendo of disasters was imminent on the edge and eve of the world's annihilation. Hence the next series of visions is full of material and military troubles, delineated partly in supernatural colours which are borrowed from the fanciful astro-theology of eschatological tradition. From this point onwards the sword of the Lord is either an inch or two out of its scabbard, or showering blows upon his adversaries. In the prophet's own metaphor, before the contents of the Book of Doom (in the hands of Jesus Christ) can be read, its seven seals must be broken, and at the opening of each (vi.-vii.) some fresh woe is chronicled.[1] The woe heralded by the seventh seal drifts over, however, into another series of fearful catastrophes which are introduced by seven trumpet blasts (viii.-ix.), and it is only on their completion that the way is now clear for the introduction of the protagonists in the last conflict upon earth. These protagonists are the messiah of God, *i.e.*, Jesus

had any vivid civic consciousness, or were keenly sensitive to the historical and geographical features of their cities. The analogies sometimes drawn from the latter are interesting but for the most part specious and irrelevant coincidences. It is modern fancy which discovers in such directions any vital elements present to the mind of the prophet or his readers. Why these particular churches were selected, remains a mystery. The cities in question were not all conspicuous for a special enforcement of the imperial cultus, and the churches themselves can hardly be supposed to be in every case representative or particularly important. Even the plausible theory that they were the most convenient centres for district-groups of churches (Ramsay, *Seven Letters*, pp. 180 f.) does not work out well in detail.

[1] The longing of the martyred souls in vi. 9-11 ("lignes toutes divines, qui suffront éternellement à la consolation de l'âme qui souffre pour sa foi ou sa vertu," Renan, 463), recalls the function of the Erinnys in Greek religion, the Erinnys being primarily "the outraged soul of the dead man crying for vengeance" (*cf.* J. E. Harrison, *Prolegomena to Study of Greek Religion*, p. 214). Only, the souls in the Apocalypse are passive; they do not actively pursue their revenge upon the living. The point of the vision is in part to reiterate the deterministic conviction that God has his own way and time; he is neither to be hurried by the importunity of his own people nor thwarted by the apparent triumph of his enemies.

Christ, and the messiah of Satan, *i.e.*, the Roman empire in the person of its emperor with his blasphemous claim to divine honours upon earth. The series of tableaux which depict their entrance on the scene indicates that the prophet has now reached the heart and centre of his subject. But at this point his method alters, and the thread of purpose is less patent. Hitherto the Book of Doom, with its seven seals, has sufficed for the artistic and rather artificial presentation of his oracles. Now that the seventh seal is broken, the Book, *ex hypothesi*, is opened; we expect the secrets of divine judgment to be unbared. Instead of describing what follows as the contents of this book, however, the prophet relates how he absorbed another and a smaller volume (x.), containing the sum and substance of the final oracles which bear on the world's fate.[1] He then proceeds, in terms of current and consecrated mythological traditions, to portray the two witnesses (xi.) who herald the advent of the divine messiah (xii.) himself, in the latter days. Messiah's rival, the dragon or Satan, is next introduced, together with the dragon's commission of the Roman empire and emperor (xiii.) as the supreme foe of God's people. Here is the crisis of the world! And surely it is a *nodus dignus vindice;* God must shortly and sternly interfere. The imperial power, with its demand for worship, is confronted by a sturdy nucleus of Christians who will neither palter nor falter in their refusal to give divine honours to the emperor. Characteristically, the prophet breaks off to paint, in proleptic and realistic fashion, the final bliss of these loyal saints (xiv.), and the corresponding tortures reserved by God for the enemy and his deluded adherents. But at this point, just as the closing doom might be expected to crash down upon the world, the kaleidoscope of the visions again alters rather abruptly. The element of fantasy

[1] The distinctive and Jewish characteristics of the following oracles (xi.-xiv., xvii. f.) suggest, as Sabatier was almost the first to see, that the contents of this **βιβλαρίδιον** are to be found here; so Weyland (a Jewish Neronic source in x.-xi. 13, xii.-xiii., xiv. 6-11, xv. 2-4, xvi. 13, 14, 16, xix. 11-21, xx.-xxi. 8), Spitta (a Jewish source, *c.* 63 B.C., in most of x.-xi., xiv. 14 f., xv. 1-8, xvi. 1-12, 17, 21, xvii. 1-6, xviii., xix. 1-8, xxi. 9-27, xxii. 1-3, 15), Pfleiderer (Jewish source, Neronic and Vespasianic, in most of xi.-xiv., xvii.-xix.), and J. Weiss (Jewish source, Neronic, in xi. 1-13, xii. 1-6, 14-17, xiii. 1 7, xv.-xix., xxi. 4-27). But the first editor has worked over the contents of the **βιβλαρίδιον** so thoroughly that it is impossible to be sure that it ever was a literary unity. The probability is that xi.-xiii. at least reproduce fragments from it; the evidence hardly warrants us in postulating the incorporation of any coherent source. After chap. x. the symmetry of the Apocalypse is impaired by rapid and bewildering alterations of standpoint to which no satisfactory clue can be found.

becomes still more lurid and ornate. The world of men and nature is drenched by a fresh series of chastisements (xv.-xvi.), which prove unavailing; no repentance follows (xvi. 11, 21), and the climax of history is eventually reached through a succession of mortal penalties inflicted upon the city and empire of Rome (the vices of the empire being ascribed to the city, on the O.T. view which identified capital and kingdom, *cf.* Nah. iii. 1 f.), the votaries of the imperial cultus, and the devil himself (xvii.-xx). To the mind of an early Christian (*cf.* Tert., *Scap.*, 2)[1] it was inconceivable that the world could long survive the downfall of the Roman empire. "And when Rome falls, the world." All that the prophet sees beyond that ruin is the destruction of the rebels employed by God to crush the capital; then—thanks to the survival of an O.T. idea, quickened by later tradition—a desperate recrudescence (xx. 7 f.) of the devil. His defeat ushers in the general resurrection and the judgment. *Earth and sky flee from the face of God*, but men cannot fly. They must stand their trial. Then follows the advent of a new heaven and earth (xxi.-xxii.) for the acquitted and innocent, with the descent of the new Jerusalem and the final bliss of God and of his loyal people.

The cycles of seven (ii.-iii., vi. f., viii. f., xv.-xvi.) apparently formed the nucleus of the book, as the author conceived it, the seals representing the certainty, the trumpets the promulgation, and the bowls the actual execution of the doom. They may have been composed at different times and re-arranged in their present order, like the books of the *Aeneid*, but, as they stand, they are closely welded together. The introductory Christophany leads up to ii.-iii., while these chapters again anticipate the visions of iv.-v., which are independently linked to i. (*cf.* i. 4 = iv. 5, v. 6; i. 5, 6 = v. 9). Chapters vi.-ix. are interwoven, and, although the last cycle of seven (xv.-xvi.) seems abruptly introduced, it is really prepared for by x. (see notes). Like the Fourth Gospel, the Apocalypse has been edited, possibly after the author's death, by the local Johannine circle in Asia Minor (*e.g.*, i. 1-3, xxii. 18 f.); one or two cases of transposition by copyists also occur (*cf.* notes on xvi. 15, xviii. 14, xix. 9, xx. 14-xxii. 6 f.), and glosses may be suspected occasionally (*e.g.*, i. 18, iii. 8, ix. 9, xvii. 5; see § 8). But substantially it bears the marks of composition by a single pen; the blend of original writing and editorial re-setting does not impair the impression of a literary unity. This may be seen from the following analysis or outline:—

[1] The author of the Daniel-Apocalypse similarly believed that the resurrection of loyal Jews would follow the downfall of Antiochus Epiphanes (xii. 2, 13).

i. 1-8. Prologue.
i. 9-20. A vision of Jesus the messiah, introducing
ii.-iii. Seven letters to Asiatic churches :—
(1 Ephesus.
(2) Smyrna.
(3) Pergamos.
(4) Thyatira.
(5) Sardis.
(6) Philadelphia.
(7) Laodicea.
iv.-v. A vision of heaven : the throne of God, the Lamb, the book of Doom or Destiny, introducing the plagues of the
vi. Seven seals :—
(1) The white horse.
(2) ,, red ,,
(3) ,, black ,,
(4) ,, pale ,,
(5) ,, souls of the slain.
(6) ,, earthquake and eclipse, etc.
Intermezzo :—
vii 1-8. the sealing of the redeemed on earth.
vii. 9-17. the bliss of the redeemed in heaven.
viii. 1. (7) ,, silence or pause.
viii. 2-5. A vision of heaven : an episode of angels, introducing
viii. 6-ix. 21. Seven trumpet blasts for
(1) earth.
(2) sea.
(3) streams : the star Wormwood.
(4) an eclipse.
(5) a woe of locusts.
(6) a woe of Parthian cavalry.
Intermezzo :—
x. episode of angels and a booklet.
xi. 1-13. the apocalypse of the two witnesses.
xi. 14-19. (7) voices and visions in heaven, introducing
xii. A vision of (*a*) the dragon or Satan as the anti-Christ ; a war in heaven.
xiii. 1-10. (*b*) the Beast or Imperial power } A war on earth.
xiii. 11-18. (*c*) the false prophet or Imperial priesthood. }
Intermezzo :—
xiv. 1-5. the bliss of the redeemed in heaven.
xiv. 6-20. episode of angels and doom on earth.
xv. A vision of heaven : the triumph of the redeemed, introducing
xvi. Seven bowls with plagues for
(1) earth.
(2) sea.
(3) waters.
(4) the sun.

(5) the realm of the Beast.
(6) the Euphrates : an Eastern invasion.
(7) the air: a storm, introducing
A vision of Doom upon

xvii. (*a*) The realm of the Beast, or Rome, at the hands of the Beast and his allies.
xviii. a song of doom on earth:
xix. 1-10. ,, ,, triumph in heaven.
xix. 11-21. (*b*) The Beast and his allies, and the false prophet.
xx. 1-10. (*c*) The Dragon or Satan himself, with his adherents.

A vision of the new heaven and earth: including

xx. 11-xxi. 8. The judgment of the dead.
xxi. 9-xxii. 5. The descent of the new Jerusalem.
xxii. 6-21. Epilogue.

§ 3. *Literary Structure*.—This general unity of conception as well as of style is a unity of purpose, however, rather than of design.[1] Once we descend into details another series of features emerges into view. Even upon the hypothesis that it was written by one author, it cannot have been the product of a single vision, much less composed or dictated under one impulse. Furthermore, inconsequence of a certain kind is one of the psychological phenomena of visions; a change comes over the spirit even of religious dreams, as they drift through the mind of the seer. But more than this is required to account for incongruities and differences of climate, as *e.g.*, in xi. 1, 2, 19 and xxi. 22, xi. 8 and xviii. 24, the various descriptions of the second advent (i. 7, xiv. 14 f., xix. 11 f.), of the judgment (xx. 11 f., xxii. 12), or of heaven (vii. 11 f., xv. 2, xix. 7 f., xxi. 1 f., xxii. 1-5, etc.), the isolated allusions to Michael, Gog and Magog, the four angels of vii. 1-4, the carnage of xiv. 20, etc., the unrelated predictions which are left side by side, the amount of repetition, the episodical and conflicting passages of vii. 1-8, 9-17, x., xi. 1-13, xiv. 1-5, 6-13, 14-20, xix. 11 f., etc. Such phenomena are too vital and numerous to be explained upon the same principle as the contradictions and discrepancies which are to be found in many great works of ancient

[1] "It is of the nature of an epic poem describing what a Christian Homer might describe as 'the good news of the accomplishment of the righteousness and wrath of God'" (Abbott, p. 75). *Cf.* Rom. i. 16-18, Apoc. vi. 17, x. 7, xi. 17, 18. The dramatic hypothesis, favoured by a series of students from Milton to Archbishop Benson, is worked out elaborately by Palmer and Eichhorn. The latter, after the prelude (iv. 1.-viii. 5), finds the first act in viii. 6-xii. 17 (overthrow of Jerusalem in three scenes), the second in xii. 18-xx. 10 (downfall of paganism), and the third in xx. 11-xxii. 5 (the new Jerusalem). But all such schemes are artificial.

literature, or even as the free play of a poetic mind; they denote in several cases planes of religious feeling and atmospheres of historical outlook which differ not simply from their context but from one another. This feature of the book's structure, together with the absence or comparative absence of distinctively Christian traits from certain sections, the iteration of ideas, the differences of Christological climate, the repetitions and interruptions, and the awkward transitions at one point after another, has given rise to the whole analytic movement of literary criticism upon the Apocalypse. The earlier phases are surveyed by A. Hirscht (*Die Apocalypse u. ihre neueste Kritik*, 1895), Dr. Barton (*Amer. Journ. Theol.*, 1898, 776-801), and the present writer (*Hist. New Testament*, 1901, 677-689); for the later literature, see Dr. A. Meyer's articles in the *Theologische Rundschau* (1907, 126 f., 182 f.), and an article by the present writer in the *Expositor* for March, 1909. The legitimacy of this method is denied by Dr. William Milligan (*Discussions on the Apocalypse*, 1893, pp. 27-74), Zahn in his *Einleitung in das N.T.* (§§ 72-75), and Dr. M. Kohlhofer (*Die Einheit der Apocalypse*, 1902), amongst others, but, although both attack and defence have too often proceeded upon the false assumption that the Apocalypse contains a balanced series of historical and theological propositions, or that it can be treated with the ingenuity of a Dante critic, the storm of hypotheses has at least succeeded in laying bare certain strata in the book, as well as a teleological arrangement of them in their present position. The Apocalypse is neither a literary conglomerate nor a mechanical compilation of earlier shreds and patches. There is sufficient evidence of homogeneity in style and uniformity in treatment to indicate that one mind has been at the shaping of its oracles in their extant guise (*cf.* G. H. Gilbert in *Biblical World*, 1895, 29-35, 114-123, and Gallois in *Revue Biblique*, 1894, 357-374). But the prophet has worked occasionally as an editor of earlier sources or traditions, as well as an original composer. These leaflets or traditions are stones quarried from foreign soils; it is no longer possible[1] to ascertain with any great certainty when or how or even why they were gathered. The main point is to determine approximately the object of the watch-tower which the apocalyptist built by means of them, and the direction of his outlook. In some cases it is probable that, alike as a poet and a practical religious seer, he was indifferent to

[1] The state of the extant literature leaves our knowledge of early eschatological tradition full of gaps. It is less exhilarating but more critical to mark the extent of the gaps than to attempt to fill them up or to bridge them with more or less airy guesswork.

their origin, and in every case the important thing is to learn not the original date or shape of a source, or the particular mythological matrix of a tradition, but the new sense attached to it by the prophet himself and the precise object to which he adapted it. This consciousness of a purpose is the least obscure and the most Christian feature of the Apocalypse. Strictly speaking, it is an apocalypse not of John but of Jesus as the Christ[1] (i. 1), and it is the triumphant adoration of Christ which gives an inner clue to the choice and treatment of the various messianic categories. Where the problems of structure arise, and where source-criticism of some kind[2] is necessary, in order to account satisfactorily for the literary and psychological data—is in the juxtaposition of disparate materials (*cf.* notes on vii., x., xi., xii., xiii., xiv., xvii., xviii.).

The results reached in the following commentary outline a theory of the Apocalypse, in its literary aspect, which falls under (*a*) the incorporation hypothesis. According to this view, the Apocalypse is substantially a unity, due to one hand, but incorporating several older fragments of Jewish or Jewish-Christian origin. So Weizsäcker (ii. 173 f.), Sabatier (*Les origines littéraires et la composition de l'Apocalypse*, 1888: Jewish fragments in xi. 1-13, xii., xiii., xiv. 6-20, xvi. 13-14, 16, xvii. 1-xix. 2, xix. 11-xx. 10, xxi. 9-xxii. 5), Schön (*L'origine de l'Apocalypse*, 1887: Jewish fragments in xi. 1-13, xii. 1-9, 13-17, xviii. [except ver. 20]), Bousset, Jülicher (*Einleitung in das N. T.*, § 22), C. A. Scott, F. C. Porter, A. C. M'Giffert (*History of*

[1] The anti-Jewish note of the Apocalypse is as distinct as, though less loud than, the anti-Roman. *Cf.* notes, *e.g.*, on i. 6, 19 f., ii. 9, iii. 7-10, v. 9, 10, x. 7, xi. 19, xxi. 22, xxii. 18. The Christian church was the new and true Israel, and thus served herself heir to great traditions and to high destinies which were only inferior to her own in that they formed a lower slope on the same hill. One of the minor effects (which differentiates the Apocalypse from the Fourth Gospel) of this conception is that Christians are not invited by John to love God or Christ; the temper of their vocation is defined in Jewish terms as a reverent fear of God (*cf.* xi. 18, xiv. 7, xv. 4, xix. 5). Another is the avoidance of ἐκκλησια as a collective term for the church and the ignoring of ἐπίσκοποι, διάκονοι, πρεσβύτεροι, etc.—for the twenty-four celestial πρεσβύτεροι, of course, have nothing whatever to do with the officials of the same name.

[2] English criticisms of Völter's first essays by Warfield (*Presbyterian Review*, 1884, 228-265), and A. Robertson (*Critical Review*, Jan., 1895), of Vischer and Sabatier by Salmon (*Introd. N.T.*, pp. 232 f.), of Vischer and of Völter's earlier theory by Simcox (pp. 215 f.), and of Vischer by Thomson (*Books which influenced Our Lord*, pp. 461 f.). Northcote once told Hazlitt that he believed the Waverley novels were written by several hands, on account of their inequalities. "Some parts are careless, others straggling; it is only when there is an opening for effect that the master-hand comes in." There are several criticisms of the Apocalypse which, with their quasi-reasons, recall this perverse and hapless verdict of a clever man.

Apostolic Age, pp. 633 f.), A. Meyer (*Theol. Rundschau*, 1907, pp. 132 f.), Abbott, Baljon, Wrede (*Entstehung der Schriften des N. T.*, 103, 104), Schmiedel and Calmes. Pfleiderer's two Jewish fragments ie in xi.-xiv., xvii.-xviii., and in xxi. 10-xxii. 5. Those who are unwilling to admit the use of any Jewish sources fall back, as a rule, upon (*b*) the revision hypothesis of an Apocalypse which has been re-edited and brought up to date. This is represented best by Erbes (*Die Offenbarung des Johannes*, 1891), who regards the original work as Johannine (before A.D. 70, incorporating one fragment of a Caligula apocalypse = xii.-xiii.), with editorial additions (Domitianic) in i. 1-3, 20, vii. 4-8, 13-17, ix. 12, xi. 14, xiii. 12, 14, xiv. 4, 8-9*a*, xv. 1, 5-xix. 4, xix. 9*b*-xx. 10, xxi. 5-xxii. 2 (18-19 ?). Similarly, but very elaborately, Briggs (*Messiah of Apostles*, pp. 285 f.) discovers a fourfold process of editing, or rather of materials successively gathering round an original nucleus, while Dr. Barth, in his recent *Einleitung in d. N. T.* (1908, pp. 250-276) goes to the opposite extreme of simplicity by conjecturing (partly along the lines followed by Grotius) that John simply revised, under Domitian, an earlier apocalypse of his own (written under Nero). Either (*a*) or (*b*) is preferable to the over-precision and disintegration of (*c*), the compilation hypothesis, according to which two or more large sources, fairly complete in themselves, have been pieced together by a redactor or redactors. So Weyland (*Omwerkings-en compilatie-hypothesen*, etc., 1888: two Jewish sources, with Christian editorial additions (*c.* A.D. 100) in i. 1-9, 11, 18, 20, ii.-iii., v. 6-14 (vi. 1, 16), ix. 18, x. 7, xi. 8*b*, 19, xii. 11, 17*c*, xiv. 1-5, xv. 1, 6-8, xvi. 1-12, 15, 17*a*, 21, xvii. 14, xix. 7-10, 13*b*, xxii. 7*a*, 12, 13, 16-21), K. Kohler (*E. J.*, x. 390-396: two Jewish sources, one from seventh decade, the other slightly later = x. 2-xi. 13, xii. 1-xiii. 10, xiv. 6 f.), Ménégoz (*Annales de bibliog. Théol.*, 1888, 41-45; two Jewish sources), Bruston (*Études sur Daniel et l'Apocalypse*, 1908, summarising his earlier studies: two Hebrew apocalypses, one Neronic = x. 1, 2, 8-11, xi. 1-13, 19*a*, xii.-xiv. 1, xiv. 4-end, xv. 2-4, xvi. 13-16, 19*b*, xvii.-xix. 3, xix. 11-xx.; the other *c.* A.D. 100 = i. 4 f., ii-iii., iv.-ix., x. 1, 2*b*-7, xi. 14-19, xiv. 2-3, 12, 13, xix. 4-10, xxi. 1-8, xxii. 6-13, 16, 17, 20, 21), Spitta (*Offenbarung des Johannes*, 1898: two Jewish sources, one B.C. 63 and one *c.* A.D. 40, with a Christian apocalypse by John Mark *c.* A.D. 60), Schmidt (*Anmerkungen*, etc., 1891: three Jewish sources, iv. 1-vii. 8, viii. 2-xi. 15 [except x. 1-xi. 13], xii. 1-xxii. 5), Eugène de Faye (*Les Apocalypses Juives*, 1892, pp. 171 f.: two Jewish apocalypses, one from Caligula's reign in vii. 1-8, viii. 2-ix. 21, x. 1*a*, 2*b*-7, xi. 14-15*a*, 19, xii.-xiv. 11, etc.; another = A.D. 69-70),

J. Weiss (*die Offenbarung des Johannes*, 1904: two sources, one Christian [A.D. 65-70] = i. 4-6, 9-19, ii.-iii., iv.-vi., vii., ix., xii. 7-12, xiii. 11-18, xiv. 1-5, 14-20, xx. 1-15, xxi. 1-4, xxii. 3-5; one Jewish, *c.* A.D. 70), etc. Upon similar lines O. Holtzmann (in Stade's *Gesch. Israel*, ii. 658 f.) detected two Jewish sources, one imbedded in the other, the earlier from Caligula's period (xiii., xiv. 6 f.), the later from Nero's. The coast of reality almost disappears from view in Völter's latest theory (*die Offenbarung Johannis, neu untersucht u. erklärt*, 1904), which is a combination of (*b*) and (*c*); it postulates an apocalypse of John Mark (*c.* A.D. 65) and an apocalypse of Cerinthus (*c.* A.D. 70 = x. 1-11, xvii. 1-18, xi. 1-13, xii. 1-16, xv. 5, 6, 8, xvi. 1-21, xix. 11–xxii. 6), both edited under Trajan and under Hadrian. Least successful of all, perhaps, in dealing with the complex literary and traditional data, is (*d*) the Jewish and Christian hypothesis, which is really a simplified variant of (*b*); *e.g.*, Vischer (*Texte u. Untersuchungen*, ii. 3, 1886, 2nd ed. 1895) finds the groundwork of the apocalypse to be an Aramaic Jewish writing (mainly) from A.D. 65-70, which was translated, re-set, and edited by a Christian (in the "Lamb"-passages, with i.-iii., v. 9-14, vii. 9-17, xii. 11, xiii. 9-10, xiv. 1-5, 12, 13, xvi. 15, xvii. 14, xix. 9, 10, 11, 13, xx. 4-6, xxi. 5*b*-8, xxii. 6-21, etc.). Similarly Harnack (*ibid.*), Martineau (*Seat of Authority*, 217-227), and independently, an anonymous writer in the *Zeitschrift für alt. Wiss.* 1887, 167-171, as well as Dr. S. Davidson (*Introd. to N. T.*, ii., pp. 126-233: the Apocalypse an Aramaic Jewish work translated, with additions and interpolations). Von Soden's theory (*Early Christian Literature*, pp. 338 f.), which finds in viii. 1-xxii. 5 of the Johannine Apocalypse under Domitian, a Jewish apocalypse written between May and August of A.D. 70, lies, like C. Rauch's (*Offenbarung des Johannes*, 1894: Jewish composite nucleus, worked up by Christian editor) between (*d*) and (*b*).

The unsatisfactory result of many of these hypotheses is due to the use of inadequate criteria or to the inadequate use of right criteria. The distinction of Jewish and Christian elements is particularly hazardous in a book which deals with eschatology, where no Christian could work without drawing upon Jewish traditions. And these were neither stereotyped nor homogeneous. A given passage in the Apocalypse may not be couched in Christian language, but this does not necessarily prove that it was not written by a Christian; we know far too little about Jewish Christianity in the first century to be sure, apart from certain fundamental beliefs about Jesus, how far it diverged from cognate Jewish conceptions. A failure to appreciate either the poetic freedom of the Apocalyptist or the characteristic phenomena of apocalyptic writing in general has also turned some literary analysts into theorists of the narrowest *parti pris*. But such extravagances do not invalidate the legitimacy of the method in question; without some application of it, the phenomena of the book present a hopeless literary and psychological enigma, and it may fairly be concluded as well as argued that this apocalypse, like most others of its class, is composite to some degree.

§ 4. *Characteristic Features.*—In spirit as well as in form the Apocalypse of John has affinities to the apocalyptic literature of the later Judaism.[1] An apocalypse was the word for a crisis, and for a crisis which bordered on the end. Whenever such epochs of dire emergency recurred, the faith of Israel rose in poignant hope that by breasting this wave of suffering they would soon be past the worst, and lie safe out of the swing of the sea. Since the exile, Israel's foe had been some foreign power, whose policy threatened the religious conscience and whose annihilation was eagerly awaited by the faithful. Apocalypses frankly doomed the State and the world alike; they maintained an irreconcilable and pessimistic attitude towards both. Hence their speculation upon empires and emperors. Hence their constant appeal for courage, based on a conviction that God would intervene ere long in the political sphere to inaugurate a reign of the saints on earth. For the apocalypse was a programme of the immediate future on earth, or of a new earth, as well as a brilliant panorama of celestial mysteries vouchsafed to men in dreams or visions. Its subject was invariably ἃ δεῖ γενέσθαι ἐν τάχει. Apocalyptic always spread its gorgeous pinions in the dusk of the national fortunes, but it strained to the near dawn of relief.

Our concern, however, is with the genius rather than with the genus of John's Apocalypse. It rises above its class *quantum lenta solent inter uiburna cupressi*. The *uiburna* are not to be ignored, indeed. Their order is the general order of the Apocalypse, and when the latter is approached from the side of the early Christian literature, it seems often to include material of little or no specific Christian value. There is a certain foreign air and shape about its foliage. But when it is approached through the tangled underwoods of apocalyptic writings in general, with their frigid speculations upon cosmic details, their

[1] For the characteristics of apocalyptic literature, and for the relation of apocalypse to prophecy, *cf.* §§ 6-19 of Lücke's epoch-making *Versuch einer vollständigen Einleitung in die Offenbarung Joh. und in die gesammte apok. Literatur* (sec. ed. 1822); English summaries and surveys by Dr. Torrey (*E. J.* i. 669-675); L. Hassé in *Inaugural Lectures* (Manchester, 1905, 126-159); Dr. Driver ("Daniel," 1900, pp. lxxxvi. f.); Dr. A. C. Zenos in *Dict. of Christ and Gospels*, i. 79-94: and Dr. R. H. Charles (*E. Bi.* 213-250, also 1338-1392 on Eschatology).

wearisome and fantastic calculations, their tasteless and repulsive elements, and the turgid rhetoric which frequently submerges their really fine conceptions, the Apocalypse of John reveals itself as a superior plant. Its very omissions are significant. There is no allusion, *e.g.*, to the prevalent category of the *two æons*, or to the return of the ten tribes, or to the contemporary Jewish wail over the cessation of sacrifice after A.D. 70 (*e.g.* in *Apoc. Bar.* x. 10), or to the martyrs' death as expiatory (*cf.* 2 Macc. vii. 37 f., 4 Macc. vi. 29, xvii. 21, etc.), or to any intercession of the prophet on behalf of the church (*cf.* 4 Esdras viii.). There is no cosmogony, no self-satisfied comparison of God's people with pagans, no reference to the law[1] (in contrast to the contemporary glorification, *e.g.*, in 4 Esdras iii.-ix., *Apoc. Bar.* xv.-lxix. [*cf.* Charles' note on xv. 5], where it rivals even the messiah as a medium of fellowship and a nucleus of future bliss). There are no parables (as in 4th Esdras) or allegories; above all, there are no querulous complaints from the living. Carlyle describes the Girondist pamphlets as far too full of long-drawn out ejaculations, "Woe is me, and cursed be ye!" Even 4 Esdras, for all its noble pathos, partakes of this self-pity and fury; it is half-anger and half-agony. But the Apocalypse of John usually breathes another air, mitigating upon the whole the brusque temper of its class. Though the oppression which makes a wise man mad may also make a good man sad, for all the feelings of exasperation and indignation stirred by the empire, the prophet John has not yielded to any pessimism about the cause of God. He never attempts to justify the ways of God, like his Jewish contemporaries, or to explain how *the devil gave his power to the beast.* His faith in Jesus as the messiah inspires a simple hope which enables him to remain unintimidated by the last threats and terrors of a foe whose end is near. The quarrel with Rome, *e.g.*, is God's affair. His people have merely to stand still and witness their enemy's rout.

It is this faith, this Christian consciousness, with its moral steadiness, which differentiates John's Apocalypse from the other members of its class. To write an apocalypse meant, like the composition of a drama or a sonnet, conformity to certain literary rules or standards as well as approximation to a certain spirit and temper. It justified, if it did not necessitate, the use of earlier fragments, which were only partially intelligible, since the agony of their hour had long passed by. Apocalyptic modified and adapted such sources to the needs of a later generation. There was a sequacity about apocalyptic

[1] This is all the more remarkable as contemporary Christians were being led, for ethical reasons, to view their religion more and more from a nomistic standpoint.

literature.[1] An author in this province could not start *de novo;* not merely had conventional designs or traditions to be followed, but earlier products were commonly treasured and reset. John followed this method, but his regulative principle was unique, and one fascination of his Apocalypse lies in the fact that we have here a Christian prophet half-mastering and half-mastered by the literary exigencies[2] of apocalyptic, uttering his convictions in strange and hardly relevant terms which had hitherto been appropriated to alien ends. His vision of Jesus came to him through an atmosphere of truculent and fantastic messianism, which was scarcely lucid at all points and which tended to refract if not to blur the newer light; yet the Christian messianic belief generally managed to overpower the inadequate, archaic, and incongruous categories of tradition, through which it had often to pass. It is this juxtaposition which helps to explain the occasional awkwardness and artificiality in the symbolism of the Apocalypse. No doubt the author himself, whether as editor or composer, is partly responsible for this. A certain stiffness of structure pervades the book. There is a lack of sustained interest, and at several points the dove-tailing is defective, while, by a favourite Semitic device, repetition (*cf.* Augustine, *Civ. Dei*, xx. 17) is made to serve the purpose of emphasis. But such inconsistencies and inequalities are mainly due to the fact that the writer's Christian consciousness repeatedly tends to break through forms too narrow for its fulness. Probably the materials at the author's disposal would have been better arranged, had this been anything less than the presentation of a living Redeemer in heaven as the messiah of God's people upon earth. The mere fact that the messiah had lived, involved a readjustment of messianic categories; the further fact that he had suffered and risen meant that many had to be reshaped, There are things in the Apocalypse which show a careful study of earlier prophetic scriptures and rabbinic traditions; but there are

[1] This applies to traditions (*S. C.* 252 f.) as well as to literature (Selwyn, 59 f.). A political and religious crisis promoted the resetting of older eschatological traditions and the resumption of such elements from the common fund or circle of apocalyptic teaching as had acquired special impressiveness (*S. C.* 221 f.). The different interpretations of Jeremiah's prediction about the 70 years by the authors of Daniel and En. lxxxix. 59 f., are a case in point.

[2] One of the clearest instances of this may be found in the *angelus interpres* (*cf.* note on i. 1), which also illustrates, by the way, the difference between the Fourth Gospel and the Apocalypse. The Fourth Gospel scrupulously avoids connecting angels with Jesus. The only allusion to them, during his life-time, is the popular mistake (xii. 29 f.) which misinterpreted God's voice to him as if it had been an angel's voice. The Apocalypse, on the other hand, swarms with angels.

other things which could only have been taught and learned within the school of Jesus Christ, and these are really the telling sentences throughout the book.

At the same time it must be remembered that some of the very features which have lost much if not all of their significance for later ages, ornate and cryptic expressions, allusions to coeval hopes and superstitions, grotesque fantasies and glowing creations of an oriental imagination, the employment of current ideas about antichrist, calculations of the immediate future, and the use of a religious or semi-mythical terminology which was evidently familiar to some Asiatic Christians in the first century—these more or less ephemeral elements combined to drive home the message of the book. They signify to us the toll which had to be paid to contemporary exigencies; without them the book could not have made its way at all into the conscience and imagination of its audience. The momentum of its message lay, however, in the deep sincerity and lofty outlook of the prophet himself, and this broke out occasionally in passages of unexampled splendour and dignity. Sublimity, as a contemporary critic of literary style observed (Pseudo-Longinus, περὶ ὕψους), has always a moral basis; it is, he declared, the echo of a great soul (μεγαλοφροσύνης ἀπήχημα)—or, we might add, of a great soul exercised upon a great issue. The same critic makes another remark, which is apposite to a passage like ch. xviii. of the Apocalypse. One avenue to sublimity, he notes, lies through imitation of and devotion to great writers of an earlier age: Ἔστι δὲ οὐ κλοπὴ τὸ πρᾶγμα, ἀλλ' ὡς ἀπὸ καλῶν εἰδῶν ἢ πλασμάτων ἢ δημιουργημάτων ἀποτύπωσις. This canon throws a ray of light upon the special psychological problem of the Apocalypse's relation to its O.T. and extra-canonical models. Some great writers in every period of literature are only to be understood in the light of a long series of predecessors, and the prophet John is one of these. His apocalypse in one aspect is the final and brilliant flash of the red light which had gleamed from Amos down to the Maccabees. His affinities in point of form, treatment, and general aim are with the line of literary prophets who, from Ezekiel to the authors of Daniel, 4th Esdras, and Baruch, applied themselves to the statement and restatement of apocalyptic eschatology. John's Apocalypse is flecked with allusions to Ezekiel, Zechariah,[1] and above all Daniel.

[1] In two aspects John resembles his prototype Zechariah: (*a*) in the employment of an intricate symbolism, which makes it difficult to be sure where intuition ends and literary decoration begins, (*b*) in the use of schematism to explain providence. For the latter, *cf.* Giesebrecht's *Die Berufsgabung der alttest. Propheten*

But his use of Daniel especially is more than that of a *littérateur* reproducing impressive and poetic conceptions from the study of a classic. For all the artistic and even artificial literary shape of the book, we should weigh it in the wrong scales were we to estimate it as the work of an author who simply drew upon such earlier models for his own later purposes. As contemporary rabbis not only pondered over passages like the Egyptian plagues, the prophecy of Gog and Magog, and the opening vision of Ezekiel, but even had ecstatic visions of heaven granted them (*cf. R. J.*, 350, 379), so the prophet John was not a mere literary artist or a student of prophecy or an editor of earlier fragments. He was that, but he was more. Two features of his book differentiate him from such a class of writers; (*a*) he was a prophet in his own way, and (*b*) his consciousness had been so powerfully affected by the post-exilic Judaism, as well as by contemporary beliefs, that it is not possible to derive his conceptions exclusively from those of the canonical Old Testament.[1] These two features partially coalesce. As a prophet, no less than as a student of the prophetic and apocryphal scriptures, John believed that the predictions of Daniel were at last on the point of being fulfilled. This was the assurance which dominated his whole treatment of the O.T. in general. It explains how he appropriated and applied time-honoured messianic predictions which he considered relevant to Jesus the true messiah, and it also serves to account psychologically for the form of several visions (*e.g.*, that of ch. i.), which imply a mind already brooding over some of these passages. A well-known instance of this suggestion of visions occurs in Tertullian's *De anima*, ix.: "Est hodie soror apud nos reuelationum charismata sortita, quas in ecclesia inter dominica sollemnia per

(1897), pp. 60 f. (p. 68: bei Amos drängt ein Lebendiges zum Lichte, bei Sacharja herrscht das Programm). On Ezekiel as a prophet who foretold the coming of Christ, *cf.* Clem. Rom., xvii. 1. The typical and eschatological significance of the Egyptian plagues especially seems, from Irenæus (iv. 27, 28), to have impressed the Asiatic πρεσβύτεροι.

[1] The author knows the Hebrew original as well as the LXX (or, at any rate, some of his sources do), but the LXX quotations, or rather references (Swete, pp. cxxxv.-cxlviii.) and reminiscences—for no formula of citation occurs—occasionally (*cf.* i. 7, ix. 20, x. 6, xii. 7, xiii. 7, xix. 6, xx. 4, 11) mark a deliberate divergence, not unexampled in the N.T., towards what was apparently a pre-Christian Greek version of the Hebrew, approximating to the version of Theodotion (particularly in Daniel). They thus anticipate the later preference of writers like Origen for the Theodotionic Daniel (*cf.* Salmon's *Introd. to N.T.*, pp. 547 f., and Swete's *Introd. to the O.T. in Greek*, pp. 46 f.), or else they prove that he was translating directly from the Hebrew text (so *e.g.* in i. 6, xi. 4 ?, xiv. 8, 18). For instances of composite O.T. reminiscences *cf.* Selwyn, pp. 62-64.

ecstasin in spiritu patitur; conuersatur cum angelis, aliquando etiam cum Domino, et uidet et audit sacramenta, et quorundam corda dinoscit, et medicinas desiderantibus submittit. Iam uero prout scripturae leguntur aut psalmi canuntur aut allocutiones proferuntur aut petitiones delegantur, ita inde materiae uisionibus subministrantur". When John's soul is stirred to creative vision or prediction, it is usually something he has heard or read in Daniel or Ezekiel which is moving on the face of the waters. But the form taken by some of the oracles cannot be explained simply from the sacred scriptures, and it is therefore necessary to define separately and more precisely each of the features which have been just mentioned, even though the former necessarily involves the latter.

(*a*) The mind of a prophet like John is, in Wordsworth's phrase, "a feeling intellect," which instinctively embodies ideas in symbols. Thought rises before it in pictorial shape. Symbols are idea and picture at once; they embody beliefs and are also realities of a kind. Conceptions clothe themselves in vivid representations which are effective either on account of their traditional associations or from the aptness of their contemporary allusions, though it is often difficult for a modern reader to fathom their origin in the writer's mind or to estimate the precise relation between the figurative element and the definite idea which that element is intended to enshrine.[1] The difficulty is doubled when, as in the present case, we have occasionally to deal with an ecstatic experience. The material to be interpreted includes the reflective working of the prophet's mind upon a previous mental condition, the literary presentment (with some expansions, rearrangement and embellishment) of what he remembers to have seen in the exalted moments of rapture, together with the impressions produced by these upon his later consciousness. The Apocalypse is not a continuous vision. In parts, it is not a vision at all. There are rhapsodies in it, but it is not a rhapsody. Occasionally the prophet speaks as a counsellor, or writes as an editor of earlier fragments, or calculates the future in terms of traditional eschatology. The very elaboration with which the details and design of the book are worked out precludes any idea of it as a mere transcript of visions written when the seer's memory was fresh, even though some phrases were set down as reflective or editorial glosses. At the same time, the nucleus and the origin of the book are inexplicable apart from the presupposition of

[1] On this power of the poetic Eastern imagination, at certain stages of culture, to fill sensuous forms with a higher content, see some admirable remarks in Caird's *Evolution of Religion*, i. 287 ff.

a definite religious experience which assumed in part the form of a trance or rapture. Vision here, as elsewhere, in apocalyptic literature is occasionally the literary form of allegory and tradition; but not always. The psychological problem is to explain the relation between this inner consciousness of inspiration and the curious imaginative forms in which the prophet seemed to think it needful to embody his Christian conceptions. He employs a large number of suggestive figures and metaphors, drawn from the Old Testament and elsewhere, in spite of their literal inadequacy; these phantasmagoria it is impossible to regard as mere symbols, but on the other hand they are hardly to be taken literally in the case of John any more than that of the later prophets of Judaism (*cf.* Riehm's *Messianic Prophecy*, pp. 228 f.) from whom he borrowed many of them. Often the best way to explain them is to let them appeal to the religious imagination, since it is in this way that they are likely to disclose any permanent truth of which they may be at once the vesture and the vehicle. But whatever they are, they are suggestive, not dogmatic; they are poetic coefficients rather than logical definitions of the author's faith.

The comparative independence with which, like the psalmists (*cf.* Cheyne's *Origin of the Psalter*, pp. 285, 286), he occasionally employs "anthropomorphic, or, let us say at once, mythic expressions, is a consequence of the sense of religious security which animates" him. These expressions helped out his Christian consciousness by their vivid realism and their time-honoured associations in the circles for which he wrote. He could embody in them some deeper truths of his own faith. In this weird world of fantasy, peopled by a rich Oriental imagination with spectral shapes and uncouth figures,[1] where angels flit, eagles and altars speak, and monsters rise from sea and land—in a world of this kind many Asiatic Christians of that age evidently were at home, and there the prophet's message had to find them. Often the point of an allusion lies in some half-forgotten contemporary belief; the terms of it may be superstitious enough, but the aim is predominantly spiritual. An apt illustration of this procedure in the sphere of popular religion is afforded by Luther's well-known use of the superstition about the wood of the cross. "The cross of Christ," he writes in one of his letters, "is parted throughout all the world, and every one meets with his portion. Do not you therefore reject it, but rather accept it as the

[1] Even grotesque symbols of an Oriental cast would appeal to Hellenic readers who were familiar, *e.g.*, with the Ἄρτεμις πολύμαστος of Ephesus, on whose statue winged bulls and rams appear (*cf.* Apoc. iv. 5 f.).

most holy relic, to be kept, not in a gold or silver chest, but in a golden heart, that is, a heart imbued with gentle charity." Here we have a Christian message couched poetically and effectively in terms of a familiar superstition which neither Luther nor his readers any longer shared. A similar explanation may fairly be applied now and then to John's poetic use of the superstitions about amulets, talismans, secret names,[1] and the like, although it is often a fair question how far his language is faded metaphor, and whether he did not sincerely attach himself to some of the current beliefs which underprop his imagery. Otherwise we must allow that details are often used for their poetical impressiveness, which depends on the power of starting old associations and of suggesting dim, mysterious beliefs.

His relation to history is equally free. Nothing could well be more jejune than to suppose that he is covertly conveying political information to his readers, or laboriously spelling out the course of providence from the politics, warfare, and meteorology of his age. History does not move in neat systems of seven, and even apocalyptic prophecy—for all its artificial dogmas and tendency to produce an impression by means of prediction—forms no calendar of exact events to come, much less any chronicle of recent happenings. It is the dogmatic programme which is uppermost in apocalyptic. The seer, by virtue of his inherited ideas, knew how external events must move; his schematism was more to him than anything else, and this accounts for the large haggadic element in such writings (*cf.* Baldensperger, 100, 117 f.). But John's prophetic impulse in the revelation of Jesus to his spirit overbore the tendency to rest the weight of his message on exact disclosures of the future. "For the mass of his audience," George Eliot says of Savonarola (*Romola*, ch. xxv.), "all the pregnancy of his preaching lay in his strong assertion of supernatural claims, in his denunciatory visions, in the false certitude which gave his sermons the interest of a political bulletin." John's forecasts, such as they were, did not aim, at any rate, at the gratification of curiosity, and even his dogmatic programme was little more than a traditional form of expressing his absolute certainty that the God of Jesus Christ would conquer evil.

(*b*) As a product of Asiatic Christianity towards the close of the first century, no less than as a member of a literary class which was usually heterogeneous in eschatology, the Apocalypse further reflects the religious syncretism which prevailed especially in Phrygia and

[1] Thus in ii.-iii., especially, Christians are promised a real initiation into the privileges of the Divine cult after death, instead of the pagan cults which they abjure.

the surrounding districts. The visions of the book are frequently put in terms of local and contemporary religion. Even the contour of what are apparently Old Testament reminiscences is occasionally modified by the collateral foreign tendencies which permeated post-exilic Judaism, especially along apocalyptic lines (*cf.* Cheyne's *Bible Problems*, 70 f.). Thus (*a*) the Babylonian background of several conceptions[1] is now recognised on all hands (see notes on i. 4, 20, iv. 7, 8, v. 6, vi. 1 f., xiii. 11, xiv. 6, xix. 7, 16, xxi. 1-2, 18, xxii. 1, 16). The gnosticism of Asia Minor during the second century reveals the survival and adaptation of more than one feature which was ultimately due to Babylonian mythology or astro-theology, and the previous developments of Judaism had already assimilated ideas from the older speculations of the Babylonians. (*b*) Along with this, traits corresponding to analogous conceptions in Egyptian religion are fairly common (see notes on i. 8, ii. 7, 11, 17, 26 f., iv. 3, 9, v. 13, vii. 16, xii., xiv. 5, xv. 6, xxii. 4, 16). This is hardly surprising, as Egyptian prophecy probably affected Hebrew prophecy (*cf.* Wilcken in *Hermes*, 1905, 544 f.), as the relations between Asia Minor and Egypt were close, and as the latter country was the natural home of eschatology.[2] (*c*) The Hellenic traits, though fewer and fainter, are not inconspicuous (*cf.* notes on ii. 17, iv. 11, vii. 9, 16, viii. 5, ix. 11, xii., xv. 6, xx. 8 f.), but specifically Orphic features (*cf.* Maas, *Orpheus*, 1895, pp. 250-261) are scarcely recognisable. (*d*) The Zoroastrian[3]

[1] Especially behind xii. (*cf.* Calmes, *Rev. Biblique*, 1903, 52-68, and Jeremias pp. 34 f.). But cosmological traits or traditions from Babylonia will not explain the entire form of this oracle (*cf.* Cheyne's *Bible Problems*, 195-207, and Kohlhofer, pp. 72 f.), and even elsewhere they break down. Thus it is extremely questionable if the Babylonians had any conception of the millennium or of the resurrection of the dead; the accusing function of the devil is absent from Babylonian theology, as are the features of xiii. 11-17; and the Babylonian origin of the heavenly temple seems to be highly doubtful (*cf.* Prof. G. B. Gray in *Expos.*, 1908, May-June).

[2] Hermas, the next apocalypse of the early church, is tinged at one point by this influence (*cf.* Reitzenstein's *Poimandres*, 12 f.). The occupation of the Cyclades led to the introduction of many Egyptian deities into the local cultus between 308 and 146 B.C. (*cf.* F. Hiller von Gaertringen's *Beiträge zur alten Gesch.*, i., 1902, pp. 218 f.), including not only Isis but that worship of the Ptolemies which, *e.g.* in Thera (*cf.* the same writer's *Thera*, i., pp. 237 f.) fostered the later Imperial cultus of Rome. Some further Egyptian parallels are collected by Miss A. Grenfell in *The Monist* (1906), 179-200.

[3] The English reader may consult Prof. Moulton's article on "Zoroastrianism" in Hastings' *Dict. B.*, vol. iv., *E. Bi.* iv. 5428-5442, Lightfoot's *Colossians*, pp. 385 f.), and Renan (pp. 470 f.). I have stated and discussed the general evidence in *H. J.*, 1903-1904. The best investigations are in the *Jahr. für protest. Theologie*, Hübschmann (1879, pp. 203-245) and Brandt (1892, pp. 405 f., 575 f.) respectively., *Cf.* also Böklen and Stave (§ 10).

influence is strongly marked, though not so strongly as Völter, in his latest volume (pp. 29 f., 63 f., 86 f., 116 f.), would make out. This, like that of Babylonia, reaches back not simply to the indirect channel of the post-exilic Judaism, but apparently to an almost direct relationship. In Zoroastrian angelology and eschatology alone, for example, does anything adequate correspond to the sort of conceptions which in their present shape are peculiar, or almost peculiar, to the Apocalypse: *viz.* (i.) the binding or noosing of the fiend (xx. 1 f., *cf. S. B. E.*, v. 19), (ii.) the blasting of the third part of the earth (viii. 7 f., *cf. S. B. E.*, v. 164, where the climax of the evil spirit's work is that "he took as much as one-third of the base of the sky in a downward direction, into a confined and captive state"), (iii.) the seven spirits of God (i. 4, *cf. Encycl. Religion and Ethics*, i. 384-385, and *S. B. E.*, iv. pp. lxxi. f.), (iv.) the guardian *fravashis* of the churches (see note on i. 20—quite an Avestan touch), (v.) the recrudescence of evil genii before the consummation (xx. 7 f., *cf.* Stave, pp. 227 f.), (vi.) the emphasis on the millennium-period,[1] and (vii.) the renewal of the universe. See, further, notes on i. 13, ii. 5, iv. 3, vii. 17, xi. 5 f., xiv. 17 f., xvi. 13, 20. Upon the other hand, no distinct references to Mithraism (as, *e.g.*, against Barns in *Expos.*, iii. 220 f.: Titan, the number of the Beast = Mithra as sun-god) can be detected, while the Buddhistic or Indian parallels are scanty and as a rule remote.

Nothing is more deceptive than such coincidences between primitive religions. *Si duo faciunt idem, non est idem.* They may simply be due in certain cases to analogous but independent movements of the religious feeling in different quarters. Here as elsewhere inferences have to be drawn with extreme caution, yet there is good reason to believe that a number of the special traditions and paraphernalia used in the Apocalypse owed part of their form, if not of their content, to ideas which were current in Jewish and pagan circles during the first century in Asia Minor. The coincidences with Oriental religious conceptions (*cf.*, *e.g.*, J. Brandis in *Hermes*, 1867, pp. 259-284) are too numerous and too striking to be dismissed in every case as accidental. Even when the cord is Christian, it may be spun out of several variegated threads, though it is often diffi-

[1] Plutarch (*De Iside*, 46 f.), in describing the Zoroastrian doctrines of the Magi as these were known to Romans and Greeks of the first century A.D., closes by sketching the final doom of Ahriman, when the earth lies smooth under a single ruler and a single language, and "at the end Hades shall fail and men be happy" (Apoc. xx. 6-14). Similarly, the fierce doom of Apoc. xix. 17-18, where birds are summoned to eat the flesh of messiah's victims, is probably a reflex of the supreme penalty inflicted on the carcases of those who resist Mazdeism, *viz.*, that they be devoured by birds of prey (*S. B. E.*, iv. 27, 131).

cult and sometimes impossible to determine where the threads were drawn from. Clemen's *Religionsgeschichtliche Erklärung des Neuen Testaments* (1909) is a convenient handbook to the whole subject of these highways and byways of the apocalyptic fairy-land.

§ 5. *The Nero-redivivus Myth.*—The most central of these co-efficients, drawn from a mixture of supernatural and political legends, is the belief in the return of a Nero-antichrist from the underworld.

The massacre of A.D. 64 had invested Nero with such peculiar infamy for the early Christians, that it is not surprising to find Satan's chief agent in the final attack upon God's kingdom depicted by the prophet John as an infernal Nero, issuing from the under-world to head a coalition of the East against Rome and then against the Christ. Both the Jewish and the Christian literature of this period show traces of the successive phases of the Nero-redivivus anticipation (Suet. *Nero*, 47).[1] The legend sprang up on Roman soil. People could hardly credit the tyrant's death, so sudden and secret had been its circumstances. A curious mixture of relief and regret prevailed after the removal of the last member of the Julian dynasty at the age of thirty-two. For some time, indeed, a more or less sincere belief (Tacit., *Hist.* ii. 8, 9) prevailed, that he could not have died, but must be lying hidden somewhere in the East. This idea was suggested by his friendly relations with Parthia, and perhaps corroborated by the wide-spread notion, which he had encouraged in his own life-time, that he would reign over the East from Jerusalem, or that Rome was to be supplanted by an Eastern empire (Suet. *Nero,* 40, *Vesp.* 4, Tacit. *Ann.* xv. 36, *Hist.* v. 13, 3: pluribus persuasio inerat antiquis sacerdotum litteris contineri eo ipso tempore fore ut ualesceret Oriens profectique Judaea rerum potirentur; *cf.* Joseph. *Bell.* vi. 5, 4). On the strength of this superstition, edicts were actually issued in Nero's name, 'quasi uiuentis et breui magno inimicorum malo reuersuri' (Suet. *Nero*, 57). The East was disturbed by pretenders, who exploited this superstition. One

[1] In *Sib.* iv. 119 f. the great king (*i.e.*, Nero) flies away wounded across the Euphrates into Parthian territory, while in *Sib.* iv. 137-139 (after 80 A.D.) the eruption of Vesuvius is taken as a portent of Nero's immediate return from the East with a huge retinue to wreak vengeance on Rome. In another of these Asiatic oracles (v. 143-147, dating 71-74 A.D.) the flight of the detested and unpopular Nero from Babylon (*i.e.*, Rome) to the Parthians is described. He reaches the kingdom of the Medes and Persians, to return in the last days (361 f.) for a bloody conquest of the earth (κοσμομανὴς πόλεμος). *Cf.* Geffcken's studies "Zur älteren Nero-sage" in *Nachrichten d. Götting. Gesellschaft d. Wissensch.* (1899), pp. 443 f. The presence of the Nero-myth in the Apocalypse seems to have been first re-discovered by a Spanish Jesuit, Juan Mariana, who commented on the book in 1619.

appeared shortly (Tac. *Hist.* ii., 8-9) after Nero's death; another (Terentius Maximus) came forward in 80 A.D., who bore a physical resemblance to the emperor, and was only surrendered by the Parthians to Domitian after some years of power; a third emerged in 88 A.D. (Suet. *Nero*, 57). This created disaffection, especially in the Eastern provinces (Tacit. *Hist.* i. 2: "mota prope etiam Parthorium arma falsi Neronis ludibrio"), where revolutionary hopes and dislike of the existing *régime* were only too easily excited. Even under Trajan, Nero was believed by some to be still alive somewhere (Dio Chrysost. *Orat.*, xxi.), but by that time the illusion had been broken for most people, or rather it had been transmuted into the shuddering belief that Nero would return from the under-world. The political expectation thus became semi-supernatural or transcendental.[1] In certain Jewish and early Christian circles towards the close of the first century, particularly throughout Asia Minor, Nero-redivivus became fused with the other weird figures of Beliar and the antichrist. To some of the Romans Domitian was another Nero. To the Christians who shared John's view, Nero was to come again in another form. The Apocalypse passes over the Beliar-myth of a Satanic accuser who thwarts and seduces God's people (*cf.* Introd. to 2 Thessalonians); incidentally, it assigns this function to the dragon, Satan (xii. 10). But it follows one cycle of Jewish tradition in associating antichrist with some political or foreign persecuting power (Antiochus Epiphanes, *Daniel;* Pompey = dragon, *Ps. Sol.* ii. 29; head of Roman Empire, *Apoc. Bar.*, xxxix.-xl.). The dragon Satan delegates his authority on earth to the Roman empire and emperor. The supreme enemy on earth, however, is the weird, spectral figure of this *revenant* Nero, who reappears in history (*A. C.* pp. 184 f.; *cf.* for contemporary Jewish evidence, Dr. L. Ginzberg in *E. J.*, i. 625-627 on Nero as the devil-antichrist). Thus it is that the saga is doubled, not in xiii. 1-10, 11-18, so much as in xvii., and this doubling seems to be anticipated even in xi. 7 (compare xiii. 1 f.). The seduction of the Jews by antichrist proper (xi. 7 f.) is subordinated by the prophet John to the seduction of the pagan nations (xiii.-xiv., xvi.-xviii.), the latter being regarded as a far more ominous sign of the end. On the other hand, Nero-redivivus is employed, quite in Old Testament fashion, as the unconscious instrument of the divine vengeance upon Rome-Babylon; then he falls as a just victim to God's wrath.

[1] On the apocalypse as a means of transition from political to transcendental messianism, see Dr. Shailer Mathews' scholarly pages (pp. 25 f.) in his *Messianic Hope in the New Testament* (1906).

The eschatological portent of Nero-redivivus, however, was bound up with the pressing claim of the Roman emperors to be worshipped as divine, and it was the latter peril which formed at once the occasion and the theme of John's Apocalypse.

§ 6. *The Imperial Cultus.*—Over two centuries earlier the great exemplar of apocalyptic literature had been issued in order to nerve the faithful who were persecuted for refusing to admit the presumptuous divine claims of Antiochus Epiphanes. The Apocalypse of John is a latter-day pamphlet thrown up by a similar crisis. The prophet believed that the old conflict had now revived in its final form; Daniel's predictions were on the way to be fulfilled at last in an age when the Roman emperor insisted upon being worshipped as the august lord and god of men!

Since the days of Augustus, the emperor had been viewed as the guardian and *genius* of the empire, responsible for its welfare and consequently worthy of its veneration. It was a convenient method of concentrating and expressing loyalty, to acknowledge him as entitled to the prestige of a certain sanctity, even during his lifetime. There were no monarchical traditions available to strengthen the sense of imperial patriotism, and it was a politic step of the emperor to permit a certain adoration to gather round his official figure, an adoration which was generally the outcome of gratitude to the dead and deference to the living ruler for his εὐεργεσίαι (*cf.* Rushforth's *Latin Historical Inscriptions,* pp. 46 f., and A. J. H. Greenidge's *Roman Public Life,* pp. 440, 444, with Gwatkin's article in Hasting's *D.B.,* iv., pp. 293-295). The imperial cultus in this aspect was instinctive rather than deliberate, developing out of certain germs within the ancient mind, such as the blend of religion and patriotism among the Persians, the custom of hero-worship[1] (ἀφηρωΐξαι, especially prevalent in the Ionian islands, *e.g.,* at Thera, *cf. CIG,* 2467—2473, Usener's *Götternamen,* 1896, pp. 249-250), and the worship of the Ptolemies which shocked the pious Plutarch. Its primary aim was to foster patriotism by presenting a symbol of

[1] For the Latin germs of Caesar-worship, prior to Augustus, see Mr. E. Fiddes in *Historical Essays* (Manchester), 1902, pp. 1-16. Many heroes were **πάρεδροι θεοί,** associated with specific gods in a cult as **σύνναοι** or **σύνθρονοι** of the gods (*cf.* E. Kornemann's essay "Zur Gesch. der antiken Herrscherkulte" in *Beiträge zur alten Gesch.,* i. 51 f.); *e.g.,* the later Attalidae at Pergamum had statues in the temple dedicated to them as divine (pp. 85 f.). The shrinking of the Christian conscience from this deification or apotheosis reveals the significance of the divine honours paid to Jesus in the Apocalypse. The position assigned him by Christian faith was no result of apotheosis.

the solidarity and unity of the empire. Its political convenience, however, lent it increasing momentum. Gradually, on the worship of the *Lares Augusti* in Italy and the capital (Rushforth, pp. 59 f.) and on the association of the imperial cultus with that of *dea Roma* (to whom a temple had been erected at Smyrna as far back as 195 B.C.), the new canonisation rose to its height, never jealous of local cults, but thriving by means of its adaptability to the religious syncretism of the age. It was the religious sanction of the new imperialism.[1] It had temples, sacrifices, choirs (as at Smyrna), and even a priesthood (the *sodales Augustales*) of its own.

For obvious reasons the cult flourished luxuriantly in the provinces, particularly in Asia Minor,[2] where the emperor was often regarded as an incarnation of the local god or named before him. Distance lent enchantment to the provincial view of the emperor. Any sordid traits or idiosyncrasies retired into the background before the adoration felt for the divinity which hedged this unseen, powerful figure, who was hailed with a mixture of servility and real gratitude as "the Saviour," "the Peace," "the αὐτοκράτωρ" of the world, or as the lord of men (κύριος, dominus; *cf.* Kattenbusch, ii. pp. 612 f.). Asia Minor became a hotbed of the cultus. The mere recognition of an abstract empire with its authority providentially vested in the emperor passed often into a religious adulation of the latter, as θεός (*cf.* Thieme's *Inschriften von Magnesia am Mäander u. das N.T.*, pp. 28 f.). The annual festival or diet of the nine Asiatic townships, which served as an organ of government throughout the province, readily coalesced with an annual festival in honour of the reigning

[1] Full investigations by Boissier (*La Religion Romaine*, i. 184 f.), Friedländer (iii. 455 f.), and Mr. B. W. Henderson (*Nero*, pp. 347 f., 434 f.), to be supplemented by Otto Hirschfeld's essay in *Sitzungsberichte d. Akademie d. Wissensch. zu Berlin* (1888), 833 f, the articles in Roscher's *Griech. u. Röm. Mythologie* (ii. pp. 902-919) and in *Prot. Real-Encykl.* (1901), x. 539 f., Wendland's *Hellen.-Römische Kultur in ihren Bezieh. zu Jud. u. Christ.* (1907), §§ 5 and 7, and especially by J. Toutain's pages on the cult of *Roma* (37 f.) and the spread of the imperial cultus generally (pp. 43 f.) in his notable work on *Les cultes païens dans l'Empire Romain* (première partie, tome i. Paris, 1907). Popular sketches in English in L. Dyer's *Studies of the Gods in Greece* (1891, pp. 37, 45); Lecky's *History of European Morals* (i. 257 f.), Westcott's *Epistles of St. John* (235-269), Iverach *H.J.* (1906, 262 f.), Workman's *Persecution in the Early Church* (1906, pp. 94 f.), and Harnack's *Mission and Expansion of Christianity* (1908), i. book ii. chap. ix.

[2] With the title of Jesus (ἡ ἀρχὴ τῆς κτίσεως τοῦ θεοῦ), in Apoc. iii. 14, contrast the servile language of the decree issued (*c.* 9 B.C.) by the Asiatic κοινόν, fixing New Year's Day as the emperor's birthday: ἣν τῇ τῶν πάντων ἀρχῇ ἴσην δικαίως ἂν εἶναι ὑπολάβοιμεν (τοῦτο αὐτῷ ἀρχὴν τοῦ βίου καὶ τῆς ζωῆς γενονέναι). *Cf.* Dittenberger's *Orientis Graeci Inscript. Selectae*, 458.

emperor (Mommsen, *Provinces*, i., 344 f.). The Asiarchs probably organised and pushed the new religion, even more than the local magistrates (*cf.* xiii. 11 f.). At any rate the cultus, attaching itself like mistletoe to institutions and local rites alike, shot up profusely; polytheism found little trouble in admitting the emperor to a place beside the gods, and occasionally, as in the case of Augustus and Apollo, or of Domitian and Zeus, "the emperor was represented as the deity incarnate in human form" (*C. B. P.* i. 53 f.). The islands also shared in this cult, as they had previously shared in the worship of the Ptolemies. At Thera, for example, a pagan altar has been found which was dedicated "to the almighty Caesar, the son of God" (contrast Apoc., ii. 18). This *divi filius* title was one of the most common and least conventional of what John called **βλασφημίας ὀνόματα.**

The inevitable clash between this cult and the sensitive monotheism of Judaism was struck during the latter years of the insane madcap, Caligula (39-41 A.D.). His pretensions to divinity would have been ridiculous, if they had not been dangerous. But he deified himself in literal earnest by means of incense, gestures, and clothing (*cf.* Joseph. *Antiq.* xviii. 7-8, xix. 1-2; Suet. *Calig.* 22); and the climax of his insults to Judaism—the proposed erection of his statue in the temple at Jerusalem—was only averted by the prudent temporising of Petronius and the murder of the emperor himself. Under Claudius matters righted themselves. Still, the shock of the crisis (*cf.* Eus. *H. E.* ii. 5-6) left a deep impression on the conscience of the Jews. It revived the worst memories of Antiochus Epiphanes, and the dread remained, as Tacitus allows, that some other emperor might attempt what Caligula had failed in (*cf.* Spitta 490 f.). Echoes of this are to be heard possibly in 2 Thess. and the synoptic apocalypse as well in Apoc. xiii., which (according to many critics)[1] is based upon a source either Christian (Erbes 19 f., Bruston, Briggs) or Jewish (Spitta, Pfleiderer, de Faye, O. Holtzmann, Rauch adding xvi. 13-14, 16), dating from this period. On this view, the general tenor

[1] Otherwise, xii. 18 - xiii. 7 is held to contain a Jewish fragment (Kohler, J. Weiss), concluded in xix. 11-21, which dates from 70 A.D. Similarly Schmidt, Weyland. Wellhausen, and others (Neronic). "Caligula", in Hebrew (Gaskulgas = קסר גסקלגם) as in Greek (ΓΑΙΟΣ ΚΑΙϹΑΡ) is equivalent by gematria to 616, the variant to which Irenæus objected (*cf.* on xiii. 18); but so is ΚΑΙϹΑΡ ΘΕΟϹ (Deissmann: *Licht vom Osten*, 199 f.) as well as the shortened form of "Nero Caesar". For a discussion of the Beast's number, see the recent symposium by Clemen, Corssen, Bruston, and Vischer in Preuschen's *Zeitschrift für die neutest. Wiss.* 1901-1904.

of the oracle required only a few alterations to render it applicable to the later situation, when Nero and Domitian had become for Christians what Caligula had been for the Jews half a century earlier. The arguments for this literary hypothesis, however, are not oxen strong enough to pull the plough (*cf.* notes on xiii.).

Hitherto Christians had been out of the fray. Even Nero's massacre of them was a freak of personal violence, justified by their reputation for hostility to the State, and apparently prompted by Jewish malevolence. It had nothing whatever to do with the imperial cultus. The latter was not seriously enforced until the second part of Domitian's reign. Like Caligula[1] formerly and Diocletian afterwards, this emperor (*cf.* Schoener, in *Acta Semin. Philologici Erlang.* 1881, pp. 476 f.) laid claim to the title of *dominus et deus*, and though his claim was not official, it was none the less serious. Hence, while he proved a "second Nero" to the Christians no less than to his own restive subjects, the former had special reasons for remembering the reign of terror,

> "When Vespasian's brutal son
> Cleared Rome of what most shamed him."

The strict and harsh enforcement of the poll-tax (Suet. *Domit.* 12) pressed heavily upon the Jews, indeed, but otherwise they were generally undisturbed, since normally, under the semi-tolerant policy of the empire, they were not obliged to erect or worship statues of the emperor (Joseph. *Apion.* ii. 6). They sacrificed for him, not to him. As a national religion, Judaism had its own rights like the rest.[2] But Christianity was not a *religio licita*, and the Nazarene faith, by the sheer force of its principles and the success of its contemporary propaganda, had soon to face the exercise of the law against illicit cults (especially when these refused the test of swearing by the emperor's genius). The very differentiation of Christianity from Judaism, which had become increasingly plain ever since Nero's outburst,[3] deprived the

[1] The bisellium, a splendid double throne, was assigned as a divine honour to Caligula alone after Caesar. Contrast Apoc. xxii. 1.

[2] They suffered under Domitian not for their personal faith but for the success of their propaganda in making proselytes; *cf.* S. Gsell's *Essai sur le Règne de l'Empereur Domitien*, pp. 313 f.

[3] The most recent discussion is by Klette in *Die Christen-Katastrophe unter Nero* (1907; *cf.* the present writer's review in *H. J.*, 1908, 704-707). Renan's coloured pages (pp. 124 f.) and Hausrath's graphic outline (*Hist. of N.T. Times. The Apostles* iv. 168 f.) must be checked by the statements of Ramsay (*Church in Roman Empire*, ch. xi.) and of Mr. B. W. Henderson in his *Life and Principate of the Emperor Nero* (1903).

former of its right to the shelter of the imperial aegis and rendered it liable to the religious and patriotic tax of the Caesar-worship which Domitian's claim now emphasised. The growth of the new faith and the deepening need of the imperial cultus as a national bond of loyalty made a collision between the church and the State inevitable; and, although no literary record exists of the opening movement in the campaign, the correspondence of Trajan and Pliny is now recognised pretty generally to presuppose an earlier stage in the policy of the empire towards Christianity—a stage most probably associated with the later years of Domitian (*cf.* Neumann's *der Röm. Staat u. die allgemeine Kirche bis auf Diocletian*, 1890, i. pp. 7 f. 11-15).[1] Then the conflict became more than sporadic (οἱ πολλοὶ ἐπὶ Δομετιανοῦ διωγμοί, *Mart. Ign.* 1). Domitian not only permitted but encouraged and enforced the payment of divine honours to himself; compliance with the rites of the Caesar cultus was made the convenient test of loyalty for Christians who had hitherto been arraigned for the most part upon criminal charges (*flagitia cohaerentia nomini*) such as anarchy; confession of the Name of Christ now involved a refusal to give the emperor the name of *deus* or *divus*, and, as John put it, all who refused to *worship the image of the beast* or to be *marked by his name* were liable to death. The religious recusant was naturally suspected of *lése majesté*. When his religious susceptibilities were outraged by the quasi-deification of the emperor, his protest was viewed as a veiled pretext for rebellion, as well as an assertion of ἀθεότης or sacrilege (*cf.* for Domitian's reign, Lightfoot's *Clem. Rom.* i. pp. 104-115). But whether *obstinatio* or ἀθεότης or *maiestas*, the crime was visited with the same penalties.

This conflict of loyalties is the business of the Apocalypse. At

[1] The connexion of the Apocalypse with this Domitianic phase is also worked out by A. Matthaei (*Preussische Jahrb.* 1905, 402-479) from the Roman standpoint. He argues (477 f.) that the first θηρίον of ch. xiii. is the imperial cultus itself, while the second symbolises the provincial authorities especially in Asia Minor. Ramsay (*Seven Letters*, p. 97) partly agrees with the latter identification, taking the θηρίον of xiii. 11 f. to mean "the Province of Asia in its double aspect of civil and religious administration," but the probability (see notes) is that the writer is thinking of the Asiatic priests of the imperial cultus, who may have played a part like that of the Buddhist and Taoist priests during the Boxer rising in China, or like that of the officials of the Russian Church in the recent campaign against the Milkist sectaries. It is noticeable that there is no Christian antithesis, in the way of priesthood, to Satan's embodiment in the priesthood of the imperial cultus (xiii. 11 f.), whereas the latter in the sense of *false prophet* is implicitly contrasted with the true prophetic order of Christianity, as are the official ὑμνῳδοί of the cultus at Pergamos and elsewhere with the singers of hymns to God and Jesus in the Apocalypse.

the first shock of persecution in Asia Minor over the principle of the imperial cultus, John grasped with moral power the truth that this was not a local skirmish but a matter of life or death to the church. The issue between ΚΥΡΙΟΣ ΙΗΣΟΥΣ and ΚΥΡΙΟΣ ΚΑΙΣΑΡ was to be neither compromised nor confused; the worship of the emperor, even as a form of patriotism, and the adoration of Jesus as the Christ of God were incompatible. The State did not realise this until afterwards, when the dimensions and irrepressible vigour of the Christian movement revealed it as a menace to the older civilisation of the empire. As yet the Nazarene faith was little more than one of the numerous Oriental weeds which had to be rooted out as immoral, anti-social, and unpatriotic; it was mainly notable for its tenacity of life. The State did not dream as yet of regarding these atheists and anarchists as a rival power. It was contemptuous rather than distrustful of the new faith. That this sect within a sect, or rather this struggling offshoot of the Jewish superstition, would outlive the empire which treated it as the legions treated the daisies on their line of march, must have seemed then the infatuation of a narrow-minded fanatic. History, by justifying this expectation, has proved that it was more than a magnificent reach of the religious instinct, that it was in fact what men have agreed to label rather than define as "inspired". It is true that the messianic and apocalyptic traditions, with which the prophet worked, tended to foreshorten his view of the campaign. The host of martyrs were not crowded into a brief interval, and the triumph of the church over the empire came in a very different way from what the prophet or any of his contemporaries imagined. But the Apocalypse penetrated to the heart of the issue. The resolve which it knit and the hope which it kindled were substantially the faith which nerved the later church, from Ignatius and Polycarp onwards. What "faithfulness to death" (*cf.* ii. 10) involved may be illustrated from the normal procedure of the pro-consul in Bithynia, where Pliny, as he tells us, had people brought before him who were accused, sometimes anonymously and sometimes erroneously, of being Christians. They included persons of both sexes, all ages, and varying health. After being thrice warned, those who still adhered to their confession of faith were, in consequence of the *cognitio* or preliminary investigation, either imprisoned and killed (if provincials, *cf.* Apoc. ii. 13) or deported to Rome (if Roman citizens, *cf.* Apoc. xvii. 6, Ignatius, etc.). Others, however, were not so loyal to their Lord.[1] When an

[1] There were the δειλοὶ and ἄπιστοι, *e.g.*, of Apoc. xxi. 8. Cowardice was particularly dangerous on account of its infectious nature. For the bad example of the

opportunity of recantation was offered, some denied any recent connexion with Christianity, telling the proconsul that they had been (some twenty years ago, *i.e.*, *c.* 93 A.D., the period of the Apocalypse), but no longer were, Christians. Some also had no objection to offer incense before the image of the emperor or to curse publicly the name of Christ. This was the criterion applied to the suspect,[1] and it was largely due to the propagation of such resolute ideas as are expounded in the Apocalypse that Christians were kept loyal to their faith, and that, without a tear in their eye or a sword in their hand, they were able eventually to change the face of the world by enforcing the recognition of their claims at the hands of the empire. Like the conventicles of the Scottish Covenanters, the primitive Christian churches were accused of immorality and sedition, but, unlike them, they succeeded by passive resistance pure and simple. The Apocalypse is a call to arms, but the arms are only patience and loyalty to conviction.[2]

It is unnecessary to assume that any widespread persecution under Domitian, or indeed any "persecution" in the later and technical sense of the term, was before the prophet's mind, in order to account for the language and spirit of the Apocalypse. John himself had only been banished or imprisoned, like some of his friends (ii. 10, *Clem. Rom.* ix. and *cf.* on i. 9). But from the position of matters he already argued the worst. The few cases of repressive interference and of martyrdom in Asia Minor (and elsewhere)

δειλοὶ spies, *cf.* Joseph. *Antiq.*, iii. 15, 1. Ep. Lugd. describes ten renegades "who occasioned us much grief and immeasurable sorrow and impaired the ready zeal of those who had not yet been arrested". "Some remained **ἔξω** (*cf.* Apoc. xxi. 8, xxii. 15), **οἱ μηδὲ ἴχνος πώποτε πίστεως, μηδὲ αἴσθησιν ἐνδύματος νυμφικοῦ, μηδὲ ἔννοιαν φόβου θεοῦ σχόντες**" (*cf.* Apoc. xi. 18).

[1] Pliny's idea of repentance was that Christians should give up their faith. He thought that a number would be willing to recant if they got the opportunity, and Trajan confirmed his suggestion by ordering that *whoever denies himself to be a Christian and makes that plain by his actions, i.e., by worshipping our gods, shall gain forgiveness.* Contrast Apoc. ix. 20, xvi. 9 f. At Vienne and Lyons the Roman citizens in the church were beheaded (*cf.* Apoc. xx. 4, and the cases of John the Baptist and James, Ac. xii. 1). The rest were thrown to the wild beasts or tortured to death in other ways. It must always be remembered that **μάρτυς**, in its sombre sense, did not necessarily imply that a Christian had suffered the death-penalty (*cf.* Tert. *de Fuga* 12, Eus. *H. E.* v. 18, etc.).

[2] *Cf.* xiii. 10, xiv. 12. In spite of the Cameronian touch of xiii. 17, this is the normal temper of the book; it is a Christian expression of the passivity shown already by the Quietists in Judaism, but the controlling motive is the spirit of Jesus as recorded in his own saying (Matt. xxii. 21) and in the reply of his relatives to Domitian (Eus. *H. E.*, ii. 32): "His kingdom is not of this world or of this earth, but heavenly and angelic, to arrive at the consummation of this age".

were enough to warn him of the storm rolling up the sky, though as yet only one or two drops had actually fallen. Eusebius probably exaggerates when he speaks of "many others" along with Clemens and Domitilla (iii. 18), and the period of terror was admittedly short (H. E., xx. 9-11, *cf.* Tert. *Apol.* 5), but the crisis was sufficiently acute to open John's mind to the issues at stake. It is this sense of the irreconcilable antagonism between the imperial cultus and Christianity, not any specific number of martyrdoms, which accounts for the origin of the Apocalypse during the latter years of Domitian. A cursory glance will show that its language presupposes a situation more definite and serious than any covered by earlier references to persecution for *The Name* or *My Name*, which in all likelihood, as 1 Peter indicates, obtained more or less generally after the crisis of 64 A.D. in Rome. John sees another name set up against the name of Christ, and he stamps it as the essence of blasphemy to recognise any such title. What Christians were summoned by him to do was to say "No". Their positive confession of the Christian name resolved itself practically into a refusal to admit the legitimacy of the emperor's divine names.

This power of penetrating to the eternal issues underneath the conflict of the day is one note of the true prophet, and in touching the Apocalypse we touch the living soul of Asiatic Christendom. The book comes forward as a work of prophecy (*cf.* notes on i. 1, 3; xi. 18; xviii. 20, 24; xxii. 6-7, etc.). As such it is designed for the instruction and encouragement of the Christian society (1 Cor. xiv. 3 f.). It fulfils this design by means of visions depicting (*a*) the approach and certainty of the Christ's return, (*b*) the warnings and comfort of God for the churches during the interval, and (*c*) the bliss and terror of the world to come. Ordinarily the revelation takes the form of rapture or vision. This, again, may pass into an address in which the prophet leaves the *rôle* of seer for that of spiritual adviser. Or, rhapsody may become a song (ψαλμός), reflecting the antiphonal outbursts of melody (*E. Bi.* 2138-2140, 3242) in the congregation (*cf.* the responsive *Amen* in v. 14, vii. 12, the Trisagion in iv. 8, and the Hallelujah in xix. 1 f.) which were based in part upon earlier Jewish psalms of the synagogue (as Pliny found in Bithynia: "carmen Christo quasi deo dicere secum inuicem"). Finally, the prophet may work along the lines of traditional apocalyptic oracles which were more or less familiar to his hearers, just as the author of Daniel took Jeremiah's seventy weeks as one of his texts. All these varieties are represented in the Apocalypse of John. But, whatever *rôle* he assumes, the seer or speaker is pre-eminently a prophet, and the Christian prophet is ranked beside Moses and the angels as the *servant of God* κατ' ἐξοχήν. The order of prophets is second only to the apostles.

If it is the vocation of the prophet to reveal and emphasise the faith, it is the corresponding duty of the martyr to be loyal at all costs to that faith in the killing times. Hence the martyr or confessor is, next to the prophet, the most prominent figure in the landscape of the Apocalypse. One of the tests proposed (most unfairly) by an anti-Montanist in the second century as a criterion of Montanist prophecy was its capacity for producing martyrs. Did it inspire a faith equal to the stress of persecution? Was the religion it fostered strenuous enough to provoke persecution? The crisis of the imperial cultus under Domitian seemed to John at any rate to demand an attitude of passive resistance[1] on the part of Christians which involved the risk of death. Neither rebellion nor suicide was to be contemplated as a means of escape, and flight was out of the question. Whither could one flee from the Caesar? The Christian must be prepared to be *faithful unto death*, and if there is any distinction among Christians drawn by the prophet's mind it lies not between Jewish and Gentile Christians, but between the martyrs on the one hand and the rank and file of the church upon the other. The martyr is *primus inter pares*; an exceptional place and space is assigned him for his persistent fidelity. At the same time the extravagant prerogatives of the martyrs and the confessors in later Christian belief lie outside the purview of the Apocalypse. The prophet's homage to them is partly due to the exceptional circumcumstances of the "killing" time, and the permanent element underlying it is the truth (witnessed by Zoroastrianism in its own way, *cf. Encycl. Rel. and Ethics*, i. 210) that history is neither caprice nor blind fate, but a moral order in which sacrifice for the sake of Christ and loyalty to God are not water spilt upon the ground—a moral order, too, whose end is bound up with the person of Jesus Christ as Lord and Redeemer. It was perhaps inevitable that the expression of this great religious conception should, by its very emphasis, lead to some exaggeration. The flood-tide which submerges some truths isolates others in a position of abnormal prominence. Thus the Apocalypse, which is a tract for the bad times of persecution, views the philosophy of history as catastrophe rather

[1] With xiii. 9-10 compare the Jewish high-priest's prayer on the day of atonement (Jer. Jom. v. 42 c.), that "neither this day nor through this year may any captivity come upon us. . . . And as for Thy people Israel, let no enemy exalt himself against them."

than as growth; the virtues of asceticism and even celibacy (*cf.* on xiv. 4) acquire unwonted prominence; sensuous aspects of the messianic reign tend to predominate; the impulse of propaganda is checked by the sombre and fore-shortened view of the world which the presentiment of approaching judgment fostered; religion tends to be bound up with a hatred and fear of the civil power;[1] and God is a dazzling, silent, enthroned figure of majesty, who has men warned and wounded, not (as in the fourth gospel) a Father who is in direct touch with his children upon earth. The passion for moral retribution regards material and political convulsions more and more as the proper dynamic of providence. To John's eyes, the cause of affairs in the empire of his day was running straight to the edge of a precipice. He saw in history not any τύχη or εἱμαρμένη but the justice and irony of providence abroad, and his puritanic temper expressed itself in a mixture of spiritual resignation with an imperious and vindictive expectation:—

> Rome shall perish! write that word
> In the blood that she has spilt.

This expectation is only a heightened form of the traditional belief (*cf.* 4th Esd. xii. 11 f., Apoc. Bar. iv. 4-5) that the fourth kingdom of Daniel's vision was the Roman empire, which was to be overthrown at the advent of messiah's reign. Josephus prudently evades this interpretation, though he is well aware of it. His business, he protests, is not to explain the future (*Antiq.* x. 10. 4). But the interpretation was widespread in apocalyptic circles, and a Christian had special reasons for sharing it. John expresses it with characteristic vigour. He will encourage no fifth-monarchy tendencies among Christians in Asia Minor, but he has no word of showing loyalty to the empire as distinguished from worshipping the emperor. He makes no attempt, such as Agrippa made before Caligula (*Leg. ad Gaium*, 36), to disprove the charge of treason, and no considerations of patriotism qualify his threats of doom against the Roman empire.[2]

[1] It cannot be too strongly insisted that the tone of the Apocalypse here was neither normal nor final. Indeed the subsequent history of the church bears out this verdict. The Asiatic idiosyncrasies of its eschatology, and above all of its relation to the State are thrown into relief against the "loyalist" tone of a contemporary Roman writing like that of *Clemens Romanus*. The moderation of this fine epistle is attributed by Lightfoot (*Clem. Rom.*, i. pp. 27 f. 60 f. 382 f.) to the fact that its author and bearers were connected with the imperial household.

[2] Dr. Selwyn actually conjectures (pp. 124 f.) that the prophet was banished for having written the seditious oracles of iv.-xxii., and that when he re-edited the work (adding i.- ii.) during Galba's reign it was only the strong anti-Neronic feeling at Ephesus which saved him from capital punishment as a traitor (pp. 214 f.).

§ 7. *The Date.*—When the motive of the Apocalypse is thus found in the pressure upon the Christian conscience exerted by Domitian's emphasis of the imperial cultus, especially as that was felt in Asia Minor, any earlier date for the book becomes almost impossible (*cf.* Mommsen's *Provinces of Rom. Empire*, ii. 175 f.). The traditional alternative, *i.e.*, the reign of Claudius, is absurd. The Neronic date (*i.e.*, soon after Nero's death) exerts most of its fascination on those who cling to too rigid a view of the book's unity, which prevents them from looking past passages like xi. 1 f. and xvii. 9 f. But (*a*) the phase of the Nero-redivivus myth which is represented in the Apocalypse cannot be earlier than at least the latter part of Vespasian's reign; (*b*) the church of Smyrna, as we know from Polycarp (ad Phil. xi.) was not founded by 64 A.D., and it is impossible to crush the development implied in ii. 8-11 into a few years; (*c*) the conception of the new Jerusalem implies a post-70 date (*cf.* notes on xxi.-xxii.); (*d*) no worship of the emperor, adequate to explain the data of the Apocalypse, was enforced under Nero; and (*e*) the allusions to the martyrs (ii. 13, and especially vi. 10-11—the *How long?* of the Neronic victims, and their subsequent comrades in martyrdom) surely presuppose a much longer period than three or four years. For recent English statements of the Neronic date, see Selwyn (pp. 215 f.) and Mr. B. W. Henderson (*op. cit.* pp. 439 f.). The Vespasianic date (*cf.* V. Bartlet, *Apostolic Age*, 388-408; Scott, 48-56), which has rather a better case in the internal evidence of the book, is ruled out of court by (*d*). The lack of any traditional reference to persecution under this emperor would not indeed be a decisive argument by itself; it is only by the letters of Pliny that we happen to know anything of the troubles experienced by Asiatic Christians under Trajan, and a similar outburst under Vespasian might have passed unnoticed by Christian or pagan writers. But this is unlikely.[1] In any case, Vespasian did not take his inherited and official divinity seriously. Christians had a temporary and comparative immunity under him, and "so rapidly did their influence grow that they even made converts in the imperial family itself" (*cf.* Lightfoot, *Clem. Rom.* ii. 507). Parts of the Apocalypse, taken singly (*e.g.*, in xiii.), might be referred to Vespasian's reign, but, unlike Domitian, he does not seem to have interfered with Oriental

[1] An even stronger term might be used, in view of the researches by critics like Matthaei, Gsell, Neumann and Ramsay. The extreme unlikelihood of the Apocalypse being elicited by anything during the reigns of Titus or Vespasian is also recognised by Linsenmayer in his *Bekämpfung des Christentums durch den römischen Staat* (1905), pp. 66 f.

cults. Thus, since the general intensity of John's language about martyrdom cannot be explained altogether as either a reminiscence of the Neronic outburst or as a prophetic anticipation of what was to be expected at the hands of the world-power during the latter days—for some concrete occasion is necessary to account for the prophet's standpoint—the most probable solution is that Christians were being persecuted here and there in Asia Minor for what Domitian (as Neumann and others rightly point out) regarded as a cardinal offence, *viz.*, the refusal to acknowledge him as the divine head of the empire. The religious development of the churches is often held to presuppose a considerable length of time, but this argument must be used with caution. Worldliness and error and uncharitable feelings did not require decades to spring up in the primitive churches of Asia Minor and elsewhere. No great stress can be laid on this feature. Still, the character of the heresies described in ii.-iii. certainly presupposes an acquaintance with incipient gnosticism which requires a later period than 70 A.D. for its development.

The one passage (apart from vi. 6, where see note) which appears to be a water-mark of the date is unfortunately ambiguous (see notes on xvii.), as it contains an earlier Vespasianic source. But in xvii. 10-11 so much at least seems clear. The numbers are literal, not symbolical. The reckoning probably begins with Augustus as the first emperor; the three usurpers (Galba, Otho and Vitellius) are passed over (*cf.* Suet. *Vesp.* 1: rebellione trium principum et caede incertum diu et quasi uagum imperium suscepit firmauitque tandem gens Flavia), as was only natural to a provincial, who would be specially apt to regard their struggle as a brief nightmare. The sixth and reigning emperor (ὁ εἷς ἔστιν) is Vespasian (69-79 A.D.), with whom the Flavian dynasty took up the imperial succession, after Nero's death, which ended the Julian dynasty, had well-nigh broken up the empire (*cf.* xiii. 3 f.). Vespasian's successor (Titus, 79-81 A.D.) is to have a very brief reign.[1] As a matter of fact it only lasted for a couple of years. After him, the deluge! Nero-redivivus (τὸ θηρίον), incorporating the full Satanic power of the empire, who had already reigned on earth (ὃ ἦν) but who meanwhile was

[1] This might be (*a*) a *uaticinium ex euentu*, or (*b*) an eschatological inference (a writer, composing under the sixth emperor of a series which was only to number seven, would naturally argue that, as the end was near, the seventh emperor could not have long to reign), or (*c*) a reflection of the widespread feeling (*cf.* Schiller's *Gesch. d. Röm. Kaiserzeit*, i. 520) that the poor health of Titus would not permit him to reign for very long.

invisible (καὶ οὐκ ἔστιν) was to reappear from the abyss, only to be crushed finally (καὶ εἰς ἀπώλειαν ὑπάγει). In its present form the oracle announces that the downfall of the empire is to be heralded by the reappearance after Titus of one belonging to the seven emperors (ἐκ τῶν ἑπτά ἐστιν) who, on the traditional scheme of the *heads*, were to see the rise and ruin of the State. Here a literary problem of some nicety emerges, for, while ver. 10 implies the reign of Vespasian, ver. 11 points to an eighth emperor (evidently Domitian). The solution is either that the writer of both throws himself back in thought into Vespasian's age, representing history under the form of apocalyptic prophecy, or that ver. 11 (Domitian recalling and playing the part of Nero) represents a later addition,[1] inserted in order to bring the source up to date. In either case the final standpoint is Domitianic, however, and this tallies with the general evidence of the rest of the book.[2]

It also tallies with second-century tradition. In describing the persecution of Christians by Domitian, that worthy successor of Nero, Eusebius (*H. E.* iii. 18) quotes the following words from Irenaeus on the name of Antichrist; εἰ δὲ ἔδει ἀναφανδὸν ἐν τῷ νῦν καιρῷ κηρύττεσθαι τοὔνομα αὐτοῦ, δι᾽ ἐκείνου ἂν ἐρρέθη τοῦ καὶ τὴν ἀποκάλυψιν ἑορακότος. οὐδὲ γὰρ πρὸ πολλοῦ χρόνου ἑωράθη, ἀλλὰ σχεδὸν ἐπὶ τῆς ἡμετέρας γενεᾶς, πρὸς τῷ τέλει τῆς Δομετιανοῦ ἀρχῆς. The attempts to turn the force of this passage by supposing that Irenaeus confounded Domitian's actual reign with his temporary regency in 70 A.D., or by referring ἑωράθη to the seer instead of to the vision, are ingenious but quite unconvincing. The tradition must be taken as it stands. Originally, as πρὸς τῷ τέλει

[1] "To me it seems that there are two distinct notes of time in the passage, and that we are almost compelled to suppose that what was written at one date has been adapted to another" (Dr. Sanday in *Journ. Theol. Studies*, viii. 492).

[2] This kind of elusive, enigmatic reckoning is illustrated by the Jewish Domitianic apocalypse in 4 Esd. iii-.xiv. and by Barn. iv. In the former, the Roman empire is an eagle with three heads (*i.e.* the Flavian dynasty: Vespasian, Titus, and Domitian), the first of which rules the earth oppressively, the second of which is devoured by the third (alluding to the belief that Domitian had made away with his brother), while the third is to be challenged and vanquished by messiah (a parallel to John's prediction). The Christian writing, in order to prove the nearness of the end, quotes Dan. vii. 7-8 and 24 for the purpose of showing that *from the beast* (*i.e.* the Roman empire) *ten horns* were to spring (*i.e.* the Caesars from Julius to Vespasian or Domitian) and *from them a little horn by way of excrescence* (παραφυάδιον, *i.e.* Nero antichrist) which will abase *three of the great horns* (*i.e.* the Flavian dynasty) Similarly Daniel's addition of the 11th horn to the traditional 10 illustrates John's apocalyptic revisal of the 7 heads. The only σοφία of the Apocalypse is the knack of solving puzzles in this province of religious arithmetic (xiii. 18, xvii. 9).

suggests, it was more precise and extended. It was held by Hippolytus, Clement of Alexandria, Jerome, and Victorinus, possibly even by Hegesippus at an earlier date, if Dr. Lawlor is correct in his argument (*Journ. Theol. Studies*, viii. 436 f.) that the statements of Eusebius (*H.E.* iii. 11-20) were borrowed from that writer's *Hypomnemata;* indeed, no other early tradition has anything like the same support or plausibility. Irenaeus, of course, is no great authority by himself on matters chronological, but he is reporting here what there was no obvious motive for inventing. The internal and the external evidence thus converge upon the latter part of the reign of Domitian as the period of the book's composition or publication. Little more than half a century later, one of its first commentators, bishop Melito of Sardis, protested to Marcus Aurelius that "of all the emperors it was Nero and Domitian alone who, at the instigation of certain slanderous persons," assailed the Christian church (so Lact. *De Morte Persec.* 3). Whether Melito knew this independently of the Apocalypse or not, we need have very little hesitation (*cf.* Stephan Gsell's *Essai sur le règne de l'Empereur Domitien*, 1894, pp. 307 f.) in collating this persecution with the book in question.

§ 8. *The Author.*—The settlement of the date clears up the problem of the authorship to this extent, that it confirms the disjunctive canon of Dionysius (*cf.* Lücke, § § 39-42 ; Simcox xxiii. f. xxxiii. f.), Origen's thoughtful pupil, who saw, upon grounds of internal evidence, that it was impossible for the Apocalypse and the Fourth Gospel to have come from the same pen. Were the Apocalypse dated earlier, it could be supposed that John had matured during the interval, since twenty or twenty-five years' residence in a Greek city might be conjectured to have improved his style and widened his outlook. But when the Apocalypse has to be dated in the same decade as the Fourth Gospel, the hypothesis of a single author collapses. While the data of vocabulary, style, and thought suggest that both writings originated in a school or circle of Asiatic Christians, they differentiate the one book from the other unambiguously.[1]

Hardly any writing in the New Testament loses so little, or gains so much, by translation as the Apocalypse, for almost any version

[1] Recent, though rather extreme, statements are to be found in J. Réville's *Le Quatr. Évangile* (1901), pp. 26-47, 333 f. in Selwyn (pp. 81 f. 114 f., 222 f., 258 f., the Fourth Gospel = a correction not only of the synoptists but of the Apocalypse), and in Schmiedel's article (*E.B.* ii. ii. 2515-2518). As Alford admits, "the Greek of the Gospel and Epistle is not that of the Apocalypse in a maturer state".

serves to obliterate most of the exceptionally numerous and glaring irregularities of its syntax. But one drawback of this advantage is that the distinctive characteristics of the book are less vividly felt; the further one goes from the original, the less visible are those idiosyncrasies of conception, style, and construction which mark off the Apocalypse from the rest of the early Christian literature and notably from the Fourth Gospel. The psychological difference by itself should not be pressed too far. One has only to recollect men like Samuel Rutherford and Keble, to understand how vindictiveness to religious opponents is compatible with a sweet and even devout spiritual tone in certain natures. But the disjunctive canon in the present case proceeds from a wider induction. Thus *e.g.* the weil-known resemblances of the Lamb and the Logos are both specious and secondary. The former (τὸ ἀρνίον Apoc.; ὁ ἀμνὸς τοῦ θεοῦ, Gospel, ἀρνίον being reserved for Christians) does not exist in the original, nor is it peculiar to the Johannine literature. The latter again (ὁ λόγος τ. θεοῦ, Apoc.; ὁ λόγος, Gospel) is verbal (*cf.* note on xix. 13); the two ideas are adapted from totally different soils in pre-Christian Judaism and for alien ends. Some closer analogies, such as (*a*) the relation of God, Christ, and the believer (*cf.* on ii. 27, iii. 19 f.), (*b*) the use of the partitive ἐκ, ἵνα, δείκνυμι (of revelation), etc., (*c*) the explanation of Hebrew terms, (*d*) formulas like μετὰ ταῦτα, and (*e*) phrases about witnessing or keeping God's word (commandments), do not necessarily imply more than a common *milieu* of thought and expression such as contemporary writers belonging to the same school might naturally employ. A common religious dialect often produces similar instances of corresponding or coincident expression in different authors of the same period. On the other hand, the Apocalypse has a vocabulary of its own, whose peculiarities are not to be explained simply from the subject matter; *e.g.* δοῦλοι θεοῦ (in explicit contrast to Joh. xv. 15), λατρεύειν, οἰκουμένη, παντοκράτωρ, πίστις, ὑπομονή, etc. besides cases of the multiplied genitive (xiv. 8, etc.). It ignores many favourite and even characteristic terms of the Fourth evangelist, *e.g.* ἀλήθεια, ἀληθής, ἀληθῶς, ἀπεκρίθη κ. εἶπεν, ἀφιέναι τὰς ἁμαρτίας, θεᾶσθαι, ἴδε, ἴδιος, καθὼς, μετὰ τοῦτο, πάντοτε, παρρησία, πώποτε, ὑψοῦσθαι, χάρα, sonship (*cf.* on xxi. 7) asking (ἐρωτάω) God, *darkness*, μὲν . . . δέ, μένειν (except in xvii. 10, historically), πονηρός or ἄρχων τοῦ κόσμου (of the devil), to be of God or to be born of God, love to God or Christ, ὑπέρ with genitive, ἀντί, ὑπό (accus.), μέντοι, etc., etc. Even where the Apocalypse uses certain terms or ideas of the Fourth Gospel, it is in a different sense; *e.g.* αἰώνιος (only in xiv. 6, never with ζωή), *light* and *the world* (physically not spiritually), ἐκεῖνος (never substantival), ἐμός (only once), οὖν of logical appeal[1] (not of historical transition), Ἱερουσαλήμ not Ἱεροσόλυμα, νικᾶν (never transitive, and in special sense *cf.* on ii. 7), judgment (outward and dramatic, not inward), *the Spirit* (wholly prophetic, in contrast to the inward Comforter of the Gospel), σημαίνειν, ὑπάγειν, etc. Furthermore, the Fourth Gospel ignores, often deliberately, a large number of words or phrases used not only by the Apocalypse (once at least) but by the earlier synoptic Gospels; *e.g.* ἀναγινώσκω (of Scriptures), ἀποδίδωμι, ἀπόστολοι, ἄρσην, ἀφαιρέω, βασανίζειν, βδέλυγμα, βίβλος, γαστήρ, γρηγορεῖν, γυνή (wife), δαιμόνια, δένδρον, διαθήκη, δίκαιος (of men), δῶρον, ἔθνη (=Gentiles), εἰκών, ἔλαιον, ἐνδύειν, ἑπτά, ἐσθίω, ἔσχατος, ἔσωθεν (ἔξωθεν), εὐαγγέλιον (*cf.* on xiv. 6), ἑξήκοντα, ἐχθρός, ἥλιος, θρόνος, ἰσχύς, ἰσχυρός, κληρονομεῖν, κλίνη, κηρύσσειν, κόπτω, λιμός, λοιπός, λυχνία, μακρόθεν, μαρτύριον, μάρτυς, μηδείς, μετρέω, μικροί, μυστήριον, νεφέλη, ὀλίγος, ὀμνύειν, ὀδούς, οὐαί, οὖς (contrast John xviii. 10, 26), πάσχω, πατάσσειν, περί (accus.), πέτρα, πίστις, πλοῦτος (-σιος), ποτίζειν, πόλεμος, πρεσβύτεροι, προσευχή, πρόσωπον, ῥάβδος, ῥίζα, σεισμός, σελήνη, σκηνή, σοφία, σταυρόω, σφόδρα, ὑψηλός, φυλακή, ψευδοπροφήτης, and χήρα. The Apocalypse also substitutes ἔρχου for ἐλθέ, and uses phrases like ἄξιος with infin. for ἄξιος with ἵνα. The eschatological differences of conception, which are too patent to require comment or to admit of harmonising, corroborate the impression made by this argument from words. Such features, linguistic and mental (*cf. e.g.* on i. 4, ii. 7, iii. 21, vii. 15), are not due to literary versatility, nor to an imaginary growth in the same writer's vocabulary and soul, nor even to a common editorial revision. The argument from solecisms (*cf.* § 1) and regular irregularities of style, from the special vocabulary, and above all from the realistic type of religious feeling, may be cumulative, but it is none the less able to support the contention that whilst the Fourth Gospel and the Apocalypse must have sprung from the same circle of Asiatic Christianity, they could not have been written by the same person within a few years of each other; the divergences of eschatology, angelology, and Christology—which represent the crucial points of comparison between the two books—are almost as clearly cut in Apoc. i.-iii., where the Apocalypse is least apocalyptic, as in the later oracles. In general, it would not be irrelevant to apply to the Fourth Gospel and the Apocalypse the terms used by Dionysius of Halicarnassus to characterise the works of Herodotus and Thucydides respectively; the one is radiant (ἱλαρόν), the other is awe-inspiring (φοβερόν).

[1] This is particularly significant, since, as the Apocalypse "is largely made up of narrative, we might have expected narrative οὖν in abundance if it had been written by the hand that wrote the Fourth Gospel" (Abbott, *Joh. Grammar*, p. 479).

While the author of the Apocalypse cannot have been the author of the Fourth Gospel, his personality is partially disclosed by the internal evidence of the book, which shows that it was the work of a Jewish Christian prophet called John (i. 1, 9, etc.) who was in close touch with the Asiatic churches. It is a προφητεία, and as such it is ranked by the first Christian writer of the second century who definitely mentions it (*cf.* Justin's *Dial.*, 81, 82). It was intended to be read aloud in the worship[1] of those Christian congregations, primarily but not exclusively, to which its opening messages were addressed. In reality it is a sort of catholic epistle as it stands (*cf.* ii. 7, etc., xxii. 16, 21), an open letter or manifesto to the churches. The authority claimed by John is that of a prophet, not of an apostle. The seven Asiatic communities may have lain within his circuit or diocese, but the data of Apoc. ii.-iii. do not suggest any specifically concrete relations between the prophet and the churches. He does not seem to have founded any of them, nor does he promise to re-visit them. Upon the other hand, John claims no special relation to Jesus Christ, and there is no distinct evidence that he had been an eye-witness of Jesus the messiah upon earth. None of the visions implies any such personal intimacy; indeed that of i. 9 f. tells against it, for the apocalyptic categories which dominate the opening vision are not such as might be expected from one who had been among the Galilean disciples.[2] It may be replied that an apocalypse is not a gospel, and that in an apocalypse it was the qualities of a προφήτης which would naturally be prominent. But this only raises the further psychological problem: how should a primitive disciple adopt such categories? The reference in xviii. 20 does not absolutely exclude the possibility of John having been an apostle, for ἀπόστολος is here employed in its wider sense, and in any case the addition of προφῆται shows that this προφήτης might have equally well referred objectively to the class or order to which he

[1] Passages like i. 3, ii. 7, etc., xiii. 9, 18, xxii. 7, reflect this ecclesiastical use, while the explanatory comments in iv. 5 (ἅ εἰσιν . . . θεοῦ); v. 6 (οἵ εἰσιν . . . γῆν), v. 8 (ἅ εἰσιν . . . ἁγίων), xviii. 24, xix. 8 (τὸ γὰρ . . . ἐστίν), xix. 10 (ἡ γὰρ . . . προφητείας), xix. 13 (καὶ κέκληται . . . θεοῦ), xx. 14 (οὗτος . . . πυρός), sound often like prose glosses which in some cases may have been inserted by the author himself or a general editor, but in others were probably due to the interpretative reading in the churches. A partial analogy is furnished by the influence of the players on the text of Shakespeare's plays.

[2] The seer never says, *I saw the Lord Jesus*, or, *Behold, the Lord Jesus.* Contrast Acts vii. 55, 56, etc. "Jesus speaks through His Spirit under various forms or without any form, and is never beheld in the form He wore in Galilee" (Abbott, p. 214). *Cf.* Prof. A. S. Peake, in Mansfield College Essays (1909), pp. 89-106.

belonged. The unique allusion in xxi. 14 to *the twelve apostles of the Lamb*, however, has an objective and retrospective tinge, which, though it does not absolutely rule out apostolic authorship, points in that direction. It is not a subtle anti-Pauline touch, for even Paul did not number himself among the twelve (1 Cor. xv. 5), but when it is collated with such discrepancies as that between xi. 1-2 and Mk. xiii. 2 (*cf.* also iii. 21 with Mk. x. 37-40) or that between Ac. i. 6-8 and the apocalyptic calcu ations of the end (see further, on iii. 21, vii. 1-3, 14, ix. 15) the result is a cumulative argument in favour of some primitive Christian who sat looser to the synoptic tradition than a disciple such as the son of Zebedee would have done. During last century the apostolic authorship of the book, in conjunction with the Neronic date, was urged by Baur (*cf. Church Hist. of First Three Centuries*, i. 84 f., 153 f.) and his school, on the double ground that it represented a type of narrow Jewish Christianity in the apostolic church, and that it contained an overt polemic against the apostle Paul. Neither of these arguments is seaworthy at the present day, although the anti-Pauline reference becomes a much more serious question, when the Nero or Galba date is chosen, than some recent defenders of the latter hypothesis appear to realise. The Apocalypse has the Pauline teaching behind it (*cf.* iii. 14, xxii. 17), but it neither reproduces any of the Pauline idiosyncrasies nor opposes Paul personally. It goes back to the popular Jewish Christianity of the primitive churches, whose "theology" consisted primarily in a belief that Jesus, the true messiah, had secured the forgiveness of sins for his people and would return presently to establish the divine βασιλεία. The writer ignores any problem of the law or of the resurrection of the body. Echoes of the synoptic tradition are audible enough, particularly of its Lucan form, and one feature of the teaching of Jesus is preserved carefully, *viz.*, the belief in the catastrophic advent of the βασιλεία; but no evidence is available to prove a literary filiation between it and any of the synoptic gospels.[1]

[1] So far as the local colour is not derived from O.T. traditions, it may be ascribed, as, *e.g.*, by Mr. Theodore Bent (*Nineteenth Century*, 1888, 813-881, *cf.* also *Historical New Testament*, p. 688) to a personal acquaintance with Palestine and Asia Minor (see on iv. 2, vi. 12 f., viii. 8 f., ix. 16, 18, xxii. 2). Thus, *e.g.*, the references to the appearance or the disappearance (*cf.* the case of Chrysê near Lemnos, told by Pausanias, viii. 33-4) of islands reflect the insular situation of Patmos, from which several of the Ægean islands were at least visible (Tozer: *Islands of the Aegean*, pp. 178-95), as well as the volcano of Santorin. The crater of some Mediterranean volcano may have lent special point to *the lake of fire and brimstone.* But John's imagination is stronger than his susceptibility to his environment, though

Who was this John? Was he some otherwise unknown figure (ἄλλον τινα τῶν ἐν Ἀσίᾳ γενομένων, Dionysius) in the primitive church of Asia Minor (so *e.g.*, J. Reville, F. C. Porter, Jülicher)? This is possible, for the name was common enough. But, if it is felt that the work must be connected with a more authoritative personality, tradition offers us the choice of three figures. (*a*) That of John Mark (so *e.g.*, Hitzig, Weisse, and Hausrath), whom Dionysius of Alexandria mentions in this connection but only to set aside on the score of his un-Asiatic career, need not be seriously discussed, though Beza favoured his claims ("quod si liceret ex stylo conjecturam facere, nemini certe potius quam Marco tribuerim qui et ipse Johannes dictus est"). The real alternative lies between (*b*) John the son of Zebedee, and (*c*) John the presbyter, both of whom have strong traditional claims. The latter is not to be emended out of existence by any manipulation of the text of Papias, and we have no reason to regard the one as the *doppelgänger* of the other. Whether Eusebius was right in arguing from that text or from other evidence that Papias was one of his hearers, John ὁ πρεσβύτερος was an important Christian disciple; his authority was so great that he could be called ὁ πρεσβύτερος without any further designation. There is strong and early support for (*b*) in tradition, but the internal evidence, as we have seen, is at best neutral and in certain lights unfavourable. It is impossible here to analyse that tradition in its bearings upon the Apocalypse, but it may be said that there were special reasons which contributed to its popularity (*cf.* § 9). Internal evidence weighed less with the early church than other considerations. The wavering position of the Apocalypse required nothing short of apostolic sanction to keep it within the canon, and indeed apostolic authorship came more and more to be tantamount to inspiration. Under these circumstances it was not easy for any theory or tradition of unapostolic authorship to keep its footing. Mr. Conybeare puts this succinctly (*The Armenian Text of Revelation*, pp. 161 f.): "Between 350 and 450 Greek texts of Revelation were rare in the Eastern half of the empire. The best minds of the Greek Church, men such as Eusebius Pamphili and Dionysius of Alexandria, denied its Johannine authorship. Living in an age when

sometimes it is not fanciful to trace a special significance in some conventional phrase, *e.g.*, the boom of the Mediterranean in i. 15, or in vi. 15-16—an allusion to the Sipylus range, north of the Gulf of Smyrna, where cisterns and holes cut in the rocks afforded temporary shelter to the population during the frequent panics caused by earthquakes on the coast (*cf.* Perrot and Chipiez, *History of Art in Phrygia*, Eng. tr., 1892, pp. 61-62).

old Greek was still the language of every-day life, they were too conscious of the contrasts of style which separate it from the Fourth gospel to accept the view that a single author wrote both. Having to accept John the apostle as author of one or the other, they decided in favour of the gospel. In the West, on the other hand, where both documents circulated only in a Latin dress, men were unconscious of these contrasts of style, and so found no difficulty in accepting both as writings of the apostle John." Hence, taking the Apocalypse by itself on the one hand and the tradition of John the presbyter on the other, we find both converging on the conclusion that, even if John the apostle did survive till the end of the first century in Asia Minor, it was not he but his namesake who wrote the Johannine Apocalypse. καὶ οἱ πρεσβύτεροι ὑμῶν ἐνυπνίοις ἐνυπνιασθήσονται (Acts ii. 17), under the influence of the prophetic spirit. In this case, the term πρεσβύτερος (as in 2 John ver. 3, and 3 John ver. 1) is the Christian term of honour and authority (*cf.* Deissmann, 154 f., 233 f.), not the Jewish term[1] for a member of the Sanhedrin (πρεσβύτης). Occasionally, as in the case of John, the presbyter must have had prophetic gifts; the fragments preserved by Irenæus from the tradition of the Asiatic presbyters point unmistakably to prophetic and even chiliastic tendencies, though they are more sensuous than in the corresponding features in the Apocalypse. John was also a μαθητὴς τοῦ κυρίου in the wider sense of the term. He was one of the most important authorities who were in touch with apostolic tradition, and it is easier to credit him with the rabbinic erudition and apocalyptic lore of the Apocalypse than one who was ἀγράμματος καὶ ἰδιώτης (Acts iv. 13).

A further possibility (recognised by Erasmus) lies in the direction of pseudonymity. Apocalypses were almost invariably pseudonymous, and it is held by some (*e.g.*, S. Davidson, Weizsäcker, Wernle, Forbes, and Bacon in *Expositor*, 1907, 233 f.), that the presumption is in favour of John's Apocalypse also belonging to the pseudepigrapha. This would be rendered more probable, were it taken to include fragments or traditions which were really due to John Mark (Spitta, Völter), John the son of Zebedee (Erbes, Bruston), or John the presbyter (J. Weiss, so differently Bousset and Schmiedel). But it does not follow that an early Christian apocalypse must necessarily be pseudonymous. Hermas is not. Besides, one *raison d'être* for pseudonymity is absent, *viz.*, the consciousness that the prophetic

[1] So Selwyn (127 f.), holding that the author of the Apocalypse retained his earlier Jewish title. But it is prosaic to see that semi-circular court reflected in iv. 2 f., or to find evidence of special legal knowledge in v. 1 and xii. 10.

spirit was no longer present in the church. The amount of antedated prediction in the Apocalypse (*i.e.*, in xiii. xvii.), too, is barely adequate, of itself, to support this theory. And it may be argued that a pseudonymous writer would probably have been more explicit upon the apostolic authority of John, *i.e.*, if John the apostle was the John under whose name he issued the Apocalypse. The case for the latter form of the hypothesis would be strengthened, of course, if it could be shown, as many critics have recently attempted to prove, that the tradition of John's early martyrdom is reliable. In any case the ardent and even vindictive spirit of the Apocalypse is not to be connected necessarily with Luke ix. 55. Such a passionate, unpatriotic temper would be as much due to the apocalyptic traditions and to the local exigencies of the period as to any personal idiosyncracy, and if John retained this feeling till the end of the century, or even till the seventh or eighth decade, he must have profited very little by the lesson which Jesus had read him long ago. When he is connected with the tradition or authorship of the Fourth gospel, the supposition that he was responsible for the attitude of the Apocalypse becomes doubly, trebly difficult.

To sum up. The Apocalypse was a product of the "Johannine" school or circle in Asia Minor, towards the close of the first century. Beyond the disjunctive canon that it was not composed by the author of the Fourth Gospel, but that it may have been written by the presbyter whose name appears in the address of 2 and 3 John, we can hardly go, in our comparison of the Johannine writings. The data of tradition are unfortunately ambiguous and contradictory, but, whether or not the son of Zebedee resided in Asia Minor, the presbyter John seems on the whole to suit the requirements of the Apocalypse better than any other contemporary figure, and, unless we are content with Castellio and others to share the pious reticence of Dionysius (ὅτι μὲν οὖν Ἰωάννης ἐστὶν ὁ ταῦτα γράφων, αὐτῷ λέγοντι πιστευτέον· ποῖος δὲ οὗτος, ἄδηλον), the balance of probability is in favour either of pseudonymity or of the hypothesis that the prophet John who composed the Apocalypse was the presbyter John of early Christian tradition (so after Dionysius, from various standpoints,[1] Eichhorn, Wittichen, De Wette, Mangold, Credner, Bleek, Ewald, Keim, Havet, Düsterdieck, Selwyn, Erbes, O. Holtzmann, Harnack, Kohler, Von Soden, Heinrici (*Das Urchristenthum*, 1902, 126 f.), and Von Dobschütz (*Probleme d. apost. Zeitalters*, 1904, 91 f.).

[1] Grotius: "Credo autem presbytero, apostoli discipulo, custoditum hunc librum; inde factum, ut eius esse opus a quibusdam per errorem crederetur". Loisy (*Le*

§ 9. *The Reception of the Apocalypse.*—No immediate traces of the Apocalypse (*cf.* Zahn's *Geschichte des N. T. Kanons*, i., pp. 201 f., and Leipoldt's *Gesch. d. N. T. Kanons*, i., pp. 32 f., 58 f., etc.), are to be found in early Christian literature; the two or three apparent allusions in Clemens Romanus, Barnabas, and Hermas, imply nothing but common oral tradition or the independent use of the O.T., if not of apocryphal sources. Ignatius, however, seems to have known it (see on iii. 12, xxi. 3); certainly Papias and Justin did. Melito of Sardis (*c.* 170 A.D.) wrote a commentary upon it, while Apollonius and Theophilus of Antioch were acquainted with it; so were the Valentinians, and of course the chiliasts. Irenæus and the *Ep. Lugd.* attest its circulation in southern Gaul (*c.* 177 A.D.). Clement also read it in Alexandria as a sacred scripture. The evidence of the martyrdoms and of Tertullian proves that in Africa, as well as in southern Gaul and Egypt, it was widely circulated before the close of the second century, and the Muratorian canon witnesses to its authority in Rome. But it did not escape sharp criticism (τί με ὠφελεῖ ἡ ἀποκάλυψις Ἰωάννου, λέγουσά μοι περὶ ἑπτὰ ἀγγέλων καὶ ἑπτὰ σαλπίγγων;) and even repudiation not only from Marcion, with his antipathy to the O.T., but from the anti-Montanists, alike in Asia Minor and in Rome,[1] who disliked the sensuous elements in its prophecies and repudiated ecstasy as a form of true prophecy. The predilection for Hellenistic eschatology also helped to throw it into disfavour, as compared with, *e.g.*, *The Apocalypse of Peter*, which even the Muratorian canon ranks alongside of it. Another feature which probably told against its popularity was its unpatriotic attitude to the empire. When prayers were offered in the churches for the emperor, and when the empire had come to be viewed, as Paul had taught, in the

Quatr. Evangile, p. 134), Swete, M'Giffert, Peake (*Introd. N.T.*, 1909, 152 f.), and some others incline to this hypothesis with hesitation, as does Jacoby (*Neutestam. Ethik*, 1899, 444-455). It was admitted by Vogel (*Commentationes*, etc., 1811-1816), who was almost the first to suggest the composite origin of the Apocalypse.

[1] The controversy between Hippolytus and Gaius the Roman presbyter, in the beginning of the third century, shows that the latter, like the Alogi, possibly ascribed the Apocalypse to Cerinthus (*cf.* Schwartz's essay, *Ueber den Tod d. Söhne Zebedaei*, 1904, pp. 33-45). Hippolytus feels that Caius has gone too far in his wholesale repudiation of the Apocalypse along with its Montanist exploiters. One of the objections urged by the Alogi was that there was no church at Thyatira, and consequently that John was no true prophet, which probably means that the local church had become Montanist (*cf.* Corssen in *Texte u. Unters.*, xv. 1, 52-56), and therefore had ceased to exist as a church, from the standpoint of catholic Christianity. For the most part, as Dionysius says, they went through every chapter of the book, with a keen scent for its Oriental phantasy (ἄγνωστόν τε καὶ ἀσυλλόγιστον ἀποφαίνοντες).

light of a providential bulwark, it is not surprising that John's Apocalypse had a hard struggle to retain its place in the canon, and that except in times of sore persecution it did not appeal to the majority of Christians. The result was that before very long the only means of preserving it for ecclesiastical edification was to allegorise it freely. This naturally threw the interpretation of the book quite out of focus, so that the fortunes of the Apocalypse really form a chapter in the history of the canon or of the church (*cf.* Lücke, §§ 30-36, 50-59). But even prior to, or independent of, the allegorical interpretation, the book had vitality. It is paradoxical to claim that the apocalypses of the early church, including that of John, were the first Christian scriptures to be canonised, owing to their prophetic origin, which ranked them with the O.T. Their place in the series of prophetic writings is obvious, but the treatise *de aleatoribus*, from which the main evidence for this theory is drawn, is of too uncertain a date to be used safely in this connexion. Still, the Apocalypse did retain its vogue in many circles of the early church, especially throughout the west. Often this was due to a vague and correct instinct for John's great religious message in spite of its archaic paraphernalia and its fantastic elements (*cf.* Renan, 479, 480). Yet even its literal prophecies still maintained an appeal of their own. It was the chiliasm of the book, not its unfulfilled predictions, which proved a difficulty. The prediction which went soonest out of date (*i.e.*, xvii. 8-11) seems to have occasioned as little trouble to the church as the Sibylline oracles or the similar passages of the O.T. prophets. The Apocalypse evidently was not final any more than normal.[1] Besides, against the failure of its historical programme to correspond with the subsequent trend of history, must be set the fact that the number of the Beast could be interpreted as Trajan, Hadrian, or Marcus Aurelius, that the expectation[2] of a Nero-antichrist lingered down to the fifth century in certain corners of the popular religious mind, that Gog and Magog were repeatedly expected in the form of savage hordes (Huns, Goths, etc.), and that the dread (*cf.* Lightfoot's *Ignatius,* i., 644 f.) of a Parthian invasion did not become obsolete till the third century. In several respects the book could still be taken reasonably as a prediction of near events. Thus, by the time that Constantine's policy had antiquated the Apocalypse's view of

[1] *Cf.* A. B. Davidson on this point in Hastings, *D.B.*, i. 736, 737, iv. 126.

[2] Though "it was during the continuance of the Flavian dynasty that the expectation was at white heat," yet it "lingered on for many centuries" (Lightfoot, *Clem. Rom.*, ii., pp. 511, 512).

the Roman State, the position of the book was fairly secure. New systems of interpretation, allegorical (*e.g.*, that of Tyconius) and semi-historical, were devised to vindicate its rights as a scripture of the church, and these were the more cordially welcomed, as the book itself was enigmatic and in parts ambiguous. All sense of its original object had faded from the uncritical mind of the church. Dogmatic prepossessions underlay its rejection as well as its reception; it was exposed to extravagant censure and extravagant praise, but the growing belief in its apostolic origin helped to save it, like Hebrews, from ultimate exclusion or depreciation. In the case of the one book as of the other, the instinct which determined the judgment of the councils and the churches was sounder than the political reasons which they adduced. *Nostra res agitur*, they felt. The authentic note of loyalty to Jesus Christ at all costs was audible enough to prevail with them over their antipathy to the crashing discords of Christian apocalyptic.[1]

§ 10. *Literature, etc.*—In addition to abbreviations which are already noted (page 284), or which are obvious enough, the following may be mentioned:—

Abbott = E. A. Abbott's *Notes on N. T. Criticism* (1907), pp. 75 f., 175 f.

AC = Bousset's *der Antichrist* (Eng. Tr. by Keane, 1896).

Baldensperger = sec. ed. (1892) of Baldensperger's *das Selbstbewusstsein Jesu.*

Blass = *Grammatik des NTlichen Griechisch* (2nd ed. 1902; Eng. Tr. 1905).

Böklen = B.'s *die Verwandtschaft d. jüdisch-christlichen mit der Parsischen Eschatologie* (1902).

Burton = E. de W. Burton's *New Testament Moods and Tenses* (2nd ed. 1894).

C.B.P. = W. M. Ramsay's *Cities and Bishoprics of Phrygia*, vol. i. part i. (1895), part ii. (1897).

Dalman = Dalman's *Worte Jesu* (Eng. Tr. *The Words of Jesus*).

Dieterich = A. Dieterich's *Nekyia* (1893).

[1] "If a great man interprets a national crisis so as to bring home to the nation its true ideals and destination, he remains a true prophet even if his forecast was mistaken. Without the critical situation it is probable that the great man could never have brought so much truth to such powerful expression. So an eschatology is not to be judged by a simple rule of agreement with facts, but rather by its fitness under the circumstances to quicken faith in God, to stir the conscience and put men's wills under the domination of ideal motives, to give a living sense of God and eternity' (F. C. Porter, *Messages of the Apoc. Writers*, p. 73).

Dobschütz = Von Dobschütz's *die urchristlichen Gemeinden* (1902; Eng. Tr., "Christian Life in the Primitive Church," 1904).

E.B.D.—"The Egyptian Book of the Dead" (ed. E. Wallis Budge; the translation, 1898).

E.Bi. = *The Encyclopædia Biblica.*

E.J. = *The Jewish Encyclopædia* (1901 ff.).

Ep. Lugd. = "The epistle of the churches at Vienne and Lyons," 177 A.D. (Eus. *H.E.* v. 1).

Friedländer = *Darstellungen aus der Sittengeschichte Roms* (1888, 6th ed.), by L. Friedländer.

Gfrörer = Gfrörer's *das Jahrhundert des Heils* (1838).

Grill = J. Grill's *Untersuch. über die Entstehung d. vierten Evglms* (1902).

Grotius = Grotius's *Annotationes*, viii. 234 f. (1839 ed.).

Helbing = R. Helbing's *Grammatik der Septuaginta* (1907).

Gregory = C. R. Gregory's *Textkritik des N.T.* (1900-1909).

Jastrow = Prof. Morris Jastrow's *The Religion of Babylonia and Assyria* (1898).

Jeremias = A. Jeremias' *Babylonisches im N. T.* (1905).

Kattenbusch = K., *das apostolische Symbol*, vol. ii. (1900).

Lueken = Lueken's *Michael* (1898).

Moulton = J. H. Moulton's *Gramm. N. T. Greek*, vol. i. (sec. ed., 1906).

Pausanias = Pausanias' "Description of Greece" (ed. J. G. Frazer, 1898).

Pfleiderer = *das Urchristentum* (1902), vol. ii., pp. 281 f.

P.W. = Pauly's *Real-Encycl. der class. Altertumswissenschaft* (ed. Wissowa, 1894 f.).

Renan = Renan's *L'antéchrist* (1871).

R.J. = Bousset's *die Religion des Judentums im neutest. Zeitalter* (1903; the references are to the first edition).

R.S. = W. Robertson Smith's *Religion of the Semites.*

S.B.E. = "The Sacred Books of the East" (Oxford).

S.C. = Gunkel's *Schöpfung und Chaos* (1895): with his essay (1903) *Zum religionsgesch. Verständnis des N. T.* (*cf. The Monist*, 1903, 398-455).

Selwyn = E. C. Selwyn: "The Christian Prophets and the Prophetic Apocalypse" (1901).

Stave = *Ueber d. Einfluss d. Parsismus auf d. Judentum* (1898).

Thumb = *Die Griechische Sprache im Zeitalter d. Hellenismus* (1901).

Titius = Dr. A. Titius: *die vulgäre Anschauung von d. Seligkeit im Urchristentum* (1900).

Viteau = Viteau's *Étude sur le grecque du nouveau Testament*, vol. i. (1893), vol. ii. (1896).

Volz = P. Volz: *Jüdische Eschatologie* (1903).

Weinel = Weinel's *die Wirkungen des Geistes u. der Geister im nachap. Zeitalter* (1899).

Weizsäcker = *The Apostolic Age* (Eng. Tr., 1894-1895).

Win. = Winer's *Grammatik* (8th ed., by P. W. Schmiedel).

In order to save space, most of the citations from the O.T. and the N.T. have been relegated to the margin; often the substance of a note has been crushed into a handful of such references. It has been impossible to give any register of opinion or history of interpretation, and I have abstained from furnishing such grammatical, philological, or geographical information as may be found in any concordance, grammar, or dictionary of the Bible. For fuller details on questions of introduction I must refer the reader to the relevant sections in my forthcoming *Introduction to the Literature of the New Testament.*

The English student is now excellently served by the articles of Bousset (*E.Bi.* i. 194-212, summarising the results of his *editio princeps* in Meyer [1896, 1906]) and Dr. F. C. Porter (Hastings' *Dict. of the Bible*, iv. pp. 239-266, an invaluable introduction), and by Dr. Swete's full edition of the Greek text (3rd. ed. 1909). Manual editions by W. H. Simcox (Cambridge Greek Testament, 1893), C. A. Scott (Century Bible, 1902), and H. P. Forbes (*Intern. Handbks to N. T.*, iv., 1907, pp. 86-149). The main English contributions, since Alford, are those of Farrar (*Early Days of Christianity*, 1882, ch. xxviii.), Lee (*Speaker's Comm.* 1881), Wordsworth (1875), Randall (*Pulpit Comm.*, 1890), Milligan (*Discussions on the Apocalypse*, 1893; also his edition in the fourth vol. of Schaff's Commentary), E. W. Benson (*The Apoc.*, 1900), Selwyn, and Briggs (*Messiah of the Apostles*, pp. 285-461); *cf.* further G. H. Gilbert (*The First Interpreters of Jesus*, 1901, pp. 332-397), F. Palmer's *The Drama of the Apocalypse* (1903), H. Berg's *The Drama of the Apocalypse* (1894), Dr. F. C. Porter's *Messages of the Apoc. Writers* (1905, pp. 169-296), the English translations of Beyschlag's *Neutest. Theol.* (vol. ii., 247-361) and Wernle's *Die Anfänge*, pp. 256-274 ("The Beginnings of Christianity," 1901, vol. i., pp. 360 f.), Sir W. M. Ramsay's *Letters to the Seven Churches* (1904), Hort's posthumous fragment (*Apoc.* i.-iii., 1908), and Canon J. J. Scott's *The Apocalypse* (1909).

German edd.—De Wette (1848), Bleek (Eng. tr. 1875), Düsterdieck (1887), B. Weiss (2nd ed. 1902), J. Weiss (*die Schriften des N. T.*, 1907), Bousset, and H. J. Holtzmann (*Hand-Commentar*, 3rd. ed., 1908). Schmiedel's *Volksbuch* (1906) is included in the English edition of his *Johannine Writings* (1908). There is a competent Dutch commentary by J. M. S. Baljon (Utrecht, 1908); besides French works by Havet (*Le Christ. et ses origines*, iv. 314-344), Reuss (Paris, 1878), A. Crampon (Tournai, 1904), and Th. Calmes (Paris, 1905), with the last-named scholar's pamphlet, *L'Apoc. devant la tradition et devant la critique*[3] (1907). Baljon's critical introduction is given in his *Geschiedenis van de Boeken des nieuwen Verbonds* (1901), 241-265.

Of the commentaries which preceded Alford, almost the only English works which retain any critical value are those of Moses Stuart (Andover, 1845: on the lines of Lücke) and Trench (*Commentary on the Epp. to the Seven Churches*, 1861, sixth edition, 1897).

Since the present commentary was drafted, six years ago, a number of monographs, including some of those just mentioned, have been issued. I have occasionally inserted references to them in the text, for the sake of convenience and completeness, but, for the sake of independence, the notes have otherwise been left untouched.

ΑΠΟΚΑΛΥΨΙΣ ΙΩΑΝΝΟΥ.[1]

I. 1. [a] **ἈΠΟΚΑΛΥΨΙΣ Ἰησοῦ Χριστοῦ, ἣν [b] ἔδωκεν αὐτῷ ὁ θεὸς**
[c] **δεῖξαι τοῖς δούλοις αὐτοῦ,[2] ἃ δεῖ γενέσθαι ἐν τάχει, καὶ ἐσήμανεν**

a Sc. ἥδε ἐστιν (article absent as from Matt. i. 1, *cf.* Win. § 19, 10). For eschat. connotation, *cf.* Rom. ii. 5, viii. 19. b John xii. 49, xiv. 10: constr. John vi. 52. c John v. 20, x. 32.

[1] Om. with ℵC, etc. (edd.), from the title the **του θεολογου** of Q and (with expansions) many cursives, which was a description of the apostle John in the fourth century as the author of the fourth gospel, and applied to him here as the exponent of divine oracles (**θεολογος = προφητης,** Philo, de Vit. Mos., ii. 11; Luc., *Alex.*, 19, 22) or as the herald of God (*cf.* Chrys., *Orat.*, 36). Inscriptions show that **θεολογοι** were sacred officials in Pergamum, Ephesus, Smyrna, etc. (Deissm., 231-232, *Licht vom Osten*, 252 f.), who were frequently **υμνωδοι** as well.

[2] Punctuate **Θεος δειξαι τ. δ. αυτου,** with WH, Ws., Bs., Hort. On the alternative form **Ιωανει** (ℵ*), *cf.* Win. § 5, 26c, Schmiedel (*E. Bi.*, 2504-2505), Thumb 20 f., Helbing 29-30.

Chapter I.—Vv. 1-3. The superscription. **Ἀπ. Ἰωάννου** is the ecclesiastical title (distinguishing it from the apocalypse of Peter, or of Paul, etc.) of what professes in reality to be an **ἀπ. Ἰησοῦ Χριστοῦ** (subjective genitive), *i.e.*, a disclosure of the divine **μυστήρια** (Dan. ii. 19, 22, 28, Theod.) in the immediate future (**ἃ δεῖ γ. ἐν τάχει**) which has been communicated (**ἔδωκεν,** *cf.* on iii. 9) by God to Jesus (*cf.* v. 7) and which in turn is transmitted by Jesus (Gal. i. 12) to John as a member of the prophetic order.

Ver. 1. **δούλοις,** in specific sense of x. 7, xi. 18, after Dan. ix. 6, 10; Zech. i. 6, and Amos iii. 7 (**ἀποκαλύψῃ παιδείαν πρὸς τοὺς δούλους αὐτοῦ τοὺς προφήτας**). *Jesus Christ* is used only in i. 1-5 (xxii. 21 ?), *Lord Jesus* only in xxii. 20, *Lord* (*i.e.*, Jesus) only in xi. 8 and xiv. 13; elsewhere either **ὁ Χριστός** (xx. 4, 6) **αὐτοῦ** (xi. 15, xii. 10) or (as in Hebrews) the simple *Jesus*. **ἃ δεῖ κ.τ.λ.** (from Dan. ii. 28-29), either object of **δεῖξαι** (Vit. ii. 229) or more probably in opposition to **ἥν. ἐν τάχει** = "soon" (as in Clem. Rom. xxiii. 5 and the instructive logion of Luke xviii. 8). This is the hinge and staple of the book. When the advent of Jesus is hailed as a relief, it is no consolation to say that the relief will come suddenly; sudden or not, it must come soon (x. 7), if it is to be of any service. The keynote of the Apocalypse is the cheering assurance that upon God's part there is no reluctance or delay; His people have not long to wait now. **καὶ ἐσήμανεν** (so of what is future and momentous, Ezek. xxxiii. 3, Acts xi. 26, etc.: Heracleitus on the Delphic oracle, **οὔτε λέγει οὔτε κρύπτει ἀλλὰ σημαίνει**) **ἀποστείλας** (from seventh heaven, in Asc. Isa. vi. 13), a loose Heb. idiom for "he (*i.e.*, Jesus here and in xxii. 16, God in xxii. 6) sent and signified it". **διὰ** (as in Asc. Isa. xi. 30, etc.) **τοῦ ἀγγέλου αὐτοῦ** (*cf.* Test. Jos. vi. 6). Jesus is the medium of all revelation, but **ἀποκάλυψις** is further conceived of as transmitted through the *angelus interpres*, a familiar and important figure in rabbinic (*cf.* *E. J.* i. 592, 593) and apocalyptic tradition (see reff. and on Acts vii. 30), who stands here between Jesus and the prophet as a sort of *double* of the former. Like Hermas (*Mand.* xi. 9), the post-exilic tradition required the executive function of this angel, in order to (*a*) satisfy the yearning for some means of divine communication, and (*b*) at the same time to maintain reverence for the divine glory (Baldensperger, 48 f.). But John's Christian consciousness here and elsewhere is

ἀποστείλας διὰ τοῦ [d] ἀγγέλου αὐτοῦ τῷ δούλῳ αὐτοῦ Ἰωάννῃ, 2. ὃς ἐμαρτύρησεν τὸν [e] λόγον τοῦ θεοῦ καὶ τὴν μαρτυρίαν Ἰησοῦ Χριστοῦ, ὅσα [f] εἶδεν. 3. μακάριος ὁ [g] ἀναγινώσκων καὶ οἱ ἀκούοντες τοὺς

d Zech. i. 9, 13, ii. 3, Dan. viii. 16, ix. 21 f., Ap. Bar. lv. 3 (Ramiel), etc.: Dieterich's *Mithras Liturgie*, 47 f. e Ver. 9. f *i.e.*, in present apocalypse. g 2 Cor. iii. 15, Acts xv. 21, Matt. xxiv. 15, 1 Tim. iv. 13, Clem. Hom. xix.

too large for the traditional and artificial forms of its expression. Unless this angel is identified with that of x. 1 f., he plays only a scanty and tardy rôle (xvii. 1 f., xxi. 5 f.) in the series of visions; the prophet's sense of direct experience (*e.g.*, in i. 9 f.) bursts through the cumbrous category of an intermediate agent between himself and Christ. It is by a conventional form of religious symbolism prevalent in this *genre* of literature, that Jesus, like Yahweh in Ezekiel (*cf.* x. 1, 3, xliv. 2), is represented both as addressing the prophet directly and as instructing him indirectly. The latter mode of expression (*cf.* Milton's *Uriel* and 4 Esd. iv. 1) was due to a hypostatising tendency which was not confined to Judaism. As Plutarch points out (*cf.* below on viii. 5 and xv. 8), the daemons in Hellenic religion are a middle term between the divine and the human; they prevent the former from being disturbed or contaminated by direct intercourse with men, and they also act as interpreters who communicate the divine will to men (*cf. De Iside* 25; Oakesmith's *Religion of Plutarch*, pp. 121 f., 163 f.). Wherever the reaction against materialism prevailed, especially in the popular religion of the empire, the belief in daemons or spirits as intermediate agents gave expression to the conviction that human weakness could not come into direct touch with the divine glory (*cf.* Friedländer, iii. 430 f.; Hatch's *Hibbert Lectures*, 245 f.).

Ver. 2. **ἐμαρτ.** (epistol. aor., *cf.* Phlm. 19, *cf.* further Thuc. i. 1 **ξυνέγραψε**). **λόγ. τ. θ.**, like דבר יהוה (LXX **λόγος τοῦ θεοῦ**, *e.g.*, Jer. i. 2), a collective term for God's disclosures to men (**τοὺς λόγους**, 3), or as here for some specific revelation more exactly defined in **ὅσα εἶδεν**, all that was seen or even heard (Amos i. 1) in visions being described by this generic term. The double expression *the word of God and the testimony borne by Jesus Christ* (xxii. 16, 20; *cf.* xix. 10) is an amplified phrase for the gospel. The subject upon which Jesus assures men of truth is the revelation of God's mind and heart, and the gospel is that utterance of God—that expression of His purpose—which Jesus unfolds and attests. The book itself is the record of John's evidence; he testifies to Christ, and Christ testifies of the future as a divine plan. For the revelation of God, in the specific form of prophecy, requires a further medium between Jesus and the ordinary Christian; hence the rôle of the prophets. On the prophetic commission to write, *cf.* Asc. Isa. i. 4-5 and i. 2, **παρέδωκεν αὐτῷ τοὺς λόγους τῆς προφητείας οὓς αὐτὸς εἶδεν, κ.τ.λ.** The primitive sense of **μαρτ.** (= oral confession and proclamation of Jesus by his adherents) thus expands into a literary sense (as here) and into the more sombre meaning of martyrdom (ii. 13, John xviii. 37-39, xix. 19; *cf.* Lightfoot on Clem. Rom. v.). It is significant that the **λόγος τ. θ.** of Judaism was not adequate to the Christian consciousness without the **μαρτυρία Ἰησοῦ.**

Ver. 3. The first of the seven beatitudes in the Apocalypse (xiv. 13, xvi. 15, xix. 9, xx. 6, xxii. 7, 14), endorsing the book as a whole. In the worship of the Christian communities one member read aloud, originally from the O.T. as in the synagogues, and afterwards from Christian literature as well (apostolic epistles, Col. iv. 16, and sub-apostolic epistles), while the rest of the audience listened (Eus. *H. E.* iv. 23). In its present form the Apocalypse was composed with this object in view. *Cf.* Justin's description of the Christian assemblies on Sunday, when, as the first business, **τὰ ἀπομνημονεύματα τῶν ἀποστόλων ἢ τὰ συγγράμματα τῶν προφητῶν ἀναγινώσκεται** (Apol. i. 67). The art of reading was not a general accomplishment in the circles from which the Christian societies were for the most part recruited, and this office of reader (**ἀναγνώστης**), as distinct from that of the president, soon became one of the regular minor positions in the worship of the church. Here the reader's function resembles that of Baruch (*cf.* Jer. xxii. 5, 6). **τηροῦντες τὰ, κ.τ.λ.**, carefully heeding the warnings of the book, observing its injunctions, and expecting the fulfilment

λόγους [h]τῆς προφητείας καὶ [i]τηροῦντες τὰ ἐν αὐτῇ γεγραμμένα· [k]ὁ γὰρ καιρὸς ἐγγύς.

4. Ἰωάννης ταῖς ἑπτὰ ἐκκλησίαις ταῖς ἐν τῇ Ἀσίᾳ· [l]χάρις ὑμῖν

h Cf. xxii. 10.
i Lk. xi. 28, John xiii. 17; contrast below, xxii. 18-19.
k After Dan. vii. 22 (Lk. xxi. 8-9), cf. Ap. Bar. xxiii. 7.
l Sc. εἴη (primit. Christ. salutation).

of its predictions, instead of losing heart and faith (Luke xviii. 8). *Cf.* Hipp. *De Antich.* 2 and En. civ. 12, "books will be given to the righteous and the wise to become a cause of joy and uprightness and much wisdom". The content of the Apocalypse is not merely prediction; moral counsel and religious instruction are the primary burden of its pages. The bliss of the obedient and attentive, however, is bound up with the certainty that the crisis at which the predictions of the book are to be realised is imminent; they have not to wait long for the fulfilment of their hopes. This, with the assurance of God's interest and intervention, represented the ethical content of early Christian prediction, which would have been otherwise a mere satisfaction of curiosity; see on ver. 19.

[*Note on* i. 1-3. If this inscription (absent from no MS.) is due to the author, it must have been added (so Bruston, Jülicher, Hirscht, Holtzm., Bs.), like the **προοίμιον** of Thucydides, after he had finished the book as a whole. But possibly it was inserted by the later hand of an editor or redactor (Völter, Erbes, Briggs, Hilg., Forbes, Wellhausen, J. Weiss, Simcox = elders of Ephesus, John xxi. 24) rather than of a copyist (Spitta, Sabatier, Schön), who reproduced the Johannine style of the Apocalypse proper. At the same time, the change from the third to the first person (ver. 9) is not unexampled (*cf.* Jer. i. 1-3, 4 f.; Ezek. i. 1-4; Enoch repeatedly), and forms no sure proof of an original text overlaid with editorial touches; nor is a certain sententious objectivity (*cf.* Herod. i. 1, ii. 23, etc.) unnatural at the commencement of a book, when the writer has occasion to introduce himself. The real introduction begins at ver. 4 (*cf.* xxii. 21).]

Vv. 4-8. The prologue.

Ver. 4. **ταῖς ἑπτὰ ἐκκλ.,** seven being the sacred and complete number in apocalyptic symbolism (*E. Bi.* 3436). The **ταῖς** must refer proleptically to to ver. 11; for other churches existed and flourished in proconsular Asia at this time, *e.g.*, at Troas, Magnesia, Hierapolis and Colossae, with which the prophet must have been familiar. These seven are selected by him for some special reason which it is no longer possible to disinter (see above, Introd., § 2). **ἀπὸ ὁ ὢν, κ.τ.λ.,** a quaint and deliberate violation of grammar (Win. § 10, 1c.; Moult. i. 9) in order to preserve the immutability and absoluteness of the divine name from declension, though it falls under the rule that in N.T. and LXX parenthetic and accessory clauses tend to assume an independent construction. The divine title is a paraphrase probably suggested by rabbinic language (*e.g.*, Targum Jonath. apud Deut. xxxii. 39, ego ille, qui est et qui fuit et qui erit); the idea would be quite familiar to Hellenic readers from similar expressions, *e.g.*, in the song of doves at Dodona (**Ζεὺς ἦν, Ζεὺς ἔστιν, Ζεὺς ἔσσεται**) or in the titles of Asclepius and Athene. Simon Magus is said to have designated himself also as **ὁ ἑστὼς, ὁ στὰς, ὁ στησόμενος,** and the shrine of Minerva (= Isis) at Sais bore the inscription, *I am all that hath been and is and shall be: my veil no mortal yet hath raised* (Plut. *de Iside*, 9), the latter part eclipsed by the comforting Christian assurance here. **ἦν,** another deliberate anomaly (finite verb for participle) due to dogmatic reasons; no past participle of **εἰμί** existed, and **γενόμενος** was obviously misleading. **ὁ ἐρχ.,** instead of **ὁ ἐσόμενος,** to correspond with the keynote of the book, struck loudly in ver. 7. In and with his messiah, Jesus, God himself comes; **ἐρχ.** (the present) acquires, partly through the meaning of the verb, a future significance. For the emphasis and priority of **ὢν** in this description of God, see the famous passage in Aug. *Confess.* ix. 10. **τ. ἑπτὰ πνευμάτων**: a puzzling conception whose roots have been traced in various directions to (*a*) an erroneous but not unnatural interpretation of Isa. xi. 2-3, found in the Targ. Jonath. (as in En. lxi. 11, sevenfold spirit of virtues) and shared by Justin (*Dial.* 87, *cf. Cohort. ad Graec.*, c. 32, **ὥσπερ οἱ ἱεροὶ προφῆται τὸ ἓν καὶ τὸ αὐτὸ πνεῦμα εἰς ἑπτὰ πνεύματα μερίζεσθαί φασιν**), or—more probably—to the later Jewish

καὶ εἰρήνη ἀπὸ [m] ὁ ὢν καὶ ὁ ἦν καὶ ὁ [n] ἐρχόμενος· καὶ ἀπὸ τῶν
ἑπτὰ πνευμάτων ἃ ἐνώπιον τοῦ θρόνου αὐτοῦ· 5. καὶ ἀπὸ Ἰησοῦ
Χριστοῦ, [o] ὁ μάρτυς ὁ [p] πιστός, ὁ [q] πρωτότοκος τῶν νεκρῶν, καὶ ὁ
[r] ἄρχων τῶν βασιλέων τῆς γῆς· τῷ ἀγαπῶντι ἡμᾶς καὶ λύσαντι [1] ἡμᾶς

m i. 8, iv. 8, Ex. iii. 14 f.
n From Hab. ii. 3, Zech. ii. 14, etc.
o 1 Tim. vi. 13, Heb. xii. 1-2. John xviii. 37. Clem. Rom. xxiv.
p ii. 10, 13, *cf.* Ps. lxxxviii. 38 (LXX).
q 1 Cor. xv. 20, Col. i. 18,
r Isa. lv. 4 (LXX), only here in Apoc.

The **λουσαντι . . . απο** of PQ, min., vg., Me., Aeth., Areth. (so Bg., Trench, Ew., de W., Balj., Sp., Bs., Burgon: *Corruption in Trad. Text*, 59-60; for constr. *cf.* Deissm., 227) is a corruption of **λυσαντι εκ** (ℵAC, 1, etc., Syr., Arm., Anda, Pr., edd., *cf.* xx. 7), probably due to misconception of Heb. use of **εν** (WH), and to the association of the two ideas (*cf.* Iren. iv. 27, 1: qui abluit et emundat eum hominem qui peccato fuerat obstrictus, and Plato's *Cratylus*, 405 B **ὁ ἀπολούων τε καὶ ἀπολύων τῶν κακῶν**).

notion (*b*) of the seven holy angels (Tobit xii. 15; *cf.* Gfrörer, i. 360 f.) which reappears in early Christianity (*cf.* Clem. Al. *Strom.* vi. 685, **ἑπτὰ μέν εἰσιν οἱ τοῦ μεγίστου δύναμιν ἔχοντες πρωτόγονοι ἀγγέλων ἄρχοντες**), modified from (*c*) a still earlier Babylonian conception, behind (*b*), of the seven spirits of the sky—the sun, the moon, and the five planets. The latter is not unknown to Jewish literature before 100 A.D. (*cf.* Jub. ii. 2 f.; Berachoth, 32, *b*), corresponding to the Persian Amshaspands (Yasht, xix. 19, 20, *S. B. E.* xxxi. 145) and reflected in "the seven first white ones" or angelic retinue of the Lord in Enoch xc. 21 f. (Cheyne, *Orig. Ps.* 281-2, 327 f., 334 f.; Stave, 216 f.; Lüken, 32 f.; *R. J.* 319). Whether the prophet and his readers were conscious of this derivation or not, the conception is stereotyped and designed to express in archaic terms the supreme majesty of God before whose throne (*i.e.*, obedient and ready for any commission, *cf.* v. 6) these mighty beings live. They are not named or divided in the Apocalypse, but the objection to taking the expression in the sense of (*a*) denoting, as in Philo (where, *e.g.*, **ὁ κατὰ ἑβδομάδα ἅγιος** or **κινούμενος** is a characteristic symbol of the divine Logos), the sevenfold and complete energy of the Spirit in semi-poetic fashion, is the obvious fact that this is out of line with the trinity of the apocalypse, which is allied to that of Luke ix. 26; 1 Tim. v. 21; Just. Mart. *Apol.* i. 6. The Spirit in the Apocalypse, as in Jude, 2 Peter and the pastoral epistles, is wholly prophetic. It has not the content of the Spirit in Paul or in the Fourth Gospel. Since the writer intends to enlarge upon the person of Jesus, or because the seven spirits stood next to the deity in the traditional *mise-en-scène*, he makes them precede Christ in order.

Ver. 5. **ἀπὸ, κ.τ.λ.**, another grammatical anomaly; as usual the writer puts the second of two nouns in apposition, in the nominative.—**ὁ μ. ὁ π.** Jesus not merely the reliable witness to God but the loyal martyr: an aspect of his career which naturally came to the front in "the killing times". **ὁ πρωτότοκος** (a Jewish messianic title by itself, Baldensperger, 88) **τ. ν.**, his resurrection is the pledge that death cannot separate the faithful from his company. The thought of this and of the following trait (*cf.* Matt. iv. 8 f.) is taken from Ps. lxxxviii. 28, **κἀγὼ πρωτότοκον θήσομαι αὐτόν, ὑψηλὸν παρὰ τοῖς βασιλεῦσιν τῆς γῆς.** On the two allied functions of ruling and witnessing (Isa. lv. 4) *cf.* the different view of John xviii. 37. At the inspiring thought of Christ's lordship the prophet breaks into adoration—**ἀγαπῶντι κ.τ.λ.** The eternal love (*cf.* iii. 19) which Christ bears to his people is proved by his death, as a revelation of (*a*) what he has done for them by his sacrifice, and (*b*) what he has made of them (so Eph. v. 25-26 = Apoc. xix. 7, 8). The negative deliverance from sins (*cf.* Ps. cxxix. 8) at the cost of his own life (**ἐν** instrumental) is a religious emancipation which issues in (*b*) a positive relationship of glorious religious privilege.—**βασιλείαν, ἱερεῖς,** a literal (*cf.* Charles on Jub. xvi. 18) and inaccurate rendering of ממלכת כהנים (Exod. xix. 6) to emphasise the royal standing of the Christian community in connexion with their Christ as **ἄρχων, κ.τ.λ.**, and also (Tit. ii. 3) their individual privilege of intimate access to God as the result of Christ's sacrificial death.

ἐκ τῶν ἁμαρτιῶν ἡμῶν [s] ἐν τῷ αἵματι αὐτοῦ· 6. καὶ ἐποίησεν ἡμᾶς
[t] βασιλείαν [1] ἱερεῖς τῷ θεῷ καὶ [u] πατρὶ αὐτοῦ· [v] αὐτῷ ἡ δόξα καὶ τὸ
κράτος εἰς τοὺς αἰῶνας τῶν αἰώνων. ἀμήν.

7. [w] Ἰδοὺ ἔρχεται [x] μετὰ τῶν νεφελῶν, καὶ ὄψεται αὐτὸν [y] πᾶς
ὀφθαλμὸς, καὶ οἵτινες αὐτὸν ἐξεκέντησαν· καὶ [z] κόψονται ἐπ' αὐτὸν
πᾶσαι αἱ φυλαὶ τῆς γῆς. [a] ναί· ἀμήν.

s v. 9, 1 Pet. i. 18-19. t v. 10, 1 Pet. ii. 9; *cf.* 2 Macc. ii. 17, Jos. *Ant.* xx. 9, Jub. xvi. 13. u *Cf.* on xxi. 7 (Ps. lxxxviii. 27) (LXX). v Resuming τῷ ἀγ. Same doxology as in 1 Pet. iv. 11; see also Mk. xiii. 26, 2 Thess. i. 9, and Chase in *Camb. Texts and Stud.* i. (1891) 168 f. w xvi. 15. x Mk. xiii. 26, xiv. 62, 4 Esd. xiii. 3; *cf.* on Apoc. xiv. 14. y "The world," Did. xvi.; *cf.* Matt. xxvi. 64. z xviii. 9; from Hab. iii. 10, LXX. a John xi. 27

[1] **βασιλεις και** (P, 1, 28, 36, etc., And.) is one of several glosses introduced (like **ιεραν** or **ιερατικην** of Syr., S. for **ιερεις**, or **ημων** of C, Lat. for **ημας**) to ease the difficulty of the original **βασιλειαν** (א*AC, etc., vg., Syr., Areth., edd.) [like **ιερατευμα** 1 Pet. ii. 5, 9].

καὶ ἐποίησεν, the harsh anacolouthon breaks up the participial construction. **ἡμᾶς,** emphatic. "We Christians are now the chosen people. In us the Danielic prophecy of a reign of the saints is fulfilled and is to be fulfilled." This is a characteristically anti-Jewish note. Persecution (*cf.* 1 Peter ii. 5) deepened the sense of continuity in the early Christians, who felt driven back on the truth of election and divine protection; they were the true successors of all noble sufferers in Israel who had gone before (*cf.* the argument of Heb. xi. 32—xii. 2). In the Apocalypse the Christian church is invariably the true Israel, including all who believe in Christ, irrespective of birth and nationality. God reigns over them, and they reign, or will reign, over the world. In fact, Christians now and here are what Israel hoped to become, *viz.*, priest-princes of God, and this position has been won for them by a messiah whom the Jews had rejected, and whom all non-Christians will have to acknowledge as sovereign. According to rabbinic tradition, the messianic age would restore to Israel the priestly standing which it had lost by its worship of the golden calf; and by the first commandment (Mechilta on Exod. xx. 2), "slaves became kings". There may also be an implicit anti-Roman allusion. We Christians, harried and despised, are a community with a great history and a greater hope. Our connection with Christ makes us truly imperial. The adoration of Christ, which vibrates in this doxology (*cf. Expos.*[6] v. 302-307), is one of the most impressive features of the book. The prophet feels that the one hope for the loyalists of God in this period of trial is to be conscious that they owe everything to the redeeming love of Jesus. Faithfulness depends on faith, and faith is rallied by the grasp not of itself but of its object. Mysterious explanations of history follow, but it is passionate devotion to Jesus, and not any skill in exploring prophecy, which proves the source of moral heroism in the churches. Jesus sacrificed himself for us; **αὐτῷ ἡ δόξα.** From this inward trust and wonder, which leap up at the sight of Jesus and his grace, the loyalty of Christians flows.

This enthusiasm for Jesus naturally carries the prophet's mind forward (7, 8) to the time when the Lord's majesty will flash out on mankind. He resumes the line of thought interrupted by the doxology of 5*b*-6.

Ver. 7. A reminiscence and adaptation of Dan. vii. 13 (Theod.) and Zech. xii. 10-14. The substitution of **ἐξεκέντησαν** (so John xix. 37, Justin's *Apol.* i. 52, *Dial.* xxxii., *cf.* lxi., cxviii., adding **εἰς**) for **κατωρχήσαντο** (LXX mistranslation in this passage, though not elsewhere, of דקרו)—shows that the original text was used (though Lücke and Ewald hold that **ἐξ.** was the LXX reading till Origen), and that it was interpreted in some (Johannine? Abbott, *Diatessarica*, 1259-1262, 2317) circles as a prophecy of the crucifixion. Only, the reference is no longer to repentance (Zech.), but, by a turn of characteristic severity, to remorse and judgment. There is a remarkable parallel in Matt. xxiv. 30, where patristic tradition (*cf.* *A. C.* 233-36) early recognised in **τὸ σημεῖον τ. ὐ. ἀ.** the cross itself, made visible on the day of judgment. The first of the three signs preceding Christ's advent in the clouds, acc. to Did. xvi. 6 (*cf.* Zech. ii. 13 LXX), is **σημεῖον ἐκπετά-**

8. "Ἐγώ εἰμι [b] τὸ ἄλφα καὶ τὸ ὦ," λέγει κύριος ὁ θεός, [c] ὁ ὢν
καὶ ὁ ἦν καὶ ὁ ἐρχόμενος, ὁ [d] παντοκράτωρ.
9. Ἐγὼ [e] Ἰωάννης, ὁ ἀδελφὸς ὑμῶν καὶ συγκοινωνὸς ἐν τῇ θλίψει

b *Cf.* Riedel (*S. K.* 1901, 295 f.). The patristic reference of this verse to Jesus is defended by Abbott, 182 f., *cf.* Isa. xli. 4, xliii. 10, etc.

c Ver. 4.

d Isa. xliv. 6, Amos iv. 13; except (Cit.) 2 Cor. vi. 18, only in Apoc. (?) in N.T. Here, as 3 Macc. vi. 17 f., in connection with retribution; *cf.* *R. J.* 305, and Kattenbusch (ii. 533 f.).

e xxii. 8. Dan. vii. 2, Ex. xii. 3, 4 Esd. ii. 42, etc.

σεως ἐν οὐρανῷ (Christ with outstretched arms, as crucified?); and, acc. to Barn. vii. 9, "they shall see him on that day wearing about his flesh **τὸν ποδήρη κόκκινον**". Note (*a*) that the agreement with John xix. 37 is mainly verbal; the latter alludes to the crucifixion, this passage to an eschatological crisis. (*b*) No such visible or victorious return of Christ is fulfilled in the Apocalypse, for visions like xiv. 14 f., xix. 12 f., do not adequately correspond to i. 7, xxii. 12, etc. (*c*) No punishment of the Jews occurs at Christ's return, for the vengeance of xix. 13 f. falls on pagans, while xi. 13 lies on another plane. **καὶ, κ.τ.λ.**: the monotonous collocation of clauses (Vit. i. 9-16) throughout the Apocalypse with **καί**, is not necessarily a Hebraism; the syntax of Aristotle (*e.g.*, *cf.* Thumb, 129) betrays a similar usage. **καὶ οἵτ. κ.τ.λ.**, selected as a special class (**καὶ τότε μετανοήσουσιν, ὅτε οὐδὲν ὠφελήσουσι,** Justin). The responsibility of the Jews, as opposed to the Romans, for the judicial murder of Jesus is prominent in the Christian literature of the period (Luke-Acts, *cf.* von Dobschütz in *Texte u. Unters.* xi. 1, pp. 61, 62), though the Apoc. is superior to passages like 2 Clem. xvii. **πᾶσαι κ.τ.λ.** = the unbelieving pagans, who are still impenitent when surprised by the Lord's descent (**ἐπὶ** = "because of," *cf.* xviii. 9 in diff. sense); a realistic statement of what is spiritually put in John xvi. 8, 9.—This forms an original element in the early Christian apologetic. To the Jewish taunt, "Jesus is not messiah but a false claimant: he died," the reply was, "He will return in visible messianic authority" (Mark xiv. 62 = Matt. xxvi. 64, significant change in Luke xxii. 69). In several circles this future was conceived not as a return of Jesus, nor in connexion with his historical appearance, but as the first real manifestation of the true messianic character which he had gained at the resurrection (*cf.* Titius, 31, 32). See on xii. 4 f. **ναί, ἀμήν**: a double (Gk. Heb.) ratification of the previous oracle.

Ver. 8. Only here and in xxi. 5 f. is God introduced as the speaker, in the Apocalypse. The advent of the Christ, which marks the end of the age, is brought about by God, who overrules (**παντοκράτωρ** always of God in Apocalypse, otherwise the first part of the title might have suggested Christ) even the anomalies and contradictions of history for this providential climax. By the opening of the second century **πατὴρ παντοκράτωρ** had become the first title of God in the Roman creed; the Apocalypse, indifferent to the former epithet, reproduces the latter owing to its Hebraic sympathies. **ἐγώ εἰμι**: Coleridge used to declare that one chief defect in Spinoza was that the Jewish philosopher started with *It is* instead of with *I am.* **τὸ ἄλφα καὶ τὸ ὦ**: not the finality (Oesterley, *Encycl. Relig. and Ethics*, i. 1, 2), but the all-inclusive power of God, which comes fully into play in the new order of things inaugurated by the second advent. The symbolism which is here put in a Greek form had been developed in rabbinic speculation upon אמת. With this and the following passage, *cf.* the papyrus of Ani (*E. B. D.* 12): "He leadeth in his train that which is and that which is not yet. . . . Homage to thee, King of kings, and Lord of lords, who from the womb of Nut hast ruled the world and Akert [the Egyptian Hades]. Thy body is of bright and shining metal, thy head is of azure blue, and the brilliance of the turquoise encircleth thee." For the connexion of a presentiment of the end (7, 8) with an impulse to warn contemporaries (9 f.) see 4 Esd. xiv. 10 f., where the warning of the world's near close is followed by an injunction to the prophet to "set thine house in order, reprove thy people, console the humble among them"; whereupon the commission to write under inspiration is given.

i. 9-iii. 22, an address to Asiatic Christendom (as represented by seven churches) which in high prophetic and oracular style rallies Christians to their genuine oracle of revelation in Jesus and his prophetic spirit. At a time when local oracles (for the famous one of Apollo near Miletus, see Friedländer, iii.

καὶ βασιλείᾳ καὶ [f] ὑπομονῇ ἐν Ἰησοῦ, ἐγενόμην ἐν τῇ νήσῳ τῇ καλουμένῃ Πάτμῳ [g] διὰ τὸν λόγον τοῦ θεοῦ καὶ τὴν μαρτυρίαν

f Keynote of age, Heb. vi. 12, x. 36, Lk. xxi. 19, Clem. Rom. xxxv., etc.

g In sense of vi. 9, xx. 4, *cf.* Epict. *Diss.* iii. 24, 113. διὰ = ἕνεκεν practically (*cf.* Eus., *H. E.*, iii 18, 1-3).

561 f.), besides those in Greece and Syria and Egypt, were eagerly frequented, it was of moment to lay stress on what had superseded all such media for the faithful. *Cf.* Minuc. Felix, *Oct.* 7, "pleni et mixti deo uates futura praecerpunt, dant cautelam periculis, morbis medelam, spem afflictis, operam miseris, solacium calamitatibus, laboribus leuamentum".

i. 9-20, introductory vision.

Ver. 9. The personality of the seer is made prominent in apocalyptic literature, to locate or guarantee any visions which are to follow. Here the authority with which this prophet is to speak is conditioned by his kinship of Christian experience with the churches and his special revelation from God. **ἀδελφός** (*cf.* vi. 11, xii. 10): for its pagan use as = fellow-member of the same (religious) society, *cf. C. B. P.* i. 96 f., and Dittenberger's *Sylloge Inscr. Graec.* 474, 10 (**ἀδελφοὶ οἷς κοινὰ τὰ πατρῷα**). **θλίψει,** put first as the absorbing fact of their experience, and as a link of sympathy between writer and readers; **καὶ βασιλείᾳ,** the outcome of **θλίψις** in the messianic order: distress no end in itself; **καὶ ὑπομονῇ,** patient endurance the moral condition of participation in **ἡ θλίψις** and **ἡ βασιλεία,** by which one is nerved to endure the presence of the former without breaking down, and to bear the temporary delay of the latter without impatience. While **μακροθυμία** is the absence of resentment at wrong, **ὑπομονή** = not giving way under trials. See Barn. ii., "the aids of our faith are fear and patience, long-suffering and self-control are our allies"; also Tertullian's famous aphorism, "ubi Deus, ibi et alumna eius, patientia scilicet". —**ἐν Ἰησοῦ** (a Pauline conception, only repeated in Apocalypse at xiv. 13), either with all three substantives or merely (*cf.* 2 Thess. iii. 5) with **ὑπομονή.** In any case **ὑπ.** is closely linked to **ἐν Ἰ.**; such patience, as exemplified in Jesus, and inspired by him, was the cardinal virtue of the Apocalypse and its age. In the early Christian literature of this period "we cannot name anything upon which blessedness is so frequently made to rest, as upon the exercise of patient endurance" (Titius, 142). **ἐγενόμην ἐν** ("I found myself in": implying that when he wrote he was no longer there), not by flowing waters (as frequently, *e.g.*, En. xiii. 7), but in the small, treeless, scantily populated island of Patmos, one of the Sporades, whither criminals were banished sometimes by the Roman authorities (Plin. *Hist. Nat.* iv. 12, 23). *Relegatio* to an island was not an infrequent form of punishment for better-class offenders or suspects under the black *régime* of Domitian, as under Diocletian for Christians (*cf.* Introd. § 6). No details are given, but probably it meant hard labour in the quarries, and was inflicted by the pro-consul of Asia Minor. Why John was only banished, we do not know. As "the word of God and the witness of Jesus" are not qualified by any phrase such as **ὅσα εἶδεν** (ver. 2, and thereby identified with the present Apocalypse), the words indicate as elsewhere (*cf.* **διὰ, κ.τ.λ.,** reff.) the occasion of his presence in Patmos, *i.e.*, his loyalty to the gospel (*cf.* **θλίψις**), rather than the object of his visit. The latter could hardly be evangelising (Spitta), for Patmos was insignificant and desolate, nor, in face of the use of **διὰ,** can the phrase mean "for the purpose of receiving this revelation" (Bleek, Lücke, Düsterdieck, Hausrath, B. Weiss, Baljon, etc.). Either he had voluntarily withdrawn from the mainland to escape the stress of persecution (which scarcely harmonises with the context or the general temper of the book) or for solitary communion (*cf.* Ezek. i. 1-3), or, as is more likely, his removal was a punishment (*cf.* Abbott, 114-16). The latter view is corroborated by tradition (*cf.* Zahn, § 64, note 7), which, although later and neither uniform nor wholly credible, is strong enough to be taken as independent evidence. It can hardly be explained away as a mere elaboration of the present passage (so, *e.g.*, Reuss, Bleek, Bousset); the allusion to **μαρτύριον** is too slight to have been suggested by the darker sense of martyrdom, and it is far-fetched to argue that the tradition was due to a desire to glorify John with a martyrdom. Unless, therefore, the reference is a piece of literary fiction (in which case it would probably have been

Ἰησοῦ. 10. ἐγενόμην [h] ἐν πνεύματι ἐν τῇ κυριακῇ ἡμέρᾳ· καὶ

h (From Zech. i. 6, vii. 12, etc. LXX), *cf.* iv. 2, xxi. 10; condition of vision, Acts vii. 55; = ἐν ἐκστάσει (Acts xi. 5, xxii. 17), contrast γεν. ἐν ἑαυτῷ Acts xii. 11.

elaborated) it must be supposed to be vague simply because the matter was perfectly familiar to the circle for whom the book was written. It is to those exercised in prudence, temperance, and virtue that (according to Philo, *de incorrupt. mundi*, § 1, *cf.* Plutarch's discussion in *defect. orac.* 38 f.) God vouchsafes visions, but John introduces his personal experience in order to establish relations between himself and his readers rather than to indicate the conditions of his theophany.

Ver. 10. Ecstasy or spiritual rapture, the supreme characteristic of prophets in Did. xi. 7 (where the unpardonable sin is to criticise a prophet **λαλοῦντα ἐν πνεύματι**), was not an uncommon experience in early Christianity, which was profoundly conscious of living in the long-looked for messianic age (Acts ii. 17 f., *cf.* Eph. iii. 5), when such phenomena were to be a matter of course. Throughout the Apocalypse (xxi. 5, etc.) John first sees, then writes; the two are not simultaneous. While the Apocalypse is thus the record of a vision (**ὅρασις**, ix. 17), the usual accompaniments of a vision—*i.e.*, prayer and fasting—are significantly absent from the description of this inaugural scene, which is reticent and simple as compared, *e.g.*, with a passage like *Asc. Isa.* iv. 10-16. It is possible, however, that the prophet was engaged in prayer when the trance or vision overtook him (like Peter, Acts x. 9-11, *cf.* Ign. *ad Polyc.* ii. 2, **τὰ δὲ ἀόρατα αἴτει, ἵνα σοι φανερωθῇ**), since the day of weekly Christian worship is specially mentioned on which, though separated from the churches (was there one at Patmos?), he probably was wrapt in meditations (on the resurrection of Christ) appropriate to the hour. The *Imperial* or Lord's day, first mentioned here in early Christian literature (so Did. xiv., Gosp. Peter 11, etc.) contains an implicit allusion to the ethnic custom, prevalent in Asia Minor, of designating the first day of the month (or week?) as **Σεβαστή** in honour of the emperor's birthday (see Thieme's *Inschr. Maeander*, 1906, 15, and Deissmann in *E.Bi.* 2813 f.). Christians, too, have their imperial day (*cf.* Introd. § 2), to celebrate the birthday of their heavenly king. With his mind absorbed in the thought of the exalted Jesus and stored with O.T. messianic conceptions from Daniel and Ezekiel, the prophet had the following ecstasy in which the thoughts of Jesus and of the church already present to his mind are fused into one vision. He recalls in spirit the usual church-service with its praises, prayers, sudden voices, and silences. (Compare Ign. *Magn.* ix. **εἰ οὖν οἱ ἐν παλαιοῖς πράγμασιν ἀναστραφέντες εἰς καινότητα ἐλπίδος ἦλθον, μηκέτι σαββατίζοντες ἀλλὰ κατὰ κυριακὴν ζῶντες, ἐν ᾗ καὶ ἡ ζωὴ ἡμῶν ἀνέτειλεν δι' αὐτοῦ καὶ τοῦ θανάτου αὐτοῦ . . . καὶ διὰ τοῦτο ὑπομένομεν.**) John's service of God (ver. 2) involved suffering, instead of exempting him from the trials of ordinary Christians; the subsequent visions and utterances prove not merely that in his exile he had fallen back upon the O.T. prophets for consolation but that (*cf.* 2 Cor. xi. 28, 29) he was anxiously brooding over the condition of his churches on the mainland. *Cf.* Dio Chrys. *Orat.* xiii. 422, where the philosopher dates the consciousness of his vocation from the period of his exile. Upon the other hand, the main criterion of a false prophet (Eus. *H. E.* v. 17, 2), apart from covetousness, was speech **ἐν παρεκστάσει**, *i.e.*, the arrogant, ignorant, frenzied rapture affected by pagan Cagliostros, who were destitute of any unselfish religious concern for other people. **ὀπίσω μου**, the regular method of spiritualistic voices and appearances: **σάλπιγγος**, loud and clear, not an unusual expression for voices heard in a trance (*cf. Martyr. Polyc.* xxii. 2, Moscow MS). The following Christophany falls into rhythmical expression. As a revelation of the Lord (ver. 1, *cf.* 2 Cor. xii. 1), with which we may contrast Emerson's saying ("I conceive a man as always spoken to from behind and unable to turn his head and see the speaker"), it exhibits several of the leading functions discharged by Jesus in the Apocalypse, where he appears as (*a*) the revealer of secrets (i. 1 f., v. 5), (*b*) the guardian and champion of the saints (ii., iii., etc.), (*c*) the medium, through sacrifice, of their relationship to God, (*d*) associated with God in rewarding them, and (*e*) in the preliminary overthrow of evil which accompanies the triumph of righteousness. Compare the main elements of the divine

ἤκουσα [i] ὀπίσω μου φωνὴν μεγάλην [k] ὡς σάλπιγγος 11. [l] λεγούσης,
“Ὃ βλέπεις γράψον εἰς βιβλίον καὶ πέμψον [m] ταῖς ἑπτὰ ἐκκλη-
σίαις, εἰς Ἔφεσον καὶ εἰς Σμύρναν [1] καὶ εἰς Πέργαμον καὶ εἰς Θυάτειρα
καὶ εἰς Σάρδεις καὶ εἰς Φιλαδελφίαν καὶ εἰς Λαοδικίαν”.
12. Καὶ ἐπέστρεψα [n] βλέπειν τὴν φωνὴν ἥτις ἐλάλει μετ’ ἐμοῦ·
καὶ ἐπιστρέψας εἶδον ἑπτὰ [o] λυχνίας χρυσᾶς,
13. καὶ ἐν μέσῳ [2] τῶν λυχνιῶν ὅμοιον [p] υἱὸν ἀνθρώπου

i *Cf.* Ezek. iii. 12.
k Sc. *φωνήν*; *cf.* Exod. xix. 6 and Apoc. iv. 1, where voice recurs, also Soph. *Ajax*, 17.
l = *λεγοῦσαν*, false attract. to *σ* instead of *φ*.
m ii. 8, etc., xxii. 16. For ἐκκλ. *cf.* on 1 Thess. i.2.
n *Cf.* Jos., *Ant.*, ix. 4, 5.
o Exod. xxxvii. 23 (*cf.* Abbott, 194 f.).
p *Cf.* xiv. 14, Ez. i. 26, from Dan. vii. 13 (*cf.* Abbott, 175).

[1] For the orthography of **Σμυρναν** (**ζμυρναν** א, vg.) see on ii. 8.

[2] Almost invariably AC, like A (LXX), write **εμμεσω** for **εν μεσω** (*cf.* Meisterhans, *Gramm. d. att. Inschr.*, 110 f.): the original **υιον** (of אQ, 1, etc., And[c], so Ti., WH, Simcox, Bj., Swete, Bousset) has been corrected, as at xiv. 14, into **υιω** by ACP, etc., Cyp., Ar. (so Al., Ws., WH marg.): the **μαστοις** (**απ. λεγ.** in this sense) of CPQ, min., Ar. (edd.) has also been corrected into **μασθοις** (א, min., Ti.) or even **μαζοις** (A, min., so Lach., Ws.); **μαζους** uirorum **μαστους** (Luke, xxiii. 29) mulierum: **χρυσαν**, an irregular contraction, is smoothed out in א[c]PQ into **χρυσην** (for the papyri-usage, *cf. Class. Rev.*, 1901, 35).

nature as conceived by the popular religion of contemporary Phrygia, *viz.*, (*a*) prophetic power, (*b*) healing and purifying power, and (*c*) divine authority (symbolised by the axe): *C. B. P.*, ii. 357.

Ver. 11, **γράψον** (*cf.* Herm. *Vis.* II. iv. 3); this emphasis put upon the commission to compose and circulate what he sees in the vision, is due to the author's claim of canonical authority and reflects a time when a literary work of this nature still required some guarantee, although at an earlier date smaller oracles had been written and accepted (*e.g.*, that which determined the flight of the early Christians to Pella, Eus. *H. E.*, iii. 5, 3). John's rôle, however, is passive in two senses of the term. He seldom acts or journeys in his vision, whereas Jewish apocalypses are full of the movements of their seers; nor does his vision lead to any practical course of action, for—unlike most of the O.T. prophets—he is not conscious of any commission to preach or to reform the world. The prophet is an author. His experience is to be no luxury but a diffused benefit; and as in Tob. xii. 20 (“and now . . . write in a book all that has taken place”) and 4 Esd. xii. 37 (“therefore write in a book all thou hast seen, and thou shalt teach,” etc.), the prophet is careful to explain that composition is no mere literary enterprise but due to a divine behest. The cities are enumerated from Ephesus northwards to Smyrna (forty miles) and Pergamos (fifty miles north of Smyrna), then across for forty miles S.E. to Thyatira, down to Sardis, Philadelphia (thirty miles S.E. of Sardis), and Laodicea (forty miles S.E. of Philadelphia). *Cf.* on ver. 4 and Introd. § 2. Except Pergamos and Laodicea, the churches lay within Lydia (though the writer employs the imperial term for the larger province) which was at that period a by-word for voluptuous civilisation.

Ver. 12. The seven golden lamp-stands are cressets representing the seven churches (20), the sevenfold lamp-stand of the Jewish temple (*cf. S. C.* 295-99) having been for long used as a symbol (Zech. iv. 2, 10). The function of the churches is to embody and express the light of the divine presence upon earth, so high is the prophet's conception of the communities (*cf.* on ii. 4, 5); their duty is to keep the light burning and bright, otherwise the reason for their existence disappears (ii. 5). Consequently the primary activity of Jesus in providence and revelation bears upon the purity of those societies through which his influence is to reach mankind, just as his connexion with them on the other hand assures them of One in heaven to whom out of difficulties here they can appeal with confidence.

Ver. 13. The churches are inseparable from their head and centre Jesus, who moves among the cressets of his temple with the dignity and authority of a high priest. The anarthrous **υ. α.** is the human appearance of the celestial mes-

ἐνδεδυμένον [q] ποδήρη καὶ περιεζωσμένον πρὸς τοῖς μαστοῖς
ζώνην χρυσᾶν.

14. ἡ δὲ κεφαλὴ αὐτοῦ καὶ αἱ τρίχες λευκαὶ ὡς ἔριον λευκόν,
[t] ὡς χιών· [1]
καὶ οἱ ὀφθαλμοὶ αὐτοῦ ὡς [u] φλὸξ πυρός·

q Only here in N.T.: Sir. xxvii. 8.
r Like angels in xv. 6.
s From Dan. vii. 9, En. xlvi. 1.
t From En. xiv. 20 (cvi. 2, 10), *cf.* Matt. xxviii. 3, Slav. En. i. 5, xxxvii. 1.
u ii. 18, xix. 12, Sir. xxiii 19-20, Hom. *Iliad*, xiii. 474.

[1] For a late variant (**αι τρ. λ. ωσει ερ. και το ενδ. αυτου λ. ως χιων**), conforming the words to Daniel, *cf.* Simcox in *Expos.*[3] iv. 316-318.

siah, as in En. xlvi. 1-6 (where the Son of man accompanies God, who, as the Head of Days, had a head "white as wool") and *Asc. Isa.* xi. 1. The difficult **ὅμοιον** is to be explained (with Vit. ii. 127, 223, 227) as = **ὡς** (ii. 18, vi. 14, ix. 7, 8, xxi. 11) or **οἷον**, "something like," a loose reproduction of the Heb. ("un être semblable à nous, un homme"). The whole passage illustrates the writer's habit of describing an object or person by heaping up qualities without strict regard to natural or grammatical collocation. **ποδήρης** (sc. **χιτὼν** or **ἐσθής**), a long robe reaching to the feet, was an oriental mark of dignity (*cf.* on i. 7, and Ezek. ix. 2, 11, LXX), denoting high rank or office such as that of Parthian kings or of the Jewish high priest who wore a purple one. High girding (with a belt?) was another mark of lofty position, usually reserved for Jewish priests, though the Iranians frequently appealed to their deities as "high-girt" (*i.e.*, ready for action = *cf.* Yasht xv. 54, 57, "Vaya of the golden girdle, high-up girded, swift moving, as powerful in sovereignty as any absolute sovereign in the world"). The golden buckle or **πόρπη** was part of the insignia of royalty and its **φίλοι** (1 Macc. x. 8, 9, xi. 58). The author thus mixes royal and sacerdotal colours on his palette to heighten the majesty of Christ's appearance. *New*, *golden* (as in Iranian eschatology), *shining*, *white*—are the usual adjectives which he employs throughout the book for the transcendent bliss of the life beyond and its heavenly tenants; "golden" had been used already in Greek as a synonym for precious, excellent, divine.

Ver. 14. **ὡς χ.**; another conventional simile for celestial beings. **ἡ κ. κ. αἱ τ.**, a pleonastic expression; either = "his head, *i.e.* his hair," or "his forehead and his hair"; scarcely a hendiadys for "the hair of the head" (Bengel). Jewish tradition rationalised the white hairs into a proof of God's activity as a wise old teacher (Chag. 14, *cf.* Prov. xx. 27 f.), and the Daniel-vision might suggest the fine paradox between the divine energy and this apparent sign of weakness. But such traits are probably poetical, not allegorical, in John's vision; they body forth his conception of Jesus as divine. In Egyptian theology a similar trait belongs to Ani after beatification. The whole conception of the messiah in the Apocalypse resembles that outlined in Enoch (Similitudes, xxxvii.-lxxi.), where he also possesses pre-existence as Son of man (xlviii.) sits on his throne of glory (xlvii. 3) for judgment, rules all men (lxii. 6), and slays the wicked with the word of his mouth (lxii. 2); but this particular transference to the messiah (i. 14, 17, 18, ii. 8, xxii. 12, 13), of what is in Daniel predicated of God as the world-judge, seems to form a specifically N.T. idea, unmediated even in Enoch (xlvi. 1), although the association of priestly and judicial attributes with those of royalty was easy for an Oriental (it is predicated of the messiah by Jonathan ben Usiel on Zech. iv. 12, 13). **ὡς φλὸξ πυρός**, like Slav. En. i. 5, from Dan. x. 6; *cf.* Suet. *August.* 79, "oculos habuit claros et nitidos, quibus etiam existimari uoluit inesse quiddam diuini uigoris; gaudebatque si quis sibi acrius contuenti quasi ad fulgorem solis uultum submitteret". Divine beauty was generally manifested (Verg. *Aen.* v. 647 f.) in glowing eyes (insight and indignation), the countenance and the voice; here also (ver. 15) in feet to crush all opposition. The messiah is not crowned, however (*cf.* later, xix. 12). **χ.** = some hard (as yet unidentified) metal which gleamed after smelting. The most probable meaning of this obscure hybrid term is that suggested by Suidas: **χαλκολίβανον· εἶδος ἠλέκτρου τιμιώτερον χρυσοῦ, ἔστι δὲ τὸ ἤλεκτρον ἀλλότυπον χρυσίον μεμιγμένον ὑέλῳ καὶ λιθείᾳ** (**ἤλ.** actually occurring in LXX, Ezek. i. 27).

15. καὶ οἱ πόδες αὐτοῦ ὅμοιοι [v] χαλκολιβάνῳ, ὡς ἐν καμίνῳ πεπυρωμένης·[1]
καὶ [w] ἡ φωνὴ αὐτοῦ ὡς φωνὴ ὑδάτων πολλῶν·
16. καὶ [x] ἔχων ἐν τῇ δεξιᾷ χειρὶ αὐτοῦ ἀστέρας ἑπτά·
καὶ [y] ἐκ τοῦ στόματος αὐτοῦ ῥομφαία δίστομος ὀξεῖα ἐκπορευομένη·
καὶ [z] ἡ ὄψις αὐτοῦ ὡς ὁ ἥλιος φαίνει ἐν τῇ δυνάμει αὐτοῦ.
17. Καὶ ὅτε εἶδον αὐτόν, [a] ἔπεσα πρὸς τοὺς πόδας αὐτοῦ ὡς
νεκρός· καὶ [b] ἔθηκεν τὴν δεξιὰν αὐτοῦ ἐπ' ἐμὲ λέγων, "Μὴ φοβοῦ·

v ii. 18, *cf.* Ezek. i. 7 (LXX).
w Ezek. i. 24, xliii. 2 (Heb.), 4 Esd. vi. 17.
x Pres. ptc. = pres. indic. (Heb. idiom ?) as often.
y 2 Thess. ii. 8, *cf.* 4 Esd. xiii. 4, 10, and Isa. xlix. 2.
z Judg. v. 31, Slav. En. i. 5, xix. 1.
a Isa. vi. 5, Dan. viii. 17-18, x. 17-19, En. xiv. 13-14, 19, 24-25, Slav. En. i. 7-8, Tob xii. 16, Add. Esth. xv. 15, Matt. xxviii. 4.
b Dan. x. 10, 12.

[1] **πεπυρωμενοι** (PQ, etc., And., Ar., so Al., WH marg.) and **πεπυρωμενῳ** (א, min., vg., Sah., Syr., S., Aeth., Vict., so Ti, Bj., Bs., Holtzm.) seem variant corrections of the original genitive **πεπυρωμενης** (AC, so Lach., Tr., WH, Ws., Sw.)—Pr. = sicut de fornace ignea.

The reference then is to amber or to some composition like brass or (copper) bronze; only, it contains gold (*cf.* vulg. = aurichalcum, a valuable and gleaming metal). Abbott (201) sees a corruption of some phrase like **χαλκὸν ἐν κλιβάνῳ,** while others suggest **χαλκός** and לבן (*i.e.*, glowing white brass). Haussleiter would upon inadequate grounds omit **ὡς ἐκ. κ. πεπ.** (219-24).

Ver. 16. The care and control exercised by Christ over the churches only come forward after the suggestions of majesty and authority (13-15) which followed the initial idea of Christ's central position (**ἐν μέσῳ**) among the churches. *Cf.* v. 6 (**ἐν μέσῳ**) for another reference to Christ's central authority—**ἔχων, κ.τ.λ.** For the astrological background of this figure, *cf.* Jeremias 24 f. The traditional symbol, of which an interpretation is given later (ver. 20), probably referred to the seven planets rather than to the Pleiades or any other constellation. If the description is to be visualised, the seven stars may be pictured as lying on Christ's palm in the form of the stars in the constellation of Ursa Major—**ῥομφαία, κ.τ.λ.** By a vivid objectifying of the divine word (corresponding to that, *e.g.*, in Isa. ix. 8 f., ix. 4, and suggested by the tongue-shaped appearance of the short Roman sword or dagger), the figure of the sharp sword issuing from the mouth is applied (in Ps. Sol. xvii. 27, 39, as here) to the messiah, as in Jewish literature to God (Ps. cxlix. 6, etc.) and to wisdom (Sap. xviii. 15), elsewhere to the **λόγος τοῦ θεοῦ** (Heb. iv. 12, *cf.* Apoc. xix. 13-15): Christ's power of reproof and punishment is to be directed against the church (ii. 12 f.) as well as against the world of heathen opposition (xix. 21, where the trait is artistically more appropriate). As a nimbus or *coronata radiata* sometimes crowned the emperor ("image des rayons lumineux qu'il lance sur le monde," Beurlier), so the face of Christ (**ὄψις** as in John xi. 44, *cf.* below, x. 1) is aptly termed, as in the usual description of angelic visitants (reff.), bright as sunshine unintercepted by mist or clouds. This is the climax of the delineation.

Ver. 17. **ἔπεσα κ.τ.λ.**, the stereotyped behaviour (*cf.* Num. xxiv. 4) in such apocalyptic trances (Weinel, 129, 182, *R. J.* 375 f.; for the terror of spiritual experience *cf.* Schiller's lines: "Schrecklich ist es Deiner Wahrheit | Sterbliches Gefäss zu seyn"); Jesus, however, does here what Michael (En. lxxi. 3) or some other friendly angel does in most Jewish apocalypses. There is no dialogue between the prophet and Christ, as there is afterwards between him and the celestial beings—**μὴ φ.** The triple reassurance is (1) that the mysterious, overwhelming Figure reveals his character, experience and authority, instead of proving an alien unearthly visitant; (2) the vision has a practical object ("write," 19) bearing upon human life, and (3) consequently the mysteries are not left as baffling enigmas. All the early Christian revelations which are self-contained, presuppose the risen Christ as their source; the Apocalypse of Peter, being fragmentary, is hardly

ἐγώ εἰμι [c] ὁ πρῶτος καὶ ὁ [d] ἔσχατος, 18. καὶ [1] ἐγενόμην νεκρός καὶ ἰδοὺ ζῶν εἰμὶ εἰς τοὺς αἰῶνας τῶν αἰώνων· [e] καὶ ἔχω τὰς κλεῖς [f] [g] τοῦ θανάτου καὶ τοῦ ᾅδου. 19. Γράψον οὖν ἃ εἶδες, καὶ ἃ εἰσὶ καὶ ἃ

c Isa. xliv. 6, xlviii. 12, *cf.* below on iii. 14.
d *Cf.* xxii. 3, 16 f.
e Job xxxviii. 17, Sap. xvi. 13. f = κλεῖδας (Helbing 40). g Gen. obj. For Hades = θαν. or the grave, see Rohde's *Psyche* (1894), 491 f., 673 f.

[1] Om και ο ζων, after εσχατος, with primitive Latin text (Pr., Tic., Beatus, etc.), Haussl. 218-220, Wellh. The words (a marginal gloss., from και ι. ζ. ε.?) are more likely to have been added (and retained for their bearing on Christ's pre-existence) than omitted; they add nothing to the sense or continuity of the passage. The expression is used of God in iv. 9-10, as of Yahveh in O.T. א om. και ("If ο ζων was a marginal note, it would enter the text at first without και," Simcox).

an exception to the rule. The present vision presents him as superhuman, messianic, militant and divine. But the writer is characteristically indifferent to the artistic error of making Christ's right hand at once hold seven stars and be laid on the seer (16, 17). *Cf.* the fine application of the following passage by Milton in his "Remonstrant's Defence". The whole description answers to what is termed, in modern psychology, a "photism".

Ver. 18. Not "it is I, the first and the last" (which would require ἐγώ εἰμι before μὴ φοβοῦ), but "I am, etc." The eternal life of the exalted Christ is a comfort both in method and result; ἐγενόμην νεκρός (not ὡς; really dead), his experience assuring men of sympathy and understanding; καὶ ἰδοὺ, κ.τ.λ., his victory and authority over death = an assurance of his power to rescue his own people from the grim prison of the underworld (Hades, *cf.* 3 Macc. v. 50, the intermediate abode of the dead, being as usual personified in connexion with death). A background for this conception lies in the primitive idea of Janus, originally an Italian sun-god, as the key-holder (*cf.* Ovid's *Fasti*, i. 129, 130, Hor. *Carm. Sec.* 9, 10) who opens and closes the day (sun = deus clauiger), rather than in Mithraism which only knew keys of heaven, or in Mandæan religion (Cheyne's *Bible Problems*, 102-106). The key was a natural Oriental symbol for authority and power (*cf.* in this book, iii. 7, ix. 1, xx. 1). Jewish belief (see Gfrörer, i. 377-378) assigned three keys or four exclusively to God ("quos neque angelo neque seraphino committit"); these included, according to different views, "clauis sepulchorum," "clavis uitae," "clauis resurrectionis mortuorum". To ascribe this divine prerogative to Jesus as the divine Hero who had mastered death is, therefore, another notable feature in the high Christology of this book. For the whole conception see *E. B. D.* ch. lxiv. (fifth century B.C.?): "I am Yesterday and To-day and To-morrow . . . I am the Lord of the men who are raised again; the Lord who cometh forth from out of the darkness." It is based on the theophany of the Ancient of Days in Dan. vii. 9 f. (yet *cf.* x. 5, 6), who bestows on the ideal Israel (ὡς υἱὸς ἀνθ.) dominion. John changes this into a Christophany, like the later Jewish tradition which saw in υἱὸς ἀ. a personal, divine messiah. When one remembers the actual position of affairs, the confident faith of such passages is seen to have been little short of magnificent. To this Christian prophet, spokesman of a mere ripple upon a single wave of dissent in the broad ocean of paganism, history and experience find unity and meaning nowhere but in the person of a blameless Galilean peasant who had perished as a criminal in Jerusalem. So would such early Christian expectations appear to an outsider. He would be staggered by the extraordinary claims advanced on behalf of its God by this diminutive sect, perhaps more than staggered by the prophecy that imperial authority over the visible and invisible worlds lay ultimately in the hands of this deity, whose power was not limited to his own adherents.—Christophanies were commissions either to practical service (Acts x. 19, etc.), or, as here, so composition.

Ver. 19. οὖν, at the command of him who has authority over the other world and the future (resuming ver. 11. now that the paralysing fear of ver. 17 has been removed). Like the author of 4th Esdras, this prophet is far more interested in history than in the chronological speculations which engrossed many of the older apocalyptists. The sense of γράψον

μέλλει γενέσθαι[1] μετὰ ταῦτα. 20. [h] τὸ μυστήριον τῶν ἑπτὰ ἀστέρων
οὓς εἶδες ἐπὶ τῆς δεξιᾶς μου, καὶ τὰς ἑπτὰ λυχνίας τὰς χρυσᾶς—

h Anacolouthon, μ = nom. pendens, λ. irreg. attracted into case of οὗς after εἶδες

[1] For **γινεσθαι** [Luke xxi. 36] (ℵ[c]A, 1, 38, etc., And[c], Areth., WH, Bs., Bj., Sw., Lach.) read **γενεσθαι** (ℵ*CQP, etc., And[pal], Al. Ti., Ws.).

κ.τ.λ. is not, write the vision already seen (**ἃ εἶδες,** i. 10-18), the present (**ἃ εἰσὶν,** i. 20-iii. 20, the state of the churches, mainly conceived as it exists now and here), and the future (**ἃ μέλλει γενέσθαι μετὰ ταῦτα,** *i.e.*, iv. 1 f.), as though the words were a rough programme of the whole book; nor, as other editors (*e.g.*, Spitta) unconvincingly suggest, is **ἃ εἰσὶν** = "what they mean," epexegetic of **ἃ εἶδες,** or **εἶδες** (*cf.* x. 7, xv. 1) in a future perfect sense (Selwyn). The following chapters cannot be regarded merely as interpretations of i. 10-18, and the juxtaposition of **μέλλει γεν.** (from LXX of Isa. xlviii. 6) fixes the temporal meaning of **εἰσίν** here, even although the other meaning occurs in a different context in ver. 20. Besides, i. 10-18 is out of all proportion to the other two divisions, to which indeed it forms a brief prelude. The real sense is that the contents of the vision (**εἶδες,** like **βλέπεις** in ver. 11, being proleptic) consist of what is and what is to be, these divisions of present and future underlying the whole subsequent Apocalypse. The neut. plur. with a plural verb and a singular in the same sentence, indicates forcibly the indifference of the author to the niceties of Hellenistic grammar. For the whole see Dan. ii. 29, 30, also Barn. i.: "The Lord (**δεσπότης**) hath disclosed to us by the prophets things past and present, giving us also a taste of the firstfruits of the future"; v.: "We ought, therefore, to be exceedingly thankful to the Lord for disclosing the past to us and making us wise in the present; yea as regards the future even we are not void of understanding". Moral stimulus and discipline were the object of such visions: as Tertullian declares of the Mortanist seers: "uidunt uisiones et ponentes faciem deorsum etiam uoces audiunt manifestas tam salutares quam occultas" (*de exhort. cast.* 10).

Ver. 20. **μυστ.** (as in Dan. ii. 27, LXX; see below on x. 7) = "the secret symbol". These two symbols, drawn from the lore of contemporary apocalyptic, are chosen for explanation, partly as an obscure and important element in the foregoing vision which had to be set in a new light, partly because they afford a clue to all that follows (especially the opening section, ii. 1, 5). The seven-branched lamp-stand was a familiar symbol, frequently carved on the lintel of a synagogue. Along with the silver trumpets and other spoils of the temple it now lay in the temple of Peace at Rome. The fanciful symbolism, by which the cressets shining on earth are represented — in another aspect — as heavenly bodies, corresponds to Paul's fine paradox about the Christian life of the saints lying hidden with Christ in God; even unsatisfactory churches, like those at Sardis and Laodicea, are not yet cast away. Note also that the light and presence of God now shine in the Christian churches, while the ancestral Jewish light is extinguished (4 Esd. x. 22): "The light of our lamp-stand is put out"). It is curious that in Assyrian representations the candelabrum is frequently indistinguishable from the sacred seven-branched tree crowned with a star (*R. S.* 488); Josephus expressly declares (*Ant.* iii. 6. 7, 7. 7) that the seven lamps on the stand signified the seven planets, and that the twelve loaves on the shew-bread table signified the signs of the zodiac (*Bell.* v. 5, 5), while Philo had already allegorised the lamp-stand (=seven planets) in *quis haeres*, § xlv. This current association of the **λύχνοι** with the planets is bound up with the astral conception of the angels of the churches (**ἀγγ.** = "angels" as elsewhere in Apocalypse), who are the heavenly representatives and counterparts or patron angels of the churches, each of the latter, like the elements (*e.g.*, water xvi. 5, fire xiv. 18; see further in Baldensperger, 106, and Gfrörer, i. 368 f.), the wind (vii. 1), and the nether abyss (ix. 11), having its presiding heavenly spirit. The conception (*E. J.* i. 593, 594) reaches back to post-exilic speculation, in which Greece, Persia and Judæa had each an influential and responsible angelic prince (Dan. x. 13, 20-21, xii. 1), and especially to the Iranian notion of *fravashis* or semi-ideal prototypes of an earthly personality

i Similar explanations, xiii. 18, xvii. 7, 9, Mk. xiii. 14, 1 Cor. xv. 51, Rom. xi. 25 (*cf.* 1 Cor. xiv. 1 f.).

[i]οἱ ἑπτὰ ἀστέρες ἄγγελοι τῶν ἑπτὰ ἐκκλησιῶν εἰσί· καὶ αἱ λυχνίαι αἱ ἑπτά, ἑπτὰ ἐκκλησίαι εἰσί.

II. 1. "Τῶι ἀγγέλῳ τῆς ἐν Ἐφέσῳ[1] ἐκκλησίας γράψον. Τάδε λέγει

[1] The variant τω (AC, Pr., τω της 36, *cf.* Ws., 64-65) for the της (τω εν εκκλησια Εφεσου = S) of ℵQP, Arm., And., Areth. is preferred by Lach., Tr., Naber, WH (136-137), Sx., Sw., and Hort (38-40): for χρυσων (ℵQP, etc., Ti., WH, Bj., Bs.) Lach., Tr., Ws., Sw. (after AC) substitute χρυσεων (*cf.* Helbing, 84 f).

(here, a community), associated with reminiscences of the Babylonian idea that certain stars were assigned to certain lands, whose folk and fortunes were bound up with their heavenly representatives (*cf.* Rawlinson's *Cuneif. Inscript. West. Asia Minor*, ii. 49, iii. 54, 59, etc.). Afterwards (*cf.* Tobit) individuals were assigned a guardian spirit. This belief (Gfrörer, i. 374 f.) passed into early Christianity (Matt. xviii. 10, Acts xii. 15, where see note), but naturally it never flourished, owing to Christ's direct and spiritual revelation of God's fatherly providence. The association of stars and angels is one of the earliest developments in Semitic folklore, and its poetic possibilities lent themselves effectively as here to further religious applications; *e.g.*, Enoch (i. 18) had long ago represented seven stars, "like spirits," in the place of fiery punishment for disobedience to God's commands. As Dr. Kohler points out (*E. J.* i. 582-97), the determining factors of Jewish angelology were the ideas of "the celestial throne with its ministering angels, and the cosmos with its evil forces to be subdued by superior angelic forces," which corresponds to the punitive and protective rôles of angels in the Johannine Apocalypse. But in the latter they are neither described at length nor exalted. They are simply commissioned by God to execute his orders or instruct the seer. The supreme concern of God is with the earth and man; angels are but the middle term of this relationship, at most the fellow-servants of the saints whose interests they promote (see below on xix. 9, 10, xxii. 8, 9). Christians, unlike the Iranians (*e.g. Bund.* xxx. 23, etc.), offer no praises to them; they reserve their adoration for God and Christ. However graphic and weird, the delineation of demons and angels in this book is not grotesque and crude in the sense that most early Jewish and Christian descriptions may be said to deserve these epithets. Here the guardian spirit who is responsible for a church's welfare, would, roughly speaking, be identified with itself; his oversight and its existence being correlative terms. Hence there is a sense in which the allied conception of ἀγγ. is true, namely, that the ἀγγ. is the personified spirit or genius or heavenly counterpart of the church, the church being regarded as an ideal individual (so Andr., Areth., Wetst., Bleek, Lücke, Erbes, Beyschlag, Swete, etc.) who possesses a sort of Egyptian *Ka* or double. By itself, however, this view lies open to the objection that it explains one symbol by another and hardly does justice to the naïve poetry of the conception. The notion of guardian angels was widespread in the early church (Hermas, Justin, Clem. Alex., Origen, etc.), independently of this passage. Statius (*Silv.* i. 241) says that Domitian "posuit sua sidera" (*i.e.*, of his family) in the heaven, when he raised a temple to the Flavians—a contemporary parallel upon a lower level of feeling, but indicating a similar view of the heavenly counterpart (*cf.* Ramsay, *Seven Letters*, 68 f.) The Apocalypse, though presupposing the exercise of discipline and the practice of reading, prayer, and praise within the Christian communities, entirely ignores officials of any kind; and the following homilies are directly concerned with the churches (ii. 7, ἐκκλησίαις, not the angels), their different members (*cf.* ii. 24) and their respective situations. Hence the poetic idealism of the ἄγγελοι soon fades, when the writer's practical sense is brought to bear. As the scene of revelation is ἐν πνεύματι and its author the heavenly Christ, the writer is instructed to address not τοῖς ἁγίοις (*e.g.*, ἐν Ἐφέσῳ), but their patron spirit or guardian angel. The point of the address is that the revelation of Jesus is directly conveyed through the spoken and written words of the prophets, as the latter are controlled by his Spirit.

CHAPTER II. 1-CHAPTER III. 20. The

ὁ κρατῶν τοὺς ἑπτὰ ἀστέρας ἐν τῇ δεξιᾷ αὐτοῦ, ὁ [a] περιπατῶν ἐν
μέσῳ τῶν ἑπτὰ λυχνιῶν τῶν χρυσῶν· 2. Οἶδα τὰ [b] ἔργα σου, καὶ
τὸν κόπον καὶ τὴν ὑπομονήν σου, καὶ ὅτι οὐ δύνῃ [c] βαστάσαι κακούς,
καὶ [d] ἐπείρασας τοὺς λέγοντας ἑαυτοὺς εἶναι ἀποστόλους [e] καὶ οὐκ

a Lev. xxiv. 4, xxvi. 12 (LXX).
b Not in ii. 9, 13.
c (*Cf.* Epict. Diss. i. 3, 2 οὐδεὶς σου τ. ὀφρὺν βαστάσει), "Thou canst not so much as tolerate".
d 1 John iv. 1, *cf.* 2 Cor. xiii. 5: "tested, put to the proof".
e *Cf.* on i. 6.

seven open letters or pastorals (in the modern and ecclesiastical sense of the term) are appeals for vigour and vigilance which reflect a mind in which imaginative, even mystic fervour was accompanied by shrewd penetration into the existing state of morals and religion in the Asiatic communities. Their disorders and difficulties do not escape the notice of the prophet. He will neither spare nor despair of the churches. He speaks in the name of a Lord who knows not only who are his, but what they are, One who is keenly alive to their plight and struggles (**οἶδα**, ii. 1, etc.) alike against inward corruption and the external pressure of the Empire, one to whom their obscure provincial conflict is a matter of infinite moment.

ii. 1-7, to Ephesus.

Ver. 1. The political and commercial primacy of Ephesus, conjoined with its prestige as a centre for the Imperial cultus which flourished beside the local cult of Diana, lent it œcumenical importance in the Eastern Empire. Christianity had for about half a century already made it a sphere and centre, and its position was enormously enhanced after the crisis of 70 A.D. in Palestine, when Asia Minor became one of the *foci* of the new faith (*cf.* von Dobschütz, pp. 100 f.). The description of the speaker is carried on from i. 12, 16, 20, with **κρατῶν** for **ἔχων** (the church is neither to be plucked nor to be dropped from his hand) and the addition of **περιπατῶν** to **ἐν μέσῳ** (activity and universal watchfulness, *cf.* Abbott, pp. 196 f.), touches which make the sketch more definite, but which are too slight to be pressed into any significance, unless one supposes a subtle general contrast between the ideal of the churches—"a star shining by its own inherent light"—and their actual condition upon earth which, like the lamp, requires constant replenishing and care, if its light is not to flicker or fade.

Ver. 2. **οἶδα**: nothing escapes his notice, neither the good (2-3, 6) nor the bad (4, 5) qualities. **ἔργα** = the general course and moral conduct of life, exemplified more especially in its active and passive sides, as exertion and endurance, by **κόπος** and **ὑπομονή**, which are knit together by the final **σου** as epexegetic of **ἔργα**. The **κόπος**, or hard work, is further specified in the text of ver. 2 (the church's vigorous dealing with impostors), while the **ὑπομονή** is developed in ver. 3. For a parallel, verbal rather than real, see 1 Thess. i. 3. Here duty follows privilege (ver. 1), and communion with Christ involves practical energy and enterprise on earth. The remarkable prominence of **ἔργα** in this book corresponds to its O.T. conception of the *fear of God* which, as a religious principle, manifests itself effectively in *works*. The phrase has nothing to do with the special sense in which Paul had employed it during a bygone controversy. *Works* here are the result of an inner relation to God (xii. 11).—Patient endurance (2, 3, 7) wins everything and triumphs over opposition, as in the case of the Maccabean martyrs (4 Macc. i. 11) who are lauded for their courage, **καὶ τῇ ὑπομονῇ . . . νικήσαντες τὸν τύραννον τῇ ὑπομονῇ.**—**βαστάσαι,** the weak are a burden to be borne (Gal. vi. 2): the false, an encumbrance to be thrown off. Patience towards the former is a note of strength: towards the latter, it is a sign of weakness. The prophet is thoroughly in sympathy (*cf.* 2 John 10, 11) with the sharp scrutiny exercised at Ephesus over *soi-disant* missioners; he gladly recognises the moral vigour and shrewdness which made the local church impatient of itinerant evangelists whose character and methods would not stand scrutiny. Pretensions, greed and indolence were the chief sins of this class, but the prophet does not enter into details. He is content to welcome the fact that uncomplaining endurance of wrong and hardship has not evaporated the power of detecting impostors and of evincing moral antipathy to them, upon the principle that **ὑπομονή,** as Clem. Alex. finely explained (*Strom.* ii. 18), is the knowledge of what is to be endured and of what is not. The literature of this

εἰσί, καὶ [f] εὗρες αὐτοὺς ψευδεῖς, 3. καὶ ὑπομονὴν ἔχεις, καὶ
ἐβάστασας διὰ τὸ ὄνομά μου, καὶ οὐ [f] κεκοπίακες. 4. Ἀλλ' ἔχω
[g] κατὰ σοῦ ὅτι τὴν [h] ἀγάπην σου τὴν πρώτην ἀφῆκας.[1] 5.
[i] μνημόνευε οὖν πόθεν πέπτωκες,[2] καὶ μετανόησον καὶ τὰ πρῶτα

f For these uneducated forms in -ες, *cf.* Moulton, i. 52.
g For phrase, *cf.* Matt. v. 23.
h 1 Thess. iii. 12, iv. 9, 2 Thess. i. 3; Clem. Rom. xxxiii. 1, xlix. 7. *Cf.* Eph. iii. 17, v. 2, 1 Tim. i. 5.
i See Acts xxvi. 20.

[1] For the perfective flexion (Helbing, 103-104) **αφηκας** (ℵccAPQ, etc., Al. Lachm., Bs., Ws.) [Matt. xxiii. 23] some (Ti., Tr., WH, Bj., Sw.) substitute **αφηκες** (ℵ*C).

[2] For the **εκπεπτωκας** of P, 1, etc., S., Andpal, vg., Vict., read either **πεπτωκες** (ℵ, Ti., WH, Bj., Sw.) or **-ας** (ACQ, etc., Andc, Areth., Cyp., Pr., Al. Lachm., Tr., Ws.).

period (1 John, Didachê, etc.) is full of directions upon the moral and religious tests which a community should apply to these itinerant evangelists and teachers called "apostles". The popularity and spread of Christianity rendered precautions necessary on the part of the faithful against unscrupulous members of this order, which had already attracted men of quite inferior character as well as of heretical beliefs. The *evil men* here includes these pseudo-apostles as well as the Nikolaitan libertines of ver. 6 (*cf.* 15) with whom perhaps the "apostles" were in sympathy; **ἐπείρ.** and **εὗρ.** denote some definite and recent crisis, while **μισ.** reflects the permanent obstacles of the local situation. This temper of the church is warmly commended by Ign. (*ad Eph.* ix.) at a later period; "I have learned that certain folk passed through you with wicked doctrine (**κακὴν διδαχήν**), but you would not allow them to sow seed in you". With equal loftiness and severity of tone, John like Ignatius might have added: **τὰ δὲ ὀνόματα αὐτῶν, ὄντα ἄπιστα, οὐκ ἔδοξέν μοι ἐγγράψαι** (*Smyrn.* v.).

Ver. 3. The tenses as in ver. 2 denote a general attitude still existing, the outcome of some special stage of persecution for the sake of the Christian name. **κεκοπίακες,** *cf.* **κόπον** (ver. 2), a slight play on words; "noui laborem tuum, nec tamen laboras, *i.e.*, labore non frangeris" (Bengel). Tired in loyalty, not of it. The Ephesian church can bear anything except the presence of impostors in her membership.

Ver. 4. Brotherly love, an early and authentic proof of the faith; as in ver. 19, 2 John 5-6, 3 John 6, and the striking parallel of Matt. xxiv. 12 (see 10) where, as at Corinth (see also Did. xvi. 3) party-spirit and immorality threatened its existence. Jealous regard for moral or doctrinal purity, and unwavering loyalty in trial, so far from necessarily sustaining the spirit of charity, may exist side by side, as here, with censoriousness, suspicion, and quarrelling. Hence the neglect of brotherly love, which formed a cardinal fault in contemporary gnosticism (*i.e.*, 1 John ii. 9; 1 Tim. i. 5 f.), may penetrate the very opposition to such error. During any prolonged strain put upon human nature, especially in a small society driven jealously to maintain its purity, temper is prone to make inroads on affection and forbearance; it was inevitable also that opportunities for this should be given in early Christianity, where party-leaders tended to exaggerate either the liberal or the puritan element in the gospel. When Apollonius of Tyana visited Ephesus, one of the first topics he raised was the duty of unselfish charity (*Vit. Apoll.* iv. 3). The historical reference here is probably to the temporary decline of the Ephesian church after Paul's departure (see Acts xx. 29 f., etc.) Its revival took place under the ministry of the Johannine circle, who—carrying on the spirit of Paulinism with independent vigour—made it the most prominent centre of Christianity in the East. With vv. 2-4, compare Pliny, *H. N.* ii. 18: "deus est mortali iuuare mortalem, et haec ad aeternam gloriam uia"; also Pirke Aboth, ii. 15, where R. Jehoshua, a contemporary Jewish sage, says: "an evil eye [*i.e.*, envy, niggardliness], and the evil nature, and hatred of mankind put a man out of the world" (*cf.* 1 John iii. 15). This emphasis upon brotherly love as the dominant characteristic of the church and the supreme test of genuine faith, is early Christian, however, rather than specifically Johannine (see the account of the young aristocratic martyr Vettius Epagathus, *Ep. Lugd.*). The purity which is not peaceable cannot be adequate to the demands of Jesus, and nowhere did this need reinforcement more than in the townships of Asia Minor, where factiousness and division constantly spoiled their guilds and mutual relations.

Ver. 5. **πόθεν,** from what a height. Contrast Cic. *ad Attic.* iv. 17: "non

ἔργα [i]ποίησον· εἰ δὲ μή, ἔρχομαί [k]σοι καὶ [l]κινήσω τὴν λυχνίαν
σου ἐκ τοῦ [l]τόπου αὐτῆς, ἐὰν μὴ μετανοήσῃς. 6. Ἀλλὰ τοῦτο

k ii. 16, iii. 3.
l For phrase see vi. 14.

recordor unde ceciderim, sed unde resurrexerim". To realise that a decline has taken place, or to admit a lapse, is the first step and stimulus to amendment (see the fine passage in Bunyan's preface to *Grace Abounding*, and the "Hymn of the Soul," 44, 45, in *Acts of Thomas*). Once this is brought home to the mind (**μνημόνευε**, a prolonged effort), repentance quick and sharp (**μετανόησον,** aor.) will follow, issuing in a return to the first level of excellence (**καὶ τὰ πρῶτα ἔργα ποίησον**), *i.e.*, to the initial charity (2 John 6, 8; love shown in deeds). The way to regain this warmth of affection is neither by working up spasmodic emotion nor by theorising about it (Arist. *Eth. Nic.* ii. 4), but by doing its duties. ("The two paracletes of man are repentance and good works," Sanhed. 32). It is taken for granted that man possesses the power of turning and returning; the relation of Christ's redeeming death to the forgiveness of sins throughout the Christian life, although implied, is never explicitly argued (as in Hebrews) by this writer. The present (**ἔρχ.**) emphasises the nearness of the approach, while the future (**κιν.**) denotes a result to follow from it. **σοι** either a dat. incommodi or (more probably) a local dat. (rare in classical literature, *cf.* Aesch. *Pr. V.* 360) with "the sense of motion to a place" (Simcox, *Lang. N. T.* 81), if not an incorrect reproduction of Heb. לָךְ (as Matt. xxi. 5, Blass). *Cf. Journ. Theol. St.* iii. 516. **κινήσω κ.τ.λ.**, ("efficiam ut ecclesia esse desinas," Areth.); not degradation but destruction is the threat, brotherly love being the *articulus stantis aut cadentis ecclesiae.* So, in a remarkable parallel from Paul (Phil. ii. 14-16), quarrelsomeness forfeits the privileges of Christ's care and service, since the function of being **φωστῆρες ἐν κόσμῳ, λόγον ζωῆς ἐπέχοντες** depends upon concord and charity in the church (**πάντα ποιεῖτε χωρὶς γογγυσμῶν καὶ διαλογισμῶν**). A slackened sense of the obligation to mutual love formed the cardinal sin at Ephesus; to repent of this was the condition of continued existence as a church; utility or extinction is the alternative held out to her. The nature of the visitation is left unexplained; the threat is vague, but probably eschatological. The Apocalypse, however, knows nothing of the Jewish idea that Israel's repentance would bring the advent of messiah (*cf.* Schürer's *Hist.* II. ii. 163, 164), as though the transgressions of the people hindered his appearance.

Ver. 6. The message ends with a tardy echo of 2 *b*. The prophet admits that one redeeming feature in the church is the detestation of the N. Not all the spirit of animosity at Ephesus is amiss. When directed, as moral antipathy, against these detestable Nikolaitans (corresponding to the Greek quality of **μισοπονηρία**), it is a healthy feature of their Christian consciousness. The Nikolaitans have been identified by patristic tradition, from Irenæus downwards, with the followers of the proselyte Nikolaos (Acts vi. 5, where see note), who is alleged, especially by Tertullian and Epiphanius, to have lapsed into antinomian license, as the result of an overstrained asceticism, and to have given his name to a sect which practised religious sensuality in the days before Cerinthus. The tenets of the latter are in fact declared by Irenæus to have been anticipated by the Nicolaitans, who represented the spirit of libertinism which, like the opposite extreme of legalism at an earlier period, threatened the church's moral health. But if the comment of Vict. were reliable, that the N. principle was merely *ut delibatum exorcizaretur et manducari posset et ut quicumque fornicatus esset octauo die pacem acciperet*, the representation of John would become vigorously polemical rather than historically accurate. The tradition of the N.'s origin may of course be simply due to the play of later imagination upon the present narrative taken with the isolated reference to Nikolaos in Acts vi. 6. On the other hand it was not in the interest of later tradition to propagate ideas derogatory to the character of an apostolic Christian; indeed, as early as Clem. Alex. (*Strom.* ii. 20, iii. 4; *cf. Constit. Ap.* vi. 8), a disposition (shared by Vict.) to clear his character is evident. Whatever was the precise relation of the sect to Nikolaos, whether some tenet of his was exploited immorally or whether he was himself a dangerously lax teacher, there is no reason to doubt the original connexion of the party with him. Its accommodating principles are luminously indicated by the comment of Hippolytus

ἔχεις, ὅτι [m] μισεῖς τὰ ἔργα τῶν Νικολαϊτῶν, [n] ἃ κἀγὼ μισῶ. 7. [o] Ὁ ἔχων οὖς ἀκουσάτω τί τὸ Πνεῦμα λέγει ταῖς ἐκκλησίαις· Τῷ

m Ps. cxxxix. 21, *cf.* on Rom. xii. 9.
n *Cf.* Polyk. *Phil.* ii. 2.
o Mk. iv. 23, etc., fr. Ezek. iii. 27.

(ἐδίδασκεν ἀδιαφορίαν βίου) and the phrase attributed to him by Clem. Alex. (παραχρήσασθαι τῇ σαρκὶ δεῖ), a hint which is confirmed, if the Nikolaitans here and in ver. 15 are identified with the Balaamites (νικο-λαος, in popular etymology, a rough Greek equivalent for בלע עם, perdidit uel absorpsit populum). This symbolic interpretation has prevailed from the beginning of the eighteenth century (so Ewald, Hengstenberg, Düst., Schürer, Julicher, Bousset). The original party-name was probably interpreted by opponents in this derogatory sense. It was thus turned into a covert censure upon men who were either positively immoral or liberally indifferent to scruples (on food, clubs, marriage, and the like) which this puritan prophet regarded as vital to the preservation of genuine Christianity in a pagan city. A contemporary parallel of moral laxity is quoted by Derenbourg, *Hist. de la Palestine* (1867), p. 363. If Nikolaos was really an ascetic himself, the abuse of his principles is quite intelligible, as well as their popularity with people of inferior character. Pushed to an extreme, asceticism confines ethical perfection to the spirit. As the flesh has no part in the divine life, it may be regarded either as a foe to be constantly thwarted or as something morally indifferent. In the latter case, the practical inference of sensual indulgence is obvious, the argument being that the lofty spirit cannot be soiled by such indulgence any more than the sun is polluted by shining on a dunghill.

Ver. 7. A stringent demand for attention (πίστις, ὦτα ψυχῆς: Clem. Alex.) to the utterances of prophets who were inspired by the Spirit (of prophecy, *cf.* on xix. 10). These as usual are ejaculatory, positive and brief—ἐκκλ. scattered local communities, and not a Catholic organisation, being the conception of the Apocalypse, it is for use in their public worship that this book is written (i. 3). It is a subordinate and literary question whether the seer means in such phrases as this to designate himself (Weinel, 84 f.) liturgically as the speaker, or whether (as the synoptic parallels suggest) they form an integral part of the whole menage. In any case the prophet represents himself simply as the medium for receiving and recording (*cf.* i. 19) these oracles of the Spirit (*cf.* xiv. 13, xix. 9, xx. 17). Unlike other writers such as Paul and the authors of Hebrew and 1 John, he occupies a passive rôle, throwing his personal rebuke and counsels into the form *Thus saith the Spirit:* but this really denotes the confidence felt by the prophet in his own inspiration and authority. The Spirit here, though less definitely than in Hermas, is identified with Jesus speaking through his prophets: it represents sudden counsels and semi-oracular utterances (*cf.* on i. 10), not a continuous power in the normal moral life of the saints in general. The seven promises denote security of immortal life (positively as here and ver. 28 or negatively as ver. 11), privilege (personal, ver. 17, or official, ver. 27), honour (iii. 5, 21), or increased intimacy (iii. 12). As usual, (*cf.* 1 Cor. ii. 9f.), the higher Christian γνῶσις is connected with eschatology.

Observe the singling out for encouragement and praise of each soldier in the host of the loyal. The effect resembles that produced by Pericles in his panegyric over the Athenians who had fallen in the Peloponnesian war: "together they gave up their lives, yet individually they won this deathless praise" (Thuc. ii. 43, 2). νικῶν (a quasi-perfect), in Herm. *Mand.* xii. 2, 4 f., 5. 2, 4, 6. 2, 4 (over sin and devil), might have its usual Johannine sense, the struggle being obedience in face of the seductions and hardships which beset people aiming to keep the divine commandments (*cf.* on John xvi. 33). For a special application of the term, see xv. 2. But behind the general usage lies the combination of "to be pure or just" and "to conquer or triumph" in the Hebrew *ṣédeḳ* and the Syriac *zedhā*. Furthermore, νικῶν throughout is equivalent to the Egyptian eschatological term "victorious," applied to those who passed successfully through life's temptations and the judgment after death. Its generic sense is illustrated by 4 Esd. vii. [128]: "here is the intent of the battle to be fought by man born upon earth: if he be overcome, he shall suffer as thou hast said; but if he conquer, he shall receive the thing of which I speak" (*i.e.*, paradise and its glories). The Essenes

[p] νικῶντι δώσω αὐτῷ [r] φαγεῖν ἐκ τοῦ ξύλου τῆς ζωῆς, ὅ ἐστιν ἐν τῷ [s] παραδείσῳ τοῦ θεοῦ.

"8. Καὶ τῷ ἀγγέλῳ τῆς[1] ἐν Σμύρνῃ ἐκκλησίας γράψον· Τάδε

p En. I, 2. q Redundant, Moult. i. 85, Win. § 22, 5a.

r xxii. 2, 14, 19. s Ezek. xxxi. 8, 2 Cor. xii. 4, Lk. xxiii. 43: Deissm. 148.

[1] For της ℵCPQ (Ti., Al. Ws., Bs., Bj.) Lach., WH, Sw. prefer τω (A, *cf.* ii. 1, 18): Ζμυρνη (ℵ, am., fuld., S., Ti.), an orthography which ceases on coins towards end of Trajan's reign (according to Waddington, *Fastes des provinces asiatiques*, i. 158).

according to Josephus (*Ant.* xviii. 1, 5), held the soul was immortal, **περιμάχητον ἡγούμενοι τοῦ δικαίου τὴν πρόσοδον**—eternal life the reward of an untiring, unsoiled fight against evil. The imagery of the metaphor is drawn from Jewish eschatology which anticipated the reversal of the doom incurred in Eden; *cf. Test. Levi*, 18, **καὶ δώσει τοῖς ἁγίοις φαγεῖν ἐκ τοῦ ξύλου τῆς ζωῆς,** also En. xxiv. 1-11, xxv., xxxi. 1-3, etc., and (for Egyptian ideas) below on iii. 21. The garden-park of God (**π.** = a garden with fruit-trees, Wilcken's *Griech. Ostraká*, i. 157) is one of the intermediate abodes, possibly (as in Slav. En. viii. 1, and Paul) the third heaven where the favoured saints live after death in seclusion and bliss, So Iren. v. 5. 1 (abode of translated) and v. 36, 1-2, where heaven is for the Christians of the hundredfold fruit, paradise for the sixty-fold, and the heavenly city for the thirty-fold (a very ancient Christian tradition). The tree of life blooms in most of the apocalypses (*cf.* on xxii. 2). Philo had already allegorised it into **θεοσέβεια ὁ τῆς τελείας ἀρετῆς χαρακτήρ.** But the allusion corresponds to the general eschatological principle (borrowed from Babylonia, where cosmological myths passed into eschatological) that the end was to be a transcendently fine renovation of the original state (Barn. vi. 8). **μου** a deliberate addition to the O.T. phrase; Christ's relation to God guarantees his promise of such a privilege (iii. 12). God's gift (Rom. vi. 23) is Christ's gift. He is no fair promiser like Antigonus II., whom men dubbed **δώσων** for his large and unfulfilled undertakings (Plut. *Coriol.* xi.).

Vv. 8-11. The message (shortest of the seven) to the Christians in Smyrna, "one of the first stars in the brilliant belt of the cities of Asia Minor" (Mommsen), a wealthy and privileged seaport, and like Sardis a constant rival of Ephesus for the title of primacy which properly belonged to Pergamos, the real capital of the province. It is probably owing to the petty jealousies of these urban communities that the prophet refrains from speaking of one to the other (as Paul did, with his churches), by way of example.

Ver. 8. The title from i. 17-18, with special reference to ver. 10 and its situation, also to the promise of ver. 11. The Smyrniote Christians, in peril of death, are addressed and encouraged by One who himself has died—and risen to life. He is familiar [ver. 9] with the rough brake and briars through which faith must struggle to win its crown, and this familiarity is as usual put forward as the first element of encouragement. The other notes of help are (i.) the unapproachable wealth of a devoted life, (ii.) the justice of their claim in spite of their opponents' prestige and pretensions, (iii.) the providential limit assigned to their trial, and (iv.) its ample reward, besides the fact that Christ does not conceal from them the worst.—**πτωχ.** Contrast R. Jochanan's aphorism: "Whosoever fulfils the Torah in poverty will at length fulfil it in wealth; and whosoever neglects the Torah in wealth, will at length neglect it in poverty" (Pirke Aboth, iv. 13). The subsequent allusion to Jews acquires fresh point from a comparison with (Chagigah, 9*b*) another contemporary rabbi's comment on Isa. xlviii. 10: "this means that the Holy One sought for all good qualities to give to Israel, and found only poverty".—**Ἰουδ.** Does the prophet resent (see on this, von Dobschütz, *Texte u. Unters.* xi. 1. 35 f.) the Jewish claim to the title of God's people, declaring in so many words (as Matt. xxi. 43), that Judaism, so far as it is genuine, is now inside the church, and that the Jewish nation has forfeited its privilege and is now a pseudo-church (Harnack, *H. D.* i. 177-179)? If the passage does not breathe this common antipathy, the calumnies may be supposed to have taken the form of taunts upon the Christian delusion of believing that a Palestinian peasant and criminal was messiah, or of slanders upon Christian morals and mo-

[t] *Cf.* xiii. 14. [u] Vernacular genitive (as in ii. 19, iii. 1, 8, 15), *cf.* Abbott, *Diat.* 2781. [v] Result of θλῖψις (Heb. x. 33-34)?

λέγει ὁ πρῶτος καὶ ὁ ἔσχατος, ὃς ἐγένετο νεκρὸς καὶ [t] ἔζησεν· 9.
Οἶδα [u] σου τὴν θλίψιν καὶ τὴν [v] πτωχείαν· ἀλλὰ [w] πλούσιος εἶ· καὶ
τὴν [x] βλασφημίαν [y] ἐκ τῶν λεγόντων [z] Ἰουδαίους εἶναι ἑαυτούς, καὶ
οὐκ εἰσὶν, ἀλλὰ συναγωγὴ [a] τοῦ Σατανᾶ. 10. Μηδὲν[1] φοβοῦ ἃ μέλλεις
πάσχειν. ἰδοὺ μέλλει βάλλειν ὁ διάβολος [b] ἐξ ὑμῶν εἰς φυλακὴν

[w] 2 Cor. vi. 10, viii. 9, Jas. ii. 5, *cf.* Ps. xxxiv. 10-11, and espec. Tobit iv. 21. [x] *Cf.* 1 Pet. iii. 16, iv. 4. [y] John iii. 25. [z] Constr. iii. 9, Rom. ii. 19, Lk. xx. 20 (Blass, § 72, 2). [a] iii. 9, 2 Cor. xi. 14-15. [b] 2 John 4, partitive by harsh Hellenistic usage.

[1] For **μηδεν** (אP, etc., vg., Syr., Aeth., And^ac bav, Areth., Cypr., Pr., Ti., Sx., Bs.) Lach., Al., Düst., Tr., WH, Ws., Bj., Sw. read the easier and less probable **μη** (ACQ, 8, 38, 49, Arm, And^pal).

tives (reff.), or of malicious, anonymous accusations laid before the Roman authorities with reference to revolutionary designs on the part of the churches. "Les Orientaux prennent d'ordinaire la religion comme un prétexte de taquineries" (Renan). Judaism was strong at Smyrna, and its hostility to the Christians (see Otto's notes on Just. *Dial.* xvi. 11, xxxv., etc.) would not be lessened by the accession of converts from the old faith to the new (Ign. *ad Smyrn.* i. 2, describes the saints and faithful folk of Christ **εἴτε ἐν Ἰουδαίοις εἴτε ἐν ἔθνεσιν**); the reasons for such social animosity and interference are analysed in Jowett's note on 1 Th. iii. 13, in E. G. Hardy's *Christianity and the Roman Government*, pp. 45-53, and in Ramsay's *Seven Letters*, 272 f. At the martyrdom of Polykarp in Smyrna, some years after the Apocalypse was written (as later still at the death of Pionius, 250 A.D.) the Jews made themselves conspicuous by denouncing him with the pagan mob before the Asiarch (**ἀκατασχέτῳ θυμῷ καὶ μεγάλῃ φωνῇ**), eagerly assisting to heap faggots on his pile (**προθύμως, ὡς ἔθος αὐτοῖς**), and helping to prevent the Christians from obtaining the martyr's body (**ὑποβαλλόντων καὶ ἐνισχυόντων τῶν Ἰουδαίων**: Mart. *Polyk.* xii., xvii.). The name of "Jew," ancient and honourable, is claimed (**καὶ οὐκ εἰσί**) for believers in Jesus the messiah, who constitute the real people of God with a legitimate claim to the privileges and titles of the O.T. community. "Now by our faith we have become more than those who seemed to have God" (2 Clem. ii. 3).—**συν. σατ.** a bitter retort to the contemporary claims of Judaism with its **σ. τοῦ κυρίου** (*cf*, Num. xvi. 3, xx. 4, Ps. Sol. xvii. 18, **σ. ὁσίων**). The allusion here is to Jewish, in ver. 13 (throne of S.) to pagan, and in ver. 24 (depths of S.) to heretical, antagonism.

Ver. 10. **μη. φοβοῦ, κ.τ.λ.** "Thou orderest us to endure, not to love, trials. A man may love to endure, but he does not love what he endures" (Aug. *Conf.* x. 28). Ill-treatment, as well as misrepresentation, is traced back to a diabolic source, in the common early Christian manner (Weinel, 13 f.). The Imperial authorities (**διάβολος** as in 1 Peter v. 8), although often instigated by the Jews, had the sole power of inflicting imprisonment, in this case for a refusal to worship the emperor's image; the prophet here predicts an imminent persecution of this kind (compare Acts ix. 16, and above Introd. § 6) lasting for a short and limited time (**δέκα ἡμ.** see reff., originally due to the rough Semitic division of a month into decades). The local intensity of feeling upon the Imperial cultus may be gathered from the fact that in 23 A.D. Smyrna had secured from Tiberius and the senate, after keen competition, the coveted distinction of possessing the second temple decreed by the province to the Imperial cultus. Hence the struggle anticipated here is desperate (**ἄχ. θ.**); martyrdom is no remote contingency. Compare Ep. Lugd., where the martyr-crisis is taken as an anticipation of the final persecution (*cf.* Apoc. iii. 10, xiii. 7-15): "with all his might the adversary assailed us, giving us a hint of what his unbridled advent would be like at the end"; the martyrs "endured nobly all the assaults heaped on them by the mob. They were shouted at, struck, haled about, robbed, stoned, imprisoned; in fact they suffered all that an infuriated mob likes to inflict on enemies and opponents."—Then follows a commandment with promise: **γίνου** (not **ἴσθι**), "show thyself" throughout all degrees of trial and in any emergency. It is more than doubtful if this is a subtle local allusion to the loyalty and local patriotism upon which Sardis prided her-

ἵνα πειρασθῆτε· καὶ ἕξετε θλίψιν ἡμερῶν [c] δέκα. γίνου πιστὸς
[d] ἄχρι θανάτου, καὶ δώσω σοι τὸν [e] στέφανον τῆς [f] ζωῆς. 11. Ὁ
ἔχων οὖς ἀκουσάτω τί τὸ Πνεῦμα λέγει ταῖς ἐκκλησίαις· Ὁ νικῶν οὐ
μὴ ἀδικηθῇ ἐκ τοῦ [g] θανάτου τοῦ [g] δευτέρου.

"12. Καὶ τῷ ἀγγέλῳ τῆς ἐν Περγάμῳ ἐκκλησίας γράψον. Τάδε
λέγει [h] ὁ ἔχων τὴν ῥομφαίαν τὴν δίστομον τὴν ὀξεῖαν· 13. Οἶδα
ποῦ κατοικεῖς, ὅπου ὁ θρόνος τοῦ Σατανᾶ, καὶ κρατεῖς [i] τὸ ὄνομά μου,

c Gen. xxiv. 55, Num. xi. 19, Dan. i. 12, 14.
d xii. 11, Acts xxii. 4, Phil. ii. 8, Sib. Or ii. 47, Ign., *Polyk.* ii. 3.
e 1 Pet. v. 4, 2 Tim. iv. 8, Jas. i. 12.
f Gen. epexeg.
g See on xx. 6, 14.
h xix. 15, Heb. iv. 12, En. lxii. 2; its stroke = Sir. xxi. 3. The spiritual *jus gladii*.
i *Cf.* on ver. 10, and iii. 8.

self and which she had urged as her plea to Tiberius (Tacit. *Ann.* iv. 56). On the honours subsequently paid to martyrs in Smyrna, *cf. Mart. Polyk.* xvii. **τοῦτον μὲν γὰρ υἱὸν ὄντα τοῦ θεοῦ προσκυνοῦμεν, τοὺς δὲ μάρτυρας ὡς μαθητὰς καὶ μιμητὰς τοῦ κυρίου ἀγαπῶμεν** (also Euseb. *H. E.* iv. 15. 46, 47), with the contemporary cry of 4 Esd. viii. 27: "Look not at the deeds of the impious but at those who have kept Thy covenants amid affliction" (*i.e.*, the martyrs), also the subsequent Christian honour paid by Hermas (*Vis.* iii. 1, 2), who reserves the right hand of God for the martyrs who have "suffered for the sake of the Name," enduring "stripes, imprisonments, great afflictions, crosses, wild beasts". For **καὶ** with fut. after imperative, see Eph. v. 14, James iv. 7.—**στέφ. ζ.** *Life*, the reward assigned in ver. 7 to the triumph of faith is here bestowed upon the loyalty of faith. To hold one's ground is, under certain circumstances, as trying and creditable as it is under others to win positive successes. The metaphor of **στέφ.** with its royal, sacerdotal, and festal (Cant. iii. 11, Isa. xxviii. 1, Herm. *Sim.* viii. 2) associations, would call up civic and athletic honours to the local Christians, the latter owing to the famous games at Smyrna, the former from the fact that **στ.** frequently occurs also in inscriptions as = public honour for distinguished service (paid, *e.g.*, to Demosthenes and Zeno), whilst the yearly appointment of a priest at Eumeneia to the temple of Zeno was termed **παράληψις τοῦ στέφανου** (*C. B. P.* ii. 358). Compare, with the **ἄξιοι** of iii. 4, the sentence in Ep. Lugd. upon the martyrs: **ἐχρῆν γοῦν τοὺς γενναίους ἀθλητὰς, ποικίλον ὑπομείναντας ἀγῶνα καὶ μεγάλως νικήσαντας, ἀπολαβεῖν τὸν μέγαν τῆς ἀφθαρσίας στέφανον**, and the Greek phrase for noble deeds, **ἄξια στεφάνων** (Plut. *Pericl.* 28).

Ver. 11. **οὐ μὴ** (emphatic): no true Christian, much less one who dies a martyr's death, need fear anything beyond the pang of the first death. The second death of condemnation in the lake of fire leaves the faithful scatheless, no matter how others may suffer from the terrors (*cf.* on iii. 12) which haunted the ancient outlook (especially the Egyptian) upon the dark interval between death and heaven. *Cf.* the sketch of Ani, seated on his throne and robed in white, holding sceptre and staff, and crying: "I am not held to be a person of no account, and violence shall not be done me. I am thy son, O Great One, and I have seen the hidden things that belong to thee. I am crowned king of the gods, and shall not die a second time in the underworld" (*E. B. D.* 99). If a Christian keep himself loyal till death, the prophet here guarantees that Christ will keep him safe after death. After the promise of ver. 10 however, this sounds like an anticlimax. The general tenor of the message indicates that John was rather more cordial and sympathetic to the Smyrniote church than to the Ephesian.

Vv. 12-17. The message to Pergamos, the Benares or Lourdes of the province.

Ver. 12. The title is apt in view of ver. 16.

Ver. 13. Two features in the local situation menaced Christianity. Pergamos, besides forming a legal centre for the district (ad eam conueniunt Thyatireni aliaeque inhonorae ciuitates, Plin. v. 33), was an old centre of emperor-worship in Asia Minor; in 29 B.C. a temple had been erected to the divine Augustus and the goddess Roma, and a special priesthood had been formed (**ὑμνῳδοὶ θεοῦ Σεβαστοῦ καὶ θεᾶς Ῥώμης**). Another feature, shocking to early Christian feeling, was the local cult of Aesculapius (*cf.* Zahn, § 73, note 2), whose favourite symbol (*e.g.*, on coins) was a serpent ("the god of Pergamos, Mart. ix. 17); so Pausan. *Cor.* 27, (iii. 402), **κάθηται δὲ ἐπὶ θρόνου βακτηρίαν κρατῶν, τὴν δὲ ἑτέραν τῶν χειρῶν**

καὶ οὐκ ἠρνήσω τὴν [k] πίστιν [1] μου καὶ ἐν ταῖς ἡμέραις Ἀντίπας [1] ὁ
μάρτυς μου, ὁ [m] πιστός μου, ὃς ἀπεκτάνθη παρ' ὑμῖν, ὅπου ὁ σατανᾶς
κατοικεῖ. 14. Ἀλλ' ἔχω κατὰ σοῦ ὀλίγα. ἔχεις ἐκεῖ κρατοῦντας τὴν
διδαχὴν Βαλαάμ, ὃς ἐδίδασκεν [n] τῷ Βαλὰκ [o] βαλεῖν σκάνδαλον

k 1 Tim. v. 8.
l xiv. 12: "in me".
m Christ's own title (i. 5, iii. 14).
n Heb. dat. (Job xxi. 22 למד ל); correct constr. in ver. 20.
o Peculiar to Apocalypse; for *τίθεναι* or *ποιεῖν*.

[1] As an alternative to taking **Αντιπας** as indeclinable, WH (after Lachm.) suggest the genit. **Αντιπα** (final **C** taken up from following **O**); so Nestle, Zahn, Schmiedel, Bj., Sw. With **εν αις** or **αις** (before **Αντιπας**, so Ws., Bs.), supply either *exstitit* (Haym) or *occisus est* (*Quaestt.*, 102, 2950). The **αντειπας** of S. might suggest a significant appellation rather than any personal noun (Gwynn).

ὑπὲρ κεφαλῆς ἔχει τοῦ δράκοντος. In addition to these fashionable cults, a magnificent throne-like altar to Zeus Soter towered on the Acropolis (Paus. ii. 73, 75, iii. 556, 557) commemorating the defeat of the barbarian Gauls by Attalus two centuries earlier, and decorated by a famous frieze of the gods warring against the giants (the latter, a brood of vigorous opponents, having often human bodies and serpentine tails, *cf.* below, ix. 19). No wonder Pergamos was called "a throne of Satan" by early Christians who revolted against the splendid and insidious paganism of a place where politics and religion were firm allies. Least of all at this cathedral centre of the Imperial cultus could dissent be tolerated. The Asiarch, *e.g.*, who condemns Polykarp is the local high priest of the altar, and the animus against Cæsar-adoration which pervades the Apocalypse easily accounts for the last phrase **ὁ θ. τ. σ.**, particularly as the symbol of the serpent in the Aesculapius cult would come vividly home to pious Jewish Christians in the church, as a reminder of Satan (*e.g.*, xii. 9 and *passim*). The priesthood of this cult, "a vast college, believed to be in possession of certain precious medical secrets," came "nearest, perhaps, of all the institutions of the pagan world, to the Christian priesthood," its rites being "administered in a full conviction of the religiousness, the refined and sacred happiness, of a life spent in the relieving of pain" (Pater, *Marius the Epicurean*, i. 30; see Usener's *Götternamen*, 1896, pp. 147 f., 350, and Dill's *Roman Soc. from Nero to M. Aur.* 459 f.). **κρατεῖς, κ.τ.λ.**, "And the magistrate pressed him hard, saying, 'Swear the oath [by the genius of Cæsar] and I will release thee; curse the Christ.' But Polykarp replied, 'For eighty-six years I have served him, and he has never injured me. How then can I blaspheme my King, who has saved me?'" (*Mart. Polyc.* ix., Jewish analogies in 2 Macc. viii. 4, *Ass. Mos.* viii. etc.). Some definite outburst of persecution at Pergamos is in the writer's mind (**ἠρνήσω**). To disown or abjure faith in Jesus, saying **Κύριος Καῖσαρ**, implies here as in the gospels the moral fault of cowardice, elsewhere (*e.g.* 1 John, Jud. 4, 2 Peter ii. 1) erroneous doctrine. The circumstances and surroundings of the local church are taken into account, as usual, in the prophet's estimate; they either claim some allowance to be made, or reflect additional credit and lustre on the particular community. **ὁ μάρτυς, κ.τ.λ.** He is faithful who retains his faith. Antipas (= **Ἀντίπατρος**, Jos. *Ant.* xiv. 1, 3; the name occurs in a third century inscription of Pergamos, Deissm. 187), is mentioned by Tertullian (*adv. Gnost. scorp.* 12); otherwise he is unknown. His Acts appear to have been read by Andreas and Arethas, and, according to Simon Metaphrastes, he was an old, intrepid bishop of Pergamos whose prestige drew upon him the honour of being burned to death in a brazen bull during Domitian's reign. The sober truth is probably that he formed the first prominent victim in the local church, possibly in Asia Minor, to the demands of the Imperial cultus. Carpus, Papylus, and Agathonikê, the other martyrs of Pergamos named by Eusebius (*H. E.*, iv. 15, 48), died at a later period. On the whole verse see Ep. Lugd., "then did the holy martyrs endure indescribable torture, Satan eagerly striving to make them utter **τι τῶν βλασφήμων**". The textual variants arose from a failure to see that **Ἀντίπας** (or **-α**) was a genitive and that **μάρτυς** was in characteristic irregular apposition to it. The name is neither a personification nor typical.

Ver. 14. **ὀλίγα**, the errorists are a mere minority; they do not represent or

ἐνώπιον τῶν υἱῶν Ἰσραήλ, ᵖφαγεῖν εἰδωλόθυτα καὶ ᵍπορνεῦσαι. p 1 Cor. viii. 7-13 x. 20-30.
15. οὕτως ἔχεις καὶ σὺ κρατοῦντας τὴν διδαχὴν τῶν Νικολαϊτῶν q xiv. 8, xvii. 1-2, 4-5, xviii. 3, 9.
ὁμοίως.[1] 16. Μετανόησον· εἰ δὲ μή, ʳἔρχομαί σοι ταχὺ καὶ r ii. 5, iii. 3

[1] Al., Düst., Lachm., WH, Sw. (after ACQ, Arm.) om. των before Νικ.

affect the main body of the church, whose fault is not sympathy but indifference. This carelessness arose probably from contempt or fear rather than through ignorance.—**ἐκεῖ** (in the midst of loyalty and martyrdom). **κρατ.** (not **τὸ ὄνομά μου**, but) lax principles worthy of a Balaam, the note of a pupil of Balaam being (according to Pirke Aboth, v. 19), an evil eye, a proud spirit, and a sensual soul. Contemporary opponents of Gnostic tendencies evidently found it an effective weapon to employ O.T. analogies or identifications such as this or the similar ones in 2 Tim. iii. 8, Jud. 11. In the Hexateuch (JE = Num. xxv. 1-5, P = Num. xxv. 6-18, xxxi. 8-16, Josh. xiii. 22) Balaam is represented as a magician who prompts the Moabite women to seduce the Israelites into foreign worship and its attendant sensualism; but in the subsequent Jewish Midrash (followed here) his advice is given to Balak (Joseph. *Ant.* iv. 6, 6; *cf.* iv. 6, 11 for Zimri, and Philo's *Vit. Mos.* i. 48-55), and the sorcerer comes to be regarded as the prototype of all corrupt teachers and magicians (for this sombre reputation, see *E.J.* ii. 467), as of this party at Pergamos who held—to John's indignation—that it was legitimate for a Christian to buy food in the open market, which had already been consecrated to an idol. This problem, which had occurred years before in a sharp form at Corinth, was certain to cause embarrassment and trouble in a city like Pergamos, or indeed in any pagan town, where entertainments had a tendency towards obscenity. It is a curious instance of how at certain periods a scruple may assume the rank of a principle, and of how the ethical inexpediency of some practices lies in their associations rather than in their essential elements. Such questions of religious conscience in the East were frequently connected with food; for the association of the latter with sexual vice, see the notes on Acts xv. 20 (also 1 Cor. x. 4, 8, in its context). The literal sense is preferable, although the usage of the Apocalypse makes the metaphorical sense of **πορν.** possible, as a general description of pagan religions viewed under the aspect of unfaithfulness to the true God (*cf.* John viii. 41, Philo *de migr. Abr.* § 12) For the connexion between certain forms of popular religion in Phrygia and prostitution, see *C.B.P.*, i. 94 f. Such burning questions arose from the nature of the early Christian society, which never aspired to form a *ghetto*, and consequently, in a pagan township, had to face many nice problems with regard to the prudence and limits of conformity or the need of nonconformity (*cf.* 2 Cor. vi. 16, 17). In social and trading pursuits the individual Christian met and mingled with fellow-citizens outside his own religious circle, and these relationships started serious points of ethical principle (Dobschütz, 26 f., 188 f.). The line was drawn, but not always at the same place; and naturally laxity lay on the borders of enlightenment.

Ver. 15. **οὕτως κ.τ.λ.** Are the N. put parallel to, or identified with, the Balaamites? The latter becomes more probable when the symbolical sense of N. and B. (see above, on ver. 6, and Kalisch's *Bible Studies*, i. 23) is adopted. In this event a single class of errorists is in view; they are instigating and seducing the local Christians much as Balaam managed (by means of Balak, in rabbinic tradition, *cf.* the slight play on **βαλεῖν**) to get the Israelites enticed to ruin (*Sanh.* 105 a). Josephus explains that Balaam showed Balak how to win a victory over the Israelites (**νίκην τινὰ . . . κατ' αὐτῶν κερδᾶναι**) by enticing them to lust, and such a symbolic allusion is quite in the manner of the Apocalypse. The Nikolaitans, who probably resembled Cerinthus or Carpokrates in their tenets, are no better than a Balaam. And the Jewish dictum was (*Sanh.* 106 b) that whenever one discovered anything bad in Balaam's life, one should preach about it.

Ver. 16. The church as a whole must repent of her too tolerant attitude to these errorists, but the threatened visitation is directed against the errorists themselves in the shape of some physical malady or mortal sickness, according to the current belief in early Christianity

s xii. 7, xiii. 4, xvii. 14 (Hebraism = עם נלחם); *cf.* Isa. lxiii. 10.

t Sib. vii. 149, John vi. 31-32; partit. gen.

[s] πολεμήσω μετ' αὐτῶν ἐν τῇ ῥομφαίᾳ τοῦ στόματός μου. 17. Ὁ
ἔχων οὖς ἀκουσάτω τί τὸ Πνεῦμα λέγει ταῖς ἐκκλησίαις· Τῷ νικῶντι
δώσω αὐτῷ τοῦ [t] μάννα τοῦ κεκρυμμένου, καὶ δώσω αὐτῷ ψῆφον

(*cf.* on 1 Cor. v. 4-5, 13, xi. 30, Everling: *die paul. Angelologie*, etc., 20 f.). Grotius refers the threat to the prophetic order ("prophetas suscitabo in ecclesia"). But the ethnic conscience generally regarded pestilence or any physical calamity as a punishment inflicted by the god for some offence against his ritual or some breach of morals. In the Hexateuch, the sword opposes (Num. xxii. 23, 31) and finally slays (xxxi. 8) Balaam. The run of thought in the verse is that if the church does not repent, *i.e.*, if she does not act on her own initiative and expel the wrongdoers (in the hope of them ultimately coming to a better mind, 1 Cor. v. 4, 5), she must submit to having them cut out of her, and thus being irretrievably lost by death. The church is responsible for her erring members, and the exercise of discipline is viewed as a duty to them as well as to herself and God. Weak laxity is false kindness, the prophet implies; it merely exposes offenders to an alternative far more dreadful than discipline itself. The sword, Vict. remarks on i. 16, is used to punish deserters as well as to win victory for the faithful. For instrumental ἐν in the pre-Christian vernacular, see *Tebtunis Papyri* vol. i. (p. 86) ἐν μαχαίρῃ-αις.

Ver. 17. The reward for those who deny themselves pagan pleasures in this world is (as in ver. 26) participation in the privileges (*Pereq Meir* 5), reserved for God's people in the latter days (here = a victor's banquet, Gen. xiv. 18), not as hitherto (7, 11) simply participation in eternal life. The imagery is again rabbinic (2 Macc. ii. 4-6, Apoc. Bar. vi. 7-9). Previous to the destruction of Jerusalem, Isaiah or the prophet Jeremiah was supposed to have hidden the ark of the covenant (*cf.* on xi. 19) with its sacred contents, including the pot of manna. At the appearance of the messiah, this was to be once more disclosed (*cf.* Mechilta on Exod. xvi. 25, etc.). It is significant how the writer as usual claims for his messiah, Jesus, the cherished privileges and rights to which contemporary Judaism clung as its monopoly, and further how he assumes that all the past glories of O.T. religion upon earth—as well as all the coming bliss, which in one sense meant the transcendent restoration of these glories—were secured in heaven for the followers of Jesus alone (vii. 17, xxi. 2, etc.). See Apoc. Bar. xxix. 8, where "the treasury of manna will again descend from on high," at the messianic period, that the saints may eat of it; the Fourth Gospel, on the other hand, follows Philo (*quis rer. div.* 39, *leg. allegor.* iii. 59, 61, etc.) in using manna as a type of the soul's nourishment in the present age. There does not seem to be any allusion to the rabbinical legend underlying Sap. xvi. 20.—The strange association of manna and white stones, though possibly a reminiscence of the rabbinic notion preserved in Joma 8 (cadebant Israelitis una cum manna lapides pretiosi), cannot be explained apart from the popular superstitions regarding amulets which colour the metaphor. White stones represented variously to the ancient mind acquittal, admission to a feast (tessera hospitalis), good fortune, and the like. But the point here is their connexion with the new name. This alludes to the mysterious power attached in the ancient mind to amulets, stones (*cf. E.J.* i. 546-550, where vignettes are given; also Dieterich's *Mithras-Liturgie*, 31 f.) marked with secret and divine names (Jeremias, 79-80, Pfleid. *Early Christ. Conc. of Christ*, 112 f.), the possession of which was supposed to enable the bearer to pass closed gates, foil evil spirits, and enter the presence of the deity. If the new name (*cf.* Heitmüller's *Im Namen Jesu*, 128 f.), is thus regarded as that of Jesus—the irresistible, invincible name above every name—the promise then offers safe entrance through all perils into the inner bliss and feast of God; the true Christian has a charmed life. But when the new name is taken to apply to the individual, as seems more likely here, another line of interpretation is required, and the origin of the phrase (though tinged still with this amulet-conception of a stone, the more potent as it was hidden somewhere on the person, *cf.* Prov. xvii. 8, etc.), is best approached from a passage like Epict. i. 19, where the philosopher is trying to dissuade a man from undertaking the duties of priesthood in the Imperial cultus at Nikopolis. What good will it do him

λευκήν, καὶ ἐπὶ τὴν ψῆφον ὄνομα [u] καινὸν γεγραμμένον, ὃ οὐδεὶς u Isa. lxii. 2, lxv. 15.
οἶδεν εἰ μὴ ὁ λαμβάνων. v Cf. on Acts xvi.
"18. Καὶ τῷ ἀγγέλῳ τῆς ἐν [v] Θυατείροις[1] ἐκκλησίας γράψον, 14.

[1] On the variant τω (Lach., WH, Sw.) for της, *cf.* ii. 1, 8. The singular form, Θυατειρη (Q, vg., etc.), is less well supported; similar collocations of singular (i. 11) and plural are not uncommon (*E. Bi.*, 4538*b*, 5064*b*).

after death, to have his name used to mark his year of office in public documents? "My name will remain," replies the man. "Write it on a stone and it will remain," is the retort of Epictetus—plainly a colloquial expression for permanence. This would fit in with the Apocalyptic saying excellently (see Schol. on Pind. *Olymp.* vii. 159). Still more apposite, however, is an ancient ceremony of initiation (as among the aborigines of New South Wales: Trumbull, *Blood-Covenant*, 1887, pp. 335-337), by which each person, on the close of his novitiate, received a new name from the tribe and at the same time a white stone or quartz crystal. The latter was considered to be a divine gift, and was held specially sacred, never to be surrendered or even shown. These boons formed part of the religious covenant which marked the entrance of a man into the closest relation with the deity of his tribe and also into the full enjoyment of manhood's privileges. Hence, if we suppose some such popular rite behind the language here, the idea is apt: the victor's reward is the enjoyment of mature and intimate life with his God (so Victor.). For the symbolism of a name as evidence of personal identity (and inferentially of a new name as proof of a renovated, enduring nature), see *E.B.D.* 75: "May my name be given to me in the Great House, and may I remember my name in the House of Fire. . . . If any god whatsoever should advance to me, let me be able to proclaim his name forthwith" (the latter clause illustrating Apoc. iii. 12). The significance attached by the Egyptian religion especially to the *reu* or name was due to the belief that its loss meant the extinction of a man's existence. The idea in the prophet's mind is little more than that developed, *e.g.*, in Mrs. Browning's sonnet, "Comfort": "Speak low to me, my Saviour, low and sweet, From out the hallelujahs sweet and low, Lest I should fear and fall, and miss Thee," etc. As the succeeding chapters are full of the state and splendour of heaven, with royal majesty predominating, the prophet finds place here for the more intimate and individual aspect of the future life, depicting God in touch with the single soul (*cf.* xiv. 1). In addition to this, he conveys the idea that outside the Christian experience no one can really know what God is or what He gives; the redeemed and victorious alone can understand what it means to belong to God and to be rewarded by him.—Wünsch has recently pointed out (*Excav. in Palestine*, 1898-1900, p. 186) that, as in Egypt the sacred paper (χάρτης ἱερατικὸς) was used for solemn appeals to the gods (*Brit. Mus. Papyri*, xlvi. 308), "in like manner, doubtless, in Palestine, limestone had some superstitious significance, but of what special kind we do not know. Perhaps it is in this connexion that in Apoc. ii. 17 "he that overcometh" is to receive "a white stone" inscribed with a "new" spell, evidently as an "amulet". There may also be a further local allusion to the ψῆφοι and names which were supposed to be received by votaries of Asclepius as they lay in a trance or dream (Aristides, i. 352, 520). For the initiation-custom, *cf.* Spence and Gillen's *Native Tribes of Central Australia*, pp. 139-140, where the secret, individual name is described as given only to those who are "capable of self-restraint" and above levity of conduct. Clem. Alex. (*Strom.* i. 23) preserves a Jewish tradition that Moses got three names—Joachim, Moses, and Melchi (*i.e.*, king), the last-mentioned ἐν οὐρανῷ μετὰ τὴν ἀνάληψιν, ὥς φασιν οἱ μύσται.

Vv. 18-29. The longest message of the seven is to a church in the least important of the cities (judged from the historical standpoint) Thyatira, a township of Northern Lydia, the holy city of Apollo Tyrimnaios, adjacent to the high road between Perg. and Sardis. It soon became a centre of Montanism.

Ver. 18. χαλκολιβ. Some local allusion to the bronze-work for which Thyatira was famous. *Son of God* (*cf.* Kattenbusch ii. 563 f.) is practically an equivalent for messiah (Luke iv. 41), or for the superhuman personality of Jesus as divinely commissioned (*cf.* Grill,

Τάδε λέγει [w] ὁ υἱὸς τοῦ θεοῦ, ὁ ἔχων τοὺς ὀφθαλμοὺς αὐτοῦ ὡς
[x] φλὸξ[1] πυρός, καὶ [y] οἱ πόδες αὐτοῦ ὅμοιοι χαλκολιβάνῳ· 19. Οἶδα
σου τὰ ἔργα καὶ τὴν [z] ἀγάπην καὶ τὴν πίστιν καὶ τὴν διακονίαν καὶ
τὴν [a] ὑπομονήν σου, καὶ τὰ ἔργα σου τὰ ἔσχατα [b] πλείονα τῶν
πρώτων. 20. Ἀλλ᾽ ἔχω κατὰ σοῦ ὅτι ἀφεῖς τὴν γυναῖκα[2] [c] Ἰεζάβελ
ἡ λέγουσα [d] ἑαυτὴν προφῆτιν, καὶ διδάσκει καὶ πλανᾷ τοὺς [e] ἐμοὺς

w Like vv. 26-27, from Ps. ii. 7-9; only here in Apoc. In inscript. = *diui filius*, of Augustus (Deissm. 166-167; *Inscript. Maris Ægei*, iii. 174, etc.). x i. 14, *cf.* ἐραυν. ver. 23. y i. 15, *cf.* ὡς . . . συντ. ver. 27. z ii. 4. a ii. 2. b Contrast ii. 4-5, Matt. xii. 45, 2 Pet. ii. 20, *cf.* Ruth iii. 10. c From 2 Kings ix. 22, *cf. Sams. Agon.* 1034-1045. d Constr. i. 5. e Possess. pron. only here in Apoc.

[1] For **φλογα** (ACQP, etc., Lach., Al., WH, Ws., Sw.) read the harder **φλοξ** (א 12 am., fuld., Pr., Ti., Bs., Bj., sc. **εστιν**).

[2] The well-attested **σου** after **γυναικα** (AQ, min., Syr., Areth., Pr., etc., so Grot., Al., Zahn, and J. Weiss) may have arisen from the repeated **σου** previously or from 1 Kings xix.-xx. But any such allusion to the wife of the local bishop is untenable, and to retain it as = "thy woman" (Ramsay, *Seven Letters*, 341) is harsh in the extreme. It is to be omitted with אCP, min., g., vg., Me., Arm., Aeth., Tert.

pp. 76-77) to carry out God's purpose for his people (*cf.* John x. 36). But the expression has pagan as well as Jewish colouring; and there is undoubtedly an apologetic allusion to the similar terminology of the Imperial cultus (*cf.* Introd. § 6).

Ver. 19. Instead of being retrograde like Ephesus, Thyatira has steadily progressed in *the works* of Christianity. The sole flaw noted (see Ramsay's discussions in *D. B.* iv. 758 f., *Seven Letters*, 338 f.) is an undue laxity shown to certain members (not, as at Pergamos, a mere minority) who, under the sway (*cf.* Zahn, § 73, n. 7) of an influential woman, refused to separate themselves from the (ἐργασίαι) local guilds where moral interests, though not ostensibly defied, were often seriously compromised. The prophet takes up a puritan attitude, corroborated by that of the leading church of the district (ii. 6); he demands in the name of Christ that such inconsistent members should withdraw—a severe and costly step to take, amid the social ties and interests of an Asiatic city, where social clubs were a recognised feature of civic life and appealed forcibly to several natural instincts, especially when backed by the approval of an oracular and impressive leader in the local church.

Ver. 20. Women (*cf.* Acts xxi. 9; 1 Cor. xi. 5, and the later Ammia in Philadelphia: Eus. *H. E.* v. 17. 2) occasionally prophesied in the early church, and false prophetesses were as likely to exist as false prophets. This "Jezebel of a woman, alleging herself to be a prophetess," seems to have been some influential female (as the definite imagery of vv. 21-23 indicates); her lax principles or tendencies made for a connexion with foreign and compromising associations which evidently exerted a dangerous charm upon some weaker Christians in the city. The moral issue corresponds to that produced by the Nikolaitan party at Pergamos (**εἰδ. φαγεῖν, πορνεῦσαι**), but the serious nature of the heresy at Thyatira appears from the fact that it was not simply propagated within the church but also notorious (ver. 23) and long-continued (**τέκνα**), thanks to obstinacy among the Ahabs and adherents of this prominent woman (ver. 21). They prided themselves on their enlightened liberalism (ver. 24). The definiteness of her personality, the fact of her situation within a Christian church which had jurisdiction over her, and the association of her practices with those of the Nikolaitans, who were members of the church, render it impossible to identify this libertine influence of J. with a foreign institution such as the famous shrine of the Chaldean Sibyl at Thyatira (Schürer: *Theol. Abhandlungen*, pp. 39 f., a theory suggested by Blakesley, in Smith's *DB*), or with the wife of the local Asiarch (Selwyn, 123). Besides it was not the cults but the trade-guilds that formed the problem at Thyatira. Jastrow points out (p. 267) that for some occult reason female sorcerers were preferred to men among the Babylonians; "the witch appears more frequently than the male sorcerer". Hillel (Pirke Aboth, ii. 8; see Dr. C. Taylor's note) had already de-

[f] **δούλους πορνεῦσαι καὶ φαγεῖν εἰδωλόθυτα. 21. Καὶ ἔδωκα αὐτῇ**
χρόνον ἵνα μετανοήσῃ, [g] καὶ οὐ θέλει μετανοῆσαι ἐκ τῆς πορνείας
αὐτῆς. 22. ἰδοὺ βάλλω αὐτὴν εἰς [h] κλίνην, καὶ τοὺς [i] μοιχεύοντας
μετ' αὐτῆς εἰς θλίψιν μεγάλην, ἐὰν μὴ μετανοήσουσιν ἐκ τῶν ἔργων
αὐτῆς, 23. καὶ τὰ [k] τέκνα αὐτῆς ἀποκτενῶ ἐν [l] θανάτῳ· καὶ
γνώσονται πᾶσαι αἱ ἐκκλησίαι ὅτι ἐγώ εἰμι [m] ὁ ἐραυνῶν[1] [n] νεφροὺς

f vii. 3, xix. 2, 5, xxii. 3, 6 = Christians in general.
g ii. 22, ix. 20 f., xvi. 11, *cf.* Sap. xi. 23—xii. 2.
h See Jud. ix. 2-3.
i Mal. iii. 5, *cf.* Isa. lvii. 3.
k 2 Kings x. 7, Sir. xxiii. 24-25, En. x. 9.
l Jer. xiv. 12, xxi. 7, Ezek. xxxiii. 27, Ps. Sol. vii. 4, etc.; LXX (θ. = דבר).
m Clem. Rom. xxi.
n ἅπ. λεγ. N.T.

[1] For **ερευνων** (אQP, etc., Al. Bs.) read (with AC, etc., edd.) the Egyptian (Thumb pp. 176-177; Helbing, 7) form **εραυνων**.

clared, "more women, more witchcraft". For the connexion of women and sorcery *cf.* Blau's *Altjüd. Zauberwesen* 18 f., 23 f. —**ἡ λέγουσα κ.τ.λ.,** an irregular nomin. absolute, characteristic of the writer. This LXX peculiarity of a detached participle thrown into relief, which is not confined to the Apocalypse (*cf.* Phil. iii. 16-19, etc.), renders the participle almost a relative (Vit. I., 202); but indeed any word or group of words, thus singled out as characteristic of some preceding noun tends to become independent and to take its own construction (II. 8f). See Zeph. i. 12 (LXX).

Ver. 21. The immorality was flagrant; more flagrant still was the obstinate persistence in it, despite admonitions and forbearance (*cf.* Eccles. viii. 11; Bar. Ap. xxi. 20; 2 Peter iii. 9). This allusion to an abuse of God's patience and to a warning given already (hardly in some writing like Jud. 2 Peter, Spitta) is left quite indefinite; it was probably familiar enough to the first readers of the book. Interests and old associations had proved hitherto too strong for this prophetic counsel to be followed. Membership of a trade-guild, although it necessarily involved the recognition of some pagan deity and often led to orgies, "was a most important matter for every tradesman or artisan; it aided his business, and brought, him many advantages socially" (Ramsay).

Ver. 22. **κλίνην** (bed, not a couch of revelry) aegritudinis non amoris; disease or sickness (*cf.* for the phrase, 1 Macc. i. 5) the punishment of error, especially of error accompanied by licentiousness. The inscriptions from Asia Minor abound with instances of the popular belief that impurity, moral and even physical, was punished by disease or disaster to oneself, one's property, one's children. Sickness might even go the length of death (1 Cor. xi. 29-30). The prophet, however, seems to avoid calling Jesus or God **σωτὴρ** or **σώζων**, a term appropriated by the popular religions of Phrygia and lavished on many deities as healers and helpers (*C. B. P.* i. 262 f.). —**μοιχ.,** men and women who imitate her licentiousness. **θλ.,** physical distress, illness.—**μετανοήσουσιν,** the fut. indic., expresses rather more probability than subj. with **ἐὰν μή** (*cf.* Blass, § 65, 5). For tense of **βάλλω** see Zech. viii. 7, LXX, etc.

Ver. 23. **τέκνα,** literally, perhaps with an indirect allusion to the killing of Ahab's seventy sons. **ἀποκτ. θ.** (Hebraism), "I will utterly slay"; see on vi. 8. If any particular form of death is meant, it may be pestilence (the inscriptions often mention fever), which represented to an Oriental mind the punishment of God on man's unfaithfulness. The curious difference between the treatment of the **μοιχ.** and the **τέκνα** is due to the fact that (*cf.* Dan. vi. 24), a parent's sin was visited upon his family, both in Jewish and in contemporary pagan belief (*cf.* the Phrygian inscription, cited by Mayor on Jas. v. 12, **κατηράμενος ἤτω αὐτὸς καὶ τὰ τέκνα αὐτοῦ**). Yet even when both classes are allegorised into active coadjutors and deluded victims, the relative punishment looks unequal. John, unlike Ezekiel (xiii. 17-23), holds that the victims of the false prophetess are willing and responsible for their position.—**πᾶσαι αἱ ἐκκλ.,** the judgment was to be as notorious as evidently the scandal had been. The idea recalls one of Ezekiel's favourite conceptions.—**ἐγώ κ.τ.λ.** "I know the abysses," and "discerner of hearts and searcher of the reins" were old Egyptian titles for divine beings. This intimate knowledge of man (*cf.* 16 c) pierces below superficial appear-

καὶ [o] καρδίας· καὶ [p] δώσω ὑμῖν ἑκάστῳ κατὰ τὰ ἔργα ὑμῶν. 24.
Ὑμῖν δὲ λέγω τοῖς λοιποῖς τοῖς ἐν Θυατείροις, ὅσοι οὐκ ἔχουσι τὴν
διδαχὴν ταύτην, οἵτινες οὐκ ἔγνωσαν τὰ [q] βαθέα τοῦ Σατανᾶ, ὡς
λέγουσιν, [r] Οὐ βάλλω ἐφ' ὑμᾶς ἄλλο βάρος· 25. πλὴν ὃ ἔχετε

o Ps. vii. 9, xxvi. 2, etc. p Ps. lxii. 13, *cf.* Apoc. xx. 12, xxii. 12, 2 Clem. xviii. 4, etc. Fresh clause, indep. of ὅτι, begins here. q 1 Cor. ii. 10. r *Cf.* 1 John v. 3.

ances, *e.g.*, connexion with the church, prophetic zeal, and plausible excuses. As in Jer. xvii. 10, xx. 12 (*cf.* Ps. Sol. viii. 8), the divine acquaintance with man's real, secret life forms the basis of unerring and impartial judgment; while, as in Jer. iv. 16, 17 (*cf.* Acts iv. 1 f., 1 Tim. i. 20, 1 Cor. v. 4, etc.) the prophetic denunciation or imprecation has a direct effect upon the person denounced (*cf.* von Dobschütz, 270 f.). The former would be a fairly novel idea to most of those accustomed to the Roman *religio*, which was "one of observance, sacrifice, and outward act, that in no way searched the heart of the worshipper—a system of rules which covered the circumstances of Roman life" (H. O. Taylor, *Ancient Ideals*, i. 417, 418).

Ver. 24. To know "the depths" of the divine being and counsel was a characteristic claim of the Ophites and the later Gnostics; *cf.* Iren. *adv. Haer.* ii. 22, 1 (qui profunda bythi adinuenisse se dicunt; *cf.* 3), and Tertullian's sarcastic description (*adv. Valent.* 1), "Eleusinia Ualentiniana fecerunt lenocinia, sancta silentio magno, sola taciturnitate coelestia. Si bona fide quaeris, concreto uultu, suspenso supercilio *Altum est* aiunt." "The depth of knowledge" was a phrase of Herakleitus, the famous Ephesian philosopher, and in the creed of the Dukhobortsui, a sect in modern Russia, the Holy Spirit is Depth, the Father being Height and the Son Breadth. Since **ὡς λέγουσιν** refers to the errorists themselves, the quoted phrase about "knowing the depths of Satan" may (i.) contain an indignant and sarcastic retort; "depths of —Satan," not "God," as they boast (**τοῦ σ.** being substituted for **τοῦ θεοῦ**); such teaching and principles are simply infernal. Or (ii.) as is more probable the words may voice the actual claim of the errorists, who considered that some accommodation to pagan practices gave them a necessary acquaintance with the meaning of evil (so *e.g.*, Spitta, Pfleiderer, Zahn, Jülicher, Bousset). Their higher standing gave them immunity from any risks. They could fathom securely what the immature orthodox called immorality. Devil-study, or even devil-worship (xiii. 4 is quite different) was not uncommon in some of the Gnostic sects throughout Asia Minor, *e.g.*, the Cainites, the Naassenes, and the Ophites (the earliest Gnostics, **φάσκοντες μόνοι τὰ βάθη γινώσκειν**, Hipp. *adv. Haer.* v. 6). The idea was that as the principle of evil would ultimately be redeemed, it might be used meantime for the advantage of the initiated. Compare Mansel's *Gnostic Heresies*, pp. 73, 96, 105. In En. lxv. 6 the unrighteous are punished for their acquaintance with "all the secrets of the angels and all the violence of the Satans and all their hidden power and all the power of those that practise sorcery, and the power of witchcraft." The influence of a movement like Gnosticism, whose motto was *eritis sicut deus scientes bonum et malum*, gave wide opportunities to immorality, in its more popular applications. It produced the same sort of union between subtlety and sensualism which can sometimes be traced within Hinduism. In contrast to this unwholesome temper of speculation, the prophet substitutes for speculative flights the obedience of the normal Christian praxis (*cf. Parad. Lost*, viii. 170-197, xii. 561-589), with a plain allusion to the Jerusalem concordat of the early church which is recommended tacitly as a safe, wise rule of conduct. In the case of the **βαθέα τοῦ σατανᾶ**, ignorance is bliss. John is totally unsympathetic to the local liberals. He does not combat the theoretical principles at the root of their movement. Like the prophets who wrote Jude and 2 Peter, he attacks instead of arguing, quite content to judge it by its moral fruits of libertinism. He bitterly declares that such occasional results are the deliberate object of the party. The strange collocation of this error with the habit of partaking of sacrificial food is probably due to the prophet's stern conviction that the latter, with its friendly and liberal attitude to pagan customs, fostered the former, in the case of people who took an ultra-spiritual view of Paul's principle of Christian freedom.

κρατήσατε, [s] ἄχρι οὗ ἂν ἥξω. 26. Καὶ ὁ νικῶν καὶ ὁ [t] τηρῶν ἄχρι
τέλους τὰ ἔργα μου, δώσω [u] αὐτῷ ἐξουσίαν ἐπὶ τῶν ἐθνῶν. 27. καὶ
ποιμανεῖ αὐτοὺς ἐν [v] ῥάβδῳ σιδηρᾷ, ὡς τὰ σκεύη τὰ κεραμικὰ
[w] συντρίβεται, [x] ὡς κἀγὼ εἴληφα παρὰ τοῦ πατρός μου· 28. [y] καὶ
δώσω αὐτῷ τὸν ἀστέρα τὸν πρωϊνόν. 29. Ὁ ἔχων οὖς ἀκουσάτω
τί τὸ Πνεῦμα λέγει ταῖς ἐκκλησίαις.

"III. 1. Καὶ τῷ ἀγγέλῳ τῆς ἐν Σάρδεσιν ἐκκλησίας γράψον,

s "Till such time as I come" (eschat., as iii. 11): ἥξω aor. subj. from ἧξα.
t i. 3, suggested by κρατ. 25.
u Resuming nom. absol.
v *Cf.* Mic. v. 5, Isa. x. 24-26. w xii. 5, xix. 15, *cf.* Bar. iv. 25. x *Cf.* John xiv. 6 f., etc.
y Double promise here only (exc. iii. 12 ?).

Ver. 26. Triumph here consists in unflagging attention to the duties of a Christian vocation. The **ἔργα** are (xiv. 12, xix. 8) the normal activities of this calling, viewed as the outcome of a personal relation to Jesus; they are "his," as commanded by him and executed in his strength. The general idea of this and the following verse is that the only irresistible force is the force of a life which is able to resist seduction and compromise, because it holds to faith and purity. The promise of reward, preceding (as in iii. 5, 12, 21) the appeal for attention, is couched in terms of messianic conquest (from Ps. ii. 8, 9). In a more or less figurative form, the rule of the saints, a cherished hope of Jewish eschatology, had its own attraction for some circles of early Christianity (see on v. 10 and 1 Cor. vi. 3; and for **ῥάβδῳ**, the well-known flail wielded by Horus, the Egyptian god of requital or warfare): evidently it appealed to their eagerness for a righting of present wrongs and a reversal of the immoral sway of captain ill over captive good. The **ἐξουσία ἐπὶ τῶν ἐθνῶν** (by which they are not governed but shivered in irreparable ruin; *cf.* Isa. xxx. 14, Jer. xix. 11) is defined with ferocious detail in 27; the whole description is modelled on a traditionally messianic application of (LXX) Ps. ii. 8, 9. For the shepherd's staff as a royal sceptre see *E. Bi.* 4317. **ὡς κἀγὼ κ.τ.λ.**, God, Christ, and the individual Christian as in iii. 21 (John xvii. 16-22). "Illud **ὡς** aliquam similitudinem, non paritatem significat" (Rosenmüller). John xxi. 15-17 is not "a deliberate correction of this terrible sentence" (Selwyn, 195), but the mature expression of Christian solicitude in a different province, from which messianic incongruities have been wholly purged.

Ver. 28. To "grant the morning-star" (a characteristically loose usage of **δίδωμι**) means, not to invest him with its glory, nor to give him possession of Christ himself, but (so Bleek, after Victor.) to make the dawn of salvation or of life eternal shine on him after his dark afflictions. The victor shares in the divine life (with its punitive government) and honour above, or rather in the new messianic era of Jesus himself (see note on xxii. 16, where by a further application the metaphor is directly connected with Jesus). Staunch adherence to the truth on the part of leaders and confessors is similarly rewarded in Dan. xii. 3, En. civ. ii. Semitic folklore found some mystic connexion between the countless brilliant stars in heaven and the departed faithful, who became immortal (4 Esd. vii. [97]), and the sense here might be that the loyal Christian was sure of shining like a star in immortality; *cf.* Ign. *ad Rom.* ii. 2, **καλὸν τὸ δῦναι ἀπὸ κόσμου πρὸς Θεὸν, ἵνα εἰς αὐτὸν ἀνατείλω** (and passage cited on i. 10). But xxii. 16 (*cf.* Job iii. 9) tells against this, as does Ign. *ibid.* vi. 2 (speaking of his martyrdom) **ἄφετέ με καθαρὸν φῶς λαβεῖν· ἐκεῖ παραγενόμενος ἄνθρωπος ἔσομαι.** The collocation of the morning star and the judicial authority over the nations may have been suggested to the prophet's mind (*cf.* 14, 20) by the prophecy, read in a messianic sense, of Num. xxiv. 17. The sequence and the Christian spirit of the whole promise are certainly improved if we omit 27 *a* with Selwyn (194) and Jacoby (*Neutest. Ethik*, 1899, p. 446) and Wellhausen (with 23-28 *a*), since the doubled promise and the later use of the metaphor do not justify any suspicion of 28 as a gloss (so Könnecke, p. 34). But it is as likely that the author himself (*cf.* xvii. 14) added this co-operation with the vindictive messiah (*cf.* xii. 5, xix. 15), as that an early copyist was responsible for the insertion.

CHAPTER III.—Vv. 1-6. The message to Sardis. The title of the speaker (drawn from i. 4, 16, 20), as general as

Τάδε λέγει ὁ ἔχων τὰ ἑπτὰ πνεύματα τοῦ Θεοῦ καὶ τοὺς ἑπτὰ
ἀστέρας· Οἶδά σου τὰ ἔργα, ὅτι [a] ὄνομα ἔχεις ὅτι ζῇς, καὶ [b] νεκρὸς
εἶ. 2. Γίνου [c] γρηγορῶν, καὶ [d] στήρισον τὰ λοιπὰ ἃ ἔμελλον ἀπο-
θανεῖν· οὐ γὰρ εὕρηκά σου ἔργα[1] πεπληρωμένα ἐνώπιον τοῦ
Θεοῦ μου. 3. [e] μνημόνευε οὖν πῶς [f] εἴληφας καὶ ἤκουσας, καὶ τήρει
καὶ μετανόησον. ἐὰν οὖν μὴ γρηγορήσῃς, [g] ἥξω ὡς [h] κλέπτης, καὶ
οὐ μὴ γνῷς[2] [i] ποίαν ὥραν ἥξω ἐπὶ σέ. 4. Ἀλλὰ ἔχεις ὀλίγα

a Herod. vii. 138 οὔνομα εἶχε, ὡς ἐπ᾽ Ἀθήνας ἐλαύνει, Pl Hipp. Maj. 281c.
b Jas. ii. 17, 1 Tim. v. 6: Philo, *de pro-fug.* § 10.
c Eph. v. 14.
d Ezek. xxxiv. 4, 16 (Helbing 85). e See Gal. iii. 2 f., Heb. x. 32 f. f John iii. 11, 33, xiv. 17, xvii. 8. g ii. 5, 16. h Jer. xlix. 9, Matt. xxiv. 43 = Lk. xii. 39, see on 1 Thess. v. 2. i Temporal acc. as xi. 2, 6, 9, xii. 6.

[1] **τα** bef. **εργα** is om. by Lach., WH, Ws., Sw. (AC, 1 mg.).

[2] For **γνως** (ACP, 1, etc., Areth., Al., Ws., Bs., Sw., Bj.) Lach. Ti. Tr. WH (marg.) read the correct **γνωσῃ** with ℵQ, vg., Aeth., Syr., And[c], Pr.,

in the similar letter to Ephesus, has no special bearing on the subsequent address, unless an antithesis be implied between the plenitude of the divine spirit and the deadness of a church which had the name or credit of being "alive". The sweeping verdict of ver. 1 upon the formalism of the local church —which had lapsed from its pristine vitality, just as the township of S. had by this time declined from its old historical prestige—is modified by the recognition of better elements not yet too far gone in decay to be recovered (2) and of a goodly nucleus of members. The metaphor is paralleled by a Jewish estimate of orthodoxy (Kidd. 71 *b*) which dubbed Mesene as "dead," Media as "ill," Elymais as "in extremis," and the strict inhabitants of the Ghetto between the Tigris and the Euphrates as "healthy".

Ver. 2. **ἔμελλον**, epistol. impf.—**σου ἔργα**, "any works of thine". Judged from the Divine standpoint (**ἐνωπ. θ.**), no matter how satisfactory is the verdict of outsiders upon her or of her own complacency, her condition is decadent.

Ver. 3. Memory again the lever for repentance (as at ii. 5); **εἴληφας** aoristic pf. (*cf.* v. 7, Burton 88) rather than pf. of existing result (Weiss, Bs.); **πῶς** = our colloquial "how" (practically equivalent to "that"). The melancholy feature about contemporary indifference at S. was that it had a fine beginning behind it: yet this very circumstance afforded hopeful ground for an appeal. **καὶ τήρει** (the primitive deposit of the faith) **καὶ** (to secure this steadfast adherence) **μετανόησον** (aor., sharp and decisive act of repentance). As ver. 4 (compared with ver. 2) implies, positive stains were visible in the local church no less than sins of mere omission. Sardis and Laodicea, which apparently were the only members of this group untroubled by outside persecution or inward error, were the least satisfactory of all the seven. **ἐὰν οὖν μὴ γρηγορήσῃς,** although the need is so desperate (*cf.* below on xvi. 15). The sudden and signal visitation of punishment threatened in the following words (for **ὥραν** in acc. *cf.* Moult. i. 63, Abbott's *Diat.* 2013) is left vaguely impressive. It may be that (as in Jude 4, 18, and 2 Peter) local libertinism meant a slackening of belief in the second Advent.

Ver. 4. **ὀλ. ὀν.** "quasi paucos nominatos, *i.e.*, bonos qui nominatione digni sunt" (*cf.* the use of **πρόσωπα** = persons or individuals, in Clem. Rom. and Ignat.). **ἐμόλ.** (*cf. Fragment of Uncanonical Gospel*, *Oxyrhyn.* 2 cent. A.D., line 16 **μεμολυμμένος ἐπάτησας, κ.τ.λ.**) the sullied garment an emblem of moral stains, including but not identical with that of **πορνεύειν** (xiv. 4, *cf.* Sir. xxii. 1, 2). The language reflects that of the votive inscriptions in Asia Minor, where soiled clothes disqualified the worshipper and dishonoured the god. Moral purity qualifies for spiritual communion (note the dramatic contrast of this **ἄξιοι** [*cf.* on ii. 16] with that of xvi. 6); the apocalyptic beatitude is: blessed are the pure in life, for they shall join God (see on xiv. 14, xix. 8). Note here only in the seven messages an eschatological promise unintroduced by the phrase **ὁ νικῶν**, although ver. 5 really repeats the same idea. **οὕτως** = "as being victor" (*i.e.*, accordingly). The idea of heavenly raiment is distinctively Persian (Brandt, 575, 580; Lüken, 122), but permeates Jewish eschatology from Enoch

[k] ὀνόματα ἐν Σάρδεσιν ἃ οὐκ [l] ἐμόλυναν τὰ ἱμάτια αὐτῶν· καὶ περιπατήσουσι μετ' ἐμοῦ ἐν λευκοῖς, [m] ὅτι ἄξιοί εἰσιν. 5. Ὁ νικῶν οὕτως περιβαλεῖται ἐν ἱματίοις λευκοῖς· καὶ οὐ μὴ [n] ἐξαλείψω τὸ ὄνομα αὐτοῦ ἐκ τῆς [o] βίβλου τῆς ζωῆς, καὶ [p] ὁμολογήσω τὸ ὄνομα αὐτοῦ [p] ἐνώπιον τοῦ πατρός μου καὶ ἐνώπιον τῶν ἀγγέλων αὐτοῦ.
6. Ὁ ἔχων οὖς ἀκουσάτω τί τὸ Πνεῦμα λέγει ταῖς ἐκκλησίαις.
"7. Καὶ τῷ ἀγγέλῳ τῆς ἐν Φιλαδελφίᾳ ἐκκλησίας γράψον,

k xi. 13, see on Acts 15, etc., En. lxx. 1
l Jude 23 (Isa. lxiv 6).
m *Cf.* Ignat. *Smyrn.* ix. 2; Herm. *Sim.* viii 2.
n *Cf.* Jos. *Ant.* vi. 6, 1, xvii. 5, 2, etc. See Herm. *Vis.* I. 3, 2, *Sim.* ix. 24, 4, Clem. Rom. xlv. 8, etc.
o v. 1, xiii. 8 xvii. 8, xx. 12, 15, xxi. 27, En. cviii. 2.
p Reminisc. of syn., Matt. xii. 32, Lk. xii. 8.

(lxii. 15, 16, the elect clothed after the resurrection in eternal "garments of glory") down to Slav. En. xxii. 8; 4 Esd. ii. 39, 45 (*cf.* Herm. *Sim.* viii. 2) and *Asc. Isa.* iv. 16 (garments = spiritual bodies in which the saints are vested at the last day, stored up in seventh heaven; *cf.* viii. 26, ix. 24 f., uidi stolas multas et thronos et coronas jacentes). **περιβαλεῖται κ.τ.λ.,** like Joshua (Zech. iii. 3 f.); or (as others suggest) like priests acquitted before the Sanhedrin, who were robed in white. In the Apoc., as in En. lxxxv.-xc., white is the colour of righteousness, associated with innocence (and joy? Eccles. ix. 8), just as black with evil. In Apoc. Pet. 5, the dwellers in Paradise are clothed in **ἔνδυμα ἀγγέλων φωτινῶν,** whilst the angels who (ver. 6) chastise the wicked are robed in black. All such metaphors reflect the primitive notion that clothing somehow could form almost a part of a man's personality, corresponding to his identity and character (*E. Bi.* 1140, 1141), rather than the Roman custom of assuming a white *toga uirilis* to mark entrance upon manhood's privileges ("uitae liberioris iter," Ovid).—**τῆς βίβλου τῆς ζωῆς,** this favourite symbol of the Apocalypse which goes back even to pre-exilic Judaism (Isa. iv. 3, *cf.* Exod. xxxii. 32 f., etc.; for the Babylonian background, *cf.* Jeremias, 69 f.), had through the influence of Dan. (xii. 1) a great vogue in apocalyptic dreams as an apt image no longer of a share in the temporal felicity of God's reign but of personal salvation. For a name to be erased from the book of life (one's deeds not corresponding, upon scrutiny, to one's position; *cf.* xx. 12, Jub. xxxvi. 10) meant condemnation, or exclusion from the heavenly kingdom. To have one's name retained ("and never will I blot out," etc.) on the list of heavenly citizens was by this time a current metaphor for eternal fellowship with God and his people, and (by a natural inference drawn in xiii. 8) for predestination, the belief in which formed then as always a vivid inspiration in distress and conflict. For the erasure of names from the civic register, consequent upon their owner's condemnation, *cf.* Dio Chrys. xxxi. 336 *c*, **ὅταν δημοσίᾳ τινὰ δέῃ τῶν πολιτῶν ἀποθανεῖν ἐπ' ἀδικήματι, πρότερον τὸ ὄνομα αὐτοῦ ἐξαλείφεται**; Xen. *Hell.* ii. 3, 51, and Arist. *Pac.* 1180. Also Dittenberger's *Sylloge inscript. Graec.*[2] 439[20] (iv. B.C.) **ὃς δ' ἂν δόξηι μὴ ὢν φράτηρ ἐσαχθῆναι, ἐξαλειψάτο τὸ ὄνομα αὐτô ὁ ἱερεύς,** and *Orientis Græci Insc. Sel.* 218[129] (iii. B.C.) **ἐξαλείψαντας τὸ ὄνομα τὸ ἐκείνου.** The special comfort of this verse is intelligible when one reads the prayer offered in contemporary Jewish worship (*cf.* Shmone-Esreh xii. Palest. recension): "for apostates let there be no hope, may the kingdom of the haughty quickly collapse in our days, and may the Nazarenes and the Minim suddenly perish, may they be blotted out of the book of Life and not enrolled along with the righteous".

The message to Sardis, the most vehement of the seven, has some interesting resemblances to that addressed to Ephesus; *cf.* ii. 1 = iii. 1, ii. 5 (**μνημ.**) = iii. 3, ii. 5 (visitation) = iii. 5, ii. 6 = iii. 4. The hope described in ver. 5 is burlesqued by Lucian (*Peregr.* xl.) who describes his pseudo-Christian hero as seen after death **περιπατοῦντα ἐν λευκῇ ἐσθῆτι, φαιδρόν, κοτίνῳ τε ἐστεμμένον.** The metaphorical references to raiment gain point in view of the local trade in woollen goods and dyed stuffs.

Vv. 7-13. The message to Philadelphia.

Ver. 7. **ἐν Φ.** Less than twenty years later an equally favourable account of the local church was given by Ignatius (*ad Phil.* 3, 5, 10). **ἅγιος κ.τ.λ.,** Jesus is a messiah indeed, one deserving that honoured name and realising its meaning. The favourite Johannine term **ἀληθινός** (= "true," in the wider sense

Τάδε λέγει ὁ [q] ἅγιος ὁ ἀληθινός, ὁ ἔχων τὴν [r] κλεῖν τοῦ [s] Δαυείδ, ὁ
ἀνοίγων καὶ οὐδεὶς κλείσει καὶ κλείων καὶ οὐδεὶς ἀνοίγει· 8.
[Οἶδά σου τὰ ἔργα·][1] ἰδοὺ δέδωκα ἐνώπιόν σου [t] θύραν [t] ἠνεῳγμένην,
ἣν οὐδεὶς δύναται κλεῖσαι [u] αὐτήν· ὅτι μικρὰν ἔχεις δύναμιν, καὶ

q Only here = Christ (*cf.* Acts iii. 14, iv. 27, 30, John vi. 69, etc.), in Apoc. Hendiadys = ὁ ἀληθῶς ἅγιος (Grot.)? "Holy and true," of God vi. 10, *cf.* iv. 8. r i. 18. s On such orthographical forms in ει or ι, see Win. § 5, 13, 32, generally (§ 9, 7). t 1 Cor. xvi. 9, 2 Cor. ii. 12, Col. iv. 3. u Constr. vii. 2, 9, xiii. 8, 12, xx. 8, *cf.* xii. 6, 14, xvii. 9; redundant Heb. use, Win. § 22, 7.

[1] Pr. om. **οιδα σου τα εργα** (so Hauss. i. 211-212, breaking connection and harmonistic).

of "genuine," opposed to unreal rather than to untruthful, *cf.* Justin's *Dial.* cxvi., Athen. vi. 253 c: no pseudo-messiah, as local Jews asserted, *cf.* 8 *c* and 9) is here grouped with **ἅγιος** (*i.e.*, not merely = legitimately messianic as in John x. 36, Clem. Rom. xxiii. 5, but freed from creaturely weakness and imperfection, his nature in intimate touch with the divine fulness, Issel: *der Begriff der Heiligkeit im N.T.*, 1887, pp. 70, 110, *R.J.* 305), as in iii. 14, xix. 11, xxi. 5, xxii. 6 with **πιστός,** and in xv. 3, xvi. 7, xix. 2 with **δίκαιος.** Slightly otherwise, Apoc. Bar. lxvii. 7: "He is true, so that he shall do you good and not evil," and below at xvi. 7 (though this sense might suit here also, as an amplification of **ἅγιος**). **κλεῖν κ.τ.λ.** (based on Isa. xxii. 22) the messiah, as Davidic scion, possesses the absolute power of admission to and exclusion from the divine realm. This part of the title (*cf.* Job xii. 14, **ἐὰν κλείσῃ κατὰ ἀνθρώπων τίς ἀνοίξει**;) alludes to what immediately follows as well as to the arrogant claim mentioned in ver. 9. Christ alone, the heavenly **κλειδοῦχος,** has the right to excommunicate. Compare Savonarola's brave reply to the bishop of Vasona who had pronounced his sentence of degradation (*separo te ab ecclesia militante atque triumphante*):—*Militante, non triumphante: hoc enim tuum non est.*

Ver. 8. **οἶδά . . . ἔργα,** as in the case of Smyrna implying unqualified approval. The reward of this steadfastness (8 *c*, 10) is threefold: (*a*) security in their relation to God (8 *b*), through the love of Christ for them (9); (*b*) ultimate triumph over their foes (9), and (*c*) deliverance in the final crisis (10). The open door, here as in Paul (for the ethnic use of the term on sepulchres *cf. C. B. P.*, ii. 395) is usually taken to denote facilities for preaching and advancing the faith among outsiders, in which case the sense would be that the extension of the gospel depends upon, as it forms a high reward of, open confession and a decided stand for Christ. But in view of a passage written by Ignatius to this very church (*ad Philad.* 3, where Christ himself is termed **θύρα τοῦ πατρὸς, δι' ἧς εἰσέρχονται** the patriarchs, prophets, apostles, **καὶ ἡ ἐκκλησία**) and of Clem. Rom. xlviii. (where the gate of righteousness is described as open in Christ), the phrase is better connected with Christ himself, not with any good opening for Christian activity. He makes access to God through himself sure; despite trials and temptations (vv. 8, 9, 10) his church's standing is guaranteed by his authority (as in John x. 7, 9, Christ **ἡ θύρα τῶν προβάτων**). **θύρα** here is the open heart of God for man; in ver. 20, man's open heart for God. Jesus, then, equipped with the O.T. attributes of divine authority, assures the church how futile are such excommunications as the Jews were levelling against them. The latter have nothing to do with the conditions of the kingdom. Faith in Jesus constitutes a relation to God which cannot either be impaired or rivalled. Only, the perseverance of the saints is needed; an assured position with God depends not merely on Christ's will and power but on Christian loyalty as the coefficient of grace. The church at P. is not blamed for the slenderness of her equipment, which evidently is due to causes outside her control. She is praised for having made good use of the slight resources she possessed (*cf.* Mark xiv. 8). Otherwise, though less well, a full stop might be placed after **αὐτήν,** and **ὅτι . . . τὸ ὄνομα μου** taken as the reason for the promise **ἰδοὺ . . . σε,** just as in ver. 10 **ὅτι . . . μου** is followed by **κἀγὼ . . . γῆς.—αὐτήν,** pleonastic use of pron. after relative, a Semitic idiom with Greek affinities (Vit. ii. 138, Thumb 128, Blass § 50, 4) confined to Apoc. (exc. cit. fr. LXX,

ἐτήρησάς μου τὸν λόγον, καὶ οὐκ ἠρνήσω τὸ ὄνομά μου. 9. ἰδοὺ [v]
[v] διδῶ ἐκ τῆς συναγωγῆς τοῦ [w] Σατανᾶ, τῶν λεγόντων ἑαυτοὺς
Ἰουδαίους εἶναι, καὶ οὐκ εἰσὶν ἀλλὰ ψεύδονται· ἰδοὺ [x] ποιήσω
αὐτοὺς [x] ἵνα ἥξουσι καὶ [y] προσκυνήσουσιν ἐνώπιον τῶν ποδῶν σου,
καὶ γνῶσιν [1] ὅτι ἐγὼ [z] ἠγάπησά σε. 10. Ὅτι ἐτήρησας τὸν [a] λόγον

v Irreg. form, WH 174, Deissm. 192.
w ii. 9, = "hypocrites," Did. viii. 1.
x Constr. John iv. 35, v. 42, etc., ἵνα = infin. of conseq. as ix. 20, xiii. 13.
y Isa. xlix. 23, xlv. 14, lx. 14.
z John xi. 36, *cf.* Ps. lxii. 8, Zech. viii. 20 f., John xvii. 23. See on xxi. 9.
a i. 9, *cf.* Sir. ii. 14, Dan. xii. 3.

[1] For **γνωσιν** ACPQ, etc., Syr., Arm., Aeth., Andr., Areth. (edd.), the variant **γνωση** (א, 14, Sah., Pr.) is preferred by Wellh. (*cf.* ii. 23 and Isa. xlix. 23).

Acts xv. 17) in N.T. In Enoch (xxxviii. 2, and *passim*) to deny the Lord of Spirits is the capital crime, as opposed to "believing in his name".

Ver. 9. **διδῶ ἐκ** (partit. gen., the construction being dropped and resumed in a rather harsh anacolouthon, **ἵνα κ.τ.λ.**). The absence of **ἐκ** before **λεγ.** does not prevent it from being interpreted as in apposition to **συναγωγῆς** rather than as directly dependent on **διδῶ**. On the forms of **δίδωμι** in Apocalypse see Jannaris' *Hist. Gk. Gramm.* 996, 51; the wide usage of the verb is carried on through the LXX from the equally extended employment of the Hebrew equivalent in the later stages of O.T. literature. The Jewish synagogue is denounced as Satanic, owing to its persecuting habits (Satan being regarded as the final source of persecution as of error, *cf.* above ver. 8 and on ii. 9). Ignatius corroborates the malign activity of Jews at Philadelphia, who were in the habit of molesting the church (*ad Philad.* 6); he also refers them to the malicious cunning of Satan. Apparently Judaizing tendencies were rife among Christians of Gentile birth at Philadelphia. As in writing to Smyrna, the prophet therefore claimed the ancestral title "Jew" for the Christian church. Faith in Christ, not mere nationality, constituted true Judaism; the succession had passed to Christianity. The prominence assigned to this phase of polemic is characteristic of the period, though already presaged by Paul (in Rom. ix. 6-7, ii. 28, 29). The supercilious contempt of these churchmen for all Christian dissenters from Judaism was to be changed one day into humble respect. The former would find out their grievous mistake when it was too late. **καὶ προσκυνήσουσιν, κ.τ.λ.**, in the spirit and realistic language of post-exilic Judaism (see reff.), denoting abject submission and homage before the glory of the church in the future messianic reign (slightly otherwise in 1 Cor. xiv. 25). What they fondly expected from the Gentiles, they were themselves to render to Christians—such would be the grim irony of providence. Compare with what follows, the earlier expectation of Jub. i. 25: "and they shall all be called children of the living God, and every angel and spirit will know, yea they will know that these are my children, and that I love them". **καὶ γνῶσιν, κ.τ.λ.**, still Isaianic in colouring (from xliii. 4, xlix. 23). Christ's love to his church (**ἠγ.** = "I have loved") will be proved by her triumphant survival of perils. Her final position, when the conditions of earth are reversed, will throw light upon the divine affection which underlay her previous perseverance, and which meantime is a secret save to those who experience it. The promise of dominion over the Jews here corresponds to that of authority over the Gentiles in ii. 26, 27, except that the latter is definitely eschatological. The Jews tardily awaken to the privileges of the church as to the claims of Jesus (see on i. 7). Probably they scoffed at the claim of the Philadelphian Christians to be objects of the true God's love. The answer is that faith in Jesus means a revelation of Divine love (*the* revelation of it), apart from which no Christian life can be accounted for.

Ver. 10. The position of **μου** shows that it belongs not to **τὸν λόγον τῆς ὑπομονῆς** as a whole, but to **ὑπομονῆς** (2 Thess. iii. 5). The precise sense therefore is not "my word about patience" (*i.e.*, my counsel of patience as the supreme virtue of these latter days, so Weiss, Bousset, etc.), but "the word, or the preaching, of that patience which refers to me" (*i.e.*, the patient endurance with which, amid present trials, **Christ is to be served; so Alford, Spitta, Holtzm.**).

τῆς ὑπομονῆς μου, κἀγώ σε τηρήσω ἐκ τῆς ὥρας τοῦ [b] πειρασμοῦ
τῆς [b] μελλούσης ἔρχεσθαι ἐπὶ τῆς οἰκουμένης ὅλης, πειράσαι τοὺς
κατοικοῦντας ἐπὶ τῆς γῆς. 11. [c] ἔρχομαι ταχύ· [d] κράτει ὃ ἔχεις, ἵνα
μηδεὶς λάβῃ τὸν στέφανόν σου. 12. [e] Ὁ νικῶν, ποιήσω αὐτὸν
[f] στύλον ἐν τῷ ναῷ τοῦ Θεοῦ μου, [g] καὶ ἔξω οὐ μὴ ἐξέλθῃ ἔτι, καὶ

b Matt. xxiv. 21 f. *cf.* Apoc. vii. 3, ix. 4, Jer. xxx. 7 f.
c A comfort (xxii. 7, 20) not a threat (ii. 16), *cf.* xxii. 12.
d ii. 25, *cf.* 4 Macc. vi. 18-21, Heb. x. 36.
e Nom. pendens, as ii. 7. For constr., Win. § 22, 5*a*, Abbott, *Diat.* 1920.
f Gal. ii. 9 (see Lgft.'s note), Isa. xxii. 23, Jer. i. 18.
g Emphatic, as opposed to Isa. xxii. 25.

See Ps. xxxviii. (xxxix.), 8: **καὶ νῦν τίς ἡ ὑπομονή μου; οὐχὶ ὁ κύριος;** The second reason for praising the Philadelphian Christians is their loyal patience under persecution, as well as the loyal confession of Christ (ver. 8) which had possibly brought on that persecution. **κἀγὼ κ.τ.λ.** ("I in turn"; *cf.* similar connection in John xvii. 6-8), a reproduction of the saying preserved in Luke xxi. 36. The imminent period **τοῦ πειρασμοῦ** refers to the broken days which, in eschatological schemes, were to herald messiah's return. Later on, this period is specifically defined as a time of seduction to imperial worship (*cf.* xiii. 14-17, vii. 2, with Dan. xii. 1, LXX). The Philadelphian Christians will not only triumph over the contempt and intrigues of their Jewish foes but also over the wider pagan trial (which is also a temptation), inasmuch as their devotion, already manifested in face of Jewish malice, will serve to carry them through the storm of Roman persecution. The reward of loyalty is in fact fresh power to be loyal on a higher level: "the wages of going on, and ever to be". This seems better than to take the world-wide trial as the final attempt (viii. 13, xi. 10, etc.) to induce repentance in men or to punish them, from which the P. Christians (*cf.* vii. 1-8, and Ps. Sol. xiii. 4-10, xv. 6, 7) would be exempt; but it is impossible from the grammar and difficult from the sense, to decide whether **τηρεῖν ἐκ** means successful endurance (pregnant sense as in John xvii. 15) or absolute immunity (*cf.* 2 Peter ii. 9), safe emergence from the trial or escape from it entirely (thanks to the timely advent of Christ, ver. 11). Note the fine double sense of **τηρεῖν**: unsparing devotion is spared at least some forms of distress and disturbance. It is like Luther's paradox that when a man learns to say with Christ, "The cross, the cross," there is no cross. Rabbinic piety (*Sanh.* 98 *b*) expected exemption from the tribulation of the latter days only for those who were absorbed in good works and in sacred studies.

Ver. 11. "You have not long to wait and suffer now"; a fresh motive for tenacity of purpose. Compare with what follows the tradition of R. Simon (in Tract. Shabb. bab. 88 *a*) that on the occasion of Exod. xxiv. 7, the Israelites were each crowned with two crowns by 600,000 angels—one when they said *we will do*, the other when they said *we will be obedient*; but on the occasion of Exod. xxxiii. 6 these crowns were snatched off by 1,200,000 devils. In the last day, at the messianic age, God restores these crowns (according to Isa. xxxv. 10). The sense is not altered if **ἵνα . . . σου** (like Luke xii. 20) is taken as a vivid form of the passive "lest thou be deprived of thy crown" (*cf.* Col. ii. 18 with 2 Tim. iv. 8), forfeiting it through misconduct.

Ver. 12. The reward of steadfastness here is a stable relation to God and absolute (trebly verified) assurance of eternal life, permanence **ἐν τῷ ναῷ** (verbally inconsistent with xxi. 22) **τοῦ θεοῦ μου** (four times in this verse). From Strabo (xii. 868 B, **ἥ τε Φιλαδελφία . . . οὐδὲ τοὺς τοίχους ἔχει πιστούς, ἀλλὰ καθ' ἡμέραν τρόπον τινὰ σαλεύονται καὶ διΐστανται**: xiii. 936 B, **πόλις Φιλ. σεισμῶν πλήρης· οὐ γὰρ διαλείπουσιν οἱ τοῖχοι διϊστάμενοι, καὶ ἄλλοτ' ἄλλο μέρος τῆς πόλεως κακοπαθῶν, κ.τ.λ.**) we learn that the city was liable to frequent and severe earthquakes, one of which had produced such ruin a while ago (Tac. *Ann.* ii. 47) that the citizens had to be exempted from Imperial taxation and assisted to repair their buildings. These local circumstances (*cf.* Juv. vi. 411; Dio Cass. lxviii. 25; Renan, 335) lend colour to this promise, which would also appeal to citizens of a city whose numerous festivals and temples are said to have won for it the sobriquet of "a miniature Athens" (*E. Bi.* 3692). The promise is alluded to in Ep. Lugd., where God's grace is said to have "delivered the weak and set them up as **στύλους ἑδραίους**

γράψω ἐπ' αὐτὸν τὸ ὄνομα τοῦ θεοῦ μου καὶ τὸ ὄνομα τῆς πόλεως τοῦ θεοῦ μου, [h] τῆς καινῆς Ἰερουσαλήμ, ἡ [i] καταβαίνουσα [1] ἐκ τοῦ

h Gal. iv. 26, Heb. xi. 10, xii. 22, xiii. 14.
i See on xxi. 2, 10; false apposition.

[1] The ungrammatical η καταβαινουσα (ℵ*AC) has been corrected into η καταβαινει (Q, Andr., Ar.) and της καταβαινουσης (ℵ[ca]).

able by means of their patience to stand all angry onsets of the evil one," and Attalus of Pergamos is termed a **στύλον καὶ ἑδραίωμα** of the local Christians. Permanent communion with God is further expressed in terms of the widespread ethnic belief that to be ignorant of a god's name meant inability to worship him, whereas to know that name implied the power of entering into fellowship with him. "Just as writing a name on temple-walls puts the owner of the name in continual union with the deity of the temple, so for early man the knowledge, invocation and vain repetition of the deity's name constitutes in itself an actual, if mystic, union with the deity named" (Jevons' *Introd. Hist. Religion*, 1896, p. 245; *cf.* Jastrow, p. 173). **καὶ γράψω, κ.τ.λ.**, inscriptions upon pillars being a common feature of Oriental architecture, *cf.* Cooke's *North Semitic Inscriptions*, p. 266, names on pillars; also Reitzenstein's *Poimandres*, 20. The provincial priest of the Imperial cultus erected his statue in the temple at the close of his year's official reign, inscribing on it his own name and his father's, his place of birth and year of office. Hence some of the mysterious imagery of this verse, applied to Christians as priests of God in the next world. This is more probable than to suspect an allusion to what was written on the high priest's forehead (Exod. xxviii. 36, *cf.* Apoc. vii. 3, xiv. 1, xvii. 5, xxii. 4). Pillars were also, of course, sculptured now and then in human shape. For the first (*a*) of the three names, *cf. Baba Bathra*, 75, 2: R. Samuel ait R. Jochanan dixisse tres appellari nomine Dei, justos (Isa. xliii. 7), Messiam (Jer. xxiii. 6), Hierosolyma (Ezek. xlviii. 35); also Targ. Jerus. on Exod. xxviii. 30, quisquis memorat illud nomen sanctum [*i.e.*, **τετραγράμματον**] in hora necessitatis, eripitur, et occulta reteguntur. Where a name was equivalent in one sense to personality and character, to have a divine name conferred on one or revealed to one was equivalent to being endowed with divine power. The divine "hidden name" (*Asc. Isa.* i. 7 Jewish: "as the Lord liveth whose name has not been sent into this world," *cf.* viii. 7) was (according to En. lxix. 14 f.) known to Michael, and had talismanic power over dæmons. Perhaps an allusion to this also underlies the apocalyptic promise, the talismanic metaphor implying that God grants to the victorious Christian inviolable safety against evil spirits (*cf.* Rom. viii. 38, 39). The second (*b*) name denotes (*cf.* Isa. lvi. 5, Ezek. xlviii. 35) that the bearer belongs not merely to God but to the heavenly city and society of God. Since rabbinic speculation was sure that Abraham had the privilege of knowing the mysterious new name for Jerusalem in the next world, John claims this for the average and honest Christian. On the connexion between the divine name and the temple, see 3 Macc. ii. 9, 14, Judith x. 8, etc. The third (*c*) "my own new name" (xix. 12) is reflected in *Asc. Isa.* ix. 5 (the Son of God, *et nomen eius non potes audire donec de carne exibis*); it denotes some esoteric, incommunicable, pre-existent (LXX of Ps. lxxi. 17, En. lxix. 26, *cf. R. J.* 249, 344) title, the knowledge of which meant power to invoke and obtain help from its bearer. The whole imagery (as in ii. 17, xix. 12) is drawn from the primitive superstition that God's name, like a man's name, must be kept secret, lest if known it might be used to the disadvantage of the bearer (Frazer's *Golden Bough*, 2nd ed. i. 443 f.). The close tie between the name and the personality in ancient life lent the former a secret virtue. Especially in Egyptian and in Roman belief, to learn a god's name meant to share his power, and often "the art of the magician consisted in obtaining from the gods a revelation of their sacred names". The point made by the prophet here is that the Christian God bestows freely upon his people the privilege of invoking his aid successfully, and of entering into his secret nature; also, perhaps, of security in the mysterious future across death. See the famous ch. cxxv. of *E. B. D.* where the successive doors will not allow Nu to pass till he tells them their names (*cf.* chapters cxli. f.). Ignatius tells the Philadelphians (obviously referring to this passage, *ad Phil.* 6) that people unsound upon the truth of

οὐρανοῦ ἀπὸ τοῦ θεοῦ μου, καὶ τὸ [k] ὄνομά μου τὸ καινόν. 13. Ὁ
ἔχων οὖς ἀκουσάτω τί τὸ Πνεῦμα λέγει ταῖς ἐκκλησίαις.
"14. Καὶ τῷ ἀγγέλῳ τῆς ἐν Λαοδικίᾳ ἐκκλησίας γράψον, Τάδε
λέγει ὁ [l] Ἀμήν, ὁ [m] μάρτυς ὁ πιστὸς καὶ [n] ἀληθινός, ἡ [o] ἀρχὴ τῆς
κτίσεως τοῦ θεοῦ· 15. Οἶδά σου τὰ ἔργα, ὅτι οὔτε ψυχρὸς εἶ οὔτε

k *Cf.* Isa. xliii. 7, lxii. 2.
l Isa. lxv. 16 (LXX ὁ θεὸς ὁ ἀληθινός).
m *Cf.* on i. 5, Ps. lxxxix. 37.
n = *Genuine*, Did., xiii. 1-2.
o See on Col. i. 15 f., also Just. *Apol.* ii. 6, Diognet. vii.

Jesus Christ are to him **στῆλαι καὶ τάφοι νεκρῶν, ἐφ' οἷς γέγραπται μόνον ὀνόματα ἀνθρώπων.** The **μόνον** is emphatic. In the survival of P. during the later conquests which left the other six towns of the Apocalypse more or less ruined, Gibbon (ch. lxiv.) irrelevantly finds "a pleasing example that the paths of honour and safety may sometimes be the same".

Vv. 14-22. The message for Laodicea, where a church existed by 60 A.D. (Col. iv. 16).

Ver. 14. Jesus is *the Amen* because he guarantees the truth of any statement, and the execution of any promise, made by himself. He is consequently *the faithful and true witness*, whose counsel and rebuke (18, 19) however surprising and unwelcome, are therefore to be laid to heart as authoritative. A faithful witness is one who can be trusted never to misrepresent his message, by exaggeration or suppression, (**ἀληθινός** practically = **ἀληθής** as often, since a real witness is naturally a truthful and competent one) his veracity extending not only to his character but to the contents of his message. In point of sincerity and unerring insight (as opposed to "false" in both senses of the term), Jesus is the supreme moral critic; the church is the supreme object of his criticism. He is also absolutely trustworthy, and therefore his promises are to be believed (vv. 20, 21), or rather God's promises are assured and realised to men through him (*cf.* **π. καὶ ἀ.** in 2 Macc. ii. 11). Compare the fine Assyrian hymn of Ishtar (Jastrow, p. 343): "Fear not! the mind which speaks to thee comes with speech from me, withholding nothing. . . . Is there any utterance of mine that I addressed to thee, upon which thou couldst not rely?" (also, Eurip. *Ion* 1537). The resemblance of **ἡ ἀρχὴ κ.τ.λ.**, to a passage in Colossians is noteworthy as occurring in an open letter to the neighbouring church of Laodicea (Philonic passages in Grill, pp. 106-110). Here the phrase denotes "the active source or principle of God's universe or creation" (**ἀρχή**, as in Greek philosophy and Jewish wisdom-literature, = **αἰτία** or origin), which is practically Paul's idea and that of John i. 3 ("the Logos idea without the name Logos," Beyschlag). This title of "incipient cause" implies a position of priority to everything created; he is *the first* in the sense that he is neither creator (a prerogative of God in the Apocalypse), nor created, but creative. It forms the most explicit allusion to the pre-existence of Jesus in the Apocalypse, where he is usually regarded as a divine being whose heavenly power and position are the outcome of his earthly suffering and resurrection: John ascribes to him here (not at xii. 5, as Baldensperger, 85, thinks) that pre-existence which, in more or less vital forms, had been predicated of the messiah in Jewish apocalyptic (*cf.* En. xlviii.). This pre-existence of messiah is an extension of the principle of determinism; God foreordained the salvation itself as well as its historical hour. See the Egyptian hymn: "He is the primeval one, and existed when as yet nothing existed; whatever is, He made it after He was. He is the father of beginnings. . . . God is the truth, He lives by Truth, He lives upon Truth, He is the king of Truth." The evidence for the pre-existence of messiah in Jewish Christian literature is examined by Dr. G. A. Barton, *Journ. Bibl. Lit.* 1902, pp. 78-91. *Cf.* Introd. § 6.

Ver. 15. The moral nausea roused by tepid religion. It is best to be warm, and energetic; but even a frank repudiation of religion is at least more promising from an ethical standpoint (Arist. *Nik. Eth.* vii. 2-10) than a half-and-half attachment, complacently oblivious of any shortcoming. The outsider may be convinced and won over; there is hope of him, for he is under no illusion as to his real relation to the faith. But what can be done with people who are nominal Christians, unable to recognise that they need repentance and that Jesus is really outside their lives (ver. 20)? *Cf.* Dante's *Inferno*, iii. 30 f. For such homely metaphors and their effectiveness, compare the criticism of Longinus in **περὶ ὕψους**

[p] ζεστός· [q] ὄφελον ψυχρὸς ἦς ἢ ζεστός· 16. οὕτως ὅτι [r] χλιαρὸς εἶ,
καὶ οὔτε ζεστὸς οὔτε ψυχρός, μέλλω σε [r] ἐμέσαι ἐκ τοῦ στόματός
μου. 17. ὅτι λέγεις, [s] ὅτι [t] πλούσιός εἰμι καὶ [u] πεπλούτηκα καὶ οὐδὲν [1] χρείαν ἔχω, καὶ οὐκ οἶδας ὅτι σὺ εἶ [v] ὁ ταλαίπωρος καὶ ἐλεεινὸς
καὶ πτωχὸς καὶ τυφλὸς καὶ γυμνός· 18. συμβουλεύω σοι ἀγοράσαι

p ἅπ. λεγ. N.T., *cf.* Rom. xii. 11.
q *Cf.* Moult. i. 200, Helbing, 73-74, Win. § 12, 5. For idea, Matt. xii. 33? Epict. iii. 15, 13.
r ἅπ. λεγ. N.T.
s John i. 32, *cf.* Plato's *Symp.*, 204A.
1 Cor. iv. 8, 2 Cor. viii. 9.
u Hos. xii. 8 (9), Zech. xi. 5.
v Art. as in Lk. xviii. 13.

[1] **ουδενος** (אPQ, 1, Areth, etc.) is a correction of the difficult and original **ουδεν** ("like *nil opus est*," Simcox: *cf.* Epict. iii. 7) AC, 12, Andbav, edd.

(xxxi.): "Sometimes a plain expression like this tells more forcibly than elegant language; being drawn from common life, it is at once recognised, whilst its very familiarity renders it all the more convincing". The spirit of the verse resembles that which pervaded Christ's denunciation of the religious authorities in his day for their **ὑπόκρισις,** and his more hopeful expectations with regard to the harlots and taxgatherers (*Ecce Homo*, ch. xiii.); the former condition of religious life was to Jesus a sickening feature in the situation. Just as spiritual death, in the case of the Sardis Christians, meant a lost vitality, so in the case of Laodicea lukewarmness implies that a condition of religious warmth once existed. "He who was never fervent can never be lukewarm." In his analysis of this state (*Growth in Holiness*, ch. xxv.), Faber points out not only that its correlative is a serene unconsciousness and unconcern (*cf.* ver. 17 *b*), but that one symptom is a complacent attention to what has been achieved (*cf.* 17 *a*) rather than sensitiveness to what is left undone, with "a quiet intentional appreciation of other things over God" (*cf.* ver. 20), which is all the more mischievous that it is not open wickedness.

Ver. 16. The divine disgust at lukewarm religion. Christ, says the prophet, is sick of the lukewarm: as the purpose (**μέλλω**) of rejection does not exclude the possibility of a change upon the part of the church which shall render the execution of the purpose needless, advice to repent immediately follows upon the threat. The latter is unconditional only in form. Exclusion from God's life forms one side of the penalty, humiliating exposure before men the other (18).

Ver. 17. Priding herself not merely on the fact but (as is implied) on the means by which it had been secured (*viz.*, personal skill, merit) and finally on the independent self-reliant position thus attained: a profuse certificate of merit, self-assigned. To conceit and self-deception the prophet wrathfully ascribes the religious indifference at Laodicea. "No one," says Philo (*Fragm.* p. 649, Mang.), "is enriched by secular things, even though he possessed all the mines in the world; the witless are all paupers." The reference is to spiritual possessions and advantages. It is irrelevant to connect the saying with the material wealth and resources of Laodicea, as exemplified in the fact that it was rebuilt by its citizens after the earthquake in 60-61 A.D. without help from the imperial authorities (Tacit. *Ann.* xiv. 27). For one thing, the incident is too far back; for another, the Apocalypse is concerned not with the cities but with the Christian churches. Such an allusion may have been in the writer's mind, especially if the church included in its membership prosperous and influential citizens, since complacency and self-satisfaction are fostered by material comfort. "If wealthily then happily," in Laodicea as in Padua. Still, these weeds spring from other soils as well. An inefficient ministry (*cf.* Col. iv. 17) and absence of persecution or of special difficulties at Laodicea probably helped to account for the church's languid state. As John suggests, the church which is truly rich in spiritual and moral qualities does not plume itself upon them (ii. 9). **οὐκ οἶδας,** *cf.* the echo of this in *Oxyrhynchite Logia*, i. 3: **τυφλοί εἰσιν τῇ καρδίᾳ αὐτῶν καὶ οὐ βλέπ[ουσιν, πτωχοὶ καὶ οὐκ οἴδασιν τ]ὴν πτωχιαν** (?), where blindness and poverty and unconsciousness of both occur. **σύ,** emphatic; **ἐλεεινός,** "needing pity" rather than (as Dan. ix. 23, x. 11, LXX) "finding pity"; **ταλ.** (*cf.* with ver. 19, Sap. iii. 11: **σοφίαν γὰρ καὶ παιδείαν ὁ ἐξουθενῶν ταλαίπωρος**), only here and Rom. vii. 24 in N. T., two passages representing the extremes of misery—unconscious and conscious. **ὁ κ.τ.λ.** = "the embodiment of".

Ver. 18. The counsel is conveyed in the

[w]παρ' ἐμοῦ χρυσίον [w]πεπυρωμένον [x]ἐκ [x]πυρὸς ἵνα πλουτήσῃς, καὶ
[y]ἱμάτια [y]λευκὰ ἵνα περιβάλῃ καὶ μὴ φανερωθῇ ἡ [z]αἰσχύνη τῆς
γυμνότητός σου· καὶ [r]κολλούριον [a]ἐγχρῖσαι[1] τοὺς ὀφθαλμούς σου
ἵνα βλέπῃς. 19. ἐγὼ [b]ὅσους ἐὰν φιλῶ [c]ἐλέγχω καὶ παιδεύω·

w A forgotten lesson, *cf.* Col. ii. 3, iv. 16. x Zech. xiii. 9. For constr. ii. 11, viii. 11 = dative. y iii. 4, vii. 9, 14, xix. 14. z See on xvi. 15. a 1 John ii. 20, 27. b Prov. iii. 11-12 = Heb. xii. 5-6, Ps. Sol. x. 2, 1 Cor. xi. 32. c John iii. 20, xvi. 8 (*R.J.* 365), Sir. xviii. 13.

[1] For **εγχρισον** (P, 1, 92 marg., 96, etc.) read **εγχρισαι** (infin. not imper; the technical term; **ἅπ. λεγ.** in N.T.) with ℵAC, etc., vg., Pr., And[a], edd.

dialect of the local situation. **ἀγοράσαι** in the poor man's market (Isa. lv. 1, *cf.* Matt. vi. 19, 20), significant words as addressed to the financial centre of the district. "From me," is emphatic; the real life is due to man's relation with Christ, not to independent efforts upon his own part. Local Christians needed to be made sensitive to their need of Christ; in Laodicea evidently, as in Bunyan's Mansoul, Mr. Desires-awake dwelt in a very mean cottage. "Refined" = genuine and fresh, as opposed to counterfeit and traditional (*cf.* Plato, *Rep.* iii. 413 *e*, 416 *e*). For **παιδεία** wrought upon the people of God by a divine Davidic king whose words are **πεπυρωμένα ὑπὲρ χρυσίον τίμιον,** see Ps. Sol. xvii. 47, 48.—**ἱμάτια.** Laodicea was a famous manufacturing centre, whose trade largely consisted of tunics and cloth for garments. The allusion is (*cf.* below, on ver. 20 and xvi. 15) to careless Christians caught off their guard by the suddenness of the second advent. **κολλούριον** or **κολλύριον** (*cf.* the account of a blind soldier's cure by a god [Aesculapius?] who bade him **κολλύριον συντρῖψαι,** Dittenberger's *Sylloge Inscript. Graec.* 807, 15 f.), an eye-salve for tender eyes: an allusion to the "Phrygian powder" used by oculists of the famous medical school at Laodicea (*C. B. P.* i. 52). To the Christian Jesus supplies that enlightenment which the Jews found in the law (Ps. xix. 8); "uerba legis corona sunt capitis, collyrium oculis" (*Tract. Siphra* fol. 143, 2); "uerba legis corona sunt capitis, torques collo, collyrium oculis" (Vajikra R., fol. 156, 1). True self-knowledge can be gained only by the help of Christ, *i.e.*, in the present case mediated by Christian prophecy. Like Victor., Lightfoot (*Colossians*, p. 44) interprets this allusion by the light of Eph. i. 8, Col. i. 27, as a rebuke to the vaunted intellectual resources of the Church; but there is no need thus to narrow the reference. It is to be observed that John does not threaten Laodicea with the loss of material wealth (*cf. Pirke Aboth*, cited above on ii. 9) in order to have her spiritual life revived.

Ver. 19. The prophet now relents a little; the church has still a chance of righting herself. Such a reproof as he has given in Christ's name, and the discipline it involves (**παιδεύω,** wider than **ἐλ.**) are really evidence of affection, not of antipathy or rejection. This is the method of God at least (**ἐγώ,** emphatic; "whatever others do"), with whom censure does not mean hostility. **φιλῶ,** the substitution of this synonym (contrast Heb. xii. 6) for the LXX **ἀγαπᾷ** is remarkable in view of the latter term's usage in the Apocalypse; the other variation **ἐλέγχω καὶ παιδεύω** (**ἐλ.** B, **παιδ.** ℵA, LXX) is probably ornate rather than a duplicate. The love of Christ for his people is mentioned in the Apocalypse only here (with a reminiscence if not a quotation of O.T.), in i. 5, and in iii. 9 (incidentally). In the latter passage, the divine love sustains and safeguards those who are loyal; here it inflicts painful wounds upon the unworthy, to regain their loyalty. **ζήλευε** (pres.) = a habit, **μετανόησον** (aor.) = a definite change once for all. The connexion (**οὖν**) seems to be: let the foregoing rebuke open your eyes at once to the need of repentance, and also to the fact that it is really love on my part which prompts me thus to expose and to chastise you; such a sense of my loving concern, as well as of your own plight, should kindle an eager heat of indignation (2 Cor. viii. 11, **ἀλλα ζῆλον**) gathering into a flame of repentance that will burn up indifference and inconsistency (*cf.* Weinel, 188 f.). The urgent need of immediate repentance rests not only on the special character of the temptation to which the local Christians were succumbing ("It is a great grace to find out that we are lukewarm, but we are lost if we do not act with vigour. It is like going to sleep in the snow, almost a pleasant, tingling feeling at the first, and then—lost for

ζήλευε οὖν καὶ μετανόησον. 20. Ἰδοὺ ἕστηκα ἐπὶ τὴν θύραν καὶ
κρούω· [d] ἐάν τις [e] ἀκούσῃ τῆς [e] φωνῆς μου καὶ ἀνοίξῃ τὴν θύραν,
καὶ εἰσελεύσομαι [1] πρὸς αὐτὸν καὶ [f] δειπνήσω μετ' αὐτοῦ καὶ αὐτὸς
μετ' ἐμοῦ. 21. Ὁ [g] νικῶν, δώσω αὐτῷ [h] καθίσαι μετ' ἐμοῦ ἐν τῷ

d And not?—then fate of Matt. xxvi. 64. e Constr. xiv. 13, xvi. 1, xxi. 3; crying "open" (*aperi*), *cf.* John x. 3. f Gen. xxvi. 29-31, En. lxii. 14-15. g Ver. 12, Suspended nom. (Abbott, *Diat.* 2421). h 1 Macc. x. 63, *cf.* Lk. xxii. 30, a reminiscence of Col. iii. 1, Eph. ii. 6?

[1] Before **εισελευσομαι** add (Hebraistic, introd. apodosis, x. 7, xiv. 10) **και** ℵQ, etc., Andc, Pr. (Ti., WH marg., Bj., Bs.): the apparent absence of **ακουσῃ της φωνης μου και** from the text used by Orig., Hil., Epiph. might suggest that the words were a natural though (as their excellent textual attestation shows) an early gloss upon **ανοιξῃ**. S. reads **και ανοιξει** (thus beginning the apodosis).

ever," Faber), but on the fact that this warning was their last chance.

Ver. 20. The language recalls Cant. v. 2 (**φωνὴ ἀδελφιδοῦ μου κρούει ἐπὶ τὴν θύραν· ἄνοιξον μοι**, for contemporary evidence of the allegorical use of Canticles see Gunkel's note on 4 Esdras. v. 20 f. and Bacher's *Agada d. Tannaiten*, i. 109, 285 f. 425, etc.) interpreted in the eschatological sense (**γινώσκετε ὅτι ἐγγύς ἐστιν ἐπὶ θύραις** Mark xiii. 29 = Matt. xxiv. 33) of the logion in Luke xii. 35-38 upon the servants watching for their Lord, **ἵνα ἐλθόντος καὶ κρούσαντος εὐθέως ἀνοίξωσιν αὐτῷ** (whereupon, as here, he grants them intimate fellowship with himself and takes the lead in the matter). To eat with a person meant, for an Oriental, close confidence and affection. Hence future bliss (*cf.* En. lxii. 14) was regularly conceived to be a feast (*cf.* Dalman i. § 1, C. 4 *a* and Volz 331), or, as in Luke xxii. 29, 30 and here (*cf.* ver. 21), feasting and authority. This tells against the otherwise attractive hypothesis that the words merely refer to a present repentance on the part of the church or of some individuals in it (so *e.g.* de Wette, Alf., Weiss, Simcox, Scott), as if Christ sought to be no longer an outsider but a welcome inmate of the heart (*cf.* Ruskin's *Sesame and Lilies*, § 95). The context (*cf.* 18 and 21), a comparison of xvi. 15 (which may even have originally lain close to iii. 20), and the words of Jas. v. 9 (**ἰδοὺ ὁ κριτὴς πρὸ τῶν θυρῶν ἕστηκεν**) corroborate the eschatological interpretation (so *e.g.* Düsterdieck, Pfleid., Bousset, Forbes, Baljon, Swete, Holtzmann), which makes this the last call of Christ to the church when he arrives on the last day, though here Christ stands at the door not as a judge but as a friend. Hence no reference is made to the fate of those who will not attend to him. In ii. 5 and 16, **ἔρχομαι σοι** need not perhaps be eschatological, since the coming is conditional and special, but **ἔρχομαι** by itself (iii. 11) and **ἥξω** (ii. 25) must be, while iii. 3 probably is also, in view of the context and the thief-simile. The imminent threat of iii. 16 is thus balanced by the urgency of iii. 20. For the eschatological **ἰδού** *cf.* i. 7, xvi. 15, xxi. 3, xxii. 7, 12. **φωνῆς**, implying that the voice is well-known. To pay attention to it, in spite of self-engrossment and distraction, is one proof of the moral alertness (**ζήλευε**) which means repentance. For the metaphorical contrast (reflecting the eternal paradox of grace) between the enthroned Christ of 21 and the appealing Christ of 20, *cf.* the remarkable passage in Sap. ix. 4, 6 f., 10 f., where wisdom shares God's throne and descends to toil among men; also Seneca's *Epp.* xli. (quemadmodum radii solis contingunt quidem terram, sed ibi sunt unde mittuntur; sic animus magnus et sacer conuersatur quidem nobiscum, sed haeret origini suae [Apoc. v. 6]: illinc pendet, illuc spectat ac nititur, nostris tanquam melior interest). By self-restraint, moderation, and patience, with regard to possessions, a man will be some day a worthy partner of the divine feast, says Epictetus (*Enchir.* xv.): "but if you touch none of the dishes set before you and actually scorn them, **τότε οὐ μόνον ἔσει συμπότης θεῶν ἀλλὰ καὶ συνάρχων.**

Ver. 21. **δώσω κ.τ.λ.**, To share Christ's royal power and judicial dignity is a reward proffered in the gospels, but Jesus there (*cf.* Mark x. 40) disclaimed this prerogative. God's throne is Christ's, as in xxii. 1. **νικῶν** = the moral purity and sensitiveness (*cf.* 18 and on ii. 7) which succeeds in responding to the divine appeal. The schema of God, Christ, and the individual Christian (*cf.* on ii. 27) is characteristically Johannine (*cf.* John xv. 9 f., xvii. 19 f., xx. 21), though here as in ver. 20 (contrast John xiv. 23) the eschatological emphasis makes the parallel one of diction rather than of thought.

The scope and warmth of the promises

θρόνῳ μου, ὡς κἀγὼ ἐνίκησα καὶ ἐκάθισα μετὰ τοῦ πατρός μου
ἐν τῷ θρόνῳ αὐτοῦ. 22. Ὁ ἔχων οὖς ἀκουσάτω τί τὸ Πνεῦμα λέγει
ταῖς ἐκκλησίαις."

to Laodicea seem rather out of place in view of the church's poor religion, but here as elsewhere the prophet is writing as much for the churches in general as for the particular community. He speaks **ταῖς ἐκκλησίαις**. This consideration, together with the close sequence of thought in 19-21 forbids any attempt to delete 20, 21 as a later editorial addition (Wellhausen) or to regard 20 (21) as an epilogue to the seven letters (Vitringa, Alford, Ramsay) rather than as an integral part of the Laodicean epistle. Such a detachment would be a gratuitous breach of symmetry. But, while these closing sentences are not a sort of climax which gathers up the menaces of ii.-iii., ver. 21 (with its throne-reference) anticipates the following visions (iv.-v.). To the prophet the real value and significance of Christ's life were focussed in his sacrificial death and in the rights and privileges which he secured thereby for those on whose behalf he had suffered and triumphed. This idea, already suggested in i. 5, 6, 17, 18, forms the central theme of the next oracle.

The **ἐκκλησίαι** now pass out of sight till the visions are over. During the latter it is the **ἅγιοι** who are usually in evidence, until the collective term **πόλις** is employed in the final vision (*cf.* iii. 12). John knows nothing of any catholic **ἐκκλησία**. To him the **ἐκκλησίαι** are so many local communities who share a common faith and expect a common destiny; they are, as Kattenbusch observes, colonies of heaven, and heaven is their mother-country. Partly owing to O.T. associations, partly perhaps on account of the feeling that an **ἐκκλησία** (in the popular Greek sense of the term) implied a city, John eschews this term. He also ignores the authority of any officials; the religious situation depends upon the prophets, who are in direct touch with God and through whom the Spirit of God controls and guides the saints. Their words are God's words; they can speak and write with an authority which enables them to say, *Thus saith the Spirit.* Only, while in the contemporary literature of Christianity the prophetic outlook embraces either the need of organisation in order to meet the case of churches which are scattered over a wide area and exposed to the vagaries of unauthorised leaders (Pastoral Epistles and Ignatius), or contention among the office-bearers themselves (a sure sign of the end, *Asc. Isa.* iii. 20 f.), John's apocalypse stands severely apart from either interest.

NOTE on i. 9-iii. 22. We have no data to show whether the seven letters or addresses ever existed in separate form, or whether they were written before or after the rest of the visions. All evidence for such hypotheses consists of quasi-reasons or precarious hypotheses based on some *a priori* theory of the book's composition. The great probability is that they never had any rôle of their own apart from this book, but were written for their present position. As the Roman emperors addressed letters to the Asiatic cities or corporations (the inscriptions mention at least six to Ephesus, seven to Pergamos, three to Smyrna, etc.), so Jesus, the true Lord of the Asiatic churches, is represented as sending communications to them (*cf.* Deissmann's *Licht vom Osten*, pp. 274 f.). The *dicit* or **λέγει** with which the Imperial messages open corresponds to the more biblical **τάδε λέγει** of ii. 1, etc. Each of the apocalyptic communications follows a fairly general scheme, although in the latter four the appeal for attention follows (instead of preceding) the mystic promise, while the imperative *repent* occurs only in the first, third, fifth, and seventh, the other churches receiving praise rather than censure. This artificial or symmetrical arrangement, which may be traced in or read into other details, is as characteristic of the whole apocalypse as is the style which—when the difference of topic is taken into account—cannot be said to exhibit peculiarities of diction, syntax, or vocabulary sufficient to justify the relegation of the seven letters to a separate source. Even if written by another hand or originally composed as a separate piece, they must have been worked over so thoroughly by the final editor and fitted so aptly into the general scheme of the whole Apocalypse (*cf. e.g.* ii. 7 = xxii. 2, 14, 19; ii. 11 = xx. 16; ii. 17 = xix. 12; ii. 26 = xx. 4; ii. 28 = xxii. 16; iii. 5 = vii. 9, 13; iii. 5 = xiii. 8, xx. 15; iii. 12 = xxi. 10, xxii. 14; iii. 21 = iv. 4; iii. 20 = xix. 9; etc.), that it is no longer possible to dis-

IV. 1. [a] ΜΕΤΑ ταῦτα [a] εἶδον, [b] καὶ ἰδοὺ θύρα ἠνεῳγμένη ἐν τῷ
οὐρανῷ, καὶ ἡ φωνὴ ἡ [c] πρώτη ἣν ἤκουσα ὡς σάλπιγγος [d] λαλούσης

a vii. 1, 9, xv. 5, xviii. 1, xix. 1, *cf.* i. 12.

b xiv. 14, xix. 11, *Zech.* v. 9. c i. 10. d Loose appos. to σ. instead of φωνή, *cf.* ix. 13, etc.

entangle them (or their nucleus). The special traits in the conception of Christ are mainly due to the fact that the writer is dealing here almost exclusively with the inner relation of Jesus to the churches. They are seldom, if ever, more realistic or closer to the messianic categories of the age than is elsewhere the case throughout the apocalypse; and if the marjoram of Judaism or (as we might more correctly say) of human nature is not wholly transmuted into the honey of Christian charity—which is scarcely surprising under the circumstances—yet the moral and mental stature of the writer appears when he is set beside so powerful a counsellor in some respects as the later Ignatius. Here John is at his full height. He combines moral discipline and moral enthusiasm in his injunctions. He sees the central things and urges them upon the churches, with a singular power of tenderness and sarcasm, insight and foresight, vehemence and reproach, undaunted faithfulness in rebuke and a generous readiness to mark what he thinks are the merits as well as the failings and perils of the communities. The needs of the latter appear to have been twofold. One, of which they were fully conscious, was outward. The other, to which they were not entirely alive, was inward. The former is met by an assurance that the stress of persecution in the present and in the immediate future was under God's control, unavoidable and yet endurable. The latter is met by the answer of discipline and careful correction; the demand for purity and loyalty in view of secret errors and vices is reiterated with a keen sagacity. In every case, the motives of fear, shame, *noblesse oblige*, and the like, are crowned by an appeal to spiritual ambition and longing, the closing note of each epistle thus striking the keynote of what follows throughout the whole Apocalypse. In form, as well as in content, the seven letters are the most definitely Christian part of the book.

The scene now changes. Christ in authority over his churches, and the churches with their angels, pass away; a fresh and ampler tableau of the vision opens (*cf.* on i. 19), ushering in the future (vi.-xxii. 5), which—as disclosed by God through Christ (i. 1)—is prefaced by a solemn exhibition of God's supremacy and Christ's indispensable position in revelation. In Apoc. Bar. xxiv. 2 the seer is told that on the day of judgment he and his companions are to see "the long-suffering of the Most High which has been throughout all generations, who has been long-suffering towards all those born that sin and are righteous." He then seeks an answer to the question, "But what will happen to our enemies I know not, and when Thou wilt visit Thy works (*i.e.*, for judgment)"? This is precisely the course of thought (first inner mercies and then outward judgments) in Apoc. ii.-iii. and iv. f.; although in the former John sees in this life already God's great patience towards his people, The prophet is now admitted to the heavenly conclave where (by an adaptation of the rabbinic notion) God reveals, or at least prepares, his purposes before executing them. Chapter iv. and chapter v. are counterparts; in the former God the Creator, with his praise from heavenly beings, is the central figure: in the latter the interest is focussed upon Christ the redeemer, with his praise from the human and natural creation as well. Chapter v. further leads over into the first series of events (the seven seals, vi.-viii.) which herald the *dénouement*. Henceforth Jesus is represented as *the Lamb*, acting but never speaking, until in the epilogue (xxii. 6-21) the author reverts to the Christological standpoint of i.-iii. Neither this nor any other feature, however, is sufficient to prove that iv.-v. represent a Jewish source edited by a Christian; the whole piece is Christian and homogeneous (Sabatier, Schön, Bousset, Pfleiderer, Wellhausen). Chapter iv. is a preliminary description of the heavenly court: God's ruddy throne with a green nimbus being surrounded by a senate of **πρεσβύτεροι** and mysterious **ζῷα**. Seven torches burn before the throne, beside a crystal ocean, while from it issue flashes and peals accompanied by a ceaseless liturgy of adoration from the **πρεσβύτεροι** and the **ζῷα**, who worship with a rhythmic emotion of awe.

CHAPTER IV.—Ver. 1. **μετὰ . . . ἰδού** introducing as usual in an independent clause (instead of a simple accus., Vit. ii.

e *Cf.* 1 Kings xxii. 19.
f (Qf local position = "stood") Jer. xxiv. 1, Jo. xix. 29, etc.
g Used in Apoc. with gen., dat., and acc. indifferently.

μετ' ἐμοῦ, λέγων,[1] "'Ανάβα ὧδε, καὶ δείξω σοι ἃ δεῖ γενέσθαι μετὰ
ταῦτα". 2. εὐθέως ἐγενόμην ἐν πνεύματι·
καὶ ἰδοὺ [e] θρόνος [f] ἔκειτο ἐν τῷ οὐρανῷ,
καὶ [g] ἐπὶ τὸν θρόνον [g] καθήμενος·

[1] The **λεγουσα** of ℵ[c]P, 1, 92 marg., Areth., etc. is a correction of orig. **λεγων** ℵ*AQ, etc., And[c], edd. [an awkward *constr. ad sensum* = לאמר; *cf.* Vit. i. 204 f].

8 f., 31, 173, 174, to which he reverts in ver. 4) some fresh and weighty revelation; lesser phases are heralded by the simpler **καὶ εἶδον**. The phrase indicates a pause, which of course may have covered days as well as hours in the original experience of the seer, if we assume that his visions came in the order in which they are recorded. He is no longer in the island but up at the gates of heaven. In his trance, a heavenly voice comes after he has seen—not heaven opened (the usual apocalyptic and ecstatic symbol, *e.g.* Acts x. 11 = a vision, xi. 5, Ezek. i. 1, Matt. iii. 16, Ap. Bar. xxii. 1) but—a door set open (ready, opened) in the vault of the mysterious upper world which formed God's house. Then follows the rapture (which in i. 9 precedes the voice). The whole vision is composed by a man familiar with O.T. prophecy, in Semitic style: short clauses linked by the monotonous **καί**, with little or no attempt made at elaboration of any kind. Traits from the theophany of God as a monarch, surrounded by a triple circle (*cf.* the triple circle surrounding Ahuramazda), are blended with traits drawn from the theophany in nature. The ordinary Jewish conception (Gfrörer, i. 365 f.) tended to regard God as the royal priest, to whom angels rendered ceaseless levitical praise and service (*cf.* Apoc. iv.-v.), or as a glorified rabbi whose angels act as interpreters of the heavenly mysteries for man (*cf.* Apoc. x. and apocalyptic literature in general with its angelic cicerones). In the seven heavens of Chagiga, 12*b*, the third is the place where "the millstones grind manna for the righteous' (Ps. lxxviii. 23, 24, *cf.* Apoc. ii. 17), whilst in the fourth are the heavenly Jerusalem (*cf.* Apoc. xxi. 10) and the temple (Apoc. xv. 5 f.) and the altar (Apoc. viii. 3 f.) where the great prince Michael offers an offering, but in the fifth the ministering angels, who sing God's praise by night, are silent by day to let Israel's adoration rise to the Most High (see on ver. 8). **ἀνάβα ὧδε** (*cf.* the common phrase, **ἀναβαίνειν εἰς τὸν οὐρανόν,** of penetration into heavenly mysteries), from Exod. xix. 16, 24, **φωνὴ τῆς σάλπιγγος ἤχει μέγα . . εἶπεν δὲ αὐτῷ Κύριος . . . ἀνάβηθι.** As in the O.T. the revelation is vouchsafed spontaneously, whereas in Iranian theology (*e.g.*, in the Vendîdâd) "it is the wish of man, not the will of God, that is the first cause of the revelation" (Darmesteter, *S. B. E.* iv. p. lxxxv.). The seer does not enter the door till he is called; to know the divine will is the outcome of revelation, not of inquiry or speculative curiosity (similar idea in 1 Cor. ii. 9 f.). Enoch (xiv. 9 f.) also does not enter the palace of God with its fire-encircled walls, but sees through the open portals "a high throne, **καὶ τὸ εἶδος αὐτοῦ ὡσεὶ κρυστάλλινον . . . καὶ ὅρος χερουβίν . . .** and from underneath the great throne came streams of flaming fire so that I could not look thereon. And the great Glory sat thereon and his raiment shone more brightly than the sun and was whiter than any snow." He is finally called by God to approach but not to enter. *Cf.* Ap. Bar. li. 11, *Test. Levi.* v, "and the angel opened unto me the gates of heaven, and I saw the holy One, the Most High, seated on the throne".

Ver. 2. A fresh wave of ecstasy catches up the seer. **εὐθέως . . πνεύματι,** repeating i. 10, not because the author had forgotten his previous statement, and still less because a new source begins here (Vischer), but simply because every successive phase of this Spirit-consciousness, every new access of ecstasy, was considered to be the result of a fresh inspiration; so the O.T. prophets (*e.g.*, Ezek. xi. 1 **καὶ ἀνέλαβέν με πνεῦμα κ.τ.λ.**, followed by ver. 5 **καὶ ἔπεσεν ἐπ' ἐμὲ πνεῦμα,** ii. 2 and iii. 24; *cf.* Enoch xiv. 9 **καὶ ἄνεμοι ἐν τῇ ὁράσει μου . . . εἰσήνεγκάν με εἰς τὸν οὐρανόν** followed by ver. 14 **ἐθεώρουν ἐν τ. ὁ. μ. καὶ ἰδοὺ κ.τ.λ.**, lxxi. 1 and 5, etc.). The primitive

3. καὶ ὁ καθήμενος ὅμοιος [h] ὁράσει λίθῳ [i] ἰάσπιδι καὶ [k] σαρδίῳ· καὶ [l] ἶρις [l] κυκλόθεν τοῦ θρόνου [m] ὅμοιος ὁράσει σμαραγδίνῳ.

h "In appearance."
i *Cf.* on xxi. 11.
k xxi. 20, Exod. xxviii. 20, xxxix. 13, Ezek. xxviii. 20.
l Ezek. i. 28, ἅπ. λεγ. N.T., *cf.* x. 1, where also it is substituted for τόξον of LXX.
m *Cf.* Win. § 11, 1.

Christian conception of the Spirit was that of a sudden and repeated transport rather than a continuous experience (Acts iv. 8, 31, etc.), particularly in the region of ecstasy. The royal presence is depicted in this theophany by means of similes and metaphors (partly rabbinic) which originally were suggested in part by the marvellous atmospheric colouring of an Eastern sky during storm or sunset; several had been for long traditional and fanciful modes of expressing the divine transcendence (*e.g.*, En. xiv. 18 f. the divine glory like crystal, etc.) which dominates the Apocalypse. God is a silent, enthroned (*cf.* 1 Kings xxii. 19 etc.), eternal Figure, hidden by the very excess of light, keeping ward and watch over his people, but never directly interfering in their affairs till the judgment, when mankind appears before his throne for doom and recompense. This reluctance to name or describe God, so characteristic of the later Judaism, was allied to the feeling which mediated his action upon the world through angels or through his Christ (see on i. 1 and xv. 8). For the tendency to describe God and heaven in priestly terms, *cf.* Gfrörer, i. 276 f. The whole of the present passage is illustrated by *Pirke Elieser*, iv.: "majestas sancti benedicti est in medio quattuor classium angelicarum. Ipse insidet throno excelso eleuatus, atque solium eius sublime suspensum est sursum in aere, figura autem gloriae eius est sicut color Chasonal, juxta uerba prophetiae (Ezek. i. 27) . . . atque oculi per totum orbem discurrunt. Sagittae eius sunt ignis et grando; a dextra eius uita est, a sinistra mors, sceptrum ignitum in manu eius. Expansum est ante eum uelum, et septem angeli qui prius creati sunt, famulantur ei ante uelum . . . infra thronum gloriae eius est sicuti lapis sapphiri."

Ver. 3. The sources of the general conception lie far back in passages like Isa. vi. 1 f., Ezek. i. 26 f., Dan. vii. 9 f., Enoch xxxix., xl., xlvi., mediated by rabbinical interpretations. But it should be noted that in the palace-temple of Hatra, the Parthian capital, one well-known frieze contained a row of figures including the griffin, the eagle, the human face, the head of an ox, and an emblem on the cornice apparently representing the sun. With a sublime restraint, the author leaves the royal presence undefined, though he is more definite and explicit on the whole than (say) Ezekiel. The latter's advance in this respect upon his predecessors was explained by the rabbis (*cf.* Streane's *Chagiga*, p. 73) as a needful counteractive to the Jewish belief that visions were impossible outside Canaan, and as a help to men of the captivity who needed "special details to support them in their trials" (*cf.* above, i. 9 f.). The **σάρδιον,** a flesh-coloured, semi-transparent, often golden or ruddy gem, answers to our red jasper or cornelian, so-called perhaps from Sardis, whence the stone was originally exported. **ὅμοιος,** adj. only here with two terminations. "The striking simile **ὅμ. ὁρ. λ. ἰ. κ. σ.** recalls the portrait statues of Roman emperors and others, in which the raiment is worked out in hard-coloured stones—a fashion introduced in the last years of the republic from Ptolemaic Egypt" (Myres, *E. Bi.*, 4812).—**ἶρις.** The nimbus or halo round the throne is green, **σμ.** (*cf.* Deissm. 267) being malachite or more probably an emerald (xxi. 19), to which the ancients attributed a talismanic power of warding off evil spirits. "Thou hast made heaven and earth bright with thy rays of pure emerald light" (hymn to Ra, *E. B. D.* 8). The rabbis (*Chagiga*, 16 *a*) discouraged any study of the rainbow, as it symbolised the glory of God. As the symbol of God's covenant, it may be here a foil to the forbidding awe of ver. 5 *a* (which develops 3 *a*, as 5 *b* develops 3 *b*-4); "Deus in judiciis semper meminit foederis sui" (Grotius.) But, like the parabolic details of Jesus, these traits are mainly descriptive. The association of jasper, sardius, and emerald is a genuinely Hellenic touch: *cf. Phaedo*, 110, where Plato describes the real earth under the heavens of paradise as a place where in perfection lie such things as exist here but in fragmentary beauty—for example, the pebbles esteemed here, **σάρδιά τε καὶ ἰάσπιδας καὶ σμαράγδους.** Flinders Petrie, taking **σμ.** as rock-crystal, argues that the rainbow here is of the prismatic colour which a hexagonal prism of that colourless stone would throw (Hastings, *D. B.* iv. 620).

n Sc. εἶδον from ἰδού.
o On the forms τεσσερ. τεσσαρ. throughout, *cf.* Win. § 5, 20c.
p Sap. v. 15-16, 2 Macc. xiv. 4, *cf.* Jos. *Ant.*, iii. 7, 7.

4. Καὶ κυκλόθεν τοῦ θρόνου[1] ⁿ θρόνους εἴκοσι ᵒ τέσσαρας·
καὶ ἐπὶ τοὺς θρόνους εἴκοσι τέσσαρας πρεσβυτέρους καθημένους,
περιβεβλημένους ἐν ἱματίοις λευκοῖς·
καὶ ἐπὶ τὰς κεφαλὰς αὐτῶν ᵖ στεφάνους χρυσοῦς.

[1] θρονοι (PQ, etc., Areth., Bg., Al. Bs.) after θρονου seems a correction of (anacoluthon) θρονους ℵA, 34, 35, And[c], etc. (Lach., Ti., WH marg., Bj., Sw., Ws.).

Ver. 4. This verse breaks the continuous description of 3 and 5; it is evidently an original touch of the writer introduced into the more or less traditional scenery of the eternal court where "all the sanctities of heaven stood thick as stars" (*cf.* v. 11). The conception of twenty-four πρεσβύτεροι royally (i. 6) enthroned as divine assessors, with all the insignia of state, reaches back in part to a post-exilic apocalypse (Isa. xxiv. 23, βασιλεύσει κύριος ἐν Σιὼν καὶ εἰς Ἱερουσαλὴμ καὶ ἐνώπιον τῶν πρεσβυτέρων δοξασθήσεται), in part to the historic gerousia. But their attire (golden crowns, white robes) and functions are royal rather than judicial or sacerdotal. They are heavenly beings, angelic figures corresponding to the θρόνοι of Col. i. 16 (*cf.* Isa. lxiii. 9 οὐ πρεσβὺς οὐδὲ ἄγγελος). The significance of the doubled 12 has been found in the twelve patriarchs or tribes + the twelve apostles (Andr., Areth., Vict., Alford, Weiss, etc.), in Jewish and Gentile Christianity (Bleek, de Wette, Weizsäcker, Swete), or in the twenty-four classes of the post-exilic priests with their "elders" (Schürer, *H. J. P.* i. 216 f., so from Vitringa to Ewald, Hilg., Renan, Spitta, Wellh., Erbes, Briggs). But the notion of the church as a fusion or combination of the old and the new covenants is alien to primitive Christianity, and the "elders" are not the ideal or celestial representatives of the church at all. They pertain to the heavenly court, as in the traditional *mise-en-scène* of the later Judaism, which had appropriated this and other imaginative suggestions of the heavenly court (Schrader,[3] pp. 454 f.), or judicial council from the Babylonian astro-theology, where μετὰ τὸν ζῳδιακὸν κύκλον were ranged four-and-twenty stars, half to the north, and half to the south, of which the visible are reckoned as belonging to the living, the invisible to the dead, οὓς δικαστὰς τῶν ὅλων προσαγορεύουσιν (Diod. Sic. ii. 31, quoted by Gunkel in *S. C.* 302-308, who rightly finds in the same soil roots of other symbols in this passage, such as the four ζῷα and the seven λαμπάδες). In Slav. En. iv. 1, immediately after "the very great sea" in the first heaven is mentioned (*cf.* Apoc. iv. 6), Enoch is shown "the elders and the rulers of the orders of the stars;" so in *Judicium Petri*, εἴκοσι γὰρ καὶ τέσσαρές εἰσι πρεσβύτεροι, twelve on the right hand of God and twelve on the left, as in *Acta Perpet.* The twenty-four star-deities of the Babylonian heaven had thus become adoring and subordinate angelic beings (*cf.* ἡμῶν, ver. 11) in the apocalyptic world of the later Judaism, and our author retains this Oriental trait, together with the seven torches, the halo, etc., in order to body forth poetically his conception of the divine majesty (so, after Gunkel, Jeremias, and Bousset, Bruston, J. Weiss, Scott, Forbes, Porter). A partial anticipation of this feature, as well as of some others, in the Apocalypse occurs not only in the "sacred council" of Doushara, the Nabatean deity (*cf.* Cook's *North Semit. Inscr.*, pp. 221 f., 443 f.), but in Egyptian mythology, as, *e.g.*, in the following inscription from the tomb of Unas (5th dynasty, 3500 B.C.) "His place is at the side of God, in the most holy place; he himself becomes divine (*neter*), and an angel of God; he himself is triumphant. He sits on the great throne by the side of God [Apoc. iii. 21]. He is clothed with the finest raiment of those who sit on the throne of living right and truth. He hungers not, nor thirsts, nor is sad, for he eats daily the bread of Ra, and drinks what He drinks daily, and his bread also is that which is spoken of by Seb, and that which comes forth from the mouth of the gods [Apoc. vii. 16, 17, xxi. 4]. Not only does he eat and drink of their food, but he wears the apparel they wear—the white linen and sandals, and he is clothed in white . . . and these great and never-failing

5. Καὶ [q] ἐκ τοῦ θρόνου ἐκπορεύονται ἀστραπαὶ καὶ φωναὶ καὶ
[q] βρονταί·
καὶ [r] ἑπτὰ [r] λαμπάδες πυρὸς καιόμεναι ἐνώπιον τοῦ θρόνου [ἅ
εἰσιν[1] τὰ ἑπτὰ πνεύματα τοῦ θεοῦ].
6. καὶ[2] ἐνώπιον τοῦ θρόνου ὡς [s] θάλασσα [t] ὑαλίνη, ὁμοία κρυσ-
τάλλῳ.
Καὶ ἐν μέσῳ τοῦ θρόνου καὶ κύκλῳ τοῦ θρόνου τέσσερα ζῷα

q Ps. xvii. 14, xxix., Jub. ii. 1.
r i. 4, 12, 16, iii. 1, v. 6, *cf.* Ap. Bar. xlviii. 8, and Slav. En. xix. 6.
s xv. 2.
t Exod. xxiv. 10 f., Ezek. i. 22 f., ἅπ. λεγ. N.T.

[1] Either **α εισιν** (א^c P, 1, 36, 94, Syr., Ti., WH, Sw., Bj.) or **α εστιν** (A, Lach., Ws., Bs.) is to be read for **αι εισιν** (Q, etc., S., Areth.).

[2] Könnecke (*Emendationen zu Stellen N.T.*, 34) and Bs. (?) om. **και κυκλω του θρονου** as a gloss (so min., Me., Harl., Arm., Tic.), while Bruston takes **και εν μεσω του θρονου** as the mistranslation of ובתוך הכסא (= and the throne was in the midst of it, *i.e.*, of the glassy sea). For **τεσσαρα** here and in ver. 8 read **τεσσερα** (A, edd.), as generally throughout Apoc. (a **κοινή**-form, possibly Ionian: Helbing, 5-6, Thumb, 72), though "the papyri would seem to supply decisive evidence for **τεσσαρα** as the first century form" (*Class. Review*, 1901, p. 33, *cf.* 1904, p. 107).

gods give unto him of the Tree of Life [Apoc. ii. 7] of which they themselves do eat, that he likewise may live."

Ver. 5. The impression of awe is heightened by traits from the primitive Semitic theophany which, especially in judgment, was commonly associated with a thunderstorm (**φωναί** = the shrieks and roaring blasts of the storm). Thunder in the Apocalypse is either a sort of chorus in praise of God (as here) or punitive (*e.g.*, xvi. 18); in Enoch lix. 1 the seer beholds the secrets of the thunder, "how it ministers unto well-being and blessing, or serves for a curse before the Lord of Spirits". For the "torches of fire" (seven being a sacred number = collective and manifold power, Jastrow 265, Trench 62-70) *cf.* Ezek. i. 13 **ὡς ὄψις λαμπάδων συστρεφομένων ἀναμέσον τῶν ζῴων καὶ φέγγος τοῦ πυρὸς καὶ ἐκ τοῦ πυρὸς ἐξεπορεύετο ἀστραπή,** and Apoc. Bar. xxi. 6, where "holy living creatures, without number, of flame and fire" surround the throne. Fulness, intensity, energy, are implied in the figure, which reflects the traditional association (in the primitive mind) of fire and flame with the divinity, and especially with the divine purity or holiness of which they were regarded as an outward expression. There may be an allusion to the *ignes aeterni* or *sempiterni* of Roman mythology, an equivalent for the heavenly bodies; but Jewish eschatology had for over two centuries been familiar with the seven watchers of the heavenly court and their counterparts in Persian and Babylonian mythology. The combination of fire and crystal (ver. 6, see also xv. 2) goes back originally to Exod. xxiv. 9, 10, 17, and Ezek. i. 22, 27, mediated by passages like En. xiv. 9, 17 f., 21-23; while the groundwork of the symbol answers to the seven Persian councillors (Ezra vii. 14, Esth. i. 14) who formed the immediate circle of the monarch, a counterpart of the divine Amshaspands, as well as to the sacred fire of Ormuzd, which (on Zoroastrian principles) was to be kept constantly burning. Seven burning altars, evidently representing a planetary symbolism, also occur in the cult of Mithra, while in the imageless temple of Melcarth at Gades fires always burned upon the altar, tended by white-robed priests.—5 *c* reads like an editorial comment or a liturgical gloss; the **πρεσβύτεροι,** *e.g.*, are undefined.

Ver. 6. For a sea in heaven, *cf.* above (on ver. 4). In *Test. Patr. Levi.* 2 the sea lies within the second (first) heaven **ὕδωρ κρεμάμενον ἀνάμεσον τούτου κἀκείνου,** and in the Egyptian paradise the triumphant soul goes to "the great lake in the Fields of Peace," where the gods dwell. The description, "a sea of glass, like crystal" (*i.e.*, transparent, ancient glass being coarse and often semi-opaque, and **ὕαλος** being primarily = transparent, not vitreous) borrowed partly from archaic tradition (coloured by Egyptian and Assyrian ideas), is intended to portray the ether, clear and calm, shimmering and motionless. Rabbinic fancy compared the shining floor of the temple to crystal,

u From Ezek. i. 10, x. 12.
v Num. xxiii. 22, xxiv. 8.
w "apiece" (distribut. as John ii. 6, etc.)
x Isa. vi. 3, *cf.* Slav. En. xi. 2, xxi. 1.
y Not in Isa. vi. 3 (LXX), *cf.* on i. 8.

[u] γέμοντα ὀφθαλμῶν ἔμπροσθεν καὶ ὄπισθεν. 7. καὶ τὸ ζῷον τὸ πρῶτον ὅμοιον λέοντι, καὶ τὸ δεύτερον ζῷον ὅμοιον [v] μόσχῳ, καὶ τὸ τρίτον ζῷον ἔχων τὸ πρόσωπον ὡς ἀνθρώπου, καὶ τὸ τέταρτον ζῷον ὅμοιον ἀετῷ πετομένῳ. 8. καὶ τὰ τέσσερα ζῷα, ἓν καθ' ἓν αὐτῶν ἔχων [w] ἀνὰ πτέρυγας ἕξ, κυκλόθεν [1] καὶ ἔσωθεν γέμουσιν ὀφθαλμῶν, καὶ [x] ἀνάπαυσιν [x] οὐκ ἔχουσιν ἡμέρας καὶ νυκτὸς λέγοντες,

"[x] Ἅγιος ἅγιος ἅγιος Κύριος ὁ Θεὸς ὁ [y] παντοκράτωρ,
ὁ ἦν καὶ ὁ ὢν καὶ ὁ ἐρχόμενος."

[1] It is arbitrary to omit (Wellh.) **κυκλοθεν . . . οφθαλμων,** and the variant addition (**και εξωθεν,** Q, Pr., etc.) after **κυκλοθεν** is an attempt to smooth out the phrase

and the hot eastern sky is likened (in Job xxxvii. 18) to a molten mirror, dry and burnished. Heaven is a sort of glorified temple (1 Kings vii. 23, the sea in the Solomonic temple being copied from the oblong or round tank which represented the ocean at every Babylonian temple, while the earth was symbolised by the adjoining zikkurat), and the crystal firmament is a sort of sea. In Slav. En. iii. 1-3 the seer observes, in the first heaven, the ether, and then "a very great sea, greater than the earthly sea". **καὶ ἐν μέσῳ, κ.τ.λ.** : "and in the middle (of each side) of the throne and (consequently) round about the throne," the four חַיּוֹת of Ezek. i. 5, 18 (*cf.* Apoc. Bar. li. 11). **γέμοντα κ.τ.λ.**, a bizarre but archaic symbol for completeness of life and intelligence rather than for Argus-like vigilance. The four angels of the presence in En. xl. 2 move out, like Milton's seven (*Par. Lost*, iii. 647 f.), on various errands (lxxi. 9, *cf.* lxxxviii. 2, 3). The **ζῷα** of John are stationary, except in xv. 7, where the context (*cf.* vi. 6) might suggest that the seer took them to represent creation or the forces of the natural world (*cf.* the rabbinic dictum: quattuor sunt qui principatum in hoc mundo tenent, inter creaturas homo, inter aues aquilo, inter pecora bos, inter bestias leo). Note also that when they worship (9), the **πρεσβύτεροι** acknowledge God's creative glory (11), and that the O.T. cherubim are associated with the phenomena of the storm-cloud. The seer does not define them, however, and they may be, like the **πρεσβύτεροι**, a traditional and poetical trait of the heavenly court.—**τέσσερα**, *cf.* Slav. En. xxx. 13, 14. The posture of the **ζῷα** may be visualised from a comparison of the Alhambra Court of the Lions.

Ver. 7. **μόσχῳ**, "an ox or steer" (as LXX). The four animals are freely compounded out of the classical figures of Ezekiel's cherubim and the seraphim in Isa. vi.; the latter supply the six wings apiece. This function of ceaseless praise (8-9) is taken from Enoch lxi. 10 f., where the cherubim and seraphim are also associated but not identified with the angelic host (though in xl. the cherubim are equivalent to the four archangels); for a possible Babylonian astral background, *cf.* Zimmern in Schrader,[3] 626-632, and Clemen's *Religionsgeschichtliche Erklärung des N. T.* (1909), pp. 74 f. Behind them lie the signs of the zodiac (the bull, the archer, the lion and the eagle, as a constellation of the North; so, *e.g.*, Gunkel, Bruston, etc.). The analogous figures of the four funerary genii before the Egyptian throne represent the four points of the compass.

Ver. 8. A description of the sounds and songs of heaven follows the picture of its sights.—**γέμουσιν**, either with **τὰ τ.ζ.** (**ἔχων** for once a real participle) or an asyndeton (if **ἔχων** here, as elsewhere in the Apocalypse, must be supplied with a copula). **κυκλ. κ. ἔ.** = "round their bodies and on the inside" (*i.e.*, underneath their wings). For the ceaseless praise, which resembles that of Nin-ib, the Assyrian deity, *cf.* on ver. 7 and ver. 11, also Enoch xxxix. 12 (the trisagion sung by the sleepless ones, *i.e.*, angels), Slav. En. xvii., and *Test. Levi* 3 (where endless praise is the function of denizens in the fourth heaven). The first line of the hymn is Isaianic, the second (**ὁ ἦν κ.τ.λ.**) is characteristic of the Apocalypse. In En. xli. 7 the sun and moon in their orbits "give thanks and praise and rest not; for to them their thanksgiving is rest". In the Apocalypse, however, the phenomena of nature are generally the objects or the scourges of the divine

9. καὶ ὅταν ᶻ δώσουσι [1] τὰ ζῷα δόξαν καὶ ᵃ τιμὴν καὶ ᵇ εὐχαριστίαν
τῷ καθημένῳ ἐπὶ τῷ θρόνῳ, τῷ ᶜ ζῶντι εἰς τοὺς αἰῶνας τῶν αἰώνων,
10. ᵈ πεσοῦνται οἱ εἴκοσι τέσσαρες ᵈ πρεσβύτεροι ἐνώπιον τοῦ καθημένου ἐπὶ τοῦ θρόνου, καὶ προσκυνήσουσιν τῷ ζῶντι εἰς τοὺς αἰῶνας
τῶν αἰώνων, καὶ ᵉ βαλοῦσιν τοὺς στεφάνους αὐτῶν ἐνώπιον τοῦ θρόνου,
λέγοντες,
11. "Ἄξιος εἶ, ὁ ᶠ Κύριος καὶ ὁ θεὸς ἡμῶν, ᵍ λαβεῖν τὴν δόξαν
καὶ τὴν τιμὴν καὶ τὴν δύναμιν·

z Cf. Moult. i. 168.
a Ps. xxviii. (xxix.) 1, 1 Tim. i. 17, Apoc. v. 13, vii. 12, cf. *Par. Lost*, iv. 677 f., vii. 600 f.
b vii. 12.
c Deut. xxxii. 40 ζῶ ἐγὼ εἰς τὸν αἰῶνα.
d v. 14, cf. 2 Chron. vii. 3.
e Verg. *Georg.* iv. 212, Mart. x. 72, Tiridates in Tac. *Ann.* xv. 29, Tigranes in Dio Cass. xxxvi., Cicero's *pro Sextio*, 27.
f Nom. practically = vocative (contrast xi. 17, xv. 3, xvi. 7), Abbott, *Diat.* 2681, Helbing, 34.
g v. 12, cf. 1 Chron. xxix. 11.

[1] For **δωσουσι** AP, min., Andᵃ (edd.), **δωσωσι** (ℵQ, min., Bs.) [*cf.* WH, app. 172] and **δωσι** (min., S., Andᶜ, Areth.) are variants (Pr. *cum dederant*, vg. *cum darent*); *cf.* Win. § 14, 9; § 13, 7—the former being an unusual conj. aor.

wrath. The precedence of **ὁ ἦν** over **ὁ ὤν** may be due to the emphasis of the context upon (ver. 11) the definite creative action of God. Since the **πρεσβύτεροι** worship God as the eternal (ver. 10), while the **ζῷα** acknowledge him as the **ἅγιος**, the latter epithet probably retains its O.T. sense, *i.e.*, absolute life and majestic power (xvi. 5). The trisagion occurs in the Babylonian recension (iii.) of the Shmone-Esreh, among the daily prayers of the Jewish community. See further *Encycl. Rel. and Ethics*, i. 117, 118.

Ver. 9. The frequentative meaning of **δώσουσι** comes from the sense rather than from the grammar of the passage. "Whenever," etc. (*i.e.*, throughout the course of this book, v. 8 f., xi. 16 f., xix. 4) is "a sort of stage-direction" (Simcox). It would be harsh to take the words as a proleptic allusion to the single occurrence at xi. 15 f. (J. Weiss). To give or ascribe **δόξα** to God is reverently to acknowledge his supreme authority, either spontaneously and gladly (as here and xix. 7, where "honour" becomes almost "praise") or under stress of punishment (xi. 13, xiv. 7, xvi. 9) and fear of judgment. The addition of **τιμή** in doxologies amplifies the idea, by slightly emphasising the expression of that veneration and awe felt inwardly by those who recognise his **δόξα.** To fear God or to be his servants is thus equivalent upon the part of men to an attitude of pious submission and homage. To "give thanks" is hardly co-ordinate with **δ.κ.τ.**, but follows from it as a corollary (*cf.* Pss. xcvi.-xcviii.). Such worship is the due of *the living God* (vii. 2, x. 6, xv. 7), whereas to eat "meat sacrificed to idols is to worship dead gods" (Did. vi. 3, *cf.* Apoc. ii. 14, 20). The Apocalypse, however, never dwells on the danger of idolatry within the Christian church; its attention is almost absorbed by the supreme idolatry of the Emperor, which is silently contrasted in this and in other passages with the genuine Imperial worship of the Christian church. "He who sits on the throne" (a title of Osiris in *E. B. D.*) is the only true recipient of worship. *Cf.* the hymn to "Ra when he riseth": "Those who are in thy following sing unto thee with joy and bow down their foreheads to the earth when they meet thee, thou lord of heaven and earth, thou king of Right and Truth, thou creator of eternity".

Ver. 10. To cast a crown before the throne was a token that the wearer disclaimed independence; an Oriental (Parthian) token of respect for royalty (reff.). *Cf.* Spenser's *Hymne of Heavenly Beautie* (141-154) and the pretty fancy in Slav. En. xiv. 2 where the sun's crown is taken from him as he passes through the fourth heaven (before God) and given to God.

Ver. 11. An implicit refutation of the dualistic idea, developed by Cerinthus, the traditional opponent of John in Asia Minor, that creation was the work of some angel or power separate from God (Iren. i. 26, iv. 32, Hippol. *Haer.* vii. 33, x. 1). The enthusiastic assent of the **πρεσβύτεροι** to the adoration of the Creator is expressed in word as well as in action. **σύ** emphatic = the usual apocalyptic (R.J., 295, 296) emphasis on creation as a proof of God's power in

b *Cf.* 4 Esd. vi. 6, and on x. 6 below.
i Constr. *cf.* xii. 11, John vi. 57, xv. 3 (dat. instrum.).

ὅτι [h] σὺ ἔκτισας τὰ πάντα,
καὶ [i] διὰ τὸ θέλημά σου ἦσαν [1] καὶ ἐκτίσθησαν."

V. 1. Καὶ εἶδον [a] ἐπὶ τὴν δεξιὰν τοῦ καθημένου ἐπὶ τοῦ θρόνου βιβλίον γεγραμμένον ἔσωθεν καὶ ὄπισθεν,[2] [b] κατεσφραγισμένον

a xx. 1. b ἅπ. λεγ. N.T., *cf.* Dan. viii. 26, xii. 4, 9 (Isa. xxix. 11).

[1] **ουκ ησαν** Q, 14, 38, 51, "created out of nothingness": A om. **και εκτισθησαν**, Pr., 36 om. **ησαν και.** For similar instances of the elision or addition of a negative, see Nestle's *Einf.*, 250-251 (E. Tr., 311-312).

[2] The strongly supported variant **εξωθεν** (PQ, min., S., gig., vg., Arm., Aeth., Hipp., Pr., etc., so Bousset) for **οπισθεν** (אA, 1, 14, Syr.) hardly alters the general sense of the passage, and is probably conformed to **εσωθεν**, *cf.* Zahn's *Einl.*, § 72, 7.

providence and claims on mankind (*e.g.* 4 Esd. iii. 4, "thou didst fashion the earth, and that thyself alone"). That God the redeemer is God the creator, forms one of the O.T. ideas which acquire special weight in the Apocalypse. Despite the contradictions of experience and the apparent triumph of Satan, the apocalypses of the age never gave way to dualism. Their firm hope was that the world, ideally God's, would become actually his when messiah's work was done; hence, as here, the assertion of his complete power over nature and nations. "Because thou didst will it (**σύ, σου** emphatic) they existed and were created" (act and process of creation). As an answer to polytheism this cardinal belief in God the creator came presently to the front in the second century creeds and apologies. But the idea here is different alike from contemporary Jewish and from subsequent Christian speculation, the former holding that creation was for the sake of Israel (*cf.* 4 Esd. vi. 55, vii. 11, ix. 13, Apoc. Bar. xiv. 18, 19, xv. 7, Ass. Mos. i. 12, etc., a favourite rabbinic belief), the latter convinced that it was for the sake of the Christian church (*cf.* Herm. *Vis.* ii. 4). Nor is there any evident trace of the finer idea (En. iii.-v, Clem. Rom. xx., etc.) which contrasted the irregularities and impiety of men with the order and obedience of the universe. The conception of the holy ones rendering ceaseless praise in heaven would be familiar to early Christians in touch with Hellenic ideas and associations; *e.g.*, Hekataeus of Abdera, in his sketch of the ideal pious folk, compares them to the priests of Apollo, **διὰ τὸ τὸν θεὸν τοῦτον καθ' ἡμέραν ὑπ' αὐτῶν ὑμνεῖσθαι μετ' ᾠδῆς συνεχῶς** (Dieterich 36 f., *cf.* Apoc. Pet. 19-20). *Test. Levi* 3 **ἐν δὲ τῷ μετ' αὐτόν εἰσι θρόνοι κ. ἐξουσίαι ἐν ᾧ ὕμνοι ἀεὶ τῷ θεῷ προσφέρονται.**

CHAPTER V.—Ver. 1. The central idea of this sealed roll or doomsday book lying open on the divine hand (*cf.* Blau, *Studien zur alt-heb. Buchwesen*, 36 f., E. J. Goodspeed, *Journ. Bibl. Lit.* 1903, 70-74) is reproduced from Ezekiel (ii. 9 f.) but independently developed in order to depict the truth that even these magnificent angelic figures of the divine court are unequal to the task of revelation. Jesus is needed. For God, a motionless, silent, majestic figure, does not come directly into touch with men either in revelation or in providence. He operates through his messiah, whose vicarious sacrifice throws all angels into the shade (*cf.* the thought of Phil. ii. 5-11). For the ancient association of a many-horned Lamb with divination, *cf.* the fragmentary Egyptian text edited by Krall (*Vom König Bokhoris*, Innsbrück, 1898) and the reference to Suidas (cited in my *Hist. New Testament*,[2] p. 687). **βιβλίον**, which here (as in i. 11, xxii. 7-18) might mean "letter" or "epistle" (*cf.* Birt's *Ant. Buchwesen*, 20, 21), apparently represents the book of doom or destiny as a papyrus-roll (*i.e.* an **ὀπισθόγραφον**, *cf.* Juv. i. 6) which is so full of matter that the writing has flowed from the inside over to the exterior, as is evident when the sheet is rolled up. Here as elsewhere the pictorial details are not to be pressed; but we may visualise the conception by supposing that all the seals along the outer edge must be broken before the content of the roll can be unfolded, and that each heralds some penultimate disaster (so 4 Esd. vi. 20). There is no proof that each seal meant a progressive disclosure of the contents, in which case we should have to imagine not a roll but a codex in book form, each seal securing one or two of the leaves (Spitta). Zahn (followed by Nestle, J. Weiss, and Bruston) im-

σφραγῖσιν ἑπτά. 2. Καὶ εἶδον ἄγγελον [c]ἰσχυρὸν κηρύσσοντα ἐν φωνῇ μεγάλῃ, "Τίς ἄξιος ἀνοῖξαι τὸ βιβλίον, καὶ λῦσαι τὰς σφραγῖδας αὐτοῦ;" 3. καὶ οὐδεὶς ἐδύνατο ἐν τῷ οὐρανῷ οὐδὲ ἐπὶ τῆς γῆς οὐδὲ ὑποκάτω τῆς γῆς ἀνοῖξαι τὸ βιβλίον οὔτε βλέπειν αὐτό. 4. Καὶ ἐγὼ ἔκλαιον πολὺ ὅτι οὐδεὶς ἄξιος εὑρέθη ἀνοῖξαι τὸ βιβλίον οὔτε βλέπειν αὐτό. 5. καὶ [d]εἷς [d]ἐκ τῶν πρεσβυτέρων

c Defined by φ. μ., *cf.* Ps. ciii. 20.

d = Genit. partit.

proves upon this theory by taking **ὄπ.** with **κατεσφρ.** and thus eliminating any idea of the **βιβλίον** being **ὀπισθόγραφον**: it simply rests on (**ἐπὶ**) the right hand, as a book does, instead of being held **ἐν** the right hand, as a roll would be. But **ἐπὶ τ. δ.** is a characteristic irregularity of grammar; to describe a sealed book as "written within" is tautological; **ἀνοῖξαι** could be used of a roll as well as of a codex; and **ἔσωθεν** would probably have preceded **γεγρ.** had it been intended by itself to qualify the participle. A Roman will, when written, had to be sealed seven times in order to anthenticate it, and some have argued (*e.g.* Hicks, *Greek Philosophy and Roman Law in the N. T.* 157, 158, Zahn, Selwyn, Kohler, J. Weiss) that this explains the symbolism here: the **βιβλίον** is the testament assuring the inheritance reserved by God for the saints. The coincidence is interesting. But the sacred number in this connexion does not require any extra-Semitic explanation and the horrors of the seal-visions are more appropriate to a book of Doom. Besides, the Apoc. offers no support otherwise to this interpretation, for the sole allusion to **κληρονομεῖν** is quite incidental (*cf.* on xxi. 7). The sealing is really a Danielic touch, added to denote the mystery and obscurity of the future (not of the past, En. lxxxix.-xc.). On the writer's further use of the symbol of the book of Doom, *cf.* below on ch. x., xi. 16-19. The silence following the opening of the last seal certainly does not represent the contents of the book (= the promised Sabbath-rest, Zahn). This would be a jejune anti-climax. Possibly the cosmic tragedies that follow that seal are intended to be taken as the writing in question. The **βιβλίον** is therefore the divine course and counsel of providence in the latter days (**ἡ πάνσοφος τοῦ θεοῦ καὶ ἀνεπίληπτος μνήμη**, Areth.). Only, while an angel read all the divine policy to Daniel (Dan. x. 21), the Christian prophet feels that Jesus alone is the true interpreter and authority, and that the divine purpose can only be revealed or realised through his perfect spiritual equipment (iii. 1, v. 6, *cf.* i. 5, ii. 27, iii. 21, xvii, 14, etc.)

Ver. 2. The **καὶ** after **ἀνοῖξαι** is either epexegetic or the mark of a hysteron proteron (*cf.* the awkward **οὔτε βλέπειν** of 3-4, unless *look* here means to look into the contents). The cry is a challenge rather than an appeal.

Ver. 3. **ὑποκάτω,** the under-world of departed spirits or of daemons. Not even angels **ἐν τῷ οὐρανῷ** (*cf.* Mark xiii. 32) can discharge this function; their rôle in the Apocalypse is prominent but limited. Gunkel prefers to think of a magical background to the whole symbolism; the book defies the necromancy of the universe, but yields to the superior power of "the new god, the lord of the book". For the mythological basis of the idea of an opened heavenly book *cf.* Winckler (*Alt-orient. Forsch.* ii. 386) and Brandis (*Hermes*, 1867, 283). The triple division of the universe was originally Babylonian but it had long ago become a popular religious idea, (*cf.* Phil. ii. 10).

Ver. 4. A naïve expression of disappointment, the expectation of iv. 1 being apparently thwarted. The sense of consolation and triumph is so strong in this book that no tears are shed in self-pity. The prophet only weeps at the apparent check to revelation.

Ver. 5. **ἀνοῖξαι . . . σφραγῖδας,** *cf.* Dittenberger's *Sylloge Inscr. Graec.* 790[47] (first century) **τὰς σφ. ἀνοιξάτω.** Christ's success is due to his legitimate messianic authority as a Davidic scion (**ῥίζα** = shoot or sprout on main stem, *cf.* Sibyll. iii. 396); the Davidic descent of Jesus was a tenet of certain circles in primitive Christianity (Dalman i. § 12). Possibly there is an allusion to the original bearing of the O.T. passage:—Jesus irresistible and courageous, yet in origin humble. In 4 Esdr. xii. 31, 32 the messiah's rebuke to the Roman empire is thus described: leonem quem uidisti de silva euigilantem mugientem et loquentem ad aquilam et arguentem eam iniquitatis . . . hic est unctus, quem reseruauit altissimus in finem [dierum, qui dicitur

λέγει μοι, "Μὴ κλαῖε· ἰδοὺ [e]ἐνίκησεν ὁ [f]λέων ὁ ἐκ τῆς φυλῆς
[f]Ἰούδα, [g]ἡ ῥίζα Δαυείδ, [e]ἀνοῖξαι τὸ βιβλίον καὶ τὰς ἑπτὰ σφραγῖδας αὐτοῦ". 6. Καὶ εἶδον ἐν μέσῳ τοῦ θρόνου καὶ τῶν τεσσάρων
ζῴων καὶ ἐν μέσῳ τῶν πρεσβυτέρων [h]ἀρνίον [i]ἑστηκὸς[1] ὡς ἐσφαγ-

e Constr. xv. 9 (iii. 21, Ps. Sol. iv. 13 ἐνίκησε σκορπίσαι), infin. of remote purpose (Blass, § 69, 3). f Gen. xlix. 9, Heb. vii. 14. g xxii. 16, Isa. xi. 1 = Rom. xv. 12, 1 Chron. xxviii. 4. h Diminut. preferred in Apoc. to *ἀμνός* of 4th gospel, etc. i Acts vii. 56, Apoc. xiv. 1.

[1] For **εστηκος** (APQ, min., Orig., Hipp., Lach., Al., WH, Bj., Sw., Ws.) Ti., Tr., Bs. read [Win. § 14, 5] **εστηκως** (א1, 7, 28, 32, 87), which probably arose from dittography. Except for xviii. 10, this is the only use of the longer participial form (*cf.* Helbing, 103) in the Apocalypse (even xiv. 1—s.v.l.—reproducing the shorter form).

ex semine David]. **ῥάβδος**, in sense of "shoot" occurs with **ῥίζα** in Isa. xi. 1 (*cf.* 10; Ezek. xix. 11, 12, 14); hence the combination with the idea of "sceptre" (**ἐνίκησεν**, *cf.* ii. 27) in a messianic connotation (*cf.* on xxii. 16). The enigma of the world's history lies with Christ, to be solved and to be controlled. Jewish eschatology (En. xlvi. 3, xlix. 1) had already proclaimed the revealing power of messiah, who is "mighty in all the secrets of righteousness . . . and who reveals all the treasures of that which is hidden". John claims that Jesus is the legitimate messiah, whose power to unfold God's redeeming purpose rests upon his victorious inauguration of that purpose. The victory of Christ in v. 5 f. follows dramatically upon the allusion in iii. 21, but it is to press the sequence too far when this scene is taken to represent his arrival in heaven "just after the accomplishment of his victory" (Briggs).

Ver. 6. Christ, crucified and risen, is in the centre. To him all things bow and sing. It is prosaic to attempt any local definition, as though the author had some architectural plan in his mind (**ἐν μ.** = "half-way up the throne," or by repetition = "between," *cf.* Gen. i. 7), or to wonder how so prominent a figure had hitherto escaped his notice. Plainly the **ἀρνίον** did not originally belong to the *mise-en-scène* of iv., though the symbol may have none the less had an astral origin (= Ram, in Persian zodiac). The prophet brilliantly suggests, what was a commonplace of early Christianity, that the royal authority of Jesus was due to his suffering for men, but the framework of the sketch is drawn from messianic dogmas which tended to make Christ here a figure rather than a personality.—**ἀρνίον** (like **θηρίον**, diminutive only in form) is not taken from Jer. xi. 19 f. (LXX) by a writer who placed it in iuxtaposition with "lion" owing to the resemblance of sound between אריה and *aries* (so variously Havet and Selwyn, 204-208), nor substituted (Vischer, Rauch) for the "lion" of the original Jewish source, but probably applied (*cf.* Hort on 1 Peter i. 19) to Jesus from the messianic interpretation of Isa. xvi. 1 or liii. 7, though the allusions elsewhere to the Exodus (xv. 2 f.) and the Johannine predilection for the paschal Lamb suggest that the latter was also in the prophet's mind. The collocation of lion and lamb is not harder than that of lion and root (ver. 5), and such an editor as Vischer and others postulate would not have left "lion" in ver. 5 unchanged. Christ is erect and living (*cf.* xiv. 1 and Abbott's *Joh. Vocabulary*, 1725), **ὡς ἐσφαγμένον** (as could be seen from the wound on the throat), yet endowed with complete power (**κέρατα**, Oriental symbol of force, *cf.* reff. and the rams' horns of the Egyptian sun-god) and knowledge. For **ἀρνίον** and **ἀμνός**, *cf.* Abbott, 210 f. In Enoch lxxxix. 44 f. (Gk.) David is **ἄρνα** prior to his coronation and Solomon "a little sheep" (*i.e.*, a lamb).—**ὀφθαλμοὺς κ.τ.λ.**, the function ascribed by Plutarch (*de defectu orac.* 13) to daemons as the spies and scouts of God on earth. The naïve symbolism is borrowed from the organisation of an ancient realm, whose ruler had to secure constant and accurate information regarding the various provinces under his control. News (as the Tel-el-Amarna correspondence vividly shows) was essential to an Oriental monarch. The representation of Osiris in Egyptian mythology consisted of an eye and a sceptre (*cf.* Apoc. ii. 27), denoting foresight and force (Plut. *de Iside*, 51), while the "eyes" and "ears" of a Parthian monarch were officials or officers who kept him informed of all that transpired throughout the country. Else-

μένον, ἔχων [k] κέρατα ἑπτὰ καὶ [l] ὀφθαλμοὺς [l] ἑπτά, οἵ εἰσι τὰ [m] ἑπτὰ
πνεύματα τοῦ Θεοῦ ἀπεσταλμένοι εἰς πᾶσαν τὴν γῆν. 7. Καὶ ἦλθεν
καὶ [n] εἴληφεν ἐκ τῆς δεξιᾶς τοῦ καθημένου ἐπὶ τοῦ θρόνου. 8. καὶ
ὅτε ἔλαβε τὸ βιβλίον, τὰ τέσσερα ζῷα καὶ οἱ εἴκοσι τέσσαρες πρεσβύτεροι ἔπεσαν ἐνώπιον τοῦ ἀρνίου, [o] ἔχοντες ἕκαστος [p] κιθάραν καὶ

k After Dan. vii. 20 f., viii. 3, En. xc. 37 f., etc.

l i. 4, iv. 6, from Zech. iv. 10 (iii. 9): eyes = stars (Ἄργος πανόπτης = starry heaven), s.c. 125, 298 f.

m iv. 5.

n viii. 5, *cf.* iii. 3, vii. 14, xix. 3, aoristic (Blass, § 59, 4).

o *i.e.* οἱ πρεσβ. (loose syntax)?

p xiv. 2, xv. 2.

where the seven spirits are identified with seven torches, but John is more concerned to express from time to time his religious ideas than to preserve any homogeneity of symbolism (seven eyes similarly varied in Zech. *cf.* reff.). The inconsistency cannot, in a writing of this nature, be taken as evidence of interpolation or of divergent sources, though it may be an editorial gloss. An analogous idea underlies Plutarch's explanation of the "travelling" power of Isis (*Iside*, 60), for which he adduces the old Greek etymology (= knowledge and movement, **θεὸς** from **θέειν** "to run"); and this etymology in turn (*cf.* Otto on Theoph. *ad Autolyc.* i. 4) reaches back to a star cultus.—N.B. In the Apoc. **ἀρνίον,** which is opposed to **θηρίον** and is always (except xiii. 11 f.) used of Jesus, denotes not only the atoning sacrificial aspect of Christ (v. 6, 9 f., 12, xii. 11) but his triumphant power (horned) over outsiders (xvii. 14) and his own people (vii. 16 f.). Neither the diminutive (*cf.* below, on xii. 17) nor the associations of innocence and gentleness are to be pressed (*cf.* Spitta, *Streitfragen der Gesch. Jesu*, 1907, 173 f.). The term becomes almost semitechnical in the Apocalypse. As a pre-Christian symbol, it is quite obscure. The text and origin of the striking passage in *Test. Ios.* xix. do not permit much more than the inference that the leader there (a **μόσχος**) becomes an **ἀμνός,** who, supported by Judah the lion, **ἐνίκησεν πάντα τὰ θηρία.** The virgin-birth is probably a Christian interpolation. No sure root for the symbolism has yet been found in astro-theology (Jeremias 15 f.). For attempts to trace back the idea to Babylonian soil, *cf.* Hommel in *Exp. Times*, xiv. 106 f., Havet, 324 f., and Zimmern in *Schrader*,[3] 597 f. One Babylonian text does mention the blood of the lamb as a sacrificial substitute for man, which is all the more significant as the texts of the cultus are almost wholly destitute of any allusion to the significance of the blood in sacrifice. But no influence of this on pre-Christian messianism, or of contemporary cults on this element of Christian symbolism, can be made out from the extant evidence. In any case, it would merely supply the form for expressing a reality of the Christian experience.

Ver. 7. A realistic symbol of the idea conveyed in John iii. 35, xii. 49, etc.

Ver. 8. A thrill of satisfaction over Christ's ability. "It is the manner of God thus to endear mercies to us, as he endeared a wife to Adam. He first brought all creatures to him, that he might first see that there was not a helpmeet for him among them" (Goodwin). John lays dramatic emphasis on *Jesus only*. **ἐνωπ. τ. ἀ.** (as before God himself, xix. 4).—**γ. θ.**, *cf.* Soph. *Oed. Tyr.* 4, **πόλις δ' ὁμοῦ μὲν θυμιαμάτων γέμει.** An essential feature in the rites of Roman sacrifice was music played on *tibicines;* the *patera*, a shallow saucer or ladle with a long handle attached, was also employed to pour wine on the altar. Harps held by living creatures who had no hands but only wings, and the collocation of a harp played by a person who is at the same time holding a bowl, are traits which warn us against prosaically visualising such visions. Hirscht compares the adoration of Rameses II. before the sun-god, the monarch's left hand holding his offering, his right grasping a sceptre and scourge. The fragrant smoke of incense rising from the hand of a worshipper or from an altar in the primitive cultus (*cf.* Ezek. viii. 2) to lose itself in upper air, became a natural symbol for prayer breathed from earth to heaven; see Philo's **τὸ καθαρώτατον τοῦ θύοντος, πνεῦμα λογικόν.—αἵ . . . ἁγίων,** probably an editorial gloss like xix. 8 *b*, suggested by the verbal parallel in viii. 3 (so, *e.g.*, Spitta, Völter, Briggs, Jülicher, J. Weiss, Wellhausen, etc.). Contrast with this verse (and ver. 4) the description of the enthusiastic seamen and passengers who "candidati, coronatique, et tura libantes," praised and blessed Augustus in the bay of Puteoli as "He by whom we live, and sail secure, and

φιάλας χρυσᾶς γεμούσας [q] θυμιαμάτων [[r] αἵ εἰσιν αἱ προσευχαὶ τῶν
ἁγίων] · 9. καὶ [s] ᾄδουσιν ᾠδὴν [t] καινὴν λέγοντες,

"[u] Ἄξιος εἶ λαβεῖν τὸ βιβλίον καὶ ἀνοῖξαι τὰς σφραγῖδας
αὐτοῦ ·
ὅτι [u] ἐσφάγης καὶ [v] ἠγόρασας τῷ Θεῷ [w] ἐν τῷ [w] αἵματί σου,
[x] ἐκ πάσης φυλῆς καὶ γλώσσης καὶ λαοῦ καὶ ἔθνους,
10. καὶ ἐποίησας αὐτοὺς τῷ Θεῷ ἡμῶν [y] βασιλείαν καὶ [y] ἱερεῖς ·
καὶ [z] βασιλεύσουσιν [1] ἐπὶ τῆς γῆς."

11. Καὶ εἶδον, καὶ ἤκουσα [2] φωνὴν ἀγγέλων πολλῶν κύκλῳ τοῦ
θρόνου καὶ τῶν ζῴων καὶ τῶν πρεσβυτέρων, καὶ ἦν ὁ ἀριθμὸς αὐτῶν

q Ps. cxli. 2.
r = ἅ, by false attraction.
s Isa. xlii. 10, Ps. xxxiii. 3, cxliv. 9, etc.
t So xiv. 3, *cf.* Judith xvi. 1 (A), 13 (15), Ps. Sol. iii. 2, etc., and Eus. *H. E.* v. 28.
u *Cf.* Isa. liii. 7.
v See on 1 Cor. vi. 20, and below xiv. 3-4.
w i. 5, *cf.* 1 Pet. i. 18-19.
x vii. 9, fr. Dan. iii. 2, 4, 7, *cf.* 4 Esd. iii. 7.
y i. 6, Briggs here also would omit the καί.
z xxii. 5.
a vii. 11, 1 Kings xxii. 19, *cf.* 1 Pet. iii. 22.

[1] For **βασιλευσομεν** (Pr., vg.), **βασιλευσουσιν** (ℵP, 1, min., S., etc., Bg., Ti., Ws., Holtzm., Bs., Bj., Briggs, etc.) is preferable to **βασιλευουσιν** (AQ, min., Syr., And[a]. Lach., Al. Tr., WH, Sw., Jacoby 448-449) in sense of Matt. v. 5.

[2] After **ηκουσα** Ti., Tr. (WH marg.), Bj., Sw. add **ως** (ℵQ**, min., Syr., Areth., etc.).

enjoy our freedom and fortunes" (Suet. *Vit. Aug.* 98.)

The scene or stage of the apocalyptical drama is occupied by an angelic and heavenly chorus, who upon this solemn and glad occasion give their *plaudite* or acclamation of glory to the Lord. The future which God rules is revealed by him through Christ; and this moves enthusiastic gratitude, till the universe rings from side to side with praise.

Ver. 9. **ᾠδὴν κ.** followed (14) by **ἀμήν**, as in the worship of the church on earth (Col. iii. 16, 1 Cor. xiv. 15, 16). **ᾄδουσιν** (historic present) no longer to God as creator (iv. 11) but to the Lamb as redeemer, for the cost and scope and issue of his redemption. This unique and remarkable passage in early Christian literature marks the growing sense and value attaching to Jesus as being far more than a mere national messiah, in fact as the one assurance of God possessed by men, as their pledge of bliss and privilege and pardon. And this is due to his redeeming function, upon which the relationship of men to God depends. It is a further stage of the Christian development when, as in *Asc. Isa.* ix. 27-32, the vision and praise of Jesus is followed by that of the Holy Spirit (35, 36) and of God himself (37-42). The prophet John's "theology" is less advanced. Universal allegiance and homage paid not, as in the contemporary sense of the **οἰκουμένη**, to a Cæsar's proud pretensions, but to the sacrifice of a Christ (see G. A. Smith, *Hist. Geogr.* 478, 479) is a new thing in the world. An undivided church, gathered from the divisions of humanity, is also a new and unexpected development, to which a foil is presented by the exclusiveness voiced at the annual Jewish paschal rite, and in the daily Shema-prayer ("For Thou hast chosen *us* from amongst all nations and tongues. . . . Blessed be the Lord that chose in love his people Israel"). For **ἀγοράζειν** (*cf.* note on i. 5) = the buying of slaves, *cf.* Dittenberger's *Orientis Gr. Inscript. Selectae*, 338[23].

Ver. 10. An allusion not so much to the idea of xx. 4, where the literal sway of the saints (= life eternal, in substance) is confined to a certain section of them, or to xxii. 5 (on the new earth, *cf.* xxi. 1), as to ii. 26. Compare the primitive patristic notion, reflected, *e.g.*, by Vict. on i. 15: adorabimus in loco ubi steterunt pedes eius, quoniam ubi illi primum steterunt et ecclesiam confirmauerunt, *i.e.*, in Judæa, ibi omnes sancti conuenturi sunt et dominum suum adoraturi. The whole verse sets aside implicitly such a Jewish pretension as of Philo, who (*de Abrah.* 19) hails Israel as the people **ὃ μοι δοκεῖ τὴν ὑπὲρ παντὸς ἀνθρώπων γένους ἱερωσύνην καὶ προφητείαν λαχεῖν.**

Ver. 11. This outer circle of myriads (the following **χιλιάδες** is an anti-climax) of angelic retainers—a favourite trait in the later Jewish pageants of heaven—does not address praise directly to the Lamb.

μυριάδες μυριάδων καὶ [b]χιλιάδες χιλιάδων, 12. [c]λέγοντες φωνῇ μεγάλῃ,

"Ἄξιός[1] ἐστιν τὸ ἀρνίον τὸ ἐσφαγμένον λαβεῖν τὴν δύναμιν καὶ [d]πλοῦτον καὶ [e]σοφίαν καὶ ἰσχὺν καὶ τιμὴν καὶ δόξαν καὶ [f]εὐλογίαν."

13. Καὶ πᾶν κτίσμα ὃ ἐν τῷ οὐρανῷ καὶ ἐπὶ τῆς γῆς καὶ [g]ὑποκάτω τῆς γῆς καὶ ἐπὶ τῆς θαλάσσης καὶ τὰ ἐν αὐτοῖς πάντα, ἤκουσα [h]λέγοντας,

"Τῷ καθημένῳ ἐπὶ τῷ θρόνῳ[2] καὶ τῷ ἀρνίῳ [i]ἡ εὐλογία καὶ ἡ τιμὴ καὶ ἡ δόξα καὶ τὸ κράτος εἰς τοὺς αἰῶνας τῶν αἰώνων."

b From Dan. vii. 10, *cf.* En. xiv. 22, xl. 1, lxxi 8, etc.
c Constr. ad sens. = λέγοντες.
d Rom. x. 12, xi. 33. Phil. iv. 19, Eph. iii. 8.
e *Cf.* on vii. 12.
f vii. 12, Sir. l. 20.
g Phil. ii. 10, Eph. i. 21, *cf.* ver. 3 and Ps. cxlv. 4, Ign. *Trall.* ix. 1.
h Irreg. apposition like xvii. 10, xix. 14, etc.
i On art. *cf.* Win. § 18, 42.

[1] **αξιος** A (Bg., Ti., WH marg., Ws.), *constr. ad sensum* [**αξιος ει**, S.], is preferable to the easier **αξιον** of ℵQ, min., Syr.

[2] **τω θρονω** AQ, min., Andc (edd.) is preferable to **του θρονου** of ℵP, 1, etc., S., Areth. (WH text, Bj.).

Ver. 12. For similar arrangements in Jewish doxologies, see Gfrörer, ii. 146-8; and, for **ἰσχ. τιμ. δόξ.** see Dan. ii. 37 (LXX). **τήν** groups together the seven words of the panegyric; honour and glory and praise are due to one whose victorious death has won him the power of bestowing incalculable riches on his people and of unriddling the future, against all opposition (Weiss). The refrain of **δύν.** is heard in xi. 17, and **δόξα** had been already associated with "wealth" and "power" (Eph. i. 18 f.) or "wisdom" (2 Cor. iii. 7 f., iv. 4, etc.) in Christ (contrast Isa. liii. 2 LXX). The act of taking the book (ver. 7) suggests the general authority and prestige of the Lamb, which is acknowledged in this doxology. The order in 12, 13 is the same as in Ps. ciii. 20-22, where the angels are followed by creation in the worship. When God's creatures and servants magnify, praise, and bless him, yielding themselves to his dominion, and acknowledging that to him all the strength and wealth and wisdom of life rightly belong, God is honoured. Christ was glorified by God (*cf.* Acts iii. 13, Rom. vi. 4, John xvii. 1) at the resurrection, when God's power raised him to eternal life; he is glorified by men in their homage and submission to him as the sole medium of redemption and revelation.

Ver. 13. From the whole creation a third doxology rises, catching up the last word (**εὐλογίᾳ**) of the preceding, and addressed—as in the primitive and distinctive confessions of early Christianity (*e.g.*, John xvii. 3, 1 Tim. ii. 5) to God and Jesus alike (vii. 10). In this chorus of praise (i. 6), by a sweep of the poet's imagination, even departed spirits and sea-monsters (**ἐπὶ τ. θαλ.**, rather than seafaring men) join—"even all that is in" earth and sea and heaven (*cf.* the title of the sun in the Rosetta inscription of 196 B.C., **μέγας βασιλεὺς τῶν τε ἄνω κ. τ. κάτω χωρῶν**). Sacrifice is on the throne of the universe; by dying for men, Jesus has won the heart and confidence of the world. Thus the praise of God the creator (ch. iv.) and the praise of Jesus the redeemer (ch. v.) blend in one final song, whose closing words indicate that the latter's prestige was not confined to a passing phase of history. The crime for which the messiah dethrones the rulers (in Enoch xlvi.) is just "because they do not praise and extol him, nor thankfully acknowledge whence the kingdom was bestowed upon them, . . . because they do not extol the name of the Lord of Spirits". In the papyrus of Ani (*E. B. D.* 3) Rā is worshipped by the gods "who dwell in the heights and who dwell in the depths"; whilst Isis and Osiris, as possessing supreme power, received honour "in the regions under the earth and in those above ground" (Plut. *de Iside*, 27). Compare the fine rabbinic saying of Rabbi Pinchas and R. Jochanan on Ps. c. 2: "though all offerings cease in the future, the offering of praise alone shall not cease; though all prayers cease, thanksgiving alone shall not cease".

k iv. 10, xix. 4.
l Detached "Amen" (so often in O.T.), *cf.* 1 Cor. xiv. 16, Just. *Apol.* i. 65, 67.

14. Καὶ τὰ τέσσερα ζῷα ἔλεγον, [k] "Ἀμήν". [l] καὶ οἱ πρεσβύτεροι ἔπεσαν καὶ προσεκύνησαν.

VI. 1. ΚΑΙ εἶδον ὅτε ἤνοιξεν τὸ ἀρνίον [a] μίαν [a] ἐκ τῶν ἑπτὰ σφραγίδων, καὶ [b] ἤκουσα ἑνὸς ἐκ τῶν τεσσάρων ζῴων λέγοντος ὡς φωνὴ [1]

a See v. 5, etc. b See v. 11.

[1] For **φωνης** (P, 1) read **φωνη** [harsh ex. of nom. indep.] ACQ., etc., And., Areth. Bg., Lach., Ti., Tr., Bs., Düst., Bj. [**φωνῇ** 7, 87, 93, WH, Sw., Ws.].

Ver. 14. The prologue is brought to a splendid close by "amen" from the four **ζῷα,** who have the last as they had the first word (iv. 8), followed by silent adoration from the **πρεσβύτεροι.** As in the liturgical practice of early Christian assemblies, so in the celestial court, the solemn chant of praise to God is succeeded by the "amen" ("ad similitudinem tonitrui . . . *amen* reboat," Jerome); Q, Areth., etc. Alf., bring this out by reading here **τὸ Ἀμήν.** By prefacing the struggle on earth (vi. f.) with a vision of the brilliant authority and awe of heaven (iv., v.), the prophet suggests that all the movements of men on earth, as well as the physical catastrophes which overtake them, are first fore-shadowed in heaven (the underlying principle of astrology, *cf.* Jeremias, 84 f.) and consequently have a providential meaning. In iv., v. the writer takes his readers behind the scenes; the whole succeeding tide of events is shown to flow from the will of God as creator of the universe, whose executive authority is delegated to Jesus the redeemer of his people. This tide breaks in two cycles of seven waves, the seventh (viii. 1) of the first series (vi. 1-vii. 17) issuing in a fresh cycle (viii. 2-xi. 19) instead of forming itself (as we should expect) the climax of these preliminary catastrophes in nature and humanity, disasters which were interpreted (*R. J.* 237-239) as the premonitory outbursts of an angry deity ready to visit the earth with final punishment. Observe that throughout the Apocalypse wind and fire are among God's scourges handled by angels in order to punish the earth and the waters, according to the conception preserved in Apol. Arist. 2: "Moreover, the wind is obedient to God, and fire to the angels; the waters also to the daemons, and earth to the sons of men" (*Ante-Nicene Library*, ix. 257 f.). The visitation is divinely complete, sevenfold like Ezekiel's oracles against the nations (xxv.-xxxii.). Apoc. vi.-ix. has, for its staple, little more than a poetic elaboration of Mark xiii. 8 (*cf.* 24, 25), international complications due to the scuffling and strife of peoples, and physical disasters as a fit setting for them.

The vision of the seven seals opened (vi. 1-viii. 2): vi. 1, 2, a Parthian invasion.

CHAPTER VI.—Ver. 1. The command or invitation **ἔρχου** is not addressed to Christ (as xxii. 17, 20). If addressed to the seer, it is abbreviated from the ordinary rabbinic phrase (*ueni et uide*) used to excite attention and introduce the explanation of any mystery. The immediate sequel (omitted only in ver. 4), **καὶ εἶδον,** does not, however, forbid the reference of **ἔρχου** to the mounted figures; hearing the summons, John looked to see its meaning and result. The panorama of these four dragoons ("ad significandum iter properum cum potentia") is partly sketched from Semitic folk-lore, where apparitions of horsemen (*cf.* 2 Macc. iii. 25, etc.: "the Beduins always granted me that none living had seen the angel visions . . . the meleika are seen in the air like horsemen, tilting to and fro," Doughty, *Arab. Deserta*, i. 449) have been a frequent omen of the end (*cf. Jos. Bell.* vi. 5; *Sib. Or.* iii. 796), partly reproduced from (Persian elements in) Zech. i. 7 f., vi. 1-8, in order to bring out the disasters (*cf.* Jer. xiv. 12, xxi. 7) prior to the last day. The direct sources of vi. and ix. lie in Lev. xxvi. 19-26; Ezek. xxxiii. 27, xxxiv. 28 f., and Sir. xxxix. 29, 30 ("fire and hail and famine and **θάνατος**, all these are created for vengeance; teeth of wild beasts and scorpions and serpents and a sword taking vengeance on the impious to destroy them"). An astral background, in connection with the seven tables of destiny in Babylonian mythology, each of which was dedicated to a planet of a special colour, has been conjectured by Renan (472); *cf.* Chwolson's *Die Ssabier*, iii. 658, 671, 676 f. For other efforts to associate these horsemen with the winds or the planets, see Jeremias (pp. 24 f.) and M. W. Müller in *Zeitr. f. d. neutest.*

βροντῆς, [c] "Ἔρχου". 2. Καὶ εἶδον, καὶ ἰδοὺ ἵππος [d] λευκός, καὶ
ὁ καθήμενος ἐπ' αὐτὸν ἔχων [e] τόξον· καὶ ἐδόθη αὐτῷ στέφανος, καὶ
ἐξῆλθε νικῶν καὶ ἵνα νικήσῃ. 3. Καὶ ὅτε ἤνοιξε τὴν σφραγῖδα τὴν δευτέραν, ἤκουσα τοῦ δευτέρου ζῴου λέγοντος, "Ἔρχου".
4. Καὶ ἐξῆλθεν ἄλλος ἵππος [f] πυρρός· καὶ τῷ καθημένῳ ἐπ' αὐτὸν
ἐδόθη αὐτῷ λαβεῖν τὴν εἰρήνην ἐκ τῆς γῆς καὶ [g] ἵνα [h] ἀλλήλους
[g] σφάξουσιν· καὶ ἐδόθη αὐτῷ μάχαιρα μεγάλη. 5. Καὶ ὅτε

c xvii. 1, xxi. 9, John i. 39, 46.
d Sib. Or. iii. 176, Verg. *Aen.* iii. 537 f. (Servius).
e ἅπ. λεγ. N.T.
f xii. 3, ἅπ. λεγ. N.T.
g *Cf.* on iii. 9.
h Mk. xiii. 8, etc., Ap. Bar. lxx. 3, 4 Esd. vi. 24, xiii. 31, Sib. Or. ii. 156.

Wiss. (1907), 290-316. But the proofs are fanciful and vague, though they converge upon the view that the colours of the steeds at least had originally some planetary significance. The series, as usual, is divided into the first four and the second three members. The general contents of vi. 1-8 denote various but not successive phases of woe (only too familiar to inhabitants of the Eastern provinces) which were to befall the empire and the East during the military convulsions of the final strife between Rome and Parthia. The "primum omen," for John as for Vergil, is a white horse, ridden by an archer.

Ver. 2. White = royal and victorious colour, *cf.* the white horse of the Persian kings (Philostr. *Vit. Ap.* i.). The triumphant figure of the mounted bowman is by no means to be identified with that of the Christian messiah or of the gospel. It would be extremely harsh and confusing to represent the messiah as at once the Lamb opening the seal and a figure independently at work. The initial period of the gospel was not one of irresistible triumph, and matters have become too acute for John to share the belief voiced in Mark xiii. 10. Besides, the messiah could hardly be described as preceding the signs of his own advent, nor would he be on the same plane as the following figures. The vision is a tacit antithesis, not an anticipation, of xix. 11 f.; the triumph of the world which opens the drama is rounded off by an infinitely grander triumph won by Christ.—**νικῶν κ. κ.τ.λ.** John was too open-eyed to ignore the fact that other forces, besides the Christian gospel, had a success of their own on earth. What is this force? Not the Roman Empire, as if the four steeds represented the first four emperors (so, variously, Renan, Spitta, Weizsäcker), but a raid of the Parthians (so most edd. from Vitringa to Erbes, Völter, Holtzm., Bousset, Bruston, Ramsay, Scott), which represented war in its most dreaded form for inhabitants of the Eastern provinces. There is no need to find any definite reference to the raid of Vonones (Wetstein) or of Vologesus who invaded Syria in 61-63 A.D. The simple point of the vision is that the Parthians would be commissioned to make a successful foray, carrying all before them. The bow was the famous and dreaded weapon of these oriental cavalry; **Νικήτωρ** was a title of Seleucus, and **νικητής** of the Persian satrap. One plausible hypothesis (developed by Erbes) refers the basis of the seal-visions to (*a*) the triumphs of Augustus and Tiberius, (*b*) the bloody feuds in Palestine under Caligula, (*c*) the famine in Syria under Claudius (Ac. xi.), (*d*) the subsequent pestilence, (*e*) the Neronic martyrs, and (*f*) the agitations of the empire under Galba, etc. (for portents *cf.* Plin. *Ep.* vi. 16, 20; Tacit. *Hist.* i. 4). But a similar collocation of portents is found in the reign of Titus; and apart from the misinterpretation of the first seal, it is arbitrary and jejune to suppose that this prophet's splendid, free reading of providence was laboriously spelt out from details of more or less recent history.

Vv. 3, 4. *The second seal opened:* A swordsman representing (red = martial colour) war and bloodshed, "is permitted to make men slay one another". The allusion to the merciless weapon (Plut. *de Iside*, 11) of the sword as Rome's national arm thus places the Parthian and Roman empires side by side (**τῆς γῆς** generally, not Judaea in particular), but the vision of war is also connected directly with the two following visions of famine (5, 6) and mortality (from pestilence, 7, 8). The seven punishments drawn up by rabbinic theology (*Pirke Aboth*, v. 11 f.) were: three kinds of famine, pestilence, noisome beasts, and captivity or exile.

Vv. 5, 6. The third seal opened = *famine.*

Ver. 5. The spectral figure of Hunger

ἤνοιξε τὴν σφραγῖδα τὴν τρίτην, ἤκουσα τοῦ τρίτου ζῴου λέγοντος,
“Ἔρχου”. Καὶ εἶδον, καὶ ἰδοὺ ἵππος μέλας, καὶ ὁ καθήμενος ἐπ᾽
αὐτὸν ἔχων [k] ζυγὸν ἐν τῇ χειρὶ αὐτοῦ. 6. καὶ ἤκουσα ὡς φωνὴν
ἐν μέσῳ τῶν τεσσάρων ζῴων λέγουσαν,

[l] “Χοῖνιξ σίτου [m] δηναρίου, καὶ τρεῖς χοίνικες κριθῶν [h] δηναρίου·
καὶ τὸ ἔλαιον καὶ τὸν οἶνον μὴ [n] ἀδικήσῃς.”

7. Καὶ ὅτε ἤνοιξε τὴν σφραγῖδα τὴν τετάρτην, ἤκουσα φωνὴν τοῦ
τετάρτου ζῴου λέγοντος, “Ἔρχου”. 8. καὶ εἶδον, καὶ ἰδοὺ ἵππος
[o] χλωρός, καὶ ὁ καθήμενος ἐπάνω αὐτοῦ,[1] ὄνομα αὐτῷ ὁ Θάνατος,

i *Cf.* Lam. iv. 8-9 (bloodlessness): *cf.* the Greek terms αἰανής and αἴθοψ for λιμός.
k Prov. xvi. 11, Ezek. iv. 16, v. 1, xlv. 10.
l = ἡμερήσιος τροφή (Diog. Laert. 8, 18, *cf.* Herod. vii. 251).
m Gen. price (sc. πωλεῖται): *cf.* Matt. xx. 2.
n Thuc. ii. 71, iv. 98, aor. of prohibition.
o Hom. *Il.* viii. 479.

[1] Read **αυτω** (אQ, 5, And., Areth., Tr. marg.: *cf.* xiv. 4, 9, xix. 14) for **μετ αυτου** (edd.), and, after **εδοθη, αυτω** (Q, min., vss., Bg., Bs.) for the correction **αυτοις** (אACP, edd.). [In any case, the **αυτοις** refers to Death and Hades, not to the second, third, and fourth riders (Wellh.)].

holds a balance or pair of scales (**ζ.** literally = the beam, see reff.) for measuring bread by weight, to personify (ver. 6) bad times, when provisions became cruelly expensive. One **χοῖνιξ** of wheat, the usual rations of a working man for a day, is to cost twelve times its normal price, while the labourer's daily pay will not command more than an eighth of the ordinary twenty-four measures of the coarser barley. Grain is not to disappear entirely from the earth, otherwise there would be no famine. But food-stuffs are to be extremely scanty and therefore dear (*cf.* Lev. xxvi. 26; Ezek. iv. 16). These hard times are aggravated (**καὶ** adversative) by the immunity of oil and wine, which are, comparatively speaking, luxuries. One exasperating feature of the age would be the sight of wine and oil flowing, while grain trickled slowly into the grasp of the famishing. The best explanation of this realistic exception is to regard it as a water-mark of the Domitianic date (for details see the present writer's study in *Expos.* Oct. 1908, 359-369). In 92 A.D. Domitian had made a futile attempt to injure the cultivation of the vine in the provinces, which led to widespread agitation throughout Ionia. His edict had soon to be withdrawn, but not till it had roused fear and anger. Hence the words *hurt not the wine* have the force of a local allusion to what was fresh in his readers' minds. The point of the saying lies in the recent events which had stirred Smyrna and the surrounding townships, and which provided the seer with a bit of colour for his palette as he painted the final terrors. It is as if he grimly said: “Have no fears for your vines! There will be no Domitian to hurt them. Comfort yourselves with that. Only, it will be small comfort to have your liquid luxuries spared and your grain reduced almost to starvation point.” Or, the prophet's meaning might be that the exemption of the vine would only pander to drunkenness and its attendant ills. The addition of **τὸ ἔλαιον** is probably an artistic embodiment, introduced in order to fill out the sketch. The cultivation of the olive accompanied that of the vine, and the olive meant smooth times. It is no era of peace; far from that, the prophet implies. But the olive, “the darling of Peace” (as Vergil calls it), flourishes unchecked, so mocking and awry are the latter days. For **ἀδικεῖν** = “injure” (a country), see reff., vii. 2, and Dittenberger's *Sylloge Inscr. Graec.* 557. This Domitianic reference of vi. 6 was first worked out by S. Reinach (*Revue Archéolog.* 1901, 350 f.) and has been accepted by Harnack, Heinrici, Bousset, J. Weiss, Abbott, Holtzmann, Baljon, and others. There is no allusion to Jos. *Bell.* v. 13, 6, or to the sparing of gardens during the siege of Jerusalem (S. Krauss, in Preuschen's *Zeitschrift*, 1909, 81-89).

Vv. 7, 8. The fourth seal opened: *pestilence and mortality.*

Ver. 8. **χλωρός,** pale or livid as a corpse.—**ἐπάνω αὐτοῦ,** for the ordinary **ἐπ᾽ αὐτόν,** a grammatical variation which has no special significance. In this Durersque vignette the spectre of Hades, bracketed here as elsewhere with Death, accompanies the latter to secure his booty

καὶ ὁ [p] ᾍδης [q] ἠκολούθει [q] αὐτῷ· καὶ ἐδόθη αὐτῷ ἐξουσία ἐπὶ τὸ
τέταρτον τῆς γῆς ἀποκτεῖναι [r] ἐν ῥομφαίᾳ καὶ ἐν λιμῷ καὶ ἐν
[s] θανάτῳ καὶ [t] ὑπὸ τῶν θηρίων τῆς γῆς.
9. Καὶ ὅτε ἤνοιξε
τὴν πέμπτην σφραγῖδα, εἶδον ὑποκάτω τοῦ θυσιαστηρίου τὰς [u] ψυχὰς
τῶν ἐσφαγμένων [v] διὰ τὸν λόγον τοῦ Θεοῦ καὶ διὰ τὴν [u] μαρτυρίαν
ἣν εἶχον,
10. καὶ ἔκραξαν φωνῇ μεγάλῃ, λέγοντες, "Ἕως πότε, ὁ

i. 18, xx. 13-14, Hos. xiii. 14, Isa. xviii. 5.
q xiv. 13, *cf.* Luke ix. 49.
r Instrum. Abbott, *Diat.* 2332*a*.
s xviii. 8; = pestilence (LXX).
t Rare with act. verb.
u xx. 4 (*cf.* Heb. xii. 23).
v i. 9, xii. 17.

of victims. So Nergal, the Babylonian Pluto, is not content with ruling the regions of the dead but appears as an active personification of violent destruction, especially pestilence and war, inflicting his wounds on large masses rather than on individuals (Jastrow, 66, 67). A similar duality of conception, local and personal, obtained in Semitic and Hellenic mythology (*cf. e.g.*, ix. 11); only, Death is not here personified as an angel (with Jewish theology, *cf.* Eisenmenger's *Eindecktes Jud.* i. 854 f., 862 f.). As the chief partner in this grim league, he is given destructive power over a certain quarter of the earth (**τὸ τέτ.** colloquially); his agents are the usual apocalyptic scourges (*cf.* Ezek. xiv. 21, Ps. Sol. xiii. 2 f., with Plut. *Iside*, 47 for the Iranian expectation of **λοιμὸς καὶ λιμός** as inflictions of Ahriman) against which the Jewish evening prayer was directed ("keep far from us the enemy, the pestilence, the sword, famine and affliction"). War, followed by famine which bred pestilence, was familiar in Palestine (Jos. *Antiq.* xv. 9) during the first century A.D. Indeed throughout the ancient world war and pestilence were closely associated, while wild beasts multiplied and preyed on human life, as the land was left untilled. In Test. Naphth. 8, etc., Beliar is the captain of wild beasts. Note that the prophet sees only the commissions, not the actual deeds, of these four dragoons: not until vi. 12 f. does anything happen. The first four seals are simply arranged on the rabbinic principle (Sohar Gen. fol. 91), "quodcunque in terra est, id etiam in coelo est, et nulla res tam exigua est in mundo quae non ab alia simili quae in coelo est dependeat". The four plagues (a Babylonian idea) are adapted from Ezek. xiv. 12 f. Contemporary disasters which may have lent vividness to the sketch are collected by Renan (pp. 323 f.).

Vv. 9-11. The fifth seal opened.

Ver. 9. The scene changes from earth to heaven, which appears as a replica of the earthly temple with its altar of burnt offering. As the blood of sacrifices flowed at the base of the altar (xvi. 7), the blood representing the life, the symbolism is obvious. It was mediated by rabbinic ideas of the souls of the just (*e.g.*, of Moses) resting under the divine throne of glory; *cf.* R. Akiba's saying, "quicumque sepelitur in terra Israel, perinde est ac si sepeliretur sub altari: quicumque autem sepelitur sub altari, perinde est ac si sepeliretur sub throno gloriae" (*Pirke Aboth*, 26). The omission of **Ἰησοῦ** after **μ.** may suggest that the phrase is intended to include not so much the heroic Jews who fell in the defence of their temple against Rome (Weyland) as pre-Christian Jewish martyrs (*cf.* Heb. xi. 39, 40) who are raised to the level of the Christian church, and also those Jews who had been martyred for refusing to worship the emperor (*cf.* vii. 9, xvii. 6, and Jos. *B. J.* vii. 10, 1). But the primary thought of the Christian prophet is for Rome's latest victims in the Neronic persecution and the recent enforcement of the cultus under Domitian. The general idea is derived from Zech. i. 12, Ps. lxxix. 10, and En. xxii. 5 ("and I saw the spirits of the children of men who were dead, and their voice penetrated to the heaven and complained," from the first division of Sheol).

Ver. 10. Like Clem. Rom., John is fond of **δεσπότης** as implying the divine might and majesty (3 Macc. iii. 29, v. 28). This severe and awe-inspiring conception (*cf.* Philo, *quis rer. div. haer.* 6) means that God will vindicate his holiness, which had been outraged by the murder of the **δοῦλοι** for whom he is responsible. In contemporary pagan religions throughout Asia Minor, the punishment of wrong-doing is often conceived in the same way, *viz.*, as the answer to the sufferer's appeal (*cf.* Introd. § 2), not simply as a spontaneous act of divine retribution. "How long wilt thou refrain from charging and avenging our blood upon (**ἐκ** as in 1 Sam. xxiv. 13, Ps. xlii. 1) those who dwell on the earth" (*i.e.*, pagans)? The bleeding heart of primitive Christendom stands up and cries, "I

[w] δεσπότης ὁ ἅγιος καὶ ἀληθινός, οὐ [x] κρίνεις καὶ [x] ἐκδικεῖς τὸ [y] αἷμα ἡμῶν ἐκ τῶν κατοικούντων ἐπὶ τῆς γῆς;" 11. καὶ ἐδόθη αὐτοῖς ἑκάστῳ [z] στολὴ [z] λευκή, καὶ [a] ἐρρέθη αὐτοῖς ἵνα ἀναπαύσωνται ἔτι

w = φοβερὸς κύριος (Philo), Plato, *Euthyd.* 302: *cf.* on Luke ii. 29, Acts iv. 24, Did. x. 3, Dan. iii. 37, ix. 8, etc. x 2 Kings ix. 7, 2 Chron. xxiv. 22, *cf.* Hab. i. 2, Deut. xxxii. 43, etc. y John xvi. 2. z iii. 4, 5, 18. a As ix. 4 for ἐρρήθη Attic.

have suffered". For **ἐκδικεῖν αἷμα** *cf.* Dittenberger's *Sylloge Inscript. Graec.* 816^{12} (1 cent. A.D.) **ἵνα ἐγδικήσῃς τὸ αἷμα τὸ ἀναίτιον**, etc.; for **ἐκδ. ἐκ.** (= מִן) of vengeance, *cf.* Luke xviii. 3-8 (**ἀπὸ**), a close parallel in thought, though this pathetic, impatient thirst for blood-revenge, which has "the full drift of Ps. xciv. below it" (Selwyn) is inferior not only to 1 Peter ii. 23 but to the synoptic wail. The Jewish atmosphere is unmistakable (*cf.* 2 Macc. vii. 36; also Deissmann's *Licht vom Osten*, 312 f.), but this does not mean that the passage was necessarily written by a Jew. In that case we should have expected some allusion to the vicarious, atoning power of the martyrs' death (*R. J.* 181). The prophet evidently anticipated further persecution, since he wrote on the verge of the end precipitated by the Domitianic policy (*cf.* on ii. 13). Such persecution follows natural disturbances, as in the synoptic apocalypse (Matt. (xxiv. 6-7, 21 f.), but the outline of the fifth seal is taken from Enoch, where (xlvii.) the prayer and blood of the martyred saints "rise from the earth before the Lord of Spirits," while the angels rejoice that such blood has not been shed in vain. In En. xcvii. 3-5 the prayer of the righteous for vengeance overtakes their persecutors on the day of judgment with woeful issues (xcix. 3, 16). "Persist in your cry for judgment, and it shall appear unto you; for all your tribulation will be visited on the rulers, and on all their helpers, and on those who plundered you" (civ. 3, *cf.* xxii. 6, 7, where Abel's spirit complains of Cain).—**κατ. κ.τ.λ.** always in Apocalypse opposed to the saints, almost as "the world" to "the pious" in modern phraseology. This usage is largely paralleled by that of the Noachic interpolations in Enoch (see Charles on xxxvii. 5), where the phrase has either unfavourable or neutral associations. **ἅγιος** here (as John xvii. 11 = Did. x. 3, **πανάγιος** Clem. Rom. xxxv. 3, lviii. 1) applied by a comparatively rare usage (1 Peter i. 15 and Apoc. iv. 8 being dependent on O.T.) to God, whose intense holiness must be in antagonism to the evil and contradictions of the world (Titius, 9-11).

Ver. 11. The white robe assigned each (Blass, § 32, 4) of these martyr-spirits as a pledge of future and final glory (vii. 9) and a consoling proof that no judgment awaited them (xx. 4-6), is a favourite gift in the Jewish heaven (*cf.* Enoch lxii. 15 f., and *Asc. Isa.* ix. 24 f.). The intermediate state was a much debated question in apocalyptic literature, and early Christian thought fluctuates between the idea of a provisional degree of bliss (as here and, *e.g.*, Clem. Rom. i. 3, "those who by God's grace have been perfected in love possess the place of the pious, and they shall be manifested at the visitation of God's kingdom") and a direct, full entrance into heavenly privileges—especially, though neither uniformly nor exclusively, reserved for martyrs (Clem. Rom. v., Polyk. *ad Phil.* ix. 2, Heb. xii. 23, etc.); *cf.* Titius, 44-46. A cognate idea is reproduced in *Asc. Isa.* ix. 6 f., where in the seventh heaven Abel, Enoch and the Jewish saints appear all clothed "in the garments of the upper world" (*i.e.*, in their resurrection-bodies) but not yet in full possession of their privileges, not yet seated on their thrones or wearing their crowns of glory. These are not theirs, till Christ descends to earth and ascends to heaven again.—"And they were told to rest (or wait quietly) for a little while yet," as they had been doing till the successive shocks of providence stirred them to an outburst of eager and reproachful anticipation. To rest implies to cease crying for vengeance (*cf.* iv. 8). Gfrörer (ii. 50) cites a rabbinic tradition that the messiah would not come until all souls in גּוּף (an intermediate resting-place of the departed?) were clothed with bodies. **ἕως κ.τ.λ.**, this is closely and curiously reproduced, not so much from ideas preserved in the contemporary Apoc. Bar. xxiii. 4, 5 (where the end of the world comes when the predestined number of human beings is completed) as from the religious tradition also used in Clem. Rom. ii., lix., Justin (*Apol.* i. 45), and the contemporary 4th Esdras (iv. 36 f., quoniam in statera ponderauit

χρόνον μικρόν, ἕως πληρωθῶσιν[1] καὶ οἱ σύνδουλοι [b]αὐτῶν καὶ οἱ
[c]ἀδελφοὶ [b]αὐτῶν οἱ μέλλοντες [d]ἀποκτέννεσθαι ὡς καὶ αὐτοί. 12.
Καὶ εἶδον ὅτε ἤνοιξε τὴν σφραγῖδα τὴν ἕκτην· καὶ [e]σεισμὸς μέγας
ἐγένετο, καὶ ὁ ἥλιος ἐγένετο [f]μέλας ὡς σάκκος [g]τρίχινος, καὶ ἡ
σελήνη ὅλη ἐγένετο ὡς αἷμα, 13. καὶ οἱ [h]ἀστέρες τοῦ οὐρανοῦ
ἔπεσαν εἰς τὴν γῆν, ὡς συκῆ βάλλει τοὺς [g]ὀλύνθους αὐτῆς ὑπὸ
ἀνέμου μεγάλου σειομένη· 14. καὶ ὁ οὐρανὸς ἀπεχωρίσθη ὡς

b Note repet. of poss. gen. ix. 21.
c For ethnic use (= fellows of same religious community) *cf.* *C. B. P.* i. 96 f.
d On Aeolic form, *cf.* Helbing, 73-74.
e viii. 5, xi. 13, xvi. 18, Matt. xxiv. 7, 4 Esd. vi. 14, Ap. Bar. lxx. 8, Dio Cass. lxvi. 23, etc.
f Isa. xiii. 10, l. 3, Joel ii. 3, 10, 30-31. Matt. xxiv. 29, Ass. Mos. x. 4 f.
g ἅπ. λεγ. N.T.
h Isa. xxxiv. 4, Ezek. xxxii. 7-8, *cf.* Sib. Or. iii. 82, viii. 238, 413 (190).

[1] For **πληρωσονται** (Areth.) read **πληρωθωσιν** (AC, 29, vg., S., Cypr., Bg., Düst.. Lach., WH, Ws., Bj., Sw., Bs.) [**πληρωσωσιν** ℵPQ, etc., And., Ti., Al. Tr., Holtzm.).

saecula et mensura mensurauit tempora et non commouit nec excitauit, usquedum impleatur praedicta mensura . . . quando impletus fuerit numerus similium uobis) which thinks not of mankind but of the righteous (*cf.* Apoc. Bar. xxx. 2, and Heb. xi. 40). The atmosphere of this belief goes back to the first century B.C., as in Enoch (xlvii., *cf.* ix. xxii.) "and the hearts of the holy were filled with joy that the number of righteousness had drawn nigh, and the prayer of the righteous was heard, and the blood of the righteous required, before the Lord of Spirits" (*cf.* below, ch. xi. 15 f.). The thought is repeated in Ep. Lugd. from this passage ("day by day those who were worthy were seized, filling up their number, so that all the zealous people and those through whom our affairs here had been especially established, were collected out of both churches"). It had been already developed otherwise in 4th Esdras iv. 35 f., where the seer's impatience for the end is rebuked and God's greater eagerness asserted. "Did not the souls of the righteous question thus in their chambers, saying, 'How long are we still to stay here? et quando ueniet fructus areae mercedis nostrae?' And the archangel Jeremiel answered them and said, 'When the number of your fellows is complete'." Substituting martyrs for the righteous, the author of our Apocalypse has exploited the idea thus familiar to him as a devout Jew; his first four visions come mainly through Zechariah; for the next he adapts this later post-exilic notion. The Neronic victims and their fellows occupied in his mind the place filled by the early Jewish saints in the reverent regard of contemporary Jews. As Renan notices (317 f.), this thirst for vengeance was in the air after Nero's death, shared even by Romans; one legend (Suet. *Nero*, xlviii., Dio Cass. lxiii. 28) told how, as Nero fled to his last retreat, during a thunderpeal the souls of his victims burst from the earth and flung themselves upon him.—As the safety of the physical universe rested on the safety of the righteous, according to the Jewish notion, so any massacres of the latter at once affected the stability of the world. Hence the sequence of vv. 11 and 12 f. There is no hint that these physical aberrations were temporary. Yet the following catastrophes (vii. f.) plainly presuppose a universe in its original and normal condition. It depends upon the theory adopted of the book whether this points merely to such discrepancies as are not unfamiliar in literature (especially imaginative literature), or to recapitulation, or to the presence of different sources.

Vv. 12-17. *The sixth seal opened* (*cf.* Crashaw's *To the Name of Jesus*, 220-234).

Vv. 12-14. The earthquake (reff.), darkening of sun by atmospheric disturbances, (Verg. *Georg.* i. 463 f., Lucan i. 75 f., 522 f. Compare Ass. Mos. x. 4 f.: et tremebit terra. Usque ad fines suas concutietur . . . sol non dab it lumen et in tenebras conuertet se, etc.; for Babylonian background *cf.* Schrader,[3] 392 f.), reddening of the full moon as in a total eclipse (*cf.* reff.), the dropping of stars, the removal of the sky, and the displacement of mountain and island (En. i. 6, see below on xiv. 20) are all more or less stereotyped features of the physical situation in apocalyptic eschatology, where naturally (*cf.* Jos. *Bell.* iv. 4, 5) agonies and distortions of the uni-

βιβλίον ἑλισσόμενον, [i]καὶ πᾶν ὄρος καὶ νῆσος[1] ἐκ τῶν τόπων
αὐτῶν ἐκινήθησαν· 15. καὶ οἱ βασιλεῖς τῆς γῆς καὶ οἱ [k]μεγισ-
τᾶνες καὶ οἱ [l]χιλίαρχοι καὶ οἱ [m]πλούσιοι καὶ οἱ ἰσχυροὶ καὶ πᾶς
δοῦλος καὶ ἐλεύθερος [n]ἔκρυψαν ἑαυτοὺς εἰς τὰ σπήλαια καὶ εἰς τὰς
πέτρας τῶν [o]ὀρέων, 16. [n]καὶ λέγουσι τοῖς ὄρεσι καὶ ταῖς πέτραις,

i Jer. iv. 24, Ezek. xxxviii. 20, Nah. i. 5, *cf.* Sen. *Nat. Quaes.* iv. 26.
k xviii. 23 = the Parthian chiefs (Macedonian term)? *cf.* Dan. v. 23, LXX, Ps. Sol. ii. 36.
l On form see Win. § 8, 9.
m Jas. v. 1.
n From Hos. x. 8, Isa. ii. 10 f., vi. 16, Ezek. xxxix. 17-20, Luke xxiii. 30; a characteristic of the wicked in En. xcvii. 3, c. 4, cii. 1.
o For uncontracted form, *cf.* Helbing, 41.

[1] The **πασα** prefixed to **νησος** by S. smoothes out the constr. of **παν**.

verse precede some divine punishment of men (Verg. *Georg.* i. 365 f.).

Vv. 15-17. Note the sevenfold description of the effect produced on humanity (xix. 18, *cf.* xiii. 16), the Roman **χιλίαρχοι** (=tribuni), the riches and rank of men (**ἰσχ.** a dramatic touch=defiant authority, like Mrs. Browning's Lucifer: "strength to behold him and not worship him, Strength to be in the universe and yet Neither God nor God's servant"; see especially Ps. Sol. xv. 3, 4), the distinction of slaves and free as a pagan, never as an internal Christian, division; also the painting of the panic from O.T. models (reff.). Those who are now the objects of dread, cower and fly to the crags and caves—a common sanctuary in Syria (*cf.* Introd. § 8). Mr. Doughty describes a meteoric shock in Arabia thus: "a thunder-din resounded marvellously through the waste mountain above us; it seemed as if this world went to wrack. . . . The most in the mejlis were of opinion that a 'star' had fallen" (*Ar. Des.* i. 462, 463). The Hosean citation (*cf.* Jer. viii. 3) here, as in Luke, gives powerful expression to the dread felt by an evil conscience; even the swift agony of being crushed to death is preferable to being left face to face with the indignation of an outraged God. To stand (*cf.* Luke xxi. 36) is to face quietly the judgment of God (1 John ii. 28), which is impossible except after a life which has resolutely stood its ground (Eph. vi. 13) amid reaction and served God (Apoc. vi. 10, 11). The panic of kings, etc., is taken from the description of the judgment in Enoch lxii.-lxiii., where before the throne of messiah "the mighty and the kings" in despairing terror seek repentance in vain; "and one portion of them will look on the other, and they will be terrified, and their countenance will fall, and pain will seize them," at the sight of messiah. In Apoc. Bar. xxv. also the approach of the end is heralded by stupor of heart and despair among the inhabitants of the earth, while a similar stress falls (in Sap. vi. 1-9) on kings, etc., and (in En. xxxvii.-lxxi. generally) on the earth's rulers. There is no need to suspect **καὶ . . . ἀρνίου** (16) as an editorial gloss (Vischer, Spitta, Weyland, de Faye, Völter, Pfleiderer, von Soden, Rauch, J. Weiss, Briggs); it may be a characteristic touch designed to point the O.T. citation (for **αὐτοῦ** in 17 or in xxii. 3 *cf.* 1 Thess. iii. 11, 2 Thess. ii. 16, 17), rather than a scribal or editorial insertion in what was originally a Jewish source.

The great day of God's wrath has come, but the action is interrupted by an *entre-acte* in vii., where as in x. 1-xi. 13, the author introduces an intermezzo between the sixth and the seventh members of the series. A change comes over the spirit of his dream. But although this oracle is isolated by form and content from its context, it is a consoling rhapsody or rapture designed to relieve the tension by lifting the eyes of the faithful over the foam and rocks of the rapids on which they were tossing to the calm, sunlit pool of bliss which awaited them beyond. They get this glimpse before the seventh seal is opened with its fresh cycle of horrors. The parenthesis consists of two heterogeneous visions, one (1-8) on earth and one (9-17) in heaven. The former (and indeed the whole section, *cf.* the **ἑστῶτες** of 9) is an implicit answer to the query of vi. 17, **τίς δύναται σταθῆναι**; it is an enigmatic fragment of apocalyptic tradition, which originally predicted (*cf.* Ezek. ix. 1 f.) God's safeguarding of a certain number of Jews, prior to some catastrophe of judgment ("Cry havoc, and let slip the winds of war!") upon the wicked. The chapter is not a literary unit with editorial touches (Weyland, Erbes, Bruston, Rauch), nor is

"Πέσετε ἐφ' ἡμᾶς καὶ κρύψατε ἡμᾶς
ἀπὸ προσώπου τοῦ καθημένου ἐπὶ τοῦ θρόνου,
καὶ ἀπὸ τῆς ὀργῆς τοῦ ἀρνίου,
17. [p] ὅτι ἦλθεν ἡ ἡμέρα ἡ μεγάλη τῆς ὀργῆς αὐτοῦ,[1]
καὶ τίς δύναται [q] σταθῆναι;"

p (Luke xxiii. 30), xvi. 14, Nah. i. 6, Mal. iii. 2, Zeph. i. 14, 18, etc.
q Win. § 14, 4.

αυτων (אC, 38, vg., Syr., S., Haym., etc., Ti., Tr., WH, Sw., Bj.) is an emendation of the original and difficult **αυτου** (APQ, min., Me., Arm., Aeth., And., Areth., Pr., Lach., Al., Ws., Bs.).

9-17 a continuation of vi. (Spitta). Vv. 1-8 are a Jewish fragment incorporated by the author, who writes 9-17 himself (so, *e.g.*, Vischer, Pfleiderer, Schmidt, Porter, Bousset, von Soden, Scott, Wellhausen). The fact that a selection, and not the whole, of the Jews are preserved, does not (in view of 4 Esdras) prove that a Jewish Christian (Völter, J. Weiss) must have written it. The scenery is not organic to John's proper outlook. After ver. 8 he shows no further interest in it. The winds are never loosed. The sealing itself is not described. The sealed are not seen. An apparent allusion to this remnant does occur (xiv. 1), but it is remote; John makes nothing of it; and the detached, special character of vii. 1-8 becomes plainer the further we go into the other visions. The sealed are exempted merely from the plague of the winds, not from martyrdom or persecution (of which there is no word here); one plague indeed has power to wound, though not to kill, them (ix. 4, 5). The collocation of the fragment with what precedes is probably due in part to certain similarities like the allusions to the wind (vi. 13), numbering (vi. 11), and the seals (vi. 1 f.). The real problem is, how far did John take this passage literally? This raises the question of the relationship between 1-8 and 9-17; either (*a*) both are different forms of the same belief, or (*b*) two different classes of people are meant. In the former event (*a*) John applies the Jewish oracle of 1-8 to the real Jews, *i.e.*, the Christians, who as a pious remnant are to be kept secure amid the cosmic whirl and crash of the latter days (vi. 12-17, *cf.* iii. 10 and the connexion of Nahum i. 5, 6, and 7). The terror passes and lo! the saints are seen safe on the other side (9-17). This interpretation of Christians as the real Israel or twelve tribes is favoured not only by early Christian thought (*cf.* 1 Peter i. 1, Jas. i. 1, Herm. *Sim.* ix. 17), but by the practice of John himself (*e.g.*, xviii. 4). Here as elsewhere he takes the particularist language of his source in a free symbolic fashion; only, while the archaic scenery of 1-8 suffices for a description of the safeguarded on earth, he depicts their beatified state (9-17) in ampler terms. The deeper Christian content of his vision implies not deliverance from death but deliverance through death. His saints are not survivors but martyrs. Hence the contrast between 1-8 and 9-17 is one of language rather than of temper, and the innumerable multitude of the latter, instead of being a supplement to the 144,000, are the latter viewed after their martyr-death under a definitely Christian light. The O.T. imagery of 1-8 mainly brings out the fact that the true Israel (Gal. vi. 16) is known and numbered by God; not one is lost. The alternative theory (*b*) holds that in taking over this fragment and adding another vision John meant Jewish Christians by the 144,000. The latter identification (so, *e.g.*, Prim., Vict., Hausrath, Vischer, Spitta, Hirscht, Forbes, Bousset) is less probable, however, in view of the general tenor of the Apocalypse (*cf.* Introd. § 6), for the usual passages cited as proof (*cf.* notes on xiv. 1 f., xxi. 12 and 24) are irrelevant, and while John prized the martyrs it is incredible that 9-17 was meant to prove that martyrdom was required to admit Gentile Christians even to a second grade among the elect (Weizsäcker, Pfleiderer). A Jewish Christian prophet might indeed, out of patriotic pride, regard the nucleus of God's kingdom as composed of faithful Jews, without being particularist in his sympathies. Paul himself once held this nationalist view (Rom. ix.-xi.), but it is doubtful if it represented his final position, and in any case the general conception of the Apocalypse (where Christians are the true Jews, and where particularist language is used metaphorically, just because literally it was obsolete) tells on the whole in favour of the view that 9-17 represents 1-8 read in the light of v. 9 (so, *e.g.*, de Wette, Bruston,

a In a net? (like Tiamat, En. xviii. s.c.411 f.).
b Jer. xlix. 36, Ezek. xxxvii. 9, Dan. vii. 2.

VII. 1. Μετὰ τοῦτο εἶδον τέσσαρας ἀγγέλους ἑστῶτας ἐπὶ τὰς τέσσαρας γωνίας τῆς γῆς, [a]κρατοῦντας [b]τοὺς τέσσαρας [b]ἀνέμους τῆς γῆς, ἵνα μὴ πνέῃ ἄνεμος ἐπὶ τῆς γῆς, μήτε ἐπὶ τῆς θαλάσσης,

Porter, Wellhausen, and Hoennicke: *das Judenchristentum*, 194 f.). Only, the general description of redeemed Christians in v. 9 is specifically applied in vii. 14 to the *candidatus martyrum exercitus*. Here as elsewhere John apparently conceives the final trial to be so searching and extensive that Christians will all be martyrs or confessors. The wonderful beauty of 9-17, whose truth rises above its original setting, requires no comment. It moved Renan (479, 480), after criticising "le contour mesquin" of the Apocalypse in general, to rejoice in the book's "symbolical expression of the cardinal principle that God is, but above all that He *shall be*. No doubt Paul put it better when he summed up the final goal of the universe in these words, *that God may be all in all*. But for a long while yet men will require a God who dwells with them, sympathises with their trials, is mindful of their struggles, and *wipes away every tear from their eyes*."

CHAPTER VII.—Ver. 1. As on the synoptic scheme (Matt. xxiv. 31), physical convulsions and human terrors are followed by a pause during which the saints are secured. It is impossible and irrelevant to determine whether the winds' blast and the sealing were already conjoined in the fragment or oral traditions which lay before this editor, or whether their combination is due to himself. They reflect the tradition underlying the synoptic apocalypse (Mark xiii. 24-27, etc., *cf.* Apoc. vi. 12-vii. 3), but here the safeguarding of the elect comes before, instead of after, the advent, and the four winds are agents of destruction instead of mere geographical points; besides, the rôle of messiah is omitted altogether. It is assumed not merely that these angels are the spirits of the four winds (Zech. vi. 5, and repeatedly in Enoch, *e.g.*, lxix. 22, "the spirits of the waters and of the winds and of all zephyrs"), but that some onset of the winds is imminent (ver. 2, *cf.* En. xviii. 22), as part of the horrors of the last catastrophe (for punitive winds, see Sir. xxxix. 28). Stray hints proving the existence of such a tradition (*cf.* Dan. vii. 2) have been collected (*cf. S. C.* 323 f.; *A. C.* 246, 247) *e.g.*, from Sibyll. viii. 203 f., etc., where a hurricane is to sweep the earth previous to the resurrection of the dead (trees being here singled out as most exposed to a storm's ravages). If such allusions are not mere echoes of the present passage, they would appear to indicate a runlet of eschatological tradition flowing behind more important ideas. Or are the saints like trees of God (Ps. Sol. xiv. 2, 3) never to be uprooted by a wind or onset of foes (*ibid.* viii. 6, xvii. 13)? It is no longer possible to be sure. In En. xviii 1 f. by a semi-Babylonian touch, the four winds are identified with the four pillars of the heaven and the foundations of the earth; in Apoc. Bar. vi. 4, 5, four angels with lamps are restrained by another angel from lighting them (*cf.* also *E. Bi.* 5303). There seems to be no allusion to the notion of a blast (from the sea) as a form of mortal fate (*e.g.*, Oed. *Col.* 1659, 1660; *Iliad*, vi. 345 f.); on the contrary, the idea goes back to Zech. vi. 8 (LXX), whence the prophet had already developed vi. 1-8. As xiv. 1 f. roughly answers to vii. 9 f., so the appearance of wild beasts out of the agitated sea of the nations (in Dan. vii. 1-8) corresponds to the sequence of Apoc. vii. 1-4, and xiii. 1 f.

The earth is a rectangular plane or disc on which John looks down from heaven's dome resting on it, to observe (ver. 2) a fifth angel "ascending" from the sun-rising (the east as the source of light, *cf.* on xvi. 20, the site of paradise, the sphere of divine activity?). **ζῶντος**, here (as in xv. 7; *cf.* Heb. x. 31) in O.T. sense (*cf* Deut. xxxii. 39 f.; Ezek. xx. 33; Jer. x. 10, etc.) of vitality to succour and to punish, God's "life" being manifested in his effective preservation of the saints and chastisement of their enemies or of the world in general. He lives and keeps alive. Here, as in the parent passage, Ezek. ix. 4-6 (*cf.* Exod. xii. 13 f. and the "Egyptian" character of the plagues in chap. viii.), the true **δοῦλοι** of God are distinguished by a mark denoting God's ownership. Before the crisis good and evil must be discriminated (Spitta, 80 f.). *Cf.* Ps. Sol. xv. 6 f. on the immunity of the righteous, **ὅτι τὸ σημεῖον τοῦ θεοῦ ἐπὶ δικαίους εἰς σωτηρίαν, λιμὸς καὶ ῥομφαία καὶ θάνατος μακρὰν ἀπὸ δικαίων**; where-

[c] μήτε ἐπὶ πᾶν[1] δένδρον. 2. Καὶ εἶδον ἄλλον ἄγγελον ἀναβαίνοντα
ἀπὸ [d] ἀνατολῆς ἡλίου, ἔχοντα σφραγῖδα Θεοῦ [e] ζῶντος· καὶ ἔκραξε
φωνῇ μεγάλῃ τοῖς τέσσαρσιν ἀγγέλοις οἷς ἐδόθη [f] αὐτοῖς ἀδικῆσαι
τὴν γῆν καὶ τὴν θάλασσαν, λέγων, 3. "Μὴ [g] ἀδικήσητε τὴν γῆν
μήτε τὴν θάλασσαν, μήτε τὰ δένδρα, ἄχρι [h] σφραγίσωμεν τοὺς
[i] δούλους τοῦ Θεοῦ [i] ἡμῶν ἐπὶ τῶν [k] μετώπων αὐτῶν". 4. Καὶ
ἤκουσα τὸν ἀριθμὸν τῶν ἐσφραγισμένων· ἑκατὸν τεσσεράκοντα τέσσαρες [l] χιλιάδες, ἐσφραγισμένοι ἐκ πάσης [m] φυλῆς υἱῶν [m] Ἰσραήλ·

c *Cf.* Jos. *Bell.* iii. 7, 8 and below ix. 4.
d *Cf.* xvi. 12 and on xxi. 13: Isa. xli. 2, Ezek. xliii. 2, Bar. iv. 36, v. 5.
e En. v. 1, Jub. xxi. 4.
f *Cf.* on iii. 8.

g Aor. subj. "action not yet begun," Burton, 164. h *i.e.* the angels, as Matt. xxiv. 31. For the more common ἄχρις οὗ or ἂν *cf.* Blass, § 65, 10. i vii. 11-12, xix. 5. k Only (in N.T.) in ix. 4, xiii. 16, xiv. 1, 9, xvii. 5, xx. 4, xxii. 4. l Irreg. indep. nom. after accus., as often in Apoc., *cf.* ix. 11, ii. 18, etc. m Only here in Apoc., except xxi. 12 (also an interpolated source ?).

[1] For **παν** (ℵP, 1, etc., Ti., Bj., Sw., WH) Lach., Tr., Al. Düst., Ws. read **τι** (CQ, min., vg., Pr.) [**επι δενδρου** A, Me., Syr. Arm., Aeth. (Bs = **δενδρον** ?): conj. Naber (deleting also **μ. τα δενδρα** in ver. 3) **επι ανυδρου**].

as these plagues hunt down the wicked, **τὸ γὰρ σημεῖον τῆς ἀπωλείας ἐπὶ τοῦ μετώπου αὐτῶν.** This royal, sacred sign, which in Ezekiel is the cross or Tau as the symbol of life and is here probably ליהוה, authenticates the bearers as God's property (*cf.* Herod. ii. 113, vii. 233) and places them beyond risk of loss. It identifies them with his worship and also (*cf.* on ii. 17) serves to protect them as an amulet against harm (see Deissm. 351, 352 on **φυλακτήρια** as protective marks and amulets). In *Test. Sol.* (tr. Conybeare, *Jew. Quart. Rev.* 1898, p. 34) an evil spirit declares he will be destroyed by the Saviour "whose number (**στοιχεῖον**), if anyone shall write it on his forehead, he will defeat me". Mr. Doughty also describes (*Ar. Des.* i. 171) a false Christ in Syria who declared he had God's name sculptured between his eyebrows; *i.e.* the wrinkles resembled the Arabic hieroglyph for Allah. For the religious significance of such tattooing as a mark of divine ownership see *R. S.* 316; and, for the connection of vi. 12 f. and vii. 1 f., the basal passage in Dan. xi. 40, 44, xii. 1. The parallel device of Antichrist later on (xiii. 16, etc.) shows that this sealing is something special, baptism or the possession of the Spirit (as in Paul) as the guarantee of destined bliss. A contemporary expression of the idea occurs in Clem. Rom. lix., lx.: "We will ask that the Creator of all things preserve intact to the end the appointed number of his elect throughout all the world, etc.". As Apoc. vi. 1-8 and 12 f. are free reproductions, with a special application, of the ideas underlying Mark xiii. 7, 8, 24, 25, so Apoc. vii. 1 f. is an imaginative sketch on the lines of Mark xiii. 27. The Apocalypse, however, has no room for the false messiahs of Mark xiii. 6, 22, etc. (*cf.* on Apoc. xiii. 11 f.) as a peril. See further 4 Esd. vi. 5, "Ere they were sealed who laid up the treasure of faith," and Melito (Otto ix. 432, 476) the apologist, who preserves a dual tradition of the end, including wind as well as fire = et selecti homines occisi sunt aquilone uehementi, et relicti sunt iusti ad demonstrationem ueritatis, (whilst at the deluge of fire) seruati sunt iusti in arca lignea iussu dei. But the Apocalypse like Philo, stands severely apart from the current Stoic notion, adopted in Sib. iv. 172 f.; 2 Peter, etc., of a destruction of the world by means of a final conflagration.

Ver. 4. After a pause, in which the sealing is supposed to have taken place, the writer hears that the number of the sealed is the stereotyped 144,000, twelve thousand from each of the twelve tribes of Israel (a "thousand" being the primitive subdivision of a clan or tribe, like the English shire into "hundreds"). The enumeration of these tribes (5-8) contains two peculiarities, (*a*) the substitution of Joseph for Ephraim, a variation to which we have no clue, and (*b*) the omission of Dan. The latter reflects the growing disrepute into which Dan fell; it either stands last (*e.g.* in P.; Josh. xix. 40 f.; Jud. i. 34) or drops out entirely, while it is curiously connected in the Talmud, as already in *Test. XII. Patr.* (Dan. 5), with Beliar, and in Irenæus (v. 30, 32) as in Hippolytus (*de Antichr.* 5, 6) with the

5. ἐκ φυλῆς Ἰούδα δώδεκα χιλιάδες ἐσφραγισμένοι·
ἐκ φυλῆς Ῥουβὴν δώδεκα χιλιάδες·
ἐκ φυλῆς Γὰδ δώδεκα χιλιάδες·
6. ἐκ φυλῆς Ἀσὴρ δώδεκα χιλιάδες·
ἐκ φυλῆς Νεφθαλεὶμ δώδεκα χιλιάδες·
ἐκ φυλῆς Μανασσῆ δώδεκα χιλιάδες·
7. ἐκ φυλῆς Συμεὼν δώδεκα χιλιάδες·
ἐκ φυλῆς Λευεὶ δώδεκα χιλιάδες·
ἐκ φυλῆς Ἰσσαχὰρ δώδεκα χιλιάδες·
8. ἐκ φυλῆς Ζαβουλὼν δώδεκα χιλιάδες·
ἐκ φυλῆς Ἰωσὴφ δώδεκα χιλιάδες·
ἐκ φυλῆς Βενιαμεὶν δώδεκα χιλιάδες· ἐσφραγισμένοι.
9. ΜΕΤΑ ταῦτα εἶδον ὄχλον πολύν,[1] ὃν ἀριθμῆσαι [n] αὐτὸν οὐδεὶς
ἐδύνατο, ἐκ [o] παντὸς ἔθνους καὶ φυλῶν καὶ λαῶν καὶ [o] γλωσσῶν,
[p] ἑστῶτες ἐνώπιον τοῦ θρόνου καὶ ἐνώπιον τοῦ ἀρνίου, περιβεβλημένους στολὰς λευκάς, καὶ [q] φοίνικες ἐν ταῖς χερσὶν αὐτῶν· 10. καὶ
κράζουσιν φωνῇ μεγάλῃ λέγοντες,
"Ἡ [r] σωτηρία [s] τῷ Θεῷ ἡμῶν τῷ καθημένῳ ἐπὶ τῷ θρόνῳ καὶ [s] τῷ
ἀρνίῳ."
11. [t] Καὶ πάντες οἱ ἄγγελοι [u] εἱστήκεισαν κύκλῳ τοῦ θρόνου καὶ
τῶν πρεσβυτέρων καὶ τῶν τεσσάρων ζῴων, καὶ [v] ἔπεσαν ἐνώπιον τοῦ

n *Cf.* on iii. 8.
o *Cf.* v. 9.
p Irreg. appos. to plur. sense of ὄχλος.
q Nom. after (sc.) ἰδοὺ; *cf.* John xii. 13, Lev. xxiii. 40.
r See on xix. 1 and xii. 10.
s v. 13, xii. 10, xix. 1.
t v. 11-12.
u *Cf.* Win. § 13, 20.
v xi. 16.

[1] Read, for και ι. οχλος πολυς, the οχλον πολυν of A, vg., Me., Aeth., Cypr., Pr. (Lach.) [Syr. = κ. μ. τ. ειδον οχλυν πολυν ον, κ.τ.λ.].

origin of Antichrist. This sinister reputation (*cf. A.C.* 171-174, Selwyn 200-204, Erbes 77 f.), current long before Irenæus' day, rested on the haggadic interpretation of passages like Gen. xlix. 17; Deut. xxxiii. 22; and Jer. viii. 16. Andreas, commenting on xvi. 12, thinks that Antichrist will probably come from Persia, ἔνθα ἡ φυλὴ τοῦ Δάν.

Ver. 9. ἔθν. κ. φ. curious and irregular change from singular to plural. ἑστῶτες = erect, confident, triumphant. For the white robes, see on vi. 11 (the number of the martyrs being now completed). Certain religious processions in Asia Minor consisted of boys robed in white and bearing crowns of leafy boughs (Deissm. 368 f.); and in some Asiatic inscriptions νίκη is associated with the palm branch, which in one case is placed alongside of the *meta* or goal (*C. B. P.* ii. 496). The carrying of palm-branches was a sign of festal joy in the Greek and Roman (= victory at the games Liv. x. 47, Verg. *Aen.* v. 109), as well as in the Jewish world (1 Macc. xiii. 51; 2 Macc. x. 7), accompanied by the wearing of wreaths of green leaves. For the robes, see Liv. xxiv. 10: "Hadriae aram in coelo, speciesque hominum circum eam cum candida ueste visas esse". Here = "scilicet de antichristo triumphales" (Tertullian). For the numberless multitude, see Enoch xxxix. 6, where "the righteous and the elect shall be for ever and ever without number before" the messiah, in the mansions of bliss; white raiment and crowns of palm in Herm. *Sim.* viii. 2-4.

Ver. 10. "Salvation" (or, if ἡ be pressed, the salvation we enjoy) be ascribed "to our God and to the Lamb". The subordinate nature of the seven spirits (i. 4, iv. 5) is shown by the fact that no praise is offered to them throughout the Apocalypse, although in Iranian theology (Bund. xxx. 23): "all men become of one voice and praise aloud Aûharmazd and the archangels in the renovated universe".

Vv. 11-12. The angels standing around once again adore God, catching up the previous praise with "Amen," and uttering a sevenfold ascription of praise upon their own behalf, closed with another

θρόνου ἐπὶ τὰ πρόσωπα αὐτῶν καὶ προσεκύνησαν τῷ Θεῷ, 12. λέ- [w]
γοντες,

[w] "Ἀμήν· ἡ εὐλογία καὶ ἡ δόξα καὶ ἡ [x] σοφία καὶ ἡ εὐχαριστία
καὶ ἡ τιμὴ καὶ ἡ δύναμις καὶ ἡ [y] ἰσχὺς τῷ Θεῷ ἡμῶν εἰς τοὺς αἰῶνας
τῶν αἰώνων. ἀμήν."

13. Καὶ [z] ἀπεκρίθη εἷς ἐκ τῶν πρεσβυτέρων λέγων μοι, "Οὗτοι
οἱ περιβεβλημένοι τὰς στολὰς τὰς λευκάς, τίνες εἰσὶν καὶ πόθεν
ἦλθον;" 14. καὶ [a] εἴρηκα αὐτῷ, "Κύριέ μου, σὺ [b] οἶδας". Καὶ
εἶπέ μοι, "Οὗτοί εἰσιν οἱ ἐρχόμενοι [c] ἐκ τῆς θλίψεως τῆς μεγάλης,

w Initial Amen, xix. 4, xxii. 20.
x *Cf.* v. 12; σ. and δύναμις Job xii. 13 (*cf.* Dan. ii. 20).
y As in 1 Chron. xxix. 11.
z Constr. Matt. xi. 25, Cant. ii. 10.
a Aoristic pf., v. 7.
b Ezek. xxxvii. 3, Job xxi. 15.
c Contrast Rom. ii. 8-9, and compare Apoc. iii. 10.

"Amen". The article is repeated before each substitute, as in v. 13. The divine "wisdom" is shown in the means devised by the divine power to redeem (v. 12) and deliver (vii. 14) men, in straits where no human prudence could prevail. See Clem. Rom. lx. and Ps. Sol. xvii. 25.

Ver. 13. "And one of the elders addressed me, saying"; for similar openings of a dialogue, see Jer. i. 11, Zech. iv. 2. Perhaps, like Dante (*Parad.* iv. 10-12), John although silent showed desire painted on his face. The form of inquiry resembles Homer's **τίς πόθεν εἰς ἀνδρῶν; πόθι τοι πόλις,** or Vergil's qui genus? unde domo?, more closely still the similar sentences which recur in Hermas. See throughout, Zech. iv. 1, 6, and *Asc. Isa.* ix. 25, 26 (and I said to the angel "For whom are these robes and thrones and crowns reserved?" And he said to me: "They shall be missed by many who believe the words of him of whom I told thee [*i.e.*, Antichrist]"; also xi. 40, uos autem uigilate in sancto spiritu ut recipiatis stolam uestram et thronos et coronas gloriae in caelo iacentes). It is the origin and character, not the number, of the company which interests the prophet.

Ver. 14. **κύριέ μου** ("Sir") the respectful address of an inferior to his superior in age or station, the **πρεσβύτεροι** being conceived as angelic beings (as in Dan x. 17, 19, 4 Esd. iv. 3, etc.).—"Thou knowest" (and I fain would know also). The great distress is plainly the period of persecution and martyrdom (vi. 11) predicted (*e.g.*, Matt. xxiv. 21, from Dan xii. 1) to herald the final catastrophe. It is still expected by Hermas (*Vis.* ii. 2. 7, iv. 2. 5, 3. 6); but he less religiously attributes the white garments (*i.e.*, purity of soul) to the virtues. As the crisis with its outcome of faith and loyalty in all nations (ver. 9) is to be world-wide, this passage seems to imply, although in a characteristically vague and incidental fashion (*cf.* v. 9, xiv. 6, etc.), the idea of Mark xiii. 10. But the situation of the Apocalypse is so acute, that mission operations are at a standstill. Instead of the gospel invading and pervading the pagan world, the latter has closed in upon the churches with threatening power, and in the brief interval before the end practically nothing can be looked for except the preservation of the faithful. Those "who come out of the great distress" are further described as having washed their robes and made them white in the blood of the Lamb; which portrays their character and conduct and at the same time explains the secret of their triumphant endurance. "Mehr gedacht als geschaut ist das Bild" (J. Weiss). The great thing is not to emerge from trial, but to emerge from it with unstained faith and conscience. And this is possible, not to man's unaided efforts, but to the sacrificial power of Christ, the experience of which forms the last line of defence in the struggle. The confessors and martyrs owed their moral purity to what they obtained through the sacrifice of Jesus. But moral purity became in this case something more intense (as the context and the emphatic language of this verse imply) than the normal Christian experience of forgiveness and holiness. By a turn of thought which is developed later by Ignatius and Tertullian (*Scorp.* xii. sordes quidem baptismate abluuntur, maculae uero martyrio candidantur), it is suggested that in their martyrdom (*cf.* Dan. xii. 10) these saints were able to make the redeeming power of Jesus peculiarly their own; the nature of their cruel sufferings identified them especially with their Lord. It is noticeable that the mystic union of the individual Christian with Christ mainly comes for-

καὶ ἔπλυναν τὰς στολὰς αὐτῶν καὶ ἐλεύκαναν αὐτὰς ἐν τῷ αἵματι τοῦ ἀρνίου.
15. [d] διὰ τοῦτό εἰσιν ἐνώπιον τοῦ θρόνου τοῦ Θεοῦ,
καὶ λατρεύουσιν αὐτῷ ἡμέρας καὶ νυκτὸς ἐν τῷ ναῷ αὐτοῦ·
καὶ ὁ καθήμενος ἐπὶ τοῦ θρόνου [f] σκηνώσει ἐπ' αὐτούς.
16. οὐ πεινάσουσιν ἔτι, οὐδὲ διψήσουσιν ἔτι,
[g] οὐδὲ μὴ πέσῃ ἐπ' αὐτοὺς ὁ ἥλιος, οὐδὲ πᾶν [h] καῦμα·
17. ὅτι τὸ ἀρνίον τὸ ἀνὰ μέσον [1] τοῦ θρόνου [i] ποιμανεῖ αὐτούς,
καὶ [g] ὁδηγήσει αὐτοὺς ἐπὶ [k] ζωῆς πηγὰς [k] ὑδάτων,

d Reward and glory (*e.g.* Jer. xxxi. 9-12); Levitic privilege (Deut. x. 8, etc., *cf.* Ps. Sol. ii. 40). e xi. 19, xxii. 3 (worship). f Divine favour and protection, Ps. Sol. vii. 1, 5; *cf.* xxi. 3, John i. 14, also Lev. xxvi. 11, Isa. iv. 5, Ezek. xxxvii. 27, etc. g Ps. cxxi. 6; from Isa. xlix. 10. h xvi. 9. i Ezek. xxxiv. 23, Ps. xxiii. 1, John x. 1 f.; not Death, Clem. Rom. li. k xxi. 6, xxii. 1, 17, John iv. 10, vii. 8 (Jer. ii. 13), Cant. iv. 15.

[1] **ανα μεσον,** the true reading, is not a subtle allusion to mediatorship (Abbott, 198-199) but a loose synonym for **εν μεσω** (*cf.* Weymouth, *Journ. Philol.*, 1869, ii. 318-322): the **ζωσας** of min., Me., Syr. (**ζωην και επι** S.) is a correction of the orig. gen. of quality **ζωης** (MSS., edd.), which is thrown to the front (like **σαρκος** in 1 Pet. iii. 21) for emphasis.

ward in the Apocalypse (*cf.* xiv. 13) when the martyrs and confessors are mentioned, as if the writer held that such an experience alone could yield the deepest consciousness of communion with One who was conceived essentially as *a Lamb who had been slain*, *a faithful witness*, etc. (*cf.* Titius, 216, 217). On the high respect for martyrs, of which this forms an early trace, see Weinel, 142-144. At the same time it is to *the blood of the Lamb*, not to their own blood, that they owe their bliss and triumph; redemption, not martyrdom, is the essential basis of their deliverance. People might be redeemed without becoming martyrs; as, for example, either recreant Christians or those who happened to die a natural death. But no one could be a martyr without having the strength of redemption behind him.

Ver. 15. Ritual as well as pastoral traits from the O.T. fill out the conception of this final bliss with its favoured position (**ἐνώπ. θρόν.**). Note the singular tenderness of the oxymoron—*he that sitteth on the throne* (the majestic almighty God) *shall overshadow them* with a presence of brooding, intimate, care; followed by **ποιμανεῖ** here (as opposed to ii. 27) in its literal sense of tender shepherding on the part of Jesus. The messiah as shepherd was an ancient and familiar conception. This verse is partly adapted from Enoch xlv. 4-6. Unlike John i. 14, it reflects a Christian fulfilment of the Jewish anticipation (*cf.* xiii. 6, xxi. 3; Zech. ii. 10 f.; Sir. xxiv. 8 f.) that the Shekinah would return in the era of final bliss.

Ver. 16. **οὐ μή** with both fut. indicative and subjunctive (=ii. 11), in emphatic assertions. For the absence of scorching as a trait of the Hellenic Utopia, *cf.* Dieterich, 31-33. If **καῦμα** corresponds here to the sense of the Isaianic equivalent **καύσων,** the reference is to the scorching sirocco. So the Egyptian dead yearned for a cooling breeze in the next world—"Let me be placed by the edge of the water with my face to the north, that the breeze may caress me, and my heart be refreshed from its sorrows" (see Maspero, *Dawn of Civil.* p. 113).

Ver. 17. **ζωῆς** goes with **ὑδάτων** ("living waters") though prefixed for emphasis, like **σαρκὸς** in 1 Peter iii. 21 (*cf.* xvi. 3 **πᾶσα ψυχὴ ζωῆς**); a favourite Johannine idea. In Enoch xlii, xlviii, the fountains contain wisdom which is drunk by all the thirsty, though in the centre there is also "a fountain of righteousness which was inexhaustible"; elsewhere in the division of Sheol assigned to the spirits of the righteous there is "a bright spring of the water of life" (xxii, 9) in accordance with the Pythagorean belief that the dead suffered from thirst in the underworld (Luke xvi. 24, *cf.* Dieterich, 97 f.). In the familiar vignette of ancient Egyptian eschatology, the deceased kneels before Osiris who pours out to him the water of life (the motto being *that the soul may live*); *cf.* Renouf's "Hibb. Lect.," p. 141, and for "living" waters as divine, *R. S.* 127. In the ideal

καὶ [l]ἐξαλείψει ὁ Θεὸς πᾶν [m]δάκρυον ἐκ τῶν ὀφθαλμῶν αὐτῶν."

VIII. 1. ΚΑΙ ὅταν [a]ἤνοιξε τὴν σφραγῖδα τὴν ἑβδόμην, ἐγένετο
[b]σιγὴ ἐν τῷ οὐρανῷ ὡς ἡμιώρον. 2. Καὶ εἶδον τοὺς [c]ἑπτὰ ἀγγέ-

l Isa. xxv. 8.
m Form (*cf.* xxi. 4) of nom. peculiar to Apoc. in N.T.
a ὅταν irreg. equiv. for ὅτε (Blass, § 65, 9): indic. with ὅταν (iv. 9, Mark ii. 20, Luke xiii. 28); a relative clause conditional in form but definite in force (Burton, 316).
b 4 Esd. vii. 29 f., Zech. ii. 13 (17), Hab. ii. 20.
c En. xx., Luke i. 19, etc.

realm of the good Shepherd-King Yima, Iranian belief saw neither hunger nor thirst for the faithful, and found no place for death (*cf.* Apoc. xxi. 4) or falsehood (Apoc. xxi. 8) of any kind (passages and parallels in Böklen, 133 f.).—**ὁδηγήσει,** a touch of local colour for Asiatic Christians, since sheep and shepherds were a common feature in the Lycos valley (*C. B. P.* i. 40-42); but the heaven of the Apocalypse is, in Semitic fashion, pastoral or civic, with touches of Babylonian splendour, unlike some later apocalypses, *e.g.*, that of Peter (15 f.) where the Hellenic conception of God's garden in the next world predominates (Dieterich, 19 f.).—Briggs explains the variants **σκηνώσει ἐπ' αὐτούς** (vii. 15) and **σκ. μετ' αὐτῶν** (xxi. 3), **ἀπὸ τῶν ὀφθ.** (xxi. 4) and **ἐκ τῶν ὀφθ.** (vii. 17) as variant translations of בקרבם ישכן and מעיניהם; but, like **ἐπὶ τὸ μέτωπον** (xiii. 16), **ἐπὶ τῶν μετώπ.** (vii. 3, etc.), these are probably nothing more than rhetorical variations. Unlike the synoptic tradition (*e.g.*, Matt. ii. 6) and the fourth Gospel (x. 1, 18), the Apocalypse confines Christ's shepherding to the future life (see also ii. 26, 27). In Isa. liii. 6, 7, the wayward roving habits of sheep express the temper of God's people, whilst the patient submissiveness of a lamb for sacrifice denotes the function of God's servant; in the Apocalypse, the latter (not the former) occurs. The saints are God's flock in heaven, not on earth (contrast 1 Peter ii. 25, v. 2 f.).

Whatever elements have been employed in the following series (viii.-xi.) of trumpet-visions, no adequate data exist to prove that John has edited a Jewish or Jewish-Christian source here any more than in vi. The vision, which forms the result of the breaking of the seventh seal (viii. 1, 2), opens, after a prelude (2-5), in viii. 6 and does not close till xi. 19 (*cf.* viii. 5).

CHAPTER VIII.—Ver. 1. The opening of the seventh seal is followed by half an hour's silence in heaven: "he opened" looks back to vi. 12, the absence of subject showing that vii. is a parenthesis foreign to the seal-series in its original shape. Probably this series, like each of the others, was originally a separate oracle upon the latter days. When woven by the author into his large work, they suffered a literary treatment which has interrupted but not altogether obliterated their original form and sequence. The book of destiny is now open; what follows (viii. 6 f.) is the course of the future, which naturally corresponds at some points to the predictions already sketched proleptically in chap. vi. A brief interval, not of exhaustion but of expectation, of breathless suspense (a pause in the ecstasy, LXX of Dan. iv. 16), ushers in a preliminary series of judicial plagues heralded by seven trumpet-blasts (viii. 2-xi. 19). Half an hour (**ἡμ.**, *cf.* Win. § 5, 22 *a* for form) may have been an ominous period; Josephus (*B. J.* vi. 5, § 3) describes a portent at the siege of Jerusalem which consisted of a bright light shining at twilight for half an hour, and the collocation of silence with reverence is illustrated by the LXX version (**εὐλαβείσθω πᾶσα σάρξ**) of Zech. xii. 13 and Zeph. i. 7 f. The following trumpet-series has been woven into the frame of the work by the device of making it take the place of the climax which (after vi. 17, vii. 1, 2) one would naturally expect to occur at this point. When the dénouement should take place, nothing happens; the judgment is adjourned.

Ver. 2. "The seven angels who stand before God" are introduced as familiar figures (*cf.* Lueken 36 f., *R. J.* 319 f.); they belonged to pre-Christian Judaism (Tobit xii. 15, "I am Raphael, one of the seven holy angels, which present the prayers of the saints, and go in before the glory of the Holy One"), and are associated with trumpets (1 Thess. iv. 16). According to the Targ. on 2 Chron. xxxiii. 13 when Manasseh prayed, all the angels who superintend the entrance of prayers went and closed every approach, to prevent his petition reaching heaven; in Chag. 13 *b* the prayers of the righteous are offered by Sandalphon (*cf.* Longfellow's *Sandalphon*, and contrast Heb. vii. 25).

λους οἱ ἐνώπιον τοῦ Θεοῦ ἑστήκασι, καὶ ἐδόθησαν αὐτοῖς ἑπτὰ
[d] σάλπιγγες. 3. καὶ [e] ἄλλος ἄγγελος ἦλθε καὶ ἐστάθη [f] ἐπὶ τοῦ
θυσιαστηρίου, ἔχων λιβανωτὸν [g] χρυσοῦν· καὶ ἐδόθη αὐτῷ θυμιάματα πολλά, ἵνα δώσει [1] [h] ταῖς προσευχαῖς τῶν ἁγίων [i] πάντων ἐπὶ τὸ
[k] θυσιαστήριον τὸ χρυσοῦν τὸ ἐνώπιον τοῦ [l] θρόνου. 4. καὶ ἀνέβη ὁ
καπνὸς τῶν θυμιαμάτων [h] ταῖς προσευχαῖς τῶν ἁγίων ἐκ χειρὸς τοῦ
ἀγγέλου ἐνώπιον τοῦ Θεοῦ. 5. καὶ [m] εἴληφεν ὁ ἄγγελος τὸν λιβα-

d 1 Thess. iv. 16, 1 Cor. xv. 52, Matt. xxiv. 31, 4 Esd. v. 4, vi. 23; cf. Josh. vi. 4, Jer. iv. 19, Zeph i. 15-16.
e As vii. 2.
f iii. 20, vii. 1, etc. (= "at altar of burnt offering") Amos ix. 1.
g 1 Kings vii. 50.
h Dat. commodi? cf. Moult. i. 75. = "in aid of".
i Cf. Win. § 20, 11 f.
k Num. iv. 11, inner altar of incense.
l I. e. God (ix. 13).
m Aoristic pf., v. 7.

[1] The variants **δωση** and **δω** are corrections of the original **δωσει** (ℵAC, 1, edd.) —**ινα** with fut. indic. as iii. 9, etc. (Win. § 5, 17, § 13, 7, § 14, 9).

This septet of distinguished angels belongs to the circle of ideas behind i. 4, iv. 5, v. 6; but the author as usual prefers vividness and variety to homogeneity. He uses them for minatory purposes, assigning to "another angel" their characteristic function (ver. 3) in Jewish tradition. The alteration of figure at this point is deliberate. The certainty of divine decrees is suggested by the figure of seals; but now that the prophet is describing the promulgation of the actual events presaged in the book of Doom, he, like the author of 4 Esdras (? *cf.* Lat. of v. 4), employs the figure of angels with trumpets of hostile summons and shattering alarm. The final series (xv.-xvi.) in which these decrees are executed, is aptly described under the figure of bowls or vials drenching the earth with their bitter contents (*cf.* Bovon, *Nouv. Test. Théol.* ii. 503). The trumpet, as a signal for war, is naturally associated with scenes of judgment (reff.). "*Power*, whether spiritual or physical, is the meaning of the trumpet, and so, well used by Handel in his approaches to the Deity" (E. Fitzgerald's *Letters*, i. 92). Trumpet to lip, the angels now stand ready. They are set in motion by a significant interlude (3-5).

Ver. 3. Between royalty and ritual the scenery of the Apocalypse fluctuates. It is assumed (as at vi. 9), after vii. 15 perhaps, that heaven is a temple, although this is not expressly stated till xi. 19; nor is it homogeneous with the throne-description in chap. iv. **λιβανωτόν** ("incense," **ἅπ. λεγ.** N.T.) is used by mistake for the classical **λιβανωτρίν** (LXX, **πυρ[ε]ιον** or **θυίσκη**) = "censer," as already in an inscription of the second century B.C. (Dittenberger's *Sylloge Inscript. Graec.* 588 [156]) **λιβανωτίς** is employed by confusion for "frankincense". Golden censers (1 Macc. i. 22) and golden bowls (**φιάλαι**) were among the furniture of the temple (1 Esd. ii. 13). On prayers as an offering, see Acts x. 4. The symbolism is borrowed from the temple-ritual; when the saucer of incense had been emptied over the burning coals placed on the altar of incense, the people bowed in prayer, as the fragrant cloud of smoke rose up. Wellhausen's deletion of 3 *b*, 4 as a gloss is therefore unnecessary. John is consoling the church (*cf.* on vi. 10) by the assurance that their prayers for the coming of the kingdom are not breathed in vain.

Ver. 4. As an agent of God, the angel is commissioned to ratify with Divine approval the petitions of the saints for the end; this involves retribution on the impenitent and hostile world. The prophet is sure such aspirations are in harmony with God's will.

Ver. 5. The censer, having offered incense to heaven, is now used to hurl fire upon the earth (adopted from Ezek. x. 2-7; *cf.* Lev. xvi. 12). As at the close of the trumpets (xi. 19) and the bowls (xvi. 18), physical disturbances here accompany the manifestation of God's wrath and judgment. In answer to the prayers and longings of the saints (Renan, 393), God at last visits the impenitent pagan world with a series of catastrophes (viii., ix., *cf.* ix. 4), which herald the end and also give (though in vain, ix. 20, 21) an opportunity for repentance.

Note on viii. 3-5. This episode (in dumb show) of angel and incense, though apparently isolated, is an overture for the seri s of judgments, of which the successive trumpet-blasts are precursors. The prayers of all the saints, which, like those of the martyrs in vi. 10, crave punishment upon God's enemies through-

νωτὸν καὶ ἐγέμισεν αὐτὸν ἐκ τοῦ πυρὸς τοῦ θυσιαστηρίου καὶ ἔβαλεν [n] εἰς τὴν [n] γῆν· καὶ [o] ἐγένοντο βρονταὶ[1] καὶ φωναὶ καὶ ἀστραπαὶ καὶ σεισμός.

6. Καὶ οἱ ἑπτὰ ἄγγελοι ἔχοντες τὰς [p] ἑπτὰ σάλπιγγας ἡτοίμασαν

n vi. 13.
o Exod. xix. 16, Ezek. x. 2.
p Seven trumpets in Levitical orchestra, Neh. xii. 41, etc.

[1] **βρονται και αστραπαι και φωναι** A, 16, 38, Me., Syr. (Lach., WH marg., Al., Ws.), text ℵQ, min., vg., Arm., S., And[c], Pr., etc. (Ti., Tr., WH, Bj., Sw., Bs.).

out the earth, are supported and reinforced by the ministry of this angel, and answered at once by the succession of incidents beginning with ver. 5. This object of Christian prayers, *i.e.*, the final crisis, when Christ returns to crush his enemies and inaugurate his reign, pervaded early Christianity as a whole. At special periods of intolerable persecution, it assumed under the stress of antagonism as here a more sensuous and plastic form than the ordinary consciousness of the church would have been usually disposed to cherish; yet the common prayer of the church in any case was for the speedy end of the world (**ἐλθέτω χάρις καὶ παρελθέτω ὁ κόσμος οὗτος**, Did. x.). In Apoc. Mos. (tr. Conybeare, *Jewish Quart. Rev.*, 1895, 216-235) xxxiii., when the angels intercede for Adam at his ascension to heaven, they take golden censers and offer incense; whereupon smoke overshadows the very firmament. The intercession of angels on behalf of the saints, a result of their function as guardians, goes back to post-exilic Judaism with its inarticulated conception of the angels as helpful to mankind (Job v. 1. xxxiii. 23; Zech. i. 12); subsequently the idea developed into a belief that the prayers of the pious won special efficacy as they were presented to God by angels such as Gabriel, Raphael, Michael, or the seven archangels (*cf.* Tobit, *loc. cit.*; Slav. En. vii. 5; En. ix. 2-11, xv. 2, xl. 6, xlvii. 2, xcix. 3, 16, civ. 1). In Christianity this rôle was naturally absorbed by Christ, who alone ratified and inspired his people's supplications. But the old belief evidently lingered in pious circles of Jewish Christianity (*cf.* Test. Lev. 3, 5), side by side with a complete acceptance of Christ's heavenly function. The latter did not immediately or universally wither up such survivals of the older faith; popular religion tended then as now to be wider at several points than its theoretical principles (as in Origen, *Cels.* v. 4; and Tertull. *de Orat.* xii.). Plato, in *Sympos.* 202 E., makes the **δαίμονες** present men's prayers and offerings to the gods, and mediate the latter's commands and recompence to men (*cf.* Philo, *de Somniis*, i. 22, and on i. 1). See further xvii. 1, xxi. 9, for a similar state of matters in primitive Christianity with regard to the corresponding function of Jewish angels as intermediaries of revelation.

Ver. 6 f. The fresh series of disasters does not advance matters any further than the previous seal-series. Both lead up to the final catastrophe, and upon the edge of it melt into a further development which practically goes over the same ground once more. This reflects of course literary artifice, not any successive or continuous scheme of events; it is iterative not historically chronological. It is doubtful if the prophet intended to suggest the idea which occurs to a modern mind, *viz.*, that such apparent cycles seem to recur in history. At certain epochs everything seems to be working up to some mighty climax for which men look in dread or hope, and yet the world rights itself for another epoch; the dénouement fades for the time being into the far horizon; the powers of evil gather themselves afresh in other forms. Neither here nor in the previous seven cycles can the astrological reference (to the colours and characteristics of the planets, cp. *Exp. Ti.* xx. 426-427) be worked out with any plausibility.

Vv. 6-12. *The first four trumpets.*

Ver. 6. In the scheme of the trumpet-visions, as of the seal-visions, the first four are differentiated from the next three; the fifth and sixth in both cases stand by themselves and are separated by a considerable interlude from the closing seventh. It is remarkable that even the final trumpet of xi. 15 f. does not correspond to the loud trumpet-blast which according to Jewish and early Christian tradition, was to awaken the dead to resurrection or to rally the saints (Matt. xxiv. 31) at the close of the world. The Apocalypse knows nothing of this fea-

αὐτοὺς ἵνα σαλπίσωσι. 7. Καὶ ὁ πρῶτος ἐσάλπισεν, καὶ
ἐγένετο [q] χάλαζα καὶ [q] πῦρ μεμιγμένα ἐν [r] αἵματι, καὶ ἐβλήθη εἰς
τὴν γῆν· καὶ τὸ τρίτον τῆς γῆς κατεκάη, καὶ τὸ [s] τρίτον τῶν [t] δένδρων κατεκάη, καὶ πᾶς χόρτος χλωρὸς κατεκάη. 8. Καὶ ὁ
δεύτερος ἄγγελος ἐσάλπισεν, [u] καὶ ὡς ὄρος μέγα πυρὶ καιόμενον
ἐβλήθη εἰς τὴν θάλασσαν· καὶ ἐγένετο τὸ τρίτον τῆς θαλάσσης
[v] αἷμα, 9. καὶ ἀπέθανε τὸ τρίτον τῶν κτισμάτων τῶν ἐν τῇ θαλάσσῃ, τὰ [w] ἔχοντα ψυχάς, καὶ τὸ τρίτον τῶν [x] πλοίων [y] διεφθάρησαν.

q xi. 19, xvi. 21 only, in N.T. See Ovid's *Met.* xv. 788, Exod. ix. 24, Isa. xxviii. 2, Ps. xviii. 12.
r *Cf.* Dan. v. 7, LXX.
s Ezek. xxxviii. 22, Joel ii. 30 (iii. 3).
t 4 Esd. v. 8, Isa. ii. 13. u En. xviii. 13 f., xxi. 3, cviii. 4, from Jer. ii. 25? v Exod. vii. 20-21. w False apposition (ii. 20, etc.) or ptc. used (Weiss) as a relative clause. x Isa. ii. 16. y Irreg. as ix. 12, 18.

ture, nor of the tradition (preserved by R. Akiba) that the process of the resurrection would be accompanied by seven trumpet-peals from God. The first four trumpets set in motion forces of ruin that fall on natural objects; in Sap. v. 17-23 (xvi. 17-24) the world of nature is used directly by God to punish men. The closing three concern human life, *i.e.*, the godless inhabitants of the earth. The general idea is that of the Jewish tradition (see on xv. 2) which prefaced the second great redemption by disasters analogous to those preceding the first: *cf. e.g.*, Sohar *Exod.* 4 *b*, tempore quo se reuelabit rex Messias, faciet Deus omnia ista miracula, prodigia et divinae uirtutis opera coram Israele, quae fecit olim in Aegypto, quemadmodum scriptum est Mic. vii. 15; also Jalkut *Sim.* i. 56 *b*, Targ. Jon. on Zech. x. 11, etc. The disasters remind one now and then of the Egyptian plagues (*cf.* Jos. *Ant.* ii. 14-1; also Amos iv. 4 f., Isa. ix. 7 f.). The first four visit earth, sea, waters, and the sky. Hail-showers were a traditional scourge and weapon of the divine armoury; on their association with thunderstorms see G. A. Smith's *Hist. Geog.* 64, 65.

Ver. 7. Hail and fire, as in the fourth Egyptian plague, but with the added O.T. horror (see reff.) of a shower of blood instead of rain (see Chag. 12 *b*, where the sixth heaven is the storehouse of hail, storm, and noxious vapours, enclosed within gates of fire; and specially Sibyll. v. 377, **πῦρ γὰρ ἀπ' οὐρανῶν . . . βρέξει . . . πῦρ καὶ αἷμα**). For similar atmospheric phenomena, see on vi. 8, 12. Portents of this abnormal nature are recorded for the seventh decade of the first century by Roman historians, but there is no need to see specific historical allusions in prophecy upon this grand scale. The sight of atmospheric fire always signified to the ancients the approach of various disasters, especially when stars fell. Wetstein cites *Bara Mezia*, 59, 1; dixit R. Eliezer, percussus est mundus, tertia nempe pars olearum, tertia pars tritici, et tertia hordei. The third is a primitive Semitic (Babylonian: Jastrow, 107 f.) division, which has its roots also in Iranian religion (Yasht, xiii. 3, Yasna, xi. 7, etc.), where the tripartite division of earth, derived originally from the threefold division of earth, atmosphere, and universe, is older than the sevenfold.—**δένδρων**, see Schol. (**τὰ δένδρα δηλονότι**) on Thuc. ii. 19 **καθεζόμενοι ἔτεμνον . . . τὸ πεδίον.** Pausan. ii. 365 (*cf.* iv. 166 f.) mentions among the phenomena attending earthquakes heavy rain or prolonged drought, the discolouring of the sun's disc, etc.; "springs mostly dry up. Sudden gusts sometimes sweep over the country, blowing the trees down. At times, too, the sky is shot with sheets of flame. Stars are seen of an aspect never known before, and strike consternation into all beholders."

Vv. 8, 9. A fiery mass, huge as a mountain, is flung into the sea—a description which would recall the fiery volcanic bombs familiar to inhabitants of the Egean. The catastrophe includes, as in the first Egyptian plague, the turning of water into blood and the destruction of marine animals (4 Esd. v. 7, Verg. *Georg.* iii. 541 f.), besides havoc among the shipping. Volcanic phenomena (*cf.* Introd. § 8) in the Egean archipelago (*e.g.*, at Thera) are in the background of this description, and of others throughout the book; features such as the disturbance of islands and the mainland, showers of stones, earthquakes, the sun obscured by a black mist of ashes, and the moon reddened by volcanic dust, were the natural consequences of eruption in some submarine volcano, and Thera—adjoining

10. Καὶ ὁ τρίτος ἄγγελος ἐσάλπισεν, [a]καὶ ἔπεσεν ἐκ
τοῦ οὐρανοῦ ἀστὴρ μέγας καιόμενος ὡς λαμπάς, καὶ ἔπεσεν ἐπὶ τὸ
τρίτον τῶν ποταμῶν καὶ ἐπὶ τὰς [a]πηγὰς τῶν ὑδάτων. 11. καὶ τὸ
ὄνομα τοῦ ἀστέρος λέγεται ὁ [b]Ἄψινθος· καὶ [c]ἐγένετο τὸ τρίτον τῶν
ὑδάτων [c]εἰς ἄψινθον, καὶ πολλοὶ τῶν ἀνθρώπων ἀπέθανον ἐκ τῶν
ὑδάτων, ὅτι ἐπικράνθησαν. 12. [d]Καὶ ὁ τέταρτος ἄγγελος
ἐσάλπισεν, καὶ [e]ἐπλήγη τὸ τρίτον τοῦ ἡλίου καὶ τὸ τρίτον τῆς
σελήνης καὶ τὸ τρίτον τῶν ἀστέρων, ἵνα σκοτισθῇ τὸ τρίτον αὐτῶν,
καὶ ἡ ἡμέρα μὴ [f]φάνῃ τὸ τρίτον αὐτῆς, καὶ ἡ νὺξ ὁμοίως.
13. Καὶ εἶδον, καὶ ἤκουσα ἑνὸς ἀετοῦ [1] πετομένου ἐν [g]μεσουρανήματι,
λέγοντος φωνῇ μεγάλῃ, [h]"Οὐαί, οὐαί, οὐαὶ [i]τοὺς κατοικοῦντας ἐπὶ
τῆς γῆς, [k]ἐκ τῶν λοιπῶν φωνῶν τῆς σάλπιγγος τῶν τριῶν ἀγγέλων
τῶν μελλόντων σαλπίζειν".

a *Cf.* Sib. Or. v. 158-xvi. 4, *cf.* Ps. Sol. xvii. 21, Test. Levi. 4.
b Jer. ix. 15, xxiii. 15.
c Luke xiii. 19, *cf.* Win. § 29, 2*a*.
d Exod. x. 21-22; *cf.* on vi. 12, with 4 Esd. v. 4.
e ἅπ. λεγ. N.T.
f *Cf.* xviii. 23, Win. § 13, 12.
g xiv. 6, xix. 17: ἅπ. λεγ. N.T.

h Imitated in 4 Esd. xv. 14-15. i xii. 12. k *Cf.* ver. 11; = ἀπό Matt. xviii. 7.

[1] The curious and inferior variant **αγγελου** (P, 1, etc., Arm., Vict., And., Vitringa; *unus ut aquilam*, Pr.) probably arose from a copyist's recollection of xiv. 6. Könnecke (*Emendationen zu Stellen N.T.*, 34-35) prefers the complete (so 13) reading **αγγελου ως αετου**.

Patmos—was in a state of more or less severe eruption during the first century. All this suggested the hideous colours in which the final catastrophe was painted by the imagination of pious contemporaries. In the eruption of 1573, the sea round Thera was tinted for twenty miles round, and even when the submarine volcano is quiescent, "the sea in the immediate vicinity of the cone is of a brilliant orange colour, from the action of oxide of iron". In 1707 a large rock suddenly appeared in the sea, during the eruption, and owing to noxious vapours "all fish in the harbour died".

Vv. 10, 11. The third part of all drinking waters is poisoned by a huge, noxious, torch-like meteor shooting down from the sky (Vergil's "de coelo lapsa per umbras stella facem ducens multa cum luce concurrit," Aen. ii. 693, 694). Wormwood, a bitter drug typical of divine punishment, was apparently supposed to be a mortal poison; thus Pliny (*H. N.* ii. 232) ascribes the bitterness of Lake Sannaus (Anava) in the Lycos valley to the *circa nascente apsinthio.* But this feature of the vision is taken from Iranian or Mandaean eschatology (Brandt, 584 f.), where among the signs of the end are famine, wars, a star falling from heaven and making the sea red [*cf.* Apoc. xvi. 3], and a cyclone with a dust-storm. *Cf.* 4 Esd. v. 9, et in dulcibus aquis salae inueniuntur. Rivers and fountains were associated in the ethnic mind (*cf.* Neh. ii. 13) with supernatural spirits and curative properties; hence upon them this stern prophet of monotheism sees the doom of God falling. **ἐγένετο . . . εἰς**, a Hebraistic constr., common in Apocalypse and in quotations from O.T., but "decidedly rare elsewhere" in N.T. (Simcox). Springs (like those, *e.g.*, near Smyrna) and fountains naturally appeared to the ancient mind somewhat mysterious and separate; their lack of visible connexion with rivers or lakes suggested the idea that they sprang from the subterranean abyss or that they were connected with daemons. Hence their rôle in the final convulsions of nature (4 Esd. vi. 24 uenae fontium stabunt, Ass. Mos. x. 8 et fontes aquarum deficient). *Cf.* Rohrbach's *Im Lande Jahwehs und Jesu* (1901), 30 f.; for their connexion with dragons, *R. S.*, 157, 161 f., and for their bubbling as a mark of sacred energy, *ibid.* 154 f.

Ver. 12. "So as to darken a third part of them, and (*i.e.*) to prevent a third of the day from shining (**φάνῃ**, or **φανῇ**, Win.) and of the night likewise". Daylight is shortened by a third, and the brightness of an Eastern night correspondingly lessened (*cf.* the Egyptian plague of darkness). The writer either forgets or ignores the fact that he has already cleared the heaven of stars (vi. 13).

Ver. 13. An ominous introduction to the last three trumpets. An eagle, here as in Apoc. Bar. lxxvii. 17-22, lxxxvii. 1 (*cf.*

a viii. 10, xii. 9, Isa. xiv. 12, Luke x. 18.
b xi. 7, xvii. 8, xx. 1, 3, En. x., Luke viii. 31, *cf.* Gen. xxix. 2.
c Gen. xix. 28, Exod. xix. 18, Joel ii. 2, 10.
d xvi. 10.
Only here in N.T. in literal sense.
in final clause.

IX. 1. ΚΑΙ ὁ πέμπτος ἄγγελος ἐσάλπισεν, καὶ εἶδον [a] ἀστέρα ἐκ
τοῦ οὐρανοῦ [a] πεπτωκότα εἰς τὴν γῆν, καὶ ἐδόθη αὐτῷ ἡ κλεὶς τοῦ
[b] φρέατος τῆς ἀβύσσου, 2. καὶ ἤνοιξε τὸ φρέαρ τῆς ἀβύσσου, καὶ
ἀνέβη [c] καπνὸς ἐκ τοῦ φρέατος ὡς καπνὸς καμίνου μεγάλης, καὶ
[d] ἐσκοτώθη ὁ ἥλιος καὶ ὁ ἀὴρ ἐκ τοῦ καπνοῦ τοῦ φρέατος. 3. [e] Καὶ
ἐκ τοῦ καπνοῦ ἐξῆλθον ἀκρίδες εἰς τὴν γῆν, καὶ ἐδόθη αὐτοῖς ἐξουσία, ὡς ἔχουσιν ἐξουσίαν οἱ σκορπίοι τῆς γῆς· 4. καὶ ἐρρέθη
αὐτοῖς ἵνα μὴ ἀδικήσουσιν τὸν χόρτον τῆς γῆς, [f] οὐδὲ [f] πᾶν χλωρὸν,
οὐδὲ πᾶν δένδρον, εἰ μὴ τοὺς ἀνθρώπους [g] οἵτινες οὐκ [h] ἔχουσι τὴν

e *Cf.* Schol. on Arist. *Acharn.* 150. f Hebraistic = οὐδέν; οὐδέ synt. irreg- g i. 7. h vii. 4-8.

Rest of Words of *Bar.* vii.) a messenger and herald of catastrophe (its associations are punitive and bodeful, Deut. xxviii. 49, Hos. viii. 1, Hab. i. 8, Eurip. *Rhes.* 528-536) flies in the zenith, *i.e.*, swooping exactly over the heads of men. For the eagle (Simurgh in Zoroastrianism) as the servant of Deity in ancient (Syrian) mythology, see *E. Bi.* "Cherub," § 8, and *Acts of Thomas* (Hymn of Soul, 51).—"Woe . . . for the rest of the trumpet voices." The first woe finishes at ix. 12, the second (after the interlude of x. 1-xi. 13) at xi. 14, the third apparrently at xii. 12—though as usual one series of phenomena melts irregularly at the close into another.

CHAPTER IX.—Vv. 1-12: *The fifth trumpet.*

Ver. 1. Stars (as σώματα ἐπουράνια) drop from heaven in the form of beasts (Enoch lxxxvi. 1 f.) and men (*ibid.* lxxxviii.) throughout Jewish apocalyptic (*cf. ibid.* xviii. 16, xxi. 1, 6, xc. 21, 24); even earlier (Judges v. 20, Job xxxviii. 7) they had been personified. On falling stars, associated as evil portents with death or divine displeasure, see Frazer's *Golden Bough* (2nd ed.), ii. 18 f. From what follows, it is possible that this angelic being who had fallen is conceived as an evil agent (reff.), permitted (ἐδόθη) to exercise malicious power on earth in furtherance of divine judgment. "The pit of the abyss" is the abode of the devil and daemons (reff. *cf. Aen.* vii. 583 f., viii. 243 f.), a subterranean chasm or waste underworld, located sometimes in the middle of the earth (Slav. En. xxviii. 3), and represented here (*cf.* xx. 1) as covered by a lid or great stone. To judge from xiii. 1, this abyss seems to contain, as in O.T., the flow of waters formerly upon the earth, and now confined (according to Jewish folk-lore) by God's decree and the magical potency of His name (*cf.* on xx. 4 and ii. 17 also *Prayer of Manasseh*, "O Lord Almighty . . . Who hast shut up the deep, τὴν ἄβυσσον and sealed it by thy terrible and glorious name".) A fearsome cavity ("ditis spiraculum") emitting poisonous exhalations once existed near Hierapolis (Pliny, *H. N.* ii. 95). Such chasms (throughout Italy, Greece and Asia) seemed, to the superstitious, local inlets into Hades and outlets for infernal air in the shape of mephitic vapours. In Phrygia itself springs of hot vapour and smoke are a feature of the Lycos valley (*C. B. P.* i. 2, 3), and the volcanic cone in the harbour of Thera was believed to be such an aperture of hell. Fire belching from this subterranean furnace was a sure portent of the final catastrophe (4 Esd. v. 8); *cf.* Renan, 330 f., 396, *R. S.* 127, and Jeremias, 116 f.

Ver. 2. For the following description of this destructive horde of weird locusts, see Joel ii. with Driver's notes and excursus (*C. B.*) to which add the famous description of a locust-plague in Newman's *Callista* (ch. xv.). Naturally the sketch is far more idealised than that given by Joel; it often recalls the monstrous associates created by Tiamât out of the primeval abyss (Jastrow, pp. 419 f.); *i.e.*, strong warriors, "great serpents, merciless in attack, sharp of tooth. With poison instead of blood she filled their bodies. Furious vipers she clothed with terror, made them high of stature."

Vv. 3, 4. The dense smoke resolves itself into a swarm of infernal demons in the form of locusts but rendered more formidable by their additional power of stinging like scorpions. Instead of preying on their natural food (Exod. x. 15), already plagued (viii. 7) they are let loose upon men unmarked by the Divine

σφραγῖδα τοῦ ᵍ Θεοῦ ἐπὶ τῶν μετώπων. 5. καὶ ἐδόθη αὐτοῖς[1] ἵνα
μὴ ἀποκτείνωσιν αὐτούς, ἀλλ' ἵνα βασανισθήσονται ⁱ μῆνας ⁱ πέντε·
καὶ ὁ βασανισμὸς αὐτῶν ὡς βασανισμὸς σκορπίου, ὅταν παίσῃ
ἄνθρωπον.
6. καὶ ἐν ταῖς ἡμέραις ἐκείναις ᵏ ζητήσουσιν οἱ ἄνθρωποι τὸν
θάνατον,
ˡ καὶ οὐ μὴ εὕρωσιν[2] αὐτόν·
καὶ ᵏ ἐπιθυμήσουσιν ἀποθανεῖν,
καὶ φεύγει ὁ θάνατος ἀπ' αὐτῶν.
7. Καὶ τὰ ὁμοιώματα τῶν ἀκρίδων ὅμοια ᵐ ἵπποις ἡτοιμασμένοις
εἰς ⁿ πόλεμον,

i Full season locusts' activity, April to August.
k Progressive fut. Burton, 60. Contrast Phil. i. 23.
l Job iii. 21 Jer. viii. 3 see Anacr. *fr.* 51, Soph. *El.* 1007-1008 Ovid: *Ibis* 123-124, Aesch. *fr.* 314, *cf.* Sib. Or. viii. 353, Herod. vii. 46, and Eur. *Hipp.* 1047.
m Joel ii. 4.
n xii. 17

[1] Read αυτοις (ℵA, 1, Pr.) as in vv. 3 and 4 (ℵQ), with Ti., Ws., Bs., Bj. (Lach. WH marg., Sw., ver. 5).

[2] Read ου μη (ℵAPQ, 1, etc., And., Areth.) ευρωσιν (AP, min., etc.) with Lach., Düst., WH marg., Ws., Bs., Bj. [ευρησουσιν ℵQ, min., vg., And^pal, Areth., Ti., Tr. Al. Sw., WH].

seal (though the expected blast of winds is dropped), the idea being similar to that reproduced in Ps. Sol. xiii. 1-3, 4, 5, xv. 1, 9 (see above, on vii. 3). The nations under command of Holofernes (Jud. ii. 20) are also likened by the Jewish romancer to a swarm of innumerable locusts; and from the mouth of the beast in Hermas issue ἀκρίδες πύριναι to persecute the virgin church. Josephus, too, compares the army of Simeon to locusts (*B. J.* iv. 9 7). Why are trees (vii. 1) exempted? For the reason suggested in Ps. Sol. xi. 6, 7?

Ver. 5. παίσῃ here, like ἐπάταξεν Jas. iv. 7, represents LXX, tr. of נכה in sense of reptile's bite; the scorpion with its long-fanged tail stings the prey which it has already gripped with its claws (*cf.* Sen. *Hercul.* 1218). Scorpions were a natural symbol for vicious and dangerous opponents (*cf.* Ezek. ii. 6, Luke x. 9), whose attacks were always painful and might be mortal. "The sting is not perilous. . . . The wounded part throbs with numbness and aching till the third day, there is not much swelling" (Doughty, *Ar. Des.* i. 328). But the effects were not always so mild (Arist. *H. N.* ix. 29).

Ver. 6. The withholding of death, instead of being an alleviation, is really a refinement of torture; so infernal is the pain, that the sufferers crave, but crave in vain, for death (Sibyll. iii. 208: καὶ καλέσουσι καλὸν τὸ θανεῖν καὶ φεύξετ' ἀπ' αὐτῶν). It is singular that suicide is never contemplated, although it was widely prevalent at this period in certain circles of the Empire (see Merivale's *Romans under the Empire*, ch. lxiv; Lecky's *Europ. Morals*, i. 212 f.). For its un-Jewish character see Jos. *Bell.* iii. 8. 5.

Ver. 7. Arabian poets compare locusts in head to the horse, in breast to the lion, in feet to the camel, in body to the snake, in antennæ to a girl's long, waving hair. The resemblance of the head in locusts and in horses has been often noticed (*Cavalleta, Italian*), and their hard scales resemble plates of equine armour. The rest of the description is partly fanciful ("crowns gleaming like gold," human faces; yet *cf.* Pl. *H. N.* vi. 28, Arabes mitrati degunt, aut intonsa crine), partly (vv. 8-9) true to nature (woman's hair [*i.e.*, abundant and flowing, a well-known trait of the Parthians and Persians], and lion-like teeth, scaly plates on the thorax, and rustling or whirring noises), partly (ver. 10) recapitulatory (=ver. 5; note ὁμοίας σκορπίοις, an abbreviated comparison like Homer's κόμαι Χαρίτεσσιν ὁμοῖαι), partly (ver. 11) imaginative (*cf.* Prov. xxx. 27). The leader of these demons is the angel of the inferno from which they issue. His name is Abaddon (*cf.* *Exp. Times*, xx. 234 f.), a Heb. equivalent for שאול personified like death and Hades. The final syllable of the name is taken to represent as in Greek, a personal ending. Hence the LXX rendering ἀπώλεια pro-

καὶ ἐπὶ τὰς κεφαλὰς αὐτῶν ὡς στέφανοι ὅμοιοι χρυσῷ,
καὶ τὰ πρόσωπα αὐτῶν ὡς πρόσωπα ἀνθρώπων·
8. καὶ [o] εἶχαν τρίχας ὡς τρίχας γυναικῶν·
καὶ οἱ [p] ὀδόντες αὐτῶν ὡς λεόντων ἦσαν·
9. καὶ εἶχον θώρακας ὡς θώρακας σιδηροῦς·
καὶ ἡ [q] φωνὴ τῶν πτερύγων αὐτῶν ὡς φωνὴ ἁρμάτων [1] πολλῶν
τρεχόντων εἰς πόλεμον.

10. καὶ ἔχουσιν [r] οὐρὰς [s] ὁμοίας [2] σκορπίοις καὶ κέντρα, καὶ ἐν
ταῖς οὐραῖς αὐτῶν ἡ ἐξουσία αὐτῶν ἀδικῆσαι τοὺς ἀνθρώπους μῆνας
πέντε. 11. ἔχουσιν ἐπ᾽ αὐτῶν [t] βασιλέα τὸν ἄγγελον τῆς ἀβύσ-
σου· ὄνομα αὐτῷ Ἑβραϊστὶ [u] "Ἀβαδδών," καὶ ἐν τῇ [v] Ἑλληνικῇ
ὄνομα ἔχει [w] "Ἀπολλύων".
12. [x] Ἡ οὐαὶ ἡ μία ἀπῆλθεν·
ἰδοὺ [y] ἔρχεται ἔτι δύο οὐαὶ μετὰ ταῦτα.
13. Καὶ ὁ ἕκτος ἄγγελος ἐσάλπισεν· καὶ ἤκουσα φωνὴν [z] μίαν ἐκ
τῶν κεράτων τοῦ [a] θυσιαστηρίου τοῦ [a] χρυσοῦ τοῦ ἐνώπιον τοῦ [b] Θεοῦ,
14. λέγοντα τῷ ἕκτῳ ἀγγέλῳ ὁ ἔχων τὴν σάλπιγγα, "Λῦσον τοὺς
τέσσαρας ἀγγέλους τοὺς δεδεμένους [c] ἐπὶ τῷ ποταμῷ τῷ μεγάλῳ
[d] Εὐφράτῃ". 15. Καὶ ἐλύθησαν οἱ τέσσαρες ἄγγελοι οἱ [e] ἡτοιμα-

o For form, *cf.* x. 9, xi. 12. Abbott (90) compares the feminine garb of the fanatics in Jerusalem (Jos. *Bell.* iv. 9, 10).
p Joel i. 6, Sir. xxi. 2, xxxix. 30.
q Jer. xlvii. 3, Joel ii. 5.
r Ver. 19, xii. 4: ἅπ. λεγ. N.T.
s Constr. xiii. 11, Matt. v. 20.
t *Cf.* Job xviii. 14.
u Job xxvi. 6, xxviii. 22.
v ἅπ. λεγ. N.T.
w Constr. Blass, § 33, 1, Win. § 29, 1*b*.
x *Cf.* xi. 14, rare and irreg. Win. § 28, 2*d*.
y *Cf.* Ezek. vii. 25-26: irreg. due to Heb. fem. = Gk. neut.? Vit. ii. 98 f.
z = indef. art. viii. 13, Dan. viii. 13.
a Exod. xxx. 1-10 1 Kings ix. 23, Ezek. xli. 22.
b *i.e.*, θρόνου (viii. 3).
c "At," or "beside," John iv. 6.
d xvi. 12.
e Providential sense, xii. 6, *cf.* Dan. vii. 12.

[1] After **αρματων** om. **ιππων** (so Sah., Bousset, Baljon, Könnecke p. 35) as a gloss introduced by a copyist to smooth out the sense of the O.T. citation.

[2] **ομοιας** PQ, min., And., Areth., vg. (edd.) [**ομοιοις** ℵA, 14 (Tr., WH marg.)] prim. corrupt. of **ομοια** as adverb, like **ομοιον = οιον** i. 13, xiv. 14 (WH)?

bably suggested the synonym **Ἀπολλύων**, containing a (sarcastic?) gibe at Apollo with whom the locust was associated ("uelut proprium nomen Caesaribus," Suet. *Oct.* 29); *cf.* Schol. on Aesch. *Agam.* 1085 and Plato's *Cratylus*, 404, 405. Both Caligula and Nero aped the deity of Apollo, among their other follies of this kind, as Antiochus Epiphanes had already done.

Ver. 12. A parenthetical remark of the author. **ἔρχεται** with plur. subj. following is not an irregularity due to Greek neut. as equiv. to Heb. fem. (Viteau, ii. 98-100), but an instance of the so-called "Pindaric" anacoluthon (*cf.* Moult. i. 58).

Vv. 13-21. *The sixth trumpet blast.*

Ver. 13. The golden altar of incense stands before God, as in the original tabernacle and temple; the specially solemn invocation of the angel shows that the Parthian-like invasion constitutes the climax of this series of disasters. **φωνήν**, as i. 10, x. 4, etc., the "bath qol" (Gfrörer, i. 253 f., Dalman, viii. 1).

Ver. 14. The sixth angel takes part in the action. The Euphrates had been the ideal Eastern boundary of Israel's territory: it now formed the frontier between Rome and her dreaded neighbour, the Parthian Empire (Philo, *leg. ad C.* § ii.; Verg. *Georg.* i. 509; Tac. *Hist.* iv. 51).

Ver. 15. This quartette of angels (= complete ruin, Zech. i. 18 f.) has been kept in readiness, or reserved for this occasion, though they are not to be connected (as by Spitta) with the four moments of time—*hour*, *day*, *month*, and *year*. Like the use of **δεῖ**, **μέλλει**, and **ἐδόθη**, this touch of predestined action brings out the strong providential belief running through the Apocalypse. On the rôle of destructive angels in Jewish eschatology *cf.* Charles on Slav. En. x. 3 and for the astrological basis (En. lxxxi. 10 f.) of this tradition see Fries in *Jahrb*

σμένοι εἰς [f] τὴν ὥραν καὶ ἡμέραν καὶ μῆνα καὶ ἐνιαυτόν, [g] ἵνα
ἀποκτείνωσι τὸ [h] τρίτον τῶν ἀνθρώπων. 16. καὶ ὁ ἀριθμὸς τῶν
στρατευμάτων τοῦ [i] ἱππικοῦ δισμυριάδες μυριάδων· ἤκουσα τὸν
ἀριθμὸν αὐτῶν. 17. Καὶ [k] οὕτως εἶδον τοὺς ἵππους ἐν τῇ [l] ὁράσει,
καὶ τοὺς καθημένους ἐπ᾽ αὐτῶν, ἔχοντας θώρακας [l] πυρίνους καὶ
[m] ὑακινθίνους καὶ [l] θειώδεις· καὶ αἱ κεφαλαὶ τῶν ἵππων ὡς κεφαλαὶ
[n] λεόντων, καὶ ἐκ τῶν στομάτων αὐτῶν [o] ἐκπορεύεται πῦρ καὶ καπνὸς

f Constr. i. 9, v. 12, xiv. 6, article grouping several substantives.
g With ἐλυθ. rather than ἡτ. despite viii. 6.
h Zech. xiii. 9, Sib. Or. iii. 544, v. 103.
i Only here in N.T.
k *i.e.*, "As is now to be described".
l Diff. sense in iv. 2. Only in Acts ii. 17 (O.T. quot.), elsewhere in N.T.
m Nah. ii. 3: on the curious variant *spineas* (= ἀκανθίνους) Pr. see Nestle's *Einführ.* 264.
n 1 Chron. xii. 8.
o (Constr. as in 1 Tim. vi. 4, Jas. iii. 10), *cf.* xi. 5, Job xli. 19-21, Joel ii. 3.

f. d. klass. Alterth. (1902) 705 f. Probably the author means that the angels set in motion the hordes of cavalry (two hundred million) described in the semi-mythical, semi-historical pageant of the next passage. But he does not directly connect the two, and it is evident that here as at vii. 1 f., we have "dream-like inconsequences" (Simcox), or else two fragments of apocalyptic tradition, originally heterogeneous, which are pieced together (at ver. 16). The four angels here do not correspond in function or locality to the four unfettered angels of vii. 1; they rather represent some variation of that archaic tradition in which four angels (perhaps angel-princes of the pagan hordes) were represented as bound (like winds?) at the Euphrates—a geographical touch due to the history of contemporary warfare, in which the Parthians played a rôle similar to that of the Huns, the Vikings, or the Moors in later ages. Since the first century B.C. a Parthian invasion of some kind had formed part of the apocalyptic apparatus so that there is no particular need to allegorise the Euphrates into the Tiber or to find the four angels in Ps. lxxviii. 49 (LXX). The bloody and disastrous Parthian campaign of 58-62 (*cf.* on vi. 2) may account for the heightened colour of the scene, whether the fragment was composed at that period, or (as is most probable) written with it in retrospect. But the entire vision is one powerful imaginative development of a tradition preserved in a Syriac Apocalypse of Ezra (published by Baethgen) which may be based on old Jewish materials: "and a voice was heard, Let those four kings be loosed, who are bound at the great river Euphrates, who are to destroy a third part of men. And they were loosed, and there was a mighty uproar." Could this be reckoned as proof of an independent tradition it would help to illumine the application of the idea in John's Apocalypse, especially if one could accept with Köhler the attractive conjecture of Iselin that **ἀγγέλους** represents a confusion (or variety of reading, *cf.* 2 Sam. xi. 1, 1 Chron. xx. 1) between מלאכים (=ἀγγ.) and מלכים in a Hebrew original of Apoc. ix. 15 (*Zeits. aus der Schweis*, 1887, 64). The conjecture (Spitta, de Faye, J. Weiss) **ἀγέλαι** (=hosts, as in 2 Macc. iii. 18, etc.) is less likely, and **ἐπὶ** cannot be taken with **λῦσον** (Bruston). Cavalry formed a standing feature of the final terror for the Jewish imagination ever since the Parthians loomed on the political horizon (Ass. Mos. iii. 1). The whole passage was one of those denounced by the Alogi as fantastic and ridiculous (*cf.* Epiph. *Haer.* li. 34). Gaius also criticised it as inconsistent with Matt. xxiv. 7.

Ver. 16. The second woe is an irruption of fiendish cavalry.

Ver. 17. Here only the writer refers to his "vision". **ἔχοντας** (horse and rider regarded as one figure: in the Persian heavy cavalry horses as well as men were clad in bright plate) **κ.τ.λ.,** "they wore coats of mail, the colour of fire and jacinth and brimstone," *i.e.*, gleaming red, dark blue, and yellow, unless **ὑακ.** (a favourite Oriental military colour) is meant to denote the colour of dull smoke. Plutarch, in his life of Sulla, describes the Medes and Scythians with their **πυροειδῆ καὶ φοβερὰν ὄψιν** (*cf.* Sir. xviii. 9).—**πῦρ, κ.τ.λ.,** like Job's leviathan, Ovid's bulls (Metam. vii. 104), or Diomede's horses (Lucret. v. 29, *cf. Aen.* vii. 281). They are also as destructive as Joel's locusts. The description is a blend of observation and fantastic popular beliefs. Brimstone was a traditional trait of divine wrath among people who "associated the ozonic smell which often so perceptibly accompanies lightning

p Plur. vb. with sing. noun (in collective sense); *cf.* on viii. 9.
q xiv. 10, xix. 20, xxi. 8.
r *Cf.* above on ver. 10.
s Sir. xxv. 15.
t xvi. 11, 21.
u Deut. iv. 28, Mic. v. 13, Ps. cxxxiv. 15, Isa. ii. 8, 20: = "idols". Philo. *vit. contempl.* § 1.

καὶ θεῖον. 18. ἀπὸ τῶν τριῶν πληγῶν τούτων [p] ἀπεκτάνθησαν τὸ τρίτον τῶν ἀνθρώπων, ἐκ τοῦ [q] πυρὸς καὶ τοῦ καπνοῦ καὶ τοῦ [q] θείου τοῦ ἐκπορευομένου ἐκ τῶν στομάτων αὐτῶν. 19. ἡ γὰρ ἐξουσία τῶν ἵππων ἐν τῷ στόματι αὐτῶν ἐστιν καὶ ἐν ταῖς οὐραῖς αὐτῶν· αἱ γὰρ οὐραὶ αὐτῶν [r] ὅμοιαι ὄφεσιν, ἔχουσαι [s] κεφαλάς, καὶ ἐν αὐταῖς ἀδικοῦσι. 20. Καὶ οἱ λοιποὶ τῶν ἀνθρώπων οἳ οὐκ ἀπεκτάνθησαν ἐν ταῖς πληγαῖς ταύταις, [t] οὐ [1] [t] μετενόησαν ἐκ τῶν [u] ἔργων τῶν [u] χειρῶν αὐτῶν, [v] ἵνα [v] μὴ προσκυνήσουσι τὰ δαιμόνια καὶ τὰ εἴδωλα [w] τὰ χρυσᾶ καὶ τὰ ἀργυρᾶ καὶ τὰ χαλκᾶ καὶ τὰ λίθινα καὶ τὰ [w] ξύλινα, [w] ἃ οὔτε βλέπειν δύνανται οὔτε ἀκούειν οὔτε [w] περιπατεῖν· 21. [x] καὶ

v Constr. iii. 9, Matt. xxi. 32, etc.; ἵνα μὴ of conceived result. w From Dan. v. 4, 23, also from Ps. cxv. 4-7, etc., En. xcix. 7. x *Cf.* xxii. 15, Apoc. Pet. 25, Ezek. xliii. 9.

[1] For (before μετεν.) ουτε (AP, 1, 36, etc., Bg., Lach.) read ου C, min., And[c, pal], Areth., WH, Bs., Bj. [ουδε ℵQ, 14, 38, 92, vg., Copt., Pesh., Syr., Cyp., Pr., etc., Ti., Al. Sw., Ws.].

discharges with the presence of sulphur" (*E. Bi.* 611). The symbolism is coloured by actual Parthian invasions (*cf.* vi. 1 f.) and by passages like Sap. xi. 18 where God punishes men by sending "unknown, newly-created wild beasts full of rage, breathing out a fiery blast or snorting out noisome smoke or flashing dread sparkles from their eyes." Mr. Bent recalls the curious superstition of the modern Therans, who during the eruptions of last century saw "in the pillars of smoke issuing from their volcano, giants and horsemen and terrible beasts".

Ver. 19. Heads attached to their serpentine tails are an allusion not only to the well-known tactics of the Parthians (*cf. Parad. Regained*, iii. 323 f.) but to a trait of ancient Greek mythology; on the altar of Zeus at Pergamos (*cf.* note on ii. 12) the giants who war against the gods are equipped with snakes (instead of limbs) that brandish open jaws. The amphisbaena of ancient mythology was often described as possessing a headed tail ("tanquam parum esset uno ore fundi uenena," Pliny: *H. N.* viii. 35).

Vv. 20, 21. The impenitence of the surviving two-thirds of men, who persist in worshipping daemons and idols (Weinel, 3, 4). Hellenic superstition (Plut. *de defectu orac.* 14) attributed to malignant daemons these very plagues of pestilence, war, and famine. Plutarch is always protesting against the excessive deference paid to such powers, and on the other hand against the rationalists and Christians who abjured them entirely. **δαιμ.**, either the gods of paganism (LXX) or the evil spirits of contemporary superstition. In Enoch xix. 1, the spirits of the fallen angels "assuming many forms defile men and shall lead them astray to offer sacrifices to demons as to gods"; *cf.* xlvi. 7 (of the kings and rulers) "their power rests on their riches, and their faith is in the gods which they have made with their hands". (See Clem. *Strom.* vi. 5. 39, 40)—**ἀργυρᾶ**, contracted form, as in 2 Tim. ii. 20 (Helbing, pp. 34 f.).—**φαρμ.**, here in special sense of magic spells inciting to illicit lust (Artemid. v. 73), a prevalent Asiatic vice (*cf.* Greg. Naz. *Orat.* iv. 31). But in the imprecatory (*c.* 100 B.C.) inscription of Rheneia (Dittenberger, *Syll. Inscript. Graec.*[2] pp. 676 f.), punishment is invoked from **τὸν κύριον τῶν πνευμάτων** (*cf.* Apoc. xxii. 6) upon **τοὺς δόλωι φονεύσαντας ἢ φαρμακεύσαντας** the hapless girl. The three vices of the decalogue occur here (as in Matt.) in the Hebrew order, not in that of the LXX (Rom. xiii. 9; Mark x. 19; Luke xviii. 20). *Cf.* on xxi. 8, and, for the connexion of polytheism and vice, Harnack's *Mission and Exp. of Christianity*, i. (1908), pp. 290 f. Repentance here (as in xvi. 9. 11) is primarily a change of religion, but the prophet has evidently little hope of the pagan world. There is no polemic against the Egyptian worship of animals, and, in spite of the Jewish outlook upon the *dolores Messiae*, the Apocalypse ignores family disturbances and false messiahs as harbingers of the end.—Once more (*cf.* vii. 1 f.) between the sixth (ix. 13-21) and the seventh (xi. 15-19) members of the series,

οὐ μετενόησαν ἐκ τῶν [x] φόνων αὐτῶν οὔτε ἐκ τῶν [y] φαρμακειῶν αὐτῶν
οὔτε ἐκ τῆς πορνείας αὐτῶν οὔτε ἐκ τῶν [z] κλεμμάτων αὐτῶν.

X. 1. ΚΑΙ εἶδον ἄλλον ἄγγελον ἰσχυρὸν καταβαίνοντα ἐκ τοῦ
οὐρανοῦ, [a] περιβεβλημένον [a] νεφέλην, καὶ ἡ [b] ἶρις ἐπὶ τὴν κεφαλὴν
αὐτοῦ καὶ τὸ [c] πρόσωπον αὐτοῦ ὡς ὁ ἥλιος, καὶ οἱ [d] πόδες αὐτοῦ ὡς
στύλοι πυρός· 2. καὶ [e] ἔχων ἐν τῇ χειρὶ αὐτοῦ [f] βιβλαρίδιον ἠνεῳγ-
μένον· καὶ [g] ἔθηκε τὸν πόδα αὐτοῦ τὸν δεξιὸν ἐπὶ τῆς θαλάσσης, τὸν
δὲ εὐώνυμον ἐπὶ τῆς γῆς, 3. καὶ ἔκραξε φωνῇ μεγάλῃ ὥσπερ [h] λέων
[i] μυκᾶται· καὶ ὅτε ἔκραξεν, ἐλάλησαν αἱ ἑπτὰ βρονταὶ τὰς ἑαυτῶν

y *Cf.* xvii. 2 with xviii. 2, 23, En. xcv. 4, also Isa. xlvii. 9 f., Mal. iii. 5, 2 Kings ix. 22.
z ἅπ. λεγ. N.T.
a i. 7, xiv. 14, from Dan. vii. 13: = "cloud-wrapt" (like Horace's *Augur Apollo*). b iv. 3. c i. 16, *cf.* Matt. xvii. 2. d i. 15, *cf.* Exod. xiv. 19 (LXX). e As if ἄλλος ἄγγ. had preceded (ver. 1). f Corrupt form of class. dimin. βιβλιδάριον. g Sap. xviii. 16. h Am. i. 2, iii. 4, 8, Hos. xi. 10, etc. i ἅπ. λεγ. N.T.; of thunder Aesch. *Prom.* 1062, Arist. *Clouds*, 292.

a passage (this time of some length) is intercalated (x. 1-xi. 13), in which the personality of the seer now re-emerges (on earth, instead of in heaven). The object of x. 1-11 is to mark at once a change of literary method and a transition from one topic to another. The passage, which certainly comes from the prophet's own pen (so Sabatier, Schön, and others), looks backward and forward. Now that the preliminaries are over, all is ready for the introduction of the two protagonists (xi.-xiii.) whose conflict forms the closing act of the world's history (xv. 1-xx. 10). One of these is Jesus, the divine messiah, who has hitherto (v.-ix.) been depicted as the medium of revelation. Since his rôle is now to be more active, the prophet expressly alters the literary setting of his visions. The subsequent oracles are not represented as the contents of the book of Doom (which is now open, with the breaking of its last seal). Dropping that figure (contrast v. 2 and x. 1) the writer describes himself absorbing another roll of prophecy received from an angel. Evidently he intends to mark a new departure, and to introduce what follows as a fresh start. This new procedure is accompanied by an explicit assurance—intended to whet the reader's interest—that the Apocalypse has now reached the verge of the final catastrophe; the prophet apparently makes this eagerness to reach the goal the reason for omitting a seven-thunders vision (or source) which otherwise he might have been expected to include either at this point or subsequently. It is quite in keeping with the wider outlook and rather more historical atmosphere of xi. f., that a freer and less numerical method pervades these oracles. In short, x. 1-11 is a digression only in form. It serves to introduce not simply the Jewish fragment (xi. 1-13)—whose strange contents probably required some express ratification—but the rest of the oracles (xiii. f.), which are thus awkwardly but definitely connected with the foregoing design (through the closing trumpet-vision: x. 7 = xi. 15 f.).

CHAPTER X.—Ver. 1. **ἄλλον,** referring to v. 2, where another strong angel was mentioned, also in connexion with a book. The position of the seer is implied (since viii. 2?) to be no longer in heaven (*cf.* verses 4 and 8), but on earth, as the gigantic angel of light descends to him. The face and feet are described in stereotyped fashion. In Ezekiel's description of God (i. 28) the appearance of a rainbow surrounds the divine throne, as an element of the theophany in nature. Here also it is an æsthetic detail. Suetonius describes (*Vit. Aug.* 95) Augustus seeing suddenly "in a clear and bright sky a circle like a rainbow in heaven, surrounding the sun's disc".

Ver. 2. "And in his (left? *cf.* ver. 5) hand a small booklet open" (in contrast to the larger closed book of v. 1), after Ezek. ii. 9. This colossal figure, like an Arabian jin, bestrides earth and sea. His message is for the broad world.

Ver. 3. **ὥσπερ λέων** (of God in O.T. reff.; of the messiah 4 Esd. xi. 37, xii. 31) **μυκᾶται** Theokr. *Id.* xxvi. 21, **μύκημα λεαίνης,** properly of cattle = "to bellow". **ἐλάλησαν κ.τ.λ.** = "uttered what they had to say" (*i.e.*, spoke articulately). **αἱ** (the well-known or familiar) **βρονταί** "of the apocalyptic machinery" (Alford), **or** a popular piece of apocalyptic prophecy (see below). *Cf.* **the sevenfold voice of**

φωνάς· 4 καὶ ὅτε ἐλάλησαν αἱ ἑπτὰ βρονταὶ ἤμελλον[1] γράφειν·
καὶ ἤκουσα [k] φωνὴν ἐκ τοῦ οὐρανοῦ, λέγουσαν [l] Σφράγισον ἃ ἐλάλησαν αἱ ἑπτὰ βρονταί, καὶ μὴ αὐτὰ γράψῃς. 5. Καὶ ὁ ἄγγελος, ὃν
εἶδον ἑστῶτα ἐπὶ τῆς θαλάσσης καὶ ἐπὶ τῆς γῆς, [m] ἦρε τὴν χεῖρα
αὐτοῦ τὴν δεξιὰν εἰς τὸν οὐρανόν, 6. καὶ [n] ὤμοσεν [n] ἐν τῷ ζῶντι εἰς
τοὺς αἰῶνας τῶν αἰώνων, [o] ὃς ἔκτισε τὸν οὐρανὸν καὶ τὰ ἐν αὐτῷ καὶ
τὴν γῆν καὶ τὰ ἐν αὐτῇ καὶ τὴν θάλασσαν καὶ τὰ ἐν αὐτῇ, "Ὅτι
[p] χρόνος οὐκέτι ἔσται· 7. ἀλλ᾽ ἐν ταῖς ἡμέραις τῆς φωνῆς τοῦ ἑβδό-

k i. 10 f., 19 xiv. 13, etc.
l Dan. viii. 26, xii. 4, *cf.* Apoc. Bar. xx. 3.
m Gen. xiv. 19, 22, Deut. xxxii. 40, Ezek. xx. 5. (Hebraic) Matt. v. 34, 36, xxiii. 16, 18, 20-22.
o Neb. ix. 6, Ps. cxlv. (cxlvi.) 6.
p = respite, ii. 21, Jos. *Bell.* iv. 3, 10, *cf.* Ezek. xii. 23-24.

[1] The double augment of ημελλον (ACQ, min., so Lach., Tr., WH, Ws., Swete) is better attested here than in iii. 2, *cf.* Helbing 71-72.

the Lord in thunder, Ps. xxix. The seven thunders here may be conceived loosely as the echoes of the angel's voice reverberating through the universe (Spitta, Weiss), thunder, throughout the ancient world, being especially venerated as a divine voice or warning.

Ver. 4. To seal or shut up a vision is to keep it secret from mankind, *i.e.*, in the present case (by a sequence of thought which is scarcely logical) to leave it unwritten. In a similar passage (Apoc. Bar. xx. 3) "seal" means to lay up fast in one's memory (because the realisation is not immediate); but this meaning is suggested by the context, although it might suit the present passage. The seer describes himself as prohibited by a heavenly voice (which reverence leaves as usual undefined, 4 Esd. vi. 17: Dalman viii. 1) from obeying his impulse. No reason is assigned; but the plain sense of the passage is that the author wishes (Weizs., Schön, Bs., Holtzm., Pfleid.) to justify his omission of a seven-thunder source or set of visions circulating in contemporary circles of prophecy (x. 7). In view of the authoritative character of such fragments or traditions John justifies his procedure by the explanation that he felt inspired to do so, and also to substitute other oracles. Thus in the middle, as at the opening and end of his book, he reiterates his prophetic authority. The episode may further indicate that the written contents of the Apocalypse represents merely a part of the author's actual vision (*cf.* John xxi. 25), or it may serve to heighten the effect of what is now to be introduced, or it may suggest that while the seer is to write (i. 11), he is to write only what is revealed through the medium of angels. In Slav. En. xxiii. 3, 6 the seer spends thirty days in writing the remarks of his angel-instructor. To hear ἄρρητα ῥήματα, ἃ οὐκ ἐξὸν ἀνθρώπῳ λαλῆσαι was not incompatible, however, with an ἀποκάλυψις κυρίου (2 Cor. xii. 1-4), *cf.* Weinel, 162 f. There was an inspiration of restraint as well as an inspiration of impulse. Thus Hermas (*Vis.* i. 3) listens with wonder to glories of God which he could not remember, "for all the words were awful, such as man cannot bear. The last words, however, I did remember; they were fit for us and mild". Possibly the seven-thunders source was of a severely punitive character (viii. 5), traversing ground which had been already (vi.-ix.) and was to be again (xv.-xvi.) covered.

Vv. 5-6. Modelling from Dan. xii. 7, the writer describes the angel's oath (by the *living* God as usual in O.T.; *cf.* Matt. xxvi. 63), with its native gesture (*cf.* Trumbull's *Threshold-Covenant*, 78 f.) and contents. In the ancient world oaths were usually taken in the open-air (Usener, *Götternamen*, 181), before the all-seeing deities of the upper light. But here, as at iv. 17 and xiv. 7, the eschatological and the creative acts of God (the latter an outcome of His living might, as Sir. xviii. 1, En. v. 1, Acts xiv. 15, etc.) are deliberately conjoined; God's activity in creation and providence would culminate in judgment. "There shall be no further delay," or time lost. The interval of vi. 11 (Dan. xii. 7) is over: all is ripe now for the end, ἡ συντέλεια καιροῦ. The parallels in Slav. En. xxxiii. 2, lxv. 7, upon the abolition of seasons and periods of time are merely verbal. What engages the writer here is the usual point of importance in apocalyptic literature, *viz.*, "Is it long to the end? Is the future longer than the past" (4 Esd. iv. 44-50)?

Ver. 7. Vav consec. with the Heb.

μου ἀγγέλου, ὅταν μέλλῃ σαλπίζειν, καὶ [q] ἐτελέσθη τὸ μυστήριον
τοῦ Θεοῦ, [r] ὡς [s] εὐηγγέλισεν τοὺς ἑαυτοῦ δούλους τοὺς προφήτας".
8. Καὶ ἡ φωνὴ ἣν ἤκουσα ἐκ τοῦ οὐρανοῦ, πάλιν λαλοῦσαν
μετ' ἐμοῦ καὶ λέγουσαν, "[t] Ὕπαγε [u] λάβε τὸ βιβλίον[1] τὸ [v] ἠνεῳγμένον ἐν τῇ χειρὶ τοῦ ἀγγέλου τοῦ ἑστῶτος ἐπὶ τῆς θαλάσσης καὶ
ἐπὶ τῆς γῆς". 9. Καὶ [w] ἀπῆλθα πρὸς τὸν ἄγγελον, λέγων αὐτῷ

q xv. 1, John xix. 30. r Zech. i. 6, Amos iii. 7, Dan. ix. 6, 10, etc., *cf.* Acts iii. 21. Favourite thought of sub-primitive Christianity, Col. i. 26 = Eph. iii. 1-12 = 1 Pet. i. 10-12 = Rom. xvi. 25. s *Cf.* Gal. iii. 8. εὐαγ. as act. vb. only here and xiv. 6 (ἐπὶ accus.) in N.T.: late Greek usage. t xvi. 1. u v. 7: like ἀνάβα (iv. 2) an Attic form. v Double augment, Blass, § 15, 7; Win. § 12, 7. w *Cf.* ix. 8, xi. 12, for form.

[1] For **βιβλιδαριον** (Q, etc., And[a, c], Areth.) or **βιβλαριδιον** (אP, 1, etc., Al., Ti., Bs., Bj.) read **βιβλιον** AC, 6, 14 (Lach., Tr., WH, Sw., Ws.). The two former readings are corrections.

pf. (LXX = **καὶ** and fut. indic.) here by an awkward solecism (*cf.* on iii. 20) = "Then is (*i.e.*, shall be) finished the secret of God." The final consummation (inaugurated by the advent of messiah, xii.) is to take place not later than the period of the seventh angel's trumpet-blast, which *ex hypothesi* is imminent. The **μυστήριον** is plainly, as the context implies, full of solace and relief to God's people. —**εὐηγγ.** The total (exc. xiv. 6) omission of **εὐαγγέλιον** and the restricted use of its verb in the Apocalypse may have been due to the fact that such terms had been soiled by ignoble usage in the local Ionian cult of **εὐάγγελος** (*e.g.*, at Ephesus), with its oracular revelations and fellowship of *Euangelidae*. The Asiatic calendar of Smyrna contained a month called **εὐαγγέλιος**.—The connexion between **μυστήριον** = "secret purpose or counsel" (as here) and **μ.** = "symbol, or symbolic representation" (i. 20, xvii. 7) is due to the fact that in the primitive world the former was enigmatically conveyed by means of symbolic-representations in word, picture, or deed. As "every written word was once a **μυστήριον**," it was natural that the word used for the sign came to be employed for the thing signified (Hatch, *Essays in Bibl. Greek*, 61). The near approach of the end had been for years a matter of confidence and joy to the Christian prophets—for it is they and not their predecessors who are specially in view. The special and solemn contribution of John's Apocalypse is to identify certain events in the immediate future with the throes out of which the final bliss was to be born. These throes include the downfall of the dragon from heaven, the subsequent climax of the Beast's influence on earth, and the assertion of God's authority over his own and against his foe's adherents (xii.-xiv. 20). The great and glad revelation is God seen in action, with his forces deployed for the final campaign which, with its issues of deliverance and triumph (xv.-xxii.), forms the climax of this book. The apotheosis of the Cæsars in their life-time—above all, of Domitian—marked the pitch of human depravity; divine intervention was inevitable.

Up to the end of ch. ix., the Apocalypse is fairly regular and intelligible; thereafter, criticism enters upon an intricate country, of which hardly any survey has yet succeeded in rendering a satisfactory account. The problem begins with ch. x. Although vv. 1-7 complete the preceding oracles by introducing their finale (7 = xi. 14 f.), while 8-11 connect more immediately with ch. xi., this forms no reason for suspecting that the oracle is composite. Spitta takes 1*a*, 2*b*-7 (except 4) as the continuation of ix., followed by xi. 15, 19, while the rest is substantially a prelude to xi. 1-13; Briggs similarly views 1*a*, 3-7 as the original transition between ix. and xi. 14, 15 *a*, 19, while x. 1 *b*-2, 8-11 (a vision of messiah) introduces the new source of xi. 1-13, xii. 18; and Rauch regards x. 1 *b*, 2 *a*, 5-7, 4, 9-11 as the opening of xi. 1-13, xii. 1-17, with x. 1-4 *a* (substantially) as the preface to xii. 18-xiii., xvi. 13-16. These analyses are unconvincing. The alleged signs of a Hebrew original (*e.g.*, ver. 7, also **λέγουσί μοι** and **λέγει μοι** in vv. 9, 11 = variant versions of ואמר לי) are not decisive.

Ver. 8. **ἡ φωνὴ** (*cf.* ver. 4) left ungrammatically without a predicate, the two participles being irregularly attracted into the case of **ἣν** (*cf.* i. 1, iv. 11).

Vv. 9-10. The prophet absorbs the

"δοῦναί μοι τὸ βιβλαρίδιον". Καὶ λέγει μοι, [x] "Λάβε καὶ κατάφαγε αὐτό· καὶ πικρανεῖ σου τὴν κοιλίαν, ἀλλ' ἐν τῷ στόματί σου ἔσται γλυκὺ ὡς μέλι". 10. Καὶ ἔλαβον τὸ βιβλαρίδιον ἐκ τῆς χειρὸς τοῦ ἀγγέλου, καὶ κατέφαγον αὐτό· καὶ ἦν ἐν τῷ στόματί μου ὡς μέλι, γλυκύ· καὶ ὅτε [y] ἔφαγον αὐτό, ἐπικράνθη ἡ κοιλία μου. 11. Καὶ [z] λέγουσίν μοι, "Δεῖ σε πάλιν προφητεῦσαι [a] ἐπὶ [b] λαοῖς καὶ ἔθνεσι καὶ γλώσσαις καὶ [b] βασιλεῦσι πολλοῖς".

x For basis of this passage, *cf.* Ezek. ii. 8—iii. 3, Ps. cxix. 103, and 4 Esd. viii. 4 (absorbet ergo anima sensum et deuoret quod sapit). See Dieterich's *Mithras-Liturgie*, p. 101. y In sense of κατέφαγον which it echoes (*cf.* Moulton, i. 111, 115). z = "I was told" (like xi. 1, xvi. 15 impers. plur.). a *Cf.* xxii. 16, John xii. 16: = "of," "concerning". b Pleonastic, as v. 9, vii. 9, Dan. iii. 4, vii. 14, *cf.* xiii. 7.

word of God; in our phrase, he makes it his own or identifies himself with it (Jer. xv. 16). To assimilate this revelation of the divine purpose seems to promise a delightful experience, but the bliss and security of the saints, he soon realises, involve severe trials (*cf.* xi. 2, xii. 13 f., etc.) for them as well as catastrophes for the world. Hence the feeling of disrelish with which he views his new vocation as a seer. The distasteful experience is put first, in ver. 9, as being the unexpected element in the situation. (The omission of *bitterness* in LXX of Ezek. iii. 14 renders it unlikely that this additional trait of unpleasant taste is due, as Spitta thinks, to an erroneous combination of Ezek. iii. 2 and 14). The natural order occurs in ver. 10. The only analogous passage in early Christian literature is in the "Martyrdom of Perpetua" (iv. *cf.* Weinel, 196, 197). Wetstein cites from Theophrastus the description of an Indian shrub **οὗ ὁ καρπὸς . . . ἐσθιόμενος γλυκὺς. οὗτος ἐν τῇ κοιλίᾳ δηγμὸν ποιεῖ καὶ δυσεντερίαν.** Before the happy consummation (ver. 7), a bitter prelude is to come, which is the subject of national and political prophecies. In order to underline his divine commission for this task of punitive prediction, he recalls his inspiration.

Ver. 11. **λέγ. μοι,** an oblique, reverential way of describing the divine impulse, due to Aramaic idiom and common in later Biblical Hebrew (*cf.* Dalman, i., viii. 11). The series of oracles, thus elaborately inaugurated, is concerned increasingly (" again," in view of iv. 4, 15, vii. 4, 9, viii. 13, ix. 6, 16 f.) with those international movements ("kings" = **φυλαί,** or those in xvii. 10, 12) which a prophet related to the course of the divine kingdom. Strictly speaking, the revelation assimilated in x. 10, 11 opens in xii., but the intervening passage is linked to both (see below). The first part of this passage (xi. 1-2, 3-13) evidently forms part of the **βιβλαρίδιον** (*cf.* Introd. § 2). Its enigmatic contents, interrupting the trumpet-visions with edges which do not fit into the context or the rest of the Apocalypse, point to the incorporation of a special and disparate source. Any analysis is more or less hypothetical, but the writer is evidently not moving with absolute freedom. He has his own end in view, but he reaches it, here as elsewhere (*cf.* vii. 1 f.) by means of stepping-stones which originally lay in different surroundings. This is widely recognised by critics and editors, who commonly take 1-2 and 3-13 as separate oracles. Each indeed might be the torso of a larger source. But, in spite of the different descriptions of Jerusalem, the hypothesis of their original unity has much in its favour. How could so tiny a scrap of papyrus as that required for 1, 2 be preserved? Besides ver. 3 goes with ver. 2 (the prophetic mission as a counterpart to the punishment), the two periods are alike, the strange **δίδωμι**-construction occurs in both (here only in Apoc.), and the inversion of object and verb is common to both (2, 5, 6, 9, 10). To discover an oracle of the Zealots in 1, 2 (Wellhausen, Bousset, Baljon, J. Weiss) is precarious, for even if we could suppose that these passionate citizens took time to write oracles, they had not a monopoly of belief in the temple's inviolability. The latter belief conflicts with Mark xiii. 1, 2 (Ac. vi. 14); but, while this makes it extremely unlikely that the passage was adopted, or at least composed, by one of the Twelve, it does not necessarily disprove a Jewish Christian origin for the fly-leaf. Patriotism must have often swayed hope, even in face of authoritative logia. Still, a Jewish origin is more probable (so from Vischer and Sabatier to Baljon, Forbes, von Soden, Wellhausen and J. Weiss), in which case 8 *c* (**ὅπου . . . ἐσταυρώθη**), with possibly 9 *a* and

XI. 1. Καὶ ᵃἐδόθη ᵃμοι ᵇκάλαμος ὅμοιος ᵇῥάβδῳ, λέγων, a x. 11. b xxi. 15-16, Ezek. xl. 3-6, xlii. 16-19, Zech. ii. 1.

12 *b*, must be Christianising touches by the editor. As 8 *c* is the only place in the Apocalypse where Jesus is thus designated (contrast 4), and as the unexampled **αἱ . . . ἑστῶτες** occurs in 4, the editor may be using a previous translation of the fly-leaf. Otherwise, the repeated traces of Hebraistic idiom suggest that he translated it from an Aramaic or Hebrew original (so especially Weyland, Briggs, and Bruston) which was a Jewish (or Jewish Christian) oracle, composed towards the end of the siege in 70 A.D. between May and August (*cf.* Joseph. *Bell*, v. 12, 3) by a prophet who anticipated (*cf. S. C.*, 219, 220) that the temple and a nucleus of the God-fearing would be kept inviolate during the last *times of the Gentiles*, at the end of which anti-Christ or the pseudo-messiah would blasphemously re-assert himself in the temple (hence its preservation, 1, 2), according to one cycle of tradition (2 Thess. ii. 3, etc., *cf. A. C.* 160 f.), after murdering the two heralds of messiah. The motives and further career of the beast are omitted, if not in the source, at least by the editor. He resumes the subject afterwards (*cf.* xiii. 6), when the eschatological monster is specially identified with the imperial power. Here his main concern is with the fate of the two witnesses. Probably it was this feature of the oracle which primarily led him to adopt and adapt it, as showing how the beast or anti-christ was foiled in his attack on messiah's forerunners, just as (in xii.) the dragon is foiled in his attack on messiah himself. The other details are left standing; in their present setting they have much the same pictorial and dramatic interest as the minutiæ of the parables, and it is perhaps doubtful whether the editor linked any symbolic or allegorical meaning to them, although such can easily be attached in a variety of ways, *e.g.*, to the language of 1, 2 in the light of Barn. iv. 11, Ign. *ad Magn.* 7, etc. (so Weiss, Simcox, Swete, and others). Even the two witnesses are not to be identified with any historical figures of contemporary life, much less taken as allegorical or as typifying aspects of the church's testimony. "The vision . . . is of the nature of a superimposed photograph showing traces of many pasts" (Abbott). The original Jewish tradition which lay behind the source expected only Elijah, who should preach repentance to the pagan world, but he was occasionally furnished with a companion in Moses (on the basis of Deut. xviii. 15; *cf.* Mal. iv. 4, 5, the transfiguration-story, and possibly the two radiant saints of Apoc. Pet. 6 f.). The only other serious rival is Enoch, a grand figure in Jewish and early Christian eschatological tradition (for the curious Sir. xliv. 16, *cf. E. Bi.* 1295). Later tradition, indeed, thinking mainly of Elijah and Enoch (Gfrörer ii. 261 f.; *A. C.* 203, 211), whom antichrist in wrath slays for their witness against him, and whom God (or Michael and Gabriel) resuscitates, suggests a fairly apposite cycle of belief which may reproduce the earlier Jewish expectation out of which the materials of this fragmentary oracle have been drawn. The unique character of this expectation is illustrated, not so much by Anu and Nudimmut, Marduk's predecessors in the fight against Tiamât, as by the Zoroastrian belief that the temporary triumph of the evil spirit would be followed by the appearance of two reformers or prophets, Hushêdar and Hushêdarmâh (*S. B. E.* xxiii. 195; *cf.* Hübschmann, 227), who would act each for a millenium on earth as the precursors and heralds of their Lord, the Persian messiah. This belief is much older than the sources in which it occurs, and like several other Zoroastrian traits, it may have fused with the Jewish expectation in question, though the Zoroastrian heralds do not appear simultaneously (*cf. Encycl. Relig. and Ethics*, i. 207). Here at any rate the appearance of the two anonymous and mysterious witnesses precedes the final outburst of evil (xi. 7, xii. f.) and the manifestation of messiah (xi. 15 f., xiv. 14f.)—an idea for which no exact basis can be found in the strictly Jewish eschatology of the period. It may have grown up under the influence of this kindred trait in the adjoining province of Zoroastrian belief, unless the doubling of the witnesses was simply due to the side-influence of the Zechariah-trait (in ver. 4). Wellhausen argues from the singular **πτῶμα** (8, 9) that the two witnesses were a duplication of the original single witness, *i.e.*, Elijah; but the singular is collective, and there is no trace of any conflation with Jonah.

CHAPTER XI.—Vv. 1, 2. "And I wa given a rod (קְנֵה הַמִּדָּה) like a staff,

[c] Ἔγειρε καὶ [c] μέτρησον τὸν [c] ναὸν τοῦ Θεοῦ, καὶ τὸ θυσιαστήριον, καὶ
τοὺς προσκυνοῦντας [d] ἐν αὐτῷ· 2. καὶ τὴν αὐλὴν τὴν ἔξωθεν τοῦ
ναοῦ ἔκβαλε ἔξωθεν, καὶ μὴ αὐτὴν μετρήσῃς, ὅτι [e] ἐδόθη τοῖς ἔθνεσι·
καὶ [f] τὴν πόλιν τὴν [f] ἁγίαν [g] πατήσουσι μῆνας τεσσεράκοντα δύο.
3. Καὶ [h] δώσω τοῖς δυσὶ μάρτυσί [i] μου, [h] καὶ [k] προφητεύσουσιν
[l] ἡμέρας χιλίας διακοσίας [l] ἑξήκοντα, περιβεβλημένοι[1] [m] σάκκους.
4. [n] Οὗτοί εἰσιν αἱ δύο ἐλαῖαι καὶ [o] αἱ δύο λυχνίαι αἱ ἐνώπιον τοῦ
κυρίου τῆς γῆς [p] ἑστῶτες.

c Ezek. xli. 1-2. d John viii. 20. e See on xvii. 17, prophetic perfect. f xxi. 2, xxii. 19, Matt. xxvii. 53 (title of Jer. in later Judaism). g Ps. Sol. vii. 2, xvii. 25, Luke xxi. 24; see wail of 4 Esd. vi. 56 f. h *Cf.* on ix. 5. i ii. 13. k As 1 Cor. xiv. 3, 24. l ver. 2, xii. 6. m Isa. xxii. 12, Jer. vi. 26, Jas. iii. 5. n From Zech. iv. 3, 11-14. o *Cf.* Win. § 23, 5*b*. p Grammat. irregularity, to emphasise personality of witnesses.

[1] For **περιβεβλημενοι** (אcC, 1, S., vg., And., Areth., Vict., Hipp., etc., so Al., Ti., Ws., Bs., Bj., Sw.) Lach., Tr., WH read the primitive corruption **περιβεβλημενους** (א*AQP, min.), though WH suggest it may be an early error for **περιβεβλημενοις**.

with the words" (**λέγων** by a harsh attraction, *cf.* LXX of 1 Kings xx. 9, Josh. ii. 2, is left in apposition to the subject implied in **ἐδόθη**), "Up (or come = קוּם) and measure the temple of God and the altar (of burnt-offering, which stood outside the inner shrine) and (sc. number) those who worship there" (*i.e.*, in the inner courts, xiii. 6; for constr. *cf.* 2 Sam. viii. 3). The outer court (Ezek. x. 5) is to be left out of account (**ἐκβ.** = "omit" or exclude as unworthy of attention), "for it has been abandoned (or, assigned in the divine counsel) to the heathen, and (indeed) they shall trample on the holy city itself (emphatic by position, = Jerusalem) for two and forty months." In *Asc. Isa.* iv. 12 antichrist's sway lasts for three years, seven months, and twenty-seven days, but three and a half years is the conventional period for the godless persecutor to get the upper hand (*cf.* xiii. 5, after Daniel's "time, and times, and the dividing of time," *i.e.*, three and a half years, vii. 25, xii. 7). Originally this broken seven as the period of oppression reflected the Babylonian three and a half winter months (*S. C.* 309 f.; Cheyne's *Bible Problems*, 111 f.), preceding the festival of Marduk in the vernal equinox, a solstice during which Tiamât reigned supreme. Here it is the stereotyped period of the **καιροὶ τῶν ἐθνῶν** (Luke xxi. 24), extending to the second advent.—**μετρήσῃς.** To measure is here not a prelude to ruin but a guarantee of preservation and restoration (Zech. ii. 1 f.). Failure to satisfy God's standard or test means calamity for men, but when he surveys their capacities and needs in peril, it implies protection. As the context implies, this is the idea of the present measuring. It is not to be identified prosaically with "orders given to the Roman soldiers, who were encamped in Jerusalem after its destruction, not to set foot in what had been the Holy of Holies" (Mommsen).

Ver. 3. **σάκκους,** the simple, archaic garb of prophets, especially appropriate to humiliation (reff.). The faithful prophets who withdraw from the local apostacy to the desert in company with Isaiah (*Asc. Isa.* ii. 9 f.) are also clothed in this black hair-cloth. The voice of the divine speaker here "melts imperceptibly into the narrative of the vision" (Alford, *cf.* ver. 12). Contemporary Jewish belief (4 Esd. vi. 26) made these "witnesses" (men "who have not tasted death from their birth," *i.e.*, Enoch, Elijah) appear before the final judgment and preach successfully, but the only trace of any analogous feature in rabbinical prophecy seems to be the appearance of Moses and Messiah during the course of the Gog and Magog campaign. The reproduction of this oracle, long after its original period in 70 A.D., would be facilitated by the fact that the visions of Ezekiel and Zechariah, upon which it was modelled, both presupposed the fall of the city and temple in ancient Jerusalem (Abbott, pp. 84-88).

Ver. 4. They are further described in the terms applied by Zechariah to the two most prominent religious figures of his day, except that they are compared to two lampstands, not to one which is septiform. The idea is that their autho-

5. καὶ εἴ τις αὐτοὺς θέλει ἀδικῆσαι,
[q] πῦρ ἐκπορεύεται ἐκ τοῦ στόματος αὐτῶν καὶ κατεσθίει
τοὺς ἐχθροὺς αὐτῶν·
καὶ εἴ[1] τις αὐτοὺς [r] θελήσῃ ἀδικῆσαι,
οὕτω δεῖ αὐτὸν ἀποκτανθῆναι.
6. οὗτοι ἔχουσιν τὴν ἐξουσίαν [s] κλεῖσαι τὸν [s] οὐρανόν,
ἵνα μὴ ὑετὸς βρέχῃ τὰς ἡμέρας αὐτῶν τῆς προφητείας
αὐτῶν,
καὶ ἐξουσίαν [t] ἔχουσιν ἐπὶ τῶν [t] ὑδάτων,
στρέφειν αὐτὰ εἰς αἷμα,
καὶ [t] πατάξαι τὴν γῆν ἐν πάσῃ πληγῇ,
ὁσάκις ἐὰν θελήσωσιν.
7. Καὶ ὅταν τελέσωσι τὴν μαρτυρίαν αὐτῶν, τὸ θηρίον τὸ ἀναβαῖνον ἐκ τῆς [u] ἀβύσσου [v] ποιήσει μετ' αὐτῶν πόλεμον καὶ νικήσει
αὐτοὺς καὶ ἀποκτενεῖ αὐτούς. 8. καὶ τὸ πτῶμα αὐτῶν ἐπὶ τῆς

q ix. 17, 2 Kings i. 10 f., Luke ix. 54, (Moses) Num. xvi 35.
r For subj. with εἰ, *cf.* 1 Cor xiv. 5 (Deissm. 118).
s 1 Kings xvii., Sir. xlviii. 3, Jub. xxiii. 18.
t See feats ascribed to Moses in Exod. vii. 19-21; 1 Sam. iv 8 (Apoc. viii. 8, xvi. 3), *cf.* Jos. *Bell.* v. 9. 4.
u *Cf. Encycl. Relig. and Ethics*, i. 53-55.
v From Dan. vii. 21; divine permission (Apoc. xiii. 7)?

[1] For και ει Bl. conj. καν (from καιη ℵ*C, 1).

rity and influence are derived from God. As in ver. 7, the function of the two witnesses (*cf.* Deut. xvii. 6, xix. 15) is defined as "prophecy," but no details are given.

Vv. 5, 6. In this description, borrowed from traditional features of Moses and Elijah (whose drought lasted for three and a half years, according to Luke iv. 25; James v. 17), the metaphorical expressions of passages like Jer. v. 14 and Sir. xlviii. 1 are translated into grim reality (see reff.), as in Slav. En. i. 5 and the thaumaturgic practices chronicled by Athen. iv. 129 D and Lucian (*Philopseud.* 12). These are no meek apostles of the Christian faith. To stop rain was equivalent to a punishment for iniquity (Ps. Sol. xvii. 20-22, En. c. 11, etc.)

Ver. 7. The influence of Hebraic idiom helps to explain (*cf.* xx. 7-9) the translator's "transition from futures through presents to preterites" here (Simcox). τελέσωσι (Burton, 203) indicates no uncertainty. When their work is done, they are massacred—not till then; like their Lord (Luke xiii. 31 f.), they are insured by loyalty to their task. The best comment upon this and the following verses, a description coloured by the famous passage in Sap. ii. 12-iii, 9, is Bunyan's description of the jury in Vanity Fair and their verdict. This beast "from the abyss" is introduced as a familiar figure—an editorial and proleptic reference to the beast "from the abyss" in xvii. 8 or from "the sea" (xiii. 1; the abyss and the sea in Rom. x. 7 = Deut. xxx. 13) which was (*cf. Encycl. Rel. and Ethics*, i. 53 f.) the haunt and home of daemons (Luke viii. 31, etc.), unless he is identified with the supernatural fiend and foe of ix. 2, 11. (Bruston heroically gets over the difficulty of the beast's sudden introduction by transferring xi. 1-13 to a place after xix. 1-3). The beast wars with the witnesses (here, as in ix. 9 and xii. 17, Field, on Luke xiv. 31, prefers to take πόλεμον = μάχην, a single combat or battle, as occasionally in LXX [*e.g.*, 3 Kings xxxii. 34] and Lucian), and vanquishes them, yet it is the city (ver. 13) and not he who is punished. The fragmentary character of the source is evident from the fact that we are not told why or how this conflict took place. John presupposed in his readers an acquaintance with the cycle of antichrist traditions according to which the witnesses of God were murdered by the false messiah who, as *the abomination of desolation* or *man of sin*, was at feud with all who opposed his worship or disputed his authority.

Ver. 8. God's servants rejected and cast aside, as so much refuse! See *Sam. Agonistes*, 667-704. The "great city" is Jerusalem, an identification favoured

πλατείας τῆς [w] πόλεως τῆς [w] μεγάλης, ἥτις καλεῖται πνευματικῶς
Σόδομα καὶ [x] Αἴγυπτος,[1] ὅπου καὶ ὁ Κύριος αὐτῶν ἐσταυρώθη. 9.
καὶ βλέπουσιν [y] ἐκ τῶν λαῶν καὶ φυλῶν καὶ γλωσσῶν καὶ ἐθνῶν τὸ
[a] πτῶμα αὐτῶν ἡμέρας τρεῖς καὶ ἥμισυ, καὶ τὰ [b] πτώματα αὐτῶν οὐκ

w xiv. 8, xvi. 19, xvii.-xviii.
x Ps. cv. 38.
y *Cf.* on ii. 10 (partitive).
a Here as in 8 = collective term ("corpses"), as *πρόσωπον* Gen. xlviii. 20, *κεφαλή* Lev. x. 6.
b *Cf.* Isa. lxxviii. (lxxix.) 3, Ps. Sol. ii. 31, En. xxii. 10; 2 Kings ix. 10, and Jer. xxiii. 19.

[1] Pr. om. **και Αιγυπτος** (an early gloss, Haussleiter 213). Further editorial Christian additions are suspected in **ητις . . . εσταυρωθη** (so *e.g.*, Weyland, S. Davidson, Wellh.) or **οπου . . . εσταυρωθη** (so *e.g.*, Sabatier, Schön, Vischer, Pfleid., Rauch, Völter, Baljon, Bs., de Faye, Kohler, von Soden).

by (*a*) incidental O.T. comparisons of the Jews to Sodom (Isa. i. 9; Jer. xxiii. 14; so *Asc. Isa.* iii. 10), (*b*) the Christian editor's note **ὅπου καὶ ὁ κύριος αὐτῶν ἐσταυρώθη**, (*c*) a passage like Luke xiii. 33, (*d*) the reference in xvi. 19, and (*e*) passages in Appian (*Syr.* 50 **μεγίστη πόλις Ἰ.**), Pliny (*H. N.* xiv. 70), Josephus (*Apion*, i. 22), and Sib. Or. (v. 154, 226, 413, written before 80 A.D.), all of which confirm this title (*cf.* the variant addition **μεγάλην** in Apoc. xxi. 10): it is indeed put beyond doubt by the peculiar antichrist-tradition upon which the Jewish original was based (*A. C.* 19 f., 134 f., *E. Bi.* i. 179, 180). The obscurity and isolated character of this eschatology, "an exotic growth upon the soil of Judaism" and much more in early Christianity, may be accounted for perhaps by the historical changes in the later situation, which concentrated the antichrist in anti-Roman rather than in anti-Jewish hostility. As yet, however, the seduction of the Jews by a false messiah (*cf.* John v. 43 and its patristic interpretation) was quite a reasonable expectation: see the evidence gathered in *A. C.* 166 f. Victorinus, following the Apocalypse literally (xi. 7 = xvii. 11), makes Nero redivivus beguile the Jews. The alternative to this theory has won considerable support (especially from Spitta and Wellhausen) upon various grounds; it regards *the great city* as Rome, where the two prophets are supposed to preach repentance to the heathen world and eventually to be killed. But although this suits some portions of the language well (*e.g.*, ver. 13, conversion to *God of heaven*), it is not exegetically necessary; it introduces Rome abruptly (8 *c* being of course taken as a gloss) and irregularly: nor does it explain the general contour of the oracle as happily as that advocated above. Bruston's ingenious attempt to take **τ. μεγάλης** with **πλατείας** (= Jewish justice) is quite untenable, and *the great city* is not likely to be a translator's error (Weyland), גדולה for קדושה.—**πνευματικῶς** (*cf.* Gal. iv. 24 f.) as opposed to **σαρκικῶς** ("literally," Just. Mart. *Dial.* xiv. 231 *d*) is "allegorically, or mystically."—**καὶ Αἴγυπτος,** not as the home of magic (*cf.* Blau's *Altjüd. Zauberwesen*, 39 f.) but as a classical foe of God's people (and Moses of old?). The connexion with the water-dragon of xii. 15 (*cf.* Ezek. xxix. 3, xxxii. 2) is obvious. Philo allegorises E. usually as a type of the corporeal and material.—**ὅπου κ.τ.λ.,** no wonder if Christians suffer, after what their Lord had to suffer (*cf.* Matt. x. 22-25, 28 f.) at the hands of impious men. There is none of the modern's surprise or indignation at the thought of "Christian blood shed where Christ bled for men".

Ver. 9. *Cf.* 2 Chron. xxiv. 19 f., Matt. xxiii. 34 f., Job. i. 12.—**ἀφίουσιν,** for other N.T. assimilations of irreg. to reg. verb (Win. § 14. 16; Blass, § 23. 7), *cf.* Mark i. 34, Luke xi. 4. In Ep. Lugd. the climax of pagan malice is the refusal to let the bodies of the martyrs be buried by their friends, **ὑπὸ γὰρ ἀγρίου Θηρὸς ἄγρια καὶ βάρβαρα φῦλα παραχθέντα δυσπαύστως εἶχε.** The rendering of burial honours to the dead was a matter of great moment in the ancient world; to be denied pious burial meant ignominy in the memory of this world and penalties in the next. The two witnesses are treated as the murdered high priests, Ananus and Jesus, were handled by the Jewish mob in the seventh decade (Jos. *Bell.* iv. 5, 2).—**βλέπουσιν,** the onlookers, who evidently sympathise with antichrist (*cf.* on xvi. 12), include pagans as well as Jews (Andr.).—**ἡμέρας, κ.τ.λ.,** three and a half as the broken seven (*cf.* on ver. 2) here in days. This trait (*cf.* on ver. 12) shows that their fate was not originally modelled on that of Jesus.

ἀφίουσιν [b] τεθῆναι εἰς μνῆμα. 10. καὶ οἱ κατοικοῦντες ἐπὶ τῆς γῆς
χαίρουσιν ἐπ᾽ αὐτοῖς καὶ εὐφραίνονται· καὶ [c] δῶρα πέμψουσιν [1]
ἀλλήλοις, ὅτι οὗτοι οἱ δύο προφῆται [d] ἐβασάνισαν τοὺς κατοικοῦντας
ἐπὶ τῆς γῆς. 11. [e] Καὶ μετὰ τρεῖς ἡμέρας καὶ ἥμισυ [f] πνεῦμα ζωῆς
ἐκ τοῦ Θεοῦ εἰσῆλθεν ἐν αὐτοῖς,[2] καὶ ἔστησαν ἐπὶ τοὺς πόδας αὐτῶν,
καὶ [g] φόβος μέγας [g] ἐπέπεσεν ἐπὶ τοὺς [h] θεωροῦντας αὐτούς. 12.
καὶ ἤκουσαν[3] [i] φωνῆς μεγάλης ἐκ τοῦ οὐρανοῦ λεγούσης αὐτοῖς,
"[k] Ἀνάβατε ὧδε". Καὶ [l] ἀνέβησαν εἰς τὸν οὐρανὸν ἐν τῇ [m] νεφέλῃ,
καὶ ἐθεώρησαν αὐτοὺς οἱ ἐχθροὶ αὐτῶν. 13. Καὶ ἐν ἐκείνῃ τῇ ὥρᾳ
ἐγένετο [n] σεισμὸς μέγας, καὶ τὸ [o] δέκατον τῆς πόλεως ἔπεσε, καὶ
ἀπεκτάνθησαν ἐν τῷ σεισμῷ [p] ὀνόματα ἀνθρώπων χιλιάδες ἑπτά·
καὶ οἱ λοιποὶ ἔμφοβοι ἐγένοντο καὶ [q] ἔδωκαν δόξαν [r] τῷ Θεῷ τοῦ
οὐρανοῦ.

14. [s] Ἡ οὐαὶ ἡ δευτέρα ἀπῆλθεν·
ἰδοὺ ἡ οὐαὶ ἡ τρίτη ἔρχεται ταχύ.

15. Καὶ ὁ ἕβδομος ἄγγελος ἐσάλπισεν, καὶ ἐγένοντο φωναὶ μεγάλαι ἐν τῷ οὐρανῷ, [t] λέγοντες,

c Ps. cv. 38, Neh. viii. 10, 12, Esth. ix. 19, 22.
d Sap. ii. 12 14-15, 1 Kings xviii. 17.
e From Ezek. xxxvii. 5, 10.
f xiii. 15, = רוח היים (Gen. vi. 17).
g Gen. xv. 12.
h Only here in Apoc.
i *Par. Lost*, vi. 29-36.
k Win. § 13, 22. Such unusual -α forms of sec. aor. are textually untenable however in vi. 16, xvii. 6, and xviii. 19.
l 2 Kings ii. 11.
m Acts i. 9.
n vi. 12, Matt. xxvii. 51.
o ἅπ. λεγ. N.T.
p *Cf.* on iii. 4, Num. i. 20, 28; Deissm. 196-197, Abbott 91-93.
q xvi. 9, 11, Jer. xiii. 16, Dan. ii. 18, 44, Isa. xxv. 3.
r *Cf.* as ix. 12, and xii. 12.
s Only here and xvi. 11 (citation from Dan. ii. 19), in N.T.: = אלה שמיא.
t Constr. ad sensum.

[1] Ti., Bs., Bj. read πεμπουσιν (א*P, Arm., Tic., Spec., etc.). The vss. on the whole favour the futures in 9-10.

[2] Read εν (om. εν CP, 1, etc., Tr., WH ?) αυτοις A, min. (5), Arm., vg., And[a], Lach., Al. Ti., Ws., Bs. (*cf.* Luke ix. 46), which has been early improved into εις (אQ, etc., Bj.) or επ (min. 5) αυτους.

[3] For ηκουσαν (א*ACP, vg., Ti., Tr., WH, Ws., Sw., Bj.) ηκουσα (א[c]Q, etc., Me., And., Areth., Tic.) is read by some (*e.g.*, Al., de Wette, Düst., Bs., Lind., Wellh.).

Ver. 10. So far from laying it to heart that the godly perish, men are hyperbolically represented as congratulating one another on getting rid of these obnoxious prophets with their vexatious words (3) and works (6), which hitherto had baffled opposition (4, 5). Another naive Oriental touch is that their victims exchange presents in order to celebrate the festive occasion.

Ver. 12. After being resuscitated, they ascend in a cloud (like Enoch and Jesus) before the eyes of their enemies (unlike Jesus).

Ver. 13. On earthquakes as a punishment for sin, *cf.* Jos. *Ant.* ix. 10, 4 = Zech. xiv. 5, and (for Sodom) Amos iv. 11. The beast, as in 2 Thess. ii. 9-12, gets off scatheless in the meantime, though his tools are punished or terrified into reverence (Jonah iii. 5-10).—ὀνόματα ἀ. Briggs ingeniously conjectures that this is a clumsy version of אנשי שמות = men of name or fame (*cf.* 1 Chron. v. 24, Num. xvi. 2). From this point till xvi. 19 and xx. 9 Jerusalem seems to be ignored among the wider political oracles, except incidentally at xiv. 20 (see note), where another erratic block from the same or a similar cycle of eschatological tradition breaks the surrounding strata of prediction.

The ample and proleptic style of the next passage shows that the author has left his source in order to resume matters with (14-18) the seventh trumpet-blast or third woe, which ushers in the final stage (1 Cor. xv. 52) of the divine purpose (x. 7 = xii.-xx). But what immediately follows is, by anticipation, a celestial reflex of the last judgment which is characteristically deferred till "the various underplots of God's providence" (Alford) are worked out. The announcement of it starts an exultant song of praise in heaven.

Ver. 15. The rout of Satan (xii. 10 and xx. 4-10) means the absolute messianic

"Ἐγένετο ἡ [u] βασιλεία τοῦ [u] κόσμου τοῦ [v] Κυρίου ἡμῶν καὶ τοῦ [w] Χριστοῦ αὐτοῦ,
Καὶ [x] βασιλεύσει εἰς τοὺς αἰῶνας τῶν αἰώνων."

16. [y] Καὶ οἱ εἴκοσι τέσσαρες πρεσβύτεροι οἳ ἐνώπιον τοῦ Θεοῦ
κάθηνται[1] ἐπὶ τοὺς θρόνους αὐτῶν, [z] ἔπεσαν [a] ἐπὶ τὰ πρόσωπα αὐτῶν
καὶ προσεκύνησαν τῷ Θεῷ, λέγοντες,

17. "[b] Εὐχαριστοῦμέν σοι, [c] Κύριε ὁ Θεὸς ὁ παντοκράτωρ,
ὁ ὢν καὶ ὁ ἦν,
ὅτι [d] εἴληφας τὴν δύναμίν σου τὴν μεγάλην,
καὶ [d] ἐβασίλευσας.

18. καὶ τὰ ἔθνη [e] ὠργίσθησαν,
καὶ ἦλθεν ἡ ὀργή σου,
καὶ ὁ [f] καιρὸς τῶν νεκρῶν [f] κριθῆναι,
καὶ [f] δοῦναι τὸν [g] μισθὸν [h] τοῖς δούλοις σου τοῖς [h] προφήταις,
καὶ τοῖς [i] ἁγίοις καὶ τοῖς [k] φοβουμένοις τὸ [k] ὄνομά σου, [l] τοῖς
μικροῖς καὶ τοῖς μεγάλοις,[2]
καὶ [m] διαφθεῖραι τοὺς διαφθείροντας τὴν γῆν."

u Sing. only here: = β. ἐπὶ τ.κ., xvii. 18, *cf.* Obad. 21.
v (Possess. genit.) from Ps. ii. 2, 6, quot. also in Acts iv. 26; *cf.* Ps. xxii. 29, and Isa. lii. 7-8; God's reign again in Apoc. xix. 6.
w Ps. (x.) 16; *cf.* on Acts iii. 18, Dalman i. § 11, 1.
x Dan. ii. 44, vii. 14, quot. in Luke i. 33.
y *Cf.* Isa. xxv. 9.
z iv. 10, v. 8, 14.
a vii. 11. xix. 6.

b Common at open. of votive inscriptions (Asia Minor). c i. 8, xvi. 7, xviii. 8, d Inceptive aor. *cf.* Luke xv. 32, 1 Cor. iv. 8, Burton 54. From Ps. xcii. xciii.) 1 where, as 2 Sam. xvi. 8, ἐβασ. = "is king". e xii. 17. From Ps. ii., xcviii. xcix., *κύριος ἐβασίλευσε, ὀργιζέσθωσαν λαοί.* f Constr. Rom. ix. 21 (*ἐξουσία . . . ποιῆσαι*); = *ἵνα κριθῶσιν κ.τ.λ.* See Esth. ii. 12 *οὗτος δὲ ἦν ὁ καιρὸς κορασίου εἰσελθεῖν.* g xxii. 12 (not elsewhere in Apoc.). h x. 7; prophets and saints = Christendom, as i. 1-2, *cf.* on xviii. 20 and 24. From Dan. ix 6, 10, etc. i Always in Apoc. = Christians, never angels (*cf.* xiv. 10). k Here only, N.T.; *cf.* xiv. 7, xv. 4, and on xix. 5; also 2 Cor. vii. 1. l Ps. cxv. 13: quot. in xiii. 16, xix. 5, xx. 12. m viii. 9, *cf.* on xix. 2. For double sense of word("destroy" and "corrupt") compare Eng. usage of "ruin".

[1] For **καθημενοι** (AP, 1, etc., Al. Lach., WH, Sw., Ws., Bs.) Ti., Tr., Bj. rightly read (οι) **καθηνται** ℵ*CQ, etc., Syr., S., And[c], Areth., vg., Pr.

[2] Lach., Tr., WH, Sw. read **τους μικρους και τους μεγαλους** (ℵ*AC).

(ὁ Χ. only in these sections = "messiah" in the eschatological sense) authority of God, as the destruction or submission of paganism (*cf.* ver. 13) means the true coming of the eschatological **βασιλεία** (*cf.* xix. 1-6, after Rome's downfall). The apocalyptic motto is not so much "The Lord reigns," as "The Lord is to reign". Meanwhile he overrules, and every preliminary judgment shoots the pious mind forward to anticipate the final triumph. Linguistically **τοῦ Χριστοῦ** might mean here as in Hab. iii. 13 God's chosen people, but the usage of the Apocalypse puts this out of the question. There is no need to delete the words here as a gloss (so, *e.g.*, Baljon, von Soden, Rauch) or the similar phrase in En. xlviii. 10 (with Dalman).

Ver. 17. **ὁ ἐρχόμενος** is naturally omitted from this paean; God has already come! The variation of order in i. 4 and iv. 8 has no occult significance. The phrase *Lord God* is considered by Philo (on Gen. vii. 5) specially applicable to seasons of judgment; *Lord* precedes *God*, since the former signifies not beneficence but "royal and destructive power".

Ver. 18. **ὠργ.** = defiant rage (*cf.* xvi. 11), not the mere terror of vi. 17, at the messianic **ὀργή**. The prophets are as usual the most prominent of the **ἅγιοι**. If the **καὶ** after **ἁγίοις** is retained, it is epexegetic (as in Gen. iv. 4, Gal. vi. 16), not a subtle mark of division between Jewish and Gentile Christians (Völter) or (in a Jewish source) saints and proselytes. The same interpretation (for **φοβ.** *cf.* Introd. § 6) must be chosen, if **καὶ** is omitted (as, *e.g.*, by Bousset and Baljon), but the evidence is far too slight to justify the deletion.—**διαφθ.** "When Nero perished by the justest doom/Which ever the destroyer yet destroyed" (Byron). Contrast the exultant tone of this retrospective thanksgiving with the strain

19. Καὶ [n] ἠνοίγη ὁ ναὸς τοῦ Θεοῦ ὁ ἐν τῷ οὐρανῷ,
καὶ ὤφθη ἡ [o] κιβωτὸς τῆς διαθήκης αὐτοῦ ἐν τῷ ναῷ αὐτοῦ·

n On form, see Deissm. 189.
o Heb. ix. 4: elsewh. = Noah's ark in N.T.

of foreboding which is sounded in xii. 12 before the actual conflict.

Ver. 19 introduces xii. 1-18; all that the prophet can speak of, from his own experience (*cf.* xiii. 1, 11, **εἶδον**), are the two **θηρία** on earth, but their activity in these latter days is not intelligible except as the result of mysterious movements in heaven. The latter he now outlines (*cf.* **ὤφθη** xi. 19, xii. 1, 3. By whom?) in order to comfort Christians by the assurance that the divine conqueror of these **θηρία** was in readiness to intervene. The celestial (contrast xi. 1) **ναός**, presupposed in the scenery of iv.-vi., is now mentioned for the first time; its opening reveals the long lost **κιβωτὸς τῆς διαθήκης**, and is accompanied by the usual storm-theophany, marking a decisive moment. Jewish tradition had for long cherished the belief (*cf.* on ii. 17) that the restoration of the people (gathered by God, *cf.* xiv. 1 f.) in the last days would be accompanied by the disclosure of the sacred box or ark (in a cloud; *cf.* here the lightning and thunder) which, together with the tabernacle and the altar of incense, had been safely concealed in Mount Nebo. So, *e.g.*, Abarbanel (on 1 Sam. iv. 4: haec est arca quam abscondit ante uastationem templi nostri et haec arca futuro tempore adueniente messia nostro manifestabitur). Epiphanius repeats the same rabbinical tradition (**καὶ ἐν ἀναστάσει πρῶτον ἡ κιβωτὸς ἀναστήσεται**). The underlying idea was that the disappearance of the ark from the holy of holies (Jer. iii. 16; 4 Esd. x. 22; Jos. *Bell.* v. 5. 5) was a temporary drawback which had to be righted before the final bliss could be consummated. This legend explains the symbolism of the Jewish Christian prophet. The messianic crisis is really at hand! The dawn may be cold and stormy, but it is the dawn of the last day! The spirit and content of the passage are transcendental; it is prosaic to delete **ἐν τ. ὀ.** (Spitta, and Cheyne in *E. Bi.* i. 309) and refer the vision to the earthly temple in Jerusalem. Like the author of Hebrews, this writer views heaven under the old ritual categories; besides, the originals of the sacred things were supposed to exist in the heaven of God (Heb. viii. 5).

This overture leads up to two sagas (xii. and xiii.) which explain that the present trouble of Christians was simply a final phase of the long antagonism which had begun in heaven and was soon to be ended on earth. It is the writer's task "not only to announce the future but also (i. 19) to convey a right understanding of that present on which the future depends" (Weiss). Hence the digression or retrospect in xii. 1 f. is only apparent. Hitherto only hints of persecution have been given; now the course, methods, and issues of the campaign are unfolded. The messianic position of Jesus is really the clue to the position of affairs, and it is of the utmost (**μέγα**, ver. 1 = weighty and decisive) moment to have all events focussed in the light of the new situation which that position has created. So much is plain. But that the source (or tradition) with its goddess-mother, persecuting dragon, celestial conflict, and menaced child, did not emanate from the prophet himself is evident alike from its style and contents; these show that while it could be domiciled on Jewish Christian soil it was not autochthonous (*cf.* Vischer, 19 f.; Gunkel, *S. C.* 173 f.). The imagery is not native to messianism. It bears traces of adaptation from mythology. Thus, where it would have been apposite to bring in the messiah (ver. 7), Michael's rôle is retained, even by the Christian editor, while the general oriental features of the mother's divine connexion and her flight, the dragon's hostility and temporary rout, and the water-flood, are visible through the Jewish transformation of the myth into a sort of allegory of messiah, persecuted by the evil power which he was destined to conquer. "In reality it is the old story of the conflict between light and darkness, order and disorder, transferred to the latter days, and adapted by spiritualisation . . . to the wants of faithful Jews" (Cheyne, *Bible Problems*, 80). While the vision represents the messianic adaptation of a sun-myth, it is uncertain what the particular myth was, and whether the vision represents a Jewish source worked over by the prophet. In the latter case, the Christian redactor's hand is visible perhaps in 4 *a* and 5 (**πρὸς τ. θ. αὐτοῦ**, *cf.* v. 6), certainly in 11 (which, even apart from *the Lamb*, interrupts the sequence) and 17 *c*, if not

καὶ ἐγένοντο [p] ἀστραπαὶ καὶ φωναὶ καὶ βρονταὶ καὶ [q] σεισμὸς
καὶ χάλαζα μεγάλη.

p iv. 5, viii. 5 f., xvi. 18-21.
q Individual (as vi. 14, etc.), not generic as Mark xiii. 8.

also in the whole of 10-12. If, in addition to this, the source was originally written in Hebrew, traces of the translator are to be found (so Gunkel, Kohler, and Wellhausen, after Ewald, Bruston, Briggs, and Schmidt) in 2 (**βασ. τεκεῖν**, *cf.* 1 Sam. iv. 19 חרה ללדת), 5 (**υἱὸν ἄ.** = בן זכר), 6 (**ὅπου . . . ἐκεῖ** = אשר שם), 8 (**κ. οὐκ ἴ.** = ולא יכל *cf.* 14 and on iii. 8), 9 (*the old serpent* = הנחש הראשון or הקדמוני), possibly 10 (**κατήγωρ** = קטיגור), and 12 (**κατέβη**, *cf.* **ἐβλήθη** of 10 = ירד). But whether the source was written or not, whether (if written) it was in Greek or not, and whether it was Jewish or Jewish-Christian, the clue to the vision lies in the sphere of comparative religion rather than of literary criticism. Its atmosphere has been tinged by the international myth of a new god challenging and deposing an older, or rather of a divine hero or child menaced at birth—a myth which at once reflected the dangers run by the seed sown in the dark earth and also the victory of light (or the god of light) over darkness, or of light in the springtide over the dead winter. The Babylonian myth of Marduk, which lacks any analogous tale of Marduk's birth, does not correspond so aptly to this vision (*cf.* Introd. § 4 *b*), as does the well-known crude Egyptian myth (Bousset); Isis is a closer parallel than Ishtar, and still closer perhaps at one point is the **κουροτρόφος** of Hellenic mythology, who was often represented as *uirgo coelestis*. But, if any local phase of the myth is to be assumed as having coloured the messianic tradition used by John, that of Leto would be particularly intelligible to Asiatic readers (*cf.*, *e.g.*, Pfleiderer, *Early Christ. Conception of Christ*, 56 f., after Dieterich's *Abraxas*, 117 f.; Maas, *Orpheus*, 251 f.). The dragon Python vainly persecuted her before the birth of Apollo; but she was caught away to a place of refuge, and her divine child, three days later, returned to slay the monster at Parnassus. This myth of the pregnant and threatened goddess-mother was familiar not only in Delos but throughout the districts, *e.g.*, of Miletus and Magnesia, where the fugitive goddess was honoured on the local coinage. Coins of Hadrian's reign associate the myth with Ephesus (ΕΦΕϹΙΩΝ ΛΗΤΩ). At Hierapolis, "the story of the life of these divine personages formed the ritual of the Phrygian religion" (*C. B. P.* i. 91 f.); the birth of a god is associated with Laodicea, one coin representing an infant god in the arms of a woman (Persephone); while in the legend of Rhea, as Ramsay points out (*C. B. P.* i. 34), Crete and Phrygia are closely allied (*cf.* also *Sib. Orac.* v. 130 f.). All this points decisively to the Hellenic form of the myth as the immediate source of the symbolic tradition (so, *e.g.*, J. Weiss, Abbott, 99), though here as elsewhere in the Apocalypse the obscurity which surrounds the relations between Jewish or early Christian eschatology and the ethnic environment renders it difficult to determine the process of the latter's undoubted influence on the former. Fortunately, this is a matter of subordinate importance. The essential thing is to ascertain not the soil on which such messianic conceptions grew, but the practical religious object to which the Christian prophet, as editor, has freely and naively applied them. His design is to show that the power of Satan on earth is doomed. Experience indeed witnesses (12-17) to his malice and mischief, but the present outburst of persecution is only the last campaign of a foe whose efforts have been already baffled and are soon to be crushed in the inexorable providence of God. The prophet dramatically uses his source or tradition to introduce Satan as a baffled opponent of the messiah (*cf.* on xi. 7), who is simply making the most of his time (ver. 12). *Moriturus mordet.* Once this cardinal aim of the piece is grasped—and the proofs of it are overflowing—the accessory details fall into their proper place, just as in the interpretation of the parables. In all such products of the poetical and religious imagination, picturesque items, which were necessary to the completeness and impressiveness of the sketch, are not to be invested with primary significance. Besides, in the case of an old story or tradition which had passed through successive phases, it was inevitable that certain traits should lose much if not all of their meaning.

XII. 1. Καὶ [a] σημεῖον μέγα ὤφθη ἐν τῷ οὐρανῷ, γυνὴ [b] περιβεβλημένη τὸν [b] ἥλιον—καὶ ἡ σελήνη ὑποκάτω τῶν ποδῶν αὐτῆς,

a Matt. xxiv. 30, parll. Matt. ii. 2.
b Ps. civ. 2.

"These ancient *traits*, fragments of an earlier whole, which lack their proper connexion in the present account, and indeed are scarcely intelligible, as they have been wrested from the thought-sequence of the original writer, reveal to the expert the presence of an earlier form of the story" (*S. C.* p. 6.)

CHAPTER XII.—The procedure of the writer here is very much the same as in ch. xi. (see above). The oracle of xii. is not an allegorising version of history, nor an exegetical construction of O.T. texts, nor a free composition of the author, but the Christianised reproduction of a Jewish source (possibly from the same period as the basis of xi. 1-13, or at least from the same **βιβλαρίδιον**), or at any rate a tradition, which described the birth of messiah in terms borrowed from such cosmological myths as that of the conflict between the sun-god and the dragon of darkness and the deep. The psychological origin of such a Jewish adaptation would be explained if we presupposed a tradition similar to that of the later Talmud (Jer. *Berach.* fol. 5, 1) which described the messiah as born at Bethlehem and swept away from his mother by a storm-wind, just after the fall of Jerusalem. But this messiah is merely removed, not raised to heaven. And as we have no clear evidence that the stress of 68-70 A.D. excited such a messianic hope among the Pharisees, it is hazardous to use this (as *e.g.*, Jülicher and Wellhausen still do) to prove that the date of the source is the same as that of xi. 1 f. The structure of the passage is equally ambiguous. 4 *a* presupposes something equivalent to ver. 7-9, while 13-16 is an expansion or variant of 6; and yet 13 is the natural sequel to 9 (12). These features have led to a variety of literary reconstructions. Spitta, *e.g.*, takes ver. 6 as the Christian editorial anticipation of 13 f., and finds another Christian touch in ver. 11 (Weyland in 11 and 17 *c*). J. Weiss puts 1-6 and 13-17 together, regarding 7-12 as an independent continuation of the third woe (editorial notes in 3, 11, and 17). Wellhausen (*Analyse*, 18 *f*) bisects the oracle into two parallel but incomplete variants (A=1-6, B=7-9, 13, 14), with 15-17 as an editorial conclusion. Others (*e.g.*, Schön and Calmes) find a Christian editor only in 10-12 (with 17 *c* of course)' while Weizsäcker regards 13-18 as the expansion of 1-12 (a Jewish-Christian fragment of 64-66 A.D.). Some of the incoherencies of the description are due, however, to the alterations necessitated by messianic belief in the circle of such ethnic traditions. The latter made the mother's flight precede the child's birth (as in 4, 5). But, on the messianic scheme, it was the child's birth which roused the full fury of the enemy and turned it into an outburst of baffled revenge upon the mother (6, 13 f.), after the child's escape. Furthermore, this activity of the devil on earth had to be accounted for by his dislodgement from heaven, as a result of the messianic child's elevation to heaven (7 f.). Hence the apparent inconsistencies, the shifting standpoint, and the amount of repetition and confusion are due to the presence of a messianic conception employing terms of earlier and inadequate mythology for its own purposes, rather than to any literary rearrangement such as the transposition of part of the trumpet-visions to 7-12 (Simcox, J. Weiss). The interest of the prophet in this source or tradition, as in that of xi. 1-13, centres in the outburst of the evil power which shows that the end is imminent. There the beast's attack on messiah's heralds is ultimately foiled. Here the dragon's attack on messiah himself is not only defeated but turned into a rout which obliges him to shift the scene of his campaign to a field where his deputies are presently to be annihilated.

Vv. 1-2. **ἐν τ. οὐ.** almost="in the sky" (*cf.* ver. 4.). A Greek touch: *cf.* Hom. *Iliad*, ii. 308, ἔνθ' ἐφάνη μέγα σῆμα· δράκων ἐπὶ νῶτα δαφοινός (*i.e.* fiery-red). Here as elsewhere mythological traits of the original source are left as impressive and decorative details. The nearest analogy is the Babylonian Damkina, mother of the young god Marduk and "queen of the heavenly tiara" (*i.e.*, the stars, *cf.* Schrader, pp. 360, 361). For Hebrew applications of the symbolism *cf.* Gen. xxxvii. 9, 10 and Test. Naph. 5 (καὶ Ἰούδας ἦν λαμπρὸς ὡς ἡ σελήνη καὶ ὑπὸ τοὺς πόδας αὐτοῦ ἦσαν ιβ´ ἀκτῖνες). The Egyptian Osiris was also wrapt in a flame-coloured robe—the sun being the "body" of deity (Plut. *de Iside*,

καὶ [c] ἐπὶ [c] τῆς [c] κεφαλῆς αὐτῆς στέφανος ἀστέρων δώδεκα—2. καὶ ἐν γαστρὶ ἔχουσα· καὶ [d] κράζει [1] [d] ὠδίνουσα καὶ βασανιζομένη [e] τεκεῖν. 3. Καὶ ὤφθη ἄλλο σημεῖον ἐν τῷ οὐρανῷ, καὶ ἰδοὺ [f] δράκων [g] πυρρὸς μέγας, ἔχων [h] κεφαλὰς ἑπτὰ καὶ [i] κέρατα δέκα· καὶ ἐπὶ τὰς κεφαλὰς αὐτοῦ ἑπτὰ [k] διαδήματα· 4. καὶ ἡ οὐρὰ αὐτοῦ σύρει τὸ τρίτον τῶν ἀστέρων τοῦ οὐρανοῦ, καὶ ἔβαλεν αὐτοὺς εἰς τὴν γῆν. καὶ ὁ δράκων [l] ἕστηκεν ἐνώπιον τῆς γυναικὸς τῆς μελλούσης [m] τεκεῖν,

c Only here in Apoc. is ἐπί with gen. of κεφαλή.
d Isa. xxvi. 17, Mic. iv. 10.
e Obj. infin. of "desire implied in preced. ptcc" (Burton, 389).
f Ezek. xxix. 3; only in Apoc. in N.T.
g cf. vi. 4.
h Ps. lxxiv. 13-14.
i From Dan. vii. 7.
k Only in Apoc. in N.T., cf. xix. 12, xiii. 1.
l For form cf. Win. § 14, 14.
m τεκεῖν incorrectly for τίκτειν; τέκῃ (cf. xi. 7), on mood see Burton, 303, 305.

[1] Read και (ℵC, Aeth., Pr., S., etc.) κραζει (ℵAP, 1, etc., Hipp.), edd.

51). The original figure was that of Israel personified as a pregnant goddess-mother, but it probably represented to the prophet the true Israel or Zion of God (Wernle, 276-288) in which his Christ had been born (*cf.* John xvi. 21, with John xiv. 30, also En. xc. 37). The idealisation was favoured by the current conceptions of Zion as pre-existent in heaven (*cf.* xix. 8, xxi. 8, and Apoc. Bar. iv. = widow) and as a mother (4 Esd. ix. 38-x. 59). The prophet views the national history of Israel as a long preparation for the anguish and woe out of which the messiah was to come. "Tantae molis erat *Christianam* condere gentem" (Grotius). The idea is echoed in Ep. Lugd., where the church is "the virgin mother". The virgin-birth falls into the background here as in the Fourth Gospel, though for different reasons. The messiah of Apoc. xii. is not the son of Mary but simply born in the messianic community, and the description is no more than a transcendental version of what Paul notes in Rom. ix. 4, 5. The editor's interest lies not in the birth of messiah so much as in the consequences of it in heaven and earth. At the same time the analogies discovered between Cerinthus and this passage (by Völter and others) are wholly imaginary (Kohlhofer, 53 f.).

Ver. 3. **πυρρός**: Vergil's serpents which attack Laokoon have blood-red crests, and Homer's dragon has a blood-red back, but here the trait (*cf.* above) is reproduced from the red colour of Typhon, the Egyptian dragon who persecuted Osiris (Plut. *de Iside*, 30-33). The seven heads are taken from the seven-headed hydra or mušmaḫḫu of Babylonian mythology. The devil's deputy in xiii. 1 (= the composite mušruššu of Babylonia) has the same equipment of horns and heads, but the diadems adorn his horns. Here, to John's mind at any rate (*cf.* ver. 9), the dragon is not equivalent to any contemporary pagan power like Pompey (Ps. Sol. ii. 29) or the king of Babylon.

Ver. 4. The symbolism is a reminiscence of an ætiological myth in astrology (*cf.* the *cauda* of the constellation Scorpio) and of the primitive view which regarded the dark cloud as a snake enfolding the luminaries of heaven in its hostile coils (Job iii. 8, xxvi. 13, with A. B. Davidson's notes). Thus the Iranians (*S. B. E.* iv. p. lxxiii., Darmesteter) described the fiend as a serpent or dragon not on the score of craftiness but "because the storm fiend envelops the goddess of light with the coils of the cloud as with a snake's fold". The same play of imagination would interpret eclipses and falling stars, and, when the pious were compared to stars (as in Egyptian theology, Plut. *de Iside*, 21), it was but a step to the idea of Dan. viii. (*cf.* Sib. Or. v. 512 f., the battle of the stars), where Antiochus Epiphanes does violence to some devout Israelites who are characterised as stars flung rudely down to earth (*i.e.*, martyred, 1 Macc. i.) Originally, this description of the dragon lashing his tail angrily and sweeping down a third of the stars probably referred to the seduction of angels from their heavenly rank (so 8-9) to serve his will (Weiss). But John, in recasting the tradition, may have thought of the Danielic application, *i.e.*, of the devil succeeding in crushing by martyrdom a certain number of God's people. In this event, they would include at least, if they are not to be identified with, the pre-Christian martyrs of Judaism (*cf.* Heb. xi. 32 f. Matt. xxiii. 35).—**ἕστηκεν**, a conventional posture of the ancient dragon *cf. e.g.*, Pliny, *H. N.* viii. 3, "nec flexu multiplici ut reliquae serpentes cor-

ἵνα ὅταν [m] τέκῃ τὸ τέκνον αὐτῆς [n] καταφάγῃ. 5. Καὶ ἔτεκεν υἱόν
ἄρσενα,[1] ὃς μέλλει [o] ποιμαίνειν πάντα τὰ ἔθνη ἐν ῥάβδῳ [o] σιδηρᾷ·
καὶ [p] ἡρπάσθη τὸ τέκνον αὐτῆς πρὸς τὸν θεὸν καὶ πρὸς τὸν θρόνον
αὐτοῦ. 6. καὶ ἡ γυνὴ [q] ἔφυγεν εἰς τὴν ἔρημον, ὅπου ἔχει ἐκεῖ
τόπον ἡτοιμασμένον ἀπὸ τοῦ θεοῦ, ἵνα ἐκεῖ [r] τρέφωσιν αὐτὴν [s] ἡμέρας
χιλίας διακοσίας ἑξήκοντα.

n Matt. ii. 16-20, Luke xiii. 30-31, Acts iv. 25-27. o ii. 27, xix. 15; *cf.* Sib. Or. viii. 196 f. p Acts viii. 39, 1 Thess. iv. 17, 1 Cor. xii. 2, 4. q Matt. ii. 13, *cf.* Ps. Sol. xvii. 9. r (= τρέφεται, 14) for constr. see x. 11, Win. § 5, 20 f., Moult. i. 58-59. How? with heavenly food, like ancient Israel (Ps. lxxviii. 24, cv. 40)? s *Cf.* on xi. 2-3.

[1] Read **αρσενα** P, 95, Meth., And[bav] (Ws., Bs.) for the solecistic **αρσεν** (AC' Lach., Ti., Tr., Al. Sw., WH) [**αρρενα** (the Attic form, Thumb 77, Helbing 20) ℵQ, 1, etc., Areth., Bj.]: **α.** (Vict.) or **υ.** (Pr.) a redundant gloss? Wetstein cites a verbal parallel from Aristoph., *Eccles.*, 549-550 (**ἄρρεν γὰρ ἔτεκε παιδίον. ἠκκλησία;**). *Cf.* Cooke's *North Semitic Inscript.*, 221-222.

pus impellit, sed celsus et erectus in medio incedens"; *ibid.* viii. 14, for serpents devouring children. The mother of Zoroaster had also a vision of wild beasts waiting to devour her child at its birth. This international myth of the divine child menaced at birth readily lent itself to moralisation, or afforded terms for historical applications, *e.g.*, the abortive attack on Moses, the prototype of messiah (Baldensperger, 141, 142) at his birth (Ac. vii. 20 f.) and the vain efforts of Herod against the messiah. The animosity of Pytho for Leto was due to a prophecy that the latter's son would vanquish him.

Ver. 5. In accordance with the rabbinic notion which withdrew messiah for a time, the infant, like a second Moses, is caught up out of harm's way. He has no career on earth at all. This is intelligible enough in a Jewish tradition; but while no Christian prophet could have spontaneously depicted his messiah in such terms, even under the exigencies of apocalyptic fantasy, the further problem is to understand how he could have adopted so incongruous and inadequate an idea except as a pictorial detail. The clue lies in the popular messianic interpretation of passages like Ps. ii. where messiah's birth is really his inauguration and enthronement. The early application of this to Jesus, though not antagonistic to an interest in his historic personality, tallied with the widespread feeling (*cf.* note on i. 7) that his final value lay in his return as messiah. *Natiuitas quaedam eius ascensio*: "The heavens must receive him" (Acts iii. 21) till the divine purpose was ripe enough for his second advent. This tendency of primitive Jewish Christianity serves to explain how John could refer in passing to his messiah in terms which described a messiah, as Sabatier remarks, *sans la croix et sans la mort*, and which even represented his ascension as an escape rather than a triumph. The absence of any allusion to the Father is not due so much to any reluctance on the prophet's part to call Jesus by the name of *Son of God* (*cf.* ii. 18), which pagan usage had profaned not only in such mythical connexion but in the vocabulary of the Imperial cultus, as to the fact that the mythical substratum always gave special prominence to the mother; the goddess-mother almost invariably displaced the father in popular interest, and indeed bulked more largely than even the child.

Ver. 6. **ἀπὸ κ.τ.λ.**, = ὑπό of agent (so Acts ii. 22, iv. 36, etc., Ps. Sol. xv. 6, and a contemporary inscription in Dittenberger's *Sylloge Inscr.* 655^8 **συντετηρημένα ἀπὸ βασιλέων καὶ Σεβαστῶν**) only here in Apocalypse. On the flight of the faithful to the wilderness, a stereotyped feature of the antichrist period, *cf.* *A. C.* 211 f. Apocalyptic visions, particularly in the form of edited sources or adapted traditions, were not concerned to preserve strict coherency in details or consistency in situation. Thus it is not clear whether the **ἔρημος** was conceived to exist in heaven, or whether heaven is the background rather than the scene of what transpires. What follows in 7-12 is the description (from the popular religious version of the source) of what John puts from a definitely Christian standpoint in iii. 21, v. 5, where (as in *Asc. Isa.* Gk. ii. 9-11) the downfall of Satan is ascribed to Jesus himself.

t Foll. by loose infin. of explanation (*cf* Moult. i. 217-218). u From Dan. x. 13, 21, xii. 1, *cf.* Jude 9. v Matt. xxv. 41; evil beings in heaven, Asc. Isa. vi. 9 f.

7. Καὶ ἐγένετο [t] πόλεμος ἐν τῷ οὐρανῷ· ὁ [u] Μιχαὴλ καὶ οἱ
ἄγγελοι αὐτοῦ τοῦ πολεμῆσαι μετὰ τοῦ δράκοντος, καὶ ὁ δράκων
ἐπολέμησε καὶ [v] οἱ ἄγγελοι αὐτοῦ, 8. [w] καὶ οὐκ ἴσχυσεν,[1] οὐδὲ
[x] τόπος [x] εὑρέθη αὐτῶν ἔτι ἐν τῷ οὐρανῷ. 9. καὶ ἐβλήθη ὁ δράκων
ὁ μέγας, [y] ὁ ὄφις ὁ ἀρχαῖος, [z] ὁ καλούμενος "Διάβολος," καὶ "ὁ
Σατανᾶς," ὁ [a] πλανῶν τὴν οἰκουμένην ὅλην, [b] ἐβλήθη εἰς τὴν γῆν,
καὶ οἱ ἄγγελοι αὐτοῦ μετ᾽ αὐτοῦ ἐβλήθησαν. 10. καὶ ἤκουσα
[c] φωνὴν [c] μεγάλην ἐν τῷ οὐρανῷ λέγουσαν

w *εἰς οὐδὲν δέον συνέβη τελευτῆσαι τὴν τάξιν αὐτῶν* (Papias, cit. Andr.). x xx. 11, *Par. Lost*, vi. 56 f. y Isa. xxvii. 1. z xx. 2. a ii. 20, xx. 3, 8, 10. b From Slav. En. xxix. 5. c xi. 15, xix. 1.

[1] Read **ισχυσεν** (Ps. xii. 5, LXX) A, etc., Me., Aeth., And[c] (WH, Ws., Sw., Bs.), [verb agreeing as in LXX with principal subject, *cf.* Vit., ii. 114 f.].

Ver. 7. **ἐγένετο . . . τοῦ π.** (= ותהי מלחמה בשמים להלחם), the nomin. makes this rare use of the genit. infin. even more clumsy and irregular than the similar constr. with accus. in Acts x. 25 (where see note). The sense is plain, and it is better to put the constr. down to syntactical laxity than to conjecture subtle reasons for the blunder or to suggest emendations such as the addition of **ἐγένετο** to **πόλεμος** (Vit. i. 168), or of **ἦσαν** or **ἐγένετο** before **ὁ Μ. κ. οἱ ἄγ. αὐτοῦ** (Ws., Bousset), the latter being an irregular nomin., or the alteration of **πολ.** to **ἐπολέμησαν** (Düst.) or the simple omission of **πόλεμος . . . οὐρανῷ.** For **πολ. μετὰ** *cf.* Thumb 125 (a Copticism ?). In the present form of the oracle, the rapture of messiah seems to have stimulated the devil to fresh efforts, unless we are meant to understand that the initiative came from Michael and his allies. The devil, as the opponent of mankind had access to the Semitic heaven, but his rôle here recalls the primitive mythological conception of the dragon storming heaven (*A. C.* 146-150). Michael had been for over two centuries the patron-angel or princely champion of Israel (**ὁ εἷς τῶν ἁγίων ἀγγέλων ὃς ἐπὶ τῶν τοῦ λαοῦ ἀγαθῶν τέτακται,** En. xx. 5; *cf. A. C.* 227 f.; Lueken 15 f.; Volz 195; *R. J.* 320 f., and Dieterich's *Abraxas*, 122 f.). As the protector of Israel's interests he was assigned a prominent rôle by Jewish and even Christian eschatology in the final conflict (*cf.* Ass. Mos. x. 2). For the theory that he was the prince-angel, *like a son of man* (Dan. vii. 13) who subdued the world-powers, *cf.* Grill 55 and Cheyne 215 f. More generally, a celestial battle as the prelude of messiah's triumph on earth, forms an independent Jewish tradition which can be traced to the second century B.C. (*cf.* Sibyll. iii. 795-807, 2 Macc. v. 2-4; Jos. *Bell.* vi. 5, 3).—**καὶ οἱ ἄγγελοι αὐτοῦ.** The only allusion in the Apocalypse (*cf.* even xx. 11 with Matt. xxv. 41) to the double hierarchy of angels, which post-exilic Judaism took over from Persia (Bund, iii. 11). In the Leto-myth, Pytho returns to Parnassus after being baffled in his pursuit of the pregnant Leto.

Ver. 9. **Δράκων** and **ὄφις** are in the LXX interchangeable terms for the leviathan or sea-monster of mythology, who is here defined as *the old serpent* (a rabbinical expression, *cf.* Gfrörer, i. 386-389); so Tiâmat, the primaeval rebel, as dragon and serpent (*cf.* Rohde's *Psyche*, 371) had been identified in JE's paradise-story with the malicious and envious devil (Sap. ii. 24; En. xx. 7; Test. Reub. 5). The opponent of God was the adversary of man (*cf.* Oesterley's *Evol. of Mess. Idea*, 176 f.). Two characteristic traits of Satan are blended here: (*a*) cunning exercised on men to lure them into ruin (**πλανῶν, κ.τ.λ.,** *cf.* 2 Cor. ii. 11, xi. 3), and (*b*) eagerness to thwart and slander them before God (ver. 10, *cf.* En. xl. 7; Zech. iii. 1 f.). The second is naïve and archaic, of course, in a Christian apocalypse.

Ver. 10. **κατήγωρ** (קטיגור) is the counterpart to the rabbinic (Lueken 22) title of **συνήγορος** given to Michael as a sort of Greatheart or advocate and protector of men (En. xl. 9). The Aramaic derivation of the word (Win. § 8. 13) is not absolutely necessary, as the papyri show that it might have sprung up on Greek soil (*cf.* Thumb, 126; Rademacher,

"Ἄρτι ἐγένετο ἡ [d] σωτηρία καὶ ἡ δύναμις
καὶ ἡ βασιλεία τοῦ θεοῦ ἡμῶν καὶ ἡ ἐξουσία τοῦ [e] Χριστοῦ αὐτοῦ·
οτι ἐβλήθη ὁ κατήγωρ τῶν ἀδελφῶν ἡμῶν,
ὁ [f] κατηγορῶν αὐτοὺς ἐνώπιον τοῦ θεοῦ ἡμῶν ἡμέρας καὶ νυκτός.
11. καὶ αὐτοὶ [g] ἐνίκησαν αὐτὸν [h] διὰ τὸ αἷμα τοῦ ἀρνίου,
καὶ διὰ τὸν [i] λόγον τῆς [i] μαρτυρίας αὐτῶν,
καὶ [k] οὐκ ἠγάπησαν τὴν ψυχὴν αὐτῶν ἄχρι [k] θανάτου.
12. [l] διὰ τοῦτο [m] εὐφραίνεσθε [n] οὐρανοὶ καὶ οἱ ἐν αὐτοῖς [n] σκηνοῦντες.
[o] οὐαὶ τὴν γῆν καὶ τὴν θάλασσαν,
ὅτι κατέβη ὁ διάβολος πρὸς ὑμᾶς ἔχων θυμὸν μέγαν,
εἰδὼς ὅτι [p] ὀλίγον καιρὸν ἔχει."

13. Καὶ ὅτε εἶδεν ὁ δράκων ὅτι ἐβλήθη εἰς τὴν γῆν, ἐδίωξε τὴν
γυναῖκα [q] ἥτις ἔτεκε τὸν ἄρσενα. 14. καὶ [r] ἐδόθησαν τῇ γυναικὶ
αἱ δύο πτέρυγες τοῦ [s] ἀετοῦ τοῦ μεγάλου, ἵνα πέτηται εἰς τὴν ἔρημον

d *Cf.* on xix. 1; here alm.= "victory" (1 Sam. xix. 5, Ps. xx. 7, and Luke i. 71) ישׁוּעָה
e xi. 15, *cf.* xx. 4, 6 (final editor's hand).
f From Jub. xlviii. 15, 18.
g 1 John ii. 13-14. Rom. viii. 33-34, 37-39.
h iv. 11.
i i. 2, vi. 9.
k ii. 10, John xii. 25, Acts xx. 24.
l *i.e.*, over 9-10, not 11.
m Isa. xlii. 10 f., xliv. 23, xlix. 13.
n xviii. 20, Ps. xcvi. 11; only here (Apoc.) in plural.
o viii. 13, *cf.* Sib. Or. iii. 323.
p = 3½ years (6, 14), *cf.* xx. 3.
q *Cf.* on i. 7.
r viii. 2, xi. 1, etc., *cf.* Arist. *Hist. Nat.* x. 1, Hor. *Od.* iv. 4. 1, 9, Plut. *Timol.* xxvi., Jos. *Ant.* xii. 4, 10, Aesch. *Choeph.* 239 f., and Dan. vii. 4.

Rhein. Mus. lvii. 148). On the accuser's rôle *cf. Sohar Levit.* fol. 43 (ille semper stat tanquam delator coram rege Israelis) and the prayer of Jub. i. 20: "let not the spirit of Beliar rule over them to accuse them before thee and to turn them deceitfully from all the paths of righteousness" (where both traits are combined, *cf.* above on 9).

Ver. 11. This sentence, like ver. 7, suggests that earth's history is the reflex and outcome of transactions in heaven, on the common principle of Jalkut Rub. (on Exod. xiv. 7): "there was war above (in heaven) and war below (on earth), and sore was the war in heaven". Satan's dislodgment from heaven is another (*cf.* on xi. 19) sign of messiah's approaching victory (*cf.* Yasna xxx. 8). What Jesus had already seen in his own victory over daemons (Matt. xii. 24 f.; *cf.* J. Weiss, *Predigt Jesu*, 28 f., 89 f.), John hails from another standpoint, as inaugurating the messianic age. *Vexilla regis prodeunt.* How readily the mythological trait could be moralised is evident from a passage like Rom. viii. 33 f., of which Apoc. xii. 11 is a realistic variant. In the background lie conceptions like that of En. xl. 7 where the fourth angel of the Presence is heard "fending all the Satans and forbidding them to appear before the Lord of Spirits to accuse men". Ver. 11 chronologically follows ver. 17, but the author, by a characteristic and dramatic prolepsis, anticipates the triumph of the martyrs and confessors, who refute Satan's calumnies and resist his wiles. In opposition to the contemporary Jewish tradition (Ap. Bar. ii. 2, xiv. 12; 4 Esd. vii. 77, etc.), it is not reliance on works but the consciousness of redemption which enables them to bear witness and to bear the consequences of their witness. This victory on earth depends on Christ's previous defeat of evil in the upper world (Col. ii. 15; *cf.* above on ii. 10, also xxi. 8) which formed its headquarters.

Ver. 12. **εὐφραίνεσθε**, *cf.* the Egyptian hymn in honour of Rā, the sun-god: "Rā hath quelled his impious foes, heaven rejoices, earth is delighted".—**οὐαὶ κ.τ.λ.** This desperate and last effort of Satan is a common apocalyptic feature (*cf. e.g.*, 4 Esd. xiii. 16 f.; Ap. Bar. xxviii. 3, xli. 1, lxxv. 5; Mark xiii. 21; Did. xvi.), which John identifies later with the Imperial cultus.

The dragon's pursuit of the woman (13-17) resumes and expands the hint of ver. 6.

Ver. 14. "The two wings of a huge griffon-vulture" (**τοῦ** either generic ar-

εἰς τὸν τόπον αὐτῆς, [s]ὅπου τρέφεται [s]ἐκεῖ καιρὸν καὶ [t]καιροὺς
καὶ ἥμισυ καιροῦ [u]ἀπὸ προσώπου τοῦ ὄφεως. 15. καὶ ἔβαλεν
ὁ ὄφις ἐκ τοῦ στόματος αὐτοῦ ὀπίσω τῆς γυναικὸς ὕδωρ ὡς ποταμόν,
ἵνα αὐτὴν [v]ποταμοφόρητον ποιήσῃ. 16. καὶ ἐβοήθησεν ἡ γῆ τῇ
γυναικί, καὶ ἤνοιξεν ἡ γῆ τὸ στόμα αὐτῆς καὶ κατέπιε τὸν ποταμὸν
ὃν ἔβαλεν ὁ δράκων ἐκ τοῦ στόματος αὐτοῦ. 17. καὶ [w]ὠργίσθη ὁ
δράκων ἐπὶ τῇ γυναικί, καὶ ἀπῆλθε [x]ποιῆσαι [x]πόλεμον μετὰ τῶν
λοιπῶν τοῦ [y]σπέρματος αὐτῆς, τῶν [z]τηρούντων τὰς ἐντολὰς τοῦ θεοῦ
καὶ [a]ἐχόντων τὴν μαρτυρίαν Ἰησοῦ.

s. ver. 6. t Dan. vii. 25 (Theod.), xii. 7; = dual (Win. § 27, 5). u Hebraism (מפני הנחש) = "safe from". v ἅπ. λεγ. N.T. With ἐποίησεν = ἀπόερσεν (Hesych. on *Iliad*, vi. 348). "To get her swept away by the stream". w xi. 18 = "waxed wroth". x xi. 7. y *Cf.* 2 John 1, 4, 13; also 1 Pet. i. 1-2, iv. 12 f. z 1 John ii. 3, iii. 22, 24, 1 Cor. vii. 19. a vi. 9, xiv. 12, xix. 10, etc.

ticle, or a Hebraism, or more likely an allusion to the mythological basis). In traditional mythology the eagle opposed and thwarted the serpent at all points (*cf.* reff.). In the Egyptian myth the vulture is the sacred bird of Isis (Hathor). Any allusion to Israel's deliverance (as in Exod. xix. 4; Deut. xxxii. 11) is at best secondary.

Ver. 15. Another mythological metaphor for persecution or persecutors, like "torrents of Belial" (Ps. xviii. 4). As the primaeval dragon was frequently a sea-monster, from Tiâmat onwards, his connexion with water (*cf.* on viii. 10) was a natural development in ancient (*cf.* Pausan. v. 43 f.) and even Semitic (*e.g.*, Ps. lxxiv. 4; Ezek. xxix., xxxii.) literature. The serpent in the river was, for Zoroastrians, a creation of the evil spirit (Vend. i. 3).

Ver. 16. The dragon is unexpectedly baffled by the earth, as the woman's ally, which swallows the persecutors like Korah, Dathan, and Abiram (Num. xvi. 30-32). This enigmatic detail has not yet been paralleled from Jewish or early Christian literature, for *Protev. Jacobi*, 22 (cited by Selwyn, 7-9) is even more remote than 4 Esd. xiii. 44. Probably it was retained from the astrological setting of the original myth: Cetos, the aquatic dragon of the southern heavens, which astrologically is a watery region, casts forth the river of Êridanos, which is swallowed up in the zodiac as it flows down the heavens into the underworld.

Ver. 17. The baffled adversary now widens his sphere of operations.—**τ.λ.** an apocalyptic term = the *derelicti* or *relicti* of 4 Esdras (*cf.* Volz, 319). These represent to the Christian editor the scattered Christians in the Empire; by adding this verse (or at least **καὶ ἐχ. . . . Ἰησοῦ**) to the source, he paves the way for the following saga of xiii. which depicts the trying situation of Christians exposed to the attack of the devil's deputies. The devil keeps himself in the background. He works subtly through the Roman power. This onset on the faith and faithfulness of Christians by the enforcement of the Imperial cultus is vividly delineated in Ep. Lugd. which incidentally mentions the experience of Biblias who, like Cranmer, repented of a recantation. "The devil, thinking he had already swallowed up B., one of those who had denied Christ, desired to condemn her further by means of blasphemy, and brought her to the torture [*i.e.*, in order to force false accusations from her lips]. . . . But she, reminded by her present anguish of the eternal punishment in Gehenna [*cf.* Apoc. xiv. 9 f.], contradicted the blasphemous slanderers, confessed herself a Christian, and was added to the order of the martyrs." Blandina, the heroic slave-girl, survived several conflicts **ἵνα νικήσασα τῷ μὲν σκολιῷ ὄφει ἀπαραίτητον ποιήσῃ τὴν καταδίκην.**

The keynote of the situation hinted in xii. 17 f. is struck in xiii. 2. *The dragon* has given *his authority to the beast*; what God's people have now to contend with is no longer the O.T. Satan merely (xii. 9, 10) but his powerful and seductive delegate on earth. In the Imperial cultus the Christian prophet could see nothing except a supreme and diabolically subtle manœuvre of Satan himself (*cf.* on xiii. 1 and 5). The Danielic prophecy was at last on the verge of fulfilment! Mythological and cosmological elements (*S. C.* 360 f.) were already present in the Danielic tradition, but the prophet (or the source which he edits) readapted them to the historical situation created by the ex-

18. Καὶ [b] ἐστάθην [1] ἐπὶ τὴν ἄμμον τῆς θαλάσσης, XIII. 1. καὶ
εἶδον ἐκ τῆς θαλάσσης θηρίον ἀναβαῖνον, ἔχον κέρατα δέκα καὶ
κεφαλὰς ἑπτά, καὶ ἐπὶ τῶν κεράτων αὐτοῦ δέκα διαδήματα, καὶ
ἐπὶ τὰς κεφαλὰς αὐτοῦ [a] ὀνόματα βλασφημίας. 2. καὶ τὸ θηρίον
ὃ εἶδον ἦν [b] ὅμοιον [c] παρδάλει, καὶ οἱ πόδες αὐτοῦ ὡς [d] ἄρκου, καὶ
τὸ στόμα αὐτοῦ ὡς στόμα λέοντος. [e] καὶ ἔδωκεν αὐτῷ ὁ δράκων
τὴν δύναμιν αὐτοῦ καὶ τὸν θρόνον αὐτοῦ καὶ ἐξουσίαν μεγάλην.
3. καὶ [f] μίαν ἐκ τῶν κεφαλῶν αὐτοῦ ὡς ἐσφαγμένην εἰς θάνατον.

b On form, *cf.* Helbing, 98-99.
a *Cf.* xvii. 3.
b From Dan. vii. 4-6.
c Here only, N T.: *cf.* Ign. *Rom.* v. λεοπάρδοις, ὅ ἐστιν στρατιωτικὸν τάγμα.
d On form, *cf.* Win. § 5, 31, Helbing, 21-22.
e Dan. vii. 6, *cf.* Matt. iii. 8, 9, etc.
f xvii. 7-8.
Sc. εἶδον.

[1] For **εσταθην** (PQ, Me., S., etc., And., Areth. so Ti., Al., S. Davidson, Ew., Ramsay, Briggs, Gunkel, J. Weiss, Bs., Bj., etc.), Lach., Tr., Düst., Hofm., WH, Ws. (p. 5), Sw., Holtz., Hirscht, read **εσταθη** (אAC, 87, 92, vg., Arm., Aeth., Spec., Haym., Tic.), as if the dragon awaited the rise of the beast. But of this there is no hint in the context. A new start is made here, and what follows is (unlike xii.) a personal vision of the seer who is now dealing with present-day actualities. The variant seems due to an erroneous attempt to deepen the continuity of the two oracles (which is expressed in xii. 17*a* and xiii. 2*c*).

pectation of Nero's return from the under world and the enforcement of the Imperial cultus. For the hypothesis of a Caligula-source in this chapter, *cf.* Introd § 6.

xii. 18-xiii. 18: the saga of the woman and the red dragon (a war in heaven) is followed by the saga of the two monsters from sea and land (a war on earth), who, with the dragon, form a triumvirate of evil. First (xii. 18-xiii. 10) the monster from the sea, *i.e.*, the Roman Empire.

Ver. 18. The scene is the sea-shore, *ex hypothesi*, of the Mediterranean (*Phædo*, 109 *b*, 111 *a*, etc.), *i.e.*, the West, the whole passage being modelled on Dan. vii. 2, 3, 7, 8, 19-27, where the stormy sea from which the monsters emerge is the world of nations (*cf.* 4 Esd. xi. 1: ecce ascendebat de mari aquila, also xiii. 1).

Chapter XIII.—Ver. 1. His ten horns first become visible. The prophet has shifted the diadems from the heads to the horns (thereby altering their number, of necessity), since he wishes to stamp the heads (*i.e.*, the Roman emperors, *cf.* Sib. Or. iii. 176; Tac. *Ann.* xv. 47) with the blasphemous names. Hence the ten horns (successive monarchs in the Danielic oracle) are superfluous here, except as an archaic, pictorial detail in the sketch of this polycephalous brute. Such grotesque, composite monsters were familiar figures in Persian and Babylonian mythology. The blasphemous title of *divus*, assumed by the emperors since Octavian (Augustus = **σεβαστός**) as a semi-sacred title, implied superhuman claims which shocked the pious feelings of Jews and Christians alike. So did **θεός** and **θεοῦ υἱός** which, as the inscriptions prove, were freely applied to the emperors, from Augustus onwards. The imperial system, especially with its demand for imperial worship, appeared the embodiment of irreverence and profane infatuation (ver. 6). This calm usurpation of divine honours was inexplicable except on the supposition (ver. 2) that the empire was a tool or agent of the devil himself. Much had happened since Paul wrote Rom. xiii. 1-6, and even since Asiatic Christians had received the counsel of 1 Peter ii. 13 f.

Ver. 2. The empire gathered up all the obnoxious qualities of Israel's former oppressors: craft, lust of blood, and vicious energy. Hence the combination of traits from Daniel's four beasts: general appearance that of a fierce panther, feet like a bear's (*i.e.*, plantigrade), jaws like a lion's (of devouring strength)—a Palestinian (Hos. xiii. 7, 8) picture of a perfect beast of prey, raging and ravening, before whom the church, like Dryden's milk-white Hind, "was often forced to fly, And doom'd to death, though fated not to die".—**καὶ ἔδωκεν κ.τ.λ.**, connecting the empire with the dragon of xii. and stamping it as Satanic (*cf.* Lueken, 22 f.; Weinel, 11-12), as a weird and wild messiah of the devil on earth.

Ver. 3. The prophet sees in the empire an extraordinary vitality which adds to its fascination. Disasters which would suffice to ruin an ordinary state, leave

[f] καὶ ἡ πληγὴ τοῦ θανάτου [g] αὐτοῦ ἐθεραπεύθη, καὶ [h] ἐθαυμάσθη ὅλη ἡ γῆ [h] ὀπίσω τοῦ θηρίου. 4. καὶ προσεκύνησαν [i] τῷ δράκοντι ὅτι ἔδωκεν τὴν ἐξουσίαν τῷ θηρίῳ,[1] καὶ προσεκύνησαν τῷ θηρίῳ λέγοντες,

"τίς [k] ὅμοιος τῷ θηρίῳ;

"καὶ τίς δύναται πολεμῆσαι μετ' αὐτοῦ;"

5. καὶ ἐδόθη αὐτῷ στόμα [l] λαλοῦν μεγάλα καὶ βλάσφημα·[2]

καὶ ἐδόθη αὐτῷ ἐξουσία [m] ποιῆσαι μῆνας [n] τεσσαράκοντα δύο·

6. καὶ ἤνοιξε τὸ στόμα αὐτοῦ εἰς βλασφημίας πρὸς τὸν θεόν,

g *i.e.*, the person denoted by *μίαν* or the beast. h xvii. 8; pregn. constr. "went after him in wonder". *Cf.* Acts viii. 9-11. Antithesis to John xi. 48-49. i Apart from this verse, *προσκ.* in Apoc. takes the dative only with God or angels (xix. 10). k xviii. 18, Exod. xv. 11, Jud. vi. 2, Ps. cxiii. 5, etc. l *Cf.* En. v. 4, xcviii. 7-8, ci. 3, cii. 6, 4 Esd. xi. 43, Ps. xii. 4. m From Dan. viii. 12, 24, xi. 28, 30, 32; pregn. Heb. use = "exercise" or "practise" (intrans.), with ἐξ. not *μῆνας* (Jas. iv. 13). n xi. 2.

[1] For **το θηριον** (A 79, And[a], Ws., WH marg., Bs.) read **τω θηριω** (ℵCPQ, etc., And[c], Areth., edd.). [The acc. is conformed to general usage of **προσκ.** with **θηριον**, see ver. 8, 12, xiv. 9, 11, xx. 4.]

[2] Read **βλασφημα** A, 12, 28, 34, 35, 47, 79, 87, And., etc. (Lach. Al. Ws.): the idiomatic **ποιησαι** has been early improved by the addition of **ο θελει** (ℵ) or **πολεμον** (Q, And[c], Areth.), and Naber conj. **σημεια ποιησαι.**

Rome as strong as ever, thanks to her marvellous recuperative power. The allusion is not to the murder of Cæsar (so *e.g.*, Bruston, Gunkel, Porter), nor to the illness of Caligula (Spitta), but (so Düsterdieck, O. Holtzmann, B. Weiss, etc.) to the terrible convulsions which in 69 A.D. shook the empire to its foundations (Tac. *Hist.* i. 11). Nero's death, with the bloody interregnum after it, was a wound to the State, from which it only recovered under Vespasian. It fulfilled the tradition of the wounded head (Dan. viii. 8). So 4 Esd. xii. 18 (where the same crisis is noted) "post tempus regni illius [*i.e.*, Nero's] nascentur contentiones non modicae et periclitabitur ut cadat et non cadet tunc, sed iterum constituetur in suum initium"; also Suet. *Vesp.* 1 and Joseph. *Bell.* iv. 11, 5, vii. 4, 2 (Rome unexpectedly rescued from ruin by Vespasian's accession). The vitality of the pagan empire, shown in this power of righting itself after the revolution, only added to its prestige. The infatuation of loyalty, expressing itself in the worship of the emperor as the personal embodiment of the empire, grew worse and worse. A comparison of 3 *a* with 12 (*cf.* 18) shows, however, a further allusion, *viz.*, to the Nero redivivus belief (*cf.* Introd. § 5). This is not developed until xvii., but already the beast is evidently identified in a sense with one of its heads, who is a travesty (3 *a* = v. 6) of the Lamb, *i.e.*, an antichrist. The context would certainly read quite naturally without 3 *a*, but it is implied in 12 (and 18), and none of the numerous attempts to analyse the chapter into source and revision is of any weight, in view of the general style and characteristics. These indicate the author's own hand. Even the translation-hypothesis (*e.g.*, Bruston, Gunkel) leads to arbitrary handling. See Introd. § 6.

Ver. 4. All that had transpired—Nero's own death heralding a return, and the collapse of his dynasty proving no fatal blow to the empire—had simply aggrandised the influence of Rome. The Caesar-cult which characterised it is dubbed a worship of Satan by the indignant prophet. The hymn to the incomparable and invincible beast is a parody of O.T. hymns to God. In the following description (vv. 5-8) two traits are blended: insolent blasphemy towards God and almost irresistible powers of seduction over men. Both are adapted from the classical sketch of Antiochus Epiphanes (in Dan. vii. 8, 20, 25, xii. 7), the prototype of that anti-divine force whose climax had been reached, as the prophet believed, in the divine pretensions of the Caesars.

Ver. 5. "Big and blasphemous (or abusive; 2 Peter ii. 11) words." So Apoc. Bar. lxvii. 7: "surget rex Babylonis qui destruxit nunc Sionem et gloriabitur super populo et loquetur magna in corde suo coram Altissimo".

Ver. 6. The days of Antiochus (Dan. viii. 10-12) have returned. On the claims

βλασφημῆσαι τὸ ὄνομα αὐτοῦ καὶ τὴν σκηνὴν αὐτοῦ [τοὺς ἐν ° Cf. John
τῷ οὐρανῷ σκηνοῦντας].
7. καὶ ° ἐδόθη αὐτῷ ᵖ ποιῆσαι πόλεμον μετὰ τῶν ἁγίων καὶ
νικῆσαι αὐτούς·
καὶ ἐδόθη αὐτῷ ᑫ ἐξουσία ἐπὶ πᾶσαν φυλὴν καὶ γλῶσσαν καὶ
ᑫ ἔθνος.[1]
8. καὶ προσκυνήσουσιν ʳ αὐτὸν πάντες οἱ κατοικοῦντες ἐπὶ τῆς
γῆς,
ˢ οὗ οὐ ᵗ γέγραπται τὸ ὄνομα αὐτοῦ ἐν τῷ βιβλίῳ τῆς ζωῆς [τοῦ
ἀρνίου τοῦ ἐσφαγμένου] ἀπὸ καταβολῆς κόσμου.
9. ᵘ εἴ τις ἔχει οὖς, ἀκουσάτω.

o Cf. John xix. 10-11, and below on xvii. 17.
p xi. 7. Fulfilment of Dan. vii. 21.
q Dan. v. 19, vii. 23.
r Constr. ad sensum, "the beast, or his Imperial representative *pro tem.*" *Cf.* Tiridates to Nero (Dio Cass. lxiii.): "I come to worship thee, my God, as Mithras".
s Referring to each individual of πάντες.
t Dan. xii. 1; *cf.* Ep. Jer. 6, Addit. Esth. xiii. 14, xiv. 3-10.
u ii. 7, etc.

[1] The omission of 7*a* in ACP, 1, 12, 14, 92, Arm. (zoh.), Iren., Andᵖ, Andᵇᵃᵛ (so Spitta) is due to homoioteleuton.

of the emperor, see Introd. § 6, and Sib. Or. v. 33, 34 (Nero **ἰσάζων θεῷ αὐτόν**), Asc. Isa. iv. 6-8, x. 13, etc.—**τοὺς . . . σκηνοῦντας,** an exegetic gloss defining **σκήνη** (*cf.* xii. 7, 12). The temple in Jerusalem is no longer the scene and object of the beast's blasphemy.

Ver. 7. In Enoch xlvi. 7 the rulers and kings "make themselves masters of the stars of heaven [*i.e.*, the righteous], and raise their hands against the Most High". The beast's world-wide authority goes back to the dragon's commission (2) but ultimately to divine permission (so in 5). There is a providence higher even than the beast.

Ver. 8. Standing on the verge of this crisis (note the change to the future tense), the prophet anticipates the almost universal success of the Cæsar-cult (*cf.* iii. 10). Only the elect will be able to resist its appeal (*cf.* Matt. xxiv. 25). As in the O.T., the consciousness of predestination is made a moral lever (*cf.* xvii. 8). The rest of mankind who succumb to the cult are plainly not on the celestial burgess-roll or register. *Cf.* the instructive second-century gloss on Acts v. 39. As a rule the faithless in life are deceived (2 Th. ii. 2-10; *Asc. Isa.* iv. 7, 8), but here the Imperial cultus occupies the place of the false prophet in Mark xiii. 12, etc,—**τοῦ ἀ. τοῦ ἐσφαγμένου,** which transfers to Christ the possession of the divine register of citizens in the heavenly state, is usually taken as a scribe's gloss (after xxi. 27 where the position of **ἀρνίου** is less difficult). Elsewhere *the book of life* appears by itself. In any case, **ἀπὸ κ. κ.** goes with **γέγραπται**, not **ἐσφαγμένου.**

Ver. 9. The prophet's *nota bene* introduces (ver. 10) what is either (*a*) a demand for patience and non-resistance, or (*b*) an encouragement to it. (*a*) "Be patient. If captivity is your destiny from God, accept it. *If any one is* (destined) *for captivity, to captivity he goes* (in God's order, **ὑπάγει** in a future sense). Show your patient faith in God by abstaining from the use of force" (*cf.* Matt. xxvi. 52). This interpretation (rejecting **συνάγει** or **ἀπάγει** in 10 *a*) is preferable to (*b*) that which reads (or even understands; with B. Weiss) **συνάγει, ἀπάγει,** or **ὑπάγει** (so some cursives and versions) in 10 *a*, and thus finds in the words a promise of requital rather than an appeal for endurance. The fate inflicted on Christians will recoil on their persecutors (*cf.* xiv. 12). Imprisonment or captivity and death were the normal fates of the age for criminals who refused to invoke the emperor's genius (*cf.* Jos. *Bell.* iii. 10. 10, vi. 8. 2, Philo: *de Flacc.* 11, *leg. ad Gaium*, 32). A variation of this meaning would be: use force, and you (Christians) will suffer for it. The whole stanza is written for saints who, like Sigurd, are not born for blenching.—**ὧδε κ.τ.λ.** Josephus (*Bell.* iii. 5. 8, etc.) had just given, from prudential motives, a similar warning to Jews against participating in any anti-Roman movement. It was always hard to disabuse the Oriental mind of the idea that religious faith must be bound up with fate and fighting. *Cf.* Introd. § 6.

10. [v]εἴ τις εἰς αἰχμαλωσίαν,
εἰς αἰχμαλωσίαν ὑπάγει·
εἴ τις ἐν [w]μαχαίρῃ ἀποκτενεῖ,
δεῖ αὐτὸν ἐν [w]μαχαίρῃ ἀποκτανθῆναι·
[x]ὧδέ ἐστιν ἡ [y]ὑπομονὴ καὶ [z]ἡ πίστις τῶν ἁγίων.
11. Καὶ εἶδον ἄλλο θηρίον ἀναβαῖνον ἐκ τῆς γῆς, καὶ εἶχε κέρατα
δύο [a]ὅμοια ἀρνίῳ, καὶ [b]ἐλάλει ὡς δράκων. 12. καὶ τὴν ἐξουσίαν
τοῦ πρώτου θηρίου [c]πᾶσαν ποιεῖ [d]ἐνώπιον [e]αὐτοῦ· καὶ [f]ποιεῖ τὴν
γῆν καὶ τοὺς [g]ἐν αὐτῇ κατοικοῦντας [f]ἵνα προσκυνήσουσι τὸ θηρίον
τὸ πρῶτον, οὗ ἐθεραπεύθη ἡ πληγὴ τοῦ θανάτου [e]αὐτοῦ· 13.
καὶ ποιεῖ [h]σημεῖα μεγάλα ἵνα καὶ [i]πῦρ ποιῇ ἐκ τοῦ οὐρανοῦ καταβαίνειν εἰς τὴν γῆν ἐνώπιον τῶν ἀνθρώπων. 14. καὶ [k]πλανᾷ τοὺς
κατοικοῦντας ἐπὶ τῆς γῆς [l]διὰ τὰ σημεῖα ἃ ἐδόθη αὐτῷ ποιῆσαι
[m]ἐνώπιον τοῦ θηρίου, λέγων τοῖς κατοικοῦσιν ἐπὶ τῆς γῆς ποιῆσαι

v Gen. ix. 6 Jer. xv. 2 (LXX).
w Ionian form (Win. § 8, 1; *cf.* Thumb, 68 f.)?
x *Cf.* ver. 18; Win. § 23, 1. "Here is room for."
y See on i. 9, also xiv. 2. "Et quo contemptius abuteretur patientia hominum" (Suet. *Dom.* 11).
z Sec. article usually omitted. Win. § 18, 7*b*. For idea, *cf.* 4 Macc. xvi. 18-23, etc. For form, *cf.* *Class. Rev.* 1904, 108-109, Helbing, 31-32.
a Chap. ix. 10; from Dan. viii. 3; *cf.* Matt. vii. 15, of which this passage forms an apocalyptic application.
b Gen. iii. 15, *cf.* 1 Macc. i. 30.
c *Cf.* Win. § 20, 11 f.
d Ver. 14, xix. 20.
e *Cf.* on iii. 8.
f *Cf.* iii. 9 (xiii. 15).
g With ἐν, here only.
h xvi. 14, xix. 20, so (Beliar) Sib. Or. iii. 63-74, 2 Thess. ii. 9, Mark xiii. 22, etc.
i xi. 5; as false Elijah.
k ii. 20, Deut. xiii. 2-4. En. lxvii. 7.
l *Cf.* xii. 2 (διὰ=dat. instrum.).
m By his authority, or at his instigation (*cf.* Num. iii. 6, etc.).

Vv. 11-18: the Imperial *alter ego* or the second beast, a monster from the land (identified afterwards with the traditional "false prophet," xvi. 13, xix. 20, xx. 10). This mythological figure is not any individual like Simon Magus or Alexander of Abonoteichos or Apollonius of Tyana or Balaam redivivus, but a personification of some order or institution devoted to the interests of the empire on its religious side, *i.e.*, the priests of the Cæsar-cult in the provinces and especially (*cf.* Introd. § 6) in Asia Minor, where the local dignitaries acted through the Diet of Asia in order to superintend and popularise the cult (so Holtzm., Pfleid., Charles, Bartlet, Porter, Bousset, Forbes, Swete). The following description brings out the cunning, suavity, and arrogance of this sacerdotal power.

Ver. 11. **ἐκ τῆς γῆς**—the mythological trait is applied geographically to Asia Minor (*i.e.*, the East). Here again the cosmological antithesis has been transformed into a political application. The marine monster cannot exercise dominion over the land except through an intermediary **ἐκ τῆς γῆς**. *Cf.* Apoc. Bar. xxix. 4, where the two beasts, leviathan and behemoth, rise from the sea and the land, as in the ancient Semitic and Babylonian mythology the dry land and the deep were the habitations of the two primeval monsters (En. lx. 7 f., 4 Esd. vi. 49 f.), who represented the chaos-opponent of heaven. The mild appearance of the beast (**ὁμ. ἀρν.** does not mean that he deceived men with the name of the Lamb) is accompanied by a plausible appeal (*cf.* Weinel, 21 f.). The allusion (ver. 12), borrowed from the older dragon-myth, is to the seductive inducements held out by the Beast to Christians, such as considerations of loyalty, patriotism, self-interest, and the like. These are backed by (ver. 13) miracles, which together with magic are also connected with Nero redivivus in *Asc. Isa.* iv. 9-11 (*cf. A. C.* 175 f.). The deceptive influence of miracles was a sure sign of the end, in early Christian literature (*cf.* the lines of the **πρεσβύτης** cited by Irenæus, i. 15, 6). Most Oriental cults practised such tricks lavishly, and constant warnings against them were heard (*cf.* Weinel 9; Friedländer, iii. 458 f., 521 f.).

Ver. 14. As Beliar sets up "his image before him in every city" (*Asc. Isa.* iv. 11, after 10="and there will be the power of his miracles in every city and region"), so here the **εἰκών** or bust of the emperor as the Neronic antichrist representing the empire (*cf.* the hint repeated from ver. 12 *c*) is brought forward along with the statues of the gods to receive offerings of wine and incense

εἰκόνα τῷ θηρίῳ [n] ὃς ἔχει τὴν πληγὴν τῆς μαχαίρης καὶ ἔζησε. 15.
καὶ ἐδόθη αὐτῷ δοῦναι πνεῦμα τῇ εἰκόνι τοῦ θηρίου, ἵνα καὶ
[o] λαλήσῃ ἡ εἰκὼν τοῦ θηρίου, καὶ [p] ποιήσει [1] ἵνα [q] ὅσοι ἂν μὴ προσ-
κυνήσωσι τὴν εἰκόνα τοῦ θηρίου [p] ἀποκτανθῶσι. 16. καὶ [p] ποιεῖ
πάντας, τοὺς μικροὺς καὶ τοὺς μεγάλους, καὶ τοὺς πλουσίους καὶ
τοὺς πτωχούς, καὶ τοὺς ἐλευθέρους καὶ τοὺς δούλους, [p] ἵνα [r] δῶσιν
αὐτοῖς [s] χάραγμα ἐπὶ τῆς [t] χειρὸς αὐτῶν τῆς [t] δεξιᾶς, ἢ ἐπὶ
τὸ [u] μέτωπον αὐτῶν, 17. [καὶ] [v] ἵνα μή τις δύνηται [2] [w] ἀγοράσαι ἢ
πωλῆσαι, εἰ μὴ ὁ ἔχων τὸ χάραγμα, τὸ ὄνομα τοῦ θηρίου, [x] ἢ τὸν
ἀριθμὸν τοῦ ὀνόματος αὐτοῦ. 18. [x] ὧδε ἡ [y] σοφία ἐστίν. ὁ ἔχων

n Cf. on αὐτόν (8).
o Acts xvi. 16.
p Cf. ver. 12. Double use of ποιεῖν, the ἵνα . . . ποιῇ (epexeg. of μεγάλα) of ver. 13 (with πῦρ displaced for emphasis) = ὥστε ποιεῖν of result (Burton, 322).
q Dan. iii. 5-7, 15.
r Indef. plur. as x. 11, xvi. 15 (= "they get").
s xiv. 9-11, xvi. 2, xix. 18-20 (vii. 3, ix. 4), cf. Ps. Sol. xv. 30.
t Cf. Assuan Papyri (K, 4. 6).
u Cf. Jos. Ant. iii. 7. 6. Or neck? Ps. Sol. ii. 6.
v = Infin. epexeg. 1 John v. 20, etc. Burton, 198, 213.
w 1 Macc. xiii. 49.
x xvii. 9, cf. 4 Esd. vi. 10 ζήτει, Ἔζρα.
y only here in Apoc., of human quality; cf. v. 12, vii. 12.

[1] **ποιησει** ℵ (min.), Syr., Tr. marg., WH marg., Ws.: for **την εικονα** (A, min., Lach. Al. Bs.) Ti., Tr., WH, Ws., Bj., Sw. read **τη εικονι** (ℵPQ, etc., Hipp., Areth.). Little is to be said for WH's conj. that **τη γη** has been either lost after or displaced by **αυτη (αυτω)**.

[2] Lach., Ti., Bj. om., Al. WH, Bs. Sw. bracket, the **και** of ℵcAPQ, etc., vg., Arm., Aeth., Areth., Haym.: the irreg. **δυναται** is read by PQ, min. (Ws., WH marg., Bs.).

from the citizens. For the naïve identification of such images with the deities they represented see Friedländer, iii. 500 f.—**λέγων = κελεύων** (Blass § 72, 5).

Ver. 15. The statue is made to speak, in order to work on the credulity and awe of the worshippers. The trick was well within the reach of contemporary magic (*cf.* Valer. Maxim. i. 8. 3-5), and later tradition attributed it to Simon Magus (Clem. *Recogn.* iii. 47, *cf.* Clem. *Hom.* ii. 32), while similar ventriloquism was practised by Apollonius of Tyana and Egyptian sorcerers at Caligula's court. *Cf.* Lucian's **αὐτόφωνοι χρησμοὶ** (*Alex.* 26).—**ἀποκτανθῶσιν**, *cf.* the scutcheon of Captain Pope in Bunyan's *Holy War*—"the stake, the flame, and the good man in it".

Vv. 16, 17. Detection was inevitable, for the very coins were stamped (Matt. xxii. 19) with the head of the Cæsar, the gods, or Rome itself, and the prophet apparently expected that genuine Christians would refuse to sanction idolatry and condone blasphemy by handling such emblems of profanity (*cf.* Ign. *ad Magn.* 5, **δύο νομίσματα, ὃ μὲν θεοῦ, ὃ δὲ κόσμου**). Only abject, servile devotees of the cultus will stoop to that! Irenæus has a similar allusion (iv. 30. 2) to those who carried money "cum inscriptione et imagine Cæsaris".—**μέτωπον**. This highly figurative allusion is to the habit of marking soldiers and slaves with a conspicuous tattoo or brand (*cf.* Lucian, *Dea Syra;* 3 Macc. ii. 29, where the Alexandrian Jews are branded with the mark of Dionysius; also on Gal. vi. 17); or, better still, to the religious custom of wearing a god's name as a talisman (*cf.* Deissmann, 349 f.). The general sense of the prediction is that the faithful will be shut up to the alternative of starving or of coming forward to avow their prohibited faith, so subtly and diabolically does the cultus of the emperor pervade all social life. Another solution is to think of the **χάραγμα** or red stamp, which was essential to all documents of exchange (Deissmann, 240 f.); it consisted of a red seal with tho emperor's name or effigy. Ramsay (*Seven Letters*, pp. 106 f.) takes the whole description as a symbolic and rather sarcastic way of referring to a boycotting demand that every Asiatic Christian should somehow "stamp himself overtly and visibly as loyal, or be disqualified from participation in ordinary social life and trading". Probably the passage is a figurative and unqualified expression for conspicuous loyalty to the Imperial cult. In Ep. Lugd. the devil is said to work against Christ by "excluding us from houses, baths, and markets, and also by forbidding any one of us to appear anywhere".

Ver. 18. "Now for wisdom"—skill to penetrate the secret of the cryptogram

νοῦν ψηφισάτω τὸν ἀριθμὸν τοῦ θηρίου· ἀριθμὸς γὰρ ἀνθρώπου ἐστί, καὶ ὁ ἀριθμὸς αὐτοῦ ἑξακόσιοι [1] ἑξήκοντα ἕξ.

[1] **χξϛ'**, *i.e.*, **εξακοσιοι (-αι) εξηκοντα εξ** (ℵAPQ, etc., Iren., Vict., Pr.), but **χιϛ'**, *i.e.*, **εξακοσιοι δεκα εξ** (C, 5, 11, Tic., Spec., "quidam sequentes idiotismum" apud Iren.). See on xiv. 20, and Zahn, § 75, n. 5. "There is no doubt but that 616 given in the Jerusalem codex is the original Armenian reading" (Conybeare).

which would reveal the features of the dread opponent. This cryptic method was a favourite apocalyptic device, due partly to prudential reasons, partly to the desire for impressiveness; Orientals loved symbolic and enigmatic modes of expression in religion (*cf.* Apoc. Bar. xxviii. 1, 2; Sib. Or. i. 141 f.; Barn. ix. 8, burlesqued by Lucian in *Alex.* 11). The prophet here drops the rôle of seer for that of hierophant or cabbalist. He invites his readers to count the name or number of the Beast, *i.e.*, to calculate a name whose letters, numerically valued on the fanciful principles of Gematria, would amount to 666. For John and his readers the Beast was primarily the foreign power which opposed the divine kingdom, *i.e.*, in this case, the Roman empire. But the drift of the present oracle is the further identification of the empire with the emperor, or rather (ver. 3) with one emperor in particular. Hence the prophet throws out the hint which will solve his riddle: the number of **τοῦ θηρίου** is **ἀριθμὸς ἀνθρώπου**, *i.e.*, of a historic personality. **'Ανθρώπου** does not require **τινός** or **ἑνός** before it to bring this out. The only intelligible sense of the words is "a human number," *i.e.*, not a number which is intelligible (for no other kind of number would be worth mentioning) but one which answered to an individual. Hence it is a matter of comparative indifference what the number of the Beast originally meant —TEITAN (so recently Abbott 80 f. = Titus, Teitous), Η ΛΑΤΕΙΝΗ (ΙΤΑΛΗ) BACILEIA (Clemen), ΛΑΤΕΙΝΟC, רום קיסר (=616), קיסר רומים (=666), Nimrod (נמרד בר כש, Bruston), or any other (*cf.* Cheyne's *Traditions and Beliefs of Anc. Israel*, p. 248). This generic number is expressly identified or equalised by John with the number of an individual, *viz.*, Nero Cæsar (קסר נרון), the Greek letters of which yield 666. The defective writing of קסר (without the yod) is not unexampled. Besides, the abbreviated form would gain, at a very slight expense, this telling and symetrical cipher. Furthermore, when the last letter of Neron is dropped, this Latinised spelling brings the total value of the name to 616, the very variant which puzzled Irenæus. Gunkel's proposal תהום קדמוניה (primal chaos = Tiâmat) suffers from several flaws; it omits the article, it employs a feminine ending which is not used in adjectives of this type, and "primal" is not a conventional epithet of mystery (*cf.* G. F. Moore in *Journ. Amer. Oriental Society*, 1906, 315 f.). Besides, as Gunkel admits, there are no Babylonian parallels to xiii. 11-17. Thus, while the application of the term is obvious, its origin is obscure. The basis of such contrivances (which became popular in Gnostic circles) was twofold: (*a*) *gematria*, which, using Greek and Hebrew letters to denote numbers, could often turn a name into a suggestive cipher; (*b*) *isopsephia*, which put two words together of the same numerical value (*cf.* for instances of **ἰσόψηφα**, Farrar 468 f. and Corssen). Probably the number of the Beast belonged to tradition. John plays upon it in order to disclose the shuddering climax of his oracle, that the final foe of the saints was Nero redivivus. The particular number 666 was specially apt as a symbol for this anti-divine power, since it formed a vain parody of the sacred number seven (Gfrörer notes further the ominous usage of 18 = 6 + 6 + 6 in Judges iii. 14, x. 8; Jerem. xxxii. 1, lii. 29; Luke xiii. 1, etc.), always falling short of it. In Sib. Or. i. 324 f. 888 represents Christ, and Origen (on Ezek. iv. 9) remarks, apropos of the present passage, **ἐστὶν ὁ ἀριθμὸς οὗτος πάθους σύμβολον καὶ κακώσεως τοῦ σωτῆρος τῇ ἕκτῃ ἡμέρᾳ πεπονθότος.** Irenæus explains the suitability of the number as "in recapitulationem uniuersae apostasiae eius, quae facta est in sex millibus annorum" (*adv. Haer.* v. 28, 2). Thus the very number 666 by itself, may have been significant of the anti-divine power. The Neronic application would intensify and concentrate its meaning for John's readers who were initiated. And such calculations, as the Pompeii *graffiti* prove, were familiar even

XIV. 1. Καὶ εἶδον, καὶ ἰδοὺ τὸ [a] ἀρνίον [a] ἑστὸς ἐπὶ τὸ ὄρος Σιών, [a] v. 6.
καὶ μετ᾽ αὐτοῦ [b] ἑκατὸν τεσσεράκοντα τέσσαρες χιλιάδες ἔχουσαι τὸ [b] vii. 4; *cf.* Zech. xiv. 5:
ὄνομα αὐτοῦ καὶ τὸ ὄνομα τοῦ πατρὸς αὐτοῦ [c] γεγραμμένον ἐπὶ τῶν [c] iii. 12, Ezek. ix. 4.
μετώπων αὐτῶν. 2. [d] καὶ ἤκουσα φωνὴν ἐκ τοῦ οὐρανοῦ ὡς φωνὴν
ὑδάτων πολλῶν καὶ ὡς φωνὴν βροντῆς μεγάλης· καὶ ἡ φωνὴ ἣν [d] i. 15, xix. 1, 6.
ἤκουσα ὡς [e] κιθαρῳδῶν κιθαριζόντων ἐν ταῖς κιθάραις αὐτῶν. 3. [e] ἅπ. λεγ. NT. xviii. 22.

to Greek-speaking inhabitants of the empire. The Pergamos-inscriptions furnish analogous instances.

Chapter XIV. The prophet again breaks off to point his readers across the sombre vista opened up by this oracle of the **θηρίον**, not to the church as an oasis and asylum on earth but to the glad sure hope of the faithful after death. How can the **θηρίον** be met? Who (ver. 8) can hold out against such seductions? By way of answer to such doubts and fears the prophet raises the veil of the future for a moment to reveal the heavenly (*cf.* xiii. 15, xiv. 3) survivors of the conflict (xiv. 1-5); whereupon he rapidly sketches the doom of Rome and the pagan world by way of contrast (6-20). The latter passage, in its present form and site, gives a proleptic outline of catastrophes described later on (*cf.* xiv. 7 = xix. 1-6, xiv. 8 = xviii. 2, 3, etc.). The two supreme motives for patient loyalty on the part of the saints (ver. 12) are, (*a*) negatively, fear of the fate reserved for the unbelieving (xiv. 8-11), and, (*b*) positively, the bliss in store for the loyal (ver. 13, *cf.* 1-5).

Vv. 1-5, introduced as a foil to what precedes and as an anticipation of xxi.-xxii., is "a sort of Te Deum" (Wellhausen), a vision of the Lamb no longer *as slain* but triumphant (militant on the mount of Olives, Zech. xiv. 3 f., against the nations = Apoc. xi. 8, 18), attended by the *élite* of the redeemed who had worshipped him, not the Emperor, during their life-time. The Jewish tradition underlying this oracle seems to have been cognate to that of En. i. 4 f. (Greek), reflected already in vii. 1-8; it showed the rallying of the faithful remnant at mount Zion (Joel ii. 32; Isa. xi. 9-12) after the throes of the latter days (*cf.* on xi. 19). In terms of this John pictures the Christians who appear with Jesus their messiah upon earth (*cf.* v. 10, xx. 4-6). Verses 1-5 thus hint faintly and fragmentarily at the belief that, before the general judgment and recompense of the saints (xi. 18, xx. 11 f.), the vanguard who had borne the brunt of the struggle would enjoy a special bliss of their own. The prophet does not stop to elaborate this independent anticipation of xx. 4-6, but hurries on (6 f.) to depict the negative side, *viz.*, the downfall of the enemy. When Caligula first attempted to enforce his worship on the Jews, the pious flung themselves on the ground, "stretching out their throats" in their readiness to die sooner than let their God be profaned (Jos. *Bell.* ii. 10, 4; *Ant.* xviii. 8, 3). John desiderates an equally dauntless temper in Christians, though they could not hope to avert, as the Jews had done, the imperial propaganda of the false prophet (xiii. 16 f.; *cf.* 2 Thess. ii.). Martyrdom (xiv. 13, *cf.* xiii. 15) was all that the majority could expect. But loyalty would bring them ultimate triumph. The passage is not simply Christian but from the hand of the prophet himself.

Ver. 1. Instead of the beast, the Lamb; instead of the beast's followers and their mark, the Lamb's followers with the divine name; instead of the pagan earth, mount Zion. The vision is based on an old Jewish apocalyptic tradition, copied by the Christian editor of 4 Esdras (ii. 42) but already present in the Jewish original (xiii. 35: ipse [*i.e.*, Messias] stabit super cacumen montis Sion, 39 et quoniam uidisti eum colligentem ad se aliam multitudinem pacificam, hae sunt decem tribus), which apparently described (*cf.* Joel ii. 32) a further cycle of the tradition underlying vii. 1-8. The appearance of this manlike messiah on mount Zion was accompanied by the manifestation of the celestial Zion (postponed here till xxi.). Thus, xiv. 1-5 is, in some respects, a companion panel to vii. 9 f., though the retinue of messiah are painted in more definitely Jewish colours. They are distinguished for their testimony borne against the Imperial cultus and the contaminations of the pagan world.

Ver. 3. Who sing the new song? angels or the redeemed? In v. 9 it is chanted not before the living creatures and elders but by them; here it is not originally sung by the redeemed (as in xv. 3 and 4 Esd. ii. 42) but is intelligible to them and to them alone. Their experi-

καὶ [f] ᾄδουσιν [g] ᾠδὴν[1] καινὴν ἐνώπιον τοῦ θρόνου καὶ ἐνώπιον τῶν τεσσάρων ζῴων καὶ τῶν πρεσβυτέρων· [h] καὶ οὐδεὶς ἐδύνατο μαθεῖν τὴν ᾠδὴν εἰ μὴ αἱ ἑκατὸν τεσσεράκοντα τέσσαρες χιλιάδες, [i] οἱ ἠγορασμένοι ἀπὸ τῆς γῆς.

4. [k] οὗτοί εἰσιν οἳ μετὰ γυναικῶν οὐκ ἐμολύνθησαν· παρθένοι γάρ εἰσιν.

[k] οὗτοι οἱ [m] ἀκολουθοῦντες τῷ ἀρνίῳ ὅπου ἂν [n] ὑπάγει.

[k] οὗτοι [o] ἠγοράσθησαν ἀπὸ τῶν ἀνθρώπων [p] ἀπαρχὴ τῷ θεῷ [καὶ τῷ ἀρνίῳ].

5. καὶ [q] ἐν τῷ στόματι αὐτῶν οὐχ [q] εὑρέθη ψεῦδος· [r] ἄμωμοί εἰσιν.

f *i.e.*, the angels. g Jud. xvi. 13. h *cf.* ii. 17, xix. 12. i constr. ad sensum (as v. 13, xi. 4, etc.) k Triple οὗτοι an apoc. formula (*cf.* Jude 12, etc.). l *cf.* Just. *Apol.* i. 15, Matt. xix. 12, Eus. *H.E.* v. 24 (Melito τὸν εὐνοῦχον), 2 Clem. xii. 2, *C.I.G.* 3098 (παρθένοι ἱερατείας, in ethnic sense). m Matt. xvi. 24-25, Joh. xxi. 19, 1 Pet. ii. 21-22. Quoted (in *Ep. Lugd.*) of the martyr Vettius Epagathus. n as in Mark vi. 56 (indic.). o 2 Pet. ii. 1. p *cf.* Schol. on Eurip. *Orest.* 96. q 1 Pet. ii. 22, Isa. liii. 9, Zeph. iii. 13, Ps. xiv. 1 f., xxx. 2. r Jude 24; *cf.* Col. i. 22, 1 Pet. i. 19, Heb. ix. 14 (sacrificial).

[1] Ti. (Al.), Ws., Bj. rightly om. **ως** (with אPQ, etc., Me., Pesh., Aeth., Arm., Orig., Method., And[c, pal], Areth., Pr.) before **ωδην**, as an echo of ver. 2.

ence enabled them to enter into its meaning. This privilege is due to (vv. 4-5) their previous character and conduct, This inner circle are ascetics, **παρθένοι**. *i.e.*, not merely unmarried or free from sexual vice but celibates (*cf.* Cheyne, *Orig. Psalter*, 446; Hoennicke, *das Judenchristentum*, 1908, 130 f.; Baldensperger, 109; von Dobschütz, 39 f., 228, 261); *cf.* 1 Cor. vii. 32. The prevailing Jewish respect for marriage did not check a tendency to celibacy which was by no means confined to the Essenes or Therapeutae. Even Methodius, who allegorises the seven heads of xii. 3 into the seven deadly sins and the stars of xii. 2 into heretics, takes this phrase literally, in the sense of virginity not simply of purity (so Epiph. *Hær.* xxx. 2); and, although the touch is too incidental to bear pressing, it is unmistakable (*cf.* Introd. § 6). In the popular religion of Phrygia there was a feeling (expressed in the eunuchism, *e.g.*, of the priests at Hierapolis) that one came nearer to the divine life by annihilating the distinction of sex, while in the votive inscriptions of Asia Minor (*C. B. P.* i. 137) marriage is not recognised as part of the divine or religious life. This atmosphere of local feeling, together with the lax moral conscience of the popular religion, would foster the religious tendency to regard celibates as pre-eminently near to God.—**ἀκολουθοῦντες**: either a historic present to secure vividness (**ἀκολουθήσαντες**, syr. S), in which case the allusion is to their earthly loyalty (reff.), or, more probably (in view of **ὑπάγει**, pres.), a description of their heavenly privilege and position (*cf.* vii. 17), borrowed from Egyptian religion where the "followers of Horus," the divine and victorious son of Osiris, were a series of celestial kings who were supposed to have reigned during the earlier dynasties. To be among the "followers of Horus" was an equivalent for immortal life. *Cf.* *E. B. D.* 101: "Let me rise up among those who follow the great God; I am the son of Maūti, and that which he abominateth is the spirit of falsehood [*cf.* Apoc. xiv. 5]. I am in triumph!"—**ἀπό** in 3, 4 is equivalent to the partitive **ἐκ** (*cf.* v. 9).—**ἀπαρχή**: they form the firstfruits of mankind for God; others are to follow, but these are the *élite*, they have a prestige all their own. The idea of priority shades into that of superiority, though in a very different way from that of Rom. xi. 16. Dr. Rendel Harris (in *Present Day Papers*, May, 1901) describes the interest and excitement at Jerusalem during the early days of summer when "the first ripe figs were in the market. When one's soul desires the vintage or the fruitage of the summer . . . the trees that are a fortnight to the fore are the talk and delight of the town."—**καὶ τ. ἀ.**, usually taken as a scribe's gloss. Elsewhere the saints are redeemed by, not for, the Lamb (v. 9).

Ver. 5. **ἄμωμοι**, "unblemished" (a ritual term), possibly contains a sacrificial tinge, like **ἀπαρχή** in some of the inscriptions (= gift to deity), *cf.* Thieme's *Inschriften von Magnesia*, 26. These

6. Καὶ εἶδον [s]ἄλλον[1] ἄγγελον πετόμενον ἐν [t]μεσουρανήματι,
ἔχοντα [u]εὐαγγέλιον αἰώνιον [v]εὐαγγελίσαι ἐπὶ τοὺς [w]καθημένους ἐπὶ
τῆς γῆς [x]καὶ ἐπὶ πᾶν ἔθνος καὶ φυλὴν καὶ γλῶσσαν καὶ λαόν,
7. [y]λέγων ἐν φωνῇ μεγάλῃ,

"[z]φοβήθητε τὸν θεὸν καὶ [a]δότε αὐτῷ δόξαν,
ὅτι ἦλθεν ἡ ὥρα τῆς κρίσεως αὐτοῦ·

s here and 15, 17 f., perhaps like the idiomatic use of ἀ. in Plato, = προσέτι, *cf.* use of ἕτερος in Dan. viii. 13, etc.

t viii. 13. u a genuine gospel (*cf.* Gal. i. 8). v 1 Pet. i. 25; for contr. John xvi. 12. w *Cf.* Luke xxi. 35. x x. 11, xiii. 7, and (for καί epexeg.) xi. 18, xiii. 12. y *cf.* iv. 1, etc. z xi. 18, Fear *God*, not the beast, *cf.* Xen. *Mem.* iv. 19. a xi. 13.

[1] **αλλον** is more likely to have been omitted (so ℵ*Q, Orig., etc., Bs.), owing to the difficulty of reference (x. 1, xi. 15) than to have been inserted. For **αγγελον** J. Weiss conj. **αετον.**

adherents are redeemed. But in another aspect their qualities of purity and guilelessness form a sweet sacrifice to God. A Christian not only may be redeemed but may sacrifice himself in the interests of the Redeemer.—**ψεῦδος.** In view of xxi. 8, 27, xxii. 15 it is superfluous to think of prophets or teachers specially (Weinel, 146-148) in this connexion, although the gifts of utterance and prophecy were particularly associated with asceticism (En. lxxxiii., cviii., etc.) in the early church of the first century; *e.g.*, "the whole yoke of the Lord" in Did. vi. may refer to celibacy (in which case **τέλειος** would be equivalent to **ἄμωμος** here). *Cf.* the discussion of reasons, in a Babylonian incantation (Zimmern, *die Beschwörungstafeln Shurpu*, 5, 6), why the sufferer was punished. "Has he for 'no' said 'yes', | For 'yes' said 'no'? . . . Was he frank in speaking | but false in heart? | Was it 'yes' with his mouth | but 'no' in his heart?" The Assyrian idiom for loyalty is "true speech in the mouth of the people," neither rebellious nor seditious talk.

Vv. 6-20: the fearful doom of the impenitent pagans is announced in a triple vision of angels (ver. 6-13), whereupon a proleptic summary of the final judgment on the world follows (ver. 14-20). In 6-13, 12-13 and **καὶ ἐν τ. ἀ.** (10) are the only specifically Christian touches; but the latter need not even be a scribal gloss, and 6-11 is intelligible as the outburst of a vehement Jewish Christian apocalyptist. The stylistic data do not justify any hypothesis of an edited source. The first angel (6-7) announces (**εὐαγγελίσαι** here, and perhaps also in x. 7, in neutral sense of LXX, 2 Sam. xviii. 19-20; Dio Cass. lxi. 13) to the universe the news that the divine purpose is now to be consummated, but that there is still (*cf.* xi. 3) a chance to repent (implicit, *cf.* Mark i. 15). The sterner tone of viii. 13-ix. 21 is due to the fact that men were there accounted as strictly responsible for their idolatry and immorality. Here the nations are regarded in the first instance as having been seduced by Rome into the Imperial cultus (8-9); hence they get a warning and a last opportunity of transferring their allegiance to its rightful object. The near doom of the empire, of which the prophet is convinced even in the hour of her aggrandisement (xiii. 8), is made a motive for urging her beguiled adherents to repent in time and her Christian victims to endure (xiv. 12). The substance of this proclamation is not much of a gospel, and the prophet evidently does not look for much result, if any. Its "pure, natural theism" (Simcox) is paralleled by that of Rom. ii. 5 f.

Ver. 6. **πετόμενον**: angels begin to fly in the Jewish heaven about the beginning of the first century B.C. (En. lxi. 1).

Ver. 7. **ποιήσαντι κ.τ.λ.** Since he who has created has the right to judge his creatures, as well as to receive their worship (*cf.* iv. 11 f., etc.).—**ὥρα** = the fixed (*cf.* 15), **καιρός** the fit, moment for action. Contrast with this summons Lucan's fulsome appeal to Nero (i. 57 f.): "librati pondera cœli Orbe tene medio," etc. The second angel of the trio announces the faults and fall of (ver. 8) Rome as a second Babylon. The prophet quotes from the postexilic oracle appended to Jeremiah (Jer. li. 7-8).—**θυμός** has probably the double sense carried by the English term "passion". As history proves, the Cæsar cult fairly intoxicated people, especially in the East. In Asia Minor it became a perfect passion with many communities. They will find it a different kind of passion, the prophet

b Emphatic; as against xiii. 4, 12, 15, *cf.* above on x. 6, and further, Ps. cxlvi. 6, Deut. xxxii. 3; with Acts iv. 24, xiv. 15.
c viii. 10, xvi. 4. an irreg. omission of article, see Win. § 18, 7d.
d aor. of "what has just happened" (so xviii. 2), Moult. i. 135; *cf.* Isa. xxi. 9.
e 1 Pet. v. 13.
f Dan. iv. 27 (30), Jer. li. 58.
g Seductive influence of idolatry (as in xiii. 2, Jer. l. 2).
h xiii. 12-17.
i gen. as vii. 3, etc.
k he, as well as Babylon; *cf.* on iii. 20.
l Jer. xxv. 17-19, 27-29, xxxii. 1, also Ps. lxxv. 9, Ps. Sol. viii. 15. See below at xvi. 19, xix, 15.
m *cf.* Jos. *Ant.* xvii. 6, 1, xviii. 9, 8, etc.
n *Cf.* on ix. 18.
o As Mark viii. 38, Acts x. 22, etc.

καὶ προσκυνήσατε τῷ [b] ποιήσαντι τὸν οὐρανὸν καὶ τὴν γῆν καὶ [c] θάλασσαν καὶ [c] πηγὰς ὑδάτων."
8. καὶ ἄλλος ἄγγελος δεύτερος [1] ἠκολούθησε λέγων,
"Ἔπεσεν [d] ἔπεσε [e] Βαβυλὼν ἡ [f] μεγάλη·
[g] ἣ ἐκ τοῦ οἴνου [τοῦ θυμοῦ] τῆς πορνείας αὐτῆς πεπότικε πάντα τὰ ἔθνη."
9. καὶ ἄλλος ἄγγελος τρίτος ἠκολούθησεν αὐτοῖς λέγων ἐν φωνῇ
μεγάλῃ, "Εἴ τις προσκυνεῖ [h] τὸ θηρίον καὶ τὴν εἰκόνα αὐτοῦ καὶ
λαμβάνει χάραγμα ἐπὶ [i] τοῦ μετώπου αὐτοῦ ἢ ἐπὶ τὴν χεῖρα [h] αὐτοῦ,[2]
10. [k] καὶ αὐτὸς [l] πίεται ἐκ τοῦ οἴνου τοῦ θυμοῦ τοῦ θεοῦ, τοῦ
κεκερασμένου [m] ἀκράτου ἐν τῷ ποτηρίῳ τῆς ὀργῆς αὐτοῦ, καὶ
βασανισθήσεται ἐν πυρὶ καὶ [n] θείῳ ἐνώπιον ἀγγέλων [o] ἁγίων

[1] The tautological **δευτερος** goes either before (AQ, 1, etc., Areth., Lach., Tr., Al., WH, Sw., Bj.) or after (א^ccCP, min., Me., Pesh., Arm., etc., Ti., Ws.) **αγγελος**. **του θυμου** (om. fuld. 1, 96, Tic., Pr., Cassiod.) as at xviii. 3 (om. S., Pr.) a gloss [Bl., § 35, 6]? Cp. xvii. 2.

[2] **η . . . αυτου** (om. S.) a gloss? (Bj., *cf.* xiii. 16).

grimly writes, drawing on a powerful O.T. figure; the passion of God's hot indignation will be forced down their throats, like a bitter draught (ver. 10). **θυμός**, however, besides translating a Hebrew equivalent for "fury" (Isa. li. 17 f.), is occasionally a LXX rendering for the analogous idea of "venom" or "poison" (חֵמָה or רֹאשׁ, *cf.* Job xx. 16), and this would yield a good sense here.

Vv. 9-11. The third angel proclaims that the deliberate adherents of the Imperial cultus are to be held responsible for their actions, and punished accordingly. The object is that these votaries may be "scared into faith by warning of sin's pains". The plea of force (xiii. 12) is no excuse (*cf.* Matt. x. 28).

Ver. 10. **κεκερασμένου** here as in xviii. 6 by oxymoron = "poured out," the original meaning of "mixed" (with water) being dropped. The torture (depicted from Isa. xxxiv. 9, 10) is inflicted *before the holy angels* (who evidently sit as assessors at the judgment, En. xlviii. 9), **ἁγίων** being either an *epitheton ornans* or an allusion to xii. 8-9. Normally the prophet refrains from introducing such spectators of doom (xix. 20, xx. 10-14). "Fire is the divine cruelty of the Semitic religions" (Doughty), but the torment which Judaism designed for fallen angels and apostates is assigned here to the worshippers of the Cæsars. The Apocalypse is silent upon agents of torture; they are not the angels, much less the devil (who is himself punished, xx. 10). But, like 4 Esd. vii. [ver. 36] ("the furnace of Gehenna shall be disclosed and over against it the paradise of delight"), John locates the place of torment over against the place of rest. For such grim popular fancies Enoch (xxvii. 2, 3, xlviii. 9, xc. 26, 27) is mainly responsible; there (as in Clem. *Hom.* xvii.) the tortures proceed under the eyes of the righteous, though (especially in the later fragments, as in John's Apoc.) the moralisation of the idea has advanced, until Gehenna vanishes from the scene of bliss. "It is impossible for us to understand how such a sight could be compatible with heavenly happiness" (Stanton, *Jewish and Christian Messiah*, p. 344; *cf.* Lecky's *European Morals*, ii. 225 f.), but the psychological basis of the ghastly expectation can be verified in the cruder types of primitive and modern religion. Most critics delete **καὶ ἐνώπιον τοῦ ἀρνίου** as another gloss (*cf.* on ver. 4); the position of Jesus after the angels is not unexampled (*cf.* i. 4, 5), even if *before the holy angels* were not

[καὶ ἐνώπιον τοῦ ἀρνίου]· 11. καὶ ὁ καπνὸς τοῦ [p] βασανισμοῦ
αὐτῶν [q] εἰς αἰῶνας αἰώνων [r] ἀναβαίνει· καὶ οὐκ ἔχουσιν [s] ἀνάπαυσιν
ἡμέρας καὶ νυκτὸς οἱ προσκυνοῦντες τὸ θηρίον καὶ τὴν εἰκόνα αὐτοῦ,
καὶ [t] εἴ τις λαμβάνει τὸ χάραγμα τοῦ ὀνόματος αὐτοῦ." 12. Ὧδε
ἡ [u] ὑπομονὴ τῶν ἁγίων ἐστίν· οἱ [v] τηροῦντες τὰς ἐντολὰς [w] τοῦ θεοῦ
καὶ τὴν [x] πίστιν Ἰησοῦ.
13. καὶ ἤκουσα φωνῆς ἐκ τοῦ οὐρανοῦ [y] λεγούσης "Γράψον,
Μακάριοι οἱ νεκροὶ οἱ [z] ἐν Κυρίῳ ἀποθνήσκοντες ἀπάρτι·

Ναί, [a] λέγει τὸ Πνεῦμα, [b] ἵνα [c] ἀναπαήσονται ἐκ τῶν κόπων αὐτῶν·
[d] τὰ γὰρ ἔργα αὐτῶν ἀκολουθεῖ μετ' αὐτῶν."

p by metonymy = βασάνου (*cf.* xviii. 7, 10, 15). q xx. 10. r xviii. 9, xix. 3, Isa. xxxiv. 10. s Grim contrast to iv. 8. t = ὅστις (ὃς ἄν), Win. § 24, 16. u xiii. 10. v xii. 17; nom. indep., as i. 5, etc. w not of men (Acts iv. 19). x ii. 13; *cf.* Rom. iii. 22, 26, Mark xi. 22, etc. (object. gen.), *cf.* Seeberg's *der Katech. d. Urchrist.* 167 f. y Contrast x. 4. z 1 Th. iv. 16, 1 Cor. xv. 18; *cf.* Sap. iv. 7-12. Frequentative (Moult. i. 114). a ii, 7, etc.; *cf.* x: ii. 16-17. b Pract. = ὅτι (*cf.* John viii. 56, ix. 2, etc.), xxii. 14. c (Isa. lvii. 1-2) like sec. fut. pass. of *καίω*. *cf.* Jannaris, *Hist. Greek Gramm.* 1991. d *Cf.* Sir. xiv, 19.

taken (Bs., Baljon) as a periphrasis for the divine presence (Luke xii. 8, 9, xv. 10).

Ver. 12. The prospect of this fearful and imminent retaliation is not only a warning to weak-minded Christians but a consolation to the loyal. To be a saint is to obey God and to believe in Jesus at all costs. Contemporary Jews took a similar encouragement: "if ye endure and persevere in his fear, and do not forget him, the times will change over you for good, and ye will see the consolation of Zion" (Apoc. *Bar.* xliv. 7). John's words **τηρ. τ. ἐντολὰς τ. θ.** are an answer to the complaint and claim that God's commandments were being neglected by every one except the Jews (*cf.* the plaintive cry of 4 Esd. iii. 33: "I have gone hither and thither through the nations and seen their abundance, though they remember not thy commandments"; 32, "Is there any other nation that knoweth thee save Israel? yet their reward appeareth not, and their labour hath no fruit").

Ver. 13. The approaching climax of retribution upon pagan Rome affects the dead as well as the living. The latter are encouraged to hold on in hope; the former are brought nearer their reward (*cf.* vi. 11, xi. 18). **Ἀπάρτι** goes with **μακάριοι** (note here and in Clem. Rom. xlvii. the first application of **μ.** to the dead saints) rather than with **ἀποθνήσκοντες,** and **οἱ ἐν κ. ἀποθ.** (which is timeless, like **προσκ. τ. θ.** in ver. 11) denotes all who die in the faith, loyal to their Lord, *i.e.*, primarily martyrs and confessors (*cf.* xiii. 8, 15). They die "in His fellowship, as it were in His arms" (Beyschlag). Like Paul (in 1 Thess. iv. 15), though on different grounds, the writer is controverting a fear (*cf.* 4 Esd. xiii. 24) that at the advent of messiah those who survived on earth would have some advantage over those who had already died. "Yea, saith the Spirit"—ratifying what has been said—"happy to rest from their labours" (*i.e.*, their Christian activities, not the special form of their death for the faith). So far as the sense is concerned, it matters little whether **ἵνα κ.τ.λ.** depends on **μακάριοι** or **ἀποθνήσκοντες.** Both constructions are grammatically legitimate, though the former is perhaps closer. The point of the passage (note **πνεῦμα** and **γράψον,** as in i.-iii., xxii. 6 f.) is that the bliss of death for a Christian consists not in mere rest from labour but in a rest which brings the reward of labour. While death brings the rest, the reward cannot be given till the final judgment. Consequently the near prospect of the latter is welcome, among other reasons, because it means the long-deferred recompense (xi. 18) for the faithful dead. So far from being forgotten (ii. 2 f., 19, 23, etc.), their **ἔργα** accompany them to judgment and —it is implied—receive their proper reward there (*cf.* Milton's fourteenth sonnet). The bliss of the departed therefore depends upon two grounds: their **ἔργα** are not to be overlooked, and the interval of waiting is now (**ἀπάρτι**) brief. The fourth degree of bliss in 4 Esd. vii. [95] is that the departed spirits of the just understand "the rest which, gathered in their chambers [*cf.* Apoc. vi. 9-11] they can enjoy now with deep quietness, guarded by angels, as well as the glory

e *Cf.* Abbott, 206 f.
f i. 13; *cf.* Dalman i. § ix. 2.
g *Cf.* on ii. 20, iii. 12, and λέγων (η) or οἱ τηρ. (12) above.

14. καὶ εἶδον, καὶ ἰδοὺ νεφέλη ᵉλευκή, καὶ ἐπὶ τὴν νεφέλην καθήμενον ᶠὅμοιον υἱὸν ἀνθρώπου, ᵍἔχων ἐπὶ τῆς κεφαλῆς αὐτοῦ

which still awaits them in the latter days". John does not share the current pessimistic belief (*cf.* Apoc. *Bar.* xi.-xii. 4, Verg. *Aen.* i. 94 f., with Isa. lvii. 1 f.) that death was preferable to life, in view of the overwhelming miseries of the age. His thought is not that death is happier than life under the circumstances, but that if death came in the line of religious duty it involved no deprivation. The language reflects Gen. ii. 2 (with **κόπων** put for **ἔργων**), but while it is true enough, it is hardly apposite, to think of the dead as resting from works (Heb. iv. 9), no more being needed. The root of the passage lies not in the Iranian belief (Brandt, 423 f., Böklen, 41) that the soul was escorted by its good deeds to bliss in another world (*cf.* Maas, *Orpheus*, 217 f.), but in the closer soil of Jewish hope (*cf.* Bacher's *Agada d. Tannaiten*,[2] i. 399 f.; Volz 103) as in En. ciii. 2, 3, Apoc. Bar. xiv. 12, 13, and Pirke Aboth vi. 9 (hora discessus hominis non comitantur eum argentum aut aurum aut lapides pretiosi aut margaritae, sed lex et opera bona). In 4 Esd. vii. 35 (where, at the resurrection of the dead, "the work shall follow and the reward be disclosed") *opus* may be a Hebraism for "recompense" (Ps. cix. 20 **ἔργον**, *cf.* 1 Ti. v. 25). Contemporary Jewish eschatology also took a despairing view of the world (*cf.* 4 Esd. iv. 26-33). But while the dead are pronounced "blessed," *e.g.*, in Apoc. Bar. xi. 7, it is because they have not lived to see the ruins of Jerusalem and the downfall of Israel. Better death than that experience! Death is a blessing compared with the life which falls upon times so out of joint (x. 6 f.). The living may well envy the dead. In John's Apocalypse, on the other hand, the dead are felicitated because they miss nothing by their martyrdom. Yet life is a boon. No plaintive, weary cry of *Weltschmerz* rises from the pages of this Apocalypse.—**ἀναπαύω** in the papyri means relief from public duties or the "resting" of land in agriculture (*cf.* U. Wilcken's *Archiv f. Papyrusforschung*, i. pp. 157 f.).

Vv. 14-20, in their present position, are a proleptic and realistic summary of the final judgment, representing as a divine catastrophe what xvi.-xvii. delineate as the outcome of semi-political movements (*cf.* xviii. after xvii.). The strange picture of messiah (14 f., contrast i. 10 f., xix. 11 f.), the absence of any allusion to the Beasts (9-11) or to the Imperial cultus, the peculiar angelology, and the generally disparate nature of the scene as compared with the context, point to the isolated character of the episode. The abrupt mention of *the city* (20) suggests that the tradition belonged to the cycle underlying xi. 1-13 (*the city*, 13), and several critics (*e.g.*, Spitta, Erbes, Weyland, Völter, Schön, Briggs, Rauch) regard it variously as a finâle to the oracles of that chapter. But the connexion is one of tradition rather than of literary unity. The data of style and content leave it uncertain even whether the episode goes back to a source or a tradition, whether it is Jewish (so especially Sabatier, Pfleiderer, and Rauch) or Jewish Christian (Schön, Erbes, Bruston, J. Weiss, etc.), and, if Jewish Christian, whether it was written by the author of the Apocalypse (Weizsäcker) or not. The least obscure feature is the victory of the messiah over antichrist and his legions (not of an angelic judgment on Israel, J. Weiss) in the vicinity of Jerusalem (*cf.* xi. 13, xiv. 1 f., and xx. 9) at the end of the world, an expectation of which we have another variant apparently in xix. 11 f. Probably the prophet inserts the episode here in order to repeat, in a graphic and archaic, although somewhat incongruous fashion, the final doom of which he has just been speaking and to which he is about to lead up (xv.-xx.) through a fresh series of catastrophes. "If one might venture to wish to discard as an interpolation any part of the attested text of the Apocalypse, it would be this passage. How can it be understood of anything but the final judgment? Yet it comes here as anything but final. . . . The earth goes on just as before" (Simcox). But here, as often elsewhere, the clue lies partly in the vivid inconsequence of dream-pictures, partly in the preacher's desire to impress his hearers, and partly in the poetic, imaginative freedom of his own mind.

Ver. 14. This royal, judicial figure is evidently the messiah (drawn from Dan. vii. 13, which had been already interpreted thus in En. xxxvii.-lxxi. and 4

[h] στέφανον χρυσοῦν καὶ ἐν τῇ χειρὶ αὐτοῦ δρέπανον ὀξύ. 15. καὶ
ἄλλος ἄγγελος ἐξῆλθεν [i] ἐκ τοῦ ναοῦ, κράζων ἐν φωνῇ μεγάλῃ τῷ
καθημένῳ [k] ἐπὶ τῆς νεφέλης,

"Πέμψον [l] τὸ δρέπανόν σου καὶ θέρισον,
ὅτι ἦλθε ἡ [m] ὥρα [m] θερίσαι,
ὅτι ἐξηράνθη ὁ θερισμὸς τῆς γῆς."

16. καὶ ἔβαλεν ὁ καθήμενος ἐπὶ τῆς νεφέλης τὸ δρέπανον αὐτοῦ
ἐπὶ τὴν γῆν, καὶ ἐθερίσθη ἡ γῆ.

17. καὶ ἄλλος ἄγγελος ἐξῆλθεν ἐκ τοῦ ναοῦ τοῦ ἐν τῷ οὐρανῷ,
ἔχων καὶ αὐτὸς δρέπανον ὀξύ. 18. καὶ ἄλλος ἄγγελος ἐξῆλθεν ἐκ
τοῦ [n] θυσιαστηρίου, ὁ ἔχων [1] ἐξουσίαν [o] ἐπὶ τοῦ πυρός, καὶ ἐφώνησε
φωνῇ μεγάλῃ τῷ ἔχοντι τὸ δρέπανον τὸ ὀξὺ λέγων,

h xix. 12.
i xi. 19 (heavenly temple).
k *Cf.* Dalm. ix. 2.
l Mark iv. 29.
m Constr. ix. 10, xi. 6, *cf.* Mark xiii. 28 parl. Herm. *Sim.* iv. 2, Sib. Or. i. 387.
n viii. 3-5: prayers of martyrs?
o Angels of snow, hail, thunder, lightning, fire, etc., in Jub. ii. 2. Here = viii. 5, the angel of fire.

[1] Before εχων Lach., Al., Tr. (marg.), Ws. [WH], [Sw.] add the ο of AC, vg., Syr., S.

Esd. xiii.). The crown (omitted in i. 13 f.) was a familiar appurtenance of deity in Phrygia (*e.g.*, of Apollo); for the cloud as the seat of deity, *cf.* Verg. *Aen.* ix. 638-640, etc.

Ver. 15. **ἄλλος ἄγγελος**, as in ver. 6. The alternatives are (*a*) to translate "another, an angel" (אחר מלאך) which might be the sense of the Greek (*cf. Od.* i. 132, Clem. *Protrept.* ix. 87. 3) but is harsh, or (*b*) to take the figure of ver. 14 as an angel (Porter) and not as the messiah at all (which, in the face of i. 13, is difficult). The subordinate and colourless character of the messiah is certainly puzzling, and tells against the Christian authorship of the passage. Messiah is summoned to his task by an angel, and even his task is followed up by another angel's more decisive interference. He seems an angelic figure (*cf.* on xix. 17), perhaps *primus inter pares* among the angels (so En. xlvi. 1: "and I saw another being [*i.e.*, the Son of Man] whose countenance had the appearance of a man, and his face was full of graciousness, like one of the holy angels"). The conception was inconsistent with John's high Christology, but he may have retained it, like so much else, for its poetic effect, or as part of a time-honoured apocalyptic tradition. That the messiah should receive divine instructions through one of his comrades (Heb. i. 6, 9; *cf.* Zech. ii. 3, 4) was perhaps not stranger than that he should require an angel in order to communicate with men (i. 1). **πέμψον κ.τ.λ.** The double figure of judgment (harvest and vintage) is copied from the poetic parallelism of Joel iii. 13; the independent rendering of שלח by **πέμψον** and **ἔβαλεν**, and the change of agent from messiah (14-16) to an angel (17-20, so Mark xiii. 39 f.), show that the writer is using the Hebrew of that passage (where God does the reaping).

Ver. 16. The **δρέπανον** (only here, xiv. 14-19, in Apocalypse; *cf. C. B. P.* ii. 652 f. for a Phrygian inscription **καὶ τὸ ἀρᾶς δρέπανον εἰς τὸν ὗκον αὐτοῦ**) is represented as a living thing, probably like the **δρέπανον πετόμενον** of Zech. v. 1 (Wellhausen). The classical use of reaping to symbolise death and destruction is too common to need illustration. "The harvest of the earth is ripe and dry," but this ripeness of paganism for judgment (Jer. li. 33) is re-stated dramatically (17-20) in a parallel O.T. symbol from the wine-press. The angelic *mise-en-scène* recalls that of viii. 3-5. Unlike the harvest-symbol, the vintage-symbol is worked out vividly (*cf.* Gen. xlix. 11; Isa. lxiii. 1 f.).

Ver. 18. **πυρός.** The figure of this angel (=Jehuel in rabbinic tradition, Gfrörer, i. 369) has an Iranian tinge. The justice of the punishment is attested by its origin in the purpose of one who corresponded to the Persian Amshaspand (*cf.* on i. 4), Ashem Vahishtan, who presided over fire and at the same time symbolised the closely allied conceptions of goodness, truth, and right in Zoroastrian mythology (*cf. H. J.*, 1904, 350).

"Πέμψον σου τὸ δρέπανον τὸ ὀξύ,
καὶ [p] τρύγησον τοὺς βότρυας τῆς ἀμπέλου τῆς γῆς,
ὅτι ἤκμασαν αἱ σταφυλαὶ αὐτῆς."
19. καὶ ἔβαλεν ὁ ἄγγελος τὸ δρέπανον αὐτοῦ εἰς τὴν γῆν, καὶ
ἐτρύγησε τὴν ἄμπελον τῆς γῆς καὶ ἔβαλεν εἰς [q] τὴν [r] ληνὸν τοῦ
θυμοῦ τοῦ θεοῦ τὸν μέγαν. 20. καὶ [q] ἐπατήθη ἡ ληνὸς [s] ἔξωθεν τῆς
πόλεως, καὶ ἐξῆλθεν [t] αἷμα ἐκ τῆς ληνοῦ ἄχρι τῶν χαλινῶν τῶν
ἵππων, [u] ἀπὸ σταδίων χιλίων ἑξακοσίων.[1]

p Lk. vi 44.
q xix. 15, *cf.* Ezek. xxxv. 6.
r = an oblong trough or tub, *cf.* Zech. xiv. 10.
s *cf.* Jos. *Bell.* iv. 6, 3, vi. 2, 1, vi. 6, 3, etc.
t The red juice of the vine (Deut. xxxii. 14). (only here in this sense in Apoc.).
u John xi. 18, xxi. 8 (*cf.* Blass, 95): at most a Latinism

[1] And. (comm.), reading (with 79) χιλ. εξακ. εξ. [διακοσιων, ℵ, 26, S.], explains the number symbolically as the perfection of wickedness; 1000 being the most perfect of numbers, the deluge occurring in the 600th year of Noah, and the creation (now stained and corrupted) being completed on the 6th day.

A similar representation of an angel speaking from the fire in connexion with providence occurs in Chag. 14 *b*.

Ver. 19. The ungrammatical τὸν μέγαν may be due to the fact that ληνός is occasionally masculine (Win. § 8. 10; Helbing, 46), or—by a rough *constr. ad sensum*—to apposition with τὸν θυμόν (understood).

Ver. 20. The heathen are stamped and crushed till their blood gushes out of the wine-press to the height of a horse's bridle and to the extent of about two hundred miles. This ghastly hyperbole, borrowed partly from Egyptian (wine = the blood of those who fought against the gods) and partly from Jewish eschatology (En. c. 3: "and the horses will walk up to the breast in the blood of sinners, and the chariot will be submerged to its height"), happens to be used later by the Talmud in connexion with the carnage at Bether (*cf.* Schlatter's *Die Tage Trajans*, p. 37; also Sib. iii. 633 f.; 4 Esd. xv. 35; Sil. Ital. iii. 704). The place is to be a veritable Senlac (sang lac).—ἀπό κ.τ.λ., probably a round number (see crit. note) compounded out 4 and its multiples (like 144,000 out of 12), to denote completeness (Vict. = per omnes mundi quattuor partes). After the fall of Rome (xiv. 8 f.), the rest of the world (*ex hypothesi* impenitent, xiv. 6-8) is ripe for the traditional (Dan. ix. 26) judgment. The same sequence is reproduced roughly and on a larger scale in xvii.-xviii. (fall of Rome) and xix.-xx. (doom of other nations). This parallelism and the sense of the Joel passage militate against the attractive idea that xiv. 14-16 is the ingathering of the saints (so Alford, Milligan, Bruston, Briggs, Titius, Gilbert, and Swete).—ἔξωθεν κ.τ.λ. This fearful vengeance is located by Jewish tradition in some valley (of Jehoshaphat = Yah judges?) near Jerusalem (Joel), on the mount of Olives (Zech. xiv. 4), or in Palestine generally (Dan. xi. 45; *cf.* below on xvi. 16), *i.e.*, as a rule in close proximity to the sacred capital, where the messiah was to set up his kingdom.

After this partial anticipation of the final catastrophe, the Apocalypse returns to a fuller and independent description of its processes (xv. 2-4 = xiv. 1-5, xv. 1, 5-xvi. = xiv. 6-11, 14-20). The panorama of the prelude is once more sevenfold, but this time seven angels (under the control of God, xvi. 9) drench the earth with plagues from seven bowls which are brimming with the divine anger. The vision is a poetical expansion of Lev. xxvi. 21 (προσθήσω ὑμῖν πληγὰς ἑπτὰ κατὰ τὰς ἁμαρτίας ὑμῶν, *cf.* 18, 24, 28). The plagues, like Habbakuk's theophany, recall the Egyptian plagues (Exod. vii.-x.), but their description is less impressive than the previous cycles of punishment. Like the seven trumpets (viii. 2-5), they are introduced by a scene in heaven (xv. 2-4); ver. 1 is merely a title or frontispiece to what follows (5 f.), since the angels do not become visible till 5 (*cf.* viii. 1-2, 6), and do not receive their bowls till 7. This θαυμαστόν (awe-inspiring) σημεῖον is the sequel (ἄλλο) to that of xii. 1 f., and the plagues are final (1 ἐσχάτας), in contrast to the trumpet-plagues (ix. 20), as they represent the wrath of God which can no longer be repressed (xvii.-xix. = the working out of these plagues, *cf.* xvi,

XV. 1. Καὶ εἶδον ἄλλο σημεῖον ἐν τῷ οὐρανῷ μέγα καὶ
[a] θαυμαστόν, ἀγγέλους ἑπτὰ ἔχοντας πληγὰς ἑπτὰ τὰς ἐσχάτας, ὅτι
ἐν αὐταῖς [b] ἐτελέσθη ὁ [c] θυμὸς τοῦ Θεοῦ. 2. καὶ εἶδον ὡς
θάλασσαν [d] ὑαλίνην μεμιγμένην πυρί, καὶ τοὺς νικῶντας ἐκ τοῦ
[e] θηρίου καὶ ἐκ τῆς εἰκόνος αὐτοῦ καὶ ἐκ τοῦ ἀριθμοῦ τοῦ [e] ὀνόματος
αὐτοῦ ἑστῶτας [f] ἐπὶ τὴν [g] θάλασσαν τὴν [g] ὑαλίνην, ἔχοντας [h] κιθάρας
τοῦ Θεοῦ. 3. καὶ [i] ᾄδουσι τὴν ᾠδὴν [k] Μωυσέως τοῦ [l] δούλου τοῦ
Θεοῦ καὶ τὴν ᾠδὴν τοῦ ἀρνίου, [m] λέγοντες,

a *Cf.* Exod. xv. 11.
b x. 7.
c vi. 17, xi. 18.
d iv. 6, same scene (*cf.* ver, 7 substantially.
e xiii. 17, xiv. 11.
f Elsewhere in Apoc. (v. 13, vii. 1, x. 2, 5, 8) ἐπὶ τῆς θ.
g *Cf.* use of δρακόντων in Ps. lxxiv. 14, LXX. (Apoc. xiii. 2, 11, and 1 Macc. iv. 6 f.).
h v. 8, xiv. 2.
i xiv. 3,
k On form, *cf.* Win. § 5, 20 c, Helbing, 59.
l *Cf.* Heb. iii. 5-6.
m From *Song of Three Child.* 4. For sequence of thought, see Jude, 5 f.

12 f., xix. 19, xvii. 1). Like ch. xvi., to which it forms an overture, xv. is not the revision of a Jewish source (so especially Spitta, Ménégoz, and Schmidt) but Christian (Briggs, Erbes) and the work of the Apocalyptist himself (Sabatier, Schön, Bousset, etc.)

Vv. 2-4. An interlude like xix. 1 f. The manifestation of divine judgment (4) evokes reverence (contrast xvi. 11) and praise from the saints in heaven.

Ver. 2. **νικ. ἐκ κ.τ.λ.,** "those who came off conquerors from"—another pregnant use of **ἐκ** (*cf.* ii. 21, viii. 11) combining the ideas of victory over (*cf.* on ii. 7) and deliverance from. A possible Latinism (*cf.* Livy viii. 8, uictoriam ferre ex aliquo; xlv. 38, aliquis est Romae qui triumphari de Macedonis nolit?)? The prophet paints the downfall of the Roman persecutor in terms of the Jewish tradition preserved, *e.g.*, in Targ. Jerus. (on Exod. xii. 42) which singled out four memorable nights, that of the creation, that on which God's promise of a son came to Abram, that of the tenth Egyptian plague, and that on which the world is ended (when Moses appears in a cloud from the wilderness and messiah in a cloud from Rome, led by the Word of the Lord). *Cf.* Schemoth Rabba on Exod. xii. 2: ex quo Deus mundum suum elegit, determinauit principium mensis redemptionis, quo liberati sunt Israelitae ex Aegypto, et quo liberabuntur futuro saeculo. In time as well as in method (*cf.* on viii. 6, and 1 Cor. x. 1-11) the two redemptions, Mosaic and messianic, are to correspond.—**πυρί,** a truly Red sea, red with the glow of God's wrath. Like Pharaoh and his host (Exod. xv. 5, 10=Apoc. xviii. 21) the persecutors of God's people in these latter days not only fail to effect their purpose, but are themselves destroyed by God's vengeance (*cf.* xvi. 2). The faithful get through their sea of troubles, resisting threats and persuasions, and now stand safe at (*i.e.*, on the shore of) the heavenly sea. "Duteous mourning we fulfil / In God's name; but by God's will / Doubt not the last word is still / victory" (D. G. Rossetti). Here, as at xii. 11 the thrill of triumph is enhanced by the fearful odds against which the saints had to contend. Apparently the world is now tenanted by pagans only, God's faithful having been removed. Hence the plagues are all-embracing (contrast vii. 1 f.). *Cf.* xx. 4.

Ver. 3. As in Exod. xiv.-xv. Moses leads Israel in a song of praise to God over the dead Egyptians, so, after Rome's downfall (xiv. 8 f., ver. 2) the faithful are led by their captain (xii. 11, xiv. 1, 4, *cf.* Heb. ii. 12), in a chant of triumph and gratitude. (Note the lack of any reference to their own sufferings. Their interest is in the great work of God.) For messiah as a second Moses in Jewish tradition, *cf.* Gfrörer, ii. 328 f. The song on the Red Sea had already been adapted to the worship of the Therapeutae (Philo, *de uit. contempl.* § xi.)—**τὴν ᾠδὴν τ. ἀ.** There is a continuity in redemption, which unites the first deliverance to the final. True to his cardinal idea of the identity of God's people (Christians being the real Israel, *cf.* on i. 6), the prophet hails Jesus as the Christian Moses who, at the cost of his life, is commissioned by God to deliver the new Israel from their bondage to an earthly monarchy. The lyric with its Hebrew parallelisms is a *Vorspiel* of the succeeding judgments; it resembles (*cf. E.Bi.* 4954) the benediction after the Shema of Judaism ("a new song did they sing to Thy name, they that were delivered, by the seashore; together did all praise and own Thee as King, saying, 'Yahveh shall reign world without end'"), and is al

"Μεγάλα καὶ [n] θαυμαστὰ τὰ ἔργα σου,
Κύριε ὁ θεὸς ὁ [o] παντοκράτωρ·
[p] δίκαιαι [q] καὶ ἀληθιναὶ αἱ [r] ὁδοί σου,
ὁ [s] βασιλεὺς τῶν ἐθνῶν.[1]
4. [s] τίς οὐ μὴ [t] φοβηθῇ, Κύριε, καὶ δοξάσει τὸ ὄνομά σου;
ὅτι μόνος [u] ὅσιος·
ὅτι [v] πάντα τὰ ἔθνη ἥξουσι καὶ προσκυνήσουσιν [w] ἐνώπιόν σου·
[x] ὅτι τὰ δικαιώματά σου ἐφανερώθησαν."

n ver. 1, 1 Chron. xvi. 8-12, etc.
o i. 8.
p From Ps cxlv. 17, Zech. viii. 8 LXX, Dan. iii. 27-28, iv. 37.
q *Cf.* on xvi. 7.
r Deut. xxxii. 4, Isa. xxvi. 8, LXX, *cf. Sam. Agon.* 293 f.
s From Jer. x. 6-7 (om. LXX), Zech. xiv. 9; *cf.* on xi. 18. An instance of Col. iii. 16.
t aor. due to "emphat. negative or rhetorical nat. of question" (Burton, 172, *cf.* Lk. xviii. 7).
u only here and xvi. 5 (N.T.) of God; *cf.* Deut. xxxii. 4, Ps. Sol. x. 6. From Ps. cxlv. 17.
v Ps. lxxxvi. 9, Mic. vii. 15 f.
w iii. 5, xvi. 9.
x = "Because;" δικ. = xix. 8 (diff. sense).

[1] The **αγιων** of the Textus Rec. represents a tr. of *sctorum* (a corruption of *sclorum*) = **εθνων** of ℵ[ca]APQ, min., Me., Arm., Aeth., And., Areth., Cypr., Amb., Pr. (edd.), which has been conformed, in **αιωνων** (ℵ*C, vg., Syr., S., so Selwyn, WH), to 1 Tim. i. 17 (*cf.* En. ix. 4, Tob. xiii. 6, 10, Clem. Rom. lv., lxi.).

most entirely composed of O.T. phrases. Adoration is its theme, stirred by the sense of God's justice. Similarly the famous hymn to Shamash, the Assyrian god of justice, which represents one of the highest reaches in ancient religious literature (Jastrow, pp. 300, 301): "Eternally just in the heavens are thou, / Of faithful judgment towards all the world art thou." Most editors take the phrase **καὶ τὴν ᾠδ. τ. ἀ.** as a gloss; but if the song has nothing to do with the Lamb, it is as silent on Moses. Since the whole section comes from the pen of the general author, and since the collocation of the two **ᾠδαί** (equivalent of course to a single hymn) is awkward mainly in appearance, while the omission of the *Lamb's Song* would leave the section incomplete, it seems better to regard it as original rather than as a scribe's addition like xiv. 10, etc. As in xiv. 1, 3, the Lamb is among his followers, yet not of them.

Ver. 4. God's holiness is the reason why his name must be feared and magnified, especially when its effects are visible in the reverent homage of all nations to God (a hyperbolical statement in view of xvi. 9, etc.) at the sight of his "deeds of judgment" (**δικαιώματα** = judicial sentences, here of condemnation and penalty) inflicted on the world (*cf.* Dan. ix. 14 f.). The absolute and unique (note the prophet's insertion of **μόνος**) reign of Yahveh was a traditional tenet of Mosaism; indeed for Orientals generally the power which formed their ideal source of righteousness and justice partook necessarily of a monarchic character (*R. S.* 74 f.). To the Semites it appeared that the perfection of their god as a just king formed a ground for his ultimate sovereignty over the nations of the world. The O.T. outlook and the phraseology warn us not to press the poetical language too closely here; otherwise (*cf.* xiv. 6, 7) it would contradict, *e.g.*, the characteristic idea of the author that the bowl-plagues, instead of producing penitence and submission, ended in defiant blasphemy.—**ἐνώπιόν σου,** here a reverential periphrasis, it being considered in the later O.T. literature, the Targums, and the N.T. (occasionally) more respectful to worship and pray *before* the royal god than directly *to* him (Dalman, i. viii. 5). For the whole conception of this dual song see Targ. Jonath. on Isa. xxvi. 1 and Targ. Schir Haschirim i. 1; the latter reckons ten songs altogether, (1) Adam's at his forgiveness, (2) that of Moses and the Israelites at the Red Sea, (3) that of the Israelites, when the spring of water was given them, (4) that of Moses at his death, (5) Joshua's at Gibeon, (6) that of Barak and Deborah, (7) Hannah's, (8) David's, (9) Solomon's, and (10) that which the children of the captivity are to sing when the Lord frees them. It tallies with this expectation that the new song of the Apocalypse (v. 9, xiv. 3) is always a song of Christ's redemption.

5. [y] καὶ μετὰ ταῦτα εἶδον, καὶ [z] ἠνοίγη ὁ ναὸς τῆς [a] σκηνῆς τοῦ
[a] μαρτυρίου ἐν τῷ οὐρανῷ· 6. καὶ ἐξῆλθον οἱ ἑπτὰ ἄγγελοι οἱ
ἔχοντες τὰς ἑπτὰ πληγὰς [b] ἐκ τοῦ ναοῦ, [c] ἐνδεδυμένοι λίνον [1] καθαρὸν
[d] λαμπρὸν καὶ [e] περιεζωσμένοι περὶ τὰ στήθη ζώνας χρυσᾶς. 7.
καὶ ἓν ἐκ τῶν τεσσάρων ζῴων ἔδωκε τοῖς ἑπτὰ ἀγγέλοις ἑπτὰ
[f] φιάλας χρυσᾶς [g] γεμούσας τοῦ θυμοῦ τοῦ θεοῦ [h] τοῦ ζῶντος εἰς
τοὺς αἰῶνας τῶν αἰώνων. 8. καὶ [i] ἐγεμίσθη ὁ ναὸς καπνοῦ ἐκ τῆς
δόξης τοῦ θεοῦ καὶ ἐκ τῆς δυνάμεως αὐτοῦ· [k] καὶ οὐδεὶς ἐδύνατο
εἰσελθεῖν εἰς τὸν ναὸν ἄχρι τελεσθῶσιν αἱ ἑπτὰ [l] πληγαὶ τῶν ἑπτὰ
ἀγγέλων.

XVI. 1. Καὶ ἤκουσα μεγάλης [a] φωνῆς ἐκ τοῦ ναοῦ λεγούσης
τοῖς ἑπτὰ ἀγγέλοις, "Ὑπάγετε καὶ [b] ἐκχέετε τὰς ἑπτὰ φιάλας τοῦ
θυμοῦ τοῦ θεοῦ εἰς τὴν [c] γῆν." 2. καὶ ἀπῆλθεν ὁ πρῶτος καὶ
ἐξέχεε τὴν φιάλην αὐτοῦ εἰς τὴν γῆν· καὶ ἐγένετο [d] ἕλκος κακὸν καὶ
πονηρὸν [e] ἐπὶ [f] τοὺς ἀνθρώπους τοὺς ἔχοντας τὸ χάραγμα τοῦ θηρίου

y Fresh stage in vision, see on iv. 1.
z already in xi. 19.
a See Acts vii. 44 (only).
b xiv. 15, 17.
c xix. 8, 14.
d *cf.* Acts x. 30 (i. 10).
e Gold belts, as i. 13.
f v. 8 f.
g xiv. 10, Ezek. xxii. 31.
h i. xviii.; *cf.* on vii. 2.
i Isa. vi. 4.
k Exod. xix. 21, xl. 34-35, 1 Kings viii. 10-11, also 2 Chron. vii. 2. (*cf.* 2 Chron. vii. 3 with ver. 2 above and iv. 10).
l ver. 1

a Of God (Isa. lxvi. 6), *cf.* xv. 8. b For form, *cf.* Win. § 13, 23. c viii. 5, Jer. x. 25, Zeph. iii. 8, Ps. lxix. 24. d Exod. ix. 10-11, Deut. xxviii. 35, Job ii. 7, Luke xvi. 21. e *Cf.* Luke i. 65, iii. 2. f xiii. 15-17, xiv. 9-10.

[1] For the λινον (λινους ℵ, λινουν min., Lat.) of PQ, Syr., S., And., Arm., Areth., etc. (Al., Ws., Ti., Bs., Bj., Sw.), Lach., Tr., Düst., WH, Sp. read the transcriptional (ΛΙΘΟΝ for ΛΙΝΟΝ) error λιθον AC, 38 mg., 48, 90, etc. (from LXX of Ezek. xxviii. 13?—λινον being commonly used of flax, not of flaxen garments. *Cf.* Nestle's *Einf.*, 263).

xv. 5-xvi. 1: the introduction to the seven bowls or plagues.

Ver. 5. The temple in heaven is here "the tent (or tabernacle) of witness," as it represents God's judicial revelation and presence; its contents and the movements of which it forms the source, are evidence of God's covenant with his people.

Ver. 6. These heavenly beings are magnificent creatures, robed in gold and light (a Hellenic conception, Dieterich, 38 f.) and linen (to denote their honourable and sacred office: so the scribe of judgment, Ezek. ix. 2, and the angel in Dan. x. 5, xii. 6). Plutarch (*de Iside*, 3, 4) explains that the linen surplice was affected by Egyptian votaries of Isis for religious reasons; *e.g.*, the bright smiling colour of flax, its freedom from lice, and the smooth, cleanly material it yielded.

Vv. 7, 8. The **φιάλαι**, shallow bowls or saucers, do not exhale a smoke (like the censer of viii. 4) grateful to God; they are filled with poisonous, hot, bitter wine, while the smoke pours from the divine majesty, whose intense holiness (ver. 4, as in O.T. theophanies) is breaking out in judgments against human sin (**δόξα** = the divine **δύναμις** in action or expression). Smouldering fires of indignation are now on the point of bursting into punishment from the arsenal of anger. Hence, till the plagues are over, God's presence is unendurable (as in Enoch xiv. 18 f.). This emphasis on the unapproachable, austere majesty of God is consonant with the general religious feeling reflected in the Apocalypse (*cf.* on i. 2).

CHAPTER XVI.—Vv. 2-21.—The series (first three **εἰς**, last four **ἐπὶ**) of these plagues as usual consists of four and three; the former, as in the seals, affecting earth (*i.e.*, votaries of the Imperial cultus), sea, waters, and the sun. The special object of the writer in this passage (*i.e.*, to introduce the doom of Rome and the worshippers of the Emperor) leads him to vary the materials drawn from the Egyptian plagues which had been already used in the corresponding series of the trumpet-visions (viii.-ix.) by defining precisely the victims of the first plague as worshippers of the Beast, by substituting the throne and realm of the Beast in the fifth plague for mankind in general, in the sixth by connecting the Parthian invasion with the Beast

καὶ [f] τοὺς προσκυνοῦντας τῇ εἰκόνι αὐτοῦ. 3. [g] καὶ ὁ δεύτερος
ἐξέχεε τὴν φιάλην αὐτοῦ εἰς τὴν θάλασσαν· [h] καὶ ἐγένετο αἷμα ὡς
νεκροῦ, καὶ πᾶσα [i] ψυχὴ ζωῆς ἀπέθανεν, [k] τὰ ἐν τῇ θαλάσσῃ. 4.
καὶ ὁ τρίτος ἐξέχεε τὴν φιάλην αὐτοῦ [l] εἰς τοὺς ποταμοὺς καὶ
τὰς [l] πηγὰς τῶν ὑδάτων· καὶ [m] ἐγένετο αἷμα. 5. καὶ ἤκουσα τοῦ
[n] ἀγγέλου τῶν [n] ὑδάτων λέγοντος,

"[o] Δίκαιος εἶ,
[p] ὁ ὢν καὶ ὁ ἦν, ὁ [q] ὅσιος,
[r] ὅτι ταῦτα ἔκρινας·
6. ὅτι [s] αἷμα [1] [t] ἁγίων καὶ [t] προφητῶν [s] ἐξέχεαν,
καὶ αἷμα αὐτοῖς ἔδωκας [u] πεῖν·
[v] ἄξιοί εἰσιν."
7. καὶ ἤκουσα τοῦ θυσιαστηρίου λέγοντος,
"Ναί, [w] Κύριε ὁ θεὸς ὁ [x] παντοκράτωρ,
[y] ἀληθιναὶ καὶ δίκαιαι αἱ κρίσεις σου."

g Exod. vii. 17, 21, *cf.* En. lx. 16. h xi. 6. The whole, not a third (as in viii. 8-9). i Gen. i. 30 (LXX); *cf.* Win. § 22, 18*b*. k *Cf.* Suet. *Calig.* 49. Irreg. oppos. to ψ. l viii. 10 f., Exod. vii. 19-24, Ps. lxxvii. 44. m Verg. *Georg.* i. 485. n John v. 4; of wind (Apoc. vii. 1) of fire (xiv. 18). o Ps. cxix. 137 f. cxlv. 17; *cf.* Job, xxxvii. 23. p xi. 17. q (vocative), *cf.* xv. 4; of Jesus, Heb. vii. 26. r God's rights, shown in judgments, Ps. Sol. ii. 16 f., 38 f., viii. 27, etc. s xvii. 6, xix. 2. Ps. lxxix. 2-3, Is. xlix. 26, Sib. Or. iii. 212, Ps. Sol. viii. 23). t xi. 18, xviii. 24. u *Cf.* John iv. 7, 9; for form in papyri, *cf.* Deissmann, 182-3, Helbing, 11. v iii. 4; from Sap. xviii. 4 (of Egyptians), asyndeton = "as they deserve". w Rare (xi. 17, xv. 3) use of vocative in Apoc. x xv. 3. y xix. 1-2, Ps. xix. 9: ἀληθ. = just, synonym for δικ. as John viii. 16, Xen. *Anab.* ii. 6, 26, So below, xix. 2, and Isa. lix. 4, LXX.

[1] The Hebraistic (= דמים) **αιματα** of א, 36, 39 is preferred here and at xviii. 24 by Ti., Bs., Swete.

itself, in the seventh by introducing Rome's fall among the physical disasters, and in the prologue by making the plagues come from God's initiative without intercession (as viii. 3 f.). How far these new touches are original or due to the influence of current traditions no longer extant, it is impossible to determine. This series of plagues is simply a free adaptation, with modifications and applications, of that in viii.-ix.; the prophet wishes to emphasise, by the genuinely Semitic method of recapitulation (*cf.* Gen. xli. 32; Ps. lxii. 11, etc.), the sure and speedy approach of judgment.

Ver. 2. The sixth Egyptian plague, "a noisome and painful ulcer" (the punishment of the impious and rebellious, according to Philo, *de Execr.* v. 6) breaks out on the adherents of the Cæsar-cult.

Ver. 3. "Coagulated blood," fatal to animal life (as in first Egyptian plague). This plague is final, as compared, *e.g.*, with that of viii. 8.

Vv. 4-7. No more drinking water. The justice of this particular plague is acknowledged by (5-6) the angel of the element in question and by (7) the altar (personified here, in line of vi. 9, 10, and viii. 3, or of xiv. 18), which echoes the angel's cry.

Ver. 5. **ὅσιος** and **δίκαιος** are used together of God in hieratic inscriptions of dedication throughout Asia Minor, possibly under Jewish influence. **Δίκαιος,** often a title of messiah (see on iii. 1 and Beer's note on En. xxxviii. 2), is reserved here for God. Retribution is the outcome of God's intense holiness or majesty (*cf.* vi. 10, xv. 4) asserting itself on behalf of his people (xv. 3, xix. 2, *cf.* iii. 7) and in self-vindication.

Ver. 6. The retribution once threatened on Jerusalem and the Jews (Matt. xxiii. 35) is now transferred apparently to Rome, the later antagonist of the faith (*cf.* on xviii. 24). Once the Romans made Christian blood run like water. Now, by the irony of providence, they shall find nothing but blood to drink. This moral vengeance (*cf.* Hawthorne's *House of the Seven Gables*), with its grim equivalence between sin and sin's punishment (xi. 18, xiii. 10, xviii. 7; *cf.* 2 Tim. ii. 12, etc.) is not pushed, however, into the grotesque and elaborately Dantesque details, *e.g.*, of the Apocalypse of Peter.—**ἐξέχεαν** (the verb runs all through this chapter, and this chapter only), *cf.* Dittenberger's *Sylloge Inscript. Graec.* 816[7] (1 cent. A.D.) **ἐγχέαντας τὸ ἀναίτιον αἷμα ἀδίκως.**—**ἁγ. κ. πρ.,** all

8. καὶ ὁ τέταρτος ἐξέχεε τὴν φιάλην αὐτοῦ ἐπὶ τὸν ἥλιον· [z]
καὶ [z] ἐδόθη [a] αὐτῷ [b] καυματίσαι [c] τοὺς ἀνθρώπους ἐν πυρί· 9. καὶ
ἐκαυματίσθησαν οἱ ἄνθρωποι [d] καῦμα μέγα, καὶ [e] ἐβλασφήμησαν τὸ
ὄνομα τοῦ θεοῦ τοῦ ἔχοντος τὴν ἐξουσίαν ἐπὶ τὰς πληγὰς ταύτας,
καὶ οὐ μετενόησαν [f] δοῦναι αὐτῷ δόξαν. 10. καὶ ὁ πέμπτος ἐξέχεε
τὴν φιάλην αὐτοῦ ἐπὶ τὸν [g] θρόνον τοῦ θηρίου· καὶ ἐγένετο ἡ
βασιλεία αὐτοῦ [h] ἐσκοτωμένη· καὶ [i] ἐμασῶντο τὰς γλώσσας αὐτῶν
[k] ἐκ τοῦ [l] πόνου 11. καὶ ἐβλασφήμησαν τὸν θεὸν [m] τοῦ οὐρανοῦ ἐκ
τῶν [l] πόνων αὐτῶν καὶ ἐκ τῶν ἑλκῶν αὐτῶν, καὶ οὐ [n] μετενόησαν [n] ἐκ
τῶν ἔργων αὐτῶν. 12. καὶ ὁ ἕκτος ἐξέχεε τὴν φιάλην αὐτοῦ ἐπὶ
[o] τὸν ποταμὸν τὸν μέγαν [o] Εὐφράτην· [p] καὶ [q] ἐξηράνθη τὸ ὕδωρ
[p] αὐτοῦ, ἵνα ἑτοιμασθῇ ἡ ὁδὸς τῶν βασιλέων τῶν ἀπὸ ἀνατολῆς
ἡλίου. 13. καὶ εἶδον [r] ἐκ τοῦ στόματος τοῦ δράκοντος καὶ ἐκ τοῦ
στόματος τοῦ θηρίου καὶ ἐκ τοῦ στόματος τοῦ [s] ψευδοπροφήτου
πνεύματα [t] τρία [u] ἀκάθαρτα, ὡς [v] βάτραχοι· 14. εἰσὶ γὰρ πνεύματα
δαιμονίων [w] ποιοῦντα σημεῖα ἃ ἐκπορεύεται ἐπὶ τοὺς βασιλεῖς τῆς

z Constr. vi. 4, etc.
a *i.e.* the sun.
b Contrast vii. 16 with this scorching.
c generic, or with ref. to 2, 6.
d vii. 16; ἅπ. λεγ. N.T.
e ix. 20-21.
f Inf. of conceived result or tendency (Burton, 371), *cf.* v. 5; usually with ὥστε. The hope of xiv. 6 f., xv. 4 is disappointed.

g xiii. 2; = kingdom, Prov. xvi. 12, xx. 28, xxv. 5. h viii. 12, Ps. cv. 28, Exod. x. 21 f. i Sc. οἱ τῆς βασ.; *cf.* Apoc. Pet. 28-29. k = ἀπό Mt. xvi. 26. l xxi. 4, Just. *Apol.* i. 8. m xi. 13, Dan. ii. 19. n ii. 21-22. o ix. 14; see Gen. xv. 18, Deut. i. 7, etc. On abs. of article, *cf.* Win. § 15, 5*b*, § 20, 9*c*. p *Cf.* Josh. iii. 17, Zech. x. 11. q Isa. xi. 15, xliv. 27. r Position of phrase "one of several traces of a tendency to attempt the rhetorical order of ordinary Greek" (Sx.). Dragon here seen by seer for first time (*cf.* xii. 1, xiii. 1). s xiii. 11. t Contrast to three angels of xiv. 6 f.? u Mark i. 26, etc. v For frogs as specially odious agents of Ahriman, *cf.* Plut. *de Iside*, 46; source of plagues and death (*SBE.* iv. 203). For irreg. constr., *cf.* ἔχων in xiv. 14. w xiii. 13, xix. 20, Matt. xxiv. 24, 2 Th. ii. 9.

prophets are **ἅγιοι,** but all **ἅγιοι** are not prophets.

Ver. 9. Failure to honour the true God, a note of the heathen spirit (as in xi. 13, xiv. 7; Rom. i. 28). See Introd., § 6. For the general idea, *cf.* 2 Clem. ix.: "while we have opportunity of being healed, let us give ourselves over to God the healer, giving him a recompense. And what recompense? Repentance from a sincere heart. . . . Let us give him eternal praise."

Vv. 10-11. The ninth Egyptian plague of darkness (due to the eclipse, *cf.* viii. 12?) falls on Rome, aggravating the previous pains of the Romans (ver. 2) and driving them into exasperation and fresh blasphemy instead of repentance. The repetition of 11 *b*, after 9, is characteristic of Oriental impressiveness (*cf.* Jer. xxx. 2, xxxi. 1, etc.), but it sums up the effect of the first four plagues.

Vv. 12-16. To facilitate the invasion of the empire (xvii. 12, 16) by the Parthians (ix. 14 f.) under Nero redivivus (*cf.* xix. 19), as in 4 Esd. xiii. 43-47 to let the ten tribes return in safety from captivity, the Euphrates is to be dried up in the latter days, like the Jordan before Joshua or the Euphrates itself when Cyrus captured Babylon (Herod. i. 191).

Ver. 13. **βάτραχοι,** perhaps a reminiscence of the second Egyptian plague, but probably an Iranian touch; the frog was a special agent of Ahriman in the final contest (*cf.* reff., *H. J.* 1904, 352, and Hübschmann, 230, 231). According to Artemidorus (ii. 15) frogs represent **γοήτας καὶ βωμολόχους,** and they were naturally associated with serpents (*cf.* Plut. *Pyth.* 12) as amphibious.

Ver. 14. "They are (not, these are) spirits of daemons". These devilish imps muster God's opponents to the final conflict. The fierce invasion of *the kings of the east* seems to give an impetus to *the kings of the world.* Antichrist's power extends to these (*cf.* xi. 10). "As the Lord sent his apostles to all the nations, so shall he (*i.e.*, Antichrist) send false apostles" (Hippol. vi. *cf. A. C.* 188 f.). The sources of the tradition lie in *Addit. Esther*, xi. 6 f., where the two dragons cry, and at their summons all nations gather to do battle against the righteous nation; also in the belief that Israel's foes muster against her in the latter days (xvii. 14, xix. 17-20,

οἰκουμένης ὅλης, συναγαγεῖν αὐτοὺς [x] εἰς τὸν πόλεμον τῆς [y] ἡμέρας τῆς μεγάλης τοῦ Θεοῦ τοῦ [z] παντοκράτορος. [15. "'Ιδοὺ [a] ἔρχομαι [1] ὡς [b] κλέπτης. μακάριος ὁ γρηγορῶν καὶ τηρῶν τὰ ἱμάτια αὐτοῦ, ἵνα μὴ [c] γυμνὸς περιπατῇ καὶ βλέπωσι τὴν ἀσχημοσύνην αὐτοῦ."] 16. καὶ [d] συνήγαγεν αὐτοὺς εἰς τὸν τόπον τὸν καλούμενον [e] Ἑβραϊστὶ [f] Ἁρμαγεδών.[2] 17. καὶ ὁ ἕβδομος ἐξέχεε τὴν φιάλην αὐτοῦ ἐπὶ τὸν [g] ἀέρα· καὶ ἐξῆλθε φωνὴ μεγάλη ἐκ τοῦ ναοῦ ἀπὸ τοῦ θρόνου

x xvii. 14, xix. 19-21.
y Only here (*cf.* i. 10, vi. 17?) in Apoc.
z Ver. 7.
a iii. 11, xxii. 7, 12, 20.
b iii. 3, 1 Th. v. 2.
c iii. 18; *cf.* Lk. xii. 36-37.
d Sc. δαιμόνια.
e ix. 11.
f *Cf.* *SC* 263 f: = הַר מְגִדּוֹ; Megiddo, a classic scene of rout for Israel's foes (*cf.* xix. 11, 14 = Judg. v. 20), like the plain of Chaeronea, an Ἄρεως ὀρχήστρα.
g ix. 2 (*Encycl. Rel. and Ethics*, i. 252 f. and Rohde's *Psyche*, 415 f., 548 f., 609 f.), haunt and home of spirits, etc., Philo, *de gig.* § 2, Eph. ii. 2, vi. 12, Yasht. xiii. 12-13, and Plut., *de Iside* 26.

[1] The variant ερχεται (ℵ*, 38, 47, S., Pr.) is an attempt to smooth out the abruptness of this interjected warning, which echoes the synoptic tradition rather than the Jewish law that it was a deadly offence for a priest to lack "complete and clean apparel" (Sanh., 83, 1, *cf.* Selwyn, 197). The extreme awkwardness of the verse in its present setting suggests that it is an interpolation or misplaced gloss, which has crept into the text owing to the above association of ideas (so, *e.g.*, Vischer, Spitta, Schön, Völter, Rauch, Weyland, von Soden, Simcox, Briggs). Beza transferred it to precede iii. 18, Könnecke (*Emendationen zu Stellen N.T.*, 35-37) to between iii. 3*a* and 3*b*, when it would complete the ἰδού series of ii. 22, iii. 9, 20.

[2] Αρ Μαγεδων (ℵA, min., And., Ar.) is preferred by WH (313) and Swete.

xx. 7-10; after Ezek. xxxviii-xxxix.; Zech. xiv. 2 f.; En. lvi, xc.; Sib. Or. iii. 310-322, 663-674). In Asc. Isa. iv. Beliar, in the guise of Nero, comes "and with him all the powers of this world, and they will hearken to him in all that he desires" (*cf.* below on xvii. 13, 17). These demonic spirits are not crushed till the day of judgment (En. xvi. 1 ἕως τῆς κρίσεως τῆς μεγάλης, Jub. x., Matt. viii. 29). The three locusts which issne from the mouth of the Beast in Hermas, *Vis.* iv. 1. 6, belong to the conception of Apoc. ix. 1.

Ver. 16. A double thread of tradition is woven into this strand of prophecy, (*a*) that of a last conflict of the world-powers with God and the messianic people (*cf.* xvii. 14, xix. 19) and (*b*) that of Rome's ruin by the Parthians under Nero redivivus. The two were originally distinct, but the apocalyptist naturally twists them together, although he never clears up their relationship. Here 13-16 is an enigmatic summary of what is variously depicted further on. But, though an erratic block in its present setting, it may have been placed here by the final editor, in his characteristically proleptic manner. Strictly speaking, the sixth plague is confined to ver. 12.—Ἁρμαγεδών, where the messianic Josiah will triumph, is (*a*) either to be located in mythology rather than in geography, as a mount where the final conflict of the gods is to be fought out (so fallen angels in En. vi. 5, 6 at mount Hermon)—in which case the phrase is a survival of some apocalyptic myth no longer intelligible to John (Gunkel, Bousset)—or (*b*) to be taken as an allusion to the hills near the plain (in the light of Judges v. 18, 19, iv. 6, 12, 14; Ezek. xxxviii. 8, 21, xxxix. 2, 17). By gematria the name is equivalent to רומה הגדולה (Ewald, Hausrath), but neither this nor the proposal to take הַר as a corruption of עִיר (city, so Hitzig, Hilgenfeld, Forbes), much less of עֲרָא (Aram. = ארץ, Völter), is natural. *Cf.* for further etymological and mythological suggestions, Nestle (Hastings, *D. B.* ii. 304, 305), Cheyne (*E. Bi.* i. 310, 311), and Legge and Cheyne in *Proc. Society of Bibl. Arch.* 1900, ii. 2. Bruston's interpretation (Ερμα = ἀνάθεμα, Γεδᾶν, *cf.* Num. xiv. 45, xxi. 3; Judges xx. 45) is far-fetched, but there may be some link between this obscure fragment of tradition and the cycle of Gog and Magog (*cf.* Cheyne in *E. Bi.* ii. 1747, 1748).

17-21: the seventh bowl and plague as the climax of all.

Ver. 17. The temple (xi. 19) and the throne (viii. 3) are again blended in one scene. In Isa. lxvi. 6 the divine ven-

λέγουσα, "[h] Γέγονε". 18. καὶ [i] ἐγένοντο ἀστραπαί καὶ φωναὶ καὶ
βρονταὶ καὶ [k] σεισμὸς ἐγένετο μέγας, [l] οἷος οὐκ ἐγένετο ἀφ' οὗ
ἄνθρωπος ἐγένετο ἐπὶ τῆς γῆς, τηλικοῦτος σεισμὸς οὕτω μέγας.
19. καὶ [m] ἐγένετο ἡ πόλις ἡ μεγάλη [m] εἰς τρία μέρη, καὶ αἱ πόλεις
τῶν ἐθνῶν ἔπεσαν· καὶ [n] Βαβυλὼν ἡ [n] μεγάλη [o] ἐμνήσθη ἐνώπιον τοῦ
θεοῦ, δοῦναι αὐτῇ τὸ [p] ποτήριον τοῦ οἴνου τοῦ [q] θυμοῦ τῆς ὀργῆς
αὐτοῦ. 20. [r] καὶ πᾶσα νῆσος ἔφυγε, καὶ [s] ὄρη οὐχ εὑρέθησαν. 21.
καὶ [t] χάλαζα μεγάλη ὡς [u] ταλαντιαία καταβαίνει ἐκ τοῦ οὐρανοῦ ἐπὶ
τοὺς ἀνθρώπους· καὶ [v] ἐβλασφήμησαν οἱ ἄνθρωποι τὸν θεὸν ἐκ τῆς
πληγῆς τῆς χαλάζης· ὅτι [w] μεγάλη ἐστὶν ἡ πληγὴ αὐτῆς σφόδρα.

h xxi. 6, *cf.* Ezek. xxxix. 8.
i iv. 5.
k viii. 5, xi. 13, 19, Jer. xxiii. 19.
l From Ass. Mos. viii. 1, Dan. xii. 1, *cf.* Matt. xxiv. 21 and Shaks. *Jul. C.* i. 3.
m *Cf.* Win. § 29, 2*b*.
n Jer. li. 58, Dan. iv. 30.
o xviii. 5, Acts x. 31. The false concord *ἐμν. δοῦναι* is due to writer's loose use of infin., *cf.* ver. 9.
p Isa. li. 17, Jer. xxv. 15.
q *Cf.* xiv. 8, 10.
r vi. 14, xx. 11.
s Judith, xvi. 15, Sir. xvi. 19, etc.
t Exod. ix. 18-25, Ezek. xiii. 11, Sib. iii. 690 f.
u ἅπ. λεγ. N.T.; figur. = "colossal".
v verr. 9-11.
w *μέγας* for the fifth time in 17-21.

geance is heralded by φωνὴ ἐκ ναοῦ, φωνὴ Κυρίου ἀνταποδιδόντος ἀνταπόδοσιν τοῖς ἀντικειμένοις.

Ver. 18. The conventional storm-theophany brings on an exceptionally severe earthquake, which (ver. 19) shatters Jerusalem into three parts and entirely overthrows the pagan cities. Rome's more awful ruin is attributed in xvii. 16 to the invasion of Oriental hordes (*cf.* xvi. 12); here the allusion to her downfall is proleptic (=xvii. 2, xviii. 6 f.), as a climax to the foregoing catastrophe. Probably *the great city* is Jerusalem (so *e.g.*, Andr., Bengel, Simcox, B. Weiss, J. Weiss), as in xi. 8. She is distinguished from the Gentile cities as Rome also is singled out from her allies and adherents. Being primarily guilty, Rome-Babylon is reserved for a special fate. The whole passage is enigmatic and obscure. Did the earthquake destroy the inhabitants of Jerusalem? and why? The allusion must be to some form of the tradition underlying xi. 1-13 and xiv. 18-20, or to that of Zech. xiv. 4, 5. Both earthquakes and invasions had been combined already in the O.T. eschatology (*cf.* Isa. xiii. 13 f.; Hag. ii. 21 f.); both perils were real, at this period; and, in delineating both dangers with a free, poetic imagination, the prophet aims as usual at impressiveness rather than at any systematic regularity. For earthquakes in Jerusalem, *cf.* G. A. Smith's *Jerusalem*, i. pp. 61 f.—ἐμνήσθη: neither magnificence nor age wins oblivion for an empire's crimes against the moral order.

Ver. 20. Here, as at vi. 14, the removal of hills tallies with the Iranian belief (shared by later Jewish Christian apocalyptic, *cf.* Böklen, 131 f.) that mountains as the work of Ahriman would disappear with him (*S. B. E.* v. 129), leaving the earth in its ideal state of a smooth plane on which mankind could dwell in unity of speech and intercourse, free from barriers. The collocation of mountain and island (so vi. 14) is possibly a relic of the ancient point of view, for which (*i.e.*, for dwellers in the West) these formed the apparent source of the sun's rising, where his light first became visible.

Ver. 21. Even an abnormal hail-shower (*cf.* the fourth Egyptian plague) fails to bring pagans to their senses. ὡς ταλ., *i.e.*, literally about sixty times the weight of even the enormous hailstones (μναααῖαι) which Diodorus Siculus (xix. 45) records. In En. lx. 17 the "spirit of the hail is a good angel," *i.e.*, amenable to God's orders.

The obscurity of chapter xvii. springs mainly from the differences of tradition and outlook which are reflected in the canonical text. The threefold interpretation of the Beast as the Imperial power (so xiii.), as Nero redivivus (ver. 8) and as (11) the eighth king (the two latter being applications of the same idea) is accompanied by a twofold explanation of the seven heads (geographical = 9, historical = 10), and of the woman's support (1, 3, 15). The eschatological tradition of Babylon as the supreme anti-divine world-power is applied to Rome, and this involves the re-interpretation of some details (*e.g.* 15, 18), while the tradition of the Beast as antichrist is further overlaid by the special tradition of Nero redivivus in that capacity. This dual Beast (as Völter first recognised; *cf.* Charles's *Ascensio Isaiæ*, pp. lx.-lxi.) is not merely the Imperial power (as in xiii. 3) but incarnate

a xxi. 9. XVII. 1. Καὶ ἦλθεν εἷς ἐκ τῶν ἑπτὰ ἀγγέλων τῶν ἐχόντων τὰς ἑπτὰ φιάλας, καὶ [a]ἐλάλησε μετ' ἐμοῦ λέγων "Δεῦρο, δείξω σοι τὸ

in an Imperial personality of infernal and supernatural character, which attacks not only the Christian messiah (14) but Rome itself (16-17). The latter trait is unmistakably due to the legend of Nero redivivus, apart from which the oracle is unintelligible. Such variations have left traces in the structure of the passage, which point to some process of editorial revision, but it is difficult to disentangle the original source or sources, or even to determine their precise character and period. Ver. 14 is certainly out of place, for the allies of the Beast could not destroy Rome after they themselves had been destroyed by the messiah and his allies. It is thus either proleptic or inserted by the Christian writer in his (Jewish) source (so *e.g.*, Vischer, Charles, Briggs, von Soden). Other traces of this editor might be found in 6 *b*, 8 (9 *a*?), and 15, and the Jewish character of the source (so Vischer, Weyland, Schmidt, Sabatier, Ménégoz, etc.), would be confirmed by the absence of any polemic against the Imperial cultus. It would be a Vespasianic oracle, inspired by a passion for revenge on Rome for her cruel, recent treatment of the Jewish people. When the source is regarded as Christian (as *e.g.*, by Erbes, Völter, and Schön), ver. 11 would be an addition inserted under Domitian to bring it up to date (so Harnack, *Texte u. Unters.* II. iii. 134 f.; *Chronologie*, 245, 246, followed by Briggs, Gunkel, J. Weiss, etc.; *cf.* Introd. § 7). But even so, the structure of the passage is involved. Vv. 9-11 are not vision but calculation or exposition (*cf.* xiii. 18). The *waters* of ver. 15 are never seen (*cf.* 1, 3), and the professed explanation (ver. 7) follows a loose order (beast = 8, heads = 9-11, horns = 12-14, waters = 15, horns again = 16-17, and finally the woman = 18). The reference to the woman, however, is thrown late in order to introduce the following doom-song (*cf. kings* in 18, xviii. 3, 9, and *great* in 18, xviii. 2), and a similar motive accounts for the irregular position of 16-17 after 14, Rome's fall, though viewed from different angles, being the main object before the writer's mind at the moment. The defeat of 14 is taken up, in its true position, afterwards (xix. 11-21). Ver. 15 (an echo of xvi. 19 *b*) is probably thrown in at this point, to contrast dramatically the revolt [16] of Rome's supporters against her. Thus, except for 9-11, there are sufficient psychological reasons to account partially for the order and contents of the oracle; but source-criticism is required to clear up the passage, in the more or less extensive theories of one source (edited in 6, 9 *a*, 14-15, so J. Weiss; or variously in 8, 12-14, with some words in 6, 9, 11, so *e.g.* Pfleiderer, Baljon, Bousset and Forbes) or even two sources (Jewish, A = 3-4, 6 *b*-7, 10, B = 11-13, 16 *b*-17, Wellhausen's *Analyse*, 26 f.), for which the linguistic idiosyncrasies (double use of **γέμειν**, 3-4, precedence of object over verb 13, 16, 18, **οἱ κ. τ. γ.** 2, and the construction **βλ. τ. θ. ὅτι ἦν**, 8) afford some basis. The main problem is to explain how the various strata of tradition overlap; *e.g.*, in 8, 12 f., the beast is Nero redivivus, an infernal power of evil, whereas in 11 Domitian seems identified with Nero the beast. It is hard to believe that one and the same writer could simultaneously regard Domitian as a second Nero and expect Nero redivivus as a semi-supernatural power. In any case the stress falls on the Beast rather than on the woman, and on the eschatological prediction, not on the historical application. It is a fairly open question whether 8 or 11 is the editorial mortar super-imposed upon the earlier tradition. Upon the whole, one of the least unsatisfactory solutions is to take 11 as a Domitianic gloss by the Christian editor, who has also added 6 *b* (if not all of 6) and 14 to a Vespasianic oracle (possibly of Jewish origin) in xvii. 4 f. which anticipated the downfall of persecuting Rome at the hands of Nero redivivus and his Eastern allies. No hypothesis is free from difficulties. But the general Domitianic reference of the Apocalypse and the presence of the Nero redivivus saga must be worked in somehow, and some hypothesis on the above lines seems to do most justice to the literary structure of this chapter as well as to the data of the book in general. It is impossible to determine how far the Christian editor worked over his source. That the difficulties of the oracle arise mainly from the presence of an earlier source (*cf.* Introd. § 7), which John has revised slightly and brought up to date, is axiomatic, however.

κρίμα τῆς [b] πόρνης τῆς μεγάλης, [c] τῆς καθημένης ἐπὶ [d] ὑδάτων
πολλῶν·

2. μεθ' ἧς ἐπόρνευσαν
[e] οἱ βασιλεῖς τῆς γῆς,
καὶ ἐμεθύσθησαν [f] οἱ [g] κατοικοῦντες τὴν γῆν
ἐκ τοῦ οἴνου τῆς πορνείας αὐτῆς."

3. καὶ [h] ἀπήνεγκέ με εἰς ἔρημον [i] ἐν πνεύματι· καὶ εἶδον γυναῖκα
καθημένην ἐπὶ θηρίον [k] κόκκινον, γέμοντα ὀνόματα [1] βλασφημίας,
ἔχον κεφαλὰς ἑπτὰ καὶ κέρατα δέκα. 4. καὶ ἡ γυνὴ ἦν [l] περιβεβλημένη [m] πορφυροῦν καὶ κόκκινον, καὶ [m] κεχρυσωμένη χρυσίῳ

b *Cf.* on xiv. 8.
c From Jer. li. 13.
d *i.e.* peoples (ver. 15).
e Visits of Herod, Tiridates, etc.
f Note irreg. change of constr., Win. § 22, 8.
g xiv. 8; omitting usual ἐπί.
h *Cf.* on xxi. 10.
i i. 10, iv. 2, xxi. 10.
k xviii. 12, 16; *cf.* Matt. xxvii. 28 (colour of Roman soldier's mantle).
l xii. 1.
m xviii. 16, ἅπ. λεγ. N.T.

[1] **γεμον ονοματων** (min., Hipp., S., And., Areth.) and **γεμον ονοματα** (ℵcQ, min., Bj.) seem corrections of the unusual (in this book) and harsh *constr. ad sensum* **γεμοντα ονοματα** ℵ*AP, Lach., Ti., WH, Sw., Bs. [**γεμον τα ονοματα,** as in ver. 4, Tr., Al., Düst., Ws.]: for the **εχον** of Q, 1, etc., Syr., And., Areth. (Lach., Al., Bj., Ws.), Ti., WH marg., Bs. read **εχοντα** (ℵP) and WH **εχων** (A, min.).

The double object of the oracle is (*a*), by a re-editing of the tradition of xiii. to represent Rome in her Imperial pride, before describing her downfall, and (*b*) to define more precisely the final appearance of the last foe. The chapter could readily be spared as isolated (Simcox), but this only proves that the author is again working upon disparate materials which he inherited. The oracle contains (1-6) a vision of the Harlot (by way of foil to xii. 1-6 and especially xxi. 9 f.) and the Beast, with (7-18) an explanation of the vision.

CHAPTER XVII.—Ver. 1. A fresh vision commences (*cf.* iv. 1), still punitive (xvi. 1), but with an exchange of angelic cicerones (as Slav. En. xxi.). The Beast which has already (in xiii.) done duty as the empire is now the support of the capital. Rome, personified (so Sib. Or. iii. 46-92, before 80 A.D.) as a feminine figure, rides on a beast of the same colour, like a Bacchante on the panther, or like the Syrian Astarte on a lion.

Ver. 2. Tyre's commercial intercourse with the nations (Isa. xxiii. 17) and Assyria's political intrigues, by which her statecraft fascinated and seduced other states (Nah. iii. 4) are both described by the same figure. Local and national cults, as a rule, were left undisturbed by the Romans; and indeed Oriental superstitions often reacted powerfully on Rome itself. But fresh conquests meant the extension of Rome's intoxicating and godless suzerainty.

Ver. 3. The wilderness was the traditional site of visions, but there may be an allusion here to Isa. xxi. 1 or even to the Roman Campagna (Erbes). The woman in xii. is in the desert to be delivered from the dragon; the woman here is in the desert to be destroyed by the Beast. **κόκκινον** "crimson or scarlet," = luxurious and haughty splendour (Mart. ii. 39; Juv. *Sat.* iii. 283 and xiv. 188 for purple). The Beast which in xiii. 1 bore the names of blasphemy upon its head, now wears them spread over all its body. Baldensperger (15-16) conjectures a similar reference to Rome in En. lii. (*seven* hills?); here at any rate the author is sketching the Roman Empire in its general magnificence and authority under the Cæsars, and the inconsistencies in his description (waters and wilderness, seat on waters, seat on the Beast) are natural to this style of fantastic symbolism. It is curious that no attack is directed against the polytheism of the Empire. *Cf.* Cebes' *Tabula*: "Do you see a woman sitting there with an inviting look, and in her hand a cup? She is called Deceit; by her power she beguiles all who enter life and makes them drink. And what is the draught? Deceit and ignorance." The mounting of divine figures on corresponding beasts is a Babylonian trait (*S. C.* 365).

Ver. 4. **κεχρυσ.** goes by an awkward zeugma with **λίθῳ** (collective) **καὶ μαργαρίταις**; "with ornaments of gold and precious stones and pearls" (like

καὶ [n] λίθῳ τιμίῳ καὶ [n] μαργαρίταις, ἔχουσα [o] ποτήριον [o] χρυσοῦν ἐν
τῇ χειρὶ αὐτῆς γέμον [p] βδελυγμάτων καὶ τὰ ἀκάθαρτα τῆς [q] πορνείας
αὐτῆς, 5. καὶ ἐπὶ τὸ μέτωπον αὐτῆς ὄνομα [r] γεγραμμένον
([s] Μυστήριον),[1] "Βαβυλὼν ἡ μεγάλη, ἡ [t] μήτηρ τῶν πορνῶν καὶ τῶν
βδελυγμάτων τῆς γῆς." 6. καὶ εἶδα τὴν γυναῖκα [u] μεθύουσαν ἐκ
τοῦ [v] αἵματος τῶν ἁγίων καὶ ἐκ τοῦ αἵματος τῶν μαρτύρων Ἰησοῦ.
καὶ [w] ἐθαύμασα ἰδὼν αὐτὴν [w] θαῦμα μέγα. 7. καὶ εἶπέ μοι ὁ ἄγγελος,
"Διατί ἐθαύμασας; ἐγὼ ἐρῶ σοι τὸ μυστήριον τῆς γυναικὸς καὶ
τοῦ θηρίου τοῦ βαστάζοντος αὐτὴν τοῦ ἔχοντος τὰς ἑπτὰ κεφαλὰς
καὶ τὰ δέκα κέρατα. 8. τὸ θηρίον [x] ὃ εἶδες ἦν καὶ οὐκ ἔστιν
καὶ μέλλει ἀναβαίνειν ἐκ τῆς [y] ἀβύσσου καὶ εἰς ἀπώλειαν [x] ὑπάγει.
καὶ [z] θαυμασθήσονται οἱ κατοικοῦντες ἐπὶ τῆς γῆς, ὧν οὐ γέγραπται
τὸ ὄνομα ἐπὶ τὸ [a] βιβλίον τῆς ζωῆς [b] ἀπὸ καταβολῆς κόσμου, [c] βλε-

n xviii. 12, 16, Ezek. xxviii. 13, 16.
o Jer. li. 7; *cf.* Milton's *Comus*, 67 f.
p xxi. 27, *cf.* Lev. xviii. 26-29, Sap. xii. 23-24 xiv. 11 (= customs of idolatry).
q *Cf.* Sap. xiv. 12.
r Sc. ἦν.
s 2 Th. ii. 7.
t Jer. l. 11-12.
u *Cf.* Isa. xxxiv. 17, xlix. 26.
v xviii. 24.
w ἅπ. λεγ. N.T. (contrast xiii. 3); for Attic ἐθαυμάσθην.
x Diabolic antithesis to divine figure of iv. 8.
y ix. 1.
z xiii. 3 (Blass, § 18, 3).
a iii. 5.
b xiii. 8.
c Irreg. gen. absol. or appos. to ὧν, as μελλ. Acts xxvi. 22.

[1] **μυστηριον** = the explanatory gloss of a reader, from ver. 7 (Könnecke, 37).

Ezekiel's doomed prince of Tyre). The harlot in *Test. Jud.* xiii. 5 was also decked **ἐν χρυσίῳ καὶ μαργαρίταις** and poured out wine for her victims. Rome is pronounced luxurious, licentious and loathsome. Here, as in the contemporary 4 Esd. iii. 2, 29, it is felt to be a mystery that prosperity and permanence should belong to a state flaunting its impiety and oppression, not merely enjoying but propagating vice.

Ver. 5. Roman *filles de joie* wore a label with their names thus (Juv. vi. 123). **μυστήριον** (which hardly belongs to the title itself) indicates that the name is to be taken **πνευματικῶς** (xi. 8), not literally; "a name written which is a symbol," or a mysteriously significant title.—**μήτηρ κ.τ.λ.**, Rome, the natural focus of Oriental cults in general, is charged with fostering all the superstitious and vicious practices of her subjects.—**βδελ.** (partly justified by a perusal of Petronius and Apuleius) is an apt rebuke if it comes from the prophet of a religion which one Roman historian classed among the *atrocia aut pudenda* which disgraced the capital (Tacit. *Ann.* xv. 44).

Ver. 6. *Cf.* Nahum's "bloody city" (of Assyrian cruelty to prisoners, iii. 1), and for the metaphor Cic. *Phil.* ii. 24, 29, or Suet. *Tiberius*, 59, or Pliny, *H. N.* xiv. 28, "quo facile intelligatur ebrius jam sanguine ciuium, et tanto magis eum sitiens," also Jos. *Bell.* v. 8, 2. When a Jewish source is postulated, **καὶ . . . Ἰησοῦ** is bracketed (*e.g.*, by Vischer, Spitta, S. Davidson, Briggs, Charles and others) as from the hand of the later Christian editor, who here, as in xviii. 24 (Mommsen), is thinking of the condemnation of provincial prisoners to fight with gladiators or wild beasts in the arena of the capital. The **ἅγιοι** of the source would thus be defined as, or supplemented by, Christian martyrs. They are not contaminated, like the rest of men, but their purity is won at the expense of their life. The Jewish martyrs would be those killed in the war of 66-70, primarily. The whole verse, however, might be (*cf.* xviii. 24) editorial; it is the contaminations, rather than the cruelties, of Rome which absorb the interest of this oracle.

Vv. 7-18. An explanation of the vision, cautiously but clearly outlining the Nero-saga.

Ver. 8. As the Beast seen by the seer cannot be described as non-existent, it must denote here (as in xiii. 3 f., though differently) not the empire but the emperor, or one of its own heads. Such an identification was natural in the ancient world especially, where a king and his capital or state were interchangeable terms. The emperor, here Nero redivivus (*cf.* the saying of Apollonius, cited in Philostr. *Vit. Apol.* iv. 38: "Regarding this wild beast," *i.e.*, Nero, "I know not how many heads he has"), embodied the empire. The Beast is a sort of *revenant*. To rise from the abyss was the conven-

πόντων τὸ θηρίον ὅτι ἦν καὶ οὐκ ἔστι καὶ παρέσται. 9. [d] ὧδε ὁ νοῦς d xiii. 18
ὁ ἔχων σοφίαν. αἱ ἑπτὰ κεφαλαὶ ἑπτὰ [e] ὄρη εἰσίν, ὅπου ἡ γυνὴ e *Cf.* Sib. Or. ii. 18, Ῥώμης ἑπταλόφοιο.
κάθηται [f] ἐπ' αὐτῶν. 10. καὶ βασιλεῖς ἑπτά εἰσιν· οἱ πέντε ἔπεσαν,
ὁ εἷς ἔστιν, ὁ ἄλλος οὔπω ἦλθε· καὶ ὅταν ἔλθῃ, [g] ὀλίγον αὐτὸν [h] δεῖ f *Cf* iii. 8 and xii. 6 also 1 Kings xiii. 25 (LXX).
μεῖναι. 11. καὶ τὸ θηρίον ὃ ἦν, καὶ οὐκ ἔστι, καὶ αὐτὸς [i] ὄγδοός
ἐστι, καὶ [k] ἐκ τῶν ἑπτά ἐστι, καὶ εἰς [l] ἀπώλειαν ὑπάγει. 12. καὶ
τὰ δέκα [m] κέρατα ἃ εἶδες δέκα [m] βασιλεῖς εἰσίν, οἵτινες βασιλείαν g vi. 11. h xx. 3. i *Cf.* 2 Pet. ii. 5.

k In and after them, so Dan. vii. 8, 24. l Ver. 8. m Dan. vii. 20, 24.

tional origin of the Beast (*cf.* xi. 7) even in the primitive tradition; the Nero-antichrist, however, introduces the fresh horror of a monster breaking loose even from death. True, he *goes to perdition* eventually, but not before all except the elect have succumbed to the fascination of his second advent. The Beast of the source here is evidently the antichrist figure of xi. 7 (also a Jewish source) transformed into Nero redivivus. There is less reason to suspect the hand of the Christian editor in 8 (Bousset) than in 9 *a* (J. Weiss).

Ver. 9. ὄρη, *cf.* Prop. iii. 11, 57 ("Septem urbs alta iugis, quae praesidet orbi"), Verg. *Georg.* ii. 534.

Ver. 11. Bruston takes **καὶ ἐκ τῶν ἑπτὰ ἐστιν** as a translation of ומן השבעה הוא, in the sense that the eighth was more (or greater) than the seven, *i.e.*, realising more fully the ideal of the Beast. But even were the case for a Hebrew original clearer than it is, such an interpretation is forced. The verse is really a parenthesis added by John to bring the source up to date. Domitian, the eighth emperor, under whom he writes, is identified with the true Neronic genius of the empire; he is a revival and an embodiment of the persecuting Beast (*cf.* Eus. *H. E.* iii. 17, Tert. *Apol.* 5: portio Neronis de crudelitate, *de pallio* 4: a sub-Nero) to the Christian prophet, as he proved a second Nero to some of his Roman subjects (*cf.* Juvenal's well-known sneer at the *calvus Nero*). This does not mean that John rationalises Nero redivivus into Domitian, which would throw the rest of the oracle entirely out of focus. Domitian, the eighth emperor, is not explained as *the Beast which was and is not and is to come up out of the abyss* (ver. 8), but simply as *the Beast which was and is not;* no allusion is made to his term of power, and the concluding phrase **καὶ εἰς ἀπ. ὑπάγει** is simply the conventional prophecy of doom upon persecutors; it need not be a post-factum reference to D.'s murder in 96. He *belonged to the seven*, as he had been closely associated with the Imperial power already (Tac. *Hist.* iii. 84, iv. 2, 3; *cf.* Jos. *Bell.* iv. 11, 4). The enigmatic and curt tone of the verse shows that either from prudence ("some consideration towards *the one who is* beseems even a prophet," Mommsen), or more probably from pre-occupation in the grim, ulterior figure of the Neronic antichrist, the prophet does not care to dwell minutely on the emperor's personality as an incarnate Nero. He does not even allude to the suspicion, voiced by his contemporaries (4 Esd. xi. 12) that Domitian had made away with Titus. His vision is strained, like that of his source, to the final and supernatural conflict; the Satanic messiah, the Beast who is to return from the abyss, bulks most prominently on the horizon. The absorbing interest of the oracle, even in its edited form, is eschatological. John simply puts in a few words, as few as possible, to bring this Vespasianic source up to date, since the death of Titus had not been followed by the appearance of the Nero-antichrist. The latter is still and soon to come however! John thoroughly shares, though he expands and applies, the prediction of his source. The addition he makes to it in ver. 11 must on no account be taken as if it meant the substitution of "Domitian = Nero redivivus" for the supernatural expectation of the latter. There is certainly some awkwardness in the juxtaposition of Domitian as a second Nero and of Nero redivivus, but this was inevitable under the circumstances.

Vv. 12-18: the campaign of Nero and his vassal-kings against Rome, which is slain by an arrow feathered from her own wings.

Vv. 12, 13. This political application of the *ten horns* probably means either the Parthian satraps of xvi. 12 reckoned

οὔπω [n] ἔλαβον, ἀλλ' ἐξουσίαν ὡς [o] βασιλεῖς μίαν ὥραν λαμβάνουσι
μετὰ τοῦ θηρίου. 13. [p] οὗτοι μίαν γνώμην ἔχουσι, καὶ τὴν δύναμιν
καὶ ἐξουσίαν αὐτῶν τῷ θηρίῳ διδόασιν.
14. [p] οὗτοι μετὰ τοῦ ἀρνίου πολεμήσουσι,
καὶ τὸ ἀρνίον νικήσει αὐτούς,
ὅτι [q] Κύριος κυρίων ἐστὶ καὶ βασιλεὺς βασιλέων—
καὶ οἱ μετ' αὐτοῦ [r] κλητοὶ καὶ [r] ἐκλεκτοὶ καὶ πιστοί."
15. καὶ λέγει μοι, "Τὰ [s] ὕδατα ἃ εἶδες, οὗ ἡ πόρνη κάθηται,
λαοὶ καὶ ὄχλοι εἰσὶν καὶ ἔθνη καὶ γλῶσσαι. 16. καὶ τὰ δέκα
κέρατα ἃ εἶδες καὶ τὸ θηρίον οὗτοι μισήσουσι τὴν πόρνην, καὶ
ἠρημωμένην ποιήσουσιν αὐτὴν καὶ [t] γυμνήν, καὶ τὰς [u] σάρκας
αὐτῆς [v] φάγονται, καὶ αὐτὴν [w] κατακαύσουσιν ἐν πυρί. 17. ὁ γὰρ
θεὸς ἔδωκεν εἰς τὰς καρδίας αὐτῶν ποιῆσαι τὴν γνώμην αὐτοῦ,
καὶ [x] ποιῆσαι μίαν γνώμην, καὶ δοῦναι τὴν βασιλείαν αὐτῶν τῷ

n = Eng. perfect, Burton, 52.
o Like Sargon's allies, Isa. x. 8 (*cf.* xxiii. 8).
p *Cf.* on xiv. 4.
q See on xix. 16; Deut. x. 17, Ps. cxxxvi. 3, Dan. ii. 37, 47, 2 Macc. xiii. 4, En. ix. 4, etc.
r *Cf.* 2 Pet. i. 10.
s Ver. 1.
t *Cf.* Ezek. xvi. 37-39, etc.
u Plur. = fleshy parts of body, 2 Kings ix. 36, etc.
v xix. 18, Ps. xxvii. 3, Mic. iii. 2 f.; on form (Hellenistic fut. of ἐσθίω) *cf.* Win. § 13, 6.
w xviii. 8, 18, Lev. xxi. 9, Nah. iii. 15.
x *Cf.* Cic. *pro Milone*, 33.

in round numbers, who occupied a royal position in the estimation of the East (so, *e.g.*, Eichhorn, de Wette, Bleek, Bousset, Scott, J. Weiss, Baljon, Wellhausen), or ("chefs d'armée," Havet) the governors of the (ten senatorial) provinces, holding office for (**μίαν ὥραν**) one year (so Ewald, Hilg., Hausrath, Mommsen, B. Weiss, Hirscht, Briggs, Selwyn, B. W. Henderson ["the number *may* be derived from Daniel. In any case it is a round number, and the seer did not go round counting the number of the Roman provinces"]), unless it is to be left as a vague description of the allies (Weizs., Holtzm., Swete). Philo (*de leg. ad Caium* xxxiv.) notes the facilities possessed by proconsuls for starting revolutions, especially if they commanded powerful armies such as those stationed on the Euphrates to protect Syria.

Ver. 14. An abrupt and proleptic allusion to xix. 11-21; the Christian messiah is the true *King of kings* (a side reference to the well-known Parthian title). This is the first time that John brings the Lamb on the scene of earthly action. He now appears at the side, or rather at the head, of his followers in the final crisis, not in a struggle preceding the sack of Rome. He and Satan (as represented by the empire) are the real protagonists. Note the share assigned to the faithful in this victory (after ii. 26, 27). The war fought on their behalf by the Lamb is their fight also (*cf.* on xix. 14); its success rests on the divine election and their corresponding loyalty (*cf.* xii. 11, xiii. 8; a Zoroastrian parallel in Yasht xiii. 48; the favourite description of the saints in Enoch as "chosen [and] righteous"; and *Passio Perpetuae*, xxi., "o fortissimi martyres! o uere uocati et electi in gloriam Domini nostri Jesu Christi"). The redeeming power of Christ, together with the adoration which he alone can rightfully claim, make his cause more than equal to the empires of the world (*cf.* the thought of Isa. liii. 12).

Ver. 15. The woman impiously rivals God (**κύριος ἐπὶ ὑδάτων πολλῶν**, Ps. xxix. 3, *cf.* 10).—**ὄχλοι** is substituted for the more common **φυλαί**, perhaps with an allusion (after Ezek. xvi. 15, 25, 31) to Rome's imperial rapacity.

Ver. 16. Rome perishes at the hands of Nero and his ruthless allies—a belief loudly echoed in the Talmud. In Sib. *Or.* iv. 145, 350 f. the East then and thus regains the treasures of which the Oriental provinces had been despoiled.—**γυμνήν . . . πυρί,** the doom of a Semitic harlot (Ezek. xxiii. 45 f., xxviii. 17, 18). But no details of the disaster are given.

Ver. 17. The remarkable unanimity and obedience of the usurping vassals, which welds them into an avenging instrument, can only be explained on supernatural grounds. A divine overruling controls all political movements (*cf.* xi. 2, xiii. 5, 7), according to the determin-

θηρίῳ, ἄχρι [y] τελεσθήσονται οἱ λόγοι τοῦ θεοῦ. 18. καὶ ἡ γυνὴ
ἣν εἶδες ἔστιν ἡ πόλις ἡ [z] μεγάλη, ἡ ἔχουσα βασιλείαν ἐπὶ τῶν
βασιλέων τῆς γῆς."

y x. 7.
z xvi. 19, xviii. 10, Verg. *Eclog.* i. 19, 24.
a Ps. ii. 2, lxxxix. 28.

ism of apocalyptic tradition (Baldensperger, 58 f.). The irony of the situation is that the tools of providence are destroyed, after they have unconsciously served their purpose (as in Isa. x. 12 f.). The Imperial power, hitherto the usual support of Rome, is to prove her deadly foe; John's stern philosophy is that one partner in this hateful union is employed to ruin the other. Not long before this prophecy appeared, Vitellius and Vespasian in the person of their partisans had ravaged Rome in the near future Nero's allies were to fight, like Coriolanus, against their "cankered country, with the spleen of all the under-fiends". —**μίαν κ.τ.λ.** The same tradition, on a simpler scale, appears in 4 Esd. xiii. 33, 34 where, at the revelation of God's Son, "every man shall leave his own land and their battles against one another; and a countless multitude shall assemble together, desiring to come and fight against him". The dualism of God and Satan is not absolute; even the latter's manœuvres are made to subserve some providential design.

Ver. 18. The dramatic climax of the oracle: the great harlot is—Rome, domina Roma, the pride and queen of the world! *Cf.* Spenser's *Ruines of Rome*, 360 f. ("Rome was th' whole world, and al the world was Rome"). For the probable position of xix. 9 *b*-10 at this point in the original form of the Apocalypse, see below (*ad loc.*).

After a prelude on the doom of this second and western Babylon (xviii. 1-3) two sublime songs follow: one of triumph in heaven (4-8) one of wailing on earth (9 f.). Both are modelled in semi-strophic style upon the earlier taunt-songs (*cf.* Introd. § 4) over Tyre and Babylon (*cf.* also Apoc. Bar. lxxxii. 3-9). But the severe invective against Rome reveals the shuddering impression which this marvel and mistress of the world made upon the conscience of her provincial subjects, Jewish or Christian. They were half fascinated, even as they felt repelled, by the sight of her grandeur. This magnificent doom song (9 f.) like that of Apoc. Bar. xii. (*cf.* xiii.), however, celebrates her downfall, partly on grounds which might be justified from contemporary pagan authors (*cf.* Renan's *Apôtres*, ch. xvii.). Vv. 24 (note the sudden change from **σοί** to **αὐτῇ**) and 20 (in whole or part) are Christian editorial insertions, (*a*) either by some scribe or editor after the Apocalypse was completed, or (*b*) by John himself in an earlier source (Jewish or from his own hand). The presence of a special source is suggested by *e.g.*, the unexampled use of **οὐαί** (*cf.* on ver. 16, and *Oxyrh. Fragment of Uncan. Gospel*, 31), the large number of **ἅπαξ εὐρημένα** (**στρήν.** 3, **διπλόω** 6, **διπλόος**, *cf.* 1 Tim. v. 17, **στρην.** 7 and 9, **σιρικοῦ**, **ἐλεφ.**,**σιδήρου**, **μαρμάρου** and **θύϊνον** in 12, **κινν.**, **ἄμωμον**, **σεμίδ.**, **ῥεδῶν**, and **σωμάτων**, [in this sense] in 13, **ἀπώλετο** (14), **ἐργάζονται** [in this sense in Apoc.] in 17, **τιμ.** 19, **ὁρμ.** 21, **μουσ.**, **σαλπιστῶν**, **κιθαρῳδῶν** [only in xiv. 2] 22, **ὀπώρα** and **λιπαρά**, 14) and rare terms, for which the special character of the contents can hardly account. Differences of outlook also emerge; *e.g.*, xviii. 9 f. is out of line with xvii. 17 and xvi. 13 f., xviii. 1-3 (Rome long desolate) hardly tallies with xviii. 9 f. (ruins still smouldering, *cf.* xix. 3), and the kings of xviii. 9, 10 lament, whereas in xvii. 16 they attack, Rome. These inconsistencies (Schön, Schmiedel) might in part be set down to the free poetic movement of the writer's imagination, working in dramatic style and oblivious of matter-of-fact incongruities like the *sauve qui peut* of 4; just as the lack of any allusion to the Imperial cultus, the Lamb, or the martyrs (exc. 20 and 24) does not necessarily denote a Jewish origin. But the cumulative effect of these features points to 20 and 24 as insertions by John in a Jewish (*cf. e.g.*, the special emphasis on the trader's point of view, 11-17) Vespasianic source which originally formed a pendant to that underlying xvii. (so variously in detail but agreeing on a source, probably Jewish—Sabatier, Rauch, Spitta, Weyland, Bousset, J. Weiss, Schmidt, Baljon, Pfleid., Wellhausen, von Soden, de Faye, Calmes). The original breathed the indignant spirit of a Jewish apocalyptist against the proud empire which had won a temporary triumph over the city and people of God. John applies it to the Rome which was also responsible for the persecutions. The tone of it

a From Zech. ix. 3-5 (Tyre), etc.
b Ezek. xliii. 2,
c See viii. 13, xvi. 11, 21.
d Cf. Acts xii. 7, and on Apoc. i. 16, iv. 1.
e xiv. 8, Jer. li. 8.
f From Isa. xxxiv. 11-15, cf. Spenser's *Ruines of Time*, 121-134.
g Cf. xix. 17-21. ἅπ. λεγ. N.T. See Deut. xiv. 12-19, Chag. 3b.
h xiv. 8, Jer. xxv. 15, 27, li. 7.
i Cf. on xiv. 8.
k xvii. 2, Isa. xxiii. 17, cf. Sib. Or. iii. 357 f.
l Ezek. xxvii. 9-25.
m Jos. *Ant.* iii. 2, 4, = "money, means".
n Acts xviii. 10: collect. subst. hence plur. vb. cf. Jo. vi. 22, etc.
o Gen. xix. 14-15, Num. xvi. 26; from Isa. xlviii. 20, Jer. l. 8, li. 45, etc.
p By succumbing to her fascinations, and thus sharing her fate.
q Cf. 1 Jo. iv. 13.
r Cf. Bar. i. 20. Suggested by Jer. li. 9. *Accumulata peruenerunt* (Bgl.).
s xvi. 19.

[a] XVIII. 1. **Μετὰ ταῦτα εἶδον ἄλλον ἄγγελον καταβαίνοντα ἐκ τοῦ οὐρανοῦ, ἔχοντα ἐξουσίαν μεγάλην· [b] καὶ ἡ γῆ ἐφωτίσθη [c] ἐκ τῆς [d] δόξης αὐτοῦ.** 2. **καὶ ἔκραξεν ἐν ἰσχυρᾷ φωνῇ λέγων,**

"Ἔπεσεν [e] ἔπεσε Βαβυλὼν ἡ μεγάλη,
καὶ ἐγένετο [f] κατοικητήριον δαιμονίων,
καὶ φυλακὴ παντὸς πνεύματος ἀκαθάρτου,
καὶ φυλακὴ παντὸς [g] ὀρνέου [g] ἀκαθάρτου καὶ μεμισημένου·
3. ὅτι ἐκ τοῦ [h] οἴνου [τοῦ [i] θυμοῦ] τῆς πορνείας αὐτῆς πέπωκαν πάντα τὰ ἔθνη,
καὶ οἱ βασιλεῖς τῆς γῆς μετ' αὐτῆς [k] ἐπόρνευσαν,
καὶ οἱ [l] ἔμποροι τῆς γῆς ἐκ τῆς [m] δυνάμεως τοῦ στρήνους αὐτῆς ἐπλούτησαν."
4. καὶ ἤκουσα ἄλλην φωνὴν ἐκ τοῦ οὐρανοῦ λέγουσαν,
"Ἐξέλθατε, ὁ [n] λαός μου, [o] ἐξ αὐτῆς,
ἵνα μὴ [p] συγκοινωνήσητε ταῖς ἁμαρτίαις αὐτῆς,
καὶ [q] ἐκ τῶν πληγῶν αὐτῆς ἵνα μὴ [q] λάβητε·
5. ὅτι [r] ἐκολλήθησαν αὐτῆς αἱ ἁμαρτίαι ἄχρι τοῦ οὐρανοῦ,
καὶ [s] ἐμνημόνευσεν ὁ Θεὸς τὰ ἀδικήματα αὐτῆς.

has been severely censured, as if it breathed a malignant orgy of revenge. "It does not matter whether Jewish or Christian materials are the ultimate source. He who takes delight in such fancies is no whit better than he who first invented them" (Wernle, p. 370). So far as this is true, it applies to xix. 17-21 (or 14-20) rather than to xviii. But the criticism must be qualified; see notes on xviii. 7 and 20. There is smoke in the flame, but a profound sense of moral indignation and retribution overpowers the mere vindictiveness of an unpatriotic fanatic who exults to see his oppressor humiliated.

Chapter XVIII.—1-3: an angelic proclamation of Babylon's fate (*cf.* xiv. 8) in terms of Isa. xiii. 19-22, xxxiv. 14 (demons of the desert, the Mazzikin of Jewish demonology, familiar to Babylonian magic), Jer. l. 30, li. 37, Zeph. ii. 15, etc. "Be of good cheer, O Jerusalem . . . Miserable are the cities which thy children served, miserable is she who received thy sons. For as she rejoiced at thy fall and was glad at thy ruin, so shall she grieve at her own desolation. Yea I will take away her delight in her great crowds, and her vaunting shall turn to mourning. For fire from the Everlasting shall come upon her for a length of days, and for long shall she be inhabited by demons" (Bar. iv. 30-35). **ἐκ κ.τ.λ.** "by (*cf.* ver. 19) the wealth of her wantonness" traders profited; *i.e.*, by the enormous supplies which the capital required to satisfy her demands (**στρῆνος, -ιάω** from the New comedy and colloquial usage).—**δόξα** in ver. 1 denotes the flashing brilliance which, according to the primitive collocation of life and light, accompanied the heavenly visitants to earth or the manifestation of a divine presence (xxi. 11, 23, xxii. 5); see the valuable paragraphs in Grill, pp. 259-271.

Vv. 4-8. A song of exulting in heaven, addressed first to the faithful (ver. 4) and then (ver. 6) to the enemies who execute God's vengeance.

Ver. 4. **ἐξέλθατε** (*cf.* Apoc. Bar. ii. 1), which in the source referred to the Jewish community at Rome, is an artistic detail, retained like several in ch. xxi., although the historical meaning and application was lost in the new situation. *Cf.* the opening of Newman's essay on *The Benedictine Centuries*.

Ver. 5. Plutarch (*de sera uindict.*

6. [t] ἀπόδοτε αὐτῇ ὡς καὶ αὐτὴ ἀπέδωκεν,
καὶ διπλώσατε τὰ [u] διπλᾶ κατὰ τὰ ἔργα αὐτῆς·
ἐν τῷ ποτηρίῳ [v] ᾧ ἐκέρασε,
κεράσατε αὐτῇ διπλοῦν.
7. ὅσα [w] ἐδόξασεν αὐτὴν καὶ [x] ἐστρηνίασε,
τοσοῦτον δότε αὐτῇ βασανισμὸν καὶ πένθος.
[y] Ὅτι ἐν τῇ καρδίᾳ αὐτῆς λέγει [z] ὅτι 'Κάθημαι βασίλισσα,
καὶ χήρα οὐκ εἰμί καὶ πένθος οὐ μὴ ἴδω,'
8. διὰ τοῦτο [a] ἐν μιᾷ ἡμέρᾳ [b] ἥξουσιν αἱ πληγαὶ αὐτῆς,
[c] θάνατος καὶ πένθος καὶ λιμός·
καὶ ἐν πυρὶ [d] κατακαυθήσεται.
ὅτι [e] ἰσχυρὸς Κύριος ὁ Θεὸς ὁ κρίνας αὐτήν.
9. καὶ κλαύσουσιν καὶ κόψονται ἐπ' [f] αὐτὴν οἱ [g] βασιλεῖς τῆς γῆς,
οἱ μετ' αὐτῆς πορνεύσαντες καὶ στρηνιάσαντες, ὅταν βλέπωσι τὸν

t Jer. xvi. 18, l. 15, 29, Ps. cxxxvii. 8.
u Æsch., *Ag.* 537: = "amply sufficient," Isa. xl. 2, lxi. 7 f., Zech. ix. 12.
v Rare attract. of rel. pron.
w Arrogance, *cf.* Ps. Sol. i. 3-6, ii. 33-35, iv. 28.
x 1 Ti. v. 11.
y = "because" (susp. ὅτι.).
z From Zeph. ii. 15, *cf.* Ovid., *Met.* vi. 193-195 (Niobe), 4 Esd. xi. 43.
a Lucret. iii. 898-899, Eur. *Herc. Fur.* 509-510, *Hec.* 285, Ovid, *Fasti*, ii. 235; *cf.* Job i. 13-19, Isa. x. 17.
b Isa. xlvii. 9, Ezek. xxviii. 18.
c *Cf.* on vi. 8.
d xvii. 16, Jer. l. 31-32.
e Jer. l. 34.
f Diff. sense, i. 7.
g xvii. 2, xviii. 3; *cf.* Isa. xxiii. 5.

15) is strong upon the solidarity of a city, which is liable to be punished at any time for past offences.—**κολλᾶσθαι** ("Heaped up to the sky are her sins") in the familiar sense of *haerere*=to follow close upon, or to cleave, the idea being that the mass of sins actually presses on the roof of heaven. The figure would be different if, as Holtzm. conjectures, **κολλ.** referred to the gluing together of the leaves composing a roll; the record of Rome's sins would form so immense a volume that when unrolled it would reach the very heavens. "Et ascendit contumelia tua ad altissimum, et superbia tua ad fortem" (4 Esd. xi. 43).

Ver. 6. The foes of Rome (unless **ἀπόδοτε κ.τ.λ.**, is a rhetorical apostrophe) are invited to serve her with the retribution promised to the first Babylon (see reff.).—**διπλώσατε**, *cf. Oxyrh. Pap.* iii. 520[6]. **Ἐν τῷ ποτηρίῳ, κ.τ.λ.** *Cf.* Apoc. Bar. xiii. 8 (to Romans), "Ye who have drunk the strained wine, drink ye also of its dregs, the judgment of the Lofty One who has no respect of persons".

Ver. 7. It is probably at this point that the passage drifts over from the conception of a voice heard (ver. 4) to that of direct utterance on the part of the prophet; unless we are to suppose that the voice speaks till the close of ver. 20 (a similar instance in ch. xi.). Imperial Rome is imperious and insolent; haughty self-confidence is the sin of the second Babylon as of the first (see Isa. xlvii. 5, 7, 8, imitated in this passage). *Cf.* (bef. 80 A.D.) Sibyll. v. 173, where the impious and doomed city is upbraided for vaunting "I am by myself, and none shall overthrow me". A similar charge of arrogance was brought by Ezekiel against the prince of Tyre (xxviii. 2 f., *cf.* xxvi., xxvii. throughout with the present passage), and by the Jewish author of Apoc. Bar. xii. 3 against Rome. To the Semitic as to the Hellenic conscience, the fall of a haughty spirit always afforded moral relief. Nothing so shocked the ancient conscience as overweening presumption in a state or an individual, which was certain ultimately to draw down upon itself the crashing anger of heaven.

Ver. 8. This drastic, ample punishment, though executed by subordinates in xvii. 16, 17, is here (as in 5, 20) regarded on its divine side. God is strong, as well as guilty, glorious Rome (ver. 10, *cf.* on vi. 15); and his strength is manifested in the huge shocks of history, as well as in creation (iv. 11, v. 13). Rome's proud disregard of all that was mutable in human conditions is visited with condign retribution. The prophet sees not a decline and fall but a sudden collapse (10, 16, 19).

Vv. 9-20: the wailing on earth, by kings (9, 10), merchants (at length, 11-16), and seafaring men (17-20), imitated from the finer and more elaborate

καπνὸν τῆς πυρώσεως αὐτῆς, 10. ἀπὸ μακρόθεν ἑστηκότες διὰ τὸν
[i] φόβον τοῦ βασανισμοῦ αὐτῆς, λέγοντες,

"Οὐαί, οὐαί, [k] ἡ πόλις ἡ [l] μεγάλη,
Βαβυλὼν ἡ πόλις ἡ [m] ἰσχυρά,
ὅτι μιᾷ ὥρᾳ ἦλθεν ἡ κρίσις σου."

11. καὶ οἱ [n] ἔμποροι τῆς γῆς κλαίουσι καὶ πενθοῦσιν ἐπ' αὐτήν,
ὅτι τὸν [o] γόμον αὐτῶν οὐδεὶς ἀγοράζει οὐκ ἔτι· 12. γόμον χρυσοῦ
καὶ ἀργύρου καὶ [p] λίθου [p] τιμίου καὶ μαργαριτῶν καὶ βυσσίνου καὶ
[q] πορφύρας καὶ [r] σιρικοῦ καὶ [s] κοκκίνου· καὶ πᾶν ξύλον θύϊνον καὶ
πᾶν [t] σκεῦος ἐλεφάντινον καὶ πᾶν σκεῦος ἐκ ξύλου τιμιωτάτου καὶ
χαλκοῦ καὶ σιδήρου καὶ [u] μαρμάρου· 13. καὶ [v] κιννάμωμον καὶ ἄμωμον καὶ θυμιάματα καὶ [w] μύρον καὶ [x] λίβανον καὶ οἶνον καὶ ἔλαιον
καὶ σεμίδαλιν καὶ σῖτον καὶ κτήνη καὶ πρόβατα καὶ [y] ἵππων καὶ

h xiv. 11. i proximus ucalegon ardet? k *Cf.* on ver. 16. l xvi. 19. m Ῥώμη robur (Bgl.); see below, ver. 21. n Isa. xlvii. 15: "merchants," not κάπηλοι "pedlars or hucksters" (Sir. xxvi. 29). o "Ship's freight" (Ac. xxi. 3), "wares". p See xvii. 4; *cf.* Plin., *H. N.* xxxvii. 12. q Friedländer, iii. 46 f. r Tac., *Ann.* ii. 33, Verg., *Georg.* ii. 121. s xvii. 4. t = "article". u Fried., iii. 65-66. v Prov. vii. 17, Lucan, x. 165 f., En. xxx. 3. w Jo. xi. 2, xii. 3, 5. x Matt. ii. 11. y Genitive depend. on γόμον (sc).

passages in Ezek. xxvi.-xxviii, where kings (xxvi. 15-18), traders (very briefly and indirectly, xxvii. 36), and mariners (xxvii. 29-36) are all introduced in the lament over Tyre's downfall. Contrast the joy of the three classes in ver. 20. A triple rhythm pervades (*cf.* 2, 3, 6, 8, 14, 16, 19) but does not dominate this grim doom-song, somewhat after the well-known structure of the Semitic elegy. But the three laments are all characteristic. The kings are saddened by the swift overthrow of power (10), and the reverse of fortune; the merchants (11, 16) by the loss of a profitable market, the mariners by the sudden blow inflicted on the shipping trade (ver. 19).

Ver. 12. **βυσσίνου** (sc. **ἱματίου**) = "of fine linen"; from **βύσσος** the delicate and expensive linen (or cotton) made out of Egyptian flax (Luke xvi. 19); **σιρικοῦ** = "silk," muslin, or gauze, chiefly used for women's attire (Paus. iv. 110 f.); **πᾶν ξύλον θύϊνον** = "all citron (citrus)-wood," a fragrant, hard, dark brown, expensive material for furniture, exported from N. Africa. Note the extensive range of Roman commerce to supply the needs of luxury (interea gustus elementa per omnia quaerunt, Juv. xi. 14; pearls, *e.g.*, from Britain as well as Red Sea), also the various demands in order: ornaments, wearing apparel, furniture, perfumes (for personal and religious use), food, and social requirements. Wets. cites a rabbinic saying: decem partes diuitiarum sunt in mundo, nouem Romae et una in mundo uniuerso.

Ver. 13. "Cinnamon," an aromatic spice (the inner bark of the tree) exported from E. Asia and S. China; **ἄμωμον**, aromatic balsam for the hair, made from the seeds of some Eastern shrub (Verg. *Ecl.* iv. 25, "assyrium uolgo nascetur amomum; from Harran, Jos. *Ant.* xx. 2, 2)—for the form, *cf.* Levy's *die Semit. Fremdwörter im Griech.* (1895), p. 37; **θυμιάματα**, "incense," in its ingredients of aromatic spices; **λίβανον** = "frankincense," a fragrant gum-resin exported from S. Arabia (Isa. lx. 6, Jer. vi. 20); enormous quantities of perfume were employed by the Romans, chiefly in the care of the body, but also to mix with wine at their banquets (*e.g.*, Juv. vi. 303, etc.; *E. Bi.* 5320); **σεμίδαλιν** = "fine flour," wheaten meal (LXX for סלת, *cf.* Deut. xxxii. 14; Ps. lxxxi. 16) of the choicest kind; wine, flour, and incense were all used in sacrifices. **ῥεδῶν**, a Gallic word = four-wheeled "carriages" used by the well-to-do (*cf.* Jerome on Isa. lxvi.). **σωμάτων** = "slaves" (later Greek, dropping the qualifying adj. **δούλων** or **οἰκετικῶν**, *cf.* Deissm. 160, Dittenberger's *Sylloge*,[2] 845, etc.). **καὶ ψυχὰς** (reverting awkwardly to accus.) **ἀνθρώπων** = "and souls of men" (from Ezek. xxvii. 13, "they traded the persons of men for thy merchandise": **ἐνεπορεύοντό σοι ἐν ψυχαῖς ἀνθρώπων**, LXX, *cf.* 1 Chron. v. 21). The double expression is strange. If **καὶ** is not to be taken as "even," identifying both, we must suppose that some distinction is intended, and that of the

ῥεδῶν καὶ [z] σωμάτων καὶ ψυχὰς ἀνθρώπων. 15. οἱ ἔμποροι [a] τούτων
οἱ πλουτήσαντες ἀπ᾽ αὐτῆς, ἀπὸ μακρόθεν [b] στήσονται διὰ τὸν φόβον
τοῦ βασανισμοῦ αὐτῆς κλαίοντες καὶ πενθοῦντες, 16. λέγοντες,

"Οὐαί, οὐαί, [c] ἡ πόλις ἡ μεγάλη,
ἡ περιβεβλημένη [d] βύσσινον καὶ πορφυροῦν καὶ κόκκινον,
καὶ [e] κεχρυσωμένη ἐν χρυσίῳ καὶ [f] λίθῳ τιμίῳ καὶ μαργαρίτῃ·
ὅτι μιᾷ ὥρᾳ ἠρημώθη ὁ τοσοῦτος πλοῦτος."

17. [g] καὶ πᾶς [h] κυβερνήτης καὶ πᾶς ὁ ἐπὶ πόντον[1] πλέων καὶ
ναῦται καὶ ὅσοι τὴν θάλασσαν ἐργάζονται, ἀπὸ μακρόθεν [i] ἔστησαν 18. καὶ ἔκραξαν βλέποντες τὸν καπνὸν τῆς πυρώσεως αὐτῆς,
λέγοντες, [k] "τίς ὁμοία τῇ πόλει τῇ μεγάλῃ;" 19. καὶ [l] ἔβαλον
χοῦν ἐπὶ τὰς κεφαλὰς αὐτῶν καὶ ἔκραξαν κλαίοντες καὶ πενθοῦντες,
λέγοντες,

"Οὐαί, οὐαί, ἡ πόλις ἡ μεγάλη,
ἐν ᾗ [m] ἐπλούτησαν πάντες οἱ ἔχοντες τὰ πλοῖα ἐν τῇ θαλάσσῃ
ἐκ τῆς [n] τιμιότητος αὐτῆς,
ὅτι μιᾷ ὥρᾳ ἠρημώθη."

20. [o] "Εὐφραίνου ἐπ᾽ αὐτῇ, [p] οὐρανέ,
καὶ οἱ [p] ἅγιοι καὶ οἱ [q] ἀπόστολοι καὶ οἱ προφῆται,
ὅτι ἔκρινεν ὁ Θεὸς [r] τὸ κρίμα ὑμῶν [s] ἐξ αὐτῆς."

z (LXX), Gen. xxxiv. 29, Tob. x. 11, 2 Macc. viii. 11, *cf.* Jos. *Ant.* xix. i. 10.
a *i.e.*, Wares mentioned in 12-13.
b Ver. 10, Ezek. xxvii. 30-31.
c Nom. for dat. after *οὐαί* (accus. viii. 13, xii. 12), *cf.* 10, 19. Here only in Apoc.
d Ver. 12, xix. 8, 14, (pecul. to Apoc. in N.T.).
e xvii. 4.
f Ver. 12.
g Isa. xxiii. 14, Ezek. xxvii. 27, 29.
h Acts xxvii. 11.
i Note change to aor. from future (9, 11, 15).
k xiii. 4 (ironical contrast).
l From Ezek. xxvii. 30, (Heb.), Jos. vii. 6 (LXX).
m Ezek. xxvii. 33.
n Abstr. for concrete, "her costly treasures" (see on ver. 3).
o Deut. xxxii. 43, Isa. xliv. 23, Ass. Mos. x. 10.
p xii. 12, *cf.* xvi. 8.
q Only here and xxi. 14, in Joh. lit.
r xvii. 1, xix. 2.
s vi. 10, Ps. cxix. 84.

[1] For the unexampled ΤΟΠΟΝ (*cf.* Ac. xxvii. 2) read ΠΟΝΤΟΝ (Nestle, *Theol. Ltzg.*, 18, 97, 274, *Einführ.*, 135, E. Tr. 168; so Baljon and Gwynn) which was apparently read in some form by Copt., Pr. (omnis super mare nauigans). A similar confusion occurs in Judith vi. 21, and conversely **κατα Ποντον** has supplanted **κατα τοπον** in Eus., *H. E.* iv. 15, 2.

two **σωμάτων** is the more specific. Prostitutes, or female slaves, or gladiators, or even grooms and drivers (**ἵπποι καὶ ἱππεῖς**, Ezek. xxvii. 14) have been more or less convincingly suggested as its meaning. Slave-dealing (Friedländer, iii. 87 f.; Dobschütz, 266-269) was a lucrative trade under the empire, with Delos as its centre, and Asiatic youths especially were in large demand as pages, musicians, and court-attendants. Thousands of captives, after the siege of Jerusalem, were sent into slavery by the Roman government; and early Christians at this period (Clem. Rom. lv.) voluntarily went into slavery either as substitutes for others or "that with the price got for themselves they might furnish others with food".

Ver. 17. **ἐργάζονται κ.τ.λ.** = "whose business is on the sea". The passage reflects the importance of Rome especially for the trade of the Levant. Pliny (*H. N.* vi. 101, xii. 84) gives the large figures of Oriental imports and their cost, adding sarcastically *tanti nobis deliciae et feminae constant* (Friedländer, iii. 48-51). The regret of the mariners for the grandeur that was Rome passes rapidly into a sense of commercial loss.

Ver. 20. This verse interrupts the sequence of 19 and 21 in which the ruin of Rome is illustrated by the dramatic action of the angel. The awkward shift from description to an apostrophe, and the evidently Christian tone of the cry, betray an editor's hand. His object is to render explicit the moral reasons why Christians should delight in the downfall of the city. He writes in the same triple rhythm as the source, and his hand is to be seen in the whole verse not simply in

21. καὶ ἦρεν εἷς ἄγγελος [t]ἰσχυρὸς λίθον ὡς μύλον μέγαν καὶ
ἔβαλεν εἰς τὴν θάλασσαν λέγων,

"Οὕτως [u]ὁρμήματι βληθήσεται Βαβυλὼν ἡ μεγάλη πόλις,
[v]καὶ οὐ μὴ εὑρεθῇ ἔτι.

22. καὶ φωνὴ [w]κιθαρῳδῶν καὶ μουσικῶν καὶ αὐλητῶν καὶ [x]σαλ-
πιστῶν

οὐ μὴ ἀκουσθῇ ἐν σοὶ ἔτι,
καὶ πᾶς τεχνίτης πάσης τέχνης
οὐ μὴ εὑρεθῇ ἐν σοὶ ἔτι,
καὶ φωνὴ [y]μύλου
οὐ μὴ ἀκουσθῇ ἐν σοὶ ἔτι,

t v. 2; see above, ver. 10.
u Neh. ix. 11, 1 Macc. iv. 8 (*cf.* Isa. xxviii. 2): "with sudden onset or impetus," suiting action to word.
v Ezek. xxvi. 21.
w xiv. 2, Isa. xxiv. 8, Ezek. xxvi. 13; *cf.* 1 Macc. iii. 45, Suet. *Nero*, 40-41, *Domit.* 4.
x Win. § 13, 4.
y Fr. Jer. xxv. 10 (Heb.), *cf. Aen.* i. 726.
Bar. ii. 22 f.

καὶ οἱ ἀπόστολοι. The voice from heaven is thus made to pass into a closing apostrophe to heaven and its inhabitants (*cf.* xi. 18), imitated from Jer. li. 48 (Heb.). John seems to assume that all had a case against Rome as victims of her cruelty, probably in the main as martyrs and confessors. "Apostles," omitted in ver. 24, has here (as in ii. 2) its wider sense (otherwise xxi. 14), but it must include Peter and Paul (Zahn, *Einleit.* § 39, n. 4).—**ὅτι κ.τ.λ.** = "for God has judged her with your judgment," *i.e.*, vindicated you (done you justice, given you your due) by exacting vengeance upon her. She who once doomed you is now doomed herself (*cf.* xvi. 6).—**εὐφραίνου.** *Cf.* En. lxii., where the kings and rulers condemned by messiah to eternal torment are to be "a spectacle for the righteous and his elect; they will rejoice over them because the wrath of the Lord of spirits resteth upon them, and his sword is drunk with their blood"; also Isa. xxx. 29, for the call to exult over a fallen oppressor. A Parisian workman, who was looking down at the corpse of Robespierre, was overheard to mutter, with relief, "Oui, il y a un Dieu".

Vv. 21-24: a rhythmic song of doom, introduced by a symbolic action partly imitated from Jer. li. 63, 64.

Ver. 21. Rome's fall will be irrevocable and sudden and violent, as a powerful angel shows dramatically by seizing a huge boulder and flinging it into the sea. *Cf.* the analogous description of Babylon's collapse in Sib. Or. v. 158, 163, 174. The reiterated emphasis on Roman luxury is notable. Later literature, as Friedländer observes (iii. 9-17), tended to a conventional exaggeration of the luxurious civilisation under the Empire; judged by modern standards, at any rate, it was not particularly extravagant. This denunciation of wealth and ease, however, is apposite in a source which reflects the age of Nero, since it was under Nero, rather than under Vespasian or Domitian, that Roman luxury during the first century of our era reached its zenith. The oracle breathes the scorn felt by simple provincials for the capital's wanton splendour, and indeed for the sins of a pleasure-loving civilisation. But it is religious poetry, not a prose transcript of the contemporary commercial situation. *Cf.* Dill's *Roman Society*, pp. 32 f., 66 f.

Ver. 22. **μουσικῶν** "minstrels or musicians" (1 Macc. ix. 41); the occurrence of the generic term among the specific is certainly awkward and would favour the rendering "singers" (Bengel, Holtzm.) in almost any other book than this. On these musical epithets see Friedländer, iii. 238 f.; the impulses to instrumental music at Rome during this period came mainly from Alexandria. For coins stamped with Nero as harpist see Suet. *Nero*, xxv. **φωνὴ μύλου,** the daily accompaniment of Oriental life. The sound of the mill meant habitation, but in the desolation of Rome no more pleasant stir of mirth or business would be heard (Isa. xlvii. 5). The fanatic Jesus, son of Ananus, who howled during the siege of Jerusalem and for four years previously (Jos. *Bell.* vi. 5, 3) "woe to Jerusalem," denounced upon her "a voice from the east, a voice from the west, a voice from the four winds, a voice against Jerusalem and the temple,

23. καὶ φῶς [z] λύχνου
οὐ μὴ φάνῃ ἐν σοὶ ἔτι,
καὶ φωνὴ [y] νυμφίου καὶ [a] νύμφης
οὐ μὴ ἀκουσθῇ ἐν σοὶ ἔτι·
14. καὶ ἡ [b] ὀπώρα σου τῆς ἐπιθυμίας τῆς [c] ψυχῆς
ἀπῆλθεν ἀπὸ σοῦ,
καὶ πάντα τὰ [d] λιπαρὰ καὶ τὰ [e] λαμπρὰ
[f] ἀπώλετο ἀπὸ σοῦ,
καὶ οὐκέτι [1] οὐ μὴ αὐτὰ εὑρήσουσιν.
23. [g] ὅτι [h] οἱ ἔμποροί σου ἦσαν οἱ [i] μεγιστᾶνες τῆς γῆς,
ὅτι ἐν τῇ [k] φαρμακίᾳ σου ἐπλανήθησαν πάντα τὰ ἔθνη.
24. [l] καὶ ἐν αὐτῇ [m] αἷμα προφητῶν καὶ ἁγίων εὑρέθη,
καὶ πάντων τῶν ἐσφαγμένων ἐπὶ τῆς γῆς."

z viii. 12. a Jer. vii. 34, xvi. 9, xxxiii. 11. b Jer. xlvii. 10, = "the ripe fruit" (on form and breathing, *cf.* Thumb, 19). c *Cf.* Win., § 22, 18*b*, and for genit., *ibid.*, § 30, 12*g*. d = "sumptuous" (living on fat of land); Isa. xxx. 23, Neh. ix. 35. e "All things rich and radiant," *cf.* Jas. ii. 2-3. f Ps. cxli. 5 Did. xvi. 5. Only here in Apoc. g From Ezek. xxvii. 21, Isa. xxiii. 8. h Predic. with article, Win. § 18, 8*g*. i vi. 15. k ix. 21, Isa. xlvii. 9-12, Nah. iii. 4. l xvi. 6; *cf.* Isa. xxvi. 21, Job xvi. 18. m xvii. 8, Ezek. xxiv. 7-9. On sing. here and xvi. 12 (v. l, *αιματα*), *cf.* Win. § 27. 4c.

[1] "Possibly S. [**ουκετι αυτα βλεψεις και αυτα**] here preserves the true text, and the rest" [*i.e.*, **αυτα ευρησουσι** = ℵACP, vg., Syr., **ευρης** = Q, min., **ευρησεις** = 1, 37, 96, etc., **αυτα** after **ευρ.** And.] "have lost the words by homoioteleuton" (Gwynn).—Here between the last **ετι** and the first **οτι** of 23 is the original place of ver. 14 (so Beza, Vitringa, Volkmar, Baljon, Weiss, and Könnecke) which got into its canonical position between 13 and 15 owing to the error of some early copyist, whose eye confused **οτι εμποροι σου** with **οι εμποροι τουτων**.

a voice against bridegrooms and brides, and a voice against the whole people".

Ver. 23. Contrast the **εὑρέθη** of 24 with the **εὑρήσουσιν** of ver. 14 which in its canonical position is an erratic boulder. **φαρμακίᾳ**, primarily in the figurative O.T. sense already noticed (harlotry and magic spells, as in Yasna ix. 32). But a literal allusion is not to be excluded, in view of the antipathy felt by pious Jews and early Christians to magic and sorcery. As Rome represented the existing authorities under whose aegis these black arts managed to flourish, and as they were generally bound up with religion, it would not be unnatural to charge the Empire with promoting sorcery (Weinel 10).—**ἐπλαν.** "Commerce, as having regard to purely worldly interests, is called harlotry" [Cheyne on Isa. xxiii. 17]. Sorcery, witchcraft, "fornication," and the persecution of the righteous, are all manifestations of the lawlessness practised by Beliar working in men and kings (Asc. Isa. ii. 4, 5).

Ver. 24. Again, as at ver. 20, the change of style (here from an apostrophe to a description) and spirit (xvii. 6) marks an insertion by the final editor, unless the verse originally lay after ver. 3. The triple rhythm corresponds to that of ver. 20. Rome has now succeeded Jerusalem (Matt. xxiii. 35, etc.) as the arch-enemy of the faithful. The climax of her iniquities is couched in terms of the primitive Semitic idea (Gen. iv. 10) that exposed and discovered blood is a cry for vengeance [2 Macc. viii. 3 f.]; blood violently shed wails till it is appeased by the punishment of the murderers. By a natural hyperbole, Rome is held responsible for the murders, judicial and otherwise, of saints and prophets and the slain of Israel in general—substituted here for the "apostles" of ver. 20, probably to include the Jews killed in the recent war as well as pre-Christian martyrs like the Maccabees of whom Augustine finely says: *nondum quidem erat mortuus Christus, sed martyres eos fecit moriturus Christus* (Heb. xi.-xii. 1). Rome here is the last and worst exponent of persecution. Her collapse is attributed to their blood drawing down God's utter retribution. "My blood be on the inhabitants of Chaldea, shall Jerusalem say" (Jer. li. 35, imprecating successfully the divine revenge, vv. 36, 49). As Chrysostom called psalm cix. a

XIX. 1. Μετὰ ταῦτα ἤκουσα ὡς φωνὴν [a] μεγάλην ὄχλου πολλοῦ
ἐν τῷ [b] οὐρανῷ [c] λεγόντων,
"Ἀλληλουϊά·
[d] ἡ σωτηρία καὶ ἡ δόξα καὶ ἡ δύναμις τοῦ [e] θεοῦ [e] ἡμῶν·
2. ὅτι [f] ἀληθιναὶ καὶ [f] δίκαιαι αἱ [f] κρίσεις αὐτοῦ·
ὅτι ἔκρινε τὴν πόρνην τὴν μεγάλην,

a Ver. 6, vii. 9.
b *Cf.* Jer. li. 48.
c Irreg. appos. to collective ὄχλου.
d vii. 10, xi. 15, xii. 10 (see note).
e *Cf.* Joh. xx. 17 Apoc. iii. 12, below 5-6.
f xv. 3; *cf.* on xvi. 7.

prophecy in the shape of a curse, this vehement, sensitive oracle against Rome's insolence and cruelty may be termed a curse in the form of a prophecy. A similar idea underlay the view of certain pious people who, according to Josephus (*cf.* Eus. *H. E.* ii. 23. 20-21), considered the fall of Jerusalem a retribution for the foul murder of James the Just nearly ten years before.

The doom-song is followed by an outburst of celestial triumph (xix. 1-8) in answer to xviii. 20. The conclusion as well as the commencement of the victory (xii. 12 f.) is hymned in heaven. The stern, exultant anthem, which is morally superior to the delight voiced by En. xlvii. 4, forms an overture to the final movement of the Apocalypse, as well as (like vii. 9 f., xiv. 1-5) a relief to the sombre context. 8 *b* is a prosaic editorial gloss, probably due to the liturgical use of the book, and the last clause of 10 (**ἡ γὰρ . . . προφητείας**) might be the same (*cf.* 1 Cor. xv. 56), as many editors think, were it not for the genuinely Johannine ring of the words. In any case it is an after-thought, probably (so Baljon, Barth, etc.) added by the author himself, in order to bring out here what is brought out in xxii. 9 by the explicit mention of the prophets, since **ἐχ. τ. μ. Ἰησοῦ** alone would mean Christians in general. The presence of 9 *b*-10 here, however, is not motived as at xxii. 8, 9, where it comes in naturally at the finalê of the revelations and after a distinct allusion (xxii. 1) to the revealing angel. Here the angel of the second **λέγει** (at least) has not been mentioned since xvii. 1, 7, 15, and no reason at all is given for the superstitious impulse to worship. The passage is certainly Johannine, but probably misplaced (like xviii. 14, etc.). Can it have originally lain at the end of xvii., where the hierophant angel is speaking (*cf.* also xvii. 17, *words of God* and xix. 9 *b*)? Such technical dislocations and derangements are common enough in primitive literature (*cf.* my *Historical New Testament*, pp. xxxix. 676, 690). The passage must have been shifted to its present site either by accident or more probably by a scribe who saw that the similar assurance in xxi. 5, xxii. 6 related primarily to future bliss rather than to judgment; perhaps he also took the first **λέγει** not as a divine saying (*cf.* xxi. 5) but as angelic (xxii. 6, *cf.* i. 10, 11, 19, and note on xxii. 10), and sought to harmonise the same order as in xiv. 13 (command to write, beatitude, asseverance). Otherwise 1-10 is a unity as it stands. The change of situation in 1-3, 4-10 does not prove any combination of sources; it is simply another of the inconsequences and transitions characteristic of the whole book. The marriage-idea of 7, 8 is a proleptic hint which is not developed till later (xxi.), while the supper (9) is only mentioned to be dropped—unless the grim vision of 17-21 (for which *cf.* Gressmann's *Ursprung d. Isr.-jüd. Eschatologie*, 136 f.) is meant to be a foil to it (so Sabatier and Schön).

CHAPTER XIX.—Ver. 1. Here only in N.T. (after the ruin of sinners, as Ps. civ. 35) the liturgical hallelujah of the psalter and synagogue worship occurs. In vv. 1, 3, and 6 it stands as usual first, an invocation = "praise Jah"; but in ver. 4 it is responsive, as in Pss. civ.-v., cxv.-cxvii. (the latter being sung at the passover; *cf.* Apoc. xix. 7).

Ver. 2. **ἔφθειρεν,** as the first Babylon had been denounced for her depraving influence by Jeremiah (li.) xxviii. 25, **τὸ ὄρος τὸ διεφθαρμένον τὸ διαφθεῖρον πᾶσαν τὴν γῆν.** The impatient cry of vi. 10 has now been answered. God "has avenged the blood (*i.e.*, the murder) of his servants at her hand (*i.e.*, on her)," the LXX rendering (*e.g.*, in 2 Kings ix. 7, **καὶ ἐκδικήσεις τὰ αἵματα τῶν δούλων Κυρίου ἐκ χειρὸς Ἰεζάβελ**) of the Heb. idiom נקם דם מיד = to exact punishment from a murderer. The idea is substantially that of Ps. Sol. iv. 9, viii. 29-31. As **ἀληθ. καὶ δικ.** are a characteris-

[g] ἥτις [h] ἔφθειρε τὴν γῆν ἐν τῇ πορνείᾳ αὐτῆς,
καὶ [i] ἐξεδίκησε τὸ αἷμα τῶν δούλων αὐτοῦ ἐκ χειρὸς αὐτῆς."
3. καὶ δεύτερον [k] εἴρηκαν,
"Ἀλληλουϊά·
καὶ ὁ [l] καπνὸς αὐτῆς ἀναβαίνει εἰς τοὺς αἰῶνας τῶν αἰώνων."
4. καὶ [m] ἔπεσαν οἱ πρεσβύτεροι οἱ εἴκοσι τέσσαρες, καὶ τὰ
τέσσαρα ζῷα, καὶ προσεκύνησαν τῷ θεῷ τῷ [n] καθημένῳ ἐπὶ τῷ θρόνῳ
λέγοντες, [o] "Ἀμήν· Ἀλληλουϊά." 5. καὶ [p] φωνὴ ἀπὸ τοῦ θρόνου
ἐξῆλθε λέγουσα,
"[q] Αἰνεῖτε τῷ θεῷ [p] ἡμῶν πάντες οἱ [r] δοῦλοι αὐτοῦ,
καὶ [s] οἱ φοβούμενοι αὐτὸν [t] οἱ μικροὶ καὶ οἱ μεγάλοι."
6. καὶ ἤκουσα ὡς φωνὴν [u] ὄχλου πολλοῦ καὶ ὡς φωνὴν [v] ὑδάτων
πολλῶν καὶ ὡς φωνὴν [v] βροντῶν ἰσχυρῶν, λέγοντες,[1]
"Ἀλληλουϊά·
ὅτι [w] ἐβασίλευσε Κύριος ὁ θεὸς ἡμῶν ὁ [x] παντοκράτωρ.

g "For that she" (i. 7, xii. 13, etc.).
h xi. 18, xviii. 23.
i vi. 10, xviii. 20, Deut. xxxii. 43, Ps. lxxix. 10.
k aoristic pf. (as v. 7, vii. 14. xix. 3), of past action with no thought of existing result (Burton, 80, Blass, § 59, 4).
l xiv. 11, xviii. 9, 18, Ps. civ. 35, Isa. xxxiv. 9-10. *cf.* Nah. i. 9.
m v. 8, 14, on form *cf.* Helbing, 63-64.
n v. 13, Isa. vi. 1.
o vii. 12, xxii. 20, From Ps. cvi. 48 (Heb.).
p Of Christ (iii. 12, Joh. xx. 17)?
q Fr. Jer. xx. 13 (*αἰνέσατε αὐτῷ*, tr. of "Hallelujah'); *αἰν.* with dat. only here in N.T.
r Ps. cxxxiv. 1, cxxxv. 1, Ps. Sol. ii. 41.
s Ps. xxii. 23, cxxxv. 20; see above xi. 18.
t xi. 18.
u Ver. 1.
v xiv. 2, Ezek. i. 24.
w xi. 15, 17, Ps. xciii., xcv.-xcix.
x i. 8.

[1] **λεγοντες** (as iv. 1) Q, min., And^c, Tic. (WH marg., Al., Ws., Bs.) [**λεγοντων** AP, min., gig., And^a, Pr., Lach., Ti., Tr., WH, Bj., Sw.].

tically ample expression for "equitable," it is in the context rather than in the language of the passage (Ritschl, *Rechtf. und Versöhn.* ii. 118, 119) that we must find the thought of God being shown to be the real and righteous Saviour of the saints by his infliction of punishment on their persecutors.

Ver. 4. After the long interlude of judgments on the earth, the **πρεσβύτεροι** and **ζῷα** (incidentally mentioned in xi. 16, xiv. 3) re-appear upon the scene, though for the last time, to take part in the chorus of praise over Rome's ruin. The cradle-song of the future is the dirge of Rome. The drama now centres mainly round the city of God, and the earlier temple-scenery of the Apocalypse (iv.-xi. xv. 5-xvi. 17) passes almost wholly out of sight.—**Ἀμήν**: the initial (and primitive) use of **ἀμήν**, social (*e.g.*, 1 Kings i. 36) as well as liturgical, which gravely assents to the preceding words of another speaker.

Ver. 5. The O.T. expression *servants of God* implied (*R. S.* 69 f.) not simply membership in a community of which God is king, but special devotion to his service and worship. It was not associated with any idea of "slavery to a divine despot," but was originally confined in the main to royal and priestly families (*cf.* i. 5) which had a special interest in primitive religion and which were near to the god of the tribe or nation. Hence, in the broader and later sense of the term, the "servants of God" are all those who live in pious fear of him, *i.e.*, yielding him honour and obedience. John, pre-occupied with judgment, views the faith of the Lord as equivalent practically to his fear; unlike most early Christian writers, who (1 Peter i. 17, 18, etc.) carefully bring forward the complementary element of love. Lowly confidence rather than warm intimacy is this prophet's ideal of the Christian life towards God. See Did. iii., iv.; Barn. iv. 11; Herm. *Mand.* x. 1, xii. 4, 6.

Ver. 6. S ingeniously but awkwardly punctuates after "Hallelujah," connecting **ὅτι κ.τ.λ.**, with the subsequent **χαίρωμεν.**—**ἐβασίλευσε κ.τ.λ.** A sublimated version of the old watchword **ΚΥΡΙΟΣ ΑΥΤΟΣ ΒΑΣΙΛΕΥΣ ΗΜΩΝ** which had been the rallying cry of pious Jews and especially of the Pharisees (*e.g.*, Ps. Sol. xvii. 1, 2, 38, 51, ii. 34-36, v. 21, 22) during the conflict with Roman aggression. This divine epithalamium is the last song of praise in the Apocalypse. At this point also the writer reverts for a moment to

7. [y] χαίρωμεν καὶ ἀγαλλιῶμεν,
καὶ [z] δώσομεν τὴν δόξαν αὐτῷ·
ὅτι [a] ἦλθεν ὁ [b] γάμος τοῦ ἀρνίου,
καὶ ἡ [c] γυνὴ αὐτοῦ [a] ἡτοίμασεν ἑαυτήν.
8. καὶ ἐδόθη αὐτῇ ἵνα [d] περιβάληται [d] βύσσινον [e] λαμπρὸν
καθαρόν [· [f] τὸ γὰρ βύσσινον τὰ [g] δικαιώματα τῶν ἁγίων ἐστίν]."
9. καὶ [h] λέγει μοι, "[i] Γράψον, [i] Μακάριοι οἱ εἰς τὸ δεῖπνον τοῦ
γάμου τοῦ ἀρνίου [k] κεκλημένοι." Καὶ λέγει μοι, "[l] Οὗτοι οἱ λόγοι

y Ps. cxviii. 24; *cf.* Mt. v. 12.
z xi. 13.
a Proleptic, as xi. 18.
b xxi. 2, 9.
c "Bride" (Mt. i. 29).
d Ver. 14, Ez. xvi. 10.
e xv. 6, *cf.* Bar. v. 1-3, and—for conn. of light and right—2 Cor. vi. 14.
f *Cf.* Matt. xxii. 11-12, vii. 12, = xxii. 37 f.
g Contrast ἀδικ. xviii. 5.
h *i.e.*, the angel of xvii. 1; implied, as in Zech. i. 7, 9 (LXX)?
i xiv. 13, Lk. xiv. 15.
k Matt. xxii. 2-3; *cf.* Dalm. i. § 1, c. 5*b*.
l xxi. 5, xxii. 6; *cf.* Dan. viii. 26, x. 1, xi. 2, xii. 7. Also Lk. xxi. 22.

the Lamb, absent since xvii. 14 from his pages, and absent again till xxi. 9.

Ver. 7. A proleptic allusion to the triumphant bliss as a marriage between the victorious messiah and his people or the new Jerusalem (*cf.* Volz, 331). The conception is primarily eschatological (Weinel, p. 137; *cf.* Mechilta on Exod. xix. 17) and is so employed here. The marriage-day of Christ and his church is the day of his second advent. This is the more intimate and tender aspect of the divine **βασιλεία**. But, as a traditional feature of the Oriental myth (Jeremias, 45 f.) was the postponement of the deity's wedding until he returned from victory (*i.e.*, after vanquishing the darkness and cold of the winter), the religious application turns first of all to the overthrow of messiah's foes (xix. 11 f.).—**ἀγαλλιῶμεν**, act. as in 1 Peter i. 8 (*cf.* Abbott, *Diatessarica*, 2,689).

Ver. 8. "Yea, she is (has been) permitted to put on" (for **διδόναι ἵνα** *cf.* ix. 5, Mark x. 37), epexegetic of **ἡτοιμ. ἑαυτήν** (Isa. lxi. 10). "Uides hic cultum gravem ut matronae, non pompaticum qualis meretricis ante (xvii. 4) descriptus," Grot. In the following gloss (see above) the rare use of **δικαιώματα** (="righteous deeds") is paralleled by Bar. ii. 19 (**τὰ δικ. τῶν πατέρων**) and by an incidental employment of the sing. in this sense by Paul (see on Rom. v. 18). Moral purity and activity, which are the conditions of future and final bliss, are (as in vii. 14, xiv. 4) defined as the outcome of human effort, although of course their existence must be referred to God (**ἐδόθη**), and their success to the aid of Christ (*loc. cit.*); see on i. 4-6. Ignatius similarly (*Eph.* x.) describes the saints as "robed entirely in the commandments of Christ". The connexion of thought is the same as that in Matt. xxi. 43, xxii. 2, 11-14. For 8 *b* see the fontal passage from Sohar (cited by Gfrörer, ii. 184, 185): traditum est, quod opera bona ab homine hoc in mundo peracta, fiant ipsi uestis pretiosa in mundo illo.

Ver. 9. The saints are the Bride, but —by a confusion inevitable when the the two cognate figures, apocalyptic and synoptic (Matt. xxii. 2 f.), are combined —they are also the guests at the wedding. (The bliss of the next world is termed "the Banquet" in rabbinic writings, which interpret Exod. xxiv. 11 as though the sight of God were meat and drink to the beholders). Like the Greek **πόλις**, the church is composed of members who are ideally distinguishable from her, just as in En. xxxviii. 1 the congregation of the righteous is equivalent to the new Jerusalem. With the idea of 7-9, *cf.* Pirke Aboth, iv. 23: This world is like a vestibule before the world to come; prepare thyself at the vestibule that thou mayest be admitted into the **τρικλίνιον**.—**ἀληθ.** either "real" as opposed to fanciful and delusive revelations, or (if **ἀληθ. = ἀληθής**) "trustworthy words of God" (Dan. ii. 9) emphasising the previous beatitude (like **ναί, λέγει τὸ πνεῦμα** xiv. 13). Originally the words (see above) gravely corroborated all the preceding threats and promises (*cf.* xvii. 17), despite their occasionally strange and doubtful look. It is a common reiteration in apocc. (*cf.* reff.), underlining as it were the solemn statements of a given passage. See, *e.g.*, Herm. *Vis.* iii 4, "that God's name may be glorified, hath this been revealed to thee, for the sake of those who are of doubtful mind, questioning in their hearts whether this is so or not. Tell them it is all true, that there is nothing but truth in it, that all is sure and valid and founded". In Sanhed. Jerus. Rabbi Joc-

ἀληθινοὶ τοῦ θεοῦ[1] εἰσίν." 10. **καὶ ἔπεσα ἔμπροσθεν τῶν ποδῶν**
αὐτοῦ προσκυνῆσαι αὐτῷ· καὶ λέγει μοι, "[m]Ὅρα [m]μή· σύνδουλός
σού εἰμι καὶ τῶν ἀδελφῶν σου τῶν [n]ἐχόντων τὴν μαρτυρίαν Ἰησοῦ·
[o]τῷ θεῷ προσκύνησον [· [p]ἡ γὰρ μαρτυρία Ἰησοῦ ἐστὶ τὸ πνεῦμα τῆς
προφητείας]."

11. **καὶ εἶδον τὸν οὐρανὸν ἠνεῳγμένον,**
καὶ ἰδοὺ [q]ἵππος λευκός,

m (xxii. 9), sc. *ποιήσῃς*, *cf.* Eur., *Phœn.* 293.
n xii. 17.
o 1 Cor. xiv. 25.
p 1 Cor. xii. 3.
q *Cf.* vi. 2 for language.

[1] Bousset and Könnecke om. **του θεου,** but if the grammatical harshness of the text is an insuperable difficulty, the solution is to read (Beng., Lachm., Ws.) **οι** before **αληθινοι** (with A, 4, 48, S.).

hanan declares, with reference to Dan. x. 1, that a true word is one which has been already revealed by God to the council of the heavenly host.

Ver. 10. Jewish eschatology at this point has much to say of the return of the ten tribes and the general restoration of Zion's children from foreign lands but these speculations were naturally of no interest to the religious mind of the Christian prophet. As hitherto the command to write has come from Christ, the seer perhaps thinks that this injunction also proceeds from a divine authority (Weiss), but his grateful and reverent attempt to pay divine homage to the *angelus interpres* (*cf.* xxii. 8) is severely rebuked. The author's intention is to check any tendency to the angel-worship which—(whether a Jewish practice or not, *cf.* Clem. Alex. *Strom.* vi. 5, 41; Lightfoot on Col. ii. 18; and Lueken, 4 f.)—had for some time fascinated the Asiatic churches here and there. If even a prophet need not bow to an angel, how much less an ordinary Christian? A contemporary note of this polemic is heard in Asc. Isa. vii. 21 (Christians): et cecidi in faciem meam, ut eum (the *angelus interpres*, who conducts Isaiah through the heavens) adorarem, nec siuit me angelus, qui me instruebat, sed dixit mihi ne adores nec angelum nec thronum. In Asc. Isa. ii. 11 the angelic cicerone even rebukes the seer for calling him Lord: **οὐκ ἐγὼ κύριος, ἀλλὰ σύνδουλός σού εἰμι.** The repetition of this scene (xxii. 8 f.), due to the Oriental love of emphasis by reduplication, is significant in a book where angels swarm (*cf.* Dan. ii. 11).—**ἡ γὰρ κ.τ.λ.,** "for the testimony or witness of (*i.e.*, borne by) Jesus is (*i.e.*, constitutes) the spirit of prophecy". This prose marginal comment (see above) specifically defines the brethren who hold the testimony of Jesus as possessors of prophetic inspiration. The testimony of Jesus is practically equivalent to Jesus testifying (xxii. 20). It is the self-revelation of Jesus (according to i. 1, due ultimately to God) which moves the Christian prophets. He forms at once the impulse and subject of their utterances (*cf.* Ignat. *Rom.* viii.; *Eph.* vi.). The motive and materials for genuine prophecy consist in a readiness to allow the spirit of Jesus to bring the truth of God before the mind and conscience (*cf.* iii. 14, 22). The gloss even connects in a certain way with **τῷ θεῷ προσκύνησον.** Since angelic and human inspiration alike spring from the divine witness of Jesus, therefore God alone, as its ultimate source, deserves the reverence of those whom that inspiration impresses. The prestige of the prophets lies in the fact that any one of them is, as Philo called Abraham, **σύνδουλος τῶν ἀγγέλων.** An angel can do no more than bear witness to Jesus. Furthermore, there is an implicit definition of the spirit of prophecy (xi. 7, etc.) in its final phase as a revelation of Jesus Christ. Even the O.T. prophetic books, with which the Apocalypse claims to rank, were inspired by the spirit of the pre-existent Christ (see on 1 Pet. i. 11; Barn. v. 6). But now, by an anti-Jewish and even anti-pagan touch, no oracular or prophetic inspiration is allowed to be genuine unless it concerns Jesus who is the Christ. Such is the triumphant definition or rather manifesto of the new Christian prophecy.

Vv. 11-21: a second vision of doom, on the Beast and his allies (in fulfilment of xii. 5). Their fate (17-21) follows a procession of the angelic troops (11-16, contrast ix. 16 f.). The connexion of this and the foregoing volume (7-9) is mediated by the idea that

καὶ ὁ καθήμενος ἐπ' αὐτὸν [r] καλούμενος [s] πιστὸς καὶ
[t] ἀληθινός,
καὶ [u] ἐν δικαιοσύνῃ κρίνει καὶ πολεμεῖ·
12. οἱ δὲ [v] ὀφθαλμοὶ αὐτοῦ φλὸξ πυρός,

r iii. 14. s In sense of Deut. vii. 9, xxxii. 4 (LXX); *cf.* Ps. Sol. xvii. 4-5, and Isa. xlii. 3 (LXX). t *Cf.* on xvi. 7, Dan. ii. 45, iii. 27 f. (LXX). u Ps. xcvi. 13: twofold function of Semitic king (1 Sam. viii. 20). v ii. 18.

the marriage of the warrior-messiah (*cf.* En. lx. 2; 4 Esd. xii. 32, xiii. 38; Apoc. Bar. xxxix., xl., lxx.) cannot take place till he returns from victory (so in the messianic psalm xlv.). Now that the preliminary movements of the enemy (xvii. 16, 17) are over, the holy war of xvii. 14 begins, which is to end in a ghastly Armageddon. This passage and the subsequent oracle of xx. 1-10 reproduce in part a messianic programme according to which the *dolores Messiae* (*cf.* Klausner: *mess. Vorstellungen d. jüd. Volkes im Zeitalter der Tannaiten*, 1904, 47 f, and Charles on Apoc. Bar. xxvii. 1) are followed by messiah's royal advent on earth (here sketched in part from Sap. xviii. 4-25) to found a kingdom of the just (*i.e.*, Israel) who are raised for this purpose. Israel supplants Rome as the world-power (Bar. xxxix.). Her period of superiority opens with the rebuilding of Jerusalem and the temple, and closes with a crushing defeat of Gog and Magog, who are led by an incarnate villain ("dux ultimus," xl.), but are finally vanquished by the aid of the ten tribes who return to take part in this campaign. Death and Satan then are annihilated, and eternal bliss ensues. Like Paul in 1 Cor. xv. 20 f., John modifies this scheme of tradition freely for his own Christian ends. He introduces a realistic expansion of the messianic age into three periods: (*a*) a victory of messiah (mounted, like Vishnu, on a white horse for the last battle) and his ἅγιοι (*cf.* xiv. 20) over the beast, the false prophet, and the kings of the world, who—as already noted—turn their attention to the saints after crushing Rome (11-21); (*b*) an undisturbed reign of Christ and his martyrs (xx. 1-6), evidently in Palestine; (*c*) the final defeat of Gog and Magog, with Satan their instigator (xx. 7-10). There is little or nothing specifically Christian in all this section (except xx. 4-6, *cf.* xix. 13), but the general style betrays the author's own hand, and there is no reason to suppose that a Jewish source in whole or part (so *e.g.*, Vischer, Sabatier, de Faye, Weyland, Spitta, von Soden) underlies it. The sequence of the passage with xvi. 13-16, 18-20 is due to a common cycle of tradition, rather than to any literary source (Schön). It is a homogeneous finalê written by the prophet, in terms of current eschatology, to round off the predictions at which he has already hinted. Moralising traits emerge amidst the realism, but it is impossible to be sure how far the whole passage (*i.e.*, 11-21) was intended to be figurative.

Vv. 11-16. messiah and his troops or retinue: Jesus to the rescue (*cf. Samson Agonistes*, 1268 f.). The following description of a semi-judicial, semi-military hero is painted from passages like Isa. xi. 3-5 (where messiah, instead of judging by appearances, decides equitably: **πατάξει γῆν τῷ λόγῳ τοῦ στόματος αὐτοῦ**: his breath slays the wicked: his loins are girt **δικαιοσύνῃ** and **ἀληθείᾳ**), the theophany of Hab. iii., and the sanguinary picture of Yahveh returning in triumph from the carnage in Idumea (*cf.* ver. 13 with Isa. lxiii. 1-6). On the connexion of this celestial Rider with the Rider in 2 Macc. iii., *cf.* Nestle in *Zeits. f. alt. Wiss.* 1905, pp. 203f.

Ver. 11. The military function of the messiah is known even to the philosophic Philo, who (*de praem. et poen.* 15-20) represents him incidentally as **καὶ στρατάρχῶν καὶ πολεμῶν ἔθνη.** The victory of messiah over the earthly foes of God's kingdom meant the triumph of the kingdom, according to Jewish and Jewish Christian hopes; but owing to the increased spiritualisation of the latter, this nationalistic tradition was laid side by side with the wider hope of an eternal, universal judgment upon dead and living. The latter was originally independent of the earlier view, which made the culmination of providence for Israel consist in the earthly subjugation of her foes. The prophet John, by dividing God's foes into the two classes of Rome and Rome's destroyers, preserves the archaic tradition and also finds room for the Gog and Magog tradition later on.

Ver. 12. **διαδήματα πολλά,** bec. he is king of kings (Ptolemy on entering Antioch put two diadems on his head, that of Egypt and that of Asia (1 Macc. xi. 13);

καὶ ἐπὶ τὴν κεφαλὴν αὐτοῦ [w] διαδήματα [w] πολλά·
[x] ἔχων [y] ὄνομα γεγραμμένον ὃ οὐδεὶς οἶδεν εἰ μὴ αὐτός·
13. καὶ [x] περιβεβλημένος ἱμάτιον βεβαμμένον [1] [z] αἵματι·
καὶ κέκληται τὸ ὄνομα αὐτοῦ, [a] "'Ο ΛΟΓΟC ΤΟΥ ΘΕΟΥ."

w Contrast xii. 3, xiii. 1.
x Loosely resuming the construction of ver. 11.

y *Cf.* on ii. 17. z Dat. *cf.* Joh. xxi. 8. a Art. with pred. irreg. after ὄνομα (as vi. 8, viii. 11, etc.).

[1] **βεβαμμενον** (AQ, min., Ar., edd.) is preferable to **ρεραμμενον** (Hort, Swete)—the conjectural origin of the variants **περιρεραμμενον** (א*) **ερραμενον, ρεραντισμενον**, etc.—which is probably a corruption of it or due to dittography with **γεγραμμενον.**

cf. the ten golden diadems of royalty in ancient Egypt). Once crowned with thorns, Jesus is now invested with more than royal rank (*cf.* Barn. vii. 9, where Jesus, once accursed, is shown crowned). Eastern monarchs wore such royal insignia when they went into battle (*e.g.*, 2 Sam. i. 10). Jesus has far more than the four (of a good name, of the law, of the high priesthood, of the divine kingdom, Targ. Jerus. on Deut. xxxiv.) 5 or three (omitting the first) which Jewish tradition assigned to Moses (see Pirke Aboth, iv. 13, vi. 5; Joseph. *Bell.* i. 2, 8, prophetic, priestly, and royal honours). — **ὄνομα κ.τ.λ.**, *cf.* Ep. Lugd., "when Attalus was placed on the iron seat and the fumes rose from his burning body, he was asked, 'What name has God?' 'God,' he answered, 'has not a name as man has." Contrast **ὃ οὐδεὶς κ.τ.λ.**, with Matt. xi. 27. The earlier words, **πιστ. κ. ἀληθ.**, are a description of the messiah's character and function, rather than a title. At this debût, which is the only event in the Apocalypse at all corresponding to the second advent (i. 7), the messiah's judicial power is practically restricted to the external work of crushing the last pagan opposition to God's cause on earth; it becomes therefore almost military. The divine commandant of the saints is "faithful and true," as he loyally executes the divine purpose and thus exhibits fidelity to the interests of the faithful. The sense remains unchanged, whether the two adjectives are taken as synonyms, or **ἀληθ.** assigned its occasional meaning of "real". Even in the latter case, to be real would mean to be trustworthy.

Ver. 13. "Dipped in blood" (*i.e.*, the blood of his foes): from the "crimsoned garments" of Yahveh in Isa. lxiii.; *cf.* also ver. 15 with "I have trodden the wine-press. . . . Yea, I trod them in mine anger (**κατεπάτησα αὐτοὺς ἐν θυμῷ μου**), and trampled them in my fury," etc. Add Targ. Palest. on Gen. xlix. 11, "How beauteous is the King Messiah! Binding his loins and going forth to war against them that hate him, he will slay kings with princes, and make the rivers red with the blood of their slain, and his hills white with the fat of their mighty ones, his garments will be dipped in blood, and he himself like the juice of the wine-press." The secret name denotes his superiority to all appeals; it indicates that the awful and punitive vigour of his enterprise made him impervious to the invocations of men. This is no Logos who dwells among men to give light and life; it is a stern, militant, figure of vengeance attacking the rebellious. Hence his name is mysterious; for "the identity, or at least the close connection between a thing and its name, not only makes the utterance of a holy name an invocation which insures the actual presence of the deity invoked, it also makes the holy name too sacred for common use or even for use at all" (Jevons' *Introd. Hist. Relig.* 361). The passage reflects certain phases of later messianic belief in Judaism, which had been tinged by the Babylonian myth of Marduk, Ea's victorious son, to whom divine authority was entrusted. Marduk's triumph was explained by Babylonian theologians as caused by the transference to him of the divine Name (so Michael, En. lxix. 14). 13 *b* may be a Johannine gloss upon the unknown name of ver. 12 (*cf.* Phil. ii. 9, 10), under the influence of passages like Heb. iv. 15, Sap. xviii. ("Thine all-powerful Logos leapt from heaven out of the royal throne, as a stern warrior into the midst of the doomed land, bearing the sharp sword of Thine unfeigned commandment"), and Enoch xc. 38 (*cp.* however Beer, *ad loc.*). —**κέκληται**, perf. of existing state, "the past action of which it is the result being left out of thought" (Burton, 75). If the above explanation of the mysterious name

b xvi. 14-16. c As in xiv. 4? differently xvii. 14 (*cf.* Yasht xiii. 12-19 for heavenly aid of certain Fravashis), *cf. Par. Lost*, vi. 880-884. d Ver. 11. e Constr. ad sensum. f Ver. 8. g From

14. καὶ τὰ [b] στρατεύματα τὰ ἐν τῷ οὐρανῷ [c] ἠκολούθει αὐτῷ ἐφ' [d] ἵπποις λευκοῖς,
[e] ἐνδεδυμένοι [f] βύσσινον λευκὸν καὶ καθαρόν.
15. καὶ ἐκ τοῦ στόματος αὐτοῦ ἐκπορεύεται [g] ῥομφαία ὀξεῖα, ἵνα ἐν αὐτῇ [h] πατάξῃ τὰ ἔθνη·
καὶ αὐτὸς [i] ποιμανεῖ αὐτοὺς ἐν ῥάβδῳ σιδηρᾷ·
καὶ αὐτὸς πατεῖ [k] τὴν ληνὸν [l] τοῦ οἴνου τοῦ θυμοῦ τῆς ὀργῆς τοῦ θεοῦ τοῦ παντοκράτορος.
16. καὶ ἔχει ἐπὶ τὸ ἱμάτιον [1] καὶ ἐπὶ τὸν [m] μηρὸν αὐτοῦ ὄνομα γεγραμμένον,
"[n] ΒΑΣΙΛΕΥΣ ΒΑΣΙΛΕΩΝ ΚΑΙ ΚΥΡΙΟΣ ΚΥΡΙΩΝ".

Dan. ix. 25; see i. 16, ii. 12. h Isa. xi. 4, (quoted Ps. Sol. xvii. 39), En. lxii. 2, *cf.* 4 Esd. xiii. 10, 27 f. i ii. 27, xii. 5. k xiv. 20, Jud. iii. 13. l xiv. 10, xvi. 19. m ἁπ. λεγ. N.T.; = "sword-belt" (Spitta). n Κυρ. κυρ. a Babylonian title of Marduk. xvii. 14, 1 Ti. vi. 15.

[1] A om. **επι το ιματιον και** (S. = "written on garments which were on his thigh"). Wellh. conj. **επι τον ιππον.** *Cf. E. Bi.*, 2517.

be correct, the author's idea was evidently forgotten or ignored by some later editor or copyist of the Johannine school, who inserted this gloss in order to clear up the obscure reference, and at the same time to bring forward the transcendent name widely appropriated by that school for Christ in a pacific and religious sense (so nearly all critical editors). In any case the two conceptions of the Apocalypse and the Fourth gospel have little or nothing in common except the word. But the introduction of this apparently illogical sequence between 12 and 13 might be justified in part by *E. B. D.* 94, "I am he that cometh forth, advancing, whose name is unknown; I am Yesterday, and Seer of millions of years is my name". The application of such titles to Jesus certainly gives the impression that these high, honourable predicates are "not yet joined to his person with any intrinsic and essential unity" (Baur); they are rather due to the feeling that "Christ must have a position adequate to the great expectations concerning the last things, of which he is the chief subject". But their introduction is due to the semi-Christianised messianic conceptions and the divine categories by which the writer is attempting to interpret his experience of Jesus. Backwards and forwards, as pre-existent and future, the redeemer is magnified for the prophet's consciousness.

Ver. 15. **αὐτός**—The victory of the messiah is single-handed ("I have trodden the wine-press alone"); *cf.* on ver. 13, and Sap. xviii. 22, Ps. Sol. xvii. 24-27, where the word of messiah's mouth is the sole weapon of his victory (an Iranian touch as in *S. B. E.* iv. p. lxxvii. f., the distinguishing excellence of Zoroaster is that his chief weapon is spiritual, *i.e.*, the word or prayer). This fine idea, taken originally from Isaiah, was reproduced, naturally in a more or less realistic shape, by the rabbis who applied it to Moses at Exod. ii. 11 (Clem. Alex. *Stron.* i. 23), and by apocalyptists (2 Thess. ii. 8; Ap. Bar. xxxvi. f., liii. f.; 4 Esd. x. 60 f., and here) who assigned an active rôle to the messiah in the latter days. The meaning of the sword-symbol is that "the whole counsel of God is accomplished by Jesus as a stern judgment with resistless power" (Baur). Thus the final rout of the devil, anticipated in xii. 12, is carried out (i.) by the overthrow of his subordinates (mentioned in ch. xiii.) here, and then (ii.) by his own defeat (xx. 10), although in finishing the torso of ch. xii. (Bousset) the prophet characteristically has recourse to materials drawn from very different cycles of current messianic tradition.

Ver. 16. "And on his garment and (*i.e.*, even) upon his thigh"; on that part of the robe covering his thigh, he has a title of honour written. Some Greek statues appear to have had a name written thus upon the thigh (Cicero mentions one of Apollo marked in small silver letters, *Verr.* iv. 43). Messiah, like many of the Assyrian monarchs, bears a double name. *King of kings*, a Persian (Æsch. *Persæ*, 24; Ezra vii. 12) and Parthian title of royalty, which in

17. Καὶ εἶδον [o] ἕνα ἄγγελον ἑστῶτα ἐν τῷ ἡλίῳ· καὶ ἔκραξε φωνῇ
μεγάλῃ λέγων πᾶσι τοῖς [p] ὀρνέοις τοῖς πετομένοις ἐν μεσουρανήματι,
"Δεῦτε συνάχθητε εἰς τὸ δεῖπνον τὸ μέγα τοῦ Θεοῦ,
18. ἵνα [q] φάγητε σάρκας βασιλέων καὶ σάρκας χιλιάρχων καὶ
σάρκας [r] ἰσχυρῶν καὶ σάρκας ἵππων καὶ τῶν καθημένων ἐπ' αὐτῶν καὶ
σάρκας πάντων [s] ἐλευθέρων τὲ καὶ δούλων καὶ μικρῶν καὶ μεγάλων."
19. καὶ εἶδον τὸ [t] θηρίον καὶ τοὺς [u] βασιλεῖς τῆς γῆς καὶ τὰ
στρατεύματα αὐτῶν συνηγμένα ποιῆσαι [v] τὸν πόλεμον μετὰ τοῦ
καθημένου ἐπὶ τοῦ ἵππου, καὶ μετὰ τοῦ στρατεύματος αὐτοῦ.
20. καὶ [w] ἐπιάσθη τὸ θηρίον, καὶ μετ' αὐτοῦ [x] ὁ ψευδοπροφήτης
ὁ [y] ποιήσας τὰ σημεῖα [y] ἐνώπιον αὐτοῦ, ἐν οἷς ἐπλάνησε τοὺς λαβόντας
τὸ χάραγμα τοῦ θηρίου καὶ τοὺς προσκυνοῦντας τῇ εἰκόνι αὐτοῦ·
ζῶντες ἐβλήθησαν οἱ δύο εἰς τὴν [z] λίμνην τοῦ [z] πυρὸς τῆς καιομένης

o viii. 13; an angel of the sun in Asc. Is. iv. 18.
p xviii. 2.
q xvii. 16.
r *Cf.* on vi. 15.
s xiii. 16.
t xiii. 1.
u xvii. 12, Ps. ii. 2.
v xvi. 14 (the final struggle of xvi. 12-16).
w Cant. ii. 15, Doric for *ἐπιέσθη*.
x xvi. 13.
y xiii. 11-17.
z xx. 10, 14, Isa. xxx. 33, Dan. vii. 11; *cf. Par. Lost*, i. 62-69.

the Apocalypse is the prerogative of messiah as the true Emperor was applied to Marduk as the conqueror of chaos and the arbiter of all earthly monarchs (*cf.* Zimmern in *Schrader*,[3] 373 f.).

Vv. 17-21: the rout and destruction of the Beast and his adherents, modelled upon Isaiah lvi. 9 f. and Ezekiel's description of the discomfiture of prince Gog (xxxix. 17-21), where beasts as well as birds are bidden glut themselves with carrion (4). This crude aspect of the messianic triumph had commended itself to Jewish speculation on the future (see En. xc. 2-4); it reflects the intense particularism of post-exilic Judaism in certain circles, and also the semi-political categories which tended to dominate the eschatology. In Asc. Isa. iv. 14, the Lord also comes with his angels and troops to drag into Gehenna Beliar and his hosts.

Ver. 17. **ἐν ἡλίῳ**, a commanding and conspicuous position.

Ver. 18. In the ancient world, this was the worst misfortune possible for the dead—to lie unburied, a prey to wild birds. On the famous "stele of the vultures" (bef. 3000 B.C.) the enemy are represented lying bare and being devoured by vultures, while the corpses of the royal troops are carefully buried.

Ver. 20. This marks the culmination of many previous oracles: the messiah meets and defeats (xvi. 13 f.) the beast (*i.e.*, Nero-antichrist, xi. 7, xiii. 1 f.) and the false prophet (*i.e.*, the Imperial priesthood = second beast of xiii. 11 f.) and their allies (*the kings of the earth*, *cf.* xi. 9, 18, xiv. 8, xvi. 14, xvii. 12 f.), according to a more specific form of the tradition reflected in xiv. 14-20. Possibly the ghastly repast of ver. 21 is a dramatic foil to that of ver. 9. At any rate there is a slight confusion in the sketch, due to the presence of heterogeneous conceptions; whilst one tradition made messiah at his coming vanquish all the surviving inhabitants of the earth, who were *ex hypothesi* opponents of God's people (*cf.* ii. 26, 27, xi. 9 f., xii. 9, xiv. 14 f., xvi. 13-16, xix. 17 f.), the prophet at the same time used the special conception of a Nero-antichrist whose allies were mainly Eastern chiefs (ix. 14 f., xvi. 12, xvii. 12 f.), and also shared the O.T. belief in a weird independent outburst from the skirts of the earth (xx. 8). Hence the rout of nations here is only apparently final. See on xx. 3. The lake of fire, a place of torment which burns throughout most of the apocalypses (Sibyll. ii. 196-200, 252-253, 286, etc.; Apoc. Pet. 8), was lit first in Enoch. (sec. cent.) where it is the punishment reserved for Azazel on the day of judgment (ix. 6) and for the fallen angels (xxi. 7-10) with their paramours. The prophet prefers this to the alternative conception of a river of fire [Slav. En. x.]. The whole passage reflects traditions such as those preserved (*cf.* Gfrörer ii., 232 f.), *e.g.*, in Targ. Jerus. on Gen. xlix. 11 and Sohar on Lev.-Exodus (miracula, uariaque et horrenda bella fient mari terraque circa Jerusalem, cum messias reuelabitur), where the beasts of the field feed for one year, and the birds for seven, upon the carcases of Israel's foes. The supreme penalty

a From Sib. Or. iii. 696-7.

ἐν θείῳ. 21. καὶ οἱ λοιποὶ ἀπεκτάνθησαν ἐν τῇ ῥομφαίᾳ τοῦ
καθημένου ἐπὶ τοῦ ἵππου, τῇ ἐξελθούσῃ ἐκ τοῦ στόματος
αὐτοῦ· [a] καὶ πάντα τὰ ὄρνεα ἐχορτάσθησαν ἐκ τῶν σαρκῶν αὐτῶν.

inflicted on the opponents of Zoroastrianism is that their corpses are given over to the corpse-eating birds, *i.e.*, ravens (Vend. iii. 20, ix. 49). *Cf.* Introd. § 4 *b*.

The messiah who forms "the central figure of this bloodthirsty scene," written like the preceding out of the presbyter's "savage hatred of Rome" (Selwyn, 83) has a semi-political rather than a transcendental role to play. The normal Christian consciousness (*cf.* xxii. 12) viewed the return of Jesus as ushering in the final requital of mankind; but in these special oracles (*cf.* xvii. 14) where a semi-historical figure is pitted against Christ on earth, the latter is brought down to meet the adversary on his own ground—a development of eschatology which is a resumption of primitive messianic categories in Judaism. The messiah here is consequently a grim, silent, implacable conqueror. There is no tenderness in the Apocalypse save for the pious core of the elect people, nothing of that disquiet of heart with which the sensitiveness of later ages viewed the innumerable dead. Here mankind are naïvely disposed of in huge masses; their antagonism to the messiah and his people is assumed to have exposed them to ruthless and inexorable doom. Nor do the scenic categories of the tradition leave any room for such a feeling as dictated Plutarch's noble description (*De Sera Uind.* 555 E. F.) of the eternal pangs of conscience. Upon the other hand, there is no gloating over the torments of the wicked.

Now that the destructive work of messiah is over, the ground seems clear for his constructive work (*cf.* Ps. Sol. xvii. 26 f.). But the idiosyncracies of John's outlook involve a departure from the normal tradition of Judaism and early Christianity at this point. Satan, who survives, as he had preceded, the Roman empire, still remains to be dealt with. The third vision of doom, therefore (xx. 1-10) outlines his final defeat, in two panels: (*a*) one exhibiting a period of enforced restraint, during which (for 2, 3 and 4-7 are synchronous) messiah and the martyrs enjoy a halcyon time of temporal and temporary bliss, (*b*) the other sketching (7-10) a desperate but unavailing recrudescence of the devil's power. The oracle is brief and uncoloured. It rounds off the preceding predictions and at the same time paves the way for the magnificent finalê of xxi.-xxii., on which the writer puts forth all his powers. But it is more than usually enigmatic and allusive. "Dans ces derniers chapitres les tableaux qui passent sous nos yeux n'ont plus la fraîcheur vivante de ceux qui ont précédé. L'imagination ayant affaire à des conceptions absolument idéales et sans aucune analogie avec les réalités concrètes de la nature, est naturellement moins sûre d'elle-même, et ne parvient plus aussi facilement à satisfaire celle du lecteur" (Reuss). Ingenious attempts have been made (*e.g.*, by Vischer, Spitta, and Wellhausen) to disentangle a Jewish source from the passage, but real problem is raised and solved on the soil of the variant traditions which John moulded at this point for his own Christian purposes. In the creation-myth the binding of the chaos-dragon or his allies took place at the beginning of the world's history (*cf.* *Prayer of Manass.* 2-4). As the dragon came to be moralised into the power of spiritual evil, this temporary restraint (*cf.* on ver. 2) was transferred to the beginning of the end, by a modification of the primitive view which probably goes back to Iranian theology (*cf.* Stave, 175 f., Baljon, Völter, 120 f., Briggs, etc.). The conception of messiah's reign as preliminary and limited on earth was not unknown to Judaism (*Encycl. Relig. and Ethics*, i. 203 f.) or even to primitive Christianity (*cf.* 1 Cor. xv. 21-28, where Paul develops it differently). But the identification of it with the sabbath of the celestial week (which was originally non-messianic, *cf.* Slav. En. xxxii. xxxiii.) and the association of it with the martyrs are peculiar to John's outlook. A further idiosyncracy is the connection between the Gog and Magog attack and the final manœuvre of Satan. The psychological clue to these conceptions probably lies in the prophet's desire to provide a special compensation for the martyrs, prior to the general bliss of the saints. This may have determined his adoption or adaptation of the chiliastic tradition, which also conserved the archaic hope of an earthly

XX. 1. Καὶ εἶδον ἄγγελον καταβαίνοντα ἐκ τοῦ οὐρανοῦ, ἔχοντα
τὴν [a] κλεῖν τῆς [a] ἀβύσσου καὶ [b] ἅλυσιν μεγάλην ἐπὶ τὴν χεῖρα αὐτοῦ.
2. καὶ [c] ἐκράτησε τὸν δράκοντα, ὁ ὄφις ὁ ἀρχαῖος, [d] ὅς ἐστι διάβολος
καὶ ὁ Σατανᾶς, καὶ ἔδησεν αὐτὸν [e] χίλια ἔτη, 3. καὶ ἔβαλεν αὐτὸν
εἰς τὴν ἄβυσσον καὶ [f] ἔκλεισεν καὶ [f] ἐσφράγισεν ἐπάνω αὐτοῦ, ἵνα μὴ
πλανήσῃ ἔτι τὰ ἔθνη, ἄχρι τελεσθῇ τὰ χίλια ἔτη· μετὰ ταῦτα δεῖ
λυθῆναι αὐτὸν [h] μικρὸν χρόνον. 4. καὶ εἶδον [i] θρόνους—καὶ ἐκάθισαν
ἐπ' αὐτούς, [k] καὶ κρίμα ἐδόθη αὐτοῖς—καὶ τὰς [l] ψυχὰς τῶν [m] πεπελεκισμένων [n] διὰ τὴν μαρτυρίαν Ἰησοῦ καὶ διὰ τὸν λόγον τοῦ θεοῦ,

a i. 18, ix. 1; *cf.* Rom. x. 7, 4 Esd. iv. 8.
b Mk. v. 3 f.
c Mk. vi. 17.
d xii. 9.
e = a Day of God, Jub. iv. 29, 2 Pet. iii. 8; *cf. E. Bi.* iii. 3096-7.
f From Dan. vi. 17 and *Bel and Dragon* (Theod.) 14.
g xiii. 14, xvi. 13, 2 Th. ii. 9-10, *cf.* Weinel, 21.
h xvii. 10.
i Never in Apoc. = "angels"; *cf.* Matt. xix. 28 = Luke xxii. 30.
k 1 Cor. vi. 2, Sap. iii. 8.
l vi. 9 = "persons," sc. εἶδον.
m Mt. xiv. 10, Acts xii. 2, Rom. viii. 35, Clem. Rom. v.-vi. (ἅπ. λεγ. N.T.).
n i. 9.

reign for the saints without interfering with the more spiritual and transcendent outlook of xx. 11 f. His procedure further enabled him to preserve the primitive idea of messiah's reign [4] as distinct from that of God, by dividing the final act of the drama into two scenes (4 f., 11 f.).—With the realistic episode of 1-3, angels pass off the stage (except the angel of xxi. 9 f. and the *angelus interpres* of xxii. 6-10), in accordance with the Jewish feeling that they were inferior to the glorified saints to whom alone (*cf.* Heb. ii. 4) the next world belonged. There is no evidence to support the conjecture (Cheyne, *Bible Problems*, 233) that ἄγγελον in ver. 1 represents "an already corrupt text of an older Hebrew Apocalypse, in which *mal'āk* was written instead of *mīkā'ēl*" (*cf.* above on xii. 7).

Chapter XX.—Vv. 1-3. The dragon is flung by an angel, not by God or messiah, into the pit of the abyss which formed his original haunt (*cf.* on ix. 1), and there locked up, like an Arabian jin, so as to leave the earth undisturbed for the millenium. The prophet thus welds together two traditions which were originally independent. The former echoes Egyptian (*E. B. D.* 4, "thine enemy the serpent hath been given over to the fire, the serpent-fiend hath fallen down headlong; his arms have been bound in chains . . . the children of impotent revolt shall never more rise up") and especially Parsee eschatology (Hübschmann, 227 f.) which held that one sign of the latter days was the release of the dragon Dahâka—once bound fast at mount Demavend—to corrupt the earth and eventually to be destroyed prior to the advent of the messiah and the resurrection of the dead. The Iranian view was that Fredûn could not kill the serpent, whose slaughter was reserved for for Sâme (Bund. xxix. 9). But John abstains from giving any reason for the devil's reappearance. He simply accepts the tradition and falls back (ver. 3) piously upon the δεῖ of a mysterious providence. Some enigmatic hints in a late post-exilic apocalypse (Isa. xxiv. 21, 22, the hosts on high and the kings on earth to be shut up in the prison of the pit but—after many days—to be visited, *i.e.*, released), upon which John has already drawn, had been developed by subsequent speculation (*cf.* the fettering of Azazel, En. x. 4 f., liv. 5 f.) into the dogma of a divine restraint placed for a time upon the evil spirit(s); see *S. C.* 91 f., Charles' *Eschatology*, 200 f.—ἔθνη. Strictly speaking, the previous tradition (xix. 18, 21) left no inhabitants on earth at all. Such discrepancies were inevitable in the dovetailing of disparate conceptions, but the solution of the incongruity here probably lies in the interpretation of ἔθνη as outlying nations on the fringe of the empire (8) who had not shared in the campaign of Nero-antichrist and consequently had survived the doom of the latter and his allies (*cf.* xviii. 9).

Vv. 4-6. The millennium.

Ver. 4. **θρόνους**, tribunal-seats for the assessors of the divine judge (as in Dan. vii. 9, 10, 22, of which this is a replica). The unnamed occupants (saints including martyrs? as in Daniel) are allowed to manage the judicial processes (so Dan. vii. 22, where the Ancient of days τὸ κρίμα ἔδωκεν ἁγίοις Ὑψίστου) which constituted a large part of Oriental government. But no stress is laid on this incidental remark, and the subjects of

[o] καὶ [o] οἵτινες οὐ προσεκύνησαν τὸ θηρίον οὐδὲ τὴν εἰκόνα αὐτοῦ
καὶ οὐκ ἔλαβον τὸ χάραγμα ἐπὶ τὸ μέτωπον καὶ ἐπὶ τὴν χεῖρα αὐτῶν·
καὶ [p] ἔζησαν καὶ [q] ἐβασίλευσαν μετὰ [r] τοῦ Χριστοῦ χίλια ἔτη· 5.
οἱ λοιποὶ τῶν νεκρῶν [s] οὐκ ἔζησαν [t] ἄχρι τελεσθῇ τὰ χίλια ἔτη. αὕτη
ἡ ἀνάστασις ἡ πρώτη. 6. Μακάριος καὶ ἅγιος ὁ ἔχων [u] μέρος ἐν
τῇ ἀναστάσει τῇ πρώτῃ· ἐπὶ τούτων [v] ὁ δεύτερος θάνατος οὐκ ἔχει
ἐξουσίαν, ἀλλ' ἔσονται [w] ἱερεῖς τοῦ Θεοῦ καὶ τοῦ Χριστοῦ· καὶ [x] βασι-

o Defining or expanding, not specifying (as i. 7) some of the previous class.
p "Came to life," as ii. 8.
q Constative aor. Moult. i. 130.
r xi. 15, xii. 10.
s Isa. xxvi. 14.
t *Cf.* Blass, § 65, 10.
u xxi. 8, Joh. xiii. 8; *cf.* Mt. xxiv. 51.
v ii. 11, xxi. 8.
w i. 6.
x v. 10, Isa. lxi. 6.

this sway are left undefined; they are evidently not angels (Jewish belief, shared by Paul). Such elements of vagueness suggest that John took over the trait as a detail of the traditional scenery. His real interest is in the martyrs, for whom he reserves (*cf.* Eus. *H. E.* vi. 42) the privilege assigned usually by primitive Christianity either to the apostles or to Christians in general. They are allotted the exclusive right of participating in the messianic interregnum.—**πεπελεκισμένων,** beheaded by the lictor's axe, the ancient Roman method of executing criminals (*cf.* Introd. § 6). Under the empire citizens were usually beheaded by the sword. The archaic phrase lingered on, like our own "execution". Here it is probably no more than a periphrasis for "put to death". Even if **καὶ οἵτινες** meant a second division, it must, in the light of xi. 7, xiii. 15, denote martyrs and confessors (who had suffered on the specific charge of refusing to worship the emperor).—**χίλια ἔτη,** tenfold the normal period of human life (Plato, *Rep.* 615), but here = the cosmic sabbath which apocalyptic and rabbinic speculation (deriving from Gen. ii. 2 and Ps. xc. 4) placed at the close of creation (*cf.* Drummond's *Jewish Messiah*, 316 f.; Bacher's *Agada d. Tann.*[2] i. 133 f.; *E. Bi.* iii. 3095-3097; *Encycl. of Religion and Ethics*, i. 204 f., 209). John postpones the **παλιγγενεσία** till this period is over (contrast Matt. xix. 28). He says nothing about those who were living when the millenium began, and only precarious inferences can be drawn. Does ver. 6 contain the modest hope that he and other loyal Christians might participate in it? or does the second (**καὶ οἵτινες**) class represent (or include) the living loyalists (so, *e.g.*, Simcox, Weiss, Bousset)? The latter interpretation involves an awkward ambiguity in the meaning of **ἔζησαν** (= *came to life*, and also *continued to live*), conflicts with **οἱ λ. τ. νεκρῶν** (5) and **ψυχὰς** (4), and is therefore to be set aside, as 5-6 plainly refer to both classes of 4. A third alternative would be to suppose that all Christians were *ex hypothesi* dead by the time that the period of xx. 1 f. arrived, the stress of persecution (*cf.* on xiii. 8 f.) having proved so severe that no loyalist could survive (*cf.* below, on ver. 11).

Ver. 6. An interpolated explanation of the preceding vision. **Ἅγιος,** if a continuation of **μακ.,** must almost be taken in its archaic sense of "belonging to God". The ordinary meaning reduces the phrase to a hysteron proteron, unless the idea is that the bliss consists in holiness (so Vendidad xix. 22, "happy, happy the man who is holy with perfect holiness"). "Blessed and holy," however, was a conventional Jewish term of praise and congratulation (*cf.* Jub. ii. 23).—**ὁ δεύτ. θάνατος κ.τ.λ.** According to the Hellenic faith recorded in Plutarch (in his essay on "the face in the moon's orb"), the second death, which gently severs the mind from the soul, is a boon, not a punishment. But John's view reflects the tradition underlying the Iranian belief (Brandt, 586 f., 592) that the righteous were exempt from the second death (defined as in xxi. 8). The clause **ἀλλ' . . . Χριστοῦ** refers to the permanent standing (i. 6, v. 10 *a*) of these risen martyrs not only during but after the millennium; otherwise it would be meaningless, since the danger of the second death (as the penalty inflicted on all who are condemned at the final assizes) does not emerge until the millennium is over. The subsequent clause **καὶ βασιλεύσουσι κ.τ.λ.** is independent, referring back to the special and temporary privilege of the first resurrection and the millennium. For this reason it is precarious to infer from **ἔσονται ἱερεῖς τοῦ θεοῦ καὶ τοῦ Χριστοῦ** (elsewhere **τῷ θεῷ**) that the occupation of these saints is the mediation of divine knowledge to the

λεύσουσι μετ' αὐτοῦ χίλια ἔτη. 7. καὶ ὅταν τελεσθῇ τὰ χίλια
ἔτη, [y] λυθήσεται ὁ Σατανᾶς [z] ἐκ τῆς φυλακῆς αὐτοῦ, 8. καὶ ἐξελεύσεται
πλανῆσαι τὰ ἔθνη τὰ [a] ἐν ταῖς τέσσαρσι γωνίαις τῆς γῆς, τὸν [b] Γὼγ
καὶ τὸν Μαγώγ, συναγαγεῖν αὐτοὺς εἰς τὸν πόλεμον, ὧν ὁ ἀριθμὸς

y Ver. 3.
z *Cf.* i. 5.
a vii. 1, *cf.* Isa. xi. 12, Ezek. vii. 2.
b *Cf.* Winckler's *Alt-Orient. Forsch.* ii. 160 f., and *E. Bi.* 4331 f.

ἔθνη whom Satan is temporarily prevented from beguiling. The likelihood is that the phrase simply denotes as elsewhere the bliss of undisturbed access to God and of intimate fellowship. John ignores the current belief that the loyal survivors on earth would be rewarded (*cf.* Dan. xii. 12; Ps. Sol. xvii. 50, etc.), which is voiced in Asc. Isa. iv. 14-16, but he reproduces independently the cognate view (Asc. Isa. iv. 16 f.) that "the saints will come with the Lord with their garments which are (now) stored up on high in the seventh heaven [*cf.* Apoc. vi. 11] . . . they will descend and be present in this world" (after which the Beloved executes judgment at the resurrection). He, retains, however, not only the general resurrection (12) but the variant and earlier idea (*cf.* 4 Esd. vii. 26 f.) of a resurrection (**ἔζησαν**, 4) confined to the saints. He calls this *the first resurrection* not because the martyrs and confessors who enjoyed it had to undergo a second in the process of their final redemption but because it preceded the only kind of resurrection with which sinners and even ordinary Christians had anything to do (Titius, 37-40; Baldensperger, 74, 79 f.).—**καὶ βασιλεύσουσι**, apparently on earth. This would be put beyond doubt were we to take the view of the risen martyrs' occupation which has been set aside above. But, even apart from this, in the light of all relevant tradition and of the context, the earth must be the sphere of the millennium; Christ might of course be conceived to execute his sovereignty from heaven, but, though ver. 9 denotes a different cycle of tradition from 4-6, it is put on the same plane, and the vision of 4 (*cf.* 1) is evidently this world. **ἐπὶ τῆς γῆς** would be more in keeping with this context than with that of v. 10, where again the refrain of xxii. 5 (**κ. β. εἰς τοὺς αἰῶνας τῶν αἰώνων**) would be more appropriate.—**χίλια ἔτη.** This enigmatic and isolated prediction has led to more unhappy fantasies of speculation and conduct than almost any other passage of the N.T. It stands severely apart from the sensuous expectations of current chiliasm (fertility of soil, longevity, a religious carnival, etc.), but even its earliest interpreters, Papias and Justin, failed to appreciate its reticence, its special object, and its semi-transcendent atmosphere. For its relevance, or rather irrelevance, to the normal Christian outlook, see Denney's *Studies in Theology*, pp. 231 f., and A. Robertson's *Regnum Dei*, pp. 113 f. When the millennium or messianic reign was thus abbreviated into a temporary phase of providence in the latter days, the resurrection had to be shifted from its original position prior to the messianic reign; it now became, as here, the sequel to that period.

Vv. 7-10: As Baligant, lord of the pagans, issues from the East to challenge Charlemagne and be crushed, Satan emerges from his prison for a short period (3) after the millennium, musters an enormous army of pagans to besiege the holy capital, but is decisively routed and flung into the lake of fire to share the tortures of his former agents. The tenses shift from future (7-8, 10 *b*) to aorist (9-10 *a*) the latter (*cf.* xi. 11) being possibly due to the influence of Semitic idiom.

Ver. 8. Satan's return to encounter irretrievable defeat upon the scene of his former successes (**ἐπ' ἐσχάτου ἐτῶν** Ezek. xxxviii. 8), is an obscure and curious feature, borrowed in part from earlier beliefs in Judaism (Gog and the Parthians both from the dreaded N. E., Ezek. xxxviii. 4), but directly or indirectly from a legend common to Persian and Hellenic eschatology: in the former the evil spirit has a preliminary and a final defeat, while in the latter the Titans emerge from Tartarus only to be conclusively worsted (Rohde, *Psyche*, 410 f.). No explanation is given of how Satan gets free. In the Iranian eschatology (Brandt, 590 f.) the serpent breaks loose at the call of Angra Mainyô (God's opponent), seduces a part of mankind and persecutes the rest, till he is overcome by the messiah, who then proceeds to raise the dead. But as John identifies the serpent with Satan, such a

[c] αὐτῶν ὡς ὁ [d] ἄμμος τῆς θαλάσσης. 9. καὶ ἀνέβησαν ἐπὶ τὸ
[e] πλάτος τῆς γῆς, καὶ [f] ἐκύκλευσαν τὴν παρεμβολὴν τῶν ἁγίων καὶ
τὴν πόλιν τὴν [g] ἠγαπημένην· καὶ [h] κατέβη πῦρ ἐκ τοῦ οὐρανοῦ καὶ

c Pleonastic (*cf.* iii. 8, etc). d Gen. xxii. 17, xxxii. 12, Heb. xi. 12, on form (omitting initial ψ) *cf.* Helbing, 22. e Hab. i. 6, Ezek. xxxviii. 11. f 2 Kings vi. 14. g See iii. 9, and on xxi. 7; Ps. lxxviii. 68, lxxxvii. 2, Jer. xi. 15. h Ezek. xxxviii. 22. xxxix. 6, 2 Kings i. 10, *Zech.* xii. 9, Isa. xxvi. 11.

theory was plainly out of the question. At any rate, Satan wins adherents for this fresh attempt from those barbarian hordes who survived the downfall of the Roman empire (xix. 17-21). They are called "Gog and Magog," after the traditional opponents who were to be defeated by the redeemed Israel of the latter days, according to the faith of Judaism (Ezek. xxxviii.-xxxix.). Jerusalem, the navel and centre of the earth (Ezek. xxxviii. 12) as messiah's residence, is besieged; but, like Gog of old, the invaders are consumed by the divine fire, whilst Satan is consigned for ever to the lake of fire, where he lies writhing among his worshippers, as a punishment for seducing men. This is at once a reminiscence of the Iranian eschatology (Hübschmann, 231), where the serpent is flung into molten metal as his final doom, in order to rid earth of his presence, and also a reflection of Enoch liv. (lxvii. 7) where the four angels grip the hosts of Azazel on the last day and "cast them into a burning furnace, that the Lord of Spirits may take vengeance on them for leading astray those who dwell on earth".

Ver. 9. **παρεμβολή**, either camp (as in O.T., *e.g.*, Deut. xxiii. 14) or army (Heb. xi. 34), the saints being supposed to lie in a circle or leaguer round the headquarters of the messiah in Jerusalem, which—by an association common in the ancient world (*e.g.*, Nineveh, "the beloved city" of her god Ishtar)—is termed his beloved city. The phrase is an implicit answer (*cf.* on iii. 9) to the claim of contemporary Judaism which held to the title of "God's beloved" as its monopoly (Apoc. Bar. v. 1, xxi. 21, *cf.* Sir. xxiv. 11). In the Hebrew Elias-apocalypse of the 3rd century (*cf.* Buttenwieser, *E. J.* i. 681-2), where Gog and Magog also appear after the millennium to besiege Jerusalem, their annihilation is followed by the judgment and the descent of Jerusalem from heaven. This tradition of xx. 4-10 therefore belongs to the cycle from which xi. 1-13 (xiv. 14-20) was drawn; Jerusalem, freed from her foes and purified within, forms the headquarters of messiah's temporary reign, tenanted not simply by devout worshippers but by martyrs (*cf.* xiv. 1-5, on mount Zion). Yet only a new and heavenly Jerusalem is finally adequate (xxi. f.); it descends after the last punishment and judgment (xi. 15 f.=xx. 10 f.). Wetstein cites from the Targ. Jonath. a passage which has suggested elements in this and in the preceding (xi. 17-21) vision: a king rises in the last days from the land of Magog, et omnes populi obedient illi; after their rout by fire their corpses lie a prey to wild beasts and birds. Then "all the dead of Israel shall live . . . and receive the reward of their works". In the highest spirit of the O.T., however, John rejects the horrible companion thought (En. lxxxix. 58, xciv. 10, xcvii. 2) that God gloats over the doom of the damned. An onset of foreign nations upon Jerusalem naturally formed a stereotyped feature in all Jewish expectations of latter-day horrors; here, however, as the city is *ipso facto* tenanted by holy citizens, the siege is ineffective (contrast xi. 1 f.). Neither here nor in xix. 21 are the rebellious victims consigned at death to eternal punishment, as are the beast, the false prophet, and Satan. The human tools of the latter die, but they are raised (xx. 11 f.) for judgment (ver. 15), though the result of their trial is a foregone conclusion (xiii. 8, xiv. 9-10). In En. lvi., from which this passage borrows, Gog and Magog are represented by the Medes and the Parthians from whom (between 100 and 46 B.C.) a hostile league against Palestine might have been expected by contemporaries. But the destruction of the troops is there caused by civil dissensions. In our Apocalypse the means of destruction is supernatural fire, as in 2 Thess. i. 8, ii. 8, 4 Esd. xii. 33, xiii. 38-39, Ap. Bar. xxvii. 10, Asc. Isa. iv. 18 (where fire issues from the Beloved to consume all the godless); the Parthians also appear some time before the end, in the penultimate stage when the Roman empire and its Nero-antichrist make their last attack. But the prophet is still left with the orthodox eschatological tradition of Gog

κατέφαγεν αὐτούς· 10. καὶ ὁ διάβολος ὁ [i] πλανῶν αὐτοὺς ἐβλήθη
εἰς τὴν [k] λίμνην τοῦ πυρὸς καὶ θείου, ὅπου καὶ τὸ θηρίον καὶ ὁ
ψευδοπροφήτης· καὶ [l] βασανισθήσονται ἡμέρας καὶ νυκτὸς εἰς τοὺς
αἰῶνας τῶν αἰώνων.

11. Καὶ εἶδον [m] θρόνον [n] μέγαν [o] λευκὸν
καὶ τὸν καθήμενον ἐπ' αὐτόν,
οὗ ἀπὸ τοῦ προσώπου [p] ἔφυγεν ἡ γῆ καὶ ὁ οὐρανός,
καὶ [q] τόπος οὐχ εὑρέθη [q] αὐτοῖς.

12. Καὶ εἶδον τοὺς νεκρούς, τοὺς μεγάλους καὶ τοὺς μικρούς,
ἑστῶτας ἐνώπιον τοῦ θρόνου,
καὶ [r] βιβλία ἠνοίχθησαν·

i = ὃς ἐπλάνα (*cf.* Eph. iv. 28).
k xix. 20, En. xc. 20-25; *cf.* Mt. xiii. 41-42, xxv. 41 (No mention of fate of devil's angels, in Apoc.).
l xiv. 11.
m *Cf.* iv. 2, Dan. vii. 9.
n As distinct from those of iv. 4, xx. 4.
o = unsullied justice?
p xvi. 20, xxi. 1, Isa. xiii. 13, xxiv. 19-20.
q From Dan. ii. 35.
r Dan. vii. 10, Mal. iii. 16, Jer. xvii. 1. *Encycl. Relig. and Ethics*, ii. 792-795.

and Magog, an episode (consecrated by the Ezekiel-prophecy and later belief) which he feels obliged to work in somehow. Hence his arrangement of Satan's final recrudescence in juxtaposition with the Gog and Magog outburst (*cf.* on xvi. 16, and Klausner's *messian. Vorstellungen d. jüd. Volkes im Zeit. d. Tannaiten*, pp. 61 f.). The latter, an honoured but by this time awkward survival of archaic eschatology, presented a similar difficulty to the Talmudic theology which variously put it before, or after, the messianic reign (Volz, pp. 175 f.). In his combination of messianic beliefs, John follows the tradition, accepted in Sib. Or. iii. 663 f., which postponed the irruption till after messiah's temporary period of power.

xx. 11-xxii. 5. The connexion of thought depends upon the traditional Jewish scheme outlined, *e.g.*, in Apoc. Bar. xxix.-xxx. (*cf.* 4 Esd. vii. 29, 30) where the messiah returns in glory to heaven after his reign on earth; the general resurrection follows, accompanied by the judgment. Developing his oracles along these current lines, the prophet now proceeds to depict his culminating vision of the End in three scenes: (i.) the world and its judgment (xx. 11-15), (ii.) the new heaven and earth (xxi. 1-8), centring round (iii.) the new Jerusalem as the final seat of bliss (xxi. 9-xxii. 5). The last-named phase was associated in eschatology (Sib. Or. v. 246 f., 414 f.) with the return of Nero redivivus and the downfall of Babylon which preceded the sacred city's rise. The destruction of hostile forces, followed by the renovation of the universe, is essentially a Persian dogma (Stave, 180 f.), and is paralleled in the Babylonian mythology, where after the defeat and subjugation of Tiâmat in the primeval age creation commences. From this point until xxi. 9 f., Jesus is ignored entirely.

Vv. 11-15. The moral dignity and reticence with which this sublime vision of the last assize is drawn, show how the primitive Christian conscience could rise above its inheritance from Jewish eschatology. The latter spoke more definitely upon the beginning of the end than upon the end itself (*cf.* Harnack's *History of Dogma*, i. 174).

Ver. 11. John hints where Isaiah is explicit (vi. 1). Nothing is said about the uselessness of intercession; *cf.* 4 Esd. vii. [102-115] 33: "and the Most High shall be revealed upon the judgment-seat, and compassion shall pass away, long-suffering shall be withdrawn". Enoch xc. 20 sets up the throne near Jerusalem, and most apocalypses are spoiled by similarly puerile details. Compare with 11 *b* the tradition in Asc. Isa. iv. 18 where the voice of the Beloved (*i.e.*, messiah) at the close of the millennium rebukes in wrath heaven and earth, the hills and cities, the angels of the sun and moon, "and all things wherein Beliar manifested himself and acted openly in this world". John's Apocalypse, however, follows (yet *cf.* xxii. 12) that tradition of Judaism which reserved the judgment for God and not for the messiah (4 Esd. vi. 1-10, vii. 33 f. anti-Christian polemic?) although another conception (En. xlv. 3, lxix. 27 etc.; Ap. Bar. lxxii. 2-6) assigning it to the messiah had naturally found greater favour in certain Christian circles.

Ver. 12. The books opened in God's court contain the deeds of men, whose

καὶ ἄλλο [s] βιβλίον ἠνοίχθη, ὅ ἐστιν τῆς ζωῆς·
καὶ ἐκρίθησαν οἱ νεκροὶ ἐκ τῶν γεγραμμένων ἐν τοῖς βιβλίοις,
[t] κατὰ τὰ ἔργα αὐτῶν.
13. Καὶ ἔδωκεν ἡ [u] θάλασσα τοὺς νεκροὺς τοὺς ἐν αὐτῇ,
καὶ ὁ [v] θάνατος καὶ ὁ [w] ᾅδης ἔδωκαν τοὺς νεκροὺς τοὺς ἐν αὐτοῖς·
καὶ ἐκρίθησαν ἕκαστος
κατὰ τὰ ἔργα αὐτῶν.

s iii. 5, xiii. 8, xvii. 8, En. xlvii. 3, cviii. 3, *cf.* Eurip. *Fragm.* 488.
t 2 Cor. v. 10, Rom. ii. 2-11. Jo. v. 28-29.
u For anc. Gk. idea of sea preventing dead from passing into Hades, *cf.* Radermacher's *Das Jenseits im Mythos d. Hellenen* (1903) 74 f.
v i. 18, Isa. xxvi. 19.
w vi. 8, *cf.* Charles on En. lxiii. 10.

fate is determined by the evidence of these "vouchers for the book of life" (Alford); the latter volume forms as it were a register of those predestinated to eternal life (*cf.* Gfrörer ii. 121 f., and below on ver. 15). The figure of books containing a record of man's career was a realistic expression of Jewish belief in moral retribution, which prevailed especially in eschatological literature (*e.g.*, Jubil. xxx.; Enoch. lxxxix.-xc.; Dan. vii. 10, etc.) after the exile. "And in these days I saw the Head of days, when he had seated himself upon the throne of his glory, and the books of the living were opened before him" (Enoch xlvii. 3; *cf.* Driver's *Daniel*, p. 86). It is obvious, from ver. 15, that the resurrection is general (as Dan. vii. 20; 4 Esd. vi. 20, vii. 32; Test. Jud. 25; Test. Benj. 10; Apoc. Bar. 7, etc.; *cf.* Gfrörer, ii. 277 f.; and Charles's *Eschatology*, 340 f.), in opposition to the primitive and still prevalent belief which confined it to the righteous (*E. Bi.* 1390). Hence the books contain not the good deeds alone of the saints (the prevalent Jewish idea, *cf.* Charles on En. li. 1; Mal. iii. 16; Jub. xxx.; Ps. lvi. 8, etc.), nor bad deeds alone (Isa. lxv. 6; En. lxxxi. 4; *cf.* En. xc. 20; Apoc. Bar. xxiv. 1) but good and bad deeds alike (as Dan. vii. 10; Asc. Isa. ix. 20 f.). This again tallies with the Iranian faith (Hübschmann, 229), according to which, at the command of Ormuzd, the righteous and the wicked alike were raised for their recompense. Here the tribunal is a throne, before which the king's subjects have to answer for their conduct; rebels are punished and the loyal get the reward of good service (*cf.* xxii. 12, etc.). **γεγραμμ.**, by whom? Jewish speculation conjectured Raphael as the recording angel (En. xx. 3) or a band of angels (Slav. En. xix. 5); but the Jewish idea of the heavenly tables (**πλάκες τοῦ οὐρανοῦ**) is omitted in the Apoc., nor is there the slightest mention of those living at the era of judgment. Did John mean that none would survive (*cf.* ver. 5)? Or were any survivors to be taken directly to heaven at the coming of Christ, as in Paul's primitive outlook (see on 1 Th. iv. 16-17)?

Ver. 13. See Pirke Aboth, iv. 32: "Let not thine imagination assure thee that the grave is an asylum" (for, like birth and life and death, judgment is appointed before the King of the kings of kings). "And the earth shall restore those that are asleep in her, and so shall the dust those that dwell therein in silence, and the secret chambers shall deliver up those souls (of the righteous, iv. 35) that were committed unto them," 4 Esd. vii. 32—reproducing, as here, Enoch li. 1, "and in those days will the earth also give back those who are treasured up within it, and Sheol also will give back that which it has received, and hell will give back that which it owes". Also En. lxi. 5 where the restoration includes "those who have been destroyed by the desert, or devoured by the fish of the sea and by the beasts". Evidently drowned people are supposed not to be in Hades; they wander about or drift in the ocean (Achill. Tat. v. 313), **μηδὲ εἰς ᾅδου καταβαίνειν ὅλως.** According to the prophet's conception (*cf.* xiii. 8, xiv. 9 f.) the fate of pagans must have been a foregone conclusion, when the Imperial cultus was made the test of character; in which case "the scene before the white throne is rather a final statement of judgment than a statement of final judgment" (Gilbert). But the broader allusion to *works* here shows that the prophet is thinking of the general ethical judgment, which embraced issues wider than the particular historical test of the Emperor-worship. —**ᾅδης κ.τ.λ.**, *cf.* Plutarch's (*de Iside*,

14. **Καὶ ὁ [x] θάνατος καὶ ὁ ᾅδης ἐβλήθησαν εἰς τὴν λίμνην τοῦ
πυρός·**

[οὗτος ὁ θάνατος [y] δεύτερός ἐστιν, ἡ λίμνη τοῦ πυρός] [1]

15. **καὶ εἴ τις οὐχ εὑρέθη ἐν τῇ βίβλῳ τῆς ζωῆς γεγραμμένος,
ἐβλήθη εἰς τὴν λίμνην τοῦ πυρός.**

x 1 Cor. xv. 26, Isa. xxv. 8, 4 Esd. vii. 31.
y Cf. on Luke xii. 4-5.

[1] Om. **ουτος . . . πυρος** with eight minn., Me., Arm. (Aug.), And[bav], Pr., Haym. as a marginal gloss [so, *e.g.*, Krüger, (*Gött. Gel. Anz.*, 1897, 34), von Soden, Bousset (?), and Wellhausen (with 14*a* and 15)], perhaps displaced from its original position after 15, where it would suit the context (Haussleiter, 212-213), since there is no question of the second death except for human beings. The misplacement was probably due to the attraction of **θανατος** in 14.

29) derivation of Amenthes, the Egyptian name for Hades, as "that which receives and gives". As in Slav. En. lxv. 6 and the later Iranian Bundehesh (*S. B. E.* v. 123 f.), the resurrection of the body is not mentioned, though it is probably implied (*cf.* En. li. 1, lxii. 14 and Matt. xxvii. 52 f.).

Ver. 14. Death as Sin's ally must be destroyed along with Sin, while Hades, the grim receptacle of Death's prey (the intermediate rendezvous for the dead, except for martyrs, *cf.* vi. 10), naturally ceases to have any function. This was the cherished hope of early Christianity as of Judaism (Isa. xxv. 8). John's idea of the second death is much more realistic and severe than the Hellenic or the Philonic (*cf. de Praem. et Poen.* § 12, etc.).

Ver. 15. In Enoch (xxxviii. 5, xlviii. 9) the wicked are handed over by God to the saints, before whom they burn like straw in fire and sink like lead in water. The milder spirit of the Christian prophet abstains from making the saints thus punish or witness the punishment of the doomed (*cf.* on xiv. 10). In Apoc. Pet. 25 the souls of the murdered gaze on the torture of their former persecutors, crying **ὁ θεός, δικαία σου ἡ κρίσις.** These features, together with those of torturing angels (Dieterich, 60 f.) and Dantesque gradations of punishment (Dieterich, 206 f.), are conspicuous by their absence from John's Apocalypse. There is a stern simplicity about the whole description, and just enough pictorial detail is given to make the passage morally suggestive. As gehenna, like paradise (4 Esd. iii. 4), was created before the world, according to rabbinic belief (Gfrörer, ii. 42-46), it naturally survived the collapse of the latter (ver. 11). Contrast with this passage the relentless spirit of 4 Esd. vii. 49 f. ("I will not mourn over the multitude of the perishing . . . they are set on fire and burn hotly and are quenched"). If John betrays no pity for the doomed, he exhibits no callous scorn for their fate. The order of xx. 13-15 and xxi. 1 f. is the same as in the haggadic pseudo-Philonic *De Biblic. Antiquitatibus* (after 70 A.D.) where the judgment ("reddet infernus debitum suum et perditio restituet paratecen suam, ut reddam unicuique secundum opera sua") is followed by the renewal of all things ("et exstinguetur mors et infernus claudet os suum . . . et erit terra alia et caelum aliud habitaculum sempiternum").

So much for the doomed. The bliss of saints occupies the closing vision (xxi.-xxii. 5). From the smoke and pain and heat it is a relief to pass into the clear, clean atmosphere of the eternal morning where the breath of heaven is sweet and the vast city of God sparkles like a diamond in the radiance of his presence. The dominant idea of the passage is that surroundings must be in keeping with character and prospects; consequently, as the old universe has been hopelessly sullied by sin, a new order of things must be formed, once the old scene of trial and failure is swept aside. This hope of the post-exilic Judaism (*cf.* Isa. lxv. 17, lxvi. 22) was originally derived from the Persian religion, in which the renovation of the universe was a cardinal tenet; it is strongly developed in Enoch (xci. 16, civ. 2, new heaven only) and 4 Esd. iv. 27 f. ("if the place where the evil is sown pass not away, there cannot come the field where the good is sown"). The expectation (*cf.* on Rom. viii. 28 f.) that the loss sustained at the fall of Adam would now be made good, is hardly the same as this eschatological transformation; the latter prevailed whenever the stern exigencies of the age seemed to demand a clean sweep of the universe, and the apoca-

a *Cf.* xx. 11, En. xlv. 4-5, lxxii. 1.

XXI. 1. Καὶ εἶδον οὐρανὸν καινὸν καὶ γῆν καινήν·
ὁ γὰρ ᵃπρῶτος οὐρανὸς καὶ ἡ πρώτη γῆ ἀπῆλθαν,
καὶ ἡ θάλασσα οὐκ ἔστιν ἔτι.

lyptic attitude towards nature seldom had anything of the tenderness and pathos, *e.g.*, of 4 Esd. viii. 42-48 (*cf.* vii. 31). The sequence of xx. 11 f. and xxi. 1 f. therefore follows the general eschatological programme, as *e.g.* in Apoc. Bar. xxi. 23 f., where, after death is ended (very mildly), the new world promised by God appears as the dwelling-place of the saints (*cf.* also xxxii. 1 f.). The earthly Jerusalem is good enough for the millennium but not for the final bliss; the new order (xxi. 5) of latter (*cf.* above) coincides, as in Oriental religion (Jeremias, 45 f.), with the new year (*i.e.*, spring) festival of the god's final victory.—The literary problem is more intricate. With xxi. 1-8, which is evidently the prophet's own composition, the Apocalypse really closes. The rest of the vision, down to xxii. 5, is little more than a poetical repetition and elaboration of xxi. 1-8, to which xxii. 6 f. forms the appropriate conclusion, just as the doublet xix. 9 *b*, 10 (in its present position) does to xix. 1-8. When xix. 9 *b*, 10 is transferred to the end of xvii. (see above), the parallelism becomes even closer. Both xvii. (the vision of the harlot-Babylon, with her evil influence on the world, and her transient empire) and xxi. 9-xxii. 5 (the vision of the Lamb's pure bride, with her endless empire) are introduced alike (*cf.* xvii. 1, xxi. 9) and ended alike, though xxii. 6-8 has been slightly expanded in view of its special position as a climax to the entire Apocalypse. As xvii. represents John's revision of an earlier source, this suggests, but does not prove, a similar origin for xxi. 9-xxii. 5. He might have sketched the latter as an antithesis to the former; certainly the "editorial" brushwork in xxi. 9-xxii. 5 is not nearly so obvious and abrupt as, *e.g.*, in xviii. Upon the other hand there are touches and traits which have been held to imply the revision of a source or sources, especially of a Jewish character (so variously Vischer, Weyland, Ménégoz, Spitta, Sabatier, Briggs, Schmidt, S. Davidson, von Soden, de Faye, Kohler, Baljon, J. Weiss, and Forbes), delineating the new Jerusalem (*cf.* xxi. 1-2). In this event the Christian editor's hand would be visible, not necessarily in xxi. 22 (see note), but in the **ἀρνίον**-allusions, in xxi. 14 *b*, 23 (*cf.* xxii. 5), 25 *b* (=xxii. 5 *a*), and 27 (=xx. 15, xxi. 8, xxii. 3 *a*). Another set of features (xxi. 12, 16, 24-27 *a*, xxii. 2 *c*, 3 *a*, 5) is explicable apart from the hypothesis of a Jewish source, or indeed of any source at all. Literally taken, they are incongruous. But since xxi. 9-xxii. 5 may be equivalent not so much to a Jewish ideal conceived *sub specie Christiana* as to a Christian ideal expressed in the imaginative terms of a Jewish tradition which originally depicted an earthly Jerusalem surrounded by the respectful nations of the world, a number of traits in the latter sketch would obviously be inapplicable in the new setting to which they were transferred. These are retained, however, not only for the sake of their archaic associations but in order to lend pictorial completeness to the description of the eternal city. The author, in short, is a religious poet, not a theologian or a historian. But while these archaic details need not involve the use of a Jewish source (so rightly Schön and Wellhausen), much less a reference of the whole vision to the millennial Jerusalem (Zahn), or the ascription of it to Cerinthus (Völter) or a chiliastic Jewish Christian editor (Bruston), may not the repetitions and parallelisms, especially in view of xxii. 6 f., indicate a composite Christian origin, as is suggested, *e.g.*, by Erbes (A=xxi. 1-4, xxii. 3-17, 20, 21, B=xxi. 5-27, xxii. 1, 2, 18, 19) and Selwyn (xxii. 16-21, the conclusion of A= xxi. 2, xxii. 3-5, xxi. 3-6 *a*, xxii. 7, xxi. 6 *b*-8, or of B=xxi. 9-xxii. 2, xxii. 6, 8-15)? Some dislocation of the original autograph or scribal additions may be conjectured with reason in xxii. 6-21 (see below), at least. But the reiterations are intelligible enough as the work of a single writer, whose aim is to impress an audience rather than to produce a piece of literature. The likelihood is that John composed xxi. 9 f. as an antithesis to the description of the evil city which he had reproduced from a source in xvii., and that he repeated the incident of xxii. 8, 9 (as xix. 9, 10 at the end of xvii.), adapting it to its position at the close of the whole book as well as of the immediately preceding oracle.

CHAPTER XXI.—Vv. 1-8: the prelude to the last vision.

Vv. 1-2, the title: 1 *a b*=xx. 11 *c*,

2. καὶ τὴν πόλιν τὴν [b] ἁγίαν Ἰερουσαλὴμ [c] καινὴν εἶδον καταβαίνουσαν ἐκ τοῦ οὐρανοῦ ἀπὸ τοῦ θεοῦ, [d] ἡτοιμασμένην ὡς νύμφην
[e] κεκοσμημένην τῷ ἀνδρὶ αὐτῆς. 3. καὶ ἤκουσα φωνῆς [f] μεγάλης [g] ἐκ
τοῦ θρόνου λεγούσης,

"Ἰδοὺ ἡ [h] σκηνὴ τοῦ θεοῦ μετὰ τῶν ἀνθρώπων,
καὶ σκηνώσει μετ' αὐτῶν·

b xi. 2, Isa. lii. 1, Heb. xi. 16, xii. 22.
c iii. 12, Gal. iv. 26.
d xix. 7-8, Isa. lii. 1, lxi. 10.
e Ezek. xvi. 11 = "full of people" (Isa. xlix. 18).
f xi. 12, xvi. 1.
g xix. 5; *cf.* xx. 11.
h xiii. 6, Ezek. xxxvii. 27, Zech. ii. 10, viii. 8, *cf.* Isa. lvii. 15.

1 *c*=xx. 13 *a*. The absence of the sea from John's ideal universe is due not to any Semitic horror of the ocean, nor to its association with Rome (xiii. 1), nor to the ancient idea of its dividing effect ("mare dissociabile," "the unplumbed, salt, estranging sea,"), but to its mythological connexion with the primitive dragon-opponent of God, the last trace of whom is now obliterated. *Cf.* Sib. v. 159, 160, 447 (ἔσται δ' ὑστατίῳ καιρῷ ξηρὸς πότε πόντος), Ass. Mos. x. 6, 4 Esd. vi. 24, Test. Levi 4, etc., for this religious antipathy to the treacherous, turbulent element of water. "La mer est une annulation, une stérilization d'une partie de la terre, un reste du chaos primitif, souvent un châtiment de Dieu" (Renan, 449). Plutarch (*de Iside*, 7 f., 32) preserves the Egyptian sacred tradition that the sea was no part of nature (παρωρισμένην) but an alien element (ἀλλοῖον περίττωμα), full of destruction and disease. The priests of Isis (32) shunned it as impure and unsocial for swallowing up the sacred Nile. One favourite tradition made the sea disappear in the final conflagration of the world (*R. J.* 289), but John ignores this view. The world is to end as it began, with creation; only it is a new creation, with a perfect paradise, and no thwarting evil (Barn. vi. 13). His omission of the ocean is simply due to the bad associations of the abyss as the abode of Tehom or Tiâmat (*cf.* Oesterley's *Evol. of Messianic Idea*, 79 f., G. A. Smith's *Jerusalem*, i. 71 f., and Hastings' *D. B.* iv. 194, 195).

Ver. 2. ἐκ=origin, ἀπὸ=originator. This conception of the new Jerusalem as messiah's bride in the latter days is an original touch, added by the prophet to the traditional Jewish material (*cf.* Volz, 336 f.). In 4 Esd. vi. 26 (Lat. Syr.) "the bride shall appear, even the city coming forth, and she shall be seen who is now hidden from the earth"; but this precedes the 400 years of bliss, at the close of which messiah dies. In En. xc. 28 f. a new and better house is substituted for the old, while in 4 Esd. ix.-xi. the mourning mother rather suddenly becomes "a city builded" with large foundations (*i.e.*, Zion). These partial anticipations lend some colour to Dalman's plea that the conception of a pre-existent heavenly Jerusalem was extremely limited in Judaism, and that John's vision is to be isolated from the other N.T. hints (see reff.). For a fine application of the whole passage, see *Ecce Homo*, ch. xxiv. The vision conveys Christian hope and comfort in terms of a current and ancient religious tradition upon the new Jerusalem (*cf.* Charles on Apoc. Bar. iv. 3). The primitive form of this conception, which lasted in various phases down to the opening of the second century, was that the earthly Jerusalem simply needed to be purified in order to become the fit and final centre of the messianic realm with its perfect communion between God and man (*cf.* Isa. lx., liv. 11=Tobit xiii. 16-17, Ezek. xl.-xlviii., En. x. 16-19, xxv. 1, Ps. Sol. xvii. 25, 33, Ap. Bar. xxix., xxxix.-xl., lxxii., lxxiv., 4 Esd. vii. 27-30, xii. 32-34, etc.). But alongside of this, especially after the religious revival under the Maccabees, ran the feeling that the earthly Jerusalem was too stained and secular to be a sacred city; its heavenly counterpart, pure and pre-existent, must descend (so here, after En. xc. 28, 29, Ap. Bar. xxxii. 3, 4, Test. Dan 5, etc.). In rabbinic theology, the vision of the heavenly Jerusalem was taken from Adam after his lapse, but shown as a special favour to Abraham, Jacob and Moses (*cf.* Ap. Bar. iv.). The Christian prophet John not only sees it but sees it realised among Christian people—a brave and significant word of prophecy, in view of his age and surroundings.

Vv. 3, 4. σκην. (chosen on account of its "assonance with the Hebrew to express the *Shekinah*," Dr. Taylor on Pirke

καὶ [i] αὐτοὶ [k] λαοὶ αὐτοῦ ἔσονται,
καὶ αὐτὸς ὁ θεὸς μετ᾽ αὐτῶν ἔσται.
4. καὶ [l] ἐξαλείψει πᾶν δάκρυον ἐκ τῶν ὀφθαλμῶν αὐτῶν,
καὶ [m] ὁ θάνατος οὐκ ἔσται ἔτι·
[n] οὔτε πένθος οὔτε κραυγὴ οὔτε [o] πόνος οὐκ ἔσται ἔτι·
[p] ὅτι τὰ πρῶτα ἀπῆλθον."
5. καὶ [q] εἶπεν ὁ καθήμενος ἐπὶ τῷ θρόνῳ, "Ἰδού, [r] καινὰ ποιῶ
πάντα." [s] καὶ λέγει "Γράψον· ὅτι οὗτοι οἱ λόγοι [t] πιστοὶ καὶ
ἀληθινοί εἰσι." 6. καὶ εἶπέ μοι, [u] "Γέγοναν.[1] [v] ἐγὼ τὸ ἄλφα
καὶ τὸ ὦ, ἡ ἀρχὴ καὶ τὸ τέλος. ἐγὼ τῷ διψῶντι δώσω αὐτῷ ἐκ τῆς
πηγῆς [w] τοῦ ὕδατος τῆς ζωῆς [x] δωρεάν. 7. ὁ [y] νικῶν κληρονομήσει

i Gen. xvii. 8, Jer. xxxi. 33, 2 Cor. vi. 16. From Lev. xxvi. 11-12.
k On plur. see Acts iv. 27.
l vii. 17, xx. 14, Isa. xxv. 8, xxxv. 10.
m *Cf.* Justin, *Dial.* xlv. 14; Volz, 348; a Persian belief (Hübschmann, 232).
n Isa. lxv. 19, Jer. xxxi. 16, Ass.-Mos. x. 1.
o = pain, only in Apoc. in N.T.
p Isa. lxv. 17.
q By itself, only here in Apoc.
r Isa. xliii. 19, 2 Cor. v. 17, vi. 16-18, Barn. vi. 13.
s Similar asseverations in Dan. ii. 45, viii. 26, etc. a feature of the apoc. style.
t In sense of Ps. xix. 7, cxi. 7, etc.
u xvi. 7: On form Deissm. (192).
v (Emphatic, ἐγώ), *cf.* i. 8, xxii. 13, Isa. xli. 4, xliv. 6, xlviii. 12.
w *Cf.* John vii. 37 f., Just. *Dial.* lxix. etc.
x xxii. 17, John iv. 10-14.
y ii. 7; emphatic (αὐτῷ, αὐτός).

[1] The unusual aoristic (*cf.* Helbing, 67) termination of **γεγοναν** (א^cA, S., Iren., edd.) has started the variants **γεγονασιν** (38), **γεγονε** (41, 94: "no doubt a conj. of Erasmus based on vg., his MS. 1 reading **γεγονα**," Gwynn), and **γεγονα** (א*PQ, Syr., Arm., And., Areth., etc.; = **ειμι**, so Buresch in *Rhein. Museum*, 1891, 206).

Aboth iii. 3) is the real tabernacle (Heb. viii. 2, ix. 11). The whole meaning and value of the new Jerusalem lies in the presence of God (En. xlv. 6, lxii. 14, Test. Jud., 25, etc.) with men which it guarantees. The O.T. promises are realised (see reff.); God is accessible, and men are consoled with eternal comfort (*cf.* Enoch x. 22, **καὶ καθαρισθήσεται πᾶσα ἡ γῆ ἀπὸ παντὸς μιάμματος καὶ ἀπὸ πάσης ἀκαθαρσίας καὶ ὀργῆς καὶ μάστιγος**). If we were to read the passage in the light of Isa. lxi. 3-10, the tears wiped away would signify that the penitents were newly espoused to the Lord; but the context here implies tears of grief and pain, not of repentance. "There shall be no more labour, nor sickness, nor sorrow, nor anxiety, nor need, nor night, nor darkness, but a great light" (Slav. En. lxv. 9).

Ver. 5. The first and only time that God addresses the seer, or indeed (apart from i. 8) speaks at all. The almost unbroken silence assigned to God in the Apocalypse corresponds to the Egyptian idea of the divine Reason needing no tongue but noiselessly directing mortal things by righteousness (Plut. *de Iside*, 75; hence the deity is symbolised by the crocodile, which was believed to be the only animal without a tongue).

Ver. 6. "'Tis done, all is over" (sc. **οὗτοι οἱ λόγοι** or **πάντα**). The perfecting of God's work is followed, as in Isa. liv.-lvi., by a liberal promise of satisfaction to all spiritual desire, and the three ideas of consolation, eternal refreshment, and Divine fellowship are thus conjoined as in vii. 14-17. Compare the fontal passage in Philo, *de migrat Abr.* § 6 **πηγὴ δὲ, ἀφ᾽ ἧς ὀμβρεῖ τὰ ἀγαθά, ἡ τοῦ φιλοδώρου Θεοῦ σύνοδός ἐστιν. οὗ χάριν ἐπισφραγιζόμενος τὰ τῶν εὐεργεσιῶν φησιν, Εσομαι μετὰ σοῦ.** The promise implies (like Isa. xliv. 3, not lv. 1) that thirst is accompanied by readiness and eagerness to accept the boon, which is free (6) and full (**πάντα**) and filial (ver. 7). The thirst for God is opposed to the unbelief and vice which quench it, just as the victorious life is contrasted with the craven spirit which shrinks from the hardships and demands of faith. Similarly the life of strenuous obedience now enters on its majority; it comes into an estate of filial confidence to the great God, bestowed on all who acquit themselves nobly in their probation. By a rare touch (since iii. 22) in the Apocalypse, the individual Christian is singled out. Usually the writer is interested in the general body of Christians. Here, however, as in ii.-iii., religious individualism aptly follows the idea of personal promise and encouragement (*cf.* xxii. 17), as afterwards of judgment (xxii. 11-12).

Ver. 7. These boons (3-7), however, are reserved for the loyal; the third (son

**ταῦτα, καὶ [z] ἔσομαι αὐτῷ θεὸς, [z] καὶ αὐτὸς ἔσται μοι υἱός. 8. τοῖς
δὲ [a] δειλοῖς καὶ ἀπίστοις καὶ ἐβδελυγμένοις καὶ [b] φονεῦσι καὶ πόρνοις
καὶ φαρμακοῖς καὶ [c] εἰδωλολάτραις καὶ πᾶσι τοῖς [b] ψευδέσι, τὸ
μέρος αὐτῶν ἐν τῇ λίμνῃ τῇ [d] καιομένῃ πυρὶ καὶ θείῳ, [e] ὅ ἐστιν
ὁ θάνατος ὁ δεύτερος.**

z 2 Sam. vii 14, Ps. lxxxix. 26-27, Zech. viii. 8, 2 Cor. vi. 18.
a Heb. x. 38-39.
b ix. 21, xxii. 15, 1 Pet. iv. 15, Jas. v. 6. Rom. i. 29, Mk. vii. 21 = Mt. xv. 19.
c Eph. v. 5; ver. 27.
d Gen. xix. 24, Isa. xxx. 33, Ezek. xxxviii. 22.
e xx. 14; constr. Win. § 24. 8*b*.

of God) was a title applied to Augustus and the emperors generally throughout the Greek and Roman world. **κληρονομήσει** (here only in Apoc.) in general sense = "enter into possession of," "partake of". ("This place" of bliss "is prepared for the righteous who endure every kind of attack in their lives from those who afflict their souls . . . for them this place is prepared as an eternal inheritance," Slav. En. ix.). This is the sole allusion, and a purely incidental one, to that central conception of the messianic bliss as a **κληρονομία**, which bulks so prominently in apocalypses like Fourth Esdras and is employed in a cosmic sense by Paul as lordship over the whole creation (see Bacon, *Biblical and Semitic Studies*, Yale Univ. 1902, pp. 240 f.). The solitary allusion to sonship expresses the close relation to God for which this writer elsewhere prefers to use the metaphor of priesthood. Partly owing to the bent of his mind, partly owing to the stern circumstances of his age, he (like Clem. Rom.) allows the majesty and mystery of God to overshadow that simple and close confidence which Jesus inculcated towards the Father (Titius, 13, 14), as also the direct love of God for his people (only in iii. 9, 19, xx. 9).

Ver. 8. The reverse side of the picture (*cf.* xx. 12-15 and below on ver. 27): a black list of those who have not conquered. **δειλοῖς** = "cowards" or apostates, who deny Christ in the persecution and worship Caesar (Introd. § 6) through fear of suffering; "**δειλία** does not of course itself allow that it is timorous, but would shelter its timidity under the more honourable title of **εὐλάβεια**" (Trench, *Synonyms*, § x.). It embraces further all those who draw back under the general strain of ridicule and social pressure (Heb. vi. 4-8; 2 Ti. iv. 16, etc.), like Bunyan's *Pliable*, but unlike his *Mr. Fearing* (*cf.* 1 Macc. iii. 16).—**ἀπίστοις** not = incredulous (so *e.g.*, Dittenberger's *Sylloge*, 802[33], 3 cent. B.C.) but, as in Luke xii. 46 (*cf.* Sir. ii. 12 f.), = "faithless," untrustworthy, those who are not **πιστός** (i. 5, ii. 10, 13, 2 Ti. ii. 13). All **δειλοί** are **ἄπιστοι** (*cf.* Introd. § 6), but not all **ἄπιστοι** are **δειλοί**. There are more reasons for disloyalty to Christ than cowardice, and some of these are hinted at in the following words, which suggest that **ἄπιστοι** includes the further idea of immorality (as in Tit. i. 15, 16, where it is grouped with **βδελυκτοί**). Lack of faith is denounced also in Apoc. Bar. liv. 21, 4 Esd. ix. 7, etc. **ἐβδελυγμένοις** for **βδελυκτοῖς** (as **εὐλογημένος** for **εὐλογητός**, etc., *cf.* Field on Gal. ii. 11; Simcox, *Lang. N.T.* 128, 129), "detestable" because "defiled and fouled" by the impurities of the pagan cults (xvii. 4, xviii. 3, etc.; *cf.* Hos. ix. 10; Slav. En. x. 4) including unnatural vice. Murder (and fornication, Jas. ii. 11) in the popular religions of the ancient world caused ritual impurity and disqualified for access to God, unless atoned for.—**φαρμακοῖς** = "poisoners" or "sorcerers" (xxii. 15), *cf.* Dan. ii. 27 LXX, and above on ix. 21, where (as here and in Gal. v. 21) witchcraft or magic is bracketed with idolatry. Idolaters, in Apoc. Pet. 18, have a special place **πλείστου πυρὸς γέμων**. **ψευδέσιν** = "liars," primarily recreant Christians who deny their faith and Lord, or worship false gods (Rom. i. 25); but also untruthful Christians who cheat (Acts v. 3) and lie to one another (Col. iii. 9, *cf.* Apoc. xiv. 5); further perhaps to be taken in its general ethical sense (Slav. En. xlii. 13; *cf.* Did. v. 2) = Oriental duplicity.—**τοῖς δὲ**: as in LXX, the subject of the principal clause is thrown forward into the dative (Viteau, ii. 41, 42). The special standpoint of the Apoc. renders the terms of exclusion rather narrower than elsewhere (*cf.* Volz, 313). Thus there is no allusion to sins of omission, especially as regards justice and kindness between man and man (as Slav. En. x., xlii. 8-9, Matt. xxv. 41 f.—the former apocalypse finely excluding from heaven all guilty of "evil thoughts" and magic, all harsh or callous men, and finally all idolaters). The parallels with the rest of

9. καὶ ἦλθεν [f] εἷς ἐκ τῶν ἑπτὰ ἀγγέλων τῶν ἐχόντων τὰς ἑπτὰ
φιάλας, τῶν γεμόντων τῶν ἑπτὰ πληγῶν τῶν ἐσχάτων, καὶ ἐλάλησε
μετʼ ἐμοῦ λέγων "Δεῦρο, [g] δείξω σοι τὴν [h] νύμφην τὴν γυναῖκα[1]
τοῦ ἀρνίου." 10. καὶ [i] ἀπήνεγκέ με ἐν πνεύματι ἐπʼ [k] ὄρος μέγα
καὶ ὑψηλόν, καὶ ἔδειξέ μοι τὴν πόλιν, τὴν [l] ἁγίαν Ἱερουσαλὴμ,
καταβαίνουσαν ἐκ τοῦ οὐρανοῦ [m] ἀπὸ τοῦ θεοῦ, 11. ἔχουσαν τὴν
[n] δόξαν τοῦ θεοῦ· ὁ φωστὴρ αὐτῆς [o] ὅμοιος [p] λίθῳ τιμιωτάτῳ, ὡς

Cf. xv. 1, xvii. 1. iv. 1, xvii. 1. xix. 7, xxi. 2. xvii. 3; cf. Weinel, 202. Not a wilderness (xvii. 3). From Ezek. xl. 2. Contrast xi. 8. m xx. 9, xxi. 2. n xv. 8, ver. 23. o Sc. ἦν. p xvii. 4.

[1] την γυναικα a gloss from xix. 7? (Bousset, Könnecke, 39-40).

the Apocalypse, as well as the general style, indicate that xxi. 1-8 comes from the pen of the prophet himself; there is no evidence sufficient to support the conjecture that 5*b*-8 is a Christian editor's gloss in a Jewish original (Vischer, von Soden, S. Davidson, Rauch = 6 *b*-8, Spitta). The catalogue of vices, not unparalleled in ethnic literature (*cf.* Dieterich, pp. 163 f., 174 f., Heinrici on 2 Cor. vi. 4 f.), diverges from those of ix. 20-21 and xxii. 15. The second agrees with Sap. xiv. 22-28 in making idolatry the fontal vice, and with Did. v. in putting theft after **πορνεία** (*cf.* Heb. xiii. 4-5, Eph. v. 5, etc.). Paul, again, invariably starts with the blighting touch of **πορνεία** or **ἀκαθαρσία** (*cf.* Seeberg's *Catechismus d. Urc.* 9-29, and von Dobschütz, pp. 406 f.) as in xxii. 15. No special significance attaches to the lists of the Apocalypse beyond the obviously appropriate selection of idolatry (ix. 20) as the outstanding vice of paganism, with cowardice (xxi. 8) as the foil to victorious confession (xxi. 7, ii. 13, 17, xv. 2); note the division of xxii. 15 into the repulsive or filthy (first three) and the wicked (second three), corresponding to xxii. 11. The **κύνες** of xxii. 15 roughly answer to the "abominable" of xxi. 8. xxi. 1-8 are a summary of what follows: xxi. 1, 2=9-21, xxi. 3, 4=xxi. 22-xxii. 5, xxi. 5-8=xxii. 16-21.

xxi. 9-xxii. 5: the new Jerusalem (resuming the thought of ver. 2, *cf.* xix. 7), corresponding to the new universe (ver. 1). The fall of Jerusalem accentuated the tendency to rise from the expectation of a new or renovated city on earth to the hope of a heavenly, transcendent city (*cf.* Apoc. Bar. iv. 2-6, etc.), though the passionate desire for a restoration of city and temple in the messianic age was still strong (*cf.* *R. J.* 226 f., Volz, 334 f.). John introduces the definitely Christian identification of the heavenly Jerusalem with the bride of the messiah, and combines the various features of a renovated, a heavenly, and a preexistent city—features which occasionally reflect the mythological background of such earlier ideas in Judaism. The whole conception, if not the passage itself, is satirised by Lucian (*Vera Hist.* ii.) in his account of the golden city with its emerald wall, its river, and the absence of night, to say nothing of vines **δωδεκαφόροι καὶ κατὰ μῆνα ἕκαστον καρποφοροῦσιν.** Vv. 11-21 describe the exterior, vv. 22-27 the interior.

Ver. 10: a fresh vision, marked by a new transport of ecstasy (*cf.* Ezek. iii. 14, xi. 1, etc.).—**ὄρος**, the vantage-ground of elevation from which the seer views the site and buildings. If the hill is the site of the city, it is a truncated cone like Cirta, or a terraced *zikkurat*. Ezra sees the vision of the descent of the new Jerusalem in a field of flowers (*cf.* 4 Esd. ix. 26 f., xiii. 35 f.), but John follows either the older tradition of Enoch (En. xxiv., xxv.) who visited a high mountain which, as his cicerone Michael explained, was the throne of God "where the great and holy One, the Lord of glory, the King of eternity, will sit when he shall descend to visit the earth with goodness," or more probably the primitive association of paradise with a mountain (*cf.* Oesterley's *Evol. of Mess. Idea*, 129 f., Volz, 375).

Ver. 11. "With the dazzling splendour of God," *cf.* on ver. 3, Ezek. xliii. 5, Isa. lx. 1, 2. *Uxor splendet radiis mariti*; **δόξα**, here, as usually in a apocalyptic literature, denotes the manifestation and realisation of the divine presence. A realistic turn is given to the expression by the "shimmering radiance" of **ὁ φωστὴρ κ.τ.λ.** (asyndeton); "her brilliance is like a very precious stone, a jasper, crystal-clear" (*i.e.*, transparent and gleaming as rock-crystal). The

λίθῳ [q] ἰάσπιδι κρυσταλλίζοντι· 12. ἔχουσα τεῖχος μέγα καὶ ὑψηλόν,
ἔχουσα πυλῶνας δώδεκα, καὶ ἐπὶ τοῖς πυλῶσιν [r] ἀγγέλους δώδεκα,
καὶ ὀνόματα ἐπιγεγραμμένα ἅ ἐστι [s] τῶν δώδεκα φυλῶν υἱῶν
Ἰσραήλ. 13. ἀπ' ἀνατολῆς, πυλῶνες τρεῖς· καὶ ἀπὸ [t] βορρᾶ,
πυλῶνες τρεῖς· καὶ ἀπὸ νότου, πυλῶνες τρεῖς· καὶ ἀπὸ δυσμῶν,
πυλῶνες τρεῖς. 14. καὶ τὸ τεῖχος τῆς πόλεως ἔχων [u] θεμελίους
δώδεκα, καὶ ἐπ' αὐτῶν δώδεκα ὀνόματα [v] τῶν δώδεκα [v] ἀποστόλων
τοῦ ἀρνίου. 15. καὶ ὁ λαλῶν μετ' ἐμοῦ εἶχε μέτρον κάλαμον
χρυσοῦν, ἵνα μετρήσῃ τὴν πόλιν καὶ τοὺς πυλῶνας αὐτῆς καὶ τὸ
τεῖχος αὐτῆς. 16. καὶ ἡ πόλις [w] τετράγωνος κεῖται, καὶ τὸ μῆκος
αὐτῆς ὅσον τὸ πλάτος. καὶ ἐμέτρησε τὴν πόλιν τῷ καλάμῳ ἐπὶ
σταδίους δώδεκα χιλιάδων· τὸ μῆκος καὶ τὸ πλάτος καὶ τὸ ὕψος
αὐτῆς ἴσα ἐστί· 17. καὶ ἐμέτρησε τὸ τεῖχος αὐτῆς ἑκατὸν τεσσεράκοντα τεσσάρων [x] πηχῶν, [y] μέτρον ἀνθρώπου, ὅ ἐστιν ἀγγέλου.

q iv. 3.
r *Cf.* 2 Chron. viii. 14 From Isa. lxii. 6.
s vii. 4-8. From Ezek. xlviii. 31 f. (*cf.* En. xxxiv.-xxxv.).
t For form *cf.* Helbing, 33, Win. § 8, 2; more common in papyri than *βορέας* (Thumb, 65, 67, 56).
u Eph. ii. 20, Heb. xi. 10; *cf.* Isa. xxviii. 16.
v As in Asc. Isa. iii. 17, ix. 17, xi. 21.
w Like orig. Babylon, Herod. i. 178; figurative Hellen. term = "perfect" (Plato, *Protag.* 344A, Arist., *Eth. Nik.* I. x. 11).
x Contracted, Hellenistic genit. for *πήχεων* (Win. § 9, 6, Deissm. 153, Helbing, 44-45).
y Nom. absol. Vit. ii. 226, 332-3.

modern jasper is an opaque tinted quartz, only partially translucent at the edges. Perhaps, in reproducing Isa. liv. 11-12 (**καὶ θήσω τὰς ἐπάλξεις σου ἴασπιν καὶ τὰς πύλας σου λίθους κρυστάλλου**), the writer regarded both clauses as complementary (Cheyne); hence **ὡς λ. ἰ. κ.** Otherwise **ἴασπις** might represent an opal, a diamond, or a topaz, any one of which answers better to the description of "transparent and valuable". Flinders Petrie, however, suggests some variety of the dark green jasper.

Ver. 12. **ἔχουσα.** The constr. becomes still more irregular, the participles agreeing with an imaginary nominative, **ἡ πόλις,** sugg. by **ὁ φωστήρ.** The inscribed names denote the catholicity of the church and its continuity with the ancient people of God. A writer who could compose, or incorporate, or retain (as we choose to put it), passages like v. 9 and xiv. 4, is not to be suspected of particularism here. Even on the score of poetic congruity, the new Jerusalem implied such an archaic and traditional allusion to the twelve tribes. The angelic guardians of the gates are an Isaianic trait added to the Ezekiel picture.

Ver. 13. In one first century inscription (*cf.* Dittenberger's *Orientis Graeci Inscript. Selectae*, 199[32]) **ἀπὸ ἀνατολῆς** and **ἀπὸ δύσεως** are East and West respectively.

Ver. 14. **ἔχων,** another rough asyndeton.—**θεμελίους κ.τ.λ.,** a symbolical and corporate expression for the historical origin of the church in the primitive circle of the disciples who adhered to Jesus (*cf.* on xxii. 19). It is not their names but their historical and apostolic position which is in the writer's mind. The absence of Paul's name is no more significant than the failure to emphasise that of Peter. For the objective and retrospective tone of the allusion, with its bearing on the question of the authorship, see Introd. § 8. Foundation-stones in an ancient building were invested with high, sacred significance. Here the twelve apostles correspond roughly to the twelve **φύλαρχοι** of the Mosaic period (Matt. xix. 28, Clem. Rom. xlii.-xliii.).

Vv. 15-17. The measures of the city are now taken, as in Ezek. xl. 3, 48, xlii. 16 f., to elucidate the vision (otherwise in xi. 1, 2). It turns out to be an enormous quadrilateral cube, like Ezekiel's ideal sanctuary, a cube being symbolical of perfection to a Jew, as a circle is to ourselves. Whether 1500 miles represent the total circumference or the length of each side, the hyperbole is obvious, but John is following the patriotic rabbinic traditions which asserted that Jerusalem would extend as far as Damascus in the latter days (Zech. ix. 1) if not to the high throne of God. In Sib. Or. v. 250 f. the heaven-born Jews who inhabit Jerusalem are to run a wall as far as Joppa. Further measurements in Baba-Bathra f. 75, 2 (*cf.* Gfrörer, ii. 245 f.; Bacher,

18. καὶ ἡ [z] ἐνδώμησις τοῦ τείχους αὐτῆς [a] ἴασπις·
καὶ ἡ πόλις χρυσίον καθαρὸν ὅμοιον [b] ὑάλῳ καθαρῷ.
19. [c] οἱ θεμέλιοι τοῦ τείχους τῆς πόλεως παντὶ λίθῳ τιμίῳ
κεκοσμημένοι· ὁ θεμέλιος ὁ πρῶτος [d] ἴασπις· ὁ δεύτερος σάπφειρος·
ὁ τρίτος [e] χαλκηδών· ὁ τέταρτος [f] σμάραγδος· 20. ὁ πέμπτος
[g] σαρδόνυξ· ὁ ἕκτος [h] σάρδιον· ὁ ἕβδομος χρυσόλιθος· ὁ ὄγδοος
[i] βήρυλλος· ὁ ἔνατος [k] τοπάζιον· ὁ δέκατος χρυσόπρασος· ὁ ἑνδέκατος [l] ὑάκινθος· ὁ δωδέκατος, [m] ἀμέθυστος.
21. καὶ οἱ δώδεκα πυλῶνες δώδεκα μαργαρῖται·
[n] ἀνὰ [n] εἷς ἕκαστος τῶν πυλώνων ἦν ἐξ ἑνὸς μαργαρίτου·
καὶ ἡ [o] πλατεῖα τῆς πόλεως χρυσίον καθαρὸν, ὡς ὕαλος διαυγής.

z Poetical form, (*cf.* Jos. *Ant.* xv. 9, 6) = "fabric" or "material". a Ver. 11. b *Cf.* on iv. 6, ὑ. like φιάλη, a genuine form of the κοινή (Thumb, 18, 75). c From Isa. liv. 11-12. d iv. 3. e Here only (N.T.). f iv. 3, *cf.* fragm. in Epiph., *Haer.* xxxi. 9. g Red and white onyx (LXX = יהלום). h iv. 3. i Pale sea-green felspar, sometimes aquamarine in colour. k Greenish-yellow gem (periodot ?) *cf.* Job xxviii. 19. l ix. 17; jacinth or sapphire. m Violet or purple. n Late and irregular idiom = καθ' εἷς (Blass, § 39, 2, § 45, 3); *cf.* Win., § 26, 9, ἀνά adverbial, like ἕως (Deissm. 139). o xxii. 2.

Agada d. Tann. i. 194 f., 392). As in the case of the tabernacle in Jerusalem of the Hexateuch, so here: the symmetry and harmony of the divine life are naïvely represented by Oriental fantasy in terms of mathematics and architecture. A wall of about 72 yards high seems oddly unsymmetrical in view of the gigantic proportions of the city, though it might refer to the breadth (Simcox) or to the height of the city above the plain. But the whole description is built on multiples of twelve, a sacred number of completeness. The wall is a purely poetical detail, required to fill out the picture of the ancient city; like the similar touches in 24, 26, xxii. 2, it has no allegorical significance whatever. *Cf.* Slav. En. lxv. 10: "and there shall be to them" (*i.e.*, to the just in eternity) "a great wall which cannot be broken down".—**μέτρον κ.τ.λ.**, another naïve reminder (*cf.* xix. 9, 10, xxii. 8, 9) that angels were not above men.

Vv. 18-21: the materials of the city. **ἐνδώμησις,** so an undated but pre-Christian inscription, **τ. ἐνδώμησιν τοῦ τεμένους** (Dittenberger's *Sylloge inscript. Graec.*[2] 583[31]), where the orthography is pronounced "nova" (see reff.).

While the city itself (or its streets, ver. 21) is supposed to be constructed of transparent gold like the house of Zeus **πολύχρυσον** (*Hippol.* 69), the wall appearing above the monoliths or foundation-stones is made entirely of jasper, which again is the special ornament assigned to the first foundation-stone (19, see on ver. 11). The Babylonian *zikkurats* were picked out with coloured bricks; but the exterior of this second city is to be what only the interior of a Babylonian sanctuary had been—brilliant as the sun—flashing with precious stones and gold and silver. In Yasht xiii. 3 the heavenly Zoroastrian palace of the sky also "shines in its body of ruby." The general sketch is suggested by Isa. liv. 11, 12, and even more directly by Tobit xiii. 16, 17 ("For Jerusalem shall be builded with sapphire and emerald, thy walls with precious stones, the towers and battlements with pure gold; and the streets of Jerusalem shall be paved with beryl and carbuncle and stones of Ophir"). The Egyptian mansion of Life is also composed of jasper, with four walls, facing the south, the north, the east, and the west (*cf.* *Records of Past*, vi. 113). The twelve gems correspond upon the whole to those set in gold (*cf.* Ezek. xxviii. 13) upon the high priest's breastplate in P (Exod. xxviii. 17-20, xxxix. 10-13), which the writer loosely reproduces from memory. What the old covenant confined to the high priest is now a privilege extended to the whole people of God (*cf.* ver. 22); for the astrological basis and the relation of the two O.T. and the present lists, *cf.* Flinders Petrie in Hastings' *D. B.* iv. 619-621; Myres in *E. Bi.* 4800 f.; St. Clair in *Journ. Theol. Studies*, viii. 213 f.; and Jeremias, 68, 88 f. No occult or mystical significance attaches to these stones. The writer is simply trying to convey the impression of a radiant and superb structure.—**σάπφειρος**=lapis lazuli (sap-

22. καὶ [p] ναὸν οὐκ εἶδον ἐν αὐτῇ·
ὁ γὰρ [q] Κύριος ὁ θεὸς ὁ [q] παντοκράτωρ ναὸς αὐτῆς ἐστί, καὶ
τὸ ἀρνίον.
23. [r] καὶ ἡ πόλις οὐ χρείαν ἔχει τοῦ ἡλίου οὐδὲ τῆς σελήνης ἵνα
φαίνωσιν αὐτῇ·
ἡ γὰρ [s] δόξα τοῦ θεοῦ ἐφώτισεν αὐτήν,
καὶ ὁ λύχνος αὐτῆς τὸ ἀρνίον.

p Matt. xxiv. 2, John, iv. 21; also Jer. iii. 16 f.
q From Amos iv. 13.
r xxii. 5, from Isa. xxiv. 23, lx. 2, Zech. xiv. 7.
s Ver. 11; *cf.* 4 Esd. vii. 42. From Zech. ii. 5 (LXX), Ps. Sol. iii. 16.

phirus et aureis punctis collucet. Caeruleae et sapphiri, raroque cum purpura, Pliny, *H. N.* xxxvii. 39), a blue stone prized in Egypt and in Assyria, where it was often "used to overlay the highest parts of buildings" (*E. Bi.* 2710).—**χαλκηδών**=either a variety of dioptase or emerald gathered on a mountain in Chalcedon (Pliny), or more probably an agate (karkedrā Pesh. rendering of שבו =LXX **ἀχάτης** Ex. xxviii. 19), *i.e.*, a variegated stone, whose base is chalcedony. The modern chalcedony is merely a translucent (grey) quartz, with a milky tinge. **χρυσόλιθος** = a gem of some (sparkling?) golden hue (LXX= תרשיש), perhaps some variety of our topaz or beryl, which ranges from emerald-green to pale blue and yellow. The modern chrysolite is merely a hard greenish mineral, of no particular value. **χρυσόλιθος** and **χρυσόπρασος** (a leek-coloured gem) are probably varieties of the ancient beryl, unless the latter is the green chalcedony, and the former the modern topaz. **μαργαρῖται κ.τ.λ.** (on their value in the ancient world, see Usener's study in *Theol. Abhand.* 203-213): the conception is simplified from an old Jewish fancy of R. Jochanan preserved in Baba-Bathra, f. 75, 1, "Deus adducet gemmas et margaritas, triginta cubitos longas totidemque latas, easque excauabit in altitudinem xx cubitorum, et latitudinem x cubitorum, collocabitque in portis Hierosolymorum". **ἡ πλατεῖα**, generic = "the streets" (like **ξύλον**, xxii. 2), unless it has the sense of "forum" or "market-place" (as 2 Chron. xxxii. 6, Job xxix. 7 LXX). But the singular may allude to the fact that "the typical Eastern city had . . . one street which led from the void place at the entering in of the gate to the court of the king's palace" (Simcox). Philo (*quis haer.* § xliv., *leg. alleg.* § xx.) had already made gold emblematic of the divine nature diffused through all the world, owing to the metal's fusible qualities.

Ver. 22-xxii. 5: the life of the city. Ver. 22. The daily prayer of Jews at this time was "restore thou the sacrificial service to the Holy of Holies of thy house". But while this may have represented the popular religion of Judaism (Schürer, *Hist.* ii. 2, 174) which tenaciously clung to a restored temple as the religious centre of all future bliss, there were finer spirits who shared the Iranian repugnance to temples, possibly under a semi-Essene influence, and who seem to have partially anticipated the more spiritual outlook of the Apocalypse (*cf.* Baldensperger, 53 f.); the second temple, owing to the debasing strifes of the first century B.C. and the growing reverence for the law, never quite absorbed the religious consciousness as the first had done. The holy City is to be unlike many Chaldean cities where the temple was a dominating and distinctive feature, often indeed the original nucleus of the town. To the seer, earth suggests heaven not only by anticipation but by contrast.

Ver. 23. Another fulfilment of the O.T. ideal (Isa. lx. 19, 20). It is a Jewish-Christian symbol for Paul's thought—*God shall be all and in all.* So in 4 Esd. vii. [42] at the last judgment there is neither sun nor moon nor any natural light, "but only the splendour of the glory of the Most High". "As the *sun of righteousness* Christ has been able to vanquish the *sol inuictus* of the Roman Cæsar-cultus" (Usener, *Götternamen*, p. 184). A cruder form of the idea occurs in the pseudo-Philonic *Biblic. Antiquit.* where "non erat necessarium lumen (for the night-march), ita exsplendebat genuinum lapidum lumen" (*i.e.*, of the jewels on the Amorite idols), jewels which were replaced by twelve precious stones each engraved with the name of one of the twelve tribes.

24. καὶ περιπατήσουσι [t] τὰ ἔθνη διὰ τοῦ φωτὸς αὐτῆς,
καὶ οἱ [u] βασιλεῖς τῆς γῆς φέρουσι τὴν δόξαν αὐτῶν εἰς αὐτήν—
25. [v] καὶ οἱ πυλῶνες αὐτῆς οὐ μὴ κλεισθῶσιν ἡμέρας·
[w] νὺξ γὰρ οὐκ ἔσται ἐκεῖ—
26. [x] καὶ οἴσουσι τὴν δόξαν καὶ τὴν τιμὴν τῶν ἐθνῶν εἰς αὐτήν.
27. [y] καὶ οὐ μὴ εἰσέλθῃ εἰς αὐτὴν πᾶν κοινὸν καὶ ὁ ποιῶν
[z] βδέλυγμα καὶ [z] ψεῦδος·
εἰ μὴ οἱ [a] γεγραμμένοι ἐν τῷ βιβλίῳ τῆς ζωῆς τοῦ ἀρνίου.
XXII. 1. καὶ [a] ἔδειξέν μοι ποταμὸν [b] ὕδατος ζωῆς, λαμπρὸν ὡς
[c] κρύσταλλον, ἐκπορευόμενον ἐκ τοῦ θρόνου τοῦ θεοῦ [d] καὶ τοῦ ἀρνίου

t Ps. lxxii. 11, Is. lx. 3 f., Ps. Sol. xvii. 34-35. u Ps. lxviii. 29, lxxii. 10; reproduced in 4 Esd xv. 20. v Isa. lx. 11, Jos. *B.J.*, vii. 10, 4. w Zech. xiv. 7, En. lviii. 3 f., Slav. En. xxxi. 2. x From. Isa. lx. 5, Tob. xiii. 11, Sib. iii. 772 f. y Isa. lii. 1, Ezek. xliv. 9. z xxi. 8, xxii. 15; *cf.* Hom. *Iliad* iii. 278. a *Cf.* xiii. 8. a xxi. 10. b vii. 17. c iv. 6, ἅπ. λεγ. N.T. d iii. 21, v., 6, 13; *cf.* En. lxii. 14.

Vv. 24-26 further traits borrowed from Isa. lx. (see reff.).

Ver. 25. νὺξ κ.τ.λ. "for no night (when even in peace they would be shut, Neh. xiii. 19) shall be there".

Ver. 26. From the tradition of En. liii. 1 and Ps. Sol. xvii. 34-35 (where the Gentile nations seek Jerusalem **φέροντες δῶρα . . . καὶ ἰδεῖν τὴν δόξαν κυρίου, ἣν ἐδόξασεν αὐτὴν ὁ θεός**); *cf.* Apoc. Bar. lxviii. 5. The idea of 24 and 26 is of course literally inconsistent with those of xix. 17 f. and xx. 12 f., since on the new earth there were no residents except the risen saints. Both ideas were current in rabbinic eschatology (Gfrörer, ii. 238 f.), but the Apocalypse is entirely free from any such complacent estimate of Gentile outsiders (*cf.* En. xc. 30). The discrepancy here, as in xxii. 5, is imaginary. These details are simply poetical and imaginative, inserted from the older symbolism, in which they were quite appropriate, in order by their archaic and pictorial fulness to fill out the sketch of the future city. They have no allegorical significance.

Ver. 27. R. Jochanan (Baba-Bathra f. 76, 2,) said the coming Jerusalem would not be like the present one: in hanc ingreditur quicunque uult, in illam uero non nisi qui ad eam ordinati sunt. Citizenship similarly in John's new city is a matter of moral character and of divine election, not of nationality. The Lord's city is like the Lord's table, as the Ep. to Diognetus finely puts it (5) **κοινὴ ἀλλ' οὐ κοινή**, *communis* but not *profanus*, "common and open to all, yet in another sense no common thing." The trait is adapted from Slav. En. ix., where the garden-paradise of the third heaven is only for those loyal to their faith, humble, just, charitable and benevolent, blameless and whole hearted, while the hell of torture (x. 4-6) is reserved for all addicted to sodomy, witchcraft, theft, lying, murder, and fornication, besides oppression and callousness to human suffering. But **βδ.** and **ψ.** may be simply "idolatry" (as in LXX); the keynote of the book being struck once more (as in En. xcix. 9). In the Egyptian litany of the nine gods (*E. B. D.* 35) every petition ends with the words, "I have not spoken lies wittingly, nor have I done aught with deceit," and in Apoc. Bar. xxxix. 6 the seer accuses the Roman Empire thus: "by it the truth will be hidden, and all those who are polluted with iniquity will flee to it, as evil beasts flee and creep into the forest".

Chapter XXII.—Ver. 1. The river is suggested partly by Ezekiel's representation of the healing stream which was to issue from the new temple and flow through the dreary Ghor of the Jordan valley (xlvii. 1-12), partly by the reference (in a later apocalypse, Zech. xiv. 8) to perennial waters issuing from Jerusalem as the dwelling-place of God in the new age. John has no use for Ezekiel's idea that the stream would assist in the messianic transformation of nature. He changes the numerous trees on either side of the wady into the (generic) single tree of life, reverting as before (ii. 7) to the ideal of the Semitic paradise. Also, he drops the notion of the river sweetening the bitter waters of the Dead Sea. *Cf.* Pirke Eliezer, 51, aquae putei ascensurae sunt e limine templi atque scaturient prodibuntque. The Babylonian origin of the idea is outlined by Zimmern in *Archiv für Relig. Wiss.* 1899, 170 f. Unlike the

2. ἐν μέσῳ τῆς πλατείας αὐτῆς· καὶ τοῦ ποταμοῦ ἐντεῦθεν καὶ
ἐκεῖθεν [e] ξύλον ζωῆς, ποιοῦν καρποὺς [f] δώδεκα, κατὰ μῆνα [g] ἕκαστον
[h] ἀποδιδοὺς[1] τὸν καρπὸν αὐτοῦ· καὶ τὰ φύλλα τοῦ ξύλου εἰς [h] θερα-
πείαν τῶν ἐθνῶν.

3. [i] καὶ πᾶν κατάθεμα οὐκ ἔσται ἔτι·
[k] καὶ ὁ θρόνος τοῦ θεοῦ καὶ τοῦ ἀρνίου ἐν αὐτῇ ἔσται·
καὶ οἱ δοῦλοι αὐτοῦ [l] λατρεύσουσιν αὐτῷ·
4. καὶ [m] ὄψονται τὸ πρόσωπον αὐτοῦ,
καὶ [n] τὸ ὄνομα αὐτοῦ ἐπὶ τῶν μετώπων αὐτῶν.

e From Ezek. xlvii. 12, and Slav En. viii. 1-4.
f = δωδεκάκις (*cf.* Matt. xviii. 22).
g Win., §20 12*b*.
h For -όν (Win., § 14, 13), *cf.* Simcox, *Lang. N.T.* 40.
i From Zech. xiv. 21; on futures, see iv. 8-11.
k "Hence": *cf.* Josh. vi. 18, vii. 12.
l vii. 15.
m Job xlii. 5, Ps. xvii. 15, 1 John iii. 2, Heb. xii. 14, *cf.* Baldensperger, 63.
n iii. 12, xiv. 1, vii. 3-4.

[1] Ti., Tr., WH (marg.), Bs. rightly read **αποδιδους** (with ℵQ, min., Areth.).

earthly Jerusalem with its inferior stream, the new city is to be richly equipped with conduits and all that makes a city prosperous and secure (Isa. xxxiii. 21).

Ver. 2. **πλατείας** ("street," or "boulevard") collective and generic (*cf.* Jas. v. 6) like **ξύλον.** Take **ἐν . . . αὐτῆς** with what precedes, and begin a fresh sentence with **καὶ τοῦ ποταμοῦ** (W. H.), **ξύλον** being governed by **ἔδειξεν** (from ver. 1). The river, which is the all-pervading feature, is lined with the trees of life. The writer retains the traditional singular of Gen. ii. 9, combining it with the representation of Ezekiel (yet note sing. in xlvii. 12); he thus gains symbolic impressiveness at the expense of pictorial coherence. Ramsay (*C. B. P.* ii. 453) observes, however, that the waters of the Marsyas were "probably drawn off to flow through the streets of Apameia; this practice is still a favourite one in Asia Minor, *e.g.*, at Denizli".—**κ. μῆνα,** the poetic imagination soars over the prosaic objection that months are impossible without a moon (xxi. 22).—**καρπὸν, κ.τ.λ.** To eat of the tree of life was, in the popular religious phraseology of the age, to possess immortality. In En. xxiv., xxv., where the prophet sees a wonderful, fragrant tree, Michael explains that it must stand untouched till the day of Judgment (**καὶ οὐδεμία σὰρξ ἐξουσίαν ἔχει ἅψασθαι αὐτοῦ**). "Then the righteous and the holy shall have it given them; it shall be as food for the elect unto life." So in contemporary Judaism; *e.g.*, 4 Esd. vii. 53 and viii. 52 ("For unto you is paradise set open, the tree of life is planted, the time to come is prepared, a city is builded and rest is established,") as already in *Test. Levi*, 18, where the messianic high-priest is to "open the gates of paradise and remove the sword drawn against Adam, and permit the saints to eat of the tree of life". For the association of God's city and God's garden, *cf.* Apoc. Bar. iv. : for the notion of healing, Apoc. Mos. vi., Jub. x. 12 f., and the Iranian idea that (Brandt, 434 f.) the tree of many seeds had curative properties. John is therefore using the realistic and archaic language of Jewish piety to delineate the bliss of Christians in a future state where all the original glories and privileges of God's life with man are to be restored. The Christian heaven is to possess everything which Judaism claimed and craved for itself. *Cf.* the Christian addition to 4 Esd. ii. 12, 34, 35, 38 f.; also the famous hymn to Osiris (*E. B. D.*, ch. clxxxiii. : "I have come into the city of God—the region which existed in primaeval time—with my soul, to dwell in this land. . . . The God thereof is most holy. His land draweth unto itself every other land. And doth he not say, the happiness thereof is a care to me?").

Ver. 3. **κατάθεμα,** a corrupt and rare form of **κατανάθεμα** = anything accursed (lit. a curse itself, Did. xvi. 8), *i.e.*, abstract for concrete, here = "a cursed person," so Ps. Sol. xvii. 29 f.—**λατρεύσουσι,** unfettered and unspoiled devotion. The interruption of the daily service and sacrifice in Jerusalem on 17th July, 70 A.D., had sent a painful thrill to the heart of all who cherished the ideal of Acts xxvi. 7. No fear of that in the new Jerusalem!

Ver. 4. The ancient ideal of intimate confidence is also to be realised (*cf.* on Matt. v. 8 and Iren. *Adv. Hær.* v. 7). With this phrase and that of xxi. 22 compare Browning's lines: "Why,

o xxi. 25.
p xxi. 23; with accus. iii. 17.
q Dan. vii. 27, *cf.* Sap. vi. 21 (= nearness to God).

5. **καὶ [o] νὺξ οὐκ ἔσται ἔτι,**
καὶ οὐχ ἕξουσι [1] [p] χρείαν φωτὸς λύχνου καὶ φῶς ἡλίου,
ὅτι Κύριος ὁ θεὸς φωτίσει ἐπ' αὐτούς·
καὶ [q] βασιλεύσουσιν [r] εἰς τοὺς αἰῶνας τῶν αἰώνων.

r Not merely for 1000 years (xx. 4).

[1] **εξουσι** (A, vg., Syr., S., gig., Tic.) Bentley, Lach., Al., Bj., is preferable to **εχουσι** (ℵP, And.), and the context, with its futures and personal pronouns, tells against the **ου χρεια κ.τ.λ.** of Q, min., S., Pr. (Ti., Düst., Bs.).

where's the need of temple when the walls | O' the world are that . . . This one Face, far from vanish, rather grows | Becomes my universe that feels and knows." The idea here is that reproduced in the seventh and supreme degree of bliss in 4 Esd. vii. [78] where the saints "shall rejoice with confidence, have boldness undismayed, and gladness unafraid, for they shall hasten to behold the face of him whom they served in life". By Oriental usage, no condemned or criminal person was allowed to look on the king's face (Esther vii. 8), In the ancient ch. lxiv. of *E. B. D.* (papyrus of Nu) the "triumphant Nu saith, 'I have come to see him that dwelleth in his divine uraeus, face to face, and eye to eye. . . . Thou art in me, and I am in thee,'" The Apocalypse, however, shuns almost any approach to the inner union of the individual Christian and Christ which distinguished both Paul and the fourth gospel; it also eschews the identification of God and man which was often crudely affected by Egyptian eschatology. No allusion occurs to the supremacy of the saints over angels (Ap. Bar. li. 12, etc.), though John is careful elsewhere to keep the latter in their place (see on xxi. 17, xxii. 9). He also ignores the problem of different degrees in bliss,—**ὄψονται.** In Chag. 5 *b* there is a story of a blind rabbi who blessed some departing visitors with the words, "Ye have visited a face that is seen and sees not: may ye be counted worthy to visit the Face which sees and is not seen". The Christian prophet has a better hope and promise. Compare, however, Plutarch's touching faith (*Iside*, 79) that the souls of men after death will "migrate to the unseen, the good," when God becomes their king and leader and where "they, as it were, hang upon him and gaze without ever wearying, and yearn for that unspeakable, indescribable Beauty".

Ver. 5. Philo (*de Jos.* 24) had already described heaven as **ἡμέραν αἰώνιον, νυκτὸς καὶ πάσης σκιᾶς ἀμέτοχον.** *Cf.* En. vi. 6.—Such teaching on heaven, though in a less religious form, seems to have been current among the Asiatic **πρεσβύτεροι.** Irenæus (v. 36, 1-2) quotes them as holding (*cf.* above on ii. 7) that some of the blessed **τῆς τοῦ παραδείσου τρυφῆς ἀπολαύσουσιν, οἱ δὲ τὴν λαμπρότητα τῆς πόλεως καθέξουσιν· πανταχοῦ γὰρ ὁ Σωτὴρ ὁρασθήσεται, καθὼς ἄξιοι ἔσονται οἱ ὁρῶντες αὐτόν, κ.τ.λ.**

The epilogue (6-21) is a series of loose ejaculations, which it is not easy to assign to the various speakers. It is moulded on the lines of the epilogue to the astronomical section of Enoch (lxxxi. f.) where Enoch is left for one year with his children—"that thou mayest testify to them all. . . . Let thy heart be strong, for the good will announce righteousness to the good, but the sinners will die with the sinners, and the apostates go down with the apostates". Two characteristic *motifs*, however, dominate the entire passage: (*a*) the vital importance of this book as a valid and authentic revelation, and (*b*) the nearness of the end. The former is heard in the definite claim of inspiration (6 f., 16) and prophetic origin (8, 9) which guarantees its contents, in the beatitude of 7 *b* (*cf.* 17), and (*cf.* 21) in the claim of canonical dignity (18, 19). The latter is voiced thrice in a personal (7, 12, 20) and twice in an impersonal (6, 10) form. Both are bound up together (*cf.* 20 and i. 3). It is as a crucial revelation of the near future and a testimony to the authority and advent of the messiah (*cf.* 20) that this apocalypse claims to be read, and honoured in the churches. This general standpoint is clear enough, but the details are rather intricate. It is characteristic of the Apocalyse, as of ep. Barnabas, that the writer often leaves it indefinite whether God or Christ or an angel is speaking. Sometimes the divine voice is recognised to be that of Christ

8. [s]κἀγὼ Ἰωάννης ὁ [t]βλέπων καὶ ἀκούων ταῦτα· καὶ ὅτε ἤκουσα
καὶ ἔβλεψα, ἔπεσα προσκυνῆσαι ἔμπροσθεν τῶν ποδῶν τοῦ ἀγγέλου
τοῦ [u]δεικνύοντός μοι ταῦτα. 9. καὶ λέγει μοι, "ὅρα μή·
σύνδουλός σού εἰμι καὶ τῶν ἀδελφῶν σου τῶν προφητῶν καὶ τῶν
τηρούντων τοὺς λόγους τοῦ βιβλίου τούτου· τῷ θεῷ προσκύνησον."
6. καὶ εἶπέν μοι, "Οὗτοι οἱ λόγοι [v]πιστοὶ καὶ ἀληθινοί· καὶ
ὁ [w]κύριος ὁ θεὸς τῶν [w]πνευμάτων τῶν προφητῶν ἀπέστειλε [x]τὸν
ἄγγελον αὐτοῦ δεῖξαι τοῖς [y]δούλοις αὐτοῦ ἃ δεῖ γενέσθαι ἐν τάχει.
7. καὶ ἰδοὺ ἔρχομαι ταχύ.

[z]μακάριος ὁ τηρῶν τοὺς λόγους τῆς προφητείας τοῦ βιβλίου τούτου."

s As in i. 9 (*cf.* Dan. xii. 5).
t 2 Cor. xii. 2.
u Win. § 14, 18.
v 4 Esd. xv. 1-2 ("Speak thou in the ears of my people the words of prophecy, and cause thou them to be written on paper, for they are faithful and true"). w *Cf.* for phrase, partial analogies in Num. xxvii. 16 (LXX), Jub. x. 3, Dan. ii. 28, 2 Macc. iii. 24, Heb. xii. 9, 1 Cor. xiv. 32. x *Cf.* i. 1-2. y *i.e.*, the Christian prophets (i. 1), *cf.* Dan. ix. 10, 4 Esd. viii. 62. z *Cf.* Luke xi. 28, En. c. 6, civ. 12-13.

(*cf.* i. 10 f., iv. 1), or may be inferred from the context to be that of an angel (*e.g.*, xvii. 15, *cf.* 1 and xix. 9), perhaps as the divine spokesman (xxi. 5, 6, *cf.* 5 and 7). But frequently, even when the seer is addressed (x. 4, xiv. 13), the voice or Bath-Qol is anonymous (*e.g.*, xi. 12, xii. 10, xiv. 2, xvi. 1, *cf.* 17). In the epilogue, as it stands, it is impossible and irrelevant to determine whether Jesus (16) begins to speak at ver. 10 (so Spitta, Holtzm, Porter, Forbes) and resumes in 18-20 *a*. But, while 6-7, and 8-9 are both intended in a sense to round off the entire Apocalypse, and not merely the immediately preceding vision, 8-9 (a replica of xix. 9-10) stands closer to xxi. 9-xxii. 5 than does 6-7. No λόγοι in the last vision justify the reference in 6, whereas the specific δεικν. μοι ταῦτα in 8 echoes the cicerone-function of the angel in xxi. 9-10, xxii. 1. Vv. 6, 7 very probably lay originally between 9 and 10 (for the juxtaposition of εἶπεν and λέγει *cf.* xvii. 7, 15), where they definitely mark the beginning of the epilogue already anticipated in 8 (*cf.* i. 4, 9) and in the broadened close of 9 (contrast xix. 10 above). It is not necessary (though perhaps a later scribe may have thought so) to account for John's action in 8-9 by supposing that he mistook the *angelus interpres* for Christ. The λόγοι of 6, when this order is adopted, acquire their natural sense (*cf.* 10), and the three successive angel-utterances (8-9, 6-7, 10-11) have a proper sequence. It is needless, in view of xvi. 15 (*cf.* iii. 11) to omit 7 *a* as an interpolation (Könnecke). But 12-13 probably have been displaced from their original order (13, 12) and position after 16 (Könnecke), where 17 echoes 12 *a*, and 14, 15 carries on the thought of 11. Vv. 18, 19 are plainly editorial, interrupting the connexion of 17 and 20. In 11 Resch (*Agrapha*, § 113) attempts to prove that some logion of Jesus is quoted. On the "inconsistent optimism" of xxii. 13 and 15, *cf.* Abbott, p. 107.

Ver. 8. There is no trace of any reluctance on the prophet's part to return to earth, as in Asc. Isa. (Gk.), ii. 33-35.

Ver. 9. The warning against any Christian θρησκεία τῶν ἀγγέλων is not, as in the parallel passage, an indirect exaltation of the prophetic order as equivalent to the angelic in religious function, but an assertion that even ordinary Christians who accept the Apocalypse are equal to the hierophant angel. Unlike Nebo, the angelic interpreter of Marduk's will in Babylonian religion, he is not to be worshipped, for all his importance. Precautions against angel-worship could hardly be more stringent. "The repetition of the scene is enough to show that it does not represent a natural ebullition of feeling and its corretction, but that the narrative has a purpose . . . and that those who observed the practice made use of" John's name, or at any rate believed they could appeal to him as sanctioning their superstition (Weizäcker, ii. 203-204).

Ver. 6. As in En. cviii. 6 (only mention of prophets in Enoch), "what God announces through the mouth of the prophets" relates to the future.—πνευμ. the plurality of spirits is an archaic detail (*cf.* i. 4) adapted also from the Enochic formula (xxxvii. 2, etc.), "God of the spirits".

Ver. 7. Here as elsewhere it is irrelevant to ask, who is the speaker? Angels

10. καὶ λέγει μοι, "Μὴ σφραγίσῃς τοὺς λόγους τῆς προφητείας
τοῦ βιβλίου τούτου· ὁ [a] καιρὸς γὰρ ἐγγύς ἐστιν.
11. [b] ὁ ἀδικῶν ἀδικησάτω ἔτι·
καὶ ὁ [c] ῥυπαρὸς ῥυπανθήτω ἔτι·
καὶ ὁ δίκαιος δικαιοσύνην ποιησάτω ἔτι·
καὶ ὁ ἅγιος ἁγιασθήτω ἔτι.[1]
14. Μακάριοι οἱ [d] πλύνοντες τὰς στολὰς αὐτῶν, [e] ἵνα ἔσται ἡ
[f] ἐξουσία αὐτῶν [f] ἐπὶ [g] τὸ [g] ξύλον τῆς ζωῆς καὶ τοῖς [h] πυλῶσιν εἰσέλ-
θωσιν εἰς τὴν πόλιν.[2] 15. [i] ἔξω οἱ [k] κύνες καὶ οἱ [l] φαρμακοὶ καὶ

a i. 3. b From Ezek. iii. 27, Dan. xii. 10 (LXX), *cf. Par. Lost*, iii. 198 f. c "Filthy" (*cf.* Mayor on Jas. i. 21): moral stains (Job xv. 16), not mere ceremonial impurity (ῥυπαρᾷ ἐσθῆτι, in votive inscriptions). d iii. 4, vii. 14. e Mixed construction (*cf.* xiv. 13). f Accus. here and vi. 8, xiii. 7, xvi. 9; genit. ii. 26, xi. 6, xiv. 18. g *Cf.* ver. 2. h Loose extension of dat. instrum. i "Out with the (or, out ye)": so Düst., Benson, J. Weiss, Wellh., *cf.* xxi. 8, 27, 1 Cor. vi. 9-10, Introd. § 6. k Matt. vii. 6, Phil. iii. 2: = "praua concupiscentia" (Gfrörer, i. 404). l ix. 21, *cf.* Deut. xxiii. 18. On their punishment in the Hellenic world, *cf.* Rohde's *Psyche*, 366 f.

[1] The ample style of the Apoc. tells against the conjecture (Zahn, Nestle's *Einf.* 264-265; Bebb, *Studia Biblica*, ii. 209-210) that the orig. reading is preserved in Ep. Lugd. **ο ανομος ανομησατω και ο δικαιος δικαιωθητω ετι,** the rest being glossematic. The v. l. **δικαιωθητω** (38, 79, vg.) has been mechanically conformed to **αγιασθητω.**

[2] Instead of the well-supported ΟΙΠΟΙΟΥΝΤΕΣΤΑΣΕ̄ΤΟΛΑΣΑΥΤΟΥ (Q, min., Syr., S., Arm., Me., Areth., And., Tert., Tic., Cyp., *cf.* 1 Jo. v. 21; so de Wette, Düst., Bs.), ΟΙΠΛΥΝΟΝΤΕΣΤΑΣΣΤΟΛΑΣΑΥΤΩΝ (ℵA, 7, 38, vg., Aeth., Pr., Haym., etc., edd.) is to be read, the variant being possibly due to the feeling that some moral characteristic was needful after 11 (Ws.).

are the envoys and mouthpieces of God here as in the O.T., and therefore entitled to speak in his name or in that of Christ. "The Oriental mind hardly distinguishes between an ancient personage and one who appears in his power and spirit" (A. B. Davidson on Ezek. xxxiv. 23). In 4 Esd. v. 31-40 the angel is also addressed as if he were the Lord—the angelic personality evidently fading into the divine, as here, and the writer being equally unconscious of any incongruity in the representation (*cf.* Zech. iii. 1-4). As the "showing" of the **ἃ δ. γ. ἐν τ.** is (i. 1) an **ἀποκ.** of Jesus, he (or a word of his) naturally breaks in (7 *a*).—**τηρῶν κ.τ.λ.**, an apocalyptic form of emphasis. *Cf. e.g.*, Slav. En. xlvii. 1-3 and xxxvi ("tell thou thy sons and all thy household before Me, that they may listen to what is spoken to them by thee . . . and let them always keep my commandments, and begin to read and understand the books written out by thee"). All apocalypses were meant to be transmitted to mankind, but the usual method of delivery is complicated (*cf.* En. lxxxii. 1, 2; Slav. En. xxxiii. 9, xlvii. 2, 3, etc.).

Ver. 10. The book of Daniel, the great classic of apocalyptic literature, is represented (*cf.* Slav. En. xxxiii. 9-11, xxxv. 3; En. xciii. 10, civ. 12, etc.) as having been providentially kept secret at the time of its composition, since it referred to a future period (viii. 26, xii. 4, 9). This was a literary device, to explain why it had not been divulged before. As John's apocalypse is for an immediate crisis, it is not to be reserved for days to come. It is not merely valid (7) but intended for the prophet's contemporaries (unlike Isa. xxx. 8, *cf.* Cheyne's note), though reserved, like most of its class, as esoteric literature for the "wise" (contrast 4 Esd. xiv. 38-48). Some interval, however, is presupposed between the vision and its fulfilment, otherwise it would be futile to write the visions down, and to arrange for their circulation throughout the churches. A certain career (7, 9, 18-19) is anticipated for the Apocalypse. But (ver. 11.) persistence in good and evil is about all the writer expects—a stereotyped feature of the apocalyptic outlook on the obduracy of the wicked and the perseverance of the saints. Apocalyptic never encouraged propaganda, and no radical or widespread change is anticipated during the brief interval before the end. As in Dan. xii. 10, 11, so here, the crisis simply accentuates and accelerates human character along previous lines. No anxiety is shown, however, as in 4 Esd. iv. 50 f., whether the prophet himself is to see the end.

Ver. 15. **κύνες, an** archaic metaphor,

οἱ πόρνοι καὶ οἱ φονεῖς καὶ οἱ εἰδωλολάτραι καὶ πᾶς [m] φιλῶν καὶ
ποιῶν ψεῦδος."

16. "Ἐγὼ Ἰησοῦς [n] ἔπεμψα τὸν ἄγγελόν μου μαρτυρῆσαι [o] ὑμῖν
ταῦτα [p] ἐπὶ ταῖς ἐκκλησίαις·

ἐγώ εἰμι ἡ [q] ῥίζα καὶ τὸ γένος Δαυείδ,
ὁ [r] ἀστὴρ ὁ λαμπρὸς καὶ ὁ πρωϊνός.

m xxi. 27, *cf.* Asc. Isa. (Gk.), iii. 3, Dan. viii. 25. See Win. § 20, 11*c*.
n *Cf.* xxii. 6 (God).
o (Dat. = Heb. x. 15) "the prophets," as in ver. 6.
p = "for" (x. 11).
q v. 5: (the scion).
r ii. 28, Sir. l, 6, Test. Levi 18, En. xxxviii. 2, Isa. xiv. 12, and Ign. *Eph.* xix, with Luke i. 78 (Dalman, i. viii. 10).

coloured by the nomad's hatred of hounds; *cf. Arabia Deserta*, i. 337, 339 ("only the dog has no citizenship in the nomad life". "It is the only life mishandled by the gentle Arab, who with spurns and blows cast out these profane creatures from the tent.") Here **κύνες** are not merely impure pagans, but the impudently impure, possibly in the special and darker sense of "sodomites" (*cf.* 1 Tim. i. 10; Deut. xxiii. 19, 20, collated with **πόρνη** and **βδέλυγμα**). *Cf.* on xxi. 8 and Cooke's *North Sem. Inscriptions*, p. 68. Such loathsome practices were not uncommon in the Oriental cults.

Ver. 16. Jesus in person now speaks in the colloquy (16, 13, 12) to ratify what has just been said. This apocalypse is not an individual fantasy (2 Peter i. 21). For the contemporary need of such accrediting, *cf.* Herm. *Sim.* ix. 22 and Asc. Isa. iii. 30, 31 (where in the last days "everyone will say what is pleasing in his own eyes. And they will make of none effect the prophecy of the prophets which were before me, and these my visions also will they make of none effect, in order to speak after the impulse of their own hearts.")—**ἄγγελον,** not John (Weiss, Wellh.) but the *angelus interpres* (*cf.* on i. 2 and 20).—**ὑμῖν,** the plural here and in ver. 6 (*cf.* i. 1) might suggest that John's apocalypse incorporated some visions of other members belonging to the prophets in the Asiatic circle or school (*cf.* the tradition about the co-operative origin of the Fourth gospel, in the Muratorian canon). But while any Jewish Christian sources may have been drawn from this quarter, the final authorship and authority is claimed by (or, for) John himself (*cf.* ver. 8).—**Δαυείδ.** Like most early Christians, John attached more weight to the Davidic descent of Jesus as messiah (Baldensperger, 82 f.), than Jesus himself allowed. Here Christ's authority in revelation is bound up with his legitimate claim to be messiah, and thus to inaugurate the new and eternal day of God. As **ἀνατολή** (the dawn = צֶמַח) was already a messianic symbol, and employed in LXX (Jer. xxiii. 5, Zech. iii. 8, vi. 12) to denote the messianic branch or stem, this double usage explains the imagery here (so Justin, *Apol.* i. 32). Jesus has not only the historic preparation of Israel behind him but the infinite future before him. In one sense he was the climax of Hebrew expectation; in another, he is of world-wide significance. In connexion with the heavenly Jerusalem it was natural that Jesus should be hailed as the scion of the David who had founded the first Jerusalem. The star-metaphor reflects the significance of the morning-star which meant the beginning of a new day for toilers in the Levant; but its eschatological outlook was taken ultimately from Babylonian astro-theology, where Nebo-Mercury (nebî = prophet), the morning-star, announced the new era, or from Egyptian theology where (*cf. E. B. D.* p. cxliii.) Pepi the dead king "goeth forth into heaven among the stars which never perish, and his guide the Morning-Star leadeth him to Sekhet-Ḥetep [the fields of peace]". The phraselogy brings out the conviction of the early church that the present trial was only the cold, dark hour before the dawn. Their faith in Jesus assured them that an eternal prospect of bliss awaited them, and that this vista of hope was bound up with the person of the risen Jesus (*cf.* ver. 13). The watchword was, sunrise and morning-star (*cf. Expos.* Dec. 1902, 424-441). Christianity was not some ephemeral Oriental cult, which had had its day; the cosmic overthrow meant a new era for its adherents. The Apocalypse thus closes, as it began (i. 5, 6) with a note of ringing emphasis upon the eternal significance of Christ in the divine plan and purpose.

13. [s] ἐγὼ τὸ [t] ἄλφα καὶ τὸ ὦ,
ὁ πρῶτος καὶ ὁ ἔσχατος,
ἡ [t] ἀρχὴ καὶ τὸ τέλος.
12. ἰδοὺ ἔρχομαι ταχύ,
καὶ ὁ [u] μισθός μου μετ᾽ ἐμοῦ,
[v] ἀποδοῦναι [w] ἑκάστῳ ὡς τὸ ἔργον ἐστὶν αὐτοῦ."
17. καὶ τὸ πνεῦμα καὶ ἡ νύμφη λέγουσιν, "Ἔρχου"·
καὶ [x] ὁ ἀκούων εἰπάτω, "Ἔρχου".
καὶ ὁ [y] διψῶν ἐρχέσθω,
ὁ [z] θέλων λαβέτω ὕδωρ ζωῆς δωρεάν.
[18. Μαρτυρῶ ἐγὼ παντὶ τῷ ἀκούοντι τοὺς λόγους τῆς προφητείας τοῦ βιβλίου τούτου·
ἐάν τις [a] ἐπιτιθῇ ἐπ᾽ αὐτά,
ἐπιθήσει ὁ θεὸς ἐπ᾽ αὐτὸν τὰς [b] πληγὰς τὰς γεγραμ-
μένας ἐν τῷ βιβλίῳ τούτῳ
19. καὶ ἐάν ἀφέλῃ ἀπὸ τῶν λόγων τοῦ βιβλίου
τῆς προφητείας ταύτης,

s God (xxi. 6, *cf.* i. 8), Christ (i. 17, ii. 8).
t *Cf.* Jos. *Ant.* viii. 11, 2, *Ap.* ii. 22, Philo: *de Somn.* 620 (of Logos), Plato, *Legg.* iv. 7. A common rabbinic symbol for God (Gfrörer, i. 285 f.).
u xi. 18, Isa. xl. 10, Sap. v. 15, 2 Pet. ii. 18, *cf.* Clem. Rom. xxxiv.
v Rom. ii. 5-6.
w *Cf.* i. 7 (πᾶς ὀφθ.). ii 23, etc.
x The individual Christian (*cf.* 1 Cor. xvi. 22).
y xxi. 6 (Isa. lv. 1).
z John iv. 14, vii. 37.
a Prov. xxx. 6, Jos. *Ap.* i. 8.
b xv. 6-xvi. 21.
c Jer. xxvi. 2, *cf.* Deut. iv. 2, xiii. 1, Barn. xix. 11, Did. iv. 13.

Ver. 13 gathers up the double thought of 16 and of 12. As the Christian **ἔργα** (ii. 2, 5, 19, etc.) are done within the sphere of faith, their recompense is a religious as well as a thoroughly moral conception (*cf.* Hastings' *D. B.* iii. 82, and Montefiore's *Hibbert Lectures*, p. 538). To the day's work, the day's wage. For the origin of this feeling on Syrian or Semitic soil, where the *fellahin's* work "was scrutinised before the wages were paid" by one who was "at once the paymaster of his dependents and their judge," *cf.* Hatch's *Hibb. Lectures*, pp. 224 f. and Dalman, i. § viii. 3. The reward, like the new Jerusalem, was safely stored in heaven. No fear of inadequate moral appreciation in the next world, at any rate!

Ver. 17. The promise of 12 *a* is caught up and answered by a deep "come" from the prophets in ecstasy (**πνεῦμα** personified, *cf.* ii. 7, etc.) and the Christian congregation.—**νύμφη.** Hitherto (xxi. 2, etc.) this term has been reserved for the church triumphant in the world to come. Now, with the memory of these oracles fresh in his mind, the prophet applies it to the church on earth, as Paul had already done.—**καὶ ὁ ἀκούων κ.τ.λ.**, a liturgical note, like Mark xiii. 14 (*cf.* Weinel, 84, 85).—**καὶ ὁ διψῶν κ.τ.λ.**, addressed to strangers who sometimes attended the Christian worship (*cf.* 1 Cor. xiv. 23, 24). For this fine turn of expression (the double use of *come*), *cf.* Did. x. 6, "may grace come and may this wórld pass away. Hosanna to the God of David! If anyone is holy let him come [*i.e.*, to the Lord's table]; if anyone is not, let him repent. Mārāna thā" (*cf.* below, ver. 20). The less likely alternative is to take **ἔρχου** here as addressed not to Jesus but to the outside world.

Vv. 18-19. Luther strongly objected to the extravagant threat of this editorial note. The curse is certainly not only an anti-climax like the editorial postscript in John xxi. 24, 25 (both indicating that either when published or when admitted to the canon, these two scriptures needed special authentication) but "an unfortunate ending to a book whose value consists in the spirit that breathes in it, the bold faith and confident hope which it inspires, rather than in the literalness and finality of its disclosures" (Porter). But the words are really a stereotyped and vehement form of claiming a canonicity equal to that of the O.T. (*cf.* Jos. *Ant.* xx. 11. 2, **τοσούτου γὰρ αἰῶνος ἤδη παρῳχηκότος οὔτε προσθεῖναί τις οὔτε ἀφελεῖν ἀπ᾽ αὐτῶν οὔτε μετα-**

ἀφελεῖ ὁ θεὸς τὸ μέρος αὐτοῦ [d] ἀπὸ τοῦ ξύλου
τῆς ζωῆς καὶ ἐκ τῆς πόλεως
τῆς ἁγίας, τῶν γεγραμμ-
ένων ἐν τῷ βιβλίῳ τούτῳ.]
20. Λέγει ὁ μαρτυρῶν ταῦτα [e] "Ναὶ· ἔρχομαι ταχύ".
[f] ἀμήν· ἔρχου, κύριε Ἰησοῦ.

21. ἡ χάρις τοῦ Κυρίου Ἰησοῦ μετὰ πάντων.[1]

d In *Apoc. Mos.* xvi. by overpowering Adam and Eve in temptation, the devil robs them "of the garden of delight and of eternal life".

e For the third time (7, 12): "Most assuredly, I am coming speedily".

f *Cf.* on xix. 4.

[1] Om. Pr.—Of the variants for **παντων υμων** (vg., Aeth.), either **παντων των αγιων** (Q, min., Me., Syr., S., Arm., And., Areth., Bs.) or preferably **παντων** (A, am., Lach., Ti., Düst., Ws.) seems more original than **των αγιων** (א, gig., Tr., Al., Simcox, WH, Bj., J. Weiss, Sw.): for a textual discussion see Nestle's *Einführung*, 125 f. (E. Tr., 157 f.) and Hastings' *D. B.*, iv. 733.—After **Ιησου, Χριστου** is added by Q, min., vg., gig., Syr., Arm., Aeth., Andr.

θεῖναι τετόλμηκεν). They are adapted from Enoch civ. 10 f. where the author expects his book to be a comfort and joy to the righteous, but exposed to perversion and alteration: "Many sinners will pervert and alter the words of uprightness" instead of refusing to "change or minish aught from my words". Similar threats to careless or wilful copyists especially in Irenæus (Eus. *H. E.* v. 20), and Rufin. pref. to Origen's **περὶ ἀρχῶν** (*cf.* Nestle's *Einführung*, 161 f.). This nervous eagerness to safeguard Christian teaching was part and parcel of the contemporary tendency to regard apostolic tradition (*cf.* xviii. 20, xxi. 14, etc.) as a body of authoritative doctrine, which must not be tampered with. An almost equally severe threat occurs in Slav. En. xlviii. 7-9, liv. (also iii. 3), so that the writer, in this jealousy for the letter rather than for the spirit, was following a recognised precedent (*R. J.* 125 f.), which was bound up with a conservative view of tradition and a juristic conception of scripture (Titius, pp. 206 f., Deissm, 113 f.). Rabbinic *librarii* got a similar warning in that age (*cf.* Bacher's *Agada d. Tann*, i. 254), and Christian copyists, if not editors, required it in the case of the Apocalypse, although apparently they paid little heed to it, for as early as the time of Irenæus there were serious discrepancies in the copies circulated throughout the churches. John had himself omitted a contemporary piece of prophecy (*cf.* on x. 4). But he explains that he was inspired to do so; this verse refuses to let others deal similarly with his book.

The prayer of ver. 17 is answered in ver. 20, which repeats the assurance of the messiah's speedy advent. This **μαρτυρία Ἰησοῦ**, in the prophetic consciousness (xix. 10), is specifically eschatological. The close and sudden aspect of the end loomed out before Judaism (*cf.* 4 Esd. iv. 26, 44 50, Apoc. Bar. xxiii. 7, lxxxiii. 1) as before the Christian church at this period, but it was held together with calculations which anticipated a certain process and progress of history. The juxtaposition of this ardent hope and an apocalyptic programme, here as in Mark xiii. 5-37 and 4 Esd. xiv. 11, 12, is one of the antinomies of the religious consciousness, which is illogical only on paper. In Sanhed. 97 *a*, a rabbinic cycle of seven years culminating in messiah's advent is laid down; whereupon "Rab. Yoseph saith, There have been many septennial cycles of this kind, and he has not come . . . Rabbi Zera saith, Three things come unexpectedly: the messiah, the finding of treasure-trove, and a scorpion" (*cf.* Drummond's *Jewish Messiah*, 220).—**Κύριε.** The Lordship of Jesus is defined as his right to come and to judge (xxii. 12), which is also the point of Rom. xiv. 9-12 (*cf.* Kattenbusch, ii. 609, 658 f.). **Ἔρχου, κύριε** is the Greek rendering of the Aramaic watchword of the primitive church (*cf.* on ver. 17), which possibly echoed a phrase in the Jewish liturgy (*cf.* on 1 Cor. xvi. 22, and *E. Bi.* 2935, 2936).

Ver. 21. A benediction at the close of the reading (i. 3, xxii. 7) before the congregation, rather than an epistolary epilogue to the Apocalypse. The epistolary form in which apocalypses, like historical and homiletical writings of the age, were occasionally cast, was connected with their use in Christian worship. Such open letters of pastoral counsel were circulated by means of public reading, and were indeed designed for that end. They were not to be rejected as merely local (*cf.* ii. 7, 23, xxii. 7-21; Mark xiii. 14 and 37), any more than their contents were to be arbitrarily treated by individuals (xxii. 18, 19) in accordance with their own predilections.